2024

GOVERNMENTAL GAAP GUIDE
FOR STATE AND LOCAL GOVERNMENTS

ERIC S. BERMAN, MSA, CPA, CGMA

Editorial Staff

Editor .... Mary P. Taylor
Production .... Jennifer Schencker, Ranjith Rajaram, and
Prabhu Meenakshisundaram

This publication is designed to provide accurate and authoritative information in regard to the subject matter covered. It is sold with the understanding that the publisher is not engaged in rendering legal, accounting or other professional service. If legal advice or other expert assistance is required, the services of a competent professional person should be sought. All views expressed in this publication are those of the author and not necessarily those of the publisher or any other person.

ISBN: 978-0-8080-5912-7

© 2023 CCH Incorporated and its affiliates. All rights reserved.
2700 Lake Cook Road
Riverwoods, IL 60015
800 344 3734
ShopTax.WoltersKluwer.com/en

No claim is made to original government works; however, within this publication, the following are subject to CCH Incorporated's copyright: (1) the gathering, compilation, and arrangement of such government materials; (2) the magnetic translation and digital conversion of data, if applicable; (3) the historical, statutory and other notes and references; and (4) the commentary and other materials.

Printed in Canada

Governmental GAAP Guide

By Eric S. Berman, MSA, CPA, CGMA

Highlights

Financial professionals who work with state and local governments must stay current with emerging governmental standards or face unfortunate consequences. This one-of-a-kind tool discusses all the promulgated principles that are applicable to accounting and financial reporting by state and local governments. CCH's *Governmental GAAP Guide* delivers a thorough analysis of GASB Statements, GASB Interpretations, GASB Technical Bulletins as well as releases of the National Council on Governmental Accounting (NCGA) that remain in effect as of the date of publication, including Statements and NCGA Interpretations. Certain AICPA Audit and Accounting Guide *State and Local Governments* concepts are also discussed. Everything is analyzed and restated in plain English and is supported by timesaving examples and illustrations.

2024 Edition

To assist preparers and auditors in meeting the requirements of generally accepted accounting principles, the 2024 edition of CCH's *Governmental GAAP Guide* includes an updated comprehensive financial statement presentation, glossary, and disclosure checklist, complete with cross-references to the applicable professional standards, and a series of practice alerts for pending GASB projects and recently issued GASB pronouncements.

This edition of the *Governmental GAAP Guide* has been updated throughout with the very latest information on the following GASB standards either recently implemented or in the process of being implemented as of the date of this publication:

GASB Statement Number	Codification Section(s) (Primary Section[s] in **Bold**)	Chapters in the Guide	Title
GASB-94	1200, 1400, 1500, 2300, **A90** (New), C65, D20, L20, **P90** (New), Bn5	10, 14	Public-Private and Public-Public Partnerships and Availability Payment Arrangements
GASB-96	1200, **1400**, 1500, 1800, 2300, D20, L20, **S80** (New), Bn5, Pe5, Po50	10, 14	Subscription-Based Information Technology Arrangements
GASB-91	1400, 1500, 2450, 2500, C50, **C65**, L20, S20, In5	12	Conduit Debt Obligations

iv *Highlights*

GASB Statement Number	Codification Section(s) (Primary Section[s] in **Bold**)	Chapters in the Guide	Title
GASB-99	1100, 1400, 1600, 1800, 2100, 2200, 2300, 2600, A90, C50, D30, D40, F60 (deleted), L20, N50, N70, P90, R30, S20, S80, Po20, Re10, 1500, 3100, C20, C50, D40, **F30 (New)** (consolidates former N30), I50	Various	*Omnibus 2022*
GASB-100	1400, 1800, 2200, **2250**, 2300, 2450, 2600, 3100, D40, I50, L10, R30, P80, Co10, In5, Po20	5, 20	*Accounting Changes and Error Corrections*
GASB-101	1500, 1600, 2200, 2300, **C60**, P20, P21, P22, P23, P24, P50, P51, P52, P53, P54, Pe5, Pe6, Po50, Po51	13	*Compensated Absences*

"Codification"-Based Guidance

Other than the analysis of the issuances of new GASB pronouncements, the primary changes in this edition relate to the removal of referencing to previously issued GASB Standards **once they have been incorporated** into the GASB's *Codification of Governmental Accounting and Financial Reporting Standards* (the *Codification*). This was done to ease the understanding for the user of this *Guide*.

> **CAUTION:** The *Codification* does *not* include certain elements of GASB Pronouncements and *Implementation Guidance*, including statuses, summaries, introductory and scope elements, most effective date and transition guidance, background, basis for conclusions, and *Codification* instructions. However, it does present a cohesive and orderly set of literature that can be easily followed by most practitioners.

Throughout the *Guide*, the nomenclature includes a reference to the GASB Codification Section [GASB Cod. Sec. ####]. The Codification also includes any related *Implementation Guide* questions as part of each section. Information from those questions and answers may be incorporated where necessary as part of the *Guide*.

Additional information on the *Codification* is included in the following Preface.

As with prior years, any GAAP superseded by the time of this release has been removed based on the timing of implementation measured as of June 30, 2023.

CCH® Accounting Research Manager®

CCH® Accounting Research Manager® is the most comprehensive, up-to-date, and objective online database of financial reporting literature. It includes all authoritative and proposed accounting, auditing, and SEC literature, plus independent, expert-written interpretive guidance.

Our Weekly Summary e-mail newsletter highlights the key developments of the week, giving you the assurance that you have the most current information. It provides links to new FASB, AICPA, SEC, PCAOB, EITF, and IASB authoritative and proposal-stage literature, plus insightful guidance from financial reporting experts.

Our outstanding team of content experts takes pride in updating the system on a daily basis, so you stay as current as possible. You'll learn of newly released literature and deliberations of current financial reporting projects as soon as they occur! Plus, you benefit from their easy-to-understand technical translations.

With **CCH® Accounting Research Manager®**, you maximize the efficiency of your research time, while enhancing your results. Learn more about our content, our experts and how you can request a FREE trial by visiting us at .

CCH® CPELink

Wolters Kluwer's goal is to provide you with the clearest, most concise, and up-to-date accounting and auditing information to help further your professional development, as well as a convenient method to help you satisfy your continuing professional education requirements. CCH® CPELink* offers a complete line of webinars and self-study courses covering complex and constantly evolving accounting and auditing issues. We are continually adding new programs to help you stay current on all the latest developments. The CCH® CPELink self-study courses are available 24 hours a day, seven days a week. You'll get immediate exam results and certification. To view our complete accounting and auditing course catalog, go to: *cchcpelink.com*.

8/23

For questions concerning this shipment, billing, or other customer service matters, call our Customer Service department at 1 800 344 3734.

© 2023 CCH Incorporated and its affiliates. All rights reserved.

---

*Wolters Kluwer is registered with the National Association of State Boards of Accountancy (NASBA) as a sponsor of continuing professional education on the National Registry of CPE Sponsors. State Boards of Accountancy have the final authority on the acceptance of individual course for CPE credit. Complaints regarding registered sponsors may be submitted to the National Registry of CPE Sponsors through its website: www.nasbaregistry.org.

Contents

Preface	ix
New Pronouncements and Outstanding Due Process Documents	xiv
Codification of Governmental Accounting and Financial Reporting Standards References	xxii
Acknowledgments	xxix
About the Author	xxxi

Part I. Basic Governmental Accounting Concepts and Standards

Chapter 1: Foundation and Overview of Governmental Generally Accepted Accounting Principles	1001
Chapter 2: Budgetary Accounting	2001
Chapter 3: Measurement Focus and Basis of Accounting	3001
Chapter 4: Governmental Financial Reporting Entity	4001
Chapter 5: Terminology and Classification	5001

Part II. Fund Accounting

Chapter 6: Governmental Funds	6001
Chapter 7: Proprietary Funds	7001
Chapter 8: Fiduciary Funds	8001

Part III. Specific Accounting and Reporting Issues

Chapter 9: Deposits, Investments, and Investment Derivative Instruments	9001
Chapter 10: Capital Assets	10,001
Chapter 11: Other Assets and Deferred Outflows of Resources	11,001
Chapter 12: Long-Term Debt	12,001
Chapter 13: Pension, Postemployment, and Other Employee Benefit Liabilities	13,001
Chapter 14: Leases and Similar Arrangements	14,001
Chapter 15: Risk Management, Claims, and Judgments	15,001
Chapter 16: Other Liabilities	16,001
Chapter 17: Revenues: Nonexchange and Exchange Transactions	17,001
Chapter 18: Expenses and Expenditures: Nonexchange and Exchange Transactions	18,001
Chapter 19: Special Assessments	19,001

Part IV. Financial Reporting by General-Purpose Governments

Chapter 20: Financial Reporting	20,001

Part V. Stand-Alone Financial Reporting by Special-Purpose Governments

Chapter 21: Public Colleges and Universities	21,001
Chapter 22: Pension and Other Postemployment Benefit Plans	22,001
Chapter 23: Public Entity Risk Pools	23,001
Chapter 24: Other Special-Purpose Governments	24,001
Chapter 25: Cross-Reference	25,001

Glossary 26,001
Accounting Resources on the Web 27,001
Index 28,001

Preface

Integrated Approach to Governmental Financial Reporting

The many sections of the GASB *Codification*, as amended, serve as the primary guidance for those who prepare, audit, and use government financial reports. In addition, the GASB continues to work on the further development and clarification of other accounting standards for state and local government entities. CCH's *Governmental GAAP Guide* provides interpretive guidance on the application of the core principles of U.S. generally accepted accounting principles (U.S. GAAP) and the other accounting and financial reporting pronouncements applicable to state and local governments.

Within each chapter, certain elements are emphasized to allow readers to focus on new standards or existing standards being implemented. Other elements are emphasized due to ongoing implementation issues. Such emphasis is contained in **PRACTICE ALERTs**, **PRACTICE POINTs**, and **OBSERVATIONs**, respectively. Examples of observations include illustrations, figures, and paragraphs demonstrating and clarifying specific accounting principles. A major **PRACTICE ALERT** follows and is discussed as applicable in various chapters:

> **PRACTICE ALERT:** The GASB is in the final stages of a wide-ranging multiple-year project reexamining the financial reporting model. A final release is expected by March 2024. As of the date of publication, the implementation provisions of a final release have not been finalized.

The GASB's proposed updates and clarifications to the *Financial Reporting Model* as of the date of publication are as follows:

Proposed Changes to the Management's Discussion and Analysis (MD&A)

- The requirement and illustrations for the analysis of year-to-year changes should emphasize the level of thoroughness of the analysis and should include the relative magnitude of the reasons for changes. The analysis of balances and transactions of nonmajor funds in the aggregate may *not* be required.

- The requirement to reference to the summary of significant accounting policies note would no longer be required.

- The section titled *Introduction* may be amended to *Overview of the Financial Statements* and the section titled *Significant Capital Asset and Long-Term Debt Activity* may be amended to *Significant Capital Asset and Long-Term Financing Activity*.

- The presentation of condensed current-year and prior-year financial information from the government-wide financial statements may be further distinguished between governmental and business-type activities.

- Most importantly to many preparers of MD&A, the discussion of significant variations between the original and final budget amounts and the final budget and actual results for the General Fund would no longer be presented. Instead, the analysis will be presented as part of a note to required supplementary information (RSI), as discussed below. Further, the requirement to present information about infrastructure assets accounted for using the modified approach would also only be presented as part of a note to RSI, as applicable.

- Clarification to the presentation of currently known facts, decisions or conditions that are expected to have a *significant* impact on financial position or results of operations may have additional examples to aid preparers.

Proprietary Activity Reporting Proposed Adjustments

A focus area for many practitioners in this project has been the definitions of operating revenues and expenses and nonoperating revenues and expenses. With slight clarifications to what was in the exposure draft as released in 2020, nonoperating revenues and expenses may be described as:

- Subsidies received and provided,
- Revenues and expenses relating to financing,
- Resources from the disposal of capital assets and inventory,
- With certain exceptions, investment income and expenses, and
- Contributions to permanent and term endowments.

The GASB is adjusting the definition of the word "subsidies" to include transfers and flows that may have a direct or indirect impact on user fees and charges. The GASB may also clarify that subsidies are noncapital subsidies unless the subsidy is for capital purposes. Once the information is assembled for financial reporting, the statement of revenues, expenses, and changes in fund net position may distinguish between operating and nonoperating revenues and expenses, with subtotals for operating income (loss) and noncapital subsidies. Then, the statistical section would be adjusted to reflect those changes, as applicable.

RSI Proposed Adjustments

As introduced in the MD&A section, the budgetary comparison information may be moved to RSI. Analysis of the variations between the original budget and final budget amounts and final budget and actual amounts will be presented in the notes to RSI.

Governmental Fund Statement Proposed Adjustments

Another element that practitioners have been following relates to the measurement focus and basis of accounting for governmental funds, which also impacts the presentation of governmental fund statements. The modified accrual basis of accounting in its current form may not be continued upon implementation of any changes provided in the *Financial Reporting Model Improvements* final standard. The basis may be renamed *short-term financial resources measurement focus and modified accrual basis of accounting*.

This change will also be reflected in the titles of the governmental fund statements. The balance sheet would be the *short-term financial resources balance sheet*. The statement of revenues, expenditures and changes in fund balances would be the *statement of short-term financial resources flows*. Sections of the flows statement would include current and noncurrent, inflows and outflows terminology.

The recognition period would be one year. The period of recognition may be quite different for some governments that use a so-called 60-day accrual period. However, as the focus would be on cash, assets available to be converted to cash and assets that are consumable in lieu of cash, the short-term recognition period of one year may not be vastly different from current practice.

The final statement may include additional guidance for governmental fund transactions including, but not limited to:

- Receivable recognition,
- Liability recognition,
- Amendments to contracts and other binding arrangements,
- Direct vendor financings,
- Escheat property,
- Irrevocable split-interest agreements,
- Land (and capital assets) held as an investment, and
- Investments not reported at fair value.

Other Changes

Unusual and infrequent items may be clarified in terms of recognition and presentation in the various basic financial statements. The Board may not include examples of unusual or infrequent items, leaving it up to professional judgment.

> **PRACTICE ALERT:** President Biden signed into law the Financial Data Transparency Act of 2022 as part of an Omnibus spending bill approved by Congress. States and local governments will be required to comply with new financial reporting provisions by 2027. The details of the provisions are uncertain other than that the mandate for reporting is to be in a machine-readable format using common data standards. The Securities and Exchange Commission (SEC) will have jurisdiction over the rulemaking for the Act which may determine the extent of the changes. CCH's *Governmental GAAP Update Service* will keep subscribers informed as the rulemaking process progresses, which appears to be required to be completed by the end of 2024. Publicly traded companies subject to SEC provisions have been required to use XBRL for financial statements phasing in from 2019 through 2021. XBRL (eXtensible Business Reporting Language) is a freely available data standard. Once the rulemaking process completes, the following edition of the *Governmental GAAP Guide* and *Governmental GAAP Practice and Disclosures Manual* will contain changes as warranted.

PRACTICE ALERT: *Revenue and Expense Recognition – Preliminary Views*

The second major project is on *Revenue and Expense Recognition*. The GASB released a *Preliminary Views* (PV) document in the spring of 2020 detailing the Board's initial views on this wide-ranging project. The project's scope includes classification, recognition, and measurement of revenues and expenses, unless specifically excluded from the project. As of the date of publication, the specific *exclusions* from the project are:

Capital asset (and related debt) activity	Purchases, sales, donations, and nonmonetary exchanges of capital assets, as well as depreciation expense, interest income or expense, and gains and losses derived from impairment or remeasurement of capital assets, inventory, or long-term debt
Certain financial instruments	Investments, financial guarantees, derivative instruments, financings such as leases, and insurance
Postemployment benefits	All guidance and projects related to pensions, OPEB, compensated absences, and termination benefits

Seven existing GASB statements are currently within scope. More statements could be added as part of further deliberations.

The Revenue and Expense model in the Board's PV assumes the following:

- Inflows and outflows are of equal importance in resource flows statements,
- Inflows and outflows should be classified independently, and not in relationship to each other,
- The government is an economic entity and not an agent of the citizenry,
- Symmetrical considerations, to the extent possible, should be included in revenue and expense recognition, and
- A consistent viewpoint, from the resource provider perspective, will be applied in the revenue and expense analysis.

Two distinct categories of revenue and expense recognition are presented, with decisions on categorization and recognition utilizing the following flow:

Revenues	Expenses
1. Identify if there is an increase in an asset	1. Identify if there is an increase in a liability
2. If not an asset, identify if there is a liability	2. If not a liability, identify if there is an asset
3. Identify if the asset meets the definition of a deferred inflow of resources	3. Identify if the liability meets the definition of a deferred outflow of resources
4. Recognize revenues	4. Recognize expenses

There are many nuances and application issues of the revenues and expense recognition model to the categories. Deliberations will continue throughout 2023 and 2024, with an Exposure Draft not expected for release until March 2025. A final Statement may not be approved until June 2027.

New Pronouncements and Outstanding Due Process Documents

Updated annually, the GASB's *Implementation Guide* (also referred to as the *Comprehensive Implementation Guide*) was developed to assist financial statement preparers and attesters in the implementation and application of GASB pronouncements. This edition includes various changes from the GASB's previous guidance. Such changes are made utilizing annual *Implementation Guidance Updates* (IGU).

Upon approval, they have been reflected where possible in the *Governmental GAAP Guide*. Other *Implementation Guides* are specific to GASB Statements that generate questions from practitioners, indicating a degree of difficulty in implementing the Statement. The most recent single-statement implementation guidance released relates to GASB Statement No. 87 (*Leases*).

> **PRACTICE POINT:** During January 2023, the GASB took the unusual step of issuing a supplemental Exposure Draft to the in-process *Implementation Guide Update* Exposure Draft. The supplement consisted of one additional question and answer relating to *Subscription-Based Information Technology Arrangements*. The final *Implementation Guide* information, including the additional question and answer are presented in Chapter 14 of the *Governmental GAAP Guide*.

The AICPA issues two annually updated guides that provide guidance for state and local governments and their auditors. The AICPA Audit and Accounting Guide *State and Local Governments* presents recommendations of the AICPA State and Local Government Audit Guide Revision Task Force on the application of generally accepted auditing standards to audits of financial statements of state and local governments.

The second guide, AICPA Audit Guide *Government Auditing Standards and Single Audits*, presents recommendations of the AICPA State and Local Government Audit Guide Revision Task Force on the application of generally accepted government auditing standards (GAGAS) to audits of financial statements of state and local governments, and audits of compliance with major federal award programs. As of the publication date of this edition of CCH's *Governmental GAAP Guide*, the AICPA had issued the March 1, 2023, edition of the Audit and Accounting Guide—*State and Local Governments*, and the 2022 edition of *Government Auditing Standards and Single Audits*.

The following GASB pronouncements, previously issued through the date of publication, are discussed in this edition and are to be implemented over the coming years along with the following implementation dates:

Preface **XV**

GASB Statement Number	*Codification* Section(s) (Primary Section[s] in **Bold**)	Title	Implementation Dates – Reporting Periods *Ending*	
			December 31,	June 30,
GASB-91	1400, 1500, 2450, 2500, C50, **C65**, L20, S20, In5	*Conduit Debt Obligations*	Should be implemented at the time of publication	2023
GASB-94	1200, 1400, 1500, 2300, **A90** (New), C65, D20, L20, **P90** (New), Bn5	*Public-Private and Public-Public Partnerships and Availability Payment Arrangements*	2023	2023
GASB-96	1200, **1400**, 1500, 1800, 2300, D20, L20, **S80** (New), Bn5, Pe5, Po50	*Subscription-Based Information Technology Arrangements*	2023	2023
GASB-99 (Paragraphs 26–31 were immediately effective).	1100, 1400, 1600, 1800, 2100, 2200, 2300, 2600, A90, C50, D30, D40, F60 (deleted), L20, N50, N70, P90, R30, S20, S80, Po20, Re10, 1500, 3100, C20, C50, D40, **F30 (New)** (consolidates former N30), I50.	*Omnibus 2022*	See explanation below.	
GASB-100	1400, 1800, 2200, **2250**, 2300, 2450, 2600, 3100, D40, I50, L10, R30, P80, Co10, In5, Po20	*Accounting Changes and Error Corrections*	2024	2024
GASB-101	1500, 1600, 2200, 2300, **C60**, P20, P21, P22, P23, P24, P50, P51, P52, P53, P54, Pe5, Pe6, Po50, Po51	*Compensated Absences*	2024	2025

For GASB-99, the effective date and transition for topics are staggered, other than for the topics effective upon issuance of the standard in April 2022. The clarifications and amendments to the standards involving leases, public-private and public-public partnerships and availability payment arrangements and subscription-based information technology arrangements became effective for fiscal years *beginning* after June 15, 2022, and all reporting periods thereafter.

For the provisions relating to financial guarantees and derivative instruments, the elements are effective for fiscal years beginning after June 15, 2023, and all reporting periods thereafter. Individual topics are permitted by the GASB to be implemented if all requirements associated with that topic are implemented at the same time.

> **PRACTICE POINT:** The GASB recently released Concepts Statement No. 7 (GASB:CS-7) (*Communication Methods in General Purpose External Financial Reports that Contain Basic Financial Statements: Notes to Financial Statements*). In this adjustment to five paragraphs of the existing conceptual framework, the GASB clarifies:
>
> - The purpose of notes to financial statements,
> - The users of notes to financial statements, including their responsibilities in using the financial statements,
> - The criteria for disclosing information items in notes to financial statements,
> - The types of information not appropriate in notes to financial statements, and
> - How notes to financial statements and reporting units should be delineated by the GASB in releasing a new standard.

As further described in Chapter 1 of the *Governmental GAAP Guide* and Chapter 17 of the *Governmental GAAP Practice and Disclosures Manual*, the conceptual framework only applies to the GASB Board. However, it signals to the profession the skeleton of financial reporting for states and local governments.

> **PRACTICE ALERT:** At the time of publication, the GASB was in the process of finalizing deliberations on a project relating to *Risks and Uncertainties Disclosures*. The GASB is proposing a requirement for governments to judge whether events that have occurred or are more likely than not to occur within 12 months of the financial statement date (or shortly thereafter—usually three months) will have a substantial impact on the government's ability to provide services at the level of the current reporting period. The judgment would include whether the government can meet its obligations as they come due within three years of the financial statement date. If criteria are met, disclosure would include a concentration or constraint on resources, the event associated with such an event and actions taken by the government prior to issuing the financial statements to mitigate the event's impact. If approved as proposed, such disclosure would be effective for fiscal years beginning after June 15, 2023. However, at least one

GASB Board Member disagreed with the proposal and provided an Alternative View.

OBSERVATION: Many new GASB standards require changes to conform to the new provisions. Such changes are to be applied retroactively by restating financial statements, if *practicable* (as opposed to practical), for all prior periods presented. If restatement of prior periods is not *practicable*, the cumulative effect, if any, of implementing a statement should be reported as a restatement of beginning net position (or fund balance or fund net position, as applicable) for the earliest period restated. In the first period that the new statement is applied, the notes to the financial statements should disclose the nature of the restatement and its effect. Also, the reason for not restating prior periods presented should be disclosed.

Other GASB Projects Discussed

The GASB also has other ongoing projects that are discussed where applicable in this *Guide*. Initial deliberations and research are occurring as of the date of publication on projects involving:

Project	Potential Preliminary Views Release	Potential Exposure Draft Release	Potential Final Statement Release
Classification of Nonfinancial Assets	None expected	August 2023	June 2024
Going Concern and Severe Financial Stress	August 2024	March 2026	April 2027

GASB Staff are also performing pre-agenda research activities on capital assets and subsequent events.

PRACTICE ALERT: The GASB is monitoring how various governments are utilizing digital assets such as cryptocurrency. Governments may be investing in cryptocurrency and / or accepting cryptocurrency for transactional activities. With the collapse of FTX Trading Ltd., that operated a cryptocurrency exchange and hedge fund prior to its collapse in November 2022, a regulatory focus is occurring from states and local governments on cryptocurrency. GASB staff are monitoring such activity and whether the GASB has a role in reporting digital assets.

Significant Changes to Chapters from the 2023 *Governmental GAAP Guide*

In addition to formatting, clarifications, updating for referencing, typographical and grammatical errors, the following significant updates were made in this edition of the *Governmental GAAP Guide*, in addition to those noted in this Introduction and Preface:

Chapter	Significant Change(s)
1	• Further background on the reasons for the issuance of GASB Statement No. 62 (*Codification of Accounting and Financial Reporting Guidance Contained in Pre-November 30, 1989, FASB and AICPA Pronouncements*) and the operations of the Financial Accounting Foundation. • Inclusion of information on the bankruptcy of Chester, Pennsylvania. • Use of the word "insignificant" in various GASB Statements. • Inclusion of GASB Concepts Statement No. 7 (GASB:CS-7) (*Communication Methods in General Purpose External Financial Reports That Contain Basic Financial Statements: Notes to Financial Statements*). • Additional **PRACTICE ALERT** on the GASB's *Classification of Nonfinancial Assets* Exposure Draft.
2	• Additional **PRACTICE ALERT** discussing the *Financial Reporting Model Improvements* Exposure Draft and the impact on budgetary reporting and analysis.
3	• Additional **OBSERVATION** on accounting and reporting within governmental funds. • Updated **PRACTICE ALERT** with recent developments from the GASB regarding the short-term financial resources measurement focus and modified accrual basis of accounting as a result of deliberations related to the *Financial Reporting Model Improvements* Exposure Draft.
4	• Added **PRACTICE ALERT** discussing the GASB's project addressing going concern and severe financial stress with mention of the potential timeline for the project. • Added **PRACTICE ALERT** discussing a change in reporting entity reporting upon implementation of GASB Statement No. 100 (*Accounting Changes and Error Corrections*). • Added **PRACTICE POINT** discussing nongovernmental component units and public colleges and universities.
5	No significant changes.
6	• Added discussion and **PRACTICE ALERT** regarding a change in qualification for a special revenue fund upon implementation of GASB Statement No. 100 (*Accounting Changes and Error Corrections*). • Added **PRACTICE ALERT** when a change from a major fund to a nonmajor fund (or vice versa) occurs and GASB Statement No. 100 (*Accounting Changes and Error Corrections*).

7	• Added **PRACTICE POINT** on the predominance of a government's participation in an Internal Service Fund and GASB Cod. Sec. 1300.705-9. • Added **PRACTICE POINT** on the importance of opinion units and fund reporting. • Added **PRACTICE ALERT** repeating the **PRACTICE ALERT** from Chapter 6 on GASB Statement No. 100, but for Enterprise Fund and Internal Service Fund reporting.
8	• Clarified discussion of "own-source revenues." • Adjusted **PRACTICE ALERT** on Internal Revenue Code Section 420 accounts and the federal SECURE 2.0 Act.
9	• Updated **PRACTICE ALERT** discussing the GASB's project on the classification of nonfinancial assets and assets held for sale. • Updated section on fund overdrafts in internal investment pools. In prior editions of the *Guide*, this was presented in Chapter 11. • Redrafted Appendix: Comprehensive Illustration of Investment Disclosures for a State changing the source to the Commonwealth of Massachusetts' Annual Comprehensive Financial Report notes to the basic financial statements.
10	• Additional **PRACTICE ALERT** on the GASB's project on *nonfinancial assets* similarly to previous chapters. • Additional clarification on the general provisions of depreciation. • Example note disclosure for capital assets including right-to-use assets. • Additional **PRACTICE ALERT** on "cloud computing" arrangements and subscription-based information technology arrangements, further discussed in Chapter 14. • **PRACTICE POINT** on materiality and capital asset reporting. • **PRACTICE POINT** on impairment of right-to-use assets, including as a result of a cyberattack.
11	• Added **PRACTICE ALERT** on prepayments relating to subscription-based information technology arrangements and incentives, also referencing Chapter 14. • Deleted discussion on escheat as it repeated information in Chapter 8. • Moved fund overdraft discussion to Chapter 9.

12	• Deleted **PRACTICE POINT** on social obligation bonds as the GASB is still in the pre-agenda research phase on such bonds. • Clarified **PRACTICE ALERT** on the impact of GASB Statement No. 99 (*Omnibus 2022*) and the sunset of London Interbank Offered Rate indexed taxable debt. • Updated example of note disclosure for outstanding long-term debt. • Updated example of note disclosure for outstanding swapped debt. • Updated example of note disclosure for defeased debt.
13	• Redrafted Part 1 for GASB Statement No. 101 (*Compensated Absences*). The former GASB Statement No. 16 guidance has been moved to an Appendix to the chapter (which will be removed in 2025). • Added **PRACTICE ALERT** regarding the bankruptcy of Chester, Pennsylvania, and the City's pension fund.
14	• Added **PRACTICE POINT** on the content of the chapter. • Amended **PRACTICE POINT** on the differences between exchange and exchange-like transactions. • Added **PRACTICE ALERT** on the GASB's project on the classification of nonfinancial assets, similar to previous chapters. • Added **PRACTICE POINT** from a GASB *Implementation Guide* question on a public university paying a lease in foreign currency [GASB Cod. Sec. L20.708-4]. • Added **PRACTICE POINT** from a GASB *Implementation Guide* question on an up-front payment for the first three years of a seven-year lease and the calculation of interest expense [GASB Cod. Sec. L20.707-2]. • Added **PRACTICE POINT** on lease modifications resulting in a short-term lease referencing GASB Cod. Sec. L20.703-11. • Added **PRACTICE ALERT** on "cloud computing" arrangements and an *Implementation Guide* question [GASB Cod. Sec. S80.702-1]. • Added **OBSERVATION** relating to the "cloud computing" **PRACTICE ALERT**. • Added **PRACTICE ALERT** on perpetual licenses for software and an *Implementation Guide* question [GASB Cod. Sec. S80.701-1]. • Added **PRACTICE ALERT** and **PRACTICE POINT** on the calculation of a term of a subscription-based information technology arrangement (SBITA) along with discussion of GASB Cod. Sec. S80.703-1. • Added **PRACTICE POINT** on the conversion of "legacy data" to new SBITAs.

15	• Added **PRACTICE POINT** on the importance of internal auditing and enterprise risk management. • Added **PRACTICE ALERT** on the GASB's upcoming Statement No. 102 (*Risks and Uncertainties Disclosures*) (to be further discussed in the 2025 *Guide*).
16	• Added **PRACTICE ALERT** as in prior chapters referencing GASB Statement No. 100 (*Accounting Changes and Error Corrections*) and estimates of landfill closure costs. • Added **PRACTICE POINT** on pollution remediation obligations and the train derailment in Eastern Ohio. • Added **PRACTICE POINT** on regulatory gaming. • Added **PRACTICE POINT** on sports betting and regulated "banked games." • Added **PRACTICE POINT** on special assessments and financial guarantees referencing Chapters 12 and 19. • Added **PRACTICE ALERT** on the National Opioid Settlement and revenue recognition.
17	• Added **PRACTICE ALERT** on the federal Inflation Reduction Act of 2022 updating Internal Revenue Code Section 6417 allowing state and local governments to receive an "applicable credit" for 12 potential energy credits through 2032.
18	• Added **PRACTICE ALERT** on a change in the useful life of a capital asset and GASB Statement No. 100 (*Accounting Changes and Error Corrections*). • Added **PRACTICE ALERT** on the change from depreciation to the modified approach for infrastructure and GASB Statement No. 100 (*Accounting Changes and Error Corrections*).
19	No significant changes.

20	• Removal of **PRACTICE POINT** on COVID-19 disclosures in MD&A. • Added **PRACTICE ALERT** on the GASB's project on the classification of nonfinancial assets, similar to previous chapters. • Redrafted basic financial statements throughout sourced from the Commonwealth of Massachusetts' Annual Comprehensive Financial Report. • Added **PRACTICE ALERT** summarizing the various changes in GASB Statement No. 100 (*Accounting Changes and Error Corrections*) and the impact on the Statement of Activities and other flows statements. • Added **PRACTICE ALERT** on the removal of reclassification language in the notes to the basic financial statements due to GASB Statement No. 100 (*Accounting Changes and Error Corrections*). • Removal of **PRACTICE ALERT** on the release of GASB *Concepts Statement* No. 7, discussed in Chapter 1. • Redrafted Notes to the RSI—Budgetary Reporting, sourced from the Commonwealth of Massachusetts. • Added **PRACTICE ALERT** on errors in RSI and GASB Statement No. 100 (*Accounting Changes and Error Corrections*).
21	• Added **PRACTICE POINT** on the complexity of operations of multicampus public colleges and university in comparison to large cities or states.
22	• Added **PRACTICE ALERT** on errors in RSI and GASB Statement No. 100 (*Accounting Changes and Error Corrections*). • Added **PRACTICE ALERT** on the provisions of the federal SECURE 2.0 Act that may impact Plans.
23	No significant changes.
24	• Added **PRACTICE POINT** on public broadcasters and leases when broadcasters surrender their licenses, but retain a tower lease and then contract with a third party in a sublease. • Added **PRACTICE POINT** on public hospitals and medical facilities and the prevalence of leases, public-private partnerships, and subscription -based information technology arrangements, referencing Chapter 14.
25	Updated chapter references throughout.
Glossary	No significant changes.

Codification of Governmental Accounting and Financial Reporting Standards References

Many practitioners use the GASB's annual *Codification of Governmental Accounting and Financial Reporting Standards*. The Codification presents another view of GASB standards, providing authoritative accounting and financial reporting guidance. However, practitioners are cautioned that the Codification may not have the most up-to-date information as it is only updated annually and for issued standards. The Codification is organized into five parts:

I. General Principles

Section	Topic
1000	The Hierarchy of Generally Accepted Accounting Principles
1100	Summary Statement of Principles
1200	Generally Accepted Accounting Principles and Legal Compliance
1300	Fund Accounting
1400	Reporting Capital Assets
1500	Reporting Liabilities
1600	Basis of Accounting
1700	The Budget and Budgetary Accounting
1800	Classification and Terminology

II. Financial Reporting

Section	Topic
2100	Defining the Financial Reporting Entity
2200	Comprehensive Annual Financial Report
2250	Additional Financial Reporting Considerations
2300	Notes to the Financial Statements
2400	Budgetary Reporting
2450	Cash Flows Statements
2500	Segment Information
2600	Reporting Entity and Component Unit Presentation and Disclosure
2700	Supplemental and Special-Purpose Reporting
2800	Statistical Section
2900	Interim Financial Reporting

III. Measurement

Section	Topic
3100	Fair Value Measurement

IV. Specific Balance Sheet and Operating Statement Items

Section	Topic
Section	Topic
A10	Asset Retirement Obligations
A90	Availability Payment Arrangements
B50	Bond, Tax, and Revenue Anticipation Notes
C20	Cash Deposits with Financial Institutions
C50	Claims and Judgments
C55	Common Stock—Cost Method
C60	Compensated Absences
C65	Conduit Debt Obligations
C75	Construction-Type Contracts—Long-Term
D20	Debt Extinguishments and Troubled Debt Restructuring
D25	Deferred Compensation Plans (IRC Section 457)
D30	Demand Bonds
D40	Derivative Instruments
E70	Escheat Property
F30	Financial Guarantees
F70	Foreign Currency Transactions
I30	Interest Costs—Imputation
I40	Inventory
I50	Investments
I55	Investments—Reverse Repurchase Agreements
I60	Investments—Securities Lending
J50	Accounting for Participation in Joint Ventures and Jointly Governed Organizations
L10	Landfill Closure and Postclosure Care Costs
L20	Leases
L30	Lending Activities
N70	Nonmonetary Transactions
P20	Pension Activities—Reporting for Benefits Provided through Trusts That Meet Specified Criteria
P21	Pension Activities—Reporting for Benefits *Not* Provided through Trusts That Meet Specified Criteria
P23	Reporting Assets Accumulated for Defined Benefit Pensions Not Provided through Trusts That Meet Specified Criteria
P40	Pollution Remediation Obligations
P50	Postemployment Benefits Other Than Pensions—Employer Reporting

Section	Topic
P70	Property Taxes
P80	Proprietary Fund Accounting and Financial Reporting
P90	Public-Private and Public-Public Partnerships
R30	Real Estate
R50	Research and Development Arrangements
S20	Sales and Pledges of Receivables and Future Revenues and Intra-Entity Transfers of Assets and Future Revenues
S40	Special Assessments
S80	Subscription-Based Information Technology Arrangements
T25	Termination Benefits
T50	Tobacco Settlement Recognition
U25	Unemployment Compensation Benefit Plans

V. Stand-Alone Reporting—Specialized Units and Activities.

Section	Topic
Bn5	Bankruptcies
Br10	Broadcasters
Ca5	Cable Television Systems
Co5	Colleges and Universities
Co10	Combinations and Disposals of Operations
Ho5	Hospitals and Other Healthcare Providers
In3	Insurance Entities—Other Than Public Entity Risk Pools
In5	Investment Pools (External)
Pe5	Pension Plans Administered through Trusts That Meet Specified Criteria—Defined Benefit
Pe6	Pension Plans Administered through Trusts That Meet Specified Criteria—Defined Contribution
Po20	Public Entity Risk Pools
Po50	Postemployment Benefit Plans Administered through Trusts That Meet Specified Criteria—Defined Benefit
Po51	Postemployment Benefit Plans Administered through Trusts That Meet Specified Criteria—Defined Contribution
Re10	Regulated Operations
Sp20	Special-Purpose Governments
Ut5	Utilities

Parts I–III are of generalized interest in accounting and financial reporting, while the remaining parts are organized similarly to an encyclopedia in alphabetical order (e.g., pensions are under "P"). Paragraphs within each section are numbered consecutively, with the following structure:

Paragraphs	Topics
Paragraphs .101—.499:	Standards
Paragraphs .501—.599:	Definitions
Paragraphs .601—.699:	GASB Technical Bulletins
Paragraphs .701—.799:	GASB Implementation Guides
Paragraphs .801—.899:	AICPA Literature cleared by the GASB
Paragraphs .901—.999:	Nonauthoritative discussion (supplemental guidance and illustrations)

Source references included in the codification are recognizable by most practitioners such as "GASBS" meaning "GASB Statement No." For GASB statements that are in the process of implementation as of the time of publication, this *Guide* not only references a GASB statement when discussing a topic, but also the codification section for clarity.

CCH's *Governmental GAAP Guide* is a single reference that discusses all the promulgated accounting principles applicable to financial reporting by state and local governments that are in use today (not superseded): GASB Statements, GASB Interpretations, GASB Technical Bulletins, NCGA Statements, and NCGA Interpretations.

These original pronouncements have been analyzed and are restated in straightforward language to allow preparers and auditors of governmental financial statements to better understand the original promulgations. To facilitate research, major topics in the text are cross-referenced to the pertinent paragraphs of the original pronouncements.

The *Guide* alerts readers to and discusses financial accounting and reporting standards necessary to prepare the basic external financial statements of a governmental entity. A companion text, CCH's *Governmental GAAP Practice and Disclosures Manual*, illustrates how governmental financial statements are prepared based on GASB standards currently effective. Every required GASB disclosure is included, including "real-world" examples. For many practitioners, both volumes could be included as part of a governmental GAAP library.

The comprehensive glossary of governmental accounting terms and acronyms continues to be updated. Although it is not meant to be all-inclusive, the glossary references every term contained in GASB standards through GASB-101.

Additional Resources

For those who are new to GAAP for state and local governments or who only desire a brief overview of their government's accounting and financial reporting, the GASB issues a user guide series. As of the time of publication, the GASB has issued the following user guides:

- *What You Should Know about the Finances of Your Government's Business-Type Activities: A Guide to Financial Statements,*
- *An Analyst's Guide to Government Financial Statements,*
- *What You Should Know about Your School District's Finances: A Guide to Financial Statements,* and
- *What You Should Know about Your Local Government's Finances: A Guide to Financial Statements.*

All are aimed at users of a state or local government's financial statements and decision-makers. Users and decision-makers can use CCH's *Governmental GAAP Guide* and the *Governmental GAAP Practice and Disclosures Manual* to supplement their understanding of the details of their state or local government's financial operations.

Acknowledgments

The preparation of this book was made possible by the efforts many of dedicated people. My thanks to Mary P. Taylor for her editing and attention to detail and Jack Georger, CPA, for his technical review of the 2024 edition.

Although other individuals played a vital role in preparing Wolters Kluwer's *Governmental GAAP Guide*, any errors or omissions are the author's responsibility. The *Governmental GAAP Guide* continues to evolve as new pronouncements are issued and as we strive to better explain governmental accounting and reporting standards. If you have suggestions that you believe will improve the quality of the material, please send them to the editor:

Mary P. Taylor
Wolters Kluwer
2700 Lake Cook Road
Riverwoods, Illinois 60015
mary.taylor@wolterskluwer.com

Eric S. Berman
Brookline, Massachusetts and Washington, DC

About the Author

Eric S. Berman, MSA, CPA, CGMA, has over 30 years of governmental accounting and auditing experience and is a Partner with Eide Bailly LLP. Before Eide Bailly LLP, he was a quality control principal with a public accounting firm in California.

Eric is the author of the *Governmental Library* for preparers for CCH. The Government Library also offers in-depth, interpretive guidance. In addition to this *Governmental GAAP Guide, users* can access CCH's *Governmental GAAP Practice and Disclosures Manual* and the *Governmental GAAP Update Service*.

Eric's public-sector experience includes being a Deputy Comptroller for the Commonwealth of Massachusetts from 1999 to 2010, and the Chief Financial Officer of the Massachusetts Water Pollution Abatement Trust from 1994 to 1999. Eric is a licensed CPA in Massachusetts. He obtained an M.S. in Accountancy from Bentley University. Eric currently serves on the Association of Government Accountants (AGA)'s Finance and Budget Committee. Eric is the immediate past National Treasurer and currently serves on the Leadership Development Committee of AGA. He recently represented the AGA as the Vice Chairman of the Government Accounting Standards Advisory Council to the GASB. He also chaired the AGA's Audit Committee and previously, the AGA's Financial Management Standards Board. He also was a previous chair of the American Institute of Certified Public Accountants' (AICPA's) Governmental Performance and Accountability Committee and is a former member of the AICPA's State and Local Government Expert Panel. Eric is a member of the GASB's task force reexamining the state and local governmental financial reporting model and has served on previous GASB task forces and working groups assisting in developing and implementing standards.

Eric is also a past member of the California Society of CPAs' Governmental Accounting and Auditing Committee and is past chair of the same committee for the Massachusetts Society of CPAs. He was also the founder and treasurer of a not-for-profit performing arts organization in Pennsylvania. Eric is frequently called upon to consult and train state and local governments throughout the country on governmental accounting and auditing. Eric shuttles between Massachusetts and Washington, DC.

PART I. BASIC GOVERNMENTAL ACCOUNTING CONCEPTS AND STANDARDS

CHAPTER 1
FOUNDATION AND OVERVIEW OF GOVERNMENTAL GENERALLY ACCEPTED ACCOUNTING PRINCIPLES

Chapter References:

GASB Statement Nos. 6, 9, 14, 33–39, 42, 51, 54, 56, 61–62, 72, 76, 78, 80, 84–85, 89–90

GASB Concepts Statement Nos. 1–7

GASB *Implementation Guide*

NCGA Statement No. 1

AICPA *Code of Professional Conduct*

INTRODUCTION

The National Council on Governmental Accounting (NCGA) in 1979 defined "generally accepted accounting principles" (GAAP) as it applied to governments in its first statement [GASB Cod. Secs. 1200.101–.102] as:

> [The] uniform minimum standards of and guidelines to financial accounting and reporting. Adherence to GAAP assures that financial reports of all state and local governments—regardless of jurisdictional legal provisions and customs—contain the same types of financial statements and disclosures, for the same categories and types of funds based on the measurement and classification criteria. Adherence to GAAP is essential to assuring a reasonable degree of comparability among the financial reports of state and local governments.

Standards have evolved dramatically since the 1970s. The NCGA was replaced by the Governmental Accounting Standards Board (GASB) five years after the original statement was released. Technology and practices have changed state and local governmental operations at breakneck speed. Yet, also unchanged is the importance of reporting entities following GAAP in the preparation of their financial statements, which is embodied in the American Institute of Certified Public Accountants (AICPA)'s *Code of Professional Conduct*, ET Section 2.320.001 (*Accounting Principles Rule*), which states:

> A member shall not (1) express an opinion or state affirmatively that the financial statements or other financial data of any entity are presented in conformity with generally accepted accounting principles or (2) state that he or she is not aware of any material modifications that should be made to such statements or data in order for them to be in conformity with generally accepted accounting principles, if such statements or data contain any departure from an accounting principle promulgated by bodies designated by

Council to establish such principles that has a material effect on the statements or data taken as a whole. If, however, the statements or data contain such a departure and the member can demonstrate that due to unusual circumstances the financial statements or data would otherwise have been misleading, the member can comply with the rule by describing the departure, its approximate effects, if practicable, and the reasons why compliance with the principle would result in a misleading statement.

Part 2 of the *Code of Professional Conduct* applies to members in *business*. ET Section 0.400.34 defines *Members in business* as members of the AICPA:

> [W]ho is employed or engaged on a contractual or volunteer basis in a(n) executive, staff, governance, advisory, or administrative capacity in such areas as industry, *the public sector*, education, the not-for-profit sector, and regulatory or professional bodies. This does not include a member engaged in public practice.

As further discussed in ET Section 0.400.44, "public practice" refers to the performance of *professional services* for a *client* by a *member* or *member's firm*. " Professional services" as defined in ET Section 0.400.42 includes:

> [A]ll services requiring accountancy or related skills that are performed by a *member* for a *client*, an employer, *or on a volunteer basis* (emphasis added). These services include, but are not limited to, accounting, audit and other attest services, tax, bookkeeping, management consulting, financial management, corporate governance, personal financial planning, business valuation, litigation support, educational, and those services for which standards are promulgated by bodies designated by *Council*.

Aggregated, these provisions mean that members of the AICPA who prepare financial statements and work for state and local governments, or who volunteer as an executive, staff, governance, advisory, or administrative capacity (e.g., serving on a school board or a city advisory committee) must follow GAAP or risk an ethics violation. If a regulatory or statutory basis of accounting is used, the departure from GAAP must be described in the notes to the basic financial statements.

Within the AICPA *Code of Professional Conduct – Revised*, appendix A, the AICPA Council has designated:

- The Federal Accounting Standards Advisory Board (FASAB) as the body to establish accounting principles for the federal government,
- The Financial Accounting Standards Board (FASB) as the body to establish accounting principles for both for-profit and not-for-profit organizations,
- Most importantly for the readers of this *Guide*, the Governmental Accounting Standards Board (GASB) as the body to establish accounting principles for state and local governments,
- The Public Company Accounting Oversight Board (PCAOB) for publicly traded entities, and
- The International Accounting Standards Board (IASB) for non-United States entities.

The Financial Accounting Foundation (FAF) was incorporated in 1972. The FAF provides funding and oversight to the FASB and the GASB. The FASB and the GASB are the standard setting bodies within the FAF.

The GASB was established in 1984. The FAF has agreed that the GASB has the authority to issue GAAP for state and local governmental units. However, based on a January 1989 report of the FAF, the GASB needed clarity on the authority of the FASB versus the GASB. Further, legacy standards released prior to the formation of the FAF and the FASB were still in use by states and local governments.

A jurisdictional determination was signed on November 30, 1989, by the FAF and various stakeholder groups providing primacy to the GASB for state and local government accounting and financial reporting. The Trustees of the FAF decided that the division between the GASB and the FASB would continue as established in the 1984 GASB *Structural Agreement*, but the hierarchy of GAAP should be changed. Each Board would have (and still has) the primary responsibility for setting standards within the respective jurisdictions. This means for state and local government practitioners that pronouncements of the FASB are not mandatory unless designated as such by the GASB. The State and Local Government Hierarchy (the hierarchy of GAAP) as established by the GASB is discussed later in this chapter.

Thus, the GASB establishes accounting principles for state and local governments, and the FASB establishes accounting principles for all other reporting entities, including not-for-profit organizations other than state and local governments. However, some crossover exists in some limited situations between FASB and GASB entities.

GASB-62 (*Codification of Accounting and Financial Reporting Guidance Contained in Pre-November 30, 1989, FASB and AICPA Pronouncements*) incorporated into the GASB's literature all former relevant FASB Statements and Interpretations, APB Opinions, and ARBs issued prior to November 30, 1989, except those that conflict with a GASB pronouncement. The omnibus statement also incorporated all relevant AICPA pronouncements also issued prior to November 30, 1989. Therefore, all non-GASB literature issued prior to November 30, 1989, that has not been codified in GASB-62, is not authoritative.

PRACTICE POINT: As discussed in Chapter 4 of this *Guide*, some *component units* (introduced later in this chapter and detailed further in Chapter 4), especially those meeting the criteria as a component unit of a primary government to be reported as a discretely presented component unit, may be a nongovernmental entity (e.g., a nonprofit organization) and follow FASB standards in their separately issued financial statements. Component units are required to apply the *definition and display provisions* of GAAP, as amended, before they are combined with the primary government. Also discussed in Chapter 4 is the possibility of a government owning a majority equity interest in a for-profit corporation, which also is required to follow FASB standards. This chapter also presents a discussion of the applicability of the FASB's Accounting Standards Codification (ASC)™ Topic 958, *Not-for-Profit Entities*.

> **OBSERVATION:** The AICPA *Code of Professional Conduct* independence rule contains an interpretation "State and Local Government Client Affiliates" (ET Section 1.224.020). Auditors should review this section carefully. A full discussion of the provisions is contained in CCH's *Knowledge-Based Audits of State and Local Governments with Single Audits Guide*, available on CCH's *Accounting Research Manager*™ Within the guidance, there are links to AICPA websites containing nonauthoritative implementation guidance for attestation engagements and an Excel template nonauthoritative tool.

Although not recognized as a standard setter for accounting principles generally accepted in the United States of America, the International Public-Sector Accounting Standards Board (IPSASB) focuses on accounting and financial reporting needs of governmental entities at an international level. The IPSASB issues and promotes benchmark guidance and facilitates the exchange of information among governmental accountants and their organizations through the issuance of International Public-Sector Accounting Standards (IPSAS) and related guidance. A key part of the IPSASB's strategy is to converge the IPSAS with the International Financial Reporting Standards (IFRS) issued by the IASB. There are no discussions under way to converge the accounting principles generally accepted in the United States of America, as established by the GASB, with the IFRS or IPSAS, even though a few standards (e.g., GASB Cod. Sec. 1400) have some elements of IPSAS.

The Unique Nature of States and Local Governments

The 10th Amendment to the Constitution of the United States of America ratified in 1791 simply states:

> The powers not delegated to the United States by the Constitution, nor prohibited by it to the states, are reserved to the states respectively, or to the people.

These important words establish the stark differences between what is part of the federal system of government, what is part of the states and what is reserved for the people of the United States. "Fiscal federalism" is a relatively new concept from the late 1950s, expanding the political strata of government to financial strata. There is a sizable portion of federal operations that are delegated to the states and to municipal governments (or directly to municipalities from federal agencies) in the form of federal grant awards. Even though there is a massive financial interrelationship between the layers of government, the federal system and the state and local system of government are vastly different.

What is a Government?

The concept of exactly *what a government is* may be difficult to apply in some circumstances. GASB Cod. Sec. 1000.801 contains AICPA literature cleared by the GASB defining a government. Governments are public corporations and bodies corporate and politic. A public corporation is defined in *Black's Law Dictionary* and referred to by the AICPA in the Audit and Accounting Guide *State and Local Governments* (Chapter 1, footnote 4) as:

An artificial person (for example, [a] municipality or a governmental corporation) created for the administration of public affairs. Unlike a private corporation it has no protection against legislative acts altering or even repealing its charter. Instrumentalities created by [the] state, formed and owned by it in [the] public interest, supported in whole or part by public funds, and governed by managers deriving their authority from [the] state. *Sharon Realty Co. v. Westlake, Ohio Com. Pl.,* 188 N.E.2d 318, 323, 25, O.O.2d 322. A public corporation is an instrumentality of the state, founded and owned in the public interest, supported by public funds, and governed by those deriving their authority from the state. *York County Fair Ass'n v. South Carolina Tax Commission,* 249 S.C. 337, 154 S.E.2d 361, 362.

Per GASB Cod. Sec. 1000.801, governments have the following characteristics:

- Popular election of officers or appointment (or approval) of a controlling majority of the members of the entity's governing body by officials of one or more state or local governments,
- The potential for unilateral dissolution by a government with the net (position) reverting to a government, and
- The power to enact and enforce a tax levy.

The AICPA's Audit and Accounting Guide *State and Local Governments* further discusses how entities are presumed to be governmental if they can issue directly (rather than through a state or municipal authority) debt that pays interest exempt from federal taxation. However, entities possessing only that ability (to issue tax-exempt debt) and none of the other governmental characteristics may rebut the presumption that they are governmental if their determination is supported by compelling, relevant evidence.

As an example, some pension and other postemployment benefit (OPEB) plans may stipulate that they are subject to the Employee Retirement Income Security Act of 1974 (ERISA) and have required filings with the United States Department of Labor (Form 5500). Filing of a Form 5500 and subjection to ERISA are not primary evidence negating a determination as a government if the characteristics are met.

As discussed in a September 2017 GASB revised white paper entitled *Why Governmental Accounting and Financial Reporting is—and Should Be—Different,* governments are structured differently than for-profit and not-for-profit entities. One central theme of the white paper is that the GASB's continued existence is vital to individuals and organizations who are interested in the financial performance of state and local governments, who have substantially different information needs than those who are interested in the financial performance of for-profit entities. For-profit entities, whose accounting standards are established by the FASB, are environmentally different from government entities. According to the white paper, governments enhance or maintain the well-being of citizens by providing services in accordance with public-policy goals. In contrast, for-profit business enterprises focus primarily on wealth creation, interacting principally with those segments of society that fulfill their mission of generating a financial return on investment for shareholders.

Governments are unique because:
- The entities serve a broader group of stakeholders, including taxpayers, citizens, elected representatives, oversight groups, bondholders, and others in the financial community.
- Most government revenues are raised through involuntary taxes rather than a willing exchange of comparable value between two parties in a typical business transaction.
- Monitoring actual compliance with budgeted public-policy priorities is central to government public-accountability reporting.
- Governments exist longer than for-profit businesses and are less subject to bankruptcy and dissolution, even during severe recessions and depressions. The city of Santa Fe, New Mexico, is the oldest state capital in the United States (settled in 1610). San Juan, Puerto Rico, was founded in 1521 and remains the oldest continuously inhabited European established settlement on United States territory. No for-profit business is nearly as old as those governments.

On this last point, GASB Cod. Sec. Bn5 (*Bankruptcies*) provides accounting and financial reporting guidance for municipal (non-state) governments that have been granted protection from creditors under Chapter 9 of the United States Bankruptcy Code. "Protection" may include modifications to the terms and conditions of certain of the government's debt issuances and relief from burdensome provisions of certain executory contracts and unexpired lease commitments. Although the number of Chapter 9 filings has been extremely limited in the 70 years since the federal legislation was passed and they only occur in the limited number of states that have approved Chapter 9, recent high-profile and threatened filings have brought the process to the public's attention, including Jefferson County, Alabama, in 2011, the City of Stockton and San Bernardino County, California, in 2012, Detroit, Michigan, in 2013 and in the Commonwealth of Puerto Rico. In 2022, the City of Chester, Pennsylvania filed for bankruptcy due to the City's ongoing deficits. This was two years after the Governor of Pennsylvania declared a fiscal emergency in the city and appointed a receiver for it.

PRACTICE ALERT: During 2022, the GASB began a project addressing issues relating to disclosures that may identify going concern uncertainties and severe financial stress. According to the GASB's *Technical Plan*, the Board is in the process of considering whether improvements are needed to existing guidance of going concern uncertainties and/or severe financial stress to address diversity in practice and clarify the circumstances under which disclosure is appropriate. The Board may develop a definition of severe financial stress and criteria for identifying when governments should disclose their exposure to severe financial stress. Based on these considerations, the GASB will consider what information about a government's exposure to severe financial stress is necessary to disclose. A Preliminary Views document is expected to be released by the end of 2023. Due to the potential issues involved, a 120-day comment period is projected. An exposure draft may not be released until April or May 2025. If the project progresses to a final statement, the pronouncement may not be released until June 2026. (Preliminary Views documents are described later in this chapter).

THE STATE AND LOCAL GOVERNMENT ACCOUNTING HIERARCHY

A governmental entity may be involved in a variety of activities that have characteristics like commercial enterprises and not-for-profit entities, as well as governmental activities. Determining which accounting standards should be observed to account for these varied activities has been confusing at times and complex. GASB Cod. Sec. 1000 (*The Hierarchy of Generally Accepted Accounting Principles for State and Local Governments*) provides fundamental guidance for determining which accounting standards governmental entities should observe to prepare their financial statements.

The GAAP hierarchy for states and local governments contains two categories of principles. The first category of authoritative GAAP consists of GASB Statements of Governmental Accounting Standards (Category A). The second category of authoritative GAAP (Category B) consists of GASB *Technical Bulletins* and *Implementation Guides*, as well as guidance from the AICPA that is specifically cleared by the GASB. Such literature contains a statement saying that it has been cleared (the majority of the GASB members did not object to its issuance) by the GASB. The GASB updates an *Implementation Guide* regularly with new or amended questions, answers, and illustrations after a public due process. Other *Implementation Guides* are issued for specific statements and after implementation of the related GASB Statement(s), are then incorporated into a future update of the *Implementation Guide*.

PRACTICE POINT: Every effort has been made to reference questions and answers in the *Implementation Guide* where it is essential to magnify, clarify, and elaborate on elements contained within the various chapters of the *Governmental GAAP Guide*. It is impossible to incorporate over 1,000 questions and answers contained in the *Implementation Guide* in this volume.

Readers should always use the GAAP hierarchy as it is intended, referencing "Category A" GAAP prior to

"Category B" and non-authoritative GAAP. Preparers of financial statements (and auditors) should also review illustrations within the *Implementation Guide* as more "background" or illustrative material than a GASB Statement—meaning, practitioners should always follow the Hierarchy to decide on the implementation to answer a practice issue, starting with GASB Statements, before referencing the *Implementation Guide* or a GASB Technical Bulletin and certainly prior to referencing nonauthoritative matter.

Exhibit 1-1 shows the state and local government accounting hierarchy in GASB-76. The hierarchy consists of two categories, with Category B subordinate to Category A. For example, if an accounting issue is addressed in both Category A and Category B, the guidance established in Category A must be followed because it is the highest source of accounting principles for the practice issue as discussed in GASB Cod. Sec. 1000.101.

EXHIBIT 1-1
STATE AND LOCAL GOVERNMENT ACCOUNTING HIERARCHY

Category A	• Officially established accounting principles—GASB Statements
Category B	• GASB *Technical Bulletins*, GASB *Implementation Guides*, and literature of the AICPA if specifically cleared by the GASB.

GASB *Interpretations* have been infrequently issued and are largely incorporated into the GASB *Codification*.

The *Codification* includes a footnote to Category A on the status of interpretations:

> All GASB Interpretations heretofore issued and currently in effect also are considered as being included within Category A and are continued in force until altered, amended, supplemented, revoked, or superseded by subsequent GASB pronouncements. Category A standards, including GASB Interpretations heretofore issued and currently in effect, are the subject of the Accounting Principles Rule of the American Institute of Certified Public Accountants' (AICPA's) *Code of Professional Conduct*, and this Statement does not affect the application of that rule.

Therefore, GASB Cod. Sec. 1000 incorporates the GASB's Interpretations by reference into Category A.

PRACTICE POINT: GASB Cod. Sec. 1000.101(b) incorporates literature of the AICPA "cleared by the GASB," inclusive of literature specifically made applicable to state and local government entities. This literature includes elements primarily found in the AICPA Audit and Accounting Guide *State and Local Governments* (*AICPA Audit Guide*) as well as the AICPA Audit and Accounting Guide *Health Care Entities* and referenced in the GASB *Codification of Governmental Accounting and Financial Reporting Standards* (the *Codification*) as follows:

Nature of Guidance in the AICPA Audit and Accounting Guide – State and Local Governments—Appendix B	GASB Codification References [GASB Cod. Secs.]
• Definition of "government"	1000.801, 1000 fn. 4
• Annual calculation of an arbitrage liability	1500.801
• Overdrafts of internal investment pools and of cash accounts	1800.801–.802
• Interfund balances relating to agency funds with negative cash balances	1800.803
• Reporting nonoperating revenue for certain nonexchange revenues for operating purposes or for operating purposes or capital outlay at the recipient's discretion	N50.802, 1800.804, 2200.801, P80.804
• When to report the issuance of debt	1500.802

Foundation and Overview of Governmental GAAP 1009

Nature of Guidance in the AICPA Audit and Accounting Guide – State and Local Governments—Appendix B	GASB Codification References [GASB Cod. Secs.]
• Reporting revenue for fees received for administering pass-through grants	N50.801
• Accounting for customer deposits for utility services	Ut5.801, P80.806
• Accounting for payments to the refunding agent for current refunding bonds as an other financing use	D20.801
• Definition of "commitment"	2300.801
• Disclosure in the notes to the financial statements if a budget is not adopted for the general or a major special revenue fund because it is not legally required when a government presents required budgetary comparison information in the basic financial statements	1700.801, 2300.802, 2400.801
• Revenues and expenses that financing authorities should report in their financial statements, including when involved with conduit debt (see discussion in Chapter 12 of this *Guide* on Conduit Debt Obligations)	P80.805, C65.801
• Reporting nonoperating revenue for appropriations for operating purposes or for operating purposes or capital outlay at the recipient's discretion	1800.804, 2200.801, N50.802, P80.804
• Accounting for lottery prize costs	P80.807, Sp20.801
• Accounting for prize liabilities for which annuities have been purchased	P80.808–.809, Sp20.802–.803
• Using present value to measure lottery prize liabilities	P80.810, Sp20.804
• Disclosure in the notes to the financial statements if a budget is not adopted for the general or a major special revenue fund because it is not legally required when a government presents required budgetary comparison information in the basic financial statements	1700.801, 2200.802, 2400.801

In addition, the *AICPA Audit Guides* contain Category B GAAP on capital asset impairment considerations for gaming entities, reporting by gaming entities, and charity care reported by public hospitals.

PRACTICE POINT: See Chapter 24 of the *Governmental GAAP Guide* for additional discussion of the accounting and financial reporting aspects of other Special-Purpose Governments such as public hospitals, public broadcasters and cable systems, insurance entities other than public entity risk pools and regulated operations.

Authoritative GAAP is incorporated annually into the *Codification*. Many practitioners reference the *Codification* as it may be easier to find information. However, due to the annual updating, there may be a time lag in between the issuance of a GASB Statement and the incorporation of the information from the new Statement into the *Codification*. Practitioners may want to initiate research by starting with the applicable GASB Statement and, if it is easier to follow, review the applicable *Codification* sections to provide an answer to a problem in accounting or financial reporting. The *Codification* also incorporates the *Implementation Guide* questions and answers.

GASB Cod. Sec. 1000.104 lists nonauthoritative literature that may be referenced, including:

- GASB Concepts Statements,
- Pronouncements and other literature of the FASB, FASAB, IPSASB, IASB, and AICPA (other than AICPA literature cleared by the GASB),
- Practices that are widely recognized and prevalent in state and local governments,
- Literature of other professional associations or regulatory agencies, and
- Accounting textbooks (including CCH's *Governmental GAAP Guide*), handbooks, and articles.

GASB Cod. Sec. 1000.105 directs practitioners to evaluate the appropriateness of nonauthoritative accounting literature by considering the consistency of the literature to GASB Concepts Statements, the relevance of the literature to circumstances, the specificity of the literature, and the general recognition of the issuer or author as an authority.

Application Guidance

The structure contained in GASB Cod. Sec. 1000 is a hierarchy. Standards established in the highest category take precedence over those contained in a lower category. As an example of this decision-making required by preparers and auditors, accounting issues related to environmental liabilities are addressed in both GASB Cod. Sec. P40 (*Accounting and Financial Reporting for Pollution Remediation Obligations*) and Statement of Federal Financial Accounting Standards (SFFAS) No. 5 (*Accounting for Liabilities of the Federal Government*), as amended. When preparing financial statements for a governmental entity, the accountant must observe the standards established in GASB Cod. Sec. P40 as GASB Statements are part of Category A of the hierarchy and Federal Accounting Standards Advisory Board (FASAB) Statements are nonauthoritative per GASB Cod. Sec. 1000.104.

When an accounting issue is not addressed in a GASB Statement, the Category B of the hierarchy must be considered. For example, if a matter is addressed in an AICPA Industry Audit and Accounting Guide that has been made applicable by the AICPA and cleared by the GASB, the guidance established in the publication should be used to prepare the financial statements of a state or local governmental entity per GASB Cod. Secs. 1000.101–.103.

> **OBSERVATION:** The state and local government accounting hierarchy does not apply to the federal government. Accounting standards for the federal government are established by the Federal Accounting Standards Advisory Board (FASAB).

Accounting Principles Other Than GAAP ("Special Purpose Framework" or "SPF")

This *Guide* focuses on accounting and financial reporting in accordance with GAAP. However, certain state and local governments that are not legally required to prepare financial statements in accordance with GAAP may elect to prepare their financial statements in accordance with a special purpose framework.

Included in the definition of an SPF are various non-GAAP bases of accounting, including the cash basis, modified cash basis, regulatory basis, and income tax basis of accounting. Some state and local laws do not recognize GASB or FASB pronouncements as the required basis for preparing their governmental financial statements. For example, a governmental unit through a charter or constitution may require that a governmental reporting entity prepare its budget and financial statements on a cash basis, modified cash basis, or regulatory basis of accounting. In addition, state regulatory requirements may specify a basis of accounting other than GAAP for the preparation and filing of a government's financial statements with a specific regulatory agency. In these circumstances, the government unit should follow the guidance applicable to SPFs in the preparation of their annual financial statements.

Many budgets prepared by state and local governments are developed based on accounting other than GAAP. As a result, the government's internal accounting records are maintained on that same non-GAAP basis to track legal compliance. Although the governmental unit maintains its accounting records on a non-GAAP basis for legal compliance purposes, the GASB has stated that the government may still adopt a supplementary accounting system that will enable it to report on a GAAP basis in its annual financial statements in accordance with GASB Cod. Sec. 1200.103.

HIERARCHY FOR PROPRIETARY FUND ACCOUNTING ACTIVITIES

From the inception of the GASB in 1984 to the release of GASB-62 in 2010, there was periodic confusion among financial statement preparers, auditors, and users over its role and that of the FASB in the promulgation of generally accepted accounting principles for governmental entities that conduct business-type activities (such as municipal utilities) or that can take the form of either a public or a private entity (such as public health care entities, colleges, and universities).

In general, proprietary funds use the same measurement focus (flow of economic resources) and accounting basis (accrual) as commercial enterprises.

Thus, governmental entities formerly had to observe all FASB Statements and Interpretations in the preparation of financial statements for proprietary funds unless the GASB has specifically addressed an accounting issue involved in one of its own pronouncements.

GASB-62 applies to proprietary funds (enterprise and internal service funds) and governmental entities that follow proprietary fund accounting, including public benefit corporations and authorities, governmental utilities, and governmental hospital or other health-care activities. Certain governmental activities also have specific provisions in GASB-62. Of the elements in GASB-62, only revenue recognition with a right of return, inventory, and regulated operations (see next section) has specific guidance for proprietary funds that may not apply to governmental activities.

Applicability of GASB Cod. Sec. Re10 "Regulated Operations" to Proprietary Fund Accounting

GASB Cod. Sec. Re10, *Regulated Operations*, applies to governmental entities that meet *all* the following criteria:

- The regulated business-type activity's rates for regulated services provided to its customers are established by or are subject to approval by an independent, third-party regulator or by its own governing board empowered by statute or contract to establish rates that bind customers.
- The regulated rates are designed to recover the specific regulated business-type activity's costs of providing the regulated services.
- In view of the demand for the regulated services or products and the level of competition, direct and indirect, it is reasonable to assume that rates set at levels that will recover the regulated business-type activity's costs can be charged to and collected from customers. This criterion requires consideration of anticipated changes in levels of demand or competition during the recovery period for any capitalized costs [GASB Cod. Sec. Re10.101].

The various provisions of the paragraphs related to regulatory operations discuss when an asset exists and when all or part of incurred costs may be capitalized and the way those costs may be recovered. Regulatory provisions may also govern asset impairment or imposition of a liability. Profits and surpluses may also be regulated.

The provisions within the various paragraphs of GASB Cod. Sec. Re10 related to regulatory accounting are not new. They are simply edited versions of FASB Accounting Standards Codification® (ASC™) Topic 980, *Regulated Operations*, as amended.

OBSERVATION: Governments that are regulated operations may have special provisions for leases. The leases must be subject to external laws, regulations, or legal rulings. GASB Cod. Sec. L20.139, cites examples of the U.S. Department of Transportation and the Federal Aviation Administration regulating aviation leases between airports and air carriers (and other aeronautical users). In such cases, airport lessors do not apply various provisions of the standard and have differing disclosure. Port authorities may have similar regulations from the Federal Maritime Commission. A further discussion of lease accounting is in Chapter 14. In addition, Chapter 24 contains a discussion on regulated operations and accounting, which primarily impact publicly regulated utilities.

Applicability of ASC™ 958, "Not-for-Profit Entities"

The GASB's guidance for component units that are not-for-profits is contained in the GASB *Implementation Guide* questions in GASB Cod. Secs. 2600.701-3, .704-12, .704-13, and .704-14.

Footnote 3 to GASB Cod. Sec. 2100 (*The Financial Reporting Entity*) discusses how component units and other related entities to a government may be organized as not-for-profit or for-profit entities. Not-for-profit entities (e.g., foundations) are typically related to public healthcare and higher education institutions. For-profit component units may be limited liability corporations related to the public healthcare, higher education, or post-employment benefit fund entities. GASB Cod. Sec. 2100.144 requires governments to apply "the definition and display provisions of this Statement." To accomplish this, translation may have to occur between accounting of the component units and the primary government.

Questions 2600.701-3 and .704-12 through 14 discuss translation between the bases of accounting and presentation. In summation, there is no requirement to change the recognition, measurement, or disclosure standards applied in a nongovernmental component unit's separately issued financial statements. Further discussion on these issues may be found in Chapter 4.

GASB Cod. Sec. 2600.113 (d) requires blending for component units that are organized as not-for-profit corporations in which the primary government is the *sole corporate member*. The effect of the change may have caused many entities related to institutions of higher education and healthcare facilities to no longer be recognized either as discretely presented component units or related organizations.

OBSERVATION: The phrase *sole corporate member* may have slight variations in practice dependent upon state law. Practitioners should review related state laws to determine the propriety of reporting such entities.

TYPES OF GOVERNMENTAL ENTITIES

According to information available from the U.S. Bureau of Census' *2017 Census of Governments*, there are 90,126 units of federal, state, and local governments in the United States that were in existence. These governmental entities can be classified into one of two categories:

- General-purpose governments, including the 50 states, territories, and the District of Columbia, over 3,000 counties, 19,500 municipalities, and 16,300 townships.
- Special-purpose governments, including nearly 13,000 independent school districts and 38,000 other special districts.

As of the date of publication, six datasets are freely available for analysis on the U.S. Bureau of Census' website. They may be found at https://www.census.gov/programs-surveys/cog/data/tables.html.

Of the largest and smallest numbers of governments, Illinois has 6,919 governmental entities. Texas has 5,344, the District of Columbia has 2, and Hawaii has 22.

General-Purpose Governments

General-purpose governments provide a wide range of services (often including both governmental and business-type activities) and include states, counties, cities, towns, villages, and similar governmental entities. Although recognized Tribal Nations may not specifically meet the criteria to be defined as a governmental entity, many Tribal Nations prepare their financial statements in accordance with the principles applicable to general-purpose state and local governments (see following **OBSERVATION**). Also included in the description of general-purpose governments are U.S. Territories and the District of Columbia.

> **OBSERVATION:** For the purposes of federal relationships and classification, Title 2, Code of Federal Regulations, Part 200, *Uniform Administrative Requirements, Cost Principles, and Audit Requirements* (2CFR200) (as amended), Tribal Nations, including Alaskan Natives, are separately defined from other governments and recipients of federal funds as long as they are recognized as eligible for the special programs and services provided by the United States to Tribal Nations because of their status (see also Title 25 United States Code (USC) Part 450(b)(e)).
>
> Throughout 2CFR200, because most Tribal Nations, including Alaskan Natives, are classified as sovereign entities, the guidance for them shares many characteristics as the guidance for states. Tribal governments may offer similar services to general-purpose governments or special-purpose governments (discussed in the next section). They may provide subsidized housing, operate a public health facility, and provide for public safety, education, sanitation, and other functions like states and other governments. Throughout this *Guide*, minimal further information specifically directed at Tribes and Alaska Natives is included. Tribal governments may follow the GASB, or they may follow the FASB, especially if they have a casino, or both.

> **OBSERVATION:** The various federal acts in response to the SARS-CoV-2 pandemic (COVID-19) included federal funds to U.S. Territories and the District of Columbia. Listed U.S. Territories include American Samoa, Guam, Northern Mariana Islands, Puerto Rico, and the United States Virgin Islands.

Special-Purpose Governments

Special-purpose governments are defined as legally separate governmental entities that perform only one or a few activities and include colleges and universities, school districts, water and other utility districts or authorities, fire protection districts, cemetery districts, public employee retirement systems, public entity risk pools, governmental hospital or health-care organizations, public housing authorities, airport authorities, and similar entities.

The accounting and financial reporting treatment for a special-purpose government depends on the type of activities conducted by the entity. For example, some special-purpose governments are engaged only in business-type activities (e.g., a water district), some are engaged only in governmental activities (e.g., a library district), and others may be involved in a combination of activities (e.g., a school district).

Accounting and financial reporting for special-purpose governments are discussed in more detail elsewhere:

- Financial Reporting (Chapter 20)
- Public Colleges and Universities (Chapter 21)
- Pension and Other Postemployment Benefit Plans (Chapter 22)
- Public Entity Risk Pools (Chapter 23)
- Other Special-Purpose Governments (Chapter 24).

GASB PRINCIPLE SETTING PROCESS

The GASB has established a due process for the promulgation of governmental generally accepted accounting principles that encourages participation by parties interested in the establishment of a principle. Once a governmental accounting issue has been identified, the due process consists of the following potential stages:

- Pre-agenda research,
- Invitation to Comment (which is a GASB Staff document),
- Preliminary Views,
- Exposure Draft, and
- Standard setting.

Pre-Agenda Research Stage

The GASB may direct its Staff to perform initial research on various accounting and reporting issues with a goal of presenting a memorandum to the GASB to decide upon whether the issue falls under its Scope of Authority and should be added to its current project agenda for further research. The research may include questionnaires, interviews with knowledgeable individuals, research of archival information from state and local government financial reports, and inquiry on industry practices. The GASB needs to vote affirmatively to add any pre-agenda research to the current agenda.

Once a project is added to the technical agenda, more research is performed by GASB Staff. Additional surveys, questionnaires, task force meetings, focus group interviews, and other information may be brought to the GASB's attention for deliberation.

Invitation to Comment

For complex projects, an Invitation to Comment document may be released. An Invitation to Comment is a document produced by the GASB's Staff designed to seek comments from interested parties at an early stage of a project before the Board has reached a consensus view. Comments are usually in writing and public hearings may take place. An Invitation to Comment is a step before a Preliminary Views document, with a goal of providing the GASB Staff and the Board additional information on a project. Invitations to Comment do not represent a consensus view of the Board.

Examples of recent Invitations to Comment have occurred in the *Financial Reporting Model Improvements—Governmental Funds* and the *Revenue and Expense Recognition* projects. In the case of the *Revenue and Expense Recognition* project, a Preliminary Views document has been issued, representing the next step in due process.

Preliminary Views Stage

A Preliminary Views document is issued by the GASB when they desire to solicit opinions from constituents on accounting and reporting alternatives and the preliminary views of the GASB members in the initial stages of accounting standards setting. This document is usually used if there is an issue that is complex or controversial. Otherwise, an Exposure Draft is developed. A Preliminary Views document may even have an Alternative View that may be shared by two or more GASB members. Comments are made by responding parties. In addition, public hearings on the issue may be held where participants can present their views orally and respond to questions raised by members of the GASB. Upon receipt of comments on the GASB's Preliminary Views, further deliberation and research occurs.

PRACTICE ALERT: The previously mentioned GASB project on going concern and severe financial stress may have a Preliminary Views document issued by August 2024.

Exposure Draft Stage

After research and GASB deliberation, or the receipt of responses from interested parties based on the description of the issue in the Preliminary Views document (if issued), an Exposure Draft may be developed. When the GASB reaches its tentative conclusion to the issue, the Board issues an Exposure Draft for public comment.

> **OBSERVATION:** Copies of current due process documents can be obtained from the GASB's website (http://www.gasb.org). Responses to Preliminary Views and Exposure Drafts are also posted on the website. The GASB may also release a "plain language" document to encourage more stakeholders to participate in commenting on the due process document.

Standard-Setting Stage

After receiving comments on the Exposure Draft, the GASB may hold another public hearing. Once the GASB reaches a consensus on the accounting issue, it promulgates a standard that becomes part of generally accepted accounting principles for state and local governments. The GASB observes due process for major governmental accounting issues.

Occasionally, the GASB revisits a previous standard and decides that an omnibus statement is needed to clarify an issue in a Statement, provide technical corrections, or more closely align an issue to current practice. The last technical corrections standard that was released was GASB Statement No. 99 (*Omnibus 2022*). If issues arise during implementation of a new Statement, the GASB may approve corrections or amendments to previously issued Statements may be placed into new Statements as they are released. Such was the case with GASB-99, which amended certain provisions of GASB Cod. Secs. 1100, 1400, 1600, 1800, 2100, 2200, 2300, 2600, A90, C50, D30, D40, F60 (which was deleted), L20, N50, N70, P90, R30, S20, S80, Po20, and Re10. Due to the staggered implementation dates of GASB Statement No. 99, further changes will occur to the June 2023 edition of the *Codification* in sections 1500, 3100, C20, C50, D40, F30 (which will be replacing N30), and I50.

> **PRACTICE POINT:** There is a provision in GASB Statement No. 99 (*Omnibus 2022*), that aligns the recission of the London Interbank Offered Rate (LIBOR) as an appropriate benchmark to decisions made beyond the GASB. Once that decision is made by the ICE Benchmark Administration (IBA), then the next edition of the *Codification* would be amended in sections I50 and D40.

In December 2010, the GASB issued a unique document suggesting guidelines on Service Efforts and Accomplishments (SEA) reporting that are voluntarily reported by governments. Suggested guidelines were used because although SEA performance reporting is not universally defined or required, the GASB believes it is an essential element of communicating basic information about a government. The GASB's extensive research and monitoring indicate that it is appropriate at this time for the Board to set forth conceptually based suggested guidelines for voluntary reporting of SEA performance information. However, it is beyond the scope of the GASB to establish the goals and objectives of state and local government services, specific nonfinancial measures or indicators of service performance, or standards of, or benchmarks for, service performance. Conversely, according to GASB:CS-1, par. 77(c), "financial reporting should provide information to assist users in assessing the service efforts, costs, and accomplishments of the governmental entity." Therefore, the GASB believes that it is proper to issue guidance, even if SEA performance reporting is voluntary.

OBSERVATION: One of the major areas of assurance involves performance auditing engagements. Many of the elements of service efforts and accomplishments reporting may be tested as part of a performance audit engagement. For example, such an engagement may involve measuring public safety response times versus staffing within a city. The SEA performance reporting would include response times by precinct for a period along with staffing and a performance audit would test the response times. Citizens may understand such reporting more than financial reporting. However, it is beyond the GASB's scope of authority to set standards in this area.

GASB Pronouncements

The GASB may express its position on a governmental accounting topic by issuing one or more of the following pronouncements:

- GASB Statements (also known as *standards* or *pronouncements*),
- GASB Technical Bulletins, and
- GASB Implementation Guides.

GASB Statement (Category A GAAP)

The GASB addresses major governmental accounting issues by issuing a GASB Statement, but only after all aspects of the due process have occurred. Statements have the following structure:

Status	Summary of Issuance Date, Effective Date provisions, Existing GASB Statements that will be amended or superseded by the Statement and the Primary *Codification* Section reference(s).
Summary	Overview of the Statement.
Introduction	Self-explanatory.
Standards of Governmental Accounting and Financial Reporting	Scope and applicability, Standards, Effective Date and Transition, materiality notice, Board member voting.
Background	Introduction into GASB's research process of the topic in the Statement.
Basis for Conclusions	How GASB deliberated and determined the Standards of Governmental Accounting and Financial Reporting, including reaction to comments provided by stakeholders.
Codification Instructions	Application of the Standards of Governmental Accounting and Financial Reporting to sections of the *Codification* (or creation of new section(s)).
Nonauthoritative Illustrations	Self-explanatory.

Illustrations are not always included with a GASB Statement. Other information or data that the GASB may determine as useful may also be included in a GASB Statement. The GASB's *Rules of Procedure* affords Board members the opportunity to dissent against issuing a Statement. The Board member(s) comments are included. At least four of the seven Board members must approve the issuance of a Statement.

PRACTICE POINT: The materiality notice is part of every GASB Statement, proclaiming: **The provisions of this Statement need not be applied to immaterial items.** The word "materiality" (and its antonym—immaterial) may have differing interpretations for preparers, auditors and users *and is undefined in GAAP*. However, materiality is not solely quantitative—it may be qualitative. Differing measures of materiality may be applied to not only assets or liabilities, but to all other elements of a set of financial statements. The word "significant" is also used in certain GASB standards, but it also is undefined in GAAP. Some consider "significant" to be more than immaterial, but less than material. Others say that "significant" is more than a 50% probability. To some, this is controversial as the GASB uses thresholds to determine recognition elements of specific transactions. As examples:

Phrase or Word	Example of When Used in GAAP
Reasonably Certain	Portions of a lessee's determination of a lease term.
Probable	Determination of the probability of a liability relating to a claim or judgment (the future claim(s) or judgment(s) are *likely* to occur).
More Likely than Not	Determination if a government may be liable for payments related to a nonexchange financial guarantee.
Material	Nearly every GASB pronouncement.
Significant	Many elements of notes to the basic financial statements, especially in the disclosure of accounting policies applicable to the government.
Insignificant	When both information technology software and tangible capital assets are included in a subscription-based information technology arrangement (SBITA), if the cost of the software component is insignificant relative to the cost of the underlying tangible capital assets, the contract may be subject to leases guidance, based on professional judgment.

These phrases or words have no mathematics or percentages aligned to them in GAAP. Therefore, one is not especially senior to another. However, some have deemed "more likely than not" to mean 50% "plus a feather."

PRACTICE ALERT: GASB Statement No. 101 *(Compensated Absences)* Footnote 1, defines the term *more likely than not* as meaning a likelihood of more than 50%.

Previously, the GASB addressed issues of lesser scope by issuing Interpretations. An Interpretation was subject to due process, although the procedures were not as formal as those for the promulgation of a Statement. Interpretations were directly voted on by the GASB and, if accepted by most of its members, became part of governmental generally accepted accounting principles. These have been included as part of Statements and are no longer being issued.

The *Codification* is typically updated annually for new statements and other matter issued by the GASB. GASB Cod. Sec. 1000.101 discusses the *Codification*, noting that upon incorporation of new statements and other matter, the information, when presented in the *Codification*, retains its authoritative status. As a reminder, the GASB Statement's Introduction, Effective Date and Transition, Background, Basis for Conclusions, and Codification Instruction sections *are not included* in the *Codification*. GASB *Concepts Statements* are nonauthoritative but are presented as an appendix (B) to the *Codification*.

GASB Technical Bulletins (Category B GAAP)

The GASB recognizes that, under certain circumstances, it may not need to follow the due process used for issuing a Statement or an Interpretation. The GASB has authorized its staff to provide timely guidance on governmental accounting issues by preparing a Technical Bulletin Series. The nature and purpose of GASB Technical Bulletins were addressed in GASB Technical Bulletin 84-1 (Purpose and Scope of GASB Technical Bulletins and Procedures for Issuance) (GASB: TB 84-1, par. 2). As GASB: TB 84-1 established procedures and not standards, that individual Technical Bulletin is not codified.

GASB: TB 84-1 states that a Technical Bulletin, rather than a Statement or Interpretation, may be issued under the following general criteria:

- The guidance is not expected to cause a major change in accounting practice for many entities.
- The administrative cost involved in implementing the guidance is not expected to be significant for most affected entities.
- The guidance does not conflict with a broad fundamental principle or create a novel accounting practice (GASB: TB 84-1, par. 5).

The GASB follows due process before it issues a Technical Bulletin. Before the GASB releases an initial draft of a Technical Bulletin to the public for comment, members of the GASB are furnished with a copy. If most of the members do not object to the initial draft, the proposed Technical Bulletin is released to interested parties. Responses from the interested parties are given to the GASB for its consideration at a public meeting. If most GASB members do not object to the proposed Technical Bulletin, the GASB will issue it as a formal Technical Bulletin. Each Technical Bulletin is published with a legend that reads, "The GASB has reviewed this Technical Bulletin and a majority of its members do not object to its issuance" (GASB: TB 84-1, pars. 6–12). Upon release, Technical Bulletins are codified within applicable sections, starting at subsection .600. As an example, the Technical Bulletin information on the Coronavirus Aid, Relief, and Economic Security Act (CARES Act) provisions are contained within GASB Cod. Sec. N50.602.

Implementation Guides (Category B)

The GASB's *Implementation Guide* is a compendium of questions and answers providing explanatory material to practitioners, assisting in understanding GASB standards. The GASB may also issue freestanding *Implementation Guides* related to specific statements. As discussed, the Board now issues *Implementation Guide* updates for any new questions and answers developed and amendments needed to previous questions and answers due to new GASB Statement issuances. All of these are collected and incorporated annually as part of the *Implementation Guide*. (See previous **PRACTICE POINT** on the usage of *Implementation Guides*, especially illustrations.) Cumulatively, over 1,000 questions and answers are included within the *Implementation Guides*.

> **PRACTICE POINT:** A more "user-friendly" way to find *Implementation Guide* questions and answers, including updates, may be in the *Codification*. In each section of the *Codification*, subsections .701–.799 contain *Implementation Guide* questions and answers for each subject. The illustrations and other nonauthoritative matter from *Implementation Guides* (and Statements) are contained in subsections .901–.999 of each section.

Post-Implementation Review Process (PIR)

The GASB has undertaken a rigorous post-implementation review process to issued standards (PIR) enhancing the quality control of the standard-setting process. The goal of a PIR is to determine if a standard achieves its objectives, provides relevant information and the costs of implementation do not exceed the benefits of the information provided.

PIRs involve three stages:

- Post-issuance date implementation monitoring of issued pronouncements,
- Post-effective date review of cost versus benefits, and
- Summarization of research and reporting.

Each stage has a project plan that is communicated to stakeholders. The GASB freely discloses that PIRs *may* result in the GASB proposing to amend existing pronouncements addressing areas that are not understandable, unforeseen or have unexpected costs.

As of the date of publication of this *Guide*, the GASB is in the process of PIRs involving:

- *Fair Value Measurement and Application* [GASB Cod. Sec. 3100 (GASB-72)],
- *Fiduciary Activities* [GASB Cod. Sec. 1300 (GASB-84, as amended)],
- *Leases* [GASB Cod. Sec. L20 (GASB-87, as amended)],
- *Other Postemployment Benefits* [GASB Cod. Secs. P50, P51, P52, P53, P54, Po50, Po51 (GASB-74 and 75, as amended)], and
- *Pensions* [GASB Cod. Secs. P20, P21, P22, P23, P24, Pe5, Pe6 (GASB-67 and 68, as amended)].

The process of a PIR may take years and if an existing pronouncement is to be amended, the standard-setting process would commence. As of the date of publication, the schedule of PIRs continues until the second quarter of 2030.

Governmental Accounting Standards Advisory Council (GASAC)

The GASB is assisted in its standards-setting process by the Governmental Accounting Standards Advisory Council (GASAC). The GASAC is responsible for consulting with the GASB on technical issues on the GASB's agenda, project priorities, matters likely to require the attention of the GASB, selection and organization of task forces, and such other matters as requested by the GASB or its chair. The GASAC is also responsible for helping to develop the GASB's annual budget and aiding the Financial Accounting Foundation in raising funds for the GASB. The GASAC has about 30 members, broadly representative of preparers, attesters, and users of financial information. In addition, the Comptroller General of the United States serves as an official observer.

GASB Resource Aids

The GASB Staff spends considerable time helping constituents to understand and implement existing standards. Highlighted below are many of the resources the GASB makes available to help constituents apply changes in U.S. generally accepted accounting principles (GAAP) for state and local governments.

Online Technical Inquiry System

A constituent with a question about GASB standards or state and local government financial statements can fill out and submit a technical inquiry form (which may be accessed through a link in the Technical Issues section of the GASB website) and gain access to input on technical matters from the GASB Staff. As resources allow, the staff responds to inquires in the interest of promoting the uniform application of GAAP and of fostering relations with the GASB constituency. Inquiries are generally responded to within a few days and are typically resolved in less than two weeks.

Governmental Accounting Research System Online

The GASB's *Governmental Accounting Research System* (GARS) is available on a subscription basis from the GASB on the internet. The complete set of original pronouncements, the GASB codification and implementation guides, and an index are included and searchable by keyword or query.

The GASB has a free, basic online version of GARS (https://gars.gasb.org), with browsing by a table of contents.

Academics have access to a subscription-based professional view, which is free for accounting program faculty and students who enroll in the program and are approved by the FAF. The professional view contains the entirety of the GASB's guidance, advanced navigation, search and connection features, the ability to go back and forth between documents, and many other features, including printing and the ability to share content through social media.

Plain Language Articles and Explanatory Videos and Webinars on Demand

Since 2005, many proposed GASB standards or new GASB standards have been accompanied by a short explanatory article that uses a minimum of technical language. The GASB is committed to communicating in plain language with constituents about its standards and standards-setting activities. All the articles, fact sheets, and publications in the Plain Language section of the GASB website are available for download free of charge. The GASB has also started to post on its website videos on demand that explain proposed standards.

Speeches

The GASB Staff, as well as its chair, board members, and director of research and technical activities, as well as GASAC members, make appearances across the country each year to provide training regarding the proper application of GASB standards and other pronouncements, and to provide updates on GASB activities.

PRACTICE POINT: Many practitioners point to speeches, webinars, and other communications from the GASB Staff, its Chairman, Board members, and others as authoritative. These communications are *not authoritative* and usually bear a "disclaimer" as part of the communication, reminding receivers of the communication that it has not been subject to due process.

Website

The GASB makes a variety of resources available through its easy-to-navigate website, which provides click-through links to the GASB News Center, free copies of all current proposals, and GASB Project Pages detailing current agenda projects and pronouncements. To be added to the GASB's constituent database, be included in GASB research and outreach activities, receive periodic e-mail updates, and be considered for GASB task forces and advisory committees, a constituent can fill out the visitors' register on the website.

User Guides

The GASB's nontechnical User Guides series, which are plain-language, nontechnical introductions to the financial reports of state and local governments, have been as useful to accountants and finance officers as they have been to users, both for understanding financial reports and explaining them to clients and elected officials. The nontechnical User Guides are designed for broad accessibility to anyone, from the government finance novice to the longtime public manager. All the editions in the series—the *What You Should Know Guides*, An Analyst's Guide, the guide to notes and supporting information, and the quick guides for elected officials—are available through the GASB store on its website.

OVERVIEW OF GOVERNMENTAL GENERALLY ACCEPTED ACCOUNTING PRINCIPLES CONCEPT STATEMENTS

As previously mentioned, NCGA-1 (*Governmental Accounting and Financial Reporting Principles*), adopted by the GASB upon its establishment in 1984, states that financial statements of a state or local government should be prepared in

1024 *Basic Governmental Accounting Concepts and Standards*

accordance with generally accepted accounting principles. Certain governments may be required or permitted to prepare their financial statements on a regulatory basis of accounting or another comprehensive basis of accounting, however, generally accepted accounting principles continue to be the primary criteria for preparation of financial statements of states and local governments. The generally accepted accounting principles that are applicable to state and local governments can be found primarily in the statements, interpretations, and other due-process documents remaining in effect of the NCGA, the GASB, and the applicable principles of the FASB and the AICPA contained in GASB-62. The framework for such principles is established in the GASB's Concepts Statements.

Although not considered generally accepted accounting principles themselves and nonauthoritative for preparers, users, and auditors, Concepts Statements are intended to provide a conceptual framework that can be used as a basis for establishing consistent accounting and financial reporting standards and serve multiple purposes, including the following:

- Identifying the objectives and fundamental principles of financial reporting that can be applied to solve numerous financial accounting and reporting issues,

- Providing the GASB with the basic conceptual foundation for considering the merits of alternative approaches to financial reporting and helping the GASB develop well-reasoned financial reporting standards, and

- Assisting preparers, auditors, and users in better understanding the fundamental concepts underlying financial reporting standards.

The GASB has issued seven Concepts Statements comprising the GASB's *Conceptual Framework*, as follows:

Concept Statement Number	Title
Concepts Statement No. 1	Objectives of Financial Reporting (GASB:CS-1)
Concepts Statement No. 2	Service Efforts and Accomplishments (GASB:CS-2)
Concepts Statement No. 3	Communication Methods in General Purpose External Financial Reports that Contain Basic Financial Statements (GASB:CS-3)
Concepts Statement No. 4	Elements of Financial Statements (GASB:CS-4)
Concepts Statement No. 5	Services Efforts and Accomplishments Reporting (an amendment to GASB Concepts Statement No. 2) (GASB:CS-5)
Concepts Statement No. 6	Measurement of Elements of Financial Statements (GASB:CS-6)
Concepts Statement No. 7	Communication Methods in General Purpose External Financial Reports That Contain Basic Financial Statements—Notes to Financial Statements (GASB:CS-7)

PRACTICE POINT: The most recent release clarifies the purpose of notes to financial statements and the users of those notes. There is also a consistent definition of the criteria for disclosing information in the notes to the basic financial statements, focusing on:

- The types of information disclosed in the notes,
- The types of information that are not appropriate for notes, and
- The degree of importance that information disclosed should possess.

The focal point on decisions to be made by the Board in the future will be whether information is *essential* in accordance with the updated framework. Determining whether a potential note would convey essential information will be the role of the GASB Staff. Staff will gather evidence if the information in the note is being utilized in users' analyses for making decisions or assessing accountability, or if the information became available, then users would modify their analyses for making decisions or assessing accountability to incorporate that information. The resulting framework is expected to be applied to all future GASB pronouncements and the reexamination of certain existing standards because of post-implementation reviews.

PRACTICE ALERT: The GASB is finalizing the update to the conceptual framework relating to the recognition and measurement of elements of financial statements. The goal of the project is to develop recognition criteria for whether information should be reported in state and local governmental financial statements and when that information should be reported. This project ultimately will lead to a Concepts Statement on recognition of elements of financial statements, with a primary focus on the basis of accounting proposed for governmental funds in the *Financial Reporting Model Improvements* project. Two paragraphs in GASB:CS-4 are proposed to be amended if the proposal is approved as drafted. A final *Concepts Statement* may be released by March 2024.

PRACTICE POINT: The importance of the term *conceptual framework* cannot be minimized. The conceptual framework of GAAP is contained in the following *Concepts Statements*, representing the guidance that the GASB uses to issue Statements and other authoritative guidance. The term is frequently used by GASB Board members and Staff. The conceptual framework is the bedrock on which all GAAP stands upon.

The following discussion describes these Concepts Statements and their accounting and reporting framework objectives.

Objectives of Financial Reporting

The purpose of financial reporting by state and local governmental entities is to provide information to facilitate decision-making by various user groups. GASB:CS-1 identifies the following primary user groups of governmental financial reports (GASB:CS-1, par. 30):

- Citizens of the governmental entity,
- Direct representatives of the citizens (legislatures and oversight bodies), and
- Investors, creditors, and others who are involved in the lending process.

Although not specifically identified in the above listing, GASB:CS-1 states that intergovernmental grantors and other users have informational needs like the three primary user groups (GASB:CS-1, par. 31).

The financial reporting objectives identified by the GASB in GASB:CS-1 are to be used as a framework for establishing accounting and reporting standards for general-purpose financial statements (GPFS) (more commonly known since the late 1990s as the basic financial statements), however, the framework may also be used by the GASB to establish standards for financial information presented outside of the GPFS. In addition, the financial reporting standards are applicable to general-purpose financial information presented in special-purpose financial reports prepared by state and local governmental entities (GASB:CS-1, pars. 8–9).

Although the governmental-type activities and business-type activities of a governmental entity can differ significantly, the GASB concluded that financial reporting objectives identified in GASB:CS-1 are applicable to both types of activities. Although financial reporting objectives are applicable to both governmental-type and business-type activities, the GASB does recognize that a specific objective may vary in its application to a reporting situation dependent on the business-type activity and the user group that is evaluating the activity. For example, both creditors and a legislative body may be interested in a business-type activity, but creditors may be more concerned with the ability of the activity to generate cash flow from operations to service future debt requirements, whereas the legislature may be more concerned with the likelihood of future operations requiring subsidies from general revenues (GASB:CS-1, par. 43).

GASB:CS-1 identifies *accountability* as the paramount objective of financial reporting by state and local governments. Accountability is based on the transfer of responsibility for resources or actions from the citizenry to another party, such as the management of a governmental entity. Financial reporting should communicate adequate information to user groups to enable them to assess the performance of those parties empowered to act in the place of the citizenry (GASB:CS-1, pars. 56–58).

The GASB states (1) that accountability is a more important concept in governmental financial reporting than in business enterprise financial reporting and (2) that all governmental financial reporting objectives are derived from the accountability concept. The objectives of governmental financial reporting identified in GASB:CS-1 are summarized in the Hierarchy of Objectives (see **EXHIBIT 1-2** later in this chapter). In addition to the overall objective of accountability, GASB:CS-1 identified the following as objectives of governmental financial reporting (GASB:CS-1, pars. 56–58):

- Financial reporting should assist in fulfilling a government's duty to be publicly accountable and should enable users to assess that accountability.

- Financial reporting should assist users in evaluating the operating results of the governmental entity for the year.

- Financial reporting should assist users in assessing the level of services that can be provided by the governmental entity and its ability to meet its obligations as they become due.

The GASB noted that although accountability is referred to only in the first objective, *accountability is implicit in all the listed objectives.*

Assessment of Accountability

The assessment of accountability is fulfilled in part when financial reporting enables user groups to determine to what extent current-period expenses are financed by current-period revenues. This reporting objective is based on the concept of communicating the extent to which the government achieved "interperiod equity," which is based on the position that the citizenry that benefits from an expense should pay for the expenses. Financial reporting should provide a basis for determining whether, during a budgetary period:

- A surplus was created (a benefit to the future citizenry),
- A deficit was incurred (a burden to the future citizenry),
- A surplus from a previous budgetary period was used to finance current expenditures (a benefit to the current citizenry),
- A deficit from a previous budgetary period was satisfied with current revenues (a burden to the current citizenry), or
- Current (and only current) expenses were financed by using current and only current revenues (interperiod equity) (GASB:CS-1, pars. 59–61).

PRACTICE POINT: As defined, interperiod equity is the concept that the citizenry that benefits from an expense should pay (fund) the expense. Many practitioners believe that the GASB conceptual framework includes the "matching principle." This is false. In for-profit and not-for-profit accounting, the "matching principle" (or concept) assumes that outflows must be paired with inflows to generate "profit" or "surplus." In the context of a government, taxation has no direct correlation with services provided. Fees and similar may have some correlation, but in many cases, the fees and similar are limited to the costs of the programs provided, including related debt service. Further, in many of these programs, the fees are only a part of the revenue stream. As an example, bus fares may only generate enough revenues to provide 20% of services provided, with the remainder in the form of *subsidies* from other levels of government. In the GASB's *Financial Reporting Model Improvements project* (see **PRACTICE ALERT**), a "subsidy" is proposed to be defined as:

1. Resources received from another party or fund to keep the rates lower than otherwise would be necessary to support the level of goods and services to be provided and
2. Resources provided to another party or fund that results in higher rates than otherwise would be established for the level of goods and services to be provided.

Financial reporting by a state or local government should provide a basis for user groups to determine whether

- The governmental entity obtained and used resources consistent with the legally adopted budget and
- Finance-related legal or contractual requirements have been met.

A budget reflects myriad public policies adopted by a legislative body and generally has the force of law as its basis for authority. The legally adopted budget is an important document in establishing and assessing the accountability of those responsible for the management of a governmental entity. While finance-related legal or contractual requirements are not as fundamental as the legally adopted budget, they nonetheless provide a basis for accountability, and financial reporting should demonstrate that accountability either has or has not been achieved with respect to the requirements (GASB:CS-1, pars. 39–41).

PRACTICE ALERT: The status of budgetary reporting is an integral part of the GASB's *Financial Reporting Model Improvements* project. The GASB is expected to determine the appropriate method of communication. Current GAAP requires presentation of comparisons of budget to actual amounts for the General Fund and each major special revenue fund with a legally adopted budget at a minimum. Current GAAP allows the budget to be reported as either basic financial statements *or* required supplementary information (RSI). (See discussion on GASB:CS-3 later in this section.) Current GAAP also presents the adopted budget, the final (amended) budget and actual amounts (using the budget's basis of accounting) with a variance column between the final and actual amounts.

The GASB has proposed in the Exposure Draft *Financial Reporting Model Improvements* to present budgetary reporting solely as required supplementary information (RSI). The reporting will include variances between the

1. Final budget and actual amounts and
2. Original budget and final budget amounts.

A discussion of significant variations between the original and final budget amounts and between the final budget amounts and actual results for the general fund are proposed to be presented as notes to budgetary comparison information, which is proposed to be presented as RSI as well. A final Statement may be issued by March 2024.

Assessing accountability of a governmental entity's management includes qualitative analysis (economy, efficiency, and effectiveness) and quantitative analysis. GASB:CS-1 states that accountability relates to service efforts, costs, and accomplishments. Financial reporting, when combined with other information, may enable user groups, for example, to determine whether certain efforts should be funded or whether elected officials should be continued in office. The information used to measure the economy, efficiency, and effectiveness of a governmental entity should be based on objective criteria. Such information may be used to compare a governmental entity's current operating results with its prior-period operating results or with other governmental entities' current operating results (GASB:CS-1, par. 79).

OBSERVATION: Accountability and the release of basic financial statements are not directly correlated, because a government may be involved in financial statement fraud. Several well-known scandals in state and local governments have involved governments changing the results of operations to make results look better than fiscal reality. Some of these governments even won awards for financial reporting disclosure only to have it be discovered that they were involved in financial statement fraud. Care must be taken to understand all a government's operations to properly gauge accountability. For many users, that understanding is nearly impossible. Many citizens may demand more transparency and immediacy in reporting in the future as a result.

EXHIBIT 1-2
HIERARCHY OF OBJECTIVES

GASB Concepts Statement No. 1 (GASB: CS-1)

OVERALL GOAL		ACCOUNTABILITY	
BASIC OBJECTIVES	Assist in fulfilling government's duty to be publicly accountable and enable users to assess that accountability	Assist users in evaluating the operating results of the government for the year	Assist users in assessing the level of services that can be provided by the governmental entity and its ability to meet its obligations as they become due.
COMPONENT OBJECTIVES:	• Sufficiency of current-year revenue	• Sources and uses of financial resources	• Financial position and condition
	• Compliance with budget and finance-related and contractual requirements	• Financing of activities and sources of cash	• Information related to physical and other nonfinancial resources
	• Assessment of governmental service efforts, costs, and accomplishments	• Effect of current-year operations on financial position	• Legal or contractual restrictions on resources and risk of loss of resources

Evaluation of Operating Results

Financial reporting should enable user groups to evaluate the operations of a state or local governmental entity. One aspect of operations evaluation is concerned with presenting information about sources and uses of financial resources. With respect to financial resource outflows, financial information presentations should identify all outflows and classify them by function (public health, public safety, etc.) and purpose (adult education, crime prevention, etc.). All financial resource inflows should be presented and identified by source (grants, bond proceeds, etc.) and type (taxes, fees, etc.). Resource inflows and outflows should be presented in a manner that enables user groups to determine the extent to which inflows are enough to finance outflows. In addition, nonrecurring inflows and outflows of resources should be disclosed in the financial report (GASB:CS-1, par. 78).

GASB:CS-1 also states that to evaluate operating results, financial reporting should enable user groups to determine how a governmental entity financed its activities and met its cash requirements (GASB:CS-1, par. 78).

OBSERVATION: To some extent, this component objective overlaps with the previous component objective (identification of sources and types of resource inflows). However, the objective of determining how cash requirements were met may require the preparation of a specific cash flow analysis, including the currently required preparation of a statement of cash flows for business-type activities.

Another element used in evaluating operations is the ability of the financial reporting to provide a basis for determining whether results of current operations improved or worsened the governmental entity's financial position as of the end of the current period (GASB:CS-1, par. 78).

Assessment of Fiscal Potential

Financial reporting should provide information concerning the financial position and condition of a state or local governmental entity. Resources should be described as current or noncurrent, and contingent liabilities should be disclosed. To assess the ability of an entity to raise resources from taxation, disclosure should include tax limitations, burdens, and sources. Likewise, the viability of issuing debt to raise revenues would require that an entity disclose debt limitations.

Disclosures in a financial report should enable user groups to assess current and long-term capital needs of the governmental entity. To this end, descriptions of physical and other nonfinancial resources with lives that extend beyond the current period should be included in the financial report. Such descriptions should include information that can be used to determine the service potential of such assets.

Finally, to allow financial statement users to assess the ability of a governmental entity to meet its obligations, the legal and contractual restrictions on resources and the potential loss of an entity's resources should be disclosed in the financial report.

Service Efforts and Accomplishments (GASB Concepts Statement No. 2—as amended by GASB Concepts Statements Nos. 3 and 5)

National Council on Governmental Accounting (NCGA) Concepts Statement 1 (*Objectives of Accounting and Financial Reporting for Governmental Units*) listed as one of its framework objectives "to provide information useful for evaluating managerial and organizational performance." The GASB was required by its 1984 structural agreement, which led in part to the Board's establishment, to recognize all NCGA statements until they were modified by the GASB. The GASB's Service Efforts and Accomplishments (SEA) reporting project has been a direct response to this mandated objective.

The GASB followed up the 1984 mandate to include in its accounting and financial reporting framework the objective "to provide information useful for evaluating managerial and organizational performance" with the issuance of Concepts Statement 2 (Service Efforts and Accomplishments) (GASB:CS-2) in 1994. GASB:CS-2 established the elements of SEA reporting, the objective and characteristics of SEA reporting, and the limitations of SEA information. The intent of GASB: CS-2 was to establish a framework for the development of "reporting standards" for performance measurement, not the establishment of the "performance standards."

Although the GASB conducted research and issued documents regarding reporting for SEA for over 20 years, several of the GASB's constituent groups expressed their opposition to the GASB's placing of SEA reporting project items on its technical agenda, citing concern that doing so would lead to the development of performance measurement standards by the GASB. One of the central issues in the SEA controversy is the contention that the GASB does not have the fundamental jurisdictional authority to provide guidance on SEA reporting, and that providing such guidance is contrary to the GASB's mission.

In response to this concern, in November 2006, the Financial Accounting Foundation (FAF) Board of Trustees, which serves as the oversight body for both the GASB and the FASB, reaffirmed that the GASB *does* have the jurisdictional authority to include SEA in its financial accounting and reporting standards-setting activities. The GASB issued a guide, *Suggested Guidelines for Voluntary Reporting: SEA Performance Information*, which contains topics on the applicability of the guidance, the essential components of SEA reports, qualitative characteristics of SEA performance information and effective communication of results. Its three appendices include illustration, background information, and board considerations.

In December 2008, the GASB issued GASB:CS-5, which amended certain portions of GASB:CS-2. The desired result of GASB SEA guidance is to provide guidelines on what might be reported regarding the foregoing categories of information and how to present or report it if a government *voluntarily* elects to do so.

GASB:CS-5 separates the "elements" of SEA performance measurement from the "related factors," clarifies the elements of SEA performance measures, and states that the elements of SEA reporting consist of three diverse types of measures:

- Measures of service efforts (i.e., inputs),
- Measures of service accomplishment (i.e., outputs and outcomes), and
- Measures that relate service efforts to service accomplishments (i.e., efficiency).

In addition, GASB:CS-5 provides examples of SEA information, which include the following performance measurement data for a governmental entity's operation:

- Inputs (e.g., tons of asphalt used to repair roads or number of teachers),
- Outputs (e.g., number of potholes filled, or number of students promoted),
- Outcomes (e.g., physical condition rating of roads or percentage of students entering college), and
- Efficiency (e.g., cost per pothole filled or cost per pupil educated).

There are other factors that affect external issues that influence the results and are related to SEA reporting but are not considered part of the basic measurement elements. The discussion of these related factors is expanded in GASB:CS-5 to address the following:

- Value of comparisons,
- Secondary effects of providing services,
- Relevance of demand for services,
- External or internal factors that influence SEA performance, and
- Explanatory information provided with SEA performance measures.

Communication Methods in Financial Reporting (GASB Concepts Statement No. 3—as amended by GASB Concepts Statements No. 7)

The GASB's Concepts Statement No. 3 (GASB:CS-3) (Communication Methods in General Purpose External Financial Reports That Contain Basic Financial Statements) provides a conceptual basis for selecting communication methods to present items of information within general-purpose external financial reports that contain basic financial statements. These communication methods include reporting in basic financial statements, disclosure in notes to basic financial statements, presentation as required supplementary information (RSI), and presentation as supplementary information (SI).

GASB:CS-3 defines the communication methods commonly used in general-purpose external financial reports, develops criteria for each communication method, and provides a hierarchy for their use. These definitions, criteria, and hierarchy should help the GASB, and all government financial statement preparers determine the appropriate methods to communicate information.

Once an item of information is considered appropriate for inclusion within general-purpose external financial reports, the appropriate communication method (placement) to be used to convey financial information should be determined. GASB:CS-3 states that this placement decision should be based on a hierarchy in the following order:

1. Recognition in basic financial statements,
2. Disclosure in notes to basic financial statements,
3. Presentation as RSI, and
4. Presentation as SI.

Recognition in the Basic Financial Statements

The financial statements provide a tabular presentation of amounts derived from the accounting records reflecting either the financial position of the reporting unit at a moment in time or inflows and outflows of resources during a period.

The criteria for financial information that is reported within the basic financial statements are as follows:

- Items are intended to provide reliable representation of the effects of transactions and other events, and
- Items are measurable with enough reliability.

   Example: Reporting a government's revenues and receivables from taxable events or transactions.

Disclosure in Notes to Basic Financial Statements (see previous **PRACTICE POINT**).

The notes to the financial statements are an integral part of the basic financial statements and are essential to users' understanding of a reporting unit's financial position and inflows and outflows of resources. Notes are to explain, describe and supplement the information contained in the basic financial statements to make decisions regarding the government. Without notes, the basic financial statements are incomplete and cannot be relied upon.

In understanding the notes, the users of the basic financial statements have a responsibility. Users need to gain a *reasonable* understanding of the government, public finance and at least the basics of state and local governmental financial reporting. Users need to utilize reasonable diligence and apply relevant analytical skills.

This does not mean that the average citizen needs to have a complete knowledge of GASB pronouncements. The framework contained in the Concepts Statement establishes the types of information to be included in the notes to the basic financial statements and the types of information to be excluded from the notes to the basic financial statements:

Included	Excluded
Descriptions of the accounting and finance-related policies underlying amounts recognized in financial statements.	*Subjective assessments* of the effects of reported information on the government's future financial position, other than expectations and assumptions about the future that are inputs to current measures in the financial statements or notes to financial statements.
More detail about or explanations of amounts recognized in financial statements.	*Predictions about the effects of future events* on future financial position.
Information about financial position or inflows and outflows of resources that does not meet the criteria for recognition.	General or educational information *that is not specific to the government.*
Other finance-related information associated with the accountability of the government.	

> **OBSERVATION:** The concept of "essentiality" should be tantamount to all note disclosure of a government. Many sections of notes to the basic financial statements are verbose or are boilerplate or have not been updated for recent events. The GASB strives to limit note disclosure to be in concurrence with the provisions of GASB:CS-3 at every discussion of new or amended note disclosure. Preparers should continuously review notes with an eye toward streamlining text for readability and clarity, updating for current events and foremost, compliance with standards. Preparers should especially review discretely presented component unit disclosures in the primary government again, asking if the notes from the discretely presented component unit are essential for the user's understanding.

As discussed, the GASB Staff will gather evidence to determine essential notes relating to a pending pronouncement. The evidence supporting this determination of essentiality is then applied to individual items. Like preparers, the GASB may use professional judgment in determining the elements to be proposed in a pronouncement. Part of the evidence obtained involves whether the perceived benefits of a proposed note disclosure exceed the costs of obtaining the information to prepare the note.

The conceptual framework for note disclosure applies to all reporting units of a government as reported in the government's basic financial statements.

Presentation as Required Supplementary Information

Required supplementary information (RSI) is supporting information that the GASB has concluded is essential for placing basic financial statements and notes in an appropriate operational, economic, or historical context.

The criteria for financial information that is reported as required supplementary information is as follows:

- Information that has a clear and demonstrable relationship to information in the financial statements or the notes to the basic statements, and
- Information that provides a context that enhances the decision-usefulness of the basic statements or notes.

Example: Ten-year schedules of net pension liability and notes to required supplementary information for defined benefit pension plans.

As is the case for the notes to the financial statements, GASB:CS-3 states that RSI should not include either subjective assessments of the effects of reported information on the reporting unit's future financial position or predictions about the effects of future events on future financial position. GASB:CS-3 also states that RSI should not include information unrelated to the financial statements.

As of the date of this publication, the GASB currently requires supplementary information as follows:

Required Supplementary Information	GASB Codification References [GASB Cod. Secs.]
Management's Discussion and Analysis	2200.106–.109.
Budgetary Comparisons (see previous **PRACTICE ALERT**)	2200.206–.207, 2400.102, .103, and .119.
Public entity risk pools—certain revenue and claims development information	Po20.147–.148.
Schedules of assessed condition and estimated and actual maintenance and preservation costs for governments that use the modified approach for infrastructure reporting	1400.118–.119.
Various pension information schedules presented by defined benefit pension plans, along with related notes	Pe5.128–.130
Various pension information schedules presented by employers that are members of defined benefit pension plans, along with related notes	P20.145, .181, .191, .197, .210, .216, .219, .229–.230.
Various pension information schedules for employers that are *not* within the scope of GASB Statement No. 68 or GASB Statement No. 78, along with related notes	P22.136, .157, .168, .180, .184–.187.
Various other post-employment benefit plan schedules presented by such plans, along with related notes	Po50.130–.132, also P53.
Various other post-employment benefit information schedules presented by employers who are members of post-employment benefit plans, along with related notes	P50 and P53—various throughout.

Presentation as Supplementary Information

Supplementary information (SI) is information that is useful for placing the financial statements and notes in an appropriate context, however, the GASB does not require the information to be presented in a reporting unit's general-purpose external financial report. However, if the government elects to prepare an annual comprehensive financial report (ACFR), certain supplemental information should be presented. See Chapter 20 for a further discussion of the ACFR.

The criteria for information that is reported as supplementary information are as follows:

- Information that is useful for placing basic financial statements and notes in an appropriate operational, economic, or historical context, and
- Information that is voluntarily included in a general-purpose external financial report.

Example: Reporting combining and individual fund financial statements for nonmajor funds.

PRACTICE POINT: Part of the determination of whether information should be presented as RSI or SI almost always includes the assurance placed on the distinct types of information. Two different sections of generally accepted auditing standards contain audit guidance related to each type of information: AU-C Section 725, *Supplementary Information in Relation to the Financial Statements as a Whole,* and AU-C Section 730, *Required Supplementary Information.* AU-C Section 730 includes additional procedures and reporting assurance due to the emphasis placed on the information required by (in this case) a GASB standard.

PRACTICE POINT: The Auditing Standards Board (ASB) recently amended the assurance provisions for *other information* (OI) (different than RSI or SI) through the release of Statement on Auditing Standards (SAS) 137. OI may be found in text, especially in introductory information in ACFRs.

PRACTICE POINT: Many governments have statutory requirements or bond covenants for continuing disclosure (see Chapter 12). Even if the schedules are in accordance with laws and regulations, they are supplementary information (SI) as they are not required by the GASB.

Elements of Financial Statements (GASB Concepts Statement No. 4)

The GASB white paper *Why Governmental Accounting and Financial Reporting Is—and Should Be—Different* makes a persuasive argument that public sector (governmental) accounting is fundamentally different from accounting outside the public sector (nongovernmental). For this reason, the elements reported within the financial statements of state and local governments and their measurement and recognition criteria deserve different consideration. To provide the framework for establishing accounting principles related to the elements of financial statements and their measurement and recognition within the financial statements, the GASB issued GASB:CS-4 (*Elements of Financial Statements*) and is deliberating another concepts statement on recognition attributes.

GASB:CS-4 identifies and defines seven elements, and it states that the definitions of the elements are to be applied to a governmental unit (i.e., a separate legal entity that is an organization created as, for example, a body corporate or a body corporate and politic). A reporting entity may include more than one governmental unit, and a governmental unit may consist of one or more reporting units. The rationale behind this entity concept is that control over resources and obligations to sacrifice resources, which are inherent characteristics of elements of financial statements, are manifested only at the governmental unit level, not at the reporting unit level. When financial statements are prepared for a reporting unit (e.g., a fund, a segment, or other subset of a legally separate entity, such as a state department of transportation), the elements of the reporting unit (e.g., the state department of transportation) are the elements of the governmental unit (e.g., the state) that have been assigned to that reporting unit for control, management, or financial reporting purposes.

The seven elements are the fundamental components of financial statements and can be organized by the specific financial statement to which they relate.

Elements of the Statement of Financial Position

GASB:CS-4 provides that the elements of a "statement of financial position" be defined as follows:

Element	Definition
Assets	Resources with a present service capacity that the entity presently controls.
Deferred Outflow of Resources	Consumption of net position by the entity that is applicable to a future reporting period.
Liabilities	Present obligations to sacrifice resources that the entity has little or no discretion to avoid.
Deferred Inflow of Resources	Acquisition of net position by the entity that is applicable to a future reporting period.
Net Position	The residual of all other elements presented in a statement of financial position.

The deferred outflow of resources and deferred inflow of resources elements were established by the GASB due to the importance placed on the concept of interperiod equity. These deferred positions can be thought of as future revenues and expenses waiting to be reported when required conditions have been met or a point in time has been reached. Although GASB:CS-4 does not provide specific examples of deferred outflow or inflow of resources, such elements are included in various transactions relating to hedging derivative instruments, defined benefit plans, other postemployment benefits, asset retirement obligations, irrevocable split-interest agreements, and other standards. Each issued GASB standard indicates whether a deferred outflow or inflow of resources may result from recognition of an accounting event.

Use of the Terms "Deferred", "Advance" or "Unearned" versus "Deferred Revenue"

This transaction does not meet the definition of a deferred inflow of resources because an acquisition of net position has not occurred. An asset (cash) increased and the liability to perform under the terms of the grant increased. Thus, net position is unchanged. The GASB believes that items such as these should be described in financial statements without using the term "deferred" in the caption. For instance, in the example, the captions "Advances from grantors" or "unearned revenue" should be used, rather than "deferred revenue." The GASB believes that financial statements would be more understandable to users if the term "deferred" was reserved for items meeting the definition of deferred inflows or outflows of resources. GAAP requires that the term "deferred" only be used in conjunction with deferred inflows of resources or deferred outflows of resources [GASB Cod. Secs. 1800.109 –.110, 2200.175 –.176, 2250.132, 2250.137, 2450.129, L30.114, N50.112 –.113, S20.110, S20.113].

Though seemingly mature in definition, the term "liability" is often misunderstood as contained within it are the concepts of obligations and, to some extent, time. An obligation is a social, legal, or moral requirement, such as a duty, contract, or promise that compels one to follow or avoid a course of action.

Obligations can be legally enforceable as exemplified when a court compels the government to fulfill its obligation. Obligations could arise from legislation or contractual obligations. They may differ, though, based on whether exchange transactions (value for value) or nonexchange transactions take place. Constructive liabilities may occur in exchange transactions when resources are transferred to a government. In this case, the government must fulfill its obligations. The concept of "little or no discretion to avoid" arises when no power exists to decline sacrificing of resources or penalty/consequences of not doing the action is more than minor.

One of the consistent themes in all these nuances is that the parties to an obligation that may be a liability are usually external to the government.

GASB Cod. Sec. 1500.118 describes "matured liabilities" in governmental funds only (not associated with proprietary or fiduciary funds) as those that are normally due and payable in full when incurred or the matured portion of general long-term indebtedness (the portion that has come due for payment).

GASB Cod. Sec. 1500.119 also lists matured liabilities including debt service on formal debt issued when due (matured) compensated absences, claims and judgments, special termination benefits, and landfill closure and post-closure care costs. All of these should be recognized as governmental fund liabilities and expenditures to the extent the liabilities are "normally expected to be liquidated with expendable available financial resources."

The GASB has considered but rejected an alternative interpretation that "other commitments" are the long-term portion of any other liabilities, provided that the government has entered into a multilateral agreement to defer payment to a future period. The GASB has concluded that there is no accrual modification that would permit deferring to a future period the recognition of fund liabilities (such as salaries and utilities) that normally are paid in a timely manner and in full, from current financial resources when incurred. Rather, the GASB proposed that such transactions should be reported as governmental fund liabilities and expenditures when incurred.

OBSERVATION: The controversy of recognition of a liability stems from the changing landscape of government operations. For example, postemployment benefits in many jurisdictions may be changed in law without collective bargaining, leading to the notion that these benefits may not be liabilities. The GASB's conclusions, mentioned above, are also leading to the interpretation (perhaps, rightfully so) that no liability would exist in a governmental fund that normally pays salary escalations that cannot be paid out of current financial resources due to economic conditions. The escalations are then renegotiated to be paid in a future period, even though in a statement of net position, a liability may be declared for the same circumstance.

PRACTICE ALERT: As previously discussed, the concept of maturity has many implications in the Exposure Draft *Financial Reporting Model Improvement* and the companion Exposure Draft *Recognition of Elements of Financial State-*

ments. Among other proposed provisions for governmental funds, the Board has proposed that the following characteristics of transactions will be required for recognition in the governmental fund financial statements:

- Payment terms should be established by the specific applicable contractual (or statutory) terms of the transaction or other event or estimated payments when there are no contractual terms.
- Items arising from long-term transactions and other events should be recognized when due—the date at which payment is scheduled or, if not scheduled, expected to be made in accordance with the recognition terms.
- The recognition period should be one year.

A final *Concepts Statement* may be released by March 2024.

Elements of the Resource Flows Statement

GASB:CS-4 provides that the elements of the "resource flows (change) statements" be defined as follows:

Element	Definition
Outflow of Resources	A consumption of net position by the entity that is applicable to the reporting period (expenses as used in nongovernmental funds and government-wide financial statements or expenditures as used in governmental funds) (see previous **PRACTICE ALERT** on *Recognition of Elements of Financial Statements*).
Inflow of Resources	An acquisition of net position by the entity that is applicable to the reporting period (revenues).

The consumption of net position (outflow) is defined as the using up of net position that results in:

- A decrease in assets more than any related decrease in liabilities or
- An increase in liabilities more than any related increase in assets.

Examples of consumption of resources include:

- Using cash resources to make direct aid payments to eligible recipients (because existing cash resources of the entity have been consumed) and
- Using the labor of employees to provide government services for which payment will be made in the next reporting period (because the entity has consumed employee labor resources that were directly acquired from the employees).

The acquisition of net position (inflow) is defined as net position coming under the control of the entity or net position becoming newly available to the entity even if the resources are consumed directly when acquired. An acquisition of net position results in:

- An increase in assets more than any related increase in liabilities or
- A decrease in liabilities more than any related decrease in assets.

Examples of acquisition of net position include:

- Imposing a tax (because the resources have newly come under the control of the entity) and
- Performing under the conditions of a grant received in advance (because liabilities of the entity have been satisfied, thereby increasing the entity's net position).

OBSERVATION: The GASB has taken an approach to defining the elements of the financial statements that is different from the approaches used by other standards-setting bodies to date. Other standard setters, such as the Financial Accounting Standards Board (FASB) and the International Accounting Standards Board (IASB), define financial statement elements in relation to each other. For example, revenues are defined as an inflow of or increase in assets, thereby making the definition of revenues dependent on the definition of assets. Because of the inherent differences between private companies and governments, and the importance of assessing interperiod equity in government, the GASB developed its financial statement elements independent of each other to the extent possible.

Measurement of Elements of Financial Statements

GASB Concepts Statement No. 6 (GASB:CS-6), *Measurement of Elements of Financial Statements*, addresses both measurement approaches and measurement attributes. A "measurement approach" determines whether an asset or liability presented in a financial statement should be either (a) reported at an amount that reflects a value at the date that the asset was acquired, or the liability was incurred or (b) remeasured and reported at an amount that reflects a value at the date of the financial statements. A "measurement attribute" is the feature or characteristic of the asset or liability that is measured.

GASB:CS-6 contains the two measurement approaches that would be used in financial statements, as follows:

- *Initial-Transaction-Date-Based Measurement (Initial Amount)* This is commonly known as "historical cost." GASB:CS-6 defines the "initial amount" as the transaction price or amount assigned when an asset was acquired, or a liability was incurred, including subsequent modifications to that price or amount, such as through depreciation or impairment.
- *Current-Financial-Statement-Date-Based Measurement (Remeasured Amount)* This is commonly known as "current value" but may be at fair value, replacement value, or settlement price. The commonality among the values is that they are defined as the amount assigned when an asset or liability is remeasured as of the financial statement date.

GASB:CS-6 established the four measurement attributes that would be used in financial statements, as follows:

- *Historical cost* is the price paid to acquire an asset or the amount received pursuant to the incurrence of a liability in an actual exchange transaction.

- *Fair value* is the price that would be received to sell an asset or paid to transfer a liability in an orderly transaction between market participants at the measurement date.
- *Replacement cost* is the price that would be paid to acquire an asset with equivalent service potential in an orderly market transaction at the measurement date.
- *Settlement amount* is the amount at which an asset could be realized, or a liability could be liquidated with the counterparty other than in an active market.

The GASB frequently must decide whether an item of information should be recognized in the financial statements, when such an item should be recognized, and at what amount it should be recognized. In the past, the GASB has relied on the conceptual framework of other standards setters and analogous examples from practice or previous standards to make such decisions. This method of making decisions can lead to certain inconsistencies in financial reporting standards and could result in too much reliance being placed on accounting concepts that were not developed for a governmental environment. The concepts statement project on recognition and measurement attributes will ultimately provide the GASB with conceptual guidance as to when elements of financial statements should be reported in which financial statements and at what amount (including the development of recognition criteria and a discussion of when elements of financial statements are recognized using different measurement focuses) (see previous **PRACTICE ALERT** on the conceptual framework for recognition).

SUMMARY OF BASIC GOVERNMENTAL ACCOUNTING PRINCIPLES

The objectives of governmental financial reporting discussed earlier in this chapter are the basis for determining specific accounting principles to be used by a governmental entity. Certain general principles of accounting and reporting are applicable to governmental entities. These principles, which are summarized in GASB Cod. Sec. 1100, provide a broad overview of financial reporting and are as follows:

- Accounting and reporting capabilities,
- Fund accounting systems,
- Fund types,
- Number of funds,
- Reporting, valuing, and depreciating capital assets,
- Reporting long-term liabilities,
- Measurement focus and basis of accounting in basic financial statements,
- To some extent, budgeting, budgetary control, and budgetary reporting,
- Transfer, revenue, expenditure, and expense account classification,
- Common terminology and classification,

- Annual financial reports, and
- Interim financial reporting.

Accounting and Reporting Capabilities

A governmental entity's accounting system should be designed to achieve the following:

- Present fairly and with full disclosure the funds and activities of the government in conformity with applicable generally accepted accounting principles, and
- Determine and demonstrate compliance with finance-related legal and contractual provisions [GASB Cod. Sec. 1100.101].

Such systems are commonly known as "the book of record." Auditors and users of a governmental entity's financial information place reliance on the internal controls contained in an accounting system to provide enough reliable evidence that the amounts and disclosures contained in the annual financial report are fairly stated. Therefore, such capabilities are vital to a governmental entity's success.

Manual Accounting Systems. In small governments, books of record may still be handwritten or may use rudimentary systems with minimal internal controls. Though the cost of these systems may be reasonable, the cost must be balanced with the integrity of the information within the books of record. Handwritten systems rely on the accuracy of transferring information from source documentation to ledgers and in many cases, performed by a single person. Even in rudimentary systems, transactions may be deleted without independent approval. Without segregation of duties, the risk of material misstatement greatly increases. A lack of segregation of duties may be alleviated somewhat with rigorous independent, timely review and oversight by a governing body such as a Board or Council. An independent audit is not meant to be the sole internal control.

Fund Accounting Systems

A "Fund" is defined as follows:

> A fiscal and accounting entity with a self-balancing set of accounts recording cash and other financial resources, together with all related liabilities and residual equities or balances, and changes therein, which are segregated for carrying on specific activities or attaining certain objectives in accordance with special regulations, restrictions, or limitations.

The detailed transactions and resulting balances of a governmental entity (the primary government as well as its blended component units) are generally recorded in individual funds, however, GAAP requires that only major funds be reported individually in a governmental entity's basic financial statements [GASB Cod. Sec. 1100.102].

Funds are the basic compliance elements of many governmental operations. Governments need to align to legal provisions in the establishment and operations of funds. A best practice is to limit the amount of funds to what is necessary to operate the government. Otherwise, budgetary and compliance activity may be obscured by movement of amounts in between funds (see the section on **Number of Funds** later in the chapter).

> **PRACTICE POINT:** The legal status of funds is one of the major differences between governments and nongovernmental entities. Due to the structure of funds in governments and the role of the budget in providing spending authority for funds, the structure of *reporting units* arises. Chapter 20 presents a section on fund financial statements and the importance of reporting major funds in governmental and proprietary fund statements (described in the following section). As further discussed in CCH's *Knowledge-Based Audits of Governmental Entities (Post SAS-134)* (found on CCH's Accounting Research Manager™), "The financial reporting model for general purpose governments is primarily based on multiple reporting units with financial statements based on different reporting models. For example, the auditor's report consists of opinions on the major governmental funds and major proprietary funds, with nonmajor funds of each presented in the aggregate. Special-purpose governments may only have one reporting unit. Therefore, each reporting unit is an opinion unit for auditors. The auditor then is required to express (or disclaim) an opinion on each opinion unit, focusing on materiality at each unit level. Therefore, 'mixed' reports may result, with an unmodified opinion for a unit and a modified (or disclaimed) opinion for another." Capturing the transactions and results of operations in funds becomes a key operation of management, legal compliance, and reporting for any government under the current financial reporting model.

Fund Types

Fund-based financial statements must be included in a governmental entity's financial report to demonstrate that restrictions imposed by statutes, regulations, or contracts have been followed. GAAP identifies the following as fund types that are to be used to record a governmental entity's activities during an accounting period:

- **Governmental Funds** (emphasizing major funds)
  — General Fund
  — Special Revenue Funds (see **PRACTICE ALERT** on the *Financial Reporting Model Improvements* project)
  — Capital Projects Funds
  — Debt Service Funds
  — Permanent Funds
- **Proprietary Funds** (emphasizing major funds)
  — Enterprise Funds
  — Internal Service Funds
- **Fiduciary Funds** (and Similar Component Units)
  — Pension (and other employee benefit) Trust Funds
  — Investment Trust Funds
  — Private-Purpose Trust Funds
  — Custodial Funds [GASB Cod. Sec. 1100.103].

> **OBSERVATION:** The fund classification provisions described in this section are for *external reporting*. The GASB does not direct how a governmental entity should construct its *internal* accounting structure to fulfill legal requirements or satisfy management strategies. For example, a government may maintain an account for a separate fund in its internal accounting system for resources administratively set aside for replacement of equipment. For external financial reporting purposes, this fund could be consolidated within the General Fund.

Governmental Funds (See Chapter 6)

Financial statements for governmental funds have a short-term emphasis and generally measure and account for cash and "other assets that can easily be converted to cash." GAAP requires fund reporting be restricted to a governmental entity's General Fund and its "major" funds.

Governmental funds primarily deal with general purpose activities and are funded largely from taxation, grants, transfers from other funds, and special assessments. In the case of a capital project, bonds are also a funding source and for permanent funds, donations are a funding source.

Below are the definitions of governmental fund type [GASB Cod. Secs. 1300.104–.108]:

Fund Type	Definition
General Fund	To account for and report all financial resources not accounted for and reported in another fund.
Special Revenue Funds	To account for and report the proceeds of specific revenue sources that are restricted or committed to expenditure for specified purposes other than debt service or capital projects (see **PRACTICE ALERT** on the *Financial Reporting Model*).
Capital Project Funds	To account for and report financial resources that are restricted, committed, or assigned to expenditure for capital outlays, including the acquisition or construction of capital facilities or other capital assets.
Debt Service Funds	To account for and report financial resources that are restricted, committed, or assigned to expenditure for principal and interest.
Permanent Funds	To account for and report resources that are restricted to the extent that only earnings, and not principal, may be used for purposes that support the reporting government's programs—that is, for the benefit of the government or its citizenry.

Proprietary Funds (See Chapter 7)

Financial statements for proprietary funds should be based on the flow of economic resources measurement focus and the accrual basis of accounting. The proprietary fund category includes Enterprise Funds and Internal Service Funds.

Enterprise Funds. This fund type may be used to "report any activity for which a fee is charged to external users for goods or services." An enterprise fund *must* be used to account for an activity *if any one* of the following three criteria is satisfied [GASB Cod. Sec. 1300.109]:

- The activity is financed with debt that is secured *solely* by a pledge of the net revenues from fees and charges of the activity.
- Laws or regulations require that the activity's costs of providing services, including capital costs (such as depreciation or capital debt service), be recovered with fees and charges, rather than with taxes or similar revenues.
- The pricing policies of the activity establish fees and charges designed to recover its costs, including capital costs (such as depreciation or debt service).

The first criterion refers to debt secured solely by fees and charges. If that debt is secured by a pledge of fees and charges from the activity and the full faith and credit of the primary government or component unit, this arrangement does not satisfy the "sole source of debt security" criterion and the activity does not have to be accounted for (assuming the other two criteria are not satisfied) in an Enterprise Fund. This conclusion is not changed even if it is anticipated that the primary government or component unit is not expected to make debt payments under the arrangement.

Unemployment Compensation Funds. Specifically for states, footnote 6 to GASB Cod. Sec. 1300.109(b) states that State Unemployment Compensation Funds meet the definition of an Enterprise Fund due to the second criterion. The third criterion should be used to account for an activity where GAAP is based on "established policies" rather than on management's intent.

The three criteria should be applied to a governmental entity's principal revenue sources. However, the criteria do not have to be applied to "insignificant activities" of a governmental entity. If none of the criteria applies, the activity can be accounted for in a governmental fund.

It should be noted that a fee-based activity can be accounted for in an Enterprise Fund even if the three criteria described above do not exist. The three criteria apply to fee-based activities that must be accounted for in an Enterprise Fund.

Internal Service Funds. An Internal Service Fund may be used to account for activities that involve the governmental entity providing goods or services within its own entity. In other words, the government is selling to itself, inclusive of component units of the government. The following are the common elements of internal service funds:

- The fund operations are for activities of the primary government or its component units, or other governments on a cost reimbursement basis and

- The reporting entity is the *predominant* participant in the activity. If the reporting entity is not the predominant participant, the activity should be reported in an Enterprise Fund [GASB Cod. Sec. 1300.110].

Fiduciary Funds (See Chapter 8)

OBSERVATION: GASB Cod. Secs. 1300.128–.136 identify the requirements for reporting an activity as a fiduciary activity focusing on whether a government is controlling the assets of the fiduciary activity and the beneficiaries with whom a fiduciary relationship exists. An activity meeting the criteria is to be reported in the fiduciary funds. An exception is provided for a business-type activity that normally expects to hold custodial assets (as defined) for three months or less. Fiduciary component units are combined with information from fiduciary funds (as described in Chapter 4).

Assets held by a governmental entity for other parties (either as a trustee or as an agent) and that cannot be used to finance the governmental entity's own operating programs should be reported in the fiduciary fund category, which includes:

- Pension (and other employee benefit) Trust Funds,
- Investment Trust Funds,
- Private-Purpose Trust Funds, and
- Custodial Funds.

Trust funds are present when the assets are:

- Administered through a trust agreement or equivalent arrangement (hereafter jointly referred to as a trust) in which the government itself is not a beneficiary,
- Dedicated to providing benefits to recipients in accordance with the benefit terms, and
- Legally protected from the creditors of the government [GASB Cod. Sec. 1300.131(a)].

Similar language is used for pension (and other employee benefit) trust funds as follows:

Pension Plans	Other Employee Benefit Plans (OPEB)
• Contributions from employers and nonemployer contributing entities to the pension plan and earnings from those contributions are irrevocable.	• Contributions from employers and nonemployer contributing entities to the OPEB plan and earnings from those contributions are irrevocable.
• Pension plan assets are dedicated to providing pensions to plan members in accordance with the benefit terms.	• OPEB plan assets are dedicated to providing pensions to plan members in accordance with the benefit terms.

Pension Plans	Other Employee Benefit Plans (OPEB)
• Pension plan assets are legally protected from the creditors of the employers, nonemployer contributing entities, and the pension plan administrator. If the plan is a defined benefit pension plan, pension plan assets also are legally protected from creditors of the plan members. The use of plan assets to pay plan administrative costs or to refund employee contributions in accordance with benefit terms is consistent with this criterion.	• OPEB plan assets are legally protected from the creditors of the employers, nonemployer contributing entities, and the OPEB plan administrator. If the plan is a defined benefit OPEB plan, OPEB plan assets also are legally protected from creditors of the plan members. The use of plan assets to pay plan administrative costs or to refund employee contributions in accordance with benefit terms is consistent with this criterion.

For pension or OPEB plans, in some circumstances, payments are made by the employer to satisfy contribution requirements that are identified by the pension plan terms as plan member contribution requirements. Those amounts should be classified as employee contributions, including for purposes of determining a cost-sharing employer's proportion. An employer's expense and expenditures for those amounts should be recognized in the period for which the contribution is assessed and classified in the same manner as the employer classifies similar compensation other than pensions (e.g., as salaries and wages or as fringe benefits) [GASB Cod. Secs. P20.101, fns. 2 and 3, P50.101, fns. 2 and 3].

Defined contribution pension and OPEB plans have similar trust language. For the purposes of such plans, refunds to an employer or nonemployer contributing entity of the non-vested portion of its contributions (not the employees') that are forfeited by employees are also consistent with the legal protection criteria stated above [GASB Cod. Secs. P21, fn. 3, P51, fn. 3].

The three trust funds are used to report resources and activities when the governmental entity is acting as a trustee (i.e., a fiduciary capacity) for individuals, private organizations, and other governments.

Pension (and other Employee Benefit) Trust Funds. This fund type is used to report fiduciary activities for pension plans and OPEB plans that are administered through trusts that meet the above criteria. They are also used for other employee benefit plans for which resources are held in a trust where the assets associated with the activity are:

- Administered through a trust in which the government itself is *not* a beneficiary,
- Dedicated to providing benefits to recipients in accordance with the benefit terms, and
- Legally protected from creditors of the government.

In addition, contributions to the trust and earnings on those contributions are irrevocable [GASB Cod. Sec. 1300.112].

> **PRACTICE POINT:** If an other employee benefit plan meets the criteria for reporting within GASB Cod. Secs. 1300.128–.136, especially if the government has control of plan assets, the plan is reported as a pension (and other employee benefit) trust fund. If the government has several plans, a combining schedule may be used.

Investment Trust Funds. An *investment trust fund* is used to report fiduciary activities from the *external* portion of investment pools and individual investment accounts that are held in a trust that meets the criteria specified in GASB Cod. Sec. 1300.134(c)(1):

- Administered through a trust in which the government itself is *not* a beneficiary,
- Dedicated to providing benefits to recipients in accordance with the benefit terms, and
- Legally protected from creditors of the government.

An *individual investment account* is an investment service provided by a governmental entity for other legally separate entities that are not part of the same reporting entity. With individual investment accounts, specific investments are acquired for individual entities and the income from and changes in the value of those investments affect only the entity for which they were acquired [GASB Cod. Secs. 1300.113, I50.138]. Small governments or other organizations that have such accounts at a larger government use the larger government's professional investing capabilities for the smaller entities' benefit.

Private-Purpose Trust Funds. These types of funds are used to report all fiduciary activities that (a) are *not* required to be reported in pension (and other employee benefit) trust funds or investment trust funds and (b) are held in a trust that meets the criteria mentioned previously on administration, dedication, and legal protection.

In some cases, *public-purpose funds* may be a term used in legislation. For financial reporting purposes, they are classified as Special Revenue Funds. Nonexpendable Trust Funds are classified as Permanent Funds. For example, a Private-Purpose Trust Fund would be used to account for escheat property as currently described in GASB Cod. Sec. E70 (*Accounting for Escheat Property*) [GASB Cod. Sec. 1300.114].

Custodial Funds. These funds are used to report fiduciary activities that are *not* required to be reported in pension (and other employee benefit) trust funds, investment trust funds, or private-purpose trust funds. The external portion of investment pools that are *not held in a trust* that meets the criteria mentioned previously should be reported in a separate *external investment pool fund* column, under the custodial fund classification. However, in practice, external investment pools not held in trust are rare [GASB Cod. Sec. 1300.115].

> **OBSERVATION:** Business-type activities and enterprise funds may report assets with a corresponding liability that otherwise should be reported in a

custodial fund in the statement of net position of the business-type activity if those assets, upon receipt, are normally expected to be held for three months or less. A business-type activity that chooses to report such assets and liabilities in its statement of net position should separately report additions and deductions, if significant, as cash inflows and cash outflows, respectively, in the operating activities category of its statement of cash flows [GASB Cod. Sec. 1300.116].

Governmental and Proprietary Fund Financial Statements—Focus on Major Funds

A governmental entity should report financial statements for its governmental and proprietary funds, but the basis for reporting these funds is not by fund type but rather by major funds [GASB Cod. Sec. 2200.157]. Major funds are reported separately within the fund financial statements. All other funds defined as nonmajor are then combined for reporting purposes. Internal service funds are not separated by major or nonmajor and are reported in one column, but they may be separate in a combining statement.

A major fund satisfies both of the following criteria [GASB Cod. Secs. 2200.158–.159]:

- Total assets, liabilities, revenues, or expenditures/expenses of the governmental (enterprise) fund are equal to or greater than 10% of the corresponding total (assets, liability, and so forth) for all funds that are considered governmental funds (enterprise funds), and

- Total assets, liabilities, revenues, or expenditures/expenses of the governmental fund (enterprise fund) are equal to or greater than 5% of the corresponding total for all governmental and enterprise funds combined.

Major fund determination calculations are performed on a yearly basis. In determining total revenues and expenditures/expenses each year, extraordinary items are excluded.

The General Fund is always considered a major fund and, therefore, must be presented in a separate column. Major fund reporting requirements do not apply to Internal Service Funds or Fiduciary Funds.

PRACTICE POINT: For governments with many funds, combining statements may be utilized as supplementary information.

If a fund does not satisfy the conditions described above, it can still be presented as a major fund if the governmental entity believes it is important to do so. All other funds that are not considered major funds must be combined in a separate column and labeled as nonmajor funds. Thus, there could be a nonmajor funds column for governmental funds and enterprise funds.

PRACTICE POINT: The importance of the major fund calculation/adjudication by the preparer cannot be underestimated. The number of major funds has a direct relationship to the amount of major funds presented in the balance sheet (or statement of fund net position) and the statement of revenues, expenditures, and changes in fund balance (or statement of revenues, expenses, and changes in fund net position) and the level of auditing of those funds. Care must be taken in the determination of these funds and the presentation to the auditor as part of the commencement of fieldwork on the engagement.

Number of Funds

A basic principle of governmental generally accepted accounting principles is that the actual number of funds used by a governmental entity should be kept to a minimum to avoid the creation of an inefficient financial system. In general, the number of funds established must be enough to meet operational needs and legal restrictions imposed on the organization. For example, only one General Fund should be maintained. In some circumstances, it may be possible to account for restricted resources in the General Fund and still meet imposed legal requirements. Also, there may be no need to establish a Special Revenue Fund unless specifically required by law [GASB Cod. Sec. 1100.104].

Reporting, Valuing, and Depreciating Capital Assets

At the fund-financial statement level, capital assets are not reported in governmental funds but are reported in proprietary funds and fiduciary funds (if any). A governmental entity's capital assets (apart from those of fiduciary funds) are reported in the government-wide financial statements and identified as related to either governmental activities or business-type activities [GASB Cod. Sec. 1100.105].

The governmental entity should report all its capital assets, based on their original historical cost, adding to the cost ancillary charges such as transportation, installation, and site preparation costs, unless there is a specific GASB pronouncement with different recognition principles. For example, donated capital assets, donated works of art, historical treasures, and similar assets as well as capital assets received in a service concession arrangement are reported at *acquisition value*, plus ancillary charges (if any) pursuant to GASB Cod. Sec. 1400.102 [GASB Cod. Sec. 1100.106].

Acquisition value is an entry price, whereas fair value is an "exit price." Acquisition value as the price that would be paid to acquire an asset with equivalent service potential in an orderly market transaction at the acquisition date, or the amount at which a liability could be liquidated with the counterparty at the acquisition date [GASB Cod. Sec. 1400, fn1].

GAAP contains an exception to acquisition value usage specifically relating to recognition and measurement of a government acquisition (a government combination) and solely where the acquired government as an asset retirement obligation (ARO). The acquiring government would use the accounting and financial reporting requirements of GASB Cod. Sec. A10, *Asset Retirement Obligations*, instead of GASB Cod. Sec. Co10, *Combinations and Disposals of Operations*, for the acceptable accounting and financial reporting in that specific circumstance. Further information on AROs is also contained in Chapter 10.

Under certain conditions, works of art, historical treasures, and similar assets do not have to be capitalized. This exception is discussed in Chapter 10.

Foundation and Overview of Governmental GAAP 1051

The cost (net of estimated salvage value) of capital assets (except for certain infrastructure assets) should be depreciated over the estimated useful lives of the assets. Inexhaustible capital assets (such as land, land improvements, and certain infrastructure assets where a government has elected to take a modified approach) should not be depreciated if the provisions of GAAP are met. These provisions are also discussed in Chapter 10.

Depreciation expense should be reported in the government-wide financial statements (statement of activities), financial statements for proprietary funds (statement of revenues, expenses, and changes in fund net position), and financial statements for fiduciary funds (statement of changes in fiduciary net position). Depreciation expense is not reported in governmental funds (the General Fund, Special Revenue Funds, and so forth).

Amortization expense for right-to-use and other intangible assets is reported similarly to depreciation. GAAP contains no provision to report amortization separately from depreciation. In practice, some governments report a combined element—*Depreciation and Amortization Expense*.

PRACTICE ALERT: As the *Guide* was in the process of publication, the GASB released an Exposure Draft, *Classification of Nonfinancial Assets*. The scope is tentatively limited to the classification of nonfinancial assets and related presentation and disclosure issues. Tangible capital assets, certain types of investments and intangible assets are within the scope of the project. The Board has tentatively concluded that intangible capital assets should be classified separately from tangible capital assets by requiring them to be reported by major class separate from major classes of tangible capital assets. Lease and other right-to-use assets would be reported similarly. The Board was deliberating the implementation provisions as the *Guide* was being published. The 2025 *Guide* will contain additional information on this project in Chapter 10.

Capital assets should also be evaluated for impairment when events or changes in circumstances suggest that the service utility of a capital asset may have been significantly and unexpectedly declined [GASB Cod. Sec. 1100.107].

PRACTICE ALERT: GASB Staff have begun pre-agenda research on whether capital asset accounting and financial reporting should change in the future.

Reporting Long-Term Liabilities

There are three distinct, major categories of long-term liabilities for most governments: the various forms of debt, defined benefit pensions, and defined benefit postemployment benefits other than pensions. Long-term liabilities related to proprietary funds should be reported both in government-wide financial statements and the fund financial statements.

> **PRACTICE POINT:** Long-term liabilities directly related to and expected to be paid from proprietary funds should be reported in the proprietary fund statement of net position as well as the government-wide statement of net position. This aspect is common in defined benefit pensions and postemployment benefits other than pensions. If a proprietary fund is separately audited and presented as a stand-alone financial statement, the fund must also present such liabilities in accordance with GAAP as applicable.

Fiduciary funds rarely have long-term liabilities due to the nature of operations in such funds. Any liabilities of pension and postemployment benefits other than pensions are liabilities of the government/employers. All other long-term liabilities that are not properly presented in either proprietary funds or fiduciary funds are general long-term liabilities and should be reported only in the governmental activities column of the statement of net position (a government-wide financial statement) [GASB Cod. Sec. 1100.108].

Measurement Focus and Basis of Accounting in the Basic Financial Statements

Government-wide financial statements provide a basis for determining (1) the extent to which current services provided by the entity were financed with current revenues and (2) the degree to which a governmental entity's financial position has changed during the fiscal year. To achieve these objectives, government-wide financial statements include a statement of net position and a statement of activities.

Accrual Basis of Accounting in Government-Wide, Proprietary, and Fiduciary Statements

The statement of net position and the statement of activities are prepared using the economic resources measurement focus and the accrual basis of accounting, similarly to a for-profit or not-for-profit entity. Revenues, expenses, gains, losses, assets, deferred outflows of resources, liabilities, and deferred inflows of resources resulting from exchange and exchange-like transactions should be recognized when the exchange takes place. Deferred outflows of resources and deferred inflows of resources may be presented if occurred and required by provisions of GAAP. Revenue from exchange transactions generally is recognized when an exchange, under normal operations, is completed. If collection on the exchange is not reasonably assured, then revenues from an exchange transaction are accounted for at the time when a transaction is completed, with provisions for uncollectable accounts [GASB Cod. Secs. 1600.103–.104].

For governments with material amounts of inventory (or materials and supplies), the consumption method is required for accounting for inventories in the government-wide statement of net position. Governments may utilize the purchase method of accounting for governmental fund statements and, therefore, must reconcile the differences between the purchase method in funds and the consumption method in the government-wide financial statements. This issue is further discussed in Chapter 11 [GASB Cod. Sec. 1600.703-1].

Modified Accrual Basis of Accounting in Governmental Fund Statements

Governmental fund-based financial statements must be included in a governmental entity's financial report to demonstrate that restrictions imposed by statutes, regulations, contracts, or similar forces of law have been followed.

Financial statements for governmental funds are based on the modified accrual accounting basis and the flow of current financial resources. Such funds have a short-term emphasis and generally measure and account for cash and "other assets that can easily be converted to cash." (See previous **PRACTICE ALERTs** on the GASB's Exposure Draft document *Financial Reporting Model Improvements* and Chapter 3.)

Expenditures of governmental funds differ from *expenses*. *Expenditures* are decreases in (uses of) governmental fund financial resources. Expenditures and transfers-out are primarily reported when measurable and when the related liability is incurred [GASB Cod. Sec. 1600.116].

Revenue and expenditure accounts thus reflect the changes in the financial condition of a governmental fund that occur during a given period except those arising from transfers and general long-term debt issuance and issuances of special assessment bonds, refunding bonds, and certain demand bonds [GASB Cod. Sec. 1800.130].

PRACTICE ALERT: If the *Financial Reporting Model Improvements* Exposure Draft is approved, the terms *revenues* and *expenditures* would no longer be applicable to governmental funds due to the proposed change in measurement focus and basis of accounting to the *short-term financial resources* measurement focus, with retention of the modified accrual basis of accounting.

Due to the differences in measurement focus and basis of accounting, the basic financial statements require a reconciliation between the government-wide and fund statements, which present financial information using different bases of accounting and measurement focuses. The process by which fund financial statements are converted to government-wide financial statements is illustrated in CCH's *Governmental GAAP Practice and Disclosures Manual*.

Budgeting, Budgetary Control, and Budgetary Reporting

In many respects, a government's budget is viewed as the most important document and activity the government releases. In many governments, the budget has a force of law. In some cases, if a manager exceeds the budgeted amount under their control, the manager may be subject to prosecution. Therefore, compliance with a legally adopted budget cannot be understated.

The following guidance should be followed as part of the budgetary process for a governmental entity:

- An annual budget (or budgets) should be adopted by every governmental entity,
- The accounting system should provide the basis for appropriate budgetary control,

- Budgetary comparisons should be provided for the general fund and each major special revenue fund that has a legally adopted annual budget, and governments are encouraged to present a comparison of amounts budgeted to amounts received or expended as part of RSI, and
- A government with significant budgetary perspective differences, such as program or organizational-based budgets rather than fund budgets, is to present budgetary comparison information consistent with the perspective that provides for comparison with its legally adopted budget [GASB Cod. Sec. 1100.111].

Beyond this guidance and the reporting guidance of budgetary perspective differences required by GAAP, GASB standards do not dictate the basis of accounting for budgets. This is due to the scope of authority of the GASB.

The Board has minimal authority over matters that have a force of law. Budgets are based upon legal definitions (not accounting principles) that are not standardized. However, GAAP does require presentation of budgetary comparison information for the general fund and major special revenue funds as RSI on the fund, organization, or program structure that the government uses for its legally adopted budget, reconciled to GAAP.

OBSERVATION: Some governments are allowed by law to approve biennial budgets. Further, some governments have a legally adopted budget for capital projects spanning multiple years. A further discussion on budgetary accounting is found in Chapter 2. (See also previous **PRACTICE ALERT** on budgetary reporting.)

Transfer, Revenue, Expenditure, and Expense Account Classification

The following guidance is followed in the preparation of governmental financial reports.

Statement of Activities. At a minimum, the statement of activities should present activities accounted for:

- In governmental funds by function, to coincide with the level of detail required in the governmental fund statement of revenues, expenditures, and changes in fund balances.
- In enterprise funds by *different identifiable activities.*

Fund Financial Statements - Flows Statements (Revenues and Expenses/Expenditures)

- Governmental fund revenues should be classified by fund and source. Expenditures should be classified by fund, function (or program), organization unit, activity, character, and principal classes of objects.
- Proprietary fund revenues should be reported by major sources, and expenses should be classified in essentially the same manner as those of similar business organizations, functions, or activities. Revenues and expenses should be distinguished as operating and nonoperating.

- Proceeds of general long-term debt issues should be classified separately from revenues and expenditures in the governmental fund financial statements (as other financing sources).

Transfers and Contributions, Special and Extraordinary Items

- Contributions to term and permanent endowments, contributions to permanent fund principal, other capital contributions, special and extraordinary items, and transfers between governmental and business-type activities should each be reported separately from, but in the same manner as, general revenues in the government-wide statement of activities.
- In the proprietary fund statement of revenues, expenses, and changes in fund net position, transfers and contributions should be reported separately after nonoperating revenues and expenses. Transfers should be classified separately from revenues and expenditures in the governmental fund statement of revenues, expenditures, and changes in fund balances.
- Special and extraordinary items should be reported separately after "other financing sources and uses" in the governmental fund statement of revenues, expenditures, and changes in fund balances [GASB Cod. Sec. 1100.112].

PRACTICE ALERT: The exposure draft to the *Financial Reporting Model Improvement* proposes to replace the current provisions for special and extraordinary items to a requirement to separately present at the bottom of a resource flows statements inflows of resources and outflows of resources that are *either* unusual in nature or infrequent in occurrence *or both*. Additional information about items that are either unusual in nature or infrequent in occurrence or both, including the program or function or identifiable activity to which the item is related and whether the item is within the control of management, are also proposed to be disclosed in the notes. Special and extraordinary items are further discussed in Chapter 5 and Chapter 20.

Common Terminology and Classification

Governmental financial information should be reported consistently in all accounts and reports of each fund or activity to enhance transparency, understanding and readability [GASB Cod. Sec. 1100.113].

Annual Financial Reports (AFRs) and Annual Comprehensive Financial Reports (ACFRs)

The GASB *recommends but does not require* that a governmental financial reporting entity prepare and publish an ACFR "as a matter of public record." ACFR include all funds and operations of the primary government, including blended component units. An overview of all discretely presented component units is also presented.

An ACFR includes multiple sections:

- Introductory section, inclusive of a letter of introduction,
- Financial section, inclusive of the independent auditor's report, management's discussion and analysis, government-wide and major fund finan-

cial statements, notes to the basic financial statements, required supplementary information other than the management's discussion and analysis, appropriate combining, and individual fund statements, schedules, and narratives, and

- A statistical section.

The ACFR is discussed in more detail in Chapter 20. The reporting entity of a government is also discussed in Chapter 4.

OBSERVATION: Governance boards, laws, or ordinances may require preparation of an ACFR.

For entities not required to produce an ACFR, the minimum external financial reporting requirements include the following:

- Management's discussion and analysis,
- Basic financial statements, consisting of:
  — Independent auditor's report,
  — Government-wide financial statements,
  — Fund financial statements, and
  — Notes to the basic financial statements, and
- Required supplementary information (other than the management's discussion and analysis).

PRACTICE POINT: The *Governmental GAAP Practice and Disclosures Manual* contains examples and explanations of every required note disclosure currently required in accordance with GAAP. This *Manual* is available on CCH's *Accounting Research Manager*.

The financial reporting entity consists of:

1. The primary government,
2. Other entities for which the primary government is financially accountable, and
3. Other entities that have a relationship with the primary government whose "exclusion would cause the reporting entity's basic financial statements to be misleading or incomplete." [GASB Cod. Sec. 1100.114].

Interim Financial Reporting

Very few governments produce publicly available interim financial reports on a GAAP basis. Usually, such reports are required by bond indentures, laws, and regulations. GAAP encourages but does not require interim financial reporting. Should interim reports be issued, GAAP requires appropriate interim financial statements, inclusive of reports of financial position, operating results, and other information to facilitate control and compliance [GASB Cod. Secs. 1100.115, 2900].

OTHER GENERAL ACCOUNTING PRINCIPLES

Three types of transactions are found in governments that may also be found in other organizations:

- Transactions with related parties,
- Subsequent events and, to a lesser extent,
- Going concern.

All three transactions have their origins in AICPA guidance repurposed for state and local governments.

Related-Party Transactions

Related-party transactions are commonly found in governments and include, but are not limited to, transactions between:

- A government and its related organizations, joint ventures, and jointly governed organizations,
- A government and its elected officials, appointed officials, management, or members of all parties' immediate families, or
- A government and trusts for the benefit of employees, such as pension and other postemployment benefit trusts that are managed by or administered by the government's management.

Such transactions may be common, especially in smaller governments or in the normal course of operations (especially involving pensions and other postemployment benefits). Related-party transactions may also involve real estate transfers, professional services, borrowing, lending, "in-kind" or donated services, and cost allocation [GASB Cod. Sec. 2250.102].

PRACTICE POINT: Many governments have laws, regulations, and ordinances for public disclosure of related-party transactions using special filings or website postings.

State and local governments are required to disclose certain related-party transactions. Generally, the accounting principle dealing with related-party transactions is that if the substance of a transaction is significantly different from its form because of the involvement of related parties, the financial statements should recognize the substance of the transaction, rather than its legal form [GASB Cod. Sec. 2250.103].

The AICPA Audit and Accounting Guide *State and Local Government* states that in a governmental entity, related parties may include members of the governing board, administrative boards or commissions, administrative officials and their immediate families, component units and joint ventures, and affiliated or related organizations that are not included as part of the financial reporting entity. Many governments require their officials and employees to periodically file statements to disclose related-party relationships and transactions.

Examples of related-party transactions that may require consideration as to whether they involve form-over-substance conditions include:

- Borrowing or lending on an interest-free basis or rate of interest well above or below prevailing market prices,
- Real estate sold at a price that differs significantly from the appraised value,
- Exchanging similar property in a nonmonetary transaction, and
- Making loans where there is no scheduled terms or plan for repayment [GASB Cod. Sec. 2250.104].

> **OBERSERVATION:** Specific guidance on leases between related parties was part of the implementation of GASB-87, *Leases* [GASB Cod. Sec. L20]. Many of these elements involving form-over-substance conditions may be present in leases between related parties. GASB-87 is discussed in detail in Chapter 14.

Even though the focus of recognition is on substance over form, such assessments may pose challenges in a governmental context. For example, governments often engage in transactions motivated by the needs of the public good or society concerns and, therefore, may not have similar characteristics to the same transactions or activities occurring in an arm's-length transaction in the nongovernmental sector or with unrelated parties. As a result, a comparison to arm's-length transactions may not be appropriate in these circumstances. For example, GASB Cod. Sec. S20 includes requirements that assets transferred within the same financial reporting entity be recognized at the carrying value of the transferor. This requirement results in a measurement that may be different from what may have occurred in an arm's-length transaction with an outside party [GASB Cod. Sec. 2250.105].

> **PRACTICE POINT:** Examples of disclosure of related-party transactions are included in the *Governmental GAAP Practice and Disclosures Manual*.

> **OBSERVATION:** GASB Cod Sec. S20.113 contains the transfer provisions of capital and financial assets between a governmental employer (or nonemployer entity) and a pension or other postemployment benefit (OPEB) plan that are within the same reporting entity. Any difference between the amount paid by the plan or OPEB plan, excluding amounts that may be refundable, and the carrying value of the assets transferred is reported as follows:
>
> - As an employer contribution (or a nonemployer entity contribution) to the pension or OPEB plan, as applicable, in the separately issued statements of the employer or nonemployer contributing entity and in the financial statements of the reporting entity, or

- As an employer contribution (or a nonemployer contributing entity contribution) in the stand-alone statements of the pension plan or OPEB plan and in the financial statements of the reporting entity.

An example of such a transaction would be when a primary government contributes a building to a pension or OPEB plan.

Subsequent Events

Events or transactions that affect financial statement amounts or disclosures sometimes occur after period-end but before the financial statements are issued. These transactions or events are referred to as "subsequent events."

Two types of subsequent events are included in GAAP, each with slightly different accounting and disclosure:

- *Recognized events*—This type of subsequent event provides additional evidence with respect to conditions that existed at the date of the financial statements and affects the estimates that were used in the preparation of the financial statements (e.g., the settlement of a lawsuit related to an event that occurred prior to the date of the financial statements). For recognized subsequent events, the financial statements should be adjusted for any changes in estimates resulting from this new evidence [GASB Cod. Sec. 2250.110].

- *Non-recognized events*—This type of subsequent event provides evidence with respect to conditions that did not exist at the financial statement date but arose after that date. These subsequent events do not result in adjustment to financial statement amounts but should be disclosed in the notes to the financial statements if considered essential to a user's understanding of the statements. For example, changes in the quoted market prices of a government's investments after year-end would generally not require adjustment to the financial statement amounts because the change in market value typically reflects a concurrent evaluation of new conditions [GASB Cod. Sec. 2250.111].

Subsequent events may need to be included in management's discussion and analysis depending on the specific facts and circumstances. Such events are currently known facts, decisions and similar which may have a significant effect on the government's financial position or the results of operations in the near future [GASB Cod. Sec. 2250.116].

PRACTICE ALERT: GASB Staff are performing pre-agenda research evaluating the effectiveness of existing guidance regarding subsequent events. The current provisions may be revised because of the research should the Board add a project to the current technical agenda. The results of the research are projected to be presented to the Board in August 2023.

Going-Concern Considerations

The continuation of a state or local government entity as a going concern is assumed in financial reporting unless significant information exists to the contrary. For governmental entities, information that would be contrary to this assumption includes evidence that indicates the government's inability to meet obligations that are due without substantial disposition of assets outside the normal course of operations, debt restructuring, required financial oversight, or similar actions.

It is the financial statement preparer's responsibility to evaluate whether there is substantial doubt about the government's ability to continue as a going concern for a reasonable period beyond the date of the financial statements. This period is defined as 12 months beyond the financial statement date. However, if information is currently known to the government that may raise substantial doubt shortly after the 12-month period (e.g., within an additional three months), it should also be considered [GASB Cod. Sec. 2250.117].

Indicators of substantial doubt about a government's ability to continue as a going concern could include the following:

- Negative trends such as recurring declines in net position or fund balances, consistent working capital deficiencies, or operating cash flow declines,
- Significant noncompliance with debt covenants, legal reserve requirements, or other requirements that can negatively affect continued operations,
- Inability to raise resources or borrow monies resulting from proximity to legal debt or revenue limits,
- Internal matters such as major work stoppages, labor disputes, or excessively burdensome contracts, significant reliance on a program's success, or the need to significantly revise operations, and
- External matters such as legal proceedings, legislative mandates, potential loss of significant intergovernmental resources or revenues, loss of principal taxpayers or customers, or the effects of natural disasters [GASB Cod. Sec. 2250.118].

If there is substantial doubt about the government's ability to continue as a going concern, GAAP requires specific note disclosures and discussion of such issues in management's discussion and analysis. GAAP also clarifies that the going-concern considerations are to be applied to the "legal entity level" or, in other words, to a "legally separate governmental entity," and not to the reporting units within the legally separate government entity. Therefore, a going concern may be assessed at a primary government that is having financial difficulties even though a component unit of a primary government may be solvent or vice versa [GASB Cod. Secs. 2250.119–.120].

PRACTICE ALERT: As previously discussed, GASB is in the process of potentially updating the provisions addressing going concern uncertainties disclosures and severe financial stress. Four areas of focus are involved with the project:

1. How should the existing guidance on going concern uncertainties (including the definition of a going concern) be clarified or improved to reduce diversity in practice in applying the guidance?

2. How should severe financial stress be defined? How should that definition differ from going concern uncertainties?

3. What are the common indicators that a government is exposed to severe financial stress? How might those indicators and other information be used to evaluate exposure to severe financial stress?

4. If a government is determined to be exposed to severe financial stress, what relevant information should a government disclose in notes to financial statements?

The GASB currently plans a Preliminary Views document for release by August 2024. During the comment period, public hearings, user forums, further deliberations, and field testing may occur until 2026. An exposure draft may not be released until March 2026. If approved, a final statement may not be released until April 2027.

CHAPTER 2
BUDGETARY ACCOUNTING

Chapter References:

GASB Statement No. 34

GASB Concepts Statement Nos. 1–6

GASB *Implementation Guide*

NCGA Statement No. 1, Interpretation 10

INTRODUCTION

A budget is a plan of financial operations that provides a basis for the planning, controlling, and evaluating of governmental activities. The budget process is a political process that usually begins with the chief executive of a governmental unit submitting a budget to the unit's legislative branch for consideration. Ultimately, the legal authority for governmental expenditures is reflected in an annual or biennial appropriations bill, act, or other form of legal adoption [GASB Cod. Sec. 1700.101].

GASB standards provide the basic guidance for budgetary accounting and reporting, but not the establishment of a consistent basis of budgetary accounting for all governments. Other than these pronouncements, GAAP contain little on budgetary accounting and reporting due to the focus on control. Control is vitally important to a government's operations. However, many recent GAAP pronouncements, notably those on derivatives, pensions and other postemployment benefits other than pensions, have migrated away from accounting transactions that primarily stem from budgetary decisions to those that are based upon accrual accounting principles. These complex transactions may result in a major budget-to-GAAP difference if the government's budget is not prepared in accordance with the economic resources measurement focus and the accrual basis of accounting ("full accrual accounting"). This chapter focuses on budgetary accounting and its role in government financial reporting. Chapter 20 discusses reporting budgetary comparison information in the annual financial report.

The budgetary process for governmental units is far more significant than it is for commercial enterprises because of the public nature of the process, the legality of a final budget and the fiduciary responsibility of public officials. Unfortunately, some members of governance may only focus on the budget, ignoring the long-term fiscal impact of decisions made for the current fiscal period.

BUDGETARY OPERATIONS AND ACCOUNTABILTY

Time Span of Budgets

Many governments issue budgets annually for operations. Some issue biennial budgets. Without some form of a legally approved continuation of a prior budget, fiscal operations for a year cannot commence without a legally approved budget. Once a budget is legally approved, it may only be amended by another legislatively approved budget.

> **PRACTICE POINT:** Some governments may approve a budget during a following year, retroactive to a prior year and based on the presence of an estimated surplus or a deficit. This practice may be indicative of lax internal controls in the budgetary establishment process.

A budget contains a control mechanism established in law providing for the financial operations of a period. A government's system of accounting needs to provide assurance of budgetary control and accountability due to the force of law. Further accountability may be established through a system of *appropriations* (individual line items) which may have allotted funds to them from the budgetary process annually or in shorter timeframes, therefore authorizing spending on programs, facilitated by cashflow.

Other budgets may be longer than one or two years. These budgets usually authorize capital spending and are funded by debt issuances or grant awards. In some jurisdictions, capital budgets do not need legislative authority, unless funded by debt or grant awards [GASB Cod. Secs. 1700.106–.108].

> **OBSERVATION:** Governments with large amounts of capital spending may control spending in a fashion like operating accounts within capital accounts. Capital spending controls have become especially important when capital spending is financed with bonds issued related to a federal program, or similar bonds, which have purpose restrictions to financing capital assets. To assure spending is in line with established laws, ordinances, and other legal requirements, a government audit might involve a large component of fieldwork centered on the control mechanisms established within a budgetary system.

Budgetary Control and Authority

Three levels of budgetary control and authority are commonly used by general-purpose governments for programs, services, and functions of governing:
- Appropriated budgets (containing individual budgetary appropriations or "line items"),
- Legally authorized, non-appropriated budgets, which allow more flexibility based on the availability of revenue or resources to facilitate spending, or
- Nonbudgeted activities, without any legal approval or review, but still subject to fiscal controls.

Nonbudgeted activities are rare in comparison to appropriated budgets. Appropriated budgets contain legal provisions providing for collections of revenues to fund services. Revenues may or may not be tied to specific spending authorizations. For example, general taxation may be apportioned to many appropriations, but a federal grant award may only have one programmatic appropriation.

The *original operating budget* is the first complete appropriated budget for the government. Reserves, transfers, allocations (also known as "allotments"), and other programmatic elements are contained in the budget which should be approved prior to the start of a period. Some budgets include amounts that were unspent from prior periods (in some situations termed "prior appropriations continued"). These amounts are legally approved to carryforward into the next year. In some cases, the approvals are automatic.

The *final budget* is the original budget, adjusted for any new sources of revenue, transfers, changes in programs and other activities, legally authorized during and prior to the end of the fiscal period(s).

Non-appropriated budgets are authorized by statute or potentially by constitution, charter or similar. Such activities are legally authorized but do not depend on legislative approval before a fiscal period starts.

Once approved by the executive branch, allocations (allotments) are established in the budgetary accounting system to facilitate spending based on cashflow. In many situations of fiscal crisis, governments may reduce allotments to curb spending [GASB Cod. Secs. 1700.113–.114].

Budgetary Accounting System

Budgetary control is enhanced when the legally adopted budget is integrated into the governmental unit's formal accounting system. The integration of the budget and accounting system is called the budgetary accounting system. Budgetary accounts are used in a budgetary accounting system. Many modern budgetary accounting systems are computerized or even "cloud-based."

A budgetary accounting system should be used by at least the General Fund and Special Revenue Funds. Other governmental funds that should employ a budgetary accounting system are those subject to the controls of an annually adopted budget, and those processing numerous revenue, expenditure, and transfer transactions through the fund. For example, it may be appropriate to use budgetary accounts in a Permanent Fund when activities are being financed annually through the investment earnings of the fund [GASB Cod. Sec. 1700.118].

Conversely, budgetary accounts may be unnecessary (or not required by law or regulation) in the following situations:

- *Debt Service Fund*—Receipts and expenditures for a period are established by the sinking fund provisions of a debt agreement or legal requirement, and few transactions are processed each period.

- *Capital Projects Fund*—Various construction projects are under contract with independent contractors who are exclusively responsible for the progress of their project (turnkey projects). However, many governments may choose to budget for capital projects individually or an entire capital program over more than one or two years.

Budgeting for Governmental Funds

Governmental funds (General Fund, special revenue funds, capital projects funds, debt service funds, and permanent funds) generally use a legally adopted fixed budget, which reflects a specific estimate for revenues and appropriations for expenditures. Once expenditures and revenues are incorporated into the budget, the total appropriation amounts usually become a legal limit for current expenditures, and the estimated revenue amounts become the basis for comparison with actual revenues [GASB Cod. Secs. 1300.102, 1700.110–.118].

To simplify the presentation and understanding of budget-and-actual comparison, the basis for preparing the budget would need to be the same as the governmental fund's GAAP basis of accounting. The modified accrual basis of accounting is the GAAP basis of accounting for governmental fund types under current GAAP. To simplify the accounting, the budget would reflect a similar basis for establishing expenditures and estimating revenues. However, many governments adopt a budget based on accounting other than GAAP, such as a cash basis, modified cash basis, or regulatory basis. When the budgetary basis and GAAP basis of accounting are different, a governmental unit usually maintains its records on the budgetary basis (legal basis) and uses supplementary information in the form of accrual adjustments to convert the budget-based information to the modified accrual basis (GAAP basis) for financial reporting purposes. Also, to facilitate the comparison of budgeted amounts and actual expenditures and revenues, similar terms and classifications should be used in the preparation of the budget and the presentation of the financial report [GASB Cod. Sec. 1700.119].

OBSERVATION: From an accounting perspective, it is preferable (but not required) that the budgetary system be on the same basis as the financial accounting system; namely, the modified accrual basis. However, some argue that a budget should be based on the cash basis, modified cash basis, or regulatory basis because those bases are more consistent with the statutory requirements and the financing of a governmental unit and are better understood by legislators. Financial reporting standards do not require a GAAP budget to be prepared. The largest state or local government to do so is New York City.

PRACTICE ALERT: The GASB's *Financial Reporting Model Improvements* exposure draft proposes no change to the measurement focus and basis of accounting of a government's budget. Budgetary reporting and analysis are proposed to transition to required supplementary information (RSI). The reconciliation of the budget to the balances and results of operation of governmental funds though may change if the governmental funds measurement focus and basis of accounting is transitioned to the short-term measurement focus and accrual basis of accounting, as proposed. Budgetary reporting is discussed later in this chapter.

Recording of a Budget

The appropriated budget for the current fiscal year may be recorded in a fund using control accounts (accounts that are closed at period-end and not reported in the financial statements) in the following manner:

	Debit	Credit
Estimated Revenues (Budgetary Control)	800,000,000	
Appropriations (Budgetary Control)		780,000,000
Fund Balance (Budgetary Control)		20,000,000
To record operating budget in control accounts.		

The above example general ledger entry for these budgetary control accounts reflects the fact that the adopted budget anticipates estimated revenues of $800,000,000, has approved appropriations of $780,000,000, and expects a $20,000,000 increase in fund balance if those estimates are achieved.

The estimated revenues control account is a budgetary account that represents the total anticipated revenues expected to be available during the fiscal year on a budgetary basis. The estimated revenues account functions as an overall control account, and the specific revenue sources, such as property taxes, fines, and intergovernmental revenues, would be recorded in revenue subsidiary ledgers.

Actual revenues are recorded in non-budgetary accounts as they are recognized throughout the accounting period. Also, as actual revenues are recorded, similar postings are made to the subsidiary ledgers. The overall control account and the subsidiary ledgers provide a basis for the subsequent comparison of the estimated revenues with the actual revenues for the period. Thus, the estimated revenues account (a budgetary account) is used to compare estimated revenues with actual revenues for the period, but it does not function as a control account for actual revenues.

The appropriations control account is a budgetary account that represents the total authorized expenditures for a current fiscal period within the budgeted fund. The appropriations account is a control account, with the details of the approved encumbrances and expenditures being recorded in appropriations subsidiary ledgers. *Encumbrances* are further discussed in a following section.

During the year, encumbrances and expenditures are recorded both in:

- Non-budgetary accounts such as public safety and health and welfare expenditures and in
- Appropriations subsidiary ledger accounts.

Throughout the fiscal year, the appropriations account and its subsidiary ledger accounts can be used to control the level of encumbrances and expenditures to avoid exceeding appropriated amounts. Thus, the appropriations control account (a budgetary account) is used for both control and comparative purposes.

OBSERVATION: To maintain fiscal balance (otherwise known as a balanced budget) in times of fiscal stress, most government executives (e.g., governors, mayors, etc.) have the power to reduce appropriations if estimated revenues decrease. If appropriations are reduced, a debit to appropriations (budgetary control) would be necessary along with a credit to estimated revenues (budgetary control). These debits and credits will likely occur at a line-item level if the government has a system with this capability.

Budgetary accounts are used exclusively for control and, therefore, only indirectly affect the actual results of operations for the accounting period as reported in the basic financial statements. Two important aspects of a budgetary accounting system are (1) budgets at various levels of appropriations and (2) accounting for encumbrances.

Budgets at Different Levels of Operations

Budgets may be established by agency, by program within an agency, by accounting period, or even by activities within a budget. Some activities may be known as *objects* and may have a code or a class for reporting purposes. Common objects are salaries, benefits, expenses of employees, employee benefits, equipment, leases, and many others. Revenues may also be by code or class, with separate elements for taxation, fees, fines, grants, and investment revenues, among others.

Accounting for Encumbrances

Encumbrances represent commitments related to contracts not yet performed, and orders not yet filled (executory contracts, open purchase orders), and they are used to control expenditure commitments for the year and to enhance cash management. A governmental unit often issues purchase orders or signs contracts for the purchase of goods and services to be received in the future. Encumbrances may or may not carry from one period to the next.

If encumbrances *do not* carry forward, they are known as "lapsing." Otherwise, they are known as "non-lapsing." Any amount that carries forward to the next period is an estimated amount of expenditures to finalize a contract. However, since the goods or services have not been provided, under most budgetary accounting principles, they do not represent expenditures or liabilities. Therefore, for accounting and *internal* financial reporting purposes, the encumbered amount that carries forward needs to be reestablished in the new period (see **OBSERVATION** below).

When these commitments are made, the following budgetary entry should be made for control purposes based on the estimated size of each encumbered contract. For example, if the annual audit of a government is estimated to cost $100,000, the following entry is made upon signing of the engagement letter with the auditor:

Budgetary Accounting **2007**

	Debit	Credit
Encumbrances (Budgetary Control)	100,000	
Reserve for Encumbrances (Budgetary Control)		100,000
To record the issuance approval of a contract for the annual audit.		

> **OBSERVATION:** Reserves for encumbrances are not accounting events for general-purpose external financial reporting purposes and are not presented. However, they are commonly used for control purposes and internal reporting to management or those charged with governance. Many governments use encumbrances for operations and contract management. Governments will need to be careful to properly translate reserves into the proper categories of fund balance for financial reporting purposes if reserves carry forward into future periods.

Significant encumbrances are required to be disclosed in the notes to the financial statements by major funds and nonmajor funds in total in conjunction with required disclosures about other significant commitments. Encumbered amounts for specific purposes for which resources already have been restricted, committed, or assigned do not result in separate display of the encumbered amounts within those classifications.

Encumbered amounts for specific purposes for which amounts have not been previously restricted, committed, or assigned should not be classified as unassigned but, rather, should be included within committed or assigned fund balance, as appropriate. This is because the encumbrances account does not represent an expenditure for the period, only a commitment to expend resources. Likewise, the account reserve for encumbrances is not synonymous with a liability account since the liability is recognized only when the goods are received, or the services performed [GASB Cod. Sec. 1700.127].

When the executed contract for audit services is completed or virtually completed, the budgetary encumbrance control accounts are liquidated or reduced, and the actual expenditure and related liability are recorded, illustrated as follows:

	Debit	Credit
Reserve for Encumbrances (Budgetary Control)	100,000	
Encumbrances (Budgetary Control)		100,000
To record the receipts of audit services and liquidation of the outstanding encumbrance, where the encumbrance was estimated at $100,000 but the final actual expenditure was only $97,000.		

	Debit	Credit
Expenditures—Professional Services	97,000	
Vouchers Payable		97,000
To record the actual expenditure for audit services.		

In the example above, because the expenditure described is the final cost to be incurred related to this purchase, the original encumbrance amount is liquidated based on the estimated cost of goods and services, which differed from the eventual cost of the item.

During the budgetary period, the governmental unit can determine the remaining amount of the new commitments that can be signed by comparing the amount of appropriations to the sum of expenditures recognized and encumbrances outstanding.

At the end of the fiscal year, some encumbrances may be outstanding. NCGA-1 states that encumbrances outstanding at the end of the year are not expenditures for the year, and the reserve for encumbrances account is not to be treated as a liability. The treatment of the two encumbrance budgetary accounts (encumbrances and reserve for encumbrances) at the end of the year depends on whether appropriations, even if encumbered at the year-end, lapse [GASB Cod. Sec. 1700.127].

Lapsing appropriations. When there are outstanding encumbrances at the end of the fiscal year, it is likely that the governmental unit will honor the open purchase orders or contracts that support the encumbrances. For GAAP-basis financial statement reporting purposes, outstanding encumbrances are not considered expenditures for the fiscal year. If the governmental unit allows encumbrances to lapse, even though it plans to honor them, the appropriations authority expires, and the items represented by the encumbrances are usually re-appropriated in the following year's budget and re-encumbered in the new budget year.

Though not required by GAAP, in practice many governments disclose the accounting policy for encumbrances due to the focus on control. To illustrate the accounting necessary to portray the lapsing appropriations process, assume that encumbrances of $100,000 are outstanding as of December 31, 20X9, but the governmental unit passes a law to commit the funds to pay for the contracts in the 20Y0 fiscal year. At the end of 20X9, the following entries should be made into the books of the government but not displayed on the face of the basic financial statements:

	Debit	Credit
Reserve for Encumbrances (Budgetary Control)	100,000	
Encumbrances (Budgetary Control)		100,000

To close control accounts for encumbrances outstanding at the end of the fiscal year.

	Debit	Credit
Fund Balance—Unassigned	100,000	
Fund Balance—Committed		100,000

To commit the fund balance by the estimated amount that will be re-appropriated in 20Y0 for outstanding encumbrance period.

The first entry closes the encumbrance budgetary controls accounts because they are strictly budgetary accounts. The second entry meets the period-end reporting requirement in GAAP portraying the committed fund balance by the government for the outstanding encumbrances to be honored in the subsequent period.

At the beginning of the next fiscal year (January 1, 20Y0), the following entries are made:

	Debit	Credit
Encumbrances (Budgetary Control)	100,000	
Reserve for Encumbrances (Budgetary Control)		100,000
To recognize outstanding encumbrances to be honored from the prior year.		

	Debit	Credit
Fund Balance—Committed	100,000	
Fund Balance—Unassigned		100,000
To reclassify fund balance in accordance with GAAP.		

In accordance with GAAP, the above entry to remove the amount for fund balance reserved for outstanding encumbrances has been replaced with an entry to debit Fund Balance—Committed or Fund Balance—Assigned, as appropriate, and credit Fund Balance—Unassigned, assuming the encumbered amounts are not already reported within the committed or assigned classifications.

Budget Adopted after a Fiscal Year Begins

GASB Cod. Sec. 1800.744-2-3 discusses the adoption of a budget and appropriation documents in a subsequent fiscal year and their effect on fund balance classification. The GASB notes that the adopted appropriation or similar legislation generally authorizes a government to spend budgeted revenues and other financing sources and does not impose constraints on existing resources.

However, if a portion of existing fund balance is included as a budgetary resource in the subsequent year's budget to eliminate a projected excess of expected expenditures over expected revenues, then that portion of fund balance (in an amount no greater than is necessary to eliminate the excess) should be classified as assigned. The amount should not be classified as committed, because the governing body does not have to take formal action to remove or modify that specific use—the purpose assignment expires with the appropriation. GASB further discusses in the next question that the assignment of fund balance terminates at the effective date of the following year's budget (the year after carryover).

The first entry reestablishes budgetary control over the outstanding encumbrances, and the next entry removes the fund balance reservation, which is no longer needed with the reestablishment of budgetary control. The appropriations control account created in the January 1, 20Y0, budget will need to include the $100,000 because an expenditure for this amount is anticipated during 20Y0.

From this point the normal entries for encumbrances and expenditures are followed. For example, if the goods or services are received on January 28, 20Y0, and the final cost is $99,000 of the $100,000 encumbered, the following entries would be made:

	Debit	Credit
Expenditures	99,000	
Vouchers Payable		99,000
To record the receipts of goods or services.		

	Debit	Credit
Reserve for Encumbrances (Budgetary Control)	100,000	
Encumbrances (Budgetary Control)		100,000
To remove encumbrances on vouchered commitments.		

The expenditures are reflected in the 20Y0 GAAP-basis financial statements.

When lapsed encumbrances are re-appropriated and treated in the manner described in the previous example, there are no differences between the budgetary accounting basis and the GAAP basis. The budgetary expenditures represented by the encumbrances are reflected in the budget in the same year that the expenditures are shown in the U.S. (GAAP) statement of revenues, expenditures, and changes in fund balances.

Non-lapsing appropriations. Appropriations for encumbrances that are outstanding at year-end and are considered non-lapsing (i.e., the legal authority to commit against them does not expire) do not require re-appropriation the following year because the appropriation authority does not expire. Typically, non-lapsing appropriations are used for long-term contracts involving construction. GAAP requires outstanding encumbrances charged against non-lapsing appropriations to be reported as a component of fund balance at period-end.

To illustrate, assume that encumbrances of $100,000 are outstanding as of December 31, 20X9. At the end of 20X9, the following entries would be made:

	Debit	Credit
Fund Balance—Unassigned	100,000	
Encumbrances (Budgetary Control)		100,000
To close encumbrances outstanding at the end of the fiscal year.		

	Debit	Credit
Reserve for Encumbrances—20X9 (Budgetary Control)	100,000	
Fund Balance — (Restricted, Committed, or Assigned)		100,000
To reserve the fund balance by the amount that represents outstanding encumbrances at the end of the fiscal year in accordance with the budget, not GAAP.		

OBSERVATION: To report in accordance with GAAP, the above entries to reserve fund balance for outstanding encumbrances are modified to debit Fund Balance—Unassigned (rather than Fund Balance—Unreserved) and credit Fund Balance—Committed or Fund Balance—Assigned, as appropriate (rather than Fund Balance—Reserved for Encumbrances), assuming the encumbered amounts are not already reported within the committed or assigned classifications.

The two entries close the encumbrance budgetary control accounts to avoid reporting budgetary accounts in the GAAP-basis financial statements. The first entry closes the encumbrances control account directly to the fund balance so that as required by GAAP they are not shown as expenditures in the current fiscal year. The second entry establishes a fund balance reserve as required by most budget systems.

At the beginning of the next fiscal year (January 1, 20Y0), the following entry would be made:

	Debit	Credit
Fund Balance — (Restricted, Committed, or Assigned)	100,000	
Reserve for Encumbrances—20Y0 (Budgetary Control)		100,000

*To recognize outstanding encumbrances from the prior year (see **OBSERVATION**, below).*

OBSERVATION: GAAP requires the above entry to recognize prior-year encumbrances to be modified to debit Fund Balance—Committed or Fund Balance—Assigned, as appropriate, rather than debiting Fund Balance—Reserved for Encumbrances, assuming the encumbered amounts are not already reported within the committed or assigned classifications.

This entry reestablishes the reserve for encumbrances account (a budgetary control account) but indicates that the reserve is applicable to amounts appropriated in the previous year's budget.

For example, if the goods or services are received on January 28, 20Y0, and the final cost is $99,000 of the $100,000 encumbered, the following entry would be made during 20Y0:

	Debit	Credit
Expenditures	99,000	
Vouchers Payable		99,000

To record the receipt of goods or services.

At the end of 20Y0, the following closing entry would be made:

	Debit	Credit
Reserve for Encumbrances—20Y0 (Budgetary Control)	100,000	
Expenditures		99,000
Fund Balance—Unreserved		1,000
To close expenditures encumbered during the prior year; see **OBSERVATION**, *below.*		

OBSERVATION: The above entry to close expenditures encumbered in the prior year will need to be modified to credit Fund Balance—Unassigned, rather than crediting Fund Balance—Unreserved upon presentation of the annual financial report. Unreserved is not used for external reporting purposes but may still be used for budgetary control purposes.

This closing entry enables 20Y0 encumbered expenditures to be reported as expenditures in 20Y0 as required by GAAP when the goods or services are received.

When encumbrances are charged against non-lapsing appropriations in the manner illustrated, there are differences between the budgetary accounting amounts and the GAAP-basis amounts. The budget-based information reflects expenditures based on liabilities incurred adjusted for the effect of encumbrances outstanding, whereas the actual (GAAP-basis) financial statements reflect expenditures that do not include amounts encumbered at the end of the fiscal year. When budget-basis revenues and expenditures differ from GAAP-basis revenues and expenditures, there must be a reconciliation between budgetary information presented with the financial statements and the actual financial statements, which must be presented on a GAAP basis. An example budgetary reconciliation is illustrated in Exhibit 20-11, "Budget-to-GAAP Reconciliation," in Chapter 20.

Once a method of accounting for encumbrances is established based on the entity's appropriation lapsing policy, it should be used on a consistent basis.

Closing a Budget Period

The difference between estimated revenues and appropriations as authorized in the budget is debited or credited to the fund's fund balance budgetary control account. The entry in the fund balance account reflects either an anticipated operating surplus (credit) or a deficit (debit) for the current budgetary period.

The use of budgetary control accounts in the general ledger does not affect the actual revenues and expenditures recognized during the accounting period. This is accomplished by reversing, at the end of the reporting period, the budgetary control accounts created when the budget was first recorded.

For example, assuming there were no budget amendments affecting the budgetary control totals, the earlier entry used to illustrate the recording of the budget would be reversed as follows:

	Debit	Credit
Fund Balance (Budgetary Control)	20,000,000	
Appropriations (Budgetary Control)	780,000,000	
Estimated Revenues (Budgetary Control)		800,000,000
To close budgetary control accounts.		

The budgetary control accounts can be grouped with related actual control accounts as part of the period closing to emphasize the comparative purpose of using the budgetary accounting system. The following example illustrates this type of closing, along with the use of other budgetary control accounts:

	Debit	Credit
Revenues (Actual)	795,000,000	
Estimated Revenues (Budgetary)		800,000,000
Appropriations (Budgetary)	780,000,000	
Expenditures (Actual)		770,000,000
Fund Balance (Budgetary)	20,000,000	
Fund Balance (Actual)		25,000,000
To close all revenue and expenditure related budgetary and actual control accounts.		

OBSERVATION: Many governments may be using systems that utilize encumbrances and are recording transactions within the various categories of fund balances. Complex enterprise resource planning (ERP) systems have very detailed accounting that may be difficult to customize. In these situations, governments would then journal voucher fund balance segregation (and many other transactions for financial reporting purposes) after the year-end, calculated by analyzing transactions and acts of those charged with governance, while leaving detailed transactions intact.

BUDGETARY ACCOUNTING BY PROPRIETARY AND FIDUCIARY FUND TYPES

Budgeting for Proprietary Funds

Generally, proprietary funds *may* adopt a flexible budget, which changes as the activity level changes. In a proprietary fund, overall activity is measured in terms of revenues and expenses and fluctuates, in part, depending on the demand for goods and services by the public (Enterprise Fund) or by other governmental departments or agencies (Internal Service Fund). The flexible budget items are generally not considered appropriations (legal spending limits) but, rather, an approved financial plan that can facilitate budgetary control and operational evaluations. A proprietary fund allows the governmental unit to prepare several budgets at different activity levels to establish an acceptable comparative basis for planned activity and actual results [GASB Cod. Secs. 1700.121–.123].

OBSERVATION: Even if several budgets are prepared, the budget ultimately used as a comparison with actual results should be based on the actual, not the anticipated, activity level. The preparation of the budget based on actual activity is feasible because the flexible budgeting approach can be expressed in terms of a formula (Total Expenses = Fixed Expenses + Variable Expenses) and should be applicable at any activity level.

The basis of accounting used to prepare a budget for a proprietary fund should generally be the same as the basis used to record the results of actual transactions. It is not appropriate to integrate the budgetary system into the proprietary fund's accounting system when a flexible budget system is used. However, if a fixed budget is used, perhaps due to a preference or legal requirement, it may be useful to integrate the budgetary system into the proprietary fund's accounting system, like governmental funds [GASB Cod. Sec. 1700.120].

Budgeting for Fiduciary Funds

Fiduciary funds include Pension and Other Employee Benefit Trust Funds, Investment Trust Funds, Private-Purpose Trust Funds, and Custodial Funds.

The first three fiduciary fund types are like proprietary funds and may use budgetary controls, although these resources are not available for governmental operations. Such controls are rare due to the nature of fiduciary activities which commonly have outflows based on demand and inflows based on investing activity or contributions based on payroll that is out of the control of the fiduciary activity. Budgets are not appropriate for Custodial Funds, because the government entity functions only as a custodial agent for resources held normally for three months or less.

Budgetary Reporting

Budgets may be approved but may not align to financial reporting, so perspective differences exist. Perspective differences exist when the structure of financial information for budgetary purposes differs from the fund structure that is defined in GAAP. For example, a government may develop a purpose-based budget that provides appropriation by project or purpose irrespective of the funds that will be used to account for those projects or purposes (in other words a cross-fund budget).

GAAP provides an alternative budgetary comparison presentation for governments that legally adopt a budget by program or purpose that may cross funds. (See an example presentation within the discussion of perspective differences for budgetary comparisons in Chapter 20.)

GASB Cod. Sec. 2200.207 discusses how budgetary comparison schedules are presented (1) using the same format, terminology, and classifications as the budget document *or* (2) using the format, terminology, and classifications in a statement of revenues, expenditures, and changes in fund balances and accompanied by a reconciliation of the budgetary information to GAAP information.

PRACTICE ALERT: GAAP requires presentation of comparisons of budget to actual amounts for the General Fund and each major special revenue fund with a legally adopted budget at a minimum. GAAP allows the budget to be reported as either basic financial statements or required supplementary information. Current GAAP also presents the adopted budget, the final (amended) budget and actual amounts (using the budget's basis of accounting) with a variance column between the final and actual amounts.

The GASB's Exposure Draft for the *Financial Reporting Model Improvements* project contains the GASB's tentative conclusion that governments should be required to present budgetary comparison information using a single method of communication—required supplementary information (RSI). Governments also would be required to present specific budget variances as part of the budgetary comparison schedule. These comparisons include analysis of variances between final budget and actual amounts as well as original and final budget amounts as part of a note to the RSI.

In some cases, special revenue funds do not meet the criteria for separate reporting in external financial statements. These funds are then reported as components of the general fund, or some other qualifying special revenue fund in accordance with GAAP. In these cases, GASB Cod. Sec. 1700.707-1 explains that the revenues and expenditures pertaining to these activities result from perspective differences and should be explained in the reconciliation between the budgetary activity and GAAP. This is due to the lack of a legally adopted budget for these activities.

In the rare circumstance when a government chooses to present its required budgetary comparison information in the basic financial statements, including disclosure that a budget is not adopted for the general fund or a major special revenue fund because it is not legally required (and, therefore, the presentation of budgetary comparison information is not required), the presentation in the notes should include an explanation why what might appear to be required information is not part of the presentation of the comparisons [GASB Cod. Sec. 1700.801] (AICPA (American Institute of Certified Public Accountants) Literature Cleared by the GASB).

CHAPTER 3
MEASUREMENT FOCUS AND BASIS OF ACCOUNTING

Chapter References:

GASB Statement Nos. 6, 14, 16, 17, 31, 33, 34, 37, 38, 51, 54, 62, 72, 81, 84

GASB Interpretation Nos. 3, 6

GASB Concepts Statement Nos. 1, 6

GASB *Implementation Guide*

NCGA Statement Nos. 1, 4

INTRODUCTION

For state and local governments, a prime area of focus of accounting and financial reporting is *accountability*. Financial reporting of state and local governments provides information to assist users in assessing accountability and making decisions. Accountability is a core element of governmental operations as the operations are funded directly or indirectly by the public. The GASB considers accountability to be the primary objective from which all other objectives are derived.

In addition to the overall objective of accountability, Governmental Accounting Standards Board Concepts Statement No. 1 (GASB:CS-1, *Objectives of Financial Reporting*) identified the following as objectives of governmental financial reporting (GASB:CS-1, pars. 76–79):

Objective of Governmental Financial Reporting	How Objective is Met in GASB Standards
Financial reporting should fulfill a government's duty to be publicly accountable and should enable users of the financial statements to assess that accountability.	• Reporting provides information to determine whether current-year revenues were enough to pay for current-year services (known as **inter-period equity**) (see Chapter 1 of this Guide). • Reporting demonstrates whether resources were obtained and used with the entity's legally adopted budget and in compliance with finance-related legal or contractual requirements. • Reporting provides information to assist users in assessing service efforts, costs, and accomplishments of the government.

Objective of Governmental Financial Reporting	How Objective is Met in GASB Standards
Financial reporting should assist users in evaluating the operating results of the governmental entity for the year.	• Reporting provides information on sources and uses of resources. • Reporting also provides information on how the government finances its activities and meets its cash requirements. • The net result of reporting determines whether the government's financial position improved or deteriorated because of the year's operations.
Financial reporting should assist users in assessing the level of services that can be provided by the governmental entity and its ability to meet its obligations.	• Reporting provides information about the financial position or condition of a governmental entity (as of a point in time). • Reporting also provides information about a government's physical and other nonfinancial resources that extend beyond the current year, including whether those resources still have a potential to provide services, or are impaired. • Finally, reporting discloses legal or other restrictions on resources and risks of potential loss of those resources.

The GASB noted that although accountability is referred to only in the first objective, accountability is implicit in all the listed objectives.

Although most interested observers may agree with the overall goal of financial reporting, implementing the goal is the subject of much debate. The overall goal of accounting and financial reporting can be summarized as providing:

1. Financial information useful for making economic, political, and social decisions and demonstrating accountability and stewardship and
2. Information useful for evaluating managerial and organizational performance. An important element in implementing this overall goal in a governmental environment is selecting a basis of accounting and a measurement focus for governmental funds.

The selection of a basis of accounting and measurement focus affects the establishment of specific accounting principles for state and local governments. As discussed in Chapters 1 and 2 of this *Guide*, a government may have a conflict between legal or statutory provisions of accounting and financial reporting. This conflict should not result in two separate accounting systems as the transfer of information between the systems may result in an increased risk of material misstatement or fraud. The accounting system may be maintained on a legal basis for day-to-day transactions but be flexible enough to permit additional information for GAAP reporting [GASB Cod. Sec. 1200.110].

An appreciation of the unique character of governmental financial reporting can be developed only when the concepts of basis of accounting and measurement focus are fully understood. For this reason, this chapter is a foundation chapter and does not discuss governmental U.S. generally accepted accounting principles (GAAP) except to illustrate basis of accounting and measurement focus.

BASIS OF ACCOUNTING

An entity's accounting basis determines when transactions and economic events are reflected in its financial statements. GASB Cod. Sec. 1600.101 states that basis of accounting refers to "when revenues, expenditures, expenses, and transfers—and the related assets and liabilities—are recognized in the accounts and reported in the financial statements."

All operating transactions are the result of expected or unexpected resource flows (usually, but not exclusively, cash flows). Because of specific contractual agreements and accepted business practices, commitments that create eventual resource flows may not coincide with the actual flow of resources. For example, goods may be purchased on one date, consumed on another date, and paid for on a third date.

The accounting basis determines when the economic consequences of transactions and events are reflected in financial statements. Generally, accounting transactions and events of state and local governments are recorded on an accrual basis or modified accrual basis in accordance with U.S. GAAP depending on the fund type involved or, for non-GAAP presentations, another comprehensive basis of accounting, such as cash, modified cash, or regulatory basis.

Flow of Economic Resources (Applied on an Accrual Basis) (also known as "Full Accrual")

GASB Cod. Sec. 1600.103 describes the measurement focus and basis of accounting of the government-wide and the proprietary (or business-type) financial statements as including revenues, expenses, gains, losses, assets, and liabilities recognized when an exchange takes place. An exchange is when value or resources is received or delivered for value or resources. Value or resources may not equate to a cash transaction. Goods and services being received or delivered may signify value.

Some of the essential elements of the accrual accounting method include the recognition of assets, liabilities, inflows, outflows and deferred inflows of resources or deferred outflows of resources when directed by GAAP in accordance with transaction type. Expenses are recognized when incurred *unless* GAAP allows deferral and amortization over an estimated number of reporting periods. For example, GAAP related to defined benefit pensions and defined benefit other postemployment benefits other than pensions allow for differences between expected amounts and actual experience to be deferred and amortized over the estimated remaining service life of an employee. However, if the difference is related to a retiree, since the retiree has no service life as an employee, then an expense is recognized immediately.

Revenues are recognized similarly unless deferred due to their applicability to a future reporting period. For example, resources that are received by a government from another government before time requirements are met (e.g., prior to a fiscal year beginning) but after all other eligibility requirements are met, are declared as a deferred inflow of resources by the receiving government.

In the accrual basis of accounting, revenues from *exchange transactions* are recognized when an exchange of value for value occurs in the ordinary course of operations. The recognition may be adjusted if the circumstances are such that the collection of the exchange price is *not* reasonably assured. The exchange would result in a credit transaction to revenue and a related debit to receivable, along with any appropriate provision for uncollectible accounts. Guidance for specific transactions may adjust recognition, including for the right of return of a product sold [GASB Cod. Sec. 1600.104].

PRACTICE ALERT: As discussed in the *Introduction*, the GASB released a *Preliminary Views* (PV) document in the spring of 2020 detailing the Board's initial views on a wide-ranging project potentially updating revenue and expense recognition. The project's scope includes classification, recognition, and measurement of revenues and expenses, unless specifically excluded from the project. There are specific exclusions from the proposed recognition and measurement proposals currently being deliberated by the Board. However, an Exposure Draft may not be released until March 2025. A final standard, if at all, may not be released until June 2027.

Current Financial Resources Measurement Focus and Modified Accrual Basis of Accounting (also known as "Modified Accrual")

The modified accrual basis of accounting is a variation of the accrual basis that adjusts the basis for certain cash flow considerations. (See **PRACTICE ALERT** later in the chapter on the GASB's Exposure Draft *Financial Reporting Model Improvements*.)

OBSERVATION: Some of the aspects of the current financial resources measurement focus and modified accrual basis of accounting are not easily understood by new practitioners, but are "second nature" to other practitioners. Some of the inconsistency with other measurement focuses and bases of accounting is evident in the presentation of a balance sheet of a Governmental Fund. The balance sheet excludes capital assets and general long-term liabilities. For the statement of revenues, expenditures and changes in fund balances, the presentation is like a traditional income statement, but the recognized elements are adjusted amounts of cash or budgetary inflows and outflows, as discussed in the following paragraphs.

Revenues

Revenues, including funds received from other governmental units, should be recorded when they are "susceptible to accrual" [GASB Cod. Sec. 1600.106]. Susceptibility is described as when revenue becomes measurable and available to finance fiscal period expenditures.

Available is defined as "collectible" within the current period *or soon enough thereafter to be used to pay liabilities of the current period.* In many ways, the concept of "susceptible to accrual" becomes highly judgmental, considering materiality of the transaction, practicality of accrual, consistency of application and, in many cases, laws and regulations.

If revenue is not available in a governmental fund, the fund should report a deferred inflow of resources until time passes and revenue is available. *As a caution,* common transactions for state and local governments which may have differing definitions of the word "available" between peer governments include, but are not limited to:

- Property taxes,
- Revenues related to governmental services,
- Intergovernmental revenues from grants (or taxation), and
- Transfers between funds.

As a practical matter, many governments accrue revenues at the end of the year only if a cash flow occurs within 60, 90, or some other number of days after the period-end date that is established by law, regulation, practice, or some other measure. In some jurisdictions, taxes collected in one period may not be able to be used until a future period, leading to a deferred inflow of resources. As further discussed below, upon the commencement of the new period, the deferred inflow of resources is debited, and tax revenue is credited.

Sales and income taxes may differ as they are dependent upon whether the taxpayer liability has been established (usually through a sale or work) and collectability is assured (or losses can be estimated). For most taxes, collectability is relatively assured as a tax lien has a force of law. If a taxpayer fails to pay taxes, property may be seized, subject to bankruptcy provisions. Other types of revenues of governments may be more related to service fees. If the service has been provided, an exchange occurs, unless there is an explicit nonexchange transaction [GASB Cod. Secs. 1600.107–.108].

OBSERVATION: There is no explicit definition of "measurable" in the pronouncements, but the term undoubtedly refers to the ability to quantify the amount of revenue expected to be collected. Thus, "measurable" can be interpreted as the ability to provide a reasonable estimate of actual cash flow.

Examples of revenue recognition under the modified accrual basis of accounting include the following:

Taxes and similar nonexchange revenue should generally be recognized as revenue when levied to the extent they are collected within the availability period as described above. Deferred inflows of resources should be reported when resources are receivable before either:

- The period for which the property taxes are levied, or
- The period when resources are required to be used, or
- When first permitted, in which a statute includes time requirements.

The word *"levy"* is not defined in GAAP as it is a legal term. In legal terms, a levy is an imposition (or collection) of a form of taxation, usually with a force of law. GASB Cod. Sec. N50.104(a) (fn. 3) discusses that *"enabling legislation authorizes the government to assess, levy, charge, or otherwise mandate payment of resources (from external resource providers)."* Once an enforceable legal claim is established, as dictated by the enabling legislation, then an asset (a receivable) may be recognized. Many governments declare this date as the *lien date*, even if a lien is not placed on a property at that date. In some governments, the phrase "assessment date" is used [GASB Cod. Sec. N50.114].

A government may levy amounts in its current property tax levy for *future* debt service payments. In other words, the government does not have an enforceable legal claim until after the lien date or assessment date. If so, there may (or may not) be a prohibition on recognizing the levy in current revenues. GASB Cod. Sec. N50.708-3 discusses that unless a legal requirement specifies otherwise, the period for which these amounts are levied is the same as the period for which the rest of the taxes are levied.

When property taxes are measurable, but not available, the collectible portion, representing taxes levied less estimated uncollectible amounts, are reported as a deferred inflow of resources in the period when an enforceable legal claim to the assets arises or when the resources or received, whichever occurs first [GASB Cod. Sec. 1500.115].

Interest and investment income, including changes in fair value of investments, should be recognized as revenue when earned and available. In many governmental fund statements of revenues, expenditures and changes in fund net position, changes in fair value of investments at the end of each period are captioned "net increase (decrease) in the fair value of investments, when identified separately as an element of investment income. In other situations, only investment income is reported on a net basis. Realized gains and losses on investments should not be displayed separately from the net increase (decrease) in the fair value of investments in the basic financial statements. However, some entities disclose realized gains and losses in the notes to the basic financial statements. Interest income should be reported at the stated interest rate, which is consistent to reporting investments at fair value. Any premiums or discounts on debt securities are not amortized in the modified accrual basis of accounting [GASB Cod. Sec. 1600.109, fn. 6].

Recreation fees, parking fees, business licenses, and similar revenue should generally be recognized when received in cash as that is likely when the exchange occurs [GASB Cod. Sec. 1600.110]. Certain adjustments may be made based on the relationship of the revenue to the period of benefit. GAAP describes business licenses as potentially relating to a fiscal year and billed before the year begins. In this case, revenue is *not recognized in advance* of the license year as the benefit period to the license holder is not until the year of actual renewal. In some cases, licenses are not renewed on a timely basis. Therefore, for many licenses, the susceptibility to accrual generally coincides with the time of payment [GASB Cod. Sec. 1600.112].

Other nonexchange revenues include taxes, grants, contributions, and fines. Each of these four classes of transactions has slightly different accounting in the modified accrual basis of accounting [GASB Cod. Sec. 1600.111]. These are further discussed in Chapter 17.

Revenues received in advance prior to the normal time of receipt are recorded as liabilities, *unless the revenues are a result of a nonexchange transaction* (such as taxes), and *all eligibility requirements* (other than the timing) have been met. For example, if a grant award has been received and eligibility is determined, but cannot be spent until a future fiscal year, then the advance is a liability [GASB Cod. Sec. 1600.114].

Expenditures

Expenditures are recorded on a modified accrual basis when they are normally expected to be liquidated with current financial resources (referred to as a governmental fund liability). Expenditures differ from expenses in that they represent a "decrease in net financial resources" (emphasis added).

Expenditures include:

- Salaries,
- Wages,
- Payments for supplies,
- Transfers to other funds,
- Capital outlays, and
- Payments for the service of debt.

Unmatured long-term indebtedness (not yet due for payment) are reported as long-term liabilities of the *government*, rather than in a governmental fund using the current financial resources measurement focus. This is a significant difference from the accrual basis of accounting.

Although most expenditures are recorded when the liability is incurred, the current financial resources measurement focus of a governmental fund significantly impacts what items are to be considered expenditures in the governmental fund. Thus, expenditures for a governmental fund cannot be equated to expenses of a business enterprise [GASB Cod. Secs. 1500.103–.104, .122, 1600.116].

Examples of expenditure recognition under the modified accrual basis of accounting include the following:

- *Capital outlay* (purchases or construction of land, buildings, improvements, infrastructure, and equipment) are not capitalized and depreciated but are recognized as expenditures in the period that the liability is incurred.
- *Debt principal and interest payments* are recognized as expenditures when due and payable from current financial resources. Interest is not accrued on the modified accrual basis.
- *Costs incurred related to accrued expenses* such as compensated-absence obligations, pension and OPEB (other postemployment benefit) liabilities, claims and judgments, termination benefits, landfill closure and post-

closure care costs, and pollution remediation obligations are not recognized as expenditures when incurred; they are only recognized when they are normally expected to be liquidated with current financial resources.

What then remains as liabilities in governmental funds are claims against current financial resources [GASB Cod. Secs. 1600.117–.118].

The major exception for expenditure accrual for most general-purpose governments includes unmatured principal and interest on debt, including special assessment debt for which the government is obligated in some way. Under the modified accrual basis of accounting, governmental fund liabilities and expenditures for debt service on general long-term debt, generally should be recognized when due. Only the extent of the portions of the debt that mature during the reporting period are recognized as expenditures and liabilities (if unpaid).

A further wrinkle occurs when financial resources are appropriated in other funds for transfer to a debt service fund in the period in which maturing debt principal and interest must be paid. Such amounts thus are not current liabilities of the debt service fund as their settlement will not require expenditure of existing fund assets. To accrue the debt service fund expenditure and liability in one period but record the transfer of financial resources for debt service purposes in a later period would be confusing and would result in overstatement of debt service fund expenditures and liabilities and understatement of the fund balance. Thus, disclosure of subsequent-year debt service requirements is appropriate, but they usually are appropriately accounted for as expenditures in the year of payment.

However, if debt service fund resources were provided during the current year for payment of principal and interest due early in the following year, the expenditure and related liability may be recognized in the debt service fund. "Early in the following year" usually refers to a short time. In many cases, this is usually a few days or a month. In other cases, this may be two or three months. An accounting policy, law or regulation dictates the period. The policy is then summarized in the notes to the basic financial statements. Accumulated financial resources that are held in a governmental fund or nondedicated financial resources transferred to a debt service fund at the discretion of management are reported as part of the debt service fund's fund balance and are not a liability [GASB Cod. Secs. 1600.120–.121, fn. 9].

The Concept of "Normally" in the Modified Accrual Basis of Accounting

As previously discussed, many governmental fund liabilities and expenditures are recognized to the extent the liabilities are *normally expected to be liquidated with expendable financial resources*. For all types of expenditures to which this applies, the criterion for modified accrual recognition is whether and to what extent the liability has matured, independent of the method and timing of resource accumulation [GASB Cod. Sec. 1600.122].

The concept of "normally" can be highly subjective and variable. For example, if a government holds bills in its desk and does not pay for years, a case may be made that it pays its bills normally over years, rather than days. This may be fiscally irresponsible to some and normal to others (see **PRACTICE ALERT** on the *Financial Reporting Model Improvements* Exposure Draft in the following section).

When Governments Accumulate Assets for Future Unmatured Liabilities

Governments may budget for future payments of unmatured liabilities. The accumulated assets in a governmental fund for such future payments for transactions such as compensated absences, claims, and judgments and similar are not outflows of current financial resources and are not recognized as governmental fund liabilities or expenditures [GASB Cod. Secs. 1600.123–.124].

Other Expenditure Recognition Issues. A few alternative expenditure recognition methods in governmental funds are acceptable as follows:

- *Inventory items* (e.g., materials and supplies) may be considered expenditures either when purchased (purchases method) or when used (consumption method), but significant amounts of inventory should be reported in the balance sheet.
- *Expenditures for insurance and similar services* extending over more than one accounting period need not be allocated between or among accounting periods but may be accounted for as expenditures of the period of acquisition.

Expenditures for Claims, Judgments and Compensated Absences in Governmental Funds

Expenditure amounts for claims, judgments and compensated absences in governmental funds are the amounts accrued during the year that are normally expected to be liquidated with expendable financial resources. As the governmental balance sheet reflects current liabilities, only the amount left unpaid at the end of the reporting period representing the current liability is reported in the governmental fund [GASB Cod. Sec. 1600.129]. This would also be true once a government implements GASB Statement No. 101, *Compensated Absences*.

PRACTICE ALERT: The *Financial Reporting Model Improvements* Exposure Draft contains proposals to change the current financial resources measurement focus and modified accrual basis of accounting. The basis may be renamed *short-term financial resources measurement focus and modified accrual basis of accounting.*

This change will also be reflected in the titles of the governmental fund statements. The balance sheet would be the *short-term financial resources balance sheet.* The statement of revenues, expenditures and changes in fund balances would be the *statement of short-term financial resources flows.* Sections of the flows statement would include current and noncurrent, inflows and outflows terminology.

The recognition period would be one year. The period of recognition may be quite different for some governments that use a so-called 60-day accrual period. However, as the focus would be on cash, assets available to be converted to cash and assets that are consumable in lieu of cash, the short-term recognition period of one year may not be vastly different from current practice.

The final statement may include additional guidance for governmental fund transactions including, but not limited to:

- Receivable recognition,
- Liability recognition,
- Amendments to contracts and other binding arrangements,
- Direct vendor financings,

- Escheat property,
- Irrevocable split-interest agreements,
- Land (and capital assets) held as an investment, and
- Investments not reported at fair value.

The Board may approve a final statement for release by March 2024.

Special-Purpose Frameworks (SPFs)

Usually to meet a regulatory requirement, many small governmental entities account for transactions and prepare their financial statements in accordance with a special-purpose framework (SPF). SPFs which are commonly used by smaller state and local governments, include the following:

- Basis of cash receipts and disbursements (cash basis);
- Cash basis with modifications having substantial support (modified cash basis); and
- Basis to comply with requirements of a regulatory agency whose jurisdiction the entity is subject to (regulatory basis).

The AICPA's Audit and Accounting Guide *State and Local Governments* provides guidance on the use of these bases of accounting for government entities.

PRACTICE POINT: The regulatory basis of accounting is discussed in Chapter 24 of this *Guide*. Some financial reports may only consist of statements for individual funds, agencies, departments, or programs. As discussed in Chapter 16 of the AICPA's Audit and Accounting Guide *State and Local Governments*, GASB pronouncements *do not* address such reporting. Auditors of such reports consider "long-established practice dictating that those presentations should apply all relevant GAAP." The presentations usually include relevant financial statements, note disclosures, management's discussion and analysis, and required supplementary information, as applicable. The auditor considers these factors as part of planning and performing the audit (par. 17.102). A further discussion on this issue is contained in Chapter 4.

PRACTICE POINT: The focus of CCH's *Governmental GAAP Guide* is on accounting and financial reporting in accordance with GAAP; therefore, it does not address the accounting and financial reporting treatment and issues for governments that account and report in accordance with an SPF. Most accounting systems record daily transactions on a cash basis or a statutory or legislative basis, with conversions performed either manually or automatically to a GAAP basis at the end of an accounting period (either monthly or yearly). CCH's *Governmental GAAP Practice and Disclosures Manual* contains entries that may be needed to convert from a modified accrual to a full accrual basis of accounting.

MEASUREMENT FOCUS

The second critical element in establishing GAAP for governments is selecting a measurement focus. Unlike the selection of an accounting basis, which is concerned with the timing of transactions and events, a measurement focus identifies what (and how) transactions and events should be recorded. The measurement focus is concerned with the inflow and outflow of resources that affect an entity. The balance sheet or statement of net position should reflect those resources available to meet current obligations and to be used in the delivery of goods and services in subsequent periods. The activity statement for the period should summarize those resources received and those consumed during the current period. The two measurement focuses recognized as generally accepted for government transactions are as follows:

- Flow of economic resources; and
- Flow of current financial resources.

Flow of Economic Resources (Applied on an Accrual Basis)

The flow of economic resources refers to the reporting of all the net positions available to the governmental unit for providing goods and services to the public. When the flow of economic resources and the accrual basis of accounting are combined, they provide the foundation for GAAP used by proprietary funds and business-type activities and in the government-wide financial statements. This approach recognizes the deferral and capitalization of certain expenditures and the deferral of certain revenues.

When the flow of economic resources is applied on an accrual basis for a fund, or for the government-wide statements, all assets, deferred outflows of resources, liabilities and deferred inflows of resources are presented in the fund's balance sheet or statement of net position. The key differences between this approach and the current financial resources measurement focus as it applies to individual governmental funds are summarized as follows:

- Capital assets are recorded in the proprietary, enterprise, or internal service fund statement of net position or the government-wide statement of net position net of accumulated depreciation.
- Long-term debts are recorded in the proprietary, enterprise, or internal service fund statement of net position or the government-wide statement of net position.
- The fund's residual represents the net position (assets plus deferred outflows of resources less liabilities and deferred inflows of resources) available to the fund rather than the fund balance. Similarly, the government-wide equity represents the net position (assets plus deferred outflows of resources less liabilities and deferred inflows of resources) available to the government rather than any cumulative fund balances.

> **PRACTICE POINT:** The term "equity" should not be presented in the basic financial statements for state and local governments unless allowed by GAAP. However, it is presented in the GASB's conceptual framework to describe net position. "Equity" may only be used when presenting interests in joint ventures and majority equity interests (see Chapter 4).

The statement of activities (or the statement of revenues, expenses, and changes in fund net position) includes all costs of providing goods and services during the period. These costs include depreciation, the cost of inventories consumed during the period, and other operating expenses. On those statements, revenues during the period are recognized along with the total cost of the segment (function) of government.

The result is a smoothing effect on those statements, rather than revenues and expenses occurring based on cash flow. For example, expenses do not include the full cost of purchasing depreciable property during the period and other financing sources do not include the proceeds from the issuance of long-term debt, as is the case in governmental funds under the current financial resources measurement focus.

Flow of Current Financial Resources (Applied on a Modified Accrual Basis)

The flow of current financial resources applied on a modified accrual basis is a narrow interpretation of what constitutes assets and liabilities for an accounting entity. Assets include only those considered current *financial resources*, such as cash and claims to cash, investments, receivables, inventory, and other similar current financial assets.

> **PRACTICE ALERT:** As part of the GASB's Basis for Conclusions to the *Financial Reporting Model Improvements* Exposure Draft, the GASB has tentatively proposed a broad definition of *financial resources* that includes assets expected to be consumed in lieu of cash or converted to cash. All investments would be reported as assets consistent with the definition of *financial assets* that includes assets available to be converted to cash.

Liabilities include those defined as governmental fund liabilities, which are liabilities normally expected to be liquidated with current financial resources under current GAAP. Deferred inflows of resources may be present in the flow of current financial resources, but only where revenue cannot be recognized but funds have been received.

Revenues, and the resulting assets, are accrued at the end of the year only if the revenues are earned and are expected to be collected in time to pay for liabilities in existence at the end of the period.

Expenditures, and the related liabilities, are accrued when they are normally expected to be paid out of revenues recognized during the current period. To determine which revenues and expenditures should be accrued, an arbitrary date after the end of the year must be established.

Due to the limitations of the flow of current financial resources, capital assets *do not* represent financial resources available for expenditure but are items for which financial resources have been used and are, thus, reported as capital outlay *of governmental funds*. However, adjustments are presented to reconcile governmental fund balances and results of operations to the statement of net position and statement of activities, respectively. These adjustments may be material.

GASB Cod. Secs. 1800.126 and 2200.166 state that debt issuance costs paid out of debt proceeds, inclusive of underwriting fees, are to be reported as expenditures of *governmental funds* and not capitalized and amortized. Issuance costs such as attorney and rating agency fees or bond insurance paid from existing resources should be reported as expenditures of a governmental fund when the related liability is incurred.

However, beyond these references, until the GASB Board finishes the *Financial Reporting Model Improvements* project, there is no finalized definition of "financial resources" or "current financial resources" as the measurement focus is referred to in the GASB literature. For example, there is little guidance on whether a long-term note receivable of a governmental fund represents a financial resource to be reported as a governmental fund asset other than the inference that fixed assets are the only assets specifically excluded from the definition (see previous **PRACTICE ALERT**).

Under the flow of current financial resources measurement focus, capital expenditures are recorded as capital outlay expenditures. In addition, prepayments and purchases of inventories may be recorded as of when the expenditures are made. Thus, the statement of revenues, expenditures, and changes in fund balances of a governmental fund reflect only those expenditures that were made during the current period, ignoring cost allocations that might arise from expenditures incurred prior to the current period. The balance sheet under the flow of current financial resources approach reflects the entity's financial resource position and includes only those assets available to pay future expenditures and the fund liabilities *normally payable* from those financial assets [GASB Cod. Secs. 1500.122, 1600.116].

Basis of Accounting/Measurement Focus Illustration

The differences and similarities of the flow of economic resources (applied on the accrual basis) and the flow of current financial resources (applied on the modified accrual basis) are illustrated in the following example, which uses the following assumptions using a fiscal Year ended June 30, 20X1 (for simplicity it is assumed that this is the first year of operations for the fund):

Activity	Amount
Revenues:	
Billed during year	$30,000
Collected during year (one-half of the remaining balance (i.e., $2,000) is expected to be collected within 60 days of the year-end and the remainder within 180 days)	26,000
Salaries:	
Paid during year	9,000
Payable (accrued) at the end of year and expected to be paid within 30 days	1,000
Property, Plant, and Equipment:	
Purchased equipment on July 1, 20X0, at a cost of $20,000, estimated four-year life, no salvage value, straight-line method for depreciation	20,000
Noncurrent Note Payable:	
Equipment purchased was financed by issuing a 10% note whereby all interest and principal are paid four years from date of issuance, but $2,000 of interest has accrued on June 30, 20X1	20,000
Supplies:	
Purchased during year	8,000
Consumed during year	6,000
Paid during year (balance to be paid 90 days after year-end date)	7,000
Pension:	
Annual required contribution	5,000
Amount funded during year	3,000

The financial statements for the governmental fund with the above financial information are presented in Exhibit 3-1.

EXHIBIT 3-1
FINANCIAL STATEMENTS

Fund Name Statement of Net Position/Balance Sheet as of June 30, 20X1

	Flow of economic resources	Flow of current financial resources*
Assets		
Current assets		
Cash	$ 7,000	$ 7,000
Receivables	4,000	2,000
Supplies	2,000	—
Total current assets	13,000	9,000
Capital assets		
Equipment	20,000	—
Accumulated depreciation	(5,000)	—
Equipment, net of accumulated Depreciation	15,000	—
Total assets	**$ 28,000**	**$ 9,000**
Liabilities and net position/fund balance		
Current liabilities		
Accounts payable	$ 1,000	—
Salaries payable	1,000	$ 1,000
Total current liabilities	2,000	1,000
Noncurrent liabilities		
Notes payable	22,000	—
Net pension obligation	2,000	—
Total noncurrent liabilities	24,000	—
Total liabilities	26,000	1,000
Net position/fund balance	2,000	8,000
Total liabilities and net position/fund balance	**$ 28,000**	**$ 9,000**

Fund Name Statement of Revenues, Expenditures (Expenses), and Changes in Fund Balance (Net position)
For the Year Ended June 30, 20X1

	Flow of economic resources	Flow of current financial resources*
Revenues	$ 30,000	$ 28,000
Expenditures/expenses:		
Capital outlays	—	—
Salaries	10,000	10,000
Interest	2,000	—
Supplies	6,000	7,000
Pensions	5,000	3,000
Depreciation expense	5,000	—
Total Expenditures/expenses	28,000	20,000
Excess of revenues over expenditures/expenses	2,000	8,000
Net position/fund balance 7/1/X0	—	—
Net position/fund balance 6/30/X1	$ 2,000	$ 8,000

* It is assumed that assets must be realizable in cash within 60 days of the end of the fiscal year to be considered available to finance current expenditures.

Basic Financial Statements: Different Measurement Focuses

Government-Wide Financial Statements

Government-wide financial statements provide a basis for determining:

- The extent to which current services provided by the entity were financed with current revenues and
- The degree to which a governmental entity's overall financial position has changed during the fiscal year.

To achieve these objectives, government-wide financial statements should include a statement of net position and a statement of activities.

Government-wide financial statements are reported on a flow of economic resources applied on the accrual basis of accounting. The flow of economic resources refers to all the assets available to the governmental unit to provide goods and services to the public.

When the flow of economic resources and the accrual basis of accounting are combined, they provide a foundation for GAAP that is like that used by business enterprises. Businesses present essentially all assets and liabilities, both current and long-term, in their balance sheet. A governmental entity's statement of activities includes all costs of providing goods and services during a period. These costs include depreciation, the cost of inventories consumed during the period, and other operating expenses. On the statement of activities, revenues earned during the period are matched with the expenses incurred for exchange or exchange-like transactions.

Nonexchange transactions are accounted for based on the standards contained in GASB Cod. Sec. N50.

As introduced in Chapter 1, a governmental entity can use (and report) three broad categories of funds: governmental funds, proprietary funds, and fiduciary funds.

- *Governmental funds.* The governmental funds grouping includes five fund types (General Fund, special revenue funds, capital projects funds, debt service funds, and permanent funds), which are used to record the normal (non-business-like) operations of a governmental entity. The financial statements for these funds have a short-term emphasis and generally measure and account for cash and "other assets that can easily be converted to cash." These fund types are accounted for using the modified accrual accounting basis and the flow of current financial resources measurement focus.
- *Proprietary funds.* Financial statements for proprietary funds are based on the flow of economic resources measurement focus and the accrual basis of accounting. The proprietary fund category includes enterprise funds and internal service funds. An enterprise fund is used to report any activity for which a fee is charged to external users for goods or services. An internal service fund may be used to account for activities that involve the governmental entity providing goods or services to other funds or activities of the primary government or its component units, or other governments on a cost-reimbursement basis where the reporting entity is the *predominant* participant in the activity. If the reporting entity is not the predominant participant, the activity should be reported in an enterprise fund.
- *Fiduciary funds.* Assets held by a governmental entity for other parties (either as a trustee or as an agent) and that cannot be used to finance the governmental entity's own operating programs should be reported in the fiduciary fund category, which includes:
  — Pension (and other employee benefit) Trust Funds,
  — Investment Trust Funds,
  — Private-Purpose Trust Funds, and
  — Custodial Funds.

Trusts are present for accounting and financial reporting purposes in accordance with GAAP when the assets are:

- Administered through a trust agreement or equivalent arrangement (hereafter jointly referred to as a trust) in which the government itself is not a beneficiary,
- Dedicated to providing benefits to recipients in accordance with the benefit terms, and
- Legally protected from the creditors of the government [GASB Cod. Sec. 1300.131(a)].

The financial statements for fiduciary funds should be reported on the flow of economic resources measurement focus and the accrual basis of accounting (except for certain liabilities of defined benefit pension plans and certain postemployment health care plans). Fiduciary fund financial statements are not reported by major fund (which is required for governmental funds and enterprise funds) but must be reported by fund type [GASB Cod. Sec. 1300.102].

GASB Cod. Secs. 1300.128–.136 identify the requirements for reporting an activity as a fiduciary activity focusing on whether a government is controlling the assets of the fiduciary activity and the beneficiaries with whom a fiduciary relationship exists. An activity meeting the criteria is to be reported in the fiduciary funds. An exception is provided for a business-type activity that normally expects to hold custodial assets (as defined) for three months or less. Fiduciary component units are combined with information from fiduciary funds (as described in Chapter 4). Further information on fiduciary funds is found in Chapter 8.

Fund financial statements may include governmental, proprietary, and fiduciary funds if they have activities that meet the criteria of using them. If no activity or legal authorization is present to use a fund, it is not presented. In summation, the fund types used in state and local governments are as follows with their respective financial statements [GASB Cod. Sec. 1300.103]:

Fund Type (Reference to chapter in this Guide)	Funds Within Type	Balance Sheet/Net Position Title	Flows Statement Title
Governmental Funds (emphasizing major funds) (Chapter 6)	• General Fund • Special revenue funds (see **PRACTICE ALERT**) • Capital project funds • Debt service funds • Permanent funds	Balance Sheet (see **PRACTICE ALERT**)	Statement of Revenues, Expenditures and Changes in Fund Balance (see **PRACTICE ALERT**)
Proprietary Funds (Chapter 7)	• Enterprise funds (emphasizing major funds) • Internal service funds	Statement of Net Position	Statement of Revenues, Expenses and Changes in Fund Net Position
Fiduciary Funds (and fiduciary component units) (Chapter 8)	• Pension (and other employee benefit) trust funds • Investment trust funds • Private-purpose trust funds • Custodial Funds	Statement of Fiduciary Net Position	Statement of Changes in Fiduciary Net Position

PRACTICE ALERT: As part of the *Financial Reporting Model Improvements* Exposure Draft, the Board has proposed renaming special revenue funds to *special resources funds*. The governmental funds financial statements are proposed to be renamed "the short-term financial resources balance sheet" and "the statement of short-term financial resource flows."

Exhibit 3-2 presents the basis of accounting and measurement focus required by GAAP accounting principles for each fund category and government-wide activity.

EXHIBIT 3-2
BASIS OF ACCOUNTING AND MEASUREMENT FOCUS

Fund Category/ Activity Type	Basis of Accounting	Measurement Focus
Governmental activities	Accrual basis	Economic resources
Business-type activities	Accrual basis	Economic resources
Governmental funds	Modified accrual basis	Current financial resources
Proprietary funds	Accrual basis	Economic resources
Fiduciary funds	Accrual basis	Economic resources

CHAPTER 4
GOVERNMENTAL FINANCIAL REPORTING ENTITY

Chapter References:

GASB Statement Nos. 14, 31, 34, 37, 39, 44, 48, 51, 61, 69, 72, 80, 84, 90, 92, 97, 100

GASB Technical Bulletin 2004-1

GASB *Implementation Guide*

INTRODUCTION

PRACTICE POINT: The importance of determining the financial reporting entity *cannot be taken too lightly*. Preparers must understand the financial reporting entity to determine what is required to be included in the annual financial report. Auditors must understand the financial reporting entity *prior* to commencing fieldwork in the audit to determine the opinion units involved in the engagement (beyond the scope of this Guide). Users need to understand the financial reporting entity in a similar vein to preparers to gauge if their investment in the government includes all elements of the government. The elements of the financial reporting entity are always among the leading areas of technical inquiry to GASB Staff and among the leading areas of audit risk.

This chapter of the *Governmental GAAP Guide* is among the more detailed chapters in the entire volume due to these issues. Practitioners should review this chapter along with related GAAP to make these decisions.

Overview of the Financial Reporting Entity

The fund is the basic unit for establishing and maintaining accountability for activities specifically established by laws, regulations, and other governmental mandates. Each fund consists of self-balancing accounts, including accounts for the fund's assets, liabilities, potentially deferred inflows of resources or deferred outflows of resources and residual fund balance or net position. A governmental unit's activities may be reflected in one or several governmental funds, proprietary funds, or fiduciary funds.

In addition, agencies, authorities, and other governmental entities exist with their various funds that may be created by a state or local government. Ultimately, financial statements of the state or local government must be prepared, which raises the question of which separate legal entities and funds should be included in these broad-based financial statements. The initial step in resolving this question is concerned with the conceptual definition of a *financial reporting entity*. Of all the foundational concepts of GAAP for state and local governments, defining what the financial reporting entity is may be among the most complex.

The financial reporting entity is defined as follows [GASB Cod. Secs. 2100.109–.111, .511, 2600.101]:

> A primary government, organizations for which the primary government is financially accountable, and other organizations for which the nature and significance of their relationships with the primary government are such that exclusion would cause the reporting entity's financial statements to be misleading or incomplete. The nucleus of a financial reporting entity usually is a primary government. However, a governmental organization other than a primary government (such as a component unit, a joint venture, a jointly governed organization, or another stand-alone government) serves as the nucleus for its own reporting entity when it issues separate financial statements (see later discussion in the section titled "The Financial Reporting Entity Concept").

GAAP contains a framework for defining a government, originally established by the AICPA that has been adopted by the GASB as "Category B" GAAP in GASB Cod. Sec. 1000.801. Governmental organizations have one or more of the following characteristics:

- Popular election of officers or appointment (or approval) of a controlling majority of the members of the organization's governing body by officials of one or more state or local governments,
- The potential for unilateral dissolution by a government with the net position reverting to a government, or
- The power to enact and enforce a tax levy.

Organizations are presumed to be governmental if they can issue debt directly that pays interest exempt from federal taxation (rather than through a state or municipal authority). However, due to the definitions in GAAP, as amended, not-for-profit organizations may indeed be included in a primary government's financial reporting entity.

What Is a Primary Government?

The focal point for preparing financial statements of a financial reporting entity is the *primary government*. Primary governments include states, general-purpose local governments, and certain special-purpose governmental entities. A primary government is defined as follows [GASB Cod. Sec. 2100.521]:

> A state government or general-purpose local government. Also, a special-purpose government that has a separately elected governing body, is legally separate, and is *fiscally independent* of other state or local governments.

The identification of a financial reporting entity is built around the concept of financial accountability. If a primary government is financially accountable for another entity, that entity's financial statements should be included in the financial statements of:

- The primary government; and
- If applicable, the primary government's *component units*.

What Are Component Units?

Component units are legally separate organizations for which the elected officials of the primary government are *financially accountable*. Component units may be a governmental organization, a non-for-profit corporation or even a for profit corporation. In addition, GAAP discusses how other organizations may also be component units based on the nature and significance of their relationship with a primary government to the point that if the organization is excluded, the reporting entity's financial statements may be misleading [GASB Cod. Sec. 2100.119].

Nongovernmental Entities May Be Component Units

An example of how a nongovernmental entity *may* be included in the definition of a governmental financial reporting entity could be when a tribal government that applies GAAP may own and operate a commercial concrete manufacturer. When the nongovernmental entity's financial information is included in a governmental financial reporting entity, the reporting standards established by GAAP should be observed. The government's intent (operational or investment) has an impact on the accounting and financial reporting treatment of the nongovernmental entity within the government's financial statements.

GAAP provides some flexibility in determining the components of the financial reporting entity. Although financial accountability is central to the identification of component units, an entity will be considered a component unit even if financial accountability does not exist. As stated previously, the organization could be a component unit the nature and significance of its entity's economic relationship with the primary government is such that its exclusion would create misleading or incomplete financial statements, or it is considered closely related or financially integrated.

To make this determination, a primary government exercises management's professional judgment if an entity should be included as part of the reporting entity if the organization that does not meet the specific financial accountability criteria. This determination should be based on the nature and significance of the organization's relationship with the primary government. In addition, other organizations should be evaluated as potential component units if they are closely related to, or financially integrated with, the primary government.

Although most GAAP are written from the perspective of a primary government, the same GAAP provisions should be used to prepare the financial statements of governmental entities that are not primary governments. This allows greater financial accountability and easier reporting.

In addition to establishing criteria for determining the scope of the financial reporting entity, GAAP also addresses accounting and reporting standards for entities that are not component units. These entities include governmental joint ventures, jointly governed organizations, pools, and certain stand-alone governmental organizations. These entities are defined as follows:

4004 Basic Governmental Accounting Concepts and Standards

Type of Entity	Definition
Joint venture (governmental)	A legal entity or other organization that results from a contractual arrangement and that is owned, operated, or governed by two or more participants as a separate and specific activity subject to joint control, in which the participants retain: (a) an ongoing financial interest or (b) an ongoing financial responsibility (see later discussion in section titled "Joint Ventures") [GASB Cod. Secs. J50.102–.104].
Jointly governed organization	A regional government or other multi-governmental arrangement that is governed by representatives from each of the governments that create the organization, but that is not a joint venture because the participants do not retain an ongoing financial interest or responsibility (see later discussion in section titled "Jointly Governed Organizations or Joint Powers Authorities"). This entity may also be known as a "joint powers authority." [GASB Cod. Sec. J50.111].
Other stand-alone government	A legally separate governmental organization that: (a) does not have a separately elected governing body *and* (b) does not meet the definition of a component unit. Other stand-alone governments include some special-purpose governments, joint ventures, jointly governed organizations, and pools (see later discussion in section titled "Other Stand-Alone Government Financial Statements") [GASB Cod. Sec. 2100.112].

The following are some examples of governmental entities, in addition to primary governments, that must follow GAAP [GASB Cod. Sec. 2600.101]:

- Commissions,
- Districts,
- Governmental enterprises,
- Public authorities,
- Public benefit corporations,
- Public employee retirement systems,
- Publicly owned utilities,
- Public owned hospitals and other health care providers, and
- Public colleges and universities.

> **PRACTICE POINT:** Some commissions, districts, trusts, authorities, and so on are not separate legal entities. Rather, they are ministerial or administrative bodies. Care must be taken to gather an understanding of an entity's legal status before making any judgment under the provisions of GAAP.

Caution: Sub-Units of Government that are Separately Presented

In some cases, so-called "sub-government" entities such as departments, agencies and programs are audited for operational, legal, regulatory, and managerial purposes. No GAAP exists for sub-government entities that are part of the reporting entity of a government. Departments, agencies, and programs may be separately audited, but they do not represent the entirety of a reporting entity.

The AICPA Audit and Accounting Guide *State and Local Governments* contains guidance on the potential audit reports for sub-units of governments within paragraph 17.102. Unless the sub-unit reports are required to use a special-purpose framework, GAAP generally must be followed as if the sub-unit was an entire reporting entity to the extent possible. To do this, practitioners consider laws, regulations, long-established practices, and other relevant procedures to follow GAAP. Financial reporting of sub-government entities then also would include all relevant financial statements in a format in accordance with GAAP (unless laws and regulations establish a special purpose framework). The management's discussion and analysis and required supplementary information that is relevant to the sub-unit would also apply.

THE FINANCIAL REPORTING ENTITY CONCEPT

At every level of government (local, state, and federal), all public resources are the responsibility of elected officials. In the context of financial reporting, once public officials are elected, the citizenry has a right to be informed as to how public resources were used during a period. To hold public officials responsible for an entity's financial affairs, care must be taken in defining the financial reporting entity. If the financial reporting entity is defined in a manner that does not represent the authority empowered in public officials, the objective of accountability cannot be achieved. Fundamentally, GAAP attempts to follow a basic rule of responsibility accounting, which reasons that one should not be held accountable for something that one cannot influence [GASB Cod. Sec. 2100.109].

The reporting entity's financial statements are structured so that a reader can differentiate between the primary government, including its blended component units, and its discretely presented component units. This is accomplished by formatting the government-wide financial statements so that balances and transactions of the primary government are presented separately from those of its discretely presented component units. In addition, the reporting entity's fund financial statements include only the primary government's governmental, proprietary, and fiduciary funds, and the first two fund categories are presented by major fund, with nonmajor funds being aggregated and presented in a single column.

The two methods used to integrate the financial information of component units into the financial statements of the reporting entity are "discrete presentation" and "blending." GAAP defines these methods as follows:

Discrete presentation method—The method of reporting financial data of component units in a column(s) separate from the financial data of the primary government. An integral part of this method of presentation is that major component unit supporting information is required to be provided in the reporting entity's basic financial statements by:

- Presenting each major component unit in a separate column in the reporting entity's statements of net position and activities,
- Including combining statements of major component units in the reporting entity's basic statements after the fund financial statements, or
- Presenting condensed financial statements in the notes to the reporting entity's basic financial statements.

PRACTICE ALERT: The GASB's *Financial Reporting Model Improvements* Exposure Draft document includes the Board's tentative view that if it is not feasible to present major component unit financial statements in a separate column(s) in the reporting entity's statement of net position and statement of activities, the financial statements of the major component units should be presented in the reporting entity's basic financial statements as combining financial statements after the fund financial statement.

For component units that are fiduciary in nature, financial information is reported only in the fund financial statements in the primary government's statements of fiduciary net position and changes in fiduciary net position. The same basis of accounting for fiduciary funds is used.

Blending method—The method of reporting the financial data of a component unit that presents the component unit's balances and transactions in a manner like the presentation of the balances and transactions of the primary government's funds. Despite legal separation, such entities are so interrelated to the primary government that they are a part of the primary government. Therefore, the balances and results of operations are reported similarly to other funds (see later discussion in section titled "Blending Component Units") [GASB Cod. Sec. 2100.110].

FINANCIAL ACCOUNTABILITY AND THE FINANCIAL REPORTING ENTITY

GAAP defines "financial accountability" as follows [GASB Cod. Sec. 2100.120]:

The level of accountability that exists if a primary government appoints a voting majority of an organization's governing board and is either able to impose its will on that organization or there is a potential for the organization to provide specific financial benefits to, or impose specific financial burdens on, the primary government. A primary government may also be financially accountable for governmental organizations with a separately elected governing board, a governing board appointed by another government, or a jointly appointed board that is fiscally dependent on the primary government.

Even though the core of a financial reporting entity usually is a primary government, a governmental organization other than a primary government (such as a component unit, a joint venture, a jointly governed organization, or another stand-alone government) serves as the core for *its own reporting entity* when it issues separate financial statements. In those cases of entities other than a primary government having component units, provisions of U.S. GAAP also apply to their separately issued basic financial statements for those governmental component units, joint ventures, jointly governed organizations, and other stand-alone governments and, therefore, those entities may present financial reports similarly to a primary government.

PRIMARY GOVERNMENTS

Definition of a Primary Government

In addition to states, Tribal Nations, and general-purpose local governmental entities, special-purpose governmental entities are considered primary governments if the entity satisfies *all* the following criteria:

- The entity has a separately elected governing body, elected by the citizenry in a general, popular election.
- The entity is legally separate from other entities, including the possession of "corporate powers." Such powers include the right to have a name, the right to sue or be sued in its own name without recourse to any other governmental unit, and the right to buy, sell, lease, or incur debt in its own name. Such powers are enumerated in enabling statutes, charters, and similar, depending upon state laws or constitution (see later discussion in section titled "Determining Separate Legal Standing").
- The entity is fiscally independent of other state and local governmental entities (see later discussion in section titled "Determining Fiscal Independence or Dependence").

Determining Separate Legal Standing

GAAP provides the following definition of "separate legal standing":

> An organization created as a body corporate or a body corporate and politic or otherwise possessing similar corporate powers. An organization that has separate legal standing has an identity of its own as an "artificial person" with a personality and existence distinct from that of its creator and others.

An entity is a legally separate organization if it is given the powers that are generally held by an individual. In effect, a separate legal entity is an artificial person having such powers as a distinct separate name, the right to be a party in litigation, and the right to finalize legal contracts. This concept is also known as the "body politic." It may also have the right to buy or sell property, have a corporate seal, establish a budget, issue debt, or set rates and charges.

For a special-purpose government to be a primary government, it must have separate legal standing. If it does not have such standing, it is part of the primary government that exercises the corporate powers related to its activities [GASB Cod. Sec. 2100.114].

PRACTICE POINT: GASB Cod. Sec. 1300.130 contains guidance that is often overlooked regarding trusts and equivalent arrangements in determining legal separation. *Generally*, pension plans that are administered through trusts that meet the criteria for an irrevocable trust (or equivalent arrangement) in GASB Cod. Secs. Pe5.101, Pe6.101 and OPEB plans that are administered through an irrevocable trust (or equivalent arrangement) that meet such criteria discussed in GASB Cod. Secs. Po50.101, Po51.101 *are legally separate entities.*

Legally separate entities may not be component units. In determining whether those legally separate entities are component units, a primary government is considered to have a financial burden relative to a defined benefit pension or OPEB plan if it is legally obligated or has otherwise assumed the obligation to make contributions to the pension plan or OPEB plan, which is common. The phrase "trusts or equivalent arrangements" is described by those referenced paragraphs as plans in which:

- Contributions from employers and nonemployer contributing entities to the plan and earnings on those contributions are irrevocable. In some circumstances, payments made by the employer to satisfy contribution requirements are identified by the plan as plan member contribution requirements. Such contributions are classified as plan member contributions for financial reporting purposes and do not eliminate this requirement.

- Plan assets are dedicated to providing pensions (or OPEB) to plan members in accordance with benefit terms. The assets may also be used for administrative costs or to refund plan member contributions in accordance with those terms, without eliminating this provision.

- Plan assets are legally protected from creditors of the employers, the nonemployer contributing entities, plan members and the plan administrator.

A related *Implementation Guide* question should be considered when a pension or OPEB plan is administered through a trust but has no governing board. Should the plans be included as a fiduciary component unit of the government?

In question 1300.716-6, the answer from the GASB is "Yes." In the case where a sponsoring government performs the duties that a governing board typically would perform (e.g., the government determines or amends the structure of the plan [vesting requirements and required contributions]). If that other government (e.g., a sponsoring government) is legally obligated to make contributions to the defined benefit pension or OPEB plan, the plan is included as a fiduciary component unit of that other government.

In accordance with GASB Cod. Sec. 2100.120(a), a government is financially accountable for a legally separate organization if it appoints a voting majority of the organization's governing body and there is a potential for the organization to provide specific financial benefits to, or impose specific financial burdens on, the government.

Some governments may not have a governing board. In those circumstances, another governing body performs the duties of a governing board. For example, a city council is the governing board of a primary government. The city's pension plan, sponsored by the city, does not have a governing board. The city council adjourns meetings and then five minutes later, reconvenes to discuss pension matters.

In those cases, a government (e.g., a sponsoring government) that performs the duties of a governing board in the absence of one *should be considered equivalent to a governing board* for which the government appoints a voting majority. Furthermore, in accordance with paragraph GASB Cod. Sec. 1300.130, a government is considered to have a financial burden if it is legally obligated or has otherwise assumed the obligation to make contributions to the pension or OPEB plan. As a result, the plan should be included as a fiduciary component unit of the other government (e.g., a sponsoring government).

However, there are plans where this does occur often. There are also employee benefit plans that are not postemployment benefit plans. As an example, Internal Revenue Code (IRC) Section 457(b) plans are *deferred compensation* plans and not pension plans. IRC Section 403(b) plans primarily offered to educators are not required by the IRC to have trust agreements or equivalent arrangements as participants are directed to tax sheltered annuities or custodial accounts, which are regulated similarly to trusts. Section 403(b) plans are also subject to rules within the IRC requiring contributions to result in benefits exclusive to participants. Yet, many practitioners view these plans to be legally separate from sponsoring governments. Governmental employer/sponsors of such plans may also contribute to the plans, in some cases on behalf of employees. As a result of the contributions, a financial burden can be thought of as occurring.

PRACTICE POINT: For Internal Revenue Code Section 457 deferred compensation plans, if such plans meet the definition of a pension plan, then the provisions of GAAP related to pension plans apply, including for Section 457 plans that are defined benefit plans (which are rare) [GASB Cod. Sec. D25.101].

A pension plan is defined in GAAP as an arrangement "through which pensions are determined, assets dedicated for pensions are accumulated and managed, and benefits are paid as they come due." [GASB Cod. Sec. Pe5.527]. If the 457 deferred compensation plan *does not* meet the definition of a pension plan, then the provisions of GASB Cod. Secs. 1300.128–.136 would apply, with a focus on GASB Cod. Secs. 1300.133–.135. As a practical matter, few such plans that are not defined benefit plans may be controlled by the sponsoring government and, therefore, may not be reported as fiduciary activities.

Determining Fiscal Independence or Dependence

The third criterion that must be satisfied for a special-purpose government to be considered a primary government is fiscal independence. For an entity to be considered fiscally independent, it must have the authority to do *all three* of the following without *substantive approval* or modification of another government:

1. Establish a budget,
2. Either levy taxes or set rates or charges, and
3. Issue bonded debt.

A special-purpose government *that is not fiscally independent* is fiscally dependent on the primary government that holds one or more of those powers. A special-purpose government may be fiscally dependent on another state or local government regardless of whether it receives financial assistance from that state or local government; fiscal dependency does not necessarily imply that a financial benefit or burden relationship exists (see discussion in this chapter on Financial Benefit or Burden) [GASB Cod. Sec. 2100.115].

If a special-purpose government does not satisfy all three criteria, the entity is fiscally dependent on the primary government that holds the power of approval or modification.

To determine whether a special-purpose government is fiscally independent, the primary government should differentiate between *substantive* approvals and *ministerial (or compliance)* approvals. Special-purpose governments typically are subject to the general oversight of their respective state governments, and sometimes to the oversight of county or other local governments as well. Often, this general oversight responsibility includes an approval process that is more ministerial or compliance oriented than substantive.

Examples of approvals that are likely to be ministerial or compliance oriented in nature rather than substantive are:

- A requirement for a state agency to approve local government debt after review for compliance with certain limitations, such as a debt margin calculation based on a percentage of assessed valuation,
- A requirement for a state agency, such as a department of education, to review a local government's budget in evaluating qualifications for state funding; and
- A requirement for a county government official, such as the county clerk, to approve tax rates and levy amounts after review for compliance with tax rate and levy limitations [GASB Cod. Sec. 2100.116].

Even though a special-purpose government may be subject to substantive approvals, such approvals are not indicative of the special-purpose government being a primary government. GAAP includes examples of when budgetary approval is substantive if a primary government has the authority to reduce or modify a special-purpose government's budget. In such a case, a transit entity that is a special-purpose government must submit a budget to a state for approval and the state has the authority to reduce or modify the transit entity's budget if the economy is in fiscal distress.

However, if a special-purpose government is *statutorily prohibited* from incurring debt, the special-purpose government may still be fiscally independent if it possesses the other two powers as the statutory prohibition does not subordinate the special-purpose government to another government for debt approval [GASB Cod. Sec. 2100.117].

GAAP acknowledges that a primary government may be temporarily subject to the financial control of another government. Usually, this involves a state government taking control or providing oversight of a municipal government or a school district because of financial difficulties. When the financial control is temporary, the governmental entity subject to the control is still considered fiscally independent for purposes of GAAP.

Of course, the government under fiscal control may also have to implement GASB Cod. Sec. Bn5 (*Bankruptcies*), if Chapter 9, Title 11 of the United States Code (U.S. bankruptcy code for municipalities) is available in the jurisdiction [GASB Cod. Sec. 2100, fn. 2]. Not all states have approved that section of the Code and therefore, oversight is used during times of fiscal emergency. In practice, if the government is expected to exit fiscal oversight in this case, it is unlikely that a continuing component unit relationship may exist with the overseeing government. In such situations, disclosure of the relationship may be warranted.

PRACTICE ALERT: The GASB is in the process of potentially updating the provisions addressing going concern uncertainties and severe financial stress. Four areas of focus are involved with the project:

1. Consideration of improvements to existing guidance for going concern considerations to address diversity in practice and clarify the circumstances under which disclosure is appropriate,

2. Developing a definition of severe financial stress and criteria for identifying when governments should disclose their exposure to severe financial stress, and

3. Are there common indicators of severe financial stress and are those indicators used to evaluate exposure to severe financial stress? And,

4. What information about a government's exposure to severe financial stress is necessary to disclose?

The GASB currently plans a Preliminary Views document for release by August 2024. After a projected 120-day comment period, further deliberations and field testing may occur throughout the remainder of 2024 and throughout 2025. An exposure draft may not be released until March 2026. If approved, a final statement may not be released until April 2027.

COMPONENT UNITS

What are Component Units?

GAAP describes component units as legally separate organizations for which the elected officials of the primary government are financially accountable. In addition, component units can be other organizations for which the nature and significance of their relationship with a primary government are such that exclusion would cause the reporting entity's financial statements to be misleading. Component units can be governmental organizations, not-for-profit corporations, or even for-profit corporations. A component unit cannot be a primary government. GAAP requires that three separate criteria be applied to an organization to determine whether it is a component unit of the primary government. These three criteria are summarized as follows and in Exhibit 4-1:

1. Financial accountability,
2. Nature and significance of relationship, and
3. How closely the entities are related or financially integrated.

Component units, therefore, are legally separate organizations for which the elected officials of the primary government are financially accountable. In addition, component units can be other organizations for which the nature and significance of their relationship with a primary government are such that exclusion would cause the reporting entity's financial statements to be misleading [GASB Cod. Sec. 2100.119] (See **PRACTICE ALERT** below).

EXHIBIT 4-1
DETERMINING WHETHER AN ORGANIZATION IS A COMPONENT UNIT OF A PRIMARY GOVERNMENT

Criterion	Methods of Integration	GASB Codification Sections
The primary government appoints the voting majority of the Board.	Blended *or* discrete presentation	2100.121–.123
The primary government is financially accountable for the other organization through financial benefits or burdens *or* imposition of will.	Blended *or* discrete presentation	2100.124–.132
The primary government may be financially accountable for a fiscally dependent government, inclusive of the potential to provide a financial benefit to or burden on the primary government. This may include special-purpose governments with separately elected governing boards, governmental organizations with boards appointed by another government or governmental organizations with jointly approved boards.	Blended *or* discrete presentation	2100.133–.136
The nature and significance of the relationship between the primary government and the other organization.	Blended *or* discrete presentation	2100.138
The other organization is a not-for-profit corporation in which the primary government is the sole corporate member as identified in the articles of incorporation or by-laws.	Blended	2600.113

PRACTICE ALERT: The method of integration may change due to changes in law, regulation, or some other change to an enabling statute. The reporting of such a change would be a change to or within the financial reporting entity in accordance with GASB Cod. Sec. 2250.127, as most recently updated by GASB Statement No. 100, (*Accounting Changes and Error Corrections*). Acquisitions, mergers, or transfers of operations that result in the addition or removal of a discretely presented component unit as well as a component unit reported as a majority equity interest would not trigger a change to or within the financial reporting entity in accordance with GASB Cod. Sec. 2250.128. If a change is triggered, GASB Cod. Sec. 2250.140 requires adjusting the current reporting period's beginning net position, fund balance, or fund net position, as applicable, for the effect of the change as if the change occurred as of the beginning of the reporting period. Note disclosure describing the change is also required. GASB Statement No. 100 became effective for periods beginning after June 15, 2023.

Financial Accountability

Accountability is not only financial in nature but also operational. Accountability flows from the notion that individuals are obliged to account for their acts, including the acts of the officials they appoint to operate governmental agencies. Thus, elected officials are accountable for an organization if they appoint a voting majority of the organization's governing board. Sometimes, however, appointments are not substantive; other governments (usually at a lower level) may have oversight responsibility for those officials.

A primary government that is financially accountable for a legally separate entity should include the financial information of that entity with its own financial statements to form the financial reporting entity. Financial accountability exists if the primary government appoints a voting majority of the entity's governing body and if either one of the following conditions exists:

- It can impose its will on that organization; or
- There is a potential for the organization to provide specific financial benefits to, or impose specific financial burdens on, the primary government, regardless of whether the organization has:
  — A separately elected governing board,
  — Governing board appointed by a higher level of government, or
  — A jointly appointed board.

Accountability is primarily demonstrated when individuals are obliged to account for their acts, including the acts of the officials they appoint to operate governmental agencies. Therefore, elected officials are accountable for an organization if they appoint a voting majority of the organization's governing board. Sometimes, however, appointments are more ministerial than substantive. In these cases, other governments (usually at a lower level) may have oversight responsibility for those officials.

In addition, financial accountability may exist when another entity is fiscally dependent (see the earlier discussion in the section titled "Determining Fiscal Independence or Dependence") on the primary government, even if the primary government does not appoint a voting majority of the entity's governing body. Therefore, fiscal accountability could exist even when the entity's governing board is separately elected, appointed by a government higher than the primary government, or jointly appointed (see the later discussion in the section titled "Financial Accountability Resulting from Fiscal Dependency") [GASB Cod. Sec. 2100.120, fns. 4–5].

OBSERVATION: GASB Cod. Sec. 2100.120 also contains guidance for financial accountability if a government holds a majority equity interest in another organization. The primary government *is* financially accountable for a legally separate organization if the primary government's holding of a majority equity interest in that organization *does not* meet the definition of an investment (see later section in the chapter).

Appointment of a Voting Majority

Financial accountability is dependent on whether a primary government appoints a voting majority of another entity's governing body. In most instances, the appointment of a simple majority is equivalent to a voting majority because the approval of financial issues is based on a simple majority vote. However, if more than a simple majority is required to approve financial issues, the appointment of a simple majority does not result in the primary government being financially accountable for the other entity.

OBSERVATION: GASB Cod. Sec. 2100, fn. 5, states that in determining whether most of the entity's governing body has been appointed, the number of appointments by the primary government would include primary government officials who are serving on the entity's governing board as required by law (also known as "*ex-officio*").

GASB Cod. Secs. 2100.121–.123 defines "appoint" as follows:

> To select members of a governing board ([if] the ability to do so is not severely limited by a nomination process) or confirm appointments made by others (provided that the confirmation is more than a formality or part of a ministerial responsibility).

The above definition recognizes that the appointment process must be more than perfunctory in that the process must demonstrate substance rather than form. In determining whether the appointment process is *substantive*, the nomination and confirmation processes should be examined.

Nomination process. The appointment process should not be significantly restricted by the nomination process. If the primary government must appoint members of the other entity's governing body who are nominated by another entity or entities, financial accountability cannot exist. What constitutes substantive appointment authority by the primary government is subjective. However, in one example, GAAP characterizes a limiting nomination process as one where the primary government must select three appointees from a slate of five candidates. In practice, the nomination process should be carefully examined to determine the degree of substantive involvement of the primary government in the nomination process.

Confirmation process. GASB takes the position that the confirmation process is not a substitute for the appointment process. Thus, if prospective members of the other entity's governing body are nominated or appointed by parties other than the primary government's officials or appointees, the primary government's right to confirm the nomination or appointment may suggest the appointment process is not substantive [GASB Cod. Sec. 2100.122].

Based on the language of GAAP, the appointment process could still be substantive even if the primary government's role in the appointment process is limited to confirmation. Although GAAP does not elaborate on this possibility, presumably the appointment process would be considered substantive if the primary government has the necessary prerequisites to conduct an effective confirmation hearing. These prerequisites could include the necessary legislative authority, enough staff to research issues, and a period that allows for reasonable investigation before nominations become effective.

Appointment authority is usually continuing and not limited to an initial appointment. Thus, the primary government may have the authority to make appointments as vacancies arise. In those circumstances where continuing authority for appointment does not exist, financial accountability between the primary government and the other entity will exist if the primary government has created the other entity (equivalent to appointing the governing body) and can unilaterally abolish the other entity [GASB Cod. Sec. 2100.123].

Substantive versus ministerial appointment authority is addressed in GASB Cod. Sec. 2100.713-8. The question and answer define a "substantive appointment" as not based on *ceremony* or *formality*. Generally, a substantive appointment is a selection that is *not significantly encumbered by a limited field of preselected candidates* (known as a "slate" in some instances.) Professional judgment should be used to determine whether the role of the primary government is substantive based on all the relevant information available about the appointment process. GASB Cod. Sec. 2100.713-9 shows the opposite effect. If the appointing official may reject all nominees, the process would not limit the primary government's appointment authority and its authority *would be considered substantive.* There is no provision in GAAP specifying the number of nominees that could be rejected before the appointment would be considered substantive.

In summation, if a primary government appoints a voting majority of the governing board of an organization, the action of its appointees alone can control the decisions of that organization. Other examples of appointment authority and outcomes in GAAP include:

Element/Fact Pattern	Outcome	GASB Codification Section
Primary government creating an organization or appointing the initial board?	• The primary government **is accountable** for that organization.	2100.713-2
Potential component unit's articles of incorporation designate *certain* primary government officials ("ex-officio") to be potential component unit board members, representing a voting majority of the potential component unit board.	• **Yes.** Accountability exists. (Example: City housing authority board has five members, three of which are the mayor, city manager and city economic development director.)	2100.713-3

Element/Fact Pattern	Outcome	GASB Codification Section
Potential component unit's articles of incorporation require board to appoint new board members from primary government's employees.	• This is different from the primary government having voting majority <u>unless employees are serving as representatives of the primary government</u>. Use professional judgment as appointment could be job-specific.	2100.713-4
Authority to appoint board of a potential component unit of a *city* rests with an elected official of a primary government, who delegates that authority to an official of the state.	• Yes. Accountability exists as the elected official still has responsibility.	2100.713-6
Housing authority is the general partner of a limited tax credit partnership which is legally separate. The limited partners have limited rights of operation for the housing authority.	• Yes. The Board of the housing authority is the general partner and is tantamount to the voting majority.	2100.713-7
A state official appoints board members for an organization from a list of nominees provided by various groups or entities. The official may reject the full list with no limit.	• Yes. This is a substantive appointment authority as it is not severely limited by nomination.	2100.713-9

PRACTICE POINT: As discussed, there are circumstances where a legally separate organization may be a potential component unit, but has no governing board. If the primary government performs the duties that a board would normally perform, the absence of a board is the same as the appointment of a voting majority of a board. There are major exceptions to this provision in the case of a potential component unit that is a defined contribution pension or OPEB plan or some other employee benefit plan. Such other employee benefit plans may include certain Section 457 plans [GASB Cod. Sec. 2100.124, fn. 7].

Imposition of Will

Imposition of will is evidenced by the primary government's ability to affect the day-to-day operations of the other entity. GAAP defines this as:

> The ability to significantly influence the programs, projects, activities, or level of services performed or provided by an organization.

The determination of whether imposition of will takes place is a matter of judgment, and the specific circumstances of each relationship must be carefully evaluated. In evaluating the imposition of will, the ability to affect day-to-day operations must be substantive and not merely procedural (see earlier discussion in the section titled "Determining Fiscal Independence or Dependence").

This determination is vital to determining the extent of the reporting entity. If the primary government appoints a voting majority of an organization's officials *and* can impose its will on the organization, the primary government *is financially accountable* for that organization.

Although the determination of whether imposition of will takes place is a matter of judgment, GAAP states that existence of *any* of the following is a clear indication of the ability of the primary government to affect the day-to-day operations of another entity:

- Appointed members can be removed at will by the primary government,
- The budget can be modified or approved by the primary government,
- Rate or fee changes that affect revenues can be modified or approved by the primary government,
- Decisions other than those related to the budget, rates, or fees may be vetoed, overruled, or modified by the primary government, and
- Management personnel may be appointed, hired, reassigned, or dismissed by the primary government [GASB Cod. Sec. 2100.125].

Many enabling statutes contain "sunset" legislation or provisions, which are dates in which the statute is no longer law. GASB Cod. Sec. 2100.714-4 addresses sunsets. *In general,* sunsets do not give the ability to impose will as defined in GAAP. A legislative body's ability to terminate agencies, programs, or organizations generally involves a formal system of due process. The ability to *unilaterally* abolish is like the ability to remove an appointed board member at *will*. Otherwise, *sunset review process* is synonymous with *removal for cause.*

The GASB notes the former is the ability to impose will, while the latter is not.

There are differences between "fiscal dependency" and "imposition of will" in GAAP that are often confusing. As stated previously in the chapter, the financial accountability of a primary government for another organization flows either from:

- The organization's fiscal dependency on the primary government; or
- The primary government's appointment of a voting majority of the governing board of the organization.

The fiscal dependency criteria previously discussed in this chapter relate to special-purpose governments with governing boards that are not appointed by the primary government. These criteria focus on the basic actions necessary for an organization to function as an autonomous government. If a special-purpose government is required to rely on another government to carry out any one of the responsibilities included in these criteria, it is not fiscally independent and is not able to function with autonomy. This would be true regardless of how the governing body of the organization is determined. In those cases, if there also is a financial benefit or burden relationship present, the special-purpose government would be included as a part of the reporting entity of the government that holds those powers.

The ability to impose will plays a different role in the determination of whether a primary government is financially accountable for an organization. Imposition of will is a means of determining whether the appointment authority granted to the primary government would result in financial accountability. Therefore, imposition of will creates financial accountability only when coupled with the authority to appoint a voting majority of the potential component unit's governing board [GASB Cod. Sec. 2100.714-1].

Other examples of imposition of will and outcomes in GAAP are summarized in the chart below:

Element/Fact Pattern	Outcome	GASB Codification Section
Potential component unit's charter requires that five of the seven members of the governing board be appointed by the city council from council members.	• *Not necessarily imposition of will.* Even though members make up most of the potential component unit's Board, they may not be the majority of city council.	2100.714-2
A primary government is required to approve any additions or changes to the component unit's facilities by statute. The potential component unit has been in the same facilities for many years and is expected to stay there indefinitely.	• **Yes.** Imposition of will exists as there is significant influence over the level of services performed or provided by the organization as the primary government has the authority over facilities. Otherwise, the primary government is like a property owner or lessor.	2100.714-6
A primary government may remove members of the governing board of a potential component unit "for cause."	• For cause does not mean "at will." Professional judgment should be used to determine whether the restriction is substantive. Removal for "inefficiency" could be considered imposition of will, unless due process is required (hearings, listing of cause, etc.)	2100.714-7
An excise tax on lodging levied by a city council is required by statute to be spent solely to make contributions to a not-for-profit convention and visitors center within the city.	• If the city has the authority to determine the rate of the excise tax or approve the tax, the city can impose its will on the potential component unit.	2100.714-8
A primary government is the principal user of a potential component unit's services. However, the transactions do not meet the financial benefit/burden criteria (see next section).	• Does not necessarily indicate imposition of will. This is like the primary government being the main resource provider of an organization.	2100.714-9

Financial Benefit to or Burden on a Primary Government

GAAP states that financial benefit or financial burden is created if *any* of the following relationships exists:

- The primary government is legally entitled to or can otherwise access the organization's resources,
- The primary government is legally obligated or has otherwise assumed the obligation to finance the deficits of, or provide financial support to, the organization, or
- The primary government is obligated in some manner for the debt of the organization.

GAAP also states that if there are exchange transactions between a primary government and a potential component unit, the transactions are *not necessarily* indicative of a financial benefit or burden. Exchange transactions are value for value. In a government, exchange transactions may appear to be funding for clean water infrastructure in exchange for clean water. But GAAP discloses that the funding aspect is not a purchase of services. Rather, it is a grant or a subsidy that usually benefits the public, not just the primary government.

In identifying financial benefits or financial burdens that create financial accountability, the benefits to or the burdens on the primary government can be either direct or indirect. For example, if the primary government is entitled to any surplus of another governmental entity, the effect is direct. On the other hand, if a component unit of the primary government is entitled to its own surplus, the effect is indirect with respect to the primary government. Either direct or indirect financial burden or benefit implies financial accountability between a primary government and another entity.

As discussed, governmental entities will engage in a variety of exchange transactions with other parties. Exchange transactions are characterized by each party giving up goods or services of approximately equivalent value. For example, a primary government may purchase used computer equipment from another governmental entity or a commercial enterprise. An exchange transaction does not create a financial benefit or financial burden relationship and therefore is not relevant in determining whether a primary government is financially accountable for another entity [GASB Cod. Secs. 2100.127–.128].

Entitlement or access to the other entity's resources. Financial benefits arise when the primary government can use the resources of another entity. The *ability* needs only to exist. There *does not need to be an actual transaction* that has occurred during the period or during previous periods to demonstrate that the primary government has received assets from the other entity.

A primary government may have a right to the residual assets of another entity if the other entity is liquidated or otherwise dissolved. An interest in the residual assets of another entity is not considered equivalent to access to the other entity's resources and therefore is not considered a benefit to the primary government for the purposes of determining financial accountability.

Access to an entity's resources may be obvious because of the relationship between the primary government and the other entity. For example, an entity may be organized specifically to collect revenue that will be remitted to the primary government (e.g., a state lottery).

Alternatively, access to an entity's resources may be based on a strategy that enables the other entity to charge a fee for its services that exceeds the amount needed to maintain its own capital, and then remit the excess to the primary government. Irrespective of the name used for such a remittance (payments in lieu of taxes, contributions, or amounts due the primary government), the relationship demonstrates that the primary government has access to the other entity's resources [GASB Cod. Secs. 2100.128–.130].

Legal or assumed obligation or responsibility for deficits or support. Specific financial burdens arise when the primary government is legally obligated or has assumed the responsibility to:

- Finance an entity's deficit, *or*
- Provide financial support to the entity.

The following are examples of this type of specific financial burden:

- An entity charges an amount for its services that will not be enough to cover the total cost of providing such services, and a primary government, either by law or by public policy, assumes the responsibility for any deficit that may arise. Examples of this include operating subsidies for a public college or university and capital grants for urban mass transit systems.
- A primary government assumes the responsibility for any deficit that another entity may incur even though a deficit has never arisen and there is no expectation that one will arise.

A special arrangement may exist whereby an entity may be fully or partially funded through tax increment financing. For example, a tax rate may be established at 7% by a primary government but another entity may receive 1% of the revenue raised to finance its operations. Tax increment financing is considered a form of financial burden irrespective of whether the incremental amount is collected by the primary government or directly by the other entity [GASB Cod. Secs. 2100.131–.132].

Responsibility for debt. The primary government may accept an obligation for the debt of another entity. The obligation may be expressed or implied. For example, an expressed obligation could arise from legislation that specifically makes a state liable for another entity's debt, or covenants contained in a bond agreement that obligate the state in case of default by the other entity. In addition, the primary government may take explicit action by assuming responsibility for the debt of another entity. An implied obligation could be based on relevant legal precedents that have occurred and may differ from state to state.

The following are example conditions any one of which would obligate the primary government for the debt of another entity:

1. The primary government is legally responsible for debt that is not paid after other default remedies have been pursued,
2. The primary government is required to provide funds to cover temporary deficiencies that will eventually be paid by primary repayment sources or by other default remedies,

3. The primary government is required either to fund reserves maintained by the other entity or to create its own reserve fund,
4. The primary government is authorized either to fund reserves maintained by the other entity or to create its own reserve fund and has established such a fund (see 6 and 7 below for guidance that is relevant when the primary entity has not established a fund),
5. The primary government is authorized either to provide financing for a reserve fund maintained by the other entity for repurchasing outstanding debt or to create its own reserve fund and has established such a fund (see below for guidance that is relevant when the primary entity has not established a fund),
6. The debt contract states that the primary government may cover defaults, although it is not required to do so, or
7. Legal precedents within a state, or actions taken by a primary government, related to actual or potential defaults make it probable that the primary government will be responsible for the other entity's defaulted debt [GASB Cod. Sec. 2100.133].

GAAP defines the term "probable," in GASB Cod. Sec. C50.155 as "the future event or events are *likely to occur.*"

Financial Guarantee of Debt. A financial guarantee transaction could signal a responsibility for the debts of another government. GASB Cod. Sec. F30 (*Financial Guarantees*) includes GAAP for accounting and financial reporting of contracts and other liabilities that are guaranteed by governments (primarily in the form of debt guarantees). Due to the implementation of GASB Statement No. 99 (*Omnibus 2022*), GAAP is inclusive of *nonexchange, exchange* and *exchange-like* transactions. (See Chapter 17 on nonexchange and exchange revenue transactions and Chapter 18 on nonexchange and exchange expenses and expenditures transactions.) In all cases, one government is providing a guarantee to another (or a private entity). Governments must consider qualitative as well as historical or quantitative factors regarding whether a liability exists at the guarantor government to provide for payment of the debts of the guaranteed government.

PRACTICE POINT: The guidance for nonexchange financial guarantees is expanded to exchange and exchange-like guarantees through the implementation of GASB Statement No. 99 (*Omnibus 2022*), pars. 4–7. Guarantees relating to special assessments, financial guarantee contracts of derivative instruments and conduit debt obligations are excluded from the guidance. The provisions became effective for reporting periods beginning after June 15, 2023. Changes adopted were to be applied retroactively by restating all prior periods presented if practicable. Upon implementation, the former GASB Cod. Sec. N30 was rescinded. The new GASB Cod. Sec. F30, *Financial Guarantees*, includes the provisions of GASB Statement Nos. 70, 91, 99, GASBTB 2020-1 and related *Implementation Guide* questions and answers.

The provisions of GASB Cod. Sec. F30 use a threshold of "more likely than not" of a likelihood that a guarantee will be exercised considering qualitative as well as quantitative aspects. As most recently described in GASB Statement No. 101, footnote 1 (*Compensated Absences*), the term *more likely than not* means a likelihood of *more than* 50 percent. If a range of probabilities of exercise is known and no amount is better than another to establish whether the more-likely-than-not standard is met, then the minimum amount will be used to measure the likelihood that a guarantee will be exercised.

In some cases, a guarantee may be provided between a primary government and a component unit. In circumstances in which a government has issued an obligation guaranteed in a nonexchange transaction by its primary government (and the government is a blended component unit of the primary government), by one of its blended component units, or by another blended component unit of the same primary government of which the government is a blended component unit, GASB Cod. Sec. F30 requires the government to recognize a receivable in the amount of any guaranteed liability recognized by the guarantor. Additional discussions on financial guarantees are contained in Chapters 12, 16, and 17.

Financial benefits and burdens may exist in many other forms. In one example, a law contains a formal agreement that establishes a temporary financial burden. GASB Cod. Sec. 2100.715-9, explains how GAAP *does not require* a legally binding financial burden relationship for a potential component unit to meet the criteria for inclusion in the reporting entity. GAAP only requires *the potential for an organization to impose financial burdens on the primary government.*

As previously discussed, GASB Cod. Sec. 2100.133(g) states that financial burden exists when *"previous actions by the primary government related to actual or potential defaults on another organization's debt make it probable that the primary government will assume responsibility for the debt in the event of default."* The fact that the primary government has entered into an agreement that creates a financial burden may indicate that it would do so again in the future, which would create the potential for financial burden and meet the criteria for inclusion. Professional judgment should be used to determine whether the facts in each situation manifest financial accountability.

Other examples of the concept of financial benefit to or burden on a primary government and outcomes of the example in GAAP include:

Element/Fact Pattern	Outcome	GASB Codification Section
City imposes a payment in lieu of taxes on various special-purpose governments to recover the cost of providing governmental services to public entities that operate as private enterprises and are exempt from property taxes.	• The special-purpose governments provide a financial benefit to the primary government. They are not taxes. They are generally subsidies.	2100.715-4
Public power authority (a potential component unit) provides electricity to a city (primary government) at no charge, or at rates that are substantially less than rates charged to other users.	• **Yes.** If the value received or sacrificed is disproportionate, it is a financial benefit/burden.	2100.715-5

Element/Fact Pattern	Outcome	GASB Codification Section
A primary government makes recurring subsidies (cash for operations or contributions of capital assets). There is no requirement for the primary government to continue to provide the subsidies.	• The pattern could be interpreted as providing financial support and the existence of a financial burden.	2100.715-7
A potential component unit is authorized to issue debt in its own name. To obtain better interest rates, the primary government issues its own general obligation bonds for the potential component unit. Amounts equal to the debt service are paid to the primary government by the potential component unit.	• Due to the legal obligation to pay the debt, the primary government has a financial benefit/burden relationship with the potential component unit.	2100.715-12
Free services are provided by a city to a public housing authority.	• **Yes.** The primary government is sacrificing resources and has a financial burden to the authority.	2100.715-14

Financial Accountability Resulting from Fiscal Dependency

A primary government is financially accountable for another entity when the other entity is fiscally dependent on the primary government. There is no difference if the entity has a separately elected governing board, a board appointed by another government, or a jointly appointed board [GASB Cod. Sec. 2100.134].

PRACTICE POINT: As previously discussed, GASB Cod. Sec. 1300.130 limits the criteria regarding fiduciary activities in the analysis of financial accountability resulting from fiscal dependency in potential component units that are fiduciary in nature only to defined benefit pension and OPEB plans that are administered through trusts.

Fiscal independence was discussed earlier in this chapter in the context of a special-purpose government considered a primary government for financial reporting purposes. An entity that is *not fiscally independent* is therefore dependent on usually a higher level of government. More specifically, fiscal dependency arises if one or more of the following activities cannot be performed by the entity without substantive approval or modification by a primary government:

- Establish a budget.
- Either levy taxes or set rates or charges.
- Issue bonded debt.

Special-purpose governments with separately elected governing boards. Many governmental entities have been established for special purposes and have separately elected governing boards. Such entities commonly are fiscally dependent on a primary government. For example, school districts often have separately elected boards, but their fiscal activities are subject to approval or modification by the municipality or county in which they serve. Entities of this nature should be presented as component units of the primary government on which they are fiscally dependent if a financial benefit or burden relationship also exists [GASB Cod. Sec. 2100.135].

> **OBSERVATION:** School boards especially may believe they are autonomous from the municipalities they may be geographically part of. The legal facts and circumstances must be analyzed to determine if the school district has some form of fiscal accountability to the municipality. Each jurisdiction may be different due to state statutes.

A common example may be in how charter schools are structured in a particular jurisdiction. In GASB Cod. Sec. 2100.716-8, a charter school does not have the constitutional or statutory authority to levy property taxes. Funding is provided by an enrollment-based formula like the formula used for public schools in the state. One component of the formula for charter schools is an allocation of the sponsoring school district's property tax levy, based on a per-student metric. In this case, the charter school *would* be fiscally dependent on the school district (or municipality) if the charter school could not levy taxes without the approval of the sponsoring district. But since the school has no tax levy of its own that would be subject to the approval of the sponsoring district, a financial burden *is* on the sponsoring school district due to the allocation formula. However, it is not necessarily an indication of fiscal dependency.

Governmental organizations with boards appointed by another government. More than one primary government may control the activities of another governmental entity. Specifically, the governing board of a governmental entity may be appointed by the state (a higher-level government) while a local government (lower-level government) is financially accountable for the governmental entity. GASB takes the position that even though the local government does not appoint the voting majority or any of the entity's governing body, that governmental entity should be considered a component unit of the local government and not the state government. In this instance, the fiscal dependency factor is considered more relevant in defining the financial reporting entity than the appointment power [GASB Cod. Sec. 2100.136]. (See also the later discussion in the section.)

Governing entities with jointly appointed boards. Various primary governments may participate jointly in the appointment of the governing boards of a governmental entity. For example, two or more states may agree to create a port authority, or a state and several local communities may agree to create a mass transit authority. In these circumstances, no one primary government may have the authority to appoint a voting majority of the entity's governing body. When this occurs, the entity should be considered a component unit of the primary government to which it is fiscally dependent, unless the entity meets the criteria to be reported as a joint venture (discussed later in this chapter). An example would be where an entity may not issue debt without a state's approval. In this case, a financial benefit or burden relationship exists. The entity should then be included within the state's reporting entity [GASB Cod. Sec. 2100.137].

> **OBSERVATION:** Common examples of jointly appointed boards usually related to large infrastructure entities. Ports, airports, public transportation systems, government councils used to fund multi-jurisdiction highway and utility projects can jointly appoint boards. Jointly appointed boards may also be at diverse levels of government. For example, a state, counties within the state, and cities within a state may all appoint members of a governing board of a water irrigation entity that spans multiple jurisdictions.

Majority equity interests. As previously discussed, there are situations where governments may hold a majority equity interest that *does not* meet the definition of an investment. As detailed in Chapter 9, investments are securities (or other assets) that the government holds primarily for the purpose of income or profit *and* has a present service capacity based solely on the investment's ability to generate cash or to be sold to generate cash [GASB Cod. Sec. I50.103].

In this case, the equity interest does not meet the definition of an investment, even though the interest in the entity is evident by the ownership of stock or having some explicit, measurable right to the net resources of the entity which is determinable. Since the interest is not an investment, the equity interest serves the government rather than for income or profit, and the interest is based on a written, explicit, ownership. The holding of the interest results in the government being financially accountable for the organization and, therefore, a component unit relationship exists (See additional discussion later in this chapter in the section titled "Investments in For-Profit Corporations—Majority Equity Interests.") [GASB Cod. Sec. 2100.138].

Potential for Dual Inclusion

It is possible that an entity could satisfy the GAAP criteria in a manner that would suggest that it is a component unit of more than one primary government. GAAP recognizes the anomaly but states that an entity can be a component unit for only one primary government. Professional judgment should be exercised to determine which primary government should report the entity as a component unit. However, that judgment should focus on fiscal dependency rather than any other factor.

The potential for dual inclusion generally occurs when:

- One government appoints the governing board of an entity, and
- The appointing government and another government provide funding for the entity.

If the funding by the appointing government is based on legislation that directs resources to the governmental entity using various formulas, it is likely that the governmental entity is a component unit of the funding government and not the appointing government. For example, most state governments mandate programs and services to be provided by local governments and in return present fiscal aid to fund these expenditures. This funding does not mean that all local governments must be reported as part of the state's reporting entity, because the state does not appoint the governing board of the entity.

Elementary and secondary education is typically financed through a combination of local taxation and state aid distributed in accordance with legislatively established formulas. In most such instances, the entity status of a school district will be clear as either a primary government or a component unit of a local government because either its governing board is separately elected, or a voting majority is appointed by the local government. In some instances, however, school district governing boards are appointed by state officials, and the state may appear to be financially accountable for the district because of the state aid distribution. Judgment needs to be exercised as to whether the district should be considered a component unit of the state or of a local government. Usually, fiscal dependency on a local government should govern in determining the appropriate reporting entity of such school districts.

In those situations where state funding is more discretionary (not based on predetermined formulas) the question of which government, state government or local government, is financially accountable for the other entity becomes more difficult. The state and local governments should communicate with one another to determine which one of them is the most appropriate primary government for the entity [GASB Cod. Sec. 2100.139].

PRACTICE POINT: Making this determination of the appropriate primary government to report the entity may be arrived at through professional judgment (or negotiation). GASB Cod. Sec. 2100.717-1 discusses a potential situation for dual inclusion by more than one reporting entity. GAAP does not suggest the level of government should be the deciding factor. Professional judgment is required to determine whether the significance of the combined fiscal dependency and financial benefit or burden relationship outweighs the financial accountability. In some cases, this judgment may be at a lower level of government than another (a city versus a state for example). Communication of this judgment may be needed with the other entity (or entities) that may be making the same decision to include to lower the risk of dual inclusion.

Nature and Significance of Relationship

GAAP states that the financial statements of governmental and nongovernmental organizations for which a primary government (or the primary government's component units) is not financially accountable should, under certain circumstances, be included in the primary government's financial statements [GASB Cod. Sec. 2100.140].

This determination is based on "the nature and significance of the relationship between the primary government and the potential component unit, including the latter's ongoing financial support of the primary government and its other component units." While that concept is broad, GAAP states that a legally separate, tax-exempt organization's financial statements are included in the primary government's financial statements if *all* the following conditions exist:

- The economic resources received or held by the separate organization are entirely or almost entirely for the direct benefit of the primary government, its component units, or its constituents.
- The primary government or its component units is entitled to, or can otherwise access, most of the economic resources received or held by the separate organization.
- The economic resources received or held by an individual organization that the specific primary government, or its component units, is entitled to, or can otherwise access, are significant to that primary government [GASB Cod. Sec. 2100.141].

When these conditions are satisfied, the other organization's financial statements are presented as a (discrete) component unit in the primary government's external financial statements.

Direct Benefit of Economic Resources

There is direct economic benefit when the other organization "obtains, seeks to obtain, or holds and invests resources that will benefit the primary government, its component units, or its constituents." This condition does not imply that there must be an actual transfer from the other organization during the year but that "the resources obtained or held are required to ultimately be used for the benefit of a specific primary government, its component units, or its constituents."

The first condition generally means that an organization that provides resources to multiple constituent groups, for example a federated fund-raising organization, would not be considered a component unit of a primary government. Under this circumstance it is possible that a significant value of resources may be provided to the primary government (or its component units or constituents) in one year but in other years other governmental or nongovernmental entities may receive a sizable portion of the other organization's resources. This situation would not satisfy the requirement that all or almost all the resources be available to the primary government.

However, a common example involves a university fund-raising foundation as detailed in GASB Cod. Sec. 2100.902, example 40. In the GASB's *nonauthoritative* example, a University Foundation is a legally separate, tax-exempt organization whose bylaws state that it exists solely to provide financial support to a university. The foundation regularly makes distributions directly to the university and pays for the maintenance of the university's football stadium and auditorium (by making payments directly to vendors and contractors rather than the university). Separately, the direct cash payments to the university and the maintenance expenses of the university paid by the foundation are not significant to the university. Combined, however, the payments are significant. Furthermore, the economic resources of the foundation that are restricted for the university's benefit are significant. In this case, the University Foundation *is a component unit* of the university and should be discretely presented. This is based on the language in the bylaws satisfying the "direct benefit" criterion and the "entitlement/ability to access" criterion as well. The funding is significant, regardless of the "in-kind" assistance to the university.

Access to Economic Resources

The second condition requires that the primary government either:

- Be entitled to most of the economic resources received or held by the separate organization, or
- Can otherwise access those resources.

There is no difficulty in applying this condition when the primary government is entitled to the resources. For example, that entitlement may be based on the legal relationship between the primary government and the separate organization, or the donations made to the separate organization may be legally restricted by donors to the benefit of the primary government.

Difficulties arise when the criterion is based on the ability to access the other organization's resources. The concept "ability to otherwise access" is broad and is not based on the narrow idea of control. GASB Cod. Secs. 2100.140–.143 state that this broad concept can be demonstrated in several ways, including the following:

- The primary government or its component units in the past have received, directly or indirectly, most of the economic resources provided by the organization,
- The organization previously has received and honored requests to provide resources to the primary government, and
- The other organization is financially interrelated with the primary government.

GAAP notes that "this criterion (access to economic resources) will further limit inclusion to organizations such as entity-specific fund-raising foundations" because these foundations:

- Have a history of providing economic resources to the primary government, or
- Honor requests for economic resources initiated by the primary government.

The third example (financially interrelated) is based on the belief that most of the "other organizations" that are evaluated in the context of the criteria established by GAAP are nongovernmental entities that follow the financial and accounting standards established fundamentally by the FASB's Accounting Standards Codification® (ASC) Topic 958 (*Financial Statements of Not-for-Profit Organizations*). GAAP uses the guidance in FASB ASC® Topic 958 by stating that the two parties are "financially interrelated" when *both* of the following two conditions exist:

1. One organization can influence the operating and financial decisions of the other. The ability to exercise that influence may be demonstrated in any of the following ways:

    a. The organizations are affiliates,

    b. One organization has considerable representation on the governing board of the other organization,

c. The charter or bylaws of one organization limit its activities to those that are beneficial to the other organization, or

d. An agreement between the organizations allows one organization to actively participate in policymaking processes of the other, such as setting organizational priorities, budgets, and management compensation.

2. One organization has an ongoing economic interest in the net position of the other. If the specified beneficiary has an ongoing economic interest in the net position of the recipient organization, the beneficiary's rights to the assets held by the recipient organization are residual rights; that is, the value of those rights increases or decreases because of the investment, fund-raising, operating, and other activities of the recipient organization. Alternatively, but less commonly, a recipient organization may have an ongoing economic interest in the net position of the specified beneficiary. If so, the recipient organization's rights are residual rights, and their value changes because of the operations of the beneficiary.

An example of this access to another organization's resources for financial benefit is in GASB Cod. Sec. 2100.902, examples 4 and 4a. In part of the examples, a city can impose a payment "in lieu of taxes" (PILOT) on certain municipal corporations, including an airport, to recover the cost of providing governmental services to public entities that are exempt from property taxes. The payment is not required to be directly related to the costs of providing specific services and the city has not assessed a payment on the airport. The airport is a discretely presented component unit. Due to the legal entitlement to the PILOT, the city has access to airport resources, despite not exercising this ability.

The opposite would be in example 8 in the same codification section. In this example, a state electric utility is a fiscally independent public benefit corporation with specific duties and powers benefitting the state's citizens. The utility determines its own budget and sets its own rates. It also issues debt in its own name. The state is not obligated to pay the utility's debt. The state also has no obligation to provide financial support to the utility and it does not have access to the utility's resources. The enabling legislation requires that certain contracts for power sales be approved by the governor. However, these contracts represent only a small fraction of the utility's outstanding contracts and the governor's approval authority is limited by financing provisions within the enabling legislation and the utility's bond covenants. In this example, the utility is *not* a component unit. However, the utility's board is appointed by the governor. As such, it is a related organization. There is no imposition of will as the board members can only be removed based on formal charges and a public hearing. There is also no financial benefit or burden relationship between the entities.

Significant Economic Support

The final condition recognizes that some governmental entities receive resources from various support groups that are clearly component units, but the GASB does not intend to require support that is insignificant to trigger the inclusion of such groups in the primary government's financial statements. This criterion is a materiality threshold. The GASB concedes that this materiality threshold is higher than that used for component units that are included in the reporting entity based on the financial accountability established in GAAP for the following reasons:

- The importance of the financial support is relative to the entire primary government rather than an individual reporting unit; and
- The criteria are applied to an individual organization rather than all organizations of a similar type (e.g., parent-teacher associations).

For example, many public-school athletic programs have separate support organizations that may pay for team trips and banquets, additional compensation for coaches, and related items. Generally, these support groups would not be presented as component units of the public-school district because the economic support to the school (not to the specific program or activity) is insignificant.

The financial statements of other organizations that are considered component units because of the nature and significance of their relationship to the primary government are to be discretely presented (not blended) in the primary government's financial statements.

Examples of Closely Related or Financially Integrated

The GASB recognizes that the three conditions listed above may be too constricting in that certain organizations that might not satisfy the three conditions listed can nonetheless be key component units of a primary government. For this reason, if the professional judgment primary government determines that the nature and the significance of a potential component unit's relationship with the primary government warrants inclusion in the reporting entity, then those organizations should also be reported as component units by the primary government.

Financial integration may be exhibited and documented through the policies, practices, or organizational documents of either the primary government or the organization being evaluated as a potential component unit.

Financial integration could be demonstrated in several ways, including the following:

- Descriptions in charters and bylaws of the primary government or the other organizations (e.g., the charter might state that the organization will lose its tax-exempt status if it fails to distribute its resources to the primary government),
- Participation by the other organization's employees in a primary government's programs or activities,
- Representation in financial aid accountability systems of work-study fellowship grants to students of a primary government for work performed for the other organization,
- Participation by the primary government's employees in the other organization's research activities and inclusion of those activities in the service effort report of the primary government, and
- Sharing of office space and administrative services by the primary government and the other organization.

The above list is not all-inclusive, and that professional judgment rather than a list of relationships is the basis for determining whether the exclusion of a potential component unit's financial statements might result in the primary government's financial statements being misleading or incomplete.

REPORTING COMPONENT UNITS

As stated in the chapter's introduction, financial statements of the reporting entity should provide an overview of the entity. The reporting distinguishes the primary government from its component units.

Some component units should be *blended* due to their closeness of their relationship to the primary government. Most component units should be discretely presented, including those meeting the criteria discussed previously where the economic resources received or held by the separate organization are entirely or almost entirely for the direct benefit of the primary government, its component units or its constituents, the primary government or its component units have access (or has the ability to access) most of the economic resources held by the separate organization or the amounts are significant [GASB Cod. Sec. 2100.143].

A complication arises when a component unit of a financial reporting entity has component units of its own (component units of component units). The component unit financial data that are incorporated into a reporting entity's financial statements should include the data from all its component units. In effect, this section should be applied in layers *"from the bottom up."* At each layer, the definition and display provisions should be applied before the layer is included in the financial statements of the next level of the reporting government. States have an especially burdensome task in understanding all the elements of component unit reporting, especially when component units of component units exist.

An example in GAAP includes when a school district may be a component unit of a municipality because the municipality appoints the governing board of the district, and the district imposes a financial burden on the municipality. If the school district is financially accountable for another organization (a building authority, for example), the district should apply the definition and display provisions of this section to the building authority. The municipality should apply the definition and display provisions of this section to the school district's "entity," which includes the building authority. The building authority is not a component unit of the municipality *per se*; however, its financial data would be included in the primary government's financial reporting entity as a part of the school district [GASB Cod. Sec. 2100.144].

As portrayed in Exhibit 4-1 (close to the beginning of this chapter), reporting may be blended or discretely presented, depending on facts and circumstances.

Discrete Presentation of Major Component Units

GASB Cod. Sec. 2600.108, requires that information related to each *major* discretely presented component unit be presented in the reporting entity's basic financial statements. To satisfy this standard, any one of the following three approaches can be used [GASB Cod. Secs. 2200.101, .209, .215, 2600.107–.108, .111]:

1. Present each major discretely presented component unit in a separate column in the government-wide financial statements,
2. Present combining statements of major component units within the basic financial statements after the fund financial statements, or
3. Present condensed financial statements in a note to the financial statements (see previous **PRACTICE ALERT** regarding the GASB's *Financial Reporting Model Improvements* Exposure Draft).

Many preparers use the same methodology of determining major component units as they do major funds. This may not always be the proper method as the major fund calculation does not include qualitative aspects.

Major component units are determined based on the nature and significance of their relationship to the primary government. This decision is based on any of the following factors:

- The services provided by the component unit to the citizenry are such that separate reporting as a major component unit is essential to financial statement users,
- There are significant transactions with the primary government, or
- There is a significant financial benefit or burden relationship with the primary government.

Nonmajor component units should be aggregated in a single column. A combining statement for the nonmajor component units is not required but may be presented as supplementary information.

Each of these three presentation approaches creates information that is part of the basic financial statements.

The requirement for major component unit information does not apply to fiduciary component units. Fiduciary component units are reported only in the statements of fiduciary net position and changes in fiduciary net position along with the primary government's fiduciary funds. In practice, states and similar complex governments with fiduciary component units and fiduciary funds often use combining statements as supplementary information, as discussed in a following subsection (see also section titled "Reporting Fiduciary Component Units," later in this chapter) [GASB Cod. Sec. 2100.110].

Separate Column(s) in Government-Wide Financial Statements

Under the presentation format using separate columns, the government-wide financial statements (statement of net position and statement of activities) have columns for:

- Governmental activities of the primary government, including blended component units,
- Business-type activities of the primary government, including blended component units, and
- Major discretely presented component units.

These financial statements should provide a total column for governmental activities and business-type activities (the primary government), but a total column for the reporting entity is optional.

Combining Statements

Rather than presenting a separate column in the government-wide financial statements for each major discretely presented component unit, combining statements for component units may be presented. The combining financial statements should be based on the accrual basis of accounting and economic resources measurement focus (as discussed in Chapter 3) and should include a statement of net position and a statement of activities.

A separate column should be used for each major discretely presented component unit. All other nonmajor component units should be aggregated into a single column. Combining statements for nonmajor component units are not required by GAAP but may be presented as supplementary information. In practice, governments that present combining information for nonmajor component units present such information after combining statements for the primary government's funds.

A total column for all discretely presented component units should be presented. Those totals should be traceable to the component unit's column in the government-wide financial statements.

OBSERVATION: If the combining-statement method is used, a combining statement for nonmajor discretely presented component units may be presented as supplementary information (but this is not a requirement).

However, if the combining-statement approach is used, GAAP requires that the aggregated total component unit information to be the total for the component unit and all its own component units, even if the component unit does not present a total column for its reporting entity within its stand-alone financial statements.

Condensed Financial Statements in Notes.

If the note disclosure method is used, the following disclosures must be made [GASB Cod. Secs. 2200.216, 2600.109] (see previous **PRACTICE ALERT** on *Financial Reporting Model Improvements* Exposure Draft):

- Condensed statement of net position, containing:
  — *Total assets* (Distinguishing between capital assets and other assets). Amounts receivable from the primary government or from other component units of the same reporting entity should be reported separately.
  — *Total deferred outflows of resources* (if any).
  — *Total liabilities* (Distinguishing between long-term debts outstanding and other liabilities. Amounts payable to the primary government or to other component units of the same reporting entity should be reported separately).
  — *Total deferred inflows of resources* (if any).

— *Total net position* (Distinguishing between restricted, unrestricted, and net investment in capital assets).

- Condensed statement of activities, containing:
  — Expenses, with separate identification of depreciation expense and amortizations of long-lived assets,
  — Program revenues (by type),
  — Net program (expense) revenue,
  — Tax revenues,
  — Other nontax general revenues,
  — Contributions to endowments and permanent fund principal,
  — Extraordinary and special items,
  — Change in net position, and
  — Beginning and ending net position.

The notes to the financial statements should also describe the nature and value of significant transactions between major discretely presented component units and the primary government and other component units [GASB Cod. Secs. 2200.217, 2600.110].

PRACTICE POINT: In practice, few governments take advantage of presenting condensed component unit information in the notes. For some governments, the length of the disclosure may be less in the notes than on the face of the basic financial statements and (if needed) in combining statements.

GASB Cod. Sec. 2600.111 states that if a discretely presented component unit does not issue a separate financial report, the primary government reporting entity's Annual Comprehensive Financial Report (if one is issued) must include fund financial statements for the component unit (major fund reporting format). This information is presented as required supplementary information. However, GAAP also requires that the fund financial statements be focused on major funds of the component unit rather than its fund types. Presentation of the fund financial statements of the individual component units is not required unless such information is not available in separately issued financial statements of the component unit. Combining financial statements for nonmajor discretely presented component units should be included in the reporting entity's Annual Comprehensive Financial Report using the same methodology as combining (and individual fund) statements of the nonmajor funds of the primary government.

Blending Component Units

A basic requirement of GAAP is to present financial information for component units separately from the financial information for the primary government. This strategy is achieved using the discrete-presentation method. However, in some circumstances (not all), the GASB believes that although a component unit is legally separate from the primary government it may simply be an extension of the primary government. Under this condition, it is more appropriate to use the blending method to incorporate the financial information of a component unit into the reporting entity's financial statements.

When the blending method is used, transactions of a component unit are presented as if they were executed directly by the primary government, normally through presentation as one or more funds within the primary government's fund financial statements. In a comparable manner, balances in a blended component unit's financial statements are merged with similar balances of the primary government in the preparation of the government-wide financial statements as either governmental activities or business-type activities so that there is no way to identify which balances relate to a blended component unit and which relate to the primary government [GASB Cod. Sec. 2600.112].

The only two circumstances that require the blending of a component unit's financial statements with those of the primary government relate to:

- Similar governing bodies, and
- Scope of services.

Similar Governing Bodies.

If the component unit's governing body is substantively the same as the primary government's governing body, then a component unit's financial statements should be blended with the primary government. The blending of financial statements should also occur when the governing body of the primary government has enough membership on the component unit's government body that the primary government controls the component unit's activities, because the two bodies are considered substantively the same.

The term "substantively the same" is exemplified as follows [GASB Cod. Sec. 2600, fn. 5]:

Example	Outcome
When a municipal component unit's governing body is composed of *all* city council members, along with the mayor serving ex-officio.	Governing bodies considered substantively the same
When a municipal component unit's governing body is composed of the mayor and only two of the ten members of the city council.	Governing bodies are *not* considered substantively the same

Because of the relatively substantial number of members of the governing body of a state government, it is unlikely that a state government would meet the "substantively the same criterion." The concept of being "substantively the same" includes two elements. First, most of the members of the governing body of the primary government must serve on the governing body of the component unit. Second, the number of primary government members on the component unit's board must be a voting majority. Thus, a situation could arise where all the members of a city council serve on the board of a component unit, but their numbers are less than half (or whatever it takes to represent a voting majority) and therefore the primary government does not control the component unit's activities.

Blending is required for a component unit when *any* of the following elements exist [GASB Cod. Sec. 2600.113]:

1. The component unit's government body is substantively the same as the governing body of the primary government and *either*
   a. There is a financial benefit or burden between the primary government and the component unit, such as the payment of debt service of the component unit by the primary government, *or*
   b. Management of the primary government has operational responsibility for the component unit, which occurs when management runs the component unit in the same manner as other programs. For example, management of a department of transportation keeps all the records and finances of a partnership to build a road, *or*,
2. The component unit provides services to the primary government in a scope of services arrangement (or in law, regulation, ordinance or similar), *or*
3. The component unit's total debt outstanding (including leases or any other types of debt), is to be repaid entirely or almost entirely by the primary government. This would include an irrevocable or general obligation pledge and appropriation to the component unit that the component unit, in turn, pledges to bondholders or lessors, *or*
4. The component unit is organized as a not-for-profit corporation in which the primary government is the sole corporate member as identified in the component unit's articles of incorporation or bylaws, and the component unit is included in the financial reporting entity pursuant to the provisions (and discussed previously in this chapter) (excluding residual equity interest ownership) [GASB Cod. Secs. 2100.120–.136].

Scope of Services Arrangement Between Blended Component Unit and Primary Government

The second circumstance that requires the blending of a component unit's financial statements depends on the scope of the services provided by the unit. If the component unit provides, either directly or indirectly, services or benefits exclusively or almost exclusively to the primary government, then blending should be used. The idea of exclusive services to or benefits for the primary government is like the purpose of an Internal Service Fund (further discussed in Chapter 7). Thus, the component unit is created to provide services or benefits not to external parties but to the primary government as the recipient of the services or benefits.

The component unit may provide similar services or benefits to governmental entities other than the primary government. If the services or benefits provided to the other entities are insignificant, the component unit's financial statements should be blended with those of the primary government.

The services or benefits provided to the primary government by the component entity may be direct or indirect. In a direct relationship, the services or benefits are provided to the primary government. For example, a component unit may be created to finance the construction of buildings for various departments or agencies of the primary government. In an indirect relationship, the services or benefits are provided to employees of the primary government. For example, a component unit may be created to administer employee benefit programs (filing claims under health insurance contracts, approving health care providers, etc.) for the primary government.

GAAP also discusses the situation in which the primary government is a business-type activity that reports in a single column. For governmental entities, if a component unit is blended, the funds of the component unit are subject to the same financial reporting requirements as the primary government's own funds. The funds of a blended component unit should be presented by including them with the primary government's other funds in the appropriate fund financial statements and combining statements, if presented. However, because the primary government's general fund is usually the main operating fund of the reporting entity and is often a focal point for report users, its general fund should be the only general fund for the reporting entity. The general fund of a blended component unit should be reported as a special revenue fund. For governments engaged only in business-type activities that use a single column for financial statement presentation, a component unit may be blended by consolidating its financial statement data within the single column of the primary government and presenting condensed combining information in the notes to the financial statements. The condensed combining information should include the details described in the following, and at a minimum, the elements discussed above when condensed financial statements are presented in the notes to the basic financial statements.

Debt Outstanding (of All Types) Is Paid for Entirely or Almost Entirely by the Primary Government.

There are many transactions that include debt issuances supported entirely or almost entirely by a lease document from a primary government. The debt issuances can be the form of any type of debt, including another lease. Repayment generally occurs from this continuing pledge. In this situation, a blended component unit automatically exists, especially if the payments from the primary government are for similar amounts, with similar dates and credit aspects. If this occurs, the component unit will appear like a fund in the primary government's basic financial statements.

The financial statements of other organizations that are component units because they are closely related to or financially integrated with the primary government may be presented in the primary government's financial statements by either blending or discrete presentation.

Special Provision for Tobacco Settlement Authorities Created by States. Tobacco Settlement Authorities (TSAs) were created as part of a Master Settlement Agreement with the major tobacco companies in the late 1990's. The TSAs were created to obtain rights to all or a portion of future tobacco resources. Typically, the TSAs have terms of legislation or enabling legislation that generally require the TSA component unit to be blended [GASB Cod. Sec. 2600.601].

Reporting Fiduciary Component Units

If the organization is fiduciary in nature *and* is identified as a component unit in accordance with the provisions of GAAP, the organization is included only in the fund financial statements with the primary government's other fiduciary funds [GASB Cod. Sec. 2600.105]. If a discretely presented component unit is not fiduciary in nature, but has fiduciary funds, such funds are *not* reported in the primary government's financial statements.

Financial data for component units that are fiduciary in nature should be reported only in the fund financial statements in the primary government's statements of fiduciary net position and changes in fiduciary net position [GASB Cod. Sec. 2600.107].

An organization *that is already judged to be a component unit* is a fiduciary activity if it is either one of the following arrangements:

- A pension or OPEB plan that is administered through a trust or equivalent arrangement (defined benefit or defined contribution), or
- A circumstance in which assets from entities that are *not* part of the reporting entity are accumulated for pensions or OPEB and *not* held in a trust or equivalent arrangement. Such activities are reported in custodial funds (see Chapter 8). The amount of assets accumulated more than liabilities for benefits due to plan members and accrued investment and administrative expenses should be reported as a liability to participating employers or nonemployer contributing entities [GASB Cod. Sec. 1300.129].

An organization *that is already judged to be a component unit* that is not a pension or OPEB arrangement described immediately preceding this paragraph, is also fiduciary activity if the assets associated with the activity have one or more of the following characteristics:

- The assets are:
  — Administered through a trust agreement or equivalent arrangement (as described previously) in which the government itself is not a beneficiary,
  — Dedicated to providing benefits to recipients in accordance with the benefit terms, and
  — Legally protected from the creditors of the government.
- The assets are for the benefit of individuals and the government does *not* have *administrative involvement* with the assets or *direct financial involvement* with the assets. In addition, the assets are *not* derived from the government's provision of goods or services to those individuals.

- The assets are for the benefit of organizations or other governments that are *not* part of the financial reporting entity. In addition, the assets are *not* derived from the government's provision of goods or services to those organizations or other governments.

"*Administrative involvement*" with the assets is described in GAAP if, for example:

- The government monitors compliance with the requirements of the activity that are established by the government or by a resource provider that does not receive the direct benefits of the activity, *or*
- The government determines eligible expenditures that are established by the government or by a resource provider that does not receive the direct benefits of the activity, *or*
- The government can exercise discretion over how assets are allocated.

A government has "direct financial involvement" with the assets if, for example, it provides matching resources for the activities. To make the determination of whether a component unit is a fiduciary component unit, control of the assets of the component unit by the primary government is *not* a factor to be considered [GASB Cod. Secs. 1300.130–.132, fn. 11].

PRACTICE POINT: Due to the provisions of GASB Cod. Secs. 1300.128–.136, few fiduciary activities that are legally separate may be reported as fiduciary component units except for defined benefit pension and OPEB plans or external investment pools, both typically reported by states and large counties with such multiple employer plans and investment pools.

For states, additional scrutiny must occur on fiduciary component units that are large employee retirement systems (PERS). Such PERS plans may also have operations that are deferred compensation or defined contribution plans where participants may have control. The primary general-purpose government that reports the PERS plan as a fiduciary component unit prior to the implementation of GASB Statement No. 84 (*Fiduciary Activities*), as amended by GASB Statement No. 97 (*Certain Component Unit Criteria, and Accounting and Financial Reporting for Internal Revenue Code Section 457 Deferred Compensation Plans—an Amendment of GASB Statements No. 14 and No. 84, and a Supersession of GASB Statement No. 32*), may have reported the combined statement fiduciary net position and the combined statement of changes in fiduciary net position of the PERS as a pension (and other employee benefit) trust fund. Yet, some of the operations mentioned may not be held in trust, nor would they be reported upon implementing GASB-97. It is inevitable that some in governance of the PERS plan may want to have accountability for these other operations. If the operations are included in the primary government and they should not be due to lack of control, a departure from GAAP may occur which may lead an auditor to qualify the opinion or express an adverse opinion, based on materiality.

A potential solution to those charged with governance who may want to have accountability for the deferred compensation or defined contribution plans where participants have control may be to present such plans in separately issued stand-alone annual financial reports from annual financial reports of the PERS.

NONGOVERNMENTAL COMPONENT UNITS

Some component units, especially those meeting the criteria as a component unit of a primary government to be reported as a discretely presented component unit, may be a nongovernmental entity (e.g., a nonprofit organization) and follow FASB standards in their separately issued financial statements.

When nongovernmental entities are reported as discretely presented component units, they should be incorporated into the reporting entity's financial statements generally in the same manner as governmental component units. There is no requirement to change the recognition, measurement, or disclosure standards applied in the nongovernmental component unit's separate financial statements. However, the financial statements of the nongovernmental component unit may need to be reformatted to comply with the classification and display requirements of GAAP.

GASB Cod. Sec. 2600.704-12 discusses how to present nongovernmental component units as part of the primary government's basic financial statements. In summary, component units are required to apply the *definition and display* provisions of GAAP, as amended, before they are combined with the primary government. For the reporting entity's statement of net position, a discretely presented component unit's financial data may be presented in a separate discrete column or combined with the financial data of other discretely presented component units. Similar treatment is afforded in the statement of activities.

If it is impractical to reformat the nongovernmental component unit's change statement data, GAAP allows the component unit to be presented on a separate following page. GASB Cod. Sec. 2600.704-14 further discusses the potential reformatting. If the component unit's statement of net assets (position) is not presented in a classified format, reclassification may be required to present current and noncurrent components based on the definitions in GAAP. The net assets may need to be redistributed utilizing net investment in capital assets, restricted expendable and restricted nonexpendable net position and unrestricted net position. The statement of activities may need to be realigned between operating and nonoperating income to conform to the approach used by the primary government. Finally, there may be different revenue and expense recognition provisions between the component unit and the primary government that may cause realignment.

PRACTICE POINT: This is a common issue with public colleges and universities with foundations that are nongovernmental. GASB Cod. Sec. 2600.704-14 details the display of such foundations where the foundation's financial statements are presented in a separate column adjacent to the public college or university's total column. If the foundation's statement of net assets is *not* presented in a classified format, its assets and liabilities should be reclassified into their current and noncurrent components. Also, the foundation's net assets should be redistributed among the three net position components as discussed in Chapters 5 and 20. Those net position components are net investment in capital assets, restricted (distinguishing between expendable and nonexpendable and between major categories of restrictions), and unrestricted. The data in the foundation's statement of activities may need to be realigned to distinguish between operating and nonoperating revenues and expenses and generally relocated to their appropriate positions in the GASB's required format. Also, because the university can present its operating expenses by either natural classification or functional categories as discussed in Chapter 21, the foundation's expenses may need to be reconfigured to conform to the approach used by the university. In addition, the foundation's revenues may need to be reduced by related discounts and allowances, if reported separately as expenses, to be consistent with the university's presentation. Chapter 21 includes a presentation of a public college or university, including a nongovernmental foundation.

Investments in For-Profit Corporations—Majority Equity Interests That Are Investments

A government may own or acquire most of the equity interest in a legally separate organization (e.g., through acquisition of voting stock of a corporation or acquisition of interest in a partnership).

Solely for this purpose, an equity interest is a financial interest in a legally separate organization evidenced by the ownership of shares of the organization's stock or by otherwise having an explicit, measurable right to the net resources of the organization that is usually based on an investment of financial or capital resources by a government. An equity interest is explicit and measurable if the government has a present or future claim to the net resources of the entity and the method for measuring the government's share of the entity's net resources is determinable.

The definition of equity interest is not intended to include a government's residual interest in assets that may (on dissolution) revert to the government for lack of another equitable claimant. This type of interest is, in substance, the same as the escheat process. That is, the reversion of property to a state resulting from the absence of any known, rightful inheritors to the property. (Escheat property is discussed in Chapter 8).

GAAP further requires for such interests:
- If a government's holding of that equity interest meets the definition of an investment, the equity interest should be reported as an investment and measured using the equity method. (See previous discussion on majority equity interests that are *not* investments, within this chapter.)
- The legally separate organization should *not* be reported as a component unit of the government.
- If a special-purpose government engaged only in fiduciary activities, a fiduciary fund, or an endowment (including permanent and term endowments) or permanent fund holds a majority equity interest in a legally

separate organization that meets the definition of an investment, that majority equity interest should be measured at fair value.
- If a government's holding of a majority equity interest in a legally separate organization does not meet the definition of an investment, the holding of the majority equity interest results in the government being financially accountable for the organization and, therefore, the government should report the legally separate organization as a component unit.
- The majority equity interest should be reported as an asset of the government or fund that holds the equity interest, measured using the equity method. However, if the component unit is blended, the asset and net position associated with the equity interest held by the government or fund should be eliminated in the blending process. In financial statements prepared using the current financial resources measurement focus, the asset representing the government's equity interest should be limited to amounts appropriately reported under the current financial resources measurement focus [GASB Cod. Sec. 2600.116, fn. 7].

REPORTING INTRA-ENTITY TRANSACTIONS AND BALANCES

Transactions between the primary government and component units are common. Such transactions may be required by law, regulation, ordinance, contract, enabling statute, even debt covenants. In some cases, nonexchange financial guarantees trigger such intra-entity transactions. If the transactions are to be repaid in the future, balances may be presented in the separate stand-alone financial statements of the component unit(s).

Intra-Entity Transactions and Balances—Blended Component Unit Reporting

Transfers of resources between the primary government and *blended* component units are internal activity in the financial statements of the reporting entity, like transactions between funds. Interfund activity within and among the three fund categories (governmental, proprietary, and fiduciary), including blended component units, should be classified, and reported as follows [GASB Cod. Sec. 1800.102]:

Basic Governmental Accounting Concepts and Standards

Type of Activity	Definitions	Categories/Explanations	Examples
Reciprocal interfund activity	The internal to the reporting entity counterpart to exchange and exchange-like transactions.	*Interfund loans:* • Amounts provided with a requirement for repayment. • Interfund loans should be reported as interfund receivables in lender funds and interfund payables in borrower funds. • This activity should not be reported as other financing sources or uses in the fund financial statements. • If repayment is not expected within a *reasonable* time, the interfund balances should be reduced and the amount that is not expected to be repaid should be reported as a transfer from the fund that made the loan to the fund that received the loan. *Interfund services provided and used:* • Sales and purchases of goods and services between funds for a price approximating their external exchange value. • Interfund services provided and used should be reported as revenues in seller funds and expenditures or expenses in purchaser funds. • Unpaid amounts should be reported as interfund receivables and payables in the fund balance sheets or fund statements of net position. • An exception is when the general fund is used to account for risk-financing activity. In such cases, interfund charges to other funds are accounted for as reimbursements per GASB Cod. Sec. C50.126.	• Due from/due to component units for amounts requiring payments. • Advances to component units. • Internal service fund transactions with component units for legal services, information technology, purchasing, fleet operations, printing and other goods and services.

Type of Activity	Definitions	Categories/Explanations	Examples
Nonreciprocal interfund activity	The internal counterpart to nonexchange transactions.	*Interfund transfers:* • Flows of assets (such as cash or goods) without equivalent flows of assets in return and without a requirement for repayment. • This category includes payments in lieu of taxes not for, and not equal in value to, services provided. • In governmental funds, transfers should be reported as other financing uses in the funds making transfers and as other financing sources in the funds receiving transfers. • In proprietary funds, transfers should be reported after nonoperating revenues and expenses as transfers.	• Transfers to/from component units in funds. • Transfers to/from component units in Statement of Activities.
		Interfund reimbursements: • Repayments from the funds responsible for these expenditures or expenses to the funds that initially paid for them. • Reimbursements should not be displayed in the financial statements.	• Like transfers to/from component units (frequently combined in practice).

Other transfers impact only the statement of net position such as loans, repayments, deferred inflows of resources and deferred outflows of resources. In many cases, these transfers are related to a sale of future revenues. GASB Cod. Sec. S20.111 requires sales of future revenues within the reporting entity to be reported by the transferor government as a deferred inflow of resources or revenue in both the government-wide and fund financial statements. Generally, revenue is recognized over the duration of the sale agreement (see Chapter 17 for further guidance).

Intra-Entity Transactions and Balances—Discretely Presented Component Unit Reporting

Transfers of resources between the primary government and *discretely presented component units* should be reported as if they were external transactions—as revenues and expenses. Timing differences may result in a receivable and payable or between component units and should be reported on a separate line from other receivables and payables [GASB Cod. Sec. 2600.117].

Transfers of Capital Assets Between a Government and a Discretely Presented Component Unit. Transfers of capital assets between a government and a discretely presented component unit requires particular care.

An example is provided in GASB Cod. Sec. S20.708-4. In the example, a county government owns a parcel of land that it classifies as a capital asset with a carrying value of $150,000. The county has agreed to transfer the land to the county redevelopment agency (RDA), a discretely presented component unit of the county. The RDA has obtained an independent appraisal valuing the land at $1.7 million. Management of the RDA believes that, after the transfer, its intent is to sell the parcel at its appraised value. When the asset is transferred, the RDA *cannot* reclassify the land as an investment measured at fair value.

Since the RDA is within the financial reporting entity, the land must continue to be reported at the county's carrying value. GASB Cod. Sec. I50.107 provides that " . . . an asset that is initially reported as a capital asset and later is held for sale should *not* be reclassified as an investment." Furthermore, the paragraph requires that the initial classification of an asset be retained for financial reporting purposes, even if the government's usage of the asset changes over time. The requirement to retain the original asset classification for financial reporting purposes applies even if the asset changes legal ownership within the financial reporting entity. In this case, the RDA should retain the classification of the land as a capital asset and should report the transferred land at its retained carrying value of $150,000.

Transfers Between Primary Governments and Pension (or OPEB) Plans (Fiduciary Component Units)

A recent trend in practice includes contributions of nonfinancial assets to pension (or OPEB) plans that are fiduciary component units. A potential goal for these transfers is to reduce a government's net pension or OPEB liability. However, care must be taken as nonfinancial assets need to be monetized to provide benefits. The result of such transfers could *increase* such liabilities as the related discount rates may lower due to the lack of financial assets.

The GASB provides an interesting fact pattern which describes the accounting and financial reporting of these transfers. In this case, a government owns a building that it reports as a capital asset. The building has a carrying value of $3 million and an appraised value of $10 million. The government transfers ownership of the building to a pension plan that it reports as a fiduciary component unit. As discussed in GASB Cod. Sec. S20.708-3, if the pension plan is part of the same reporting entity, the pension plan should report a capital asset of $3 million (the government's carrying value of the building) and an addition (a contribution) of $3 million (the carrying value of the building, less the amount paid by the pension plan—in this case, zero).

GASB Cod. Sec. S20.112 further stipulates that in such transfers within the financial reporting entity, any difference between the amount paid by the Plan (exclusive of amounts that may be refundable), and the carrying value of the assets transferred are reported as follows:

- As an employer contribution or a nonemployer contributing entity contribution to the pension or OPEB plan in accordance with the requirements of GASB Cod. Secs. P20, P21, P50, P51, as applicable, in the separately

issued financial statements of the employer or nonemployer contributing entity *and* in the financial statements of the reporting entity; and
- As an employer contribution or nonemployer contributing entity contribution in accordance with GASB Cod. Secs. Pe5, Pe6, Po50, Po51, as applicable, in the stand-alone statements of the pension or OPEB plan and in the financial statements of the reporting entity [GASB Cod. Sec. S20.112].

Intra-Entity Leasing Arrangements

GASB Cod. Secs. L20.186–.187 provide guidance on the issue of component units leasing to primary governments and vice versa. It is also customary practice for component units to lease to other component units. In a typical scenario, a building authority is a blended component unit of a county. The building authority acquires and constructs capital assets and then leases them to the county. GASB Cod. Sec. L20.735-1 further discusses how the leases with the county are eliminated and the debt and assets of the building authority are reported in the county's annual financial report as the county's debt and assets. If the building authority issues stand-alone financial statements, the leases are reported in accordance with GASB-87 as receivables, capital assets and deferred inflows of resources, as applicable.

To summarize (also see Chapter 14):

Parties to Lease	Guidance
Lessor or lessee is a blended component unit of a primary government.	• GASB Cod. Sec. L20 *does not apply*. • If *lessor* is a blended component unit, debt and assets of lessor are reported as the primary government's debt and assets.
Lease between blended component units.	• If eliminations are required, eliminations are made before the financial statements are aggregated with those of the primary government. • Remaining cash payments are inflows and outflows of resources (transfers).
Lease between primary government and discretely presented component units or between discretely presented component units.	• Treat recognition, measurement, presentation, and disclosure in accordance with GASB Cod. Sec. L20. • Related receivables and payables *are not* combined with other amounts due to or due from discretely presented component units or with other lease receivables or payables from/to third parties.

COMPONENT UNITS WITH DIFFERENT REPORTING PERIODS FROM PRIMARY GOVERNMENT

The fiscal year of the financial reporting entity's financial statements should be the same as the fiscal year of the primary government. Ideally, the primary government and its component units should have the same fiscal years, and the GASB encourages the adoption of the same fiscal year by all the units that compose the financial reporting entity.

Same Fiscal Year Impractical (Usually Codified in Law). If it is impractical for a component unit to have the same fiscal year as the primary government, a component unit's financial statements that have an ending date that occurs during the primary government's fiscal year should be incorporated into the financial statements of the reporting entity.

For example, if the primary government's fiscal year ends on June 30 and a component unit's fiscal year ends on December 31, for the fiscal year ended June 30, 20X9, the financial reporting entity should include the component unit's financial statements ended December 31, 20X8.

Exceptions. GAAP does allow one exception to the inclusion of a component unit that has a fiscal year different from, or that does not end within, that of the primary government. If a component unit's fiscal year ends *within the first quarter after* the end of the primary government's fiscal year, then the component unit's financial statements after the primary government's fiscal year financial statements may be included in the statements of the financial reporting entity.

For example, if the primary government's fiscal year ends on June 30, and a component unit's fiscal year ends on August 31, for the fiscal year ended June 30, 20X9, the financial reporting entity could include the component unit's financial statements ended August 31, 20X9 [GASB Cod. Sec. 2600.119].

Example: An example of this issue is in GASB Cod. Sec. 2600.709-2. The financial statements for the primary government for the year ending June 30, 20X4 incorporate the following information:

- Component Unit A for the year ending December 31, 20X3.
- Component Unit A's component unit B for *its* fiscal year ending June 30, 20X3 (one year old when "rolled up" into the reporting entity financial statements.
- Component Unit A would be incorporated into the financial statements of the primary government as A's year ended within the fiscal year of the primary government.

Due to the provision to "roll up" component units discussed previously in the chapter, the primary government would also include the financial data of Component Unit B after reporting in Component Unit A, even though the information is a year old.

When the financial statements of a component unit have a fiscal year different from that of the primary government, it is likely that intra-entity transactions and related balances will differ, resulting in receivables or payables that may not articulate between the statements. When the amounts differ, the nature and amount of the intra-entity transactions and related balances should be disclosed in a note to the financial statements. GASB Cod. Sec. 2600.709-3 discusses that in these cases, the internal accounts may be "out of balance" at the reporting date due to the difference in timing. It is acceptable to report the internal balance in the total primary government column and disclose this in the notes.

Once a component unit adopts a fiscal year, that date should be used consistently from year to year. If the fiscal year-end changes, the change should be disclosed in a note to the financial statements [GASB Cod. Sec. 2600.120].

Although a reporting entity's financial statements may contain financial information for component units with periods different from that of the primary government, there is no need to change the title of the reporting entity's financial statements to indicate the different dates. The financial statement titles should reflect the primary government's reporting date and period. The notes to the financial statements should disclose the fiscal period reported for component units if it is different from that of the primary government.

NOTE DISCLOSURES AND OTHER REPORTING ISSUES WITH COMPONENT UNITS

The following should be disclosed in the notes to the reporting entity's financial statements [GASB Cod. Sec. 2600.121]:

- *Brief* description of the component units,
- Relationship of the primary government with each component unit,
- Discussion of criteria or rationale used for including each component unit,
- Identification of method(s) used (discrete presentation, blending or included in the fiduciary fund financial statements) to incorporate the component unit in the financial reporting entity's financial statements. Component units may be disclosed together if they have common characteristics if each component unit is separately identified. As an example, a state department of transportation with 15 intercity bus component units that are only separated by geography and subject to the same statutes could be disclosed together as a combined "regional transportation authorities," and
- Identification of how financial statements of each component unit may be obtained.

OBSERVATION: Disclosure in this area in practice differs based on the number of component units and their operations. Some states disclose this information in a table, inclusive of fiscal year-end, the nature of transactions between the primary government and the component unit(s), rationale, links to the component unit's website to obtain information, and even whether the component unit was audited by the primary government's auditor or a separate auditor and whether the audit was performed in accordance with generally accepted government auditing standards (GAGAS).

Focus of Note Disclosures and Required Supplementary Information Regarding Component Unit Activity

GAAP requires that the financial information pertaining to the primary government, including blended component units, and similar information pertaining to discretely presented component units should be distinguishable. This philosophy is extended to disclosures in notes and the presentation of required supplementary information in the financial statements of the financial reporting entity.

Determining what should be disclosed in notes to the financial statements *is a matter of professional judgment*. The professional accountant must consider what disclosures are essential to the fair presentation of the basic financial statements. Because the financial reporting entity includes the primary government, including its blended component units, and perhaps one or more discretely presented component units, an additional dimension of professional judgment arises with regard to whether the notes related to the primary government should include relevant information from some of the discretely presented component units, all of the discretely presented component units, or none of the discretely presented component units presented in the reporting entity's financial statements [GASB Cod. Sec. 2600.122].

CCH's *Governmental GAAP Practice and Disclosures Manual* identifies numerous types of disclosures that may be made in notes to the financial statements and provides a comprehensive disclosure checklist.

Notes *essential* to fair presentation in the reporting entity's basic financial statements include:

- Governmental and business-type activities as presented in the government-wide financial statements and individually presented major funds and aggregated nonmajor funds as presented in the fund financial statements (inclusive of blended component units), and
- Major discretely presented component units considering the nature and significance of each component unit's relationship to the primary government.

For certain pension activities, if a primary government and its component units provide pensions through the same single-employer or agent pension plan, the note disclosure requirements of GASB Cod. Secs. P20.117, .136–.146 apply. In stand-alone financial statements, each government accounts for and reports its participation in the single or agent pension plan as if it were a cost-sharing employer and should apply the requirements of the related paragraphs in GASB Cod. Secs. P20.147–.182. Similar provisions also are in place for Other Post-Employment Benefits (OPEB) in GASB Cod. Sec. P50.120 [GASB Cod. Sec. 2600.123].

Issues Presenting Component Unit Information in Primary Government

Practicality or legal requirements may require a primary government to not include the financial data of component units. As GAAP applies to all entities within the reporting entity, in such cases, the financial statements of the primary government must acknowledge that they do not include the data of the component units necessary for conformity with GAAP [GASB Cod. Sec. 2600.124].

PRACTICE POINT: Such disclosure may result in a modification of the Independent Auditors' Report.

Separately Issued (Stand-Alone) Financial Statements of Component Units

GAAP is written from the perspective of a primary government in that it considers the focal point for the preparation of the financial statements of a financial reporting entity to be a primary government. However, component units may be requested or required to distribute separate financial statements, and the guidance in GAAP should also be used to prepare those statements. In effect, the focal point for the preparation of a component unit's separate financial statements is the component unit.

As discussed in the section titled "Reporting Component Units," governmental financial statements should be built in layers from the lowest-level component unit to the highest-level component unit. The bottom-up concept is important in determining which component units at which levels should be included in separately issued financial statements. From a practical perspective, if one visualizes looking down from each level or layer, then every component unit under a level should be included in the separately issued financial statements of the component unit at that level. Thus, a primary government should include all levels of component units in its separately issued financial statements, while the lowest-level component unit should present only its own financial statements because there are no component units below it.

When a component unit issues separate financial statements, there should be an acknowledgment that the governmental entity (the issuing component unit) is a component unit of another government. The other governmental entity could be a primary government or another component unit that is the focal point of separately issued financial statements. In addition, the following disclosures should be made in a note to the component unit's separately issued financial statements:

- Identify the other (higher-level) governmental entity, and
- Describe the relationship with the (higher-level) governmental entity.

An example of this in GASB Cod. Sec. 2600.713-2 for an airport that is a component unit could have the following as a title in the airport's statement of net position:

Sample County Airport
(A Component Unit of Sample County)
Statement of Net Position
December 31, 20X4

The GASB does not specify a generally accepted practice for reporting a component unit only. The AICPA's Audit and Accounting Guide *State and Local Governments* states that the notes to the financial statements and auditor's report should clearly disclose that the presentation is that of a component unit of another primary government [GASB Cod. Sec. 2600.125].

Government Acquires a 100 Percent Equity Interest in Component Unit—Reporting

Governments may acquire a 100% equity interest in an organization that remains legally separate. As discussed in the various sections of this chapter on majority equity interests, the acquisition may result in an investment or a component unit. If the acquisition results in a component unit, the measurement at acquisition of the value includes all the assets, deferred outflows of resources, liabilities, and deferred inflows of resources in accordance with the discussion later in this chapter in the section titled "Government Combinations and Disposals of Government Operations." Measurement of the consideration include:

- All the net resources exchanged to accomplish the 100% equity interest, plus
- The balances of any equity interest asset and
- The balances of any deferred outflow of resources, recognized prior to the acquisition.

The result should be equal to the net position of the component unit *after* measuring all the assets, deferred outflows of resources, liabilities and deferred inflows of resources discussed later in this chapter. After the acquisition, transactions related to the component unit are reported part of inflows and outflows [GASB Cod. Sec. 2600.126].

Other Stand-Alone Government Financial Statements

Other stand-alone governmental entities are legally separate governmental entities (see the section titled "Determining Separate Legal Standing") that have the following characteristics:

- They do not have a separately elected governing body, and
- They are not component units of another governmental entity (see section titled "Financial Accountability").

As previously discussed, examples of other stand-alone governmental entities include the following:

- Certain special-purpose governments,
- Joint ventures,
- Jointly governed organizations, and
- External investment or risk pools.

When a stand-alone governmental entity issues financial statements, GAAP should be observed to the extent applicable. Thus, *the other stand-alone governmental entity* becomes the focal point for preparing the financial statements of the financial reporting entity. For example, the other stand-alone governmental entity should follow standards established in the sections titled "Financial Accountability" and "Nature and Significance of Relationship" to determine whether it has component units for which financial statements should be incorporated into the standards of the financial reporting entity.

Other stand-alone governmental entities for which the governing board's voting majority is appointed by a primary government should disclose the accountability relationship in their separately issued financial statements (see the section titled "Related Organizations") [GASB Cod. Sec. 2600.127].

The description of the relationship between the stand-alone governmental entity and the primary government should emphasize the general concept of accountability rather than the specific criteria for financial accountability.

REPORTING RELATIONSHIPS WITH ORGANIZATIONS OTHER THAN COMPONENT UNITS

A primary government may appoint all or some of the members of the governing board of an entity that is not a component unit because it does not satisfy the criterion for component units. These organizations are broadly classified in GAAP as:

- Related organizations,
- Joint ventures and jointly governed organizations,
- Component units of another government with the characteristics of a joint venture or jointly governed organization,
- Pools,
- Undivided interests, and
- Cost-sharing arrangements [GASB Cod. Secs. 2600.128, J50.101].

Related Organizations

A "related organization" is defined as follows:

> An organization for which a primary government is not financially accountable (because it does not impose will or have a financial benefit or burden relationship) even though the primary government appoints a voting majority of the organization's governing board.

Thus, related organizations are not component units, yet there is some form of accountability, other than financial accountability, that exists between the primary government and the related organization because of the appointment authority. For this reason, the primary government should disclose in a note to the financial statements the nature of its relationship to the related organizations.

Some primary governments, especially states, have a common relationship with a group of related organizations. Rather than identify each related organization, related organizations with a common relationship can be grouped together for disclosure purposes. For example, if a state government appoints all the members of 20 local governing boards for irrigation management and there is no other relationship with the boards, a single disclosure could be made without specifically naming the 20 boards.

Due to the nature of the relationship between the primary government and related organizations, the primary government should consider whether related party transactions should be disclosed in the financial statements of the reporting entity.

Financial statements issued by a related organization should disclose the related primary government and describe the relationship between them [GASB Cod. Sec. 2600.129].

PRACTICE POINT: See the section in Chapter 1 titled "Related-Party Transactions." Related organizations may be related parties, depending on the governance of the related organization. If elected officials, appointed officials, management, or members of all parties' immediate families are part of the governance of the related organization, the organization may be a related party [GASB Cod. Secs. 2250.102–.108].

Joint Ventures

Governments may enter into a joint venture agreement or arrangement to create a separate entity to provide a service directly to the individual governments involved or the citizens served by the governments. For example, two municipalities may engage in a joint venture and create a separate entity to operate a landfill. The creation of a joint venture entity rather than a sole venture may be based on assorted reasons , ranging from economies of scale to effective risk management.

GAAP provides the following definition of a "joint venture":

> A legal entity or other organization that results from a contractual arrangement and that is owned, operated, or governed by two or more participants as a separate and specific activity subject to joint control in which the participants retain (*a*) an ongoing financial interest or (*b*) an ongoing financial responsibility.

OBSERVATION: If the agreement to jointly provide services or operate certain facilities or functions does not involve the creation of a separate legal entity or organization, the arrangement is not considered a joint venture. However, it may meet the criteria to be considered a jointly governed organization, pool, undivided interest, or cost-sharing arrangement as discussed later in this chapter.

Joint Control. One condition for a joint venture is that no one entity can unilaterally control the operational and financial policies of the commonly controlled entity. Thus, if two or more participating governments have created an entity, and each of those governments has an equal influence on it, the prerequisite condition for a joint venture exists. However, if the two or more governments do not have equal control or voting influence, then the entity is not a joint venture and may be either a component unit or some other related organization. If the joint control criterion is satisfied, but there is no ongoing financial interest or ongoing financial responsibility, the entity is a jointly governed organization and not a joint venture (see section titled "Jointly Governed Organizations or Joint Powers Authorities") [GASB Cod. Sec. J50.102].

Ongoing Financial Interest. An "ongoing financial interest" is:

> An equity interest or any other arrangement that allows a participating government to have access to a joint venture's resources.

In addition, the term "equity interest" is defined as follows:

> A financial interest in a legally separate organization evidenced by the ownership of shares of the organization's stock or by otherwise having an explicit, measurable right to the net resources of the organization that is usually based on an investment of financial or capital resources by a government. An equity interest is explicit and measurable if the government has a present or future claim to the net resources of the entity and the method for measuring the government's share of the entity's net resources is determinable.

The concept of ongoing financial interest is not limited to an existing equity interest (holding voting stock of the entity). There may be an arrangement represented by a separate contract, letter of agreement, or other document that specifically describes a participating government's right of access to the joint venture's resources.

Access to the joint venture's resources may be direct or indirect. Direct access to resources would include the participating government's right to a share of profits or surpluses earned by the joint venture or to participate in gains realized through the disposition of operating assets. Indirect access to resources enables participating governments to persuade the joint venture to use its surplus resources so that citizens are benefited directly rather than through their participating governments. For example, a regional recreation joint venture may be persuaded to build tennis courts at participating governments' playgrounds [GASB Cod. Sec. J50.103].

Ongoing Financial Responsibility. The definition of "ongoing financial responsibility" is as follows:

- When a participating government is obligated in some manner for the debts of a joint venture, *or*
- When the joint venture's existence depends on continued funding by the participating government.

For an analysis of what constitutes "obligated in some manner," see the discussion in the section (above) titled "Financial Benefit to or Burden on a Primary Government." The other component of ongoing financial responsibility deals with a participating government's financial responsibility for the continued existence of the joint venture.

In most instances, the continued existence of the joint venture is dependent on the participating governments because they or their citizens have agreed to pay for the goods used or services provided by the joint venture. GAAP relates responsibility for continued existence to a single participating government. If the number of participating governments is small (two or three), the withdrawal of any one of the three participating governments could mean the end for the joint venture. As the number of participating governments increases, it becomes more likely that no one participating government's action would mean the end of the joint venture.

Of course, there is no specific guidance as to which number of participants would invalidate the continued existence concept. For this reason, professional judgment must be exercised [GASB Cod. Sec. J50.104].

Equity Interest in a Joint Venture. Financial reporting standards for joint ventures depend on whether the joint venture is represented by a specified equity interest. If a joint venture is represented by an equity interest, a participating government should show the interest as an asset. If an equity interest is not apparent, only certain disclosures concerning the joint venture should be made in the participating government's financial statements.

A joint venture with an equity interest is demonstrated by a participating government's interest in the resources of the joint venture that is explicit and measurable. The equity interest is usually based on the contribution of resources, either financial assets or capital assets, by the participating government.

The most obvious demonstration of an explicit and measurable interest in a joint venture would be the ownership of voting stock by a participating government. For example, a participating government that has a 25% interest in a joint venture generally has a proportional interest in the net resources of the joint venture.

However, the demonstration of an equity interest in a joint venture can also be based on an arrangement other than that represented by voting stock ownership. For example, the participating governments can finalize a contract whereby the joint venture is created. The contract must be written in such a manner that the participant's interest in the joint venture's net resources is explicit and measurable. A residual interest in the net resources of a joint venture upon dissolution because there is no other equitable claimant, is not equivalent to an equity interest (see previous discussion in this chapter on "Escheat Property" and "Majority Equity Interests") [GASB Cod. Sec. J50.105].

If the reporting entity's participation in a joint venture is represented by an equity interest in the net resources of the joint venture, an asset should be reported in the financial statements of the participating government.

Equity Interest in Joint Venture Reporting in Fund Statements. The manner of presenting the asset, which represents the net equity in the joint venture's net position, depends on whether the participating government accounts for the investment in a proprietary fund or a governmental fund.

Proprietary funds. The initial investment of financial and/or capital resources in the joint venture should be recorded at cost. Whether the initial investment should be increased or decreased depends on the joint venture agreement. If the joint venture agreement states that a participating government is to share in the profits and losses of the joint venture, the investment account should be adjusted to reflect the joint venture's results of operations.

The recognition of a proportional share of the joint venture's results of operations is not dependent on whether there is an actual remittance between the joint venture and a participating government. In determining the joint venture's results of operations for a period, profits, or losses on transactions with the proprietary fund should be eliminated. Non-operating transactions, such as additional equity contributions, loans, and dividends, should be reflected as an addition or decrease to the carrying amount of the net investment in the joint venture.

The interest in the net position of the joint venture should be reported as a single asset (account) in the proprietary fund. There should be no attempt to present on a participating government's balance sheet a proportional interest in the various assets and liabilities of the joint venture. In addition, the proportional shares of the joint venture's results of operations should be presented as a single operating account on the proprietary fund's operating statement. There should be no attempt to present a proportional interest in the joint venture's operating accounts.

To show the accounting for a joint venture in which there is an equity interest, assume that the state of Pilgrim enters into a joint venture agreement with two other municipalities. In the terms of the agreement, each municipality has a one-third interest in the net position and profits/losses of the joint venture. If Pilgrim contributes $100,000 in cash and $200,000 in equipment, the following entry would be made (all entries are made in an Enterprise Fund) [GASB Cod. Sec. J50.106]:

	Debit	Credit
Equity Interest in Joint Venture	300,000	
Cash		100,000
Equipment		200,000
To record contribution to joint venture.		

If after the first year of operations, the joint venture incurs an operating loss of $90,000, the following entry would be made:

	Debit	Credit
Equity Interest in Joint Venture Operating Losses	30,000	
Equity Interest in Joint Venture		30,000
To record share of joint venture losses [$90,000 × 1/3].		

The intent of the above transactions is to eliminate "profit" on transactions within the state with itself. As discussed in GASB Cod. Sec. J50.706-1, the participant's share of net income on transactions with the joint venture would be treated as an additional equity interest in the joint venture rather than the earnings from the joint venture.

Governmental funds. The initial investment of financial and/or capital resources in the joint venture should be recorded at cost, but only to the extent the investment is evidenced by current financial resources (as defined in Chapter 3). When the investment in the joint venture is recorded in a governmental fund, only the portion of the investment considered available, and expendable should be recorded on the balance sheet. Usually, this portion of the investment is limited to amounts due to and from the joint venture. The remaining investment or payments made to the joint venture should be reported as expenditures of the governmental fund [GASB Cod. Sec. J50.107].

Government-wide financial statements. Joint ventures that are presented in proprietary funds and governmental funds should also be presented in the government-wide financial statements and should be accounted for at this level using the method described earlier for proprietary funds [GASB Cod. Sec. J50.108].

Disclosure Requirements for Joint Venture Participants. For all joint ventures (with or without equity interest), a participating government should disclose in a note to its financial statements a general description of the joint venture, including the following:

- A description of ongoing financial interest, including equity interest, if applicable, or ongoing financial responsibility, and
- Information that enables a reader to determine whether the joint venture is accumulating assets that may result in a financial benefit to the participating government or experiencing fiscal stress that may result in a financial burden on the participating government.

In addition, a participating government should disclose information about the availability of the joint venture's separate financial statements.

Finally, a participating government should disclose information concerning related party transactions between the participating governments and the joint venture [GASB Cod. Sec. J50.109].

Joint Building or Finance Authorities. Participating governments may engage in a relationship resulting in a formal joint venture, but the substance of the relationship is an undivided-interest arrangement. An undivided-interest arrangement is "an ownership arrangement in which two or more parties own property in which title is held individually to the extent of each party's interest." Thus, for accounting purposes, even though a joint venture exists, the undivided interest in property acquired through the joint venture is recorded directly by each participating government.

A joint building authority and a finance authority are examples of this type of arrangement. A joint building authority may be created to construct or acquire capital assets and in turn to lease the assets to a participating government. Under this arrangement, a participating government would have recorded a lease based on standards discussed in Chapter 14. For this reason, a participating government would reflect the effects of the lease on its financial statements [GASB Cod. Sec. J50.110]. (Also see previous section titled "Intra-Entity Leasing Arrangements.")

Jointly Governed Organizations or Joint Powers Authorities. A state may allow local governments to form regional governments or similar entities to provide goods or services to the citizens served by the local governments. For example, a state may provide for the creation of a municipal power authority that acquires, generates, and provides electrical power to participating local governments or utility districts. These entities are common, especially in the western United States. Such arrangements should be evaluated to determine whether they meet the definition of a joint venture. If an arrangement of this type does meet the criteria to be reported as a joint venture, the only disclosures that need to be made in a participating government's financial statements are those concerning its participation in the jointly governed organization and its related-party transactions [GASB Cod. Sec. J50.111].

Component Units and Related Organizations with Joint Venture Characteristics

The third type of reporting relationship with organizations other than component units concerns component units and related organizations with joint venture characteristics. A government may participate with other governments to create an organization that is either a component unit or a related organization of another government.

For example, governments #1, #2, and #3 create an organization, and assume that the organization is either a component unit or a related organization of government #1. Thus, the majority participating government (government #1) reports the organization in a manner consistent with the standards applicable to component units or related organizations. The minority participating governments (governments #2 and #3) should report their relationships with the organization based on the standards discussed in the previous sections titled "Joint Ventures" and "Jointly Governed Organizations or Joint Powers Authorities."

The organization reported as a component unit in the statements of the reporting entity that includes the financial statements of the majority participating government should present any equity interest of the minority participating governments as part of its equity section.

When participating governments jointly control an organization and it is fiscally dependent on one of the participating governments, the majority participating government should report the organization either as a component unit or as a related organization. The minority participating governments should report the jointly controlled organization in accordance with the standards discussed in the previous sections titled "Joint Ventures" and "Jointly Governed Organizations or Joint Powers Authorities" [GASB Cod. Sec. J50.112].

A common example of reporting for an entity with these characteristics is in GASB Cod. Sec. J50.711-2. A housing authority is the general partner of a limited tax credit partnership (a legally separate entity) and is financially accountable for the limited tax credit partnership. Therefore, the housing authority includes it as a component unit.

> **Example:** The limited partners have a 99.99% equity interest in the limited tax credit partnership. GAAP requires any equity interest of the minority participants to be reported as restricted net position, nonexpendable. However, other sections of GAAP require the net investment in capital assets component of net position to include capital assets, net of accumulated depreciation, reduced by outstanding obligations that are attributable to the acquisition, construction, or improvement of those assets. There is no established prioritization for the calculation of the components of net position. Because the housing authority's legal ownership is limited to 0.01% of the net position of the limited tax credit partnership, the housing authority first calculates its 0.01% of each component of net position and then report the remaining 99.99% of net position as restricted net position, nonexpendable.

Pools (Public Entity Risk Pools and Similar)

Although a pool is another example of an arrangement in which a group of governments jointly participate in a venture, GAAP states that a pool is different from a joint venture. Pools are characterized by the following:

- Membership is open (participants are free to join, resign, or alter their level of participation at will,
- Equity interest is recognized in participant's financial statements, and
- Limited disclosures are required.

An investment pool would likely give participants more flexibility in determining to what extent each participant wants to participate in the venture. In addition, a pool arrangement results in an investment being presented directly in the financial statements of a participating government, and therefore there is no need to compute and present a separate equity interest in the pool. Furthermore, because of the flexibility that characterizes each pool, it is not necessary to make the type of disclosures required for joint venture participants [GASB Cod. Sec. J50.113].

Governmental entities that participate in an external investment pool should observe the standards that apply to such investments. Further discussion of investment accounting and financial reporting is presented in Chapter 9.

Public Entity Risk Pools. GAAP requires that governmental entities that make capital contributions to or participate in the activities of a public entity risk pool should *not* account for the investment and subsequent results of operations of the pool as a joint venture. This prohibition applies to contributions to public entity pools where risk is transferred as well as where risk is not transferred. In addition, if under a retrospectively rated policy, the governmental entity's ultimate premium payments are based on the experience of the public entity risk pool, this relationship does not create a joint venture relationship for financial reporting purposes [GASB Cod. Sec. J50.113]. Chapter 23 contains further information on pools and reporting.

Undivided Interests

Participating governments may join with one another in a type of joint venture in which no new joint entity is created. Such an arrangement results in an undivided interest (joint operation). An undivided interest arises when two or more parties own property that is held individually because of each party's interest in the property. In addition, liabilities related to the operation of the undivided interest are obligations of each participating government.

In an undivided interest, no separate entity is created and, therefore, accounts and transactions related to the operations of the undivided interest must be recorded in the records of the participating governments. For this reason, there is no requirement to make disclosures like those described in the section titled "Disclosure Requirements for Joint Venture Participants."

Governments may participate in arrangements that have characteristics of both a joint venture (separate entity) and an undivided interest. Under this arrangement, the undivided interest should be accounted for as described in the previous paragraph and the equity interest related to the joint venture should be accounted for as described in the section titled "Reporting Participation in Joint Ventures in Which There Is an Equity Interest" [GASB Cod. Sec. J50.114].

Cost-Sharing Arrangements

Cost-sharing projects, such as the financing of highway construction by the federal, state, and local governments, are not joint ventures because there is no ongoing financial interest or responsibility by the participating governmental entities.

In addition, joint purchasing agreements or shared-services arrangements that commit participating governments to purchase a stated quantity of goods or services for a specified period are not joint ventures [GASB Cod. Sec. J50.115].

There are no specific financial reporting or disclosure requirements related to a government's participation in a cost-sharing arrangement.

GOVERNMENT COMBINATIONS AND DISPOSALS OF GOVERNMENT OPERATIONS

Governments may have various transactions called mergers, acquisitions, and operations transfers. The GASB distinguishes between mergers and acquisitions by the degree of "consideration" that is exchanged in conjunction with the transaction. Assets and liabilities involved in the combination are measured at carrying value when involved in a merger. However, in an acquisition, assets and liabilities are measured at their acquired value with certain exceptions.

Combinations also include transfers or disposals of operations. Disposals of operations occur when a government discontinues or transfers specific activities.

Combinations occur in legally separate entities, such as a governmental entity with other governmental entities. Combinations may also occur between a governmental entity and a not-for-profit or for-profit entity if the new or continuing organization is a government. Government combinations also include mergers and acquisitions of activities that comprise less than an entire legally separate entity and involve only the assets and liabilities previously used by an entity to provide specific goods or services [GASB Cod. Sec. Co10.101].

Portions of governments are "operations." The GASB describes an "operation" as an integrated set of activities conducted and managed to provide identifiable services with associated assets or liabilities. For example, an operation may include the assets and liabilities specifically associated with the activities conducted and managed by the fire department in a city. Conversely, fire engines donated to or acquired by a fire department would comprise only a portion of that activity and, therefore, would not constitute an operation. Anything that constitutes less than an operation (e.g., a process) has no defined GAAP as of the date of publication.

Government combinations must result in a continuation of a substantial portion of the services provided by the previously separate entities or operations after the transaction. The legal instrument (law, ordinance, contract, etc.) that provides the basis for the combination will contain information, including whether services should be continued after the combination or whether assets (and/or liabilities) have been acquired. If the legal instrument is not specific regarding the continuation of services, GAAP allows for professional judgment to determine whether a combination has occurred [GASB Cod. Sec. Co10.106].

Government Mergers

Government mergers occur when legally separate entities combine in which no significant consideration is exchanged and *either* one or more governments or nongovernmental entities cease to exist, or one or more legally separate governments or nongovernmental entities cease to exist and their operations are absorbed into, and continue to be provided by, one or more continuing governments. In other words, government A plus government B can equal the new government C or government A absorbs government B and government A remains intact [GASB Cod. Sec. Co10.107].

Government Acquisition

A "government acquisition" occurs when a government acquires another entity, or the operations of another entity, in exchange for significant consideration. The consideration provided should be significant in relation to the assets and liabilities acquired (namely more than $1). The acquired entity or operation becomes part of the acquiring government's legally separate entity [GASB Cod. Sec. Co10.108].

Transfers of Operations

A "transfer of operations" occurs when a government takes a function and transfers it to another function. This may result from reorganizations, redistricting, annexation, or jurisdictional changes in boundaries. However, the standard also notes that a transfer may be present in shared service arrangements where governments agree to combine operations. Transfers of operations may occur when a function is "spun off" to create a new government [GASB Cod. Sec. Co10.109].

> **OBSERVATION:** Transfers of operations may also occur due to economic conditions or other factors. For example, assume that two adjoining cities have shared a common police department. During the year, one of the cities voted to end the contract with the adjoining city. The leaving city then issued a procurement, approving a bid by the county sheriff to provide services through a competitive process. The sheriff submitted a lower bid than several other cities that also adjoin the government. This activity is a transfer of operations.

Accounting and Financial Reporting for Various Combinations

Mergers Where Two or More Governments Combine to Form a New Government. For mergers where two or more governments combine to form a new government, the transaction date is the date on which the combination becomes effective. The initial reporting period of the new government begins on the merger date. The combined assets, deferred outflows of resources, liabilities, and deferred inflows of resources of the merging entities is recognized and measured in the statement of net position as of *the beginning* of that initial reporting period. The combination presumes that the former government followed generally accepted accounting principles. If U.S. GAAP was not followed, adjustments are necessary to make the combination effective [GASB Cod. Sec. Co10.110].

The new government measures the various accounting elements as of the merger date at the *carrying values* as reported on the separate financial statements of the merging entities. If there are no financial statements as of the date of the merger, GAAP allows for usage of the most recent financial statements if they were prepared in accordance with GAAP [GASB Cod. Secs. Co10.111–.116].

> **OBSERVATION:** Allowing for the usage of the most recent financial statements in a merger that is between fiscal year-ends is a large relief in many government combinations. It is difficult for many governments to project assets and liabilities in between fiscal year-ends and therefore from an audit and an operational standpoint, the allowance eases the transition.

Adjustments may be needed in a merger where different but acceptable bases of accounting may have been used in the various accounting elements. For example, depreciation periods may be different on similar assets. Furthermore, asset impairments may exist. For example, two city halls may no longer be needed if a single city remains.

> **OBSERVATION:** Assume that a city was spun off from a county due to a citizens' referendum. However, assume that funds were due to the new city when it formed, to be paid from a state, were never paid due to a change in a law, leaving the new city insolvent. In this very real example, the same citizens held another referendum, voting to dissolve and rejoin the county. This activity is a combination, but in reverse, as the city has voted to dissolve and rejoin the county.

Mergers Where Two or More Governments Combine and One Government Continues. In continuing governments (where one government absorbs one or more governments) the merger date is the beginning of the reporting period in which the combination occurs, regardless of the actual date of the merger. Continuing governments recognize and measure the various accounting elements of the merging entities for the reporting period in which the combination occurs as though the entities had been combined at the beginning of the continuing government's reporting period. However, the same relief is available if there are no financial statements as of the date of the merger. Similarly, adjustments and impairments may occur because of the combination. Furthermore, there may be eliminations like those that commonly occur between governments. These may involve loans between governments and other transfers. If one of the parties no longer exists, then the loan or transfer may have to be eliminated [GASB Cod. Sec. Co10.118].

OBSERVATION: Mergers may also affect the balances and results of operations in governmental funds. Fund statements may have to be adjusted and combined in those instances.

Acquisitions. In the rare instance that a government acquisition occurs, GAAP recognizes the acquisition as of the date on which the acquiring government obtains control of the assets and becomes obligated for the liabilities of an entity or its operations. Generally, the acquisition date coincides with the "closing" date because consideration is paid at that time. However, the parties may have designated another date at which the acquiring government obtains control of assets and becomes obligated for the liabilities of the former government [GASB Cod. Sec. Co10.126].

The value of the various elements involved in an acquisition is the "acquisition value" or "market price" as of the date of the acquisition. However, employee benefits, including pensions, compensated absences, other postemployment benefits, landfill post-closure care, and comparable items remain measured utilizing current provisions of GAAP. Deferred positions related to derivatives should be adjusted to reflect the difference between the acquisition value and the carrying value of acquired hedged items [GASB Cod. Secs. Co10.127–.129].

As previously discussed in this chapter, a government may acquire a 100% equity interest in a legally separate organization that is reported as a component unit. If this occurs, the component unit should measure its various accounting elements in accordance with GAAP at the date on which the government acquires the 100% equity interest. The consideration provided should include the net resources exchanged to complete the acquisition of the 100% equity interest. The flows statements of the component unit that has been acquired should include only those transactions that occurred after the acquisition of the 100%

equity interest (see also previous discussion on "Related Organizations") [GASB Cod. Sec. 2600.126].

What is Consideration? Consideration may include financial and nonfinancial assets. Cash, investments, or capital assets are likely forms of consideration. In addition, a liability incurred may represent an obligation to provide consideration to the former owners of the acquired entity. GAAP uses an example where a government issues a note payable in addition to, or in lieu of, cash to the former owners of an organization in exchange for the net position of that organization. In governments that are acquired with a negative net position, GAAP notes that relief of the negative net position is not a form of consideration.

GAAP also supposes that contingencies may be involved in consideration based on future events. If this does occur, GASB Cod. Sec. C50 contains guidance for the accounting and financial reporting of contingencies.

Since there is no element of "goodwill" in a governmental acquisition, if the consideration exceeds the various values acquired from the former government, a deferred outflow of resources is created. The deferred outflow of resources position is amortized using several possible factors largely based on the remaining estimated service lives of capital or similar long-lived assets or liabilities acquired. If the consideration is less than the various values acquired from the former government, the various values are adjusted ratably to equal the consideration. There is no provision for "bad will." In the case where consideration is in the form of economic aid, a contribution is recognized [GASB Cod. Secs. Co10.134–.138].

The deferred outflow of resources should be attributed to future periods in a systematic and rational manner, based on professional judgment, considering the relevant circumstances of the acquisition. The length of the attribution period may be determined by considering such factors as the following:

- The estimated service lives of capital assets acquired, when acquisitions are largely based on the expected use of those capital assets,
- The estimated remaining service life for acquisitions of landfills that are capacity-driven,
- The expected length of contracts acquired, or
- The estimated remaining service life of technology acquired if the acquisition is based on the expected efficiencies of a technology system.

A government should periodically review and revise its estimate of the attribution period in subsequent reporting periods.

Other Items in Acquisitions

The costs of the transaction should be expensed during the current period. Also, if the acquisition occurs within the same reporting entity, the acquiring government recognizes the various accounting elements at the carrying values of the selling entity. The difference between the acquisition price and the carrying value of the net position acquired is reported as a special item by the acquiring government in its separately issued statements and reclassified as transfers or subsidies, as appropriate, in the financial statements of the reporting entity [GASB Cod. Sec. Co10.139].

For acquisitions that are announced but not finalized as of the end of the fiscal year, estimated amounts are recognized for the items for which measurement is not complete. Once the acquisition is completed, the acquiring government should prospectively update the estimated amounts reported as of the acquisition date to reflect added information obtained about facts and circumstances that existed as of the acquisition date that, if known, would have affected the measurement of amounts recognized as of that date [GASB Cod. Sec. Co10.141].

Transfers and Disposals of Operations

The effective date of a transfer of operations is the date the transferee government obtains control of the assets and becomes obligated for the liabilities of the operation transferred. A continuing government should report a transfer of operations as a transaction in the financial statements for the reporting period in which it occurs. Alternatively, if a transfer of operations results in the formation of a new government, the new government's initial reporting period begins at the effective transfer date. In the example above regarding a police department, the county sheriff and the city would recognize the transfers as of the effective transfer date. GAAP is presumed in calculating the carrying values of the various accounting elements. However, as stated previously, adjustments and impairment testing may be needed.

In a disposal, the disposing government recognizes a gain or loss on the disposal of operations. Gains or losses on the disposal of operations are reported as a special item in the period in which the disposal occurs, based on either the effective transfer date of a transfer of operations or the date of sale for operations that are sold. The disposing government should include only those costs that are directly associated with the disposal of operations when determining the amount of the gain or loss to report. These costs may include employee termination costs calculated in accordance with GAAP for termination benefits [GASB Cod. Sec. T25]. Other contingencies may be present, including legal claims, and those should be accounted for in accordance with GASB Cod. Sec. C50 [GASB Cod. Secs. Co10.143–.151].

Note Disclosure

Note disclosure of combinations is like other GASB standards. The disclosure includes a brief description of the combination, dates, and legal reason for the combination. Mergers and acquisitions will include condensed financial statements of the combination, the nature of adjustments made and the new initial amounts. It is envisioned that this disclosure would be in a table. Any consideration should be described, along with any contingencies. Disposals should disclose related items [GASB Cod. Secs. Co10.152–.155].

CHAPTER 5
TERMINOLOGY AND CLASSIFICATION

Chapter References:
   GASB Statement Nos. 6, 7, 34, 37, 46, 51, 54, 62, 63, 87, 91, 100
   GASB Interpretation No. 1
   GASB Technical Bulletin 2020-1
   GASB *Implementation Guide*
   NCGA Statement Nos. 1, 5

INTRODUCTION

A governmental reporting entity should use consistent terminology and classifications in its accounting system.

From an internal perspective, the use of a common language and classification scheme enhances management's ability to evaluate and control operations. For financial reporting purposes, the consistent use of terms and classifications in the budgeting, accounting, and reporting systems facilitates the preparation of financial statements and makes those financial statements more understandable to user groups.

It is important to distinguish the characteristics of transactions such as:

- Transfers as compared to revenues and expenditures or expenses in the basic financial statements,
- Proceeds of general long-term debt issuances and their unique reporting in governmental fund revenues and expenditures, and
- The terms *revenues* and *expenses*, as used in the government-wide financial statements and in proprietary and trust fund financial statements, which are different from the terms *revenues* and *expenditures* as used in the governmental fund financial statements [GASB Cod. Sec. 1800.101].

In many ways, these characteristics are what separates governmental accounting and financial reporting from other accounting models used.

5002 *Basic Governmental Accounting Concepts and Standards*

PRACTICE ALERT: Some of this terminology may change should the GASB's *Financial Reporting Model Improvements* Exposure Draft be approved as proposed. A major example would be the replacement of *expenditures* with *outflows of resources*. Throughout this chapter, the terminology relating to governmental fund expenditures would change. For governmental funds, revenues would be *inflows of resources*. For proprietary funds, the terminology of revenues and expenses for inflows and outflows respectively, would be unchanged.

TERMINOLOGY AND CLASSIFICATION IN REPORTING INTERFUND ACTIVITY

Reporting Interfund Activity in Fund Financial Statements

To determine how interfund transfers within and among governmental funds, proprietary funds, and fiduciary funds should be presented in the fund financial statements, transfers must be categorized in the same manner as discussed in Chapter 4, but at the primary government, between funds instead of involving component units:

Type of Activity	Definitions	Categories/Explanations	Examples
		Interfund loans: • Amounts provided with a requirement for repayment. • Interfund loans should be reported as interfund receivables in lender funds and interfund payables in borrower funds. • This activity should not be reported as other financing sources or uses in the fund financial statements. • If repayment is not expected within a *reasonable* time, the interfund balances should be reduced and the amount that is not expected to be repaid should be reported as a transfer from the fund that made the loan to the fund that received the loan.	• Due from or due to funds for amounts requiring payments. • Advances to or from funds. • On government-wide statement of net position, internal balances may be reported.
Reciprocal interfund activity	The internal to the reporting entity counterpart to exchange and exchange-like transactions.	*Interfund services provided and used:* • Sales and purchases of goods and services between funds for a price approximating their external exchange value. • Interfund services provided and used should be reported as revenues in seller funds and expenditures or expenses in purchaser funds. • Unpaid amounts should be reported as interfund receivables and payables in the fund balance sheets or fund statements of net position. • An exception is when the general fund is used to account for risk-financing activity. In such cases, interfund charges to other funds are accounted for as reimbursements per GASB Cod. Sec. C50.126.	• Internal service fund transactions with funds for legal services, information technology, purchasing, fleet operations, printing, and other goods and services.

Type of Activity	Definitions	Categories/Explanations	Examples
Nonreciprocal interfund activity	The internal counterpart to nonexchange transactions.	*Interfund transfers:* • Flows of assets (such as cash or goods) without equivalent flows of assets in return and without a requirement for repayment. • In governmental funds, transfers should be reported as other financing uses in the funds making transfers and as other financing sources in the funds receiving transfers. • In proprietary funds, transfers should be reported after nonoperating revenues and expenses as transfers.	• Transfers to or from funds. (See **PRACTICE ALERT** on GASB-100.) • Eliminated in the Statement of Activities unless between governmental and business-type activities, which would be presented as transfers.
		Interfund reimbursements: • Repayments from the funds responsible for these expenditures or expenses to the funds that initially paid for them. • Reimbursements should not be displayed in the financial statements.	• Like transfers to/from funds.

PRACTICE ALERT: GASB Statement No. 100 (*Accounting Changes and Error Corrections*) became effective for periods beginning after June 15, 2023. A change to or within the financial reporting entity does not include the addition or removal of a fund that results from the movement of continuing operations within the primary government. Had a fund change occurred as a result of discontinued operations, GASB Cod. Sec. 2250.127 (GASB-100, par. 9) requires reporting as a change to or within the financial reporting entity and a restatement of beginning balances.

"Reciprocal interfund activities" are interfund activities that have many of the same characteristics of exchange and exchange-like transactions that occur with external parties, meaning that equal value is exchanged simultaneously or near simultaneously. "Nonreciprocal interfund activities" are interfund activities that have many of the same characteristics of nonexchange transactions that occur with external parties, meaning that non-equal-value exchanges occur or only a "one way" transaction occurs [GASB Cod. Sec. 1800.102].

Interfund Loans (Reciprocal Interfund Activity). Many governments initiate advances or loans between funds. These are different from short-term amounts due to and due from funds based upon the notion that amounts due to and due from would be "repaid within a reasonable time."

The concept of a loan as envisioned by the GASB is based on the expectation that the loan will be repaid at some point. Loans should be reported as interfund receivables by the lender fund and interfund payables by the borrower fund. That is, the interfund loan should not be eliminated in the preparation of financial statements at the fund level. Thus, the proceeds from interfund loans should not be reported as "other financing sources or uses" in the operating statements in the fund financial statements.

If a loan or a portion of a loan is not expected to be repaid *within a reasonable time*, the interfund receivable or payable should be reduced by the amount not expected to be repaid and that amount should be reported as an interfund transfer by both funds that are parties to the transfer.

GASB Cod. Sec. 1800.702-8 addresses the question of what is meant by "repaid within a reasonable time" as follows:

> There is no precise definition of the provision. Professional judgment should be exercised in determining whether an interfund loan should be reclassified. The *expectation* aspect of the phrase means that the government intends to, and [can], repay the amount loaned. For example, recurring payments made to reduce the interfund loan balance may provide evidence that "repayment is expected." What constitutes a *reasonable time* for repayment is again a matter of professional judgment, but the notion is not without precedent in financial reporting standards. GASB Cod. Sec. C50 invokes a "reasonable time" consideration in paragraphs .128(b) and .130, [regarding] recovery of the full cost of internal service fund expenses.

If there is some doubt about repayment, a government may tend to want to use an allowance account against a receivable. However, the receivables, net of allowances for doubtful accounts will not balance against the offsetting payable account in the paying fund. If there is any doubt about repayment, a government should use transfers, rather than interfund loans.

Interfund Services Provided and Used (Reciprocal Interfund Activity). Interfund receivables or payables may arise from an operating activity (i.e., the "sale" of goods and services) between funds rather than in the form of a loan arrangement. If the interfund operating activity is recorded at an amount that approximates the fair value of the goods or services exchanged, the provider or seller fund should record the activity as revenue and the user or purchaser fund should record an expenditure or expense, not an interfund transfer. Any unpaid balance at the end of the period should be reported as an interfund receivable or payable in the fund balance sheet or statement of net position.

OBSERVATION: When the general fund is used to account for risk-financing activities, interfund charges to other funds must be accounted for as interfund reimbursements [GASB Cod. Secs. C50.126, 1800.102, fn. 1].

Interfund Transfers (Nonreciprocal Interfund Activity). This type of nonreciprocal transaction represents interfund activities whereby the two parties to the events do not receive equivalent cash, goods, or services. Governmental funds should report transfers of this nature in their activity statements as other financing uses and other financial sources of funds. Proprietary funds should report this type of transfer in their activity statements in a separate subsection following net income (loss) before transfers. There is no differentiation between operating transfers and residual equity transfers. Thus, equity-type transfers should not be reported as adjustments to a fund's beginning equity balance.

This area of GAAP contains guidance on payments *in lieu of taxes* from other enterprise funds to governmental funds (PILOTs). These payments should be reported as interfund transfers, *unless the payments and services received are equivalent in value based on the exchange of specific services or goods.* If the two are equivalent in value, the disbursing fund may treat the payment as an expenditure (expense) and the receiving fund may record revenue.

PILOTs are common transactions between governments. One government is usually organized as a business-type activity such as a public college or university, an airport, transit system and similar while the recipient government is usually a general-purpose government such as a city, county, or state. In some situations, the federal government makes payments to the city, county, or state where a federal facility is located such as a military facility, research center, or even a national park. The paying government is exempt from forms of taxation yet benefits from services provided by the recipient government such as utilities, public safety and so on. In practice, the payment may not be substantially equal to the value of the benefits received. However, if they are substantially equal, current GAAP has revenue recognized by the receiving government and expense by the "paying" government.

An example of differentiating amounts in lieu of taxes from interfund activity is in GASB Cod. Sec. 1800.702-7. In this case, a city government receives in its general fund an annual PILOT from the water and sewer utility fund. The PILOT is determined each year by multiplying the estimated assessed valuation of the water and sewer plant by the city's property tax rate. This transaction though does not meet the criterion for revenue or expense treatment. It is calculated like a tax, rather than a bill for goods and services. In accordance with GASB Cod. Sec. 1800.702-10, the general fund would report revenue and the water and sewer utility fund would report an expense.

OBSERVATION: Transfers are different from sales, pledges, and intra-entity transfers of assets and future revenues in accordance with GASB Cod. Secs. S20.101–.119. Collateralized borrowings may also be part of a government's activity. Determining whether a transaction should be reported as a sale rather than a collateralized borrowing requires an assessment of a government's continuing involvement with the receivables or future revenues transferred. A significant aspect of that assessment is the degree to which the selling or pledging government (the transferor) retains or relinquishes (to the transferee) control over the receivables or future revenues transferred [GASB Cod. Sec. S20.102]. Intra-entity transfers are between entities *within* the government's reporting entity. Commonly, such transactions include receivables, but may include capital assets (see **PRACTICE POINT** below). Sales, pledges, and intra-entity transfers of assets and future revenues transactions are discussed in Chapter 17.

PRACTICE POINT: Intra-entity transfers of assets may involve transfers of capital assets or financial assets between governmental or proprietary funds and fiduciary funds. GASB Cod. Sec. S20.112 discusses the accounting and financial reporting of such transfers. The transfer of capital or financial assets between a governmental employer or nonemployer contributing entity and a pension plan or other postemployment benefit (OPEB) plan that are within the same financial reporting entity, any difference between the amount paid by the pension plan or OPEB plan (exclusive of amounts that may be refundable) and the carrying value of the assets transferred should be reported as follows:

1. As an employer contribution or a nonemployer contributing entity contribution to the pension plan or OPEB plan in accordance with the requirements of GASB Cod. Secs. P20, P21, P50, P51 (*Reporting Benefits Provided Through Trusts that Meet Specified Criteria, Defined Benefit and Defined Contribution Pensions, Defined Benefit and Defined Contribution OPEB*), respectively, as applicable, in the separately issued statements of the employer or nonemployer contributing entity and in the financial statements of the reporting entity.

2. As an employer contribution or a nonemployer contributing entity contribution in accordance with the requirements of GASB Cod. Secs. Pe5, Pe6, Po50, Po51 (*Pension and OPEB Plans Administered Through Trusts That Meet Specified Criteria, Defined Benefit and Defined Contribution*), as applicable, in the stand-alone statements of the pension plan or OPEB plan and in the financial statements of the reporting entity.

Application of these provisions should be the same for both discretely presented and blended component units. That is, the standards should first be applied in the separate financial statements of the component unit.

PRACTICE ALERT: The GASB's *Financial Reporting Model Improvements* Exposure Draft proposes to change the recognition and measurement of interfund transfers. In governmental funds, two potential reporting methods are proposed:

- Transfers related to the purchase of capital assets and repayment of long-term debt (except for long-term debt issued for short-term purposes)—noncurrent activity.
- All other transfers would be reported as current activities.

In proprietary funds, transfers are proposed to be reported as noncapital subsidies or as other nonoperating revenues and expenses.

Interfund Reimbursements (Nonreciprocal Interfund Activity). A fund may incur expenditures or expenses that will be reimbursed (or paid) by another fund. Reimbursements should not be reported in the governmental entity's financial statements to avoid "double counting" revenues and expense or expenditure items. To illustrate, assume that the general fund provides $50,000 in debt service payments to a debt service fund. The transfer is recorded as follows in the general fund:

GENERAL FUND	Debit	Credit
Transfer out—debt service fund (other financing use)	50,000	
Cash		50,000
To record transfer of cash for next month's debt payments to debt service fund.		

The debt service fund then reports the transfer in for future debt service payments:

DEBT SERVICE FUND	Debit	Credit
Cash	50,000	
Transfer in—general fund (other financing source)		50,000
To record transfer of cash in from general fund for next month's debt payments.		

PRACTICE POINT: Other financing sources and other financing uses are not expenditures and revenues, respectively, and are only utilized in governmental funds. Other financing sources and uses primarily relate to debt transactions, sales of capital assets, transfers in and transfers out. A further discussion on other financing sources and other financing uses is in Chapter 6.

Reporting Eliminations and Reclassifications in Government-Wide Financial Statements

The preparation of government-wide financial statements is based on a consolidating process (like corporate consolidations) rather than a combining process. These eliminations and reclassifications related to the consolidation process are based on:

- Internal balances (statement of net position),
- Internal activities (statement of activities),
- Intra-entity activity, and
- Internal service fund balances.

Internal Balances (Statement of Net Position). The government-wide financial statements present the governmental entity and its blended component units as a single reporting entity. Based on this philosophy, most balances between funds that are initially recorded as interfund receivables and payables at the individual fund level should be eliminated in the preparation of the statement of net position within each of the two major reporting groups of the primary government (the government activities and business-type activities). The purpose of the elimination is to avoid the "grossing-up" effect on assets and liabilities presented on the statement of net position within the governmental and business-type activities columns.

For example, if there is an interfund receivable or payable between the general fund and a special revenue fund, those amounts would be eliminated to determine the balances that would appear in the governmental activities' column. Likewise, if there is an interfund receivable or payable between two proprietary funds of the primary government, those amounts would also be eliminated in the business-type activities column.

However, the net residual interfund receivable or payable between governmental and business-type activities should not be eliminated but should be presented in each column (government activities and business-type activities) and labeled as "internal balances" or a similar description. These amounts will be the same and, therefore, will cancel out when they are combined (horizontally) in the statement of net position to form the column for total primary government activities.

> **OBSERVATION:** Governments usually maintain accounting transactions using the conventional-fund approach and convert this information to a government-wide basis using the flow of economic resources and accrual basis of accounting at the time the government-wide financial statements are prepared. Thus, at the fund level the internal balance between a governmental fund (reported on the modified accrual basis) may not equal the related balance with a proprietary fund (reported on the accrual basis), however, once the governmental fund activity is adjusted to the government-wide presentation, those adjusted amounts will equal the amounts presented in the proprietary funds.

> **OBSERVATION:** Transfers between a primary government and a blended component unit are common. Some of these component units may have a different fiscal year, resulting in an out of balance condition due to the timing of the reporting dates. As explained in the GASB Cod. Sec. 1800.703-1, this situation is allowable if GASB Cod. Sec. 2600.120 is followed, stating the reason for the imbalance in the notes. Some practitioners provide a reconciliation of net position changes rather than just disclosing the imbalance due to "timing." Chapter 4 has further information on component unit transactions and differing fiscal years.

There also may be interfund receivables or payables that arise because of transactions between the primary government and its fiduciary funds. These amounts should not be eliminated, but rather should be reported on the statement of net position like receivables from and payables to external parties [GASB Cod. Sec. 1800.103] (see previous **PRACTICE POINT** on GASB Cod. Sec. S20).

As explained in GASB Cod. Sec. 2300.710-1, there is no need to explain in a note to the financial statement that internal balances with fiduciary funds are not reported as part of the internal balance. However, a governmental entity may (but is not required to) add some clarity to this difference by using one or both of the following approaches:

1. Include an explanation in the note required by GASB Cod. Secs. 2300.106, .126, with respect to the identification of the amounts due from other funds by:

    a. individual major funds,

    b. aggregated nonmajor governmental funds,

c. aggregated nonmajor enterprise funds,

d. aggregated internal service funds, and

e. fiduciary fund types, or

2. Separately present in the fund financial statements the amounts due to or from fiduciary funds from amounts due to or from other funds.

Overdrawn Funds. Cash, cash equivalents, and investments are frequently pooled by state and local governments to lower the cost of administering cashflow. AICPA literature cleared by the GASB allows an interfund liability to be reported when one fund has overdrawn its share of a cash pool (an internal investment pool). However, in the [economic resources measurement focus] financial statements, those interfund accounts should be eliminated as required for internal balances.

If a cash account for the government is overdrawn in total, the balance should be classified as a liability in the governmental fund financial statements and in the proprietary and fiduciary fund financial statements, as applicable. This issue is frequently termed "negative cash." For further information on internal cash operations, see Chapter 9.

PRACTICE POINT: The AICPA's Audit and Accounting Guide, *State and Local Governments*, pars. 5.29 and 5.31 contains the following guidance on negative cash:

> When one fund has overdrawn its share of an *internal* investment pool, that fund should report an interfund liability to the fund that the government's management deems to have lent the amount to the overdrawn fund. The fund deemed to have lent the amount should report an interfund receivable from the borrowing fund. This treatment is unaffected by whether the lending and borrowing funds are the same or different fund types or categories. However, in the government-wide financial statements, those interfund accounts should be eliminated as required for internal fund balances by GASB Statement No. 34, *Basic Financial Statements—and Management's Discussion and Analysis—for State and Local Governments*, paragraph 58 [GASB Cod. Sec. 2200.152]. If a cash account for the government is overdrawn in total, the balance should be classified as a liability in the fund and government-wide financial statements.
>
> Custodial funds may have negative cash balances because more cash has been paid out than received. The funds also may have incurred more liabilities than there are assets to pay them. In those cases, the government may have a liability to cover the shortages with amounts from other funds and should report an interfund receivable in the custodial funds.

The AICPA notes in footnote 3 to paragraph 5.29 that such overdrawn positions may represent instances of noncompliance if the government has a prohibition against interfund borrowing. Provisions of this issue are "cleared by the GASB" and contained in GASB Cod. Secs. 1800.801–.803.

Internal Activities (Statement of Activities). To avoid the "doubling-up" effect of internal activities among funds, interfund transactions should be eliminated so that expenses and revenues are recorded only once. For example, a fund (generally the general fund or an internal service fund) may charge other funds for services provided (such as insurance coverage or allocation of overhead expenses) on an internal basis. When these funds are consolidated to present the functional expenses of governmental activities in the statement of activities, the double counting of the expense (with an offset to revenue recorded by the provider fund) should be eliminated in a manner so that "the allocated expenses are reported only by the function to which they were allocated" [GASB Cod. Sec. 1800.104].

Internal activities should not be eliminated when they are classified as "interfund services provided and used." For example, when a municipal water company charges a fee for services provided to the general government, the expense and revenues related to those activities should not be eliminated [GASB Cod. Sec. 1800.105]. This type of internal activity is further discussed in Chapter 20.

Intra-Entity Activity. Transactions (and related balances) between the primary government and its blended component units should be reclassified based on the guidance discussed in Chapter 20. Transactions (and related balances) between the primary government and its discretely presented component units should not be eliminated in the government-wide financial statements. That is, the two parties to the transactions should report revenue and expense accounts as originally recorded in those respective funds. Amounts payable and receivable between the primary government and its discretely presented component units should be reported as separate line items on the statement of net position. Likewise, payables and receivables between discretely presented component units must also be reported separately [GASB Cod. Sec. 1800.106].

GAAP provides financial statement users with consistent measurement, recognition, and disclosure across governments and within individual governments relating to the accounting for sales and pledges of receivables and future revenues and intra-entity transfers of assets and future revenues. (See further discussion of accounting and reporting treatment for intra-entity transfers of assets and future revenues in Chapter 17. Chapter 4 has further information on intra-entity transactions involving component units. See also the previous **PRACTICE POINT** discussing intra-entity transactions.)

Internal Service Fund Balances. As described above, internal services and similar activities should be eliminated to avoid doubling-up expenses and revenues when preparing the governmental-activities column of the statement of activities. The effect of this approach is to adjust activities in an internal service fund to a "break-even" balance. That is, if the internal service fund had a "net profit" for the year, there should be a pro rata reduction in the charges made to the funds that used the internal service fund's services for the year. Likewise, a net loss would require a pro rata adjustment that would increase the charges made to the various participating funds. After making these eliminations, any residual balances related to the internal service fund's assets and liabilities should be reported in the governmental activities' column in the government-wide statement of net position [GASB Cod. Sec. 1800.107].

The "effect" of internal service fund activity is eliminated by a "look back" activity, adjusting the internal service fund's internal charges to break even. Internal service fund net income from internal activity would cause a pro rata *reduction* in the charges made to the participating funds or functions. Conversely, an internal service fund net loss from internal activity would require a pro rata *increase* in the amounts charged to the participating funds or functions [GASB Cod. Sec. 1800.703-4].

PRACTICE POINT: A comprehensive example of internal service fund activity and the related eliminations is portrayed in Chapter 8 of the *Governmental GAAP Practice and Disclosures Manual*. In the financial statements contained in the *Manual*, the impact of internal service fund activity is portrayed not only in governmental but also in business-type activities.

In some instances, an internal service activity of a government may not be accounted for in an internal service fund but accounted for in another governmental fund (generally the general fund or a special revenue fund). Furthermore, the internal-service transaction may not cut across functional expense categories. That is, there is a "billing" between different departments, but the expenses of those departments are all included in the same functional expenses.

Conceptually, the same break-even approach as described above should be applied so as not to gross-up expenses and program revenues of a particular functional expense, however, the GASB does not require that an elimination be made (unless the amounts are material) because the result of this non-elimination is that direct expenses and program revenues are overstated by equal values, but net (expense) revenue related to the function is not overstated.

The GASB takes the position that activities conducted with an internal service fund are generally reported as government activities rather than business-type activities, even though an internal service fund uses the flow of economic resources and the accrual basis of accounting. However, when enterprise funds account for all or the predominant activities of an internal service fund, the internal service fund's residual assets and liabilities should be reported in the business-type activities column of the statement of net position.

OBSERVATION: For internal service fund activities that are reimbursed by federal funds, the *Uniform Administrative Requirements, Cost Principles and Audit Requirements for Federal Awards* subpart E places stringent requirements on what can be charged as an "allowable cost," with an emphasis on consistent accounting no matter the source of funds. Complete coverage of the updated provisions from an auditing perspective is found in CCH's *Knowledge-Based Audits* ™ *of State and Local Governments with Single Audits.*

TERMINOLOGY AND CLASSIFICATION IN GOVERNMENT-WIDE AND PROPRIETARY FUND FINANCIAL STATEMENTS

Statement of Net Position

Assets, deferred outflows of resources, liabilities, deferred inflows of resources, and net position are presented on the statement of net position of a proprietary fund and should be classified as current and long-term, based on the guidance established in GASB Cod. Secs. 1800.109–.123. The statement of net position may be presented in either one of the following formats:

- *Net position format:* Assets + Deferred outflows of resources—Liabilities—Deferred inflows of resources = Net Position.
- *Balance sheet format:* Assets + Deferred outflows of resources = Liabilities + Deferred inflows of resources + Net position.

Governments frequently prepare classified statements of net position for accounting and financial reporting purposes. If the government prepares an *unclassified* statement of net position, there is no distinction between current assets and noncurrent assets. However, there remains a distinction between current liabilities and noncurrent liabilities.

Current Assets in a Classified Statement of Net Position. As with many other types of entities, "current assets" in a classified statement of net position is used to designate cash and other assets or resources commonly identified as those that are reasonably expected to be realized in cash or sold or consumed within one year.

Current assets generally include items such as:

- Cash available for current operations and items that are the equivalent of cash,
- Inventories of merchandise, raw materials, goods in process, finished goods, operating supplies, and ordinary maintenance material and parts,
- Trade accounts, notes, and acceptances receivable,
- Receivables from taxpayers, other governments, vendors, customers, beneficiaries, and employees if collectible within a year,
- Installment or accounts and notes receivable if they conform generally to normal trade practices and terms within the business-type activity,
- Marketable securities representing the investment of cash available for current operations, and
- Prepayments such as insurance, interest, rents, unused royalties, current paid advertising service not yet received, and operating supplies.

Prepayments are not current assets in the sense that they will be converted into cash but in the sense that, if not paid in advance, they would require the use of current assets within a year [GASB Cod. Sec. 1800.109].

Exclusions from current assets mainly include cash restricted to withdrawal for specific purposes, receivables not expected to be collected within 12 months, cash surrender value of life insurance policies and all forms of capital assets.

Unearned discounts, finance charges and interest included in receivables is a contra-asset (deduction) from the related receivables. Similar disclosures occur for asset valuation allowances [GASB Cod. Secs. 1800.110–.112].

Current Liabilities. Like commercial enterprises, current liabilities include obligations where liquidation is reasonably expected to require the use of existing resources properly classifiable as current assets, or the creation of other current liabilities. As a category in the statement of net position, the classification is intended to include obligations for items that have entered the operating cycle, such as:

- Payables incurred in the acquisition of materials and supplies to be used in providing services,
- Collections received in advance of the performance of services, and
- Debts that arise from operations directly related to the operating cycle, such as accruals for wages, salaries, commissions, rentals, and royalties.

Other liabilities whose regular and ordinary liquidation is expected to occur within one year also are intended for inclusion, such as:

- Short-term debts arising from the acquisition of capital assets,
- Serial maturities of long-term obligations,
- Amounts required to be expended (used) within one year under sinking fund provisions, and
- Certain agency obligations arising from the collection or acceptance of cash or other assets for the account of third parties.

The current liability classification also is intended to include obligations that, by their terms, are due on demand *or will be due on demand* within one year from the date of the financial statements, even though liquidation may not be expected within that period. It also is intended to include long-term obligations that are or will be callable by the creditor either because the debtor's violation of a provision of the debt agreement at the date of the financial statements makes the obligation callable or because the violation, if not cured within a specified grace period, will make the obligation callable.

Accordingly, such callable obligations should be classified as current liabilities unless *one* of the following conditions is met:

1. The creditor has waived (or subsequently lost) the right to demand repayment for more than one year from the date of the financial statements, *or*
2. For long-term obligations containing a grace period within which the debtor may cure the violation, it is *probable* that the violation will be cured within the period, preventing the call provision [GASB Cod. Sec. 1800.113].

Various other transactions may be current liabilities in an equivalent manner to commercial enterprises. These may involve rent, termination payments, and many other occurrences.

Short-Term Obligations Expected to be Refinanced. Short-term obligations are those scheduled to mature within one year after the date of a government's financial statements. *Long-term obligations* are those scheduled to mature beyond one year from the date of a government's financial statements.

Refinancing a short-term obligation on a long-term basis means either replacing it with a long-term obligation or renewing, extending, or replacing it with short-term obligations for an uninterrupted period extending beyond one year from the date of a government's financial statements. In this circumstance, even though the short-term obligation is scheduled to mature during the ensuing fiscal year, it will not require the use of working capital during that period [GASB Cod. Sec. 1800.115].

These obligations are excluded from current liabilities if:

- The government intends to refinance the obligation on a long-term basis, or
- The government can consummate the refinancing [GASB Cod. Sec. 1800.117].

The ability to consummate the refinancing is demonstrated in either of the following activities:

1. *Issuance of a long-term obligation after the date of the financial statements.* After the date of a government's financial statements but before those financial statements are issued, a long-term obligation has been issued to refinance the short-term obligation on a long-term basis, *or*
2. *Financing agreement.* Before the financial statements are issued, the government has entered into a financing agreement that clearly permits the government to refinance the short-term obligation on a long-term basis on terms that are readily determinable, *and* all the following conditions are met:
   a. The agreement does not expire within one year from the date of the government's financial statements and during that period the agreement is not cancelable by the lender or the prospective lender (and obligations incurred under the agreement are not callable during that period) except for violation of a provision with which compliance is objectively determinable or measurable.
   b. No violation of any provision in the financing agreement exists at the date of the financial statements and no available information indicates that a violation has occurred thereafter but prior to the issuance of the financial statements, or, if one exists at the date of the financial statements or has occurred thereafter, a waiver has been obtained.
   c. The lender (or the prospective lender) with which the government has entered into the financing agreement is expected to be financially capable of honoring the agreement [GASB Cod. Sec. 1800.118].

Replacement of a short-term obligation with another short-term obligation after the date of the financial statements but before the financial statements are issued is not, by itself, enough to demonstrate a government's ability to refinance the short-term obligation on a long-term basis.

If the replacement is made under the terms of a revolving credit agreement that provides for renewal or extension of the short-term obligation for an uninterrupted period extending beyond one year from the date of the financial statements, the revolving credit agreement is required to meet the conditions detailed above in GASB Cod. Sec. 1800.118 regarding financing agreements to justify excluding the short-term obligation from current liabilities. If the replacement is another short-term obligation accompanied by a "stand-by" credit agreement, the stand-by agreement is required to also required to meet the conditions in GASB Cod. Sec. 1800.118 also regarding financing agreements to justify excluding the short-term obligation from current liabilities [GASB Cod. Sec. 1800.121].

TERMINOLOGY AND CLASSIFICATION IN GOVERNMENTAL FUND FINANCIAL STATEMENTS

> **PRACTICE POINT:** The following paragraphs apply solely to governmental fund accounting and financial reporting. The major section that follows applies to proprietary funds.

Debt Issuance Proceeds

Another aspect of governmental accounting and financial reporting for many new practitioners that may not make sense involves reporting the proceeds of debt in governmental funds. In governmental funds (not proprietary funds or the government-wide statements), the proceeds from the issuance of long-term debt are recorded not as a liability, but as an "other financing source" on the statement of revenues, expenditures, and changes in fund balances. The transaction is reported using such captions as "bond issue proceeds" and "proceeds from the issuance of long-term notes (or debt)."

Why? This is due to the emphasis on the current financial resources of the governmental funds. Discounts and premiums and certain payments to escrow agents for bond refundings should also be reported as other financing sources and uses. The translation of the proceeds from the debt issuance from an other financing source to a liability occurs as one of the reconciling entries performed as part of the preparation of the government-wide statements.

Proceeds from the issuance of special assessment debt for which a government entity is "not obligated in any manner" should not be referred to as bond proceeds but instead titled as "contributions from property owners" [GASB Cod. Secs. 1800.124, S40.119].

> **PRACTICE POINT:** The treatment of debt issuance proceeds is one of the challenges that governmental funds have in the measurement focus and basis of accounting. Given the short-term focus of many governments, some believe it is understandable that debt issuance proceeds are presented as an inflow (revenue). But in theory, a liability is created, even though it may not be due for a year or more.

> **PRACTICE ALERT:** The GASB's *Financial Reporting Model Improvements* Exposure Draft proposes for governmental funds, liabilities would be recognized inclusive of short-term transactions and other events as they *occur*, and with long-term transactions or other events *when payments are due*. All liabilities recognized then would be financial liabilities. The period to determine short-term versus long-term is determined by measuring the period between the inception of the transaction and the conclusion of the transaction.
>
> Reporting in governmental funds would be as follows:
>
> 1. Short-term transactions and other events are those for which the period from inception to conclusion is *one year or less.*
>
> 2. Long-term transactions and other events are those for which the period from inception to conclusion is *greater than one year.* If payments are made or received prior to the due date, elements from long-term transactions and other events (such as debt service principal and interest) are recognized when payments are made or received.
>
> As proposed, a major exception would be long-term debt issued for short-term purposes, which would be recognized as a liability. Common examples of such debt include tax anticipation and revenue anticipation notes with maturities beyond one year from inception of the transaction. Otherwise, long-term transactions are only recognized as fund liabilities when payments are to be made, but overdue as of the reporting date.
>
> As of the date of publication, the Board was finalizing language clarifying a "short-term purpose." As currently proposed, a short-term purpose would be described as a government obtaining and consuming a financial asset or service within one year or providing financial resources to a service recipient without restricting the use of the resources to the acquisition of financial assets.
>
> Debt proceeds and payments would be presented as noncurrent activities in governmental funds should the provisions be approved as proposed. Refunding transactions as described in the next paragraph would be reported also as noncurrent activities, including payments to or from escrow agents.

Resources received based on current and advance refundings related to the defeasance of general long-term debt should be reported as an "other financing source" and presented as "proceeds of refunding bonds" to describe the transaction. Related payments to the escrow agent should be reported as an "other financing use" and identified as "payments to refunded bond escrow agent." However, when the payments are made to an escrow agent using funds other than those related to the refunding, the repayment should be reported as debt service expenditures [GASB Cod. Sec. 1800.125].

Other Debt Issuance Transactions

GAAP requires debt issuance costs to be reported as outlays for all types of funds, not just governmental funds. Debt issuance costs do not include prepaid insurance costs. Prepaid insurance costs are reported as an asset and amortized systematically and rationally over the duration of the related debt, except such costs are expended when incurred in governmental funds [GASB Cod. Sec. 1800.126].

Demand Bonds

Demand bonds may be reported as long-term debt of the government *when all the following criteria are met*:

- Before the financial statements are issued, the issuer has finalized an arm's-length financing (takeout) agreement to convert bonds "put" but not resold into some other form of long-term obligation.
- The takeout agreement does not expire within one year from the date of the issuer's balance sheet.
- The takeout agreement is not cancelable by the lender or the prospective lender during that year, and obligations incurred under the takeout agreement are not callable by the lender during that year.
- The lender or the prospective lender or investor is expected to be financially capable of honoring the takeout agreement.

Conditions Not Met. When these conditions have not been met, demand bonds must be presented as a liability of the fund that received the proceeds from the issuance of the bonds, or as a current liability if the proceeds were received by a proprietary fund. If demand bonds are issued and no takeout agreement has been executed at their issuance date or at the balance sheet date, the bonds cannot be considered a long-term liability.

If the demand bonds are presented for redemption, the redemption should be recorded as a reduction of bonds payable.

Demand bonds that were originally classified as general long-term debt because a take-out agreement existed at the issuance date of the bonds would have to be reclassified if the original takeout agreement expires.

Under this circumstance, it would be necessary to establish a liability in the fund that originally recorded the demand bond proceeds. Any actual bond redemption occurring after the debt is reclassified as the liability of a specific governmental fund should be recorded as an expenditure of the fund that accounts for the servicing of the debt [GASB Cod. Secs. 1800.127, D30.108–.109].

A full discussion on debt transactions and disclosures is contained in Chapter 12.

PRACTICE POINT: Demand bonds are separate and distinct from Conduit Debt Obligations (CDOs) in accordance with GASB Cod. Sec. C65. The discussion of these provisions is also in Chapter 12.

Lease Transactions Reported in Governmental Funds

Governmental funds often report lease transactions. If reported in a governmental fund, reporting is required to be consistent with the current financial resources measurement focus and modified accrual basis of accounting.

Government is a Lessee and Reports the Lease in a Governmental Fund. For transactions where the government is a lessee, a lease liability is calculated in accordance with GASB Cod. Secs. L20.118–.120. Due to the provisions of the governmental funds measurement focus and basis of accounting, the liability is only presented as a reconciling item between the governmental fund and the statement of net position. Instead, an expenditure and other financing source is presented for the measured amount of the liability. Future transactions relating to the lease payments are presented similarly to debt service [GASB Cod. Secs. 1800.128, L20.132–.133].

Government is a Lessor and Reports the Lease in a Governmental Fund. If a government is a lessor and reports the lease in a governmental fund, the lessor recognizes a lease receivable and a deferred inflow of resources. The initial value of the lease receivable is consistent with the other lessor provisions of GASB Cod. Sec. L20 discussed in Chapter 14. The deferred inflow of resources is amortized to revenue systematically and rationally over the term of the lease [GASB Cod. Sec. L20.153].

Capital Asset Sales

When a governmental entity sells a capital asset of a governmental fund, the proceeds from the sale should be reported as an other financing source, unless the transactions meet the definition of a special item (events within the control of management that are either unusual in nature or infrequent in occurrence, discussed later in this chapter) [GASB Cod. Sec. 1800.129].

PRACTICE ALERT: The GASB's *Financial Reporting Model Improvements* Exposure Draft proposes to amend this treatment to inflows of resources from noncurrent activities in governmental funds.

Revenue and Expenditure Classification in Governmental Funds

A governmental fund's results of operations are presented in a statement of revenues and expenditures and changes in fund balances. This statement should reflect the all-inclusive concept, and all financial transactions and events that affect the fund's operations for the period should be presented in the activity statement.

A governmental fund's activity statement is *not* referred to as an income statement because the accounting basis for its preparation is the modified accrual basis, not the accrual basis. Similarly, net income is *not* an element presented in a governmental fund's activity statement for the same reason and because the statement does not reflect allocations of various economic resources, such as the depreciation of capital assets.

Revenues. For governmental funds, revenues are "[A]n *inflow of resources* is an acquisition of (net position) by the government that is applicable to the reporting period" (GASB:CS-4, pars. 28–31). Revenues include increases to fund financial resources other than from interfund transfers and debt issue proceeds.

Revenues should be classified by fund and source. Revenues applicable to an individual governmental fund should be reflected in the fund's activity statement and should not be attributed to another governmental fund. Major revenue sources include taxes, licenses and permits, intergovernmental revenues, charges for services, fines and forfeits, and miscellaneous items.

As a supplement to the accumulation of revenues by fund and source, revenues may be classified in several ways to facilitate management evaluation and preparation of special reports or analyses, or to aid in the audit or review of accounts. For example, revenues may be classified by the operating division or branch responsible for their actual collection [GASB Cod. Secs. 1800.130–.131].

PRACTICE ALERT: The GASB's *Financial Reporting Model Improvements* Exposure Draft proposes to change the classification of revenues for governmental funds to *inflows of resources.* Further classification would occur based on the provisions of the proposed change to the short-term financial resources measurement focus and accrual basis of accounting. As previously discussed in Chapter 3 of the *Guide,* current activities are all activities other than noncurrent activities. Noncurrent activities are activities related to the purchase and disposal of capital assets and the issuance and repayment of capital-related liabilities (e.g., leases) and long-term debt except for long-term debt issued for short-term purposes.

Expenditures.

PRACTICE ALERT: The GASB's *Financial Reporting Model Improvements* Exposure Draft proposes to change the classification and terminology regarding *expenditures* for governmental funds to *outflows of resources.* Further classification would occur based on the provisions of the proposed change to the short-term financial resources measurement focus and modified accrual basis of accounting. As previously discussed in Chapter 3 of the *Guide,* similarly to revenues, current activities are all activities other than noncurrent activities. Noncurrent activities are activities related to the purchase and disposal of capital assets and the issuance and repayment of capital-related liabilities (e.g., leases) and long-term debt except for long-term debt issued for short-term purposes.

Governmental fund expenditures represent decreases in or uses of fund financial resources, except for those transactions that result in transfers to other funds and expirations of demand bond takeout agreements (see previous discussion on demand bonds). Initially, expenditures should be classified according to the fund accountable for the disbursement.

More generically, expenditures and expenses are forms of *outflows of resources,* also defined in GASB:CS-4 (pars. 24–27): "An outflow of resources is a consumption of (net position) by the government that is applicable to the reporting period."

To facilitate both internal and external analysis and reporting, expenditures may be classified further by [GASB Cod. Secs. 1800.130, .132]:

- Function (or program),
- Organizational unit,
- Activity,
- Character, and
- Object class.

Function (or program) classification. Functions refer to major services provided by the governmental unit or responsibilities established by specific laws or regulations. Classifications included as functions are, for example:

- Public safety,
- Highways and streets,
- General governmental services,
- Education, and
- Health and welfare.

Rather than use a functional classification, a governmental unit that employs program budgeting may group its expenditures by program classifications and sub-classifications. A program classification scheme groups whatever activities are related to the achievement of a specific purpose or objective. Program groupings could include activities such as programs for the elderly, drug addiction, and adult education [GASB Cod. Sec. 1800.133].

Organizational unit classification. An accounting system should incorporate the concept of "responsibility accounting" so that information reflecting a unit's responsibility for activities and expenditures will be present in the system. When an organization is responsible for certain expenditures, but the expenditures are not coded so the disbursements can be associated with the organization, it becomes difficult to hold the organizational unit responsible for the activity. Organizational unit classification generally groups expenditures based on the operational structure (department, agencies, etc.) of the governmental unit. Often, functions or programs are administered by two or more organizational units. A common example is public safety. In many governments, public safety includes police, fire, and emergency medical services departments [GASB Cod. Sec. 1800.134].

Activity classification. Function or program classifications are broad in nature and often do not provide a basis for adequately analyzing governmental operations. For this reason, expenditures may be associated with specific activities, thus allowing measurement standards to be established. These standards can be used:

- As a basis for evaluating the economy and efficiency of operations, and
- As a basis for budget preparation.

Also, grouping expenditures by activity is an important part of management accounting in which decisions may require the development of accounting data different from the information presented in the external financial reports. For example, in a make-or-buy decision, it may be necessary to consider a depreciation factor in computing a per unit cost figure (for external reporting purposes, depreciation is not generally presented) [GASB Cod. Sec. 1800.135].

Character classification. Categorizing expenditures by character refers to the fiscal year that will benefit from the expenditure. Character classifications include the following [GASB Cod. Sec. 1800.136]:

Character	Period(s) Benefited
Current expenditures	Current period
Capital outlays	Current and future periods
Debt service	Current, future, and prior periods
Intergovernmental	Depends on the nature of the programs financed by the revenue

As discussed in the following section, object classes are subdivisions of expenditure character groupings.

Object classification. Object classes represent the specific items purchased or services acquired within the overall character classifications. For example, debt service expenditures can be further classified as payments for principal and interest, while current expenditures by object class may include the purchase of supplies and disbursements for payroll.

GAAP recognizes that external reporting of expenditures by object class should be restrained because the user, on both an internal and an external basis, could be overwhelmed by voluminous information that does not enhance the decision-making process [GASB Cod. Sec. 1800.137].

> **PRACTICE POINT:** Many governments are subject to a uniform accounting system typically established by a state auditor, revenue department, or comptroller, to facilitate reporting to a legislative body. Each fund authorized by legislation may have its own numbering system solely for a consistent chart of accounts. A typical chart of accounts could be as follows for a fund:

Chart Element	Information
Fund number	100
Fund name	General Fund
Account Type Code (drop down box)	Asset (A), Deferred Outflow (DO), Liability (L), Deferred Inflow (DI), Fund Balance or Net Position (FB), Revenues and Other Financing Sources (R), Expenditures and Other Financing Uses (E)
Account Number	5 digit numeric (example—10000)
Account Name	Text—(example—Cash)
Subaccount type	Specific digits (example—2 alphanumeric)

Chart Element	Information
Subaccount name	Restricted (drop down for R)
Function	Text—(example City versus Component Unit) (to delineate areas of the reporting entity)
Subfunction	Text—(example areas of operations—general government, public safety, debt service, education, etc.)
Subfunction number	5 digit numeric (example—40000)
Subfunction name	40000 General Government
Character (expenditures)	Drop down text (Current operating expenditures, capital outlay, debt service, intergovernmental, others)
Object Class	Drop down text (Personnel, benefits, supplies, contractor charges, capital outlay, interest, transfers, others)
Object Code	Specific digits (example—3 numeric)
Object Code Name	100 Wages
Sub-object Code	Specific digits (example—3 numeric)
Sub-object name	103 Temporary employees (less than 400 hours)

Charts of accounts can be as simple or as complex based on the government's operations. In some cases, defining a new chart of accounts may take months or longer just to agree on responsibilities, security, and what reporting should look like. A best practice is to have a chart maintained centrally with clear lines of decision-making for effective internal controls and security.

TERMINOLOGY AND CLASSIFICATION IN PROPRIETARY FUNDS

PRACTICE ALERT: The GASB's *Financial Reporting Model Improvements* Exposure Draft proposes to change the definition of operating revenues and expenses by providing a description of nonoperating revenues and expenses. As proposed, nonoperating revenues and expenses are:

1. Subsidies received and provided,
2. Revenues and expenses related to financing,
3. Resources from the disposal of capital assets and inventory, and
4. Investment income and expenses.

Since the Exposure Draft was issued, the GASB has tentatively added contributions to permanent and term endowments as a fifth item separate from subsidies. They have also tentatively decided to add an exception for certain loan programs, that would classify interest revenue as operating revenue and interest expense as nonoperating expense.

Revenues and expenses that otherwise would be classified as nonoperating in most proprietary fund financial statements should be classified as operating revenues and expenses *if those transactions constitute the proprietary fund's principal ongoing operations.* For example, interest revenues and expenses should be reported as operating revenues and expenses by a proprietary fund established to provide loans to first-time homeowners. Consistent with the classifications in the statement of cash flows, revenues and expenses of certain loan programs as described in GASB Cod. Sec. 2450.116 would be reported as operating revenues and expenses.

The Exposure Draft includes a definition of "subsidies." Flows from subsidies are proposed to include:

1. Resources received from another party or fund to keep rates lower than otherwise would be necessary to support the level of goods and services to be provided, or

2. Resources provided to another party or fund that results in higher rates than otherwise would be established for the level of goods and services to be provided.

The Board has deliberated whether payments in lieu of taxes, contributions and grants, intergovernmental revenue, third-party payments, and internal scholarship allowances meet the above definition. The GASB has also deliberated further revising the definition of subsidies to indicate that:

- All transfers should be included,
- Subsidies can have a direct or indirect impact on user fees and charges, and
- Clarify that subsidies should be classified as noncapital subsidies, unless limited to capital purposes.

The Board may further deliberate on this issue before releasing a final statement tentatively expected by March 2024.

Proprietary fund statements of revenues, expenses and changes in fund net position distinguish between operating and nonoperating revenues and expenses. Revenues are reported by major sources. Separate subtotals are presented for operating revenues, operating expenses, and operating income (loss).

Nonoperating revenues and expenses should be reported after operating income. Revenues from capital contributions and additions to the principal of permanent and term endowments, special and extraordinary items, and transfers should be reported separately, after nonoperating revenues and expenses.

Under current GAAP, governments establish a policy that defines operating revenues and expenses that is appropriate to the nature of the activity being reported, disclose it in the summary of significant accounting policies, and use it consistently from period to period. A consideration for defining a proprietary fund's operating revenues and expenses is how individual transactions would be categorized for purposes of preparing a statement of cash flows [GASB Cod. Secs. 1800.138, P80.113–.115].

Chapter 7 contains a discussion on the recognition principles and presentation of proprietary funds and a further discussion on the impact of the GASB's proposed changes. (See previous **PRACTICE ALERT**.)

TERMINOLOGY AND CLASSIFICATION IN GOVERNMENT-WIDE FINANCIAL STATEMENTS

Statement of Activities

The format for the government-wide statement of activities is significantly different from any operating statement used in fund financial reporting. The focus of the statement of activities is on the *net cost* of various activities provided by the governmental entity. The statement begins with a column that identifies the cost of each governmental activity. Another column identifies revenues specifically related to the classified activities. The difference between the expenses and revenues related to specific activities computes the net cost or benefits of the activities, which "identifies the extent to which each function of the government draws from the general revenues of the government or is self-financing through fees and intergovernmental aid."

The GASB presentation format for the statement of activities is unique in part because the format provides an opportunity to provide feedback on a typical economic question that is asked when a program is adopted, namely, "What will the program cost and how will it be financed?"

OBSERVATION: A statement of activities is also presented for not-for-profit entities in accordance with FASB ASC™ 958 (*Not-for-Profit Entities*). However, support and revenue are presented at the top of the statement with expenses following. The GASB presentation is left to right, as shown later in this subsection.

The governmental entity must determine the level at which governmental activities are to be presented, however, the level of detail must be at least as detailed as that provided in the governmental fund financial statements (which are discussed later). Generally, activities would be aggregated and presented at the functional category level, however, entities are encouraged to present activities at a more detailed level, such as by programs.

Due to the size and complexities of some governmental entities, it may be impractical to expand the level of detail beyond that of functional categories. The minimum level of detail at which governmental activities can be presented is discussed in the previous sections of this chapter.

Business-type activities are reported at the level of segments. The GASB encourages governmental entities to expand the detail level from functions (which is broad) to more specific levels, such as programs and services.

An example of this is in GASB Cod. Sec. 1800.723-3. A city's water department manages four separate water districts. Separate enterprise funds are used to account for the activities in each of the four districts. The city may report each district separately in accordance with GAAP but is not required to do so. The minimum level of detail for activities accounted for in enterprise funds as *different identifiable activities*. In this case, even though there is a separate and identifiable accounting for each district, the activity in the districts is the same—

production, treatment, and distribution of water. The city can combine the four districts as, for example, "Water Utilities."

GAAP also requires presenting capital asset activity in proprietary funds and in the government-wide statement of net position with depreciation expense presented in the statement of activities. GAAP also allows a modified approach to reporting infrastructure asset systems (as described in Chapter 10) This approach may be used to account for these capital assets when they are presented in a proprietary fund. For example, a highway reported under the modified approach that is part of a toll road system could be accounted for in an enterprise fund [GASB Cod. Secs. 1800.139–.140].

Once the level of detail is determined, the primary government's expenses for each governmental activity should be presented. It should be noted that these are expenses and not expenditures and are based on the concept of the flow of economic resources, which includes depreciation expense. As noted earlier, the minimum level of detail allowed by GAAP is functional program categories. Examples of program categories include general government, public safety, parks and recreation, and public works. At a minimum, each functional program should include direct expenses, which are defined as "those that are specifically associated with a service, program, or department and, thus, are clearly identifiable to a function" [GASB Cod. Sec. 1800.141].

Example Statement of Activities. An example statement of activities in accordance with GAAP follows [GASB Cod. Sec. 2200.142]:

| | | Program Revenues | | | Net (Expense)/Revenue and Changes in Net Position | | | |
| | | | | | Primary Government | | | |
Functions	Expenses	Charges for Services	Operating Grants and Contributions	Capital Grants and Contributions	Governmental Activities	Business-Type Activities	Total	Component Units
Primary government								
Governmental activities								
Function #1	XXX	XX	X	X	X		X X	X
Function #2	XXX	XX	X	—	—		— —	—
Function #3	XXX	XX	X	X	X		X X	X
Total governmental activities	XXXX	XXX	XX	XX	XX		XX XX	XX
Business-type activities (BTA)								
BTA #1	XXXX	XXXX	—	X	X		X X	X
BTA #2	XXXXX	XXXX	—	XX	XX		XX XX	XX
Total business-type activities	XXXXX	XXXX	—	XX	XX		XX XX	XX
Total primary government	XXXXXX	XXXXX	XX	XXX	XXX		XXX XXX	XXX
Component units (CU)								
CU #1	XXXX	XXXX	XX	XX	XX		XX XX	XX
General Revenues								
General revenues (detailed)					X		X X	X
Contributions to permanent funds					X		X X	X
Special items					X		X X	X
Transfers					X		X X	X

| Functions | Expenses | Program Revenues ||| Net (Expense)/Revenue and Changes in Net Position ||||
| | | | | | Primary Government ||| |
		Charges for Services	Operating Grants and Contributions	Capital Grants and Contributions	Governmental Activities	Business-Type Activities	Total	Component Units
Total general revenues, contributions, special items, and transfers					XX	XX	XX	XX
Change in net position					XX	XX	XX	XX
Net position—beginning					XXXX	XXXX	XXXX	XXXX
Net position—end					XXXX	XXXX	XXXX	XXXX

Program Revenues and Other Programmatic Resource Inflows. A fundamental concept in the formatting of the statement of activities, as described above, is the identification of resource inflows to the governmental entities that are related to specific programs and those that are general in nature.

Program revenues. These inflows arise because the specific program with which they are identified exists, otherwise the revenues would not flow to the governmental entity. Program revenues are presented on the statement of activities as a subtraction from the related program expense to identify the net cost (or benefit) of a program. This formatting scheme enables a reader of a governmental entity's statements to identify those programs that are providing resources that may be used for other governmental functions or those that are being financed from general revenues and other resources. As shown previously, program revenues should be segregated into (1) charges for services, (2) operating grants and contributions, and (3) capital grants and contributions [GASB Cod. Sec. 1800.142].

Identifying revenues with a function does not mean that revenues must be allocated to a function. Revenues are a source of a function only when they are *directly* related to the function. If no direct relationship is obvious, the revenue is a general revenue, not a program revenue.

Charges for services. Revenues that are characterized as charges for services are based on exchange or exchange-like transactions and arise from charges for providing goods, services, and privileges to customers or applicants who acquire goods, services, or privileges directly from a governmental entity. These and similar charges are intended to cover, at least to some extent, the cost of goods and services provided to various parties. The following are common examples of charges-for-services revenue [GASB Cod. Sec. 2200.137]:

Type of Charge for Service	Common Examples
Service charges	Water usage fees, garbage collection fees, any other "fee for service."
License and permit fees	Dog licenses, liquor licenses, building permits.
Operating special assessments	Street cleaning, special-street lighting, other direct to taxpayer assessments for a specific area or jurisdiction.
Intergovernmental charges based on exchange transactions	A County charging a city for housing of short-term jailed prisoners.

Program-specific grants and contributions (operating and capital). Governmental entities may receive mandatory and voluntary grants or contributions (nonexchange transactions) from other governments or individuals that must be used for a governmental activity.

For example, a state government may provide grants to localities to reimburse costs related to adult literacy programs. These and other similar sources of assets should be reported as program-specific grants and contributions in the statement of activities, but they must be separated into those that are for operating purposes and those that are for capital purposes. If a grant or contribution can be used either for operating or capital purposes, at the discretion of the governmental entity, it should be reported as an operating contribution [GASB Cod. Sec. 2200.138]. Mandatory and voluntary nonexchange transactions are discussed Chapter 17.

Grants and contributions that are provided to finance more than one program (multipurpose grants) should be reported as program-specific grants "if the amounts restricted to each program are specifically identified in either the grant award or the grant application." (The grant application should be used in this manner only if the grant was based on the application.) If the amount of the multipurpose grants cannot be identified with a program, the revenue should be reported as general revenues rather than program-specific grants and contributions.

OBSERVATION: If a government uses a cost allocation plan (typically federal or state approved), certain costs such as general government, support services, and administration might be allocated to functions before revenues are shown in the statement of activities. Although there is no requirement to allocate these indirect costs, posting this cost allocation plan is more of a full-costing approach to expenses. These allocated costs should be shown in a separate column from the "direct" program expenses. However, in practice, this portrayal is rarely used. If it is used, a subtotal column showing total expenses is not required [GASB Cod. Sec. 2200.130].

Investment earnings of endowments or permanent fund investments. Earnings related to endowments or permanent fund investments are considered program revenues if those are restricted to a specific program use, however, the restriction must be based on either an explicit clause in the endowment agreement or contract. Likewise, earnings on investments that do not represent endowments or permanent fund arrangements are considered program revenues if they are legally restricted to a specific program. Investment earnings on endowments or permanent fund investments that are not restricted, and therefore are available for general operating expenses, are not program revenues but rather should be reported as general revenues in the statement of activities.

Earnings on investments *not related to permanent funds* but are legally restricted for a purpose should also be reported as program revenues. Also, earnings on "invested accumulated resources" of a specific program that are legally restricted to the specific program should be reported as program revenues [GASB Cod. Sec. 2200.139].

OBSERVATION: Understandably, investment earnings and related expenses are a prime focus area for fiduciary activities. A slightly different presentation of investment earnings occurs in fiduciary funds. This is further discussed in Chapters 8 and 9.

General Revenues. General revenues are provided by the reporting entity's constituencies. These include common flows from taxation (e.g., property taxes) unless specifically dedicated to a program, investment income and certain transfers.

General revenue should be reported in the lower portion of the statement of activities. Common general revenues include resource flows related to:

- Income taxes,
- Sales taxes,
- Franchise taxes, and
- Property taxes.

If material, each should be separately identified in the statement. Nontax sources of resources not reported as program revenues must be reported as general revenues. This latter group includes unrestricted grants, unrestricted contributions, and investment income that is not program revenue (as discussed previously) [GASB Cod. Secs. 1800.143, 2200.140].

General revenues are used to offset the net (expense) revenue amounts computed in the upper portion of the presentation, and the resulting amounts are labeled as excess (deficiency) of revenues over expenses before extraordinary items and special items.

OBSERVATION: All taxes, including dedicated taxes (e.g., motor fuel taxes) are considered general revenues rather than program revenues. The GASB takes the position that only charges to program customers or program-specific grants and contributions should be characterized as reducing the net cost of a specific governmental activity.

Other Revenues—Contributions to term and permanent funds, contributions to permanent fund principal. When a governmental entity receives contributions to its term and permanent endowments or to permanent fund principal, those contributions should be reported as separate items in the lower portion of the statement of activities. These receipts are not considered to be program revenues (such as program-specific grants) because, as in the case of term endowments, there is an uncertainty of the timing of the release of the resources from the term restriction and, as in the case of permanent contributions, the principal can never be expended.

Other Revenues—Transfers. Transfers should be reported in the lower portion of the statement of activities [GASB Cod. Secs. 1800.144, 2200.141]. (The standards that determine how transfers should be reported in the statement of activities were discussed earlier in this chapter.)

TERMINOLOGY AND CLASSIFICATION IN REPORTING EXTRAORDINARY AND SPECIAL ITEMS

Extraordinary and Special Items

> **PRACTICE ALERT:** The GASB's *Financial Reporting Model Improvements* Exposure Draft proposes to change the presentation and retitle these items. The retitled, *unusual, or infrequent items* would be presented individually as the last presented flow(s) of resources prior to the net change in resource flows in the government-wide, governmental funds, and proprietary funds statements of resource flows. Governments would disclose in the notes to financial statements the program or function or identifiable activity to which an unusual or infrequent item is related, if applicable, and whether that item was within the control of management. The overall definitions and guidelines of identifying items unusual or infrequent in occurrence would not change.

Extraordinary and special items are presented in the statement of activities after general revenues at the bottom of the statement. If a governmental entity has both extraordinary items and special items, they should be reported under a single heading labeled "special and extraordinary items." That is, there should not be separate broad headings for each type of item (see Chapter 20 for further discussion of special and extraordinary items) [GASB Cod. Sec. 1800.152].

Extraordinary Items. The next section of the statement of activities includes the category where extraordinary items (gains or losses) are presented. GAAP defines "extraordinary items" as both unusual in nature and infrequent in occurrence [GASB Cod. Secs. 1800.145, 2200.143, C50.121].

Extraordinary items are different from "special items." Because special items are "significant transactions or other events *within the control of management* that are either unusual in nature or infrequent in occurrence," extraordinary items are out of the control of management, while remaining unusual in nature or infrequent in occurrence.

Special Items. As previously discussed, "special items" are described as "significant transactions or other events within the control of management that are *either* unusual in nature or infrequent in occurrence." Special items should be reported separately and before extraordinary items. If a significant transaction or other event occurs but is not within the control of management and that item is either unusual or infrequent, the item is not reported as a special item, but the nature of the item must be described in a note to the financial statements [GASB Cod. Secs. 1800.146, 2200.144, 2300.107, C50.121].

GAAP allows for judgment to determine which items should be segregated in the statement of activities (or any other flows statement) for the effects of events or transactions that are special or extraordinary. Decisions about how to classify an event as either unusual in nature or infrequent in occurrence should use the following criteria, both considering the operating environment of the government making the judgment:

Unusual nature—the underlying event or transaction should possess a high degree of abnormality and be of a type clearly unrelated to, or only incidentally related to, the ordinary and typical activities of the government. Such unusual factors may be the characteristics of activities, the geographical location, the extent of regulation or oversight. There could very well be events that are unusual for one government, but not another. Unusual nature is not established by the fact that an event or transaction is beyond the control of management.

Infrequency of occurrence—the underlying event or transaction should be of a type that *would not reasonably be expected to recur* in the foreseeable future. Again, this could be operating environment specific. A specific transaction of one government might not be like another based on frequency of occurrence [GASB Cod. Secs. 1800.147–.150].

GAAP includes exceptions to these provisions based on usual, customary, and continuing operations, including, but not limited to:

- Write-down or write-off of receivables, inventories, equipment leased to others, or intangible assets,

- Gains or losses from exchange or translation of foreign currencies, including those relating to major devaluations and revaluations,

- Other gains or losses from sale or abandonment of capital assets used in operations,

- Effects of a strike, including those against major suppliers, and

- Adjustment of accruals on long-term contracts.

In some cases, one of the exceptions may be because of an extraordinary event. Typically, an impairment of assets could occur because of a natural disaster, new law, or regulation and similar [GASB Cod. Sec. 1800.151].

PRACTICE POINT: Losses due to climate change are becoming more common. It is this author's view that judgment should be used in situations where flooding and similar disasters become "the new normal" to decide whether the event is unusual or infrequent.

As discussed in GASB Cod. Sec. 1800.728-1 (and other Sections), examples of events or transactions that may qualify as extraordinary or special items may include:

Extraordinary Items	Special Items
Costs related to an environmental disaster caused by a large chemical spill in a train derailment in a small city.	Sales of certain general governmental capital assets.
Severe damage to the community or destruction of government facilities by natural disaster (tornado, hurricane, flood, earthquake, and so forth) or terrorist act. **CAUTION:** Geographic location of the government may determine if a weather-related natural disaster is *infrequent*.	Termination benefits resulting from workforce reductions due to sale of utility operations.
A large bequest to a small government by a private citizen.	Early-retirement program offered to all employees.
Reporting of a restoration or replacement of an impaired capital asset in governmental funds (separate transaction from the associated insurance recovery) (alternative could be other financing source—as appropriate). Insurance recovery in subsequent years would be similar.	Significant forgiveness of debt.
In bankruptcies, adjustments to the reported amount of governmental fund liabilities (and assets), if any.	Gains or losses on the disposal of government operations.
Claims against the government that meet the definition of extraordinary items.	Net position received or assumed by a continuing government in a transfer of operations.

PRACTICE POINT: Disclosure of the financial impact of the response to a pandemic, natural disaster and related provisions including "stay-at-home" orders on a government could be judged by some preparers as an extraordinary item for revenues and expenses (expenditures) that are unusual and/or infrequent in accordance with GASB Cod. Secs. 1800.144–.152.

However, GASB: TB 2020-1 Q.6, pars. 17–19 discusses that actions such as "stay-at-home" orders constitute management's response to events, rather than the occurrence of the event. The GASB also believes that it is reasonable to expect that coronavirus diseases will recur in the foreseeable future. Therefore, the infrequency of occurrence provision is not met to be reported as an extraordinary item. The GASB also states: "Although actions taken to slow the spread of a coronavirus disease, including stay-at-home orders, may be within the control of management of certain governments, this type of event (the appearance of a coronavirus disease) is not within the control of management." Therefore, the actions do not meet the definition in GAAP of a special item. However, it is a best practice to discuss actions taken in the Management's Discussion and Analysis as the actions are currently known facts.

Governmental fund statement reporting of extraordinary and special items. In governmental funds, extraordinary and special items are reported in the statements of revenues, expenditures, and changes in fund balances after other financing sources and uses. If both occur during the same period, special and extraordinary items should be reported separately within a "special and extraordinary items" classification.

Significant transactions or events that are either unusual or infrequent *but not within the control of management* should be separately identified within the appropriate revenue or expenditure category in the statement of revenues, expenditures, and changes in fund balances or disclosed in the notes to financial statements.

Proprietary fund reporting of extraordinary and special items. Special and extraordinary items in the proprietary fund statement of revenues, expenditures, and changes in fund net position should be reported separately, after nonoperating revenues and expenses [GASB Cod. Sec. 1800.152].

Extraordinary items and special items in fund statements vs. government-wide statements. There may be instances where extraordinary items and special items could be reported in fund statements, but not in the statement of activities. GASB Cod. Sec. 1800.729-2 has a scenario where a government sold a significant governmental capital asset for a large amount, but at a negligible gain or loss. Significant proceeds from the sale would be reported in the governmental fund financial statements, however, because the gain or loss is insignificant, it would not be reported as a special item in the statement of activities.

On the other hand, the reverse situation—a transaction is an extraordinary or special item in the statement of activities but not in the fund financial statements—also could occur. For example, a local government assumes the debt of another organization, either because it is required to as a guarantor, or because it chooses to under a "moral" obligation. There has been no flow of financial resources; thus, there is no extraordinary or special item required to be reported in the statement of revenues, expenditures, and changes in fund balances. In the statement of activities, however, the event results in a change in net position and would be reported.

TERMINOLOGY AND CLASSIFICATION IN REPORTING NET POSITION AND FUND BALANCES

Net position in government-wide statements and proprietary fund statements should be identified as:

- Net investment in capital assets,

- Restricted (distinguishing between major categories of restrictions), and

- Unrestricted.

The guidance discussed earlier (in the context of government-wide financial statements) should be used to determine what amounts should be related to these three categories of net position. Capital contributions, reserves and designations are not presented separately from these three categories, even though they are components of or transactions accumulating to the categories [GASB Cod. Sec. 1800.155].

Net Investment in Capital Assets

In a statement of net position, the net investment in capital assets consists of capital assets, net of accumulated depreciation (or amortization of intangible capital assets, reduced by:

- The outstanding balances of bonds, mortgages, notes, or other borrowings (including leases) attributable to the acquisition, construction, or improvement of those assets, and
- Deferred outflows of resources and deferred inflows of resources that are attributable to the acquisition, construction, or improvement of those assets or related debt are also included.

When debt has been used to finance the acquisition, construction, or improvement of capital assets but all or part of the cash has not been spent by the end of the fiscal year, the unspent portion of the debt should not be used to determine the amount of invested capital assets (net of related debt) amount. The portion of the unspent debt "should be included in the same net assets component as the unspent proceeds—for example, *restricted for capital projects*" in accordance with GASB Cod. Sec. 1800.732-3 [GASB Cod. Sec. 1800.156, fn. 19].

Many large general-purpose governments (such as states) construct assets and issue debt for municipalities or entities that are not part of the government's reporting entity. GASB Cod. Sec. 1800.732-5 addresses the situation where debt is issued but assets are not present. In such situations, the issuing government acquires no capital assets, and therefore, the debt is not "capital-related." The effect of the noncapital debt should be reflected in the unrestricted component of the government's net position. The fact that the bonds are related to capital assets of another entity does not make the debt "capital" debt of the issuing government—even though the assets acquired may benefit its residents in the case of a special district within a city. The government has incurred a liability, decreasing its net position, with no corresponding increase in its capital or financial assets.

The effect on the government's total net position should be the same regardless of whether it:

1. Gave the special district cash from existing resources,
2. Constructed or acquired assets and donated them to the district, or
3. Issued debt to finance the construction or acquisition.

In all the three instances, the government has decreased its net position. If the effect on unrestricted net position is significant, the government may disclose additional details of unrestricted net position in the notes to the financial statements to isolate the effect of debt issued for others. The government may also address these circumstances in the Management's Discussion and Analysis as part of either the net position or debt discussions.

A comparable situation could have the opposite outcome. In GASB Cod. Sec. 1800.733-1, the example has a county government issuing debt to finance the construction of schools for the local school district, which is a discretely presented component unit of the county. The county has the debt, and the school district has the assets. In this case, the debt is not "capital related" debt of the county. But in the reporting entity financial statements, if the county elects to present an optional "reporting entity" total column, the debt *can* be reported as capital debt in the total column as the debt *is* related to capital assets within that reporting unit. Practitioners may want to explain in the notes to the basic financial statements how the net investment in capital assets component and the unrestricted net position component of net position are not equal to the underlying calculations that can be made.

Common Errors in Calculating the Net Investment in Capital Assets.

> **PRACTICE POINT:** Many governments participate in the Government Finance Officers Association (GFOA) Certificate of Achievement (COA) program. Due to the common errors in the calculation of Net Investment in Capital Assets, the GFOA began requiring submittal of a file reconciling the Net Investment in Capital Assets reported in the government-wide statements of net position for both governmental and business-type activities, as applicable to the government in 2022. This submittal accompanies the program application. The letter to program participants notifying of the requirement is found on the GFOA website at https://www.gfoa.org.

Common errors made by financial statement preparers when calculating the net investment in capital assets component of net position include the following:

- Failure to properly reduce the "related debt" amount by the balance of unspent capital debt proceeds before it is netted against capital assets,

- Failure to include capital debt related accounts such as bond premiums and discounts in the computation,

- Failure to exclude issued debt (including leases) for noncapital assets, and

- Improper inclusion of net position restricted for capital related debt service (future debt service is not used for capital asset acquisition or construction).

In determining capital-related debt, governments are not expected to categorize all uses of bond proceeds to determine how much of the debt relates to assets that have been capitalized. Unless a significant portion of the debt proceeds is spent for non-capitalized purposes, the entire amount could be considered "capital-related." In addition, if debt is issued to refund existing capital-related debt, the new debt is also considered capital-related because the replacement debt assumes the capital characteristics of the original issue in accordance with GASB Cod. Sec. 1800.733-6.

GASB Cod. Sec. 1800.732-4 discusses the effect of bond premiums and discounts on net position. Unamortized bond premiums and discounts, and deferred amounts from debt refunding should "follow the debt" in calculating the components of net position. The following occurs:

Scenario	Presentation
Debt is capital-related	• Report as part of net investment in capital assets.
Debt is restricted for a specific purpose and the proceeds are unspent	• Report as part of restricted net position (reporting both within the same component of net position prevents one classification from being overstated while another is understated by the same amount).
Debt proceeds are not restricted for capital or other purposes.	• Report as part of the calculation of unrestricted net position.

Retainage. States and local governments commonly incorporate retainage clauses as part of long-term contracts for construction or similar acquisitions that are capital-related. In many cases, the projects are funded by capital-related debt.

GASB Cod. Secs. 1800.733.12–.13 address the issue of retainage and the net investment in capital assets calculation component of net position. As a retainage payable represents a liability usually attributable to the acquisition, construction, or improvement of capital assets and likely with a debit recognized as construction in progress, any retainage liability should be included in the calculation of the net investment in capital assets. If unspent bond proceeds are involved, the calculation of capital-related debt is adjusted including the portion of bonds payable that has been spent on capital construction, plus retainages and accounts payable attributable to that construction.

> **OBSERVATION:** In some cases, retainage is required to be accounted for in a separate fund or held in escrow with specific investments. Upon completion of the contract, the retainage and related investment earnings are released to the contractor. GASB Cod. Sec. 1300.716-14 clarifies that the retained amounts are not reported in a fiduciary fund, even though the government is withholding cash. The withholding is for the government's own benefit and therefore, a governmental (or proprietary) activity, as appropriate. The unremitted retainage is an exchange transaction between the contractor and the government. Any investments would be valued at fair value and no net investment in capital assets calculation would be presented in the fund as it only holds the investment escrow [GASB Cod. Sec. I50.701-6].

Externally Imposed Restrictions on Capital Assets. In many federal capital grants, externally imposed restrictions are placed on property constructed or property that is federal surplus property allowed to be retained by state and local governments. GASB Cod. Sec. 1800.733-3 discusses that such property should still be reported as part of the net investment in capital assets component of net position.

Capital Assets, but No Related Debt (Or Deferred Inflows of Resources). In such situations, GASB Cod. Sec. 1800.733-7 stipulates that the title net investment in capital assets may still be used.

Debt Exceeds Capital Assets (Negative Amounts). In many situations where bonds are sold in advance of construction. If the outstanding capital debt exceeds the carrying value of capital assets are reported, the "net investment in capital assets" caption should still be used, even though the amount is negative in accordance with GASB Cod. Sec. 1800.733-9.

Interfund Activity to Finance Capital Assets. Some governments finance capital acquisition through internal transfers. If this occurs, GASB Cod. Sec. 1800.733-10 reminds practitioners that interfund advances or loans are *not* considered debt for the purposes of calculating net position. Such transfers are part of unrestricted net position.

However, if a blended component unit issued bonds and loaned the proceeds to the primary government to acquire capital assets, the result of the blending process would have the component unit with a loan receivable from the primary government and the primary government would have a loan payable, both classified as internal balances. GASB Cod. Sec. 1800.733-15 discusses that the loan payable would be capital-related debt, even though, for presentation purposes, the debt has been reclassified as an internal balance. The blended component unit could regard the bonds payable as noncapital debt as the proceeds were used to acquire "the receivable" from the primary government, rather than capital assets.

A third scenario could involve a discretely presented component unit. The component unit issues bonds, remitting the proceeds to the primary government. The primary government constructs capital assets. The bonds are a liability of the component unit but secured by and payable solely from annual appropriations of the primary government. Revenues are pledged at the primary government providing resources for the appropriations. GASB Cod. Sec. 1800.733-11 discusses how the bonds do not represent capital-related debt *of the component unit* (and part of noncapital financing). But the *primary government* would present the liability to the component unit as capital-related debt, to the extent that proceeds have been spent on highway construction. Unspent proceeds are part of restricted net position.

Debt Service Funds and Debt Service Reserve Funds. In many situations, debt service funds and debt service reserve funds are established related to bonds. If resources have been set aside in a restricted account to pay for the current installment of debt, the debt meets the definition of capital-related per GASB Cod. Sec. 1800.733-16. However, debt service reserve funds are usually proceeds not related to the capital asset being acquired, constructed, etc. In accordance with GASB Cod. Sec. 1800.733-17, the resources in the debt service reserve fund are included as part of either restricted or unrestricted net position as they are unspent proceeds. (In some situations, debt service reserve funds are accumulated unrestricted net position that return to unrestricted net position once a portion of bond principal is paid.)

Example 5-1 *Net Investment in Capital Assets Calculation*

Assume a local government has the following balances within its governmental activities' assets and liabilities:

Basic Governmental Accounting Concepts and Standards

Activity	Discussion
Restricted Cash for Debt Service	$800,000 (debit balance that represents cash accumulated from property tax levies legally restricted for the debt service payments on capital-related general obligation bonds).
Restricted Cash for Capital Projects	$1,200,000 (debit balance that represents unspent proceeds from general obligation bonds to be used for capital projects).
Restricted Cash for Capital Replacement	$2,500,000 (debit balance that represents cash set aside from excess net revenues of years that is restricted by ordinance for use in replacing capital assets).
Capital Assets	$34,500,000 (debit balance that represents the historical cost of governmental activities capital assets including infrastructure).
Accumulated Depreciation	$9,500,000 (credit balance that represents the accumulated depreciation on depreciable capital assets).
Bond Issuance Costs	$500,000 (debit balance that represents the issuance expense associated with capital-related debt).
General Obligation Bonds	$10,200,000 (credit balance that represents outstanding principal balance of capital-related general obligation bonds).
Lease Payable	$1,000,000 (credit balance that represents outstanding principal balance of a five-year noncancelable equipment lease recognized in accordance with GASB Cod. Sec. L20).

Based on the above assumptions, the calculation of net position invested in capital assets, net of related debt should be as follows:

Element	Amount	
Capital-Related Assets:		
Capital assets	$34,500,000	
Accumulated depreciation	(9,500,000)	
Subtotal—capital-related assets		25,000,000
Capital-Related Debt:		
General obligation bonds	10,200,000	
Lease payable	1,000,000	
Restricted cash for capital projects—unspent bond proceeds	(1,200,000)	
Subtotal—capital-related debt		(10,000,000)
Net Investment in Capital Assets		**$15,000,000**

Note that in the above calculation the following account balances are not included:

- *Restricted Cash for Debt Service* $800,000: Excluded because the restricted cash is to be used for debt service on capital debt as opposed to the acquisition or construction of capital assets and does not represent unspent bond proceeds.
- *Restricted Cash for Capital Replacement* $2,500,000: Excluded because the restricted cash has been accumulated for net resources of the entities' operations and does not represent unspent bond proceeds.

- *Bond Issuance Costs* $500,000: Excluded because they are outlays that do not acquire, construct, or improve capital assets. This amount is expensed in accordance with the provisions of GASB Cod. Sec. I30.115.

Restricted Net Position

Restricted net position arises if *either* of the following conditions exists:
- Restrictions are externally imposed by creditor (such as through debt covenants), grantors, contributors, or laws or regulations of other governments, or
- Restrictions are imposed by law through constitutional provisions or enabling legislation.

> **OBSERVATION:** For component units with joint venture characteristics, restricted net position—nonexpendable could be presented. This is because the organization itself, when included as a component unit in the majority participant's financial reporting entity, should report any equity interests of the minority participants, which are, nonexpendable.

Net position is included in the statement of net position by major category of restriction, likely aligning to the restrictions listed previously.

Enabling Legislation. Enabling legislation is when the legislative branch of government "authorizes the government to assess, levy, charge, or otherwise mandate payment of resources (from external resource providers)" and includes a legally enforceable requirement that those resources be used only for the specific purposes stipulated in the legislation [GASB Cod. Sec. 1800.157].

In its definition of "legal enforceability," GAAP states that a government can be compelled by an external party (citizens, public interest groups, or the judiciary) to use resources created by enabling legislation only for the purposes specified by the legislation. However, enforceability cannot be proven unless it is tested through the judicial process. Therefore, professional judgment must be exercised. This definition also carries forward to governmental funds for restricted fund balances (discussed later in this chapter).

Enabling legislation also includes restrictions on asset use if established by a government utility's own government board when the utility reports in accordance with regulated operations [GASB Cod. Sec. Re10]. Regulated operations and utilities are discussed further in Chapter 24 [GASB Cod. Sec. 1800.158, fn. 21].

As enabling legislation is a law that authorizes a government to assess, levy, charge, or otherwise mandate payment of resources (from external resource providers), the way those resources are authorized or used is important. If a government passes new enabling legislation that replaces the original enabling legislation by establishing a new legally enforceable restriction on the resources raised by the original enabling legislation, then from the effective date of the legislation, the resources accumulated under the new enabling legislation should be reported as restricted to the purpose specified by the new enabling legislation.

Professional judgment should be used to determine if remaining balances accumulated under the original enabling legislation should continue to be reported as restricted for the original purpose, restricted to the purpose specified in the new legislation, or unrestricted. If resources are used for a purpose other than those stipulated in the enabling legislation or if there is other cause for reconsideration, governments should reevaluate the legal enforceability of the restrictions to determine if the resources should continue to be reported as restricted. If reevaluation results in a determination that a restriction is no longer legally enforceable, then for all periods of that year, the amounts are unrestricted. If it is determined that the restrictions continue to be legally enforceable, then for the purposes of financial reporting, the restricted net position should not reflect any reduction for resources used for purposes not stipulated by the enabling legislation [GASB Cod. Secs. 1800.159–.160].

Earmarking and Enabling Legislation. It is important to note that the earmarking of an existing resource or revenue for a specific use by the reporting government *does not* result in the reporting of restricted net position from the earmarking. GASB Cod. Sec. 1800.734-8 states that "[E]armarking an existing revenue is not equivalent to enabling legislation." The earmarking of an existing resource is like what may be called a designation of the management of the government's intent. Therefore, earmarking is different from a legal restriction established at the time the revenue was created.

Negative Restricted Net Position Should Not Be Reported. GASB Cod. Sec. 1800.734-9 discusses a scenario where liabilities and deferred inflows of resources that related to specific restricted assets, exceed those assets. If this occurs, the net negative amount should be reclassified through an adjusting journal entry to reduce unrestricted net position as a "shortfall" is created.

Restricted net position should be identified based on major categories that make up the restricted balance. These categories could include items such as net position restricted for capital projects and net position restricted for debt service. GASB Cod. Sec. 1800.734-10 discusses how net position restricted by enabling legislation should be disclosed in the notes to the financial statements, especially if restricted net position is aggregated in the statement of net position. A government can also show the major categories on the face of the statement of net position per GASB Cod. Sec. 1800.155.

In some instances, net position may be restricted permanently (in perpetuity). Under this circumstance, the restricted net position must be subdivided into expendable and nonexpendable restricted net position [GASB Cod. Sec. 1800.161].

Other Accounting Elements that May Impact Restricted Net Position. Restricted net position not only represents restricted assets and liabilities, but it may also include deferred inflows of resources and potentially deferred outflows of resources related to those assets and liabilities. GASB Cod. Sec. 1800.734-6 discusses that generally a liability relates to restricted assets if the assets resulting from incurring the liability or if the liability will be liquidated with the restricted assets.

Common Errors in Calculating Restricted Net Position. Common errors made by financial statement preparers related to reporting restricted net position include the following:

- Inappropriately classifying all restricted fund balances of governmental funds as restricted net position of governmental activities,
- Inappropriately believing that all assets reported as restricted will also be reported as restricted net position, and
- Failing to reduce restricted assets by the liabilities payable from those restricted assets or the liabilities that were incurred to generate the restricted assets.

Restricted net position will be different than restricted fund balances in governmental funds due to three conditions per GASB Cod. Sec. 1800.742-3:

1. The principal amount of a permanent fund is classified as nonspendable fund balance in the governmental fund financial statements but presented as restricted net position in the government-wide statement of net position,
2. Reconciling items that represent basis of accounting differences between the modified accrual basis of accounting in a governmental fund and the government-wide financial statements may cause a difference, and
3. Internal service fund net position is generally included with governmental activities and may be restricted net position, but not included in governmental funds.

The issue of restricted fund balance is discussed later in this chapter and in Chapter 6.

Example 5-2 *Restricted Net Position*

Assume a local government has the following balances within its governmental activities' assets and liabilities:

Activity	Discussion
Restricted Cash for Street Improvements	$500,000 (debit balance that represents the unspent portion of a state gas tax shared with the local government and restricted for street improvements pursuant to the state's enabling legislation).
Restricted Cash for Debt Service	$800,000 (debit balance that represents cash accumulated from property tax levies legally restricted for the debt service payments on capital-related general obligation bonds).
Restricted Cash for Bond Issue Capital Projects	$1,200,000 (debit balance that represents unspent proceeds from general obligation bonds to be used for capital projects).
Restricted Cash for Capital Replacement	$2,500,000 (debit balance that represents cash set aside and transferred to a capital replacement fund by the local government in the amount of 2% of annual revenues of each year that is restricted by local ordinance for use in replacing capital assets).
Restricted Investments for Museum	$1,000,000 (debit balance that represents the principal amount of a museum endowment that cannot be spent: only the interest earnings may be used for museum purposes).

Activity	Discussion
Investment in Joint Venture	$1,200,000 (debit balance representing the carrying value of an investment in a joint venture with equity interest).
Accounts Payable from Restricted Assets—Streets	$200,000 (credit balance that represents the open invoices to be paid from cash restricted for street improvements as noted above).
Accounts Payable from Restricted Assets—Bond Issue Capital Projects	$500,000 (credit balance that represents the open invoices to be paid from cash restricted for the unspent proceeds of the capital general obligation bonds as noted above).
Accounts Payable from Restricted Assets—Capital Replacement	$700,000 (credit balance that represents the open invoices to be paid from cash restricted for capital replacement as noted above).
Accrued Interest Payable on Bonds	$300,000 (credit balance that represents the amount of accrued but unpaid interest on capital-related general obligation bonds).
General Obligation Bonds Payable	$10,200,000 (credit balance that represents outstanding principal balance of capital-related general obligation bonds).

Based on the above assumptions, the calculation of restricted net position should be as follows:

Element	Amount
Assets:	
Restricted cash for street improvements	$500,000
Restricted cash for debt service	800,000
Restricted cash for bond issue capital projects	1,200,000
Restricted investments for museum	1,000,000
Subtotal—restricted assets	$3,500,000
Less related liabilities:	
Accounts payable from restricted assets—streets	200,000
Accrued interest payable on bonds	300,000
General obligation bonds payable (unspent proceeds portion)	1,200,000
Subtotal—related liabilities	(1,700,000)
Restricted net position	$1,800,000

Note that in the above calculation the following account balances are not included:

- *Restricted Cash for Capital Replacement* $2,500,000: Excluded because the restricted cash is the earmarking of existing resources and not the result of externally imposed restrictions or legal restrictions from constitutional law or enabling legislation.

- *Investment in Joint Venture* $1,200,000: GASB Cod. Sec. 1800.732-6 states that an equity interest in a joint venture is generally not restricted (even though it may be comprised of equity in capital assets) and should be included in the computation of unrestricted net position.

- *Accounts Payable from Restricted Assets—Bond Issue Capital Projects* $500,000: Although these are liabilities payable from restricted cash, the restricted cash has already been reduced to zero by netting the portion of the bonds representing unspent proceeds against the restricted asset, and further reduction would result in the reporting of negative net position for this category (see above discussion on *negative net position*).

- *Accounts Payable from Restricted Assets—Capital Replacement* $700,000: Excluded because the related asset is the result of an earmarking and is not included in the computation of restricted net position.

- *General Obligation Bonds Payable* $9,000,000 ($10,200,000 less the portion related to unspent bond proceeds in restricted cash): Excluded because this remaining long-term debt balance is considered in the computation of net position, net investment in capital assets.

The $1,800,000 of restricted net position as determined in the above example should be displayed on the face of the statement of net position in the following manner by category of restriction:

Restricted Net Position:

Restricted for street improvements	$300,000
Restricted for debt service	500,000
Restricted for permanent endowment—museum	1,000,000

Note that none of the above restricted net position is required to be disclosed in the notes to the financial statements as being restricted by enabling legislation. Although the net position restricted for street improvements represent the net position resulting from resources restricted by the state's enabling legislation, it is not restricted by the enabling legislation of the reporting government, which would require note disclosure.

Unrestricted Net Position

Unrestricted net position is the residual amount that is classified neither as net investment in capital assets nor as restricted net position.

Portions of the entity's net position may be identified by management to reflect tentative plans or commitments of governmental resources. The *tentative* plans or commitments may be related to items such as plans to retire debt at some future date or to replace infrastructure or specified capital assets. Designated amounts *are* different from restricted amounts because designations represent planned actions, not actual commitments. For this reason, designated amounts should not be classified with restricted net position but rather should be reported as part of the unrestricted net asset component. In addition, designations cannot be disclosed as such on the face of the statement of net position [GASB Cod. Secs. 1800.162–.163].

Restrictions in Proprietary Funds

The same categories of net position in the government-wide statement of net position are utilized in proprietary funds. Capital contributions are not displayed as a separate component of net position. Designated amounts are also not presented, similarly to unrestricted net position guidance in the previous section [GASB Cod. Sec. 1800.164].

Reporting Fund Balances in Governmental Funds

Fund balance is one of the most widely used elements of financial information in state and local government financial statements but in some cases one of the most misunderstood and misapplied elements. Some misunderstandings occur between the differences of budgetary accounting and reporting and financial reporting in accordance with GAAP. Budgetary accounting may still utilize designations and earmarks which are different from GAAP classifications of governmental fund balances.

Fund Balance Classifications of Governmental Funds. A hierarchy of fund balance classifications is based on how much a government is bound to observe spending constraints imposed on how resources reported in governmental funds may be used. GAAP distinguishes fund balance between amounts [GASB Cod. Sec. 1800.165]:

- Nonspendable,
- Restricted,
- Committed,
- Assigned, and
- Unassigned.

Nonspendable fund balance. Amounts that *cannot be spent* are nonspendable fund balance. They are nonspendable due to:

- The balance is not in spendable form (i.e., inventories, prepaid amounts, long-term loans and notes receivables, property held for resale) or
- The balance is legally or contractually required to be maintained intact (e.g., the corpus or principal of a permanent fund).

Although long-term loans and notes receivables and property held for resale are generally reported as part of nonspendable fund balance, if the use of the proceeds from collection of the receivables or sale of the properties is restricted, committed, or assigned, then they should be included in those appropriate fund balance classifications rather than the nonspendable classification.

The amount that should be reported as nonspendable fund balance must be determined first before classifying any remaining amounts by level of constraint (i.e., restricted, committed, or assigned). If no constraints exist, the balance is likely unassigned in the general fund, or assigned in a special revenue, capital projects, debt service or permanent fund [GASB Cod. Secs. 1800.166–.167].

Restricted fund balance. Restricted fund balances represent amounts that are constrained for a specific purpose through restrictions of external parties (i.e., creditors, grantors, contributors, or laws or regulations of other governments), or by constitutional provision or enabling legislation, like as discussed previously. The concept of legal enforceability previously discussed also applies [GASB Cod. Secs. 1800.168–.169].

Committed fund balance. Committed amounts are constrained for specific purposes imposed by *formal action* of the government's highest level of decision-making authority (i.e., amounts that have been committed by a governing body legislation, ordinance, or resolution for a specific purpose, such as an amount from specific park and recreation revenues committed by governing body resolution to be used only for park maintenance).

Committed fund balances cannot be used for other purposes *unless* the government uses the same action (i.e., legislation, ordinance, or resolution) that it took to originally commit the amounts. The authorization containing the specific purposes of the committed amounts should have the consent of both the legislative and executive branches of the government. Also, the formal action to commit resources by the government's highest level of decision-making authority should occur prior to the end of the reporting period. The actual amount committed may be determined in a subsequent period.

Fund balance "committed" by legislation is distinguished from fund balance "restricted" by enabling legislation as amounts committed by legislation may be deployed for other purposes with appropriate due process by the government, such as through changes in legislation, ordinance, or resolution. In addition, constraints imposed on the use of committed fund balances are imposed by the government "separate" from the enabling legislation that authorized the raising of the underlying revenue. Therefore, compliance with the constraints on the resources that commit the government to spend the amounts for specific purposes is not considered "legally enforceable" [GASB Cod. Secs. 1800.170–.172].

Commonly found committed fund balances include:

- Resources specifically committed for satisfying contractual obligations including leases or settlement awards [GASB Cod. Sec. 1800.743-1], and
- When a county board of supervisors, the highest level of decision-making authority for the county, passes resolutions to commit estimated amounts to long-term construction projects. The resolution, also the highest form of decision-making authority, commits the amount as the maximum and acknowledges that unneeded resources at the end of the project will be returned to the general fund or transferred to other construction projects [GASB Cod. Sec. 1800.743-4].

Assigned fund balance. Assigned fund balance consists of amounts that are constrained by the government's intent to be used for a specific purpose but are neither restricted nor committed. Intent should be expressed by:

- The governing body itself, or
- A body (e.g., a budget or finance committee), or
- An official to which the governing body has delegated the authority to assign amounts to be used for specific purposes (i.e., the amounts are

intended to be used by government for specific purposes but do not meet the criteria to be classified as restricted or committed, such as an amount set aside by management to fund a projected budgetary deficit in a subsequent year's budget).

"Assigned" fund balance is distinguished from "committed" fund balance by the fact that amounts committed must be constrained by the government's highest level of decision-making authority, whereas assigned amounts do not require this level of authority to place the assignment or remove it. For example, management of a government may be authorized by the governing body to designate fund balances for a specific purpose, such as an amount set aside to fund accrued compensated absences for terminated employees, without formal action by the governing body itself. The amounts associated with this designation by management would meet the criteria to be reported as assigned fund balances [GASB Cod. Secs. 1800.173–.174].

Assigned fund balances include all remaining amounts not reported as nonspendable, restricted, or committed in all governmental funds *other than the general fund* (i.e., special revenue, capital project, debt service, and permanent funds). By reporting amounts not restricted or committed in a special revenue, capital projects, or debt service fund, the government has assigned those amounts to the respective funds' purposes. Assignment within the general fund conveys that those amounts are intended for a specific purpose narrower than the government's general purposes.

Governments should not report an assignment for an amount to a specific purpose if the assignment would result in a deficit in unassigned fund balance. An appropriation of existing fund balance to eliminate a projected budgetary deficit in a subsequent year's budget could be classified as an assignment of fund balance [GASB Cod. Secs. 1800.175–.176].

Commonly found assigned fund balances include:

- Encumbrances (based on an executed purchase order) (unless the purchase order relates to restricted or committed resources), but *not* displayed separately on the face of the financial statements [GASB Cod. Sec. 1800.751-1],
- When a government passes a budget for the next year reflecting an excess of appropriations over revenues and the government has appropriated a portion of fund balance to eliminate the excess, as discussed previously [GASB Cod. Sec. 1800.744-5], and
- The residual of any *non-general fund* governmental fund.

Unassigned fund balance. Unassigned fund balance is the residual classification for a government's general fund; it includes all amounts that are not constrained as reported in the other classifications.

Although any governmental fund may report amounts that are nonspendable, restricted, committed, or assigned, or any combination of these four classifications, only the general fund can report a positive unassigned amount. In other governmental funds, if expenditures incurred for specific purposes exceed the amounts restricted, committed, or assigned to those purposes, the government should first reduce any assigned amounts within the fund and then, if there are no further assigned amounts to reduce, the government should report the negative residual amount as "negative unassigned" fund balances. This means that a negative residual amount *should not be reported* for restricted, committed, or assigned balances in any fund.

Governments should develop and apply an accounting policy that determines the order of fund balance reduction for committed, assigned, or unassigned fund balances when amounts are expended for purposes for which funds in any of these unrestricted classifications could be used. GAAP states that if a government does not establish such a policy, it should consider that committed amounts are reduced first, followed by assigned amounts, and then unassigned amounts [GASB Cod. Sec. 1800.177].

Stabilization Arrangements

Many state and local governments have established and reported "rainy day," "budget or revenue stabilization," "working capital needs," or "contingencies or emergencies" and similar amounts within fund balances as reserves or designations. Such amounts are generally restricted or committed as to use for meeting emergency needs, stabilizing financial position when revenue shortfalls are experienced or for other, similar purposes.

The authority to establish stabilization arrangements and set aside such resources should come from constitution, charter, statute, ordinance, or resolution provisions stating that the resources may be expended only when certain circumstances exist as defined in the formal action document. The formal action that imposes the spending parameters or criteria should identify and describe the circumstances that qualify as an appropriate use of the stabilization resources, and the circumstances should be such that they would not be expected to occur routinely.

OBSERVATION: GAAP discusses how a stabilization amount that can be accessed "in the case of emergency" would not qualify to be classified within the committed category because the circumstances or conditions that prescribe its use (i.e., what exactly constitutes an emergency) are not sufficiently detailed. Similarly, an amount set aside to "offset an anticipated revenue shortfall" would not qualify as a restricted or committed fund balance stabilization arrangement unless the shortfall was quantified and was of such magnitude to distinguish it from other revenue shortfalls that routinely occur.

GASB Cod. Secs. 1800.180–.181 treat a qualifying stabilization reserve as a specific purpose, allowing the amounts constrained to be reported as a restricted or committed fund balance in the general fund if they meet certain criteria for such classification, based on the source of the constraint on their use. "Stabilization" is regarded as a specific purpose only if circumstances or conditions that signal the need for stabilization are identified in enough detail and are not expected to occur routinely. Amounts related to stabilization arrangements that do not meet the criteria to be reported as restricted or committed fund balances should be reported as unassigned fund balance within the general fund.

If a government has not established a stabilization amount pursuant to the proposed criteria but has formally established a minimum fund balance requirement, then the minimum fund balance requirement is reported as unassigned fund balance in the general fund and is required to be disclosed in the notes to the financial statements.

Fund Balance Disclosure Requirements

GAAP requires that governments disclose in the notes to the financial statements the following information about their fund balance classification policies and procedures and other related information [GASB Cod. Secs. 1800.183–.187]:

- For committed fund balance:
  — The government's highest level of decision-making authority, and
  — The formal action that is required to be taken to establish (and modify or rescind) a fund balance commitment.
- For assigned fund balance:
  — The body or official authorized to assign amounts to a specific purpose, and
  — The policy established by the governing body granting that authorization.
- For all the classifications of fund balances:
  — Whether the government considers restricted or unrestricted amounts to have been spent when an expenditure is incurred for purposes for which both restricted and unrestricted fund balance is available, and
  — Whether committed, assigned, or unassigned amounts are considered to have been spent when an expenditure is incurred for purposes for which amounts in any of those unrestricted fund balance classifications could be used.

For nonspendable fund balance displayed in the aggregate on the face of the balance sheet, the notes should disclose amounts for the two nonspendable components, if applicable. If restricted, committed, or assigned fund balances are displayed in the aggregate, specific purposes information not portrayed on the face of the balance sheet should be disclosed.

The government should disclose the following information in the notes to the financial statements for established stabilization arrangements (see next section), even if an arrangement does not meet the criteria to be classified as restricted or committed, in addition to the authority for establishing stabilization arrangements (e.g., by statute or ordinance):

- The requirements for additions to the stabilization amount,
- The conditions under which stabilization amounts may be spent, and
- The stabilization balance if it is not apparent on the face of the financial statements.

A governing body that has formally adopted a minimum fund balance policy (e.g., specifying a percentage of annual revenue or some other amount in lieu of separately setting aside stabilization amounts) should describe it in the notes to its financial statements.

Encumbrances should be disclosed *in the notes to the financial statements* as commitments of government by major funds and nonmajor funds in the aggregate for funds that use encumbrance accounting, but not on the face of the financial statements.

PRACTICE POINT: The *Governmental GAAP Practice and Disclosures Manual* contains illustrations of fund balance reporting both in the aggregate and in the notes.

PART II. FUND ACCOUNTING

CHAPTER 6
GOVERNMENTAL FUNDS

Chapter References:
  GASB Statement Nos. 6, 14, 34, 37, 38, 51, 54, 84, 100
  GASB Interpretation No. 3
  GASB *Implementation Guide*
  GASB Concepts Statement No. 4
  NCGA Statement No. 1, NCGA Interpretation No. 9

INTRODUCTION

This chapter discusses the financial accounting and reporting standards that apply to governmental funds, which comprise the following "fund" types:

- The General Fund.
- Special revenue funds (see **PRACTICE ALERT**).
- Capital projects funds.
- Debt service funds.
- Permanent funds.

Governmental funds primarily are used to account for the sources, uses, and balances of current financial resources and often have a budgetary orientation. Current financial resources are those assets that are expendable during a budgetary period, and they are often segregated into a specific governmental fund based on restrictions imposed by outside authorities or parties, or strategies established by internal management.

Liabilities of a governmental fund are obligations that will be paid from resources held by that fund.

The difference between a fund's assets and a fund's liabilities is fund balance. ("Fund equity" is colloquially but improperly used. That phrase should not be used in a general-purpose external financial report.) Chapter 5 discusses the reporting of fund balances in governmental funds and fund balance classifications in accordance with GAAP.

Required financial statements for governmental funds are a balance sheet and a statement of revenues, expenditures, and changes in fund balances. Major funds are displayed in the basic financial statements. Nonmajor funds are found in combining schedules which are supplementary information and are not required if the government is not preparing an Annual Comprehensive Financial Report (ACFR) [GASB Cod. Secs. 1300.102(a)–.103(a)].

PRACTICE POINT: Many governments must comply with laws and regulations which require presentation of nonmajor funds, even if not preparing an ACFR.

PRACTICE ALERT: The GASB's *Financial Reporting Model Improvements* Exposure Draft contains potentially major changes to the measurement focus and basis of accounting for governmental funds as detailed in previous chapters of the *Guide* (particularly Chapter 3). Significant changes include:

- The measurement focus and basis of accounting for governmental funds are proposed to change to the *short-term financial resources measurement focus and modified accrual basis of accounting*. This measurement focus will have differences from the current measurement focus and basis of accounting as follows:
    — The terms used to classify short-term transactions or other events and long-term transactions or other events should be established by the specific applicable contractual (or statutory) terms of the transaction or other event or estimated payments when there are no contractual terms.
    — Items arising from long-term transactions or other events should be recognized when due—the date at which payment is scheduled or, if not scheduled, expected to be made in accordance with the recognition terms.
    — The recognition period should be one year measured from the inception of the transaction to the conclusion.
    — There will be certain exceptions, including long-term debt issued for short-term purposes. Effective hedges utilizing derivative instruments are proposed to be long-term transactions as will be interest related to a long-term transaction.

The Board has proposed renaming special revenue funds to *special resources funds* to reflect these changes. A final statement for the project may be released by the GASB during March 2024.

An additional related project on revenue and expense recognition is also undergoing due process. Further information on that project is in the Introduction to this *Guide* as well as in Chapter 17.

The General Fund

Every general-purpose state and local government must have a general fund to account for all the unit's financial resources except for those resources not accounted for and reported in another fund. Special-purpose governments that are entirely business-type activities or fiduciary activities would not have a General Fund.

However, the entity's fund that encompasses their operations effectively serves as a General Fund.

The General Fund is the primary fund used to account for the governmental unit's current operations by recording inflows and outflows of financial resources. Current inflows typically are from revenue sources such as property taxes, income taxes, sales taxes, grants and contributions, fines, penalties, and other general revenues. Current outflows are usually related to the unit's provision for various governmental services such as health and welfare, streets, public safety, and general governmental administration.

In addition to accounting for current operating revenues and expenditures, the general fund accounts for other sources of financial resources, such as the issuance of long-term debt and transfers from other funds and uses of financial resources such as transfers to other funds. Although a state or local government can maintain more than one fund in each fund type, it can report only one General Fund [GASB Cod. Sec. 1300.104].

When a governmental entity has a blended component unit that is a governmental activity, the general fund of the component unit must be reported as a special revenue fund.

SPECIAL REVENUE FUNDS

PRACTICE ALERT: The GASB's *Financial Reporting Model Improvements* Exposure Draft contains a proposal to change the designation of special revenue funds to *"Special Resources Funds."* The GASB acknowledges that the revenues and expenditures terminology is more familiar to stakeholders. However, the Board believes that the use of inflows of resources and outflows of resources is needed to distinguish those elements in the governmental fund financial statements from those in the government-wide financial statements. Use of the identical term *revenues* within both governmental fund financial statements and government-wide financial statements is not appropriate because the amounts recognized are different for items arising from long-term transactions and other events. With the change from revenues to inflows of resources, the Board concluded that it also was appropriate to propose to amend existing GAAP.

As currently in GAAP, special revenue funds are used to account for and report the proceeds of specific revenue sources that are restricted or committed to expenditure for specified purposes other than debt service or capital projects (see previous **PRACTICE ALERT**).

A special revenue fund must be legally mandated, in many cases through an enabling statute. (The establishment and operations of governmental funds is discussed later in this chapter.) Per GASB Cod. Sec. 1300.105, as an alternative, resources restricted to expenditure for purposes normally financed from the general fund may be accounted for through the general fund provided that applicable legal requirements can be appropriately satisfied. Therefore, the use of special revenue funds is not required unless they are legally mandated.

An example of a special revenue fund is a fund that accounts for a state gasoline tax for which distributions are made to local governments. The expenditures from the fund are restricted by state law to the maintenance of the local highway system.

GAAP provides that specific restricted or committed revenues to be expended in a special revenue fund may be initially received in another fund, such as the general fund, and subsequently distributed to the special revenue fund. In these circumstances, the amounts should not be recognized as revenue in the fund initially receiving them but instead be recognized as revenues in the special revenue fund where they will be expended in accordance with the specified purposes.

Special revenue funds may be used for a myriad of programs and services if the definition of the fund is met. GASB provides the following examples:

Summary/Fact Pattern	Codification Reference	Outcome
Are special revenue funds required in all cases?	GASB Cod. Sec. 1300.704-7	Special revenue funds are not required, except to report the General Fund of a blended component unit.
Revenue is recognized in one fund (a state lottery) and distributed to another.	GASB Cod. Sec. 1300.704-12	In this case, a lottery enterprise fund includes the revenues from lottery gaming, with the payment of prizes and the distribution of net proceeds to other state funds in accordance with constitutional provisions. The distributions are transfers. The funds that receive the transfers are not restricted revenues and therefore, *are not required* to be accounted for in special revenue funds.
A property tax levy is received in the General Fund, but amounts required to be expended in accordance with specific purposes contained in the levy or law, regulation, ordinance, court judgment, etc.	GASB Cod. Sec. 1300.704-13	Amounts are restricted or committed revenues if the revenues represent a substantial portion of the flows into the other funds.
A city council passes a resolution to accumulate resources over five years to finance required property revaluations. Annually, the Council includes an amount to be transferred into a fund created for the purpose.	GASB Cod. Sec. 1300.704-17	This fund does *not* meet the criteria for a special revenue fund as the transferred amounts do not represent restricted or committed revenues. The fund also appears not to meet the definition of a capital projects fund.

Other inflows to special revenue funds may include investment earnings, grant awards and transfers in, if the inflows are restricted, committed, or assigned to the specific purpose of the fund. Outflows of special revenue funds are only for the specific purpose of the fund. However, the use of special revenue funds is not required unless they are legally mandated.

Many governments have stabilization arrangements (commonly known as 'rainy day funds.') Stabilization arrangements may utilize a special revenue fund if the resources in the fund are generated from a specific restricted or committed revenue source. An example of a restricted or committed revenue source could be when a government establishes a requirement that 15% of tax receipts received on mineral royalties' revenues are set aside to provide for budgetary imbalances. In such a case, GASB Cod. Sec. 1300.704-6 allows the use of a stabilization fund as the foundation of the fund is a specific committed revenue source.

Special revenue funds should *not* be used to account for resources held in trust for individuals, private organizations, or other governments. Such resources are fiduciary activities.

In some cases, discerning the difference of when a special revenue fund or if the activity is a fiduciary activity may be difficult. GASB Cod. Sec. 1300.704-3 discusses when a sheriff's department collects commissions from vendors for pay telephones and other services provided to inmates. According to statute, the funds can only provide benefits to the inmates. Outflows from the fund include uniforms, meals, medical care and similar. The fund's activities should not be classified as a private-purpose trust fund as the benefits are not specific to individuals but are generalized prisoner care and welfare. Such activities *could* be reported in a special revenue fund.

Governments may be party to revenue sharing agreements that may benefit the government *and* private parties. In such cases, GASB Cod. Sec. 1300.704-4 requires the establishment of two funds *or* a special revenue fund where the resources held for the private parties should be reported as liabilities. Any remaining fund balance would be classified as restricted.

Governments must disclose the purpose of each major special revenue fund in the notes to the basic financial statements. The notes are required to also include which revenues and other resources are reported in each major special revenue fund [GASB Cod. Sec. 1300.105].

OBSERVATION: Some legislative bodies may call what is a special revenue fund a "trust" within legislation and vice versa. Care must be taken to delineate between funds with trust documents and funds with enabling legislation that meets the definition of a special revenue fund in GAAP. Because of the variability in the way that special revenue funds have been established by governments, there could be some instances of where special revenue funds in practice do not meet the definition in accordance with GAAP. Should this occur, then the fund's balances and operations should be reclassified to the general fund.

Fund No Longer Qualifies to be a Special Revenue Fund. If a special revenue fund's specific restricted or committed revenue source is no longer a substantial portion of inflows, the reporting as a special revenue fund should be discontinued by the government. Instead, the flows should be reported in the General Fund per GASB Cod. Sec. 1300.105.

PRACTICE ALERT: Such a change could trigger a change to or within the financial reporting entity in accordance with GASB Cod. Sec. 2250.127(a) (GASB Statement No. 100 (*Accounting Changes and Error Corrections*)). Changes to or within the financial reporting entity include the addition or removal of a fund that results from the movement of *continuing operations* within the primary government, including its blended component units. GASB Cod. Sec. 2250.140 requires such changes to be reported by adjusting the current reporting period's fund balance for the effect of the change as if the change occurred as of the beginning of the reporting period. In this case, the change would be to the General Fund. Note disclosure describing the change will be required. GASB Statement No. 100 became effective for accounting changes and error corrections made for fiscal years beginning after June 15, 2023, and all reporting periods thereafter.

CAPITAL PROJECTS FUNDS

A governmental entity may be involved in several capital projects, ranging from the construction of schools and libraries to the construction of storm sewers and highways. The purpose of a capital projects fund, is defined as follows:

> To account for and report financial resources that are restricted, committed, or assigned to expenditure for capital outlays, including the acquisition or construction of capital facilities and other capital assets.

Capital outlays financed by proceeds from debt issuance should be accounted for in a capital projects fund. Capital project funds also exclude those types of capital-related outflows financed by proprietary funds or assets that will be held in trust for individuals, private organizations, or other governments (see Chapter 7 and Chapter 8, respectively).

In practice, a separate capital projects fund is often established when the acquisition or construction of a capital project extends beyond a single fiscal year and the financing sources are provided by more than one fund, or a capital asset is financed by specifically designated resources. Designated resources may arise from the issuance of all forms of debt, receipts of grants from other governmental units, designation of a portion of tax receipts, or a combination of these and other financing sources.

A capital projects fund must also be used when mandated by law or stipulated by regulations or covenants related to the financing source. For control purposes, it can also be advantageous to use a separate capital projects fund for major capital facilities even though one is not legally required. As with all funds in a governmental entity, the purpose of establishing a specific fund is to establish a basis of accountability for resources provided for a purpose [GASB Cod. Sec. 1300.106].

A government may also use a capital projects fund even if an activity does not meet a capitalization threshold. GASB Cod. Sec. 1300.704-18 provides an example when a government purchases movable storage facilities (trailers) that will not meet its threshold for capitalization. A capital projects fund can be used for this purpose even though the purchases would be below the government's capitalization threshold.

> **OBSERVATION:** There may be an uncertainty as to what type of fund would be used for projects that are capital in nature, financed by bonds, but not owned by a government (e.g., construction of a municipal school by a state authority that is a governmental activity). GASB Cod. Sec. 1300.106 specifically excludes capital projects funds for capital-related outflows financed by proprietary funds or for assets that will be held as a fiduciary activity. It is the author's opinion that those sorts of projects could be accounted for in a special revenue fund.

However, GASB Cod. Sec. 1300.704-19 discusses when a state law allows school districts to establish a "capital reserve fund" into which amounts of unused appropriations (for other purposes) at year-end and unassigned amounts in the general fund may be transferred. The resources in the fund can only be used for capital improvements, the replacement of and additions to public works, and the acquisition of major equipment items. In this case, a reserve does not meet the criteria to be reported as a special revenue fund because the transfers do not represent restricted or committed revenues and the resources are restricted by state law for capital projects. A separate capital projects fund may be reported, but it is not required.

> **OBSERVATION:** To emphasize, capital projects funds are not to be used for capital projects, financed by bonds for assets held as a fiduciary activity. A similar analogy is discussed in GASB Cod. Sec. 1300.706-2. In that question's fact pattern, a county issues bonds to finance the construction of a building for its discretely presented component unit. The bonds are a liability of the county, but the building will be reported as an asset of the component unit. The county disburses funds to the component unit to pay for construction costs as they are incurred. At year-end, the county has unspent bond proceeds. The county should *not* account for the unspent proceeds in a custodial fund (a fiduciary fund) as the component unit's construction is like an expenditure-driven grant. The GASB concludes that the amounts paid to the component unit and the construction costs incurred but unreimbursed are the grants for the year. The unearned portion equates to the unspent proceeds and is an asset of the county.

DEBT SERVICE FUNDS

A debt service fund is created to account for resources that will be accumulated and used to service general debt. General long-term debt can include noncurrent bonds and notes, as well as other noncurrent liabilities that might arise from lease agreements and other long-term liabilities not created by the issuance of a specific debt instrument. The purpose of a debt service fund in accordance with GAAP is as follows [GASB Cod. Sec. 1300.107]:

> Funds that are used to account for and report financial resources that are restricted, committed, or assigned to expenditure for principal and interest.

Debt service funds *should* be used to report resources if legally mandated, and when financial resources are being accumulated for principal and interest maturing in future years.

A debt service fund operates like a sinking fund used by a commercial enterprise in that resources are accumulated for eventually retiring long-term obligations. Debt service transactions related to special assessments for which the government is *not* obligated in any manner should be reported in a custodial fund as discussed in Chapter 8 [GASB Cod. Sec. S40.119].

Like special revenue funds, debt service funds may *not always be required, nor lawful*. Unless the preparer has the legal authority to create a fund, legislative bodies must pass an enabling statute to create a fund as funds can be legal instruments. If not legally mandated, a debt service fund is not enabled. Therefore, a debt service fund is not required to be used for all debt service activities. GASB Cod. Sec. 1300.704-20 reiterates that a debt service fund must be used when legally mandated or to account for resources being accumulated for principal and interest maturing in future years. The accumulation of resources is distinguished from the annual receipt and collection of resources utilized to pay for current debt service when due.

Although separate debt service funds can be established for long-term obligations that are not based on an outstanding debt instrument (such as compensated absences and special termination benefits), these obligations are generally accounted for in other funds such as the general fund or special revenue funds.

PERMANENT FUNDS

Permanent funds are to be used when governmental entities receive resources from other parties, including individuals, private organizations, and other governments, whereby the use of the resources is restricted to the extent that only earnings, and not principal, may be used for purposes that support the reporting government's programs—that is, for the benefit of the government and its citizenry [GASB Cod. Sec. 1300.108].

The GASB provides an example of a cemetery perpetual-care fund, which could be created when the earnings of the dedicated resources can be used only for the maintenance of a public cemetery and the principal of the fund is to remain intact. GAAP requires that a permanent fund be used to report this type of resource restriction.

Comparing Permanent Funds and Private-Purpose Trust Funds. Permanent funds *are* commonly confused with private-purpose trust funds. Private-purpose trust funds are used for fiduciary activities other than those required to be reported in pension (and other employee benefit) trust funds or investment trust funds and are held in trust where the assets meet certain criteria as more fully explained in Chapter 8.

In some instances, the mandated purpose of specific resources to be accounted for in a separate fund may be such that it is not clear which fund type should be used for financial reporting purposes. For example, GASB Cod. Sec.

1300.704-1 notes that a governmental entity may need to account for financial resources that are legally restricted by enabling legislation, but a minimum balance (nonspendable) is defined by the legislation and that balance must be maintained in the fund. The nonspendable portion of the fund description would suggest that a permanent fund should be used, while the legal restriction characteristic would suggest a special revenue fund.

Permanent funds are also not permanent endowments for entities such as public colleges and hospitals. GASB Cod. Sec. Sp20 does not contain a requirement to report permanent endowments of public colleges and hospitals in governmental funds as such entities comm-only are business-type activities. If the public college or hospital is a governmental activity, then a permanent fund may be present. GASB Cod. Sec. 1300.704-2 provides guidance that the net position of a permanent endowment is reported as nonexpendable restricted net position, segregated by the purpose of the restriction.

Either fund type could be used under this circumstance. If a permanent fund is used, the portion of the fund that is expendable should be identified as a restricted, committed, or assigned fund balance depending upon the nature of the ability to spend and if the fund was created due to the implementation of an external restriction. If a special revenue fund is to be used, similar reporting may result.

Finally, unrealized gains on investments in permanent funds are included in the same fund balance classification as the related investment principal. GASB Cod. Sec. 1300.704-22 discusses when the permanent fund agreement includes the ability to "spend" appreciation, in addition to earnings, any unrealized gain would be classified as restricted for the same purpose as the earnings.

Establishing and Operating Governmental Funds

As discussed in summary form in this chapter, funds are mainly established by legal provisions. States may have funds established by constitutional provisions. Other governments may have fund establishment contained in laws, ordinances, charters, and other enabling legislation. If not in such provisions, governing bodies may create funds for administrative, control and accounting purposes. This is especially the case in accordance with grant agreements, contracts, and debt covenants [GASB Cod. Sec. 1300.117].

Number of Funds

Only one general fund can be utilized by a government. If blended component units with general funds are included in the reporting entity of the primary government, the component units' general funds are reported as special revenue funds.

Ideally, governments should have *the minimum number of governmental funds* necessary to comply with laws, regulations, and similar requirements. In addition to one general fund, many governments will not need funds of distinct types during a reporting year, or they may not be authorized to have such funds.

6010   *Fund Accounting*

Governments that establish too many funds experience complexity in administering the funds throughout the entire operating cycle. Too many funds tend to increase budgetary transparency, accounting, operating, internal controls, closing and financial reporting issues. Too few funds may not be compliant with laws, regulations, and operating requirements. A balance must be found that is ideal for operating purposes [GASB Cod. Secs. 1300.118–.120].

Other Operating Matters

A "fund" is defined as a separate self-balancing set of accounts for all accounting elements. However, GAAP does not necessary extend this requirement to *physical* separation of assets and liabilities. For example, there are no GAAP provisions for a separate fund for a separate bond issuance, or a separate bank account, receivables, or payables. Such separations are only necessary when required by law, regulation, or indenture.

Many governments utilize enterprise resource planning (ERP) systems and similar that allow sophistication including sub-funds that "close" on a periodic basis to funds to facilitate any required separation. For example, a stabilization arrangement ("rainy-day fund") may be a sub-fund of the general fund in some governments. If internal controls over financial reporting are effective and the fund structure chosen complies with laws and regulations to serve as the official books and records, provisions of GAAP have a higher probability of being met [GASB Cod. Sec. 1300.121].

Classification, Periodicity and Activity of Funds

Many governments designate an executive to implement the fund structure. This person is usually in charge of establishment, operation, classification, and reporting. The person may be a chief financial or fiscal officer, a comptroller or controller or some other similarly titled entity, such as an auditor/controller, in some governments. They may (or may not) have discretion over interpreting legislative intent.

Another important aspect is whether the fund is a periodic or a project-based fund. Periodic funds "close" at the end of an operating cycle and may include appropriations approved by a legislative body for budgetary compliance. The funds may reopen with the same information at the start of another period. Other nongovernmental funds, capital projects funds and permanent funds may continue for many periods and are more project-based. A key to this determination is whether budgetary appropriations on an ongoing basis are necessary.

In all but the simplest of general-purpose governments, more than one column is used to display funds within the basic financial statements. Governmental funds are displayed in separate statements from proprietary and fiduciary funds. Due to the differences in the measurement focus and basis of accounting as well as the different financial statements, disclosure is required in the summary of significant accounting policies of the activities accounted for in each of the following columns—major funds, internal service funds, and each type of fiduciary fund, as presented in the basic financial statements. Except for the general fund or its equivalent, the descriptions must be specific to the government, rather than general definitions that could describe any government using boilerplate language.

Finally, similar funds may have different activities. For example, some governments may have many special revenue funds for separate restricted, committed or assigned activities. The required disclosure described in the previous paragraph would include the activities of major special revenue funds to provide better understanding of these activities for users of the financial statements [GASB Cod. Secs. 1300.123–.127].

ACCOUNTING AND REPORTING FOR GOVERNMENTAL FUNDS

Measurement Focus and Basis of Accounting

The modified accrual basis of accounting and flow of current financial resources measurement focus are used to prepare the financial statements of governmental funds. These concepts are discussed in Chapter 3. (See previous **PRACTICE ALERT** on potential changes to the current financial resources measurement focus and modified accrual basis of accounting that may occur in the future with the GASB's *Financial Reporting Model Improvements* project.)

Focus on Major Funds

The basic financial statements of the primary government include separate financial statements for governmental funds from proprietary and fiduciary funds. The focus on governmental and proprietary funds is on *major* funds. The balance sheet and the statement of revenues, expenditures, and changes in fund balance for governmental funds include separate columnar information for each major fund. Proprietary funds show similar information in the statement of fund net position and the statement of revenues, expenses, and changes in fund net position. Major fund reporting does not apply to internal service funds. The nonmajor funds may be presented in combining statements as supplementary information. However, such combining statements are only required in ACFRs, or when required by law, regulation, or similar authority [GASB Cod. Secs. 2200.157–.158, fns. 27–28].

The General Fund is always a major fund. The criteria to determine a major fund for the remaining governmental and enterprise funds are based on the following provisions:

1. The total of assets and deferred outflows of resources, the total of liabilities and deferred inflows of resources, revenues, or expenditures/ expenses (excluding extraordinary items) of that individual governmental or enterprise fund are at least 10% of the corresponding element(s) total (total assets and deferred outflows of resources, total liabilities and deferred inflows of resources, and so forth) for all funds of that category or type (i.e., total governmental or total enterprise funds), *and*
2. The same element(s) that met the 10% criterion in the first provision is at least 5% of the corresponding element total for all governmental and enterprise funds *combined*.

Governments also have the flexibility to judge if any other governmental or enterprise fund should be a major fund if officials believe they are particularly important to financial statement users [GASB Cod. Sec. 2200.159].

PRACTICE POINT: Care must be taken in this decision. The independent auditor's report for a state and local government is based on "opinion units" which include each major fund and the remaining nonmajor funds in the aggregate.

PRACTICE ALERT: GASB Cod. Sec. 2250.127(b) includes a change in a fund's presentation as major or nonmajor as triggering a change to or within the financial reporting entity in accordance with GASB Statement No. 100 (*Accounting Changes and Error Corrections*). If a change occurs, the change requires an adjustment of the current reporting period's fund balance (or fund net position) as applicable, for the impact of the change as if the change occurred as of the beginning of the reporting period. The change's presentation would change the presentation of the fund balance for nonmajor funds and the individual fund as a major fund. Due to the audit concept of opinion units, the independent auditor's report would also provide disclosure of such a change. Note disclosure would be required, limited to only the nature of the change in a case where the fund's presentation no longer meets the thresholds to be a major fund. GASB Statement No. 100 became effective for periods beginning after June 15, 2023.

If a special revenue fund does not meet the percentage criteria to be considered a major fund, but is considered a major fund by the government, a budgetary comparison schedule is required to be presented if the fund has a legally adopted budget. GASB Cod. Sec. 2200.763-4 discusses that if a fund is considered a major fund (for whatever reason), then all the major fund reporting requirements must be satisfied, including those related to budgetary information. For the budgetary information to apply to a major special revenue fund, that fund must have a legally adopted annual budget.

Unlike some governmental funds, a capital projects fund is project-oriented rather than period-oriented, and for this reason it is often not necessary to record the fund's budget for control purposes. For example, the authorization of a bond ordinance by the legislature or the public will identify the fund's purpose and the balance of resources that can be used to construct or purchase the capital asset. Subsequent action by the legislature will generally not be necessary.

Unless a debt service fund budget is legally adopted, there is no requirement to record the fund's budget or to prepare financial statements that compare the results of operations for the period on a budget basis with those on an actual basis. Usually, the loan or bond indenture provision that requires the establishment of a debt service fund also controls expenditures to be made from the fund.

GOVERNMENTAL FUND FINANCIAL STATEMENTS

PRACTICE ALERT: The *Financial Reporting Model Improvements* Exposure Draft contains a proposal to change the financial statements for governmental funds to:

- The short-term financial resources balance sheet and
- The statement of short-term financial resource flows.

The proposed statement of short-term financial resource flows does not include the words "revenues" nor "expenditures" representing a major change in terminology for governmental funds.

Governmental funds must present a balance sheet and a statement of revenues, expenditures, and changes in fund balances.

Balance Sheet

The balance sheet reports information based on the current financial resources measurement focus and the modified accrual basis of accounting. Each major fund is presented along with nonmajor funds in the aggregate. A balance sheet format is used to present assets, deferred outflows of resources, liabilities, deferred inflows of resources and the various categories of fund balances, as applicable. The following formula is used:

[Assets + deferred outflows of resources] = [{Liabilities + deferred inflows of resources} + fund balances]

Totals for the assets and deferred outflows of resources and totals for the liabilities and deferred inflows of resources may be used.

Fund balance classifications should be presented as discussed in Chapter 5 [GASB Cod. Secs. 2200.161–.163].

Reconciliation to Governmental Activities Net Position. As the balance sheet presents information on a different measurement focus and basis of accounting than the statement of net position, a reconciliation of fund balances to the governmental activities total net position is required in accordance with GAAP. The reconciliation may be presented at the bottom of the balance sheet. In practice, most governments present this information on a separate schedule.

Common elements of the reconciliation include, but are not limited to:

- Capital assets at historical cost, instead of expenditures when incurred,
- Long-term liabilities not due and payable in the current period,
- Deferred inflows of resources for those amounts that were not available to pay current period expenditures,
- Internal service fund net position balances, and
- Pension and other postemployment benefit liabilities [GASB Cod. Sec. 2200.164].

> **PRACTICE ALERT:** The *Financial Reporting Model Improvements* Exposure Draft allows flexibility in the placement of the reconciliation. The reconciliation may be presented at the bottom of the short-term financial resources balance sheet or on a separate page following the balance sheet.

Presentation of Assets in Governmental Fund Balance Sheets

Assets. "Assets," as defined in GASB:CS-4, are:

> Resources with a present service capacity that the entity presently controls.

Assets of governmental funds include resources that are considered current expendable financial resources available for subsequent appropriation and expenditure (under the current model, which may change in the future as discussed in the various **PRACTICE ALERTs**). Assets other than those that are currently expendable, such as capital assets, are indeed assets, but they are not available to finance future expenditures that will be made from the governmental funds.

> **PRACTICE ALERT:** The Short-term financial resources balance sheet would include assets that arise from short-term transactions and other events. In addition to cash, assets may include inventories, prepaid expenses and other financial assets including those transactions that may be converted to cash. In addition, assets arising from long-term transactions and other events should be recognized in the governmental fund financial statements when payments to be received become due.

Classifications of Assets. The governmental funds' balance sheet is unclassified. Current and noncurrent categories are not presented. Assets of the governmental funds are primarily current assets, including cash, cash equivalents, marketable investments, inventories, various receivables, and amounts due from other funds.

Certain noncurrent assets (not currently expendable) may be reported in governmental funds, but these assets result in a restricted or non-spendable fund balance. For example, if a long-term note receivable is reported in the general fund, the general fund's fund balance should be reported as a nonspendable.

Investments. The standards contained in GASB Cod. Sec. I50, *Investments*, apply to most governmental fund investments. As defined in that code section, an investment is a security or other asset that (*a*) a government holds primarily for income or profit and (*b*) has a present service capacity based solely on its ability to generate cash or to be sold to generate cash. The accounting standards for investments are discussed in Chapter 9.

Long-Term Receivables. Governmental funds generally reflect assets that are available to finance current expenditures. However, noncurrent financial assets, such as long-term receivables, should also be presented in the governmental funds' balance sheets, along with a fund balance assigned by an equal amount. Note that management has negotiated the loan under terms delegated by the government's highest level of decision-making authority. To illustrate, if a $100,000 advance to a special revenue fund will not be repaid during the subsequent budgetary period, the transaction would be recorded as follows in the general fund:

GENERAL FUND	Debit	Credit
Interfund Loans Receivable	100,000	
Cash		100,000
Fund Balance—Unassigned	100,000	
Fund Balance—Nonspendable-Interfund Loan		100,000
To record long-term loans to special revenue fund.		

Capital Assets. General capital assets, such as land, buildings, infrastructure, and equipment, purchased and used by governmental funds should be recorded as a capital outlay expenditure in the governmental funds and not reported as a fund asset. However, the capital asset is reported in the entity's statement of net position.

The accounting for governmental funds' expenditures associated with the acquisition or construction of a capital asset is illustrated by the following transactions:

CAPITAL PROJECTS FUND	Debit	Credit
Encumbrances	400,000	
Reserve for Encumbrances		400,000
To record purchase orders and contracts of $400,000 related to the construction of an addition to a building in the capital projects fund after approval.		

NOTE: This transaction will only be carried in the ledgers during the year. For financial reporting purposes, encumbrances and reserves for encumbrances are not presented.

CAPITAL PROJECTS FUND	Debit	Credit
Reserve for Encumbrances	150,000	
Encumbrances		150,000
Expenditures—Capital Outlays	157,000	
Vouchers Payable (or Cash)		157,000
To record purchase orders and contracts that were encumbered for $150,000 that are then vouchered for $157,000 due to change orders and paid from the capital projects fund.		

NOTE: The change orders could have resulted in additional encumbrances upon approval by the government. However, encumbrance accounting might not be used by the government. Like the previous transaction, this transaction will also only be carried in the ledgers during the year. For financial reporting purposes, encumbrances and reserves for encumbrances are not presented.

Transaction recording completion of construction:

CAPITAL PROJECTS FUND	Debit	Credit
Reserve for Encumbrances	250,000	
Encumbrances		250,000
Expenditures—Capital Outlays	245,000	
Vouchers Payable (or Cash)		245,000

To record completion of construction, the remaining purchase orders and contracts are vouchered for $245,000 and paid from the capital projects fund.

Liabilities. GASB: CS-4 defines "liabilities" as:

Present obligations to sacrifice resources that the entity has little or no discretion to avoid.

Governmental fund liabilities are debts or obligations of the governmental unit that are to be met by using the governmental fund's current expendable financial resources. Liabilities that do not require the use of current expendable financial resources but will be retired later by resources made available through governmental funds, are reported as an obligation on the statement of net position. As previously discussed in this chapter, the definition of a "liability" is also unclear when considering what a "matured liability," an "obligation," and a "commitment" are due to the lack of uniformity in a definition of "current expendable financial resources" (under the current model, which may change in the future as discussed in the various **PRACTICE ALERTs**).

PRACTICE ALERT: The short-term financial resources balance sheet would include liabilities that arise from short-term transactions and other events. Long-term debt issued for short-term purposes is recognized as a liability. Liabilities arising from long-term transactions and other events are recognized when payments to be made become due except for long-term debt issued for short-term purposes, which is recognized as a short-term transaction. Payments to be made that have not yet become due on long-term transactions and other events are general long-term liabilities. Examples of long-term debt issued for short-term purposes are tax anticipation notes and revenue anticipation notes with maturities beyond one year from inception of the transaction.

Classifications of Liabilities. Although the governmental funds' balance sheet is unclassified, a liability presented on the financial statement is considered a current liability. Current liabilities of governmental funds include items such as accounts and vouchers payable, short-term notes payable, accrued liabilities, interest due and payable, and payroll withholding.

These liabilities represent debts that will be paid within a relatively brief period (i.e., a few months) after the close of the state or local government's fiscal year and are generally easy to identify as current rather than noncurrent liabilities. Liabilities must be evaluated to determine whether they are debts of governmental funds or are more appropriately reported only on the entity's statement of net position.

Bond, Tax, and Revenue Anticipation Notes. Governments may issue bond, tax, or revenue anticipation notes that will be retired when specific taxes or other specified revenues are collected by the governments. For example, a local government may issue property tax anticipation notes a few weeks or months before the anticipated receipt of property tax installments are to be paid by taxpayers. Bond, tax, and revenue anticipation notes and whether they are reported as governmental fund liabilities or only as general long-term liabilities are discussed in Chapter 12.

Demand Bonds. A bond agreement may contain a clause that allows bondholders to require a governmental unit to redeem the debt during a specified period. The demand feature, or put, and related circumstances must be evaluated to determine whether the demand bonds should be reported as a debt obligation only in the statement of net position (a government-wide liability) or also as a short-term debt (a governmental fund liability). This topic is discussed in Chapters 5 and 12.

Arbitrage. As introduced in Chapter 1, arbitrage involves the simultaneous purchase and sale of the same or essentially the same securities with the objective of making a profit on the spread between the two markets. In the context of governmental finance, this practice often occurs when a governmental entity issues tax-exempt debt and uses the proceeds to invest in debt securities that have a higher rate of return. Because of the spread between the debt securities interest rates and the tax-exempt interest rate, an entity can more effectively manage its financial resources.

However, state, and local governments must cautiously apply this indirect federal tax subsidy because the federal government has established arbitrage restrictions (requirements for how long the funds can be invested) and arbitrage rebate rules (the amount of arbitrage earnings that must be paid to the federal government).

The governmental entity must apply the rules and regulations established by the federal government to determine whether the entity has a liability that it should record in its financial statements. Such liabilities should be recorded using the general guidance contained in GASB Cod. Secs. C50.151–.168. If the governmental entity should accrue a liability, it should record the portion that represents the use of current financial resources as expenditures (although some governmental entities offset the amount against interest income) and the balance of the liability as a liability in its government-wide financial statements.

Leases. Various paragraphs of GASB Cod. Sec. L20 require reporting of leasing activity in governmental funds as follows:
- *Lessee reporting*: If a lease is expected to be paid from general government resources, the lease should be accounted for and reported on a basis consistent with governmental fund accounting principles. An expenditure and other financing source should be reported in the period the lease is

initially recognized. The expenditure and other financing source should be measured in the same manner as all other lease liabilities. Subsequent governmental fund lease payments should be accounted for in the same manner as debt service payments on long-term debt [GASB Cod. Secs. L20.132–.133].

- *Lessor reporting*: In the governmental fund financial statements financial statements, a lessor should recognize a lease receivable and a deferred inflow of resources to account for a lease. A lessor should measure the deferred inflow of resources at the initial value of the lease receivable in the same manner as other leases, plus the amount of any payments received at or before the commencement of the lease term that relate to future periods (e.g., the final month's rent). A lessor subsequently should recognize the deferred inflow of resources as inflows of resources (e.g., revenue), if available, in a systematic and rational manner over the term of the lease [GASB Cod. Sec. L20.153].

Leases are further discussed in Chapter 14.

Long-Term Debt. The proceeds from the issuance of long-term debt are recorded in the governmental funds as other financing sources; and the liability itself is not reported as debt of the governmental funds but, rather, is reported as an obligation in the government-wide financial statements. For example, the issuance of general obligation serial bonds of $10,000,000 would be recorded as follows:

CAPITAL PROJECTS FUND	Debit	Credit
Cash	10,000,000	
Other Financing Sources—Proceeds from Issuance of Serial Bonds		10,000,000
To record the issuance of general obligation serial bonds series 202Z-A.		

Bonds Issued Between Interest Payment Dates. Long-term bonds may be issued on a date that does not coincide with an interest payment date. When this occurs, the proceeds from the bond issuance include an amount of accrued interest. The accrued interest does not represent other financing sources of a governmental fund, and it should be recorded as a payable to the governmental fund responsible for servicing the long-term debt.

For example, assume that $10,000,000 of bonds carrying a 6% interest rate are issued for $10,100,000, including two months of interest ($100,000) and the proceeds are recorded in a Capital Projects Fund. The issuance of the bonds between interest payment dates would be recorded as follows, assuming a Debt Service Fund will accumulate resources to make interest and principal payments over the life of the bonds:

CAPITAL PROJECTS FUND	Debit	Credit
Cash	10,100,000	
Proceeds from Long-Term Debt Issued		10,000,000
Due to Debt Service Fund		100,000

DEBT SERVICE FUND	Debit	Credit
Due from Capital Projects Fund	100,000	
Interest Payable		100,000

To record the issuance of general obligation serial bonds series 202Z-B and related payable amounts for days between interest payments.

Alternatively, the portion of the proceeds that represents the interest that will be payable at the next interest payment date may be recorded directly in the fund responsible for servicing the debt. If this approach were chosen, the previous illustration would be recorded as follows:

CAPITAL PROJECTS FUND	Debit	Credit
Cash	10,000,000	
Proceeds from Long-Term Debt Issued		10,000,000
DEBT SERVICE FUND		
Cash	100,000	
Interest Payable		100,000

To record the issuance of general obligation serial bonds series 202Z-B and related payable amounts for days between interest payments.

Bond Premium, Discount, and Bond Issuance Costs. The face amount of the long-term debt, any related discount or premiums, and debt issuance costs should be reported separately. The debt proceeds (based on the face amount of the debt), discount, and premium must be presented as other financing sources and uses. The debt issuance costs should be presented as expenditures.

Unmatured Principal and Interest. Under the modified accrual basis, expenditures of a governmental fund are recognized when the related liability is incurred. The one significant exception to this fundamental concept is the accounting treatment for unmatured principal and accrued interest. Unmatured principal and accrued interest are not recognized as a liability of a governmental fund until the amounts are due to be paid.

For example, if long-term debt were issued on October 1, 20X8, and the first interest payment was due on April 1, 20X9, there would be no accrual of interest as of December 31, 20X8 (end of fiscal year). Likewise, if a serial bond repayment were due on April 1, 20X9, the liability would not be required to be recorded in the debt service fund's balance sheet as of March 31, 20X9, even though the amount would be due the next day.

> **PRACTICE ALERT:** This aspect of the GASB's *Financial Reporting Model Improvements* Exposure Draft is controversial to some. Liabilities arising from long-term transactions and other events are recognized when payments to be made become due, except for long-term debt issued for short-term purposes (which would be a short-term transaction). Payments to be made *that have not yet become due* on long-term transactions and other events are general long-

term liabilities. Unless the interest is due but unpaid at the end of a reporting period, the related accrued interest would be also a long-term transaction.

Current accounting standards provide for an exception to the basic concept that general long-term indebtedness is not reported as expenditures until the amount becomes due and payable. When funds have been transferred to the debt service fund during the fiscal year in anticipation of making debt service payments "shortly" after the end of the period, it is acceptable to accrue interest and debt in the debt service fund as an expenditure in the year the transfer is made. This period is also known as "the period of availability."

PRACTICE ALERT: In the GASB's *Financial Reporting Model Improvements* project, the GASB is endeavoring to standardize the period of availability for governmental funds utilizing the proposed short-term financial resources measurement focus. Currently, governments mostly utilize a period of availability of up to 60 days beyond period-end for recognition of property tax revenues. Governments are also allowed to adopt another accounting policy that reflects a different period for different revenue sources. This has led to inconsistent reporting. The period of availability within the focus is proposed to be one year from the inception of a transaction to when the transaction is concluded.

Debt Extinguishments. Scheduled debt retirements are accounted for as just described. In addition to scheduled retirements, general obligations of a governmental unit may be extinguished by:

1. Legal defeasance or
2. In-substance defeasance or debt refunding.

These transactions require special accounting treatment in governmental funds and are discussed in Chapter 12.

Zero-Interest-Rate Bonds. Zero-interest-rate bonds (often referred to as zero-coupon bonds) are issued at a deep discount, and the difference between the initial price of the bonds and their maturity value represents interest. Interest is not accrued but, rather, is recognized as an expenditure when due and payable. The interest expenditure for zero-interest-rate bonds is recorded when the bonds mature. However, the accrued interest must be recognized as part of the general debt in the governmental entity's government-wide statement of net position.

To illustrate the accounting for zero-interest-rate bonds, assume that $6,000,000 (maturity value) of non-interest-bearing term bonds are issued to yield a rate of return of 5%. The bonds mature in twenty years and are issued for $2,261,340 ($6,000,000 × 0.37689, where $i = 5\%$, $n = 20$ for the present value of an amount). The equation is as follows:

$$\text{Price} = [\text{Maturity Value} (1+\text{interest rate})^{\text{number of periods}}]$$
$$\text{Price} = [\$6,000,000 (1+5\%)^{20}]$$
$$\text{Price} = \$2,261,340$$

The issuance of the bonds, assuming the proceeds are made available to the General Fund, is recorded as follows:

GENERAL FUND	Debit	Credit
Cash	2,261,340	
Other Financing Uses—Discount on Long-Term Debt Issued	3,738,660	
Other Financing Sources—Long-Term Debt Issued		6,000,000
To record the issuance of discount bonds Series 202Z-A at 5%.		

At the end of the first fiscal year, the amount of accrued interest earned by investors on the bonds is $113,067 calculated as ($2,261,340 × 5%). Because the interest will not be paid by the debt service fund until the bonds mature, the accrued interest is not recognized as expenditures. However, the accrued interest must be included as part of general long-term debt in the government-wide statement of net position.

When the bonds mature in 20 years, assuming no change in GAAP, if enough funds have been accumulated in the debt service fund, the following entries are made:

DEBT SERVICE FUND	Debit	Credit
Expenditures—Principal	2,261,340	
Expenditures—Interest	3,738,660	
Cash		6,000,000
To record the maturity of discount bonds Series 202Z-A.		

Governmental Fund "Equity" is Presented as Fund Balance

GASB: CS-4 defines "net position" as the residual of all other elements presented in a statement of financial position. In *governmental funds*, this net position is referred to as "fund balance." Deferred inflows of resources may also be present; however, it would be rare for deferred outflows of resources to be present in a governmental fund. As a reminder, the word "equity" *should not be used in the basic financial statements.*

Statement of Revenues, Expenditures, and Changes in Fund Balances

> **PRACTICE ALERT:** As part of the GASB's *Financial Reporting Model Improvements* Exposure Draft, the GASB has proposed that the governmental fund flows statements will be retitled to "Statement of Short-Term Financial Resource Flows." The following information would be presented in the following sequence:
>
>   Inflows of resources from current activities (detailed)
>
>   Total inflows of resources from current activities
>
>   Outflows of resources from current activities (detailed)
>
>   Total outflows of resources from current activities

Net flows from current activities

Net flows from noncurrent activities (detailed)

Total net flows from noncurrent activities

Unusual or infrequent items (detailed)

Net change in fund balances

Fund balances—beginning of period

Fund balances—end of period

Each caption, subtotal, and total shown in the format above would be presented, as applicable. Current activities are all activities other than noncurrent activities. Noncurrent activities are activities related to the acquisition and disposal of capital assets and the issuance and repayment of capital-related liabilities (e.g., leases) and long-term debt, except for long-term debt issued for short-term purposes. As previously disclosed, the terms *revenues* and *expenditures* would no longer be applicable to governmental funds.

A Statement of Revenues, Expenditures and Changes in Fund Balances reports information about the flows of financial resources for each major governmental fund and nonmajor governmental funds in the aggregate using the current financial resources measurement focus and modified accrual basis of accounting. Elements of the statement include:

- Revenues (detailed).
- Expenditures (detailed).
- Excess (deficiency) of revenues over expenditures.
- Other financing sources and uses, including transfers (detailed).
- Special and extraordinary items (detailed).
- Net change in fund balances.
- Fund balances—beginning of period.
- Fund balances—end of period.

The total of the fund balances at the end of the period for each fund should articulate to the corresponding fund information in the balance sheet [GASB Cod. Sec. 2200.165].

Revenues and Other Financing Sources

PRACTICE ALERT: As introduced, revenues and other financing sources, expenditures and other financing uses would be renamed to inflows of resources and outflows of resources, respectively, should the *Financial Reporting Model Improvements* Exposure Draft be approved by the GASB as proposed. Elements of the flows would be as follows:

Governmental Funds

	Inflows of Resources	Outflows of Resources
Definition	Inflows of short-term financial resources for a reporting period in governmental fund financial statements are recognized for: a) short-term transactions and other events as they occur and b) long-term transactions and other events when payments are due (except for long-term debt issued for short-term purposes, which is recognized as a short-term transaction).	Outflows of short-term financial resources for a reporting period in governmental fund financial statements are recognized for: • short-term transactions and other events (such as use of goods and services and acquisition of capital assets) as they occur and • long-term transactions and other events when payments are due (except for long-term debt issued for short-term purposes, which is recognized as a short-term transaction).
Examples (current activities)	Taxes, intergovernmental, charges for services, licenses, fees, fines, investment earnings, transfers in.	Programs and services of government, transfers out.
Noncurrent activities	Long-term debt issuance (and related premiums), proceeds from sale of capital assets, transfers in.	Debt service, capital outlay, transfers out, payments to bond escrow agents.

GASB: CS-4 (*Elements of Financial Statements*) defines the elements of the "resource flows (change) statements" involving revenue and other financing sources and indicates that an "inflow of resources" is an acquisition of net position by the entity that is applicable to the reporting period.

The acquisition of fund balance (inflow) in governmental funds is defined as net financial assets coming under the control of the entity or net financial assets becoming newly available to the entity even if the resources are consumed directly when acquired. An acquisition of net financial assets results in:

- An increase in financial assets exceeding any related increase in fund liabilities, *or*
- A decrease in fund liabilities exceeding any related decrease in financial assets.

Examples of acquisition of fund balance in governmental funds include:

- Imposing a tax (because the resources have newly come under the control of the entity), and
- Receiving the proceeds of a bond issue (because no fund liability has been created but cash has been received, thereby increasing the entity's net position).

6024 *Fund Accounting*

Revenues and expenditures in the statement of revenues, expenditures and changes in fund balances are classified by major revenue source. Expenditures are classified (at a minimum) by function.

Other financing sources and uses include proceeds from debt issuance, payments to escrow agents, transfers, sales of capital assets and similar. Special and extraordinary items are reported separately after other financing sources and uses. (See discussion in Chapter 5.) [GASB Cod. Secs. 2200.166–.168].

Reconciliation to Statement of Activities. A summary reconciliation of the total changes in fund balance to the total changes in governmental activities net position is also required in a similar fashion to the reconciliation between the balance sheet and the governmental activities statement of net position. Common reconciling items include, but are not limited to:

- Differences in revenue recognition between the governmental funds and the governmental activities.
- Recognition of annual depreciation and amortization expense instead of expenditures for capital outlays.
- Reporting of debt proceeds in the statement of net position as liabilities instead of financial sources and debt payments as reduction of liabilities instead of expenditures.
- Conversion of other expenditures to expenses on the accrual basis.
- Additions of net revenue (expense) of internal service funds [GASB Cod. Sec. 2200.169].

PRACTICE ALERT: The *Financial Reporting Model Improvements* Exposure Draft proposes to allow flexibility in the placement of the reconciliation. The reconciliation may be presented at the bottom of the statement of short-term financial resources flows or on a separate page following the statement of short-term financial resources flows.

Revenues. Revenues represent increases in current financial resources other than increases caused by the issuance of long-term debt or the receipt of transfers from other funds. Governmental Fund revenues are recorded when they are susceptible to accrual, which means that the revenues must be both measurable and available in accordance with the modified accrual basis of accounting also stipulates that a government should report a deferred inflow of resources is assets are recorded but revenue is not available. This is common for taxation that is levied in one year, but legislation does not allow for recognition until a subsequent year. Such amounts are declared receivable where taxpayer liability has been established, with collectability assured or losses can be estimated. However, as recognition does not occur until a subsequent year, a deferred inflow of resources is recognized. As part of the opening of the subsequent year, the deferred inflow of resources is negated, and revenue recognized.

Other Financing Sources. "Other financing sources" is a classification of governmental fund resources other than those defined as "revenues." For example, when long-term debt is issued, and the proceeds are available to a governmental fund, the proceeds are recorded as other financing sources. The long-term debt is not recorded as a liability in the governmental fund but, rather, is reported as a liability only in the entity's statement of net position. Interfund transfers from other funds are also reported as "other financing sources."

> **OBSERVATION:** The face amount of the long-term debt and related discount or premium and debt-issuance costs should be separately reported in the governmental fund operating statement. The debt-issuance costs should be presented as expenditures and the other items should be presented as other financing sources and uses. GAAP requires that the "face amount," and not the proceeds (net of any discount or premium) from the issuance of the debt, be presented as other financing sources.

Classification and Disclosure. Revenues should be presented in the governmental funds' statement of revenues and expenditures and identified by major source, such as property taxes, income taxes, and so on (see Chapter 5). The revenue recognition methods used by the governmental funds should be explained in the summary of significant accounting policies.

Expenditures and Other Financing Uses

GASB:CS-4 *(Elements of Financial Statements)* defines the elements of the "resource flows (change) statements" involving expenditures and other financing uses and indicates that an "outflow of resources" is a consumption of fund balance by the entity that is applicable to the reporting period.

The consumption of fund balance (outflow) in governmental funds is defined as the using up of net financial assets that results in:

- A decrease in financial assets exceeding any related decrease in fund liabilities, or
- An increase in fund liabilities more than any related increase in financial assets.

Examples of consumption of financial resources in governmental funds include:

- Using financial resources to acquire capital assets (because existing cash resources of the entity have been consumed); and
- Using the labor of employees to provide government services for which payment will be made in the next reporting period (because the entity has consumed employee labor resources that were directly acquired from the employees).

Expenditures are accrued when incurred if the event or transaction results in a reduction of the governmental fund's current financial resources. If there is no reduction in the fund's net *current financial resources,* no expenditure is recorded. For example, a governmental unit may incur an estimated liability for compensated absences, but if the actual payments to employees are not due at period end, the expenditure would not be reflected in the governmental fund. Instead, it is reported as a liability in the entity's statement of net position.

CHAPTER 7
PROPRIETARY FUNDS

Chapter References:
   GASB Statement Nos. 1, 6, 9, 14, 34, 37, 38, 51, 62, 84, 89, 100
   GASB Interpretation No. 3
   GASB Concepts Statement Nos. 1, 6
   GASB *Implementation Guide*
   NCGA Statement No. 1, NCGA Interpretation No. 9

INTRODUCTION

A proprietary fund is used to account for a state or local government's activity that are like operations that may be performed by a commercial enterprise. For example, a hospital may be operated by a governmental unit, such as a city, or by a profit-oriented corporation. The accounting and reporting standards used by a proprietary fund and a business enterprise are similar because the activities performed are basically the same.

Proprietary activity reporting focuses on determining operating income, changes in fund net position (or cost recovery), financial position and cash flows. The proprietary fund category includes:
- Enterprise funds (focusing on major funds), and
- Internal service funds.

Proprietary fund reporting includes:
- Statements of net position, in a net position format (although a balance sheet format may be used),
- Statements of revenues, expenses, and changes in fund net position, and
- Statements of cash flows but prepared using the direct method.

The economic resources measurement focus and accrual basis of accounting is used for the accounting and financial reporting of proprietary funds [GASB Cod. Sec. 1300.101(b)]. Since the measurement focus and basis of accounting is the same as the government-wide financial statements, few reconciliation entries may be necessary to reconcile the funds to the government-wide financial statements.

ENTERPRISE FUNDS

An enterprise fund may be used to "report any activity for which a fee is charged to external users for goods or services." Activities are required to be reported as enterprise funds if any of the following criteria is met, after applying each of these criteria by considering the activity's *principal revenue sources* [GASB Cod. Sec. 1300.109]:

- The activity is financed with debt that is secured *solely* by a pledge of the net revenues from fees and charges of the activity. However, debt that is secured by a pledge of net revenues from fees and charges *as well as* the full faith and credit of a related primary government or component unit, even if that government is not expected to make any payments, is *not* payable *solely* from fees and charges of the activity.
- The pricing policies of the activity establish fees and charges designed to recover its costs, including capital costs (such as depreciation or debt service).
- Laws or regulations require that the activity's costs of providing services, including capital costs (such as depreciation or capital debt service), be recovered with fees and charges, rather than with taxes or similar revenues.

Many activities that are financed by debt are denominated as "revenue credits" or similar. As revenue credits, they are paid by a pledge of the net revenues from applicable fees and charges securing the debt. Therefore, to increase the marketability or security of the pledge, many governments place an additional pledge of the full faith and credit of the government. Therefore, the criteria may be difficult to attain in some circumstances.

GAAP does not consider the word *activity* in the same manner as *fund*. GASB Cod. Sec. 1300.705-3 reminds practitioners there could be two consequences where and *activity* does not result in a fund:

- If an activity accounted for as a separate fund meets any of the criteria, that fund should be reported as an enterprise fund, and
- If a "multiple activity" fund such as the general fund includes a *significant activity* with a principal revenue source meeting the criteria, the activity should be reclassified as an enterprise fund.

Administrative costs of the funds should be included in the general fund unless legal requirements exist that require the accounting and financial reporting of the resources in another fund. If the administrative activity *is not* required to be accounted for in an unemployment compensation enterprise fund, GASB Cod. Sec. 1300.705-8 surmises that such a requirement would invalidate the reasoning that an enterprise fund is required as the charges are not designed to recover the costs of administration. The word "depreciation" also includes amortization of intangible assets [GASB Cod. Sec. 1300, fn. 5].

State Unemployment Compensation Funds and Public Entity Risk Pools. GASB Cod. Sec. 1300, fn. 6, specifically requires state unemployment compensation funds to be reported in enterprise funds due to this criterion. Public entity risk pools must also be reported in enterprise funds in accordance with GASB Cod. Sec. Po20.115.

The above criteria have no requirements to consider *insignificant* activities of governments to be reported as enterprise funds. Fees for services are often paid as part of cost recovery of the service. For example, a building permit issuance may have a fee. But such fees are not the principal revenue source of a building department of a local government—an apportionment of taxation usually is. However, for a local government's utilities (water, sewer, electric, etc.) charges to customers are the principal revenue source for the utility and therefore, an enterprise fund is proper. If none of the criteria apply, the activity can be accounted for in a governmental fund.

The phrase *principal revenue source* is different from *major fund* as discussed in Chapter 6. GASB Cod. Sec. 1300.705-4 clarifies that determining a principal revenue source is a matter of the professional judgment of management. A government may compare pledged revenue to total revenues to make this determination or activity fees to total revenues.

Some proprietary activities do not have formal pricing policies other than an operating budget to recover budgeted costs and potentially depreciation. GASB Cod. Sec. 1300.705-6 discusses how the operating budget produces a rate scenario to comply with the recovery of costs, which derives an equivalency to a pricing policy.

PRACTICE POINT: Many enterprise funds utilizing this scenario may not include an expense for defined benefit pensions or defined benefit postemployment benefits other than pensions (OPEB). GASB Cod. Sec. P50.710-1 (among other related questions) reminds practitioners there are no specific requirements for allocation of the net OPEB or pension liability or other OPEB or pension-related measures to individual funds. Consideration needs to be made to GAAP provisions on recording liabilities in GASB Cod. Sec. 1500.102 which requires long-term liabilities that are "directly related to and expected to be paid from" those funds to be reported in the Statement of Net Position.

Some financial statement preparers raised the question about whether the three criteria listed above apply to activities that are currently accounted for in internal service funds. GAAP takes the position that an enterprise fund, not an internal service fund, must be used when external users are the predominant participants in the fund [GASB Cod. Sec. 1300, fn. 7]. (See section later in this chapter titled "Internal Service Funds.")

The first criterion refers to debt secured solely by fees and charges. If that debt is secured by a pledge of fees and charges from the activity and the full faith and credit of the primary government or component unit, this arrangement does not satisfy the "sole source of debt security" and the activity does not have to be accounted for (assuming the other two criteria are not satisfied) in an enterprise fund. This conclusion is not changed even if it is anticipated that the primary government or component unit is not expected to make debt payments under the arrangement. On the other hand, debt that is secured partially by a portion of its own proceeds does satisfy the "sole source of debt security" criterion.

The second and third criteria refer to the establishment of a pricing policy that recovers costs, including depreciation expense or debt service. In some situations, the activity might be responsible for little or no debt. GASB Cod. Sec. 1300.705-5, states that in this circumstance, the criteria are still met if the pricing policy is designed to recover *either* depreciation or debt service requirements (principal and interest). There is no assumption that there is equality between the depreciation expense and the debt service on capital debt for an activity.

The third criterion is like the previous standard for determining when an enterprise fund should be used to account for an activity except that the principles contained in GAAP are based on "established policies" rather than management's intent.

> **OBSERVATION:** If the enterprise fund also receives revenue from federal sources, special guidelines about the level of non-federal revenue required to be raised from non-federal sources may be part of the federal grant conditions. These guidelines are typically found in public transportation grants.

Commonly reported as enterprise fund activities of state and local governments include the following:

- Airports,
- Electric, gas, water, wastewater, and sanitation/landfills and similar utilities (see subsection on regulated operations discussing GASB Cod. Sec. Re10, later in this chapter and in Chapter 24),
- Golf courses,
- Hospital or other health care services,
- Institutions of higher education that do not have the power to tax separately,
- Lotteries and gaming,
- Parking and transit, and
- Unemployment insurance (States only).

Note that some lotteries are accounted for as governmental funds, following a rationale that they are mainly cash flow mechanisms for the government rather than entities that meet the criteria for an enterprise fund.

> **PRACTICE POINT:** Reporting by lotteries and gaming entities have specialized guidance in GAAP, primarily from AICPA literature cleared by the GASB. Lottery prize costs are accrued based on a percentage of ticket sales revenues. Prizes can be paid during a current period at a present value or over a period of years in an annuity funded through insurance or through U.S. Treasury securities. If a purchased annuity is in the name of a prize winner, no liability or asset is recognized as the liability has been discharged. However, a contingent liability may exist. If not in the name of the winner, then the present value of the liability is presented. The prize liability also includes prizes won but not yet claimed and anticipated prizes for games in progress at period end [GASB Cod. Secs. P80.807–.810].
>
> Gaming entities have similar accounting and financial reporting. As the games are highly specialized, entities should review GASB Cod. Secs. P80.811–.822 for applicable guidance for games in use.

Separate enterprise activities of a government may not require separate funds. GASB Cod. Sec. 1300.705-10 discusses that even in the situation where each activity issues bonds repayable solely from the activity, they may only need to be reported in the government-wide Statement of Activities as separately identifiable operations or functions. The activities may be required to be reported as "segments" though due to the provisions of the bonds. Segment information reporting is discussed later in this chapter.

Blended Component Units That Are Enterprise Activities. Blended component units are commonly enterprise activities. GASB Cod. Sec. 1300.705-11 contains a scenario where a county government creates a recreation authority component unit to construction facilities. The facilities are financed by bond issuances. The county leases the facilities from the authority, with the lease payments securing the debt service. The authority is required to be reported as an enterprise fund as the county is "external" relative to the authority's separately issued financial statements. The lease payments are fees charged to recover costs.

Special Assessment Debt. If special assessment debt is issued by a government in which the government is not obligated in any manner and the debt is secured solely from fees and charges, enterprise fund accounting and financial reporting may not apply. GASB Cod. Sec. 1300.705-16 discusses how such debt may not result in an "activity" for which external users are charged a fee for goods or services. Capital assets are constructed by special assessment debt, enhancing the value of the properties of the benefitted owners. The owners then pay the debt service on the bonds.

Alternatively, if a government *is obligated* for special assessment debt and the debt is expected to be paid from proprietary funds, all transactions related to such debt should be reported like other debt paid from proprietary funds. Assessment revenue and receivables are recognized on the accrual basis of accounting. The cost of the capital improvements financed by the special assessment debt are capitalized on the enterprise fund's Statement of Net Position. An equal amount is reported as a capital contribution in the statement of revenues, expenses, and changes in fund net position.

The liability recognized for the special assessment debt is only the amount that is a direct obligation of the fund (or if not a direct obligation, expected to be paid from the fund) [GASB Cod. Secs. S40.121-.123].

PRACTICE POINT: Governments *may* report all transactions and balances related to projects funded by special assessments, enhancing accountability. As discussed in GASB Cod. Sec. S40.123, billing and collecting of assessments, debt service, and project outlays would be reported in the fund. The assessments to owners would be recognized as a receivable at the time of levy. Debt would be reported as a liability upon issuance. Collections of assessments would reduce the receivable and debt service would reduce the debt liability. Interest income and expense would be accrued. A further discussion on special assessments is presented in Chapter 19.

INTERNAL SERVICE FUNDS

An internal service fund is a proprietary fund that may be used to report "any activity that provides goods or services to other funds, departments, or agencies of the primary government and its component units, or to other governments, on a cost reimbursement basis." An internal service fund should be used only *when the reporting government itself* is the predominant participant in the fund. When the transactions with the other governmental entities represent the predominant portion of the activity, an enterprise fund must be used [GASB Cod. Sec. 1300.110].

As discussed in GASB Cod. Sec. 1300.705-9, GASB Cod. Sec. 1300.110 does not define at what exact point a government is or is not the predominant participant. Therefore, preparer (and auditor) judgment is required.

There is no circumstance under which an internal service fund *must* be used. For example, an activity may be centralized by a governmental entity whereby all departments, programs, and so forth within the reporting entity must use the centralized activity and be billed for the service provided. That activity could be accounted for in an internal service fund. The activity could also be accounted for in another governmental fund (probably the General Fund).

PRACTICE POINT: The answer to GASB Cod. Sec. 1300.705-9 further clarifies that *usually* the *predominance* of the government will be clear. In cases where it is unclear, consideration can be made as to whether:

- The fund's primary purpose is to serve the government (and the nongovernmental activity is incidental), or
- The fund's primary purpose is to provide, and charge a fee for, goods and services and the government is a "customer" (presumably charged the same fee for goods and services that a nongovernmental "customer" would be charged).

Activities commonly reported as internal service funds of state and local governments include the following:

- Central services, such as purchasing, warehousing, information systems, and similar processes that are allocable and applicable to multiple areas of a government,
- Risk management and self-insurance, and
- Vehicle and equipment maintenance.

For internal service fund activities that are reimbursed from federal funds, the *Uniform Administrative Requirements, Cost Principles, and Audit Requirements for Federal Awards,* Subpart E places stringent requirements on what can be charged as an "allowable cost," with an emphasis on consistent accounting no matter what the source of funds is. Budgeted allocations from internal service funds are usually regularly reviewed and approved by a federal agency as part of the setting of rates and charges in accordance with an indirect (overhead) rate. Complete coverage of the *Uniform Administrative Requirements, Cost Principles, and Audit Requirements for Federal Awards* from an auditing perspective is found in CCH's *Knowledge-Based Audits™ of State and Local Governments with Single Audits*.

PROPRIETARY FUND ACCOUNTING AND REPORTING

Basis of Accounting and Measurement Focus

The economic resources measurement focus and the accrual basis of accounting are used to prepare the financial statements of a proprietary fund. These concepts are discussed in Chapter 3. Proprietary funds report based on all applicable GAAP, unless the fund is subjected to regulatory accounting as provided in GASB Cod. Sec. Re10 [GASB Cod. Secs. P80.101–.103]. As previously discussed, required financial statements for proprietary funds are:

- Statements of net position, in a net position format (although a balance sheet format may be used),
- Statements of revenues, expenses, and changes in fund net position, and
- Statements of cash flows prepared using the direct method [GASB Cod. Sec. P80.104, fn. 2].

Budgetary System and Accounts—Proprietary Funds. Although GAAP recommends that all funds adopt a budget for control purposes, it recognized that the nature of budgeting is different for governmental funds and proprietary funds. Generally, budgeted proprietary funds utilize a flexible budget, which reflects changes in the activity level. A fixed budget is inappropriate for proprietary funds because, in a fixed budget, overall activity is measured in terms of revenues and expenses and will fluctuate, in part, depending on the demand for goods and services by the public or governmental agencies. The flexible budget does not provide a basis for appropriations. It serves as an approved financial plan that can facilitate budgetary control and operational evaluations. A flexible budget approach allows the governmental unit to prepare several budgets at different activity levels to establish an acceptable comparative basis for planned activity and actual results.

The basis of accounting used to prepare a budget for a proprietary fund should be the same as the basis used to record the results of actual transactions. It is not appropriate to integrate the budgetary accounts into the proprietary fund's accounting system.

As a proprietary fund is generally not subject to a legislatively adopted budget, governmental entities are normally not required to use an encumbrance system to control executory contracts and other commitments for such funds.

Focus on Major Funds. Like governmental funds, the focus on proprietary fund financial statements is on major funds. The financial information of each major proprietary fund is presented in a separate column in the proprietary fund statements. nonmajor funds are aggregated and displayed in a single column. Only one nonmajor fund column is presented in accordance with GASB Cod. Sec. P80.704-2.

Major fund reporting requirements are not applicable for internal service funds. Combining statements for nonmajor funds may be presented as supplementary information but are only required to be presented in Annual Comprehensive Financial Reports (ACFRs).

The calculation of a major proprietary fund is the same as for governmental funds. Both use the following criteria:

1. The total of assets and deferred outflows of resources, the total of liabilities and deferred inflows of resources, revenues, or expenses (excluding extraordinary items) of that individual enterprise fund are at least 10% of the corresponding element(s) total (total of assets and deferred outflows of resources, total of liabilities and deferred inflows of resources, and so forth) for all funds of that category or type (i.e., total enterprise funds), *and*

2. The same element(s) that met the 10% criterion in (a) is at least 5% of the corresponding element(s) total for all enterprise funds combined.

The major fund determination is based on total fund revenues and expenses including both operating and nonoperating categories in accordance with GASB Cod. Sec. P80.704-9. Governments also have flexibility in determining if a proprietary fund is important to be classified as a major fund, even though it may not meet the criteria to be reported as such [GASB Cod. Secs. P80.105–.106, fns. 4–5].

PRACTICE POINT: Care must be taken in this decision. The independent auditor's report for a state and local government is based on "opinion units" which include each major fund and the remaining nonmajor funds in the aggregate.

PRACTICE ALERT: GASB Cod. Sec. 2250.127(b) includes a change in a fund's presentation as major or nonmajor as triggering a change to or within the financial reporting entity in accordance with GASB Statement No. 100 (*Accounting Changes and Error Corrections*). If a change occurs, the change requires an adjustment of the current reporting period's fund net position, as applicable, for the impact of the change as if the change occurred as of the beginning of the reporting period. The change's presentation would change the presentation of the fund balance for nonmajor funds and the individual fund as a major fund. Due to the audit concept of opinion units, the independent auditor's report would also provide disclosure of such a change. Note disclosure would be required, limited to only the nature of the change in a case where the fund's presentation no longer meets the thresholds to be a major fund. GASB Statement No. 100 became effective for periods beginning after June 15, 2023.

Reconciliation to the Government-wide Statements. As previously introduced, a reconciliation from the proprietary fund statements to the government-wide statements may be necessary. The reconciliation may be at the bottom of the financial statements or in a separate schedule following the Statement of Net Position and the statement of revenues, expenses, and changes in fund net position. In most cases where a reconciling item impacts a proprietary activity, the item involves reclassification of internal service fund information [GASB Cod. Secs. P80.107–.108].

If a reconciling item is so summarized that it obscures the nature of the individual elements of an adjustment, GASB Cod. Sec. P80.705-3 discusses how generally a note disclosure is prepared for the combined adjustment. The reconciliation may include elements of long-term liabilities that are aggregated. Therefore, in the note, disclosure is included for amounts of debt and other payables, compensated absences, claims and judgments, and other applicable items.

Separate Internal Service Fund Presentation. Major fund reporting does not apply to internal service funds. The combined totals of all internal service funds are then presented to the right of the total enterprise fund column on the face of the proprietary fund statements. Like proprietary fund statements, combining schedules may be presented as supplementary information [GASB Cod. Secs. P80.109, P80.706-2].

Eliminating internal service fund activity does not impact the major fund determination above. GASB Cod. Sec. P80.704-16 clarifies that the elimination is an adjustment and major funds are determined without the adjustment's regard and any possible look-back adjustments.

PROPRIETARY FUND FINANCIAL STATEMENTS

Statement of Net Position

GAAP require presentation of a Statement of Net Position for proprietary funds in a *classified* format, distinguishing current and long-term assets, and liabilities.

The Statement of Net Position may be presented in either one of the following formats:

- Net position format: assets plus deferred outflows of resources less liabilities less deferred inflows of resources equal net position, or
- Balance sheet format: assets plus deferred outflows of resources equals liabilities plus deferred outflows of resources plus net position.

Exhibit 20-5 in Chapter 20 illustrates a Statement of Net Position for proprietary funds using the net position format.

No matter the format used, net position is the residual of all the other elements—not net assets, fund balance or equity. Net position is inclusive of the same three components as the government-wide Statement of Net Position:

- Net investment in capital assets,
- Restricted net position, separating the major categories of restrictions), and
- Unrestricted net position.

Capital contributions and designated amounts are not displayed in the net position section [GASB Cod. Secs. P80.110–.111].

7010 Fund Accounting

Accounting and Reporting Issues—Assets in Proprietary Funds

Current assets. The definition of current assets in proprietary funds aligns to the definition of current assets as presented in the government-wide Statement of Net Position. The term is most often used to designate cash and other assets (or resources) commonly identified as those that are reasonably expected to be realized in cash or sold or consumed within a year.

Current assets generally include such resources as:

- Cash available for current operations and items that are the equivalent of cash,
- Inventories of merchandise, raw materials, goods in process, finished goods, operating supplies, and ordinary maintenance material and parts,
- Trade accounts, notes, and acceptances receivable (discounts, finance charges, and interest are deducted from these amounts),
- Receivables from taxpayers, other governments, vendors, customers, beneficiaries, and employees if collectible within a year,
- Installment or accounts and notes receivable if they conform generally to normal trade practices and terms within the business-type activity,
- Marketable securities representing the investment of cash available for current operations, and
- Prepayments such as insurance, interest, rents, unused royalties, current paid advertising service not yet received, and operating supplies.
- Prepayments are not current assets in the sense that they will be converted into cash but in the sense that, if not paid in advance, they would require the use of current assets within a year [GASB Cod. Secs. 2200.175–.178].

Reporting restrictions on asset use. In a proprietary fund it is assumed that assets (especially current assets) are unrestricted in that there are no conditions that would prevent the governmental entity from using the resources to pay existing liabilities. If the name of the asset account does not adequately explain the normally perceived availability of that asset, the item should be identified as a restricted asset on the Statement of Net Position.

For example, an amount of cash may be restricted to a specific type of expense (e.g., debt service) and therefore it would be misleading to report the restricted cash with all other unrestricted cash (classified as current assets). Under this circumstance, the cash should be reported as restricted cash in the financial statement category labeled noncurrent assets.

On the other hand, cash that is restricted for purposes related to current operations (such as cash restricted for repairs and maintenance) should be labeled as restricted cash but be reported as current assets. Equipment and other capital assets are not available to pay liabilities, but the title of the account adequately describes the availability (or lack of liquidity) of the asset and therefore there is no need to identify the asset as restricted [GASB Cod. Sec. P80.112].

For many proprietary funds, noncurrent assets commonly exclude (depending on facts and circumstances):

- Cash and claims to cash that cannot be used for current operations and that are to be disbursed to acquire or construct noncurrent assets or that are segregated for the liquidation of long-term debts,
- Receivables arising from unusual transactions (such as the sale of capital assets) that are not expected to be collected within 12 months, and
- Cash surrender value of life insurance policies.

Noncurrent assets include, but are not limited to:

- Land and other natural resources,
- Depreciable assets, and
- Long-term prepayments applicable to several years' operations or are deferred outflows of resources such as prepayments under a long-term lease.

Interest capitalization. Interest cost incurred during the construction of capital assets of a proprietary fund *is not* capitalized unless interest capitalization is required for regulated operational purposes. Interest is a period expense. GASB Statement No. 89 (*Accounting for Interest Cost Incurred before the end of a Construction Period*) superseded interest capitalization provisions upon implementation.

Infrastructure assets. GASB Cod. Sec. 1400.703-5 discusses how the modified approach may be applied to eligible infrastructure assets accounted for as either governmental activities or business-type activities. For example, an enterprise fund that owns a toll road (which is an infrastructure asset) could use the modified approach. If the enterprise fund uses the modified approach, it should be used in the preparation of both the government-wide and proprietary fund financial statements. See Chapter 10 for further discussion of infrastructure assets and the modified approach.

Customer deposits for utility services. Governmental entities that provide utility services, such as electric, water, sewer, and gas, may require deposits from customers, or a governmental entity may charge developers and/or customers system development fees (tap fees). A customer deposit is generally required to be paid before a service is turned on, and when the service is terminated, the deposit is returned to the customer. Utility services are generally accounted for as enterprise funds, and the AICPA's Audit and Accounting Guide *State and Local Governments* points out that receipts of customer deposits should be recorded as a liability and continue to be reported as such until they are "applied against unpaid billings or refunded to customers." Generally, these customer deposits are reported as restricted assets and offset with a corresponding liability payable from restricted assets [GASB Cod. Sec. P80.806].

Customer system development fees. The AICPA's *State and Local Governments* Guide also notes that the initial receipt of a customer system development fee should be recorded as a liability and recognized as revenue using the general guidance related to either an exchange transaction or a nonexchange transaction.

In an exchange transaction the governmental entity and the other party to the transaction exchange cash, goods, or services that are essentially of the same value.

A nonexchange transaction arises when the transfer of goods or services between two parties is not of equal value. See Chapter 17 for a discussion of nonexchange revenues.

Accounting and Reporting Issues—Liabilities in Proprietary Funds

Unlike governmental funds, a proprietary fund reports both current and noncurrent liabilities expected to be paid from the fund. A proprietary fund may receive the proceeds from the issuance of either general obligation bonds or revenue bonds, but in either circumstance the receipt of the proceeds coupled with the requirement to repay such debt results in a proprietary fund liability.

As previously discussed, liabilities in proprietary funds are directly related to and expected to be paid from the fund [GASB Cod. Sec. 1500.102]. Current liabilities presented in proprietary funds include accounts payable and other accrued liabilities.

The term *current liabilities* is used principally to designate obligations whose liquidation is reasonably expected to require the use of existing resources properly classifiable as current assets, or the creation of other current liabilities. The classification is intended to include obligations for items that are part of operations of the fund, commonly including:

- Payables incurred in the acquisition of materials and supplies to be used in providing services,
- Collections received in advance of the performance of services, and
- Debts arising from operations directly related to the fund's operations including accruals for wages, salaries, commissions, rentals, and royalties.

Other liabilities whose regular and ordinary liquidation is expected to occur within one year also are intended for inclusion, such as:

- Short-term debts arising from the acquisition of capital assets,
- Serial maturities of long-term obligations,
- Amounts required to be expended within one year under sinking fund provisions, and
- Certain agency obligations arising from the collection or acceptance of cash or other assets for the account of third parties [GASB Cod. Secs. 2200.180–.181].

A proprietary fund's *long-term liabilities* (alternatively presented as *noncurrent liabilities*) may include obligations other than those that arise from the issuance of a security debt instrument. These other obligations may be created from leases, claims and judgments, landfill closure and postclosure care, pollution remediation, employee termination benefits, pensions, and postemployment benefits other than pensions (OPEB).

However, the largest liability of all classifications presented in proprietary funds tends to be debt. Debt is presented with other long-term liabilities in a current portion (or a portion due or payable within one year) and a long-term portion (or a portion due or payable after one year).

Debt. A governmental entity may issue debt whereby the proceeds are used to construct capital assets reported in a proprietary fund. If the debt is directly related to and expected to be paid from the proprietary fund, both the capital asset and the debt are reported in the proprietary fund financial statements and the business-type activities column of the government-wide Statement of Net Position.

Debt may be in the form of *revenue bonds*. With revenue bonds, principal and interest is paid exclusively from the earnings of a proprietary fund. If the debt is also secured by specific capital assets of the proprietary fund, they are referred to as mortgage revenue bonds. Revenue bonds, both current and long-term portion, are recorded as a liability of the Enterprise Fund.

Statement of Revenues, Expenses, and Changes in Fund Net Position

The operating statement of a proprietary fund is the statement of revenues, expenses, and changes in fund net position. In preparing this statement:

- Revenues should be reported by major source, and
- Revenues restricted for the payment of revenue bonds should be identified.

The following categories (as applicable to the fund's operations) are presented in the statement:

Operating revenues (detailed),
    Total operating revenues,
Operating expenses (detailed),
    Total operating expenses,
    Operating income (loss),
Nonoperating revenues and expenses (detailed),
    An *Optional* Subtotal,
    Income before other revenues, expenses, gains, losses, and transfers,
    Capital contributions (grant, developer, and other),
    Additions to permanent and term endowments,
    Special and extraordinary items (detailed), and
    Transfers,
    Increase (decrease) in net position,
    Net position—beginning of period, and
    Net position—end of period.

Revenues are required to be reported net of discounts and allowances, with the discount disclosed in a parenthesis on the face of the statement of revenues, expenses, and changes in net position or in a note to the basic financial statements. Many governments report gross revenues with the related discount and/or allowances reported directly beneath the gross revenue amount [GASB Cod. Secs. P80.113–.114, fn. 6].

Operating Revenues and Expenses. Operating revenues and expenses differ from government to government. Many governments attempt to align the definition of operating revenues and expenses in a similar fashion to peer nongovernmental organizations. GASB Cod. Sec. P80.115 requires a policy defining operating revenues and expenses that is "appropriate to the nature of the activity being reported." This policy needs to be consistently applied.

PRACTICE ALERT: The GASB's *Financial Reporting Model Improvements* Exposure Draft presents a proposed revision to a government's flexibility in determining operating revenues and expenses. The Board's conclusion is that operating revenues and expenses should be defined as revenues and expenses *other than nonoperating* revenues and expenses.

Nonoperating revenues and expenses are proposed to include:

- Subsidies received and provided,
- Revenues and expenses related to financing,
- Resources from the disposal of capital assets and inventory, and
- Investment income and expenses.

Other elements of nonoperating versus operating revenues and expenses as proposed:

- Nonroutine and nonrecurring items are not included in the description of nonoperating revenues and expenses as they are self-evident,
- When investing or financing activities are the primary purpose of a proprietary fund, those revenues and expenses are operating revenues and expenses, and
- Capital contributions, additions to permanent and term endowments, and transfers are included in the definition of "subsidies" described in the next paragraph.

In an updated statement of revenues, expenses and changes in fund net position, a subtotal for operating income (loss) and noncapital subsidies should be presented before reporting other nonoperating revenues and expenses. The Board has proposed a definition of "subsidies" as resources provided by another party or fund to keep rates lower than otherwise would be necessary to support the level of goods or services provided.

Chapter 20 illustrates a statement of revenues, expenses, and changes in net position for proprietary funds.

Accounting and Reporting Issues—Revenues in Proprietary Funds

A proprietary fund should recognize revenue on an accrual basis, meaning that revenue is considered realized when:

- The earning process is complete or virtually complete, and
- An exchange has taken place.

Water, sewer, and other enterprise funds likely have unbilled revenue at the end of an accounting period. Whether revenue is billed or unbilled is not the critical issue in the recognition of revenue in a proprietary fund. When a service has been provided (e.g., the consumption of a service by a customer), the related revenue should be recognized.

Uncollectible accounts related to revenue. GASB Cod. Sec. P80, fn. 6, requires that revenues be reported net of related discounts or allowances. The amount of the discounts or allowances must be presented on the operating statement (either parenthetically or as a subtraction from gross revenues) or in a note to the financial statements. GAAP does not require that estimates of bad debt expenses be reported as an offset to revenues as GASB Cod. Sec. 2200.751-2 states that estimates of uncollectible accounts should be presented in a manner like discounts and allowances. That is, revenues should be reported net of the increase or decrease of the estimate of uncollectible accounts.

Capital contributions from governmental funds. A proprietary fund must consider the nature of a capital contribution received from another fund. For example, GASB Cod. Sec. 2200.739-1 discusses the reassignment of a capital asset between an enterprise fund and governmental activities. If the assets reassigned from governmental activities to an enterprise fund are capital assets, the transaction is not "interfund" because it involves only one fund, consequently, the enterprise fund would report the receipt of the capital assets as a capital contribution from governmental activities (in the last section of the statement of revenues, expenses, and changes in fund net position).

In the reverse situation, in which a capital asset is reassigned from an enterprise fund to governmental activities, the disposal of the capital asset would be reported by the enterprise fund as a nonoperating expense. In either case, governmental funds would not report the event because there has been no flow of current financial resources. In the Statement of Activities, the reassignment of the capital asset between governmental activities and business-type activities would be reported as a transfer, requiring a reconciling item in the governmental funds' reconciliation because a difference is created between the change in fund balances and the change in total net position.

In both cases, since the transfer consists of nonfinancial resources (a capital asset), *the governmental fund will not record the transfer* (because only financial resources are accounted for in a governmental fund), *however, the proprietary fund will record the transaction not as a transfer but as capital contribution revenue in the lower portion of its operating statement*. Even though the transfer is not presented in the governmental fund it must be presented as a transfer in the governmental activities' column in the Statement of Activities, however, the inconsistency between the treatment of the transfer at the fund financial statement level and the government-wide financial statement level would generate a reconciling item for the governmental fund's operating statement and a related note disclosure.

Proceeds from no-obligation bonds issued by a financing authority. Many governments use financing authorities to issue tax exempt debt, especially public healthcare entities and institutions of higher education. If the government has no obligation to make payments of principal and interest on the debt (or lease payments on related buildings and equipment), proceeds are reported as contributions from the sponsoring government [GASB Cod. Sec. P80.801].

See Chapter 24 on accounting and financial reporting guidance regarding such entities.

CARES Act (and Similar) Grant Programs

GASB Technical Bulletin 2020-1, *Accounting and Financial Reporting Issues Related to the Coronavirus Aid, Relief, and Economic Security Act (CARES Act) and Coronavirus Diseases* (GASB: TB 2020-1) includes a question on inflows of resources from the Coronavirus Aid, Relief, and Economic Security (CARES) Act. Question 2 discusses provider relief from the U.S. Department of Health and Human Services, the Higher Education Emergency Relief Fund from the U.S. Department of Education, the CARES Act Airport Grants from the Federal Aviation Administration, and the Formula Grants for Rural Areas and Urbanized Area Formula Grants programs from the Federal Transit Administration. A common concern from recipients of those grants programs in the CARES Act was whether those inflows are reported as nonoperating revenues. Other federal aid programs may have a similar impact.

GASB Cod. Sec. 2200.193 discusses that preparers should consider how the inflows are reported in the entity's statement of cash flows. GASB Cod. Sec. 2450.119 identifies noncapital grants as noncapital financing activities in a statement of cash flows *unless* those grants are contracts for services. Further, GASB Cod. Sec. 2450.708-5 establishes that grants, in general, should be reported as nonoperating activities, again, unless the inflows represent contracts for services.

In the instances of the grant programs in the Technical Bulletin, the GASB determined that those resources support specific activities and reimburse allowable costs like many other grants, rather than paying for specific services in the form of a contract. Further, the GASB noted that the programs are provided as subsidies, unless they constitute payment for services.

CARES Act Payments for Services. Where the grant programs *would constitute* a payment of services in the CARES Act would be in the Provider Relief Fund's Uninsured Program from the U.S. Department of Health and Human Services. In this program, payments are made for care and treatment of uninsured individuals and testing for SARS-CoV-2 (COVID-19). As the resources received for this specific program constitute payments for services provided, the resources would be reported as operating revenues [GASB Cod. Sec. P80.601].

Accounting and Reporting Issues—Expenses in Proprietary Funds

Unlike governmental funds that report expenditures related to the use of financial resources, proprietary funds report *expenses* related to the use of economic resources. For example, a proprietary fund would record a loss contingency as an expense irrespective of when the related liability is expected to be paid or financial resource used.

Defining an expense. As discussed previously in the subsection on operating and nonoperating revenues and expenses, policies are established on recognition of operating and nonoperating, which must be used consistently from period to period and disclosed in the summary of significant accounting policies in the notes to the basic financial statements. GAAP discusses considering the delineation for the purposes of preparing the Statement of Cash Flows for proprietary funds (see later in this chapter).

Transactions for which cash flows are reported as capital and related financing activities, noncapital financing activities, or investing activities normally would *not* be reported as components of operating income, *unless the transactions in those categories are the fund's principal ongoing operation*. The GASB provides an example of interest expense by a proprietary fund established to provide loans to first-time homeowners [GASB Cod. Sec. 2200.192, fn. 45].

Once defined as either operating or nonoperating, categorization may take place for proper placement in the Statement of Revenues, Expenses and Changes in Fund Net Position.

Depreciation (and amortization) expense. All depreciable capital assets of a proprietary fund must be depreciated in accordance with generally accepted accounting principles as applied by a commercial enterprise.

OBSERVATION: Any established depreciation or amortization method is acceptable if it is systematic and rational. GASB Cod. Sec. 1400.739-1, lists possible methods including:

- The straight-line method,
- Decreasing-charge methods, which include declining-balance, double-declining-balance, and sum-of-the-years' digits, among others,
- Increasing-charge methods, and
- Unit-of-production/service methods, which allocate the depreciable cost of an asset over its expected output.

In practice, the straight-line method is most common as the other methods may provide taxation advantages, which are not applicable to governments. A further discussion on capital assets is contained in Chapter 10.

PRACTICE POINT: Intangible "right-to-use" assets that may be related to leases, public-private and public-public partnerships, availability payment arrangements and subscription-based information technology (SBITA) arrangements are amortized over the shorter of the arrangement term or the useful life of the underlying asset using a systematic and rational method. The amortization of the right-to-use assets may be combined with depreciation expense related to other capital assets for financial reporting purposes. However, in such contracts, amortization does not begin until the contract term begins, which may be years removed from the effective date due to construction or SBITA implementation. In practice, most amortizations will occur using the straight-line method for such contracts.

Uncollectible accounts related to nonrevenue transactions. A governmental entity may make loans to other parties and subsequently must write off those loans as uncollectible. A change in the allowance for uncollectible accounts not related to revenue transactions must be presented as an expense rather than netted against revenue, because there is no related revenue account.

Payments in lieu of taxes (or PILOT payments). An enterprise fund, such as a housing authority fund or a transportation entity, may make a payment to a local government in lieu of the payment of property taxes. For a transaction to be presented as an expense by an enterprise fund, it must be considered an exchange or exchange-like transaction.

An exchange transaction occurs when two parties exchange assets or commitments of approximately equal value.

The GASB defines an exchange-like transaction as being "an identifiable exchange between the reporting government and another party, but the values exchanged may not be quite equal or the direct benefits of the exchange may not be exclusively for the parties to the exchange." Payments in lieu of taxes should be reported as expenses because they can be considered exchange-like transactions.

Pension (and postemployment benefits other than pensions). If compensation is paid from a proprietary fund, then employee benefits would also be declared as an expense, even if allocated.

Statement of Cash Flows

Proprietary funds should present a statement of cash flows based on the guidance contained in GASB Cod. Sec. 2450, formatted based on the *direct method* in computing cash flows from operating activities. The statement of cash flows would be supplemented with a reconciliation of operating cash flows and operating income [GASB Cod. Sec. P80.117].

Proprietary funds with no operating income or loss still must present a statement of cash flows. GASB Cod. Sec. P80.703-1 discusses how in this case, transactions other than those resulting in operating income create cash flows. The reconciliation of operating income to net cash flow from operating activities would begin with zero. Adjustments and reconciling items are then presented as additions to and deductions from zero to arrive at the amount of net cash flow from operating activities.

Chapter 20 illustrates a statement of cash flows for enterprise funds.

SEGMENT INFORMATION

Segment Information: Enterprise Funds

Segment disclosures must be made by governmental entities that report enterprise funds or that use enterprise fund accounting and reporting standards to report activities in the notes to the financial statements. Often, reporting is imposed by an external party, typically in bond indentures [GASB Cod. Sec. 2500, fn. 2].

For disclosure, GASB Cod. Sec. 2500.101 defines a segment as an identifiable activity (or grouping of activities) reported as or within an enterprise fund or an other stand-alone entity that has one or more bonds or other debt instruments (such as certificates of participation) outstanding, with a revenue stream pledged in support of that debt. In addition, the activity's revenues, expenses, gains and losses, assets and liabilities are required to be accounted for separately.

Segment disclosures are not required for an activity only with conduit debt outstanding for which the government has no obligation beyond the resources provided in the related leases and loans. Such reporting is also not required when an individual fund is *both* a segment and is reported as a major fund [GASB Cod. Sec. 2500. fn. 1].

The following segment disclosures should be made by providing condensed financial statements in a note(s) to the basic financial statements:

- A description of the goods or services provided by the segment.
- Condensed Statement of Net Position that includes the following:
  — Total assets: Distinguishing between current assets, capital assets, and other assets (amounts receivable from other funds or component units should be reported separately),
  — Total deferred outflows of resources,
  — Total liabilities: Distinguishing between current and long-term amounts (amounts payable to other funds or component units should be reported separately),
  — Total deferred inflows of resources, and
  — Total fund net position: Distinguishing between restricted, unrestricted, and amounts invested in capital assets (net of related debt), with separate identification of expendable and nonexpendable components for restricted net position, if appropriate.
- Condensed statement of revenues, expenses, and changes in net position:
  — Operating revenues by major sources,
  — Operating expenses, with separate identification of depreciation expense and amortizations of long- lived assets,
  — Operating income (loss),
  — Nonoperating revenues (expenses), with separate reporting of major revenues and expenses,
  — Capital contributions and additions to permanent and term endowments,
  — Extraordinary and special items,
  — Transfers,
  — Changes in net position, and
  — Beginning and ending net position.
- Condensed statement of cash flows:
  — Net cash provided (used by):
    • Operating activities,
    • Noncapital financing activities,

- Capital and related financing activities,
- Investing activities, and
— Beginning and ending balances of cash (or cash and cash equivalent balances).

This information is not meant to replace enterprise fund reporting for non-segments [GASB Cod. Sec. 2500.102].

GASB Cod. Secs. 2500.701-2–6 provide the following examples for determining when segment information is presented in a governmental entity's financial statements:

Fact Pattern	Suggested Guidance
A city uses a single enterprise fund to account for its water and sewer operations. Although both operations are accounted for in a single fund, the city maintains separate asset, liability, revenue, and expense accounts for each. There are outstanding revenue bonds that pertain to the water reservoir and distribution lines. The sewer operation has no long-term debt attributable to it. What are the segment reporting requirements for the Water and Sewer Fund?	Segment information for the water activity *must be disclosed* in the notes to the financial statements because that activity has "one or more revenue bonds or other revenue-backed debt instruments" outstanding. The sewer activity has no such debt and therefore segment information related to this activity does not have to be presented.
A public university has fifteen residence halls on its campus, 10 of which have individual bond debt secured by the room fee revenues of the specific dorm. Is the "identifiable activity" the entire group of 15 residence halls, or only those with revenue bonds outstanding?	As defined earlier, a segment is an activity that has an identifiable revenue stream that is dedicated to support revenue bonds or other revenue-backed debt and has identifiable expenses, gains and losses, assets, and liabilities that are related to its activities. Whether each dorm or the dorm system constitutes the segment depends on the breadth of the pledged revenue. If the pledged revenue of a specific dorm applies only to the debt of that dorm, then each dorm is considered a separate segment (ten segments). On the other hand, if the pledged revenues from all the 10 dorms apply to the dorm debt, then there is one segment (the dorm segment).

PRACTICE POINT: Recognition of the existence of a segment and presentation of the required disclosures are a frequent problem for preparers.

INTERNAL SERVICE FUND OPERATIONS

Rate Setting and Internal Service Funds (or Enterprise Funds)

Most enterprise funds and internal service funds base their operations on a rate setting process. The goal of the process is to provide enough revenues to support the full cost of operations to substantiate the operations of the fund. Determining the full cost of operations is an iterative process and in some cases is more dependent on estimations than on facts. If costs exceed budgeted amounts, a deficit may be in place and may either be carried forward and absorbed as part of the next iteration of rate setting, or a transfer occurs from the General Fund to fund the deficit. In many cases, estimated rates must be approved by a governing body prior to implementation. For example, transportation fares (a rate) may need to be approved by a local, state, or federal board.

To establish a rate, a budget must be developed with the following inputs:

- Direct salaries and wages, including overtime and other adjustments to salaries as applicable,
- Direct employee expenses that are paid from rates and charges, including pensions, OPEB and similar,
- Capital outlay applicable to the rate,
- Maintenance and supplies applicable to the rate,
- Debt service applicable to the rate, and
- Allocated indirect charges (overhead) from other funds and operations, including legal, utilities, insurance, accounting, auditing, office space, and similar.

Upon development of the estimated budget, the prior year rate is analyzed. Any estimated surplus or deficit not transferred to or from other funds is then carried forward into the new rate.

The budgeted amount is then compared to an allowable or meaningful denominator based on operations of the fund. The following could be denominators based on common enterprise or internal service funds:

Fund Operation	Denominator
Water and sewer	Gallons of flow per household per year
Airport	Parking facilities—estimated car usage in garages, takeoffs and landings, cargo tonnage, cost per square foot
Public transit	Estimated fare paying passengers (with a rate set usually at a federal minimum of 20% of total costs)
Landfill	Estimated tons per load
Dormitory	Square footage per student
Print shop	Estimated cost per page
Legal department	Estimated claims for torts
Insurance	Budgetary line item for department/agency
Information technology	Bytes of storage (or throughput)

Therefore, if $3,134,222 is estimated to be the full cost budget of a water and sewer operation and 1,970,334 gallons of flow per household is estimated for the year, then the rate would be approximately $1.59 per gallon for the year. Each billing cycle would then be based on meter readings multiplied by the $1.59 per gallon.

Differentiating between Governmental and Business-Type Activities for Internal Service Funds

The activities of an internal service fund must be analyzed to determine whether account balances and transactions of the fund must be reported as a governmental activity or a business-type activity on the government-wide financial statements.

GASB Cod. Sec. 2200.727-3 raises the issue of how the activities of a state investment board (accounted for as an internal service fund) that manages investments for several state funds (fiduciary funds, internal service funds, enterprise funds, and various governmental funds) should be reported in the government-wide financial statements. The state board's activities are financed exclusively by a fee that is charged to each participant.

The activities of the state board should be reported in the governmental activities' column in the government-wide financial statements. The fact that a high percentage of the state board's activity involved pension funds is irrelevant even though fiduciary fund financial statements are not presented at the government-wide financial statement level. The criterion to determine where to include an internal service fund's balance is based on whether the fund services governmental funds or enterprise funds. Only if enterprise funds are the predominant or only participants in the state board's activities should the balances be presented in the business-type activities column.

Activities with External Parties

When external parties are the predominant participants in the services offered by a governmental entity, an enterprise fund should be used. However, a governmental entity may establish an internal service fund that has its predominant activities with other units of the reporting entity but for simplicity purposes also makes sales (of a non-predominant amount) to external parties. Under this circumstance, the external sales and related cost of sales should not be used to determine the net profit or loss amount that is the basis for adjusting the expenses incurred in the governmental column of the Statement of Activities.

To illustrate the consolidation of an internal service fund's accounts in the government-wide financial statements when sales are made to an external party and the activities of the fund are predominantly governmental activities, assume the following pre-closing trial balances exist at the end of the fiscal year:

The following is a pre-closing trial balance for governmental activities:

	Debit	Credit
Assets	$16,000	$—
Liabilities	—	6,000
Program Revenues—General Government	—	29,000
Program Expenses—General Government	21,000	—
Program Revenues—Other	—	10,000
Program Expenses—Other	9,000	—
Interest Expense	4,000	—

	Debit	Credit
Investment Income	—	1,000
Net Position	—	4,000
Totals	$50,000	$50,000

The following is a pre-closing trial balance for the internal service fund:

	Debit	Credit
Assets	$1,500	$—
Liabilities	—	2,000
Revenues	—	4,520
Revenues—External Parties	—	480
Expenses	7,000	—
Net Position	—	1,500
Totals	$8,500	$8,500

The sales to external parties are billed at approximately 20% above the direct cost incurred by the internal service fund.

The activities accounted for in the internal service fund resulted in a net loss of $2,000 ($5,000 of revenues including revenues from external parties – $7,000 expenses). However, the revenue from external parties and the related cost ($400) is not part of the basis used to allocate the results of operations to governmental activities.

The net loss to be allocated to governmental activities per the pre-closing trial balance above is computed as follows:

	Total	Related to External Activities	Related to Internal Activities
Revenues	$5,000	($480)	$4,520
Expenses	7,000	(400)	6,600
Net loss to be allocated			$2,080

To present the residual amounts of the internal service fund into the governmental activities' columns of the government-wide financial statements, the following worksheet adjustments are made:

Fund Accounting

	Pre-closing Trial Balance for Governmental Activities		Eliminations Based on Internal Service Residual Balances		Pre-closing Trial Balance for Governmental Activities Including Internal Service Residual Balances	
	Debit	Credit	Debit	Credit	Debit	Credit
Assets	$16,000	$—	$1,500	$—	$17,500	$—
Liabilities	—	6,000	—	2,000	—	8,000
Program Revenues—General Government	—	29,000	—	480	—	29,480
Program Expenses—General Government	21,000	—	400	—	21,400	—
Program Revenues—Other	—	10,000	—	—	—	10,000
Program Expenses—Other	9,000	—	2,080	—	11,080	—
Interest Expense	4,000	—	—	—	4,000	—
Investment Income	—	1,000	—	—	—	1,000
Net Position	—	4,000	—	1,500	—	5,500
Totals	$50,000	$50,000	$3,980	$3,980	$53,980	$53,980

In the above example, it is assumed that the activity performed by the internal service fund should be classified as general governmental expenses. For example, the activity could be data processing. For this reason, the amount of revenue related to external sales ($480) is classified as program revenues from general government activities and the related expense ($400) is classified as general government expenses in the Statement of Activities. The balance of the adjustment ($2,080) is allocated to specific programs (e.g., public safety), which for simplicity are identified as "other program expenses." If the activity of the internal service fund were predominantly related to business-type activities rather than governmental activities, the residual balances of the internal service fund would be merged with other business-type activities.

Internal Service Fund Activities Impacting Fiduciary Funds

In some instances, an internal service fund provides services or goods to fiduciary funds. GASB Cod. Sec. 2200.725-14 states that in determining whether the services are predominantly provided to internal parties (therefore an internal service fund is appropriate) or predominantly provided to external parties (therefore an enterprise fund is appropriate), the activities with fiduciary funds should be considered internal. However, in folding the activities into the government-wide financial statements, activities with fiduciary funds should be treated as external transactions. In this circumstance, the external sales and related cost of sales should not be used to determine the net profit or loss amount (the lookback adjustment) that is the basis for adjusting the expenses incurred in the governmental column of the Statement of Activities.

Presentation of Internal Service Funds in the Fund Financial Statements

As previously discussed, the major fund reporting requirement does not apply to internal service funds even though they are proprietary funds. Instead, all internal service funds should be combined into a single column and presented on the face of the proprietary funds' financial statements. This column must be presented to the right of the total column for all enterprise funds. The internal service funds column and the enterprise funds total column should not be added together.

An example of the presentation of the financial statements of internal service funds can be found in Chapter 20.

Integrating Internal Service Funds into Government-Wide Financial Statements—Comprehensive Illustration

Internal service funds and similar activities should be eliminated to avoid doubling-up expenses and revenues in preparing the government activities column of the Statement of Activities. The effect of this approach is to adjust activities in an internal service fund to a breakeven balance. That is, if the internal service fund had a "net profit" for the year there should be a pro rata reduction in the charges made to the funds that used the internal service fund's services for the year. Likewise, a net loss would require a pro rata adjustment that would increase the charges made to the various participating funds. After making these eliminations, any residual balances related to the internal service fund's assets, liabilities, and net position should generally be reported in the governmental activities' column in the Statement of Net Position.

To illustrate the merging of an internal service fund's accounts in the government-wide financial statements, assume the following pre-closing trial balances exist at the end of a governmental entity's fiscal year.

The following is a pre-closing trial balance for *governmental activities*:

	Debit	Credit
Assets	$16,000	$—
Liabilities	—	6,000
Program Revenues	—	39,000
Program A Expenses	10,000	—
Program B Expenses	20,000	—
Interest Expense	4,000	—
Investment Income	—	1,000
Net Position	—	4,000
Totals	$50,000	$50,000

NOTE: These amounts include all governmental funds (general fund, special revenue funds, capital projects funds, debt service funds, and permanent

7026 *Fund Accounting*

funds) adjusted from a modified accrual basis (as presented in the fund-level financial statements) to an accrual basis (which is the basis required in the government-wide financial statements).

The following is a pre-closing trial balance for the *internal service fund*:

	Debit	Credit
Assets	$4,000	$—
Liabilities	—	2,000
Revenues	—	5,000
Expenses	4,500	—
Net Position	—	1,500
Totals	$8,500	$8,500

NOTE: The internal service fund balances are reported on an accrual basis at the fund financial statement level.

The activities accounted for in the internal service fund resulted in a "net profit" of $500 ($5,000 of revenues − $4,500 of expenses), which means that the operating expenses listed in the pre-closing trial balance of government activities are overstated by $500. To merge the residual amounts of the internal service fund into the government-activities column of the reporting entity, the following worksheet adjustments are made:

	Pre-closing Trial Balance for Governmental Activities		Eliminations Based on Internal Service Residual Balances		Pre-closing Trial Balance for Governmental Activities Including Internal Service Residual Balances (Pre-closing consolidating eliminations)	
	Debit	Credit	Debit	Credit	Debit	Credit
Assets	$16,000	$—	$4,000	$—	$20,000	$—
Liabilities	—	6,000	—	2,000	—	8,000
Program Revenues	—	39,000	—	—	—	39,000
Program A Expenses	10,000	—	—	300	9,700	—
Program B Expenses	20,000	—	—	200	19,800	—
Interest Expense	4,000	—	—	—	4,000	—
Investment Income	—	1,000	—	—	—	1,000
Net Position	—	4,000	—	1,500	—	5,500
Totals	$50,000	$50,000	$4,000	$4,000	$53,500	$53,500

> **NOTE:** For illustrative purposes only, it is assumed that during the year the internal service funds activities were provided to Program A (60%) and Program B (40%), which were reported in governmental funds. For this reason, $300 of the $500 Internal Service Fund "net profit" (surplus) is reported as a reduction of Program A expenses, while the remaining 40%, or $200, results in a reduction of Program B expenses. (The $500 is derived from $5,000 in revenues and $4,500 in expenses in the second table in this section.)

Once the government activities have been adjusted to include residual values (including assets, liabilities, net position, and operating activities), the Statement of Net Position and Statement of Activities must be formatted in accordance with GAAP.

The government-wide financial statements are divided into governmental activities and business-type activities. Generally, as illustrated above, the activities conducted by an internal service fund are related to government activities and therefore the residual amounts of the internal service fund should be consolidated with other governmental funds and presented in the governmental activities' column of the government-wide financial statements. However, the activities of an internal service fund must be analyzed to determine whether they are governmental or business-type in nature, or both. If the activities are business-type in nature, the residual amounts must be consolidated with the business-type activities in the government-wide financial statements. In addition, the operating accounts reported by the internal service fund must be analyzed to determine whether they should be used to compute the "net profit or loss" that is the basis for allocation to the governmental or business-type activities.

> **NOTE:** For a discussion of government-wide financial statements, see Chapter 20.

Activities That Are Exclusively Governmental Activities

When the activities conducted by an Internal service fund are related to governmental activities rather than business-type activities, the residual balances of the fund are allocated to the government activities columns in the government-wide financial statements. However, several accounts may appear on the internal service fund's operating statement (namely, interest expense, investment income, depreciation expense, and interfund transfers in/out) that must be considered before the residual amounts of the internal service fund are allocated to the governmental activities column that appears in the government-wide financial statements.

Investment Income. A fundamental concept in the formatting of the Statement of Activities is the identification of resource inflows to the governmental entities that are related to specific programs and those that are general in nature.

Based on the nature of an internal service fund, investment income will usually be considered general revenue and reported in the lower section of the

Statement of Activities. Therefore, when an internal service fund has investment income, only the net profit or loss before investment income should be allocated to the operating programs. The investment income should be combined with other unrestricted income and presented as a separate line item in the Statement of Activities.

To illustrate the allocation of internal service fund accounts when investment income exists for the fund, assume that in the previous example the pre-closing trial balance for the internal service fund is as follows:

	Debit	Credit
Assets	$4,000	$—
Liabilities	—	2,000
Revenues	—	4,800
Expenses	4,400	—
Interest Expense	100	—
Investment Income	—	200
Net Position	—	1,500
Totals	$8,500	$8,500

The activities accounted for in the internal service fund result in a net surplus before interest expense and investment income of $400 ($4,800 of revenues − $4,400 of expenses). The $400 amount is the basis for allocation to the program expenses, including the investment income of $200, as illustrated below and is combined with the investment income of the other governmental funds and presented as a single amount, as follows:

	Pre-closing Trial Balance for Governmental Activities Debit	Pre-closing Trial Balance for Governmental Activities Credit	Eliminations Based on Internal Service Residual Balances Debit	Eliminations Based on Internal Service Residual Balances Credit	Pre-closing Trial Balance for Governmental Activities Including Internal Service Residual Balances Debit	Pre-closing Trial Balance for Governmental Activities Including Internal Service Residual Balances Credit
Assets	$16,000	$—	$4,000	$—	$20,000	$—
Liabilities	—	6,000	—	2,000	—	8,000
Program Revenues	—	39,000	—	—	—	39,000
Program A Expenses	10,000	—	—	240	9,760	—
Program B Expenses	20,000	—	—	160	19,840	—
Interest Expense	4,000	—	100	—	4,100	—
Investment Income	—	1,000	—	200	—	1,200
Net Position	—	4,000	—	1,500	—	5,500
Totals	$50,000	$50,000	$4,100	$4,100	$53,700	$53,700

Interest Expense. Generally, interest expense on debt issued by an internal service fund is considered an *indirect expense* and should not be allocated as a direct expense to specific functional categories that appear on the Statement of Activities, rather, it should be presented as a single line item, appropriately labeled. For this reason, when an internal service fund has interest expense, only the profit or loss before interest charges should be allocated to the governmental operating programs. The interest expense should be combined with other interest expense related to governmental activities and the single amount should be presented on the Statement of Activities.

To illustrate the allocation of Internal service fund accounts when interest expense exists for the fund, assume that in the previous example the pre-closing trial balance for the internal service fund is as follows with interest expense separated from other expenses of the fund:

	Debit	Credit
Assets	$4,000	$—
Liabilities	—	2,000
Revenues	—	5,000
Expenses	4,400	—
Interest Expense	100	—
Net Position	—	1,500
Totals	$8,500	$8,500

The activities accounted for in the internal service fund result in a net profit surplus before interest expense of $600 ($5,000 – $4,400). The net surplus amount is the basis for allocation to the program expenses reported in the governmental activities' column of the Statement of Activities. The interest expense of $100 is directly allocated to the interest expense row that appears in the statement. The eliminating entry under this circumstance is illustrated as follows:

	Pre-closing Trial Balance for Governmental Activities		Eliminations Based on Internal Service Residual Balances		Pre-closing Trial Balance for Governmental Activities Including Internal Service Residual Balances	
	Debit	Credit	Debit	Credit	Debit	Credit
Assets	$16,000	$—	$4,000	$—	$20,000	$—
Liabilities	—	6,000	—	2,000	—	8,000
Program Revenues	—	39,000	—	—	—	39,000
Program A Expenses	10,000	—	—	360	9,640	—
Program B Expenses	20,000	—	—	240	19,760	—
Interest Expense	4,000	—	100	—	4,100	—
Investment Income	—	1,000	—	—	—	1,000
Net Position	—	4,000	—	1,500	—	5,500
Totals	$50,000	$50,000	$4,100	$4,100	$53,500	$53,500

Depreciation (and Amortization) Expense. GAAP requires that depreciation (and amortization) expense be reported on the Statement of Activities as a direct expense of specific functional categories if the related capital asset can be identified with the functional or program activities. Internal service funds invoice various departments. Therefore, depreciation expenses on capital assets held by the fund are directly related to the functional categories (public safety, health, sanitation, etc.) that use the services of the internal service fund. For this reason, depreciation expense should be included in the computation of the net profit or loss allocated to the various programs presented in the Statement of Activities.

Depreciation expense related to capital assets not identified with a functional category (such as the depreciation on city hall) does not have to be reported as a direct expense of specific functions. Rather, the depreciation expense may be presented as a separate line item in the Statement of Activities or included in the general governmental functional category. However, when unallocated depreciation expense is reported as a separate line in the Statement of Activities it should be indicated on the face of the statement that the amount reported as depreciation expense represents only unallocated depreciation expense and not total depreciation expense.

Interfund Transfers. As discussed in Chapter 5, GAAP requires that interfund transfers are a type of nonreciprocal transaction that represents interfund activities where the two parties to the events do not receive equivalent cash, goods, or services. Governmental funds should report transfers of this nature in their fund operating statements as other financing uses and other financial sources of funds. Proprietary funds should report this type of transfer in their activity statements after nonoperating revenues and nonoperating expenses.

Based on the nature of transfers in and out, these transfers should not be considered when determining the amount of net profit or loss that must be allocated back to the various programs reported on the Statement of Activities.

Activities That Are Exclusively Business-Type Activities

When activities conducted by an internal service fund are related to business-type activities rather than governmental activities, the residual balances of the fund are allocated to the business-type activities column in the government-wide financial statements.

To illustrate the consolidation of an internal service fund's accounts in the government-wide financial statements when its activities are exclusively related to business-type activities, the following steps need to be taken first with business-type activities.

The following is a pre-closing trial balance for *Business-Type Activities*:

	Debit	Credit
Assets	$20,000	$—
Liabilities	—	5,000
Operating Revenues	—	47,000
Operating Expenses	40,000	—
Nonoperating Revenues	—	10,000
Nonoperating Expenses	5,000	—
Interest Expense	2,000	—
Investment Income	—	1,000
Net Position	—	4,000
Totals	$67,000	$67,000

NOTE: These amounts include all enterprise funds. Because enterprise funds are presented at the fund financial statement level using the accrual basis of accounting, these totals are the basis for preparing the business-type activities columns in the government-wide financial statements.

The following is a pre-closing trial balance for the *Internal Service Fund*:

	Debit	Credit
Assets	$1,500	$—
Liabilities	—	2,000
Revenues	—	5,000
Expenses	7,000	—
Net Position	—	1,500
Totals	$8,500	$8,500

The activities accounted for in the internal service fund resulted in a net deficit of $2,000 ($5,000 of revenues – $7,000 of expenses), which means that the expenses listed in the pre-closing trial balance of business-type activities are understated by $2,000. To merge the residual amounts of the internal service fund into the business-type activities column of the reporting entity, the following worksheet adjustments are made:

Fund Accounting

	Pre-closing Trial Balance for Business-Type Activities		Eliminations Based on Internal Service Residual Balances		Pre-closing Trial Balance for Business-Type Activities Including Internal Service Residual Balances	
	Debit	Credit	Debit	Credit	Debit	Credit
Assets	$20,000	$—	$1,500	$—	$21,500	$—
Liabilities	—	5,000	—	2,000	—	7,000
Operating Revenues	—	47,000	—	—	—	47,000
Operating Expenses	40,000	—	2,000	—	42,000	—
Nonoperating Revenues	—	10,000	—	—	—	10,000
Nonoperating Expenses	5,000	—	—	—	5,000	—
Interest Expense	2,000	—	—	—	2,000	—
Investment Income	—	1,000	—	—	—	1,000
Net Position	—	4,000	—	1,500	—	5,500
Totals	$67,000	$67,000	$3,500	$3,500	$70,500	$70,500

As the internal service fund's activities exclusively support business-type activities, the results of the internal service fund are presented as part in the business-type activities column of the Statement of Net Position and the additional expense (the net loss of $2,000 incurred in the internal service fund) increases the operating expenses reported in the Statement of Activities, exclusively for the business-type activities and not the governmental activities.

Investment Income. As explained earlier, investment income earned by an internal service fund would generally not be considered in determining the amount of net surplus or deficit to be allocated to governmental activities. This concept also applies to internal service funds that exclusively service enterprise funds except the investment income is presented in the Statement of Activities as a business-type activity.

Interest Expense. When interest expense is incurred by an internal service fund that services only enterprise funds, the interest is directly related to business-type activities. That is, the funds could have been borrowed by the internal service fund or directly by the enterprise funds. For this reason, interest expense under this circumstance should be used in determining the amount of net surplus or deficit incurred by the internal service fund that should be allocated to business-type activities.

Depreciation (or Amortization) Expense. Depreciation expense of an internal service fund that exclusively services enterprise funds is directly related to the activities of the enterprise funds. For this reason, the net profit or loss incurred by an internal service fund under this circumstance should include the charge for depreciation or amortization.

Interfund Transfers. Based on the nature of transfers in and out, these transfers should not be considered when determining the amount of net profit or loss that must be allocated back to business-type activities when an internal service fund provides services only to enterprise funds. Transfers in and out by the internal service fund are reported as a business-type activity in the lower section of the Statement of Activities.

Activities That Support Predominantly Governmental Funds

When activities conducted by an internal service fund predominantly support governmental activities but also support enterprise funds, the residual balances of the internal service funds are for the most part allocated to the governmental activities' column of the government-wide financial statements. However, a portion of the net income or loss related to services provided to the enterprise funds is allocated to business-type activities.

To illustrate the consolidation of an internal service fund's accounts in the government-wide financial statements when its activities are predominantly related to governmental activities, a second step is performed.

The following is a pre-closing trial balance for *Governmental Activities*:

	Debit	Credit
Assets	$16,000	$—
Liabilities	—	6,000
Program Revenues	—	39,000
Program A Expenses	10,000	—
Program B Expenses	20,000	—
Interest Expense	4,000	—
Investment Income	—	1,000
Net Position	—	4,000
Totals	$50,000	$50,000

The following is a pre-closing trial balance for *Business-Type Activities*:

	Debit	Credit
Assets	$20,000	$—
Liabilities	—	5,000
Operating Revenues	—	47,000
Operating Expenses	40,000	—
Nonoperating Revenues	—	10,000
Nonoperating Expenses	5,000	—
Interest Expense	2,000	—
Investment Income	—	1,000
Net Position	—	4,000
Totals	$67,000	$67,000

7034 Fund Accounting

The following is a pre-closing trial balance for the *Internal Service Fund*:

	Debit	Credit
Assets	$1,500	$—
Liabilities	—	2,000
Revenues	—	5,000
Expenses	7,000	—
Net Position	—	1,500
Totals	$8,500	$8,500

During the year, the internal service fund billed the operating department of the general fund for 80% (Programs A and B) of its activities and the balance was billed to enterprise funds. The activities accounted for in the internal service fund resulted in a net deficit of $2,000 ($5,000 of revenues –$7,000 of expenses), which means that the expenses listed in the pre-closing trial balance of governmental activities and business-type activities are understated. To consolidate the residual amounts of the internal service fund into the governmental activities and business-type activities columns of the government-wide financial statements, the following worksheet adjustments are made:

	Pre-closing Trial Balance for Governmental Activities Debit	Credit	Eliminations Based on Internal Service Residual Balances Debit	Credit	Pre-closing Trial Balance for Governmental Activities Including Internal Service Residual Balances Debit	Credit
Governmental Activities:						
Assets	$16,000	$—	(a) $1,500	$—	$17,500	$—
Internal Balances	—	—	(b) 400	—	400	—
Liabilities	—	6,000	—	(a) 2,000	—	8,000
Program Revenues	—	39,000	—	—	—	39,000
Program A Expenses	10,000	—	(a) 960	—	10,960	—
Program B Expenses	20,000	—	(a) 640	—	20,640	—
Interest Expense	4,000	—	—	—	4,000	—
Investment Income	—	1,000	—	—	—	1,000
Net Position	—	4,000	—	(a) 1,500	—	5,500
Totals	$50,000	$50,000	$3,500	$3,500	$53,500	$53,500

	Pre-closing Trial Balance for Business-Type Activities		Eliminations Based on Internal Service Residual Balances		Pre-closing Trial Balance for Business-Type Activities Including Internal Service Residual Balances	
	Debit	Credit	Debit	Credit	Debit	Credit
Business-Type Activities:						
Assets	$20,000	$—	$—	$—	$20,000	$—
Liabilities	—	5,000	—	—	—	5,000
Internal Balances	—	—	—	(b) 400	—	400
Operating Revenues	—	47,000	—	—	—	47,000
Operating Expenses	40,000	—	(a) 400	—	40,400	—
Nonoperating Revenues	—	10,000	—	—	—	10,000
Nonoperating Expenses	5,000	—	—	—	5,000	—
Interest Expense	2,000	—	—	—	2,000	—
Investment Income	—	1,000	—	—	—	1,000
Net Position	—	4,000	—	—	—	4,000
Totals	$67,000	$67,000	$400	$400	$67,400	$67,400

The first entry, (a), allocates the net loss back to the funds that used the services during the period in a manner like entries discussed earlier in this section. The second entry, (b), arises because the governmental activities subsidized business-type activities through a deficit incurred in the internal service fund. In effect, the governmental activities paid some of the expenses for the enterprise fund. This is treated as an internal transaction and a "receivable" is created for the governmental activities column and a "payable" is created for the business-type activities column of the government-wide financial statements. Internal balances are presented on the face of the Statement of Net Position for both the governmental activities and the business-type activities, but they offset (net to zero) when totals are extended to the "reporting entity column" on the statement.

CHAPTER 8
FIDUCIARY FUNDS

Chapter References:

GASB Statement Nos. 3, 6, 14, 31, 34, 37, 38, 40, 51, 52, 53, 59, 62, 67, 68, 71, 72, 73, 74, 75, 79, 82, 84, 85, 92, 97

GASB Interpretation No. 3

GASB *Implementation Guide*

NCGA Statement No. 1, NCGA Interpretation No. 9

INTRODUCTION

Fiduciary funds are used to report fiduciary activities. Fiduciary funds include pension (and other employee benefit) trust funds, investment *trust* funds, private-purpose *trust* funds, and custodial funds. The word *trust* is emphasized due to the necessity of a trust *or* "equivalent arrangement." The phrase "equivalent arrangement" is undefined in GAAP, but it generally is understood to be of a nature like the Internal Revenue Code's exclusive benefit rule. The exclusive benefit rule is established in the tax code (primarily in Title 26 US Code, Section 401(a)(9)(A)) requiring plan assets to be used solely for plan participants or benefits to be a qualified trust and therefore providing an exclusive benefit.

> **PRACTICE POINT:** "Equivalent arrangement" is further discussed in the section on pension (and other employee benefit) trust funds.

Fiduciary funds utilize the economic resources measurement focus and the accrual basis of accounting. Liability recognition was updated by the implementation of the GASB's pension and postemployment benefits other than pension (OPEB) GAAP standards, as well as GASB-84.

For pension and OPEB plans, liabilities consist of benefits (including refunds of plan member contributions) due to plan members and accrued investment and administrative expenses. Pension plan liabilities for benefits are recognized when the benefits are *currently due and payable* in accordance with the benefit terms. The "due and payable" phrase does not include the entirety of a net pension liability or a net OPEB liability. Only the benefits payable are liabilities of fiduciary funds. Benefits payable from allocated insurance contracts are excluded from plan assets.

For all other fiduciary activities than pension or OPEB plans, a liability to the beneficiary of such activities is recognized when an event has occurred that *compels* the government to disburse fiduciary resources. These events may include a demand for resources where no further action or condition is required to approve the release.

Required financial statements are the Statement of Fiduciary Net Position and the Statement of Changes in Fiduciary Net Position (the word *fiduciary* distinguishing the fiduciary fund statements from other fund statements). The fiduciary fund statements include information of component units that are fiduciary in nature as well [GASB Cod. Secs. 1300.102(c), 1600.138, Pe5.118, Po50.120].

> **OBSERVATION:** Fiduciary component units are discussed in Chapter 4. Stand-alone reporting of fiduciary component units is discussed in Chapter 22 and for external investment pools in a section of this chapter as well as Chapter 9.

HOW TO IDENTIFY FIDUCIARY ACTIVITIES

Fiduciary activities may occur in many situations. Fiduciary activities can occur solely at a primary government or may occur with component units of a primary government that are fiduciary in nature. For those entities that are not component units that are fiduciary in nature, identifying a fiduciary activity from a governmental or business-type activity may be more difficult.

Component Units that are Fiduciary in Nature (Fiduciary Component Units)

To determine whether a component unit relationship is in place that is fiduciary in nature (Fiduciary Component Units), *there must already be a component unit relationship between the primary government and the potential fiduciary activity.* As a reminder of the provisions as discussed in Chapter 4, the following major provisions must be in place for a component unit, irrespective of blended or discrete reporting:

- Is there legal separation? Without legal separation, the relationship is either part of the government if the government holds the entity's corporate powers or not reported at all.
- Does the primary government appoint a voting majority of the component unit's Board? Even if not the case, is there a financial benefit or burden, or is it misleading to exclude the potential component unit?
- Finally, if there is an appointment of a voting majority of the component unit's Board, is there again financial benefit or burden *or* imposition of will?

As further discussed in Chapter 4, a primary government may identify a component unit that is fiduciary in nature in the following circumstances:

- A *defined benefit pension* or OPEB plan that is administered through a trust that meets the criteria as discussed in the section titled "Pension (and Other Employee Benefit) Trust Funds" below, or

- A circumstance in which assets from entities that are *not part of the reporting entity* are accumulated for pensions or OPEB that *are not held in trust*. These activities are most often related to multiple-employer plans *that are not held in trust* [GASB Cod. Secs. 1300.128–.129].

The word "pension" is italicized on purpose. GAAP, prior to GASB-84, relating to Internal Revenue Code (IRC) Section 457(b) plans was contained in the former GASB Statement No. 32 (*Accounting and Financial Reporting for Internal Revenue Code Section 457 Deferred Compensation Plans*) (superseded as of the implementation of GASB-97). The GASB specified in paragraph 20 in the Basis for Conclusions in the former standard:

> However, the Board *does not regard Section 457 plans as pension plans because there are no required employer contributions to the plans; they are more in the nature of tax-deferred employee savings plans.*

This sentence was written in 1997. But in practice, many governments believed such plans were pension plans, perhaps erroneously. That has led to a situation where a government employer contributes to such plans if there is a financial burden. Such plans must be held in trust according to IRC Section 457(b). But under GAAP prior to GASB-84, the Board deemed IRC Section 457(b) plans *not to be pension plans*. This situation has been remediated by the issuance of GASB Statement No. 97 (*Certain Component Unit Criteria, and Accounting and Financial Reporting for Internal Revenue Code Section 457 Deferred Compensation Plans—an Amendment of GASB Statements No. 14 and No. 84, and a Supersession of GASB Statement No. 32*).

What is a pension (or OPEB) plan? GAAP defines a pension plan as an arrangement "through which pensions are determined, assets dedicated for pensions are accumulated and managed, and benefits are paid as they come due" [GASB Cod. Sec. Pe5.527]. OPEB plans have similar wording. OPEB plans are defined in GAAP as "arrangements through which OPEB is determined, assets dedicated for OPEB (if any) are accumulated and managed, and benefits are paid as they come due" [GASB Cod. Sec. Po50.530]. It is unlikely that most deferred compensation, tax sheltered annuity, health savings and flexible spending plans fit these definitions.

In *general, defined benefit* pensions and OPEB plans that are administered through trusts are deemed by GAAP to be *legally separate entities*. Once the determination of a trust is made signaling legal separation, identification of whether a component unit that is fiduciary in nature needs to be made. GAAP stipulates that a primary government is considered to meet the financial burden criteria for determination of a component unit if the government has been legally obligated (or otherwise assumed the obligation) to make contributions relative to a defined benefit pension or OPEB plan [GASB Cod. Sec. 1300.130].

GASB Cod. Sec. 1300.130 contains guidance that is often overlooked regarding trusts and equivalent arrangements in determining legal separation. *Generally*, pension plans are administered through trusts that meet the criteria for an irrevocable trust (or equivalent arrangement) in GASB Cod. Secs. Pe5.101 and Pe6.101 and OPEB plans that are administered through an irrevocable trust (or equivalent arrangement) that meet such criteria discussed in GASB Cod. Secs. Po50.101, Po51.101 *are legally separate entities.*

However, *they may not be component units.* In determining whether those legally separate entities are component units, a primary government is considered to have a financial burden relative to a defined benefit pension or OPEB plan if it is legally obligated or has otherwise assumed the obligation to make contributions to the pension plan or OPEB plan, which is common. The phrase "trusts or equivalent arrangements" is described by those referenced paragraphs as plans in which:

- Contributions from employers and nonemployer contributing entities to the plan and earnings from those contributions are irrevocable. In some circumstances, payments made by the employer to satisfy contribution requirements are identified by the plan as plan member contribution requirements. Such contributions are classified as plan member contributions for financial reporting purposes and do not eliminate this requirement.
- Plan assets are dedicated to providing pensions (or OPEB) to plan members in accordance with benefit terms. The assets may also be used for administrative costs or to refund plan member contributions in accordance with those terms, without eliminating this provision.
- Plan assets are legally protected from creditors of the employers, the nonemployer contributing entities, plan members and the plan administrator.

A related *Implementation Guide* question should be considered when a pension or OPEB plan is administered through a trust but has no governing board. Should the plans be included as a fiduciary component unit of the government?

In question 1300.716-6, the answer from the GASB is "Yes" in the case where a sponsoring government performs the duties that a governing board typically would perform (e.g., the government determines or amends the structure of the plan [vesting requirements and required contributions]). If that other government (e.g., a sponsoring government) is legally obligated to make contributions to the defined benefit pension or OPEB plan, the plan is included as a fiduciary component unit of that other government.

There are plans where this does occur often. There are also employee benefit plans that are not postemployment benefit plans. As an example, IRC Section 457(b) plans are usually *deferred compensation* plans and not pension plans except in extremely rare circumstances where there may be a defined benefit. IRC Section 403(b) plans primarily offered to educators are not required by the IRC to have trust agreements or equivalent arrangements. Participants in Section 403(b) plans are directed to tax sheltered annuities or custodial accounts, which are regulated similarly to trusts. Section 403(b) plans are also subject to rules within the IRC requiring contributions to result in benefits exclusive to participants. Yet, many practitioners view these plans as legally separate from sponsoring governments. Governmental employers/sponsors of such plans may also contribute to the plans, in some cases on behalf of employees. Due to the contributions, a financial burden may be evident.

GASB-97 relaxed certain provisions to determine accountability for potential *defined contribution* pension, OPEB or other employee benefit plans in the case of the absence of a governing board. Such provisions are still required for defined benefit plan potential component units. It also changes the applicability for the financial burden criterion, relaxing the criteria also for defined contribution and similar arrangements. For IRC Section 457(b) plans, if such plans *meet the definition of a pension plan*, then the provisions of GAAP related to pension plans apply, including for the extremely rare circumstances where IRC Section 457(b) plans are defined benefit plans. If the 457 plan does not meet the definition of a pension plan, then the provisions of GASB-84 would apply. As a practical matter, few such plans that are not defined benefit plans may be controlled by the sponsoring government and therefore, may not be reported as fiduciary activities.

Once legal separation is determined in this regard for pensions or an OPEB plan, the type of pension or OPEB plan does not matter. They may be defined benefit or defined contribution [GASB Cod. Secs. 1300.716-1, 716-2].

Board Appointments and Fiduciary Component Units. The governmental financial reporting entity is discussed at length in Chapter 4. However, certain aspects of determining whether a component unit that is fiduciary in nature exists may cause a government to perform additional analysis.

GASB Cod. Sec. 1300.716-4 contains a fact pattern where a local government provides defined benefit pensions through a plan administered as a trust as described in this chapter. The government appoints an initial board that serves for five years. Successors are elected by retired and active plan members. The board's operations include service as trustee for the assets in the plan, approving all decisions and investment of assets. The government cannot unilaterally abolish the plan. Therefore, the government determines that fiscal dependency is *not* present, nor is financial accountability. In this case, the financial accountability provisions for a component unit are *not met* as once the initial board members retire, the government has no continuing authority. This could occur in some defined benefit plans such as those managed by organized labor (also known as "Taft-Hartley" plans).

On the other hand, if the government has a legal obligation to make contributions to the plan, even if the government cannot impose its will and is not obligated for the debt of the plan, the contributions still constitute a financial burden. If the government appoints most of the board, then the government is financially accountable. Therefore, it is likely the plan is a component unit that is fiduciary in nature [GASB Cod. Sec. 1300.716-7].

Non-Pension or OPEB Entities That Are Fiduciary Component Units

Component units that are fiduciary in nature could occur in other areas of operations than pension or OPEB arrangements. *One* (or more) of the following activities of the component unit are required to indicate presence of a component unit that is fiduciary in nature:

- The assets are administered through a trust or equivalent arrangement, in which the *government itself is not a beneficiary*. Within the trust or equivalent arrangement, the assets must provide benefits to recipients in accordance with benefit terms and are legally protected from the government, *or*
- The assets are for the benefit of individuals and the government does *not* have administrative involvement *or* direct financial involvement with the assets. Furthermore, the assets are *not* derived from the government's provision of goods or services to those individuals (see following **OBSERVATION** on administrative involvement and direct financial involvement), or
- The assets are for the benefit of organizations or other governments that are *not* part of the financial reporting entity, *nor* are the assets derived from providing goods or services to those organizations [GASB Cod. Sec. 1300.131].

OBSERVATION: Administrative involvement occurs when a government monitors compliance with the activity requirements established in a donor agreement, grant award or from some resource provider. A common indicator of administrative involvement is required subrecipient monitoring with federal awards. Other indicators of administrative involvement include, but are not limited to:

- Determining if expenses (or expenditures) are eligible based on criteria established by the government itself or by a donor, grantor or some other resource provider that does not receive the direct benefits of the activity, or
- Situations where the government can determine or can exercise discretion over how the assets are allocated [GASB Cod. Sec. 1300.131, fn. 11].

Control of the assets *is not necessary* if the primary government has determined that a component unit that is fiduciary in nature is in place. This would be a common situation where states have defined benefit plans that are component units of the state [GASB Cod. Sec. 1300.132].

A common example of when a determination of control is not necessary occurs when presenting external investment pools (described later in this chapter and in Chapter 9). If a government determines that an external investment pool meets the criteria to be a component unit, then control is not necessary as financial accountability is already present. Another common example could be legally separate private-purpose trusts.

Also, as further discussed in Chapter 9, the internal portion of an investment pool's balances are reported as assets and liabilities in the government's statement of net position and fund balance sheets and statements of net position. Flows are reported as inflows and outflows in governmental and enterprise funds as allocated [GASB Cod. Sec. 1300.716-8].

Pension and OPEB Arrangements That Are Not Component Units, but Are Fiduciary Activities

If there is a pension or OPEB arrangement that is not a component unit, the relationship could be a fiduciary activity *if the government controls the assets* in the following situations:

- A pension or OPEB plan that is administered through a trust that meets the criteria as discussed in the section titled "Pension (and Other Employee Benefit) Trust Funds,"
- A circumstance in which assets from entities that are *not part of the reporting entity* are accumulated for pensions or OPEB that *are not held in trust*. These activities are most often related to multiple-employer plans *that are not held in trust* [GASB Cod. Sec. 1300.133].

An example of this might be a county treasurer that administers a multiple-employer pension or OPEB arrangement for retirees from governments within the county borders, but not in the county's reporting entity (as the plan is not a component unit) and not held in trust.

Identifying Other Fiduciary Activities

There are other potential fiduciary activities that are not related to pensions or OPEB. The activity may or may not have a trust. The activity may be situations where funds transfer through a government. In such cases, the activity could be fiduciary if *all* the following are met:

- The assets of the activity are *controlled* by the government, *and*
- The assets of the activity are *not* derived *either*:
  - *Solely (entirely)* from the government's *own-source revenues*, or
  - From *either* of the following transactions:

Transaction	Examples
Government-mandated nonexchange transactions.	Many grants including: • Formula grants (typically block grants), • Reimbursement grants, • Expenditure-driven grants.
Voluntary nonexchange transactions (except passthrough grants where the government does not have administrative or direct financial involvement).	Reimbursement grants where there is a requirement for matching or level of effort from the government or time requirements (where revenue cannot be recognized until the requirements are met). **Caution:** Administrative involvement or direct financial involvement is commonly required due to programmatic requirements for subrecipient monitoring, determining eligible recipients or projects, having the ability to decide how funds are allocated. Grantor matching requirements or liability for disallowed costs are also indicators.

- *Or* the assets associated with the activity have *one or more* of the following characteristics:

  — The assets are administered through a trust in which the government itself is *not* a beneficiary, where the assets must provide benefits to recipients in accordance with benefit terms *and* legally protected from the creditors of the government, *or*

  — The assets are for the benefit of individuals and the government *does not have* administrative involvement or direct financial involvement with the assets, *nor* are the assets derived from providing goods or services to the individuals, *or*

  — The assets are for the benefit of organizations or other governments that are *not* part of the financial reporting entity, *nor* are the assets derived from providing goods or services to the organizations or governments [GASB Cod. Sec. 1300.134].

PRACTICE POINT: Due to the multiple levels of decisions, GASB Cod. Sec. 1300.134 is among the hardest paragraphs in GAAP. Care must be taken to understand the provisions prior to deciding on the presence of a fiduciary activity.

Student Activity (and Similar) Accounts. Decisions regarding whether a student activity account, club funds, booster club funds, and similar are fiduciary activities can be difficult. Individually, the accounts may not be material for many educational organizations. For large public institutions of higher education, the aggregated funds may be very material. Furthermore, governing bodies within the government and at higher levels of government may have compliance

Fiduciary Funds **8009**

requirements that differ from the provisions of GAAP. Frequently, these requirements are established by state boards of education.

The decisions on whether these accounts are fiduciary activities involve administrative involvement and the ultimate beneficiaries. If the ultimate beneficiary is the educational institution, chances are the activity is a governmental activity. If the ultimate beneficiaries are the students, analysis needs to be performed as to whether the activity is fiduciary. In many situations, the answer may be "it depends."

The GASB has many different scenarios on such funds and club accounts within GASB Cod. Sec. 1300.716. Not all answers result in "yes, this is a fiduciary activity" or "no, this is not a fiduciary activity." Scenarios include:

- A high school club is not legally separate. Club members fundraise for events with proceeds held in a school bank account. The assets of the club benefit the club and not the individuals of the club. Evaluation needs to be performed as to whether there is administrative involvement or direct financial involvement [GASB Cod. Sec. 1300.716-16].

- A club fee structure is established by a school board. However, no other policies and procedures are related to club fund disbursements. In this case, the school district *has administrative involvement* [GASB Cod. Sec. 1300.716-17].

- A student club is established in accordance with district guidelines and is not legally separate. Students fundraise and assets are held in a district account. The club president establishes how funds are spent. In this case, the school district *does not have administrative involvement.* The same answer would occur if parents decided how funds are spent [GASB Cod. Secs. 1300.716-18, .716-19].

- A school district holds funds raised by various clubs which pay for club activities during the year. There is no school policy on how the funds can be spent. Disbursements from the commingled account are approved by a faculty advisor representing the school district assigned to each club. The advisor has sole discretion. The school district *has administrative involvement* [GASB Cod. Sec. 1300.716-20]. Alternative answers are as follows:

  — If the policy guidelines are specific related to how club funds can be spent, there *would be administrative involvement* [GASB Cod. Sec. 1300.716-21].

  — If the policy only addresses signature authorization and prohibition for illegal activities, there would be *no administrative involvement* [GASB Cod. Sec. 1300.716-22].

  — If the state establishes specific guidelines on how resources can be spent through administrative policy, then there *would be administrative involvement*[GASB Cod. Sec. 1300.716-23].

- A university receives scholarship funds from a donor to be used for business majors with financial need. The students must maintain a minimum grade point average each semester. The university is responsible for selection and monitoring. In this case, the university *does have administrative involvement* [GASB Cod. Sec. 1300.716-27].

- A school district holds resources raised by a ski club for an annual trip. The resources can only be spent on the trip by board policy and not on any other activities. In this case, *there is administrative involvement* as the only activity that funds can be spent on is the ski trip [GASB Cod. Sec. 1300.716-26].
- A school district matches funds raised by clubs. In this case, the district has *direct financial involvement* [GASB Cod. Sec. 1300.716-28].
- A university holds funds from a foundation that is a legally separate 501(c)(3) organization for science and engineering scholarships. The foundation is not a component unit. The foundation selects the recipients based on criteria and the foundation monitors the students. Upon selection, the scholarship funds are applied to the student's account. Since the university holds the funds and the foundation is not part of the university's reporting entity, the activity *is likely fiduciary* [GASB Cod. Sec. 1300.716-29]. The same would hold for clubs that raise funds for not-for-profit disaster relief organizations separate from a school [GASB Cod. Sec. 1300.716-30].

Decisions that May Need to be Made for Other Fiduciary Activities. An example of a decision that may occur would be if a fund's operations benefit a discretely presented component unit such as taxation that is collected by the government but then passed to a discretely presented component unit mass transportation system to providing funding. In this example, the criteria above which limits the assets from benefiting organizations or other governments within the reporting entity would *not be met*. A discretely presented component unit of a government is part of the reporting entity. Therefore, it is not a fiduciary activity. As discussed in Chapter 6, this fund's operations would be best suited in a special revenue fund [GASB Cod. Secs. 1300.704-5, .706-4].

Inmates Accounts. Another example would be where a sheriff collects commissions from vendors in exchange for inmates' use of pay telephones and internet service in jails. The commissions and charges are accounted for in a fund, which is then used to provide benefits to the inmates such as uniforms, meals, medical care, law library, and other functions. The GASB also indicates that the commissions should be accounted for in a special revenue fund as the assets *are derived from providing goods and services to the inmates* [GASB Cod. Secs. 1300.704-3, 706-1].

Canteen accounts for inmates might have a different answer. If the inmates have a job and their earnings are deposited into a canteen account, the account could be a fiduciary activity. Commonly, families also deposit funds into the accounts. Even though the government is the custodian of the accounts, and the funds can only be spent at a commissary, remaining funds are returned when the inmate is released. The custodial activity is an indicator of a fiduciary activity as the government has control (see next section) [GASB Cod. Sec. 1300.716-14].

Cemeteries. Governments may be custodians for cemetery associations. Many of these associations are small not-for-profit entities that are not component units. A cemetery care trust is established with the assets from plot sales and donations used to maintain the cemetery with legal protections from creditors. There is likely a board that determines how funds are spent. In these cases, the government is controlling the assets and the assets are not derived from own-source revenues, taxation, grants, etc. as previously described and they are held in trust. As such, the arrangement is a fiduciary activity reported in a private-purpose trust as described later in this chapter [GASB Cod. Sec. 1300.716-10].

Accounting and Treasury Services. Many county and state governments perform treasury services for smaller governments and not-for-profits within their jurisdiction. The GASB provides examples of when such services could be fiduciary activities as follows:

- A county has custody of resources per an agreement with a legally separate not-for-profit for accounting, treasury, and investment services. The not-for-profit is not a component unit. This would be a *fiduciary activity* [GASB Cod. Sec. 1300.716-31].
- Under the same scenario, but fees are charged for the services. The fees would not be held in a fiduciary fund, but likely a governmental or enterprise fund [GASB Cod. Sec. 1300.716-32].

A Key Decision Is Determining Control

Other than component units that are fiduciary in nature, control of assets is an important aspect of identifying a fiduciary activity. The word "control" is described in GAAP as when a government:

- Holds the assets, *or*
- Has the ability to direct the use, exchange, or employment of the assets in a manner that provides benefits to the specified or intended recipients.

Legal or external contractual controls that are in place dictating how assets can be used for a specific purpose is not an indicator of a loss of control. A government would still be in control as it must comply with those legal or external contractual controls.

Directing the Use. A government can use an asset when it expends or consumes an asset for the benefit of individuals, organizations, or other governments, beyond the government's providing of services to them.

Employment of Assets. Governments often appoint designees, trustees, custodial financial institutions, and others to manage fiduciary funds. The government is still in control of the assets as those parties are not assuming the fiduciary duties of the government. Common examples are the use of financial institutions to manage an external investment pool's or benefit plan's investments [GASB Cod. Sec. 1300.135, fns. 14–15].

OBSERVATION: The importance of understanding "control" cannot be underestimated in some situations. A common question involves when a government establishes a slate of permitted investments for an employee benefit plan. The investments are managed by a third-party administrator such as an investment provider or similar financial institution. In paragraph B13 in the Basis for Conclusions to GASB-84, the GASB states, in part:

> In this situation, the government is imposing the restrictions on how the beneficiary can use the assets, rather than directing the use of the assets. The Board concluded that situations that do not constitute control would become more apparent by describing what is meant by a government having the ability to use the assets.

Self-directed (or participant-directed) plans are a further common nuance. There is no GASB definition of *self-directed*. One of the clearer definitions occurs in the AICPA's *Audit and Accounting Guide – Employee Benefit Plans*, par. 5.28, which describes self-directed brokerage accounts as an account "that allows participants to invest their account balances in any investment, as permitted by the plan."

PRACTICE POINT: Hopefully to answer this issue definitively, GASB *Implementation Guidance Update—2021* question 4.3 [to be codified as a replacement GASB Cod. Sec. 1300.716-31] contains a fact pattern where each participant in an employee benefit plan directs the investment of assets in their individual account from a set of investment options (more than one option). The government even can periodically change those investment options. The GASB responds that selecting the set of investment options or changing those options periodically is *not* directing the use, exchange, or employment of the assets in a manner that provides benefits to the participants. The government still does not have the ability to expend the assets, consume the assets, change one asset for another asset, or utilize the assets in another way to provide benefits to the participants in the employee benefit plan. *Rather, the plan participants have those abilities.*

Retainage, Performance Bonds, and Deposits. Control of assets is important but may not be an indicator of a fiduciary activity. Retainage, builder deposits, and performance bonds are common with construction for assets that will become a government's capital assets. If the builder does not complete the project satisfactorily, the deposits become the government's funds. In many cases, retainage and deposits are governmental or enterprise fund activities and should be reported in those funds. Even if the funds are returned to the contractor upon a satisfactory completion, the deposits are still not fiduciary activity [GASB Cod. Secs. 1300.716-11–13].

Clearing Accounts, Payroll (and Similar Withholding). A major change occurred with the implementation of GASB-84 for the financial reporting of clearing accounts, payroll, and other withholding from employees. Governments routinely reported these operations in the former agency funds. With the implementation of GASB-84, the unremitted funds became liabilities of the government. The funds are being held for the government's own benefit. Therefore, they must be reported where the expenses or expenditures were generated (governmental or enterprise funds) and not as fiduciary activity [GASB Cod. Sec. 1300.716-15].

This change in accounting and financial reporting contained in GASB-84 relating to clearing accounts, payroll, and similar withholding cannot be underestimated. It is major. Operationally, most governments will not change the computerization and control aspects of these accounts. The systems may be "hard coded" to post such transactions in the former agency funds. As a reminder, for external financial reporting, agency funds are not presented. Therefore, the withholding and clearing account activity must be presented in the paying funds. For large governments, this could mean billions of dollars in adjustments annually.

Seized Property. The public safety function of nearly every government may seize financial and nonfinancial property from individuals suspected of committing crimes. Cash is usually deposited into a separate bank account in the government's name and any other assets are held in custody by the public safety officers until a court decides on a verdict.

In the case where a law provides that the asset seizures are not the property of the government and cannot be spent until a judgment is rendered, the assets are held in custody. If the court concludes that the assets were used in the commission of the crime, the cash and other financial assets are forfeited. Upon forfeiture, seized cash and other financial assets are distributed to various law enforcement agencies (including other levels of government and the government who arrested the suspect) pursuant to the court order. If the court concludes the assets were not used in the commission of the crime, the seized assets are returned to the defendant.

In such cases, the assets are held by the government and therefore, *control is met*. The assets are not derived from the government's own-source revenues because, based on the law, resources held via asset seizures are not the property of the government until the court concludes that the assets were used in the commission of a crime; therefore, acquisition of those resources is not an imposed nonexchange revenue. The assets also are not derived from government-mandated nonexchange transactions or voluntary nonexchange transactions.

Finally, the assets are for the benefit of an individual (the defendant), and the government *does not have administrative involvement* (it is not establishing specific guidelines for how the resources can be spent until after there is a judgment) *or direct financial involvement*. As a result, the activity (financial assets and related net position) should be reported as a fiduciary activity until a judgment is rendered [GASB Cod. Sec. 1300.716-24].

PRACTICE POINT: This previous scenario can be controversial. In some situations, seized property may have never been reported in financial statements prior to the implementation of GASB-84. Care must be taken on the internal controls of the custody of such property as frequently it may be involved with illegal activity.

Internal Revenue Code Section 529 College Tuition Savings and 529A ABLE Plans

States are sponsors of college tuition savings plans and Achieving Better Life Experience (ABLE) savings plans under IRC Sections 529 and 529(a), respectively. If the plans are *not* component units and are administered by third parties hired by the state, the state might not be in control of the funds, especially if the funds are not held in a state account. The third party holding the assets and control is *not met*. The same answer would apply even if a master trust were used where individuals from other states can invest in the trust [GASB Cod. Secs. 1300.716-33, .716-35].

However, if the funds are held in a state account and, for example, the state controller is the trustee of the trust, then the state is *controlling the assets* and, therefore, a fiduciary activity may exist [GASB Cod. Sec. 1300.716-36].

Alumni and Booster Clubs. The GASB *Implementation Guide* has a scenario where a legally separate booster club of parents and other supporters is legally separate from a school district. The funds of the club are not held in district accounts and can be spent at the discretion of the club. The club is not a component unit. In such a case, the district is not holding funds and the activities are not reported in the financial statements due to the legal separation [GASB Cod. Sec. 1300.716-34].

> **PRACTICE POINT:** Many parent-teacher organizations may also fit the scenario of an alumni or booster club.

Own-Source Revenues

Own-source revenues are described in GAAP as revenues generated by the government. This includes the general or program revenues that are levied or charged by the government as well as investment earnings [GASB Cod. Sec. 1300.136].

It is self-evident that the most common own-source revenues are:

General Revenues
- Income taxes,
- Sales taxes,
- Corporate taxes,
- Motor fuel taxes,
- Other forms of general taxation,
- Investment earnings,
- Other inflows that are general to the government such as non-program specific fees.

Program Revenues
- Program-specific charges for services (fees for services),
- Operating grants and contributions to specific programs of governments,
- Capital grants and contributions to specific programs of governments.

The GASB has provided further examples of own-source revenues including:

- License fees assessed by a government and shared between governments [GASB Cod. Sec. 1300.716-37], and
- Prepaid tuition plan where participants purchase tuition credits to be used in a future year with a state investing the funds to provide the difference between the present value and future value of the credits [GASB Cod. Sec. 1300.716-39].

Should a fee be charged on such programs to provide services, the fee is not fiduciary and would likely be a governmental fund or enterprise fund revenue source [GASB Cod. Sec. 1300.716-40].

REPORTING FIDUCIARY ACTIVITIES: PENSION (AND OTHER EMPLOYEE BENEFIT) TRUST FUNDS

GAAP relating to pension (and other employee benefit) *trust* funds is codified in the following sections as discussed in this portion of the chapter:

Activity	GASB Codification Section
Defined benefit pension plans administered through trusts or equivalent arrangements	Pe5.101
Defined contribution pension plans administered through trust or equivalent arrangements	Pe6.101
Defined benefit OPEB plans administered through trusts or equivalent arrangements	Po50.101
Defined contribution OPEB plans administered through trusts or equivalent arrangements	Po51.101

In addition, there are other employee benefit plans that could be included. In such plans, resources are held in trust, and contributions to the trust and earnings on those contributions are irrevocable [GASB Cod. Sec. 1300.112].

As discussed previously, a "trust" or "equivalent arrangement" is defined in the above-referenced various pension and OPEB standards, with certain word changes for clarity as having *all* the following characteristics [GASB Cod. Secs. Pe5.101, Pe6.101, Po50.101, Po51.101]:

1. Contributions from employers and nonemployer contributing entities to the plan and earnings on those contributions are irrevocable,
2. Plan assets must provide (pensions or OPEB) benefits to plan members in accordance with benefit terms, and
3. Plan assets are legally protected from the creditors of employers, nonemployer contributing entities, and the plan administrator. If the plan is a defined benefit pension or OPEB plan, plan assets are also legally protected from the creditors of plan members.

The contribution provision may include situations where the employer "steps into the shoes" of employees and pays contributions on the employees' behalf. If the employer pays the contributions, they are termed "pick-ups" and are reported as plan member contributions. For further information on "pick ups," see Chapter 13.

The criterion of plan assets required to provide benefits to plan members in accordance with benefit terms also includes the ability to pay plan administrative costs or to refund member contributions if the activities are consistent with the provisions of the plan. This provision is somewhat derived from the aforementioned "exclusive benefit rule" within the Internal Revenue Code. Refunds to an employer or non-employer contributing entity of the uninvested portion of contributions that are forfeited by plan members in a defined contribution plan *do not* change the irrevocable status of a trust.

The legal protection provision is meant to shield the contributions and assets in the case of bankruptcy, divorce, or other litigation. However, qualified domestic relations orders (QDROs) may involve the splitting of benefits between a beneficiary and a former spouse.

> **PRACTICE POINT:** If a trust or equivalent arrangement is *not present*, custodial funds are used to report assets *not* held in trust for plan benefits as assets accumulated for these purposes are required to be reported as assets of the employer or non-employer contributing entity. Custodial funds are discussed later in this chapter.

Pension and OPEB plan reporting is similar and is contained in various GASB *Codification Sections* (see **PRACTICE POINT** following). The following table details which standards apply to which pension and other employee benefit trust fund activities:

GASB Codification Sections	Pensions		OPEB	
	Employers	Plans	Employers	Plans
Governmental GAAP Guide Chapters	8, 13	22	8, 13	22
PENSIONS:				
Pe5 Pension Plans Administered through Trusts That Meet Specified Criteria—Defined Benefit		✓		
Pe6 Pension Plans Administered through Trusts That Meet Specified Criteria—Defined Contribution		✓		
P20 Pension Activities—Reporting for Benefits Provided through Trusts That Meet Specified Criteria—Defined Benefit	✓			
P21 Pension Activities—Reporting for Benefits Provided through Trusts that Meet Specified Criteria—Defined Contributions	✓			
P23 Reporting Assets Accumulated for Defined Benefit Pensions Not Provided through Trusts That Meet Specified Criteria	✓			
P24 Reporting Assets Accumulated for Benefits Not Provided through Trusts that Meet Specified Criteria—Defined Contribution	✓			
OPEB:				
Po50 Postemployment Benefit Plans Other than Pension Plans—Defined Benefit				✓
Po51 Postemployment Benefit Plans Other than Pension Plans—Defined Contribution				✓

GASB Codification Sections	Pensions		OPEB	
	Employers	Plans	Employers	Plans
Governmental GAAP Guide Chapters	8, 13	22	8, 13	22
P50 Postemployment Benefits Other Than Pensions—Reporting for Benefits Provided Through Trusts That Meet Specified Criteria—Defined Benefit			✓	
P51 Postemployment Benefits Other Than Pensions—Reporting for Benefits Provided Through Trusts That Meet Specified Criteria—Defined Contribution			✓	
P52 Postemployment Benefits Other Than Pensions—Reporting for Benefits Not Provided Through Trusts That Meet Specified Criteria—Defined Benefit			✓	
P53 Reporting Assets Accumulated for Defined Benefit Postemployment Benefits Other Than Pensions Not Provided through Trusts That Meet Specified Criteria			✓	
P54 Postemployment Benefits Other Than Pensions—Reporting for Benefits Not Provided through Trusts That Meet Specified Criteria—Defined Contribution			✓	

The most common types of plans are:

- *Defined benefit plan*—A plan having terms that specify the amount of pension or other postemployment benefits to be provided at a future date or after a certain period; the amount specified usually is a function of one or more factors such as age, years of service, and compensation.

- *Defined contribution plan*—A plan having terms that specify how contributions to a plan member's account is to be determined, rather than the amount of retirement income or other postemployment benefits the member is to receive. The amounts received by a member will depend *only* on the amount contributed to the member's account, earnings on investments of those contributions, and forfeitures of contributions made for other members that may be allocated to the member's account.

In some instances, pension and OPEB plans have characteristics of both defined benefit pension plans and defined contribution plans. Such plans are commonly referred to as *hybrid* plans. The applicable standards refer to similar provisions that discuss if the substance of the plan is to provide a defined benefit in some form, the provisions of (the applicable standards) for defined benefit pension and OPEB plans apply.

The standards within the various standards apply to defined pension benefit and defined contribution plans irrespective of how they are funded. The following defined benefit pension plans are included:

- *Single-employer plan*—A plan that covers the current and former employees, including beneficiaries, of only one employer.
- *Agent multiple-employer plan*—An aggregation of single-employer plans, with pooled administrative and investment functions. Separate accounts are maintained for each employer so that the employer's contributions provide benefits only for employees of that employer. A separate actuarial valuation is performed for each individual employer's plan to determine the employer's periodic contribution rate and other information for the individual plan, based on the benefit formula selected by the employer and the individual plan's proportionate share of the pooled assets. The results of the individual valuations are aggregated at the administrative level.
- *Cost-sharing multiple-employer plan*—A single plan with pooling (cost-sharing) arrangements for the participating employers. All risks, rewards, and costs, including benefit costs, are shared, and are not attributed individually to the employers. A single actuarial valuation covers all plan members and the same contribution rate(s) applies for each employer.

Defined contribution plans also have variants, including, but not limited to:

- *Cash Balance Plan*—A plan with hypothetical accounts maintained for participants. The employer credits participants' accounts with funds annually and promises earnings at a specified rate. However, the rate may be different from actual earnings. Therefore, the risk is on the employer, unless the employer changes the formula for posting earnings.
- *Money Purchase Plan (IRC §401(a) Plan)*—A plan where employers can make contributions, in addition to (or instead of) employee or participants (so-called "pick-ups"). Forfeitures of contributions from employers are returned to the employer and may pay for administrative costs or to provide contributions matching other employee/participants' contributions. Investment options are usually selected by the employer, but the asset allocation may be selected by the employee. A qualified trust is required by the IRC or the plan could be offered with a defined benefit plan if forfeitures do not increase defined benefits.
- *Retirement Savings Plan (IRC §401(k) Plan)*—A plan only offered to certain tribal governments and rural cooperatives that established such plans prior to the 1986 Tax Act. Contributions are usually from employees on a pre-tax basis or can be post-income tax basis utilizing a Roth mechanism. Employers can match, but it is not required. Investment options are usually selected by the employer, but many 401(k) plans are self-directed. Trusts are required.
- *Target Benefit Plan*—A plan where employees make contributions on an actuarial basis knowing a certain date of retirement in the future. There are no guarantees of balance or return.
- *IRC §403(b) Defined Contribution Plan*—A plan that includes tax-deferred annuities funded by salary reductions. 403(b) plans are prevalent in public school systems, public institutions of higher education, and public hospi-

tals. However, certain governments are also using them to transfer lump sums from defined benefit plans at retirement into these plans managed by the new retiree. Therefore, the risk of loss shifts to the retiree. Trusts are *not* required within the IRC, but the plans are frequently managed with other defined benefit plans in master or commingled trusts. Employers can contribute on a matching basis or using "pick-ups" or just the employee.

- IRC *§457(b) Deferred Compensation Plan*—This type of plan is common in state and local governments. A plan administrator invests plan assets at the direction of plan participants. However, these are *not* pension plans. The participant has a risk of loss of value and there is not a requirement for the employer to match or contribute to the plan (see **PRACTICE POINT** on GASB-97).

- IRC *§401(h) Retiree Health Accounts*—Accounts established to help employees fund OPEB amounts. Contributions can be made by the employer or the employee or both. They can be fixed or a variable amount if they are below IRC limits that adjust annually. Investments in such accounts are usually target-date oriented based on the employee's expected retirement date. Benefits can only be drawn at retirement and only for qualifying medical expenses. Trusts are *not* required, and benefits are subordinated to other plans. In many situations, IRC Section 401(h) accounts are coupled with defined benefit pension or OPEB plans.

- IRC *§420 Excess Pension Asset Accounts*—Accounts established to facilitate the qualified transfer of excess pension assets to retiree health accounts. Only one transfer annually is permitted and is limited to the amount reasonably estimated to be that the employer maintaining the plan will pay for pension liabilities. In general, the fair value of the assets in the pension plan must be 110% of the sum of the funding target and the target normal cost in any year. The recipient account is an IRC *§401(h) Retiree Health Account*.

PRACTICE ALERT: Originally, Internal Revenue Code (IRC) Section 420 accounts were to sunset on December 31, 2025. Section 285 of the COVID-Related Tax Relief Act of 2020 afforded a one-time opportunity to end any existing transfer period and lowered the fair value of plan assets to make the transfer to 100%. However, that opportunity ended in 2021. The federal Consolidated Appropriations Act, 2023 established the so-called SECURE 2.0 Act of 2022. In that Act, the threshold for overfunding was raised to 110% and allowed a transfer of 1.75% of plan assets to pay for health and life benefits for retirees. The sunset date was then further amended to December 31, 2032.

PRACTICE POINT: Internal Revenue Code (IRC) Sections 401(h) and 420 accounts are used to pay current retiree health benefits which are obligations of a separate plan. Although the assets may be invested together with assets that are available to pay pension benefits, separate accounting must be maintained for all flows and balances. Stringent provisions are in place within the IRC regarding transfers of pension assets to fund Section 401(h) and 420 accounts and ongoing contribution and benefit provisions. Tax advice should be sought from counsel as Section 401(h) and 420 accounts are beyond the scope of this *Guide*.

PRACTICE POINT: The provisions of GASB-97 which amended GASB-84 caused some defined contribution and other employee benefit plan arrangements to no longer be reported, except, perhaps in stand-alone financial reports (separate from AFRs or ACFRs). In most situations, such plans are not fiduciary component units. Therefore, analysis of GASB Cod. Sec. 1300.134 needs to occur as discussed previously. If the government does not have control over such funds, it is unlikely such funds are fiduciary activities and therefore, not required to be reported unless the government desires to do so to enhance financial accountability by issuing a separate report. The reporting provisions of GAAP would apply as discussed further in this chapter.

It is a frequent practice for a PERS to collect a single stream of payments from an employer (or employers) and administer *both* defined benefit pensions and defined benefit OPEB within one trust. Absent IRC Section 401(h) provisions discussed above, if a PERS collects from employers and remits contributions to a separate entity for postemployment healthcare benefits administered by that separate entity, the PERS is serving as a cash conduit if it has no administrative authority for OPEB benefits. Therefore, the PERS should not follow the OPEB standards contained in GASB Cod. Sec. Po50. Instead, the separate entity would follow the OPEB standards (if they are a governmental entity) per GASB Cod. Sec. Pe5.701-19.

However, if the PERS *is an administrator* for *both* pensions and OPEB held under a common trust, two separate plans exist for reporting purposes. Either plan may or may not be held in trust and should use the provisions of GAAP as applicable per GASB Cod. Sec. Pe5.701-20. The PERS will allocate the assets between the pension and the OPEB plan based on specific circumstances, including the benefit structure and the terms and the method(s) of financing the pension and OPEB benefits. Therefore, the PERS should have an accounting policy adopted and consistently applied from period to period per GASB Cod. Sec. Po50.701-18.

INVESTMENT TRUST FUNDS

Investment trust funds are used by a governmental entity to report the external portion of an investment pool as defined in GASB Cod. Sec. I50.136 and individual investment accounts that are held in trust. Individual investment accounts include a service provided by a governmental entity *for other legally separate entities that are not part of the same financial reporting entity*. Such accounts are separated from other accounts in the investment trust and the value of the changes in the investment only benefits the separate government entity. [GASB Cod. Sec. 1300.113, fn. 8].

PRACTICE POINT: Individual investment accounts may be part of larger investment trusts. An example would be an external investment pool that manages pension investments for a statewide plan. The investment trust also manages pension investment accounts for individual cities, counties, special districts, and other governmental entities throughout the state using asset allocations determined by those entities.

Differentiating External Investment Pools from Internal Investment Pools

Internal Investment Pools. Governmental entities often pool resources for investment purposes. In some investment arrangements, the participants in the pool may be restricted to *only governmental units and departments that are part of a single governmental entity, therefore internal to the government.* This investment pooling strategy is referred to by GASB Cod. Sec. I50.533. as an "internal investment pool" and is described as follows:

> An arrangement that commingles (pools) the moneys of more than one fund or component unit of a reporting entity. (Investment pools that include participation by legally separate entities that are not part of the same reporting entity as the pool sponsor are not internal investments pools but rather are external investment pools.)

External Investment Pools. As suggested in the above description, the pooling participants may include external parties, in which case the strategy creates an "external investment pool," which is described as follows [GASB Cod. Sec. I50.522]:

> An arrangement that commingles (pools) the moneys of *more than one legally separate entity* and invests, on the participant's behalf, in an investment portfolio; in addition, one or more of the participants is not part of the sponsor's reporting entity. An external investment pool can be sponsored by an individual government, jointly by more than one government, or by a nongovernmental entity. An investment pool sponsored by an individual state or local government is an external investment pool if it includes participation by a legally separate entity not part of the same reporting entity as the sponsoring government. If a government-sponsored pool includes only the primary government and its component units, it is an internal investment pool and not an external investment pool.

An investment trust fund's main activity involves investing its resources in various assets for generating current income and capital appreciation. These investments may include investments in securities and other investments, such as real estate or limited partnerships.

Sponsoring Governments of Investment Trust Funds. The fiduciary activity portion is the external investment pool. Such pools should be used to account for "assets held in a trustee or agency capacity for others and therefore cannot be used to support the government's own programs." When an external investment pool is created, a trustee or fiduciary relationship is created between the sponsoring government and the external parties that participate in the pool. An investment trust fund (a fiduciary fund) is used when a governmental entity has an *external investment pool*, but not an internal investment pool.

Sponsoring governments may pool funds from governmental units that make up its financial reporting entity (internal portion of the pool) and from governmental units that are not part of its financial reporting entity (external portion of the pool). The internal portion of each governmental external investment pool should be allocated to the various funds and component units that make up the financial reporting entity, based on each fund's or component unit's equity interest in the investment pool as discussed in GASB Cod. Sec. 1300.716-5.

A "sponsoring government" is defined as "a governmental entity that provides investment services—whether an external investment pool or individual investment accounts—to other entities and that therefore has a fiduciary responsibility for those investments."

A sponsoring government should report the external portion of each investment pool in an investment trust fund. In the Statement of Fiduciary Net Position, the difference between the fund's assets and its liabilities should be labeled as "net position held in trust for pool participants."

Individual Investment Accounts. In addition to organizing external investment pools, a governmental entity may administer "individual investment accounts" which are defined as follows:

> An investment service provided by a governmental entity for other, legally separate entities that are not part of the same reporting entity. With individual investment accounts, specific investments are acquired for individual entities and the income from and changes in the value of those investments affect only the entity for which they were acquired.

Governmental entities that provide individual investment accounts should report those accounts in a separate investment trust fund(s) in a manner like the presentation of the external portion of an investment pool as described earlier. However, note disclosures that apply to external investment pools do not apply to individual investment accounts.

When a governmental entity offers an entity an individual investment account service as an alternative (or supplement) to participation in an external investment pool, the individual investment account should be reported in a trust fund, separate from that used to report the investment pool [GASB Cod. Sec. I50.529].

PRIVATE-PURPOSE TRUST FUNDS

Private-purpose trust funds are used to report all fiduciary activities that:

- Are *not* required to be reported in pension (and other employee benefit) trust funds, *or*
- Are Investment trust funds, *and*
- Are held in a trust where the assets are:
    — Administered through a trust in which the government itself is *not* a beneficiary,

— Dedicated to providing benefits to recipients in accordance with the benefit terms, *and*

— Legally protected from the creditors of the government [GASB Cod. Sec. 1300.114].

As previously discussed, cemetery trust accounts are frequently private-purpose trust funds. Such funds should not be used to benefit entities within the reporting entity of the government, such as discretely presented component units [GASB Cod. Sec. 1300.704-10].

A private-purpose trust fund *may* be used to account for escheat property as described in GASB Cod. Sec. E70. GASB Cod. Secs. E70.702-2 and 1300.706-5 explain that it is *optional* to use a private-purpose trust fund for escheat funds, not a requirement. Alternatives would be an agency fund (as appropriate) or in the governmental or proprietary fund in which the escheat property is otherwise reported. The reason for the variability is primarily due to the potential outcomes of the property that escheats. GASB Cod. Secs. E70.702-3, 1300.706-5, and 1300.706-6 discuss how the following alternatives may result in different funds:

Escheat Property is Held For	Type of Fund
Heirs or beneficiaries	Private-purpose trust fund
Funds that ultimately will revert to the reporting government	Governmental or proprietary fund (or both if split by law)
Other governments	Custodial fund

CUSTODIAL FUNDS

Perhaps the largest change in practice with the implementation of GASB-84 was the creation of *custodial funds*. These funds are used to report fiduciary activities not required to be reported in any other fiduciary fund. In addition, the external portion of investment pools that are *not held in trust* (as previously described with private-purpose trust funds) are also reported in custodial funds, but in a separate *external investment pool fund* column [GASB Cod. Sec. 1300.115].

Relief from Custodial Fund Presentation for Business-type Activities. Business-type activities may have custodial activities related to the operations. These activities may be part of enterprise funds. If there are custodial assets and liabilities that would otherwise be reported as part of custodial funds, if such assets, upon receipt, are *normally expected* to be held for three months or less, no separate fund is required. If the assets and liabilities are reported in the statement of net position for the activity (or fund), the additions and deductions are reported in the statement of revenues, expenses, and changes in fund net position and the flows are reported as part of operating activities in the statement of cash flows [GASB Cod. Sec. 1300.116].

As discussed in Chapter 6, custodial funds are used for special assessment debt for which the government is not obligated in any manner [GASB Cod. Sec. 1300.705-16]. As discussed with private-purpose trusts, escheat property may be reported in a custodial fund. Resources of student clubs collected for disaster relief not-for-profits (outside the reporting entity) and taxation collected by states and counties remitted to local governments on their behalf (and without any administrative involvement or direct financial involvement) might also be reported in a custodial fund.

FIDUCIARY FUND FINANCIAL STATEMENTS (INCLUDING FIDUCIARY COMPONENT UNITS)

Required financial statements for fiduciary funds and component units that are fiduciary in nature are:

- Statement of Fiduciary Net Position, and
- Statement of Changes in Fiduciary Net Position.

Fiduciary fund financial statements should include information about all fiduciary funds of the primary government, as well as component units that are fiduciary in nature. Separate columns are presented for each fund type—pension (and other employee benefit) trust funds, investment trust funds, private-purpose trusts, and custodial funds.

Basis of Accounting and Measurement Focus of Fiduciary Activities. The accrual basis of accounting and the flow of economic resources are used to prepare the financial statements of fiduciary funds. These concepts are discussed in Chapter 3. Fiduciary funds report based on all applicable GAAP.

Budgetary System and Accounting of Fiduciary Activities. Pension trust funds (and similar employment or postemployment benefit trust funds), investment trust funds, and private-purpose trust funds are accounted for in a manner like proprietary funds and may use budgetary controls. In practice, budgets are rare in these funds.

Pension and OPEB Plan Information Not Separately Issued. Financial statements for individual pension plans administered through trusts that meet the criteria in GASB Cod. Sec. Pe5.101 for pensions and for other postemployment benefit plans that are administered through trusts that meet the criteria in GASB Cod. Sec. Po50.101 should be presented in the notes to the basic financial statements of the primary government *if separate, GAAP financial reports have not been issued* [GASB Cod. Sec. 2200.756-3].

Pension and OPEB Plan Information is Separately Issued. If separate GAAP financial reports have been issued, the notes should include information about how to obtain those separate reports [GASB Cod. Sec. 2200.196]. If plan financial statements are presented in an employer's financial report, GASB Cod. Sec. 2200.756-1 provides guidance that the statements should be presented by fund type. If separate financial statements exist for each plan, the employer's report should refer readers to them. If not, the employer should include the financial statements for each plan in the notes to the financial statements [GASB Cod. Sec. 2200.197, fns. 46 and 47].

External Investment Pool Information. GASB Cod. Sec. 2200.756-2 provides similar guidance for external investment pool presentation in sponsoring governments as pension and OPEB plans. External investment pool disclosure should be

Fiduciary Funds **8025**

presented in the notes to the financial statements of sponsoring governments if separate financial statements have not been issued. GASB Cod. Sec. I50.137(c) also requires similar disclosure. If separate reports have been issued, GASB Cod. Sec. 2200.756-3 allows the use of a similar format to pension and OPEB plans. Differences in display requirements between external investment pools and pension and OPEB plans include:

- The difference between the external investment pool's assets, deferred outflows of resources, liabilities and deferred inflows of resources is captioned "net position held in trust for pool participants."
- For investments and investment income details, the level of detail for all other fiduciary funds can be used or clearly note on the face of the financial statements that summarized amounts exclude the more detailed data that is displayed.

Statement of Fiduciary Net Position

The Statement of Fiduciary Net Position should include information about the assets, deferred outflows of resources, liabilities, deferred inflows of resources, and net position for each fiduciary fund type. Amounts that are required to be reported as deferred outflows of resources should be reported in a statement of financial position in a separate section following assets.

Similarly, amounts required to be reported as deferred inflows of resources should be reported in a separate section following liabilities. The total for deferred outflows of resources may be added to the total for assets, and the total for deferred inflows of resources may be added to the total for liabilities to provide subtotals.

There is no need to divide net position into the three categories (invested in capital assets [net of related debt], restricted net position, and unrestricted net position) that must be used when preparing government-wide financial statements. All net position is restricted. Chapter 20 includes an illustration of a Statement of Fiduciary Net Position [GASB Cod. Sec. 2200.198].

> **PRACTICE POINT:** Deferred outflows of resources and deferred inflows of resources are rare in occurrence in fiduciary funds. GASB Cod. Sec. 2200.757-2 reminds practitioners that deferred outflows of resources and deferred inflows of resources should be presented in separate sections, unless in the case of hedging derivatives, there is a specific right of offset.

Assets

Fiduciary activity assets should be subdivided into:

- The major categories of assets held (e.g., cash and cash equivalents, receivables, investments, and assets used in pension or OPEB plan operations, or external investment pool assets, capital assets that are accounted for and reported in fiduciary activities); and

- Within the receivables and investments, the principal components of those activities, which are typically reported based on operational decisions, materiality and/or investment allocation and management.

Receivables. Fiduciary activity receivables generally are short term and consist of contributions due as of the end of the reporting period from employers, nonemployer contributing entities, and plan members, and interest and dividends on investments. Amounts recognized as receivables for contributions should include only those due pursuant to legal requirements.

For OPEB plans, amounts may be included for OPEB as the benefits come due and that will not be reimbursed to employers or nonemployer contributing entities using OPEB plan assets.

Receivables for contributions payable to the plan over one year after the reporting period's end (such as those from installment contracts) should be recognized in full in the period the receivable arises. If a receivable is recognized at its discounted present value, interest is accrued using the effective interest method, unless use of the straight-line method would not produce significantly different results [GASB Cod. Secs. Pe5.114–.115, Po50.116–.117].

Investments

Purchases and sales of investments should be recorded on a trade-date basis. Allocated insurance contracts should be excluded from plan assets if:

- The contract irrevocably transfers to the insurer the responsibility for providing the benefits,
- All required payments to acquire the contracts have been made, and
- The likelihood is remote that the employer or the plan will be required to make additional payments to satisfy the benefit payments covered by the contract [GASB Cod. Secs. Pe5.116–.117, Po50.118–.119].

Liabilities

Liability recognition is based upon the fiduciary activity being compelled to disburse resources. Liabilities generally consist of benefits (including refunds of plan member contributions) due to plan members and accrued investment and administrative expenses. Plan liabilities for benefits should be recognized when the benefits are currently due and payable in accordance with the benefit terms. Benefits payable from allocated insurance contracts excluded from plan assets in conformity with the previous paragraph should also be excluded from plan liabilities [GASB Cod. Secs. 2200.757-1, Pe5.118, Po50.120].

Fiduciary Net Position

Fiduciary net position is the residual of assets, plus deferred outflows of resources, less liabilities, less deferred inflows of resources. Fiduciary net position is reported as net position restricted for pensions (or OPEB), pool participants, beneficiaries, etc., as applicable [GASB Cod. Secs. Pe5.119, Po50.121].

Accumulated Assets for Fiduciary Activities but No Trust or Equivalent Arrangement. If a pension or OPEB plan, or other fiduciary activity is *not* administered through a trust as described previously, any assets accumulated for the fiduciary purposes would be reported as assets of the employer (or any nonemployer contributing entity). The assets (if any) are reported in a custodial fund. The amount of assets accumulated more than liabilities are fiduciary net position.

Statement of Changes in Fiduciary Net Position

The Statement of Changes in Fiduciary Net Position should summarize the additions to, deductions from, and net increase or decrease in net position for the year for each fiduciary fund type. In addition, GAAP requires that the statement provide information "about significant year-to-year changes in net position." Chapter 20 contains an illustration of a Statement of Changes in Fiduciary Net Position [GASB Cod. Sec. 2200.199].

A government *may* report a single aggregated total for additions and a single aggregated total for deductions if the resources within the fiduciary activity are normally expected to be held three months or less. The descriptions of the totals should be in such a manner where it is easily understandable. The GASB provides an example—*property taxes collected for (or distributed to) other governments* as a description that is understandable [GASB Cod. Sec. 2200.200].

A common example of a government holding resources for three months or less would be fundraising activities for a parks-and-recreation program. If the donations are held for three months or less and all amounts are distributed with parents in charge, the funds could show aggregated inflows and aggregated outflows if material [GASB Cod. Sec. 2200.758-1]. Flows that are insignificant but custodial could be reported as "other custodial fund collections" and "other custodial fund distributions" [GASB Cod. Sec. 2200.758-2].

Additions

Additions to statements of changes in fiduciary net position include discrete presentation of the following items, as applicable:

- Contributions from employers,
- Contributions from nonemployer contributing entities (e.g., state government contributions to a local government pension or OPEB plan),
- Contributions from plan members (active and inactive), including those transmitted by the employers; and
- Net investment income, including as applicable, the separate display of:
  — Investment *earnings* and
  — Investment costs, including investment management fees, custodial fees, and all other significant investment-related costs, and
  — Net investment earnings, which is the net of the previous elements.

Investment-related costs are reported as investment costs *if they are separable from investment earnings* and administrative costs.

Investment income includes the net increase (or decrease) in the fair value of investments and any other flows such as interest, dividends, and other income.

They may be presented in the aggregate or discretely presented [GASB Cod. Secs. 2200.199, Pe5 .120–.122, Po50.122–.124].

Deductions

At a minimum, deductions should include expenses by type, including benefit payments to plan members as they come due, refunds of contributions to all parties and amounts for administrative expenses. Benefit payments do not include amounts paid by inactive plan members.

Allocated Insurance Contracts. As allocated insurance contracts are excluded from plan assets and liabilities, purchases of annuities with amounts allocated from existing investments should be included as amounts recognized as benefit payments. Dividends from an allocated insurance contract are recognized as a reduction of benefit payments for the period. Benefit payments do not include amounts paid by the annuity contract to the annuitant. Therefore, only the flows to and from the contracts are included in the Statement of Changes in Fiduciary Net Position [GASB Cod. Secs. Pe5.122–.123, Po50.125–.126].

Net Increase (Decrease) in Fiduciary Net Position. The difference between additions and deductions is reported as the *net increase (decrease) in fiduciary net position* [GASB Cod. Secs. Pe5.124, Po50.127].

GOVERNMENT-WIDE FINANCIAL STATEMENTS EXCLUDING FIDUCIARY ACTIVITIES

The focus of government-wide financial statements is on the overall financial position and activities of the entirety of the government. These financial statements are constructed around the concept of a primary government and therefore encompass the primary government and its component units except for fiduciary funds of the primary government and component units that are fiduciary in nature. Financial statements of fiduciary funds are not presented in the government-wide financial statements but are included in the fund financial statements.

The financial statements of fiduciary funds are excluded from government-wide financial statements because resources of these funds cannot be used to finance a governmental entity's activities. The financial statements are included in the fund financial statements because a governmental entity is financially accountable for those resources even though they belong to other parties.

PART III. SPECIFIC ACCOUNTING AND REPORTING ISSUES

CHAPTER 9
DEPOSITS, INVESTMENTS, AND INVESTMENT DERIVATIVE INSTRUMENTS

Chapter References:

GASB Statement Nos. 3, 14, 28, 31, 34, 38, 40, 52, 53, 59, 62, 67, 72, 79, 81, 84, 90, 92, 93, 99

GASB Interpretation 3

GASB *Implementation Guide*

INTRODUCTION

The accounting treatment of governmental deposits with financial institutions and investments is essentially the same as accounting for deposits by private-sector businesses, with certain exceptions for unique considerations involving fund accounting and certain types of investments. Deposits, investments, and investment derivative instrument disclosures are pervasive through GASB standards and originally issued standards have been amended or superseded several times throughout the course of GASB's history in a continuously evolving process as banking practices and markets change.

Specific guidance by cash and investment topic is found in the following *Codification* sections:

Deposits with Financial Institutions or Investment Topic	GASB Codification Section
Fair value measurement	3100
Cash deposits with financial institutions	C20
Investment derivative instruments	D40
Investments	I50
Investments—Reverse Repurchase Agreements	I55
Investments—Securities Lending	I60
Irrevocable Split-Interest Agreements	I70
Investment pools—(External)	In5

Topics within the sections range from recognition and measurement to disclosure and disclosure of risks. For most governments, GASB Cod. Secs. C20 and I50 will provide the most amount of guidance. Numerous *Implementation Guide* questions are available for practitioners.

PRACTICE POINT: Hedging derivative instruments are detailed in Chapter 12.

PRACTICE POINT: This chapter of the *Governmental GAAP Guide* can be utilized focusing on individual sections for the issue at hand at the government. The sections are in order based on the listed *Codification* sections above.

An "investment" is defined as follows [GASB Cod. Sec. I50.103]:

A security or other asset:
1. That a government holds primarily for income or profit, and
2. With a present service capacity that is based solely on its ability to generate cash or to be sold to generate cash.

PRACTICE POINT: The above definition is important to remember as practitioners decide on whether an asset (or liability) is an investment or some other transaction that requires recognition and measurement.

FAIR VALUE MEASUREMENT AND APPLICATION

What is Fair Value? The definition of "fair value" is the price that may be received to sell an asset or paid to transfer a liability in an orderly transaction between market participants at the measurement date. In other words, fair value is described as an *exit* price. One party is selling without being forced to another party that is willing to buy without being forced to buy.

Fair value measurements assume a transaction takes place in a government's principal market. This assumes that the participants in the general market would act in their economic best interest—meaning the price that is most advantageous to them at a given point in time. Both parties want the "best deal" or there must be some other compelling reason to not buy or sell for the "best deal." Some call the differential between the economic best interests "bid" and "ask" with a final exit price or fair value, somewhere in the middle of the bid and ask. Fair value should not be adjusted for transaction costs [GASB Cod. Sec. 3100.102].

Measurement of fair value focuses on individual asset or liability categories. Due to the differences in how assets and liabilities are valued, disclosure may differ. Assets may have restrictions based on condition, location or contractual provisions that will affect fair value. The more restrictions on an asset, the more variability in measurement of fair value by market participants [GASB Cod. Sec. 3100.103].

GASB Cod. Sec. 3100.704-1 discusses restrictions on sales of assets in consideration of fair value. Such consideration is specific to the government holding the asset. If the restriction is a characteristic of the asset (e.g., the sale of a security in a private offering), the restriction is taken into consideration by market participants and, consequently, should be incorporated into the fair value measurement. If the restriction is a characteristic of the government and is unrelated to the asset (e.g., the asset has been pledged as collateral), the restriction should not be reflected in the fair value measurement.

Measuring Fair Value at a Unit of Account. Guidance is provided for determining a fair value measurement for financial reporting purposes along with application guidance for certain investments and related disclosures. To determine a fair value measurement, a government should consider the *unit of account* of the asset or liability.

The unit of account refers to the level at which an asset or a liability is aggregated or disaggregated for recognition and disclosure purposes as provided by the accounting standards. For example, the unit of account for investments held in a brokerage account is each individual security, whereas the unit of account for an investment in a mutual fund is each share in the mutual fund held by a government. Examples of a unit of account include but are not limited to the following [GASB Cod. Secs. 3100.104–.105, .901]:

Investment Type	Potential Unit of Account
Multiple investments	• Multiple investments may be held in one brokerage account, but the unit of account would be each individual security rather than the account in its entirety.
External investment pool	• A government holds a position in an external investment pool that is not a 2a7-like external investment pool. The unit of account is each share held, and the value of the position would be the fair value of the pool's share price multiplied by the number of shares held. The government-investor does not "look through" the pool to report a pro rata share of the pool's investments, receivables, and payables (see additional discussion on disclosures of positions in external investment pools later in this chapter).
Mutual fund	• A government holds a position in a mutual fund. The unit of account is each share held, and the value of the position would be the stated price of the mutual fund multiplied by the number of shares held.
Limited partnership	• A government owns an interest in a hedge fund organized as a limited partnership. The limited partnership owns investment assets, but the government owns an interest in the partnership itself rather than an interest in each underlying asset and liability. Therefore, the unit of account is the government's ownership interest in the limited partnership, rather than the percentage in individual assets and liabilities held by the partnership.
Government acquisition	• A government acquires another government in an acquisition. The units of account to the acquiring government are the same as they were to the acquired government, but the measurement attributes for the acquisition are prescribed by GASB Cod. Sec. Co10. Acquired assets, deferred outflows of resources, liabilities, and deferred inflows of resources are measured at acquisition value, fair value, or carrying value.

Investment Type	Potential Unit of Account
Leased Mineral Rights	• GASB Cod. Sec. 3100.705-1 discusses how there is no requirement to separate the land (in this case conservation land) from its mineral rights. If the government chooses to report the land and mineral rights aggregated in a single unit of account, the land, and the mineral rights (as one unit of account) should be classified as a capital asset. If the government separates the land and mineral rights, the land should be reported as a capital asset (the primary purpose of acquiring the land is conservation instead of income or profit). In this circumstance, the mineral rights should be evaluated in the context of whether they meet the definition of an investment in this section or should be reported as another type of asset.

The Importance of Markets to Determining Fair Value. Fair value assumes an unfettered market to conduct transactions of assets or transfers of liability. The fair value measurement would then take place in either:

- A government's principal market, or
- A government's most advantageous market if a principal market is not available, after accounting for transaction and transportation costs.

Practitioners do not need to search all possible markets to identify the principal market. For example, if an investment officer normally conducts business on the New York Stock Exchange, even if there may be variability in the exact same asset if purchased in London or Hong Kong, GAAP does not require a search for the perceived best value, or in the absence of a principal market, the most advantageous market. However, the officer should review all information that is reasonably available [GASB Cod. Sec. 3100.107]. GASB Cod. Sec. 3100.706-2 emphasizes that once a government identifies its principal market, the government cannot disregard the price of an orderly transaction in that market and instead use the price of a different market, unless the government has no access to its principal market.

If using the principal market, fair value measurement should represent the price in that market, whether it is directly observable for an identical asset, or using another valuation technique (discussed in the next section). This measurement approach should be used, even if the price may be different in a different market, or potentially more advantageous at the measurement date [GASB Cod. Sec. 3100.108].

As an example, a gallon of gasoline at a local filling station may be $3.79. To value that gasoline, someone could also calculate the cost to produce the gasoline and measure the difference. But the consumer needs to fill the tank, when necessary, at a preferred gas station. Cheaper prices may be found a short distance away at the same exact time, but the consumer chose a closer gas station. A government measuring an investment will make a similar choice. The government has access to the principal (most advantageous) market at the measurement date. From the perspective of the government, it is known there may be differences in prices [GASB Cod. Sec. 3100.109].

To determine a market, there is no need to sell an asset or transfer a liability at a measurement date to be able to measure the value based on the price in a market. For example, an assessment may be done on a commercial building held as an investment at a measurement date. There is no requirement to sell the building for that price unless an agreement to sell is in hand [GASB Cod. Sec. 3100.110].

There may be few or no observable market transactions to provide a price about the sale of an asset or the transfer of a liability at the measurement date. A fair value measurement should assume that a transaction takes place at the date of measurement, considered from the perspective of the government that controls the asset and therefore, establishing a basis determining the price to sell the asset or transfer a liability [GASB Cod. Sec. 3100.111]. In the case of the commercial building held as an investment, the building may be in an area where the building is unique in features, or few comparable transactions have occurred in recent periods. However, the assessment can still provide reasonable information about the fair value of the building.

The Importance of Market Participants to Fair Value. The fair value of an asset or a liability assumes that the potential participants in the transaction (market participants) act in their own economic best interest. Specific participants are not needed to be identified by the government. Participants may vary based on the asset or liability, the principal or most advantageous market for the asset or liability and whether the participants desire to finalize a transaction with the government or vice versa [GASB Cod. Sec. 3100.112]. Continuing with the commercial building example, a potential buyer for the building should be willing (and able) to purchase the building to determine a value. If the building is being forced on a purchaser (or the government is forcing an owner to sell a property in the case of eminent domain), the fair value will be quite different due to the unwillingness to participate.

PRACTICE POINT: The role of market participants is one of the drivers of the economy. In basic economic theory without regulatory intervention, the more the market participants with a limited supply, the higher the price (known as inflation). If market participants lessen and supply rises, the lower is the price as suppliers have too much inventory. Suppliers would need to lower production to rebalance, which may include increases in unemployment.

The Role of Transaction Costs in Pricing. GAAP requires no adjustment to the price of an asset or liability to calculate fair value. Transaction costs are not an element of the asset or liability—they are periodic expenses. However, transaction costs do not include transportation costs. If there is a requirement to transport the asset from its current location to a preferred location of the buyer, then the fair value should be adjusted.

In the case of buying a vehicle, the fair value is agreed upon between buyer and seller. However, the vehicle may not be at the location of the buyer and transportation costs are required that adjust the value [GASB Cod. Secs. 3100.113–.114].

Further examples of transaction costs are commissions and similar acquisition costs for investments. These costs are *not* part of the cost of the investment(s), even though they are outflows. The costs are separate from the investment cost and are expenses of the period. They are also not deferred and amortized with investments held for lengthy periods.

Valuation Techniques

Various valuation techniques are used to determine fair value. Governments can decide which technique is appropriate under the circumstances available to measure fair value. The goal is to utilize the most observable inputs available, rather than unobservable inputs.

A single valuation technique is appropriate in many cases. For example, common stock can be valued using quoted prices in active markets for identical shares of common stock, with the understanding there will be a "spread" between "bid" and "ask" prices. Another common example is real estate. A homeowner lists a house for sale with a realtor at a price. Depending on many factors (some of which are intangible), potential buyers may submit an offer lower than the listed price or higher than the listed price. It is up to the selling homeowner to determine the best value in the sale in accepting an offer.

In other cases, a technique using present value or market multiples can be used. In such situations, the government should use the technique that is most reasonable as there may be a range of values that result. In many of these cases, the middle value is often used in practice. If an asset or liability has multiple components, multiple valuation techniques can be used if the assumptions are well documented.

Valuation techniques should be consistent from period to period. Change in techniques may occur due to the development of new markets, availability of added information (or the retirement of previous information), valuation techniques improve, or market conditions change.

If unobservable inputs are used, the valuation technique should be adjusted so that at initial recognition, the result of the valuation equals the transaction price. In the case of the commercial building, if the building was purchased several periods ago, an assessment is a proper valuation technique. But if the building was purchased at the end of a fiscal period, the proper valuation technique is the acquisition price. From that point on, an assessment will be proper. For GAAP reporting purposes, any changes between techniques from period to period are changes in accounting estimates and therefore, no restatement is required [GASB Cod. Sec. 3100.115–.119].

Valuation Approaches

Fair value should be determined using one or more of the following widely used approaches [GASB Cod. Secs. 3100.120–.124]:

Approach	Definition
Market Approach	The market approach uses prices and other relevant information generated by market transactions involving identical or comparable assets, liabilities, or a group of assets and liabilities. Matrix pricing may be used to value some financial instruments and therefore, relying on the securities' relationship to other benchmark quoted securities.
Cost Approach	The cost approach reflects the amount that would be required currently to replace the service capacity of an asset. Buyers at market would consider a substitute comparable asset, adjusting for obsolescence.
Income Approach	The income approach converts future amounts (such as cash flows or income and expenses) to a single current (discounted) amount. The most common technique used in the income approach is present value. However, option pricing models may be used including Black-Scholes-Merton and the multiperiod excess earnings technique.

Fair Value Hierarchy

A hierarchy of inputs to valuation techniques is established to measure fair value. The hierarchy has three levels as follows:

- **Level 1** is quoted prices (unadjusted) in active markets for identical assets or liabilities,
- **Level 2** is inputs other than quoted prices included within Level 1 that are observable for the asset or liability, either directly or indirectly, and
- **Level 3** is unobservable inputs, which may assume for example an assumed rate of default on a private loan [GASB Cod. Sec. 3100.129].

Level 1 Inputs. A quotation for identical assets or liabilities in an active market is the most reliable evidence of a level 1 input. It should be used to provide fair value without adjustment whenever available with certain exceptions. Values may be easily found in exchanges, dealers, brokers, or principal to principal markets.

The following exceptions to Level 1 inputs may cause adjustments:

- *Many similar assets and liabilities may be in the transaction.* For example, a government may purchase a large block of common stock. The transaction may move the price of the stock. The seller may provide the government a discounted price due to the quantity. Conversely, if the government attempts to sell the large block at once, a "blockage factor" may be involved as the market may not have enough buyers at the same exact time. Therefore, the value of the stock may drop.
- *The quoted price may not be representative of fair value.* This may occur if a significant event occurs after the close of a market but before the measurement date. As an example, a common stock is held by a government. Period-end is on a Sunday (when the market is closed). After the close of business on Friday, the company issuing the common stock issues a

dramatic earnings warning, potentially depressing the stock value significantly when the market opens on Monday. The government may identify this issue and an adjustment may be necessary, resulting in a level 2 or 3 input.

- *Fair value of an asset not representative of fair value of a liability.* At any given time, buyer and seller pricing should equal. But adjustments may be necessary when they are not [GASB Cod. Secs. 3100.130–.136].

Level 2 and 3 Inputs. Examples of Level 2 and Level 3 inputs include but are not limited to [GASB Cod. Secs. 3100.137–.141, .901]:

Example	Potential Inputs Used
Bond valued by a pricing service that uses matrix pricing	• A level 2 input is a price or yield of a similar bond.
Pay-fixed, receive-variable interest rate swap based on a Structured Overnight Financing Rate (SOFR) swap rate	• A level 2 input is the SOFR swap rate if that rate is observable at commonly quoted intervals for substantially the full term of the swap (see **PRACTICE POINT and ALERT** on GASB-93 and GASB-99, respectively).
Three-year option on exchange-traded shares	• A level 2 input is the implied volatility for the shares derived through extrapolation to Year 3 if *both* of the following conditions exist: — Prices for one-year and two-year options on the shares are observable, and — The extrapolated implied volatility of a three-year option is corroborated by observable market data for substantially the full term of the option. In that case, the implied volatility could be derived by extrapolating from the implied volatility of the one-year and two-year options on the shares and corroborated by the implied volatility for three-year options on comparable entities' shares if correlation with the one-year and two-year implied volatilities is established.
Valuation multiple	• A level 2 input is a multiple of earnings or revenue or a similar performance measure derived from observable market data—for example, multiples derived from prices in observed transactions involving comparable (similar) businesses, considering operational, market, financial, and nonfinancial factors.
Long-dated currency swap	• A level 3 input is an interest rate in a specified currency that is not observable and cannot be corroborated by observable market data at commonly quoted intervals or otherwise for substantially the full term of the currency swap. The interest rates in a currency swap are the swap rates calculated from the respective countries' yield curves.

Example	Potential Inputs Used
Three-year option on exchange-traded shares	• A level 3 input is historical volatility, that is, the volatility for the shares derived from the share's historical prices. Historical volatility does not represent current market participants' expectations about future volatility, even if it is the only information available to price an option.
Interest rate swap	• A level 3 input is an adjustment to a midmarket consensus (nonbinding) price for a swap developed using data that are not directly observable and cannot otherwise be corroborated by observable market data.
Commercial real estate	• A level 3 input is a financial forecast (e.g., of cash flows or earnings) developed using a government's own data if there is no reasonably available information that indicates that market participants would use different assumptions.

PRACTICE POINT: In March 2020, the GASB released Statement No. 93 (*Replacement of Interbank Offered Rates*) (GASB-93). As a result of global reference rate reform, the London Interbank Offered Rate (LIBOR) was expected to cease to exist in its current form at the end of 2021, prompting governments to amend or replace financial instruments for the purpose of replacing LIBOR with other reference rates, by either changing the reference rate or adding or changing fallback provisions related to the reference rate. GASB-93 also:

- Provides for an exception for certain hedging derivative instruments to the hedge accounting termination provisions when an IBOR (interbank offered rate) is replaced as the reference rate of the hedging derivative instrument's variable payment,
- Clarifies the hedge accounting termination provisions when a hedged item is amended to replace the reference rate,
- Clarifies that the uncertainty related to the continued availability of IBORs does not, by itself, affect the assessment of whether the occurrence of a hedged expected transaction is probable,
- Removes LIBOR as an appropriate benchmark interest rate for the qualitative evaluation of the effectiveness of an interest rate swap,
- Identifies the Secured Overnight Financing Rate (SOFR) and the Effective Federal Funds Rate as appropriate benchmark interest rates for the qualitative evaluation of the effectiveness of an interest rate swap,
- Clarifies the definition of reference rate, as it is used in GASB Cod. Sec. D40, and
- Provides an exception to the lease modifications guidance in GASB Cod. Sec. L20, for certain lease contracts that are amended solely to replace an IBOR as the rate upon which variable payments depend.

9010 **Specific Accounting and Reporting Issues**

PRACTICE ALERT: GASB Statement No. 99 (*Omnibus 2022*) adjusts the impact of GASB Statement No. 93 (*Replacement of Interbank Offered Rates*), specifically regarding LIBOR as an appropriate benchmark. As stated in the above **PRACTICE POINT**, the removal of LIBOR as an appropriate benchmark interest rate was supposed to be effective for reporting periods ending after December 31, 2021. This aspect of GASB-93 became delayed as global banking regulators delayed the sunset of LIBOR due to the COVID-19 pandemic. ICE Benchmark Administrator, Ltd. (IBA – a subsidiary of the Intercontinental Exchange) is the entity responsible for independently benchmarking such indices. LIBOR is no longer an appropriate benchmark for hedging derivative instruments for *taxable debt* as LIBOR ceased to be determined by the ICE at the end of June 2023. GASB Statement No. 99 linked the implementation of this provision to that decision by IBA. The provision became effective immediately upon issuance of GASB Statement No. 99. Information on the LIBOR cessation may be found at https://www.theice.com/iba/libor.

Additional analysis may be required when the volume or level of activity for an asset or liability has significantly decreased. For example, if an investment is not publicly traded, it is far harder to value than one that has a higher volume or is publicly traded. It also requires identification of transactions that are not orderly. Non-orderly transactions are unusual or in illiquid markets [GASB Cod. Secs. 3100.142–.143].

Transactions that Are Disorderly. If there has been a significant increase or decrease in the volume of activity of an asset or a liability, the market may not be orderly. A common example is when a company may be near or in bankruptcy. Disorderly markets may also occur in the following conditions in the valuation process:

1. The period of exposure to the market before the measurement date was not adequate to allow for marketing activities that are usual and customary for transactions involving such assets or liabilities under current market conditions. An example of this is a "fire sale."
2. There was a usual and customary marketing period, but the seller marketed the asset or liability to a single market participant. This could involve a "sole source" or a private placement transaction.
3. The seller is in or near bankruptcy (i.e., the seller is distressed).
4. The seller was required to sell to meet regulatory or legal requirements (i.e., the seller was forced).
5. The transaction price is an outlier when compared with other recent transactions for the same or a similar asset or liability.

In these cases, governments should place little, if any weight (compared with other indications of fair value) on the transaction price. To determine whether a transaction is orderly, a government should consider reasonably available information. If a government is party to the transaction, it is presumed to have information to determine if the transaction is orderly [GASB Cod. Secs. 3100.146–.148].

Third Party Quotations. It is common for governments to use third party quotation services, custodial banks, or brokers. The provisions of fair value apply to those entities as well [GASB Cod. Secs. 3100.149–.151].

> **PRACTICE POINT:** Even if the government contracts with a custodial bank for pricing, the valuation of investments is the management of the government's responsibility for audit purposes. Care must be taken by practitioners not to blindly accept valuations without some form of review or testing for reasonableness. A best practice is to perform periodic testing at custodial banks or individual investment managers for valuation and may include whether the investment exists and is in the custody of the bank in the government's name. The periodic testing is also important for audit purposes as independent auditors will want to test the assumptions used by custodial banks in valuations and the reconciliations between managers' and the government's accounts.

Nonfinancial Assets that are Investments. Fair value measurement assumes the highest and best use for a nonfinancial asset. The concept of highest and best use involves considering the use of the asset that is physically possible, legally permissible, and financially feasible. As an example, when dealing with the value of a piece of commercial property:

- The location and size of the property makes it advantageous to buyers, increasing the price (physical possibility),
- The zoning of the property allows for commercially viable and robust tenants (legal permissibility), and
- The location and the zoning combine to create a financially feasible property, producing an investment return that the buyers require.

A government's current use of a nonfinancial asset is assumed to be its highest and best use, unless there are other market forces. For example, a developer may approach a city desiring to redevelop a city building, inclusive of condominiums. Therefore, the developer sees a value higher than the city does.

A fair value measurement of a liability assumes that the liability would be transferred to a market participant and not settled with the counterparty. For example, to value a liability, one would assume it would be sold to a third party that is separate from the entity receiving the payment on the liability. In the absence of a quoted price for the transfer of an identical or similar liability and when another party holds an identical item as an asset, a government should be able to use the fair value of that asset to measure the fair value of the liability [GASB Cod. Secs. 3100.152–.155].

> **PRACTICE ALERT:** The GASB is in the process of a major project on the *classification* of nonfinancial assets, but not the recognition and measurement of such assets. In scope are the following types of assets:
>
> - Tangible capital assets held for sale and tangible capital assets used for service,
> - Nonfinancial investments and financial investments,
> - Intangible capital assets and tangible capital assets,
> - Intangible lease assets and tangible owned assets,

- Contracts for the right to use intangible assets and leases of tangible assets, and
- Assets that are consumable in lieu of cash and receivables of nonfinancial assets.

Tangible capital assets held for sale tentatively may be required to be classified separately from tangible capital assets used for service by requiring them to be reported as a major class of capital asset. Intangible capital assets would be classified separately from tangible capital assets by requiring them to be reported by major class separate from major classes of tangible capital assets.

Right-to-use assets would be required to be recognized for subscription-based information technology arrangements separately from other capital assets. Assets representing the right-to-use intangible underlying assets, other than subscription-based information technology arrangements, should not be classified separately from assets representing the right-to-use tangible underlying assets. Assets representing the right-to-use intangible underlying assets would be classified separately from owned intangible assets.

Finally, nonfinancial investments would not be classified separately from financial investments on the face of the financial statements or require any new disclosures. Receivables for nonfinancial assets would not be classified separately from other receivables. The exposure draft is expected to define the term *held for sale*. Such capital assets held for sale would be required to be reclassified as used for service if the usage of the asset changes over time.

An exposure draft was in the process of release as this edition of the *Guide* was slated for publication. A final standard is expected by June 2024.

Liabilities. Some governments hold liabilities as investments. Common liabilities include interest rate swaps that are investments and not used for hedging purposes. The transfer of a liability assumes that the liability is transferred to a market participant at a measurement date. The liability would then remain outstanding with the transferee fulfilling the obligation. Even if there is no observable market for these transactions, there may be an observable market for similar liabilities if they are held by other parties as assets.

If the liability is held by another party as an asset, the government can measure the liability from the perspective of the holder of the identical item as of the measurement date. The levels and techniques detailed previously can be used.

Nonperformance Risk. There is a risk that a liability may have risks including nonperformance by the counterparty or the government's own credit rating may adjust the value of the liability (credit risk). Nonperformance risk is assumed to be the same before and after the transfer of the liability. When measuring the fair value of a liability, a government should consider the effect of its own credit risk (credit standing) and any other factors that might influence the likelihood that the obligation will or will not be fulfilled. That effect may differ depending on the characteristics of the liability, such as (*a*) whether the liability is an obligation to deliver cash (a financial liability) or an obligation to deliver goods or services (a nonfinancial liability) and (b) the terms of credit enhancements related to the liability, if any.

Restrictions Preventing the Transfer of a Liability. There may be restrictions in liabilities like restrictions in assets. Therefore, similar adjustments detailed previously may need to be made [GASB Cod. Secs. 3100.156–.160].

PRACTICE POINT: A comprehensive example of disclosures is in the *Governmental GAAP Practice and Disclosures Manual*, Chapter 17.

CASH DEPOSITS WITH FINANCIAL INSTITUTIONS

Like all enterprises, governments hold cash with financial institutions. Required disclosures of cash deposits with institutions are found later in this chapter.

Deposits may include interest-earning investment contracts such as time deposits (certificates of deposit), cash, and cash equivalents. Most governments are subject to legal or contractual provisions regarding deposits. Various risks are involved with deposits include custodial credit risk and in rare circumstances for most governments, foreign currency risk [GASB Cod. Secs. C20.101–.102].

Deposits with the U.S. Treasury for unemployment compensation, interfund loans, and equity in joint ventures are not deposits with institutions and generally are not considered investments per GASB Cod. Sec. C20.701-1.

Cash and Cash Equivalents

Cash and cash equivalents are not purely deposits, nor are they purely investments. GASB Cod. Sec. C20.701-3 discusses how they are mutually exclusive. When considering a Statement of Cash Flows in accordance with GASB Cod. Sec. 2450, the definition of a cash equivalent *overlaps* deposits and investments. A *cash equivalent*, when evaluated for purposes of whether it is a cash deposit with an institution or an investment as discussed later in this chapter, is *either* a deposit or an investment (not both except for cash flow reporting purposes of proprietary funds).

For example, a 60-day certificate of deposit is a deposit with a financial institution, and a Treasury bill purchased 60 days before its maturity is an investment. But for cash flow reporting purposes, both qualify as cash equivalents because their original maturities are three months or less. The fact that a cash equivalent is a deposit, or an investment has no effect on the presentation of the statement of cash flows of a proprietary fund.

GASB Cod. Sec. C20.701-4 discusses how to reconcile the difference between the definitions. The definition of cash equivalents for cash flow reporting purposes affects reported cash flows and beginning and ending cash and cash equivalent balances, as well as presentation of the related assets on the Statement of Net Position or Balance Sheet. The risk disclosure requirements for deposits with financial institutions and for investments primarily address disclosure in the notes to the financial statements. The financial statement presentation requirements of a statement of cash flows, as they relate to the presentation of cash equivalents, take precedence over discussions of deposits and investments. There is no requirement to reconcile the disclosures required by these sections, to the statement of cash flows or to the Statement of Net Position or Balance Sheet, however, some believe reconciliation provides useful information. As a practical matter, a reconciliation helps the user of the financial statements understand the differences.

Definition of Cash. The definition of "cash" is not contained within GASB Cod. Sec. I50 nor within GASB Cod. Sec. C20. It is contained within GASB Cod. Sec. 2450.fn.2 as follows:

> Consistent with common usage, *cash* includes not only currency on hand, but also demand deposits with banks or other financial institutions. *Cash* also includes deposits in other kinds of accounts or cash management pools that have the general characteristics of demand deposit accounts in that the governmental enterprise may deposit additional cash at any time and also effectively may withdraw cash at any time without prior notice or penalty.

Legal or Contractual Provisions for Deposits

Many governments are subject to state laws, ordinances, governance resolutions and similar guidelines regarding deposits. States may require collateral on deposits to be held by a government's independent third-party agent. GASB Cod. Sec. C20.705-1 lists potential sources of legal provisions for disclosure purposes, including those that carry the force of law. One of three forms is common:

Legal Provision or Force of Law	Common Elements
Detailed list of permissible deposits and investments (a legal list) and other requirements	Includes custody of collateral on deposits and investment securities. Many state statutes use this form.
Prudent-person or prudent-expert rule	Common in pension and other fiduciary activities and investments at lower levels of government than states. These rules are broad statements of intent, generally requiring investment selection and management to be made with prudent, discreet, and intelligent judgment and care. Additional investment objectives may be given in a prudent-person or prudent-expert rule, for example, to consider safety of principal before investment yield.
Home-rule authority	Allows governments to enact their own legislation. Sometimes local governments are given home-rule authority in some investment areas (such as investment selection) and detailed statutory requirements in others (such as a requirement to have collateral on deposits).

State investment legislation, supplemented by legal requirements established by the governing body or other oversight body of the state or local governmental entity or agency, should be used in applying the investments requirements too. For example, if state statutes provide that the investments of a pension plan should be guided by a prudent-person rule and there are no other legal requirements concerning investments for the system, the prudent-person rule should be the basis for the disclosures required. If, however, the system's board of trustees establishes detailed investment policies and board actions constitute legal requirements, the disclosures should be based on the board's policies. Similarly, local ordinances enacted by a local government with home-rule authority should be the basis for the disclosures.

Although important to an entity's portfolio management, investment policies that are *not legal requirements* are not required to be used as a basis for disclosure. For example, if state law is silent on custodial arrangements for investment securities but it is the policy of the office of the state treasurer to have independent third-party custody, that policy is not a legal provision. Therefore, although violation of that custodial policy should concern management, but GAAP does not require its disclosure in the notes to financial statements.

GASB Cod. Sec. C20.705-2 discusses how to identify *significant* violations and resulting disclosure. Recognition of a significant violation is a matter of professional judgment, connoting qualitative and quantitative factors. A significant violation would not necessarily be restricted to one that involves a large dollar investment or a large dollar risk of loss. Qualitative features to be considered include the specific wording of the legal or contractual provisions, the reason for the provisions, the current political environment, whether such a violation would affect the actions or accountability assessment of the financial statement users, and whether the lack of control that allowed a small dollar violation potentially could allow a future violation involving a much larger dollar investment or larger dollar risk of loss.

For example, suppose a government required by law to fully collateralize uninsured deposits had a small value of uncollateralized deposits during the reporting period because it has no procedures to monitor the value of collateral. This situation could be considered a significant legal violation because the lack of procedures could result in higher levels of uncollateralized deposits in the future. Moreover, some believe any violations of legal provisions relating to collateral requirements and the use of unauthorized investment types are inherently significant in a qualitative sense and should be disclosed, regardless of the dollar amount involved. Disclosure then should only be as detailed to inform users and include actions taken to address such violations.

Risks of Deposits

Deposits are subject to custodial credit risk and in rare circumstances, foreign currency risk.

Custodial Credit Risk. Deposits are exposed to custodial credit risk if they are not covered by depository insurance (Federal Deposit Insurance Corporation or FDIC) and the deposits are in the following categories:

9016 Specific Accounting and Reporting Issues

Category	Classification
1	Uncollateralized.
2	Collateralized with securities held by the pledging financial institution.
3	Collateralized with securities held by the pledging financial institution's trust department (or agent) but not in the depositor-government's name.

PRACTICE POINT: Many governments require depositing in institutions with FDIC insurance or state-sponsored insurance entities that are like FDIC. Other laws and regulations require at least 100% collateralization using securities with the least amount of risk possible.

If a government has deposits at the end of the period that are exposed to custodial credit risk, it should disclose the amount of those bank balances, the fact that the balances are uninsured, and whether the balances are exposed based on the categories above.

Foreign Currency Risk. If a government's deposits are subject to foreign currency risk, the government is required to disclose the balances of the deposit in U.S. dollars, organized by currency denomination. In practice, it would be rare that a *state or local government's* deposits would be subject to foreign currency risk. Some investment entities may have deposits subject to foreign currency risk. In many jurisdictions, deposits are required by law or regulation to be held at banks in the jurisdiction and in U.S. currency [GASB Cod. Sec. C20.108].

Finally, disclosure also includes brief summaries of policies and procedures related to the risks. If a government has no policy that addresses a risk *that it is exposed to*, disclosure is also required. Losses recognized during the period due to default by counterparties to deposits and amounts recovered from prior-period losses are part of statements of revenues, expenses (expenditures) and changes in fund balance (net position) as well as the Statement of Activities [GASB Cod. Secs. C20.109–.110].

INVESTMENT DERIVATIVE INSTRUMENTS

For many state and local government financial statement preparers, auditors, and users, the concepts and terminology associated with derivative instruments is relatively unfamiliar and difficult to fully understand.

Definition of Derivative Instruments. A derivative instrument is a financial instrument or arrangement, often complex in nature, whereby two parties agree to make payments to each other under different obligation scenarios (e.g., by utilizing an "interest rate swap"). Governments normally engage in *investment* derivative instruments to generate additional investment income (mainly with postemployment benefit plans). *Hedging* derivative instruments are used to minimize or mitigate risk related to variable rate debt issuances by:

- Fixing prices to better manage cash flows, and
- Lowering borrowing costs.

GASB Cod. Sec. D40 (*Derivative Instruments*) states that for the purposes of state and local government accounting and financial reporting, derivative standards apply to financial arrangements that have values or cash payments based on what happens in separate transactions, agreements, or rates and that has *all* three of the following characteristics:

1. The financial arrangement contains settlement factors that determine the amount of the settlement, and, in some cases, whether a settlement is required. Settlement factors include the reference rate (e.g., rate and swap indexes), the notional amount (e.g., number of currency units, shares, pounds, gallons, or bushels of a commodity), and a payment provision (e.g., a provision for a payment to be made if a reference rate behaves in a certain manner).
2. The financial arrangements are leveraged (i.e., they require no initial investment on the part of the government or an initial investment that is small relative to what would otherwise be required to obtain the same results in the market).
3. The financial arrangements have net settlement terms whereby the arrangements can be or are required to be settled net by means outside the contract such as by cash payment, or it provides for delivery of an asset that puts the recipient in a position not substantially different from net settlement [GASB Cod. Sec. D40.103].

The scope of the GASB's derivative instrument standards exclude the following types of financial instruments, some of which have provisions in other sections of GAAP:

- Derivative instruments that represent normal purchases and sales contracts (e.g., commodity purchases where it is probable the government will take or make delivery of the commodity),
- Nonperformance guarantees on contracts that are dependent on the failure of a counterparty to fulfil the contract terms,
- Insurance contracts accounted for in accordance with GASB Cod. Sec. C50 (regarding claims and judgments), or public entity risk pools in accordance with GASB Cod. Sec. Po20 (and as discussed in Chapter 23),
- Certain financial guarantee contracts unless *they are contracted as an investment derivative instrument* (Guarantees, for example, may be a loan guarantee that provides for the government to make payments if the debtor defaults or fails to meet a debt covenant. They could also include a federal guarantee that protects a university from loss in its student loans, a guarantee that a state provides for the nonpayment of debt of a private corporation or bond insurance where the government pays the premium, the bond insurance is associated with the government's debt, and the debt holder is the beneficiary),
- Certain contracts that are not exchange-traded (e.g., contracts that provide for the payment of liquidated damages if a party fails to perform under the contract),

- Revenue-based contracts that are not exchange-traded and have reference rates based on sales or service levels or volumes, and
- Loan commitments (e.g., a loan commitment extended by a government housing finance authority to potential home buyers meeting specific criteria) [GASB Cod. Sec. D40.101].

> **IMPORTANT NOTE:** These exclusions are often confused with *investment derivative instruments*, which are derivatives for income or profit and are potentially part of the scope of this section.

A "normal purchases and sales contract" is difficult to understand. GASB Cod. Sec. D40.702-4 provides the following example that would meet the normal purchases and normal sales scope exception:

- A government finalizes a take-or-pay contract for a commodity (e.g., a utility contract for an amount of electricity). Under this contract, the government agrees to pay a specified price for a specified quantity of the commodity (the electricity), without regard to whether the government ultimately takes delivery.
- The government uses the commodity in its operations, and the quantity specified in the contract is consistent with the government's activities.
- It is probable that the government will take delivery of the commodity specified in the contract.

This form of take-or-pay contract generally meets the definition of a derivative instrument if the government *does not take delivery*. However, if the government plans to take delivery and the quantity specified is consistent with what is used in the government's operations (e.g., when the government is a public utility), then the contract qualifies for the normal purchases and sales scope exception and should not be reported according to the requirements of GASB Cod. Sec. D40.

> **PRACTICE POINT:** Hedging derivative instruments are discussed in Chapter 12.

Types of Investment Derivative Instruments. A typical derivative instrument is leveraged in that it is entered into with little or no initial payment, contains settlement factors that determine the amount of settlement, can be settled with a cash payment or the transfer of an equivalent asset, and has a value based on a separate transaction or agreement. In other words, the cash flows and fair values of derivative instruments are determined by changing market prices, such as bond or commodity prices or indexes. Some investment derivative instruments may even provide an up-front cash payment to a government. Common types of investment derivative instruments used by governments include interest rate and commodity swaps, interest rate locks, options, swaptions, forward contracts, and futures contracts.

Examples of derivative instruments are as follows [GASB Cod. Secs. D40.501–.561, D40.702-1]:

Type of Derivative Instrument	Description of the Derivative Instrument
Commodity swaps	Commodity swaps are contracts that have a variable payment based on the price or index of an underlying commodity.
Forward contracts	Forward contracts are agreements to buy or sell a security, commodity, foreign currency, or other financial instrument at a certain future date for a specific price. An agreement with a supplier to purchase a quantity of heating oil at a certain future time, for a certain price, and a certain quantity is an example of a forward contract. Forward contracts are not securities and are not exchange-traded. Some forward contracts may be settled by a cash payment that is equal to the fair value of the contract rather than delivery of a commodity or financial instrument.
Futures contract	A government could enter into an agreement to buy or sell an actively traded product or commodity (e.g., fuel) for a specified price on a specific future date to protect against future commodity price increases. For example, a government-owned utility might finalize a futures contract to lock in a price for the purchase of energy (e.g., electricity or natural gas) without ever having to buy the energy.
Interest rate swap	A government may enter into an agreement to attempt to lower its borrowing costs. In this type of derivative, a government that has issued variable-rate debt also agrees to an interest rate swap in which the government agrees to pay a steady interest rate to a financial firm (usually a higher rate of interest than it currently pays on the variable-rate debt). In return, the financial firm agrees to pay the government an amount (that changes as market interest rates change), which is expected to offset the government's interest payments due to the bond or debt holders. Not only are the cash flows of an interest rate swap (i.e., the payments between the government and the financial firm) determined by changing market interest rates, but the value of the derivative also changes.
Interest rate lock	An agreement could be entered into between a government and a lender to lock interest rates to protect them from rising interest rates between the time of the agreement and the time of actual debt issuance. (This is used similarly in "rate locks" for many home mortgages.)
Options (such as calls, puts, collars, floors, and swaptions)	Options are contracts or securities that give their holders the right but not the obligation to buy or sell a financial instrument or commodity at a certain price for a certain period.

GASB Cod. Sec. D40.706-9 distinguishes insurance contracts from investment derivative instruments. Insurance contracts may resemble investment derivative instruments because they are entered to manage risk, payments are based on the occurrence of specific events, and casualty payments may be significant compared to the initial net investment (the insurance premium). An insurance contract is not a derivative instrument if it entitles the holder to be compensated only if because of an identifiable insurable event (other than a change in price) the holder incurs a liability or there is an adverse change in the value of a specific asset or liability for which the holder is at risk.

For example, the following types of contracts written by insurance enterprises, including public-entity risk pools, or held by the insured parties are not within the scope of GASB Cod. Sec. D40:

- Traditional life insurance contracts (the payment of death benefits is the result of an identifiable insurable event (death of the insured) instead of changes in a variable), and
- Traditional property and casualty contracts (the payment of benefits is the result of an identifiable insurable event (e.g., theft or fire) instead of changes in a variable).

Risks Associated with Investment Derivative Instruments. Investment derivative instruments can be effective in generating income or profit for the government, however, they also carry certain risks of loss, including credit risk, interest rate risk, and foreign currency risk, as discussed above.

Accounting and Reporting Standards Overview—Investment Derivative Instruments

With certain exceptions, GASB Cod. Sec. D40 with respect to investment derivative instruments generally requires that derivatives covered by its scope be reported in the government's accrual-based financial statements at fair value. The fair value of a derivative instrument at the end of the period is to be reported in the Statement of Net Position of the government-wide financial statements and the proprietary and fiduciary fund financial statements. Changes in fair value should be reported in the flow of resources statements (such as the Statement of Activities, Statement of Revenues, Expenses and Changes in Fund Net Position, or Statement of Changes in Fiduciary Net Position) as investment gains or losses [GASB Cod. Secs. D40.115–.116].

The GASB provided for reporting of fair value and changes in fair value for derivative instruments only in accrual-based financial statements (government-wide, proprietary, and fiduciary funds), and not in governmental funds that are reported on the modified accrual basis of accounting and current financial resources measurement focus.

Determining Fair Value of Investment Derivatives. GASB Cod. Sec. D40 provides that fair value should be measured by the market price when there is an active market for an investment derivative instrument. When an active market price is unavailable, the fair value may be estimated through an acceptable method of forecasting expected cash flows that are discounted. GASB Cod. Sec. D40 identifies several acceptable formula-based and mathematics-based methods, including matrix pricing, the zero-coupon method, and the par value method. For options, fair value may be based on a recognized option pricing model. Fair values may also be developed by pricing services, provided they are developed under acceptable methods.

Excluding an example of note disclosure, GASB Cod. Sec. D40.901 provides 19 illustrations of the accounting and financial reporting treatment application for diverse types of derivative instruments. Financial statement preparers, auditors, and users will find these illustrations extremely helpful in understanding the complexities of accounting and financial reporting for derivative instruments. An example of note disclosure for investment derivative instruments is shown in an Appendix to this chapter.

INVESTMENTS

Investments

GASB Cod. Sec. I50 is one of the more comprehensive *Codification* sections. Accounting and financial reporting standards are included for all investments, including repurchase agreements. Disclosure guidance is also included for investments.

To reiterate from the Introduction to this chapter, an "investment" is defined as follows [GASB Cod. Sec. I50.103]:

A security or other asset:
- That a government holds primarily for income or profit, and
- With a present service capacity that is based solely on its ability to generate cash or to be sold to generate cash.

PRACTICE POINT: GASB Cod. Sec. I50.702-3 makes an important point in the definition of an investment. Different governments *can* arrive at different conclusions regarding the classification of similar assets. A government's purpose for acquiring an asset is key to identifying the asset as an investment. As an example, a retirement plan may own a building whose present service capacity is based solely on its ability to generate cash. In that circumstance, the building is classified as an investment. On the other hand, a local government may own a building that is rented to individuals in the provision of low-income housing. In that circumstance, the building is not considered an investment.

As discussed in Chapter 1, GASB: CS-4 defines an *asset* as resources with a present service capacity that the entity presently controls. For many governments, investments may be one of the larger balances in the Statement of Net Position and the individual governmental fund Balance Sheets, proprietary fund Statements of Fund Net Position and certainly the fiduciary fund Statements of Fiduciary Net Position.

Present Service Capacity. Investments directly or indirectly allow a government to provide services. As an investment is an asset, the next question is related to the ability to provide services related to the government's mission and operations. Investments have value in this regard as they can be used to fund goods or services that in turn provide services directly to the citizenry. The services range from programs to capital assets used by citizens to many other forms of governance. Therefore, investments usually have present service capacity [GASB Cod. Sec. I50.104].

Held Primarily for Income or Profit. Investments are almost always acquired with the expectation of future income or profit. This does not mean an investment is risk-free. Disclosure of those risks is an important part of GAAP. The fund that reports the investment is an indicator of the holding of the asset for income or profit. In some cases, holding of a capital asset may be for income or profit, especially in endowments, pension and OPEB plans [GASB Cod. Sec. I50.105].

Ability to Generate Cash or to Be Sold to Generate Cash. Many financial instruments may generate cash to finance services. But the ability to generate cash does not mean a financial instrument is an investment. Mortgage loans are provided as an example. If the mortgage loan is part of a government's program to extend financing to first-time homebuyers, the present service capacity of the loans is not based on the loan's ability to generate cash. Therefore, the loan is part of operations and not an investment of the entity that issues the loan and receives repayment [GASB Cod. Sec. I50.106].

Indeed, some capital assets produce income, yet are classified as capital assets as the basis for determining the classification is *not* based solely on the asset's ability to generate cash (or to be sold to generate cash). GASB Cod. Sec. I50.705-1 provides examples in this regard:

- An airport serves the public with terminals and hangars that are leased,
- A water utility produces income from the sale of water,
- A transit system or toll road serves riders or users of the road in exchange for fares (tolls),
- A state owns land surrounding a waterway that produces income from easements.

An investment decision is made at acquisition. Once the government decides an asset is an investment or some other asset, the amount is presented in the financial statements based on the classification. Even if the government's usage changes over time, the asset classification remains constant [GASB Cod. Sec. I50.107].

> **PRACTICE POINT:** As introduced in this paragraph in the first example, capital assets leased could be investments. GASB Cod. Sec. L20.138 requires *lessors* (not lessees) to classify leased assets as investments *if the underlying asset meets the requirements (or definition) to be reported as an investment.* If reported at fair value (see previous and next sections), the lessor only is required to disclose the existence, terms, and conditions of options by the lessee to terminate the lease or abatement payments in the circumstance where the lessor government has issued debt for which principal and interest payments are secured by the lease payments. The remainder of disclosure may be as part of investment disclosure discussed later in this chapter. Leases are discussed in Chapter 14.

Basis of Accounting and Measurement Focus for Investments

The standards of investments apply to governmental funds, proprietary funds, government-wide financial statements, and fiduciary funds. That is, an entity must use fair value as the basis to present investments and changes in fair value of the investments in its various financial statements, no matter what type of fund as well as the government-wide financial statements, unless there is an exception provided in GAAP.

Examples of Investments at Fair Value. Examples provided by GASB of investments at fair value include:

- Common stock *not measured according to the equity method* (see following section),
- Money market investments and participating interest-earning investment contracts that do not meet the cost-based measurement,
- External investment pools that *are not* 2a7-like external investment pools (see **PRACTICE POINT**),
- Life settlement contracts,
- Open-end mutual funds,
- Land and other real estate held as investments by endowments (including permanent and term endowments) or permanent funds,
- Investment derivative instruments (as discussed in the previous section and for hedging derivatives, Chapter 12), and
- A majority equity interest in a legally separate organization held by a government engaged only in:
  — Fiduciary activities (such as a pension or OPEB plan),
  — A fiduciary fund,
  — An endowment of a public college or university or hospital (including permanent and term endowments), or
  — A permanent fund.

PRACTICE POINT: The Securities and Exchange Commission (SEC) Rule 2a7 (of the Investment Company Act of 1940) regulates money market funds. The Rule may change based on market activity, most recently as a result of the COVID-19 pandemic.

Common Stock at Fair Value. Common stock should be reported at fair value if held by:

- Governmental external investment pools,
- Pension and OPEB plans,
- Internal Revenue Code Section 457 deferred compensation plans (if reported by the state or local government or in a separately-issued stand-alone report) (see discussion of Section 457 plans in Chapter 8), and
- Endowments (including permanent and term endowments) or permanent funds.

Investments in certain entities may be calculated using net asset value (NAV) or its equivalent. Separate provisions are provided on NAV in this chapter. Equity interests in joint ventures would also be reported in accordance with the provisions discussed in Chapter 4 for joint ventures and are separate and distinct from equity interest valuation using the equity method described in the following subsection. [GASB Cod. Sec. I50.109].

The equity method is required to be used for investments only if the criteria is met in the following subsection and the investments are not specifically excluded as described in this subsection [GASB Cod. Sec. I50.110].

Equity Interests—Using the Equity Method

> **PRACTICE POINT:** The elements of the equity method contained within GASB Cod. Sec. I50 are largely adapted from FASB (Financial Accounting Standards Board) standards and applied to the governmental model. Practitioners who understand the equity method of accounting should be familiar with the accounting provisions.

Under the equity method, an investor initially records an investment in the stock of an investee at cost and adjusts the carrying amount of the investment to recognize the investor's share of the earnings or losses of the investee after the date of acquisition.

The amount of the adjustment is included in the determination of the changes in net assets by the investor. Such an amount reflects adjustments including adjustments to eliminate inter-entity gains and losses, and to amortize, if appropriate, any difference between investor cost and underlying equity in net assets of the investee at the date of investment. The investment of an investor is also adjusted to reflect the investor's share of changes in the investee's capital.

Dividends received from an investee reduce the carrying amount of the investment. A series of operating losses of an investee or other factors may indicate that a decrease in value of the investment has occurred that is other than temporary and that should be recognized even though the decrease in value is more than what would otherwise be recognized by application of the equity method [GASB Cod. Sec. I50.111].

Criteria. A key determinant for using the equity method for common stock is whether the government can exercise *significant influence* over operating and financial policies of an investee, even though the government holds 50% or less of the *voting* stock.

Influence may be indicated in several ways:

- Representation on the governing body,
- Participation in policy making,
- Significant intra-entity transactions,
- Interchange of managerial personnel, or
- Technology dependency.

Determining the ability to influence is not always clear and judgment is usually necessary. There is a presumption that holding 20% or more of *voting* stock leads to significant influence unless the influence can be shown. Care must be taken in the case of temporary influence or if the investee is in reorganization or bankruptcy. The temporary influence, reorganization, or bankruptcy are signs of questionable going concern in the investee.

An example of holding less than 20% of voting stock could occur in low-income housing tax credit entities. A government could be a general shareholder (partner) in the transaction and only hold 1% of the voting stock. The other 99% are held by limited shareholders (partners) who also receive a tax credit. By being the general shareholder (partner), the government has significant influence [GASB Cod. Sec. I50.112, fn. 3].

A government's voting stock interest is based on those currently outstanding securities where holders have present voting privileges. Other arrangements are not included. Governments then evaluate the facts and circumstances and unless there is evidence to the contrary, holding 20% of voting stock usually indicates significant influence [GASB Cod. Secs. I50.113–.114].

Problems in making the judgment of the presence of significant influence on the operations and finances of an investee on an ongoing basis include, but are not limited to:

- Opposition by the investee, including litigation, challenges, lawsuits, "proxy fights."
- There is some written agreement between the government and the investee where significant rights of the government are renounced or waived.
- The remaining ownership of the investment is held by a small group of investors who operate independently of the government's influence.
- The government requires (or asks for) financial information to prepare interim financial information, but the investee only publicly reports annual information. The investee refuses to provide the information.
- The government attempts to have a seat on the Board of Directors of the investee and is not successful.

PRACTICE POINT: Even though a government may hold a significant amount of equity in a privately held entity (also known as private equity), the government may not have influence on the operations and finances due to these factors. The same could be true in holding a significant amount of debt in a private placement (also known as private debt). These issues (and others) should be looked at over time and not on a temporary basis [GASB Cod. Sec. I50.115].

Applying the Equity Method. The equity method is calculated as follows upon purchasing the common stock and application of the equity method is required:

1. Intra-entity profits and losses should be eliminated until realized by the government or investee,
2. A difference between the cost of an investment and the amount of underlying equity in net assets of an investee should be accounted for as a deferred outflow of resources and attributed to future periods in a systematic and rational manner,

3. The investment(s) in common stock should be shown in the Statement of Net Position of a government as a single amount, and the government's share of earnings or losses of an investee(s) should be shown in the flows statement as a single amount except for the extraordinary items, which should be classified like all other extraordinary items (see Chapter 5), and

4. Sales of stock of an investee by a government should be accounted for as gains or losses equal to the difference at the time of sale between selling price and carrying amount of the stock sold.

If the financial statements of an investee are not sufficiently timely for an investor to apply the equity method currently, the government should record its share of the earnings or losses of an investee from the most recent available financial statements. A lag in reporting should be consistent.

A loss in value of an investment that is other than a temporary decline should be recognized the same as a loss in value of other long-term assets. Evidence of a loss in value might include, but would not necessarily be limited to, absence of an ability to recover the carrying amount of the investment or inability of the investee to sustain an earnings capacity that would justify the carrying amount of the investment.

The current fair value of an investment that is less than the carrying amount may indicate a loss in value of the investment. However, a decline in the quoted market price below the carrying amount or the existence of operating losses is not necessarily indicative of a loss in value that is other than temporary. All are factors that should be evaluated.

A government's share of losses of an investee may equal or exceed the carrying amount of an investment accounted for by the equity method plus advances made by the investor. The government should discontinue applying the equity method when the investment (and net advances) is reduced to zero and should not recognize additional losses unless the government has guaranteed obligations of the investee or is otherwise committed to provide further financial support for the investee.

If the investee subsequently reports net income, the government should resume applying the equity method only after its share of that net income equals the share of net losses not recognized during the period the equity method was suspended.

When an investee has outstanding cumulative preferred stock, a government should compute its share of earnings (losses) after deducting the investee's preferred dividends, whether such dividends are declared.

Transitioning from the Equity Method. An investment in voting stock of an investee company may fall below the level of ownership described in the criteria for equity method from sale of a portion of an investment by the government, sale of additional stock by an investee, or other transaction, and the government may thereby lose the ability to influence policy, as described previously.

A government should discontinue accruing its share of the earnings or losses of the investee for an investment that no longer qualifies for the equity method. The earnings or losses that relate to the stock retained by the government and that previously were accrued should remain as a part of the carrying amount of the investment.

The investment account should not be adjusted retroactively. However, dividends received by the government in subsequent periods that exceed its share of earnings for such periods should reduce the carrying amount of the investment [GASB Cod. Sec. I50.116] (see next subsection on the cost method).

Positions in Common Stock that are *Not* Investments—Cost Method

In certain circumstances, there may be some common stock that a government may hold that does not meet the definition of an investment. The position also does not meet the eligibility criteria for using the equity method as discussed previously.

The cost method is then used similarly to an individual investor's holding of stock. The equity interest in the common stock is recognized at cost. Dividends received reduce the net accumulated earnings of the company (retained earnings) since the date of acquisition by the government. The only time cost is reduced is when dividends received exceed accumulated earnings. This is known as return of capital and normally occurs during an extended period of operating losses that is more than temporary, but with the company continuing dividends in accordance with bylaws [GASB Cod. Secs. C55.101–.102].

Investment Positions in External Investment Pools as well as Cash and Investments

Amounts of cash deposits and temporary investments belonging to various funds of the government entity may be in the form of separate accounts for each fund or may be pooled with similar assets of other funds to maximize the return on invested resources. For pooled cash and investments, adequate records must be maintained to provide a basis for identifying each fund's share of the pooled assets, including interest earned and receivable at the end of the period. Each fund's portion of the pooled assets may be designated "equity in pooled cash and temporary investments" or some other, similar designation. The method of allocating interest on pooled resources to each fund should be disclosed in the financial statements.

Pooled cash and investments may be an internal or external investment pool. As discussed in Chapter 8, internal pools benefit solely the government, its funds, its component units, and its agencies. External investment pools benefit a group of governments, beyond the sponsoring government.

Certain pools may solely comprise deposits and short-term investments, including cash and cash equivalents, and other pools may solely comprise longer-term marketable investments. When reporting positions held in these cash and investment pools, a government should consider separately reporting the positions held in these diverse types of pools in the Balance Sheet or Statement of

Net Position, such as "equity in state treasurer cash and cash equivalent pool" and "equity in state treasurer investment pool."

If an external investment pool does not make the election to use amortized cost or does not meet the criteria to use amortized cost, the governments in the pool should measure their investments in the pool at fair value. Legally binding guarantees provided (or obtained) by the sponsor to support the fair value of participant's investments should be evaluated considering the creditworthiness of the sponsor. GAAP does allow an estimate of fair value if a governmental entity cannot obtain information from a pool sponsor to allow it to determine the fair value and to make required disclosures [GASB Cod. Sec. I50.117].

> **PRACTICE POINT:** For custodians, administrators or sponsors of external investment pools, the allocation of investment income and pool administrative costs between accounts is especially important for audit purposes. Allocations should be performed in accordance with applicable laws, regulations, and pool provisions. If there are no pertinent laws, regulations, or pool provisions, allocations should be performed systematically and rationally without unfairly benefiting or burdening any one or group of accounts. If accounts contain proceeds from federal awards, systematic and rational allocation is required so that program income be recognized in accordance with the federal award provisions.

Investments in pools that measure investments at amortized cost are reported at the NAV per share provided by the pool. The NAV per share is an amortized cost basis that approximates fair value [GASB Cod. Sec. I50.118].

> **PRACTICE POINT:** In practice, many external investment pools strive to report at amortized cost at the NAV per share, which approximates fair value rather than at fair value. Pools that report at fair value usually have more risk.

Life settlement contracts. Life settlement contracts are measured at fair value. Such contracts have the following elements:

- The government does not have an insurable interest (an interest in the survival of the insured),
- The government provides consideration to the policy owner that is more than the current cash surrender value of the life insurance policy,
- The contract pays the face value of the policy to the government upon the death of the insured, and
- The government is the policyholder [GASB Cod. Sec. I50.119].

Unallocated insurance contracts are interest-earning investment contracts and therefore are at fair value. These differ from *allocated insurance contracts.*

> **PRACTICE POINT:** Many practitioners confuse the reporting of insurance contracts. Unallocated contracts are in the name of the government and not the insured person. Allocated insurance contracts specifically benefit the insured person (or persons) and therefore are excluded from reporting.

Open-end mutual funds. Open-end mutual funds are funds that have limitless shares. Many of the largest mutual funds available for investment are open-end. GAAP requires investments in such funds to be at fair value determined by the current share price. These funds also include governmental external investment pools that are registered as investment companies with the Securities and Exchange Commission *and* that operate as open-end funds [GASB Cod. Secs. I50.120, .546].

Interest Earning Investment Contracts and Money Market Funds. In most cases, investments in such contracts should be at fair value. Two types of contracts are investments:

- *Participating contracts*—These contracts are investments with a value affected by market (interest rate) changes and may also be negotiable, transferable, and therefore adjusted to market rates. Examples of these contracts are adjustable-rate certificates of deposit (CDs).

- *Nonparticipating contracts*—These contracts are nonnegotiable CDs with redemption terms that do not consider market rates. These CDs are at cost, if the fair value of the contract is not affected by the creditworthiness of the issuer [GASB Cod. Sec. I50.121].

Money market funds are short-term, highly liquid debt instruments. The funds commonly include commercial paper, bankers' acceptances, and U.S. Treasury and U.S. agency obligations. They typically do not include investments with risk such as asset-backed securities, derivatives, and similar instruments.

Other than external investment pools, all other governments *may* report interest-earning investment contracts (and money-market funds) at amortized cost if these investments have a remaining maturity at time of purchase of one year or less [GASB Cod. Secs. I50.122–.123].

Investments in Land and Other Real Estate Held by Endowments. A government may acquire or receive from a donor income-producing real estate (or a partial interest in income-producing real estate) as a permanent or term endowment for the benefit of an individual, private organization, or other government and report it in a private-purpose trust fund (or for the benefit of the government itself and reported in a permanent fund).

Land and other real estate held as investments by endowments be reported at fair value at the reporting date. Any changes in fair value during the period should be reported as investment income [GASB Cod. Sec. I50.124].

Synthetic Guaranteed Investment Contracts that are Fully Benefit Responsive (SGICs) and Life Insurance Contracts. SGICs may be used in debt issuance transactions to hold construction project funds. If they are fully benefit responsive, they are measured at *contract value*. Life insurance contracts are measured at cash surrender value [GASB Cod. Secs. I50.125–.126].

Investments in Certain Entities that Calculate Net Asset Value Per Share (or its Equivalent). If an investment in a nongovernmental entity is valued by using a net asset value (NAV) per share or its equivalent, GASB Cod. Secs. I50.127–.130 allow a government to establish the fair value of an investment. These types of investments calculate NAV based on member units or an ownership interest in partners' capital, to which a proportionate share of net assets is attributed. The NAV is calculated as of the government's measurement date in a manner consistent with FASB standards.

There may be many instances where the NAV of an investment is not determined as of a government's measurement date or is not calculated in manner consistent with FASB standards. In such an event, the government may need to adjust to the most recent NAV per share. The government may determine that fair value should be applied. The method of determining fair value should be applied consistently to the fair value measurement of the government's entire position in a particular investment, *unless it is probable* at the measurement date that the government will sell a portion of an investment at an amount different from the NAV per share (or its equivalent) In those situations, the government should account for the portion of the investment that is being sold at fair value.

A sale is considered *probable* only if *all* the following criteria have been met as of the government's measurement date:

- The government, having the authority to approve the action, commits to a plan to sell the investment,
- An active program to locate a buyer and other actions required to complete the plan to sell the investment have been initiated,
- The investment is available for immediate sale subject only to terms that are usual and customary for sales of such investments (e.g., a requirement to obtain approval of the sale from the investee, or a buyer's due diligence procedures), and
- Actions required to complete the plan indicate that it is unlikely that significant changes to the plan will be made or that the plan will be withdrawn.

Recognition and Reporting of Investments and Investment Income

All investment income, including changes in the fair value of investments, must be reported as revenue on the governmental entity's operating statement. Investment income includes interest and dividend income, realized gains and losses on the sale of investments, and changes in the fair value of investments the governmental entity holds, inclusive of irrevocable split-interest agreements as discussed in this chapter. If the governmental entity elects to separately identify the change in the fair value of its investments, the change should be labeled as "net increase (decrease) in the fair value of investments," which is defined as "the difference between the fair value of investments at the beginning of the year and at the end of the year, taking into consideration investment purchases, sales, and redemptions."

Unrealized Gains and Losses. Unrealized gains and losses (from the valuation of investments at the end of the period) and *realized* gains and losses (from the sale of investments during the period) must not be reported separately on the operating statement. Realized gains and losses may be presented separately in a note to the financial statements of the governmental entity if such gains and losses are measured as the difference between the sales price of the investment and the original cost of the investment. However, governmental external investment pools that prepare separate financial reports may report realized gains and losses separately from the net increase or decrease in the fair value of investments on the face of their operating statements. If a governmental external investment pool elects this option, the unrealized gains and losses should be labeled as net increase (decrease) in the fair value of investments, as noted in the previous paragraph [GASB Cod. Sec. I50.131].

The calculation of the increase or decrease in the fair value of investments is illustrated in GASB Cod. Sec. I50.914, part of which is reproduced in Exhibit 9-1.

EXHIBIT 9-1
CALCULATION OF CHANGE IN FAIR VALUE OF INVESTMENTS

Year 1

Specific Identification Method

	Cost	A Beginning fair value	B Purchases	C Sales	D Subtotal*	E Ending fair value	F Change in fair value**
Security 1	$100	$100	—	—	$100	$120	$20
Security 2	520	540	—	—	540	510	(30)
Security 3	200	240	—	$250	(10)	—	10
Security 4	330	—	$330	—	330	315	(15)
Totals		$880	$330	$250	$960	$945	$(15)

* Column D = Columns A+B *less* Column C.
** Column F = Column E *less* Column D.

Aggregate Method	Amounts
Fair value on December 31, 20X8	$945
Add: Proceeds of investments sold in year 20X8	250
Less: Cost of investments purchased in year 20X8	(330)
Less: Fair value on December 31, 20X7	(880)
Change in fair value of investments	$ (15)

Year 2

Specific Identification Method

	Cost	A Beginning fair value	B Purchases	C Sales	D Subtotal*	E Ending fair value	F Change in fair value**
Security 1	$100	$120	—	$110	$10	$—	$(10)
Security 2	520	510	—	—	510	550	40
Security 3	330	315	—	330	(15)	—	15
Security 4	310	—	310	—	310	300	(10)
Total		$945	$310	$440	$815	$850	$35

* Column D = Columns A + B *less* Column C.
** Column F = Column E *less* Column D.

	Aggregate Method	Amounts
Fair value on December 31, 20X9		$850
Add: Proceeds of investments sold in year 20X9		440
Less: Cost of investments purchased in year 20X9		(310)
Less: Fair value on December 31, 20X8		(945)
Change in fair value of investments		$35

The calculation of the change in the fair value of investments simplifies a difficult presentation problem that arises when assets are presented at fair value and some of the assets are held for more than two accounting periods before they are sold. Specifically, the question is how to present realized and unrealized gains and losses for the same investment.

For example, assume that an investment purchased for $100 has a value of $150 at the end of the first year and is sold for $180 during the second year. The governmental entity has a $50 unrealized gain in year 1 ($150 − $100) and an $80 realized gain in year 2 ($180 − $100), however, the maximum amount of (economic) gain that can be reported on operating statements for the two years is $80.

For this reason, the effect on the operating statement in the second year is $30, because the $50 unrealized gain must be netted against the $80 realized gain. The illustrated calculation of the net change in investments simplifies the computation by not separating unrealized and realized gains and losses. The standard prohibits the presentation of realized gains and losses on the income statement, because the presentation may detract from the reporting of the change in the fair value of investments and could be misinterpreted if the reader does not understand how a realized gain may not be an economic gain in the year the investment is sold if the investment had an unrealized gain (that was equal to the realized gain in the current period) in the previous period.

Investments in Internal Investment Pools. Some governmental entities combine resources from various funds and component units into one or more "internal investment pools," defined as follows [GASB Cod. Sec. I50.132]:

> An arrangement that commingles (pools) the moneys of more than one fund or component unit of a reporting entity. Investment pools that include participation by legally separate entities that are not part of the same reporting entity as the pool sponsor are not internal investment pools, but rather are external investment pools.

Under this arrangement, for external financial reporting purposes the internal investment pool must allocate its investments to the various funds and component units based on the equity interest that each fund or component unit holds in the internal investment pool. Also, investment income and losses that the internal investment pool incurs must be allocated to the participating funds and component units based on their respective equity interests in the pool.

In some circumstances, one fund (the investing fund) may have an equity interest in an internal investment pool, while another fund (the income recipient fund) may receive the investment income from the pool. When the recipient fund's right to the investment income is based on "legal or contractual provisions," that language must be used as a basis for determining how each fund should record the allocation of investment income.

If, based on the specific language in the provision, the investment income is considered to belong to the recipient fund, then the recipient fund should record the investment income. However, if the specific language is interpreted to mean that the investment income belongs to the investing fund, the investment income should be recorded in the investing fund—and subsequently (or perhaps concurrently) recorded as a transfer by the investing fund (transfers out) and by the recipient fund (transfers in). On the other hand, when a recipient fund's right to the investment income is based on other than "legal or contractual provisions" (i.e., management's discretion), the investment income should be recorded in the investing fund, with each of the funds involved in the transfer subsequently recording an interfund transfer.

> **OBSERVATION:** As introduced above, a component unit may have a position in an internal investment pool of a primary government. GASB Cod. Sec. I50.734-7 describes the disclosure of an internal investment pool position by a component unit as being like other investments. "Looking through" to the underlying investments of the pool is *not appropriate* in *separately issued* component unit financial statements. Therefore, the component unit disclosures are limited to the position in the investment pool and not the underlying investments.

Fund Overdrafts in Internal Investment Pools. When a fund overdraws its position in an internal investment pool, GASB Cod. Secs. 1800.801–.802 and I50.721-14 require that the fund that overdrew its position report an interfund payable and the fund that is assumed (based on management's discretion) to have funded the overdraft report an interfund receivable.

For example, assume that a capital projects fund participates in an internal investment pool and withdraws $900,000 from the pool to pay for capital assets even though its equity position at the time of withdrawal is $850,000. If it is assumed that management deems the excess withdrawal to have been provided by the general fund, the following entries would be made by the two funds:

Capital Projects Fund	Debit	Credit
Capital Outlay	900,000	
Interest in Investment Pool		850,000
Due to General Fund		50,000
To record interfund payable due to overdrawn balance at fiscal year-end.		

GENERAL FUND	Debit	Credit
Due from Capital Projects Fund	50,000	
Interest in Investment Pool		50,000
To record interfund receivable due to overdrawn balance at fiscal year-end.		

The accounting for the overdraft and assumed coverage of the overdraft is the same no matter which fund types are involved. For example, an overdraft between two funds of the governmental fund category (as shown above) would be treated in the same way as an overdraft between funds that do not belong to the same fund category (e.g., the general fund may fund an overdraft by an enterprise fund).

The interfund loan would not be eliminated when the fund financial statements are prepared, however, the treatment of the interfund loan at the government-wide financial statement level would depend on the fund categories involved. For example, if the interfund loan was between two governmental funds, the interfund loan would be eliminated; however, if the interfund loan was between a governmental fund and an enterprise fund, the amounts would be reported as part of the internal balance presented on the Statement of Net Position.

Repurchase, Yield Maintenance, Reverse Repurchase, and Securities Lending Agreements. Income from such agreements is part of investment income [GASB Cod. Secs. I50.133–.135]. Repurchase and fixed coupon repurchase agreements are interest. Flows from yield maintenance repurchase agreements are purchases and sales which may have recognized gains and losses. Sections describing these transactions in more detail are found later in this chapter.

> **PRACTICE POINT:** Many governments may not be allowed to invest in these agreements.

Foreign Currency Gain and Loss Transactions. GASB Cod. Secs. F70.101–.105 contain guidance on foreign currency translation adjustments, which are extremely rare for general purpose governments. Should a foreign currency translation adjustment be required, at the date the transaction is recognized each asset, liability, revenue, expense, gain, or loss arising from the transaction should be measured and recorded in U.S. dollars by use of the exchange rate in effect at the date of transaction.

At each financial statement date, recorded balances that are denominated in a currency other than the U.S. dollar should be adjusted to reflect the current exchange rate. Exchange rates are the ratios of a unit of one currency to the amount of another currency for which that unit can be exchanged at an established date. The exchange rate to be used to translate and record foreign currency transactions is the applicable rate at which a transaction could be settled at the transaction date. At subsequent financial statement dates, the current rate is that rate at which the related receivable or payable could be settled at that date. The aggregate transaction gain or loss recognized in the period should be disclosed in the notes to financial statements.

Reporting for Governments that Sponsor External Investment Pools (States and other Large Governments)

A government that sponsors one (or more) external investment pools reports the pool as a separate investment trust fund (a fiduciary fund) that reports transactions and balances using the economic resources measurement focus and the accrual basis of accounting.

- The *external* portion of an external investment pool is the portion that belongs to legally separate entities that are not part of the sponsoring government's financial reporting entity.
- The *internal* portion of each external investment pool is the portion that belongs to the primary government and its component units and should be reported as discussed previously for the equity in internal investment pools.

The difference between the external pool assets, deferred outflows of resources, liabilities, and deferred inflows of resources should be captioned "net position—amounts held in trust for pool participants."

Separate Report Issued for the External Investment Pool. If an external investment pool issues a separate report, the annual financial report of the sponsoring government should describe in the notes to the financial statements how to obtain that report. The information is incorporated by reference.

Separate Report NOT Issued for the External Investment Pool. If an external investment pool *does not* issue such a report, the annual financial report of the sponsoring government should include the following background disclosures in the notes to the financial statements for each pool, as applicable:

- A brief description of any regulatory oversight (including whether the pool is registered with the SEC as an investment company),
- The frequency of determining the fair value of investments,
- The method used to determine participants' shares sold and redeemed and whether that method differs from the method used to report investments,
- Whether the pool sponsor has provided or obtained any legally binding guarantees during the period to support the value of shares,
- The extent of involuntary participation in the pool, if any (legally required to invest),
- A summary of the fair value, the carrying amount (if different from fair value), the number of shares or the principal amount, ranges of interest rates, and maturity dates of each major investment classification,
- The fair value disclosures (discussed later in this chapter),

- If the financial report distinguishes among different components of investment income (e.g., interest, dividend, and other income versus the net increase or decrease in the fair value of investments), the accounting policy for defining each of the components it reports should be disclosed, and
- For pools that report at amortized costs, the notes should disclose fair value as applicable and the presence of any limitations or restrictions on withdrawals (redemption notice periods, maximum transactions amounts, liquidity fees or redemption gates).
- The disclosures required by cash and investment standards.
- Condensed statements of fiduciary net position and changes in fiduciary net position. If a pool includes both internal and external investors, those condensed financial statements should include, in total, the net position held in trust for all pool participants, and the equity of participants should distinguish between internal and external portions [GASB Cod. Secs. I50.136–.137].

Reporting for Individual Investment Accounts

Governmental entities that provide individual investment accounts to other, legally separate entities that are *not part of the same financial reporting entity* should report those investments in one or more separate investment trust funds. If individual accounts are offered as an alternative to a pooled position, the individual accounts should be reported in a different investment trust from the pool. These activities might only occur in situations where a larger government is statutorily or contractually allowed to manage the individual investments for legally separate entities in their jurisdiction. Such entities may be not-for-profit entities as well [GASB Cod. Sec. I50.138, fn. 13].

ACCOUNTING AND REPORTING FOR REPURCHASE AND REVERSE REPURCHASE AGREEMENTS

Differentiating Repurchase Agreements from Reverse Repurchase Agreements

In a repurchase agreement transaction, the governmental entity (buyer-lender) transfers cash to a broker-dealer or financial institution (seller-borrower), the broker-dealer or financial institution transfers securities to the governmental entity and promises to repay the cash plus interest in exchange for the return of the *same* securities. The governmental entity should report income from repurchase agreements as interest income [GASB Cod. Sec. I50.558].

A *reverse repurchase agreement* is the opposite. The governmental entity *receives* cash from a broker-dealer or financial institution. The government transfers securities to the counterparty in exchange for the same securities, but in some cases the securities may be different [GASB Cod. Sec. I50.561].

Distinct types of repurchase and reverse repurchase agreements are available. These can be very esoteric and seldom used in practice. They include:

Deposits, Investments, and Investment Derivative Instruments

- *Dollar repurchase-reverse repurchase agreements.* This is a repurchase-reverse repurchase agreement that involves a transfer of securities where the parties agree that the securities returned will be from the same issuer, but not the exact same issues [GASB Cod. Sec. I50.517].

- *Fixed coupon repurchase-reverse repurchase agreement.* This is like the repurchase-reverse repurchase agreement, but the parties agree that the securities returned will have the same interest rates and similar maturities [GASB Cod. Sec. I50.527].

- *Yield maintenance repurchase-reverse repurchase agreement.* In this agreement, the parties agree that the securities will be returned providing the seller/borrower with a yield stipulated in the agreement [GASB Cod. Sec. I50.578].

Overview of Reverse Repurchase Agreements

Reverse repurchase agreements have significant risks and potential rewards. The major risk in such agreements is credit risk. Credit risk is defined as the risk that the counterparty to the transaction will not complete the transaction, fulfilling its obligations. The margin of a reverse repurchase agreement considers the credit risk of the agreement. The economic value of the credit risk of the agreement is the difference between the fair value of the securities involved in the transaction, less the amount of the reverse repurchase agreement and accrued interest.

The transaction may result in an economic gain or loss, which may differ from an accounting gain or loss. As discussed in footnote 3 to GASB Cod. Sec. I55, the following facts could occur in a reverse repurchase agreement:

Year-end sale of securities with accrued interest:	Accounting Impact	Economic Impact
Reported amount with accrued interest	$2,000,000	
Fair Value		$1,900,000
Obligation Including accrued interest	(1,800,000)	(1,800,000)
Counterparty defaults – loss	$(200,000)	$(100,000)

Of course, the reverse could be true if the reported amount of the securities were less than the obligation. In those situations, a gain would result.

Risks could also include the use of the securities involved in the agreement. The proceeds are likely to be invested at different yields than those involved in the agreement. Matched positions are ideal. Matched positions occur when the involved securities mature at or near the same time, lowering interest rate risk. The securities would be liquidated at the same time at similar fair values. If they are not matched, the fair value of the securities is reported at less than the reported amount and a loss is realized.

In a yield maintenance reverse-repurchase agreement, interest rate risk may be present as the seller-borrower assumes the risk that the fair value may change, taking the risk that interest rates will rise, and the securities will need to be repurchased at a price more than fair value, realizing a loss [GASB Cod. Secs. I55.103–.105, fn. 3].

Reporting Reverse Repurchase Agreements

If a government has the legal ability to sign these agreements, the assets and liabilities from fixed coupon reverse repurchase agreements are not netted in the Statement of Net Position nor the fund statements. The underlying securities are investment assets. The related liabilities are captioned "obligations under reverse repurchase agreements."

The outflows from such agreements are interest expense (or expenditures if reported in governmental funds). The interest inflows are reported as a component of investment income and again, not netted with interest expense [GASB Cod. Secs. I55.115–.116].

Internal investment pools that contain these agreements would report similarly. However, the assets and liabilities would only be reported in the Balance Sheets of the funds and activities that have a risk of loss on the assets. This could result in a separate allocation of the agreements from other investments that do not have the risk. The inflows and outflows would also differ as only the funds that are permitted to have such investments would contain the flows.

Finally, yield maintenance reverse repurchase agreement activities are sales and purchases of securities with recognized gains and losses [GASB Cod. Secs. I50.117–.119].

ACCOUNTING AND REPORTING FOR SECURITIES LENDING TRANSACTIONS

As part of the management of its cash and investments, a governmental entity may engage in a "securities lending transaction," which the GASB defines as follows:

> Transactions in which governmental entities transfer their securities to broker-dealers and other entities for collateral—which may be cash, securities, or letters of credit—and simultaneously agree to return the collateral for the same securities in the future [GASB Cod. Sec. I60.513].

The accounting standards for securities lending transactions apply to all funds and the government-wide financial statements. The standards apply to all governmental entities that have finalized securities lending transactions during the accounting period for which financial statements are being prepared.

Securities lending transactions are generally undertaken by large governmental entities, such as pension funds and investment pools that have significant resources to invest for extended periods. Due to the risk and the administration of securities lending transactions, many smaller governmental entities are precluded by law from consummating such transactions.

In a securities lending transaction, the governmental entity (lender) transfers its investments in securities, referred to as the underlying securities, to a broker-dealer (borrower), and the entity receives cash, other securities, or letters of credit. The purpose of the transaction is to enhance the return on the governmental entity's portfolio. For example, cash collateral may be received by the entity and subsequently invested. If the investment income exceeds the amount paid (interest) to the broker-dealer, the governmental entity will earn a net profit on the transaction, however, if the return is less than the amount paid, a net loss will occur. From the broker-dealer perspective, the securities are borrowed to cover short positions in specific securities.

At the end of the securities lending transaction, the governmental entity will return the collateral (the cash, securities or similar securities, or letter of credit) to the broker-dealer, and the broker-dealer will return the underlying securities (or similar securities) to the entity. Although the governmental entity can deal directly with a broker-dealer, securities lending transactions are usually executed through a "securities lending agent," which is defined as "an entity that arranges the terms and conditions of loans, monitors the fair values of the securities lent and the collateral received, and often directs the investment of cash collateral" [GASB Cod. Sec. I60.512].

Securities lending transactions raise the fundamental question of whether the governmental entity has incurred a liability that should be presented on its Balance Sheet or Statement of Net Position. GAAP addresses that fundamental question, along with disclosure requirements.

The disclosure requirements established by GAAP apply to the primary government and its blended component units. For component units that are discretely presented, the disclosure guidance also applies [GASB Cod. Sec. I60.102]. For component unit disclosures presented as part of the primary government's notes to the basic financial statements, care must be taken by the preparer to determine which disclosures are *essential*. In some cases, professional judgment may determine that such component unit disclosures are not essential [GASB Cod. Sec. I60.fn2].

Accounting and Reporting for Securities Lending Transactions

For all securities lending transactions, the governmental entity should report the underlying securities (the securities loaned to the broker-dealer) as assets in its Balance Sheet or Statement of Net Position. Although the underlying securities are transferred to the broker-dealer, they are nonetheless reported as an asset of the governmental entity. Additional accounting treatment for the transaction depends on whether the governmental entity receives:

- Cash,
- Securities that can be pledged or sold,
- Securities that cannot be pledged or sold, or
- Letters of credit [GASB Cod. Sec. I60.103].

Receipt of Cash

When a governmental entity sends securities to a broker-dealer or other entity and receives cash as collateral, the securities lending transaction should be recorded as a secured loan. A liability should be recognized, and the transferred securities should not be removed from the governmental entity's Balance Sheet and/or Statement of Net Position [GASB Cod. Sec. I60.104].

In transactions that involve cash collateral, the broker-dealer is paid interest (borrower rebate) on the amount it advances to the governmental entity. The government uses the cash to earn investment income by depositing the funds with a financial institution or by purchasing securities. The profitability of the transaction from the governmental entity's perspective depends on the rate of return on the collateral invested and the interest paid to the broker-dealer.

Based on the definition of a reverse repurchase agreement (see previous section in this chapter), the GASB states that a reverse repurchase agreement is the same (from an economic perspective, not a legal and tax perspective) as a securities lending transaction in which cash collateral is received by the governmental entity. GAAP requires that reverse repurchase agreements be accounted for as secured loans and not as sales of the securities that are the basis for the transaction. Thus, the accounting and disclosure standards for securities lending transactions involving cash collateral are like those established for reverse repurchase agreement transactions.

To illustrate securities lending transactions that involve cash collateral, assume a governmental entity holds investments in U.S. governmental securities that have a cost and fair value basis of $900,000. These securities are transferred to a broker-dealer for cash of $927,000, with the requirement that the securities be returned to the governmental entity at the end of five days. The entity would make the following entry to record the securities lending transaction:

	Debit	Credit
Cash	927,000	—
Liability under Securities Lending Transaction	—	927,000

The securities transferred to the broker-dealer remain on the Statement of Net Position or the Balance Sheet of the governmental entity. As illustrated in the example, the governmental entity records the cash collateral received from the broker-dealer and will subsequently record any securities or deposits acquired or made using the cash collateral as an asset.

The governmental entity may receive cash (collateral) from a broker-dealer that cannot be invested in securities (only deposited). When this restriction is imposed, the securities lending transactions "should be accounted for as involving securities collateral rather than cash collateral." Accounting for the receipt of securities collateral is discussed in the following section [GASB Cod. Sec. I60.fn4].

Receipt of Securities That Can Be Pledged or Sold. When a governmental entity transfers securities to a broker-dealer and receives securities that can be pledged or sold, even if the borrower has not defaulted on the transaction, the securities lending transaction should be recorded as a secured loan in a manner like a collateral transaction previously illustrated (asset and liability accounts are created). The broker-dealer pays the governmental entity a loan premium or fee for the loan of the securities [GASB Cod. Sec. I60.104].

The right to pledge or sell collateral securities without a borrower default must be stated in the securities lending transaction. However, that right could exist if the right has been previously demonstrated by pledging or selling securities under a previous contract that did not contain the explicit right. Also, the right could exist if "there is some other indication of the ability to pledge or sell the collateral securities." A borrower default would include failure to return underlying securities, pay income distributions, or make margin calls, acts of insolvency, and suspension by the Securities and Exchange Commission, an exchange, or a self-regulatory association [GASB Cod. Sec. I60.fn5].

In a securities lending transaction that involves securities as collateral, the broker-dealer receives certain incidents of ownership over the underlying securities during the term of the transaction, including the right to sell or pledge the securities. The governmental entity also receives certain incidents of ownership over the collateral securities. Although both parties have certain ownership rights over the securities they hold (the underlying securities and the collateral securities), each has income distribution rights which are described as follows [GASB Cod. Sec. I60.508]:

> Interest, dividends, stock splits, and other distributions made by an issuer of securities. Income distributions on underlying securities are payable from the borrower to the lender, and income distributions on collateral securities are payable from the lender to the borrower.

Thus, the governmental entity has distribution rights on the underlying securities and the broker-dealer has distribution rights on the collateral securities.

To illustrate this type of securities lending transaction, assume that in the previous example the governmental entity received investments in corporate fixed-income securities that have a fair value of $927,000, with the requirement that the underlying securities be returned to the governmental entity at the end of five days. The governmental entity would make the following entry to record the securities lending transaction:

	Debit	Credit
Investments in Corporate Fixed-Income Securities	927,000	—
Liability under Securities Lending Transaction	—	927,000

Both the securities transferred to the broker-dealer (underlying securities) and the securities received from the broker-dealer (collateral securities) are reported on the Statement of Net Position and Balance Sheet of the governmental entity. The reporting of underlying securities on the Balance Sheet of the governmental entity is necessary because the securities lending transaction is a loan of securities and not a sale. At the termination date of the transaction, the governmental entity receives the same or similar securities from the broker-dealer.

Reporting the collateral securities is necessary because the governmental entity is entitled to the risk and rewards of these securities during the contract term. The governmental entity can sell or pledge the securities, but at the end of the transaction it must return similar securities to the broker-dealer. If, for example, the collateral securities are sold at one price and their value rises before the governmental entity must return similar securities to the broker-dealer, the governmental entity will have an economic loss on the investment.

Receipt of Securities That Cannot Be Pledged or Sold. When a governmental entity transfers securities to a broker-dealer and receives securities that cannot be pledged or sold unless the borrower defaults, the securities lending transaction is not recorded in the general ledger by the governmental entity. Thus, investment and liability accounts are not created by the transaction. In this type of securities lending transaction, the GASB has concluded that the government's control over the collateral securities is so limited that it would be inappropriate to record the transaction as a secured loan.

Receipt of Letters of Credit. In a letter of credit, a financial institution guarantees specified payments of a customer's draft for a designated period. When a governmental entity transfers securities to a broker-dealer and receives a letter of credit, the securities lending transaction is not recorded by the governmental entity [GASB Cod. Sec. I60.105].

Securities Lending Transaction Costs. Costs incurred by a governmental entity in executing a securities lending transaction should be reported as an expenditure or expense in the governmental entity's operating statement (Statement of Revenues, Expenditures, and Changes in Fund Balances, Statement of Activities, etc.). Such costs include the following [GASB Cod. Sec. I60.106]:

- *Borrower rebates:* Payments from the lender to the borrower as compensation for the use of the cash collateral provided by the borrower. Borrower rebates are reported as interest expenditure or expense.

- *Agent fees:* Amounts paid by a lender to its securities lending agent as compensation for managing its securities lending transactions.

Transaction costs should not be netted against income (interest income, investment income, loan premiums or fees, or any other income that arises from the securities lending transaction). "Loan premiums or fees" are defined as follows [GASB Cod. Sec. I60.511]:

> Payments from the borrower to the lender as compensation for the use of the underlying securities when the borrower provides securities or letters of credit as collateral.

GAAP requires investment expenses to be reported in the additions section (as a reduction to the total of investment income) of the Statement of Changes in Fiduciary Net Position of a defined benefit plan [GASB Cod. Sec. I60.fn7].

Securities Lending Transactions in Investment Pools. Some governmental entities combine resources from their various funds into an investment pool, and the investment pool in turn may engage in securities lending transactions. Thus, such transactions may create assets and liabilities that must be reported by the governmental entity (when cash or securities that may be sold or pledged with a borrower default are received as collateral). Under this circumstance, the investment pool must allocate the assets and liabilities that arise from the securities lending transactions to the individual funds based on each fund's equity in the pool [GASB Cod. Sec. I60.107].

GAAP requires such an allocation because an internal investment pool usually is not reported as a separate fund in a governmental entity's financial statements. Thus, the investment pool must observe the standards established by GAAP so that it has enough information to make the allocation to the various funds based on the relative equity position of each participating fund. Under this approach, the fund "that has the risk of loss on the collateral assets" will report its appropriate share of assets and liabilities related to securities lending transactions completed by the governmental investment pool.

Costs incurred, and income earned based on securities lending transactions made by the investment pool should be recorded by the investment pool based on the standards. In turn, those cost and income amounts should be allocated to the participating funds based on their respective equity interest in the investment pool [GASB Cod. Sec. I60.108].

Securities Lending—Risks and Calculation of Risk. For securities lending, credit risk is the aggregate of the lender's exposures to the borrowers of its securities. Thus, the governmental entity has credit risk with respect to the broker-dealer when the amount the broker-dealer owes the governmental entity exceeds the amount the governmental entity owes the broker-dealer. To calculate credit risk, the governmental entity must consider the extent, if any, to which the right of offset exists in the case of the broker-dealer, where offset refers to the legal right a party must offset amounts due to and due from another party in the case of default.

To compute the amount owed to the governmental entity, the following must be considered:

- The fair value of the underlying securities (including accrued interest),
- Unpaid income distributions on the underlying securities, and
- Accrued loan premiums or fees due from the broker-dealer.

To compute the amount owed the broker-dealer, the following must be considered:

- The cash collateral received,
- The fair value of collateral securities received (including accrued interest),
- The face value of letters of credit,
- Unpaid income distributions on collateral securities held by the governmental entity, and
- Accrued borrower rebates payable to the broker-dealer.

The governmental entity initially does not have a credit risk because the fair value of collateral received from the broker-dealer is usually a few percentage points greater than the value of the underlying securities loaned to the broker-dealer. For purposes of the transaction (not for financial reporting), the underlying securities and the collateral securities (but not the securities purchased by cash collateral) are marked-to-market each day and the agreement may require that the broker-dealer provide additional collateral if the fair value of the collateral falls below the fair value of the underlying securities.

Collateral Securities and Underlying Securities. The carrying amounts and fair values of both collateral securities reported on the governmental entity's Balance Sheet and underlying securities that are the basis for securities lending transactions should be disclosed. Also, collateral securities reported on the governmental entity's Balance Sheet should be classified.

Collateral securities arising from securities lending transactions should be classified according to the current scheme, unless the collateral securities are part of a "collateral investment pool," which is defined as follows [GASB Cod. Sec. I60.506]:

> An agent-managed pool that for investment purposes commingles the cash collateral provided on the securities lending transactions of more than one lender.

Underlying securities are not subject to custodial credit risk if the related custodial securities are presented in the governmental entity's Balance Sheet (and therefore the related custodial securities are evaluated to determine whether they are subject to custodial credit risk). However, underlying securities are subject to custodial risk when the related custodial securities are not presented in the governmental entity's Balance Sheet or Statement of Net Position (and therefore are not subject to custodial risk disclosures), in which case the determination of whether they are subject to custodial risk is based on the type of collateral that supports the underlying securities.

Cash Collateral Held as Deposits. Deposits with financial institutions (including cash collateral held as deposits) must be evaluated for the possible need for custodial credit risk disclosures.

ACCOUNTING AND REPORTING FOR IRREVOCABLE SPLIT-INTEREST AGREEMENTS

Irrevocable split-interest agreements are structured in several different forms, including:

- When the government may be a full beneficiary of a donation,
- When the government's interest is split with the donor (i.e., split-interest),
- When the government may receive what is left after the donor dies (i.e., a charitable remainder unitrust or annuity trust),
- When a government may receive funds first for a specific period,
- Before another beneficiary receives the remainder of the funds (i.e., a charitable lead trust), or
- Several similar annuities, interests, or income funds.

The agreements are administered through trusts or similar legally enforceable arrangements. The donor must irrevocably transfer resources to an intermediary. The intermediary may be the government or a trustee that will administer the resources for the unconditional benefit of the government and at least one other beneficiary. The beneficiary can be a not-for-profit organization, a relative, some other beneficiary or even another government. Life interests in real estate are common.

Public colleges and universities, public endowments and public health care facilities are the primary recipients of one or more types of donations that are split-interest arrangements. General governments may also be recipients of irrevocable split-interest agreements, especially involving real estate of historical importance or conservation lands (open space) [GASB Cod. Secs. I70.101–.102].

Recognition of revenue on donated assets in a split-interest arrangement may be complex. Donated assets related to a split-interest agreement are proposed to be recognized at fair value and remeasured at each financial reporting date like other investments. Because there is an income stream and an asset that may involve a third party, an investment derivative instrument-like arrangement may exist. There may even be an obligation attached to the agreement in which the government may have to perform some service or duty to receive the funds in the future. GASB Cod. Sec. I70 requires that the initial recognition of this obligation would result in a liability measured at a settlement amount. Therefore, in a remainder trust in which the government would receive what is left of the assets after income is paid to a third party, the GASB has concluded that the initial value of the governmental remainder beneficiary would be the fair value of the assets, less the value of the liability. This would result in an asset to the government measured at fair value, a liability of the income stream (or the remainder amount) to the income donor at a settlement amount, and a deferred inflow of resources for the remainder (or the income benefit).

Termination provisions are contained in the agreement. There may be a *period-certain term*, culminating the agreement after a set number of years and disbursing any remaining assets. Alternatively, there may be a *life-contingent* term, which usually is the death of the donor.

Statement of Cash Flows Impact. Many irrevocable split-interest agreements are recorded in proprietary funds or in special-purpose entities that are business-type activities, both required to present statements of cash flows. Resources received related to irrevocable split-interest agreements are not divided between lead and remainder interests for cash flows reporting.

Unless there is a donor-imposed restriction for capital purposes, the resources are classified as noncapital financing activities in accordance with GASB Cod. Sec. 2450.707-5, even in circumstances if the *government's* intent to use the beneficial interest is for capital purposes. The only exception is if the *donor* restricts the resources for capital purposes. Then, the cash flows are classified as capital and related financing activities.

Irrevocable Split-Interest Agreements—Recognition and Reporting. Accounting and financial reporting for irrevocable split-interest agreements is dependent upon the facts and circumstances of the agreement.

Scenario 1 – Government Intermediary and the Remainder Interest

A government is the intermediary (trustee, fiscal agent, etc., holding and administering the donated assets) and the *remainder interest* beneficiary has the right to receive all or a portion of the resources remaining at the end of a split-interest agreement's term [GASB Cod. Sec. I70.107]:

	Debits	Credits
At the Date of the Irrevocable Split-Interest Agreement		
Resources received or receivable (assets)	XX	
Lead interest assigned to other beneficiaries (liability)		XX
Deferred inflow of resources representing the government's unconditional remainder interest		XX

In many circumstances, deciding if a government is a lead interest or a remainder interest requires a full understanding of the agreement. The GASB has examples of such situations.

In GASB Cod. Sec. I70.704-1, a university receives resources in an irrevocable split-interest agreement. At the termination of the agreement, the university is required to establish a permanent endowment. The remainder interest therefore is not recognized as revenue at inception. Revenue is only recognized when the endowment is established (at termination).

In GASB Cod. Sec. I70.705-1, a state is a lead interest and a donor's relatives are the remainder interest. The lead interest is used for park improvements for ten years. In this case, a liability exists for the amount due to the donor's relative and potentially the liability may exist in a governmental fund, if payments are to be made in accordance with the measurement focus and basis of accounting for a governmental fund.

The asset balance will change based on interest, dividends, and changes in fair value. As the assets change, the deferred inflow of resources changes. The liability is measured based on a settlement amount (the stream of payments expected to be provided to other beneficiaries). To develop the liability, assumptions may include the payment provisions in the contract, the estimated rate of return on the assets, the mortality rate (if the term of the agreement is contingent on the life of the beneficiary) and the discount rate if a present value technique is used.

Disbursements to the beneficiaries lower the liability. Upon termination of the agreement, the amount reported as a deferred inflow of resources is recognized as revenue and any remaining liability that no longer needs to be disbursed is a gain [GASB Cod. Secs. I70.108–.112].

Scenario 2 – Government is the Intermediary and the Lead Interest

A government is the intermediary (trustee, fiscal agent, etc., holding and administering the donated assets) and the *lead interest* beneficiary has the right to receive all or a portion of the resources at the beginning of a split-interest agreement's term with the remainder to the beneficiaries [GASB Cod. Sec. I70.113]:

	Debits	Credits
At the Date of the Irrevocable Split-Interest Agreement		
Resources received or receivable (assets)	XXX	
Lead interest assigned to other beneficiaries (liability)		XX
Revenue from irrevocable split-interest agreement		XX
Deferred inflow of resources representing the government's unconditional remainder interest (i.e., due in future periods)		XX

Similar accounting and financial reporting would exist. However, the liability would be much less. Revenue would be declared for any benefit received in the initial period [GASB Cod. Secs. I70.113–.118].

Scenario 3A – Government is Party to a Life Interest in Real Estate – Investment

A government is party to a life-interest in real estate that is recognized as an investment by the government in accordance with the definition of an investment. The donor retains the right to use the asset (a residence). As an investment, the residence is recognized at fair value at the date of the agreement [GASB Cod. Sec. I70.119].

	Debits	Credits
At the Date of the Irrevocable Split-Interest Agreement		
Resources received or receivable at fair value (asset)	XXX	
Various liabilities related to the residence		XX
Deferred inflow of resources (representing the difference)		XX

Liabilities related to the life-interest are dependent upon the agreement. For example, insurance, maintenance, repairs, or an outstanding mortgage may be assumed by the government. An additional receivable may be present if the donor is paying the government rent. Changes in fair value will increase or decrease the related deferred inflow of resources. At the termination of the agreement (typically at the date of the donor's death or vacating of property), revenue is recognized for any remaining portion of the deferred inflow of resources and liabilities that are no longer needed to be recognized [GASB Cod. Sec. I70.120].

Scenario 3B – Government is Party to a Life Interest in Real Estate – Capital Asset

A government is party to a life-interest in real estate that is recognized as a capital asset as it will be used for the government's programs and services. The donor retains the right to use the asset (a residence). As a capital asset, the residence is valued at acquisition value.

	Debits	Credits
At the Date of the Irrevocable Split-Interest Agreement		
Resources received or receivable at acquisition value (asset)	XXX	
Various liabilities related to the residence		XX
Deferred inflow of resources representing the difference		XX

Since the asset is recognized at acquisition value, depreciation will now occur systematically and rationally over the remaining service life of the residence [GASB Cod. Secs. I70.121–.125].

Scenario 4 – Government Has an Interest – Trustee Used

A third party is the intermediary (trustee) where a government has an interest in an irrevocable split-interest agreement. The third party acting as an intermediary is frequently a financial institution corporate trust department.

> **PRACTICE POINT:** This scenario is the most common in practice involving a government as governments that are beneficiaries are unlikely to also be intermediaries. Usually, the donor is looking for someone capable to manage the funds instead of a financial institution.

	Debits	Credits
At the Date of the Irrevocable Split-Interest Agreement		
Resources received or receivable at acquisition value (asset)	XX	
Deferred inflow of resources representing the difference		XX

To recognize assets, *all* the following must be met:

1. The government is specified by name as beneficiary in the legal document underlying the donation,
2. The donation agreement is irrevocable,
3. The donor has not granted variance power to the intermediary with respect to the donated resources (Variance power is the unilateral power to redirect the benefit of the transferred resources to another beneficiary, overriding the donor's instructions.),
4. The donor does not control the intermediary, such that the actions of the intermediary are not influenced by the donor beyond the specified stipulations of the agreement, and
5. The irrevocable split-interest agreement establishes a legally enforceable right for the government's benefit (an unconditional beneficial interest).

The assets would be recognized at fair value as of the date of the agreement and remeasured each reporting date. Changes in fair value increase or decrease the deferred inflow of resources. Revenue may be recognized initially if the government is the lead interest, reducing the beneficial interest asset to be received in the future.

If the government is the remainder interest beneficiary, the government will recognize revenue for the beneficial interest at the termination of the agreement [GASB Cod. Secs. I70.126–.131].

OBSERVATION: Irrevocable split-interest agreements that are administered by a government have operational risk as the government becomes the paying agent to beneficiaries. A good practice is to utilize a third-party administrator or trustee for this purpose, which will lower the risk of the government to default on the payment to the beneficiary (or beneficiaries).

EXTERNAL INVESTMENT POOLS ACCOUNTING AND FINANCIAL REPORTING

External Investment Pools

Many governments belong to external investment pools (commonly known as "2a7-like") that are structured like money market funds. As previously introduced, a "2a7-like" pool is not registered with Securities and Exchange Commission (SEC) as an investment company, but nevertheless has a policy that it will, and does, operate in a manner consistent with the SEC's Rule 2a-7 of the Investment Company Act of 1940.

Governmental external investment pools that are 2a7-like pools are permitted to report their investments at amortized cost. Otherwise, external investment pools should report their investments in open-end mutual funds and other external investment pools at fair value.

The net asset value (NAV) per share generally is calculated on a basis other than fair value, such as by the "amortized cost" method that provides a NAV per share that approximates fair value.

An external investment pool qualifies for that reporting if it meets *all* the applicable criteria. If an external investment pool does not meet the criteria, becomes noncompliant with the election, or fails to correct the noncompliance during the reporting period, the pool's value is fair.

The criteria for the external investment pool to use amortized cost is as follows [GASB Cod. Sec. In5.104(a)]:

1. *The pool must transact with its participants at a stable net asset value per share (e.g., all contributions and redemptions are transacted at $1.00 NAV).* Transacting at a stable net asset value per share does not necessarily mean an external investment pool can measure all its investments on an amortized cost basis. For example, many external investment pools currently transact with participants at a stable NAV but measure investments in their financial statements at fair value.

    On the other hand, many money market funds are required by the amended SEC rules to transact at a floating net asset value per share. Although there is no direct correlation between operational transactions and the measurement of an external investment pool's investments, the

GASB believes that the measurement basis should provide the most relevant reflection possible of operations. If an external investment pool is measuring all its investments at amortized cost and transacting at a floating net asset value per share, financial reporting using amortized cost would not reflect the amounts that participants would receive.

Additionally, if an external investment pool transacted with participants at a floating net asset value per share, the participants would be participating in the fair value gains and losses of the external investment pool, which suggests that fair value would be the more appropriate measure for such situations.

2. *The pool portfolio must meet stringent maturity requirements.* The underlying investments should contain securities or other investments only if the investment has a remaining maturity of 397 calendar days or less. The maturity of the investment should be the period remaining until the date on which the total or remaining principal amount is required to be unconditionally repaid in accordance with the terms of the investment, with several exceptions. If the investment has a demand feature and the pool is *not relying* on that demand feature, then the demand feature is disregarded. The exceptions are as follows [GASB Cod. Secs. In5.104(b), .108–.116]:

		Non-Governmental Securities	
Type of Investment	U.S. Government Securities and Similar	397 Days or Less	More than 397 Days
Variable interest rate investments	Measurement period is to the next readjustment of interest rate	The shorter of the period to the next readjustment of the interest rate or the date when the principal can be recovered through demand.	The *longer* length to the next readjustment of the interest rate or the date when the principal can be recovered through demand.
Floating interest rate investments based on an index or market changes	Deemed to be daily.	The remaining maturity is the shorter of the period until the interest rate resets or the maturity date of the investment.	Period remaining until the principal amount can be recovered through demand.

		Non-Governmental Securities	
Type of Investment	U.S. Government Securities and Similar	397 Days or Less	More than 397 Days
Repurchase agreements	Not specified.	Should be either: (a) the period remaining until the date on which the repurchase (or return) of the underlying securities is scheduled to occur, or (b) the duration of the notice period applicable to a demand for the repurchase (or return) of the securities, such as a put option.	Not likely in practice.
Investment in a money market fund or another external investment pool.	The period within which the fund or the pool is required to make a payment upon redemption.	Usually in practice.	Not likely in practice.

The weighted average *maturity* of the portfolio must be 60 days or less. A weighted average maturity measure expresses investment time horizons—the time when investments become due and payable—in this case, days weighted to reflect the dollar size of individual investments. Weighted average maturity includes "call features" and investment size. If a larger investment has a call feature every seven days, it will have a lower weighted average maturity than a smaller investment that did not have a call feature but matured in 30 days. Certain maturity shortening features, such as interest rate resets, should be considered, such as the variable rate securities described in the table above.

The weighted average *life* of the portfolio must be 120 days or less. A weighted average life measure expresses the average length of time that each dollar of principal remains unpaid without considering the maturity shortening features used in calculating the weighted average maturity. Therefore, no call features are used in making this calculation—only the ultimate maturity when the principal is redeemed.

3. *The pool portfolio must meet investment quality requirements.* To make the election to use amortized cost in accordance, the underlying investments must be rated by a nationally recognized statistical rating organization (NRSRO), is denominated in U.S. dollars, and has a credit rating within the highest category of short-term credit ratings (or its long-term equivalent category) or if unrated, is of similar credit quality. The Securities and Exchange Commission registers the NRSROs. As of the

date of this publication, they include firms such as A.M. Best, Fitch, Inc., Moody's Investors Service, Inc., and Standard & Poor's Ratings Services, among others.

The highest category of short-term credit ratings (or its long-term equivalent category) as established by an NRSRO may have multiple sub-categories or gradations indicating relative standing (i.e., several different ratings may constitute the single highest category). If an external investment pool is aware that a security has multiple ratings and the rating categories conflict, the following provisions apply:

- If a security has two ratings, the security is considered in the lower category.

- If a security has more than two ratings, the security is considered in the highest category of ratings as determined by at least two ratings.

- For unrated securities, they must be denominated in U.S. dollars. The pool would then determine if the investments are of comparable credit quality to securities that have been rated within the highest category of short-term credit ratings (or its long-term equivalent category) [GASB Cod. Secs. In5.117–.119].

Declines in Credit Quality. Investments may be acquired that are of the highest rating. However, they may decline in quality during the time they are held by the pool. At the reporting date, the pool would still be incompliance if the pool holds no more than 3% of its total assets in:

- Securities that have credit ratings within the second-highest category of short-term credit ratings (or its long-term equivalent category), and

- Securities that are not rated but are determined to be of comparable credit quality to securities that have been rated within the second-highest category of short-term credit ratings (or its long-term equivalent category).

As of any reporting date, the pool should not hold any security that has a credit rating below the second-highest category of short-term credit ratings or its equivalent long-term category or comparable if non-rated [GASB Cod. Sec. In50.120].

Guaranteed Securities. Securities that are guaranteed may meet the rating requirements to be qualified as securities that can be held by the pool. One of the two following criteria must be met for a guaranteed security to be allowable:

- The guarantee has received a credit rating within the highest category of short-term credit ratings (or its long-term equivalent category) or, if no credit rating is available, is determined (based upon the qualifying external investment pool's analysis) to be of comparable quality.

- The guarantor has obtained a credit rating within the highest category of short-term credit ratings (or its long-term equivalent category) or, if no credit rating is available, is determined (based upon the qualifying external investment pool's analysis) to be of comparable quality [GASB Cod. Sec. In5.121].

Other Features of Credit Quality. Demand features may also be present. The demand feature may have its own credit rating and should be considered. Securities should not be exposed to custodial credit risk as further described in this chapter. Therefore, the pool should consider the credit quality of the institution issuing or holding the security. The security may have an increase in credit quality if it is insured or collateralized to minimize or eliminate custodial credit risk.

For repurchase agreements, the credit quality of the counterparty must be analyzed. GAAP includes criteria for the counterparty of a repurchase agreement to be a primary dealer as defined by the Federal Reserve Bank of New York, in addition to credit quality. Underlying collateral of repurchase agreements must be valued at fair value and not exposed to custodial credit risk [GASB Cod. Secs. In5.122–.126].

4. *The pool portfolio must be diverse.* To qualify, the external investment pool should acquire a security or other investment only if, after acquisition, the external investment pool would hold no more than 5% of its total assets in investments of any one issuer of securities. Some securities have some form of credit support through a guarantee or demand feature. If there is credit support, or if the pool purchases an investment directly of the entity providing the support, the threshold raises to 10% of total assets.

Like to the third criteria above, if the security has a credit rating of other than the highest ratings, any one issuer is limited to 1% of total assets. If there are demand features or guarantees, the limit is 2.5% of total assets in any one issuer. U.S. government securities are exempt from these provisions [GASB Cod. Secs. In5.127–.130].

Common Control Issuers. Many issuers of securities are of similar parent companies. For example, securities may be from Megabank NA, Megabank of Delaware, Megabank of New York etc. These are often found in asset-backed securities due to the need to spread risk and local laws. GAAP requires additional analysis of commonly controlled securities as follows:

- Two or more issuers of securities are considered a single issuer if one issuer controls the other or the two issuers *are under common control.* Control is assumed to be present if one entity owns more than 50% of the issuer's voting securities.
- The acquisition of a repurchase agreement is considered the acquisition of the underlying securities if the repurchase obligation is collateralized fully without regard to maturity date.
- The acquisition of a refunded security is considered the acquisition of the escrowed securities.
- A conduit debt obligation is reported as issued by the entity responsible for the payments related to the obligation rather than the governmental issuer.
- An asset-backed security is reported issued by the entity that issued the security *except* when the obligations of a single entity constitute 10% or

more of the assets that back the security, that entity itself should be considered as the issuer of that portion of the asset-backed security.

Example: An external investment pool holds asset-backed commercial paper that is 3% of the external investment pool's total assets. 15% of the assets that back the commercial paper are receivables from a single bank. For purposes of the diversification calculation, 0.45% of the pool's total assets are issued by that bank. [0.45% = 3% × 15%]

- If some or all the assets that back the security *are themselves asset-backed securities* (secondary asset-backed securities), any entity that issues obligations constituting 10% or more of the assets that back the secondary securities is reported as the issuer of that portion of the asset-backed security.

Example: An external investment pool holds asset-backed commercial paper that is 3% of the pool's total assets. 20% of the assets that back the commercial paper are other asset-backed securities (secondary securities). 15% of the assets that back the secondary securities are receivables from a single bank. For purposes of the diversification calculation, 0.09% of the pool's total assets are issued by that bank. [0.09% = 3% × 20% × 15%]

Example: A local government external investment pool sponsored by a county treasurer has investments in a publicly available money market mutual fund *and* a state-sponsored external investment pool. The local government external investment pool is compliant and makes the election. The state-sponsored external investment pool also is compliant with the same provisions. The 5% limit does not apply to either of the investments. The 5% limit does not apply to the qualifying local government external investment pool's investments in a publicly available money market mutual fund because a money market mutual fund is subject to the Securities and Exchange Commission's money market fund requirements, including portfolio diversification requirements. The 5% limit also does not apply to the qualifying local government external investment pool's investments in the state-sponsored external investment pool in this circumstance. Given the state-sponsored pool is compliant, including the portfolio diversification requirements, the pooled investments held by the state-sponsored pool are sufficiently diversified for application of the 5% limit by the local government external investment pool to be unnecessary [GASB Cod. Sec. In5.131].

5. *The portfolio must be liquid.* Liquidity is vital in an external investment pool. There must be liquid assets enough to support reasonably foreseeable redemptions. The following are the provisions for liquidity in a qualifying external investment pool [GASB Cod. Secs. In5.132–.138]:

Deposits, Investments, and Investment Derivative Instruments

Element Limitation	Daily Liquid Assets >= 10% of Total Assets	Weekly Liquid Assets >= 30% of Total Assets	Illiquid Assets <= 5% of Total Assets
Definition	Assets that mature within one business day.	Assets that mature within five business days.	Those that cannot be sold or disposed of in the ordinary course of business at its amortized cost value within five business days.
Example(s)	Cash, including demand deposits and certificates of deposit that mature within one business day.	Cash, including demand deposits and certificates of deposit that mature within five business days and are expected to be held to maturity.	A nonnegotiable certificate of deposit that does not mature within five business days.
	U.S. Government securities that are direct obligations.	U.S. Government securities that are direct obligations.	
	Securities that will mature within one business day, without taking into account interest rate resets or call features.	U.S. Government securities that are *not* direct obligations but issued at a discount without provision for the payment of interest and have a remaining maturity of 60 days or less.	
Example(s) (continued)	Securities that are subject to demand features that are exercisable and payable within one business day.	Securities that will mature within five business days, without taking into account interest rate resets or call features.	
Example(s) (continued)	Amounts receivable and due unconditionally within one business day on pending sales of portfolio securities.	Securities that are subject to demand features that are exercisable and payable within five business days.	
		Amounts receivable and due unconditionally within five business days on pending sales of portfolio securities.	

6. *The pool must be transparent through the publication of a "shadow price."* The shadow price is the NAV per share of a qualifying external investment pool, calculated using total investments measured at fair value at the calculation date. The calculation should be performed monthly no earlier than five business days prior to and no later than the end of the month. At each date, the pool must have a shadow price within $1/2$ of 1% (0.5%) of the NAV at amortized cost.

If the external investment pool does not adhere to these provisions, *the external investment pool* must be reported at fair value [GASB Cod. Secs. In5.139–.140].

DISCLOSURE REQUIREMENTS FOR CASH DEPOSITS WITH FINANCIAL INSTITUTIONS, INVESTMENTS, AND INVESTMENT DERIVATIVE INSTRUMENTS

Disclosure Requirements for Deposits with Financial Institutions. There are dozens of potential elements on the various risks of cash deposits with institutions. In general, uninsured, and uncollateralized deposits may be exposed to custodial credit risk and should be disclosed in accordance with GAAP.

When a governmental entity has deposits in financial institutions at the end of the year that are subject to any one of the three custodial risks described in this part of the chapter, the disclosure should include:

- The amount of the bank balance,
- A statement that the balance is uninsured, and
- The nature of the custodial credit risk for each uninsured deposit (category 1, 2, or 3, as listed in the cash deposits with financial institutions section of the chapter).

The disclosure is based on the deposited amount as reported by the bank rather than the amount reported in the financial statements because the former identifies the amount of the deposit subject to custodial credit risk.

The Appendix to this chapter contains a text version of potential disclosure. Depending on the nature and complexity of the government, a table may be used.

DISCLOSURE REQUIREMENTS FOR INVESTMENT DERIVATIVE INSTRUMENTS

The disclosures for investment derivative instruments are like the disclosures of other investments. The disclosure requirements for derivative instrument activities, balances, and their related risks are quite extensive and vary depending on the distinct types of derivative instruments that a government is party to. If the government is involved in significant derivative activity and has several diverse types of derivative instruments, many of the required disclosures will likely be better presented in a tabular or columnar display.

However, GASB Cod. Sec. D40 states that the disclosures may be in a columnar display, narrative form, or a combination of both methods. To assist financial statement preparers, GASB Cod. Sec. D40.901 provides several illustrated example disclosures. In addition, the Appendix to this chapter contains disclosure for investment derivative instruments.

In addition to providing summary disclosures regarding the government's derivative instrument activities and balances (general disclosures), there are more specific disclosure requirements that depend on the type of derivative instrument.

General Disclosures. GASB Cod. Sec. D40 requires certain general disclosures that provide a summary of the government's derivatives activities and balances. These general disclosures include a summary of the government's derivative instrument activity during the period and related balances at period end that are organized by governmental activities, business-type activities, and fiduciary funds to the extent applicable.

PRACTICE POINT: Most governments with both investment derivative instruments and hedging derivative instruments report investment derivatives with other investments and hedging derivatives with other forms of debt disclosures.

The summary information about the investment derivative instruments should include:

- Notional or face amount of the derivative instrument,
- Fair value changes during the period and the location in the financial statements where the changes in fair values are reported,
- Fair values at period end and the location in the financial statements where the fair values are reported, and
- If the fair value of any derivative is based on other than quoted market prices, the method and assumptions used to estimate fair value [GASB Cod. Secs. D40.164–.165(a-c)].

For investment derivative instruments, governments should disclose their exposure to the following risks that could give rise to monetary loss. Risk disclosures are limited to investment derivative instruments reported as of the reporting period's end. Disclosures required may contain information required by other areas of GAAP. However, these disclosures should be presented in the context of an investment derivative instrument's risk as further discussed in this subsection.

Credit risk. If an investment derivative instrument exposes a government to credit risk (i.e., the government reports the investment derivative instrument as an asset), the government should disclose that exposure. That disclosure should include [GASB Cod. Secs. D40.173(a), D40.170(a)]:

- The credit quality ratings of counterparties as described by nationally recognized statistical rating organizations—rating agencies—as of the end of the reporting period. If the counterparty is not rated, the disclosure should indicate that fact.
- The maximum amount of loss due to credit risk, based on the fair value of the hedging derivative instrument as of the end of the reporting period, that the government would incur if the counterparties to the hedging derivative instrument failed to perform according to the terms of the contract, without respect to any collateral or other security, or netting arrangement.
- The government's policy of requiring collateral or other security to support hedging derivative instruments subject to credit risk, a summary description, and the aggregate amount of the collateral or other security that reduces credit risk exposure, and information about the government's access to that collateral or other security.
- The government's policy of engaging in master netting arrangements, including a summary description and the aggregate amount of liabilities included in those arrangements. Master netting arrangements are established when (*a*) each party owes the other determinable amounts, (*b*) the government has the right to set off the amount owed with the amount owed by the counterparty, and (*c*) the right of setoff is legally enforceable.
- The aggregate fair value of hedging derivative instruments in asset (positive) positions net of collateral posted by the counterparty and the effect of master netting arrangements.
- Significant concentrations of net exposure to credit risk (gross credit risk reduced by collateral, other security, and setoff) with individual counterparties and groups of counterparties. A concentration of credit risk exposure to an individual counterparty may not require disclosure if its existence is apparent from the disclosures required by other parts of this section. As an example, a government has engaged in only one interest rate swap. Therefore, concentration exists. Group concentrations of credit risk exist if several counterparties are engaged in similar activities and have similar economic characteristics that would cause their ability to meet contractual obligations to be similarly affected by changes in economic or other conditions [GASB Cod. Sec. D40.170(a)].

Interest rate risk. If an investment derivative instrument exposes a government to interest rate risk, the government should disclose that exposure consistent with the disclosures required for other investments subject to interest rate risk. Disclosures of interest rate risk information for investment derivatives should use one of the following methods:

- Segmented time distribution,
- Specific identification,
- Weighted average maturity,
- Duration, or
- Simulation model.

Governments are encouraged to select the disclosure method that is most consistent with the method they use to identify and manage interest rate risk. If a method requires an assumption regarding timing of cash flows (e.g., whether an investment is or is not assumed to be called), interest rate changes, or other factors that affect interest rate risk information, that assumption should be disclosed.

Further, an investment derivative instrument that is an interest rate swap is an additional example of an investment that has a fair value that is sensitive to interest rate changes. The fair value, notional amount, reference rate, and embedded options should be disclosed.

Terms include such information as coupon multipliers, benchmark indexes, reset dates, and embedded options. Disclosure information for similar investments may be aggregated.

Examples of sensitive investments and required disclosures are as follows:

- A variable-rate investment's coupon amount enhances or amplifies the effects of interest rate changes by greater than a one-to-one basis, such as 1.25 times a structured overnight financing rate (SOFR). (See previous **PRACTICE POINTs** on GASB-93 and GASB-99.) The multiplier makes this investment's fair value highly sensitive to interest rate changes. This investment's fair value, its coupon's multiplier, and benchmark index (1.25 times three-month SOFR), and the frequency of the coupon's reset date should be disclosed.
- A variable-rate investment's coupon amount varies inversely with a benchmark index, such as 4% minus the three-month SOFR with a floor of 1%. This investment's fair value, its coupon's multiplier, and benchmark index (4% minus the three-month SOFR with a floor of 1%), and the frequency of the coupon's reset dates should be disclosed.
- An asset-backed investment has repayments that are expected to significantly vary with interest rate changes. The variance may present itself in terms of variable repayment amounts, uncertain early or extended repayments, or in some cases, the possibility of no repayments. Interest-only and residual tranches of collateralized mortgage obligations are specific examples of such investments. This investment's fair value, the nature of

its underlying assets, and the existence of the repayment option should be disclosed [GASB Cod. Secs. D40.170(b), I50.157].

Foreign currency risk. If an investment derivative instrument exposes a government to foreign currency risk, the government should disclose that exposure based on the U.S. dollar balances of such investments, organized by currency denomination, and, if applicable, investment type [GASB Cod. Secs. D40.170(c), I50.158].

DISCLOSURE REQUIREMENTS FOR MOST OTHER INVESTMENTS

A governmental entity must disclose in notes to the financial statements the following information about its investments:

- The methods and significant assumptions used to estimate the fair value of an investment, when fair value is not based on a quoted market price,
- The policy used to identify investments that are reported at amortized cost,
- For investments in external investment pools that are not SEC-registered, a description of regulatory oversight, if any, and a statement as to whether the fair value of the investment is the same as the value of the pool shares,
- Description of involuntary participation (i.e., participation required by law) in an external investment pool,
- For positions in external investment pools for which fair value information cannot be obtained from the pool sponsor, the methods and significant assumptions used to estimate the fair value and the reasons for having to use such an estimate,
- For investments in external investment pools that report their investments at amortized cost, the presence of any limitations or restrictions on withdrawals (These may include notice periods, maximum transaction amounts and the qualifying external investment pool's authority to impose liquidity fees or redemption gates.), and
- Income from investments whereby the income from one fund has been assigned to another fund [GASB Cod. Sec. I50.143].

In some instances, external investment pools do not provide fair value information or timely information to participants in the pool. For example, the year-end date for the external investment pool might not be the same as the year-end date for the participant. Under these circumstances, the participant must estimate its fair value position in the pool, disclose the methods and significant assumptions used to compute the estimate, and disclose why an estimate must be made.

Realized Gains and Losses. In addition, if (1) a governmental entity elects to disclose in its notes any realized gains and losses from investments or (2) an

external investment pool elects to report on its operating statement any realized gains and losses from investments, the following must be disclosed:
- That the determination of realized gains and losses is independent of the determination of the net change in the fair value of investments, and
- That realized gains and losses on investments that were held by the governmental entity during a previous accounting period(s) but sold during the current period were used to compute the change in the fair value of investments for the previous year(s) as well as the current year [GASB Cod. Sec. I50.144].

Equity Method Investments in Common Stock. The following should be disclosed in the notes for equity method investments in common stock:
- The name of each investee and percentage of ownership of common stock,
- The accounting policies of the government with respect to investments in common stock,
- Regarding the accounting policies of the government with respect to investments in common stock, disclosure should include:
  — The names of any significant investee corporations in which the government holds 20% or more of the voting stock, but the common stock is not accounted for by the equity method, together with the reasons why the equity method is not considered appropriate, and
  — The names of any significant investee corporations in which the government holds less than 20% of the voting stock and the common stock is accounted for by the equity method, together with the reasons why the equity method is considered appropriate,
- The difference, if any, between the amount at which an investment is carried and the amount of underlying equity in net assets and the accounting treatment of the difference,
- For those investments in common stock for which a quoted market price is available, the aggregate value of each identified investment based on the quoted market price should be disclosed,
- When investments in common stock accounted for under the equity method are, in the aggregate, significant in relation to the financial position or results of operations of a government, it may be necessary for summarized information about assets, liabilities, and results of operations of the investees to be presented in the notes to the financial statements either individually or in groups, as appropriate, and
- Conversion of outstanding convertible securities, exercise of outstanding options and warrants, and other contingent issuances of an investee may have a significant effect on a government's share of reported earnings or losses. Accordingly, significant effects of possible conversions, exercises, or contingent issuances should be disclosed in notes to the financial statements of a government [GASB Cod. Sec. I50.145].

Other Disclosures. Governments should disclose:

- Legal or contractual provisions for investments, including repurchase agreements, and
- Investments, including repurchase agreements as of the reporting date and during the period [GASB Cod. Sec. I50.146].

Level of Detail

Investment disclosures should focus separately on (1) governmental activities, (2) business-type activities, (3) individual major funds, (4) aggregated nonmajor funds, and (5) fiduciary fund types of the primary government when the risk is significantly greater for one of the five categories than for the entirety of the government. For example, concentration of credit risk may not be great for the overall primary government, but it could be for an individual major fund because that fund invests most of its resources in the securities of a single issuer [GASB Cod. Sec.I50.147].

Investment Type Disclosures. Generally, disclosures related to investments should be formatted based on investment types, such as investments in U.S. treasuries, corporate bonds, and equities. Professional judgment must be used in order not to aggregate dissimilar investments for disclosure purposes. For example, for disclosure purposes, investments in mutual funds that predominantly invest in equities should generally not be aggregated with direct equity securities held by the governmental entity [GASB Cod. Sec. I50.148].

Investment Risk Disclosures. The additional risk disclosures required by GAAP should generally be made for the primary government, including its blended component units. The disclosures should be made for the governmental activities, business-type activities, individual major funds, nonmajor funds in the aggregate, and fiduciary fund types when the risk exposures are significantly greater for these units than for the primary government.

Interest rate risk disclosure in these types of investments is limited to investments in *debt* mutual funds, external *debt* investment pools, and other pooled *debt* instruments, which firmly relieves pressure on preparers to "look through" most mutual funds and investment pools.

Legal or Contractual Provisions for Investments. The governmental entity should disclose the types of investments that can be acquired by the primary government based on legal and contractual restrictions. There may be significantly different restrictions for component units, or the restrictions may vary significantly among funds or fund types. Under both circumstances, the different investment restrictions should be disclosed when investment activities for the component unit's individual funds or individual fund types are material in relationship to the reporting entity's investment activities. Violation of these and other investment restrictions should be disclosed in notes to the financial statements [GASB Cod. Secs. I50.149–.150].

Investment Policies. Governments are required to disclose investment policies related to investment risks. For example, if the entity holds investments denominated in a foreign currency, it should disclose its investment policy with respect to foreign currency risk, such as a policy that limits investments denominated in foreign currencies to 5% of total investments. If the entity has adopted no policy with respect to a risk, that fact should be part of the disclosure [GASB Cod. Sec. I50.151].

Basics and Examples of Risk Disclosures. Specifically, GAAP addresses disclosure issues related to the following investment risks:

- Credit risk,
- Custodial credit risk,
- Concentration of credit risk,
- Interest rate risk, and
- Foreign currency risk.

Credit Risk. A governmental entity is required to make disclosures related to investments in debt instruments about the credit risk (the risk that an issuer or other counterparty to an investment will not fulfil its obligations). Credit risk disclosure is accomplished by classifying debt investments as of the entity's Balance Sheet date by debt type and by credit quality ratings assigned by nationally recognized rating agencies (Standard & Poor's, Moody's Investors Service, and Fitch). For example, investments in commercial paper could be rated as A1 by Standard & Poor's, Aaa by Moody's Investors Service, and F-1 by Fitch. If the investment grade of a governmental entity's investment in commercial paper varies, the investment categories must be expanded to disclose the different quality of ratings by dollar amount [GASB Cod. Sec. I50.152].

The disclosure for debt investments applies to external investment pools, money market funds, bond mutual funds, and other pooled investments for fixed-income securities. If credit ratings for any of these investments are not available, the disclosure should indicate which investments are unrated.

Unless there is evidence to the contrary, investments in U.S. government debt or debt guaranteed by the U.S. government are considered to have no credit risk and therefore the credit rating for these investments is not required to be disclosed.

GASB Cod. Sec. I50.738-8 provides guidance when a debt security issued by a federal government-sponsored enterprise (GSE) that has only the implicit guarantee of the federal government and is held by a state or local government is subject to credit risk disclosures. The guarantee must only be an implicit guarantee. However, GASB also notes if the structures of financial markets change, whether a GSE has an implicit or an explicit guarantee may change. A credit risk disclosure is based on a federal guarantee's status as of the financial statements date.

Custodial Credit Risk. A governmental entity's investments are exposed to custodial credit risk when they are uninsured, unregistered, and are held by either (1) the counterparty or (2) the counterparty's trust department or agent, but not in the government's name. When investments held as of the date of the Balance Sheet are exposed to custodial credit risk the following proposed disclosures should be made:

- The type of investment,
- The reported amount, and
- How the investments are held.

Generally, investments in external investment pools and in open-end mutual funds are not subject to custodial credit risk because "their existence is not evidenced by securities that exist in physical or book entry form." Also, securities for reverse repurchase agreements are not exposed to custodial credit risk, because those securities are held by the buyer-lender.

Concentration of Credit Risk. GAAP recognizes that there is an additional dimension to credit risk that relates to the amount of investment in any one entity. For this reason, GAAP requires that a governmental entity disclose the amount invested in a separate issuer (except investments held in the U.S. government or investments guaranteed by the U.S. government) when that amount is at least 5% of total investments. The base (total investments) to be used to determine the 5% threshold must be selected consistent with the "level of disclosure criterion" [GASB Cod. Sec. I50.154].

Interest Rate Risk. Interest rate risk arises from investments in debt instruments and is defined as "the risk that changes in interest rates will adversely affect the fair value of an investment." The amount of loss in the fair value of a fixed-income security increases as the current market interest rate related to the investment rises [GASB Cod. Secs. I50.155–.157].

Governmental entities are required to provide information about debt investments so that a reader can assess to some degree the entity's exposure to interest rate risk. This disclosure is achieved by grouping investments into investment types and using one of the following methods to inform users of the level of interest rate sensitivity for debt investments:

- Segmented time distributions,
- Specific identification,
- Weighted average maturity,
- Duration, and
- Simulation model.

The disclosure method selected to demonstrate interest rate risk should be the one that the governmental entity uses to identify and manage its interest rate risk. Assumptions that are necessary to describe interest rate risk, such as the timing of cash flows (e.g., when an investment has a call provision) and changes in interest rates, should also be disclosed.

GAAP requires additional disclosures for investments in debt instruments whose fair values are "highly sensitive" to changes in interest rates. For example, a debt investment may have a variable interest rate that is 1.3 times the three-month SOFR. For debt investments that are sensitive to changes in interest rates, the governmental entity must provide (1) a description of the interest rate sensitivity and (2) contract terms (such as multipliers and benchmark indexes). (See previous **PRACTICE POINT** s on GASB-93 and GASB-99.)

Segmented Time Distributions. The segmented time distributions method of disclosing interest rate risk is simple because it groups "investment cash flows into sequential time periods in tabular form." For example, investment types could be categorized as those that mature in less than one year, between one and five years, and so on.

Example: As of the end of the fiscal year, the State had the following investments and maturities in years (amounts in thousands):

Investment Type	Less than 1 year	1 to 5 years	6 to 10 years	More than 10 years	Total
Cash equivalents	$157.9	$—	$—	$—	$157.9
U.S. Treasuries	—	7,688.6	2,259.8	1,988.5	11,916.9
Total	$157.9	$7,688.6	$2,259.8	$1,988.5	$12,074.8

PRACTICE POINT: The amounts in this (and other tables) should reconcile to the Statement of Net Position.

Specific Identification. The specific identification method does not compute a disclosure measure but presents a list of the individual investments, their carrying amounts, maturity dates, and any call options.

Example: As of the end of the fiscal year, the State had the following investments and maturities in years (amounts in thousands):

Investment Type	Maturities	Fair Value
Treasury Portfolio Fund	3.4 months weighted average	$157.9
U.S. Treasuries (by maturity date)		
Series 20Y0-Y1 (10 notes)	20Y0-20Y1	768.9
Series 20Y1-Y2 (22 notes)	20Y1-20Y2	1,537.7
Series 20Y2-Y3 (47 bills)	20Y2-20Y3	1,922.2
Series 20Y3-Y4 (18 notes)	20Y3-20Y4	2,306.5
Series 20Y4-Y5 (21 bills)	20Y4-20Y5	1,153.3
Series 20Y5-Y6 (3 notes)	20Y5-20Y6	226.0
Series 20Y6-Y7 (7 notes)	20Y6-20Y7	452.0
Series 20Y7-Y8 (12 notes)	20Y7-20Y8	565.0
Series 20Y8-Y9 (16 notes)	20Y8-20Y9	677.8
Series 20Y9-Z0 (2 notes) (both callable in 20Y5)	20Y9-20Z0	339.0
Other CUSIPS (40% callable in 20Z4)	More than 10 years	1,988.5
Total		$12,074.8

Weighted Average Maturity. When the weighted average maturity method is used to describe a governmental entity's exposure to interest rate risk, the disclosure "expresses investment time horizons—the time when investments become due and payable—in years or months, weighted to reflect the dollar size of individual investments."

For example, assume that a debt investment type comprises the following two specific investments (A and B):

Investment	Months to Maturity	Maturity Amount	Weighted Months
A	50	$100,000	16.7*
B	90	200,000	60.0
Total	140	$300,000	76.7

* 50 × ($100,000 / $300,000) = 16.7 months

Based on the above facts, the governmental entity would disclose (in tabular form, along with similar information for other investment types) that this investment type had a fair value of $300,000 and a weighted average maturity of 76.7 months.

Duration. "Duration" is defined as follows:

> A measure of a debt investment's exposure to fair value changes arising from changing interest rates. It uses the present value of cash flows, weighted for those cash flows as a percentage of the investment's full price.

Effective duration makes assumptions regarding the most likely timing and amounts of variable cash flows arising from such investments as callable bonds, prepayments, and variable-rate debt. A variety of methods can be used to compute the effective duration of an investment. GAAP does not mandate the use of a specific technique.

The following example is based on the Macaulay duration approach illustrated in GASB Cod. Sec. I50.908. To illustrate this approach, assume that a governmental entity as of December 31, 20X6 has an investment in a $100 bond that has a 7.5% coupon rate (semiannual payments) and has a yield to maturity of 7.5% that matures on December 31, 20X8. The cash flows from the investments are summarized as follows:

CASH FLOWS				Present Value Factor @4%	(A) Present Value @ 12/31/X6	(B) Periods Before Cash Flows	(C) (A) × (B)
6/30/X7	12/31/X7	6/30/X8	12/31/X8				
3.75	—	—	—	.96154	$3.61	.5	1.81
—	3.75	—	—	.92456	3.48	1.0	3.48
—	—	3.75	—	.88900	3.36	1.5	5.04
—	—	—	103.75	.85480	89.54	2.0	179.09
					$100.00		$189.41

The Macaulay duration is computed by dividing the total present values (column C) by the bond price, as follows:

$$\$189.41 \div \$100 = 1.8941 \text{ years}$$

Next, the effective duration is computed by dividing the Macaulay duration (as computed above) by 1 + the coupon rate (7.5% or 0.075) per payment period

(2 per year). Thus, the effective duration, which is to be disclosed by investment type, is 1.83 years (rounded), as follows:

$$1.8941 \div [(1+.075 / 2)] = 1.83 \text{ years}$$

Simulation Model. Finally, a governmental entity can use various simulation models to describe its exposure to interest rate risk, which "estimate changes in an investments' or a portfolio's fair value, given hypothetical changes in interest rates." For example, an investment type's fair value could be presented as of the Balance Sheet date along with estimated fair values of the same investments assuming a 100-point, 200-point, and so forth increase in the current market interest rate.

Foreign Currency Risk. Investments (as well as deposits in foreign financial institutions) denominated in a foreign currency are subject to "the risk that changes in exchange rates will adversely affect the fair value of an investment." When a governmental entity is exposed to foreign currency risk, GAAP requires that the U.S. dollar amount of the investment (classified by investment type) and the currency used to denominate the investment be disclosed [GASB Cod. Sec. I50.158].

Example: As of the end of the fiscal year, the State's exposure to foreign currency risk in U.S. dollars is summarized on the following table (in thousands):

Currency Type	Equity	Private Equity	Pending Transactions	Cash	Total Fair Value
Australian Dollar	$507.0	$—	$—	$0.1	$507.1
British Pound Sterling	1,308.7	—	0.2	0.7	1,309.6
Danish Krone	120.8	—	—	—	120.8
Euro	2,344.4	218.2	(0.3)	(0.2)	2,562.1
Hong Kong Dollar	243.0	—	—	0.4	243.4
Israeli Shekel	23.4	—	—	0.1	23.5
Japanese Yen	1,758.1	—	—	4.1	1,762.2
New Zealand Dollar	15.5	—	—	0.1	15.6
Norwegian Krone	53.9	—	—	—	53.9
Singapore Dollar	93.2	—	—	0.1	93.3
Swedish Krona	187.7	—	—	—	187.7
Swiss Franc	566.1	—	—	—	566.1
Total	**$7,221.8**	**$218.2**	**$(0.1)**	**$5.4**	**$7,445.3**

Other Disclosures. For commitments to resell securities under yield maintenance repurchase agreements, the reported amount (if applicable) and the fair value as of the reporting date of the securities to be resold, the description of the terms (settlement price ranges, yields, maturity dates, etc.) should be disclosed.

If the governmental entity has suffered losses from defaults by counterparties to investments or has recovered amounts reported as losses in previous years, those amounts should also be disclosed in the financial statements [GASB Cod. Secs. I50.159–.160].

Disclosures Related to Fair Value

Disclosures of the fair value of investments are now to be organized by type or class of asset or liability. The level of detail and how much emphasis to place on each disclosure requirement needs to consider:

- The nature, characteristics, and risks of the asset or liability. For example, GAAP disaggregates U.S. Treasury notes from U.S. Treasury separate trading of registered interest and principal securities (STRIPS).
- The level of the fair value hierarchy within which the fair value measurement is categorized. For example, more uncertainty and subjectivity may require more investments to be categorized as Level 3 of the fair value hierarchy.
- Whether a specific type or class of an asset or liability is required by another GASB statement. For example, GASB Cod. Sec. D40 requires derivative instrument disclosures by hedging derivative instruments and investment derivative instruments.
- The objective or the mission of the government may yield increased or decreased disclosures. For example, the objective of an external investment pool to achieve income or profit suggests greater disaggregation compared to a general-purpose government. Many general-purpose governments are constrained by investments due to laws, regulations, and operational practices.
- A government may be composed of governmental and business-type activities, individual major funds, nonmajor funds in the aggregate, or fiduciary fund types and component units. Additional disclosures may be appropriate when the risk exposures are significantly greater than the deposit and investment risks of the primary government. For example, a primary government's total investments may not be exposed to concentration risk. However, if the government's capital projects fund has all its investments in one issuer of corporate bonds, disclosure should be made for the capital projects fund's exposure to a concentration of credit risk.
- The relative significance of assets and liabilities measured at fair value compared to total assets and liabilities should be evaluated in terms of the government structure. If investments are immaterial, then additional disclosure may not be necessary [GASB Cod. Secs. 3100.161, D40.166, I50.140].

Recurring fair value measurements are assets or liabilities that are revalued and presented in the Statement of Net Position at the end of each reporting period. *Nonrecurring fair value measurements* are those that are permitted to be presented in the Statement of Net Position in some circumstances.

If the fair value of investments is to be disclosed after consideration of the provisions, then for both recurring and nonrecurring measurements, the following is disclosed:

- The fair value measurement at the end of the reporting period,
- The level of the fair value hierarchy within which the fair value measurements are categorized in their entirety (Level 1, 2, or 3),
- A description of the valuation techniques used in the fair value measurement, and
- If there has been a change in valuation technique that has a significant impact on the result (e.g., changing from an expected cash flow technique to a relief from royalty technique or the use of an additional valuation technique), that change and the reason(s) for making it.

For nonrecurring fair value measurements, the reason(s) for the measurement are disclosed [GASB Cod. Secs. 3100.162, D40.166, I50.141].

GASB Cod. Secs. 3100.163 and I50.142 require additional disclosures to investments in entities that:

- Calculate a NAV per share (or its equivalent), regardless of whether any other method of determining fair value has been applied,
- Do not have a readily determinable fair value, and
- Are measured at fair value on a recurring or nonrecurring basis during the period.

A government would disclose information that addresses the nature and the risks of the investments and whether the investments are probable of being sold at amounts *different from the NAV* per share. Therefore, for each type of investment that is valued at NAV per share, the following additional disclosures would be required:

- The fair value measurement of the investment type at the measurement date and a description of the significant investment strategies of the investee(s) in that type,
- For each type of investment that includes investments that can never be redeemed with the investees, but the government receives distributions through the liquidation of the underlying assets of the investees, the government's estimate of the period over which the underlying assets are expected to be liquidated by the investees,
- The amount of the government's unfunded commitments related to that investment type,
- A general description of the terms and conditions upon which the government may redeem investments in the type (e.g., quarterly redemption with 60 days' notice),
- The circumstances in which an otherwise redeemable investment in the type (or a portion thereof) might not be redeemable (e.g., investments subject to a redemption restriction, such as a lockup or gate). Also, for those otherwise redeemable investments that are restricted from redemption as of the government's measurement date, the estimate of when the restriction from redemption might lapse should be disclosed. If an estimate cannot be made, that fact and how long the restriction has been in effect should be disclosed,

- Any other significant restriction on the ability to sell investments in the type at the measurement date,

- If a government determines that it is probable that it will sell an investment(s) for an amount different from NAV per share, the total fair value of all investments that would be sold at an amount different from NAV per share and any remaining actions required to complete the sale,

- If a group of investments would otherwise be valued at NAV, but the individual investments to be sold have not been identified (e.g., if a government decides to sell 20% of its investments in private equity funds but the individual investments to be sold have not been identified), such that the investments continue to qualify for the method of estimating fair value at NAV, the government's plans to sell and any remaining actions required to complete the sale(s), and

- If a separately issued financial statement is available, disclosures may be incorporated by reference. For example, a state government may consider reduced disclosures of fair value measurements of investments in certain entities that calculate NAV per share (or its equivalent) if the financial statements of the state's pension plan include that information.

Defined benefit plans and endowments have broader disclosure due to the considerations discussed previously. The additional disclosure is detailed in Chapter 22.

Disclosures for Participating Governments in Qualifying External Investment Pools (at Amortized Cost)

For participating governments in qualifying external investment pools at amortized cost, disclosure is limited to the presence of any limitations or restrictions on withdrawals such as redemption notice periods, maximum transaction amounts and the authority to impose liquidity fees or redemption gates. This is in addition to the government's investment balance in the external investment pool as of the reporting date.

OBSERVATION: This disclosure appears not to agree with the provisions of fair value measurement and application. The GASB clarifies this disclosure in GASB Cod. Sec. I50.713-9. If the external investment pool is compliant with GAAP, and for financial reporting purposes elects to measure all its investments at amortized cost, then the investment position of a participating government is NOT at fair value. Therefore, it is not categorized as a level 1, 2, or 3 investment in the fair value hierarchy required by GASB Cod. Sec. 3100. Participating governments in this situation should first review their policy if indeed the position is really a cash equivalent. If it is not a cash equivalent, the position becomes a reconciling item to investments. In practice, the government would disclose investments as follows in accordance with GASB Cod. Sec. 3100:

Deposits, Investments, and Investment Derivative Instruments

	Fiscal Year-End 6/30/X8	Fair Value Measurements Using		
		Quoted Prices in Active Markets for Identical Assets (Level 1)	Significant Other Observable Inputs (Level 2)	Significant Unobservable Inputs (Level 3)
Investments by fair value level				
Descriptions of various types of securities held at the reporting date	$XX	$XX	$XX	$XX
Total investments by fair value level	XX	$XX	$XX	$XX
Investments measured at the net asset value (NAV)				
Descriptions of various types of securities held at the reporting date	XX			
Total investments at the NAV	XX			
Total investments at fair value	XX			
Investment Derivative Instruments	XX			
Investment in External Investment Pool	XXX			
Total Investments in Statement of Net Position	$ X,XXX			

If participating governments have restricted investments, a further reconciliation below this table may be warranted to reconcile to the amounts in the Statement of Net Position, especially if investments are contained in applicable categories such as restricted and unrestricted.

If the external investment pool generally measures its investments at *fair value* instead of at amortized cost, the local government's position is measured at fair value. This does not matter if the pool transacts with participants at a floating net asset value per share or a fixed net asset value per share (e.g., $1.00). This position should not be categorized in the hierarchy, but instead would be characterized as a NAV investment and shown in the NAV section of the above table.

Example: The State holds investments in the investment pool that are measured at fair value on a recurring basis. The State categorizes its fair value measurements within the fair value hierarchy established by generally accepted accounting principles. Investments measured and reported at fair value using Level inputs are classified and disclosed in one of the following categories:

- Level 1—Quoted prices are available in active markets for identical investments as of the reporting date. The types of investments included in Level 1 include U.S. Treasuries securities and listed equities.
- Level 2—Quoted prices for similar instruments in active markets, quoted prices for identical or similar instruments in markets that are not active, and model-derived valuations in which all significant inputs and significant value drivers are observable.
- Level 3—Valuations derived from valuation techniques in which significant inputs or significant value drivers are unobservable.

The following table presents fair value measurements as of June 30, 20Y0 (amounts in thousands):

Investments at Fair Value:	Fair Value	Level 1	Level 2	Level 3	Total
U.S. Treasuries	$11,916.9	$11,916.9	$—	$—	$11,916.9
Equities:					
Common stock	25,179.9	25,179.9	—	—	25,179.9
Preferred stock	39.8	39.8	—	—	39.8
Total equities	25,219.7	25,219.7	—	—	25,219.7
Total investments at fair value	37,136.6	$37,136.6	—	—	$37,136.6
Investments at Net Asset Value (NAV):					
Real estate investment trusts	$1,808.7				
Mutual funds	1,963.4				
Total investments at NAV	3,772.1				
Total investments as presented in the Statement of Net Position	$40,908.7				

Real estate investment trusts include domestic commercial, residential, office and retail properties. Third party appraisals are received within 90 days of the fiscal year-end. The State does not hold a controlling interest in any property held for investment. Mutual funds are publicly traded in various asset classes and are valued daily.

DISCLOSURE REQUIREMENTS FOR REVERSE REPURCHASE AGREEMENTS

Legal or Contractual Provisions for Reverse Repurchase Agreements. If reverse repurchase agreements were used during the period, the governmental entity should disclose the source of legal or contractual authorization for the transactions. Also, significant violations of restrictions related to reverse repurchase agreements should be disclosed [GASB Cod. Secs. I55.109–.110].

Disclosures for reverse repurchase agreements as of the Balance Sheet date depend on whether the transaction is based on a yield maintenance agreement [GASB Cod. Secs. I55.111–.112].

Yield Maintenance Agreements. In a yield maintenance agreement, the securities to be returned to the governmental entity provide a yield specified in the agreement. The following disclosures should be made for commitments to repurchase securities based on yield maintenance reverse repurchase agreements as of the Balance Sheet date [GASB Cod. Sec. I55.112]:

- The fair value of securities to be repurchased at the Balance Sheet date, and
- A description of the terms of the agreement.

Other Agreements. For all reverse repurchase agreements outstanding as of the Balance Sheet date, other than yield maintenance agreements, the total amounts of the obligation under the agreements (including accrued interest) and the total fair value of the securities related to the agreements should be disclosed. The difference between the two amounts is a measure of the credit risk exposure for the governmental entity in reverse repurchase agreements [GASB Cod. Secs. I55.111–.112].

Losses from reverse repurchase agreements because of defaults by counterparties, and subsequent recovery of such losses, should be disclosed either in the governmental entity's operating statement or in notes to the financial statements [GASB Cod. Sec. I55.113].

GAAP requires that a governmental entity disclose whether the maturity dates of investments made with proceeds from reverse repurchase agreements are generally matched with the maturity dates of the related reverse repurchase agreements during the accounting period. The degree to which such matching occurs as of the Balance Sheet date also must be disclosed [GASB Cod. Sec. I55.114].

DISCLOSURE REQUIREMENTS FOR SECURITIES LENDING TRANSACTIONS

Generally, governmental entities are restricted as to how resources may be invested. Restrictions may be based on legal or contractual provisions. The following be disclosed with respect to securities lending transactions [GASB Cod. Secs. I60.109–.114]:

- Basis of authorization (legal or contractual authorization) for engaging in securities lending transactions,
- Significant violations of the basis of authorization because securities lending transactions were executed during the accounting period,
- General description of securities lending transactions including:
  — Types of securities loaned by the governmental entity,
  — Types of collateral received by the governmental entity,

- Whether the governmental entity has the right to sell or pledge securities received as collateral without a borrower default,
- Amount by which the value of the securities received as collateral exceeds the value of the securities loaned by the governmental entity,
- Restrictions on the value of securities that can be loaned, and
- Carrying value and fair value of the underlying securities (the securities loaned by the governmental entity to the broker-dealer) at the Balance Sheet date,

* Description of loss indemnification (a securities lending agent's guarantee that it will protect the lender from certain losses) provided by the securities lending agent (an entity that arranges the terms and conditions of loans, monitors the fair value of the securities lent and the collateral received, and often directs the invest of cash collateral),
* Statement of whether the maturity dates of investments made with cash collateral received from broker-dealers match the maturity dates of the related securities loans,
* The extent to which maturity dates of investments made with cash collateral received from broker-dealers match the maturity date of the related securities loans as of the Balance Sheet date,
* Value of losses from default of a borrower or lending agent for the year related to securities lending transactions,
* Value of losses recovered from defaults in previous periods, and
* Value of credit risk (if any) as of the date of the Balance Sheet (if no credit risk exists, that fact should be stated in the disclosure).

The disclosure requirement relating to the matching of maturing dates can be a general description rather than a detailed listing of maturity dates. The following are three illustrative general descriptions provided in GAAP:

* The policy is to match the maturities of the collateral investments and the securities loans and that at year-end all securities loans could be terminated on demand by either the entity or the borrower and that substantially all cash collateral was invested in overnight or on-demand investments. (Disclosure explains how maturities are matched.)
* Substantially all securities loans can be terminated on demand either by the entity or by the borrower, although generally the average term of these loans is one week, cash collateral is invested in securities of a longer term, generally with maturities between one week and three months. (Disclosure explains how maturities are not matched.)
* At year-end, 50% of the collateral investments were in maturities of less than one week, and the weighted-average term to maturity of all collateral investments was 35 days. (Disclosure explains how maturities are not matched.)

DISCLOSURE REQUIREMENTS FOR IRREVOCABLE SPLIT-INTEREST AGREEMENTS

> **OBSERVATION:** GASB Cod. Sec. I70 (*Irrevocable Split-Interest Agreements*) has no separate disclosure requirements for the agreements. All other disclosure requirements in GAAP related to the underlying investments, capital assets (if applicable), and liabilities (if applicable) are required, considering materiality.

DISCLOSURE REQUIREMENTS FOR QUALIFYING EXTERNAL INVESTMENT POOLS

Disclosures for Qualifying External Investment Pools (at Amortized Cost). Qualifying external investment pools that have elected to report at amortized cost the following in the notes to the pool's basic financial statements:

- Fair value measurements, including a summary of the fair value, the carrying amount (if different from fair value), the number of shares or the principal amount, ranges of interest rates, and maturity dates of each major investment classification as referenced in the previous section. The fair value measurement would be at the end of the reporting period and separated by recurring and nonrecurring fair value measurements,
- Except for investments that are measured at net asset value (NAV) per share or its equivalent, the level of the fair value hierarchy within which the fair value measurements are categorized in their entirety (Level 1, Level 2, or Level 3),
- A description of the valuation techniques used in the fair value measurement,
- If there has been a change in the valuation technique from previous periods that has a significant impact on the result and the reasons for making the change,
- For nonrecurring fair value measurements, the reasons for the measurement,
- For investments that calculate NAV or its equivalent, the elements of disclosure discussed previously in this chapter on NAV disclosure, and
- The presence of any limitations or restrictions on participant withdrawals such as redemption notice periods, maximum transaction amounts, and the authority to impose liquidity fees or redemption gates [GASB Cod. Sec. In5.141].

APPENDIX: COMPREHENSIVE ILLUSTRATION OF INVESTMENT DISCLOSURES FOR A STATE

Source—Commonwealth of Massachusetts

PRACTICE POINT: This includes the most common disclosures as of the fiscal year ended June 30, 202X. **It is not authoritative.** Disclosures will differ from government to government based on the nature and extent of investments. The information on determining fair value is not contained herein as it is in the summary of significant accounting policies. Component units are disclosed based on professional judgment excluded for this illustration. Amounts are in thousands, except for percentages.

Summary of Significant Accounting Policies

D. CASH, CASH EQUIVALENTS, SHORT-TERM INVESTMENTS, AND INVESTMENTS

The State follows the practice of pooling cash and cash equivalents. Cash equivalents consist of short-term investments with an original maturity of three months or less and are stated at cost. Interest earned on pooled cash is allocated to the General Fund and, when so directed by law, to certain other Governmental Funds.

The Treasurer (Treasury) manages the State's short-term external mixed investment pool, the Municipal Depository Trust (MDT), which is comprised of two portfolios: a Cash Portfolio and a Short-Term Bond Portfolio. The Cash Portfolio is a money-market-like investment pool; its investments are carried at amortized cost. As of June 30, 202X, the MDT's entire cash fund is included as cash equivalents in the accompanying financial statements. The Short-Term Bond Portfolio investments are carried at fair value. As of June 30, 202X, the MDT's entire bond fund is included as short-term investments in the accompanying financial statements.

Investors in MDT are not allowed to overdraw their shares. For a complete copy of MDT's separately issued financial statements, please contact the Treasurer's Cash Management Department, at (123) 456-7890 or download the statements from the Cash Management section of the State Treasurer's website at www.money.gov/treasury. State Law Chapter X9, Section Y8 enumerates the State's investment policy for non-pension assets.

The post-employment and OPEB benefit trust funds invest in the Pension Investment Trust (PIT) Fund, a diversified external investment pool managed by the Pension Investment Management (PIM) Board and are reported at fair value in the accompanying financial statements. The State Employees,' Teachers' Public Employee Retirement Systems (PERS) and the State Retirees' Benefit Trust (SRBT) are required to invest in the PIT Fund and comprise approximately 37.4%, 38.6% and 1.9% respectively, of the net position of the PIT Fund. For a complete copy of PIT's separately issued financial statements, contact the PIM Board at 1234 Sesame Street, Money, XY 12345.

Other State investments are comprised of equities (marketable securities) and fixed income securities, as well as interests in alternative investment funds such as private equity, debt, and real estate. Marketable securities are reported at fair value based upon quoted market prices. Investments in fixed income securities, including U.S. government agency obligations, are reported at fair value using independent pricing services. In determining the price, the services may reflect such factors as market prices, yields, maturities, and ratings, supplemented by deal quotations. Alternative investments are generally reported at net asset values (NAV) reported by the investment manager for the respective securities, which are used as a practical expedient to estimate the fair value of the State's interests therein, unless it is probable that all or a portion of the investment will be sold for an amount different from NAV. As of June 30, 202X, the State had no plans or intentions to sell investments at amounts different from NAV.

Reported fair values for shares in registered mutual funds are based on share prices reported by the funds as of the last business day of the fiscal year.

Investments also include pooled investment funds with Commonfund which are valued at fair value based upon estimated net asset values provided by the management of Commonfund. These pooled investment funds are invested in marketable debt and equity securities.

Certificates of deposit and guaranteed investment or annuity contracts are carried at amortized cost.

Note 2. DEPOSITS, SHORT-TERM INVESTMENTS, AND INVESTMENTS

Primary Government

The State's cash and cash equivalents and restricted cash is comprised of the following (amounts in thousands):

	Governmental Activities	Business-Type Activities	Government Wide Total	Fiduciary Funds
Cash	$310,784	$3,677,005[1]	$3,987,789	$109,701
MDT—cash fund	16,502,464	1,419,747[1]	17,922,211	6,412,016
Restricted cash with fiscal agent	248,690	—	248,690	—
Total	$17,061,938	$5,096,752	$22,158,690	$6,521,717

[1] of which $247,256 (in thousands) is presented as restricted cash in the accompanying financial statements.

Lottery Annuity Contracts and U.S. Treasury Strips. The State Lottery Commission, a division of the State Treasurer, purchases annuity contracts from insurance companies and United States treasury strips to fund the State's liability for future installment prize obligations. These annuities and treasury strips represent obligations of the insurance companies and the custodial banks, respectively, to provide a fixed series of payments over a specified period. Only annuity investments are subject to credit risk. For the annuity contracts, risk is controlled by purchasing these investments only from insurance companies with the top two ratings issued by a national recognized ratings organization. However, due to the nature of these annuity contracts, the credit quality of the insurance company issuer is subject to change. As of June 30, 202X, the amortized cost of annuities was approximately $98 million. As of June 30, 202X, the U.S Treasury Strips have a fair value of approximately $658 million. Approximately 87.0% of these amounts are held in United States Treasury strips at a custodial bank. No insurance company has an amount of annuities over 5.9% of the overall portfolio.

State Building Authority (SBA) Deposits and Investments. The SBA is authorized to invest in obligations of the US Treasury, its agencies and instrumentalities, bonds or notes of public agencies or municipalities, bank time deposits, guaranteed investment contracts, money market accounts and repurchase agreements. These investments are recorded at fair value. The SBA has an investment policy that establishes the minimum credit quality for certain instruments, outlines investment procedures and updates for periodic reporting. The SBA investment policy does not specifically limit the amount the SBA may invest in any one issuer.

As of June 30, 202X, the SBA held the following deposits and investments which are a component of Governmental Activities above (amounts in thousands):

Cash and cash equivalents	$636,735
Restricted cash with fiscal agent	—
Restricted investments	1,076,700
Total	$1,713,435

Custodial Credit Risk – Pooled Cash. Custodial credit risk is the risk that in the event of a bank failure, deposits and investments may not be returned to the State. Cash balances represent amounts held in bank depository accounts that may be subject to custodial credit risk.

The State requires all bank deposits in excess of insurance coverage by the Federal Deposit Insurance Corporation (FDIC) to be collateralized with a perfected pledge of eligible collateral or a letter of credit. For programs created by the Treasury, such as the Small Business Banking Program, eligible collateral must be pledged in an amount equal to 102% of the amount of the deposits that exceed FDIC insurance. Sufficient collateral to cover total Commonwealth deposits in excess of the FDIC insured amount must be pledged and held in safekeeping by a custodian that is approved by and under the control of the Treasurer.

Membership by a financial institution in the Depositors Insurance Fund (DIF) or the Share Insurance Fund (SIF) will be accepted by the Treasurer's Office as alternative security, provided that the financial institution submits proof of membership in the DIF or the SIF. Membership in the DIF is limited to State chartered savings banks while membership in the SIF is limited to State cooperative banks.

Custodial Credit Risk – Higher Education. The Institutions of Higher Education have investment policies that may vary by institution for custodial credit risk. Each institution carries deposits that are fully insured by the FDIC, as well as uninsured deposits. As of June 30, 202X, the bank balances of uninsured deposits totaled $198 million.

Custodial Credit Risk – SBA. The SBA does not have a formal investment policy for custodial credit risk. The SBA carries deposits that are fully insured by the Federal Deposit Insurance Corporation (FDIC) insurance, as well as deposits that are fully collateralized. As of June 30, 202X, all SBA bank balances were fully protected against loss.

Interest Rate Risk – MDT. Interest rate risk is the extent that changes in interest rates of debt investments will adversely affect the fair value of an investment. These investments include certain short–term cash equivalents, various long-term items, and restricted assets by maturity in years. The Treasury cash portfolio minimizes the risk of the fair value of securities falling due to changes in interest rates by maintaining a dollar-weighted average portfolio maturity of 60 days or less. The Treasury cash portfolio's assets are managed to maintain a dollar-weighted average life to maturity of 120 days or less. The Cash Portfolio is operated in compliance with Governmental Accounting Standards Board (GASB) Statement No. 79, *Certain External Investment Pools, and Pool Participants.*

As of June 30, 202X, the Cash Portfolio's securities had a weighted average maturity of 49 days and a weighted average life of 65 days.

Investments in the MDT Short Term Bond Portfolio are made in investment-grade securities as defined by national statistical rating agencies. The State assesses risk for the Short-Term Bond Portfolio by using duration. Duration is the weighted maturity of the security's cash flows, where the present values of the cash flows serve as weights.

For the MDT Short Term Bond Portfolio, the June 30, 202X duration was 2.41 years. As of June 30, 202X, investments in the MDT Short Term Bond Portfolio had a total net position of $821 million with investment maturities ranging from less than one year to ten years. As of June 30, 202X, the Short-Term Bond Portfolio's effective maturity schedule was as follows:

Securities with an Effective Maturity of	Percentage of Total Net Position
Less than one year	14.8%
One to five years	78.9%
Six to ten years	3.9%
Total*	97.6%

* The remaining 2.4% consists of cash equivalents and other assets.

Interest Rate Risk – Higher Education. As of June 30, 202X, the Institutions of Higher Education had debt investments stated at fair value of approximately $482 million and had investment maturities ranging from less than one year to more than ten years, with 9.5% of the investment's fair values maturing in less than 1 year, 73.2% from one to five years, 10.9% from six to ten years, and 6.4% more than ten years.

Interest Rate Risk – SBA. The SBA's investment policy does not specifically limit investment maturities as a means of managing its exposure to fair value losses arising from interest rates. As of June 30, 202X, the SBA had approximately $200 million invested in a collateralized guaranteed investment contract and approximately $460 million invested in U.S. Treasury Bonds. These investments are included in restricted investments on the balance sheet. The guaranteed investment contract matures on July 25, 202X while the U. S. Treasury Bonds mature from May 202X to November 204Y. These investments represent approximately 70% of the SBA's total investments in debt service funds and debt service reserve funds.

Interest Rate Risk – Custodial Funds. The custodial funds hold certain debt investments in trust as collateral for regulatory purposes. As of June 30, 202X, these investments had a fair value of approximately $527 million, with investment maturities ranging from less than one year to more than ten years. Of the total fair value, approximately 28.3% has maturities of less than one year, 44.5% from one to five years, 17.2% from six to ten years and 10.0% greater than ten years.

Credit Risk – MDT. Credit risk is the risk that an issuer or other counterparty to an investment will not fulfill its obligations. The State, exclusive of Pension Trust Funds, minimizes concentration of credit risk, the risk attributed to the magnitude of the investment in a single issuer. The State's investment policy prohibits the Treasury from investing more than 5% of the total investment portfolio in any single financial institution or issuer, excluding various public entity securities and repurchase agreements. However, there are no restrictions on the amount that can be invested in public entity securities and the portfolio may be invested in U.S. Treasury and other Government Sponsored Enterprises (GSE's) obligations and repurchase agreements.

The Treasury cash portfolio is invested only in First Tier Securities as defined by the Securities and Exchange Commission's Rule 2A-7 of the Investment Company Act of 1940. The Treasury does have additional policies regarding credit ratings of investments as detailed in the Investment Circulars which can be found in the documents tab at https://www.mymoney.com/mdt/pools.do. On June 30, 202X, the Cash Portfolio's securities were all rated as First Tier.

On June 30, 202X, the Short-Term Bond Portfolio's follows:

Portfolio Composition	Percentage of Total Net Position
AAA	58.9%
AA	4.7%
A	14.2%
BBB	19.4%
BB	0.4%
Total*	97.6%

* The remaining 2.4% consists of cash equivalents and other assets.

Credit Risk – Higher Education. For the Institutions of Higher Education presented in the Business-Type Activities, fair values of debt investments were $122 million at AAA, $86 million from AA+ to A- and $274 million either unrated, BBB+ or less.

Credit Risk – SBA. The SBA's investment policy generally limits investments in fixed income products with institutions that have an investment grade rating as determined by one of the nationally recognized rating agencies. The SBA's policy requires issuers of investment contracts to be rated AA or above by at least two of the nationally recognized rating agencies or A with pledged collateral equal to 102% of the principal balance. As of June 30, 202X, the guaranteed investment contracts were not rated; however, the issuer was rated AA+ by Standard & Poor's and Aa3 by Moody's and the guaranteed investment contracts were collateralized.

Credit Risk – Custodial Funds. The custodial funds had debt investments with a fair value of $527 million, of which $358 million were in U.S Government securities, $79 million were in money market securities, $65 million were in state and local government securities, and $25 million were in corporate debt securities.

Interest Rate Risk – PIT Funds. As pension and OPEB trust funds have a longer investment horizon than many of the Commonwealth's other investments, the PIM Board manages PIT's exposure to fair value loss arising from movements in interest rates by establishing duration guidelines with its fixed income investment managers. The guidelines with each individual manager require that the effective duration of the domestic fixed income investment portfolio be within a specified percentage or number of years of the effective duration band of the appropriate benchmark index. For emerging markets fixed income investments, the portfolio must have a duration with a band ranging from three to eight years.

Effective duration is a measure of a fixed income investment's exposure to fair value changes arising from changes in interest rates. Effective duration makes assumptions regarding the most likely timing and amounts of variable cash flows. These assumptions take into consideration factors indicative of investments highly sensitive to interest rate changes, including callable options, prepayments, and other factors.

The PIM Board compares the effective duration of a manager's portfolio to their relevant benchmark including Bloomberg Barclays Capital Aggregate index, US Treasury STRIPS 20+ Year index, Bloomberg Barclays Capital Treasury 1-3 Year index, Bloomberg Barclays Capital US TIPS (Treasury Inflation Protected Securities) index, Bloomberg Barclays Capital Inflation Linked Bonds index, S&P LSTA Leveraged Loan index, JP Morgan Global Emerging Markets Bond index, and the Intercontinental Exchange Bank of America Merrill Lynch (ICE B of AML) High Yield index. The PIT Fund had fixed income and short-term investments totaling approximately $27.8 billion at fair value with an effective weighted average duration range from 1.33 to 15.12 years as of June 30, 202X.

Credit Risk – PIT Funds. The PIM Board establishes credit investment guidelines with each of its fixed income securities investment managers in establishing a diversified portfolio. These guidelines vary depending on the manager's strategy and the role of its portfolio to the overall diversification of the PIT fund. The guidelines for the PIT Fund's core fixed income portfolio establish the minimum credit rating for any security in the portfolio and the overall weighted average credit rating of the portfolio. The guidelines for the PIT Fund's high yield, fixed income portfolio establish a fair value range of securities to be held with a specific minimum credit rating and the overall weighted average credit rating of the portfolio.

Credit risk for derivative instruments held by the PIT results from counterparty risk. The PIT is exposed to credit risk resulting from counterparties being unable to meet their obligations under the terms of the derivative agreements. The weighted average quality rating of the debt securities portfolio, excluding pooled investments, investments explicitly backed by the United States Government and other nonrated investments was BBB- and BBB+ as of June 30, 202X and June 30, 202W respectively.

Credit ratings associated with the Commonwealth's investment in the PIT Fund ranged from AAA to A- investments with a fair value of approximately $2.966 billion, BBB+ to B- investments with a fair value of approximately $3.852 billion, $921 million rated CCC+ to D, $10.274 billion are unrated, and the remaining $9.988 billion are investments that are explicitly backed by the U. S. Government.

Foreign Currency Risk – PIT Funds. Foreign currency risk is the risk that changes in exchange rates will adversely affect the fair value of investments. The Treasury does not have a policy regarding foreign currency risk for the Pension Trust. The PIM Board manages PIT's exposure to foreign currencies by hedging a percentage of PIT's non-U.S. dollar denominated investments through forward foreign currency contracts. The PIT Fund's investments in foreign currency denominated investments as of June 30, 202X were approximately $190 million in cash and short-term investments, $15.246 billion in equities, $850 million in fixed income investments, $599 million in portfolio completion strategies, $1.713 billion in private equity investments and $389 million in timberland investments. An additional $4.349 billion is invested in international investments denominated in U. S. dollars.

Concentration of Credit Risk – PIT. The PIM Board manages PIT's exposure to concentration of credit risk by establishing guidelines with each investment manager that limit the percent of investment in any single issue or issuer. PIT has no investments, at fair value, that exceed 5% of PIT's net position held in trust for pool participants as of June 30, 202X.

A. INVESTMENT DERIVATIVE INSTRUMENTS

PIT may invest in investment derivative instruments. In accordance with GASB Statement No 53, *Accounting and Financial Reporting for Derivative Instruments*, PIT's derivatives are accounted for as investment derivatives and are reported at fair value.

Forward Currency Contracts. PIT enters into forward currency contracts to hedge the exposure to changes in foreign currency exchange rates on foreign portfolio holdings. The fair value of the contracts will fluctuate with changes in currency exchange rates. Risks may arise from the potential inability of counterparties to meet the terms of their contracts and from unanticipated movements in the value of a foreign currency relative to the U.S. dollar.

The contracts are marked-to-market daily and the change in fair value is recorded as an unrealized gain or loss by PIT.

When a contract is closed, PIT records a realized gain or loss equal to the difference between the cost of the contract at the time it was opened and the value at the time it was closed.

As of June 30, 202X, PIT had open foreign exchange contracts with combined net unrealized gain of approximately $888 thousand with various delivery dates.

Further information on derivative instruments can be found in the notes to PIT's basic financial statements.

Futures Contracts. PIT may purchase and sell financial futures contracts to hedge against changes in the values of securities the fund owns or expects to purchase.

Upon entering such contracts, they must pledge to the broker an amount of cash or securities equal to a percentage of the contract amount.

The potential risk is that the change in the value of futures contracts may not correspond to the change in the value of underlying instruments, which may not correspond to the change in value of the hedged instruments. In addition, there is a risk that PIT may not be able to close out its future positions due to a non-liquid secondary market. Risks may also arise from the potential inability of a counterparty to meet the terms of a contract and from unanticipated movements in the value of a foreign currency relative to the U.S. dollar.

PIT may also invest in financial futures contracts for non-hedging purposes.

PIT held contracts outstanding as of June 30, 202X with various expirations from FY2Y to FY2C. These contracts are for cash and cash equivalents, fixed income, equities, and commodities. A portion of the contracts were short contracts. The aggregated notional exposure amount as of June 30, 202X was approximately $895 million with a fair value of $887 million, yielding an unrealized net loss of approximately $8 million.

Payments are made or received by PRIT each day, depending on the daily fluctuations in the value of the underlying security and are recorded as unrealized gains or losses. When the contracts are closed, the PRIT Fund recognizes a realized gain or loss.

Swaps – PIT. PIT has entered into swap agreements to gain exposure to certain markets and actively hedge other exposures to market and credit risk. The swap contracts are reported at fair value, which represents their estimated liquidation values on costs. PIT either receives cash from the swap counterparties or pays the swap counterparties monthly depending on whether the fixed-rate interest is lower or higher than the variable-rate interest. Changes in fair value are included as part of investment income.

As of June 30, 202X, PIT had contracts in effect with an aggregated notional amount of approximately $23.052 billion to various investment banks that had maturity dates from FY2X to FY7C. The contracts have an aggregate fair value loss of approximately $84 million. PIT values these contracts using standard methods and techniques including the discounted cash flow analysis and option pricing models.

PRIT's counterparty exposure was with various major investment companies with ratings ranging from AA- to BBB+ and various other banks with other ratings. Open swap contracts as of June 30, 202X were as follows (amounts in thousands):

Counterparty	Credit Ratings	Interest Rate Swaps Gross Notional	Interest Rate Swaps Fair Value	Credit Default Swaps Gross Notional	Credit Default Swaps Fair Value	Total Return and Other Swaps Gross Notional	Total Return and Other Swaps Fair Value
BNP Paribas Securities Corp	A+	$—	$—	$184,739	$1,966	$—	$—
Citibank NA	A+	—	—	3,600	18	597,477	8,489
CME Group	AA-	344,867	(1,429)	—	—	—	—
Goldman Sachs	A+	43,358	37	1,867,722	(46,786)	—	—
Intercontinental Exchange	BBB+	—	—	100,582	1,950	—	—
LCH Ltd	AA-	130,262	(1,050)	—	—	249,751	1,935
Merrill Lynch International	A+	—	—	4,800	48	229,799	2,838
Morgan Stanley	A+	431,123	(31)	493,122	(5,294)	188,635	(221)
SMBC Capital Markets Inc.	A+	250,000	(18,429)	—	—	—	—
U.S. Bank National Association	A+	500,000	(3,255)	—	—	—	—
All others	Various	13,212,418	5,683	1,035,481	(32,336)	3,183,828	2,115
Totals		$14,912,028	$(18,474)	$3,690,046	$(80,434)	$4,449,490	$15,156

B. DISCRETELY PRESENTED COMPONENT UNIT INVESTMENTS

Component units invest in derivative transactions. Detailed information on those transactions is found in the notes to the basic financial statements of those component units.

C. FAIR VALUE MEASUREMENTS OF INVESTMENTS

In accordance with GASB Statement No. 72, *Fair Value Measurement and Application*, the Commonwealth categorizes the fair value measurements of its investments within the fair value hierarchy established by GAAP. The fair value hierarchy categorizes the inputs to valuation techniques used for fair value measurement into three levels as follows:

- Level 1—Inputs are quoted prices for identical investments in active markets.
- Level 2—Observable inputs other than quoted market prices.
- Level 3—Unobservable inputs.

The fair value hierarchy gives the highest priority to Level 1 inputs and the lowest priority to Level 3 inputs. In certain instances where the determination of the fair value measurement is based on inputs from different levels of the fair value hierarchy the level in the fair value hierarchy is based on the lowest level of input that is significant to the fair measurement.

Level 2 investments are categorized using various inputs that include, but are not limited to, pricing models, independent third party evaluated services, benchmarking yields, reported trades, broker-dealer quotes, issuer spreads and benchmarking securities among others.

The following tables present a summary of the fair value hierarchy of investments as of June 30, 2021 (amounts in thousands):

Primary government	Total	Level 1	Level 2	Level 3
Debt securities:				
US Treasury and agency securities	$1,270,498	$1,259,697	$10,801	$—
Municipal securities	33,842	30,740	3,102	—
Institutional money market funds	960,806	954,180	6,626	—
Corporate debt/bonds	124,020	6,980	116,998	42
Corporate stock	35,550	35,550	—	—
Asset backed securities	21,833	—	21,833	—
Registered investment companies	52,761	52,761	—	—
Mortgage-backed securities	33,225	—	33,225	—
Other fixed income	135,926	134,949	977	—
Total debt securities	2,668,461	2,474,857	193,562	42
Equity securities	265,782	264,147	—	1,635
Investments measured at the Net Asset Value (NAV):				
Commonfund (pooled investment funds)	446,210			
Private equity	63,244			
Private debt	16,017			
Private real estate	10,727			
Other	18,015			
Total investments measured at the NAV	554,213			
Other investments at fair value:				
MMDT—bond fund	388,836			
Total other investments at fair value	388,836			
Subtotal investments at fair value	3,877,292	$2,739,004	$193,562	$1,677
Other investments:				
Annuity contracts	97,858			
Guaranteed investment contracts	200,099			
Certificates of deposit	5,920			
Other	184,575			
Total other investments	488,452			
Total investments—primary government	$4,365,744			
Derivative instruments:				
Interest rate swaps (liabilities)	$89,997	$—	$89,997	$—

Included in the preceding schedule is approximately $7 million of various money market mutual fund investments related to the business type activities which are classified as cash equivalents in the accompanying financial statements.

Lottery annuity contracts and U.S. Treasury Strips of approximately $755 million as of June 30, 202X are presented in governmental fund and governmental activities on the Statement of Net Position.

	Total	Level 1	Level 2	Level 3
Fiduciary funds:				
Debt securities:				
US Treasury securities	$357,568	$357,568	$—	$—
Bonds	90,333	25,633	64,700	—
Total debt securities	447,901	383,201	64,700	—
Investments measured at the Net Asset Value (NAV):				
Mutual funds	79,259			
Other investments at fair value:				
MDT—bond fund	33,680			
Net investment in PIT	95,692,868			
Total other investments at fair value	95,726,548			
Total investments—fiduciary funds	$96,253,708	$383,201	$64,700	$—

10,001

CHAPTER 10
CAPITAL ASSETS

Chapter References:
GASB Statement Nos. 6, 34, 37, 42, 51, 62, 72, 83, 87, 89, 94, 96
GASB *Implementation Guide*
NCGA Statement No. 1

INTRODUCTION

Governments may have many capital assets. GAAP requires all types of governments in nearly all types of funds to report capital asset transactions. (The exception is governmental funds.) Capital assets of proprietary funds are reported in the fund statements and on the government-wide statements. Capital assets of fiduciary funds (and similar component units) are only reported in the statement of fiduciary net position. All other capital assets are for general purposes of the government [GASB Cod. Sec. 1400.101].

Capital assets are reported by governments at historical cost. The historical cost of a capital asset is like the calculation of cost in all other organizations. The cost includes all ancillary charges to place the asset in its intended location and in the condition for the asset's ultimate use. These charges range from legal fees to freight and transportation, construction, and many other potential costs. However, construction period interest is excluded.

Donated capital assets are also common, especially for public institutions of higher education, conservation districts, parks, and public healthcare facilities. Donated assets are reported at acquisition value, plus related charges to place the asset into service [GASB Cod. Sec. 1400.102].

GENERAL REQUIREMENTS FOR CAPITAL ASSETS

PRACTICE ALERT: The GASB is in the process of a major project on the *classification* of nonfinancial assets, but not the recognition and measurement of such assets. In scope are the following types of assets, excluding investments discussed in Chapter 9 of this *Guide*:
- Tangible capital assets held for sale and tangible capital assets used for service,
- Intangible capital assets and tangible capital assets,
- Intangible lease assets and tangible owned assets, and
- Contracts for the right-to-use intangible assets and leases of tangible assets.

Tangible capital assets held for sale tentatively may be required to be classified separately from tangible capital assets used for service by requiring them to be reported as a major class of capital asset. Intangible capital assets would be classified separately from tangible capital assets by requiring them to be reported by major class separate from major classes of tangible capital assets.

Right-to-use assets would be required to be recognized for subscription-based information technology arrangements separately from other capital assets. Assets representing the right-to-use intangible underlying assets, other than subscription-based information technology arrangements, should not be classified separately from assets representing the right-to-use tangible underlying assets. Assets representing the right-to-use intangible underlying assets would be classified separately from owned intangible assets.

The exposure draft is expected to define the term *held for sale*. Such capital assets held for sale would be required to be reclassified as used for service if the usage of the asset changes over time.

An exposure draft was being released as this edition of the *Guide* was slated for publication. A final standard is expected by June 2024.

Definition of Capital Assets

Capital assets include the following items that have initial useful lives extending beyond a single reporting period:

- Land and land improvements,
- Easements,
- Buildings and building improvements,
- Vehicles,
- Equipment,
- Rights to use assets related to leases longer than one year (see **PRACTICE POINT**),
- Software and technology (see **PRACTICE ALERT** in the section discussing intangible assets),
- Works of art, historical treasures, and other similar assets (see **PRACTICE ALERT** in the section discussing historical treasures),
- Infrastructure assets, and
- All other tangible or intangible assets used in operations.

PRACTICE POINT: GASB Cod. Sec. L20 (*Leases*) focuses on a "right-to-use" model for recognition of an asset by a lessee, without derecognition of a leased asset by a lessor. The asset of a lease will then be an intangible capital asset for the lessee which at inception will equate to the present value of the lease payments plus any up-front payments or deposits. See Chapter 14 for a more complete discussion of leasing activity.

PRACTICE POINT: Similar GAAP to GASB Cod. Sec. L20 is applied in two additional standards, both released in 2020. GASB Statement No. 94 (*Public-Private and Public-Public Partnerships and Availability Payment Arrangements*) (P3s) applies the framework contained in GASB Cod. Secs. L20 to P3s. Two new sections of the *Codification* have been generated from GASB-94 (P90 and A90 for availability payment arrangements).

A "right to use" asset results from a contractual relationship where a government (the transferor) engages with an operator (which may be another government or a nongovernment entity) to provide public services by conveying control of the right to operate or use infrastructure or other nonfinancial assets for a period of time in an exchange or exchange-like transaction. Availability Payment Arrangements are when a government contracts with another entity to operate or maintain the government's infrastructure or nonfinancial asset. In return, the entity receives compensation from the government based on the asset's availability for use. The availability may be based on the condition of the asset or other measures of performance (vehicle traffic per hour as an example).

There may be design, financing, construction, or other services provided. GASB-94 became effective for fiscal years beginning after June 15, 2022, and all reporting periods thereafter. Changes adopted to conform to the provisions of GASB-94 were applied by a retroactive restatement.

The implementation of GASB Statement No. 96 (*Subscription-Based Information Technology Arrangements*) also may result in an intangible asset, but conforms the existing GAAP discussed later in this chapter to so-called "cloud-computing" contracts, which may include hardware, software, a combination of both, and may even include information technology infrastructure. The statement was also effective for fiscal years beginning after June 15, 2022, and all reporting periods thereafter. Changes adopted to conform to the provisions would also be applied by a retroactive restatement. GASB-96 was codified as GASB Cod. Sec. S80. Both Statements are discussed in more detail in Chapter 14.

Infrastructure assets consist of "horizontal" assets that are in some cases, extremely long-lived. They are stationary in nature and are in use many more years than other forms of capital assets. It is common for a road, bridge, tunnel, irrigation, and drainage system, water, and sewer system, dam, and power grid to be in operation for many decades. Infrastructure assets may also have related buildings. But such related buildings are not infrastructure unless they are an ancillary part of a network of infrastructure assets [GASB Cod. Sec. 1400.103].

As an example of buildings that may be related to a network or subsystem, GASB Cod. Sec. 1400.702-13 identifies the following:

- Turnpike rest areas,
- Road maintenance buildings related to a highway system, and
- Water pumping buildings related to a water system.

A subsystem makes up a part of a network (a collection of related assets). For example, a sewer system (the network) could comprise storm drains and retention ponds.

Land Improvements. GASB Cod. Sec. 1400.702-1 defines land improvements as "betterments, other than buildings, that ready land for its intended use." Examples include the excavation of the land, utility installations, parking lots, and landscaping.

OBSERVATION: Capital assets are sometimes termed colloquially as "fixed assets." Using the term "fixed assets" in a set of basic financial statements is not proper, because capital assets may include movable assets and intangible assets. Statements of net position should only use the term "capital assets."

Inexhaustible assets include land and land improvements. Capital assets should also be evaluated for impairment if events indicate that the use of the asset has significantly and unexpectedly declined (see section discussing asset impairment) [GASB Cod. Sec. 1400.104].

Depreciation—General Provisions. Capital assets are depreciated over their estimated useful lives, unless they are inexhaustible or are infrastructure reported using the modified approach discussed in the next section. Intangible assets are amortized similarly to depreciation.

Modified Approach for Infrastructure Assets

Infrastructure assets that are part of a network (or a subsystem of a network) are not required to be depreciated if the following conditions are satisfied [GASB Cod. Sec. 1400.105]:

- An asset management system is employed that:
  — Has an up-to-date inventory of eligible infrastructure assets,
  — Performs condition assessments of the assets and summarizes the results using a "measurable scale,"
  — Estimates, on an annual basis, the annual amount needed to "maintain and preserve the eligible infrastructure assets at the condition level established and disclosed by the government," *and*
- The government is preserving and maintaining the eligible infrastructure assets "approximately at (or above) a condition level established and disclosed by the government."

The documentation of condition assessments must be carefully done so that their results can be replicated. GAAP describes results as being subject to replication as "those that are based on sufficiently understandable and complete measurement methods such that different measurers using the same methods would reach substantially similar results" [GASB Cod. Sec. 1400, fn. 7].

The condition level must be established and documented by governmental policy or legislative action, and the assessment itself may be made either by the governmental entity directly or by external parties. Professional judgment and good faith are the basis for determining what constitutes acceptable and accurate documentation of the condition of eligible infrastructure assets.

The modified approach also requires governmental entities should document the following [GASB Cod. Sec. 1400.106]:

- Complete condition assessments of eligible infrastructure assets are performed in a consistent manner at least every three years, *and*
- The results of the three most recent complete condition assessments provide reasonable assurance that the eligible infrastructure assets are being preserved approximately at (or above) the condition level established and disclosed by the government.

The condition level could be applied to a group of assets by using a condition index or "as the percentage of a network of infrastructure assets in good or poor condition." If a governmental entity identifies a subsystem of infrastructure assets as "eligible" (and therefore the computation of depreciation is optional), the documentary requirements apply only to the subsystem and not to the entire network of infrastructure assets.

GASB Cod. Sec. 1400.703-3 reminds practitioners that GAAP requires that the modified approach be applied to all assets in the network or subsystem, however, a governmental entity could decide to use the modified approach for one network but not for another network. On the other hand, if the eligible infrastructure assets are reported by two or more different departments, either all or none of the assets in the network or subsystem must be subjected to the modified approach.

GASB Cod. Sec. 1400.703-21 also recognizes that numerous asset management systems are available to governmental entities. The GASB does not sanction management systems. It is the responsibility of the management of a governmental entity to assess a management system and determine whether that system can satisfy the standards established by GAAP.

A governmental entity may perform the condition assessment annually or may use a cycle basis. If a cyclical basis is used for networks or subsystems, all assets of these groups must be assessed during the cycle. However, rather than apply the condition assessment to all assets, a statistical sample approach may be employed in the annual approach or in the cycle approach.

As eligible infrastructure assets presented using the modified approach do not have to be depreciated, all expenditures related to their maintenance should be recognized as a current expense when incurred.

Expenditures or expenses that are capital in nature (additions and improvements) should be capitalized as part of the eligible infrastructure assets because they, by definition, increase the capacity or efficiency of the related infrastructure asset [GASB Cod. Sec. 1400.107]. The adequate maintenance of the condition of eligible infrastructure assets is a continuous process and if the conditions are initially satisfied but subsequently are not, the infrastructure assets are not considered "eligible" and depreciation expense must be computed for them and reported in the Statement of Activities. The change in accounting for depreciation expense should be reported as a change in an accounting estimate [GASB Cod. Sec. 1400.108].

> **OBSERVATION:** The non-recognition of depreciation expense for eligible infrastructure assets is optional. A governmental entity can decide to depreciate all infrastructure assets that are exhaustible rather than carve out and identify "eligible infrastructure assets."

Finally, GASB Cod. Sec. 1400.702-22, clarifies the differences between infrastructure and other horizontal assets. Parks are considered land and therefore are not infrastructure assets, however, a subsystem within a park (such as roads and trails) could be considered an infrastructure asset and therefore eligible for the modified approach.

When an infrastructure asset is subject to the modified approach, the transfer of the asset from one governmental entity to another is recorded by the transferring government as a functional expense, depending on the nature of the asset transferred.

> **PRACTICE ALERT:** The GASB's *Financial Reporting Model Improvements* Exposure Draft changes the reporting of infrastructure assets utilizing the modified approach regarding analysis information in the government's Management's Discussion and Analysis. The GASB has proposed discussion of the information move to required supplementary information (RSI).

> **PRACTICE ALERT:** The GASB has added a project to the Technical Plan on Infrastructure Assets. The project will address accounting and financial reporting for such assets, including how should infrastructure be recognized and measured in the basic financial statements. The modified approach may or may not be continued to be allowed. Deferred maintenance may be addressed. A Preliminary Views document is expected by July 2024. An Exposure Draft may be released by January 2026, with a final Statement potentially a year later.

Works of Art, Historical Treasures, and Similar Assets

Works of art, historical treasures, and similar assets (that are not donated) generally must be capitalized at their historical cost, "whether they are held as individual items or in a collection." However, such assets do not have to be capitalized if they are part of a collection and all the following conditions are satisfied [GASB Cod. Sec. 1400.109]:

- They are held for public exhibition, education, or research in furtherance of public service rather than financial gain,
- They are protected, kept unencumbered, cared for, and preserved, and
- They are subject to an organizational policy that requires the proceeds from sales of collection items to be used to acquire other items for collections.

GASB Cod. Sec. 1400.704-7 discusses the situation when a governmental entity has multiple collections, works of art, and historical treasures GAAP may be applied for the entire entity or on a collection-by-collection basis. GAAP does not require the organizational policy to be formal, but there should be evidence to verify its existence.

Institutions of higher education and public schools may capitalize books due to their materiality and rare books due to their historical significance. Policies and procedures are necessary to delineate the depreciation method and useful lives of books and historical collections. A reevaluation of these policies may be necessary as increased works are being digitized.

GASB Cod. Sec. 1400.704-1 describes collections of works of art and historical treasures as "generally . . . held by museums, botanical gardens, libraries, aquariums, arboretums, historic sites, planetariums, zoos, art galleries, nature, science, and technology centers, and similar educational, research and public service organizations that have those divisions, however, the definition is not limited to those entities, nor does it apply to all items held by those entities."

For example, animals in a zoo are capital assets, and they could be considered a collection, however, GASB Cod. Sec. 1400.704-3 adds "only successful breeding colonies of zoo animals would likely meet the requirements in GAAP that collections be preserved."

In some instances, items in a collection are permanently attached to a structure and removing them might damage them or significantly reduce their value. Such items do not have to be subject to a written policy for them not to be capitalized, because the nature of how the items are displayed "demonstrates a commitment and probability that they will be maintained."

If a governmental entity capitalizes a collection that previously had not been reported, the capitalization should be reported as a change in an accounting principle (prior-period adjustment) and not as a correction of an error.

Works of art, historical treasures, and similar assets received as donations must be recorded as revenue based on the standards established by GASB Cod. Sec. N50 (see Chapter 17). If these donated items are added to a *noncapitalized* collection, the governmental entity must simultaneously record a program expense equal to the amount of the donation recorded as revenue [GASB Cod. Sec. 1400.110].

As previously discussed, works of art, historical treasures, and similar assets that are "inexhaustible" do not have to be depreciated. All other capitalized items must be depreciated [GASB Cod. Sec. 1400.111]. GASB Cod. Sec. 1400.704-8 discusses how GAAP does not provide a definition of "inexhaustible" collections or individual works of art or historical treasures. However, there is the following description of the items: "Those items with extraordinarily long useful lives that because of their cultural, aesthetic, or historical value, the holder of the asset (or assets) applies effort to protect and preserve the asset in a manner greater than that for similar assets without such cultural, aesthetic, or historical value."

REPORTING CAPITAL ASSETS IN GOVERNMENT-WIDE FINANCIAL STATEMENTS

The Statement of Net Position contains capital assets that are being depreciated and amortized, net of accumulated depreciation and amortization, respectively. Accumulated depreciation and amortization may be reported on the face of the Statement of Net Position. However, many practitioners prefer to report this amount in the notes to the basic financial statements.

Capital assets that are not being depreciated, including land and infrastructure assets using the modified approach (see previous discussion) are reported separately if significant. Additional detailed reporting is up to management [GASB Cod. Sec. 1400.112].

> **PRACTICE POINT:** Many practitioners report individual categories (buildings, vehicles, equipment, etc.) based on the asset management system used, capital budgeting, bond indentures, and other provisions.

> **PRACTICE ALERT:** Right-to-use assets should be presented in a subsection of capital asset disclosure. Additional discussions on right-to-use assets are included later in this chapter and in Chapter 14.

Depreciation and amortization expense is reported in the Statement of Activities. The expense may be identified with a function of government (police vehicles in public safety as an example) or reported as a separate line in the Statement of Activities. If reported as a separate line, it should exclude any depreciation expense reported as part of programs and activities. Depreciation of infrastructure is usually reported as part of the public works, utilities, or transportation function [GASB Cod. Secs. 2200.132–.133].

The expense is calculated by allocating the net cost of the depreciable asset (historical cost less salvage value) over the estimated service life of the asset *systematically and rationally*. Depreciation can be calculated for:

- Classes of assets (example: water reservoir infrastructure),
- Networks of assets (example: concrete dam, spillway and locks that are part of a water system),
- Subsystems of networks (example: interstate highways that are part of a statewide system), or
- Individual assets [GASB Cod. Sec. 1400.113].

Methods of calculating depreciation and amortization are discussed later in this chapter.

CAPITAL ASSET REPORTING IN GOVERNMENTAL FUNDS

The modified accrual basis of accounting and the current financial resources measurement focus should be used in accounting for assets within governmental funds. On the Balance Sheet of a governmental fund, in accordance with the modified accrual basis of accounting and the current financial resources measurement focus, assets are not classified as current or noncurrent.

However, when assets are presented on a governmental fund's Balance Sheet, it is implied that they are current. In governmental accounting, current assets represent current financial resources available for appropriation and expenditure. Financial resources are considered current when they are available for subsequent appropriation and expenditure. Examples of current financial resources include cash, various receivables, and short-term investments.

Capital assets represent past expenditures, not financial resources available to finance current governmental activities. For this reason, general capital assets (assets not related to a proprietary fund or fiduciary fund) of a governmental entity are not presented in a specific governmental fund but, rather, are reported in the entity's government-wide financial statements.

Capital assets that are acquired using the resources from a governmental fund are recorded as expenditures for the period. For example, if a governmental entity uses resources from the general fund to purchase equipment that has a cost of $10,000, the following entry would be made:

GENERAL FUND	Debit	Credit
Expenditures—Capital Outlay	10,000	
Cash		10,000
To record purchase of equipment for Mayor's office use.		

A reconciling entry would then occur to report the outlay as an addition to capital assets, becoming a component of capital assets as presented in the government-wide statements. As shown later in this chapter in the section titled "Capital Assets Disclosure in the Notes to the Basic Financial Statements," the capital outlay would be a portion of additions to capital assets.

PRACTICE ALERT: The status of capital asset transactions in governmental funds was part of the GASB's initial deliberations in the *Financial Reporting Model Improvements* project. The GASB has tentatively concluded that the current model for capital outlay transactions in governmental funds will not change as the result of the reexamination. Capital outlay will be reported as long-term transactions if purchased through governmental funds.

CAPITAL ASSET REPORTING IN PROPRIETARY FUNDS

Reporting of capital assets in proprietary funds is the same as in government-wide statements. However, the assets and depreciation are usually program-specific to the program accounted for in the fund [GASB Cod. Sec. 1400.115]. (See also Chapter 7.)

CAPITAL ASSET REPORTING IN FIDUCIARY ACTIVITIES

Capital assets *may* be reported in fiduciary activities similarly to government-wide reporting [GASB Cod. Sec. 1400.116]. (See also Chapter 8.)

PRACTICE POINT: If the capital assets are used in operations, capital asset reporting provisions are proper for pension and other postemployment benefit funds. A case can be made that if the assets are ever sold, the net proceeds are for the beneficiaries. Furthermore, if they are to be used for income or profit, reporting as an investment may be proper, especially if the capital asset is reported in a separate holding company for legal and risk aversion purposes. Reporting as an investment is common. In either case, the balances are reported in the Statement of Fiduciary Net Position. GAAP has no definitive guidance on presenting depreciation and amortization expense in a Statement of Changes in Fiduciary Net Position should the fiduciary activity have capital assets. In practice, many entities include the activity as part of administrative or other expense. Should the capital asset be reported as an investment, the corresponding depreciation or amortization would be reported as a component of investment income (as an expense, but not part of investment cost).

CAPITAL ASSETS DISCLOSURE IN THE NOTES TO THE BASIC FINANCIAL STATEMENTS

The notes to the basic financial statements have required elements detailing the capital asset disclosures in the basic financial statements. The summary of significant accounting policies is required to contain disclosure of the policy of capitalizing assets and for estimating the useful lives of those assets. It is also required to contain the method (or methods) used in computing depreciation (or amortization) of capital assets by major classes of depreciable assets. Governments that choose to use the modified approach for reporting eligible infrastructure assets are required to describe that approach [GASB Cod. Sec. 2300.106(a)(8)].

Disclosures are then required for capital asset transactions, impairment losses, idle impaired capital assets and insurance recoveries (if not apparent from the face of the financial statements). (Other disclosures may be required as applicable on impairments related to government combinations and asset retirement obligations as discussed in this chapter.)

Required Note Disclosures of Capital Assets

Required note disclosure of capital assets are divided into major classes of capital assets and further apportioned between governmental activities and those associated with business-type activities. Capital assets not being depreciated are disclosed separately from those being depreciated [GASB Cod. Sec. 2300.117].

Each major class of capital assets include disclosure of:
- Beginning and end of year balances, with accumulated depreciation presented separately from historical cost,
- Capital asset acquisitions (and transfers from other classes), inclusive of capital outlays in governmental funds and other additions and transfers,
- Sales and other dispositions, and
- Current-period depreciation (and amortization) expense, with disclosure of the amounts charged to each of the functions in the Statement of Activities [GASB Cod. Sec. 2300.118].

For collections not capitalized, disclosure includes a description of the collection and the reasons these assets are not capitalized. Otherwise, the previous required disclosures apply [GASB Cod. Sec. 2300.119].

Example Note Disclosure (including Right-to-Use Assets)

The following is an example capital asset disclosure. Business-type activities are now shown below as the display would be redundant. However, if business-type activities have capital assets, disclosure is required.

	July 1, 20X1	Additions	Deletions	June 30, 20X2
Governmental Activities:				
Capital assets not being depreciated				
Land	$—	$—	$—	$—
Construction in progress	—	—	—	—
Total capital assets not being depreciated	—	—	—	—
Capital assets being depreciated				
Land improvements	—	—	—	—
Buildings and improvements	—	—	—	—
Furniture and equipment	—	—	—	—
Total capital assets being depreciated	—	—	—	—
Total capital assets	—	—	—	—
Accumulated depreciation				
Land improvements	—	—	—	—
Buildings and improvements	—	—	—	—
Furniture and equipment	—	—	—	—
Total accumulated depreciation	—	—	—	—
Net depreciable capital assets	—	—	—	—

	July 1, 20X1	Additions	Deletions	June 30, 20X2
Right-to-use assets being amortized:				
Land improvements	—	—	—	—
Licensed software and similar technology	—	—	—	—
Buildings and improvements	—	—	—	—
Furniture and equipment	—	—	—	—
Total right-to-use leased assets being amortized	—	—	—	—
Accumulated amortization				
Land improvements	—	—	—	—
Licensed software and similar technology				
Buildings and improvements	—	—	—	—
Furniture and equipment	—	—	—	—
Total accumulated amortization	—	—	—	—
Net right-to-use assets	—	—	—	—
Governmental activities capital assets and right-to-use assets, net	$—	$—	$—	$—

Discretely Presented Component Unit Disclosures

Like other disclosures for component units, deciding which disclosures about capitalized assets is a matter of professional judgment. The decision to disclosure is based on the component unit's significance to the aggregated component units and the component unit's relationship with the primary government [GASB Cod. Sec. 2300.121].

INTANGIBLE ASSETS

An intangible asset possesses the following characteristics [GASB Cod. Sec. 1400.138]:

Characteristic	Description
The asset has a lack of physical substance.	The asset can be used, exchanged, or employed, but does not have any mass.
The asset is of a nonfinancial nature.	The asset has value, but not in a monetary form such as cash, investments securities, a claim or right to monetary assets such as receivables, or prepayments of goods and services.
The asset has a multiple period useful life.	The initial useful life extends beyond a single reporting period.

Examples of governmental intangible assets include easements, land and mineral use rights, computer software, patents, and trademarks (see **PRACTICE POINT** on *Subscription-Based Information Technology Arrangements*).

Intangible assets that are acquired or created primarily for directly obtaining income or profit should be treated and reported as investments. These may be patents or processes that the government has licensed potentially to third parties. A royalty stream may be an indicator of management's intent to obtain income or profit unless documented otherwise [GASB Cod. Sec. 1400.139].

GAAP requires that intangible assets to be reported as capital assets at historical cost. For intangible assets to be reported at historical cost in the financial statements, the asset must be "identifiable," which means the asset is separable, or the government can sell, rent, or transfer it to another party. Consequently, if the asset is not separable, the asset is comprised of contractual or other legal rights, such as water rights acquired from another government through a contract that cannot be transferred to another party [GASB Cod. Secs. 1400.140–.141].

Internally Generated Intangible Assets

Many intangible assets are purchased or received from other parties. However, certain intangible assets may be generated internally by a government itself, such as software systems that the government designs, codes, tests, and implements, rather than licensing from a vendor. Outlays related to developing such assets may be incurred over time rather than at a single point in time when a purchase occurs.

The accounting and reporting of these types of assets has been given special attention in GAAP. Three circumstances that must be met for outlays related to internally generated intangible assets to begin to be reported as a capital asset:

1. The government's specific objective for the project and the service capacity in which the asset is expected to be used upon completion of the project must be determined,

2. The feasibility of completing the project so that it can be used in that capacity has to be demonstrated, and

3. The government's intention to complete or to continue the development of the asset must be demonstrated [GASB Cod. Sec. 1400.142].

GAAP provides specific guidance for capitalizing outlays related to internally generated computer software as intangible assets. This guidance involves classifying activities in developing and installing internally generated computer software into three stages: (1) preliminary project stage, (2) application development stage, and (3) post-implementation/operation stage. Different principles apply to outlays in each of the stages. The principles are as follows:

	Preliminary Stage	Development Stage	Post-Implementation/ Operation Stage
Definition	Determination of whether a project is technologically and financially feasible.	Management authorizes and commits to funding.	Software is accepted and operating.
Characteristics of Stage	Demonstration that there is intent to complete the project Initial investigations or designs.	Software is coded, tested, implemented. INITIAL training occurs. Procurement and contracting.	Ongoing maintenance that does NOT increase useful life. (Otherwise capitalized.) Ongoing training.
GAAP Principles	Expensed.	Capitalized.	Expensed.
Additional information			Betterments are capitalized if they increase useful life or service utility of the software.

The above table can also be applied to many internally generated intangible assets other than software, including patents, trademarks, and other invented items.

> **OBSERVATION:** A government's accounting software or system needs to be flexible enough to properly account for these multiple phases and capitalize *all* related costs, including direct salaries, indirect costs, payroll, costs of consultants, and other design and build costs.

For amortization, intangible assets that have no legal, contractual, regulatory, technological, or other factors limiting their useful life are considered indefinite and should not be amortized.

> **PRACTICE ALERT:** In rare circumstances, software licenses may be perpetual, which in substance, is a transfer of ownership of the software to the licensee government. In such cases, the intangible asset provisions in GAAP would apply, rather than the provisions of GASB Statement No. 96 (*Subscription-Based Information Technology Arrangements*).

In an analogous manner to other depreciable capital assets, intangible assets are to be amortized. For example, water rights procured under a contract with no termination to the rights of the purchasing government would be considered an intangible asset with an indefinite useful life and would therefore be reported at historical cost and not be amortized. However, if an intangible asset originally considered to have had an indefinite useful life experiences an event that results in a subsequent determination that the useful life is no longer indefinite (e.g., a change in the terms of the water rights contract that provides a termination date for such rights), it must be amortized over its remaining useful life [GASB Cod. Secs. 1400.151–.152].

Outlays in governmental funds associated with intangible assets should be reported as expenditures when incurred consistent with the current financial resources measurement focus. At the government-wide level of financial reporting, these intangible asset outlays of governmental funds would be capitalized and amortized like other capital assets and be a reconciling item between the fund financial statements and the government-wide financial statements [GASB Cod. Sec. 1400.153].

PRACTICE ALERT: As discussed in *Subscription-Based Information Technology Arrangements* (SBITAs), many systems of government are so-called "cloud computing" arrangements, inclusive of a contract or software license. The user government does not take possession of the software. Instead, the software application "resides" on the vendor's, or third party's hardware and access is provided to the software on an as-needed basis over the internet or a dedicated line. SBITAs utilize the same three stages as above. SBITAs are discussed in detail in Chapter 14. "Cloud computing" arrangements should be analyzed to determine if the government has an asset by using not only the provisions in GASB Cod. Sec. 1400, but also the provisions of GASB Statement No. 96. This author thinks that if the government can use, exchange, or employ the data stored on the third party's hardware, an asset is present. As this *Guide* was nearing publication, the GASB was finalizing question 4.10 in *Implementation Guidance Update* –2023, which relates to this issue. Further details on this question are discussed in Chapter 14.

Intangible Assets and Public-Private and Public-Public Partnerships and Availability Payment Arrangements

A government could be a party to a service concession arrangement (SCA) in accordance with GASB Cod. Sec. S30. A governmental operator reports an intangible asset for the right to access the facility and collect third-party fees from its operation at cost (e.g., the amount of an up-front payment or the cost of construction of or improvements to the facility). The cost of improvements to the facility made by the governmental operator during the term of the SCA should increase the governmental operator's intangible asset if the improvements increase the capacity or efficiency of the facility. The intangible asset should be amortized over the arrangement's term in a systematic and rational manner. Service concession arrangements are also further discussed in Chapter 14.

PRACTICE ALERT: As discussed in GASB Statement No. 94 (*Public-Private and Public-Public Partnerships and Availability Payment Arrangements*) (P3s and APAs), governments may be a party to these transactions. Transactions involving SCAs potentially may be P3s. An intangible asset may result from these contracts if the government is an operator involved in a P3. Governments involved in an APA would not result in an intangible asset. The provisions of GASB Statement No. 94 are discussed in Chapter 14.

OTHER SPECIFIC ISSUES IN CAPITAL ASSETS

Capitalization Policies. A governmental entity may establish a policy whereby capital acquisitions that are less than an established amount is expensed rather than capitalized. GASB Cod. Sec. 1400.702-6 (as amended most recently by GASBIG 2021-1, Q5.1) addresses the issue of whether the threshold amount applies to the purchase of a group of assets (such as the acquisition of 100 computers) as well as to an individual asset (such as the acquisition of a single computer). Capitalization policies need to consider completeness of reporting capital assets versus the cost of keeping records and internal controls over capital assets. The amended question suggests that "(a) government *should* establish a capitalization policy that would require capitalization of assets whose individual acquisition costs are less than a threshold for an individual asset *if those assets in the aggregate are significant.*" In other words, a single computer might not be significant, but 100 may very well be significant.

PRACTICE POINT: Too often, preparers default to the phrase, "it is immaterial," rather than fully analyzing and recording a transaction or group of transactions to comply with GAAP. The concept of materiality is more of an audit construct than a preparer construct. Further, one of the main assertions from preparers to auditors is "completeness." It is impossible to determine completeness without a complete inventory of transactions comprising a balance or the result of operations. Without such a ledger prepared with effective internal controls, the risk of material misstatement rises, meaning that a materiality threshold may be misstated.

PRACTICE POINT: This issue has come to the forefront in the implementation of GASB Cod. Sec. L20 (*Leases*). As further discussed in Chapter 14, GASB Cod. Sec. L20.708-1 (GASBIG 2019-3, Q4.23) discusses when a government adopts a capitalization threshold, expensing acquisitions, including lease assets that fall under the threshold. Lease liabilities that are significant, either individually or taken together, should be recognized. As discussed, there is no specific guidance determining capitalization thresholds. But as a practical matter, governments need to consider quantitative and qualitative significance of a lease asset (and liability). If an intangible asset such as with a lease is not recognized but a liability is recognized, then the transaction would be out of balance if reported separately. A similar issue has occurred as governments have implemented GASB Statement Nos. 94 and 96.

OBSERVATION: Capitalization policies are perhaps the most important part of capital asset operations as U.S. GAAP is principles-based rather than rules-based for capital assets. Consistent and rational capitalization polices are also important for federal cost recovery. Title 2, Code of Federal Regulations, Part 200 (*The Uniform Administrative Requirements, Cost Principles, and Audit Requirements*) contains a relaxation of technology capitalization, allowing expenses of up to an established amount per unit. But the requirements also emphasize consistency in policy so that the federal government is fairly charged. Capitalization policies should at the very least stipulate construction-in-process policies, cost-accumulation methods, adjustments, transfers, impairments, betterments, and disposals.

Capital Assets Acquired through Special Assessments. Special assessments for infrastructure and other capital assets are common. Capital improvements financed through special assessments are reported at historical cost and depreciated as ultimately, the assets are likely the government's assets. Related revenues are reported as either program or general revenues in the Statement of Activities [GASB Cod. Secs. S40.124–.125]. Capital improvements financed by assessments that are proprietary activities are reported as capital contributions in the proprietary fund of the activity and reported in the statement of revenues, expenses, and changes in fund net position [GASB Cod. Sec. 1400.154]. Special assessments are further discussed in Chapter 19.

Capital Assets Funded by Federal Grants, Contributions, Nonexchange Transactions. States and local governments commonly fund capital projects through federal grants, contributions, and other forms of nonexchange transactions. Most of these transactions will be reported at historical cost (or acquisition value if donated) and then depreciated as appropriated. Life interests in real estate are an exception because the government is a beneficiary of an irrevocable split-interest agreement. In those cases, GASB Cod. Secs. I70.119–.125 require the government to classify the asset either as a capital asset or an investment based on the terms and conditions of the agreement and management's intent at the time of donation. If the capital asset is to be used for governmental programs and services, the donation is at acquisition value. If for income or profit, it should be measured in accordance with the investment provisions discussed in Chapter 9 [GASB Cod. Secs. 1400.155–.156].

In many instances, capital assets purchased by state or local government are financed or partially financed by federal awards, and the federal government can retain a reversionary interest in the asset. These assets (even though the federal government retains a reversionary interest in the asset's salvage value) should be reported by the state or local government because "the state or local government is the party that uses the assets in its activities and makes the decisions regarding when and how the assets will be used and managed." Except in the case of certain infrastructure assets (where the modified approach is used), depreciation expense should be recorded for these assets.

PRACTICE POINT: Title 2, Code of Federal Regulations, Part 200, Section 313(e), contains disposal requirements for equipment and other capital assets financed (or partially financed) by federal awards. Governments that need to dispose of capital assets in this situation must request disposition instructions from the federal awarding agency if the terms and conditions of the federal award require it.

Reporting Capital Assets Where Ownership Is Unclear. All a governmental entity's capital assets are reported in the government-wide financial statements. GASB Cod. Sec. 1400, fn. 24, discusses that a government that has the *primary responsibility for maintaining* an asset should report the asset in its financial statements. GASB Cod. Secs. 1400.729-2–6 make it clear that the footnote applies only to situations in which it is unclear who owns an asset.

For example, ambiguity of ownership commonly arises for infrastructure assets such as highways. Other examples include when localities require homeowners to repair and maintain sidewalks adjacent to their properties, and localities establish regulations to determine when and how those sidewalks are to be maintained. Because the property owners, under this arrangement, are responsible for the maintenance of the sidewalks, the sidewalks should not be reported as assets by the government. The establishment of minimum maintenance standards by the governmental entity is different from accepting responsibility for the maintenance of the asset itself.

There may be an arrangement where one governmental entity maintains an asset, but another governmental entity is responsible for the replacement of the asset. Under this arrangement, and when ownership is unclear, the government that is responsible for maintaining the capital asset should report the asset in its financial statements.

GASB Cod. Sec. 1400.729-1 addresses whether title and ownership are the same. Public assets are unique in that while title is held by the governmental entity, citizens and numerous other parties and entities have the right to use the property. Nonetheless, the governmental entity that holds title to an asset generally should report the asset in its financial statements.

Construction or Acquisition of an Asset by a Government but Not Ultimately Owned by That Government. There are many circumstances where an item that will become an asset is constructed by one government but not ultimately owned by that government. The first government may finance the construction of the ultimate asset by bonds or grants, but when it is completed, deed the finished item over to another government who will own or operate the capital asset. This frequently occurs in infrastructure construction where the infrastructure spans multiple jurisdictions, or the recipient government(s) do not have the credit or other funds or expertise to construct it. Councils of governments that are established to receive tax monies for infrastructure construction are a prime example of these arrangements. In these arrangements, a capital asset *is not* established at the constructing government, even though construction in process may be used.

Guidance provided by GASB Cod. Sec. 1300.106 implies that a capital projects fund may not be used in these arrangements, because a capital projects fund excludes "those types of capital-related outflows financed by proprietary funds or for assets that will be held as fiduciary activity." To account for these types of transactions, instead of capital outlays, which imply a capital asset in process, it is better to recognize expenditures as construction occurs within a special revenue fund. These expenditures would not need to be reclassified to construction in process as construction progresses, because construction in process is an asset. Since the constructed item is not an item with present service capacity that the government presently controls, reclassification to construction in process is not proper. Certainly, a construction journal may be maintained and is needed for the project to establish total cost. Upon completion, as expenditures have occurred in the funds, no adjustment to fund balance or net position is needed via a transfer. The total cost is then shifted to the recipient government who would then recognize the asset at cost similarly to donated assets, as discussed previously. An increase would occur to contributed assets (a revenue account) and the type of capital asset (an asset account) to record the transfer. Contributed assets would then close to the net investment in capital assets account at the end of a fiscal year.

GASB Cod. Sec. 1400.729-5 discusses when a county constructs a road that is financed by county bonds, but ultimately transitions the road to the state to manage future maintenance. If there is evidence as to which government owns the road, that government should report it. In many cases regarding infrastructure, there is no deed or title. When ownership is unclear, the government with the primary responsibility for managing an infrastructure asset reports the asset. In this case, the state reports the road. But the county would also have bonds outstanding without a related capital asset.

Calculating Depreciation and Amortization

Governments may use any established depreciation method to depreciate and amortize capital assets. Depreciation may be based on the *estimated useful life of* a class of assets, a network of assets, a subsystem of a network or individual assets. Estimated useful life information usually utilize industry or professional guidelines, comparable information from other governments, or most commonly, internal information.

PRACTICE POINT: In practice most governments depreciate and amortize on a straight-line basis.

Composite methods are also available to calculate depreciation. In a composite method, a rate is determined and applied to the cost of a group of assets to calculate the expense. The rate can be calculated on a weighted average or an unweighted average. Once determined, the rate is used throughout the life of the group of assets, only changing if the useful life changes significantly.

Example: Management has estimated a group of four assets to have useful lives of 10, 12, 14, and 16 years. To determine the rate, the following formula is used:

$$[1 \div \{(10+12+14+16) \div 4\}] = 7.6923\%$$

If the assets cost $20 million, then annual depreciation expense would be approximately $1,538,460 (rounded) ($20,000,000 × 7.6923%) [GASB Cod. Secs. 1400.175–.180].

A frequent question for practitioners is what is an acceptable method of depreciation and amortization? GASB Cod. Sec. 1400.733-1 discusses that any "rational and systematic method" can be used. This includes:

- The straight-line method, which is the most common,
- Decreasing-charge methods, which include declining balance, double-declining balance, and sum-of-the-years' digits, among others,
- Increasing-charge methods, and
- Unit-of-production or service methods, which allocate the depreciable cost of an asset over its expected output.

A consideration for practitioners could include whether the capital asset is financed by debt. If the asset was completely isolated in its own fund and financed by related debt, the method chosen may result in a temporary negative fund balance or net position as the principal on the debt may be amortized slower than the capital asset. This is known as being "upside down." Therefore, a rational and systematic method could also include amortizing or depreciating at the same amount as a principal payment so that a negative balance would not occur.

Amortization of Right-to-Use Intangible Assets

PRACTICE POINT: As previously introduced, right-to-use intangible assets are involved with leases in accordance with GASB Cod. Sec. L20 from the point of view of the lessee, GASB Cod. Sec. P90 regarding P3s, and GASB Cod. Sec. S80 regarding SBITAs. The amortization of such assets would be for the *shorter* of the contract term *or* the related asset's remaining useful life. Further discussion of the amortization is contained in Chapter 14.

PRACTICE POINT: The implementation of GASB Cod. Sec. L20 (*Leases*), also raised the question of whether amortizing the right-to-use asset using the straight-line method is systematic and rational. As discussed in the following paragraph, since GASB Cod. Sec. L20 requires amortization of a related liability using the effective interest method, due to the differences in the methods, during the early periods of amortization of the liability, the balance of the liability will be greater than the asset if the straight-line method of amortization was used on the asset. Some governments are modifying their asset amortization policy strictly for right-to-use assets to amortize based on the amortization of the related liability. Therefore, the balances may equal absent any incentives on the liability or leasehold improvements.

ACCOUNTING AND FINANCIAL REPORTING FOR IMPAIRMENT OF CAPITAL ASSETS AND FOR INSURANCE RECOVERIES

Definition of Capital Asset Impairment. Asset impairment is "a significant, unexpected decline in the service utility of a capital asset." The significant and unexpected decline is based on events or changes in circumstances that were not anticipated when the capital asset was placed into service. "Service utility" is the "usable capacity that at acquisition was expected to be used to provide service, as distinguished from the level of utilization, which is the portion of the usable capacity currently being used" [GASB Cod. Secs. 1400.181–.182].

Recognition of an asset impairment is a multiple step process. Impairments must be identified and then tested. If conditions and events identify a potential impairment on a capital asset, tests are then performed to see if a change in circumstance does indeed result in an impairment.

Most capital asset impairments are well-recognized and documented through governing board minutes, insurance engagements and the media. If impairment is recognized during normal operations, then accounting and financial reporting proceeds [GASB Cod. Secs. 1400.183–.184].

Five indicators of an impairment of a governmental capital asset are [GASB Cod. Sec. 1400.185]:

1. Evidence of physical damage, such as, for a building, damage by fire or flood, to the degree that restoration efforts are needed to restore service utility,

2. Change in legal or environmental factors, such as a water treatment plant that cannot meet (and cannot be modified to meet) new water quality standards,

3. Technological developments or evidence of obsolescence, such as that related to diagnostic equipment that is rarely used because new equipment is better,

4. A change in the manner or expected duration of usage of a capital asset, such as closure of a school prior to the end of its useful life, and

5. Construction stoppage, such as stoppage of construction of a building due to lack of funding.

The five examples listed above are identified as common indicators of impairment. The GASB recognizes that the list is not all-inclusive. Professional judgment must be used to identify other events and changes that give rise to capital asset impairments. As an example, the rapid pace of technological change may give rise to impairment as the expected duration or usage of the technology declines [GASB Cod. Sec. 1400.186].

OBSERVATION: Asset retirement obligations (AROs) are not a result of asset impairment. They are related to *legally enforceable liabilities* associated with the retirement of tangible capital assets. In an asset impairment, the impairment may only be temporary as the asset may continue to be used. The retirement of a tangible capital asset encompasses the sale, abandonment, recycling, or disposal of such assets. AROs are further discussed in Chapter 16.

Impairment Test: Two-Step Process. The common capital asset impairment indicators (and other events and changes as described above) do not have to be applied every time they arise. Such an approach would be prohibitively expensive to apply, and the resulting financial reporting benefits would be marginal. For this reason, GAAP provides for the testing of capital asset impairment by determining whether both of the following factors are present [GASB Cod. Sec. 1400.187]:

1. The magnitude of the decline in service utility is significant, and
2. The decline in service utility is unexpected.

An example of this would be a fire at a government building that significantly damages the structure. The government did not expect the fire, and a sizable portion of the building is not usable.

> **PRACTICE POINT:** Intangible assets and right-to-use assets such as those involved in SBITAs may also become impaired. The above test is referred to within GASB Statement Nos. 94 and 96. As an example, an impairment may be present if a government's data is lost due to a cyberattack and held for ransom. Undoubtedly, there is a decline in service utility and the cyberattack was unexpected. Therefore, the provisions of this section would apply. If the impairment is judged to be temporary, additional provisions would apply as discussed later in this chapter.

A significant decline is evidenced by the continuing operating expenses related to the use of the impaired capital asset or the costs to restore the asset are significant in relationship to the current service utility.

All capital assets subject to depreciation generally reflect a decline in utility with age or usage; however, asset impairment arises when that decline is *unexpected*. For example, restoration costs to the government building with a fire in the example above are generally not part of a capital asset's normal life cycle and if they were later contemplated because of an event or change, that development suggests an unexpected decline in the service utility of the capital asset. On the other hand, the incurrence of normal maintenance costs or preservation costs such as the repainting of a government building does not suggest the impairment of a capital asset. Repainting is normal maintenance.

Measuring the Impairment of Capital Assets. When a capital asset is impaired based on the criteria in GAAP, the amount of the impairment loss (based on historical cost) should be determined by using one of the following measurement approaches:

- *Restoration cost approach*—generally used to measure impairment losses from physical damage from fire, wind, and the like,
- *Service units' approach*—generally used to measure impairment losses from environmental factors, technological changes, obsolescence, or change in the manner or duration of use, and
- *Deflated depreciated replacement cost approach*—generally used to measure impairment losses from change in the manner or duration of use.

The specific method to be used should be the approach "that best reflects the decline in service utility of the capital asset." Once an approach has been used, that approach should also be used to measure subsequent impairment write-downs with similar characteristics [GASB Cod. Secs. 1400.188–.191].

Cost Approaches: Restoration Cost Approach. Under the restoration cost approach, the write-down is based on the proportion of the capital asset impaired as expressed in current restoration cost. The current restoration cost is then converted to a historical cost basis under either a cost index or a ratio approach. The following steps are used for the ratio approach:

- Step 1 Determine the restoration cost in current dollars.

- Step 2 Determine the replacement cost also in current dollars for the capital asset.

- Step 3 Determine the carrying value of the impaired capital asset before adjustment (historical cost less accumulated depreciation).

- Step 4 Determine the relationship between the restoration cost in current dollars and the replacement cost in current dollars for the capital asset.

- Step 5 Determine the impairment lost by multiplying the carrying value of the asset by the percentage computed in Step 4.

The restoration cost approach can also be implemented by using an appropriate cost index. The estimate of the restoration cost should be based on the amount of the impairment caused by the change or event and should exclude costs related to demolition, cleanup, additions, and improvements.

To illustrate the restoration cost approach, assume that the government building that had the fire in the previous example originally cost $45,000,000, had an estimated useful life of 40 years (with a nominal residual value), and was 40% depreciated, when the fire occurred. $18,000,000 of accumulated depreciation had been properly reported to that point. The cost of restoring the damaged areas is $11,000,000. The estimated current replacement cost for the building is $54,000,000. The computation of the impairment write-down is as follows in a proprietary fund (and on the government-wide statements):

Step	Amount
Step 1—Restoration Cost in Current Dollars	$11,000,000
Step 2—Replacement Cost in Current Dollars	54,000,000
Step 3—($45,000,000 - $18,000,000) (Historical cost less depreciation before adjustment)	27,000,000
Step 4—($27,000,000 ÷ $54,000,000) (Step 1 ÷ Step 2)	× 50%
Step 5—Impairment write-down	**$13,500,000**

If it is assumed that the event that caused the impairment was considered both unusual in nature and infrequent in occurrence and was not within the control of management, it would be considered an extraordinary item as discussed in Chapter 5. Recording the transaction in a proprietary fund (such as an internal service fund that maintains the accounting for the building) or government-wide financial statements would be as follows:

INTERNAL SERVICE FUND	Debit	Credit
Extraordinary Item – Impairment Loss	13,500,000	
Accumulated Depreciation – Building		13,500,000
To record impairment loss on City Hall due to fire		

An impairment loss would not be recognized in a governmental fund, because the capital assets are not reported in such funds and because the event does not reduce current financial resources of the entity.

Cost Approaches: Service Units Approach. Under the service units' approach, the write-down is based on the proportion of the capital asset, as expressed in service units, which has been lost due to the event or change that created the impairment. The total service units can be based on the maximum service units or total service units throughout the life of the capital asset and can be expressed in a variety of measurement units, including years of service, number of citizens benefited, and various outputs.

To illustrate the service units' approach, assume that waste treatment equipment has an historical cost of $5,000,000. The equipment originally had an estimated useful life of 40 years (with a nominal residual value). The depreciation expense recognized per year straight-line was $125,000.

After 10 years of use, new environmental regulations are established, and the equipment can be used for only five more years before new equipment must be acquired. The amount of the service units lost, expressed in years, is 25 years (40 years less 10 years of use and 5 more years of use prior to replacement). The amount of the impairment loss is therefore $3,125,000 [$5,000,000 × (25 ÷ 40)]. The impairment loss may be reported as part of a program or, if unusual and infrequent, as an extraordinary item. This fact pattern indicates that the regulations were outside of management's control and, therefore, could be an extraordinary item.

Cost Approaches: Deflated Depreciated Replacement Cost Approach. The computation of the impairment loss using the deflated depreciated replacement cost approach is based on determining the current cost of an asset needed for the current level of service. Based on the assumed carrying value (cost minus accumulated depreciation) of the theoretical asset, that carrying value is deflated to the historical cost basis for when the original asset was acquired. For example, assume that a building had an original cost of $5,000,000 and was 40% depreciated. The building was to be used originally as a clinic but because of the construction of a new clinic, the building will be used instead as a warehouse for a government's department of public works. A suitable (based on the new usage) warehouse costs about $1,500,000 and the clinic's replacement cost is $7,000,000. The amount of the impairment loss is computed as follows:

Step	Amount
Deflator ($7,000,000 ÷ $5,000,000)	1.4
Assumed carrying amount of a new warehouse ($1,500,000 × 60%)	$900,000
Carrying amount of old building ($5,000,000 × 60%)	$3,000,000
Deflated assumed carrying amount of a new warehouse ($900,000 ÷ 1.4)	(642,857)
= Impairment loss	$2,357,143

Temporary Impairments

The impairment of a capital asset should generally be considered permanent. If an impairment of a capital asset is considered temporary, the historical cost of the capital asset should not be written down. However, impairments can be considered temporary only when there is evidence to support such a conclusion. The following illustrates an example of a temporary impairment:

A middle school that is not being used due to declining enrollment should not be written down if future middle school enrollment projections substantiated by current elementary school enrollment demonstrate that the middle school will be needed in a few years [GASB Cod. Sec. 1400.194].

> **OBSERVATION:** The carrying amount of impaired capital assets that are idle at year-end should be disclosed, regardless of whether the impairment is considered permanent or temporary [GASB Cod. Sec. 1400.196].

> **PRACTICE POINT:** Governments should evaluate if capital assets are impaired due to discontinued operations (other than temporary), some of which came to fruition during the COVID-19 crisis as well as the shift to remote working. For example, if a building can no longer be utilized due to the lack of funds to operate the building or the building is vacant, the building may be impaired.

Insurance Recoveries. Insurance recoveries are also common related to impairments of capital assets:

- Restoration or replacement costs should be reported separately (as an expenditure) from any insurance recovery (as another financing source or extraordinary item) in the financial statements of a governmental fund.
- Restoration or replacement costs should be reported separately from the impairment loss and associated insurance recovery in the government-wide and proprietary fund financial statements.
- The impairment loss should be reported net of any insurance recovery when the recovery is realized or realizable in the same year as the impairment loss.

- Insurance recovery proceeds that are realized or realizable in a period after the recognition of the impairment loss should be reported as program revenue, non-operating revenue, or an extraordinary item [GASB Cod. Sec. 1400.197].

Storm damage cleanup could result in an insurance recovery. In some cases, the recoveries are realized or realizable in the same year as the expense/expenditures for cleanup. In those cases, the costs are netted. If the recoveries are in a subsequent year, the inflows are other financing sources or extraordinary items, as appropriate.

FEMA (Federal Emergency Management Agency) Grant Funds. In some cases, Federal Emergency Management Agency (FEMA) grant funds are received instead of insurance recoveries. FEMA grants are not insurance recoveries and are reported as program revenue in the government-wide statements and as revenue in fund statements (nonoperating in enterprise and internal service funds). As these funds are nonexchange transactions, they are *not netted* with impairment losses. FEMA awards are only provided after the event occurs and the government applies and is accepted in accordance with the grant [GASB Cod. Sec. 1400.748-1].

Net Gains. Insurance recoveries may result in a net gain in the case of when an insurance recovery is greater than the impairment loss calculated. For impairments that are special items or extraordinary items, the net gain would be reported in the same manner as a net loss. The gain may be reported as part of program revenue or operating revenue as appropriate. Gains *should not* be reported as a negative expense [GASB Cod. Sec. 1400.748-3].

Reporting Impairment Write-Down

When a capital asset impairment is determined to be permanent, the amount of the write-down must be evaluated and classified in the financial statements in one of the following categories:

- Program expense or operating expense, if not unusual or frequently occurring and part of a program's normal operations [GASB Cod. Secs. 2200.129–.134, C50.121, 2300.107, P80.114–.115],
- Extraordinary item [GASB Cod. Secs. 1800.145, .147–.151, 2200.143, .145–.149, C50.121], or
- Special item [GASB Cod. Secs. 1800.146–.151, 2200.144–.149, 2300.107, C50.121].

If the impairment write-down is related to a proprietary fund capital asset, the write-down is classified either as (1) an operating expense, (2) an extraordinary item, or (3) a special item. If the impairment is related to a governmental fund capital asset, no write-down is reported, because the write-down does not consume current financial resources of the governmental fund.

Impairments of Intangible Capital and Non-Capital Assets

Intangible assets are also subject to impairment testing. Should an intangible asset be impaired, the same guidance is followed as if the asset were tangible.

> **PRACTICE POINT:** GAAP is unclear if data has value. As previously introduced, a government's operations could be impaired if data is lost due to cyberattack. If cyber-insurance is available and funds are remitted to the government, revenue is recognized in accordance with the insurance recovery guidance discussed in the following paragraph. Information technology arrangements and similar intangible or right-to-use assets may also have a lesser adjustment due to the requirement to amortize at the *shorter* of the estimated useful life or the life of the agreement. In many situations, the pace of change in technology is such that major upgrades could occur annually. Therefore, any insurance recovery due to data loss may result in a gain.

Insurance Recoveries for Intangible Capital and Noncapital Assets. Insurance recoveries also are for noncapital assets. For example, assume a government loses $1 million due to a cyberattack on data. The loss needs to be included as part of a program or general government expense as an extraordinary item, special item, or operating expense during the year the loss is discovered. The government, however, has antifraud insurance and recovers the funds in a subsequent year. The insurance recovery would use the same methodology as part of program revenue, non-operating revenue, or an extraordinary item.

Regulated Operation Asset Impairment

Regulated business entities (mostly utilities) must determine if recovery of any allowed cost is likely to be provided with:

- Full return on investment during the period from the time the asset is impaired to the time when recovery is completed, or
- Partial or no return on investment during that period.

That determination should focus on the facts and circumstances related to the specific impairment and should consider the past practice and current policies of the applicable regulatory jurisdiction on impairment situations. Based on that determination, the regulated business-type activity should account for the cost of the impaired plant as follows:

1. *Full return on investment is likely to be provided.* Any disallowance of all or part of the cost of the impaired plant that is *both* probable and reasonably estimable should be recognized as a loss, and the carrying basis of the recorded asset should be correspondingly reduced. The remainder of the cost of the impaired plant should be reported as a separate new asset.

2. *Partial or no return on investment is likely to be provided.* Any disallowance of all or part of the cost of the impaired plant that is both probable and reasonably estimable should be recognized as a loss. The present value of the future revenues expected to be provided to recover the allowable cost of that impaired plant and return on investment, if any, should be reported as a separate new asset. Any excess of the remainder of the cost of the impaired plant over that present value also should be recognized as a loss. The discount rate used to compute the present value should be

the regulated business-type activity's incremental borrowing rate, that is, the rate that the regulated business-type activity would have to pay to borrow an equivalent amount for a period equal to the expected recovery period.

In determining the present value of expected future revenues, the regulated business-type activity should consider such matters as:

1. The probable time before such recovery is expected to begin and
2. The probable period over which recovery is expected to be provided.

If the estimate of either period is a range, the most likely period within that range should be used to compute the present value. If no period within that range is a better estimate than any other, the present value should be based on the minimum period within that range [GASB Cod. Secs. 1400.198–.199, C50.151–.168].

The recorded amount of the new asset should be adjusted from time to time as necessary if added information indicates that the estimates used to record the separate new asset have changed. Those estimates include:

- The determination of whether full return on investment will be provided and, if not, the probable period before recovery is expected to begin and the probable period over which recovery is expected to be provided, and
- The amount of any probable and reasonably estimable disallowance of recorded costs of the impaired plant. The amount of the adjustment should be recognized as a loss or gain.

The recorded carrying amount of the new asset should not be adjusted for changes in the regulated business-type activity's incremental borrowing rate.

Between the date the new asset is recognized and the date on which recovery begins, the carrying amount should be increased by accruing a carrying charge. The rate used to accrue that carrying charge should be as follows:

1. If full return on investment is likely to be provided, a rate equal to the allowed overall cost of capital in the jurisdiction in which recovery is expected to be provided should be used.
2. If partial or no return on investment is likely to be provided, the rate that was used to compute the present value should be used.

During the recovery period, the new asset should be amortized as follows:

- If full return on investment is likely to be provided, the asset should be amortized in the same manner as that used for rate-making purposes.
- If partial or no return on investment is likely to be provided, the asset should be amortized in a manner that will produce a constant return on the unamortized investment in the new asset equal to the rate at which the expected revenues were discounted [GASB Cod. Secs. 1400.200–.201].

Impairments Resulting from Combinations

GASB Cod. Sec. Co10 includes provisions for accounting and financial reporting for the capital assets involved in combinations. In a merger, impairment may occur in several ways, including a disposal of buildings and other capital assets due to redundancy. If two cities are merging, there is no need for a second city hall. Therefore, impairment is present. In this case, carrying values must be adjusted in accordance with GASB Cod. Sec. Co10.116. Similarly, in a merger where one government continues but the other does not, an impairment may also occur [GASB Cod. Sec. Co10.123].

Even in a disposal or a transfer of operations, impairment may be present. For example, if a city police force is transferred to a county sheriff, chances are there are buildings, police cars, and other assets the former city no longer needs. The transferee (receiving) government will decide if impairment is present. There may also be decisions in any type of combination to change the manner of use or duration of use, which will also potentially cause impairment [GASB Cod. Sec. Co10.146].

11,001

CHAPTER 11
OTHER ASSETS AND DEFERRED OUTFLOWS OF RESOURCES

Chapter References:
  GASB Statement Nos. 6, 16, 17, 21, 31, 33, 34, 37, 38, 62, 72, 81, 96
  GASB Interpretation No. 6
  GASB *Implementation Guide*
  NCGA Statement Nos. 1, 4

INTRODUCTION

The accounting standards that are used to determine which assets should be presented in a governmental entity's financial statements and how they should be presented vary depending on whether an asset is presented in (1) governmental funds, (2) proprietary funds and fiduciary funds, or (3) the government-wide financial statements.

NOTE: For a discussion of how cash and investments and capital assets should be presented, see Chapter 9 and Chapter 10, respectively.

GOVERNMENTAL FUNDS

The modified accrual basis of accounting and the current financial resources measurement focus should be used in accounting for assets within governmental funds.

Governmental fund assets (assets of the general fund, special revenue funds, capital project funds, debt service funds, and permanent funds) that are not considered current financial resources (e.g., capital assets) are presented only in the governmental entity's government-wide financial statements and not in the fund financial statements.

PRACTICE ALERT: The GASB's *Financial Reporting Model Improvements* Exposure Draft proposes to change the measurement focus and basis of accounting for governmental funds to the short-term financial resources measurement focus and modified accrual basis of accounting. Assets include those that result from short-term transactions and other events and are receivable at period-end, as well as cash and other financial assets that are available to be converted to cash or are expected to be consumed in lieu of cash in the subsequent period. Examples of assets that would be recognized include:

- Cash and investments,
- Accounts receivable,
- Property taxes receivable,
- Prepaid items,
- Inventory, and
- Notes and other long-term receivables that have become due, but as of the date of the basic financial statements, have not been received.

Deferred outflows of resources are recognized for outflows of resources that do not meet the definition of an asset and are inherently related to future spending. Deferred outflows would still be required to be identified by the GASB. Notes and other long-term receivables that have not become due and capital assets, including intangible assets would not be recognized as assets in governmental funds.

Materials and Supplies in Inventory

Materials and supplies in inventory are current assets of a governmental fund, but they are not considered current financial resources. As discussed in Chapter 3, governmental funds, for the most part, measure the flow of current financial resources. However, one of the exceptions to this generalization is the accounting for inventories.

Inventories may be accounted for by using either the consumption method (flow of economic resources) or the purchase method (flow of current financial resources). GASB Cod. Sec. 1600.127 states that when the inventory amount is significant, that amount must be reported in the governmental fund's Balance Sheet regardless of the method used.

Inventory is defined as tangible items that are held for sale in the ordinary course of operations, or are in process for production for sale, or are to be currently consumed in the production of goods and services to be available for sale. Property held for installation or use in the production of services of *certain* business-type activities is also usually treated as inventory. Capital assets subject to depreciation is not inventory [GASB Cod. Secs. I40.102–.103].

The value of inventory at a reporting date may be at cost or the lower of cost or market. If a government reports at cost, the cost can be determined using one of several assumptions including average cost, first-in-first-out and last-in-first-out, choosing the one method which most clearly reflects periodic cost. Whichever method is chosen is required to be disclosed in the notes to the financial statements [GASB Cod. Secs. I40.104–.114].

PRACTICE POINT: For most governments, inventory is limited to supplies consumed for services such as fuel for public works vehicles. Inventory is also usually immaterial. Inventory cost accounting for governments is the same as for for-profit enterprises (cost basis calculations, basis for determining the lower of cost or market and then stating inventories above cost). The details of the calculations are not contained in the *Governmental GAAP Guide* due to the relative immateriality of inventory to most state and local governments. The focus areas are then the methods of recognition in the basic financial statements.

Consumption Method. The consumption method of accounting for inventories is inconsistent with the fundamental governmental fund concept that only expendable financial resources should be presented in a fund's Balance Sheet. However, the consumption method is acceptable as an alternative method of expenditure recognition in governmental fund accounting. Under the consumption method, a governmental expenditure is recognized only when the inventory items are used rather than purchased. For example, if a governmental unit purchased $100,000 of supplies, the following entry is made [GASB Cod. Sec. 1600.127]:

GENERAL FUND	Debit	Credit
Supplies Inventory	100,000	
Vouchers Payable		100,000
To record purchase of inventory and related payable prior to remittance to the vendor.		

At the end of the period, an inventory of supplies would be made, and the amount of inventory consumed would be recognized as a current expenditure. To continue with the example, assume that supplies worth $25,000 remain at the end of the accounting period. The current period's expenditure for supplies would be recorded in the following manner:

GENERAL FUND	Debit	Credit
Expenditures—Supplies	75,000	
Supplies Inventory		75,000
To record consumption of inventory during the fiscal period.		

If inventories are reported as an asset (even though they do not represent expendable financial resources), it is necessary to set aside fund balance by an amount equal to the carrying value of the inventory. Thus, in the above example, the following entry would be made at the end of the accounting period:

GENERAL FUND	Debit	Credit
Fund Balance – Unassigned	25,000	
Fund Balance – Nonspendable – Supplies Inventory		25,000
To reclass fund balance for inventory remaining at the end of the fiscal period.		

GASB Cod. Sec. 1300.704-21 partially concludes that balances of inventory (and prepaid amounts) are deemed to be nonspendable because they are not expected to be converted into cash. There could be some instances where a government has inventory that would be converted into cash through a sale. For example, if prisoners make furniture for sale, the raw materials for that furniture would be inventory. However, these sorts of programs are accounted for in enterprise funds.

Purchase Method. If governments do not use the consumption method, the purchase method is used. The purchase method of accounting for inventories is consistent with the governmental fund concept of reporting only expendable financial resources. Under the purchase method, purchases of inventories are recognized as expenditures when the goods are received, and the transaction is vouchered. To illustrate, assume the same facts as those used in the consumption method example presented earlier. When the supplies are acquired, the transaction would be recorded as follows [GASB Cod. Sec. 1600.127]:

GENERAL FUND	Debit	Credit
Expenditures—Supplies	100,000	
Vouchers Payable		100,000
To record inventory purchase and related payable prior to remittance to vendor.		

Continuing with the same facts, at the end of the period, no adjustment is made to the expenditures account even though only $75,000 of goods was consumed. However, GAAP requires that an inventory item must be presented on the Balance Sheet if the amount of inventory is considered significant. If it were concluded that the ending inventory of supplies was significant, the following entry would be made at the end of the accounting period in accordance with GASB Cod. Sec. 1300:

GENERAL FUND	Debit	Credit
Supplies Inventory ($100,000 - $75,000)	25,000	
Fund Balance—Nonspendable—Supplies Inventory		25,000
To record remaining balance of inventory at the end of the fiscal period.		

Under both the consumption method and the purchase method, the nonspendable fund balance would be presented under the broad caption of fund balance in a manner like the following illustration:

PARTIAL BALANCE SHEET	
GENERAL FUND	
FUND BALANCE:	
Fund Balance—Nonspendable Supplies Inventory	$25,000
Fund Balance—Unassigned (assumed)	400,000
Total Fund Balance	$425,000

Materials and Supplies Reported at the Lower of Cost or Market—Write Down Adjustments. As discussed previously, GASB Cod. Secs. I40.101–.114, contains guidance on when materials and supplies should be reported at the lower of cost or market. GAAP requires that inventories or supplies be subjected to the lower of cost or market test for possible write-down. That is, if the replacement cost of inventories or supplies is less than the cost of the items (using FIFO, LIFO, or the average cost method) a write-down is required.

Governments should write-down inventories or supplies if they are affected by physical deterioration or obsolescence. This requirement applies to the use of either the consumption method or the purchase method. The purchase method could be affected by the need for a write-down because GASB Cod. Sec. 1600.127, requires that a governmental fund record inventories or supplies when a significant balance of inventories or supplies exist at the end of the year. Under this circumstance, a write-down would require a reduction both in the asset balance and the nonspendable fund balance for inventory or supplies.

Prepayments and Deferred Outflows of Resources

Prepaid items may include items such as prepaid expenses, deposits, and deferred outflows of resources. Like inventory items, prepayments and deferrals do not represent expendable financial resources. However, these items may be accounted for by using either the allocation method or the non-allocation method [GASB Cod. Sec. 1600.127].

> **PRACTICE ALERT:** For subscription-based information technology arrangements (SBITAs) in accordance with GASB Statement No. 96, payments before the commencement of the subscription term associated with the SBITA contract made to the SBITA vendor, as well as payments made for the capitalizable initial implementation costs before the commencement of the subscription term, should be reported as a prepayment (an asset). A prepayment to a SBITA vendor should be reduced by any incentives received from the *same SBITA vendor* before the commencement of the subscription term, if a right of offset exists (as described in GASB Statement No. 62, par. 501, as amended). That prepayment should be reclassified as an addition to the initial measurement of the subscription asset at the subscription term's commencement. If the SBITA vendor incentives are greater than the SBITA vendor prepayments made to the same vendor, the difference should be reported as a liability until the commencement of the subscription term, at which time that amount should reduce the initial measurement of the subscription asset. Certain leases may also have prepaid amounts prior to a lease term as described in GASB Cod. Sec. L20.709-1. SBITAs and leases are fully discussed in Chapter 14.

Allocation Method of Prepaid Amounts. GAAP does not specifically refer to an allocation method and a non-allocation method but describes the process of allocation regarding prepaid amounts. Like the consumption method of inventory, the allocation method is not consistent with the basic governmental fund concept that only current financial resources should be presented in the fund's Balance Sheet. However, it is acceptable and may be used.

When the allocation method is used to account for prepayments, an asset is established at the payment date and amortized over the accounting periods expected to benefit from the initial payment. For example, if a state or local government purchased a three-year insurance policy for $45,000, the transaction would be recorded as follows under the allocation method [GASB Cod. Sec. 1600.127]:

GENERAL FUND	Debit	Credit
Prepaid Insurance	45,000	
Vouchers Payable		45,000
To record purchase of three-year insurance policy prior to paying the carrier.		

At the end of each year, the partial expiration of the insurance coverage would be recorded as follows:

GENERAL FUND	Debit	Credit
Expenditures—Insurance	15,000	
Prepaid Insurance		15,000
To record amortization of prepaid insurance purchased from carrier.		

Prepayments are reported as assets of the specific governmental fund that will derive future benefits from the expenditure. In the above example, the governmental unit's fund would report prepaid insurance as an asset of $30,000 at the end of the first year of the insurance coverage.

Because prepayments are not current financial resources, the fund's fund balance should be reserved by the amount presented in the asset balance. Thus, at the end of the first year in the current example, the following entry would be made in accordance with GASB Cod. Sec. 1300:

GENERAL FUND	Debit	Credit
Fund Balance—Unassigned	30,000	
Fund Balance—Nonspendable—Prepaid Insurance		30,000
To record fund balance related to unamortized insurance policy		

Like inventory, prepaid insurance cannot be readily converted into cash and is therefore nonspendable. The balance in the nonspendable fund balance would fluctuate each year resulting from changes in the carrying value of the prepayment accounts.

Non-Allocation Method. The non-allocation method of accounting for prepayments and deferrals is consistent with the basic governmental fund concept that only expendable financial resources are reported by a specific fund. Payments for the prepaid items are fully recognized as an expenditure in the year of payment if accounted for in governmental funds. Under the non-allocation method, no asset for the prepayment is created, and no expenditure allocation to future accounting periods is required. To continue with the previous example, the only entry that will be made if the non-allocation method is used is to recognize the expenditure in the year of payment as shown in the following illustration [GASB Cod. Sec. 1600.127]:

GENERAL FUND	Debit	Credit
Expenditures—Insurance	45,000	
Vouchers Payable		45,000
To record purchase of three-year insurance policy prior to paying the carrier.		

Although GAAP requires that significant amounts of inventories be recorded in the Balance Sheet no matter which accounting method is used, no similar requirement is extended to significant amounts of prepayments. It can be assumed that significant amounts of prepayments should also be reported in a fund's Balance Sheet. If the expenditure account is closed to the fund balance account and no asset is recognized, there is no need to establish a nonspendable fund balance for prepaid insurance when the non-allocation method is used. However, if the non-allocation method is used and the decision is made to report significant amounts of prepayments at period end, a nonspendable fund balance should be recognized.

DEFERRED OUTFLOWS OF RESOURCES

Deferred outflows of resources are consumptions of net assets by the government applicable to a future reporting period. GASB standards identify which transactions are reported as Deferred Outflows of Resources. Such transactions can occur in both the funds and the government-wide financial statements in the following transactions:

Activity	Accounting and Financial Reporting Aspects
Defined benefit Postemployment benefits other than pensions (OPEB)(government-wide statements)	Defined benefit postemployment benefits other than pensions arise in the following occurrences: • Proportions change from one year to the next for a cost-sharing employer or between any type of employer and a nonemployer contributing entity in a special funding situation, • Contributions occur after the measurement date, • Differences occur between actual and expected experience due to the publication of an experience study, and • Differences occur between projected and actual investment earnings on plan investments (where projected earnings are higher than actual earnings). They may occur with trusts or equivalent arrangements or not with trusts or equivalent arrangements.
Defined benefit pensions(government-wide statements)	Deferred outflows of resources occur in similar circumstances to postemployment benefits other than pensions. For a discussion of pensions and postemployment benefits other than pensions, see Chapter 13.

Specific Accounting and Reporting Issues

Activity	Accounting and Financial Reporting Aspects
Government combinations	Existing deferred outflows of resources may be acquired or received through a merger or acquisition with another government or operation. A government may also acquire a deferred outflow of resources in increasing the holding of an equity interest to 100%. Combinations are discussed in Chapter 10.
Hedging derivative instruments	In hedging transactions, if there is a suspended loss due to a change in fair value of an effective hedge, a deferred outflow of resources is recorded. Hedging derivatives are discussed in Chapter 12.
Asset retirement obligations	When a capital asset is required to be retired in accordance with laws, regulations or similar, deferred outflows of resources is recognized while the asset is in operation. These transactions are discussed in Chapter 16.
Sales and pledges of receivables and future revenues	In intra-entity transfers of revenue, the transferee declares a deferred outflow of resources over the duration of the sale agreement. Sales and pledges of receivables and future revenues are discussed in Chapter 17.
Current refundings and advance refundings resulting in the defeasance of debt.	The difference between the reacquisition price and the net carrying amount of the old debt should be reported as a deferred outflow of resources (or a deferred inflow of resources depending on the math) and recognized as a component of interest expense in a systematic and rational manner over the remaining life of the old debt or the life of the new debt, whichever is shorter. These transactions are discussed in Chapter 12. **OBSERVATION:** The Tax Cuts and Jobs Act of 2017 changed the status of advance refunding bonds to taxable transactions.

Other Assets and Deferred Outflows of Resources   **11,009**

Activity	Accounting and Financial Reporting Aspects
Modification of a lease due to a debt refunding of a lessor. Also, sale-leaseback transactions. Both transactions are in accordance with GASB Cod. Sec. L20.	If a change to the provisions of a lease in accordance with GASB Cod. Sec. L20.172 results from a debt refunding by the lessor, including an advance refunding that results in a defeasance of debt, the *lessee* should adjust the lease liability to the present value of the future lease payments *under the revised lease* using the effective interest rate applicable to the revised lease contract. The resulting difference should be reported as a deferred outflow of resources or a deferred inflow of resources. The deferred outflow of resources or the deferred inflow of resources should be recognized as an adjustment to an outflow of resources (for example, as an increase or decrease to interest expense) in a systematic and rational manner over the remaining life of the old debt or the life of the new debt, whichever is shorter. For sale-leaseback transactions, GASB Cod. Sec. L20.181 requires the difference between the carrying value of the capital asset that was sold and the net proceeds from the sale to be reported as a deferred inflow of resources or a deferred outflow of resources and subsequently recognized in the resource flows statements in a systematic and rational manner over the term of the lease. However, if the lease portion of the transaction qualifies as a short-term lease, any difference between the carrying value of the capital asset that was sold and the net proceeds from the sale should be recognized immediately. Both transactions are discussed in Chapter 14.
Government-mandated nonexchange transactions and voluntary nonexchange transactions (provider reporting)	If resources are received by the grantee or recipient before time requirements are met, but after all other eligibility requirements have been met, the resources are reported as a deferred outflow of resources by the *provider* (and a deferred inflow of resources by the *grantee or recipient*). These transactions are also discussed in Chapter 17.
Direct loan origination costs in lending transactions	Reported as deferred outflows of resources until the underlying loan is sold, at which time the deferred outflows are expensed. Fees paid to permanent investors at origination are deferred outflows of resources until the sale, at which time the deferred outflows are expensed.

Public-private and public-public partnerships(PPP)	If an underlying PPP asset is a new asset purchased or constructed by an operator *and* the PPP *does not* meet the definition of a service concession arrangement:
	• When the underlying PPP asset is placed into service:
	  — If the operator of the PPP is a government, the operator would recognize a deferred outflow of resources for the underlying PPP asset to be transferred to the transferor government, if any.
	  — The deferred outflow of resources amount recognized by the governmental operator is equal to the *estimated* carrying value of the underlying PPP asset *as of the expected date of the transfer of ownership*.
	  — The operator then amortizes the deferred outflow of resources in a systematic and rational manner over the remaining PPP term.

Activity	Accounting and Financial Reporting Aspects
	PRACTICE POINT: These provisions apply upon implementation of GASB Statement No. 94 (*Public-Private and Public-Public Partnerships and Availability Payment Arrangements*). GASB-94 is further discussed in Chapter 14 of the *Governmental GAAP Guide*.

PROPRIETARY FUNDS, FIDUCIARY ACTIVITIES, AND THE GOVERNMENT-WIDE FINANCIAL STATEMENTS

The accrual basis of accounting and economic resources measurement focus should be used to determine which assets should be presented on the Balance Sheet or Statement of Net Position of a proprietary fund or a Statement of Fiduciary Net Position for a fiduciary fund and in the Statement of Net Position within the government-wide financial statements.

Materials and Supplies—Proprietary and Fiduciary Funds

Materials and supplies in inventory are current assets of proprietary and fiduciary funds and the government-wide financial statements under the accrual basis of accounting and economic resources measurement focus. Only the consumption method of accounting for inventories is consistent with the fundamental concept of the economic resources measurement focus. Under the consumption method, an expense is recognized only when the inventory items are used.

Prepayments—Proprietary and Fiduciary Funds

Prepaid items may include items such as prepaid expenses and inventory. As is the case for inventory items, prepayments and deferrals represent economic resources in proprietary and fiduciary funds and in the government-wide financial statements. Only the allocation method is used to account for prepayments and deferrals, with an asset established at the payment date and then amortized over the accounting periods expected to benefit from the initial payment.

OTHER TRANSACTIONS THAT MAY OCCUR IN ALL FUNDS AND FINANCIAL STATEMENTS

Interfund Receivables and Payables. Governmental entities are generally involved in a variety of interfund transactions that may give rise to an interfund receivable or payable. For a discussion of the standards that apply to the reporting of interfund receivables and payables, see Chapter 5.

Disaggregation of Receivables and Payables. Much of the information contained in governmental as well as corporate financial statements is highly aggregated in that a single balance often represents a host of individual account balances. In many instances the aggregation does not obscure the nature of the reported balance, but in some cases a reader of the financial statement may be misinformed because of the aggregation.

In a limited way, current governmental reporting standards address the aggregation issue. For example, GASB Cod. Sec. C20 requires reporting by investment type, and GASB Cod. Secs. 1400 and 1500 require reporting capital asset and long-term liabilities by class and type.

GASB Cod. Sec. 2300 requires that a governmental entity present in the notes to its financial statements the details of receivables and payables reported on the statements of net position and Balance Sheets "when significant components have been obscured by aggregation." In addition, significant receivable balances that are not expected to be collected within one year of the date of the financial statements should be disclosed.

The disclosure format depends on the complexity of the financial operations of an individual governmental entity and the amount of detail that it displays on the face of its financial statements. In some instances, there may be enough detail presented directly in the financial statements and the disclosure may simply be limited to identifying receivables that are not expected to be collected within one year, if any. In other situations, it may be necessary to present a detailed disclosure such as the following illustration [GASB Cod. Sec. 2300.903].

EXHIBIT 11-1
ILLUSTRATION OF DISCLOSURE OF DISAGGREGATION OF RECEIVABLES AND PAYABLES

NOTE—Receivables and Payables

The major components of receivables as of June 30, 20X8, were as follows:

	Accounts	Taxes	Special Assessments	Due from Other Governments	Other	Total Receivables
Governmental activities:						
General	$10,935,000	$4,457,000	$—	$5,004,000	$235,000	$20,631,000
Utilities services tax	2,676,000	—	1,990,000	—	—	4,666,000
Gas tax	347,000	—	22,000	1,841,000	—	2,210,000
Other governmental	141,000	—	—	653,000	182,000	976,000
Internal service	215,000	—	—	—	—	215,000
Total—governmental activities	$14,314,000	$4,457,000	$2,012,000	$7,498,000	$417,000	$28,698,000
Amounts not scheduled for collection during the subsequent year	$—	$—	$1,650,000	$—	$—	$1,650,000
Business-type activities:						
Wastewater	$3,789,000	$—	$1,825,000	$323,000		$5,937,000
Solid waste	1,199,000	—	—	—	—	1,199,000
Other proprietary	435,000	—	—	—	89,000	524,000
Total—business-type activities	$5,423,000	$—	$1,825,000		$412,000	$7,660,000

The major components of payables as of June 30, 20X8, were as follows:

	Vendors	Salaries and Benefits	Accrued Interest	Other	Total Payables
Governmental activities:					
General	$3,892,000	$3,651,000	$—	$415,000	$7,958,000
Gas tax	536,000	—	—	—	536,000
Community redevelopment	4,328,000	11,000	—	—	4,339,000
Other governmental	561,000	51,000	—	75,000	687,000
Internal service	1,197,000	204,000	2,169,000	—	3,570,000
Reconciliation of balances in fund financial statements to government-wide financial statements	—	—	1,681,000	—	1,681,000
Total—governmental activities	**$10,514,000**	**$3,917,000**	**$3,850,000**	**$490,000**	**$18,771,000**
Business-type activities:					
Wastewater	$6,523,000	$289,000	$3,525,000	$65,000	$10,402,000
Solid waste	870,000	132,000	—	—	1,002,000
Other proprietary	1,490,000	196,000	523,000	—	2,209,000
Total—business-type activities	**$8,883,000**	**$617,000**	**$4,048,000**	**$65,000**	**$13,613,000**

CHAPTER 12
LONG-TERM DEBT

Chapter References:

GASB Statement Nos. 6, 7, 23, 34, 35, 38, 49, 53, 54, 59, 62, 64, 65, 72, 86, 88, 91-93, 99

GASB Interpretation Nos. 1, 2, 6

GASB *Implementation Guide*

NCGA Statement No. 1

INTRODUCTION

The accounting standards that are used to determine which long-term liabilities should be presented in a governmental entity's financial statements and how they should be presented vary depending on whether a liability is presented in (1) governmental funds, (2) proprietary or fiduciary funds, or (3) the government-wide financial statements.

This chapter discusses the accounting and reporting treatment for certain long-term obligations of state and local governments, including:

- Bonds and notes [GASB Cod. Sec. 1500],
- Bond, tax, and revenue anticipation notes [GASB Cod. Sec. B50] (see **PRACTICE ALERT** on GASB's *Financial Reporting Model Improvements* Exposure Draft),
- Demand bonds [GASB Cod. Sec. D30],
- Conduit debt obligations [GASB Cod. Sec. C65] (see **PRACTICE POINT** on GASB Statement No. 91 *Conduit Debt Obligations*),
- Specific debt-related issues, including:
  — Hedging derivative instruments [GASB Cod. Sec. D40] (see **PRACTICE POINT** s on GASB Statement Nos. 92, *Omnibus 2020,* 93, *Replacement of Interbank Offered Rates* and 99, *Omnibus 2022*),
  — Arbitrage liability [GASB Cod. Sec. 1500], and
  — Extinguishment of debt and debt refunding/defeasance [GASB Cod. Sec. D20].

Certain long-term obligations and debts related to other governmental activities are discussed in other chapters as follows:

12,002 Specific Accounting and Reporting Issues

Chapter	Topic
13	Compensated absences, defined benefit pensions and other postemployment benefit obligations other than pensions [GASB Cod. Secs. C60, P20, P21, P22, P24, P50, P51, P52, P54] (see **PRACTICE ALERT**, which follows this table)
14	Leases and similar arrangements [GASB Cod. Secs. L20, S80, A90, P90]
15	Claims and judgments [GASB Cod. Sec. C50]
16	Landfill closure and post-closure obligations [GASB Cod. Sec. L10], pollution remediation obligations [GASB Cod. Sec. P40], asset retirement obligations [GASB Cod. Sec. A10]
19	Special assessments [GASB Cod. Sec. S40]

PRACTICE ALERT: The GASB released Statement No. 101, *Compensated Absences*, supersedes longstanding GAAP, including the recognition and measurement of liabilities for the distinct types of leave and related notes to the basic financial statements. One of the changes modifies the disclosure of compensated absences as part of long-term debt. Governments would not be required to present separately the increases and decreases of its compensated absences liability, only presenting the net amount as a net increase or decrease. An indication should be made that the amount is netted. Governments will also be allowed to discontinue reporting which governmental funds typically have been used to liquidate compensated absences in prior years. Implementation will occur for reporting periods beginning after December 15, 2023. Changes adopted to conform to the provisions of the new statement will be applied retroactively. A further discussion of GASB Statement No. 101 is in Chapter 13 of the *Guide*.

GASB Cod. Sec. 1500.129 and footnote 16 to that Section defines the word "debt" for purposes of disclosure in the notes to financial statements as:

[A] liability that arises from a contractual obligation to pay cash (or other assets that may be used in lieu of payment of cash) in one or more payments to settle an amount that is fixed at the date the contractual obligation is established. For disclosure purposes, debt does not include leases except for contracts reported as a financed purchase of the underlying asset, or accounts payable.

For purposes of this determination, interest to be accrued and subsequently paid (such as interest on variable-rate debt) or interest to be added to the principal amount of the obligation (such as interest on capital appreciation bonds) does not preclude the amount to be settled from being considered fixed at the date the contractual obligation is established.

A *direct borrowing* occurs when a government engages in a loan agreement with a lender, typically a financial institution. A *direct placement* occurs when a government *issues* a debt security directly to an investor. The investor may be a hedge fund or similar entity. In both types of transactions, there may be cross-default language in the agreements. Therefore, if a government defaults on a direct borrowing or direct placement with cross-default provisions, all the government's bonds and notes may be in jeopardy of default.

Since most governments finance construction and other long-term costs through debt issuances (if not borne by taxation or grants), understanding the differences and the GAAP requirements on debt is among the more important aspects of understanding governmental accounting and financial reporting.

TYPES OF LONG-TERM DEBT

General Obligation and Revenue Bonds and Notes

State and local governments generally issue long-term obligations in two forms:

- General obligation bonds, and
- Revenue bonds and notes.

Bonds are usually for periods longer than 15 years. Notes are usually for shorter periods. However, the maturities may vary due to call features (the ability of the government issuer to retire the debt prior to final maturity).

General obligation bonds represent bonded indebtedness of the government entity to which repayment is supported by the full faith and credit of the government in the form of its taxing ability. General obligation bonds normally require voter approval and are typically repaid with property or other taxes levied for such purpose.

Revenue obligation bonds and notes are obligations evidenced in the form of bonds or notes to which repayment is supported by specific revenue sources other than property taxes, such as utility revenues, hospital revenues, and other business-type activity revenue.

Some governments term revenue obligation bonds "special obligation bonds" due to a specific revenue stream. Other governments term specific portions of taxes that pay for bonds "tax allocation bonds." These are just some of the many variations of general and revenue obligation bonds. Governments that pool types of programs or uses that are bonded may issue "certificates of participation" or COPs. Within the pool, allocations are made to show the amount of debt that is attributable to the various programs or uses. Other types of obligations are in use, including "moral obligation" bonds. All have varying degrees of securitization and support.

An additional type of bond has emerged with the global focus on climate change. So-called *green bonds* are meant to secure funds from environmentally conscious or sustainability projects with the revenue stream from the project repaying the debt. For governmental accounting and financial reporting purposes, green bonds may be categorized as revenue obligations.

Bonds may have a fixed interest rate or may have variable interest. Variable interest rate bonds may have companion hedging derivative instruments to synthetically "fix" the interest rates. Hedging derivative instruments are discussed later in this chapter. Variable interest rate bonds that do not utilize hedging derivative instruments are commonly known as "floaters" or "floating rate debt."

> **PRACTICE POINT:** In some situations, COPs may be in substance, leases, or conduit debt obligations (CDOs). See Chapter 14 for a complete discussion on leases, and later in this Chapter on CDOs.

> **PRACTICE POINT:** Perpetual bonds do exist. Such bonds only mature if called and only pay interest. The interest rates never adjust for inflation (unless embedded in the bonds). As inflation is never a factor, perpetual bonds are subject to interest rate risk. Yale University holds a perpetual bond issued in 1648 by a Dutch water entity that is paying interest to this day.[1] Had the Dutch water entity been subject to GASB standards, it would likely be disclosed as a debt. It can be asked that during periods of low interest rates, why would a state or local government not issue the longest-term debt available? There may be jurisdictional laws, regulations or practical provisions that would preclude issuing debt for longer than a certain number of years. But for certain types of long-lived assets such as infrastructure that may last well longer than 40 years, an economic case can be made to issue debt for as long as possible in a low (or no) interest rate environment.
>
> [1] Ferriello, Electra, "Perpetual Bonds: Bonds that Never Mature," Yale School of Management. Retrieved at https://som.yale.edu/blog/perpetual-bonds-bonds-that-never-mature.

Tax Provisions. As discussed in Chapter 1, one of the key elements determining if an organization is a government is the ability to issue debt with interest that is tax-exempt. The Internal Revenue Code (Title 26), Subchapter B, Part IV contains sections 141 through 150 (Subparts A, B and C) discussing various aspects of bond issuances delineating whether bonds are taxable or tax-exempt. In general, bonds issued for a private purpose such as businesses, individuals and similar may be subject to taxation (also known as "private activity bonds"), with certain exceptions in federal tax law. The interest rates on the bonds may be adjusted to compensate for their taxable nature.

However, the bond's proceeds may also be invested by the issuing government in a way where the investment return is higher than the debt service to be paid. This is known as *arbitrage* (see later section on arbitrage liability in this chapter).

There are many nuances to tax-exempt status beyond private activity bonds with special provisions for mortgage revenue bonds, student loans and scholarships, pension obligation bonds, nonprofit organizations, and other aspects.

States and local governments almost always utilize either a bond counsel who specializes in this section of the Internal Revenue Code in addition to a registered municipal financial advisor (who is registered with the Securities and Exchange Commission), nationally recognized statistical ratings organizations (NRSROs) and underwriters as part of the debt issuance team. The issuance team works with the government's treasurer or chief financial officer (or both) to issue the debt. Specific due diligence procedures are used by the underwriters and bond counsel before the sale in accordance with provisions regulated by the

Securities and Exchange Commission. As part of the closing documentation, governments may have *continuing disclosure requirements* commonly including issuance of audited financial statements, meeting certain ratios and so on to secure the bonds.

Debt Issuance—Premiums and Discounts. Bonds and notes are rarely issued without a premium or discount to market rates. Some of the generation of a premium or discount is due to the difference between the date of issuance on the bonds or notes and the settlement date on the bonds or notes (when proceeds are received by the issuing government from investors or lenders).

Other aspects determining premiums or discounts may include specific coupon rates (or stated interest rates) for individual maturities versus market rates as of the date of issuance. A specific maturity may be priced at an attractive rate to an investor (or many investors) which may generate a *premium*. The result is the yield to the investor will be less than the coupon rate as the investor is paying more for the bond.

Alternatively, a bond may be priced where the interest rate to the investors is more than the coupon rate. The result is the yield to the investors that buy the bonds will be more than the coupon rate. The investor pays less for the bonds and therefore, the bonds are priced at a *discount*.

Unless directly placed, debt is effectively sold at an auction (either using a trading desk at an underwriter) or by marketing directly to the public usually through the internet, the flow of orders and interest rates may change often prior to closing. Issuers may adjust interest rates and maturities throughout the process to compensate for these flows. *Direct borrowings* and *direct placements* are discussed later in this chapter.

Accounting for debt issuance premiums and discounts is straightforward:

- Debt issuance costs and underwriter fees are expensed, even if paid out of debt proceeds.
- Bond and note premiums are "natural" credits.
- Bond and note discounts are "natural" debits.

Debt Repayment. As discussed in Chapter 6, governments *may* use a debt service fund to report debt repayments unless a proprietary fund is where the issuance and repayment occurs (which is common for revenue obligations). Most debt service is amortized using the effective interest method. However, principal maturities may not occur regularly. Often, investors (or budgetary constraints) determine how much principal matures at a given maturity. So-called "financial engineering" may be utilized by the government to devise the following:

- *Level debt service*—where principal and interest combined are relatively level for each maturity until bonds or notes are repaid. Budgeting is easier with level debt service.
- *Level principal*—where principal remains constant, but interest continuously reduces as the bonds or notes are repaid faster. In this case, principal is likely repaid faster than the effective interest method.

- *Term (or bullet) maturities*—in this case, no bonds are repaid for a certain maturity until well into the future. There may be gaps in between when serial (regularly maturing bonds at specific intervals) and term bonds mature.

Sinking funds are often used by state and local governments to sequester debt service to repay the term (or bullet) maturities. The funds are invested in an escrow fund at the bond interest rate usually using state and local government securities issued by the U.S. Treasury (see the section on arbitrage rebate later in this chapter).

Tax, Revenue, and Bond Anticipation Notes

Various forms of anticipation notes are issued with the expectation that the government will receive specific resources soon and that these resources will be used to retire the liability. Tax anticipation notes (TANs) are often issued as part of a cash management strategy that recognizes that certain taxes (such as property taxes) will not be collected evenly over the fiscal year. Bond anticipation notes (BANs) may be issued with the understanding that as soon as the proceeds from the issuance of specific long-term bonds are received, the BANs will be extinguished [GASB Cod. Secs. B50.102–.103].

PRACTICE POINT: Some governments have legislation that does not allow the issuance of anticipation notes that straddle a fiscal year. All such notes must be repaid at the end of a fiscal year. However, many governments may indeed have such legislation and retire the notes on the last day of a fiscal year only to reissue them the next day. The substance of this transaction is that a long-term debt may exist instead of a short-term debt.

For governmental funds, notes issued in anticipation of the receipt of taxes or revenues should be presented as a liability of the fund that will receive the proceeds from the issuance of the notes. The tax or revenue anticipation note (RAN) represents a governmental fund liability that will be extinguished using expendable available resources of the fund.

PRACTICE ALERT: The GASB's *Financial Reporting Model Improvements* Exposure Draft contains potential adjustments in the reporting of *tax* anticipation notes (TANs) and *revenue* anticipation notes (RANs) within governmental funds should the short-term financial resources measurement focus and modified accrual basis of accounting be approved as proposed. TANs and RANs may be examples of long-term debt issued for short-term purposes if the maturities of the notes extended beyond one year from the inception of the transaction. Therefore, TANs and RANs outstanding as of the reporting period's end would be governmental fund liabilities. The accounting and financial reporting for BANs (as discussed beginning in the following paragraph), would not be impacted.

Notes issued in anticipation of proceeds from the subsequent sale of bonds may be classified as general long-term obligations (and therefore presented only in the government-wide financial statements) when the conditions surrounding the notes satisfy the requirements contained in GAAP. GASB Cod. Secs. 1500.110–.111 state that what is typically considered a current liability may be treated as a long-term liability when:

- The intention is to refinance the debt on a long-term basis and
- The intention can be substantiated through a post-balance-sheet issuance of the long-term debt or by an acceptable financing agreement.

The actual issuance of the bonds must occur after the Balance Sheet date but before the Balance Sheet is issued to satisfy the post-balance-sheet condition for a governmental unit. The amount of the BANs that is included as long-term debt and presented in the government-wide financial statements cannot be greater than the proceeds of the actual bond sale. In addition, the maturity date of the newly issued bonds (or serial bonds) must be sufficiently later than the Balance Sheet date so as not to require the use of a fund's available expendable resources to retire the maturing bonds [GASB Cod. Sec. 1500.112].

When the intent to refinance the BANs is substantiated by a financing agreement, the maximum amount of the notes that can be presented as a long-term obligation in the entity's government-wide financial statements is the amount of the estimated bond proceeds expected to be realized under the agreement. If a portion of the actual bond proceeds is restricted for purposes other than the extinguishment of the BANs, the restricted portion must be classified as a governmental fund liability.

For example, if BANs total $10,000,000 and the actual bonds when sold under the financing agreement are expected to yield $12,000,000, but $4,000,000 of the proceeds are restricted for other purposes, only $8,000,000 of the $10,000,000 in BANs can be classified as a long-term liability. If the amount available under the financing agreement fluctuates depending on some measurable factor, the amount of the notes to be classified as long-term is based on a reasonable estimate of the minimum amount that will be available under the agreement. When a reasonable estimate cannot be made, none of the bond anticipation notes can be classified as long-term debt.

When a liability for BANs meets the criteria for classification as a long-term liability, a note to the financial statements must contain:

1. A general description of the financing agreement and
2. The terms of any new debt incurred or expected to be incurred because of the agreement.

If the criteria established by GAAP have not been satisfied, BANs must be presented as a liability in the financial statements of the governmental fund that recorded the proceeds from the issuance of the notes.

To illustrate the accounting for BANs, assume that $10,000,000 in BANs are issued and the proceeds are recorded in the capital projects fund. If the criteria are met, the following entries are made under current GAAP:

Alternative 1:

CAPITAL PROJECTS FUND	Debit	Credit
Cash	10,000,000	
Other financing sources – BANs		10,000,000
To record Issuance of Series 202X BANs		

If the criteria are not satisfied (restricted portion), the following entry is made:

Alternative 2:

CAPITAL PROJECTS FUND	Debit	Credit
Cash	10,000,000	
BANs Payable – Series 202X		10,000,000
To record Issuance of Series 202X BANs		

Demand Bonds

Demand bonds are defined as debt issuances with demand ("put") options as one of their features. These bonds allow bondholders to require a governmental entity to redeem bonds based on terms specified in the bond agreement. For example, the bond agreement may allow the bonds, based on action taken by bondholders, to be retired five years after their issuance. Often, the demand may be exercised anywhere from daily to monthly, including immediately after issuance. The redemption price is the outstanding principal with any accrued interest added [GASB Cod. Sec. D30.101].

Due to the variability in the maturity of the bond, interest rates may also be variable and adjusted daily, weekly, or monthly. Ultimate maturities on the bonds may be 30 years (or longer) [GASB Cod. Sec. D30.102].

When demand bonds are issued, the following key question arises because bondholders can redeem demand bonds on demand: should the governmental unit treat the debt as current or long-term? That is:

- Should a governmental fund account for the demand bonds in a specific fund, or
- Classify the debt as a general long-term liability (i.e., is reported only in the entity's government-wide financial statements), or
- Should a proprietary fund classify the debt as a current liability or long-term liability?

When demand bonds are redeemed, the funds needed to retire the debt may come from the governmental entity's available cash, proceeds from the resale of the redeemed bonds by remarketing agents, short-term credit arrangements, or long-term credit arrangements.

A short-term credit agreement may be based on standby liquidity agreements or other arrangements contracted by the governmental unit. In instances where the redeemed bonds are not readily resold, there may be a take-out agreement whereby a financial institution agrees to convert the bond to long-term debt, such as installment notes [GASB Cod. Sec. D30.103].

A key factor in determining the appropriate accounting for demand bonds is the existence of a "take-out agreement." In a take-out agreement, the government issuer arranges with a financial institution to convert bonds presented as part of the demand to an installment agreement that is payable sometimes for five or ten years or more. Frequently, a take-out agreement is made at the same time the bonds are sold [GASB Cod. Sec. D30.104].

Demand bonds that have an exercisable provision for redemption at or within one year of the governmental unit's Statement of Net Position date should be reported as a long-term liability in the government-wide financial statements (or excluded from current liabilities of proprietary funds) when all the following criteria are met [GASB Cod. Sec. D30.108]:

- Before the financial statements are issued, the issuer has finalized an arm's-length financing (take-out) agreement to convert bonds "put" but not resold into some other form of long-term obligation.
- The take-out agreement does not expire within one year from the date of the issuer's Statement of Net Position.
- The take-out agreement is not cancelable by the lender or the prospective lender during that year, and obligations incurred under the take-out agreement are not callable by the lender during that year.
- The lender or the prospective lender or investor is expected to be financially capable of honoring the take-out agreement.

Even when a take-out agreement is cancelable, or the obligation created by the take-out agreement is callable during the year, the demand bonds may be considered long-term debt if:

1. Violations of the agreement (if any) can be objectively determined, and
2. No violations have occurred prior to the issuance of the financial statements.

However, if violations have occurred and a waiver from the take-out agreement lender has been obtained, the debt should be considered long-term for financial reporting purposes.

When the conditions have not been met, demand bonds must be presented as a liability of the fund that received the proceeds from the issuance of the bonds. If demand bonds are issued and no take-out agreement has been executed at their issuance date or at the net position date, the bonds cannot be considered a long-term liability [GASB Cod. Sec. D30.109].

To illustrate the accounting for demand bonds in governmental funds, assume that $8,000,000 of demand bonds is issued and the proceeds are to be used by a capital projects fund. When the criteria for a long-term liability does not exist, the following entries are made under current GAAP:

12,010 *Specific Accounting and Reporting Issues*

Alternative 1:

CAPITAL PROJECTS FUND	Debit	Credit
Cash	8,000,000	
Other financing sources – proceeds from Issuance of Demand Bonds		8,000,000
To record demand bond issuance by the City Series 202Y-X.		

When the demand bonds are issued and the criteria for recognizing a liability *does exist*, the following entry is made:

Alternative 2:

CAPITAL PROJECTS FUND	Debit	Credit
Cash	8,000,000	
Bonds Payable on Demand		8,000,000
To record bond payable on demand—Series 202Y-X Demand. Bonds.		

If the demand bonds are presented for redemption, the redemption should be recorded as an expenditure of the fund from which debt service is normally paid. To illustrate, assume that the $8,000,000 demand bonds are redeemed and paid out of the debt service fund from funds transferred from the General Fund. The following entries would be made if the demand bonds were originally classified as long-term debt, and the debt is converted to long-term installment notes as determined under the terms of a take-out agreement:

GENERAL FUND	Debit	Credit
Cash	8,000,000	
Other financing sources – Proceeds from Issuance of Long-Term Notes Series 202Y-Z		8,000,000
To record Issuance of Long-Term Notes to Finance Redemption of Series 202Y-X.		

GENERAL FUND	Debit	Credit
Other financing uses—transfers out (to Debt Service Fund)	8,000,000	
Cash		8,000,000
To record funding for debt service payments to redeem Demand Bonds—Series 202Y-X.		

And then within the Debt Service Fund:

DEBT SERVICE FUND	Debit	Credit
Cash	8,000,000	
Other financing sources—transfers in (from GENERAL FUND)		8,000,000
To record funding for debt service payments to redeem Demand Bond Series 202Y-X.		

Long-Term Debt **12,011**

DEBT SERVICE FUND	Debit	Credit
Expenditures—Debt Service	8,000,000	
Cash		8,000,000
To record retirement of Demand Bonds—Series 202Y-X.		

NOTE: The debt would be removed from the government-wide financial statements since it has been retired.

If the demand bonds redeemed were originally recorded as a liability of the capital projects fund (no take-out agreement), the following entries are made to redeem the demand bonds:

GENERAL FUND	Debit	Credit
Other financing uses – transfers out (to DEBT SERVICE FUND)	8,000,000	
Cash		8,000,000
To record funding for debt service payments to redeem Demand Bonds Series 202Y-X.		

DEBT SERVICE FUND	Debit	Credit
Cash	8,000,000	
Other financing sources – transfers in (from GENERAL FUND)		8,000,000
To record funding for debt service payments to redeem Demand Bonds Series 202Y-X.		

CAPITAL PROJECTS FUND	Debit	Credit
Bonds Payable on Demand	8,000,000	
Other financing sources – Retirement of Fund Liabilities by Payments Made by Other Funds		8,000,000
To record funding for debt service payments to redeem Demand Bonds Series 202Y-X.		

The liability of the capital projects fund is reduced by simultaneously crediting other financing sources. That account would appear on the capital projects fund's statement of revenues, expenditures, and changes in fund balances.

Demand bonds that were originally classified as a long-term liability because a take-out agreement existed at the issuance date of the bonds would have to be reclassified if the original take-out agreement expires. Under this circumstance, it would be necessary to establish a liability in the fund that originally recorded the demand bond proceeds. If the $8,000,000 demand bonds illustrated earlier were originally recorded as a long-term liability (in the government-wide financial statements), the following entries would be made if the take-out agreement expires:

CAPITAL PROJECTS FUND	Debit	Credit
Other financing uses – reclassification of Demand Bonds	8,000,000	
Bonds Payable on Demand		8,000,000
To record expiration of take-out agreement related to Demand Bonds Series 202Y-X.		

NOTE: The debt is reported as a governmental fund liability and as an obligation in the government-wide financial statements.

PRACTICE POINT: The date of reclassification is not the date the take-out agreement expires. If the take-out agreement expires within one year of the date of the Balance Sheet, the debt must be reclassified as the liability of a specific governmental fund.

Conduit Debt Obligations (CDOs)

A conduit debt obligation (CDO) is debt issued in the name of the *issuer* (a government) benefitting a third party that is *primarily* liable for repayment of the debt also known as the *third-party obligor*. To be reported as a conduit debt obligation, *all* the following must be present:

- At least three parties are involved with the agreement:
  — The issuer,
  — At least one third-party obligor, and
  — A debt holder or debt trustee, or more than one debt holder or debt trustee.
- The issuer and the third-party obligor are not within the *same reporting entity*. Debt agreements issued between component units and the primary government or vice versa or between multiple component units would *not be conduit debt obligations*.
- The debt obligation is *not* a *parity bond* of the issuer, nor is it cross-collateralized with other debt of the issuer. A *parity bond* is a bond with equal rights to the collateral as other bonds contained within a common bond indenture (see **PRACTICE POINT**).
- The third-party obligor (or its agent—typically a financial institution's corporate trust department or trustee) ultimately receives the proceeds from the debt issuance. In practice, these are in the form of project or construction funds.
- The third-party obligor(s) (and not the issuer) are *primarily obligated* for the payment of all amounts associated with the debt obligation (debt service) [GASB Cod. Sec. C65.103].

PRACTICE POINT: Parity bonds and cross-collateralization provisions are common in debt issuances. They may be termed "pools" of bonds (Pool Series 1,

2, 3, . . .) or with a common obligor (ABC Hospital Series 1, ABC Hospital Series 2, and so on). Cross-collateralization occurs when one issuance is co-secured by reserve funds of other issuances. As indicated above, if parity bonds or cross-collateralization provisions are present, the issued bonds are *not* CDOs and are normal debt issuances by the issuer. The obligors would have borrowings from the issuer (liabilities).

Issuance fees are a necessity with any bond issuance, including CDOs. The issuance fees include underwriting, legal, financial advisory, and similar flows. The payment of fees commonly is made from the proceeds of the bond issuance. The arrangement still meets the definition of a CDO even though the fees may be remitted from the proceeds sent to the obligor(s) [GASB Cod. Sec. C65.702-1].

CDOs may or may not be instruments commonly known as "certificates of participation" or COPs. COPs need to be analyzed to determine if they meet the definition of CDOs (or a lease in accordance with GASB Cod. Sec. L20 as discussed in Chapter 14) prior to recognition of a liability.

Commitments Made by Issuers Associated with Conduit Debt Obligations. Commitments are commonly made in connection with CDOs by issuers. The commitments involved with a CDO involve maintenance of the debt's tax-exempt status. Otherwise, there would be limited reason for a third-party obligor to engage in a CDO. The tax-exemption affords the opportunity for third-party obligors to receive favorable interest rates and other potential economic benefits, including extended repayment terms or other forms of assistance from the issuer.

Such commitments are usually limited. The issuer assumes no responsibility for the debt service beyond the repayments made by the obligors. The repayments made by the obligors may be made directly to the issuer or through a trustee [GASB Cod. Sec. C65.104].

In practice the commitments may change over time. There could be an *additional* or *voluntary* commitment under certain circumstances described in the CDO agreement usually relating to fiscal stress at the obligor(s).

The additional commitment may be in different forms but results in debt service support only in the even the obligor(s) is (or will be) unable to make debt service payments on a timely basis. In addition to municipal aid intercept (see **PRACTICE POINT**), which is commonly embedded in CDOs, the following additional commitments may be made by an issuer:

- Moral obligation pledges made by the issuer to the obligor(s),
- Pledges of appropriation(s) (usually general obligations),
- Extended financial guarantees, or
- Pledges of property, revenues, or assets as collateral [GASB Cod. Sec. C65.105].

PRACTICE POINT: Municipal aid intercept is a common mechanism employed by state governments that are issuers for CDOs. States that provide municipal aid in the form of taxes apportioned to municipalities compare the taxes to be transferred in connection with receivables due for debt service. The aid is then garnished for the amounts due. Care should be taken though by the obligor(s) involved with a CDO that such aid does not net municipal aid revenue for accounting and financial reporting purposes. The aid is separate from debt service.

If the aid is paid directly to the trustee to pay for the debt service, it does not signify an additional commitment or a voluntary commitment from the issuer as a state is only performing an administrative function. The aid is directed to the trustee instead of the obligor on the obligor's behalf [GASB Cod. Sec. C65.703-1].

PRACTICE POINT: Note disclosure of pledged revenue or asset collateral related to all debt issuances is discussed later in this chapter.

Pledges of general obligations involve tax revenue. In the case of a general obligation pledge, should the debt service not be made, general revenues of the issuer are used to pay for the debt service like most other debt. If a general obligation is present, it is common that the CDO's credit ratings from the NRSROs are the same as the issuing government.

A *voluntary commitment* occurs when the issuer does not make an additional commitment but decides based on economic conditions to pay the CDO debt service in the event of a default by the obligor(s). Issuers would do this to not to harm the credit rating of the issuer [GASB Cod. Sec. C65.106].

Recognition and Measurement of CDOs—Issuers. If a bond issue meets the definition of a CDO as previously described, a liability is *not reported by the issuer*. Instead, the obligor(s) would report the debt as a liability.

PRACTICE POINT: There is no guidance in GASB Cod. Sec. C65 as amended for CDOs issued for multiple obligors as to how to allocate the debt service among each of the obligors in such situations. The issuer may have to engage a municipal financial advisor to allocate to the multiple obligors. The allocation process becomes especially difficult if additional commitments are involved.

If no commitments are made, there is no criteria for the issuer to recognize a liability on an ongoing basis. If an additional commitment has been made, there is an annual evaluation of whether there needs to be a liability recognized to support debt service payments. The evaluation of this support is based on qualitative factors described later in this subsection. The qualitative factors are the same as *financial guarantees* further discussed in Chapter 16.

In the situation where the issuer only agrees to maintain the CDO's tax exempt status (*limited commitment*) and assumes no responsibility for the debt service payments, if an event occurs that makes it likely that the issuer will support the debt service payment(s) for a CDO, recognition of a liability may need to be made at the issuer. Usually there are indicators of fiscal distress at the obligor(s). Each period, the issuer needs to evaluate the specific CDO for whether a liability should be reported, or if already reported, should continue to be reported [GASB Cod. Secs. C65.107–.108].

Recognition of Liabilities by Issuers in Government-Wide and Proprietary Funds Related to CDOs. In the case of where additional commitments are made to support debt service payments of obligor(s), a liability should be recognized and a related expense if *qualitative factors* indicate that it is *more likely than not* that the issuer will support one or more debt service payments in a CDO. The *more likely than not* provision is the same as discussed in Chapter 16 regarding *financial guarantees*—a threshold of more than 50%.

The qualitative factors include (but are not limited to) the following:

- An obligor initiating bankruptcy or financial reorganization, oversight, or receivership,
- An obligor breaching a debt provision in relation to the CDO. Such contractual provisions may include rate covenants, ratio thresholds, default, or delinquency,
- An obligor experiencing financial difficulty, such as failing to make timely payments to trustees, unscheduled reserve fund withdrawals, municipal aid intercept occurring (as discussed in the **PRACTICE POINT** previously), major revenue source losses and similar,
- Termination of the project financed by the CDO,
- Litigation negatively impacting the project financed by the CDO,
- The issuer becoming concerned that the default of an obligor could impact the issuer's ability to further sell debt to other obligors,
- The issuer's history of additional commitments to support other CDOs, including voluntary support, or
- The issuer's ability (or willingness) to support debt service payments.

Any of these and many others could be qualitative factors present requiring a recognition of a liability and expense [GASB Cod. Secs. C65.109–.110].

If the commitment is only limited, a liability is only recognized when there are qualitative factors that indicate that the issuer would have to voluntarily make a debt service payment instead of the obligor(s). The more likely than not threshold would also be used in such circumstances.

Measuring the Liability. The liability recognized is the discounted present value of the *best estimate* of the debt service expected to be incurred. If there is no best estimate, but a range is available, the discounted present value of the minimum amount is used [GASB Cod. Secs. C65.111–.112].

PRACTICE POINT: If the issuer is committing to pay the *entire* debt service for an obligor (or obligors) for the remainder of the period outstanding, the debt service schedule should be known as it should align to the bonds.

Recognition of Liabilities by Issuers in Governmental Funds Related to CDOs. Liabilities and expenditures are recognized by issuers also aligning to the more likely than not threshold that qualitative events are occurring which may require the issuer to remit the debt service. The liability is measured using the current financial resources measurement focus like other governmental fund liabilities [GASB Cod. Secs. C65.113–.114].

Other Arrangements Associated with CDOs—Construction (or Acquisition) of Capital Assets from Proceeds

CDOs may be used to finance the construction or acquisition of capital assets such as a new hospital, dormitory, housing complex, or similar. The CDOs involved in construction have the following attributes, in addition to aligning to the requirements of a CDO:

- The proceeds are used to finance the construction or acquisition of the capital asset,
- The *issuer* retains title to the capital asset from the initial agreement,
- The payments from the *obligor(s)* are for debt service, and
- The payment schedule aligns to the debt service schedule [GASB Cod. Sec. C65.115].

PRACTICE POINT: If the arrangement *does not* meet the definition of a service concession arrangement (SCA), as discussed in Chapter 14, the issuer should *not* report the arrangement as a lease in accordance with GASB Cod. Sec. L20 (also see Chapter 14). The documentation related to the agreement may be termed a lease, however. Care must also be taken that the arrangement is not in reality a public-private or public-public partnership in accordance with GASB Statement No. 94 (GASB-94), also discussed in Chapter 14.

Three potential outcomes may be present in these specific arrangements [GASB Cod. Secs. C65.117–.120]:

Outcome of Arrangement	Receivable for payment?	Capital Asset?	Liability for CDO?	Other Reporting?
Issuer gives up title to capital asset *at the end of the arrangement*, coinciding with the CDO being retired.	No	No	No	N/A
Issuer retains title to capital asset, but obligor has exclusive right to the capital asset until the end of the arrangement.	No	Yes—at end of arrangement at *acquisition value.*	No	N/A

Long-Term Debt 12,017

Outcome of Arrangement	Accounting and Financial Reporting—Issuer			
	Receivable for payment?	Capital Asset?	Liability for CDO?	Other Reporting?
Issuer retains title to the capital asset, but obligor may only use portions of the capital asset until the end of the arrangement. (This may include dormitory space and retail establishments where rent only is received by the issuer.)	No	Yes—at end of arrangement at acquisition value.	No	Deferred inflow of resources recognized for the capital asset amount, which is amortized systematically and rationally over the term of the arrangement.

Options. If the obligor has an *option* to purchase the debt that can only be exercised at the end of the arrangement (and therefore, unknown at the inception of the debt), the accounting follows whether the obligor exercises the option. Any of the above outcomes may occur. If the issuer retains title, but the obligor has exclusive use of the capital asset until the end of the arrangement *and then* exercises the option, the purchase price is an inflow to the issuer (revenue).

If the issuer retains title, but the obligor may only use portions of the asset, but then exercises the option to purchase, the issuer will then derecognize the capital asset, recognize revenue or expense for the difference between the carrying value of the asset (which had been depreciating) and the purchase price received. The option exercise becomes a purchase [GASB Cod. Sec. C65.708-1].

The arrangements that *do* meet the definition of an SCA by applying the accounting and financial reporting requirements are discussed in Chapter 14 regarding *Public-Private and Public-Public Partnerships and Availability Payment Arrangements* (P3s) [GASB Cod. Sec. C65.116].

SPECIFIC DEBT-RELATED ISSUES

Hedging Derivative Instruments. For many state and local government financial statement preparers, auditors, and users, the concepts and terminology associated with derivative instruments is relatively unfamiliar and difficult to fully understand.

Definition of Derivative Instruments. A derivative is a financial instrument or arrangement, often complex in nature, whereby two parties agree to make payments to each other under different obligation scenarios (e.g., by utilizing an "interest rate swap"). Governments normally engage in hedging derivatives for the following reasons:

- To fix prices to better manage cash flows,
- To lower borrowing costs, and
- To potentially minimize or mitigate a certain risk.

A derivative is a financial instrument or other contract that contains *all* three of the following characteristics:

1. The financial arrangement contains settlement factors that determine the amount of the settlement, and, in some cases, whether a settlement is required. Settlement factors include the reference rate (e.g., rate and swap indexes), the notional amount (e.g., number of currency units, shares, pounds), and a payment provision (e.g., a provision for a payment to be made if a reference rate behaves in a certain manner).
2. The financial arrangements are leveraged (e.g., they require no initial investment on the part of the government or an initial investment that is small relative to what would otherwise be required to obtain the same results in the market).
3. The financial arrangements have net settlement terms whereby the arrangements can be or are required to be settled net by means outside the contract such as by cash payment, or it provides for delivery of an asset that puts the recipient in a position not substantially different from net settlement [GASB Cod. Sec. D40.103].

The following types of financial instruments are not hedging derivatives for financial reporting purposes:

- Derivative instruments that represent normal purchases and sales contracts (e.g., commodity purchases where it is probable the government will take or make delivery of the commodity),
- Nonperformance guarantees on contracts that are dependent on the failure of a counterparty to fulfill the contract terms,
- Insurance contracts accounted for in accordance with GASB Cod. Sec. C50 (*Claims and Judgments*) or Po20 (*Public Entity Risk Pools*) or that are like contracts in accordance with a claim or a judgment,
- Certain financial guarantee contracts *unless they are engaged as an investment derivative instrument* (discussed in Chapter 9). Guarantees, for example, may be a loan guarantee that provides for the government to make payments if the debtor defaults or fails to meet a debt covenant. They could also include a federal guarantee that protects a university from loss in its student loans, a guarantee that a state provides for the nonpayment of debt of a private corporation or bond insurance where the government pays the premium, the bond insurance is associated with the government's debt, and the debt holder is the beneficiary,
- Certain contracts that are not exchange-traded (e.g., contracts that provide for the payment of liquidated damages if a party fails to perform under the contract),
- Revenue-based contracts that are not exchange-traded and have reference rates based on sales or service levels or volumes, and
- Loan commitments (e.g., a loan commitment extended by a government housing finance authority to potential home buyers meeting specific criteria) [GASB Cod. Sec. D40.101].

GASB Cod. Sec. D40.702-4 provides the following example that would meet the normal purchases and normal sales scope exception: A government contracts for a take-or-pay contract for a commodity (e.g., a utility contract for an amount of electricity). Under this contract, the government agrees to pay a specified price for a specified quantity of the commodity (the electricity), whether it takes delivery. The government uses the commodity in its operations, and the quantity specified in the contract is consistent with the government's activities. The government will likely take delivery of the commodity specified in the contract. This form of take-or-pay contract generally meets the definition of a derivative instrument. However, if the government plans to take delivery and the quantity specified is consistent with what is used in the government's operations, for example when the government is a public utility, the contract qualifies for the normal purchases and sales scope exception and should not be reported according to the requirements of GASB Cod. Sec. D40.

Types of Derivative Instruments. A typical derivative instrument is leveraged in that it is entered into with little or no initial payment, contains settlement factors that determine the amount of settlement, can be settled with a cash payment or the transfer of an equivalent asset, and has a value based on a separate transaction or agreement. In other words, the cash flows and fair values of derivative instruments are determined by changing market prices, such as bond or commodity prices or indexes. Some derivative instruments may even provide an upfront cash payment to a government. Common types of derivative instruments used by governments include interest rate and commodity swaps, interest rate locks, options, swaptions, forward contracts, and futures contracts. Examples of derivative instruments are as follows , which may be hedging derivative instruments or investment derivative instruments [GASB Cod. Secs. D40.501–.561]:

Type of Derivative	Description of the Derivative
Commodity swaps	Contracts that have a variable payment based on the price or index of an underlying commodity.
Forward contracts	Agreements to buy or sell a security, commodity, foreign currency, or other financial instrument at a certain future date for a specific price. An agreement with a supplier to purchase a quantity of heating oil at a certain future time, for a certain price, and a certain quantity is an example of a forward contract. Forward contracts are not securities and are not exchange-traded. Some forward contracts may be settled by a cash payment that is equal to the fair value of the contract rather than delivery of a commodity or financial instrument.
Futures contract	A government could enter into an agreement to buy or sell an actively traded product or commodity (e.g., fuel) for a specified price on a specific future date to protect against future increases in the commodity prices. For example, a government-owned utility might finalize a futures contract to lock in a price for the purchase of energy (e.g., electricity or natural gas) without ever having to buy the energy.

Type of Derivative	Description of the Derivative
Interest rate swap	An agreement to attempt to lower its borrowing costs. In this type of derivative, a government that has issued variable-rate debt also agrees to an interest rate swap in which it agrees to pay a steady interest rate to a financial firm (usually a higher rate of interest than it currently pays on the variable-rate debt). In return, the financial firm agrees to pay the government an amount (that changes as market interest rates change), which is expected to offset the government's interest payments due to the bond or debt holders. Not only are the cash flows of an interest rate swap (which are the payments between the government and the financial firm) determined by changing market interest rates, but the value of the derivative also changes.
Interest rate lock	An agreement could be entered into between a government and a lender to lock interest rates to protect from rising interest rates between the time of the agreement and the time of actual debt issuance. (This is used similarly in rate locks for home mortgages).
Options (such as calls, puts, collars, floors, and swaptions)	Options are contracts or securities that give their holders the right but not the obligation to buy or sell a financial instrument or commodity at a certain price for a certain period.

GASB Cod. Sec. D40.706-9 distinguishes insurance contracts from derivative instruments. Insurance contracts may resemble derivative instruments because they are entered to manage risk, payments are based on the occurrence of specific events, and casualty payments may be significant compared to the initial net investment (the insurance premium). An insurance contract is not a derivative instrument if it entitles the holder to be compensated only if because of an identifiable insurable event (other than a change in price) the holder incurs a liability or there is an adverse change in the value of a specific asset or liability for which the holder is at risk.

For example, the following types of contracts written by insurance enterprises, including public-entity risk pools, or held by the insured parties are not within the scope of GASB Cod. Sec. D40:

- Traditional life insurance contracts—These contracts require the payment of death benefits due to the result of an identifiable insurable event (death of the insured) instead of changes in a variable, and

- Traditional property and casualty contracts (the payment of benefits is the result of an identifiable insurable event such as a theft or fire at the property instead of changes in a variable).

Therefore, this section of the *Governmental GAAP Guide* is limited to *hedging derivative instruments*, which are defined as:

A derivative instrument associated with a hedgeable item that is effective by significantly reducing an identified financial risk by substantially offsetting changes in cash flows or fair values of the hedgeable item (e.g., an interest rate swap) [GASB Cod. Sec. D40.526].

PRACTICE ALERT: GASB Statement No. 99 (*Omnibus 2022*) adds a third category of derivatives. Instruments that do not meet the definition of an investment derivative instrument nor a hedging derivative instrument are termed *other derivative instruments*. This may occur if an instrument was meant to be a hedge, but is no longer effective. Reporting of other derivative instruments requires changes in fair value of such instruments to be reported separately from other investment revenue. The notes to the basic financial statements will report the information relating to such instruments separately from hedging derivative instruments and investment derivative instruments. Reclassifications from hedges to other derivative instruments would report the other derivative instrument similarly to investment derivative instruments along with the termination provisions of hedging derivative instruments. These requirements became effective for reporting periods beginning after June 15, 2023. A restatement of prior periods may be required by this implementation.

Risks Associated with Hedging Derivative Instruments. Although hedging derivative instruments can be a valuable component of the fiscal management of an entity and can help a government manage or hedge a specific risk, they can also present significant other risks to the government that could affect its liquidity and investment performance. A hedging derivative instrument significantly reduces financial risk by substantially offsetting changes in the cash flows (a cash flow hedge) or fair values (a fair value hedge) of an associated item that is eligible to be hedged. GASB Cod. Sec. D40 provides guidance in applying acceptable methods for testing whether a derivative instrument meets this effectively hedged definition. GASB Cod. Sec. D40 also provides for the deferring of changes in the fair value of the hedged derivative instrument if it is effectively hedged.

Risks associated with hedging derivative instruments include:

Risks Associated with Hedging Derivative Instruments	Explanation of Risks
Credit risk	The risk that the counterparty to the agreement will not fulfill its terms. For example, a failure to meet a promise to pay the government when required.
Interest rate risk	The risk that changes in interest rates will adversely affect the fair value of the government's financial instrument or its cash flows. For example, the longer the derivative's term, the greater the chance of a decline in its value due to changing interest rates.
Termination risk	The risk that a derivative may end earlier than originally expected, resulting in a potential termination payment requirement by the government or its asset or liability management strategy. For example, the unscheduled termination of an interest rate swap may subject the government to increasing interest rate payments.

Risks Associated with Hedging Derivative Instruments	Explanation of Risks
Basis risk	The risk that arises when variable rates or prices of the hedging derivative instrument and the hedged item are based on different reference rates. For example, the risk that the basis for the government's payment (generally from an international rate index) may cause the government's payment out to be more than its received payments from the counterparty.
Rollover risk	The risk that the derivative instrument term does not last if the maturity of the associated hedged item, thereby ending the government's risk protection when the derivative ends. For example, an interest rate swap agreement term may be 15 years and the term of the hedged debt is 30 years.
Market-access risk	The risk that a government will not be able to enter the credit markets or do so in a cost-effective manner. For example, a derivative instrument may involve the planned issuance of debt (e.g., a debt refunding) by the government at a certain time in the future, however, the government may be unable to issue the debt or doing so will become more expensive than when it was planned.
Foreign currency risk	The risk that changes in exchange rates would adversely affect the fair value of a derivative or cash flows of the government.

Accounting and Reporting Standards Overview for Hedging Derivative Instruments. Except for fully benefit-responsive synthetic guaranteed investment contracts (SGICs), GASB Cod. Sec. D40 generally requires that derivatives covered by its scope be reported in the government's accrual-based financial statements at fair value. The fair value of a derivative instrument as of the period's end is reported in the Statement of Net Position of the government-wide financial statements and the proprietary and fiduciary fund financial statements. Changes in fair value associated with *effective hedges* should be reported as deferred inflows or outflows on the statements of net position. For *ineffective hedges*, the changes in fair value should be reported in the flow of resources statements (such as the Statement of Activities, statement of revenues, expenses, and changes in net position, or statement of changes in fiduciary net position) as investment gains or losses. Changes in fair values of *other derivative instruments* are reported also in the statement of revenues, expenses and changes in net position or statement of changes in fiduciary net position, but separately from investment revenue reporting [GASB Cod. Secs. D40.115–.116]. (See also hedge termination events later in this chapter.)

The GASB provided for reporting of fair value and changes in fair value for derivative instruments only in accrual-based financial statements (government-wide, proprietary, and fiduciary funds), and not in governmental funds that are reported on the modified accrual basis of accounting and current financial resources measurement focus.

Hedge Accounting Used to Determine if Hedge Is Effective. When a derivative instrument significantly reduces financial risk by substantially offsetting the changes in the cash flows (a cash flow hedge) or fair values (a fair value hedge) of an associated item (hedgeable item) that is eligible to be hedged, the hedge is considered effective and hedge accounting should be applied. GASB Cod. Sec. D40 provides guidance in applying acceptable methods for testing whether a derivative instrument meets this definition of effectively hedged.

The GASB states that for a derivative to be considered effectively hedged (i.e., a hedging derivative instrument), *both* of the following criteria must be met:

1. The derivative is associated with an item eligible to be hedged (e.g., a hedgeable item). Association involves:

    a. A notional amount of the derivative instrument that is consistent with the principal amount or quantity of the hedgeable item.

    b. Reporting the derivative instrument in the same fund as the hedgeable item.

    c. A term or period of the derivative instrument is consistent with the term or period of the hedgeable item.

    d. A hedgeable item that is not reported in the financial statements at fair value.

2. The government demonstrates the potential hedging derivative's effectiveness using one of three approaches:

    a. Consistent critical terms,

    b. Synthetic instruments, or

    c. Quantitative techniques. In other words, the changes in cash flows or fair values of the potential hedging derivative substantially offset the changes in cash flows or fair values of the hedgeable item [GASB Cod. Sec. D40.123].

GASB Cod. Sec. D40 states that a government should evaluate the effectiveness of a potential hedging derivative instrument as of "the end of each reporting period." GASB Cod. Sec. D40.711-1 clarifies how effectiveness should be evaluated at the end of each reporting period for which financial statements are prepared in conformity with GAAP. For example, if a government issues annual GAAP financial statements, the evaluation should be performed as of the end of the year.

Consistent Critical Terms Method

The *consistent critical terms method* utilizes mainly *qualitative* analysis, allowing the practitioner to easily understand the terms and conditions of the hedgeable item (e.g., a variable rate debt issue) and the terms and conditions of the potential hedging derivative.

PRACTICE POINT: Many governments strive to have consistent critical terms as it is easiest to understand, implement and administer throughout the life of the hedging.

In the consistent critical terms method, the terms, and conditions of the hedgeable item and the potential hedging derivative instrument are the same, *or similar* in such a way that the changes in cash flows or fair values will offset. This method is commonly used for *interest rate swaps—cash flow hedges, interest rate swaps—fair value hedges* and *forward contracts*.

Type of Derivative	To Be Effective Under the Consistent Critical Terms Method—All Must Be Met
Interest Rate Swaps—Cash Flow Hedges	• The notional amount of the derivative is the same as the principal amount of the hedgeable item throughout the life of the item, even if it amortizes, • The swap must have a zero-dollar fair value upon association with the hedgeable item (no consideration has been exchanged), • The formula for computing net settlements is the same throughout the swap, • The reference rate is consistent with either a reference rate or payment of the hedgeable item (such as a cost of funds swap) or a benchmark rate (such as a percentage of an international standard rate), • The interest flows (receipts or payments) occur during the term of the hedgeable item and not after, • There are no floors or caps for the swap unless the hedgeable item has a floor or cap, • The maturity or time interval of the swap is the same as the hedgeable item (e.g., a variable rate debt that resets interest rates every seven days according to a seven-day swap index), • The frequency of the rate resets is the same (such as every seven days); and • Swap payments settle within 15 days of the payments of the hedgeable item [GASB Cod. Sec. D40.133].
Interest Rate Swaps—Fair Value Hedges	• The first four items above for cash flow hedges must be present, • The hedgeable item is not pre-payable prior to its scheduled maturity. (This does not apply to debts with call options if the derivative has a call option.), • The expiration date of the interest rate swap is on or about the maturity date of the hedgeable item to mitigate interest rate or market risk, • No floors or caps must be present; and • The reference rate on the interest rate swap resets at least every 90 days to minimize interest rate risk [GASB Cod. Sec. D40.134].
Forward Contracts	• The purchase or sale are for the same quantities between the notional item and the derivative. • A zero-dollar fair value is at the point of association with the hedgeable item. • The reference rate is consistent.

Any changes in discounts or premiums in forward contracts are excluded from the assessment of effectiveness. Such changes become part of investment revenue.

PRACTICE POINT: Variability may occur in portions of the changes in cash flows. The most common variability may occur in interest rate risk. If interest risk is the hedged risk, the evaluation of effectiveness is based on the appropriate benchmark rate. GASB Statement No. 93 (*Replacement of Interbank Offered Rates*) (GASB-93) amended this guidance. For *tax-exempt* debt, the SIFMA swap index and the AAA general obligations index are named by the GASB as appropriate benchmark rates. Because of GASB-93, for *taxable debt*, the rate required by GAAP is either:

- An interest rate on direct Treasury obligations of the U.S. government,
- The effective federal funds rate, or
- A structured overnight financing rate (SOFR).

If the benchmark rate appropriate for *taxable debt* or a percentage of a benchmark rate is used as a hedge, hedge effectiveness must be evaluated using one of the quantitative methods discussed in this section [GASB Cod. Sec. D40.135].

PRACTICE ALERT: GASB Statement No. 99 (*Omnibus 2022*) adjusts the impact of GASB Statement No. 93 (*Replacement of Interbank Offered Rates*), specifically regarding LIBOR as an appropriate benchmark. The removal of LIBOR as an appropriate benchmark interest rate was supposed to be effective for reporting periods ending after December 31, 2021. This aspect of GASB-93 became delayed as global banking regulators delayed the sunset of LIBOR due to the COVID-19 pandemic. ICE Benchmark Administrator, Ltd. (IBA – a subsidiary of the Intercontinental Exchange) is the entity responsible for independently benchmarking such indices. LIBOR is no longer an appropriate benchmark for hedging derivative instruments for *taxable debt* as LIBOR ceased to be determined by the ICE at the end of June 2023. GASB Statement No. 99 linked the implementation of this provision to that decision by IBA. The provision became effective immediately upon issuance of GASB Statement No. 99. Information on the LIBOR cessation may be found at https:/www.theice.com/iba/libor.

If the consistent critical terms method provisions cannot be met, one of three quantitative methods may be used to evaluate effectiveness. They are the synthetic instrument method, the dollar-offset method, and the regression analysis method. Other methods may be available if they meet certain criteria [GASB Cod. Sec. D40.136]. In many circumstances, if the consistent critical terms method is not available, the synthetic instrument method is commonly used given its easily understood parameters and wide latitude to judge effectiveness.

Synthetic Instrument Method

The *synthetic instrument method* relies on a combination of cash flows and the analysis of the cash flows to determine if the flows offset the potential hedging derivative flows. As such, all the following must be present to be effective:

1. The notional amount of the derivative is the same as the principal amount of the hedgeable item throughout the life of the item, even if it amortizes,
2. Upon association, the hedging derivative instrument has a zero-dollar fair value, *or the forward price is "at the market"*,
3. The formula for computing net settlements is the same throughout the swap, and
4. The interest flows (receipts or payments) occur during the term of the hedgeable item and not after [GASB Cod. Sec. D40.138].

To accomplish this method, an interest rate must also be substantially fixed (called the *actual synthetic rate*). However, interest rates are never truly fixed. Therefore, U.S. GAAP allows the variable rate debt to adjust within a "corridor" of 90% to 111% of the fixed rate of potential hedging derivative instrument to be substantially fixed [GASB Cod. Sec. D40.139].

Dollar-Offset Method

The *dollar-offset method* also utilizes changes in cash flows but allows either the current period to measure changes or life-to-date. It is a similar method to the *synthetic instrument method* but allows a corridor of 80% to 125% in absolute terms of cash flows in dollars, rather than interest rates [GASB Cod. Sec. D40.140].

Regression Analysis Method

The *regression analysis method* considers the statistical relationship between the potential hedging derivative and the hedgeable item by comparing changes in cash flows *or* fair values and whether they offset. To be effective, enough data must be analyzed and, in many cases, sophisticated software or macros are utilized to determine the effectiveness [GASB Cod. Sec. D40.141]. In practice, the regression analysis method may require a specialist to perform the calculations.

Other Methods of Measurement of Hedge Effectiveness

As introduced previously, other quantitative methods are allowable by GASB Cod. Sec. D40 if the method chosen demonstrates that the changes in cash flows or fair values substantially offset, the evaluation of effectiveness are complete and documented, and substantive characteristics of the hedgeable item and potential derivative are considered [GASB Cod. Sec. D40.144].

Hedge accounting is required if a derivative instrument is effective in significantly reducing an identified financial risk. In other words, applying hedge accounting is not optional. In practice, most governments would want an effective hedge as any changes in fair value would not be presented in the Statement of Activities or any other fund statement.

The deferral of changes in fair value for effectively hedged derivatives (and, therefore, recognizing deferred inflows of resources or deferred outflows of resources) provides a better measure of interperiod equity (taxpayer benefit or burden measurement) than recognizing the fair value changes as gains or losses in the current period, if the hedge is effective and the goal of the hedge is not to generate investment return. The deferral of changes in fair value begins in the period that a hedging derivative instrument is established and continues until a hedging termination event occurs, at which time the deferred gains or losses are to be reported as part of investment income in that period.

Illustration of Hedge Accounting. The following is an illustration of hedge accounting according to the measurement and recognition requirements of GASB Cod. Sec. D40. This illustration describes an interest rate swap hedging derivative instrument accounted for in a proprietary fund, and it comprises example assumptions, example journal entries for the related transactions or events, and pro-forma financial statement amounts for related accounts [GASB Cod. Sec. D40.901].

EXHIBIT 12-1
DERIVATIVE ILLUSTRATION: ASSUMPTIONS

Assumptions

Objective	To hedge interest rate risks that could adversely affect cash flows on variable rate demand bonds issued by the government.
Hedged item	Variable rate demand bonds issued for $100,000,000 par amount, dated 7/1/X6 with a maturity in 6/18/Y0, variable rate index is the Securities Industry and Financial Markets Association (SIFMA) swap index, plus a state tax difference 10 basis points.
Derivative instrument	Pay-fixed, receive-variable interest rate swap, with a $100,000,000 notional amount, dated 7/1/X6 with a termination date of 6/11/Y0, and pay-fixed rate of 3.807160% and variable payment based on SIFMA swap index.
Interest rate changes	From the point in time when the bonds were issued in 7/1/X6, the interest rates fell during the years the bonds were outstanding. Therefore, the fixed interest payments due to the counterparty from the government each year (3.807160%) were more than the variable payments (at the lower rates) due from the counterparty to the government.

Table of Payments and Receipts Counterparty Swap Payment

Fiscal Year Ended June 30	To	From	Net	Interest Payments to Bondholders	Total Payments
20X7	$(3,807,160)	$1,689,314	$(2,117,846)	$(1,789,314)	$(3,907,160)
20X8	(3,807,160)	1,259,205	(2,547,955)	(1,359,205)	(3,907,160)
20X9	(3,807,160)	978,661	(2,828,499)	(1,078,661)	(3,907,160)
20Y0	(3,807,160)	1,830,405	(1,976,755)	(1,930,405)	(3,907,160)
Total	$(15,228,640)	$5,757,585	$(9,471,055)	$(6,157,585)	$(15,628,640)

Fair value of swap: The fair value and changes in fair value for each of the years of the swap as determined by discounted formula-based cash flow estimates were:

	Fair Value Change	Fair Value at Fiscal Year-End
Fair value at 7/1/X6		$—
Decrease in fair value in X7	(2,984,833)	
Fair value at 6/30/X7		(2,984,833)
Decrease in fair value in X8	(1,801,798)	

Long-Term Debt **12,029**

	Fair Value Change	Fair Value at Fiscal Year-End
Fair value at 6/30/X8		(4,786,631)
Increase in fair value in X9	2,877,893	
Fair value at 6/30/X9		(1,908,738)
Increase in fair value in Y0	1,908,738	
Fair value at 6/11/Y0 (termination)		$—

Hedge effectiveness. The terms of the bonds and interest rate swap **are consistent**, and the government used the consistent critical terms method to evaluate hedge effectiveness. Because the critical terms are consistent, the hedge is effective in each year. The swap agreement is not terminated early and reaches its planned termination date.

EXHIBIT 12-2
DERIVATIVE ILLUSTRATION: EXAMPLE JOURNAL ENTRIES

Example Journal Entries

PROPRIETARY FUND (7/1/X6)	Debit	Credit
Cash	100,000,000	
Bonds Payable		100,000,000

To record sale of bonds at par value. No up-front payment related to hedging derivative instrument. The fair value of the swap is zero at inception.

6/30/X7 Entries:

PROPRIETARY FUND (6/30/X7)	Debit	Credit
Interest Expense – Bondholders	1,789,314	
Interest Expense – Swap Counterparty	2,117,846	
Cash (or interest payable)		3,907,160

To record interest expense on the bonds in 20X7, including amounts due to bondholders and the net amount resulting from the swap.

PROPRIETARY FUND (6/30/X7)	Debit	Credit
Deferred Outflow of Resources – Interest Rate Swap	2,984,833	
Derivative Instrument Liability – Interest Rate Swap		2,984,833

To record the fair value changes in the swap during 20X7, which was an effective hedging derivative.

12,030 *Specific Accounting and Reporting Issues*

6/30/X8 Entries:

PROPRIETARY FUND (6/30/X8)	Debit	Credit
Interest Expense – Bondholders	1,359,205	
Interest Expense – Swap Counterparty	2,547,955	
Cash (or interest payable)		3,907,160

To record interest expense on the bonds in 20X8, including amounts due to bondholders and the net amount resulting from the swap.

PROPRIETARY FUND (6/30/X8)	Debit	Credit
Deferred Outflow of Resources – Interest Rate Swap	1,801,798	
Derivative Instrument Liability – Interest Rate Swap		1,801,798

To record the fair value changes in the swap during 20X8, which was an effective hedging derivative.

6/30/X9 Entries:

PROPRIETARY FUND (6/30/X9)	Debit	Credit
Interest Expense – Bondholders	1,078,661	
Interest Expense – Swap Counterparty	2,828,499	
Cash (or interest payable)		3,907,160

To record interest expense on the bonds in 20X9, including amounts due to bondholders and the net amount resulting from the swap.

PROPRIETARY FUND (6/30/X9)	Debit	Credit
Derivative Instrument Liability – Interest Rate Swap	2,877,893	
Deferred Outflow of Resources – Interest Rate Swap		2,877,893

To record the fair value changes in the swap during 20X9, which was an effective hedging derivative, but recorded an annual loss in fair value.

6/30/Y0 Entries:

PROPRIETARY FUND (6/30/Y0)	Debit	Credit
Interest Expense – Bondholders	1,930,405	
Interest Expense – Swap Counterparty	1,976,755	
Cash (or interest payable)		3,907,160

To record interest expense on the bonds in 20Y0, including amounts due to bondholders and the net amount resulting from the swap.

PROPRIETARY FUND (6/30/Y0)	Debit	Credit
Derivative Instrument Liability – Interest Rate Swap	1,908,738	
Deferred Outflow of Resources – Interest Rate Swap		1,908,738

To record the fair value changes in the swap during 20Y0, which was an effective hedging derivative, but matured as of 6/11/Y0.

| | | Long-Term Debt | **12,031** |

PROPRIETARY FUND (6/30/Y0)	Debit	Credit
Bonds Payable	100,000,000	
Cash		100,000,000
To record bond retirement as of 6/11/Y0		

OBSERVATION: Notice how the inflows to and outflows from the counterparty are netted, which exemplifies the net settlement nature of derivative contracts. Some preparers may want to account for the net flows on a disaggregate basis to prepare an investment section or financing section of a direct method statement of cash flows. However, the disaggregation is not GAAP.

EXHIBIT 12-3
DERIVATIVE ILLUSTRATION: PRO-FORMA FINANCIAL STATEMENT BALANCES

Pro-Forma Financial Statement Balances

PROPRIETARY FUND:	Assets	Deferred Outflow of Resources	Liabilities	Income	Deferred Inflow of Resources	Expense
6/30/X7:						
Cash	$96,092,840	—	—	—	—	—
Deferred Outflow Interest Rate Swap	—	$2,984,833	—	—	—	—
Derivative Instrument Liability—Interest Rate Swap	—	—	$2,984,833	—	—	—
Bonds Payable	—	—	$100,000,000	—	—	—
Investment Income (Loss)	—	—	—	—	$0	—
Interest Expense	—	—	—	—	—	$3,907,160
6/30/X8:						
Cash	$92,185,680	—	—	—	—	—
Deferred Outflow Interest Rate Swap	—	$4,786,631	—	—	—	—
Derivative Instrument Liability—Interest Rate Swap	—	—	$4,786,631	—	—	—
Bonds Payable	—	—	$100,000,000	—	—	—
Investment Income (Loss)	—	—	—	—	$0	—
Interest Expense	—	—	—	—	—	$3,907,160
6/30/X9:						
Cash	$88,278,520	—	—	—	—	—
Deferred Outflow Interest Rate Swap	—	$1,908,738	—	—	—	—

Specific Accounting and Reporting Issues

PROPRIETARY FUND:	Assets	Deferred Outflow of Resources	Liabilities	Income	Deferred Inflow of Resources	Expense
Derivative Instrument Liability—Interest Rate Swap	—	—	$1,908,738	—	—	—
Bonds Payable	—	—	$100,000,000	—	—	—
Investment Income (Loss)	—	—	—	—	$0	—
Interest Expense	—	—	—	—	—	$3,907,160
6/30/Y0:						
Cash	$(15,628,640)	—	—	—	—	—
Deferred Outflow Interest Rate Swap	—	$0	—	—	—	—
Derivative Instrument Liability—Interest Rate Swap	—	—	$0	—	—	—
Bonds Payable	—	—	$0	—	—	—
Investment Income (Loss)	—	—	—	—	$0	—
Interest Expense	—	—	—	—	—	$3,907,160

NOTE: For this illustration's purposes, only the journal entries and pro-forma financial information for the proprietary fund are shown. The presentation in the business-type activities column in the government-wide financial statements is not included.

Hedge Termination Events. As previously discussed, if a derivative instrument is effectively hedged, GASB Cod. Sec. D40 provides for the deferring of changes in its fair value. If the derivative is terminated or ceases to be effective prior to its expected ending date, the accumulated deferrals are eliminated from the Statement of Net Position and reported as gains or losses in investment revenue or income in the resource-flow statements.

Termination events include the following:

- The hedging derivative instrument is no longer effective,
- The hedged expected transaction occurs (such as commodities are purchased or bonds are sold),
- It is no longer *probable* that the hedged expected transaction will occur,
- The hedged asset or liability is sold or retired but not reported as a debt refunding resulting in defeasance,
- A current or advanced refunding that results in defeasance is executed, and
- The hedging derivative instrument is terminated.

PRACTICE POINT: GASB-93 amended certain provisions of hedge termination guidance. Due to the replacement of the former London Interbank Offered Rate (LIBOR) with other reference rates, a termination may occur. An exception criterion was added by GASB-93 allowing hedge accounting to continue to be applied to a hedging derivative instrument that is effective as of the end of the reporting period, assuming the hedging derivative instrument's variable payment is an Interbank Offered Rate (IBOR) or an IBOR multiplied by a coefficient or adjusted by addition or subtraction of a constant. However, all the following criteria must be met:

- The hedging derivative instrument is amended or replaced to change the reference rate of the hedging derivative instrument's variable payment or to add or change fallback provisions related to the reference rate of the variable payment.
- The reference rate of the amended or replacement hedging derivative instrument's variable payment essentially equates the reference rate of the original hedging derivative instrument's variable payment by one or both of the following methods:
  - The replacement rate is multiplied by a coefficient or adjusted by addition or subtraction of a constant; the amount of the coefficient or constant is limited to what is necessary to essentially equate the replacement rate and the original rate. (A reference rate replaced in the current reporting period may have previously replaced another rate. Therefore, *original rate* is the same as replacement rate for this purpose).
  - An up-front payment is made between the parties; the amount of the payment is limited to what is necessary to essentially equate the replacement rate and the original rate.
- If the replacement of the reference rate is effectuated by ending the original hedging derivative instrument and finalizing a replacement hedging derivative instrument, those transactions occur on the same date.
- The terms that affect changes in fair values and cash flows in the original and amended or replacement hedging derivative instruments are identical, except for the term changes, that may be necessary for the replacement of the reference rate.

To meet these qualifications, term changes may be necessary. GASB-93 limited those changes to the frequency with which the rate of the variable payment resets, the date on which the rate resets, the methodology for resetting the rate and the dates on which periodic payments are made. If all these factors are met, hedge accounting may continue.

The accounting treatment for the deferred inflows or outflows at the time a terminating event occurs depends on the type of terminating event. Generally, the treatment involves eliminating the deferred amount from the Statement of Net Position and reporting it as gains or losses in investment revenue or income in the resource-flow statements.

Many diverse types of derivatives terminations may occur depending on the facts and circumstances of the transaction. Should a current refunding occur, both GASB Cod. Sec. D40.708-4 and GASB Cod. Sec. D40.901, illustration 6, describe the circumstance when a fair value of a swap is a liability at a point of a refunding and requires a termination payment. The amount of the payment needs to be included as part of the calculation of the deferred amount on refunding as an offset to the net carrying amount. Therefore, the deferred amount on refunding would be lowered because of the termination payment.

GASB Cod. Secs. D40.118–.121 specifically address termination of hedge accounting. Termination may occur when a government enters into an interest rate swap agreement, a commodity swap agreement, or some other hedge in which a swap counterparty, or the swap counterparty's credit support provider, commits or experiences either an act of default or a termination event as described in the swap agreement.

As amended by GASB Statement No. 99 (*Omnibus 2022*), if the terminating event occurs, the balance of any deferred outflows of resources or deferred inflows of resources is reported separately from investment revenue in the various applicable statements of the government. The event is captioned "*increase (decrease) upon hedge termination*" [GASB Cod. Sec. D40.122].

Governments then replace their swap counterparty, or swap counterparty's credit support provider, either by amending existing swap agreements or by entering into new swap agreements. An effective hedging relationship continues when *all the following* criteria are met:

- Collectability of swap payments is *probable*,
- The swap counterparty of the interest rate swap or commodity swap, or the swap counterparty's credit support provider, is replaced with an assignment or in-substance assignment, and
- The government finalizes the assignment or in-substance assignment in response to the swap counterparty, or the swap counterparty's credit support provider, either committing or experiencing an act of default or a termination event as both are described in the swap agreement.

An assignment occurs when a swap agreement is amended to replace an original swap counterparty, or the swap counterparty's credit support provider, but all the other terms of the swap agreement remain unchanged. Therefore, assignments are different than terminations. An in-substance assignment occurs when *all the following* criteria are met:

- The original swap counterparty, or the swap counterparty's credit support provider, is replaced,
- The original swap agreement is ended, and the replacement swap agreement is agreed to on the same date,
- The terms that affect changes in fair values and cash flows in the original and replacement swap agreements are identical. These terms include, but are not limited to, notional amounts, terms to maturity, variable payment terms, reference rates, time intervals, fixed-rate payments, frequencies of rate resets, payment dates, and options, such as floors and caps, and
- Any difference between the original swap agreement's exit price and the replacement swap's entry price is attributable to the original swap agreement's exit price being based on a computation specifically permitted under the original swap agreement. Exit price represents the payment made or received because of terminating the original swap. Entry price represents the payment made or received because of engaging in a replacement swap.

The differential between the exit price and the entrance price is deferred and amortized [GASB Cod. Secs. D40.118–.121].

An example of a terminating event is as follows utilizing the previous example. The result of this early termination is recorded in the following journal entry:

EXHIBIT 12-4
DERIVATIVE ILLUSTRATION: EXAMPLE EARLY TERMINATION JOURNAL ENTRY

PROPRIETARY FUND (12/31/X8)	Debit	Credit
Investment Income (Loss)	1,908,738	
Deferred Outflow of Resources – Interest Rate Swap		1,908,738

To reclassify the deferred outflow balance as an investment loss at the time of the hedge is no longer considered effective due to early termination.

After the early termination and the reclassification, all further changes in fair value to the derivative would be recorded as investment income or loss.

Determining Fair Value of Derivatives. GASB Cod. Sec. D40 provides that fair value should be measured by the market price when there is an active market for a derivative instrument. When an active market price is unavailable, the fair value may be estimated through an acceptable method of forecasting expected cash flows that are discounted. Several formula-based and mathematics-based methods, including matrix pricing, the zero-coupon method, and the par value method are acceptable in GAAP. For options, fair value may be based on a recognized option pricing model. Fair values may also be developed by pricing services, provided they are developed under the acceptable methods.

PRACTICE POINT: Many governments utilize third-party service providers to calculate the fair value of derivatives. Care must be taken to understand the assumptions used and results of the calculation as the government is ultimately responsible for the fair value determination and hedge effectiveness calculation in accordance with auditing standards.

Arbitrage Liability

Arbitrage involves the simultaneous purchase and sale of the same or essentially the same securities with the object of making a profit on the spread between two markets. In the context of government finance, arbitrage describes the strategy of issuing tax-exempt debt and investing the proceeds in debt securities that have a higher rate of return. However, state, and local governments are subject to rules and regulations established by Internal Revenue Code Section 148 and the U.S. Treasury that under certain conditions create an arbitrage rebate to be paid to the federal government.

Care must be taken in investing the proceeds of tax-exempt bonds to avoid arbitrage unless a government can successfully navigate the various exceptions to paying an arbitrage rebate. The rebate tax is based on the differential of the interest yields and can be an up to 50% tax on the earnings payable every five years. Penalties for failing to calculate this spread include the loss of tax-exempt status.

In general, state, and local governments should use the guidance contained in GASB Cod. Secs. C50.151–.168 and GASB Cod. Sec. 2300.106, to determine whether an arbitrage liability must be recognized. The AICPA's Audit and Accounting Guide *State and Local Governments* requires that the arbitrage analysis be made annually "to determine whether it is material and thus should be reported in the financial statements."

Subsidized Bonds (Issued Prior to December 31, 2017)

The federal government has authorized various forms of subsidized bonds at the state and local levels (Build America, Recovery Zone Economic Development Bonds, Qualified Zone Economic Development Bonds, etc.). Although they are not guaranteed by the federal government, the bonds are subsidized by a revenue stream that reduces overall interest costs. GASB Cod. Sec. N50.710-3 notes that these subsidies should not reduce interest expense. Rather, the federal reimbursement is a separate nonexchange transaction and should be recognized as nonexchange revenue when all eligibility requirements are met. Thus, the payment of interest on the qualifying bonds is reported gross, not netted with the federal reimbursement.

The 2017 Tax Cuts and Jobs Act eliminated the ability to sell qualified tax credit bonds after December 31, 2017.

EXTINGUISHMENT OF DEBT, -DEBT REFUNDING AND DEFEASANCE

A governmental unit may extinguish debt in a manner where the unit:
- Has no further legal responsibilities under the original debt agreement, *or*
- Continues to be legally responsible for the debt, but the extinguishment is considered an in-substance defeasance (retirement).

Extinguishment of Debt

Debt is *extinguished* under the following circumstances for financial reporting purposes [GASB Cod. Sec. D20.103]:
- Using financial resources *that did not arise from debt proceeds* (in other words, using existing cash), the debtor pays the creditor and is relieved of all its obligations with respect to the debt. This includes the debtor's reacquisition of its outstanding debt securities in the public securities

markets, regardless of whether the securities are cancelled or held as so-called treasury bonds.

- The debtor is *legally released* from being the primary obligor under the debt, either judicially or by the creditor, and it is *probable* that the debtor will not be required to make future payments with respect to that debt under any guarantees. The legal release is usually because nonrecourse debt is assumed by a third-party in conjunction with the sale of an asset that is the collateral for the debt. (This occurs with certain mortgages).

Refunding Transactions

Extinguishment of debt is different than a debt refunding. Refunding transactions occur often based on interest rate fluctuations and the terms and conditions of outstanding bond issuances. Two distinct types of refunding transactions occur resulting in a *defeasance* of some outstanding debt:

- The new debt proceeds may be used to repay the old debt *immediately*. This is known as a *current refunding*.

- The new debt proceeds are held in escrow, invested at a yield, and utilized to pay principal and interest on the old debt in the future as the debt matures. This is known as an *advance refunding*.

A third type of refunding occurs. A "crossover refunding" issuance is secured similarly to other refunding bonds, but even though the original bonds are refunded, the original revenue stream continues to pay for them until a call date. Effectively, the government is taking advantage of lower interest rates on new debt at the point of sale of these bonds. But not all the criteria for a defeasance are met. What usually occurs is that the new refunding bonds escrow is not enough to meet the debt service of the old debt until a future date. At that time, the pledged revenues "crossover" or swap to pay debt service on the refunding bonds and escrowed securities are used to pay the refunded bonds.

During the period when both the refunded and the refunding bonds are outstanding, debt service on the refunding bonds is paid from interest earnings on the invested proceeds of the refunding bonds. However, for accounting purposes, because an accounting defeasance has not occurred, both issues are shown as outstanding debt and the related escrow is shown as part of restricted investments. GASB Cod. Sec. 2200.709-14 discusses that in a crossover refunding bond issuance, the refunding debt is not capital related until it refunds (defeases) the old debt at the crossover date and therefore, reported in the Statement of Net Position.

Before that, the refunding bond liability and cash and investments balances should be about equal, so the net position is not affected. After the defeasance occurs (after the crossover date), the refunding debt assumes the characteristics of the old debt and would be included in the calculation of net investment in capital assets.

Defeasance

A defeasance of debt is either *legal* or *in-substance*. Legal defeasance occurs as the debt is satisfied based on the provisions in the old debt's indenture (contractual agreement), even though the debt may not be repaid. An *in-substance* defeasance occurs when the debt is considered defeased *for accounting and financial reporting purposes*, but a legal defeasance has *not occurred*. When a prior debt is defeased, it no longer is reported as a liability on the face of the financial statements. Only the new debt is reported [GASB Cod. Sec. D20.105].

When debt is extinguished as an in-substance defeasance transaction, only monetary assets can be contributed to the irrevocable trust. The monetary assets must be (1) denominated in the same currency in which the debt is payable, and (2) essentially risk free with respect to the timing, amount, and collection of principal and interest. The following are examples of essentially risk-free assets as denominated in U.S. dollars [GASB Cod. Sec. D20.106]:

- Direct obligations of the U.S. government,
- Obligations guaranteed by the U.S. government, and
- Securities backed by U.S. government obligations as collateral under an arrangement by which the interest and principal payments on the collateral generally flow immediately through to the holder of security, commonly known as "SLGS" or "slugs." The yield on the "basket" of securities does not exceed IRS arbitrage limits. (See previous section on Arbitrage.)

The monetary assets must generate cash flows that approximate the debt service requirements of the original debt. That is, cash must be available from the trust to pay interest and make principal repayments as they become due. The cash flows must be enough to meet trustee fees and similar administrative expenditures if these expenditures are expected to be made from the assets of the trust. If the administrative expenditures are to be paid directly by the governmental unit, a liability for the total expected administrative expenditures should be recognized in the period in which the debt is considered extinguished.

In-Substance Defeasance of Debt Using Only Existing Resources. Debt is also considered defeased for accounting and financial reporting purposes if the government *irrevocably* places cash and other monetary assets from existing resources into an escrow account solely used to satisfy scheduled payments of both interest and principal of the defeased debt. The transaction occurs without issuing new debt. The trust must be funded so that the possibility of the government being required to make future payments on the defeased debt is remote. The trust is also restricted to owning only the monetary assets that meet the risk-free requirements and cash flow requirements [GASB Cod. Sec. D20.121].

PRACTICE POINT: Some of the securities may be callable and subject to interest rate risk. They may also not be perfectly timed to mature when debt is due. If some securities can be paid before their scheduled maturities, they are not essentially *risk-free* regarding their timing of the collection of interest and principal. If the securities are callable, there is no assurance that the reinvested funds would provide the yields necessary to meet the required debt service schedule.

The liability recognized based on the expected administrative expenditures financed by the governmental unit may be classified as general long-term debt and therefore presented only in the government-wide financial statements if the expenditures do not require current appropriation and expenditure of governmental fund financial resources.

The concept of in-substance defeasance was established in for-profit GAAP, where debt could be removed from an entity's financial statements (even though it is not legally retired) by creating an irrevocable trust and transferring certain types of assets to the fund that will be used to meet debt service requirements of the obligation over its remaining life. The GASB incorporated the standards established by for-profit GAAP with respect to in-substance defeasance and thus enabled governmental entities to remove debt from their financial statements even when the debt instrument is not legally surrendered by an investor.

Accounting and Financial Reporting of Advance and Current Refunding Transactions

Refunding transactions occur for many reasons, including:

- To take advantage of lower interest rates,
- To extend maturity dates,
- To revise payment schedules,
- To modify restrictions contained in old indentures, or
- To achieve short-term budgetary savings by extending debt maturities in the future.

In some cases, debt service requirements for the life of the debt may be higher because of the refunding, resulting in an *economic loss*. In other cases, the debt service requirements will be lower, resulting in an *economic gain*. The calculation of economic gain or economic loss utilizes the present value of the difference in total cash flows between the old debt and the new debt, discounted at a specific interest rate [GASB Cod. Secs. D20.107–.108].

Advance refunding transactions may occur in governmental funds or proprietary funds. As a reminder, such transactions are *taxable* under tax law as of the date of publication.

Accounting and Reporting for Advance Refundings—Governmental Funds. Under current GAAP, when debt is defeased through an advance refunding, the proceeds from the issuance of the new debt should be recorded as "Other Financing Source—Proceeds of Refunding Debt" in the governmental fund that receives the proceeds from the issuance of the new debt. The newly issued debt should also be recorded as a liability in the governmental unit's government-wide financial statements. When payments to the escrow agent to defease the old debt are made from the proceeds of the newly issued debt, the payments should be recorded as "Other Financing Use—Payment to Refunded Debt Escrow Agent." The defeased debt should be removed from the governmental unit's government-wide financial statements [GASB Cod. Sec. D20.109].

For example, if a government defeased $500,000 of long-term notes by issuing $500,000 of long-term bonds and placed the proceeds in an irrevocable escrow, the following entries would be made assuming that the proceeds from the issuance of the new debt were recorded in the debt service fund:

DEBT SERVICE FUND	Debit	Credit
Cash	500,000	
Other Financing Source – Proceeds of Refunding Debt		500,000
To record the issues of refunding bonds series 202A		

DEBT SERVICE FUND	Debit	Credit
Other Financing Use – Payment to Refunded Debt Escrow Agent	500,000	
Cash		500,000
To record the escrowing of proceeds from refunding bonds series 202A to defease previously outstanding debt series 19X8 and 19YL per schedule.		

In the government-wide financial statements, long-term notes payable would be removed and bonds payable would be presented. If the cash is never deposited to the governmental entity's accounts, the first two entries may be combined to show only the source and use of the proceeds.

When payments made to the escrow agent to defease the debt are made from the governmental unit's resources and not from proceeds generated from the issuance of new debt, the payments should be recorded as a debt service expenditure and not as an other financing use.

For example, if it is assumed in the previous illustration that the $500,000 debt was defeased by issuing $400,000 of bonds and using $100,000 from the General Fund, the following entries would be made:

DEBT SERVICE FUND	Debit	Credit
Cash	400,000	
Other Financing Source – Proceeds of Refunding Debt		400,000
To record issuance of refunding bonds series 202B		

DEBT SERVICE FUND	Debit	Credit
Other Financing Use – Payment to Refunded Debt Escrow Agent	400,000	
Cash		400,000
To record the escrowing of proceeds from refunding bonds series 202B to defease previously outstanding debt series 19X8 and 19YL per schedule.		

Long-Term Debt **12,041**

GENERAL FUND	Debit	Credit
Expenditures—Principal	100,000	
Cash		100,000
To record debt extinguishment of the remainder of series 19YL per schedule using cash from the General Fund.		

In the government-wide financial statements, long-term notes of $500,000 would be removed and bonds payable of $400,000 would be presented. Payments made to the escrow agent from current governmental resources that represent accrued interest on the defeased debt should be recorded as a debt service expenditure (interest) and not as an other financing use.

Accounting and Reporting for Advance Refundings—Proprietary Funds

GASB Cod. Sec. D20.111 requires that the difference between the reacquisition price and the net carrying amount of the old debt be recognized as a deferred inflow of resources or deferred outflow of resources and amortized as a component of interest expense in a systematic and rational manner over the remaining life of the old debt or the life of the new debt, whichever is shorter.

When a governmental entity that uses proprietary fund accounting refunds debt (either a current refunding or an advance refunding), the difference between (1) the book value of the refunded (old) debt and (2) the amount required to retire the debt should be accounted for as a deferred inflow of resources or a deferred outflow of resources and should not be reported as a gain or loss on the fund's operating statement.

The book value of the retired debt includes its maturity value and any related unamortized discount or premium. The amount required to retire the old debt (*reacquisition price*) depends on whether the transaction is a current refunding or an advance refunding. In current refundings, the reacquisition price is the amount paid to debt holders (face value of the debt plus the premium amount, if any). For advance refundings, the reacquisition price is the amount of assets that must be placed in escrow to satisfy the in-substance defeasance criteria originally established by for-profit GAAP.

Transaction costs related to the issuance of the new debt that is the basis for the refunding are not considered when determining the difference between the book value of the old debt and the reacquisition price. For an advance refunding, for-profit GAAP, states that if "it is expected that trust assets will be used to pay related costs, such as trustee fees, as well as to satisfy scheduled interest and principal payments of a specific debt, those costs shall be considered in determining the amount of funds required by the trust. On the other hand, if the debt incurs an obligation to pay any related costs, the debt shall accrue a liability for those probable future payments in the period that the debt is recognized as extinguished" [GASB Cod. Sec. D20.112].

In the latter circumstance (accrual of future payments), the amount accrued should be used to determine the amount of the deferred inflow or outflow of resources, but not reported as a current expense. The deferred inflow or outflow of resources is presented separately from the balance of the refunding debt in the Statement of Net Position.

GASB Cod. Secs. D20.111–.112 characterize the differential between the reacquisition price of the previously issued debt and the net carrying amount of the old debt to deferred inflows or deferred outflows of resources, depending on if the differential is positive or negative. This may also occur in the case of a lease refunded by using tax-exempt debt prior to the lease term's expiration.

Subsequently, the deferred outflow (or inflow) of resources is amortized over the original remaining life of the old debt or the life of the new debt, whichever is less. The amount is amortized in a "systematic and rational manner" as a component of interest expense. If the amount is a deferred outflow of resources, interest expense is increased because of the periodic amortization. If the amount is a deferred inflow of resources resulting in an eventual gain, interest expense is decreased.

Amortization methods that satisfy the systematic and rational guideline include:

- The effective interest method,
- The straight-line method for term bonds, and
- The proportion to stated-interest requirements method.

In financial accounting, it is generally accepted that periodic interest expense should be determined based on the effective interest method or the straight-line method if the results from applying the latter method are not materially different from the use of the effective interest method. GAAP does not use the effective interest method as the benchmark for determining the acceptability of periodic amortization. Because of the structure of the refunding and of the bonds that are refunded, other methods may reflect more of a fiscal reality than either the effective interest or the straight-line method.

Other methods can include amortizing when groups of principal amounts mature. This is preferable when the maturities are uneven. What constitutes "systematic and rational" is a matter of judgment. GASB does not attempt to provide a general definition of "systematic and rational" in any literature regarding amortization of interest, discount or premium, other than for depreciation and amortization as discussed in Chapter 10 of this *Guide*.

The accounting for gains or losses that arise from refundings are significantly different from the standards applicable to similar transactions in the private sector. For government entities, any loss will be deferred, while in the private sector, a loss must be reported immediately on an entity's statement of operations.

Current Refundings of Prior Refundings and Advance Refundings of Prior Refundings. Debt used to refund previously issued debt may also be later refunded. Any gain or loss from the subsequent refunding should be deferred and combined with any unamortized deferred inflows of resources or deferred outflows of resources related to the original refunding. The combined deferred position should be amortized over the shorter of (1) the remaining period used in the original refunding or (2) the life of the newly issued debt. The standard applies to current and advance refundings. However, refunding debt that has been previously refunded may result in a taxable debt issuance [GASB Cod. Sec. D20.112].

Accounting and Reporting—Current Refunding

In a current refunding, proceeds from the newly issued debt are used to immediately retire the old debt. For proprietary funds, the computation of the deferred outflow of resources arising from a current refunding is contained in the following comprehensive example, including the involvement of an effective derivative hedge that will be terminated.

Example: Castle Rock County retires $20,000,000 in variable rate debt, paying $400,000 of a call premium. The county had an interest rate swap as an effective hedging derivative instrument that is also terminated as part of the transaction. As of the interest rate swap's termination date, the fair value of the swap represents a liability of $1,500,000, and the deferred outflow of resources amount is $1,500,000 (an effective hedge). The termination requires a $1,500,000 payment to the counterparty by the government. Costs of the transaction are immaterial to this discussion. New fixed-rate debt was issued for $20,000,000 to fund the transaction.

To record the transactions the following must occur:

1. The termination payment is a cash outflow of $1,500,000.
2. The net carrying amount of the refunded debt determined to calculate the deferred outflow of resources or deferred inflow of resources on the refunding should include the deferred outflow of resources or deferred inflow of resources amount related to the terminated hedging derivative instrument—a $1,500,000 deferred outflows of resources, computed as of the date of refunding. In many cases, the deferred outflow of resources or deferred inflow of resources approximates the hedging derivative instrument's termination payment.
3. The deferred outflow of resources on refunding in the circumstances described in the fact pattern is calculated as follows:

REACQUISITION PRICE:		
Old bonds outstanding	$20,000,000	
Call premium on bonds	400,000	
Funds required to retire old bonds		$20,400,000
NET CARRYING AMOUNT OF OLD BONDS:		
Old bonds outstanding	(20,000,000)	
Balance of related deferred outflows of resources – interest rate swap	1,500,000	
Net Carrying Amount of Old Bonds		(18,500,000)
Deferred Outflows of Resources on Bond Refunding		$1,900,000

To record the current refunding, the following entries would be made in the proprietary fund, irrespective of interest accruals on the new debt:

	Debit	Credit
Interest Rate Swap	1,500,000	
Cash		1,500,000
To record termination of swap payment to counterparty		

	Debit	Credit
Variable rate bonds	20,000,000	
Deferred outflow of resources – refunding bonds	1,900,000	
Deferred outflow of resources – interest rate swap		1,500,000
Cash (retired call premium on old bonds)		400,000
Fixed rate bonds – Series 202C		20,000,000
To retire variable rate debt and associated hedge, to record call premium and issue Series 202C fixed rate bonds		

In a current refunding, a difference between the reacquisition price and the carrying amount of the old debt usually results from one or more factors, all related to the old debt: call premium and unamortized premium or discount because the new bonds effectively incorporate those factors into their pricing structure.

In a refunding transaction, if there is a deferred inflow of resources or a deferred outflow of resources related to a derivative transaction that hedged the prior bonds, the balance of the deferred account should be included in the net carrying amount of the old debt for purposes of calculating the difference between that amount and the reacquisition price of the old debt. This method must be used whether (or not) a termination of the related hedging derivative instrument occurs. The balance of the deferred account also is part of the economic gain or loss calculation.

Based on the above analysis, the deferred outflow of resources arising from the early retirement of debt is $1,500,000. This amount is recorded as a deferred outflow of resources and be amortized in a systematic and rational manner over the lesser of the original remaining life of the old bonds or the life of the new bonds, whichever is shorter.

If the deferred outflow of resources amount is amortized using the straight-line method, the annual amortization is $300,000 ($1,500,000 ÷ 5 years). The amortization would be part of the interest expense the proprietary fund recognizes each year. However, the effective interest method may also be preferable.

If an Assignment Occurred. GAAP requires instead of recognizing investment revenue immediately because of the release of the accumulated deferred outflows of resources (or deferred inflows of resources) when a derivative terminates, the derivative may not terminate when certain circumstances occur, as discussed in this chapter previously. If those criteria are met, the loss would continue to be deferred outflow of resources. The swap agreements would terminate and be replaced immediately with identical terms and conditions. Many of these instances occurred when the credit markets failed during the fall of 2008 and 2009 and during the COVID-19 pandemic. In the above example, should an in-substance assignment have occurred, the $1,500,000 would not have been released.

Example of Determining Information Needed to Understand Refunding Transactions

Difference in Cash Flow Requirements. The cash flow requirements of the old debt are simply the sum of all future interest and principal payments that would have to be paid by the governmental entity if the debt remained outstanding until its maturity date. The cash flow requirements of the new debt are the sum of all future interest and principal payments that will have to be paid to service the new debt in the future, and other payments that are made from the governmental entity's current resources rather than from proceeds from the issuance of the new debt. Any proceeds from the issuance of the new debt that represent accrued interest (when the bonds are sold between interest payment dates) should not be included as cash flow requirements related to the new debt but should include the effects of a hedging derivative instrument, as applicable [GASB Cod. Secs. D20.114–.117].

When new debt is issued in an amount that exceeds the amount needed to defease the old debt, only the portion of the new debt needed to defease the old debt should be included as cash flow requirements related to the new debt, again, including the effects of a hedging derivative instrument, as applicable.

Determining Economic Gain or Loss. The economic gain or loss is computed by determining the difference between the present value of cash flow requirements of the old debt and the present value of cash flow requirements of the new debt. The interest or discount rate used to determine the present value of the cash flows is a rate that generally must be computed through trial and error, either manually or by using a computer software package. The objective is to identify an interest rate that, when applied to the cash flow requirements for the new debt, produces an amount equal to the sum of the:

- Proceeds of the new debt (net of premium or discount), and
- Accrued interest, less the underwriting spread.

Issuance costs related to the advance refunding may include such transaction costs as insurance, legal, administrative, and trustee costs. These costs may be recoverable through the yield in the escrow fund or may likely be expensed. The U.S. Treasury Department regulations establish the maximum allowable yield of the escrow fund, and certain issuance costs (allowable costs) may be used to reduce the amount defined as proceeds from the issuance of the new debt. The Treasury Department regulations increase the allowable amount that can be legally earned in the escrow fund. Although issuance costs may be allowable under the Treasury Department regulations, they may not be recoverable through the escrow fund because:

- The interest rate on securities purchased by the escrow fund may be less than the legal maximum rate allowed by the Treasury Department, *or*

- The escrow fund may be used to liquidate the old debt on a call date and the investment period may be too short to allow for the full recovery of the allowable costs through escrow earnings.

When issuance costs are considered allowable costs by the Treasury Department and they are recovered through the escrow fund, the result is that such costs are not an actual cost to the governmental entity. These are referred to as *recoverable costs* and are not used to compute the interest or discount rate used to determine the present value of the cash flow requirements related to the old debt and new [GASB Cod. Sec. D20.115].

Steps to Determine the Required Refunding Disclosures. To clarify the computation of the differences in cash flow requirements and the economic gain or loss arising from an advance refunding, GASB Cod. Sec. D20 presents detailed examples in exhibits and illustrations. The following sections present the steps that may be followed to compute the required disclosures. The following are four suggested steps can be applied to a specific set of circumstances.

- *Step 1.* Compute the value of resources that will be required to
  - Make a payment to the escrow agent to defease the debt and
  - Pay issuance costs (to be expensed).

  The resources may be generated entirely from the issuance of new debt, or the refunding may be partially financed by using other resources of the governmental unit.

  The payment to the escrow agent must be large enough to make all interest payments and the principal payment based on either the call date or maturity date of the old debt. Either the call date or the maturity date is used, depending on which is specified as the retirement date in the escrow fund agreement. The amount of the required payment to the escrow agent is also dependent on the rate of return that can be earned in the escrow fund. The escrow rate of return is determined by the market investment conditions and the allowable yield on the escrow investment as determined by Treasury Department regulations.

  The amount of the issuance costs must be added to the amount paid to the escrow agent to determine the total amount of resources required to defease the debt.

- *Step 2.* Compute the effective interest rate target amount. The effective interest rate target amount is computed by subtracting the amount of non-recoverable issuance costs from the amount of the resources required to defease the old debt and to pay issuance costs (computed in Step 1). By reducing the amount required to defease the old debt (and to pay issuance costs) by the non-recoverable issuance costs, the effective interest rate (to be computed in Step 3) will be decreased. If all issuance costs are recoverable and the new debt is sold at par, the coupon rate on the new debt will be the same as the effective interest rate.

- *Step 3.* Compute the effective interest rate. The effective interest rate is the interest rate used to discount the debt service requirements on the new debt so that it is exactly equal to the effective interest rate target amount (computed in Step 2). The computation of the effective interest rate is relatively easy if you have access to a computer and a software program. If you do not have access to a computer, the computation of the effective interest rate is tedious because it must be determined through trial and error and by using interpolation.

- **Step 4.** Compute
  - The difference between the cash flow required for service the old debt and the cash flow required to service the new debt and
  - The economic gain or loss resulting from the advance refunding.

The difference between the cash flow requirements can be computed as follows:

ELEMENTS	AMOUNTS	
Total interest payments on old debt (using the maturity date of old debt)	$X	
Principal payment to retire old debt	X	
Total cash flow requirements to service old debt (cash)		$X
Total interest payments on new debt	$X	
Other resources to defease old debt	X	
Principal payments to retire new debt	X	
Less: Accrued interest on new debt at date of issuance	(X)	
Net cash flow requirements to service new debt		(X)
Difference in cash flow requirements		$NET

The economic gain or loss on the advance refunding can be computed as follows:

ELEMENTS	AMOUNTS	
Present value of cash flow requirements to service old debt		$X
Present value of cash flow requirements to service new debt	$X	
Other resources used to defease old debt	X	
Less: Accrued interest on new debt at date of issuance	(X)	
Economic gain (loss) on advance refunding		$NET

Many underwriters and financial advisers will compute these amounts and provide them for a government.

FINANCIAL REPORTING OF DEBT BALANCES AND TRANSACTIONS

Governmental Funds

The measurement focus for governmental funds is the flow of current financial resources. Liabilities that will consume current financial resources of the fund responsible for payment during the fiscal period are presented in that fund's balance sheet. No explicit current liability classification exists on a fund's Balance Sheet (the financial statement is unclassified) unless the debt has matured and remains unpaid as of the reporting date.

The presentation of the liability in the Balance Sheet of the government's fund implies that the debt is current and will require the use of expendable financial resources. In summation, the outstanding balance of long-term debt is not a liability in a governmental fund, unless it is to be liquidated with current financial resources.

Demand Bonds. If the take-out agreement is cancelable or callable because of violations that can be objectively determined by both parties and no violations have occurred prior to issuance of the financial statements, the demand bonds are classified as general long-term liabilities. Otherwise, violations would cause the demand bonds to be reported in the governmental funds as liabilities. This would also occur if the take-out agreement were cancelable or callable because of violations that cannot be objectively determined by both parties [GASB Cod. Sec. D30.108].

Refunded Debt. Under current GAAP, in governmental funds, for current and advance refundings resulting in defeasance of general long-term debt, the face amount of the new debt should be reported as an "other financing source—refunding bonds" in the governmental fund receiving the proceeds. For advance refundings, payments to the escrow agent from resources provided by the new debt should be reported as an "other financing use—payment to refunded bond escrow agent." Payments to the escrow agent made from other resources of the entity should be reported as debt service expenditures [GASB Cod. Sec. D20.109].

Defeasance with Existing Resources. In governmental funds, payments to the escrow agent using only existing resources (and not the issuance of debt) are reported as debt service expenditures [GASB Cod. Sec. D20.123].

PROPRIETARY FUNDS

The accrual basis of accounting and economic resources measurement focus is used to determine which liabilities should be presented on the Statement of Net Position of a proprietary or fiduciary fund. In general, a proprietary fund should report liabilities comparable to a commercial enterprise if the presentation is consistent with standards established by the GASB. It is unlikely that fiduciary activities have long-term debt as the funds are being held for others.

Bond, Tax, and Revenue Anticipation Notes. A previously discussed, GAAP stipulates that a proprietary fund must determine whether bond, tax and revenue anticipation notes should be presented on the proprietary fund's Balance Sheet as a current or long-term liability.

Demand Bonds. GAAP is applicable to demand bonds accounted for in a proprietary fund that have an exercisable provision for redemption at or within one year of the fund's Balance Sheet date. Such bonds may be reported as a long-term liability in the proprietary fund when all the criteria are met. When the conditions recognizing a long-term liability have not been met, demand bonds must be presented as a current liability if the proceeds were received by a proprietary fund. If demand bonds are issued and no take-out agreement has been executed at their issuance date or at the Balance Sheet date, the bonds cannot be considered a long-term liability.

GOVERNMENT-WIDE FINANCIAL STATEMENTS

The accrual basis of accounting and the economic resources measurement focus are used to determine which liabilities should be presented in a governmental entity's Statement of Net Position. Liabilities should be presented in the Statement of Net Position based on their relative liquidity. The liquidity of liabilities is based on maturity dates or expected payment dates. Because of the significant degree of aggregation used in the preparation of government-wide financial statements, the GASB notes that the liquidity of an asset or liability account presented in the Statement of Net Position should be determined by assessing the average liquidity of the class of assets or liabilities to which it belongs, "even though individual balances may be significantly more or less liquid than others in the same class and some items may have both current and long-term elements" [GASB Cod. Secs. 2200.116, B50.103, C50.120, C60.109, D30.110].

Both governmental activities and business-type activities should be presented in the Statement of Net Position.

Bond, Tax, and Revenue Anticipation Notes. Bond, tax, and revenue anticipation notes should be presented in the government-wide financial statements. Tax and revenue anticipation notes are considered current liabilities (liabilities due within one year).

Demand Bonds. Demand bonds should also be presented in the government-wide financial statements. To determine the liquidity of this type of debt, the criteria established by GAAP must be used to determine whether the demand bonds are current or noncurrent (due in more than one year).

Hedging Derivative Instruments. As discussed previously in this chapter, hedging (or investment) derivative instruments should be reported in the Statement of Net Position at fair value. They may be assets or liabilities. They may be in the government-wide Statement of Net Position or in a proprietary fund Statement of Net Position [GASB Cod. Sec. D40.115]. Changes in fair value of hedging derivatives are recognized through the application of hedge accounting. If effective hedges, the change in fair value of hedging derivative instruments are reported as either deferred inflow or deferred outflows of resources in the Statement of Net Position. In proprietary fund statements, the fund that reports the hedged items should do so. Hedge accounting is applied beginning in the period that a hedging derivative instrument is established until a termination event occurs [GASB Cod. Sec. D40.116]. Termination events that are not assignments result in the release of any unamortized deferred positions to investment revenue (or expense).

Refunded Debt. If the defeasance occurs in a proprietary fund, for both current refundings and advance refundings resulting in defeasance of debt, the difference between the reacquisition price and the net carrying amount of the old debt should be reported as a deferred outflow of resources or a deferred inflow of resources and recognized as a component of interest expense in a systematic and rational manner over the remaining life of the old debt or the life of the new debt, whichever is shorter [GASB Cod. Sec. D20.111]. This same presentation is in the government-wide statements as well [GASB Cod. Sec. D20.113]. The only exception is in crossover refunding transactions, which do not result in a defeasance. If there is no defeasance, then both the old debt and the new debt remain in the Statement of Net Position until the crossover date(s).

Defeasance with Existing Resources. For government-wide statements and proprietary fund statements, like other refundings, when a government places cash and other monetary assets acquired with only existing resources with an escrow agent in a trust that meets the criteria for an in-substance defeasance, the debt should no longer be reported as a liability in the financial statements. Any difference between the reacquisition price and the net carrying amount of the debt, together with any deferred outflows of resources or deferred inflows of resources from prior refundings, should be recognized as a separately identified gain or loss in the period of the in-substance defeasance [GASB Cod. Sec. D20.122].

NOTE DISCLOSURE OF DEBT

Note disclosure of debt information is among the more important sections of the notes to the basic financial statements. Governments are required to separate information in debt disclosures regarding direct borrowings and direct placements from other debt. Required details include:

- Principal and interest requirements to maturity, presented separately, for each of the five subsequent fiscal years and in five-year increments thereafter. Interest requirements on variable-rate debt are determined using the rate in effect at the date of the financial statements.
- The terms by which interest rates change for variable rate debt.

Governments should also disclose in the notes to the financial statements *summarized* information about the following, separating information regarding direct borrowings and direct placements of debt from other debt:

1. Amount of unused lines of credit,
2. Assets pledged as collateral for debt, and
3. Terms specified in debt agreements related to *significant*:
   - Events of default with finance-related consequences,
   - Termination events with finance-related consequences, and
   - Subjective acceleration clauses [GASB Cod. Secs. 1500.129–.130].

Long-Term Debt **12,051**

EXAMPLE: NOTE X—OUTSTANDING LONG-TERM DEBT

As of June 30, 202X, debt service requirements to maturity for principal and interest are as follows (amounts in thousands):

Fiscal Year Ended June 30	Public Offered Debt Principal	Public Offered Debt Interest	Direct Placements Principal	Direct Placements Interest	Total Governmental Activities Principal	Total Governmental Activities Interest	Revenue Obligation Principal	Revenue Obligation Interest
202B	$1,346,587	$1,235,406	$—	$9,000	$1,346,587	$1,244,406	$2,444,606	$180,030
202C	1,365,981	1,177,059	—	9,000	1,365,981	1,186,059	225,012	174,780
202D	1,291,446	1,105,880	—	9,000	1,291,446	1,114,880	206,862	167,635
202E	1,312,000	1,045,308	—	9,000	1,312,000	1,054,308	203,561	160,631
202F	1,281,476	985,740	—	9,000	1,281,476	994,740	198,705	153,050
202G–203A	5,660,220	4,107,549	100,000	38,500	5,760,220	4,146,049	1,049,637	631,098
203B–203F	4,564,507	2,911,085	100,000	23,500	4,664,507	2,934,585	964,825	413,056
203G–204A	4,701,145	1,944,476	50,000	11,750	4,751,145	1,956,226	911,795	216,511
204B–204F	4,652,810	1,008,271	50,000	3,950	4,702,810	1,012,221	484,688	73,909
204G–205A	2,572,285	230,912	—	—	2,572,285	230,912	152,739	13,781
Total long-term debt	28,748,457	15,751,686	300,000	122,700	29,048,457	15,874,386	6,842,430	2,184,481
Less: current portion	(1,346,587)	(1,235,406)	—	(9,000)	(1,346,587)	(1,244,406)	(2,444,606)	(180,030)
Long-term debt	$27,401,870	$14,516,280	$300,000	$113,700	$27,701,870	$14,629,980	$4,397,824	$2,004,451

Other debt disclosure requirements are discussed in Chapter 20.

If a governmental entity has debt that carries a variable interest rate, the debt service disclosures should be based on the interest rate in effect as of the date of the current Statement of Net Position or Balance Sheet. In addition, the conditions that affect the determination of the variable interest rate should be disclosed. The notes to the financial statements should focus on the primary government (which includes its blended component units) and support the information included in the government-wide financial statements and the fund financial statements. Note disclosures related to discretely presented component units should be presented based on the concept of essentiality as further discussed in Chapter 4 [GASB Cod. Secs. 2300.105, 2600.123].

OBSERVATION: Controversy has ensued as to how much debt disclosure to incorporate for discretely presented component units within a primary government's notes to the basic financial statements. GASB Cod. Secs. 2300.105 and 2600.123 stipulate that for discretely presented component units, notes essential to fair presentation in the reporting entity's basic financial statements encompass only major discretely presented component units considering the nature and significance of each component unit's relationship to the primary government. Determining which discretely presented component unit disclosures are essential to fair presentation is a matter of professional judgment and should be done on a component unit-by-component unit basis. A specific type of disclosure might be essential for one component unit but not for another depending on the individual component unit's relationship with the primary government. For example, if a primary government is obligated in some manner for the debt of an individual component unit, it is likely that debt-related disclosures should be made for that component unit. On the other hand, for nonmajor component units, debt-related disclosures do not always need to be included in the primary government's notes to the basic financial statements if the primary government is not obligated in some manner for that debt. It is up to professional judgment and the policies and practices of the primary government.

Anticipation Notes and Other Forms of Short-Term Debt

GAAP requires that the activity in long-term debt presented in the Statement of Net Position be summarized in a note to the financial statements. This requirement includes providing details in the notes to the financial statements about short-term debt activity during the year, even if no short-term debt is outstanding at year-end.

Like other forms of debt, for this purpose, debt is defined as a liability that arises from a contractual obligation to pay cash (or other assets that may be used in lieu of cash) in one or more payments to settle an amount that is fixed at the date the contractual obligation is established. For this purpose, short-term debt does not include leases, except for contracts reported as a financed purchase of the underlying asset, or accounts payable. A government should separate information in debt disclosures regarding direct borrowings and direct placements of debt from other debt. Short-term debt results from borrowings characterized by anticipation notes, use of lines of credit, and similar loans. Details should include:

1. A schedule of changes in short-term debt, disclosing:
   a. Beginning-and end-of-year balances,
   b. Increases, and
   c. Decreases, and
2. The purpose for which the short-term debt was issued [GASB Cod. Sec. 2300.124].

The following is potential note disclosure:

Note X—Short-Term Debt

During the year, the County issued bond anticipation notes to begin the reconstruction of a major bridge that had been heavily damaged by floodwaters. The proceeds from the short-term debt were needed immediately to begin the project, and these notes were paid off approximately three months later, when long-term bonds were issued to finance the capital project. Short-term debt activity for the year ended June 30, 20X7, is summarized as follows:

	Beginning Balance	Proceeds	Repayment	Ending Balance
Bond anticipation notes	$—	$12,000,000	$(12,000,000)	$—

Demand Bonds

In addition to the other notes for debt, entities with demand bonds outstanding should disclose:

- A general description of the demand bond program,
- Terms of any letters of credit or other standby liquidity agreements outstanding,
- Commitment fees to obtain the letters of credit,
- Any amounts drawn on them outstanding as of the Balance Sheet date,
- A description of the take-out agreement including its expiration date, and
- Commitment fees to obtain that agreement, and the terms of any new obligation under the take-out agreement (regardless of when the demand provisions are exercisable).

The notes should also disclose the debt service requirements that would result if the take-out agreement were to be exercised. Like other debt disclosures, for demand bonds, a government should separate information regarding (*a*) direct borrowings and direct placements of debt from (*b*) other debt [GASB Cod. Sec. D30.111].

If a take-out agreement has been exercised converting the bonds to an installment loan, the installment loan should be reported as general long-term debt and the payment schedule under the installment loan should be included as part of the schedule of debt service requirements to maturity [GASB Cod. Sec. D30.112].

Conduit Debt

The following information should be disclosed in the financial statements of the issuing entity related to conduit debt obligations:

- A general description of the issuer's conduit debt obligation(s),
- A general description of the issuer's limited commitment(s),
- A general description of the issuer's voluntary commitment(s),
- A general description of the issuer's additional commitment(s), including:
  — The legal authority and limits for extending the commitment(s),
  — The length of time of the commitment(s),
  — Arrangements, if any, for recovering payments from the third-party obligor(s), and
- The aggregate outstanding principal amount of all conduit debt obligations that share the same type of commitment(s) at the end of the reporting period.

If an *issuer* has recognized a liability, it should disclose the following information:

- A brief description of the timing of recognition and measurement of the liability and information about the changes in the recognized liability, including the following:

- Beginning-of-period balances,
- Increases, including initial recognition and adjustments increasing estimates,
- Decreases, including payments made and adjustments decreasing estimates,
- End-of-period balances,

- Cumulative amounts of payments that have been made on the recognized liability at the reporting date, if any, and
- Amounts expected to be recovered from those payments, if any [GASB Cod. Secs. C65.122–.123].

Hedging Derivative Instruments

GASB Cod. Sec. D40 requires the objectives, terms, and risks of hedging derivative instruments to be disclosed, in addition to a summary of derivative instrument activity that provides the location of fair value amounts reported on the financial statements.

The disclosure requirements for hedging derivative instrument activities, balances, and their related risks are extensive and vary depending on the distinct types of hedging derivative instruments that a government is party to. If the government is involved in significant derivative activity and has several diverse types of hedging derivative instruments, many of the required disclosures will likely be better presented in a tabular or columnar display.

In addition to providing summary disclosures regarding the government's derivative instrument activities and balances (general disclosures), there are more specific disclosure requirements that depend on the type of derivative instrument.

General Disclosures for Hedging Derivative Instruments. GASB Cod. Sec. D40 requires certain general disclosures that provide a summary of the government's hedging derivative instrument activities and balances. These general disclosures include a summary of the government's derivative instrument activity during the period and related balances at period end that are:

- Organized by governmental activities, business-type activities, and fiduciary funds to the extent applicable, and
- Separated into categories for hedging derivative instruments and investment hedging derivative instruments; and within each category, aggregated by type of derivative (e.g., receive-fixed swaps, pay-fixed swaps, swaptions, and futures contracts).

The summary information about the hedging derivative instruments should include:

- Notional or face amount of the derivative instrument,
- Fair value changes during the period and the location in the financial statements where the changes in fair values are reported,

- Fair values at period end and the location in the financial statements where the fair values are reported,
- If the fair value of any derivative is based on other than quoted market prices, the method and assumptions used to estimate fair value, and
- Fair values of any hedging derivative instruments reclassified to an investment derivative instrument during the period and the deferral amount reported within investment income upon reclassification.

GASB Cod. Sec. D40 *does not* require a government to disclose the identities of the counterparties to the government's hedging derivative instruments. In addition, the credit quality rating of hedging derivative instruments does not need to be separately disclosed and may be aggregated by derivative instrument type or by credit quality rating. A portfolio, for example, consisting of swaps and forward contracts with differing credit quality ratings may be aggregated and displayed by credit quality.

Should the government have a policy requiring collateral or other security to support hedging derivative instruments subject to credit risk, a summary description, and the aggregate amount of the collateral or other security that reduces credit risk exposure, and information about the government's access to that collateral or other security should also be included.

If the government has a policy of engaging in master netting arrangements, included should be a summary description and the aggregate amount of liabilities included in those arrangements. Master netting arrangements are established when:

- Each party owes the other determinable amounts,
- The government has the right to set off the amount owed with the amount owed by the counterparty, and
- The right of setoff is legally enforceable.

Specific Disclosures for Hedging Derivative Instruments. Although hedging derivative instruments can be a valuable component of the fiscal management of an entity and can help a government manage or hedge a specific risk, they can also present significant other risks to the government that could affect the entity's liquidity and investment performance. GASB Cod. Sec. D40 requires unique disclosures about a government's use of hedging derivative instruments. The disclosures for each type of derivative instrument outstanding at period end should include:

- The government's objective for engaging in the hedging derivative instrument, and
- The significant terms of the hedging derivative instrument.

GASB Cod. Sec. D40 also requires that the following risks associated with hedging derivative instruments be disclosed to the extent the government has exposure to those risks as previously described (*credit risk, interest rate risk, termination risk, basis risk, rollover risk, market access risk, and foreign currency risk*). (See Chapter 9 for examples of such disclosure for investments.)

Other Derivative-Related Disclosures. GASB Cod. Sec. D40 also requires certain other disclosures when specific circumstances are met. These include:

- Disclosure of contingent features that are included in hedging derivative instruments held at period end (such as a government's obligation to post collateral if credit quality declines),
- The net debt service requirements of the hedged debt considering the hedging derivative instrument,
- Disclosure of embedded derivatives or other hybrid instruments (such as an interest rate swap embedded in a borrowing), and
- Disclosure of descriptive and fair value information about any synthetic guaranteed investment contracts the government is a party to [GASB Cod. Secs. D40.164–.176].

Variable Interest Rate Debt Disclosure When Coupled with a Hedging Derivative Instrument. Many governments can legally sell variable rate debt either with a corresponding derivative hedge or without a hedge (commonly known as "naked" variable rate debt). The purpose of issuing the debt is to lower interest costs and satisfy bondholders' needs. Typically, the bondholders for this type of debt are tax-exempt money market mutual funds.

Due to the variability in interest rates, disclosure is slightly different than fixed rate debt disclosure. GASB Cod. Sec. 1500.129 stipulates that the schedule of debt service requirements to maturity for variable rate debt should use interest determined using the rate in effect at the financial statement date and the terms by which interest rates change for variable rate debt.

The following is an example of variable interest rate debt disclosure with an effective hedge, excluding the derivatives disclosure detailed previously:

EXAMPLE: *Outstanding Swapped Debt*

Security for Interest Rate Swap Agreements. Under legislation approved by the then Governor in 20X8, scheduled, periodic payments to be made by the State pursuant to swap agreements in existence or entered into after such date shall constitute general obligations of the State for which its full faith and credit is pledged.

Future bond interest payments are calculated using rates applicable to the scheduled payment nearest to June 30, 20Y2 for variable rate bonds. The net swap payments are calculated by subtracting the projected future variable rate interest payment per the swap agreement from the projected future fixed rate payment per the swap agreement. Projected future variable rate payments on the swap agreements are based on variable rates applicable to the scheduled payment nearest to June 30, 20Y2. The actual amount of variable rate interest paid to bondholders and net swap payments made to counterparties are affected by changes in variable interest rates, changes in inflation (CPI), as well as changes in the London Interbank Offered Rate (LIBOR) and the Securities Industry and Financial Markets Association (SIFMA) floating rate indices. Changes in the amounts paid to bondholders versus amounts paid to counterparties are largely offsetting.

Long-Term Debt **12,057**

Debt service requirements to maturity for variable-rate bonds hedged by interest rate swap agreements and projected future net settlement payments on interest rate swap agreements as of June 30, 20Y2 are provided below:

Fiscal Year Ending June 30	Variable-Rate Bonds Principal	Interest	Interest Rate Swaps, Net	Total
20Y3	$74,955,000	$4,097,732	$21,409,976	$100,462,708
20Y4	75,405,000	2,257,714	19,256,400	96,919,114
20Y5	126,385,000	1,655,365	15,668,498	143,708,863
20Y6	131,780,000	863,641	11,115,685	143,759,326
20Y7	52,185,000	331,518	7,814,499	60,331,017
20Y8–20Z2	106,070,000	684,096	22,995,725	129,749,821
20Z3–20Z7	49,875,000	65,815	2,212,342	52,153,157
Total	$616,655,000	$9,955,881	$100,473,125	$727,084,006

Business-Type Activities—Swapped Debt. The business-type activities have various swaps. As of June 30, 20Y2, the fair value liability of the outstanding interest rate swaps was $1 million.

Refunding Disclosures. GASB Cod. Sec. D20 contains the following required disclosures for advance refunding transactions, at a minimum [GASB Cod. Secs. D20.114–.117]:

- The difference between (*a*) the cash flow requirements necessary to service the old debt over its life and (*b*) the cash flow requirements necessary to service the new debt and other payments necessary to complete the advance refunding, and

- The economic gain or loss that arises because of the advance refunding.

The life of the old debt is based on its stated maturity date and not on its call date, if any.

OBSERVATION: The two disclosures described above are the only disclosure requirements for advance refunding transactions. Additional information could include (1) amounts of the old and new debt, (2) additional amounts paid to the escrow agent, and (3) management's explanation for an advance refunding that results in an economic loss. The GASB also states that ultimately the specific disclosures by a governmental entity are dependent on "such things as the number and relative size of the entity's advance refunding transactions, the fund structure of the reporting entity, and the number and type of refundings of its component units."

For periods after an in-substance debt defeasance has occurred, the amount of the defeased debt outstanding should be disclosed with a distinction between amounts that apply to the primary government (including blended component units) and discretely presented component units [GASB Cod. Sec. D20.117].

PRACTICE POINT: The required disclosures for defeased debt outstanding are applicable only to in-substance defeased debt and not to legally defeased debt.

The following are examples of notes to a financial statement that provide disclosures for (1) an advance refunding resulting in defeased debt and (2) prior-year defeasance of debt outstanding.

EXAMPLE: *Note X—Defeased Debt.* The State defeased certain general and special obligation bonds by purchasing securities from the proceeds of advance refunding bonds or from surplus operating funds and placing them in irrevocable trusts to provide for all future debt service payments on the defeased bonds in years prior to 20Y2. The trust account assets and the liabilities for the defeased bonds are not included in the financial statements. As of June 30, 20Y2, approximately $2.079 billion of bonds outstanding from advance refunding activities is considered defeased.

Business-Type Activities. The State University and the State Building Authority (SBA) defeased various bonds by issuing refunding bonds and placing the proceeds in irrevocable trusts to provide for all future debt service payments on the defeased bonds. The trust assets and the liabilities of the defeased bonds are not included in the business-type activity financial statements. As of June 30, 20Y2, approximately $619 million and $634 million of bonds outstanding from advanced refunding transactions are considered defeased for the State University and SBA, respectively.

If a government accomplished a defeasance during the current year using existing resources, the note would be as follows:

EXAMPLE: *Note X—Defeased Debt Related to Sale of Convention Center.* On December 31, 20X8, Castle Rock County sold the Castle Rock County Convention Center. As of that date, the Convention Center had $100 of outstanding noncallable bonds that mature on December 31, 20Y0. No outstanding insurance was connected to the bonds. To fund the payment of the outstanding noncallable bonds and related interest, the County placed $99.50 into an irrevocable debt defeasance trust held by the County's third-party trustee. The amount placed into escrow plus accrued interest will be enough to pay the entirety of principal and interest on the noncallable bonds at maturity. The assets held in escrow contain obligations guaranteed by the U.S. government denominated in U.S. dollars that are essentially risk free as the escrow's cash flows approximately coincide as to timing and amount with the scheduled interest and principal payments of the defeased debt. Due to the defeasance, the outstanding debt was removed from the liabilities of the County's government-wide financial statements.

CHAPTER 13
PENSION, POSTEMPLOYMENT, AND OTHER EMPLOYEE BENEFIT LIABILITIES

Chapter References:

GASB Statement Nos. 16, 34, 47, 68, 69, 71, 73, 75, 78, 82, 85, 97, 101

GASB Interpretation No. 6

GASB *Implementation Guide*

INTRODUCTION

A state or local government employer often provides several pension, postemployment, and other employee benefits to its employees, the most common ones are:

PART 1:
- Termination benefits,
- Compensated absences,

PART 2:
- Defined benefit pension and other forms of pension benefits, and

PART 3:
- Postemployment benefits other than pensions (OPEB).

PRACTICE ALERT: GASB Statement No. 101 (*Compensated Absences*) replaces GASB Statement No. 16 of the same title upon implementation for periods beginning after December 15, 2023. For those governments that have *not* implemented GASB Statement No. 101, the former discussion in Part 1 has been moved to an Appendix to this chapter.

A common theme among the accounting requirements of these types of benefits is the measurement and recognition of the costs of the benefits at the time the employee works and earns them rather than when they are paid. This chapter addresses the accounting and financial reporting issues related to these types of benefits.

PART 1 TERMINATION BENEFITS AND COMPENSATED ABSENCES

Termination Benefits

GASB Cod. Sec. T25 provides for the accounting and reporting of all forms of employment termination benefits for state and local governments, such as early-retirement incentives, severance pay, and other voluntary or involuntary benefits [GASB Cod. Sec. T25.101].

Termination benefits are specifically excluded from the definition of "pensions." However, termination benefits effectively increase a defined benefit pension liability immediately as no service life remains on the employee, assuming the employee is eligible to receive a defined benefit pension.

OPEB excludes terminating benefits or similar payments usually for sick leave (see also section titled "Compensated Absences" later in this part). But the economic impact of a termination benefit would also increase a defined benefit OPEB liability, as applicable. Terminating employees may also be offered to convert unused sick leave to enhance defined benefit OPEB. This conversion may result in an increase or decrease in defined benefit OPEB. In some situations, this conversion would occur through a pension plan. If through the pension plan, the conversion *would not* be OPEB, but would be pensions [GASB Cod. Secs. P50.104, P52.104].

Termination benefits could be provided in several ways to departing employees. For example, employees could be offered extended healthcare-related termination benefits for a specified period or enhanced defined pension benefits in exchange for early retirement.

GASB Cod. Sec. T25 makes a distinction between "voluntary" and "involuntary" termination benefits. Financial reporting requirements for unemployment compensation programs have separate provisions, which require the programs to be presented in enterprise funds. Compensated absences are also not termination benefits as the employee is continuing service, unless, because of the termination, additional leave is granted. (See also compensated absences provisions.) Benefits are determined based on the nature and circumstances of the separation, including the employer's intent, the plan of termination, whether a retirement age is a factor in the termination and the length of time the benefits are available.

Voluntary Termination Benefits. Voluntary termination benefits are defined as benefits provided by employers to employees as an inducement to hasten the termination of services or because of a voluntary early termination. Examples of voluntary termination benefits include the following:

- Cash payments (one-time or installments), and
- Healthcare coverage when none would otherwise be provided.

Involuntary Termination Benefits. Involuntary termination benefits are defined as benefits arising from the involuntary early termination of services, such as layoffs. Examples of involuntary termination benefits include the following:

- Career counseling,
- Continued access to health insurance through the employer's group plan,
- Outplacement services, and
- Severance pay.

Measurement and Recognition of Termination Benefits

Measurement: Healthcare-Related Termination Benefits. Generally, the measurement criteria require the employer to measure the cost of termination benefits by calculating the discounted present value of expected future benefit payments in accordance with the following requirements, as applicable:

1. Projection of benefits,
2. Healthcare trend rate, and
3. Discount rate.

In certain circumstances, the benefit cost may be based on unadjusted premiums.

Projection of Healthcare Incentive Benefits in an Age-Related Program. Some terminations are large-scale age-related programs, commonly resulting in healthcare incentives for the most senior employees to terminate early. GAAP requires apportionment of benefits provided to terminated employees (and their beneficiaries as applicable) from benefits that will remain provided to active employees. The employer's expected future benefit payments are based on the projected total claims costs, or age-adjusted premiums approximating claims costs for the terminated employees, calculated as follows:

Projected claims costs (or age-adjusted premiums approximating claims costs)	$XX,XXX
Less: Payments (if any) to be made *by the terminated employees for those claims*	(x,xxx)
Employer's expected future benefit payments related to termination	$X,XXX

PRACTICE POINT: This calculation is not utilized if the healthcare-related termination benefit affects the employer's obligation to provide defined benefit OPEB.

Projection of Healthcare Incentive Benefits Not in an Age-Related Program. Other terminations are simply a reduction in labor force without regard to age. In these cases, the apportionment of benefits provided to terminated employees from active employees does not use projected claims costs or age-adjusted premiums. Instead, unadjusted premiums are used for the basis of projection of expected future benefit payments, calculated as follows:

Projected unadjusted premiums	$XX,XXX
Less: Payments (if any) to be made *by the terminated employees*	(x,xxx)
Employer's expected termination benefit payments	$X,XXX

To make the projection, an assumed healthcare cost trend rate is utilized for the periods involved in the employer's commitment to provide the benefits. Factors in the rate may include inflation, probability of utilization of the service, plan provisions, and other elements. A discount rate is also used for the same period, if investments will fund the benefits and excluding investments that are dedicated to fund other services [GASB Cod. Sec. T25.105].

> **PRACTICE POINT:** The provisions of the healthcare cost trend rate and discount rate are discussed later in this chapter regarding defined benefit OPEB and pensions. The rate-setting process is similar and usually involves an actuarial calculation.

> **PRACTICE POINT:** In practice, investments are rarely apportioned to specifically fund termination programs. Also, the payments made by the terminated employees are often zero.

The formulae include a reduction in the employer's cost for payments to be made (if any) by the terminated employees. GASB Cod. Sec. T25.704-1 addresses the effect of the Consolidated Omnibus Reconciliation Act (COBRA) when the former employee may continue to participate in an employer's active employee healthcare plan if the former employee pays 100% of the blended premium rate.

For financial reporting purposes. COBRA benefits are considered a form of healthcare-related termination benefits, which are included in the calculations. If the termination is not part of a large-scale, age-related termination event, GASB Cod. Sec. T25 also allows the government to use blended premium rates as the basis for projection of benefits. The employer would have no expected future benefit payments as the former employee is expected to pay 100% of the blended premium rate. Therefore, no liability would be calculated. But if there were a large-scale layoff and the age-adjusted premium approximating claims costs is different than the former employee's contributions, a liability may be present.

Measurement: Non-Healthcare–Related Termination Benefits. If the benefit terms establish an obligation to pay specific amounts on fixed or determinable dates, the cost of the benefits are required to be measured at the discounted present value of expected future payments. However, if the terms do not establish such an obligation to pay on fixed or determinable dates, the benefit cost may, alternatively, be measured at the undiscounted total of estimated future payments at current cost levels or the discounted present value of expected future benefit payments, including an assumption regarding changes in future cost levels during the period the employer commits to providing the benefits.

If the employer uses discounting, the discount rate considers the estimated yield on investments that will fund the benefits during the period of the benefits, including current and expected asset allocation mix. As previously discussed, in practice, investments to fund termination benefits are rarely apportioned from other operating funds [GASB Cod. Secs. T25.106–.107].

Recognition of Termination Expense and Termination Liabilities in the Government-Wide and Proprietary Fund Financial Statements. An employer is required to recognize a liability and expense for *voluntary* termination benefits, on the accrual basis of accounting, when the employees accept an offer, and the amount can be estimated. The liability is updated with each period the benefits are in effect, adjusting expense (positively or negatively).

> **PRACTICE POINT:** Termination benefits are often a result of a government combination, typically a disposal of an operation. The expense is a period expense and utilized to calculate the gain or loss for the disposal of operations.

An employer is required to recognize a liability and expense for *involuntary* termination benefits, on the accrual basis of accounting, when a plan of termination has been approved by those in authority to commit the employer to the plan, the plan has been communicated to the employees, and the amount can be estimated.

Like voluntary termination benefits, the liability and expense are adjusted each period the benefit is provided.

To have a plan of termination, the following must be communicated:

- At a minimum, the number of employees to be terminated, job classifications, functions, locations, and timing, and
- The terms of the termination in enough detail to allow the employees involved in the termination to determine the value of benefits they will receive if they are involuntarily terminated [GASB Cod. Secs. T25.108–.110].

In rare circumstances, there may be a requirement for the employee to provide future service to receive the termination benefits. These may be related to a work requirement for up to half time work for a specific transition period. The liability and expense for the involuntary portion are then recognized ratably over this future service period, beginning when the plan of termination is approved and communicating to the employees, assuming the amounts may be estimated [GASB Cod. Sec. T25.111].

Recognition in Governmental Fund Financial Statements. In governmental fund financial statements prepared on the modified accrual basis of accounting, termination benefit liabilities and expenditures are recognized to the extent that the liabilities are normally expected to be liquidated with expendable available financial resources like other governmental fund liabilities. If a governmental operation is terminated, the benefit expenditures associated with the termination would be included as part of a special item related to the disposal of operations [GASB Cod. Sec. T25.112].

A reminder that care must be taken regarding termination benefits funded by federal grants. Federal agencies scrutinize termination benefits because many governments will want to charge termination benefits to federal awards so that these benefits have a separate funding source. However, unless an employee worked predominantly for a federally funded program, these costs are not chargeable to a federal award, causing a questioned cost and potentially a refund of the costs to the federal program.

Termination Benefit Impact on Employer's Defined Benefit Pension or OPEB

Termination benefits may enhance defined benefit pension or OPEB payments. For example, an early retirement incentive may provide additional service credits (instead of the employee working X years, additional Y years are credited to service providing an enhancement). If the benefits are provided in this manner, then the calculation of defined benefit pension or OPEB is adjusted, irrespective of whether a trust or equivalent arrangement is utilized [GASB Cod. Sec. T25.113]. (See sections on pensions and OPEB in this chapter).

Note Disclosure of Termination Benefits

GAAP requires the footnotes to include description of:

- The termination benefits arrangements,
- The costs of termination benefits in the period in which the employer becomes obligated if that information is not otherwise identifiable from information displayed on the face of the financial statements, and
- Significant methods and assumptions used in determining the termination benefit liabilities and expenses.

If an employer provides termination benefits that affect defined benefit pension or OPEB liabilities, the employer should disclose the change in those liabilities attributable to the termination benefit. If a termination benefit is not recognized as the expected benefits are not estimable, the event is disclosed with that fact, likely as a contingency [GASB Cod. Secs. T25.114–.117]. The enhanced benefits would also be part of all pensions (or OPEB) elements reported by the employer, note disclosures, and required supplementary information [GASB Cod. Sec. T25.708-1].

COMPENSATED ABSENCES

PRACTICE ALERT: GASB Statement No. 101 (*Compensated Absences*) is discussed in this subsection of Part 1. The Statement recodifies GASB Cod. Sec. C60. The effective date for GASB-101 is for reporting periods beginning after December 15, 2023 (January 1, 2024). Changes required to conform the provisions of GASB-101 are applied through a retroactive restatement of all prior periods presented. For provisions in accordance with GASB Statement No. 16, as amended, please see the Appendix to this chapter. The *Codification* references in the Appendix are the former GASB Cod. Sec. C60.

The provisions of the GAAP for compensated absences contained within GASB Statement No. 101 of the same name, modernize standards for accounting and financial reporting for:

- Compensated absences, and
- Associated salary-related payments, including certain defined *contribution* pensions and other postemployment benefits (which are discussed in Part 2 and Part 3, respectively) [GASB Cod. Sec. C60.101].

Definition of Compensated Absence. Such absences involve leave for which *current* employees may receive one or more of the following:

- Cash payments when the leave is used for time off (which is the most common payment),
- Other cash payments, such as payment for unused leave upon termination of employment (see previous section), or
- Noncash settlements, such as conversion to defined benefit postemployment benefits (see Parts 2 and 3).

The payment or settlement could occur during employment or upon termination of employment. Compensated absences generally do not have a set payment schedule.

Examples of compensated absences include:

- Vacation (or annual) leave,
- Sick leave,
- Paid time off (PTO),
- Holidays,
- Parental leave,
- Bereavement leave, and
- Certain types of sabbatical leave [GASB Cod. Sec. C60.102].

What is Sabbatical Leave? Sabbatical leave is common for tenured employees primarily in public colleges and universities as well as certain employees in other governments. The employee is not required to perform any *significant* duties for the government during the leave [GASB Cod. Sec. C60.103].

PRACTICE POINT: If the duties during a sabbatical are significant, the provisions of GASB Cod. Sec. C60 do not apply. The GASB gives an example of performing research instead of teaching during a sabbatical. Temporary assignments and details would also not be compensated absences. They are not sabbaticals as duties are being performed in separate locations or positions.

PRACTICE POINT: The *termination* of employment provisions in GASB Statement No. 101 links to the provisions in GASB Cod. Sec. T25, which is discussed in the first subsection to this Part [GASB Cod. Sec. C60.104].

Recognition and Measurement of Compensated Absences

> **PRACTICE POINT:** The former recognition and measurement provisions in GASB Statement No. 16 allowed a probable threshold of recognition and two different measurement methods for the compensated absences liability. The probable threshold and measurement methods no longer apply upon implementation of GASB Statement No. 101. Governments with large groups of employees may need to engage an actuary to make the calculations described in this section.

GASB Cod. Sec. C60.106 requires measurement of compensated absences using the economic resources measurement focus (full accrual basis of accounting) as it applies to:

- Leave that has *not* been used, and
- Leave that has been used, *but not settled or paid* (e.g., when someone is paid biweekly or monthly).

If there are applicable salary-related payments coinciding with the leave, they are included in those liabilities [GASB Cod. Sec. C60.106] (see discussion later in this subsection on salary-related payments).

Recognition of Leave That Has Not Been Used. With certain exceptions, a liability is generated if *all* the following occur:

Requirement	Definition
Leave is generated for services rendered,	The employee has performed the services required to earn the leave.
Leave accumulates,	The balance of leave carries forward from one period to another in the future until it is used for paid time off or settled through noncash means.
The leave is *more likely than not* to be used for a compensated absence, or paid in cash, or settled in some noncash means (more likely than not is more than 50%).	Governments will be required to evaluate if the leave will be taken, settled in cash, or through noncash means using potential factors that are relevant.

> **PRACTICE POINT:** The GASB has a nonauthoritative illustration of applying the recognition criteria to leave that has not been used as follows [GASB Statement No. 101, Illustration 1]:

Type of Leave Occurrence	Explanation of Impact on Compensated Absences Liability
PTO carries over without limits, unused paid upon termination.	Some governments offer their employees general PTO that can be used for vacation time, sick time, or other time off, at the discretion of the employee. The leave is attributable to services already rendered because employees earn a certain number of hours or days for each month that they are employed. The leave accumulates because it carries over at the end of the fiscal year. Because there are no limits on carrying over unused leave and any unused leave is paid upon termination of employment, all PTO is more likely than not to be used or paid. *Accordingly, all PTO is recognized as a liability for compensated absences.*
SICK LEAVE carries over without limits, unused paid upon termination.	Governments often offer leave to employees that can be used only when an employee is sick. Some governments allow employees to accumulate sick leave during their employment, but any unused amounts are forfeited upon termination of employment. Such leave is attributable to services already rendered because employees earn a certain number of hours or days for each month that they are employed. The leave accumulates because it carries over at the end of the fiscal year. *The government estimates how much of the leave is more likely than not to be used as paid leave and recognizes that portion as a liability for compensated absences.*
Sick leave that is earned each month, *does not carry over* at the end of the fiscal year, and *is not paid upon termination of employment*. (forfeited).	<u>Leave is not recognized as a liability</u> for compensated absences in annual financial statements.
Similar to previous (no carryover), but forfeited at calendar year-end.	Usually occurs if accumulation is for a number of hours or days each month employed. If the government's fiscal year does not coincide with the calendar year, sick leave accumulates because it does carry over at the end of the fiscal year, even though employees may only have until the end of the calendar year to use it. *The government estimates how much of the leave is more likely than not to be used as paid leave before the leave is forfeited at the end of the calendar year and recognizes that portion as a liability for compensated absences.*

Specific Accounting and Reporting Issues

Type of Leave Occurrence	Explanation of Impact on Compensated Absences Liability
Vacation leave that is made available on the first day of the fiscal year (or at inception of employment) and added to the employee's time bank, but is earned throughout the fiscal year and the balance is reconciled if an employee terminates during the year, carries over at the end of the fiscal year without limits, and is paid upon termination of employment.	Some governments add leave for the entire year into employees' time banks on the first day of the fiscal year (or, for new hires, on their first day of employment) as an *advance* for the year to provide flexibility with regard to when employees may use their paid leave. If an employee terminates during the year, the government reconciles the amount of leave that has been used by the terminating employee against the amount of leave that has been earned by that employee. Therefore, such leave is considered to be attributable to services already rendered only as it is earned by an employee throughout the year. At the beginning of the fiscal year, even though leave has been added to employees's time banks, the leave is not yet attributable to services rendered and, therefore, is not recognized as a liability for compensated absences. By the end of the fiscal year, the unused portion of leave is fully attributable to services rendered because it has been earned by employees throughout the year. Because that leave carries over at the end of the fiscal year, it accumulates. Because there are no limits on carrying over unused leave and any unused leave is paid upon termination of employment, all of the vacation leave is more likely than not to be used or paid. *The vacation leave at the end of the year is recognized as a liability for compensated absences.*
Compensatory time that is earned as employees work overtime and carries over at the end of the fiscal year. Per state statute, unused compensatory time is not forfeited and is required to be paid upon termination of employment.	Some governments offer employees compensatory time (often referred to as "comp time") if they work overtime or on holidays or weekends. Such leave is attributable to services already rendered because it is earned as the employees work overtime or on holidays or weekends. The leave accumulates because it carries over at the end of the fiscal year. Because there are no limits on carrying over unused compensatory time and any unused compensatory time is paid upon termination of employment, *all of the compensatory time is more likely than not to be paid.* Thus, *all compensatory time is recognized as a liability for compensated absences.*

Type of Leave Occurrence	Explanation of Impact on Compensated Absences Liability
Parental Leave	Many governments allow employees to take extended periods of paid leave due to the birth or adoption of a child. Parental leave is not subject to the recognition criteria. Instead, GASB Cod. Sec. C60.112 states that parental leave is recognized when the leave commences. A liability for the entire leave is recognized at the time an employee goes on leave.

Recognition of Relevant Factors to Determine if Leave Will be Used or Settled. A more likely than not threshold is used (more than 50%). To determine if leave may be used, governments may want to review the following factors:

- The government's employment policies related to compensated absences,
- Whether leave that has been earned is, or will become, eligible for use or payment in the future,
- Historical information about the use, payment, or forfeiture of compensated absences, and
- Information known to the government that would indicate that historical information may not be representative of future trends or patterns [GASB Cod. Secs. C60.107–.110].

PRACTICE POINT: Governments may allow the balance of accumulated leave to be valued on a regular basis and deposited as an employee contribution to a defined benefit plan. Commonly, these are termed "sick leave" conversions. Typically, they are used to convert to OPEB plans. Such conversions are not included in the liability for compensated absences [GASB Cod. Sec. C60.111].

Sporadic Leave and Other Exceptions. Many absences occur on a haphazard basis due to parental leave, jury duty, military call ups and similar. Sick leave and unrestricted sabbatical leave are not sporadic due to their accumulation factors. The GASB provides an exception for the liability accumulation provisions for sporadic leave as it cannot be determined in advance. No liability is declared until the leave occurs but is unpaid [GASB Cod. Sec. C60.112].

Other exceptions in GASB Cod. Sec. C60 include:

- *Unlimited Leave*—leave with no specific time limits, and
- *Holiday Leave*—which is taken on a specific date, but *not* at the discretion of employees (known as "floating holidays" which would generate a liability) [GASB Cod. Sec. C60.113].

Measurement of Compensated Absences if Required to be Calculated. For recognized leave recognized due to GASB Cod. Secs. C60.106–.110 and .112, the employee's pay rate is used *as of the date of the financial statements*, unless one of the following exceptions occurs:

- Some (or all) of the leave is to be paid at a different rate to the employee at the time the payment is made. For example, sick leave is paid at 50% of current compensation upon termination (sometimes termed "the golden handcuffs"), or
- Leave is part of a shared leave pool, in which case, the liability would be at an estimated rate using the eligible population, or
- If some (or all) of the leave is settled through noncash means, *other than conversion to a defined benefit OPEB plan*. In such cases, only the amount that is more likely than not to be settled is used [GASB Cod. Secs. C60.114–.117].

Pay Rate Used in Measurement of Liability Changes from Period to Period. Rates of pay commonly change. If the rate changes during a period, the change is recognized in the period of change [GASB Cod. Sec. C60.118].

Leave that Has Been Used but Unpaid. Leave is commonly used outside of alignment to pay periods. Leave that has been used generates a liability if unpaid in cash or settled by noncash means. The liability is measured using the amount of cash paid or noncash settlement used for the leave [GASB Cod. Sec. C60.119].

Salary-Related Payments (including Social Security and Medicare Taxes). As an employee renders services, salary-related payments are generated. Such payments can be fixed, or variable based on an hourly amount. The payments are included with the compensated absences liability if they are *directly* and *incrementally* associated with the leave with certain exceptions. This is explained as follows:

Related Payment	Explanation
Directly Associated	Payment is a function of the salary paid (rises or falls depending on the salary).
Incrementally Associated	Payment is *in addition* to the salary to be paid.

These payments add to the compensated absence liability at the rate of pay in effect as of the date of the financial statements. Changes to the rate of pay are period expenses.

Like other payments, the salary-related payment may be associated with only a portion of the leave. For example, there may be a "cap" or "floor" (limit or minimum, respectively) to the salary-related payment. There may also be a limit to when the salary-related payment can occur, such as upon termination. If upon termination, then only the amount that is more likely than not to be used for time off is included as part of the liability.

If the salary-related payment is contributed to a defined contribution pensions or OPEB plan, the liability is recognized and reported as a pension or OPEB expense, as applicable, and as further discussed in Parts 2 and 3. Salary-related payments for defined benefit plans are excluded in the measurement of compensated absences [GASB Cod. Secs. C60.120–.124].

Relationship to Defined Pensions and OPEB. The impact of compensated absences does not impact defined benefit postemployment benefits liabilities and vice versa. But some governments do allow sick leave conversions upon termination for payment of the employee's share of future healthcare premiums. If the leave has not been used but is required to be recognized and is more likely than not to be paid, then the liability is measured in accordance with GASB Cod. Secs. C60.114–.115 [GASB Cod. Secs. C60.125–.126].

Recognition in Governmental Funds

Under *current GAAP*, the liability would be recognized in a governmental fund in accordance with the current financial resources measurement focus and modified accrual basis of accounting. For example, if the liability was incurred before the end of the period, but paid in the future period, a liability would be recognized [GASB Cod. Sec. C60.127].

Required Notes to the Basic Financial Statements for Compensated Absences

Compensated absence liability amounts are presented as part of the schedule of long-term liabilities in the notes to the basic financial statements. Liabilities presented within this schedule include:

1. Beginning-and end-of-year balances (regardless of whether prior-year data are presented on the face of the government-wide financial statements),
2. Increases and decreases (separately presented),
3. The portions of each item that are due within one year of the statement date, and
4. Which governmental funds typically have been used to liquidate other long-term liabilities (such as pension liabilities) in prior years [GASB Cod. Sec. 2300.120].

The increase and decrease provisions are amended by GASB Statement No. 101, *solely for compensated absences*. The GASB allows a net increase or decrease if it is captioned as a net amount. Further, the provision of which governmental funds typically have been used to liquidate compensated absences no longer is required to be presented due to the provisions of GASB Statement No. 101.

PRACTICE POINT: The updated disclosure is contained in Chapter 17 of the *Governmental GAAP Practice and Disclosures Manual*.

PART 2 EMPLOYER PENSION AND OTHER FORMS OF PENSION BENEFITS

Governmental employers may provide postemployment benefits through a defined benefit pension plan, a defined contribution plan or in some cases, a hybrid. For the most part, the standards address issues related to defined benefit pension or defined benefit other postemployment benefit (OPEB) plans, which are common types of plans adopted by state or local governmental employers. *OPEB benefits are discussed in Part 3.*

> **PRACTICE POINT:** The GASB has published several hundred questions related to pensions and other forms of benefits in the *Implementation Guide* covering many scenarios. Many sections to this chapter could have been added for the various scenarios and are therefore not included due to their granularity. OPEB has similar largess of questions and answers.

> **PRACTICE POINT:** Pension and OPEB *plan* reporting is discussed in Chapter 22.

The following GASB *Codification* sections are applicable for various pension liabilities:

	Pensions				
GASB *Codification* Section	P20	P21	P22	P23	P24
GASB Statement Nos.	68, 73, 78, 82, 85	68, 85	73, 82, 85	73	73, 85
Situation:					
Employer that is a member or sponsor of a defined benefit plan	Yes				
Employer that is a member or sponsor of a defined contribution plan (see **PRACTICE POINT** on defined contribution plans, GASB-97)		Yes			
Employer that is a member or sponsor of a defined benefit plan *not provided through a trust or equivalent arrangement*			Yes		
Reporting of assets accumulated for defined benefit *not provided through a trust or equivalent arrangement*				Yes	
Reporting of assets accumulated for defined contribution *not provided through a trust or equivalent arrangement*					Yes
Special funding situations	Yes	Yes	Yes		

As indicated above, all the statements in some capacity also provide guidance for defined contribution plans. In a defined contribution plan, future payments to an employee are based on the amounts contributed to the plan, earnings on those investments, and forfeitures allocated to an employee's account. A defined contribution plan does not create the difficult accounting and reporting issues raised by a defined benefit plan.

> **PRACTICE POINT:** In a special funding situation, a participating non-employer may have more than one liability. Typically, this occurs in teachers' retirement systems where a state pays some (or all) of the pension benefits.

PENSIONS

The Basic Provisions of Pensions

A *pension plan* is

> [A]n arrangement through which pensions are determined, assets dedicated for pensions are accumulated and managed, and benefits are paid as they come due [GASB Cod. Sec. P20.537].

This definition is extremely important in delineating what a pension is, especially for a defined contribution pension or other employee benefit arrangement.

Defined Benefit Pensions. These pensions are arrangements for which the income or other benefits that the plan member will receive at or after separation from employment are defined by the benefit terms. Those terms may include not being able to receive funds from the Plan until the participant reaches retirement age as defined in the plan. The pensions may be stated as a specified dollar amount or as an amount that is calculated based on one or more factors such as age, years of service, and compensation [GASB Cod. Sec. Pe5.517]. Many traditional pension plans of state and local governments are defined benefit plans. However, some are closing to new entrants in order to manage liabilities. *Defined contribution plans* and other employee benefit arrangements are increasing in prevalence as a result.

The Importance of Trusts. For a defined benefit pension as provided to the employees of state and local government employers from a pension plan that are administered through trusts or equivalent arrangements (jointly referred to as trusts), all the following must be present:

- Contributions from employers and nonemployer contributing entities to the pension plan and earnings on those contributions are irrevocable. In some instances, payments are made by the employer to satisfy contribution requirements identified in plan documents normally from plan members. Those amounts are classified as *employee* contributions, including for determining a cost-sharing employer's proportion. They may be classified as salaries, wages, or fringe benefits on the employer's records.

- Pension plan assets are dedicated solely to provide pensions to plan members in accordance with the benefit plan terms. Pension plan assets used for administrative costs or to refund employee contributions in accordance with the plan terms is also allowable.

- Pension plan assets are legally protected from the creditors of employers, nonemployer contributing entities, the pension plan administrator, and the creditors of the plan members [GASB Cod. Sec. P20.101].

The advantages to using a trust or equivalent arrangement are primarily monetary and security. If assets are accumulated in the trust, investment earnings are generated that may in the long-term, offset a portion, if not all, of a related pension (or OPEB) liability. As the assets are protected from creditors, shielding occurs in bankruptcy.

> **PRACTICE ALERT:** During November 2022, the City of Chester, Pennsylvania filed for municipal bankruptcy in the United States Bankruptcy Court in the Eastern District of Pennsylvania (Philadelphia) (Petition 22-13032-amc). The largest creditor in the filing was the City of Chester Aggregate Pension Fund with an unsecured claim of $103,200,000 at the time of filing for police, plus an additional $16,900,000 claim as part of the filing for firefighters and $7,100,000 for officers and employees. Other governments within the Commonwealth of Pennsylvania are also creditors. Under GAAP, if a trust is in place, any assets should be shielded from creditors. It is unclear at the time of publication how and will the City's Pension Fund will be made whole by the bankruptcy.

The components of a defined benefit pension are:

- Retirement income, and
- Postemployment benefits other than retirement income (death benefits, life insurance and disability), *only if provided through the pension plan*. Otherwise, such benefits are OPEB benefits.

The benefits are received at (or after) separation from employment are defined by benefit terms. Common factors determining the benefits are compensation, years of service, age and whether survivors of the beneficiary are entitled to the benefit. The basic benefit plan is usually well-documented in law, regulation or even state constitutional provisions. Variations may occur due to collective bargaining or early retirement incentive programs [GASB Cod. Secs. P20.106–.107].

Defined Contribution Pensions. These pensions have terms that include:

- An individual account for each employee,
- The contributions that an employer is required to make (or the credits that it is required to provide) to an active employee's account are for periods in which that employee renders service, and
- There are provisions that the pensions an employee will receive will depend *only* on:
  — The contributions (or credits) to the employee's account,
  — Actual earnings on investments of those contributions (or credits), and
  — The effects of forfeitures of contributions (or credits) made for other employees, as well as
  — Pension plan administrative costs, that are allocated to the employee's account [GASB Cod. Sec. P20.108].

Defined benefit pension plans are classified according to:

- The number of employers whose employees are provided pensions through the pension plan; and
- Whether pension obligations and pension plan assets are *shared*.

Classification of Pension and OPEB Arrangements. The following are the classification of employers regarding pensions and OPEB:

1. *Single employers* are those whose employees are provided with defined benefit pensions through single-employer pension plans—pension plans in which pensions are provided to the employees of *only one employer*. An example of this is where a city public safety force has its own pension plan.
2. *Agent employers* are those whose employees are provided with defined benefit pensions through agent multiple-employer pension plans. Agent-multiple-employer pension plans are entities where plan assets are pooled for investment purposes, but separate accounts are maintained for each individual employer so that each employer's share of the pooled assets is legally available to pay the benefits of *only the employer's employees and no other employer in the plan*. Many local governments are members of larger statewide plans that are agent-multiple-employer plans.
3. *Cost-sharing employers* are those whose employees are provided with defined benefit pensions through cost-sharing multiple-employer pension plans. These pension plans are where the pension obligations to the employees of more than one employer are pooled and plan assets can be used to pay the benefits of the employees *of any employer* that provides pensions through the pension plan. Some local governments are members of countywide cost-sharing plans [GASB Cod. Sec. P20.109–.111].

Certain governments may have employees who are provided with defined benefit pensions through a cost-sharing plan that:

- Is not a state or local governmental pension plan,
- Is used to provide defined benefit pensions *both* to employees of state or local government employers *and* to employees of nongovernmental employers, and
- Has no predominant state or local governmental employer (either individually or collectively with other governmental employers through the pension plan).

These plans are colloquially known as "Taft-Hartley" plans and are typically administered by unions on behalf of their members. Specific note disclosure provisions are for employers with members in such plans due to the plan not being a government [GASB Cod. Sec. P20.112].

PRACTICE POINT: Two *Implementation Guide* questions discuss situations when a pension or OPEB plan is administered through a trust but has no governing board, which is common in defined contribution plans. Should the plans be included as a fiduciary component unit of the government? Generally, pension and OPEB plans that are administered through trusts are legally separate entities. In determining whether those legally separate entities are component units, a primary government is considered to have a financial burden relative solely to a *defined benefit* plan (pension or OPEB) if it is legally obligated or has otherwise assumed to have the obligation to make contributions to such plans.

13,018 *Specific Accounting and Reporting Issues*

In accordance with GASB Cod. Sec. 2100.120(a), a government is financially accountable for a legally separate organization if it appoints a voting majority of the organization's governing body and there is a potential for the organization to provide specific financial benefits to, or impose specific financial burdens on, the government. For purposes of that paragraph, a government (e.g., a sponsoring government) that performs the duties of a governing board in the absence of one *should be considered equivalent to a governing board* for which the government appoints a voting majority, but only in the case of a defined benefit plan.

Internal Revenue Code Section 457(b) Deferred Compensation Plans and 403(b) Tax Sheltered Annuity Plans—Overview. There are also employee benefit plans that are not postemployment benefit plans. As an example, IRC Section 457(b) plans are *deferred compensation* plans (see later in this Part), and not a pension plan. IRC Section 403(b) plans primarily offered to educators are not required by the IRC to have trust agreements or equivalent arrangements as participants are directed to tax sheltered annuities or custodial accounts, which are regulated similarly to trusts. IRC Section 403(b) *tax sheltered annuity* plans are also subject to rules within the IRC requiring contributions to result in benefits exclusive to participants. Yet, many practitioners view these plans to be legally separate from sponsoring governments. Governmental employers or sponsors of such plans may also contribute to the plans, but due to the provisions of GASB Cod. Secs. 1300 and D25, such plans may not be reported within the basic financial statements.

For Internal Revenue Code Section 457 plans, if such plans meet the definition of a pension plan, then the provisions of GAAP related to pension plans apply, including for Section 457 plans that are defined benefit plans (which are rare). If the 457 plan does not meet the definition of a pension plan, then the provisions of GASB Cod. Sec. 1300 would apply. As a practical matter, few such plans that are not defined benefit plans may be controlled by the sponsoring government and therefore, may not be reported as fiduciary activities

Due to these provisions, for many general-purpose governments:

- Unless a component unit that is fiduciary in nature that is a defined benefit pension or OPEB plan held in trust exists in accordance with GASB Cod. Secs. 1300 and 2100, other arrangements may not be reported as pension and other employee benefit trust funds.

- Defined contribution plan reporting would be limited to those situations where the government is a pension plan held in trust, or in the case of a circumstance in which assets from entities that are not part of the reporting entity are accumulated for pensions (held in a custodial fund) and in both cases, where the government controls the assets of the arrangement. If the investments in the plan are self-directed by the participants, the government would not have control and the plan would not be reported as a pension and other employee benefit trust fund, or a custodial fund.

The Number of Defined Benefit Plans Reported by an Employer. Determining how many defined benefit plans to report may be difficult for an employer. If assets accumulated in a defined benefit pension plan for the payment of benefits may be legally used to pay benefits (and refunds) to *any* employee, the total assets are in *one plan*. This is even the case if separate reserves, funds, accounts, groups, benefit provisions or similar are maintained.

Separate actuarial valuations may be performed for different classes of employees or groups resulting in different contribution rates, benefits, or other formulas. This is most commonly the case for public safety or other hazardous duty employees. Even if assets are pooled with other assets for investment purposes, a separate defined benefit plan should be reported based on meeting *both* the following criteria:

- The portion of assets accumulated is solely for the payment of benefits to those classes or groups of employees or to the active or inactive employees of those classes or groups, and

- The portion of assets *may not* be legally used to pay benefits to other classes or groups of employees or other entities' employees.

If the asset portion meets *both* criteria, it is a separate plan for reporting purposes [GASB Cod. Sec. P20.113].

PRACTICE POINT: A common misnomer is when a plan includes an employer and a discretely presented component unit. In some cases, preparers judge such a plan to be a multiple-employer plan. GAAP requires a primary government *and* its component units be considered *one employer* for both pensions and OPEB.

What are Special Funding Situations? Special funding situations are circumstances in which a nonemployer entity (typically a state) is *legally responsible* for making contributions *directly* to a pension (or OPEB) plan that is used to pay pensions (or OPEB) of another entity (or group of entities) and certain circumstances exist as follows:

Special Funding Situation Exists with EITHER of These Circumstances	Special Funding Situation DOES NOT Exist
The value of contributions for which the nonemployer entity legally is responsible *is not dependent upon one or more events* or circumstances unrelated to the pensions (or OPEB). Examples of conditions that meet this criterion include: 1. A circumstance in which the nonemployer entity is required by statute to contribute a defined percentage of an employer's payroll directly to the pension (or OPEB) plan, and	Examples of situations in which the value of contributions *is* dependent upon an event or circumstance that is unrelated to pensions (or OPEB) include: • A circumstance in which the nonemployer entity is required to make contributions to the pension (or OPEB) plan based on a specified percentage of a given revenue source, such as taxation, and

Specific Accounting and Reporting Issues

Special Funding Situation Exists with EITHER of These Circumstances	Special Funding Situation DOES NOT Exist
2. A circumstance in which the nonemployer entity is required by the terms of a pension plan to contribute directly to the pension (or OPEB) plan a statutorily defined proportion of the employer's required contributions to the pension (or OPEB) plan.	• A circumstance in which the nonemployer entity is required to make contributions to the pension (or OPEB) plan equal to the amount by which the nonemployer entity's ending fund balance exceeds a defined threshold amount, such as a percentage of a so-called "rainy-day fund" or stabilization account.
The nonemployer entity is the *only entity* with a legal obligation to make contributions *directly* to a pension (or OPEB) plan.	Resources are provided directly to the employer and not the plan, regardless of purpose.

The most common special funding situations are related to teachers' pensions (and OPEB). For example, municipal aid is provided to school districts by a state for general purposes, including the school district's contributions to a statewide teacher retirement system. But GAAP stipulates that special funding situations do *not* include circumstances where resources are provided to the *employer* and not to the plan regardless of the purpose for which those resources are provided. In that case, the aid is not indicative of a special funding situation. The aid is presented as revenue by the school district [GASB Cod. Sec. P20.114].

DEFINED BENEFIT PENSIONS—SINGLE AND AGENT EMPLOYERS

Recognition and Measurement with No Special Funding Situation

The Net Pension Liability. Employers recognize a liability for the *net pension liability*. To calculate this number, actuaries measure the portion of the actuarial present value of projected benefit payments that is attributed to every employee's past period of service in accordance with the plan's benefit terms. The resulting present value is the *total pension liability*. The total pension liability is then netted by the pension plan's fiduciary net position. The fiduciary net position determination uses the same valuation methods used by the plan to prepare its statement of fiduciary net position.

> **PRACTICE POINT:** Plans with no fiduciary net position (usually without a trust) report only the total pension liability.

The Importance of Dates. The net pension liability is determined as of a date known as the *measurement date*. This date can be no earlier than the end of the *employer's prior fiscal year* and consistently applied from period to period.

> **Example:** An employer's fiscal year-end is June 30, 20Y0. The measurement date can be no earlier than June 30, 20X9 (one year prior) and consistently applied from period to period.

PRACTICE POINT: If the measurement date changes, a new actuarial valuation would be necessary (see following discussion). For financial reporting purposes, a beginning balance restatement would be required. Choice of a measurement date needs to be extremely precise.

Many employers present multiple plans. Different pension plans may be displayed in the aggregate in the Statement of Net Position. However, if some plans are in asset positions (net pension assets), they should be displayed separately from plans in liability positions (net pension liabilities) [GASB Cod. Secs. P20.119–.120].

Actuarial Valuations and Assumptions. The *total pension liability* is determined by:

- An actuarial valuation as of the measurement date (explained previously), or
- Using update procedures to "roll-forward" to the measurement date amounts from an actuarial valuation performed as of a date no more than 30 months plus 1 day earlier than the employer's most recent fiscal year-end.

PRACTICE POINT: The reason one day was added to the actuarial valuation limit is due to many plans allowing for additional creditable service if serving one day into the next period. For example, some plans may allow for an additional month or even an additional year by serving just one day into the next period. Therefore, the actuarial valuation would potentially be materially misstated if many employees retire as of the first day of a period without this adjustment.

Example: An employer's fiscal year-end is June 30, 20Y0. The measurement date can be no earlier than June 30, 20X9 (one year prior) and consistently applied from period to period. An actuarial valuation can be performed as of a date no more than 30 months plus 1 day earlier than June 30, 20Y0, which would be no earlier than 12/31/20X7.

If update procedures are performed and changes occur in the period of updating to the plan, management should use judgment to determine the nature and extent of procedures needed to update the actuarial valuation.

PRACTICE POINT: If a change in the plan occurs that could be material, a new actuarial valuation may be needed. A material change is usually due to legislation or major collective bargaining agreement. Management may also determine a new valuation is needed due to a major change in a discount rate.

GAAP requires actuarial valuations at least every two years. Once set, the valuation must occur on the same day in the same pattern. For example, if a government has the valuations every two years as of December 31st, December 31st must be used for the valuations in the future or else a change in accounting principle will occur, requiring a beginning balance restatement for all periods presented. More frequent valuations are encouraged [GASB Cod. Sec. P20.121]. The "as of" date of the valuation is known as the *actuarial valuation date* [GASB Cod. Sec. P20.506]. Many practitioners shorten the term to *valuation date*.

PRACTICE POINT: Most large plans perform valuations annually.

GAAP only allows the entry-age actuarial cost method to be used *for financial reporting purposes*. Any other method may be used for operating purposes, however, translation between the two methods may be needed for decision makers to understand their differences. These differences are known as *deviations*.

Benefit projections must be based on the plan provisions existing at the measurement date. Actuarial standards of practice as established by the Actuarial Standards Board (not GASB) are used to calculate the total pension liability and related pension elements required to be disclosed [GASB Cod. Sec. P20.122].

Benefit provisions may be in contract or law. The effects of projected salary changes, projected service credits, and projected automatic benefit changes (including cost of living adjustments (COLAs)) are included in the calculations. If COLAs are not automatically provided, if there is a pattern of granting that is "substantially automatic," then these "ad hoc" COLAs are also included to the extent of their granting.

In some cases, an *allocated insurance contract* is used to stabilize benefit payments. In an allocated insurance contract, the beneficiary's name is included. The insurer has an irrevocable responsibility to provide the benefits to the beneficiary. If all payments are made to acquire the contract have been made by the employer and the likelihood is *remote* that the employer (or the pension plan) will be required to make additional payments to satisfy the benefit payments covered by the contract, the allocated insurance contract is excluded from projected benefit payments and therefore, not part of the pension liability [GASB Cod. Sec. P20.124].

Benefit payments are discounted to their actuarial present value using a formula comprising a single discount rate that is derived from:
- A long-term expected rate of return on pension plan investments to the extent that the pension plan's fiduciary net position is projected to be enough to pay benefits and pension plan assets are expected to be invested using a strategy to achieve that return, and
- A tax-exempt, high-quality municipal bond rate to the extent that the conditions for use of the long-term expected rate of return are not met.

These two rates are compared using cash flows to the point where funds available to pay benefits in the future are insufficient to pay benefits. At that point, the high-quality (typically AA or better) municipal bond rate is used [GASB Cod. Sec. P20.125].

Pension, Postemployment, and Other Employee Benefit Liabilities

> **PRACTICE POINT:** During periods of economic uncertainty, the discount rate setting process may be problematic and under pressure. A key element is the *long-term* expected rate of return on plan assets. The more cash flow needed to fund benefits, the less plan assets earning a rate of return. The volatile markets could have a significant impact on this equation. Care must be taken in the selection of reasonable assumptions.

The two rates are then solved together to provide one stream of cash flows at the updated discount rate until all benefits are paid as of the measurement date. Determining the discount rate is an iterative process performed by actuaries that will build a table consisting of:

- *Payroll*—Current employees with projected salary increases and future employees expected to be hired with *their* salary increases into the future.
- *Employee Contribution percentages*—Employee contribution percentages are based on current statute or plan provisions (which may be different for current versus future employees that have different rates dependent upon date of hire). If employees are noncontributory, zero would be used. The percentages contributed would be multiplied by the payroll amounts.
- *Employer Contribution percentages*—Similarly to employee contributions, the percentages are based upon current statute or plan provisions.
- *Benefit payments*—These would be projected by the actuary in accordance with the entry age actuarial cost method, as described previously.
- *Service costs*—This is the annual expense that an employee earns based upon service and the current statute or plan provisions.
- *Beginning plan fiduciary net position*—This would be the beginning balance held in trust for the payment of benefits.
- *Administrative expense*—This would be the current administrative expense and projected forward with increases into the future.
- *The long-term expected rate of return on plan assets*—This would be used to provide an estimate of investment rate of return on plan assets (must be held in trust).
- *The tax-exempt high-quality general obligation rate*—This needs to be known if indeed the plan will run out of funds to pay remaining benefits to be paid as of the valuation date.

A very high-level view of the calculation is as follows:

- Beginning fiduciary net position, *plus*
- Projected total contributions from employers, including nonemployer contributing entities, along with current as well as future employees (if applicable) based upon the rates, *less*
- Projected benefit payments, *less*
- Projected administrative expense, *plus*
- Projected investment earnings, *equals*
- Ending fiduciary net position.

For each year into the future, the projected beginning fiduciary net position and the projected benefit payments are then compared. If the projected benefit payment for the year is *less than* the beginning fiduciary net position, then it is "funded" with plan assets. This calculation continues the same way until the fiduciary net position is insufficient to fund projected benefits however many years into the future. The point when fiduciary net position is *insufficient* to fund benefit payments that are remaining is known as the "cross-over" point. The remainder of the benefit payments must then be funded by investments at the tax-exempt high-quality general obligation rate.

Both streams of projected benefit payments are then discounted at the present value of each rate until all projected benefits are paid for current and future employees, which may be many decades into the future. GASB Cod. Sec. P20.901, Illustration 1 contains a thorough example of how to calculate the discount rate [GASB Cod. Secs. P20.126–.130].

PRACTICE POINT: An example of the calculation is not shown in the *Governmental GAAP Guide* due to its complexity. GASB's OPEB standards use a similar calculation for the discount rate (however for OPEB, the discount rate in many cases is not a large driver of the OPEB liability due to projected healthcare claims costs). In practice, actuaries usually perform the calculation, but management is ultimately responsible for its reasonableness.

PRACTICE POINT: If a plan has a significant amount of fiduciary net position in relation to its total pension liability, the "cross-over" point is well into the future. In some cases where law stipulates "full funding," the cross-over point may never occur, allowing the use of the long-term expected rate of return on plan assets. If a plan does not have a significant amount of fiduciary net position, the "cross-over" point will be more current, therefore lowering the discount rate and raising the pension liability. If there is no trust present, there is no fiduciary net position (assets), necessitating a lower discount rate and higher total pension (or OPEB) liability.

The present value of the projected benefit payments is then required to be attributed to periods of employee service using the entry age actuarial cost method with each period's service cost determined as a level percentage of pay. The actuarial present value is required to be attributed for each employee individually, from the period when the employee first accrues pensions through the period when the employee retires.

The elements of the projections are applied as follows using the entry age actuarial cost method:

- Attribution should be made on an employee-by-employee basis rather than on an entire group.

- Service costs should be level as a percentage of an employee's projected payroll. If an employee does not have projected pay, the projected inflation rate can also be used instead of a projected rate of change in salary.
- The beginning of the attribution period should be the period in which the employee was hired.
- A single exit age, based on retirement, should be used for all benefits. For DROP plans (described elsewhere in this chapter), the date of entry into the drop is the date of retirement.
- The service costs attributed to all periods should be based on a single measure of the present value of the employee's projected benefit payments. Differences between actual and expected experience should reduce or increase the total pension liability of the employer(s) [GASB Cod. Sec. P20.131].

Single and Agent-Multiple-Employers: Financial Reporting, Notes, and Required Supplementary Information

Pension Expense, Deferred Outflows of Resources, Deferred Inflows of Resources, Support of Non-employers. Annual pension expense is calculated by the summation of work multiplied by the items contained within the benefit plan structure and resulting in changes to the components of the net pension liability. Deferred outflows of resources and deferred inflows of resources change by amortization of changes between estimated amounts and actual amounts of various aspects of the liability, including investments, demographics, and plan structure.

Succinctly, the following are elements of pension expense:

Element of Pension Expense	Does Element Increase or Decrease Pension Expense?
Service cost, excluding employee contributions	Increases
Employee contributions	Decreases
Interest on beginning total pension liability	Increases
Changes in benefit terms	May increase or decrease
Plan administrative costs	Increase
Projected earnings on plan investments	Decreases
Amortization of deferred outflows of resources (or deferred inflows of resources) for differences between expected and actual experience, changes in assumptions, net differences between projected and actual earnings	Increases (or decreases in the case of amortizations of deferred inflows of resources)
Other adjustments	May increase or decrease
Employer contributions to the plan	No impact to expense as contributions increase fiduciary net position
Contributions to the pension plan from nonemployer contributing entities *that are not in a special funding situation*	Does *not* adjust pension expense, reported as revenue (Example: intergovernmental revenue or aid)

Most changes to the net pension liability will occur in the period of change, especially in a change of a plan that only affects retirees or beneficiaries with no remaining service to the employer. Current-period service cost, interest on the total pension liability also is expensed immediately. However, projected earnings on the pension plan's investments are also included in the determination of the annual pension expense.

Demographic and economic assumption changes and differences between expected and actual experience are recorded as deferred inflows of resources or deferred outflows of resources and amortized to pension expense annually in a systematic and rational manner over a closed period equal to the average of the expected remaining service lives of all employees that are provided with benefits through the pension plan (active employees and inactive employees), beginning with the current period.

The effect on the net pension liability of differences between the projected earnings on pension plan investments and actual experience regarding those earnings is required to be included in pension expense in a systematic and rational manner over a closed period of five years, beginning with the current period. Changes in the net pension liability not included in pension expense are required to be reported as deferred outflows of resources or deferred inflows of resources related to pensions.

Finally, if employer contributions are made after the measurement date of the net pension liability, they are required to be reported as deferred outflows of resources not only in the government-wide financial statements, but potentially in the fund financial statements that paid the contributions [GASB Cod. Secs. P20.132–.133].

OBSERVATION: One of the major changes in mindset with the implementation of the updated pension standards, which occurred long ago, was the annual required contribution (ARC). The ARC may still be prepared for management (internal) purposes and in terminology used by management (or in law). In its basis for conclusions to GASB-68, the GASB explained that by (a) requiring employers to report measures such as the ARC introduced and the extent to which they contributed the ARC and (b) establishing parameters (including a maximum amortization period for unfunded actuarial liabilities) for the calculation of those measures, the GASB was viewed as having established de-facto contribution policy standards. Many governments accepted this and even had the calculation of an ARC written into law or similar ordinance, even though it was not meant to be required and with the ability to do biennial actuarial valuations as a component of prior GAAP, the ARC was certainly not meant to be an annual requirement.

GASB made clear the separation between its objectives related to establishing standards for the financial reporting of pensions by employers, on the one hand, and public policy matters such as pension contribution policy, on the other. Consistent with this distinction, GASB did not establish an ARC or similar measure in the updated standards. As a result, the GASB did not believe that it would be appropriate to require disclosures about a standardized measure of the amount an employer would need to contribute to a pension plan each year as part of a systematic contribution pension plan to reach projected objectives.

PRACTICE POINT: For agent-multiple employers, receiving the information from an agent-multiple employer plan to record in the basic financial statements, notes to the basic financial statements, and required supplementary information appears to be a challenge. The plans need to present each employer with a financial statement, the note disclosure, and required supplementary information. If the plan has hundreds of employers and performs allocations of investment revenues and administrative expenses to the various employers, the timely presentation of this information is a challenge.

The AICPA's Audit & Accounting Guide, *State and Local Governments*, Chapter 13, Part II and especially Appendix A to Chapter 13, contain guidance requiring the information to be transmitted from the plans to the employers to be audited separately from the audit of the plan's financial statements. As an alternative, an internal controls engagement may be performed in accordance with AT-C Section 320 (*Reporting on an Examination of Controls at a Service Organization Relevant to User Entities' Internal Control Over Financial Reporting*). Controls may be required to be tested based on management's assertion that internal controls are suitably designed and have been operating effectively for an entire year under audit (also known as a Type 2 report). For single employer plans, increased testing on census data and the information transfer occurs. Therefore, in both cases time can be saved by accomplishing some of these elements off-cycle to the date of the basic financial statements.

Within governmental fund statements, a net pension liability may be recorded, but only to the extent that it would be liquidated with current financial resources (potentially the accrued amount for the next fiscal period). Pension expenditures include the amounts that have been paid by the employer to the pension plan and the change in the beginning and ending net pension liability as recorded in the funds, not on the government-wide financial statements.

Governmental funds may also report revenue from the support of nonemployer contributing entities. The revenue is the total of amounts paid during the period by nonemployer contributing entities to the plan and the change between nonemployer contributing entities beginning and ending balances of amounts *normally* expected to be liquidated with expendable available financial resources [GASB Cod. Secs. P20.135–.136].

Notes to the Basic Financial Statements for Single and Agent Employers. For single and agent-multiple employers, the notes to the basic financial statements include disclosure of all pension-related elements applicable to the employer if not otherwise identifiable from information contained in the basic financial statements. The information is disclosed by the plan in which the employer participates but avoids unnecessary duplication.

For component units provided through pensions through the same single-employer or agent plan, the note disclosures should separately identify the elements associated with the primary government with its blended component units and those associated with discretely presented component units.

> **PRACTICE POINT:** Discretely presented component unit disclosure in this area may not be deemed essential by management. See Chapter 4 on discretely presented component unit disclosure in a primary government's notes to the basic financial statements.

The notes commence with descriptive information about the pension plan through which benefits are provided, as applicable:

1. The name of the pension plan, identification of the public employee retirement system (PERS) or other entity that administers the pension plan, and identification of the pension plan as a single-employer or agent pension plan.
2. A brief description of the benefit terms, including:
   a. The classes of employees covered,
   b. The types of benefits, and
   c. The key elements of the pension formulas.

   The terms of policies, if any, with respect to automatic postemployment benefit changes, including automatic COLAs, and ad hoc postemployment benefit changes, including ad hoc COLAs, and

   The authority under which benefit terms are established or may be amended. If the pension plan is closed to new entrants, that fact should be disclosed.
3. The number of employees covered by the benefit terms, separately identifying numbers of the following:
   a. Inactive employees (or their beneficiaries) currently receiving benefits,
   b. Inactive employees entitled to but *not yet receiving benefits*, and
   c. Active employees.
4. A brief description of contribution requirements, including:
   a. The basis for determining the employer's contributions to the pension plan (for example in statute, contract, an actuarial basis, or some other manner),
   b. Identification of the authority under which contribution requirements of the employer, nonemployer contributing entities, if any, and employees are established or may be amended, and
   c. The contribution rates (in dollars or as a percentage of covered payroll) of those entities for the reporting period.

   Also, the value of contributions recognized by the pension plan from the employer during the reporting period (measured as the total of amounts recognized as additions to the pension plan's fiduciary net position resulting from actual contributions and from contributions recognized by the pension plan as current receivables), if not otherwise disclosed should be disclosed.

5. Whether the pension plan issues a stand-alone financial report (or the pension plan is included in the report of a PERS or another government) that is available to the public and, if so, how to obtain the report (e.g., a link to the report on the PERS website).

In many situations, much of this information can be presented in the form of a table.

The next section in the notes contain information about the net pension liability, including assumptions and other inputs, the pension plan's fiduciary net position and finally information about the changes in the net pension liability for the period. These elements can also be incredibly detailed. Tables are often used by practitioners.

The assumptions and other inputs include inflation measures, salary changes, ad hoc postemployment benefit changes (including ad hoc COLAs). Mortality assumptions are included, including the source of the assumptions and the dates of the latest experience study.

> **PRACTICE POINT:** Mortality assumptions are often based on federal census data and often are apportioned by gender. Different rates may be assumed for different periods. They should be updated in accordance with Actuarial Standards of Practice.

The discount rate-setting process and sensitivity of the rate is then included in the notes, consisting of:

- The discount rate applied in the measurement of the total pension liability and the change in the discount rate since the prior measurement date, if any,
- Assumptions made about projected cash flows into and out of the pension plan, such as contributions from the employer, nonemployer contributing entities, and employees,
- The long-term expected rate of return on pension plan investments and a brief description of how it was determined, including significant methods and assumptions used for that purpose,
- If the discount rate incorporates a municipal bond rate, the municipal bond rate used and the source of that rate,
- The periods of projected benefit payments to which the long-term expected rate of return and, if used, the municipal bond rate applied to determine the discount rate,
- The assumed asset allocation of the pension plan's portfolio, the long-term expected real rate of return for each major asset class, and whether the expected rates of return are presented as arithmetic or geometric means, if not otherwise disclosed, and
- Measures of the sensitivity of the net pension liability calculated using a discount rate that is 1-percentage-point higher than that required because of the discount rate setting process described previously.

The pension plan's fiduciary net position is then disclosed, including all the elements of the plan, such as assets, deferred outflows of resources, liabilities, deferred inflows of resources, and fiduciary net position.

> **PRACTICE POINT:** This information is commonly on the internet either as a stand-alone financial report or as a fiduciary fund of another government (typically a state). The employer may reference how to obtain the report in these circumstances. Disclosure then includes that the information in the employer's financial statements is on the same basis of accounting as the plan. Such disclosure is usually in the summary of significant accounting policies.

A table of the changes in the net pension liability is then disclosed in the notes, including the following elements:

- The beginning balances of the total pension liability, the pension plan's fiduciary net position, and the net pension liability,
- The effects during the period of the following items, if applicable, on the balances:
  — Service cost,
  — Interest on the total pension liability,
  — Changes of benefit terms,
  — Differences between expected and actual experience in the measurement of the total pension liability,
  — Changes of assumptions or other inputs,
  — Contributions from the employer,
  — Contributions from nonemployer contributing entities,
  — Contributions from employees,
  — Pension plan net investment income,
  — Benefit payments, including refunds of employee contributions,
  — Pension plan administrative expense, and
  — Other changes, separately identified if individually significant, and
- The ending balances of the total pension liability, the pension plan's fiduciary net position, and the net pension liability.

If the employer has a special funding situation, the above should be presented for the collective net pension liability (not separately for each employer). In addition, if the employer has a special funding situation, the following is disclosed:

- The nonemployer contributing entities' total proportionate share of the collective net pension liability, and
- The employer's proportionate share of the collective net pension liability.

Employers should also disclose, as applicable:

- The measurement date of the net pension liability, the date of the actuarial valuation on which the total pension liability is based, and any update

procedures used to roll forward the total pension liability to the measurement date,
- If a special funding situation is in place, the employer's proportion (percentage) of the collective pension liability, the basis on which the proportion was determined, and the change in its proportion since the prior measurement date,
- A brief description of changes of assumptions or other inputs that affected measurement of the total pension liability since the prior measurement date,
- A brief description of changes of benefit terms that affected measurement of the total pension liability since the prior measurement date,
- The amount of benefit payments in the measurement period attributable to the purchase of *allocated insurance contracts*, a brief description of the benefits for which allocated insurance contracts were purchased in the measurement period, and the fact that the obligation for the payment of benefits covered by allocated insurance contracts has been transferred from the employer to one or more insurance companies,
- A brief description of the nature of changes between the measurement date of the net pension liability and the employer's reporting date that are expected to have a significant effect on the net pension liability, and the amount of the expected resultant change in the net pension liability, if known,
- The amount of pension expense recognized by the employer in the reporting period,
- The employer's balances of deferred outflows of resources and deferred inflows of resources related to pensions, classified as follows, if applicable:
  — Differences between expected and actual experience in the measurement of the total pension liability,
  — Changes of assumptions or other inputs,
  — Net difference between projected and actual earnings on pension plan investments,
  — If the employer has a special funding situation, changes in the employer's proportion and differences between the employer's contributions (other than those to separately finance specific liabilities of the individual employer to the pension plan) and the employer's proportionate share of contributions,
  — The employer's contributions to the pension plan after the measurement date of the net pension liability,
- A schedule presenting the following:
  — For each of the subsequent five years, and in the aggregate thereafter, the net amount of the employer's balances of deferred outflows of resources and deferred inflows of resources in that will be recognized in the employer's pension expense,

- If the employer does not have a special funding situation, the amount of the employer's balance of deferred outflows of resources that will be recognized as a reduction of the net pension liability,
- If the employer has a special funding situation, the amount of the employer's balance of deferred outflows of resources that will be included as a reduction of the collective net pension liability, and
- The amount of revenue recognized for the support provided by nonemployer contributing entities [GASB Cod. Secs. P20.137–.145].

Required Supplementary Information and Notes to Required Supplementary Information—All Single and Agent Employers. The required supplementary information (RSI) and notes to the RSI are presented separately for each single-employer and agent plan reported by the employer. The following information is reported as of the *measurement date* and reported in a single schedule:

1. A 10-year schedule of changes in the net pension liability that separately presents the information required above in the notes for each year.
2. A 10-year schedule presenting the following for each year, as applicable:

If the employer *does not* have a *special funding situation*:	If the employer *does* have a *special funding situation*, information about the *collective net pension liability*:
• The total pension liability,	• The total pension liability,
• The pension plan's fiduciary net position,	• The pension plan's fiduciary net position,
• The net pension liability,	• The collective net pension liability,
• The pension plan's fiduciary net position as a percentage of the total pension liability,	• The nonemployer contributing entities' total proportionate share (amount) of the collective net pension liability,
• The covered payroll, and	• The employer's proportionate share (amount) of the collective net pension liability,
• The net pension liability as a percentage of covered payroll.	• The covered payroll,
	• The employer's proportionate share (amount) of the collective net pension liability as a percentage of covered payroll, and
	• The pension plan's fiduciary net position as a percentage of the total pension liability.

The next 10-year schedule is determined as of the employer's *most recent fiscal year-end.*

If an *actuarially determined contribution is calculated*, a *schedule presenting the following for each year*:	If an *actuarially determined contribution is not calculated* and the *contribution requirements of the employer are statutorily or contractually established*, a *schedule presenting the following for each year*:
• The actuarially determined contribution of the employer. For purposes of this schedule, actuarially determined contributions should exclude amounts, if any, associated with payables to the pension plan that arose in a prior fiscal year and those associated with separately financed specific liabilities of the individual employer to the pension plan,	• The statutorily or contractually required employer contribution. For purposes of this schedule, statutorily or contractually required contributions should exclude amounts, if any, associated with payables to the pension plan that arose in a prior fiscal year and those associated with separately financed specific liabilities of the individual employer to the pension plan,
• The value of contributions recognized by the pension plan in relation to the actuarially determined contribution of the employer. For purposes of this schedule, contributions should include only amounts recognized as additions to the pension plan's fiduciary net position during the employer's fiscal year resulting from actual contributions and from contributions recognized by the pension plan as current receivables,	• The value of contributions recognized by the pension plan in relation to the statutorily or contractually required employer contribution. For purposes of this schedule, contributions should include only amounts recognized as additions to the pension plan's fiduciary net position during the employer's fiscal year resulting from actual contributions and from contributions recognized by the pension plan as current receivables,
• The difference between the actuarially determined contribution of the employer and the value of contributions recognized by the pension plan in relation to the actuarially determined contribution of the employer,	• The difference between the statutorily or contractually required employer contribution and the value of contributions recognized by the pension plan in relation to the statutorily or contractually required employer contribution,
• The covered payroll, and	• The covered payroll, and
• The value of contributions recognized by the pension plan in relation to the actuarially determined contribution of the employer as a percentage of covered payroll.	• The value of contributions recognized by the pension plan in relation to the statutorily or contractually required employer contribution as a percentage of covered payroll.

In the situation where the primary government reports component units, the information on both schedules is presented for the *whole reporting entity*.

Notes to Required Supplementary Information. Notes to the required schedules include significant methods and assumptions in calculating actuarially determined contributions (as applicable). Other disclosures may include changes in benefits or assumptions. Any investment related changes are only included where the employer has influence [GASB Cod. Secs. P20.146–.147].

DEFINED BENEFIT PENSIONS—COST-SHARING EMPLOYERS

Proportionate Share of Net Pension Liability

The major difference between cost-sharing employers and all other employers is the concept of *proportionality*. The employer is only responsible for its proportionate share of the collective net pension elements measured as follows:

- A measure of the proportionate relationship of:
  - The employer and nonemployer contributing entities that provide support but are not in a special funding situation (otherwise that employer would have its own proportionate share) to
  - All employers and all nonemployer contributing entities.

The proportion is consistent in the way contributions to the pension plan are determined. The proportion excludes contributions for an individual employer's separately financed specific liabilities to the pension plan.

The proportionate share of the employer is then used as a percentage to multiply against all the applicable pension elements.

Different contribution rates may be utilized for different classes or groups of employees. There may be an internal calculation performed to account for these variations. The proportion is established as of the measurement date, unless the proportion is actuarially determined. In those cases, the actuarial valuation date is used [GASB Cod. Secs. P20.148–.150].

Like single and agent employer presentations, if an employer contributes to multiple plans resulting in net pension assets and net pension liabilities, the net pension assets are presented separately from the net pension liabilities [GASB Cod. Sec. P20.151].

Cost Sharing Employers: Financial Reporting, Notes, and Required Supplementary Information

Pension Expense, Deferred Outflows of Resources, and Deferred Inflows of Resources. All the elements related to pensions are similar for cost-sharing employers as single and agent employers with one major difference. Cost-sharing employers are required to present their *proportionate share* of the elements of the plan, *as determined by the plan.*

An additional deferred outflow of resources or deferred inflow of resources may occur due to the change in the employer's proportionate share from one measurement date to the next, determined as of the *beginning of the measurement period*. The change in proportion is recognized beginning in the current period and amortized over a closed period using a systematic and rational method, using *expected average remaining service lives of all employees that are provided pensions* (active *and* inactive) (EARSL) determined as of the beginning of the measurement period. Any remainder is reported as part of deferred inflows of resources or deferred outflows of resources [GASB Cod. Sec. P20.154].

> **PRACTICE POINT:** Some plans calculate this proportionate share change. Others do not. Ultimately, the employer is responsible for recognizing this change and determining if the amounts are material in conjunction with their auditor.

Contributions during the measurement period occur similarly to single and agent employers. Specific liabilities of an individual employer or nonemployer contributing entity to the plan are reported separately from other employers (discussed in the next paragraph). If there are differences between the total amount of the contributions from the employer and amounts associated with the individual employer from nonemployer contributing entities that are not in a special funding situation versus the amount of the employer's specific proportionate share of contributions from all employers and all nonemployer contributing entities, any difference is deferred and amortized in a separate deferral. This begins in the current measurement period and expensed also over the EARSL. In many cases, this does not occur as the employers will unlikely over or underfund contributions due to budgetary constraints, laws, and regulations [GASB Cod. Sec. P20.155].

If there are separately financed specific liabilities of individual employers to the plan, the difference during the measurement period between the contributions and the proportionate share of the total of contributions is expensed. If the contributions are made by others to the plan, excluding the amounts that are not in a special funding situation, the contributions immediately reduce pension expense. The contributions from others could be in the form of a special financial "bailout" that is separate from other forms of municipal aid. As the specific liabilities of individual employers are likely contractual for unfunded prior contributions arising from joining a plan, in practice, differences are also rare [GASB Cod. Secs. P20.156–.157].

Components of pension expense are like single and agent employers with the major exception of proportional differences discussed previously.

Element of Pension Expense	Does Element Increase or Decrease Pension Expense?
Service cost, excluding employee contributions	Increases
Employee contributions	Decreases
Proportionate share of interest on beginning total pension liability	Increases
Proportionate share of changes in benefit terms	May increase or decrease
Proportionate share of plan administrative costs	Increase
Proportionate share of projected earnings on plan investments	Decreases

Specific Accounting and Reporting Issues

Element of Pension Expense	Does Element Increase or Decrease Pension Expense?
Proportionate share of amortization of deferred outflows of resources (or deferred inflows of resources) for differences between expected and actual experience, changes in assumptions, net differences between projected and actual earnings	Increases (or decreases in the case of amortizations of deferred inflows of resources)
Changes in proportion	May increase or decrease
Differences between actual contributions and proportionate share	May increase or decrease
Other adjustments	May increase or decrease
Employer contributions to the plan	No impact—contributions increase fiduciary net position
Contributions to the pension plan from nonemployer contributing entities *that are not in a special funding situation*	Does *not* adjust pension expense, reported as revenue (Example: intergovernmental revenue or aid)

AICPA Schedule of Employer Allocations and Schedule of Pension Amounts by Employer (Not Contained in GASB Pronouncements). Employers should always be concerned about the ability obtain information from the cost-sharing plan for audit purposes. The AICPA Audit and Accounting Guide *State and Local Governments*, Chapter 13, discusses how information from a cost sharing plan should be communicated to employers. The schedules are separately audited. A "Schedule of Employer Allocations" details by employer the allocation percentages based on contributions, including when a nonemployer funds a portion of the liability in a special funding situation.

The AICPA's example Schedule of Employer Allocations is presented as follows:

	Contributions	Allocation
Employer 1	$2,143,842	36.3748%
Employer 2	268,425	4.5544%
Employer 3	322,142	5.4658%
Employer 4	483,255	8.1994%
Employer 5	633,125	10.7423%
Employer 6	144,288	2.4481%
Employer 7	95,365	1.6181%
Employer 8	94,238	1.5989%
Employer 9	795,365	13.4950%
Employer 10	267,468	4.5382%
Employer 11	403,527	6.8467%
Employer 12	165,886	2.8146%
Employer 13	68,454	1.1615%
Employer 14	6,240	0.1059%
Employer 15	2,144	0.0364%
Total	**$5,893,764**	**100.0000%**

Each employer could create a similar schedule within the government and for component units that contribute through the government to the plan to properly allocate the pension elements to those funds/employers that are expected to contribute to funding the government's pension elements in accordance with GASB Cod. Secs. 1100.108 and 1500.102 (see "*Allocations of Pension Elements within Reporting Entities*" later in this chapter).

The AICPA's example "Schedule of Pension Amounts by Employer" has two alternative presentations. Alternative 1 lists all employers in the plan and the allocation for every accounting element that needs to be transferred to the employers, based on the allocations in the previous schedule. For large cost-sharing multiple employer plans with more than a handful of employers, Alternative 1 yields a very onerous schedule for plans with many employers.

> **PRACTICE POINT:** This schedule may have hundreds of employers listed with datapoints for each accounting element. For statewide plans, such a schedule may last for many pages.

A second alternative contains only the *aggregated amounts* for each accounting element, including:

- Net pension liability,
- Deferred outflows of resources, including, but not limited to:
  - Differences between expected and actual experience,
  - Net difference between projected and actual investment earnings on pension plan investments,
  - Changes of assumptions,
  - Changes in proportion and differences between employer contributions and proportionate share of contributions, and
  - Total deferred outflows of resources,
- Deferred inflows of resources, including, but not limited to:
  - Differences between expected and actual experience,
  - Changes of assumptions,
  - Changes in proportion and differences between employer contributions and proportionate share of contributions, and
- Total deferred inflows of resources,
- Proportionate share of plan pension expense,
- Net amortization of deferred amounts from changes in proportion and differences between employer contributions and proportionate share of contributions, and
- Total employer pension expense.

13,038 *Specific Accounting and Reporting Issues*

It is up to the employer to use the information in the allocation schedule and multiply the allocation against the aggregated amounts for each element. Upon receipt of each of the schedules, the employers can then rely on this information to be placed in their basic financial statements, notes to the basic financial statements, and required supplementary information because it will contain an audit opinion. Like agent multiple-employer plan information, time should be increased to prepare this data, unless it can be prepared off-cycle to the date of the basic financial statements. Further discussion of these schedules is found in Chapter 22.

As summarized above, changes in the employer's proportion of the collective net pension liability as well as differences between the individual employer's contributions and the employer's proportionate share of total contribution from all employers must be determined. The effect of this is declared as a deferred inflow of resources or a deferred outflow of resources and amortized to pension expense over the remaining service lives of all employees (active and inactive) GASB Cod. Sec. P20.901, Illustration 3b portrays how to calculate this amount.

EXHIBIT 13-4
ILLUSTRATION: CALCULATION OF CHANGES IN PROPORTION OF A COST-SHARING EMPLOYER AND RELATED JOURNAL ENTRIES

To illustrate the calculation of changes in proportion for a cost-sharing employer, the following information must be used [adapted from GASB Cod. Sec. P20.901, Illustration 3b]:

Step 1: Collective balances on December 31, 20X7 and 20X8, are as follows:

Measurement Date	12/31/20X7	12/31/20X8
Collective deferred outflows of resources for the plan	$1,373,691	$2,185,960
Collective deferred inflows of resources for the plan	$1,538,565	$1,233,001
Collective net pension liability	$6,178,023	$7,455,024
District's proportion	0.19%	0.20%

The collective pension expense for the measurement period ended December 31, 20X8, is $1,163,898. The average of the expected remaining service lives (ERSL) of all employees that are provided pensions through the pension plan (active and inactive employees) determined as of the beginning of the measurement period (January 1, 20X8) is 9.3 years.

Step 2: Additional information for the fiscal year ended *June 30, 20X9* is as follows:

- Contributions from the school district to the plan from January 1, 20X8 to June 30, 20X8 were $1,030, reported as a deferred outflow of resources in the prior year, due to the provisions of GASB Cod. Sec. P20.157. From July 1, 20X8 to December 31, 20X8, contributions were also $1,030. From

January 1, 20X9 to June 30, 20X9, contributions after the measurement date but prior to the district's year-end were $1,065.

- The beginning deferred outflows related to changes in proportion and contributions in prior periods was $170. The amount to be recognized as an increase to pension expense in the next measurement period (ended December 31, 20X9) is $30.

- The beginning deferred inflows of resources related to changes in proportion and contributions in prior periods was $192. The amount to be recognized as a *decrease* to pension expense for the next measurement period (ended December 31, 20X9) is $36.

Step 3: The following amounts would be recognized as debits and credits related to the change in proportionate share:

	Proportionate Share on 12/31/20X7 (0.19%)	Proportionate Share on 12/31/20X8 (0.20%)	Adjustments to Natural Debits	Adjustments to Natural Credits
Deferred outflows of resources	$2,610 = ($1,373,691 × 0.19%)	$4,372 = ($2,185,960 × 0.20%)	$1,762	
Deferred inflows of resources	$2,923 = ($1,538,565 × 0.19%)	$2,466 = ($1,233,001 × 0.20%)		($457)
Net pension liability	$11,738 = ($6,178,023 × 0.19%)	$14,910 = ($7,455,024 × 0.20%)		$3,172

NOTE: The ($457) is the result of a lowering of a "natural credit"—the deferred inflows of resources. This would be a debit. As the deferred outflows of resources increases a "natural debit," a further debit is needed. Finally, the net pension liability increases a "natural credit" resulting in a further credit. The above debits and credits are not meant to balance as further information is needed in Step 4.

Step 4: Journal entries for the district for the fiscal year ended June 30, 20X9 (December 31, 20X8 measurement date)

The pension expense for the measurement period ended December 31, 20X8 is $2,327, which would be $1,163,898 × 0.20%. The beginning balances as of 12/31/20X7 for the period reflected $137 in debit balances for deferred outflows of resources, $154 in deferred inflows of resources and $618 in net pension liability related to the change in proportion.

As the $154 + $618 equals total credits of $772, $635 must be the amount recognized as the net effect of the change in proportion on beginning balances ($772 – $137 = $635). Therefore, this difference of $635 would have to be deferred and amortized over the remaining service lives of active and inactive members, beginning with this year ($635 ÷ 9.3 years = $68 in pension expense, the remaining $567 would be a deferred outflow of resources).

13,040 Specific Accounting and Reporting Issues

Finally, contributions from employers to the plan during the period ending December 31, 20X8 were $1,004,730. The district's proportionate share (0.20%) should have been $2,009. However, the district contributed $2,060 ($1,030 from January 1, 20X8 to June 30, 20X8 and another $1,030 from July 1, 20X8 to December 31, 20X8). Therefore, a difference exists of $51 that would need to be deferred and amortized over the remaining service lives of active and inactive members ($51 ÷ 9.3 years = $5 in pension expense, the remaining $46 would be a deferred outflow of resources).

Therefore, the journal entries for the district for the fiscal year ended June 30, 20X9 (December 31, 20X8 measurement date) would be:

GOVERNMENT-WIDE STATEMENT OF NET POSITION (OR PROPRIETARY FUND)	Debits	Credits
Deferred outflows of resources—proportionate share of collective deferred outflows of resources (from Step 3)	$1,762	
Pension expense ($2,327 + 68 + 5 all from Step 4)	2,400	
Deferred inflows of resources—proportionate share of collective deferred inflows of resources (from Step 3) (proportion lowered)		457
Deferred outflows of resources—($567 + 46 from Step 4)		613
Proportionate share of net pension liability (from Step 3)		$3,172
Deferred outflows of resources—District contributions from 1/1/X8–6/30/X8		1,030
Cash (likely already recorded)—District contributions from 7/1/X8–12/31/X8		1,030

NOTE: The only pension element that is not presented in the Statement of Net Position on the government-wide financial statements is "pension expense." Therefore, the results of Steps 1 through 3 all "close" to pension expense. This closing may change pension expense as reported in the schedule of pension amounts by employer.

A second set of journal entries would recognize the amortization of deferred outflows of resources and deferred inflows of resources for the year calculated in Step 2:

GOVERNMENT-WIDE STATEMENT OF NET POSITION (OR PROPRIETARY FUND)	Debits	Credits
Deferred inflows of resources (from Step 2)	$36	
Deferred outflows of resources (from Step 2)		$30
Pension expense		6

Finally, per GASB Cod. Sec. P20.157, the district's contributions from 1/1/X9 to 6/30/X9 would be recognized as deferred outflows of resources to be adjusted to net pension liability in the next measurement period:

GOVERNMENT-WIDE STATEMENT OF NET POSITION (OR PROPRIETARY FUND)	Debits	Credits
Deferred outflows of resources – district contributions from 1/1/X9 to 6/30/X9 (from Step 2)	$1,065	
Cash		$1,065

Like single and agent-multiple employer plans, governmental fund statements include the cost-sharing employer's proportionate share of the net pension liability that will be liquidated with current financial resources. Pension expenditures are calculated similarly [GASB Cod. Sec. P20.173]. Support of nonemployer contributing entities in governmental funds are also reported similarly to single and agent employer governmental fund support—revenue as adjusted for amounts receivable at the beginning of the year and the end of the year [GASB Cod. Secs. P20.174–.175].

The notes to the basic financial statements of cost-sharing employers include similar descriptive information and annual information to single and agent employers, however including proportionate share information. [GASB Cod. Secs. P20.176–.182].

Required Supplementary Information—Cost-Sharing Employers. RSI is like what is required for single and agent employers except it focuses on the proportionate share information. The initial 10-year schedule is prepared as of the measurement date and includes each year:

If the employer *does not have a special funding situation*:	If the employer *has a special funding situation*:
• The employer's proportion (percentage) of the collective net pension liability,	• The employer's proportion (percentage) of the collective net pension liability,
• The employer's proportionate share (amount) of the collective net pension liability,	• The employer's proportionate share (amount) of the collective net pension liability,
• The employer's covered payroll,	• The portion of the nonemployer contributing entities' total proportionate share (amount) of the collective net pension liability that is associated with the employer,
• The employer's proportionate share (amount) of the collective net pension liability as a percentage of the employer's covered payroll, and	• The total of the amounts in the previous two elements,
• The pension plan's fiduciary net position as a percentage of the total pension liability.	• The employer's covered payroll,
	• The employer's proportionate share (amount) of the collective net pension liability as a percentage of the employer's covered payroll, and
	• The pension plan's fiduciary net position as a percentage of the total pension liability.

The contributions schedule is as of the employer's most recent fiscal year-end. It includes the same information required for single and agent employers, adjusted for either statutorily or contractually required contributions.

The required notes to the RSI are also like what is required for single and agent employers [GASB Cod. Secs. P20.183–.184].

Special Funding Situations and Other Issues

If the employer is involved in a "special funding situation," the amount that a nonemployer entity is legally and irrevocably required to fund (e.g., a state on behalf of a school district) becomes a liability of the nonemployer entity rather than that of the employer. If a state funds 50% of a school district's pension liability on an ongoing basis, then 50% of the liability is recorded on the state's Statement of Net Position, while the remainder is recorded on the school district's Statement of Net Position. Special funding situations may occur in all types of plans and funding may be received from nongovernmental employers.

The proportionate share of the nonemployer entity is calculated like being a cost-sharing employer. Pension expense, changes in proportion, and contribution adjustments for amounts contributed after the measurement date are also like cost-sharing provisions [GASB Cod. Secs. P20.185–.191].

The support provided by a nonemployer contributing entity is recognized as revenue by the employer receiving the support as the total of:

- The nonemployer contributing entities' total proportionate share of collective pension expense, reduced by the total amounts, if any, recognized by the nonemployer contributing entities as a reduction of expense related to separately financed specific liabilities, *plus*
- The portion associated with the employer of the nonemployer contributing entities' *additional expense* recognized for contributions to the plan to separately finance specific liabilities of the individual nonemployer contributing entity to the plan.

The support provided is included as part of note disclosure, RSI, and notes to RSI as applicable [GASB Cod. Secs. P20.192–.199].

The nonemployer contributing entity recognizes its proportionate share of all accounting elements, including net pension liability, deferred outflows of resources, deferred inflows of resources, and pension expense. Changes in proportionate share may occur at each measurement date. The pension expense should then be reported to each employer in the plan in *their proportion*, which would result in additional expense and subsidy revenue to that employer. Note disclosure, RSI and notes to RSI, provisions all apply, as applicable [GASB Cod. Secs. P20.200–.211].

In many cases, especially in teachers' pensions, nonemployer contributing entities recognize a *substantial* portion of the collective net pension liability. Disclosures of this situation may be combined to avoid unnecessary duplication. For example, a state may contribute a substantial portion to teachers' pensions to a PERS, but also have its own liability in the same PERS for its active and inactive members.

Therefore, the many of the required disclosures and RSI can be combined [GASB Cod. Secs. P20.212–.219]. If less than a substantial proportion, the amount of disclosure and RSI required by nonemployer contributing entities is diminished [GASB Cod. Secs. P20.220–.221].

An employer's reporting of receiving funds in a special funding situation is contained in Exhibit 13-5.

EXHIBIT 13-5
ILLUSTRATION: SPECIAL FUNDING SITUATION AND RELATED JOURNAL ENTRIES

To illustrate a special funding situation, based upon contributions in the prior year, School District #19080 has a 0.063% employer proportionate share of total statewide teachers cost-sharing multiple employer plan calculated employer contributions. However, the state has a special funding situation and contributes 37.65% of total statewide teachers cost-sharing multiple employer plan calculated employer contributions.

The plan reports a pension expense that would be recognized by all employers of $1,389,000,000 (rounded). Therefore, School District #19080 would recognize a pension expense of $875,070 as follows:

Element	Amount
Annual pension expense reported by the plan	$1,389,000,000
School District #19080's proportion	× 0.063%
School District #19080's proportion of annual pension expense	**$875,070**

However, the District would not recognize the same amount in revenue. 0.063% is 0.101043% of the total statewide teachers' contributions, *without* the state's portion. Therefore, they must recognize revenue as follows:

Element	Amount
Annual pension expense reported by the plan	$1,389,000,000
State's portion of annual pension expense	× 37.65%
Aggregated state's proportion of annual pension expense (to be reported by all school districts as the state participates in a special funding situation) (the state would report this as pension expense)	$522,958,500
School District #19080's proportion	0.063%
The total of the proportions of all employers for which support is provided by the state (aggregated employer contributions) (1–37.65%)	62.350%
Proportion of the state's total proportionate share of collective pension expense associated with School District #19080 (0.063% ÷ 62.350%)	× 0.101043%
In conformity with GASB Cod. Secs. P20.196–.197, the District recognizes revenue and pension expense that is associated with School District #19080 ($522,958,500 × 0.101043%) (Debit pension expense, credit revenue—state aid)	**$528,410**

13,044   Specific Accounting and Reporting Issues

The school district also needs to record its share of deferred outflows of resources, deferred inflows of resources, and net pension liability. Using the 0.063%, the following is its share of other accounting elements as reported by the plan:

Element	Plan Amounts	District #19080 (0.063%) Amounts
Net pension liability	$58,437,000,000	$36,815,310
Deferred outflows of resources	–	–
Deferred inflows of resources – representing unamortized differences between projected and actual earnings on plan investments	$14,390,000,000	$9,065,700

Any contributions made after the measurement date by the District to the plan would be recognized as a deferred outflow of resources, reducing pension expense. At the next measurement date, the contributions previously reclassed to deferred outflows of resources would be recognized as part of the net pension liability.

Therefore, pension expense would be recognized as part of a reversing entry of the reclassed deferred outflows of resources. Then, to record the expense and subsidy as of the end of the year:

GOVERNMENT-WIDE STATEMENT OF NET POSITION (OR PROPRIETARY FUND)	Debit	Credit
Pension expense ($875,070 + $528,410)	$1,403,480	
Revenue—state aid		$528,410
Cash (or payables that already adjusted net position)		875,070

If an employer receives funds *not in a special funding situation*, the amount is reported as revenue and the provisions of measurement and recognition may or may not apply. The amount that is reported by the nonemployer contributing entity is like any other intergovernmental transfer, aid, or grant [GASB Cod. Secs. P20.222–.223].

Payables to a plan may arise under normal circumstances. The full amount of the payable is recognized in the reporting period the payable arises, equating to the contribution to the plan. The payable is reported separately from the net pension liability. If paid from a governmental fund, amounts that are normally expected to be liquidated with expendable available financial resources are declared as a payable [GASB Cod. Secs. P20.224–.225].

OBSERVATION: Special funding situations are different than separately financed specific liabilities. A section on separately financed specific liabilities occurs later in this chapter.

Allocations of Pension Elements within Reporting Entities

Since 1979, U.S. GAAP has required long-term liabilities directly related to and expected to be paid from proprietary and fiduciary funds to be presented in said funds [GASB Cod. Secs. 1100.108, 1500.102]. Recording the accounting elements required by GASB Cod. Sec. P20 in funds that are in the full accrual basis of accounting presents a challenge for preparers and auditors. GAAP contains no specific guidance for allocation of the net pension liability or other pension related measures to individual funds.

Amounts are required to be allocated to component units. GASB Cod. Secs. P20.707-1–3 discuss the issue of allocating to component units as follows:

Fact Pattern	Guidance
A single-employer defined benefit pension plan is used to provide pensions to the employees of a state government and several governments that are component units of the state. In their stand-alone financial reports, should each of the component units report as a single employer?	No. Component units would apply the cost-sharing employer requirements for GASB Cod. Sec. P20 for their own stand-alone reports. Therefore, each government would report their own proportionate share of the collective net pension liability (or asset), considering if a special funding situation is present. The reporting entity (the state and component units) would include just note disclosures and RSI for a single employer.
If the component units do not issue stand-alone financial reports, is a portion of the accounting elements required to be allocated to the component units as if they were cost-sharing employers for the purposes of the reporting entity's financial report?	Yes. Regardless of whether the financial data (in this case, the net pension liability, and related measures) is issued in stand-alone financial reports of the component units, the reporting entity's financial report should include that data as if it had been. GASB Cod. Sec. P20 requires that in stand-alone financial statements, the component units account for and report their participation in the pension plan as if they were cost-sharing employers. Therefore, the financial report of the reporting entity should include the primary government's and the component units' proportionate shares of the collective net pension liability and related measures as if the entities were cost-sharing employers.
In a single employer or agent multiple-employer plan, does it matter if the component unit is discretely presented or blended?	No. Each should account for and report its participation in the plan as if it were a cost-sharing employer, regardless of status.

As there is minimal guidance as to the allocations, employers need to consider if a basis of allocation is systematic and rational. For example, if a cost-sharing multiple employer plan uses employer contributions as a basis for allocations, the employers should use the same and using the same measurement period information in allocating to enterprise, internal service, or fiduciary funds.

As a reminder, if proportions change from year to year, if material, a deferred inflow of resources or deferred outflow of resources may result, requiring a "due to" or "due from" entry between funds. This also presents a problem for separately audited departments or funds. U.S. GASB standards rightfully do not discuss separately audited departments that present GAAP-based departmental financial statements. The AICPA Audit & Accounting Guide, *State and Local Governments*, recommends consideration of long-established practices in these presentations applying all relevant GAAP.

PRACTICE POINT: Allocating to fiduciary funds raises a further problem. There are no provisions in fiduciary fund reporting to declare deferred inflows of resources nor deferred outflows of resources, Furthermore, for plans that are fiduciary component units, allocating pension elements back to the plan may result in a circular accounting entry or an inability to post pension-related information. Plans routinely expense administrative expense including employee benefits. These expenses are funded from investment return or in some cases budgetary funding. Therefore, there is inconsistent U.S. GAAP for this issue. For most plans and fiduciary funds, an allocation of pension elements would likely be immaterial to the rest of the reporting entity. In most cases, the reporting government may be better served to report the information in the governmental activities and note disclose the allocation stating as part of the summary of significant accounting policies regarding pensions: "amounts that would normally be allocated to fiduciary funds have been reported as part of governmental activities" or something similar.

Separately Financed Specific Liabilities. GASB Cod. Sec. P20.546 describes separately financed specific liabilities regarding a cost-sharing pension plan. A *separately financed specific liability* to a defined benefit pension plan is a *one-time* assessment to an *individual employer or nonemployer contributing entity* of an amount resulting from an increase in the total pension liability due to:

- An individual employer joining a pension plan,
- A change in benefit terms to an individual employer, or
- A contractual commitment for a nonemployer contributing entity to make a one-time contribution to finance a reduction in the net pension liability.

Examples of separately financed liabilities to the pension plan include cash payments or long-term payables for amounts assessed to an individual employer upon joining the pension plan or for increases in the total pension liability for changes of benefit terms specific to the employer.

If a long-term installment contract is used to finance an employer joining a plan, GASB Cod. Sec. P20.732-2 requires for the portion of past service cost associated with employees that exceeds assets to the plan, the amount of the installment contract is a payable to the new plan. Both the amount of the installment contract and the amount of assets to the new plan should be accounted for as contributions from the employer for a separately financed specific liability of the individual employer.

GASB Cod. Sec. P20.145(c) requires separately financed specific liabilities to be excluded from required supplementary information if the liabilities are related to actuarially determined contributions and contributions made from single and agent employers. Similarly, the value of contributions presented in relation to the actuarially determined or statutorily or contractually required contribution, as applicable, should exclude amounts recognized as additions to the pension plan for separately financed specific liabilities of the individual employer to the pension plan.

Separately financed specific liabilities are also required to be excluded from determining a cost-sharing employer's proportion [GASB Cod. Sec. P20.147]. For the cost-sharing employer, pension expense must also be adjusted. For contributions to the pension plan to separately finance specific liabilities of the individual employer to the pension plan, the difference during the measurement period between both elements below derives the employer's pension expense as follows:

- The amount of such contributions from the employer (and amounts associated with the employer from nonemployer contributing entities that are not in a special funding situation), and
- The amount of the employer's proportionate share of the total of the contributions determined using the employer's proportion of the collective net pension liability.

This is a similar calculation for determining the contributions to recognize to the pension plan for a cost-sharing employer with separately financed specific liabilities. It is also similar for governmental nonemployer contributing entities in the calculation of their proportionate share of the collective net pension liability.

Accordingly, the governmental nonemployer in a special funding situation contributing to an entity for separately financed specific liabilities also generates revenue at the employer receiving the benefits. Therefore, the proportionate shares would be affected.

Employer Contributions to Nongovernmental Defined Benefit Pension Plans with a Trust

As discussed previously, reporting in these situations is greatly diminished from other defined benefit plan reporting. In the government-wide and proprietary fund statements, pension expense is recognized equal to the employer's contributions for the reporting period with a payable recognized for any unpaid contributions required. In the governmental funds, again, payables are determined to the extent of expendable resources. Expenditures are the total of amounts paid by the employer to the plan plus the change between the beginning and ending balances payable to the plan [GASB Cod. Secs. P20.228–.229].

Note Disclosure and RSI

Due to the minimized accounting and financial reporting, for these circumstances, note disclosure and RSI is minimal:

- Name of the pension plan, identification of the entity that administers the pension plan, and identification of the pension plan as a cost-sharing pension plan that is not a governmental plan,
- Whether the pension plan issues a publicly available financial report and, if so, how to obtain the report,
- A brief description of the benefit terms, including:
  — The number of the government's employees covered,
  — The types of benefits provided,
  — The authority under which benefit terms are established or may be amended,
- A brief description of contribution requirements, including:
  — The basis for determining the employer's contributions to the pension plan (e.g., pursuant to a collective-bargaining agreement),
  — Identification of the authority under which contribution requirements of the employer and its employees are established or may be amended,
  — The required contribution rates of the employer and its employees for the reporting period,
  — The amount, in dollars, of the employer's required contributions for the reporting period,
  — The expiration date(s) of the collective-bargaining agreement(s) requiring contributions to the pension plan, if any,
  — A description of any minimum contributions required for future periods by the collective-bargaining agreement(s), statutory obligations, or other contractual obligations, if applicable,
  — Whether the employer is subject to any provisions regarding withdrawal from the pension plan,
- The following information about the employer's payables, if any:
  — If not otherwise identifiable, the balance of payables,
  — Significant terms related to the payables, and
  — A description of what gave rise to the payables (e.g., required contributions to the pension plan or a contractual arrangement for contributions to the pension plan related to past service upon entrance into the arrangement).

RSI includes only the employer's contributions for each of the 10 most recent fiscal years. Notes to the required schedules would only pertain to any factors that affect trends reported. They may likely include changes in contribution rates or related items [GASB Cod. Secs. P20.230–.232].

DEFINED BENEFIT PENSIONS—NON-TRUST SITUATIONS

As discussed previously, a trust or equivalent arrangement is present when all the following occur:

- Contributions from employers and nonemployer contributing entities to the pension plan and earnings on those contributions are irrevocable.

- Pension (or OPEB) plan assets exclusively provide pensions (or OPEB) to plan members in accordance with the benefit terms.

- Pension (or OPEB) plan assets are legally protected from the creditors of employers, nonemployer contributing entities, and the pension (or OPEB) plan administrator. If the plan is a defined benefit pension (or OPEB) plan, plan assets also are legally protected from creditors of the plan members.

Even without a trust, many of the pension provisions contained in GASB Cod. Sec. P20 apply. The same provisions of GASB Cod. Sec. P20 discussed in most of this chapter previously apply to non-trust situations, including:

Provisions	Exceptions
Types of pensions	None—the same as trust provisions
Types of defined benefit plans	Exception for *insured plans*
Special funding situations	None—the same as trust provisions
Actuarial valuation process	Discount rate setting process is different due to the more likely lack of assets. The result from the actuarial valuation is a *total pension liability*. No fiduciary net position is held in trust to offset the total pension liability and derive a net pension liability.
Pension expense, deferred outflows of resources, deferred inflows of resources and support of nonemployer contributing entities	Exception for deferred outflows of resources and deferred inflows of resources related to projected investment return versus actual return due to a likely lack of assets
Recognition in government-wide and funds	Total pension liability is used.
Notes to the financial statements	Lack of disclosure of fiduciary net position as no fiduciary net position available
RSI	Likely no contribution schedules
Proportionate share calculations when pensions provided through same plan for both primary government and component units	Proportionate share based on benefit payments, which derives liability rather than on a contribution or some other effort
Support of nonemployer contributing entities	None—the same as trust provisions

As indicated above, without a trust, there is only a minimal chance of assets available to pay for plan benefits (fiduciary net position). Without fiduciary net position, the discount rate is much lower as there are no assets to generate a long-term expected rate of return. Therefore, the related pension liability may be much higher than a plan with similar characteristics using a trust as it is reported on a total basis (the *total pension liability*).

Insured Plans

Defined benefit plans may be insured without trusts if they have the following provisions:

- Pensions are financed through an arrangement whereby premiums are paid to an insurance company while employees are in active service, and
- The insurance company *unconditionally* undertakes an obligation to pay the pensions as defined in the pension plan terms.

The pensions provided through insured plans are classified as insured benefits. Employers with both provisions have limited disclosure [GASB Cod. Sec. P22.107].

Discount Rate (Without a Trust)

As there is no trust and no fiduciary net position, the discount rate is required to be a yield or index rate for the 20-year tax-exempt general obligation bonds. The bonds must have a rating of AA/Aa or higher (or equivalent quality on another scale) [GASB Cod. Sec. P22.122].

Pension Expense, Deferred Outflows of Resources, Deferred Inflows of Resources, and Support of Nonemployer Contributing Entities (Without a Trust)

As indicated above, without fiduciary net position (without assets), elements of deferred outflows of resources and deferred inflows of resources are not calculated in pensions without a trust. The calculation of pension expense previously shown in this chapter now is as follows:

Element of Pension Expense Without a Trust	Does Element Increase or Decrease Pension Expense?
Service cost	Increases
Interest on beginning total pension liability	Increases
Changes in benefit terms	May increase or decrease
Plan administrative costs	Increase
Amortization of deferred outflows of resources (or deferred inflows of resources) for differences between expected and actual experience, changes in assumptions	Increases (or decreases in the case of amortizations of deferred inflows of resources)
Other adjustments	May increase or decrease
Employer contributions to the plan	No impact as contributions increase fiduciary net position
Contributions to the pension plan from nonemployer contributing entities *that are not in a special funding situation*	Does *not* adjust pension expense, reported as revenue (Example: intergovernmental revenue or aid)

For employers contributing to plans after the measurement date, but prior to the end of a fiscal year, a deferred outflow of resources is declared, just like a defined benefit plan with a trust [GASB Cod. Secs. P22.124–.125].

Determining Proportionate Share of Collective Total Pension Liability in Situations where Primary Governments and Component Units Are Part of the Same Defined Benefit Plan (Without a Trust)

A liability is required to be declared for the primary government's or the component unit's proportionate share of the total pension liability on the measurement date no earlier than the end of the government's prior fiscal year *and* no later than the end of the current fiscal year. Like defined benefit plans with a trust, the measurement date must be consistent from year to year.

To determine the government's proportionate share of the collective total pension liability:

- Measure the proportionate relationship of:
  - The government (and to the extent that the government nonemployer contributing entities provide support, if any, but are not in a special funding situation) to
  - All entities that make *benefit payments*, consistent with the way the amounts that are paid as benefits come due are determined.
- Multiply the proportion to the collective total pension liability [GASB Cod. Secs. P22.139–.142].

Changes in proportion are more likely to occur due to the variability of benefit payments. If there is a change in the government's proportion of the collective total pension liability since the prior measurement date, the change is deferred and amortized in the same manner as illustrated in **Exhibit 13-4**.

Insured Benefits Accounting, Disclosure, Note Disclosure

In the accrual basis of accounting, insured plans recognize an expense equal to the amount of premiums or other payments required for the reporting period in accordance with the agreement with the insurance company and a change in the liability to the insurer equal to the difference between the amount of pension expense and the amount paid to the insurer. For governmental fund financial statements, the amounts would be similar as they would likely be only amounts expended with current available financial resources.

Required notes to financial statements for insured plans only include:

- A *brief* description of the insured benefits, including the benefit provisions, and the authority under which the benefit provisions are established or may be amended,
- The fact that the obligation for the payment of benefits has effectively transferred from the employer to one (or more) insurance companies, and
- Whether the employer retains an obligation for benefits in the event of the insurance company's insolvency, and the current year pension expense or expenditure for the insured benefits [GASB Cod. Secs. P22.192–.194].

PRACTICE POINT: Many practitioners confuse insured plans. If the employer makes payments to insurance entity for OPEB, the payments *do not* signify an insured plan. An insured plan only occurs when premiums are paid to an insurance company while employees are in active service, in return for which the insurance company *unconditionally* undertakes an obligation to pay the OPEB of those employees as defined in the plan terms [GASB Cod. Sec. Po50.104].

Assets Accumulated for Defined Benefit Pensions Not Provided through Trusts

If assets are accumulated without the benefit of a trust, the assets are reported as *assets of the employer* or the nonemployer contributing entity. The assets are reported in a custodial fund. The amount of assets accumulated more than liabilities for benefits due to members and accrued expenses are a liability to the other employer(s) or nonemployer contributing entities. The amounts in the custodial fund should exclude the amounts due to the reporting entity employer. Instead, those amounts will be reported as assets of the employer [GASB Cod. Secs. P23.105–.106].

> **PRACTICE POINT:** Assets may be held aside for future pension contributions in similar funds. If they are not held at the plan (or in an irrevocable trust), the assets are part of the employer's operating funds and should not be in a custodial fund.

PENSIONS—DEFINED CONTRIBUTION PLAN REPORTING AT EMPLOYERS AND OTHER EMPLOYEE BENEFIT PLANS (DEFERRED COMPENSATION)

> **PRACTICE POINT:** In some situations, the employer may not have control of defined contribution plans, especially if participants direct investments, even from a slate of investments. In such situations, unless a law, regulation or contract requires reporting, such plans may not be reported, unless reported as an optional stand-alone report. In situations where the arrangement is *not a fiduciary activity*, the accounting and financial reporting of the arrangements may be limited to recognition of employee benefit expense or expenditures in the payroll-generating fund and any related payable amounts to the plan.

Defined Contribution Plans

Defined contribution reporting is far simpler than defined benefit reporting due to the nature of the plan. Irrevocable trusts are used in most cases with similar provisions to defined benefit plan trusts, including irrevocable contributions from employers and nonemployer contributing entities, dedication of assets to providing pensions to plan members and legal protection from creditors, including the plan administrator. Non-trust defined contribution reporting is later in this chapter [GASB Cod. Secs. P21.101–.103].

PRACTICE POINT: Defined contribution *plan* reporting is found in Chapter 22.

Special funding situations could occur in like the situations in defined benefit plans. The determination of existence of a special funding situation is the same as well [GASB Cod. Secs. P21.107–.108].

In financial statements prepared using the economic resources measurement focus and accrual basis of accounting, pension expense includes the value of contributions or credits to employees' accounts that are defined by the benefit terms as attributable to employees' services in the period. This amount is reported net of forfeited amounts that are removed from employees' accounts. Amounts that are reallocated to the accounts of other employees should not be considered forfeited amounts for this purpose. A change in the pension liability is then recognized equal to the difference between amounts recognized as pension expense as calculated above and amounts paid by the employer to the pension plan [GASB Cod. Secs. P21.109–.110].

Under current GAAP, for governmental funds, pension expenditures are the total of amounts paid by the employer to the plan and the change in the beginning and ending balances of amounts normally expected to be liquidated with expendable available financial resources. A fund liability is then declared for any unpaid contributions expected to be liquidated with expendable available financial resources. These liabilities are due and payable in accordance with the plan and legal requirements [GASB Cod. Sec. P21.111].

Also, due to the type of plan, the notes to the financial statements for plans where the employer contributes include the following:

- Name of the plan and identification of the administrator of the plan and the plan as a defined contribution plan,
- Brief description of the benefit terms (including vesting, forfeitures, and the policy related to the use of forfeited amounts) and establishment and amendment of benefit terms authority,
- The contribution (or crediting) rates (dollars or percentages) for employees, the employer, and nonemployer contributing entities, if any, and the authority under which those rates are established or may be amended, and
- The pension expense, forfeitures reflected in pension expense, and the amount of the employer's liability outstanding at the end of the period (if any) [GASB Cod. Sec. P21.112].

In special funding situations, the recognition of additional expense and revenue by the employer and the nonemployer contributing entity is also like defined benefit provisions [GASB Cod. Secs. P21.113–.118].

If a trust is not used in a defined contribution situation, defined contribution pensions are recognized by employers that do not have a special funding situation as follows:

- Pension expense is the value of credits to the employee's accounts defined by the benefit terms as attributable to employees' services in the period, net of forfeited amounts removed from the accounts;
- Amounts reallocated to other accounts of employees are not forfeited; and
- A change in the pension liability is equal to the difference between amounts recognized as pension expense and amounts paid by the employer as the benefits come due for the period.

For governmental funds, under current GAAP, pension expenditures are the amounts paid by the employer for pension benefits as the benefits come due as adjusted for a change in a beginning and ending pension liability, if any and normally expected to be liquidated with expendable available financial resources [GASB Cod. Secs. P24.108–.109].

Even if a trust is not used, the note disclosure for a defined contribution plan is similar but with additional reporting that there are no assets accumulated in a trust [GASB Cod. Sec. P24.111]. Special funding situation accounting, financial reporting, and note disclosure are also like defined benefit plans.

Other Employee Benefit Plans—Deferred Compensation—Internal Revenue Code Sections 457(b) and 403(b)

If reported, the types of postemployment benefit plans that are not defined benefit plans may continue to be reported by some entities for accountability purposes. However, if the participants in such plans are in control of the assets, such as through the ability to change investments, even from a slate provided by a government, the other employee benefit plan may not be reported by the government. (See Chapter 8 titled "Fiduciary Funds.")

The types of plans vary by law or contract. The most prevalent ones used in state and local governments include the following:

- *Internal Revenue Code Section 457(b) plans*—These plans are common in government. A plan administrator invests plan assets at the direction of plan participants. Due to the plan's provisions, the participant has the risk of loss of value.
- *Internal Revenue Code Section 403(b) plans*—These tax deferred annuity plans (or mutual funds) are funded by salary reductions. They are usually found in public institutions of higher education and hospitals. However, some governments use them to receive lump-sum payments at retirement from defined benefit plans. The risk of having enough funds at retirement then shifts to the retiree. Elementary and secondary public and private school systems also often offer Internal Revenue Code (IRC) Section 403(b) plans to their employees. *Caution*: These plans are *not* required to be held in trust due to IRC provisions. However, the benefits are restricted to beneficiaries of the plan. Due to the restriction, the plan may be deemed an "equivalent arrangement." GAAP has no specific definition of the phrase "equivalent arrangement" however.

So-called "hybrid plans" may also be found in state and local governments. These plans include the following:

- *Cash balance plans*—In these plans, hypothetical accounts are maintained for participants. The government then credits the accounts with funds

annually and promises earnings at an established rate. The rate may be different than actual earnings and the formula may be changed annually.
- *Money purchase plans*—In these plans, contributions are determined for and allocated for specific individuals as a percentage of compensation. The employer's contributions are based on a formula.
- *Target benefit plans*—In these plans, the employees contribute on an actuarial basis knowing a certain date of retirement. There is no guarantee of a balance or return. Many mutual funds sell these types of plans.
- *Deferred Retirement Option Program (DROP)*—It allows an employee to elect a calculation of benefit payments based on service credits and salary as of a certain date (the DROP date). The employee continues to provide service to the employer and is paid for that service by the employer after the DROP entry date, however, the pensions that would have been paid to the employee (if the employee had retired and not entered the DROP) are credited to an individual employee account within the defined benefit pension plan until the end of the DROP period.

PRACTICE POINT: In some cases, governments may offer IRC Section 401(k) plans and may even file a Form 5500, *Annual Return/Report of Employee Benefit Plan*, with the United States Department of Labor. The governments that offer such plans are mainly Tribal Nations, educational institutions, and similar entities. The AICPA Audit and Accounting Guide *State and Local Governments*, Chapter 13, notes: "Although many of the audit objectives for governmental plans are like those for private-sector pension plans, the Employee Retirement Income Security Act of 1974 (ERISA) does not apply to most governmental entities." In such cases where a non-Tribal Nation, educational institutions, and similar entities offer an IRC Section 401(k) plan to employees, the offering is likely a plan that existed prior to 1974 and has continued to the current time. If the plan was established after 1974 and does not have the aspects of the "grandfathered" entities (Tribal Nations, etc.), the filing of a Form 5500 is usually not necessary.

PART 3 EMPLOYER REPORTING OF OTHER POSTEMPLOYMENT BENEFITS

In addition to pension benefits, postemployment benefits may include payments to retirees or their beneficiaries for life insurance benefits, health insurance benefits, and other related benefits (OPEB). The liability related to these postemployment benefits in many cases is significant and may exceed the amount related to an employer's pension liability.

Overview of GAAP Provisions

OPEB related GAAP mirrors the provisions of defined benefit and defined contribution situations for pensions. In practice, more often than defined benefit plans, a trust is *not* present. OPEB plan terms and conditions are not as well-defined as pension plans, and they may vary based on collective bargaining agreement. Legislative bodies have far more latitude to change OPEB provisions than pension provisions. In many OPEB situations, OPEB plans are not well-funded, if funded at all.

To have a trust or equivalent arrangement, like the pension provisions, the following must be present:
- Contributions from employers and nonemployer contributing entities to the OPEB plan and earnings on those contributions must be irrevocable. Refunds to an employer or nonemployer contributing entity of the nonvested portion of contributions that are forfeited by plan members in a defined contribution OPEB plan do not violate this requirement.
- OPEB plan assets must be utilized to provide OPEB to plan members in accordance with benefit terms. It is common that OPEB plan assets pay OPEB administrative costs or to refund plan member contributions consistent with benefit terms. The payment of administrative costs and refunds do not violate this criterion.
- Plan assets are legally protected from the creditors of employers, nonemployer contributing entities and the OPEB plan administrator. In a defined benefit OPEB plan, plan assets are also legally protected from the creditors of the individual plan members [GASB Cod. Sec. P50.101].

Major differences between pensions and OPEB have to do with healthcare provisions. A major source of the total OPEB liability is in the projected cost of retiree healthcare benefits comprised largely of medical benefit claims. The liability can vary widely due to the variations of retiree healthcare costs, the availability of a trust, and changes in healthcare provisions from period to period from legislation or contract. Due to the differences in plan provisions, governments in the same geographical area can have vastly different plans. Insurance does play a significant role in healthcare, but more in the management of healthcare costs and not in the overall assumption of a liability. However, insured plans do exist.

The following GASB Statements focus on OPEB as aligned to sections of the *Codification*:

	OPEB				
GASB Codification Section	P50	P51	P52	P53	P54
GASB Statement Nos.	75, 85	75, 85	75, 85	74	75, 85
Situation:					
Employer that is a member or sponsor of a defined benefit plan	Yes				
Employer that is a member or sponsor of a defined contribution plan		Yes			
Employer that is a member or sponsor of a defined benefit plan *not provided through a trust or equivalent arrangement*			Yes		
Reporting of assets accumulated for defined benefit *not provided through a trust or equivalent arrangement*				Yes	
Reporting of assets accumulated for defined contribution *not provided through a trust or equivalent arrangement*					Yes
Special funding situations	Yes	Yes	Yes		

Types of OPEB and OPEB Plans. The most common form of OPEB is postemployment retiree healthcare benefits. These include, but are not limited to:

- Medical, (including prescription drugs and supplies),

- Dental,

- Vision,

- Hearing and other health-related benefits whether provided separately from a pension plan or included as part of a pension plan.

- Death benefits,

- Life insurance,

- Disability and

- Long-term care.

There are also plans where legal services and other forms of postemployment benefits are made available to members.

OPEB does not include termination or sick leave benefits as discussed earlier in this chapter. However, the effects of either may be included in measures of OPEB liabilities as frequently, they may be used as contributions on the employees' behalf.

Defined benefit OPEB plans and defined contribution OPEB plans have similar definitions to pensions and similar structures. The most common OPEB plan is for a single employer. Multiple-employer OPEB plans may use an agent-multiple employer or a cost-sharing employer model. Again, trusts may or may not be used. Should a trust *not* be utilized, the funds are likely passed through custodial funds in a method termed *pay-as-you-go* (or PAYGO). In PAYGO, assets are rarely accumulated [GASB Cod. Secs. P50.102–.106].

Most OPEB plans (and employers) are likely single-employer plans. As such, this section of the chapter focuses primarily on single employer provisions, noting any changes for agent-employer and cost-sharing employer situations. Employers may also have employees who are provided with defined benefit OPEB through a cost-sharing OPEB plan that, like defined benefit pensions, is:

- Not a state or local governmental OPEB plan,

- Used to provide defined benefit OPEB both to employees of state or local governmental employers, and

- Without a predominant state or local governmental employer (either individually or collectively with other state or local governmental employers that provide OPEB through the OPEB plan).

Such plans are health and welfare benefit plans, usually administered by a labor organization. GASB Cod. Sec. P50 does apply in such situations, but with similar, limited disclosure to Taft-Hartley plans discussed previously [GASB Cod. Secs. P50.107–.114].

Special Funding Situations. As with defined benefit pensions, special funding situations are circumstances when a nonemployer entity is *legally responsible* for providing financial support of OPEB of the employees of another entity by making contributions *directly to an OPEB plan*. Having a trust is not as important as making the contributions or making the payments when due. The value of contributions or benefit payments must not be dependent upon events or circumstances unrelated to OPEB. Like pensions, examples of dependency and non-dependency are as follows [GASB Cod. Secs. P50.115–.116].

Not Dependent— Special Funding Situation Likely	Dependent– Special Funding Situation Unlikely
• Nonemployer entity is required by statute to contribute a defined percentage of an employer's payroll directly to an OPEB plan that is administered through a trust.	• Nonemployer entity is required to make contributions to an OPEB plan that is administered through a trust based on a specified percentage of a given revenue source or equal to the amount by which the nonemployer entity's ending fund balance exceeds a defined threshold amount.
• Nonemployer entity is required to pay retiree health insurance premiums as the premiums come due.	• The amount of benefit payments required to be made by the nonemployer entity as OPEB comes due is limited by a given revenue source or by the amount by which the nonemployer entity's fund balance exceeds a defined threshold.
• Nonemployer entity is required by the terms of an OPEB plan to contribute directly to the OPEB plan a statutorily defined proportion of the employer's required contributions to the OPEB plan.	• Resources provided to the employer, regardless of the purpose for which those resources are provided.

Defined benefit and defined contribution OPEB may have special funding situations.

OPEB Provided to Employers through OPEB Plans Administered through Trusts (but Are Not Health and Welfare Benefit Plans). Like defined benefit pensions, defined benefit OPEB includes the following to be reported by employers:

- Liabilities to employees for OPEB (or on rare occasion, assets), and
- Payables to a defined benefit OPEB plan that is administered through a trust.

PRACTICE POINT: Health and welfare benefit plans are subject to the Employee Retirement Income Security Act of 1974 (ERISA). As discussed in the AICPA's Audit and Accounting Guide *Employee Benefit Plans* Chapter 7, they include provisions for:

- Medical, dental, prescription drugs, vision, psychiatric, long-term health care, life insurance, or accidental death or dismemberment benefits,

- Benefits for postemployment (benefits for former or inactive employees after employment but before retirement), such as Consolidated Omnibus Budget Reconciliation Act (COBRA) benefits, severance, or long-term or short-term disability,
- Other benefits, such as sick leave, vacation, holiday, apprenticeship, tuition assistance, day care, dependent care, housing subsidies, or legal services,
- Postretirement benefits, such as medical, dental, prescription drugs, vision, and life insurance benefits, and
- Supplemental unemployment benefits.

As states and local governments are generally *not* subject to ERISA, the provisions in the Act related to such plans do not apply. However, some governments may have (or are participants in) plans subject to ERISA. ERISA provisions are beyond the scope of this *Guide*.

In the basic financial statements, liabilities to employees for defined benefit OPEB provided through different OPEB plans may be displayed in the aggregate, but not aggregated with pension liabilities. Net OPEB assets can be displayed similarly, if applicable [GASB Cod. Secs. P50.117–.118].

Number of OPEB Plans. If assets accumulated in a plan that is administered through a trust are used to pay benefits (and refunds of employee contributions) to *any* employee, the total assets are one plan, even if separate reserves, funds, or accounts are present.

PRACTICE POINT: It is common to have separate actuarial valuations performed for individual bargaining unit groups due to variations in collective bargaining agreements, especially for teachers and public safety employees. Different contribution rates and benefit provisions may exist. Separate actuarial valuations do not necessarily mean a multiple-employer plan.

GAAP requires a separate defined benefit OPEB plan reported for a portion of the total assets, even if the assets are pooled for investment purposes, if the portion of assets meets *both* of the following criteria:

- The portion of assets is accumulated *only* for the payment of benefits to certain classes or groups of employees or to the active or inactive employees of certain entities (for example, state government employees), *and*
- The portion of assets may not legally be used to pay benefits to other classes or groups of employees or other entities' employees (for example, local government employees) [GASB Cod. Sec. P50.119].

DEFINED BENEFIT OPEB—SINGLE AND AGENT EMPLOYERS

Net OPEB Liability

Measurement of the OPEB liability raises can be different than the measurement of the net pension liability in the following areas:

13,060   Specific Accounting and Reporting Issues

Actuarial Assumption	Pensions	OPEB
Long-term rate of return	A main driver of the discount rate in the calculation of the net pension liability.	Many OPEB plans are not funded (PAYGO) or only provide subsidies as pass-through transactions. Therefore, the long-term rate of return is not a large concern.
Mortality	This vital assumption determines the payment period of benefits.	Mortality is not as vital as the liability is largely driven by claims. Furthermore, if the retiree is required to transfer to a Medicare plan at an eligible age, mortality is unlikely an issue as the risk has shifted to Medicare.
Salary inflation	Salary is a large driver of benefits and therefore, inflation is a factor.	Salary is not a driver of benefits and therefore, not a factor.
Retirement age or retirement rate	Like salary level, payments may be based on age at retirement.	The rate of retirement is a major factor in terms of eligibility to receive benefits and the calculation of cash flow to determine the liability.
Cost of living adjustments (COLAs) and healthcare cost trends	COLAs are only applicable if offered by the plan.	The healthcare cost trend rate is the main driver of OPEB, even more so than other assumptions.
Plan options	Options chosen by participants are dependent upon law, regulations, and plan provisions.	Many plans have multiple options of healthcare providers, limits, plans, deductibles and similar. Many plans only provide subsidies.
Utilization rate (rate that plan resources are used to pay benefits)	Applicable, but pension plans tend to have more assets to pay benefits, even if benefits adjust, than OPEB plans.	A large factor as the beneficiary ages, the more healthcare is needed.
Participation rate (the likelihood that a participant will retire based on plan provisions and for OPEB, select healthcare coverage)	Based on vesting requirements.	Retirees are often required to pay into the plan. Higher premiums may result in lower participation as the beneficiary can pay for their own healthcare, including Medicare (if eligible).

The following GAAP provisions of OPEB are like those discussed for pensions:

- Timing and frequency of actuarial valuations (measurement date and actuarial valuation date),
- Selection of assumptions,
- Discount rate setting process (see long-term rate of return, above), and
- Attribution of the actuarial present value of projected future projected benefit payments to periods.

Projections of benefit payments for defined benefit OPEB has a slightly different process than defined benefit pensions. Usually, a written document is the best evidence of benefit terms, but the *substantive plan* (the one understood by employees) may be different than the written document. The plan may also change at a greater frequency than pensions due to legislation or contract agreement.

Projections of benefits may also include taxes or other assessments *expected to be imposed* on benefit payments using rates in effect at the measurement date, or rates approved by the assessing government to be applied in future periods.

> **PRACTICE POINT:** The assessing government may be the federal government.

The projection is based on claims costs, or age-adjusted premiums approximating claims costs, in accordance with actuarial standards of practice.

> **PRACTICE POINT:** Projecting claims costs should be performed by an actuary experienced in healthcare. Pension actuaries may not have this skill. Age-adjusted premiums approximating claims costs was formerly known as the *implicit rate subsidy* under prior GAAP. The subsidy is a component of benefit payments and contributions and therefore, is not required to be disclosed separately.

There may be legal or contractual caps on benefit payments for OPEB which need to be considered. For example, it is common for an employer to be only responsible for a certain dollar amount or percentage of a retired employee's premiums. Another example is known as a *"Medicare toggle."* Once a beneficiary reaches eligibility for Medicare, the beneficiary shifts to Medicare. The effect of the shift is a major reduction in the potential OPEB liability for the state or local government as future claims are now shifted to Medicare (a federal program).

Finally, there may be *allocated* insurance contracts present for OPEB. *Allocated* insurance contracts are excluded from the projection of benefit payments if:

- The contract *irrevocably* transfers the responsibility for providing benefits to the insurer,

- All required payments to acquire the contract have been made, and

- The likelihood is remote that the employer (or nonemployer contributing entities, if any or an OPEB plan) will be required to make additional payments to satisfy the benefit provisions in the contract.

Allocated insurance contracts are in the name of the insured (Jane Smith) and not the government employer [GASB Cod. Secs. P50.120–.138].

OPEB Expense, Deferred Outflows of Resources, Deferred Inflows of Resources, and Support of Nonemployer Contributing Entities

Calculating various elements of OPEB is like pensions for single and agent employers. For cost-sharing employers, the concept of proportionality also is used in calculating the elements. An exception would be when the *alternative measurement method* is used, which is discussed later in this chapter.

Amortization of existing deferred outflows of resources and deferred inflows of resources for OPEB, as applicable, are components of OPEB expense, beginning in the current reporting period. Like pensions, the amortization uses a systematic and rational method over a closed period equal to the average of the expected remaining service lives of all employees that are provided OPEB through the OPEB plan (active and inactive) determined as of the *beginning* of the measurement period. Therefore, the following are components of OPEB expense:

Element of OPEB Expense with a Trust	Does Element Increase or Decrease OPEB Expense?
Service cost	Increases
Interest on beginning total OPEB liability	Increases
Changes in benefit terms	May increase or decrease
Plan administrative costs	Increase
Amortization of deferred outflows of resources (or deferred inflows of resources) for differences between expected and actual experience, changes in assumptions	Increases (or decreases in the case of amortizations of deferred inflows of resources)
Other adjustments	May increase or decrease
Employer contributions to the plan (may be unlikely in OPEB)	No impact as contributions increases fiduciary net position
Contributions to the pension plan from nonemployer contributing entities *that are not in a special funding situation*	Does *not* adjust OPEB expense, reported as revenue (Example: intergovernmental revenue or aid)

Amortizations of the differences between projected and actual earnings on OPEB plan investments (if any) are also amortized over a five-year period like pensions. Also, like pensions, contributions to the OPEB plan from the employer after the measurement date of the net OPEB pliability and before the end of the reporting period (excluding amounts associated with the employer from nonemployer contributing entities that are *not* in a special funding situation) are reported as deferred outflows of resources [GASB Cod. Secs. P50.139–.140].

Financial Reporting of OPEB by the Employer

Governmental Funds. Under current GAAP and similarly to defined benefit pensions, an OPEB liability is only recognized to the extent that it would be liquidated with expendable available financial resources. In most circumstances unless the plan was closed, and a final payment is being made, the OPEB liability would not be reported. However, amounts may be payable to a plan if due and payable. OPEB expenditures are recognized similarly to pensions: amounts paid by the employer during the reporting period (and by nonemployer contributing entities, if any) to the plan, including those amounts for benefits as they come due (PAYGO), as adjusted for the change in the payable amounts to the plan at the beginning and the end of the period.

Support of nonemployer contributing entities is revenue. The revenue may include amounts paid for OPEB as the benefits come due and the change in the receivable amounts at the beginning and the end of the period.

Government-Wide Statements. The Statement of Net Position reports the employer's portion of the net OPEB liability (or asset), and any unamortized deferred outflows of resources and deferred inflows of resources related to OPEB separately from pension-related amounts. OPEB expense is reported as a component of programmatic expenses on the Statement of Activities, like employee benefits [GASB Cod. Secs. P50.141–.143].

Note Disclosures—Single and Agent Employers

Note disclosures for OPEB information is like the information required by single and agent employers related to pensions. GAAP allows information to be aggregated wherever possible to avoid unnecessary duplication.

However, OPEB information should not be included in the same footnote element as pension information. The total (aggregate for all OPEB, regardless of the type of OPEB plans through which the OPEB is provided and whether the OPEB plans are administered through a trust) of the employer's OPEB liabilities, net OPEB assets, deferred outflows of resources and deferred inflows of resources related to OPEB, and OPEB expense or expenditures for the period associated with defined benefit OPEB liabilities to employees, as applicable, should be disclosed if the total amounts are not otherwise identifiable from information presented in the financial statements. If note disclosures include the primary government and component units, the note disclosures should separately identify the primary government inclusive of blended component units from discretely presented component units [GASB Cod. Secs. P50.144–.146].

For single and agent employers, note disclosures include:

- OPEB plan description, name and type of plan, the benefit terms, classes of employees covered, types of benefits, contribution information, key elements of OPEB formulas, changes in terms, COLAs, the number of employees covered by benefit terms and their classes, contribution requirements and the availability of a stand-alone report from the plan.
- Information about the NOL including assumptions and other inputs, healthcare cost trend rate, discount rate, mortality, experience studies and a sensitivity analysis of the healthcare cost trend rate as discussed previously.
- Information about the OPEB Plan's fiduciary net position (largely from the plan's financial statements).
- Changes in the NOL for the year (likely formatted as a table or schedule in the notes). If the employer has a special funding situation, the non-

employer's proportionate share information should be included in this section.
- Information on the measurement of the NOL including the actuarial valuation information, expense and similar information presented for pensions. As with pensions, separately financed specific liabilities to the OPEB plan are excluded from employer's contributions.
- Schedules showing the balances and amortization of deferred inflows and outflows of resources similarly to pensions [GASB Cod. Secs. P50.147–.153].

Required Supplementary Information and Related Note Disclosure—Single and Agent Employers

Required supplementary information for single and agent employers for OPEB is like that of pensions. The following should be provided as of the *measurement date of the net OPEB liability* is most often found in a single schedule:

- A 10-year schedule of changes in the net OPEB liability that separately presents the information required in the notes for each year,
- A 10-year schedule presenting the following for each year:

If the employer *does not* have a special funding situation:	If the employer *has* a special funding situation, information about the collective net OPEB liability:
The total OPEB liability,	The total OPEB liability,
The OPEB plan's fiduciary net position,	The OPEB plan's fiduciary net position,
The net OPEB liability,	The collective net OPEB liability,
The OPEB plan's fiduciary net position as a percentage of the total OPEB liability,	The nonemployer contributing entities' total proportionate share (amount) of the collective net OPEB liability,
The covered payroll, if contributions to the OPEB plan are based on pay, otherwise, the covered-employee payroll, and	The employer's proportionate share (amount) of the collective net OPEB liability,
The net OPEB liability as a percentage of the covered payroll.	The covered payroll, if contributions to the OPEB plan are based on pay, otherwise, the covered-employee payroll,
	The employer's proportionate share (amount) of the collective net OPEB liability as a percentage of the payroll in the previous disclosure, and
	The OPEB plan's fiduciary net position as a percentage of the total OPEB liability.

The following 10-year schedules are presented as of the employer's most recent fiscal year-end, as applicable [GASB Cod. Sec. P50.154]:

If an actuarially determined contribution is calculated:	If an actuarially determined contribution *is not* calculated *and* the contribution requirements of the employer are statutorily or contractually established:
The actuarially determined contribution of the employer. For purposes of this schedule, actuarially determined contributions should exclude amounts, if any, associated with payables to the OPEB plan that arose in a prior fiscal year and those associated with separately financed specific liabilities of the individual employer to the OPEB plan.	The statutorily or contractually required employer contribution. For purposes of this schedule, statutorily or contractually required contributions should exclude amounts, if any, associated with payables to the OPEB plan that arose in a prior fiscal year and those associated with separately financed specific liabilities of the individual employer to the OPEB plan.
The value of contributions recognized by the OPEB plan in relation to the actuarially determined contribution of the employer. For purposes of this schedule, contributions should exclude amounts resulting from contributions recognized by the OPEB plan as noncurrent receivables.	The value of contributions recognized by the OPEB plan in relation to the statutorily or contractually required employer contribution. For purposes of this schedule, contributions should exclude amounts resulting from contributions recognized by the OPEB plan as noncurrent receivables.
The difference between the actuarially determined contribution of the employer and the value of contributions recognized by the OPEB plan in relation to the actuarially determined contribution of the employer.	The difference between the statutorily or contractually required employer contribution and the value of contributions recognized by the OPEB plan in relation to the statutorily or contractually required employer contribution.
The covered payroll, if contributions to the OPEB plan are based on pay, otherwise, the covered-employee payroll.	The covered payroll, if contributions to the OPEB plan are based on pay, otherwise, the covered-employee payroll.
The value of contributions recognized by the OPEB plan in relation to the actuarially determined contribution of the employer as a percentage of the payroll.	The value of contributions recognized by the OPEB plan in relation to the statutorily or contractually required employer contribution as a percentage of the payroll.

Note disclosure mirrors that of pensions. The disclosure is inclusive of significant methods and assumptions used in calculating the actuarially determined contributions, if any. Information should be presented about factors that significantly affect trends in the amounts reported (e.g., changes of benefit terms, changes in the size or composition of the population covered by the benefit terms, or the use of different assumptions).

Information about investment-related factors that significantly affect trends in the amounts reported should be limited to those factors over which the OPEB plan or the participating governments have influence (e.g., changes in investment policies). Information about external, economic factors (e.g., changes in market prices) should not be presented. (The amounts presented for prior years should not be restated for the effects of changes—for example, changes of benefit terms or changes of assumptions—that occurred after the measurement date of that information). [GASB Cod. Sec. P50.155].

DEFINED BENEFIT OPEB—COST SHARING EMPLOYERS (WITH A TRUST)

As summarily discussed earlier in this chapter, most OPEB employers are single employers. Much of the cost-sharing employer guidance replicates pension guidance, adjusting where necessary for the characteristics of OPEB.

Proportionate Share of the Collective Net OPEB Liability

If a trust is used, employers that do not have a special funding situation recognize a liability for the employer's proportionate share of the collective net OPEB liability no earlier than the end of the employer's prior fiscal year and no later than the current fiscal year, applied consistently. This determination of the proportionate share is likely provided by the OPEB plan and is measured by:

1. Determining the employer's proportion—a measure of the proportionate relationship of:

    a. The employer (and, to the extent associated with the employer, nonemployer contributing entities, if any, that provide support for the employer but that are not in a special funding situation) to

    b. All employers and all nonemployer contributing entities. The basis for the employer's proportion should be consistent with the way contributions to the OPEB plan, excluding those associated with separately financed specific liabilities of an individual employer to the OPEB plan, are determined. The use of the employer's projected long-term contribution effort to the OPEB plan (including that of nonemployer contributing entities that provide support for the employer but that are not in a special funding situation) as compared to the total projected long-term contribution effort of all employers and all nonemployer contributing entities to determine the employer's proportion is encouraged.

2. Multiplying the collective net OPEB liability by the employer's proportion calculated.

PRACTICE POINT: If employer contributions are not made to the OPEB plan, an actuarial model is likely used based on benefit payments.

Once the proportion is determined, all other accounting elements follow suit—OPEB expense (adjusting for employer contributions to the OPEB plan after the measurement date, but prior to the fiscal year-end), deferred outflows of resources and deferred inflows of resources. Changes also occur similarly to pensions and follow similar GAAP. Adjustments may need to be made if the *alternative measurement method* is used (see section later in this chapter).

All other presentation provisions and most of the notes and required supplementary information is like single and agent-employers [GASB Cod. Secs. P50.156–.198].

OPEB—OTHER ISSUES

Special Funding Situations

For single and agent employers, if a special funding situation is present, only the proportionate share of the OPEB accounting elements is presented as it is in pensions. The nonemployer contributing entity will recognize the remainder.

The support of the nonemployer contributing entity in a special funding situation is recognized as revenue by the employer. The revenue equates to the total nonemployer contributing entity's total proportionate share of collective OPEB expense, reduced by the total amounts, if any, recognized by the nonemployer contributing entity as a reduction in expense. Added to this amount is any additional expense recognized for contributions to the OPEB plan to separately finance specific liabilities of the individual governmental nonemployer contributing entity to the OPEB plan.

If the employer receives funds from a nonemployer, but not in a special funding situation, only revenue is recognized [GASB Cod. Secs. P50.199–.209]. For the nonemployer, it is an expense or expenditure and reported similarly to other grants or aid [GASB Cod. Secs. P50.242–.243].

Reporting of Cost Sharing Employers that Contribute to OPEB Plans in Governmental Funds

GASB Cod. Sec. P50.601 contains a technical bulletin question and answer regarding expenditure recognition in governmental funds for such employers. For cost-sharing employers that have contractually required contributions to OPEB plans, expenditures are reported in governmental funds attributable to the periods of time for which the contributions are *assessed* by the plan. The period(s) may be different from the fiscal year.

Expenditures presented in governmental funds (as applicable) are the sum of amounts paid during the period as contractually required contributions for pay periods within that period *plus* any unpaid contractually required contributions for one (or more) pay periods within that period. The section contains an example where contributions are contractually required to a cost-sharing OPEB plan for the first six months of the employer's fiscal year totaling $700,000. $800,000 is due the second six months but paid after year end. Expenditures are then $1,500,000 with $800,000 as a payable [GASB Cod. Sec. P50.601].

Impact of Medicare Part D Subsidies from the Federal Government

Retiree drug subsidies (RDS) are reported by employers as a voluntary nonexchange transaction, like a grant. Employers recognize an asset and revenue for the payment received in accordance with GASB Cod. Sec. N50.104. The payment should not be netted as it is separate from salaries, benefits, and retiree drug benefits among the employer, employees, and retirees. Therefore, the calculation of the net OPEB liability is *not* reduced for the effect of the RDS related to Medicare Part D [GASB Cod. Sec. P50.602].

Alternative Measurement Method

In place of a full actuarial valuation small employers may measure the total OPEB liability utilizing a mathematical model if there are fewer than 100 members (both active and inactive) which receive OPEB from the plan as of the beginning of the measurement period.

Modifications are made to the measurement process including:

- Assumptions are based on the actual experience of the covered group, to the extent available, emphasizing long-term trends,
- The expected point in time to which benefits will begin to be made for active employers may be a single assumed age or an assumption attaining a specific amount of service,
- The expected time when employees will exit active service reflects experience and expectations of the group,
- Marital and dependency status are based on the status of members or historical data,
- Mortality is based on current published tables,
- Turnover is based on a probability of assumed age for benefits, or historical age-based turnover,
- The healthcare cost trend rate is derived from an objective source,
- Health insurance premiums may be used to project healthcare benefit payments, but should be obtained from the insurer,
- Coverage options are based on experience and may include Medicare options, and
- Grouping can be used by common demographics [GASB Cod. Secs. P50.244–.246].

PRACTICE POINT: It is the author's view that the alternative measurement method may be more difficult to use and to audit than to have an actuary prepare the information, except for the very smallest employers. Though it is U.S. GAAP, the information that is calculated may be very suspect. Luckily, for the very smallest employers, it is likely that the amounts calculated by the alternative measurement method may be immaterial.

OPEB Provided through OPEB Plans Not Administered through Trusts

Many employers provide OPEB outside of a trust for many reasons. The total OPEB liability, timing and frequency of actuarial valuations, assumptions, and projection of benefit payments, OPEB expense calculation and other items are all the same as previously discussed regarding OPEB and pensions.

A major difference is in the discount rate setting process. As no fiduciary net position is available without a trust, in this situation, the discount rate is a yield or index rate for 20-year tax-exempt general obligation municipal bonds with an average rating of AA/Aa or higher (or equivalent quality on another rating scale) [GASB Cod. Sec. P52.123].

For reporting in the Statement of Net Position, the liability is recognized as the total OPEB liability. All other elements are recognized the same as with a trust.

Note Disclosure for OPEB Provided through OPEB Plans Not Administered through Trusts

Note disclosure is like the previously mentioned OPEB, dependent upon the type of plan. However, it must be noted that there are no assets accumulated in a trust. Each criterion for a trust previously described should be noted that the OPEB plan does not meet the provisions of having a trust [GASB Cod. Secs. P52.131–.138].

Required Supplementary Information and Notes for OPEB Provided through OPEB Plans Not Administered through Trusts

As there are no assets or fiduciary net position, the 10-year schedules for required supplementary information are limited. They include the 10-year schedule of changes in the total OPEB liability and related notes to the required schedule. No contribution schedule is necessary [GASB Cod. Secs. P52.139–.140].

Insured Benefits

As with pensions, defined benefit OPEB plans in which benefits are financed through an arrangement whereby premiums are paid to an insurance company while employees are in active service, in return for which the insurance company unconditionally undertakes an obligation to pay the OPEB of those employees as defined in the OPEB plan terms, are insured plans, and the OPEB provided through those plans is classified as insured benefits) [GASB Cod. Sec. P52.106].

The accounting and financial reporting for insured benefits is simplified. In the government-wide or business-type activity financial statements, an employer that provides OPEB through an insured plan should recognize OPEB expense equal to the amount of premiums or other payments required for the reporting period in accordance with the agreement with the insurance company for such OPEB and a change in the liability to the insurer equal to the difference between amounts recognized as OPEB expense and amounts paid by the employer to the insurer.

For governmental funds, OPEB expenditures related to insured benefits should be recognized equal to the total of the amount of premiums paid or other payments made by the employer to the insurer and the change between the beginning and ending balances of amounts normally expected to be liquidated with expendable available financial resources. A liability for insured benefits is normally expected to be liquidated with expendable available financial resources to the extent that the payments are due and payable pursuant to legal requirements, including contractual arrangements.

Notes to the financial statements for insured benefits only require a brief description of the benefits, the fact that the obligations are insured by one or more insurance companies, details of retained obligations and the current-year OPEB expense or expenditure for the insured benefits [GASB Cod. Secs. P52.203–.205].

PRACTICE POINT: Many practitioners confuse insured plans. If the employer makes payments to insurance entity for OPEB, the payments do not signify an insured plan. An insured plan only occurs when premiums are paid to an insurance company while employees are in active service, in return for which the insurance company unconditionally undertakes an obligation to pay the OPEB of those employees as defined in the plan terms [GASB Cod. Sec. Po50.104].

Reporting Assets Accumulated for Defined Benefit OPEB Without a Trust

Without a trust, assets are rarely accumulated to pay future benefits for OPEB. If an OPEB plan is not administered through a trust, any assets accumulated for OPEB purposes are assets of the employer or nonemployer contributing entity.

The government that holds assets accumulated for OPEB purposes in a fiduciary capacity reports the assets in a custodial fund. The amount of assets accumulated that exceeds the liabilities for benefits due to plan members and accrued investment and administrative expenses is reported as a liability to participating employers or nonemployer contributing entities.

If the custodial fund is included in the financial report of an employer whose employees are provided with benefits through the OPEB plan or a nonemployer contributing entity that makes benefit payments as OPEB comes due, balances reported by the custodial fund should exclude amounts that pertain to the employer or nonemployer contributing entity that reports the custodial fund [GASB Cod. Secs. P53.107–.108].

Defined Contribution OPEB

Defined contribution OPEB is similar to defined contribution pension reporting. OPEB expense is equal to the value of contributions or credits to employees' accounts defined by the plan terms as attributable to employees' services in the period, net of forfeited amounts removed from the employees' accounts. Amounts that are reallocated to the accounts of other employees should not be considered forfeited amounts for this purpose. Trusts may or may not be present. Special funding situations may or may not be present.

Added to the expense is a change in the OPEB liability. If a trust is used, the difference between the amounts recognized as OPEB expense and the amounts paid is added to the expense. If no trust is used, the difference between amounts recognized as OPEB expense and amounts paid by the employer as the benefits come due during the fiscal year is added to expense.

Governmental fund reporting is like governmental fund reporting for pensions. OPEB expenditures equal the total of amounts paid by the employer for OPEB as the benefits come due and the change between the beginning and ending balances of amounts normally expected to be liquidated with expendable available financial resources. A liability for defined contribution OPEB is recognized to the extent the liability is normally expected to be liquidated with expendable available financial resources. A liability for defined contribution OPEB is normally expected to be liquidated with expendable available financial resources to the extent that contributions are due and payable pursuant to legal requirements, including contractual arrangements.

For multiple defined contribution OPEB plans, aggregated OPEB liabilities should be displayed separately from aggregated OPEB assets.

The notes to financial statements about each defined contribution OPEB plan to which an employer is required to contribute include:

- The name of the OPEB plan, identification of the entity that administers the OPEB plan, and identification of the OPEB plan as a defined contribution OPEB plan,

- A brief description of the benefit terms (including terms, if any, related to vesting and forfeitures and the policy related to the use of forfeited amounts) and the authority under which benefit terms are established or may be amended,

- If the OPEB is provided through a defined contribution OPEB plan that is administered through a trust the contribution (or crediting) rates (in dollars or as a percentage of salary) for employees, the employer, and nonemployer contributing entities, if any, and the authority under which those rates are established or may be amended,

- If the OPEB is provided through a defined contribution OPEB plan that is not administered through a trust, disclosure includes the fact that there are no assets accumulated in a trust that meets the criteria. If OPEB is provided through an OPEB plan *that is* administered through a trust and that trust does not meet the criteria for a trust, each criterion that the trust does not meet should be disclosed,

- Identification of the authority under which requirements for the employer and nonemployer contributing entities, if any, to pay OPEB as the benefits come due are established or may be amended. Also, the amount paid by the employer for OPEB as the benefits came due during the reporting period, if not otherwise disclosed,

- The amount of OPEB expense recognized by the employer in the reporting period,

- The value of forfeitures reflected in OPEB expense recognized by the employer in the reporting period, and

- The amount of the employer's liability outstanding at the end of the period, if any [GASB Cod. Secs. P51.101–.110, P54.101–.120].

PRACTICE POINT: As discussed in Chapter 8, in some situations, defined contribution arrangements for employees may not be fiduciary activities.

In situations where the arrangement is a fiduciary activity, reporting of assets, liabilities, fiduciary net position, inflows, and outflows would be in a pension (and other employee benefit trust fund). In situations where the arrangement is *not a fiduciary activity*, the accounting and financial reporting of the arrangements may be limited to recognition of employee benefit expense/expenditures in the payroll-generating fund and any related payable amounts to the plan.

An example of a plan which may require analysis to determine if a fiduciary activity is in place would be a retirement health savings account (or program), which may only be open to eligible employees. For those employees, participation is mandatory and determined by the employer. However, the employer *may not* have any financial burden to the plan. The employer *may not* have control of the plan. In such cases, the account *is not a fiduciary activity*. Care must be also taken not to confuse retirement health savings accounts or programs with IRC Section 401(h) accounts which are commonly paired with IRC Section 401(a) plans, which are money purchase plans. Section 401(h) accounts are subordinated to other types of pension plans and are established in a separate account.

APPENDIX—COMPENSATED ABSENCES PRIOR TO GASB STATEMENT NO. 101

NOTE: The following paragraphs are for provisions *prior to implementing GASB Statement No. 101*. See Part 1 for the new provisions.

Many state and local governments provide a variety of compensated absences for their employees such as paid vacations, paid holidays, sick pay and especially in the case of public institutions of higher education, sabbatical leaves. Due to the nature of these commitments, most compensated absences programs generally create a liability for a governmental entity.

The elements of vacation and sick leave often differ. In some cases, unused vacation or sick leave carries forward and becomes a component of compensation at retirement or termination at the rate of pay (or a percentage of pay) at that time based on the accumulation of past service. Accrued vacation or sick leave is earned as a component of daily work. Paid compensation occurs for sick leave because of an illness that is unplanned and out of the control of the employer and employee.

In some cases, employees are "capped" in the number of hours of sick and vacation resulting in a "use or lose" decision made by the employee. There may be other nuances, including when furloughs occur, employers may offer additional vacation time in exchange for unpaid hours. In other circumstances, employers allow for interchangeable sick and vacation time also utilizing an annual cap, except in the case of catastrophic illness [Former GASB Cod. Secs. C60.101–.102].

Measurement and Recognition of Compensated Absences

A liability for compensated absences should be recorded when future payments for such absences have been earned by employees as a condition of services rendered if the benefits are not contingent on an event outside the control of the employer and employee. The liability is generated by the employee's right to the benefit.

Therefore, there should be no accrual for compensated absences that are dependent on the performance of *future* services by employees, or when payments are dependent on future events that are outside the control of the employer and employees.

The accrual concept in the context of the following compensated absences:

- Vacation leave, and other compensated absences with similar characteristics,
- Sick leave and other compensated absences with similar characteristics, and
- Sabbatical leave [Former GASB Cod. Sec. C60.103].

Vacation Leave and Other Compensated Absences with Similar Characteristics

Compensated absences for vacation leave and benefits with similar characteristics should be recorded as a liability when earned by employees if the following conditions are satisfied:

- Compensated absence is earned based on services *already performed* by employees.
- It is *probable* that the compensated absence will be paid (payment may be in the form of paid time off, cash payments at termination or retirement, or some other means) in a future period.

Fringe-benefit arrangements may allow employees to earn compensated absences, but employees may not be entitled to benefits until certain minimum conditions (such as minimum time of employment) are met. For example, the employee must work at least half time (20 hours per week) for a minimum of three months.

Under this arrangement, a governmental entity should accrue for compensated absences that are probable (i.e., likely to take place). Thus, a governmental entity must determine whether it is likely that benefits earned, but not payable until certain conditions are met, will be paid. On the other hand, benefits related to compensated absences that have been earned, but are expected to lapse, should not be accrued. As previously introduced, some benefits may lapse due to a cap on the number of vacation days that can be carried forward from period to period.

Although the standards are discussed in the context of vacation leave, those standards are equally applicable to compensated absences that have characteristics like vacation leave. Thus, any compensated absence benefit that is not

13,074 *Specific Accounting and Reporting Issues*

dependent on an event outside of the control of the employer or the employee should be accounted for in a manner like vacation leave benefits.

Generally, these types of benefits are granted to employees solely based on the length of their employment. For example, a governmental entity that provides its employees with one personal day for each 180-calendar day period worked is providing a compensated absence benefit that should be accrued, because it is based on length of employment. On the other hand, an entity that provides its employees with military-leave benefits should not accrue this compensated absence, because the benefit will be paid only if an employee serves in the military at a future date [Former GASB Cod. Sec. C60.104]. An example of accruing vacation leave is in Exhibit 13-1.

EXHIBIT 13-1
ILLUSTRATION: VACATION LEAVE

To illustrate the use of compensated absences for vacation leave, assume the following based on Former GASB Cod. Sec. C60.901, example 1:

- Each employee earns one day of vacation for each month worked starting with the hire date.
- An employee is entitled to use vacation leave after one year of employment.
- If an employee is terminated, all earned (but unused) vacation leave is paid at the employee's current pay rate. (Employees with less than one year of service receive no payment.)

The estimated liability for vacation leave is based on the following information: Number of current employees by length of service:

Employee Category	Members of the Category	Number of Members in Category
1	Employees who have worked for more than one year	70
2	Employees who have worked for less than one year	30

Characteristics of employee categories:

	Category 1	Category 2
Current average daily pay rate	$400	$250
Average number of vacation days accumulated	25	7

Based on prior experience, it is estimated that approximately 30% of employees with less than one year of experience will work at least one year and therefore be entitled to termination pay for accumulated vacation days.

The estimated liability for compensated absences liability for vacation leave is computed below:

Category	Number of Employees		Average Pay Rate		Average Vacation Days Accumulated		Probability Factor		Extended Amounts
1	70	×	$400	×	25	×	100%	=	$700,000
2	30	×	250	×	7	×	30%	=	15,750 |//
Estimated liability for vacation leave									**$715,750** *

* The estimate should also include a provision for additional salary-related payments (see the section entitled "Liability Calculation").

The accrual of compensated absences for vacation leave is usually straightforward. Most governmental entities impose few, if any, restrictions on an employee's right to take vacation days earned or to receive accumulated vacation pay when termination occurs. Thus, in most instances, the number of vacation days earned to date should be the basis for the accrual for compensated absences for vacation leave.

However, in some cases, the right to receive vacation leave may depend on some unfulfilled condition. As previously discussed, a new employee may have to work a minimum of six months before vacation days are earned. In this case, the governmental entity must determine whether it is probable that newly hired employees eventually will meet the minimum work criterion. If so, the entity must include these employees' past work experience in the calculation of the compensated-absence accrual. Including this type of work experience could be contrary to the basic premise that accrual is appropriate only when payments do not depend on events outside the control of the employer and employee. As future employment is a condition controlled by the employer and employee, a contingency is present: the employer could fire the employee, or the employee could quit.

Sick Leave and Compensated Absences with Similar Characteristics

Sick leave benefits often differ from other compensated absences in that sick-pay benefits are dependent on employee illness (a future event). However, sick leave programs often allow employees to accumulate sick days. If the leave days are not used, employees may be paid for all or perhaps a maximum number of the accumulated sick days on termination or retirement, referred to as termination payments.

Due to the unique characteristics of sick leave programs, the GASB addresses the issue separately from other compensated absences. Thus, compensated absences for sick leave and other compensated absences with similar characteristics should be accrued only when it is probable that the employer will have to make termination payments. Sick-pay benefits that have been earned, but probably will be used only for sick leave, should not be accrued, but rather recorded as an expenditure or expense when employees are paid for days not worked due to illness.

Other compensated absences are considered like sick leave when the benefit is based on a specific future event *that is not subject to control by the employer or employees*. Examples of other compensated absences with this characteristic include leaves for military service, jury duty, and close-family funerals.

Two methods are contained in the former GASB Cod. Sec. C60 that can be used to calculate the liability related to compensated absences for sick leave: the *termination payment method* and the *vesting method*. Neither method allows for the accrual of non-vesting (rights that cannot or will not vest) sick leave.

Termination Payment Method. Under the termination payment method, a governmental entity generally estimates its sick pay liability based on history, adjusted for changes in pay rates, administrative policies, and other relevant factors. Thus, the accrual applies historical information or trends to a governmental entity's current workforce [Former GASB Cod. Sec. C60.105]. An example of this method is in Exhibit 13-2.

EXHIBIT 13-2
ILLUSTRATION: SICK LEAVE (TERMINATION PAYMENT METHOD)

To illustrate the termination payment method, assume the following:

- Sick leave can be used only for personal sickness or close-family sickness.
- Sick leave accumulates with no limit, and sick leave not taken before termination or retirement will be paid to an employee at the rate of 80% of the employee's current pay rate if the employee has 10 years or more of service.
- Each employee earns one day of sick leave for each month worked, and when sick leave is taken, the employee is paid at his or her current rate of pay.

The estimated liability for sick leave is based on the following governmental entity's experience over the past five years:

Factor	Amount
Number of employees terminated or retired during past five years	10 employees
Number of sick days paid on termination or retirement for employees during past five years	90 sick days
Total number of years worked by all employees terminated or retired during past five years (all employees × hours worked past 5 years ÷ 365) (rounded)	180 years
Current average daily pay rate	$400

Currently, the governmental entity's active labor force includes 100 employees who have accumulated 1,200 person-years of work. The estimated liability for sick leave compensated absences is computed below:

Operation	Amount
Number of sick days paid on termination or retirement for employees during past five years	90
Multiply by average current pay rate	× $400
Subtotal	$36,000
Multiply by final payment percentage of current pay	× 80%
Subtotal	$28,800
Divide by number of years worked by retired and terminated employees	÷ 180 years
Equals	= $160
Multiply by number of years worked by current labor force	× 1,200
Estimated liability for sick leave	**$192,000** *

*The estimate should also include a provision for additional salary-related payments.

Although termination payments for sick leave are usually paid in cash to employees, some governmental entities allow an employee to forego direct payments for additional service credit in determining the amount of pension benefits or as a contribution to the cost of postemployment health care due to the employee. Such arrangements are not termination payments. However, they should be considered in determining the actuarial valuation of the governmental entity's pension liability [Former GASB Cod. Sec. C60, fn. 4].

The estimation methodology is based on an example presented in the former GASB Cod. Sec. C60.901. However, there is no prescribed method that must be used to compute the estimate. A governmental entity must determine the most appropriate method to compute the estimate. For example, the former GASB Cod. Sec. C60.901, example 4, notes that a governmental entity could estimate the liability by "developing a ratio based on historical data of sick leave paid at termination compared with sick leave accumulated and by applying that ratio to the sick leave accumulated by current employees as of the (Statement of Net Position) date."

Vesting Method. The termination payment method may be difficult for some governmental entities to apply. For example, in some instances, relevant historical information may not be available or the workforce may be too small to successfully apply historical ratios or trends. The vesting method focuses on those employees who have a right to sick leave based on some form of longevity. Vesting sick-leave rights include vested rights and those rights that will eventually vest, generally after a minimum number of years have been worked. The vesting method differs in the termination payment method using a probability factor and weighting to different classes of employees. Differences in classes of employees are almost always in collective bargaining agreements, which may make the vesting method more fairly stated than the termination method. An example of this method is in Exhibit 13-3.

EXHIBIT 13-3
ILLUSTRATION: SICK LEAVE (VESTING METHOD)

To illustrate the vesting method, assume the following:

- Sick leave can be used only for personal sickness or close-family sickness.
- Sick leave accumulates with no limit, and any sick leave accrued but not previously taken by the time of termination or retirement will be paid to an employee at the rate of 80% of the employee's current pay rate if the employee has 10 years or more of service.
- Each employee earns one day of sick leave for each month worked, and when sick leave is taken, the employee is paid at his or her current rate of pay.

The estimated liability for sick leave is based on the following estimates:

Number of current employees by classification:

Employee Category	Members of the Category	Number of Members in Category
1	Administrative or professional	10
2	Uniformed	20
3	Clerical or secretarial	70
	Total	**100**

Characteristics of employee-categories:

		Amounts	
Factor	Category 1	Category 2	Category 3
Current average daily pay rate	$300	$260	$120
Average number of sick days accumulated	13	16	8
Probability employee will work at least 10 years	90%	95%	25%

The estimated liability for compensated absences liability for sick leave is computed below:

Category	Number of Employees		Average Pay Rate		Average Sick Days Accumulated		Probability Factor		Extended Amounts
1	10	×	$300	×	13	×	90%	=	$35,100
2	20	×	$260	×	16	×	95%	=	79,040
3	70	×	$120	×	8	×	25%	=	16,800
							Subtotal		$130,940

Multiply by percentage of final payment 80%
Estimated liability for sick leave **$104,752** *

* Estimate should also include a provision for additional salary-related payments (see the section entitled "Liability Calculation"). The vesting method includes all vesting sick leave amounts for which payment is probable, not just the vesting amounts that will result in terminal payment. The vesting method is based on accumulated benefits as of a Statement of Net Position date, not on amounts accruing over expected periods of services.

Sabbatical Leave

Governmental fringe benefits may include earning sabbatical leaves, especially in public institutions of higher education and healthcare facilities. In determining whether compensated absences for sabbatical leaves should be accrued, the criteria discussed earlier must be satisfied (see discussion in section titled "Vacation Leave and Other Compensated Absences with Similar Characteristics").

In applying those criteria, the purpose of the leave must be evaluated. If sabbatical leave provides employees with unrestricted time off, a liability for compensated absences should be accrued. The amount of the accrual should be based on the periods during which the rights to sabbatical leaves are earned and the probable amounts that will be paid (through paid time off or by other means) to employees under the sabbatical program.

Some sabbatical leave benefits provide restricted leaves. The nature of the duties performed by governmental personnel change, but the governmental entity dictates the services or activities to be performed by employees on sabbatical. For example, employees may be required to perform research or participate in continuing professional education programs. Compensated-absences liability for sabbatical-leave programs based on restricted leaves should not be accrued. Instead, it should be reported as a current expenditure or expense during periods that employees perform their directed duties as required under sabbatical programs [Former GASB Cod. Sec. C60.106].

Liability Calculation

The accrual of compensated absences should be based on pay rates that are in effect as of the Statement of Net Position date, unless a specific rate is established by contract, regulation, or policy. For example, some governmental contract agreements may entitle employees to sick-pay termination settlements at one-half of employees' current pay rates [Former GASB Cod. Sec. C60.107].

In addition to the basic pay rate, the accrual of compensated absences should include estimated employer payments related to the payroll. The former GASB Cod. Sec. C60 describes these payments as items for which a government is "liable to make a payment directly and incrementally associated with payments made for compensated absences on termination" (incremental salary-related payments).

To meet the standard of being directly and incrementally associated with payment of termination payments for compensated absences, the related payroll payments must be:

- A function of the employee's salary amount, and
- Payable as part of salary for compensated-absences balances at the date an employee takes time off, retires, or is terminated.

Common salary-related payments include the employer's share of Social Security and Medicare payroll taxes because those taxes are a function of an employee's level of salary and are also paid to the federal government when employees receive payments for compensated absences. However, all of an employee's salary may not be subject to payroll taxes, a fact the employer should take into consideration when estimating the compensated absences accrual.

> **PRACTICE POINT:** In general, whatever payroll withholding is required to be remunerated while an employee is working should also be a salary-related payment calculated as part of the compensated absences accrual. Union dues, wage garnishments, transit passes, deferred compensation, and many other payments may all be salary-related.

Another salary-related payment is the employer's share of contributions to pension plans. When the pension plan is a defined contribution plan or a cost-sharing, multiple-employer defined benefit pension plan, the employer's share of the contribution should be part of the accrual for compensated absences if the employer is liable for contributions to the plan based on termination payments made to employees for compensated absences. The salary-related pension contribution must be part of the accrual, as it is included in the base used to determine the employer's share of contributions to the pension plan. On the other hand, the accrual should not include contributions to single-employer plans and agent multiple-employer defined benefit plans, in which case, the actuarial computation for employer contributions takes into consideration termination payments for compensated absences [Former GASB Cod. Sec. C60.108].

> **OBSERVATION:** The former GASB Cod. Secs. C60.707-1-2 clarify the situation when a government includes cash payments to retiring employees for unused compensated absences (vacation leave and sick leave to the extent settled by means of a termination payment) as part of the employee's compensation for the final year of service for the purposes of determining employees' defined pension benefits and the employer's contractually required contributions to the cost-sharing pension plan. The former GASB Cod. Sec. C60.108 *does not apply*. Instead, the projected effects of the termination payment for compensated absences in an employee's compensation in the final year of service on benefit payments is required to be included in the projection of benefit payments for determining the employer's pension liability. Defined benefit pensions are discussed later in this chapter.
>
> The former GASB Cod. Sec. C60 does not attempt to address all compensated absences that might be part of a governmental entity's fringe-benefit package. If a governmental entity has such fringe benefits, those benefits should be accounted for using the broad concepts contained in GASB Cod. Sec. C60. Also, each compensated absence benefit should be accounted for based on the substance of the benefit plan, not on its name. For example, a fringe benefit may be labeled as sick leave when in fact employees can be absent from work for reasons other than illness. In this case, standards related to vacation-leave absences should be observed rather than the standards related to sick leave.

Reporting Compensated Absences

Presentation in Government-Wide Financial Statements. The accrual basis of accounting and the economic resources measurement focus should also be used to determine the amount of the liability related to compensated absences that should be presented in a governmental entity's Statement of Net Position. Liabilities should be presented in the Statement of Net Position based on their relative liquidity. Compensated absences that are long-term liabilities would be shown as such in the Statement of Net Position. This establishes the potential for a disclosure of amounts estimated due within one year and an amount due in more than one year [Former GASB Cod. Sec. C60.109].

> **PRACTICE POINT:** Because the occurrence and dollar amounts are generally not known reliably in advance, the former GASB Cod. Sec. C60.708-1 allows governments to estimate the current portion of compensated absences due. Most governments base this amount on historical trends, budgeted amounts, and policy adjustments.

Presentation in Proprietary and Fiduciary Fund Financial Statements. The accrual basis of accounting should be used to determine the amount of the liability related to compensated absences that should be presented on the Statement of Fund Net Position of a proprietary fund or the Statement of Fiduciary Net Position of a fiduciary fund. In determining the amount of the liability, the guidance discussed earlier should be followed, except the total amount of the estimated debt should be presented as a liability (not just the portion of the debt that will use expendable financial resources) [Former GASB Cod. Sec. C60.110].

Presentation in Governmental Fund Financial Statements. While the former GASB Cod. Sec. C60 contains standards for the measurement of the compensated absences liability, the amount that should be reported as an expenditure in a governmental fund is based on the modified accrual basis of accounting and current financial resources measurement focus. Thus, *only* the portion of the estimated future payments for compensated absences *that will use current expendable resources should be reported as a liability of a governmental fund* presented in a Balance Sheet. However, the entire amount would be presented in the governmental entity's Statement of Net Position [Former GASB Cod. Sec. C60.111].

CHAPTER 14
LEASES AND SIMILAR ARRANGEMENTS

Chapter References:
GASB Statement Nos. 14, 34, 65, 72, 87, 92–94, 96, 99
GASB *Implementation Guide*

INTRODUCTION

PRACTICE POINT: This chapter provides guidance for leases in accordance with GASB Cod. Sec. L20, public-private and public-public partnerships and availability payment arrangements in accordance with GASB Cod. Secs. P90 and A90, respectively (P3's), and subscription-based information technology arrangements (SBITAs) in accordance with GASB Cod. Sec. S80.

Basic Provisions of Leasing

GASB Cod. Sec. L20 defines a lease as:

A contract that conveys the right to use a nonfinancial asset (the underlying asset) for a defined period in an exchange or exchange-like transaction.

"Exchange" and "exchange-like" transactions have the same definitions as presented in GASB Cod. Sec. N50 (*Nonexchange Transactions*) [GASB Cod. Sec. L20–.102, fn. 1].

PRACTICE POINT: See Chapters 17 and 18 of the *Governmental GAAP Guide* for further information on exchange and "exchange-like" transactions. As defined in GASB Cod. Sec. N50.503, "the difference between exchange and exchange-like transactions is a matter of degree." In contrast to a "pure" exchange transaction, an exchange-like transaction is one in which the values exchanged, though related, may not be quite equal or in which the direct benefits may not be exclusively for the parties to the transaction. Nevertheless, the exchange characteristics of the transaction are strong enough to justify treating the transaction as an exchange for accounting recognition. These definitions are referred to repeatedly throughout the chapter as part of the framework for leases, P3's and SBITAs.

PRACTICE ALERT: The GASB is in the process of a major project on the *classification* of nonfinancial assets, but not the recognition and measurement of such assets. In scope are the following types of assets, excluding investments discussed in Chapter 9 of this *Guide*:

- Tangible capital assets held for sale and tangible capital assets used for service,
- Intangible capital assets and tangible capital assets,
- Intangible lease assets and tangible owned assets, and
- Contracts for the right-to-use intangible assets and leases of tangible assets.

Tangible capital assets held for sale tentatively may be required to be classified separately from tangible capital assets used for service by requiring them to be reported as a major class of capital asset. Intangible capital assets would be classified separately from tangible capital assets by requiring them to be reported by major class separate from major classes of tangible capital assets.

Right-to-use assets would be required to be recognized for subscription-based information technology arrangements separately from other capital assets. Assets representing the right-to-use intangible underlying assets, other than subscription-based information technology arrangements, should not be classified separately from assets representing the right-to-use tangible underlying assets. Assets representing the right-to-use intangible underlying assets would be classified separately from owned intangible assets.

The exposure draft is expected to define the term *held for sale*. Such capital assets held for sale would be required to be reclassified as used for service if the usage of the asset changes over time.

An exposure draft was being released as this edition of the *Guide* was slated for publication. A final standard is expected by June 2024.

Differentiating Exchange and Exchange-Like Transactions in Leasing. It may be difficult to discern if a lease is present in many situations. For example, the situation where a government obtains the right to use land which has a market rent that is far above what the government is paying in the arrangement. If a government does not give up essentially equal value (or not quite equal value), it would not be a lease as it is not an exchange or exchange-like transaction.

Another example is when a government agrees to use a facility, but only for a few days of the week, with unrelated parties using the same facility for the remainder of the week. The GASB discusses how uninterrupted control is not necessary if the government has the right to use the facility in accordance with the contract. During the days of use, the government is in control [GASB Cod. Sec. L20.701-2].

However, in the case of where a government leases land to a rancher for grazing, but the agreement allows access to the public and even allows the government to construct other assets on the land without permission from the rancher, then what results is a rights agreement, not a lease. The key difference is *control* [GASB Cod. Sec. L20.701-4].

> **PRACTICE POINT:** As further discussed in the *Exclusions from Leasing Framework* subsection, care must be taken on farmland and "live" assets. Contractual exchanges of biological assets are excluded from GASB Cod. Sec. L20 as discussed in the subsection on exclusions.

Easements and Rights Easements present a further problem. Some do meet the definition of a lease, others do not. Permanent easements last indefinitely without cancellation. Therefore, they do not meet the defined period criteria contained in GASB Cod. Sec. L20 [GASB Cod. Sec. L20.701-5].

Cell phone towers are common on government property especially buildings and land. Cell phone towers and similar are leases if the arrangements meet the definition of a lease, including control. The control criteria are met if the placement agreement allows the company control of the right to use the land or building on which the tower is placed or the connection point to which the antenna is positioned [GASB Cod. Sec. L20.701-8].

A government has a right to use a *nonfinancial asset* if the government has *both*:

- The right to obtain the present service capacity from use of the underlying asset as specified in the contract, and
- The right to determine the nature and manner of use of the underlying asset as specified in the contract.

The rights may be identified as a lease or not identified as a lease in the contractual arrangement. However, the substance of the arrangement meets the characteristics of a lease. Some contracts have both a lease component and a service component, which may (or may not) be in accordance with GASB Cod. Sec. L20 or the provisions of GASB Cod. Sec. P90 (*Public-Private and Public-Public Partnerships and Availability Payment Arrangements*) or GASB Cod. Sec. S80 (*Subscription-Based Information Technology Arrangements*), both discussed later in this chapter [GASB Cod. Secs. L20.103–.104].

> **PRACTICE POINT:** The American Institute of Certified Public Accountants (AICPA) has released a nonauthoritative appendix in the Audit and Accounting Guide *States and Local Governments* including an emphasis point on *embedded leases*. The contracts that may be embedded leases do not use the word "rent" or "lease" in them but meet the characteristics of a lease. The emphasis point mentions common contracts that may contain embedded leases including:
> - "As-a-service" contracts,
> - Sales contracts,
> - Advertising contracts,
> - Transportation and construction arrangements, and
> - Related-party contracts.

In implementations of the leasing pronouncements, a best practice may be to perform a search for contracts that may have recurring payments to the same counterparties at similar frequencies for similar values to find such potential lease contracts.

PRACTICE POINT: In the AICPA's nonauthoritative appendix on leasing in the Audit and Accounting Guide, *States and Local Governments*, the completeness assertion will be a key audit focus area in the auditing of leases presented in accordance with GASB-87 by either lessees or lessors.

Financial assets are defined in GASB Cod. Sec. 3100.517 as cash, evidence of an ownership interest in an entity, or a contract that conveys to one entity a right to do either of the following:

- Receive cash or another financial instrument from a second entity, or
- Exchange other financial instruments on potentially favorable terms with the second entity (e.g., an option).

Under current GAAP, the opposite of financial assets are nonfinancial assets. Examples of nonfinancial assets include buildings, land, vehicles, and equipment [GASB Cod. Sec. L20.105].

Exclusions from Leasing Framework

GASB Cod. Sec. L20 specifically excludes the following types of assets:

- Lease contracts for intangible assets such as:
  — Lease contracts concerning the rights to explore for or to exploit natural resources such as oil, gas and similar,
  — Licensing contracts (most notably computer software) (discussed later in this chapter), and
  — Other than sublease contracts for intangible right-to-use lease assets,
- Leases of biological assets,
- Leases where the underlying asset in a lease meets the definition of an investment in accordance with GASB Cod. Sec. I50 (See Chapter 9 of the *Governmental GAAP Guide*.),
- Contracts that meet the definition of a service concession arrangement (as discussed later in this chapter), and
- Leases in which the underlying asset is financed with outstanding conduit debt, unless both the underlying asset and the conduit debt are reported by the lessor (see discussion on *Conduit Debt Obligations* in Chapter 12).

Certain regulated leases have limited treatment, most notably aviation leases between airports and airlines that are regulated by the U.S. Department of Transportation. The concessions at airports do not include the airlines and are subject to the provisions of GASB Cod. Sec. L20 [GASB Cod. Sec. L20.106]. Contracts involving the Federal Maritime Commission at ports and the Nuclear Regulatory Commission may also be regulated.

Leases and Similar Arrangements **14,005**

Other aspects and facts may determine whether a contract or agreement should be considered for inclusion as a lease in accordance with GASB Cod. Sec. L20. As examples:

Fact Pattern	Guidance	GASB Cod. Sec.
Five-year agreement signed with a nongovernmental entity with the right to use the government's land. The entity uses the land for hunting and has sole access during season.	*It is a lease.* The contract conveys control of the right to use the land during the agreement. Uninterrupted control not required.	L20.701-3
Government contracts with a private party for control of a portion of a power plant for parts of a year for three years. The government makes fixed payments and variable payments based on usage and output.	*It is a lease.* Control of the underlying asset is obtained. (Variable payments are outflows as discussed later in this chapter.)	L20.701-6
Government contracts with a private party to design and build a solar farm based on the government's specifications. The farm is on the government's property, but the equipment is maintained by the private party who determines its manner and use. The contract requires the government to purchase the power generated and make payments based on the power generated. At the end of the contract, the equipment is removed.	*Not a lease.* The government does not have the right to determine the nature and manner of use. The design/build function could be a lease (see later in this chapter on public-private and public-public partnerships and availability payment arrangements).	L20.701-7
Substitution of an underlying asset with an essentially identical asset still a lease?	Yes. (See discussion later in this chapter on *Contract Combinations*.)	L20.701-9
Government conveys control of the right to use parcel of land for oil and gas production.	Still a lease even though the right to *explore* is excluded. The production of such assets indicates that extraction is certain.	L20.701-10

Determining the Lease Term

One of the more important provisions of GASB Cod. Sec. L20 involves the determination of the lease term. The lease term is determined as follows:

1. The period during which a lessee has a non-cancellable right to use an underlying asset, *plus*

2. Periods covered by a *lessee's* option to *extend* the lease *if it is reasonably certain, based on all relevant factors,* that *the lessee will* exercise that option, *plus*

3. Periods covered by a *lessee's* option to *terminate* the lease *if it is reasonably certain*, based on all relevant factors, that the *lessee will not* exercise that option, *plus*
4. Periods covered by a *lessor's* option to *extend* the lease *if it is reasonably certain*, based on all relevant factors, that *the lessor will* exercise that option, *plus*
5. Periods covered by a *lessor's option* to *terminate* the lease *if it is reasonably certain*, based on all relevant factors, that *the lessor will not* exercise that option.

The Importance of Options. The word "option" is vital in this determination. During timeframes for which *both* the lessee and the lessor have an option to terminate the lease *without permission from the other party*, or if both parties must agree to extend, the lease has cancelable periods, and those periods are excluded from the lease term. This is common in so-called rolling (or month-to-month) leases where the lease continues during a "holdover period" until a new contract is signed. Since the lessee and the lessor have an option to terminate during this period, the period is not included in the calculation of the lease term. Also excluded from termination options would be provisions that allow for termination of a lease due to:

- Purchase of the underlying asset (lease with an option to buy, which would be a financing or a borrowing),
- Payment of all sums due (prepayment on leases), or
- A default on payments [GASB Cod. Sec. L20.109].

PRACTICE POINT: GASB Statement No. 99 (*Omnibus 2022*) amended the lease term provisions. If a provision in a lease allows for the termination of a lease due to the action (or inaction) of another party, the provision is not a termination option for the purposes of determining a lease term. The GASB provides examples of violations of lease terms and conditions or payments of sums due, or default on payments as potential occurrences that would not be termination options.

Lease Inception, Control and Month-to-Month Leasing. There are many caveats to the lease term as can be plainly seen in this subsection. Determination of the lease term may include understanding when a lease begins.

For example, if the underlying asset is being constructed and the lessee has no access to the asset until a certificate of occupancy of a building, the lease term does not commence until the lessee has an unconcealable right to use the underlying asset. Since the lessee has no control over the asset and cannot obtain service from the asset, the lease does not start to amortize [GASB Cod. Sec. L20.702-1].

At the end of the lease, if both lessor and lessee have the right to cancel or continue a lease *using the same terms* on a month-to-month basis, the month-to-month basis also *is not* included in the lease term as the term is cancelable by both parties [GASB Cod. Sec. L20.702-2].

Bargain Renewals and Lease Terms. A lease may have *incentives* embedded in the contract. (Incentives are discussed in a later subsection in this chapter.) The initial lease term may be at a market rate. However, an option to extend may be at a significant discount. The significant discount is the hallmark of an incentive. The government then must make an assessment that the lessor will exercise the extension (or termination) based on the significant discount. If the extension is reasonably certain to be exercised, then the period of extension is added to the noncancelable period.

The language in the option then becomes key. Of course, there may also be a disincentive to exercise the option. If the government were the lessor in this case and the government holds the option to give the lessee a significant discount, it would be presumed that it is *not* in the government's interest to extend.

PRACTICE POINT: The concept of *reasonably certain* was considered by the GASB as part of the deliberations for what became the new leasing provisions. The Board could have used *probable* in a similar vein to contingencies. Many practitioners consider it *probable* to have a 75% certainty. The GASB believes *reasonably certain* is a higher threshold than *probable* and is analogous to *reasonably assured*. Professional judgment is likely needed to determine a threshold for this amount of certainty.

A portion of GASB Cod. Sec. L20.901, Illustration B1 contains a calculation (in text form) of a lease term, which is reproduced in the following table for ease of understanding:

Factor	Facts
Lessee	City government
Lessor	Unnamed counterparty in example
Begin date of contract	January 1, 20X1 (first day of the city's fiscal year)
Noncancelable period	60 months
Option to extend?	The city has the option for 24 months.
Reasonably certain?	No—the city is unsure whether it will exercise the option to extend the lease.
Month-to-month potential?	Yes. At the end of the noncancelable period, if the city does not extend the lease or 84 months (if the City extends the lease), the lease may be continued on a month-to-month basis *which either* the City *or* the lessor can cancel.
Lease term?	**60 months—noncancelable period.** Because the city is not reasonably certain that it will exercise the option to extend the lease for an additional 24 months, it should not include those months in the lease term. The potential month-to-month extensions also would not be included in the lease term because these periods are not enforceable (either the city or the lessor can cancel). Therefore, the lease term should include only the noncancelable period—60 months.

A fiscal funding or cancellation clause would be considered in determining the lease term only when it is *reasonably certain* that the clause will be exercised (where the government fails to appropriate funds to pay for the following period under lease).

Relevant Factors within Options. All relevant factors need to be considered to determine the likelihood that the lessee will exercise an option to extend the lease. These are embedded in the contract or may be dependent upon the asset, the market for similar property, or government-specific reasons. The factors required to be considered include, but are not limited to:

- A significant economic incentive, such as contractual terms and conditions for the optional periods that are favorable compared with current market rates. The GASB provides an example of a bargain rate in GASB Cod. Sec. L20.702-3 where a five-year renewal is available at a 30% discount from market.
- A significant economic disincentive, such as costs to terminate the lease and sign a new lease (e.g., negotiation costs, relocation costs, abandonment of significant leasehold improvements, costs of identifying another suitable underlying asset, costs associated with returning the underlying asset in a contractually specified condition or to a contractually specified location, or a substantial cancellation penalty).
- The lessee's history of exercising renewal or termination options, and
- The extent to which the lease is essential to the provision of government services [GASB Cod. Sec. L20.111].

Reassessment of the Lease Term. The lease term may change for many reasons. Some of the reasons are in control of the lessee and some are within the control of the lessor. If the lease term changes, a re-amortization is triggered, or a termination. One (or more) of the following factors will trigger a reassessment of the lease term:

- The lessee *or* lessor elects to exercise an option even though it was previously determined that it was reasonably certain that the lessee or lessor *would not* exercise that option, or
- The lessee *or* lessor elects not to exercise an option even though it was previously determined that it was reasonably certain that the lessee or lessor *would* exercise that option (the opposite), or
- An event specified in the lease contract that requires an extension or termination of the lease takes place [GASB Cod. Sec. L20.112].

An example of this reassessment might be when a lessee has a bargain renewal option, involving a 20-year lease at a market rate with the lessee having the option to renew the lease for an additional five years at a 30% discount. This bargain would be a relevant factor if the lessee determines that it is reasonably certain it will be exercised. If it will be reasonably certain, then the lease term would be for 25 years instead of 20 [GASB Cod. Sec. L20.702-3].

Alternatively, if a contract allows for cancellation by either party at any time, but subject to penalties at such a level that it is *reasonably certain* that neither

Leases and Similar Arrangements **14,009**

party will cancel, then the cancelable periods *are excluded*. In this case, if it is *reasonably certain* that neither party will terminate, then the lease term would be for the entire noncancelable period [GASB Cod. Sec. L20.702-4].

However, if only one party can terminate in the instance of large cancelation penalties to the point where it is *reasonably certain* that that party will *not* terminate the lease, then the periods covered by the lessee's option to terminate *are included* in the lease term. The penalties and which party has the risk become major factors in this calculation [GASB Cod. Sec. L20.702-5].

> **PRACTICE POINT:** A government as a lessee may default on payments due to economic conditions or changes in law, regulation and similar. Alternatively, a government lessor may have a nongovernmental lessee default on payments. This is currently common in the case of economic development entities leasing retail space or public housing entities with tenants in default. Lease contracts usually have default provisions, but per GASB Cod. Sec. L20.109 as previously discussed, provisions that allow for termination of a lease due to default on payments, are not considered termination options.

Short-Term Leases

A short-term lease will be extremely difficult to encounter in practice except in the situation where at the beginning of the lease term, the maximum possible term under the contract is 12 months or less, *including any option to extend*. Probability or certainty has no bearing on this definition. For month-to-month leases or a year-to-year lease, the maximum possible term is the noncancelable period, including any periods of notice.

Short-Term Leases—Lessees. If a short-term lease is in place, lessees recognize outflows of resources (expenses) based on the payment terms. Lessees recognize assets if payments are made in advance or a liability if payments are in due but unpaid. Rent holidays (free rent) are not expensed.

Short-Term Leases—Lessors. Lessors recognize the opposite of lessees. Inflows of resources are recognized (revenue) based on the contract terms. Liabilities are recognized for payments in advance and assets (receivables) for payments due but unpaid. Like lessees, free rent does not trigger revenue [GASB Cod. Secs. L20.113–.115].

Again, the word *option* is key. The following are examples provided by the GASB of how important this is [GASB Cod. Secs. L20.703-1–.703-3, .703-9–.703-10]

14,010   *Specific Accounting and Reporting Issues*

Fact Pattern	Lease Term
Government agrees to a 12-month noncancelable lease in which the lessee has options to renew for 12 months at a time for 49 times.	The lease is for 50 years, as it includes options to extend. *Not* a short-term lease.
Government agrees to a six-month noncancelable lease with an option to extend it for 12 months after the initial six months. The government is not reasonably certain it will extend.	*Not* a short-term lease, but the lease term would be for six months requiring an asset and a liability to be reported. Reassessment would occur at six months.
Government agrees to a 16-month lease but can cancel it after six months. The lessor cannot cancel the lease.	*Not* a short-term lease as the lessee can cancel. The maximum possible term is 16 months. Since the lease can only be cancelled by the lessee, it is not a short-term lease.
The lease contract states that it will remain in effect for three years unless terminated prior to that point. The contract allows the lessee to terminate the lease with 60 days' notice. The contract allows the lessor to terminate with the same notice, but only in the case of a default by the lessee.	*Not* a short-term lease. Although the lessee has an unconditional right to terminate, the lessor does not have an unconditional right to terminate because the lessor is allowed to terminate the lease only on the condition that the lessee defaults on payments. Accordingly, there are no periods for which both the lessee and lessor have an option to terminate and, therefore, no cancellable periods to exclude from the maximum possible term, which is three years.
A lease has a noncancellable period of 36 months, and the lessee has an option to extend the lease for an additional 12 months. At the outset of the lease, it is *not* reasonably certain that the lessee will exercise that option. At the end of the noncancellable period, the lessee exercises the option to extend.	The maximum possible term *does not change*. The term at commencement includes all options to extend, regardless of their probability of being exercised. At the commencement of the lease, the lease term is 36 months, and the maximum possible term is 48 months. As a result, although the reassessed lease term is only 12 months *from the exercise date*, the maximum possible term remains 48 months when the option is exercised. In addition, although some lease modifications are accounted for as separate leases for which the maximum possible term would be assessed separately, exercising an existing option is not a lease modification (which is discussed later in this chapter).

PRACTICE POINT: As part of the previously mentioned GASB Statement No. 99 (*Omnibus 2022*), for periods for which *both* the lessee *and* the lessor have an option to terminate the lease *without the permission of the other party* (or for which both parties have to agree to extend the option to terminate) *are cancellable periods* and should be excluded from the calculation of the noncancelable lease term. In addition, a short-term lease that has been modified to extend the initial maximum possible term under the lease contract should be reassessed *from the inception of the lease.* If the reassessed maximum possible term is greater than 12 months, the lease would no longer be considered a short-term lease. The lease term is then assessed from the date of the modification to the new date of the noncancelable term to calculate either the lease receivable for lessors or lease liability for lessees.

Contracts That Transfer Ownership Are Not Leases

If a lease transfers ownership from lessor to lessee and does not contain termination options, a financed purchase exists (a borrowing). A note payable would be recognized along with a transfer of the asset from the lessor [GASB Cod. Sec. L20.116].

If the government is the receiver in a transfer of ownership, financed purchases are like any other capital asset purchase. A capital asset is acquired using debt. If the contract is accounted for in a governmental fund, capital outlay occurs. An acquisition would then be shown as an addition to a capital asset. The financing would also indicate an additional long-term debt. Therefore, the accounting and financial reporting provisions in Chapters 10 and 12 of the *Governmental GAAP Guide* would apply to the capital asset transaction and the debt transaction, respectively.

> **PRACTICE POINT:** Contracts that transfer ownership are common. Some are even titled "tax-exempt lease purchases" (TELPs). The GASB includes an example of computers leased by a school district in the *Implementation* guidance. At the end of the lease term, students may purchase the computers from the district, but even if the students do not purchase them, the district is required to purchase the computers and cannot terminate the contract. This would be a financed purchase by the school district. The potential sale to the students is a different transaction [GASB Cod. Sec. L20.706-2].

LEASE ACCOUNTING MODEL—LESSEES

Lessee Recognition and Measurement

Lessees account for a lease by recognizing a lease liability and a right-to-use intangible lease asset at the beginning of a lease unless it is a short-term lease or transfers ownership of the underlying asset. The lease liability will be measured at the present value of payments to be made for the lease term.

> **PRACTICE POINT:** Governments should be careful in utilizing the same policy in recognizing a capital asset for recognition of a liability. Even though there is no specific guidance in current GAAP for materiality or significance, capitalization thresholds for assets are usually much greater than liabilities. Lack of recognizing a significant liability either individually or in the aggregate is an audit risk [GASB Cod. Sec. L20.708-1].

The leased asset is measured at the amount of the initial measurement of the lease liability plus any payments made to the lessor at or before the beginning of the lease and certain indirect costs. The lease liability is reduced as payments are made and an outflow of resources for interest on the liability is recognized. The lessee would amortize the lease asset in a systematic and rational method over the term of the agreement. Notes to the financial statements will include a description of leasing arrangements, the amount of lease assets recognized, and a schedule of future lease payments to be made.

Calculating the Lease Liability—Lessees. The following elements are used to determine the initial value of the lessee's liability:

- Fixed payments, less any lease incentives (such as a cash payment or reimbursement of moving costs) receivable from the lessor,

- Variable lease payments that depend on an index or a rate (such as the Consumer Price Index or a market interest rate), initially measured using the index or rate as of the beginning of the lease,

- Variable lease payments that are fixed in substance,

- Amounts that are reasonably certain of being required to be paid by the lessee under residual value guarantees,

- The exercise price of a purchase option if it is reasonably certain that the lessee will exercise that option,

- Payments for penalties for terminating the lease, if the lease term reflects the lessee, exercising an option to terminate the lease or a fiscal funding or cancellation clause, and

- Any other payments that are reasonably certain of being required based on an assessment of all relevant factors.

Variable payments based on future performance or usage are not included. Common variable payments based on usage may include copies made, miles driven and other use factors. Instead, they are an expense for the period.

> **Example:** A coffee stand at an airport leases space in the terminal lobby. The lease is based on 3% of sales, paid monthly 15 days after each monthly period and subject to audit by airport internal audit staff. The lessee will record the monthly payment as an expense. However, if the coffee stand pays the lesser of a minimum monthly payment, or 3% of sales, then the payment is in substance fixed at the minimum monthly payment.

> **PRACTICE POINT:** Copier contracts may have minimums for supplies that require delivery. The contract should be analyzed carefully to determine reasonableness and if the minimums should be included in the liability [GASB Cod. Sec. L20.708-3].

As discussed, the variable payment may include adjustments for the consumer price index or sales. Copies made, miles driven, hours used could all constitute variable payments. For government lessees, such payments would be outflows, unless coupled with a minimum payment.

> **PRACTICE POINT:** The GASB provides an example of a public university leasing a building in Europe for a payment of 5,000 Euros monthly. As the lease payment is required to be made in euros, the amount of the payment in U.S. dollars is subject to change throughout the lease as exchange rates fluctuate. Such payments are not considered variable as the currency in which lease payments are made does not affect whether those payments are considered fixed. Since the contract requires a fixed payment amount in euros, the lease payments should be considered fixed payments. The increase or decrease in expected U.S. dollar cash flows is a foreign currency transaction gain or loss. Foreign currency transaction gains and losses are discussed in Chapter 9 [GASB Cod. Sec. L20.708-4].

For space leases, taxes, insurance, and utilities may need to be paid to a nongovernmental lessor. These are *components*, which are discussed later in this chapter.

The payments that are reasonably certain of being required could also include termination penalties if the penalties are expected to be paid.

> **PRACTICE POINT:** The previously mentioned *Omnibus 2022* includes a clarification that variable payments *other than those that depend on an index or rate*, such as payments based on future performance of the lessee or usage of the underlying asset would not be included in the measurement of the lease liability. The lease liability would also not be remeasured solely for a change in an index, or a rate used to determine variable payments, nor would the rate be reassessed solely for a change in the lessee's incremental borrowing rate (as discussed in the *Discount Rate* section that follows).

Discount Rate. The lease payments are discounted using the interest rate the *lessor* charges the lessee, which may be explicitly disclosed in the lease or implicitly. If the interest rate is not explicitly disclosed, then the lessee's incremental borrowing rate may be used as an estimate of the lease rate. Imputation of interest [GASB Cod. Sec. i30] is not required but can be used as a practical expedient for determining the rate.

To use the implicit rate, the fair value of the leased asset needs to be known as of the inception of the lease. The difference between the lease payments and the fair value can be construed as interest. Software may be used to determine the discount rate by solving for the present value difference.

Example: GASB provides an example of determining the implicit rate summarized as follows:

Total of 30 monthly payments over term	$1,100,000
Fair value of underlying asset (half of useful life)	$1,000,000 ($2 million fair value)
Difference	$100,000

Using software, knowing the payment would be $36,667 (rounded) monthly with a future value of $1,000,000, depending on when the payment would be at the beginning of each month or the end of each month. The solved interest rate is approximately 7.5% [GASB Cod. Sec. L20.708-9].

> **PRACTICE POINT:** In the absence of frequent debt issuances to determine an incremental borrowing rate, a policy needs to be effective in not only establishing the discount rate but using the discount rate for the contracts in scope during a period. Governments should not use a peer government's rate as it would not be specific to their own debt profile. As governments implemented GASB Cod. Sec. L20, practical expedients have emerged including, but not limited to, the U.S. Treasury state and local government securities (SLGS) rates plus a factor or the government's specific incremental borrowing rate (if the government issues debt throughout the year). Using the incremental borrowing rate though is also problematic as the term of the debt needs to align to the term of the lease contract.

Liability Amortization

The amortization of the liability uses the effective interest method, recognizing interest expense first and then a reduction of principal. For proprietary funds, the interest is a financing activity. The interest liability is reported separately from the principal as in any other amortization of a borrowing or debt.

> **PRACTICE POINT:** The GASB provides an example where a government leases a building for a 10-year term. The government makes an "up-front" payment for the entire first three years of the term and then recognizes a liability for the remaining seven years, with payment commencing in year four. Interest expense would be recognized during the first three years even though the government retired that liability at inception. The interest is generated in the remaining seven years. The interest liability will continue to accrue until the government starts making payments in the fourth year [GASB Cod. Sec. L20.707-2].

Liability Remeasurement Triggers. During the period under lease, the lease may require remeasurement if any of these changes individually or in the aggregate impact the liability since the previous (or initial) measurement:

- There is a change in the lease term.
- An assessment of all relevant factors indicates that the likelihood of a residual value guarantee being paid has changed from reasonably certain to not reasonably certain, or vice versa.
- An assessment of all relevant factors indicates that the likelihood of a purchase option being exercised has changed from reasonably certain to not reasonably certain, or vice versa.
- There is a change in the estimated amounts for payments already included in the measurement of the lease liability (with certain exceptions).
- There is a change in the interest rate the lessor charges the lessee, if used as the initial discount rate.

- A contingency, upon which some or all the variable payments that will be made over the remainder of the lease term are based, is resolved such that those payments now meet the criteria for measuring the lease liability. For example, an event occurs that causes variable payments that were contingent on the performance or use of the underlying asset to become fixed payments for the remainder of the lease term.

If the lease liability is required to be remeasured, the liability may also need to be adjusted for any change in rates or indexes to determine variable payments if the change *significantly* impacts the liability since the last measurement. However, a lease liability is not required to be remeasured just for a change in index.

Due to these changes, the discount rate may need to change, especially in the instances of a change in lease term or a purchase option being exercised (or not exercised). But a change in the incremental borrowing rate would also not solely require a remeasurement of the liability [GASB Cod. Secs. L20.117–.126].

Leased Asset

The initial measurement of the lease asset is based on the date of obtaining service capacity. Payments made relating to a leased asset that is still being constructed would *not* be part of the lease payment as the government lessee would not have occupancy or control of the asset. Such payments would be prepayments though and not part of the leased asset [GASB Cod. Sec. L20.709-1].

The measurement uses the following formula:
- The amount of the initial liability, *plus*
- Lease payments made to the lessor prior to the lease term, *less*
- Lease incentives *received from the lessor* at or before the lease term, *plus*
- Initial direct costs that are ancillary to placing the asset into service such as moving costs.

Initial direct costs are expensed unless they are required to place the asset into service.

Asset Amortization. The asset is then amortized systematically and rationally over the useful of the leased asset or the lease term, whichever is shorter. Exceptions would occur to the amortization in cases where:
- There is reasonable certainty the asset will be purchased by the lessee, and
- The underlying asset is non-depreciable such as land.

Amortization expense may be combined with depreciation. If there is any remeasurement activity to the liability, the asset may also need to be remeasured as the lease liability is the largest factor in the asset capitalization. However, if the asset reduces to zero (or below) due to the remeasurement, then any further change may result in a gain [GASB Cod. Secs. L20.127–.131].

Composite or group methods may be used to amortize leased assets, especially in the cases of many pieces of equipment or similar assets leased at the same time from the same lessor with the same terms and conditions. Some leases may include provisions to allow for substitutions of leased assets, especially with technology or vehicles in the case of failure without impacting the terms and conditions of the lease [GASB Cod. Sec. L20.709-2].

PRACTICE POINT: The asset may also be impacted by asset impairment. The measurement and reporting of asset impairment is discussed in Chapter 10. An example of impairment on leased assets is contained in GASB Cod. Sec. L20.709-5. At the end of year nine of a ten-year lease, a flood damages a leased building. The leased asset's unamortized value prior to the flood was $275,000 with a liability of $300,000. The lessor reduces the remaining payments by $20,000 to $280,000. The government determines the remaining service utility of the lease asset to be only $100,000. The lessee would reduce the liability and the asset by the $20,000 reduction provided by the lessor. However, an additional impairment reduction needs to occur in the asset for $155,000 equating to $275,000 – $20,000 – $100,000. Unfortunately, in this case, the remaining liability will be more than the remaining leased asset. The annual amortization of the liability may be more than the amortization of the leased asset. Had the opposite occurred, where the liability was reduced below the leased asset value, the reduction in the liability would be an inflow (likely a gain).

Lessee Financial Reporting

Governmental Funds. Lessees report lease activity as other financing sources and expenditures upon initial recognition. Lease payments are reported like debt service payments on long-term debt (see **PRACTICE ALERTs** on the GASB's *Financial Reporting Model* project in the introduction to this *Guide*) [GASB Cod. Secs. L20.132–.133].

Note Disclosure—Lessees. The notes to the basic financial statements for lessees for leasing activity are presented in an aggregated fashion, not by individual leases. Short-term leases do not have any required notes. The following is required to be disclosed:

- A *general* description of leasing arrangements, including:
  - The basis, terms, and conditions on which variable payments not included in the measurement of the lease liability are determined,
  - The existence, terms, and conditions of residual value guarantees provided by the lessee not included in the measurement of the lease liability,
  - The total amount of lease assets, and the related accumulated *amortization, disclosed separately from other capital assets* (but in practice may be disclosed near the capital assets section),
  - The amount of lease assets by major classes of underlying assets, disclosed separately from other capital assets,
  - The amount of outflows of resources recognized in the reporting period for variable payments not previously included in the measurement of the lease liability,
  - The amount of outflows of resources recognized in the reporting period for other payments, such as residual value guarantees or termi-

nation penalties, not previously included in the measurement of the lease liability,

— Principal and interest requirements to maturity, presented separately, for the lease liability for each of the five subsequent fiscal years and in five-year increments thereafter,

— Commitments under leases before the commencement of the lease term, and

— The components of any loss associated with an impairment recognized on the lease asset during the period.

PRACTICE POINT: The lease assets are included in the disclosure of capital assets which includes the beginning balance, additions, deductions, transfers, and ending balance [GASB Cod. Sec. L20.711-5].

A common question is whether amortization expense may be included with depreciation expense in the disclosure of such expenses by function. GASB Cod. Sec. L20.711-1 does allow such disclosure for clarity.

Relevant disclosures are also provided for sublease, sale-leaseback, and lease-leaseback transactions, discussed later in this chapter. Collateral pledged as security for a lease is not required to be disclosed if that collateral is solely the asset underlying the lease [GASB Cod. Secs. L20.134–.136]. In the case of a lease that has payments dependent solely on the use of the asset, the lease is still required to be disclosed, even though not asset or liability is recognized [GASB Cod. Sec. L20.711-3].

Example of The Accounting Model for Lessees

Assume that a government is leasing a piece of equipment. The initial term is five years with two options to renew at two years each. Payments are $1,000 a month for the initial term and do not rise upon renewal. The estimated useful life of the equipment is seven years. It is reasonably certain that the government will lease the equipment for seven years, using one renewal period. This is based on all relevant factors, including the useful life of the equipment and the history of the government's pattern of leasing equipment. Similar pieces of equipment from the same source have a 6% borrowing rate, determined using the provisions for imputation of interest (see further discussion below on implicit interest). The entry for the lessee at inception would be:

Proprietary Fund	Debit	Credit
Right-to-Use Asset—Equipment	$68,453	
Lease Liability		$68,453

To record the value of the right to use the equipment at inception and the present value of the liability (present value of $1,000 per month for [5 + 2 years] at 6%).

In the first month, the entry would be:

PROPRIETARY FUND	Debit	Credit
Amortization expense	$815	
Lease liability	658	
Interest expense	342	
Accumulated amortization—Right-to-Use Asset—Equipment		$815
Cash		1,000
To record the straight-line amortization of the right to use the equipment ($68,453 ÷ 84). The interest expense is [$68,453 x (6% ÷ 12 months)]. The payment on the lease liability is $1,000 less the interest expense and both the interest and the principal will adjust monthly using the effective interest method.		

If the lease were to occur in a governmental fund, the following would be the initial entry under current GAAP, even though there is no capital asset that results, but there is an intangible asset:

GENERAL FUND	Debit	Credit
Capital outlay—(expenditure)—leased equipment	$68,453	
Other financing source—leased equipment		$68,453
To report new lease contract for equipment.		

The first month's entry in a governmental fund would be:

GENERAL FUND	Debit	Credit
Other Financing Use—lease payments	$658	
Interest expenditures	342	
Cash		$1,000
To report lease payments on equipment for the year from the General Fund.		

LEASE ACCOUNTING MODEL—LESSORS

Lessor Recognition and Measurement for Leases (Other than Short-Term Leases and Contracts that Transfer Ownership)

Governments may be lessors to parties beyond the reporting entity (see subsection on intra-entity leases later in this chapter). Governmental lessors recognize a lease receivable and a deferred inflow of resources at the beginning of a lease, with certain exceptions (such as a short-term lease or a lease that transfers ownership of the underlying asset, leases that are investments, and certain leases subject to regulation). Lessors do not derecognize the asset underlying the lease unless the property transfers to the lessee because of a financed purchase.

Initial Direct Costs. Initial direct costs borne by the lessor are expensed. These include:

- Costs to originate a lease incurred in transactions with independent third parties that:
  - Result directly from and are *essential* to acquiring that lease, *or*
  - Would not have been incurred had that leasing transaction not occurred.
- Certain costs directly related to specified activities performed by the lessor for that lease. Those activities include:
  - Evaluating the prospective lessee's financial condition such as obtaining a credit rating,
  - Evaluating and recording guarantees, collateral, and other security arrangements,
  - Negotiating lease terms,
  - Preparing and processing lease documents, or
  - Closing the transaction [GASB Cod. Sec. L20.712-2].

The lease receivable is measured at the present value of lease payments to be received for the lease term. The deferred inflow of resources will be measured at the value of the lease receivable plus any payments received at or prior to the beginning of the lease that relate to future periods.

PRACTICE POINT: Government owners of assets that are leased may use administrators, leasing, or management companies to operate the leased assets. Frequently, the assets may be held in separate title holding companies (or similar legal constructs) to shield the government from liability. The government usually is the sole shareholder in such companies. The government is still the lessor in these transactions, despite using administrators and holding companies (see also following discussion on leased assets that are investments).

Leased Assets that are Investments. Many defined benefit plans and similar fiduciary activities report leased assets as investments. If the underlying asset is reported as an investment, the leasing accounting and financial reporting provisions *do not apply*. Only note disclosure of the existence, terms, and conditions of options by the lessee to terminate the lease or abate payments (if the government has issued debt secured by the lease payments) is disclosed related to such leases.

Leases Regulated by External Laws, Regulations, Court Rulings. Most of the leasing provisions do not apply if laws, regulations, or court rulings establish *all* the following requirements:

- Lease rates cannot exceed a reasonable amount, with reasonableness being subject to determination by an external regulator.
- Lease rates should be similar for lessees that are similarly situated.
- The lessor cannot deny potential lessees the right to initiate leases if facilities are available, provided that the lessee's use of the facilities complies with generally applicable use restrictions.

If the preceding provisions all apply, then only revenue is recognized in accordance with the lease contract and disclosure is limited to the following (other than short-term leases):

- A general description of its agreements,
- The extent to which capital assets are subject to preferential or exclusive use by counterparties under agreements, by major class of assets, and by major counterparty,
- The total value of inflows of resources (e.g., lease revenue, interest revenue, and any other lease-related inflows) recognized in the reporting period from these agreements, if that amount cannot be determined based on the amounts displayed on the face of the financial statements,
- A schedule of expected future minimum payments under these agreements for each of the subsequent five years and in five-year increments thereafter,
- The value of inflows of resources recognized in the reporting period for variable payments not included in expected future minimum payments, and
- The existence, terms, and conditions of options by the lessee to terminate the lease or abate lease payments if the lessor government has issued debt for which the principal and interest payments are secured by the lease payments [GASB Cod. Secs. L20.137–.140, .154(d), .157].

Regulated contracts may have nonregulated uses, especially involving the airlines with the lessor being an airport entity. The resulting contracts with nonregulated uses become a separate component and would be accounted for and reported by the lessor like any other leasing activity (components are discussed later in this chapter) [GASB Cod. Sec. L20.714-1].

PRACTICE POINT: Regulated operations are discussed in more detail in Chapter 24.

Lease Receivable Calculation. The lease receivable is measured at inception using the present value of the lease payments expected during the lease term, adjusted for amounts estimated to be uncollectible. The following elements are used to determine the initial value of the lessor's receivable:

- Fixed payments,
- Variable lease payments that depend on an index or a rate (such as the Consumer Price Index or a market interest rate), initially measured using the index or rate as of the beginning of the lease,
- Variable lease payments that are fixed in substance,
- Amounts that are reasonably certain of being required to be paid by the lessee under residual value guarantees, and
- Any lease incentives payable to the lessee.

Variable payments to be received from lessees based on future performance or usage are not included. Instead, they are revenue for the period and recognized as such in accordance with U.S. GAAP.

GASB Cod. Sec. L20.715-1 contains an example of calculating the lease receivable from a vendor involved in a three-year lease, showing the amounts are fixed in-substance:

Leases and Similar Arrangements 14,021

Fact	Amount
Payment in the first year—minimum annual guarantee	$100,000
Payment in the second year depends on sales in the first year. *If sales exceed $1,000,000—minimum annual guarantee is the amount shown (otherwise remains at the first year)*	$110,000
Minimum annual guarantee for the third year	$90,000
Recognized Receivable ($100,000 + $100,000 + $90,000)	**$290,000**

> **PRACTICE POINT:** The previously mentioned GASB Statement No. 99 (*Omnibus 2022*) also includes a clarification that variable payments *other than those that depend on an index or rate*, such as payments based on future performance of the lessee or usage of the underlying asset would not be included in the measurement of the lease receivable. The lease receivable would also not be remeasured solely for a change in an index, or a rate used to determine variable payments (as discussed in the *Discount rate* section that follows).

Discount Rate. The lease payments are discounted using the interest rate the *lessor* charges the lessee, which may be explicitly disclosed in the lease or implicitly. Imputation of interest [GASB Cod. Sec. i30] is not required but can be used as a practical expedient for determining the rate.

Lessors will likely know the rate more than the lessee may know the rate and the rate may be adjusted for risk factors in the lease such as the lessee's credit rating. Lessors should use professional judgment to determine the best rate that reflects the market and credit risk.

> **PRACTICE POINT:** Often, managers of leases may turn to treasurers or finance officers to determine leasing rates and how often they need to be changed. Such policies should be documented as to which party sets rates and how they are reassessed. The policies will likely then be used for tests of compliance by auditors as a key focus area.

Discount Amortization. The amortization of the discount on the lease receivable uses the effective interest method, recognizing interest revenue first and then a reduction of the receivable. For proprietary funds, the interest is a financing activity. Straight-line amortization *should not be used* due to the provisions of GAAP [GASB Cod. Sec. L20.715-3].

> **PRACTICE POINT:** Even if the principal ongoing operation of a proprietary fund is leasing, interest revenues are not operating revenue under current GAAP. However, this may change in the future should the provisions of the GASB's *Financial Reporting Model Improvements* Exposure Draft be approved.

Receivable Remeasurement Triggers. During the period under lease, the lease may require remeasurement if any of these changes individually or in the aggregate impact the receivable since the previous (or initial) measurement:

- There is a change in the lease term.
- There is a change in the interest rate the lessor charges the lessee.
- A contingency, upon which some or all the variable payments that will be received over the remainder of the lease term are based, is resolved such that those payments now meet the criteria for measuring the lease liability. For example, an event occurs that causes variable payments that were contingent on the performance or use of the underlying asset to become fixed payments for the remainder of the lease term.

If the lease receivable is required to be remeasured, the receivable may also need to be adjusted for any change in rates or indexes to determine variable payments if the change *significantly* impacts the receivable since the last measurement. A receivable is not required to be remeasured just for a change in index, however.

The lessor should adjust the discount rate as an integral part of the remeasurement if either (or both) the lease term changes and there is an interest rate change made by the lessor to the lessee. The revised discount rate is then used for the remeasurement.

PRACTICE POINT: Government lessors need to evaluate the uncertainty on a lessee's ability to pay. Receivables need to be evaluated if there are uncollectible amounts.

Deferred Inflow of Resources. The lessor records a deferred inflow of resources as the credit to the receivable at the initial signing of the lease. The deferred inflow of resources equals:

- The amount of the initial measurement of the lease receivable, *plus*
- Lease payments received from the lessee at or before the commencement of the lease term that relate to future periods (e.g., the final month's rent), *less*
- Any lease incentives paid to, or on behalf of, the lessee at or before the commencement of the lease term.

The deferred inflow of resources is then amortized systematically and rationally to revenue over the lease term. In practice, this will likely use the effective interest method (see previous section on discount amortization) [GASB Cod. Sec. L20.715-3]. If the lease term is reduced due to asset impairment, modification, or termination (see discussion later in this chapter), the deferred inflow would also adjust by the reduction of the receivable.

In a previous paragraph, a fact pattern was discussed on payments made by a lessee during a construction period recognized as a prepayment. For a government lessor, the lessor would recognize such payments as a liability until the lease term commences. Upon commencement of the lease term, the liability is debited, and the related deferred inflow of resources is credited [GASB Cod. Sec. L20.716-1].

Security and other deposits are liabilities unless for the first (or last) month's rent. Upon commencement of the lease, a deposit for the first month's rent would be recognized as revenue. A last month's rent would be part of the deferred inflow of resources.

Underlying Leased Asset

The underlying leased asset remains a capital asset at the lessor. All existing guidance for the capital asset continues (see Chapter 10). The only instance where depreciation would cease would be if the lessee must return the leased asset in as good or better condition than when leased. In practice, this might be rarely present [GASB Cod. Secs. L20.141–.152].

Lessor Financial Reporting

Governmental Funds. Lessors report lease activity as a receivable and deferred inflow of resources at initial value as calculated previously. The deferred inflow of resources would adjust by any payments received that benefit future periods (prepayments) (Also see **PRACTICE ALERT** s on the GASB's *Financial Reporting Model* project in the introduction to this *Guide.*) [GASB Cod. Sec. L20.156].

Note Disclosure—Lessors. The notes to the basic financial statements for lessors for leasing activity is presented in an aggregated fashion, not by individual leases. Short-term leases do not have any required notes and regulated leases were discussed previously. For all other leasing activity, the following is required to be disclosed by lessors:

- A *general* description of leasing arrangements, including the basis, terms, and conditions on which variable payments not included in the measurement of the lease receivable are determined,
- The value of inflows of resources (lease revenue, interest, etc.) recognized in the period from leasing *if the activity is not presented on the face of the basic financial statements,*
- The value of inflows of resources recognized in the reporting period for variable payments not previously included in the measurement of the lease receivable, such as residual value guarantees or termination penalties, not previously included in the measurement of the lease receivable, and
- The existence, terms, and conditions of options by the *lessee* to terminate or abate payments if the lessor has issued debt which is secured by the lease payments.
- Additional disclosures may be required for:
  — Leases of assets that are investments (discussed previously),
  — Certain regulated leases (discussed previously),
  — Sublease transactions, and
  — Sale-leaseback and lease-leaseback transactions (discussed later in this chapter).

Special Provisions for Entities that Have Primarily Leasing Operations (Public Housing). The disclosures vary for entities that primarily have leasing for operations.

For those entities, a principal and interest schedule for the first five years and five-year aggregates after is disclosed [GASB Cod. Secs. L20.154–.156].

Example of Accounting Model for Governmental Lessors

For a governmental lessor, the accounting model for the same piece of equipment discussed previously, leased by a government to another government not in the same reporting entity would be as follows, assuming no uncollectable amounts, no transfer of ownership and no down payment:

PROPRIETARY FUND	Debit	Credit
Lease Receivable—Equipment	$68,453	
Deferred Inflow of Resources—Leased Equipment		$68,453
To record the value of equipment leased to ABC at inception and the present value of the receivable (present value of $1,000 per month for [{5 + 2 years} × 12 months = 84 months] at 6%).		

In the first month, the entry would be:

PROPRIETARY FUND	Debit	Credit
Cash	$1,000	
Depreciation Expense—Equipment	815	
Deferred Inflow of Resources—Leased Equipment	658	
Lease Receivable—Equipment		$658
Revenue—Leases		658
Interest revenue		342
Accumulated Depreciation		815
To record aggregated lease receipts on leased equipment to ABC.		

Depreciation on the equipment would continue as it is still owned by the government ($68,453 ÷ 84). Amortization is not used as the equipment remains a capital asset of the government. The interest expense is ($68,453 × [6% ÷ 12 months]).

If the governmental lessor accounts for the lease in a governmental fund, the entry would be like above, except for the depreciation expense and accumulated depreciation entries.

LEASES—OTHER ISSUES

Impact of Lease Incentives, Components, and Combinations

Lease incentives are:

- Payments made to (or on behalf of), the lessee where the lessee has a right of offset with its obligation to the lessor (reducing the lease payment to be made), or
- Other concessions granted to the lessee by the lessor, such as free rent (also known as a rent holiday).

Lease incentives are common. They could include rebates, discounts, or assumptions of existing lease obligations to a third party, payment of utilities

Leases and Similar Arrangements 14,025

and similar fees usually borne by the lessee. In some cases, they may include reductions of interest or principal amounts due to the lessor during periods of recession.

The incentives reduce the amount that is required to be paid in the contract. If incentives are in the lease, the following adjustments may need to be made to the assets and liabilities (or deferred inflows of resources) because of a lease incentive [GASB Cod. Secs. L20.158–.159]:

Incentive	Result
Payments made to (or on behalf of) a lessee at or before start of the lease term	• Reduce the amount of the lease asset recorded by the lessee
Payments made *after the start of the lease term*	• Reduce lease payments for the periods in which the incentives are provided. If fixed or fixed in-substance, include in initial measurement. If variable or contingent—do not include in initial measurement. — Lessees—measure consistently with lease liability. — Lessors—measure consistently with lease receivable.

Example: The GASB provides an example in GASB Cod. Sec. L20.901-B2 of a building lease with a lease incentive. A utility signs a lease with a noncancelable term of 10 years. Fixed payments of $15,000 are due at the beginning of each year. At the end of the first year, the utility receives a rebate of $5,000. The discount rate is 6%. As the rebate is provided at the end of year 1, the amount reduces the payment due immediately following the start of year 2. The calculation of the liability (and the lease asset) then is:

Year	Payment	Present Value (a)	Incentive	Present Value (b)	Total (a-b)
1	$15,000	$15,000	$–	$–	$15,000
2	15,000	14,151	(5,000)	(4,717)	9,434
3	15,000	13,350	–	–	13,350
4	15,000	12,594	–	–	12,594
5	15,000	11,881	–	–	11,881
6	15,000	11,209	–	–	11,209
7	15,000	10,574	–	–	10,574
8	15,000	9,976	–	–	9,976
9	15,000	9,411	–	–	9,411
10	15,000	8,878	–	–	8,878
			Initial lease liability		**$112,307**

Lease Incentives—Lessees. Lease incentive payments may occur prior to a lease term. As an example, if a government is leasing a fleet of vehicles near the end of the model year, the dealer may offer an incentive such as a rent holiday to consummate the lease. GASB Cod. Sec. L20.721-1 discusses that such incentives would reduce any lease prepayments made by the lessee (such as a deposit to order the vehicles). If there are no lease prepayments, the incentives effectively are a liability until the delivery of the vehicles. Upon delivery, the incentive reduces the lease asset per the amortization schedule prior to this paragraph.

Lessors may assume a lessee's preexisting lease obligation to a third party as a further incentive. However, the lessee should *not* reduce the lease liability to the third party unless the third party has legally released the government lessee.

Lease Incentives—Lessors. Lease incentive payments would also need to be recognized by governmental lessors. In the case of assuming a lessee's lease to a third party as discussed in the previous paragraph, the payment is an asset to the lessor if made prior to the lease term at the time the payments are made. Once the lease term commences, the asset is credited, and the related deferred inflows of resources is debited [GASB Cod. Sec. L20.722-1].

PRACTICE POINT: GASB Statement No. 99 (*Omnibus 2022*) also clarifies lease incentives. A lease incentive is equivalent to a rebate or discount and includes an assumption of, or an agreement to pay, a lessee's preexisting lease obligations to a third party, other reimbursements of lessee costs, rent holidays, and reductions of interest or principal charges by the lessor.

Contracts with Multiple Components

Leases commonly contain components consisting of the core elements of the lease terms and conditions, along with non-lease components including leases involving multiple assets (such as hundreds of computers or dozens of sheriff's vehicles). Non-lease components may include maintenance, security, utilities even taxes that are to be paid by the lessee.

The lease and non-lease components are required to be accounted for separately as separate contracts unless pricing for the individual components is not available in the contract or if any of the prices appear to be unreasonable. The allocation of the contract price to the different components follows these steps [GASB Cod. Secs. L20.160–.165]:

Step	Guidance	Example
1	Use any prices for individual components that are included in the contract, if the price allocation does not appear to be unreasonable based on the terms of the contract and professional judgment, maximizing the use of observable information. Adjust for quantity discounts readily observable if not unreasonable.	• Use readily available observable stand-alone prices such as contracts for maintenance, utilities, or security unrelated to the lease.
2	If the contract does not include individual prices for components or if prices are unreasonable, use professional judgment using observable information.	• Use similar contracts and quantities and allocate. For multiple floors of a building, an allocation of common area costs could be by square foot.
3	If it is not practicable to determine the best estimate for some (or all) components, account as a **single lease unit** (pricing cannot be separated).	• No allocation can be made due to variability of pricing or lack of comparable information.

If the contract results in a single lease unit, then the accounting for that unit is based on the primary lease component. The following are indicators of the primary lease component:

- The component performs a function that is the government's primary objective in entering into the contract.

- The component's fair value is substantial relative to the fair values of the other components.

- The lease term of the component is longer than the lease terms of the other components.

- The component's benefit to the government is substantial relative to the benefits of the other components [GASB Cod. Sec. L20.723-5].

As discussed previously, initial direct costs should not be confused with components. For example, if the government pays a lessor to install leased equipment, the payments are generally a non-lease component, unless they are required to be installed to put the leased asset into service. In such cases, the equipment would be part of the leased asset [GASB Cod. Sec. L20.723-1].

PRACTICE POINT: Separating the costs of the component services becomes most of the burden in this section of GASB Cod. Sec. L20. The lease contract may not specify an amount or a percentage of costs. Of course, the services may be variable based on usage, or may be subject to monthly fixed charges to the lessor, who then passes those charges ratably to lessees. Of course, the lessee may ask the lessor for a reconciliation of charges. But in some cases, the GASB discusses how it may not be practicable for such a reconciliation to separate or estimate the costs. If not practicable, then the costs are included in the lease liability for lessees [GASB Cod. Sec. L20.723-5].

Discount rates may also need to be separated for lease components that have different lease terms. The GASB provides an example of a building lease for 30 years and an attached parking garage for 15 years that are presented in one lease document. Due to the differing terms, different discount rates may be present [GASB Cod. Sec. L20.723-4].

Contract Combinations

Leases commonly have combinations. Combinations are contracts finalized at or near the same time with the same counterparty. Common combinations involve technology, vehicle fleets, and other equipment, or potentially, office space. Even if multiple contracts are in place, the contracts are considered the same contract if *either* of the following criteria are met:

- The contracts are negotiated as a package with a single objective.
- The amount of consideration to be paid in one contract depends on the price or performance of the other contract.

In such cases, the contract may need to be evaluated for the existence of components as discussed in the previous subsection [GASB Cod. Secs. L20.166–.167].

PRACTICE POINT: States commonly issue master vendor agreements to lower pricing on equipment, especially technology. The equipment is then purchased from the vendor by the individual agencies or other governments. Since the master vendor agreement does not automatically result in the delivery of the underlying equipment, the contracts *are not* combinations unless the criteria are met [GASB Cod. Sec. L20.724-2].

Lease Modifications and Terminations

Amendments occur to lease contracts during the term for a multitude of reasons. Lengthening (or shortening) the term is the most common reason. Underlying assets may be added or removed and in some cases the contract price changes.

When the right to use the underlying asset decreases, an amendment occurs, which results in a partial (or full) termination. This is different from exercising an option which results in remeasurement, as previously discussed.

Amendments during the reporting period resulting in a modification to a lease contract are reported as a *separate lease* from the most recent lease if *both* of the following occur:

- The lease modification gives the lessee an additional lease asset by adding one or more underlying assets that were not included in the original lease contract, and
- The increase in lease payments for the additional lease asset *does not appear to be unreasonable* based on:

1. The terms of the amended lease contract, and
2. Professional judgment, maximizing the use of observable information (e.g., using readily available observable stand-alone prices).

OBSERVATION: Variable payments may be adjusted based on the London Interbank Offered Rate (LIBOR). GASB Statement No. 93 (*Replacement of Interbank Offered Rates*) contains guidance if the rate terminates. The provisions of a lease contract may be amended while the contract is in effect. Amendments modify the provisions of the lease contract and the change in a LIBOR-based rate is an example. If variable payments of a lease contract depend on an IBOR, an amendment of the contract solely to replace the IBOR with another rate (that is adjusted, as necessary, to essentially equate the replacement rate and the original rate) by either changing the rate or adding or changing fallback provisions related to the rate, is not a lease modification.

An example is provided by the GASB of a modification relating to a 10-year lease contract with an option to extend if *both* the lessor and lessee agree. Since both must agree, the extension is cancelable and therefore excluded from the lease term calculation discussed in this chapter. Once the parties agree, the extension becomes noncancelable and therefore, a modification occurs if the original terms and conditions in the lease are extended. If not, a new lease occurs [GASB Cod. Sec. L20.725-2].

Modifications—Lessees. Unless a separate lease occurs, the lease liability is remeasured. Lessees adjust the difference between the new and the prior liability. The lease asset also adjusts in the same manner. If the change reduces the carrying value of the lease asset below zero, the remainder of the adjustment results in a gain.

The change to a lease term may be a result of a debt refunding by the lessor. If the economic advantages pass to the lessee because of the refunding (likely due to a defeasance of debt) (see Chapter 12), lessees should:

- Adjust the lease liability to the present value of the future lease payments under the revised lease using the effective interest rate applicable to the revised lease contract.
- The resulting difference should be reported as a deferred outflow of resources *or* a deferred inflow of resources.
- The deferred outflow of resources or the deferred inflow of resources should be recognized as an adjustment to an outflow of resources (e.g., as an increase or decrease to interest expense) in a systematic and rational manner over the remaining life of the old debt or the life of the new debt, *whichever is shorter.*

If the provisions of a lease are changed in connection with an advance refunding by the lessor that results in a defeasance of debt and *the lessee is obligated to reimburse the lessor for any costs* related to the refunded debt that have been or will be incurred (such as an unamortized discount or a call premium), the lessee should recognize those costs in a systematic and rational manner over the remaining life of the old debt or the life of the new debt, *whichever is shorter.* The amortization would be like discounts or premiums.

Modifications—Lessors. For lessors, the modification results in an adjustment of the lease receivable and the deferred inflow of resources, unless amounts relate to the current period. In such cases, the amount is either a revenue or expense for the period. If the transactions involve a debt refunding, similar treatments occur for lessors as lessees, except the adjustments are deferred inflows of resources and revenue.

> **PRACTICE POINT:** GASB provides an example which may be common during times of economic uncertainty. In this case, a government lessor leases one floor of an office building to a nongovernmental entity. An economic downturn occurs, and the government renegotiates the lease payments for the remainder of the lease, which the lessee intends to fulfill. The lease receivable is reduced by $230,000. In addition, the deferred inflow of resources would also be reduced by the same amount if it is for future periods. Any current period reduction would reduce revenue [GASB Cod. Sec. L20.728-1].

> **PRACTICE POINT:** As discussed in GASB Cod. Sec. L20.703-11, there are two circumstances when a lease modification results in a short-term lease:
> - If the lease was a short-term lease before the modification and the maximum possible term after the modification to extend the lease (reassessed from inception as a result of the clarified guidance within GASB-99), is 12 months or less, then the lease remains a short-term lease.
> - Regardless of whether the lease was a short-term lease before the modification, if the modification meets the criteria to be accounted for as a separate lease and the maximum possible term of that separate lease is 12 months or less, then the modification results in a separate short-term lease.

Terminations—Lessees. Terminations end a lease. If the right to use the underlying asset is decreased during the period, lessees reduce the carrying value of the asset and liability, resulting in a gain or loss for the difference. The exception would be if the lessee decides to purchase the underlying asset, which would result in a reclassification of the class of asset from leased to owned capital assets.

Terminations—Lessors. Lessors would reduce the receivable and deferred inflow of resources if a termination occurs, recognizing a gain or loss for the difference. Again, the exception would be if the lessee purchases the asset in which case, the asset would be derecognized, and an additional gain (or loss) would occur [GASB Cod. Secs. L20.168–.176].

Subleases

Of the areas changed by the implementation of GASB-87, subleases and subletting were a major change. Prior GAAP netted sublease activity, even though different dates and counterparties are involved.

Three parties are involved in a subleasing:
- The original lessor,
- The original lessee, who is now the lessor, and
- The new lessee.

The government as the original lessee and now a lessor would account for the transactions separately using the lessee and lessor guidance in this chapter. They are not offset. Disclosure is required of the transactions, separating transactions as a lessee and those as a lessor [GASB Cod. Secs. L20.177–.178].

Sale-Leaseback Transactions

Sale-leasebacks include a qualifying sale of the underlying asset by the owner to a buyer that is unrelated to the seller and the buyer leasing the same property back to the seller. Activity that does not qualify as a sale is a borrowing by the seller/lessee and lending for the buyer/lessor.

What are Qualifying Sales? Sales are not qualified until:
- The parties are bound by the terms of a contract,
- All consideration has been exchanged,
- Any permanent financing for which the seller is responsible has been arranged, and
- All conditions precedent to closing have been performed.

Usually, those four conditions are met at the time of closing or after closing, not when an agreement to sell is signed or at a preclosing. The sale should not be subject to subordination. Further, the seller should not have risk retained that is associated with owning the property.

PRACTICE POINT: These provisions are common with the sale of real estate by governments. For further information, see Chapter 17 which contains a further discussion on sales.

Two separate transactions occur in sale-leaseback transactions, which are self-evident. The sale transaction results in a deferred inflow of resources or a deferred outflow of resources representing the difference between the carrying value of the asset sold and the net proceeds from the sale. The related lease term will determine the amortization period. Amortization is to either revenue or expense in a systematic and rational manner. The exception would be for a short-term lease in which case, there would be no deferred amount. The net would be a revenue or expense.

If there are off-market terms such as a bargain sale, the substance of the transaction may be quite different than a sale-leaseback. A borrowing or a nonexchange transaction (advance lease payment) may result depending on the provisions of the transactions.

> **PRACTICE POINT:** Care must be taken to understand the parties and flow to these transactions. The GASB provides an example of a government selling a building to a third party and leasing a *different* (but equivalent building) *from the same party*. The government receives rent concessions for the leased building. This would not be a sale-leaseback due to two different underlying assets. The rent concessions are part of the consideration of the sale and not a lease incentive [GASB Cod. Sec. L.20.733-2].

Regulated Sale-Leasebacks. For these transactions, the regulatory language determines the accounting. Likely, the inflows or outflows may be an allowable cost for rate-making purposes and may result in a regulatory asset or deferred inflow of resources [GASB Cod. Secs. L20.179–.183].

Lease-Leaseback Transactions

Lease-leaseback transactions involve a lease to a counterparty and then the counterparty leasing the asset back to the original lessor. The property may be an entire asset or only a part of an asset. These transactions are netted but have required note disclosure [GASB Cod. Sec. L20.184].

Intra-Entity Leases

Intra-entity leases are common in government. Frequently, governments establish building authorities and similar component units. If the lessee or lessor is a blended component unit, the entirety of this Chapter does not apply. If the lessor is blended, the assets and debt are reported as the primary government's assets and debt.

Leases between blended component units are eliminated as part of presentation of the blended component unit financial statements in the primary government's financial statements. Any remaining flows are still presented (likely as transfers) [GASB Cod. Sec. L20.735-1].

Leases involving discretely presented component units (or between) are treated the same manner as any other lease as discussed in this chapter. Related receivables and payables are not combined with other receivables and payables [GASB Cod. Secs. L20.185–.186].

Related Party Leases

Leases between related parties are shown with the same classification and accounting as if the parties were unrelated unless there are off-market terms. With off-market terms, reclassification may be necessary to adjust the substance to the provisions discussed in this chapter, rather than legal form. The most common adjustment involves reclassifying from a short-term lease to not a short-term lease. Additional disclosure is required. Equity method adjustments may also be necessary for controlling interests [GASB Cod. Secs. L20.187–.188].

> **PRACTICE POINT:** Leasing between related parties may be subject to laws, regulations, and grant award provisions. Care must be taken that these provisions are followed due to the risk of fines, fees, or disallowed costs.

Public-Private and Public-Public Partnerships and Availability Payment Arrangements

Basic Provisions of Public-Private or Public-Public Partnerships and Available Payment Arrangements

Like leases, a Public-Private or Public-Public Partnership (PPP or PPPs) is an arrangement in which a government (the transferor) contracts with an operator to provide public services by conveying control of the right to operate or use a nonfinancial asset, such as infrastructure or other capital asset (the underlying PPP asset), for a period of time in an exchange or exchange-like transaction [GASB Cod. Sec. P90.102].

> **PRACTICE POINT:** Operators may be non-governments (in the case of a public-private partnership) or another government (in the case of a public-public partnership). In practice, public-private partnerships are prevalent if tax incentives are involved. A major thrust of infrastructure financing in recent years is the use of PPPs in airports, toll infrastructure and similar. Public-public partnerships are common in relationships beyond shared services, such as datacenters.

Some (not all) PPPs meet the definition of a service concession arrangement (SCA), which GASB Cod. Sec. P90 defines as a PPP in which:

- The operator collects and is compensated by fees from third parties,
- The transferor determines or can modify or approve which services the operator is required to provide, to whom the operator is required to provide the services, and the prices or rates that can be charged for the services, and
- The transferor is entitled to significant residual interest in the service utility of the underlying PPP asset at the end of the arrangement [GASB Cod. Sec. P90.103].

An Availability Payment Arrangement (APA) is an arrangement in which a government compensates an operator for services that may include designing, constructing, financing, maintaining, or operating an underlying nonfinancial asset for a period in an exchange or exchange-like transaction [GASB Cod. Sec. A90.102].

> **PRACTICE POINT:** PPPs may involve existing assets or newly constructed or acquired assets. The *transferor* government is ostensibly the lessor. As discussed, the operator may be a nongovernmental entity or a governmental entity. If the *operator* is a governmental entity, it is ostensibly the lessee. Therefore, this section of the chapter focuses on the differences between PPP accounting and financial reporting and the lease framework discussed previously.

PRACTICE POINT: GASB Statement No. 99 (*Omnibus 2022*) contains conforming provisions of the PPP provisions to those made to leases by the same Statement. If a provision in a PPP allows for the termination of a PPP due to the action (or inaction) of another party, the provision is not a termination option for the purposes of determining a PPP term. The GASB provides examples of violations of PPP terms and conditions or payments of sums due, or default on payments as potential occurrences that would not be termination options.

Which Framework to Use—PPPs or Leases?

PRACTICE POINT: If the PPP meets the definition of a lease as well *but does not meet the definition of a service concession arrangement*, nor is the operator required to make improvements on the underlying asset(s), then the provisions of GASB Cod. Sec. L20 apply as applicable, as discussed throughout this chapter. If improvements *are required* to be made to the underlying asset, then the provisions of GASB Cod. Sec. P90 apply, as applicable. This is illustrated in this subsection.

GASB has circulated a *non-authoritative* decision illustration, if a contract meets *both* lease and PPP definitions as follows:

Scenario	Accounting
PPP meets the definition of a lease as discussed in this chapter and is an SCA.	Use the accounting and financial reporting provisions of GASB Cod. Sec. P90.
PPP meets the definition of a lease, but not an SCA	If the underlying assets are *not* existing assets of the transferor government (being acquired or constructed), use GASB Cod. Sec. P90.
	If the underlying PPP assets involve existing transferor assets, then if improvements are made, use GASB Cod. Sec. P90.
	If the underlying PPP assets involve existing transferor assets, but *no improvements are made by the operator*, **then follow the leasing guidance in the first section of this chapter**[GASB Cod. Sec. P90.105].

Differences Between PPP Accounting and Financial Reporting and Lease Framework

Underlying PPP Asset is a New Asset Purchased or Constructed—Transferor Recognition and Measurement. It is common that new assets are purchased or constructed when a PPP is used. If the PPP does *not* meet the definition of an SCA, when the PPP asset is placed into service, the transferor government recognizes a receivable for the underlying asset purchased or constructed to be received. An additional receivable is recognized for installment payments (if any), to be received in conjunction with the PPP (in a comparable manner to a receivable recognized by a lessor) and a deferred inflow of resources offsetting both receivables [GASB Cod. Sec. P90.112].

The receivable for the underlying PPP asset is calculated based on an estimated carrying value of the underlying PPP asset as of the expected date of the transfer from the operator. Like other leased assets, if there is an impairment, modification or termination, the amount may require adjustment as necessary [GASB Cod. Sec. P90.127].

> **PRACTICE POINT:** GASB Statement No. 99 also amends the PPP receivable provisions. The receivable for installment payments would not be required to be remeasured solely for a change in an index or a rate used to determine variable payments. The receivable for the underlying PPP asset would be remeasured if there is a change in the PPP term and the change is expected to *significantly* impact the amount of the operator's estimated carrying value on the underlying PPP asset as of the date of transfer of ownership.

> **PRACTICE POINT:** The date of transfer may be many years from the inception of the PPP. Depending on the structure of the agreement, the estimated carrying value may be zero.

Underlying PPP Asset is a New Asset Purchased or Constructed—Governmental Operator Recognition and Measurement. If the underlying asset is a new asset that is either purchased or constructed by the governmental operator *and* the PPP *does not meet the definition of an SCA*, the governmental operator recognizes the PPP until ownership of the underlying PPP asset is transferred to the transferor government.

Like lessees, the governmental operator would apply the provisions for capital assets as discussed in Chapter 10 of the *Governmental GAAP Guide*. Once the underlying asset is acquired or constructed and placed into service, the governmental operator then:

- Declares a liability for the underlying PPP asset to be transferred back to the transferor government,
- Declares a liability (if any) for the installment payments to be made in relationship to the PPP, and
- Offsets the liability for the underlying PPP asset to be transferred back to the transferor government with a deferred outflow of resources [GASB Cod. Sec. P90.135].

Liability for Underlying PPP Asset. For a governmental operator that is required to transfer the underlying PPP asset to the transferor during or at the end of the PPP term, the measurement of the liability is at estimated carrying value as of the estimated date of transfer in ownership to the transferor. If there is a change in term or other form of modification or termination, the liability is remeasured, if the change significantly impacts the carrying value [GASB Cod. Sec. P90.148].

> **PRACTICE POINT:** As with the PPP asset, the date of transfer may be many years from the inception of the PPP. Depending on the structure of the agreement, the estimated carrying value may be zero.

Deferred Outflow of Resources. The governmental operator records a deferred outflow of resources equal to the estimated carrying value if the operator is required to transfer the underlying PPP asset during or at the end of the PPP term equal to the estimated carrying value as of the expected date of the transfer. Throughout the term of the PPP (or until the transfer), the governmental operator recognizes an outflow (and expense) for the amortization of the deferred outflow. The amortization should be made systematically and rationally [GASB Cod. Sec. P90.149].

> **PRACTICE ALERT:** GASB Statement No. 99 (*Omnibus 2022*) includes a provision clarifying the treatment of the deferred outflow of resources for governmental operators. The deferred outflow of resources should be adjusted by the same amount as any change resulting from the remeasurement of the liability for the underlying PPP asset. However, if that change reduces the deferred outflow of resources to zero, any remaining amount should be reported in the Statement of Activities or the Statement of Revenues, Expenses and Changes in Fund Net Position, as applicable.

Multiple Components. As can be seen, the underlying PPP asset may have many components, especially if the asset involves infrastructure. PPP and non-PPP components may also be present. Governmental operators should account for each underlying PPP asset as separate PPP components. Components may also involve different asset classes.

Allocations of the contract price may be needed for the different components as follows:

1. Use any prices for individual components that are explicit in the contract, if the prices for the individual components do not appear to be *unreasonable* based on professional judgment, using observable information to the greatest extent possible, including stand-alone prices that are readily available. The impact of discounts for multiple components in one contract needs to be considered, again, based on reasonableness. Or,
2. If a contract does not include individual component prices, or they are unreasonable, the transferor government or the government operator needs to use their professional judgment to determine the estimated allocation. Or,
3. If neither is reasonable, then a single PPP is in place and accounted for using the primary PPP component's term [GASB Cod. Secs. P90.155–.160].

> **PRACTICE POINT:** The importance of components in PPPs cannot be underestimated. Consider a PPP toll road—there could be dozens of different

components in the road from open-road tolling infrastructure, the roadbed, bridges, tunnels, lighting, computer servers, and so on. The servers and open-road tolling infrastructure may have quite different terms than the road infrastructure, which may be considered one class of asset. More so than leases, the allocation of each of the components may also result in different discount rates due to the different terms.

APAs and the Lease Framework

As discussed, APAs are arrangements in which a government compensates an operator for services that may include designing, constructing, financing, maintaining, or operating an underlying nonfinancial asset for a period in an exchange or exchange-like transaction. Like leases and PPPs, multiple components may exist in APAs.

Unlike leases and PPPs, payments associated with APAs only occur based exclusively on the asset's availability for use rather than measures of revenue or demand. Only when the asset is used is a payment generated. There may be specific criteria for the condition of the asset, construction, or many other measures.

Due to the variable payment, the compensation is almost a contractual fee for service arrangement, but not quite. The counterparty in the APA generates compensation from the government based totally on the *availability to perform* and not the performance of the services [GASB Cod. Sec. A90.102].

Example: GASB Cod. Sec. A90.901 illustrates an APA:

Facts and Assumptions: On January 2, 20X0, a State, through its State Department of Transportation, the transferor, finalizes an arrangement with a corporation to design, build, and finance the construction of the Spare Bridge. The corporation will collect all tolls for the bridge for 40 years and remit them to the State. The State will remit to the corporation $10 million at the start of the project, $10 million on the date the bridge is placed into service, and $2 million annually for each of the 40 years the corporation will operate the bridge to compensate the corporation for designing, building, and financing the bridge, beginning in the period in which the bridge is placed into service. The State also will remit $100,000 per month during the 40 years to compensate the corporation for collecting the tolls. In addition, if the bridge is placed into service prior to December 31, 20X1, the State will remit an additional $1 million for each month prior to December 31, 20X1, the bridge is in service to compensate the corporation for operating the bridge and as an incentive to complete the project sooner.

The bridge is placed into service on October 31, 20X1. After payment of the $10 million for completion of the project and $2 million for completing the project two months early, the present value of future payments to the corporation is $40 million.

Accounting at the commencement of the APA: The State should report an asset for the initial payment of $10 million to the corporation.

Accounting in future years: On the date the Spare bridge is placed into service, the State should recognize a capital asset for the bridge in the amount of $61.8 million ($10 million at the start of the project, $10 million at the date the bridge is placed into service, $40 million present value of future payments, and $1.8 million for two months of payments of $1 million for the bridge opening early, less the $100,000 portion of those payments for collecting tolls) and should apply existing capital asset guidance, including depreciation, to the bridge. The State also should recognize a liability in the amount of $40 million to the corporation for the present value of the future annual payments to the corporation. The State also should recognize an expense for $100,000 per month for payments related to toll collection.

Subscription-Based Information Technology Arrangements

GASB-96, *Subscription-Based Information Technology Arrangements* (SBITAs), also utilizes the lease model but applies it to information technology (IT) arrangements such as software as a service, platform as a service, infrastructure as a service and similar involving hardware, software, or a combination of both.

Basics of SBITAs

For many governments, SBITAs may be more common than leases, especially since the onset of remote working environments. For many, remote working is the norm, not the exception. Data, the infrastructure that creates, transmits, and stores data and applications all may be SBITAs. End users of SBITAs (governments, nongovernmental entities, and individuals) do not own SBITAs. SBITAs are *licensed*.

Like GASB Cod. Sec. L20, assets and liabilities resulting from SBITAs should be recognized and measured using the facts and circumstances that existed at the beginning of the fiscal year in which the provisions are implemented. Governments are permitted, but not required to, include in the measurement of the SBITA subscription asset capitalizable outlays associated with the initial implementation stage and the operation and additional implementation stage incurred prior to the implementation of GASB-96.

The most common structures of SBITAs include:

Abbreviation	Definition	Explanation	Examples (all ™ or ®)
SaaS	Software as a Service	Customer can use software through a "cloud" infrastructure.	Microsoft Office 365, Zoom, Workiva, Salesforce, Mimecast, CCH Accounting Research Manager, CCH Axcess
PaaS	Platform as a Service	Customer can use tools or coding language to create applications that will run on a SBITA vendor's cloud infrastructure.	Apple iOS, Android, Windows Azure
IaaS	Infrastructure as a Service	Customer may remotely access the SBITAs network, server, and other tools to process, store and operate the customer's data.	IBM, Oracle, Cisco, Citrix

Abbreviation	Definition	Explanation	Examples (all ™ or ®)
DwaaS	Data Warehouse as a Service	Outsourcing of storage of a customer's data for data security, continuity, and instant retrieval.	Amazon Web Services, Snowflake, Google Cloud

PRACTICE ALERT: The GASB *Implementation Guide Update* – 2023 includes a question on whether cloud computing arrangements are SBITAs. A cloud computing arrangement may *or may not* meet the definition of a SBITA. Cloud computing arrangements have three common deployment models: Software as a Service, Platform as a Service, and Infrastructure as a Service (as identified in the table above). All three deployment models provide the customer with the right to use a combination of another party's IT software and tangible capital assets. The definition of a SBITA requires, in part, that a contract conveys control of the right to use another party's IT software, alone or in combination with tangible capital assets (the underlying IT assets). Therefore, as part of its determination of whether a cloud computing arrangement meets the definition of a SBITA, governments should evaluate whether the contract conveys control of the right to use the underlying IT assets [GASB Cod. Sec. S80.702-1].

OBSERVATION: The above question and answers require the preparer to perform the analysis. In many cases, DwaaS contracts allow digital storage space, which to this author, allows the government to use, exchange and employ that space for operations. Therefore, the space would be an asset. Valuing the space would then require the calculation of the SBITA liability and related asset.

The provisions of GASB-96 exclude the following arrangements:

- Contracts that convey control of the right to use another party's combination of IT software and tangible capital assets that meets the definition of a lease in which the software component is *insignificant* when compared to the cost of the underlying tangible capital asset (e.g., a computer with operating software or a smart copier that is connected to an IT system),
- Governments that provide the right to use their IT software and associated tangible capital assets to other entities through SBITAs (as a passthrough and therefore not the end user),
- Contracts that meet the definition of a PPP as described in the previous section, and
- Licensing arrangements that provide a perpetual license to governments to use a vendor's computer software, which are subject to GASB Cod. Secs. 1400.126–.137 (*Internally Generated Intangible Assets*) (See Chapter 10.) [GASB Cod. Secs. S80.101–.102].

PRACTICE POINT: Perpetual licenses that transfer software are rare. In these rare cases, the software code ownership fully transfers to the government in exchange for payment to the vendor. If this transaction occurs, the software becomes an intangible asset of the government and is subject to the intangible asset provisions discussed in Chapter 10.

Most license agreements have no transfer of ownership provisions. Even if the vendor allows customization of the code, the customization is provided by the vendor.

PRACTICE ALERT: The GASB 2023 *Implementation Guide Update* contains a question further clarifying the issue of perpetual licenses. In the case of when a licensing agreement for software automatically renews until cancelled, the agreement has an option to terminate at *each renewal date*. An agreement that includes an option to terminate is not a purchase. This is different from a perpetual license, which is a purchase in which a government is granted a permanent right to use the vendor's computer software. Therefore, a licensing agreement for a vendor's computer software that automatically renews until cancelled does not provide a perpetual license. The issue of automatic renewal is widespread with the prevalence of well-known "Office" suites of programs, which automatically renew annually with a 30-or 60-day cancellation period. In those cases, the software would be a short-term SBITA [GASB Cod. Sec. S80.701-1].

Definition of a SBITA. Applying the leases framework, an SBITA is a contract that conveys control of the right to use another party's (an SBITA vendor's) IT software, alone or in combination with tangible capital assets (the underlying IT assets), as specified in the contract for a period of time in an exchange or exchange-like transaction. However, it only applies to the end-user. Governments that provide the right to use *their software* and similar through SBITAs are excluded from the SBITA accounting and financial reporting provisions contained in GASB-96.

SBITAs also exclude contracts for strictly IT support services but may include contracts that contain *both* a right-to-use IT asset component and IT support services [GASB Cod. Secs. S80.103, .105].

PRACTICE POINT: The provisions to calculate the term of an SBITA are from the lease framework. Discerning the term may be difficult as once a government engages in an SBITA, the cost of changing to a competing SaaS, IaaS, PaaS or DwaaS needs to be addressed. Like the lease framework, the noncancelable period should be in the license agreement as should be renewal provisions.

PRACTICE POINT: GASB Statement No. 99 also amends the SBITA term provisions. If a provision in an SBITA allows for the termination of an SBITA due to the action (or inaction) of another party, the provision is not a termination option for the purposes of determining an SBITA term. The GASB provides examples of violations of SBITA terms and conditions or payments of sums due, or default on payments as potential occurrences that would not be termination options. It is unclear when the implementation of these provisions would occur.

Further, the provisions for short-term SBITAs that are modified to extend the initial maximum possible term under the SBITA contract would be reassessed from the inception of the SBITA. If longer than 12 months, the SBITA would no longer be considered short-term.

> **PRACTICE ALERT:** The GASB provides an example of the difficulty of calculating a term for a SBITA. In the GASB *Implementation Guide Update*, a government signs a contract for a six-year SBITA with no options to extend or terminate the contract. The government begins making semiannual subscription payments to the SBITA vendor immediately after the contract takes effect. The initial implementation stage is not completed until the end of the second year after the contract takes effect (see following section). The subscription term is *four years*. The initial implementation stage is completed at the end of the second year of the contract. Therefore, the subscription term commences at the beginning of the third year and ends at the conclusion of the sixth year when the SBITA contract ends [GASB Cod. Sec. S80.703-1].

> **PRACTICE POINT:** The above **PRACTICE ALERT** and the following section illustrate that the SBITA term may result in vastly different asset balances from liability balances with SBITAs. Further, the amortization of the SBITA underlying asset is required to be the *shorter* of the useful life of the SBITA or the contract. Amortizations of SBITA underlying assets may be shorter than a similar intangible asset.

Outlays Other Than Subscription Payments, Including Implementation Costs

In addition to the subscription liability, governments with SBITAs may have additional assets. The accounting and financial reporting provisions for deriving these additional assets are from GASB Cod. Secs. 1400.126–.137. The same three stages of capitalization (or expense) are utilized as described in Chapter 10 for internally generated intangible assets, but now applied to an SBITA environment:

Stage	Discussion
Preliminary Project Stage	Activities in this stage include the conceptual formulation and evaluation of alternatives, the determination of the existence of needed technology, and the final selection of alternatives for the SBITA.
Initial Implementation Stage	Activities in this stage include ancillary charges related to designing the chosen path, such as configuration, coding, testing, and installation associated with the government's access to the underlying IT assets. Other ancillary charges necessary to place the subscription asset into service also should be included in this stage. The initial implementation stage for the SBITA is completed when the subscription asset is placed into service.

Stage	Discussion
Operational and Additional Implementation Stage	Activities in this stage include maintenance, troubleshooting, and other activities associated with the government's ongoing access to the underlying IT assets. Activities in this stage also may include additional implementation activities, such as those related to changes to the SBITA that occur after the subscription asset is placed into service, unless the changes extend the service life or add functionality [GASB Cod. Sec. S80.123].

Often, SBITAs have more than one module implemented at separate times (also known as *waves*) (see additional discussion on *modifications to SBITA*). The initial "core" implementation is in service, but the additional modules depend on the "core." The additional modules are subsequent implementations and are capitalized if the nature and timing of the activity increases the functionality of the SBITA or increases the level of service of the SBITA [GASB Cod. Sec. S80.124].

Data Conversion. Data conversion costs are considered part of the initial implementation stage as the conversion is necessary to place the SBITA into service. Data conversion that is ancillary to place the SBITA into service is part of the operation and additional implementation stage [GASB Cod. Sec. S80.125].

PRACTICE POINT: As discussed in the following subsection, the operational and additional implementation stage activities are expensed. This includes the conversion of "legacy" data that is not needed to "go-live."

Accounting for Each Stage. As with GASB Cod. Secs. 1400.126–.137, each stage has specific accounting provisions [GASB Cod. Secs. S80.126–.132]:

Stage	Accounting	When Stage is Completed
Preliminary Project Stage	Expensed	Final selection of alternatives for the SBITA made *and* management implicitly (or explicitly) authorized and commits to funding the SBITA, at least for the current fiscal year in the case of a multiyear project. In practice, this would be upon finalizing of a contract.
Initial Implementation Stage	Capitalized as part of subscription asset unless a short-term SBITA (unlikely in practice)	In practice, explicitly stated in a contract (also known as "go-live"). The SBITA contract may have multiple milestones.
Operational and Additional Implementation Stage	Expensed	Normal operations of SBITA.

Training Costs. The most controversial aspect of the operational and additional implementation stage are training costs. GASB-96 requires training costs to be expensed as incurred, regardless of the stage in which they are incurred [GASB Cod. Sec. S80.133].

The GASB discusses at great length within the Basis for Conclusions to GASB-96 as to why training costs are expensed:

- The expensing of training aligns to the existing provisions of GASB Cod. Sec. 1400.133.
- The answer to GASB Cod. Sec. 1400.717-5 states: "Although the skills obtained by the employees through the training may facilitate the development of the computer software, the training itself does not further the development of the software and does not otherwise contribute to putting the software in condition for use. Therefore, this training should not be considered an activity of the application development stage, and the related outlays should be expensed as incurred."
- The GASB does acknowledge that initial training is required by some SBITA contracts as part of the initial implementation. They also state: "However, in the context of a SBITA, even though certain employees may be required by the contract to obtain training and show a certain aptitude with the SBITA vendor's IT assets before the vendor considers the government to have obtained the necessary skills to use its IT assets, the training itself does not contribute to the present service capacity of the subscription asset."

Modifications to SBITA

Once an SBITA is in service, additional outlays may occur including legacy data conversion. Generally, conversion is expensed. But other outlays are capitalized, if they add to an existing SBITA (in practice—*wave* modules). To capitalize, the modules must:

- Increase in the functionality of the subscription asset, that is, the subscription asset allows the government to perform tasks that it could not previously perform with the subscription asset, or
- Increase in the efficiency of the subscription asset, that is, an increase in the level of service provided by the subscription asset without the ability to perform additional tasks [GASB Cod. Sec. S80.134].

The remainder of the accounting and financial reporting provisions contained in GASB-96 aligns to the lease framework from the point of view of a lessee. This includes:

- Impairment,
- Incentives provided by a SBITA vendor,
- Contracts with multiple components (which will be common),
- Contract combinations,
- SBITA modifications and terminations,
- Financial statements prepared using the current financial resources measurement focus, and
- Notes to financial statements.

CHAPTER 15
RISK MANAGEMENT, CLAIMS, AND JUDGMENTS

Chapter References:
  GASB Statement Nos. 1, 10, 14, 17, 30, 34, 53, 62, 65, 72, 92
  GASB Interpretation Nos. 4, 6
  GASB *Implementation Guide*
  NCGA Statement No. 4

INTRODUCTION

State and local governments encounter the same accounting and reporting issues as commercial enterprises that purchase insurance coverage (insured). GASB Cod. Sec. C50 (*Claims and Judgments*) was issued to provide guidance for governmental entities that assume the role of the insurer and the role of the insured. For public entity risk pools, GASB Cod. Sec. Po20 contains guidance on reporting.

> **PRACTICE POINT:** For a discussion of the accounting standards that apply to governmental entities that assume the role of an insurer and pool resources of other governments, see Chapter 23.

Most governmental entities are exposed to a variety of risks that may result in losses. These risks may be wide-ranging. GASB Cod. Sec. C50 addresses risk of loss that arises from events where the government (not a pool) bears the risk, such as:

- Torts (wrongful acts, injuries, or damages—not involving breach of contract—for which a civil action can be brought),
- Theft of, damage to, or destruction of assets,
- Business interruptions,
- Errors and omissions (such as the publication of incorrect data or the failure to disclose required information),
- Job-related illnesses or injuries to employees (but not a pool for workers' compensation), and
- Acts of God (events beyond human origin or control—natural disasters such as lightning, windstorms, and earthquakes).

Governments are also exposed to claims and judgments with contingent losses (and in some circumstances gains). This chapter focuses on risk financing, insurance-related activities of state and local government entities (other than risk pools) and other claims and judgments, including breaches of contract. [GASB Cod. Secs. C50.101–.103].

> **PRACTICE POINT:** Governments may be exposed to Landfill Closure and Postclosure Care Costs [GASB Cod. Sec. L10], Pollution Remediation [GASB Cod. Sec. P40], and Asset Retirement Obligations [GASB Cod. Sec. A10] (ARO). All these are discussed in Chapter 16.

Risk management is the process of a government's procedures and activities to minimize the effects of certain types of losses. Risk management includes two elements:

1. *Risk control*—The policies and procedures to minimize losses that impact a government, and
2. *Risk financing*—The financial policies and procedures used to finance the restoration of damages occurring from those losses.

> **PRACTICE POINT:** From an internal audit perspective, risk management may be termed *enterprise risk management* (ERM). For any organization, the ERM process is important. The basic question is asked: "*What Could Go Wrong?*" But then a follow up is asked: "*What would be the impact and likelihood of risks?*" The potential impact and likelihood are then scored by some internal audit programs to derive a risk rating. From there, a point person or entity is then named along with strategies to mitigate the risks. Upon mitigation, monitoring occurs. This is known as a component of the ERM COSO (Committee of Sponsoring Organizations) Framework.

Some large governments only self-insure, and only up to a certain dollar threshold set in law (e.g., $100,000). This affords some relief from frivolous lawsuits and exorbitant billing by legal teams. Self-insurance means that settlements and judgments are paid out of current appropriated funds rather than out of a trust or pool of funds. In certain circumstances, the settlement or judgment is structured to pay out over years and the court orders such amounts be appropriated annually.

On certain large construction projects, one way to mitigate risk is to have all construction contractors pool their resources and have the government control the pool (known as an owner-controlled insurance program, or OCIP). OCIPs may be effective in reducing workers' compensation losses. Depending on how the law is written creating the OCIP, any unspent assets may inure to the government, with the government assuming risk after a certain time, or the assets may inure to a private insurance carrier or the contractors. If the sponsoring government assumes the risk, then the provisions discussed in this chapter and in Chapter 23 (if a public entity risk pool) may apply.

From an accounting perspective, potential losses related to these events require that a governmental entity consider whether an accrual for losses should be recognized at the end of an accounting period. Again, the consideration for an accrual for losses by a governmental entity is no different from the evaluation that a commercial enterprise must make [GASB Cod. Sec. C50.104].

Transferring Risk

A key question for a state or local government involves whether risk has been transferred to another entity, or has it been retained, even if an insurance provider or other third party is involved. Even if an insurance provider is involved, risk may not absolutely transfer. Premiums (or similar required contributions) may be paid by a government to an insurer (or a risk pool) based on claims or loss experience. If the government's losses exceed the initial charge, additional amounts are assessed to the government by the insurer to recover those losses. But if the premium charges are more than the losses, the government (hopefully) will receive a refund. If this activity or pattern occurs, the government retains the risk. The annual premium is merely a deposit. The insurer is providing a service to pay the claims.

But if the insurer is assessing premiums based on coverage of *all claims* without adjusting future premiums (additional premiums or refunds), risk may be pooled with other governments (or nongovernmental entities) and the risk of the reporting government *may* be transferred. If the insurer does not have enough assets to pay the claims though (in the case of a catastrophe, for example), the government remains liable. Risk *has not* transferred [GASB Cod. Secs. C50.105–.107].

The accounting standards that are used to determine the amount of the liability that should be presented in a governmental entity's basic financial statements vary depending on whether a liability is presented in a (1) governmental fund, (2) proprietary and fiduciary funds, or (3) the government-wide basic financial statements.

ACCOUNTING FOR RISK MANAGEMENT LIABILITIES

General Principles of Liability Recognition

Unless the risk has been transferred to another entity, governments report an estimated loss from a claim as an expenditure in a governmental fund (or an expense in all other funds and the government-wide basic financial statements) along with a corresponding liability, if *both of the following conditions are met*:

- Information is available to the government *before the basic financial statements are issued* that it is *probable* that an asset has been impaired, or a liability has been incurred at the date of the basic financial statements, and
- The amount of loss can be *reasonably* estimated.

The themes of *probable* and *reasonably estimated* occur often throughout this Chapter and are benchmarks of liability recognition for most GAAP transactions. The *reasonable estimation* process may be a range of potential losses. When an amount within the range appears (based on management judgment) to be a better estimate than any other amount in the range, the better estimate amount is accrued. When no amount within a range is a better estimate than any other, the *minimum amount* is accrued.

> **PRACTICE POINT:** If a financial guarantee transaction is evident, a measurement technique of probability is added involving a "more likely than not" (MLTN) scenario. MLTN can be explained by having a probability of any amount more than 50%. Some have also explained that MLTN is a probability of 50% "plus a feather." A further discussion on nonexchange financial guarantees is contained in Chapter 16. The MLTN threshold is also used in compensated absences, which are discussed in Chapter 13.

> **PRACTICE POINT:** GASB Cod. Secs. L20 (*Leases*), P90 (*Public-Private and Public-Public Partnerships*) (P3s) and S80 (*Subscription-Based Information Technology Arrangements*) (SBITAs) add another potential scenario for probability measurement. These types of contracts require measurement of the applicable term based on being "reasonably certain" that the contract will be renewed based on the terms and conditions embedded in the contract and may include some qualitative aspects. "Reasonably certain" is indicated by the GASB to be more than probable. For further information on these contracts, see Chapter 14.

These phrases or words have no mathematics or percentages aligned to them in GAAP. Therefore, one is evident, a measurement technique of probability is added involving a measurement technique not especially senior to another.

Exceptions to this process include when an internal service fund is used, for pollution remediation obligations, for municipal solid waste landfill obligations and for nonexchange financial guarantees, all of which are discussed later in this chapter. Asset retirement obligations are discussed in Chapter 16 with an accrual generated from a similar process to pollution remediation obligations [GASB Cod. Secs. C50.110–.111].

The accrual of a loss in a current period implies that an event will occur in a subsequent period that will substantiate the recognition of the accrual. The accrual of a loss due to an event that suggests that the governmental entity will be held liable for the loss will eventually be confirmed when the entity agrees (or is forced) to pay the injured party. Of course, the accrual of a loss is based on a prediction that the future event will in fact occur. GAAP uses the following definitions to describe the various probabilities of whether a loss will eventually be confirmed by a future event [GASB Cod. Sec. C50.112]:

- Probable—The future event or events confirming the fact that a loss has occurred are likely to occur.

- Reasonably possible—The chance of the future event or events occurring is more than remote but less than likely.

- Remote—The change of the future event or event occurring is slight.

PRACTICE POINT: The importance of these three definitions cannot be underestimated. A sizable portion of a government's presentation of liabilities are presented based on the decision if the potential for loss is probable, reasonably possible, or remote. Unfortunately, there are no steadfast equations to determine if a potential is probable, reasonably possible, or remote. Therefore, the decision is qualitative and based on discussions with the government's independent auditor and confirmation with the government's legal counsel. As discussed in Chapter 1, there are seemingly uses for additional probabilities, including:

Phrase or Word	Example of When Used in GAAP
Reasonably Certain	Portions of a lessee's determination of a lease term.
Probable	Determination of the probability of a liability relating to a claim or judgment (the future claim(s) or judgment(s) are *likely* to occur).
More Likely than Not	Determination if a government may be liable for payments related to a nonexchange financial guarantee.
Material	Nearly every GASB pronouncement.
Significant	Many elements of notes to the basic financial statements, especially in the disclosure of accounting policies applicable to the government.
Insignificant	When both information technology software and tangible capital assets are included in a subscription-based information technology arrangement (SBITA), if the cost of the software component is insignificant relative to the cost of the underlying tangible capital assets, the contract may be subject to leases guidance, based on professional judgment.

The criterion that the loss must be subject to reasonable estimation before an accrual is appropriate does not imply that there must be only a single amount that is likely to be incurred. A reasonable amount can be expressed in terms of a range of possible losses. If one specific amount within the range is the most likely to occur, that amount should be accrued as a loss and the excess (the maximum amount in the range minus the amount accrued), as discussed later, should be disclosed in the basic financial statements. This is often the case in pending litigation.

When no single amount within the range of possible losses is most likely to occur, the minimum amount in the range should be accrued as a loss and the excess should be disclosed in the basic financial statements.

Incurred but Not Reported (IBNR) Claims. A governmental entity must evaluate its exposure to *incurred but not reported* (IBNR) conditions. IBNR claims are claims that have not yet been asserted, as of the basic financial statements' issuance date, even though they may have occurred before the date of the Statement of Net Position. These types of claims are common in Medicaid, earthquake, or hurricane insurance and similar programs. The valuation of the claims is discussed in the next section.

If the governmental entity concludes that it is not probable that IBNR claims will be asserted, the loss should not be accrued or disclosed in the basic financial statements. On the other hand, if the entity concludes that it is probable that an IBNR claim will be asserted by another party, the loss should be accrued if a reasonable estimate of the loss can be made [GASB Cod. Sec. C50.113].

IBNR claims include three components:

1. Known loss events that are expected to be presented as claims,
2. Unknown loss events that are expected to become claims, and
3. Expected future development on claims already reported.

IBNR is an estimate of loss and is (for the most part) based on historical data and patterns of loss. A footnote to GASB Cod. Sec. C50.113 fn. 5 uses the following fact pattern to explain the differences in each of the components: "After reviewing historical claims experience, (a government) finds that only 40 percent of all claims are normally reported during the year of occurrence. Another 50 percent the next year and the remainder in the third year. This pattern would be used to estimate the IBNR amounts and the timing of those amounts for financial reporting purposes."

Governmental entities must evaluate their exposure to liabilities related to unpaid claims costs, which includes both (1) claims that have been reported and (2) claims incurred but not reported. GAAP requires that the liability for unpaid claims costs should be based on the following factors:

- Total ultimate costs of settling a claim, including provisions for inflation and other societal and economic factors,
- Experience of settling claims, and
- Factors needed to make experience trends consistent with current conditions.

Valuation of Claims Cost Liabilities. The estimated liability for claims costs should include all costs related to the ultimate settlement of claims. In addition to an estimate for actual payments to claimants, the estimated liability for claims costs should include specific, incremental claims adjustment expenditures or expenses. Specific claims adjustment expenditures or expenses represent costs incurred by a governmental entity only because it is attempting to dispose of a specific claim. For example, a claim may require the governmental entity to hire an individual with a certain type of expertise to evaluate the government's legal responsibility as it relates to the claim. In this example, salaries of administrative personnel in the department that processes claims, and other similar overhead costs, would generally not be considered incremental. Other allocated or unallocated claim adjustment expenditures or expenses may be included in the estimated liability for claims costs, but GAAP does not require their inclusion.

The estimated liability for claims costs for a public entity risk pool must include a provision for other allocated or unallocated claim adjustment expenditures or expenses. The GASB implied that expenditures or expenses are conceptually part of the estimated liability for claims costs for entities other than pools. GAAP includes a provision for allocated or unallocated claim adjustment expenditures or expenses in the accrual for claims costs to be optional. The composition of the accrual must be disclosed in the basic financial statements.

The estimated liability for claims costs should be reduced by estimated recoveries that may arise from unsettled claims. GAAP refers to two broad categories of recoveries, "salvage" and "subrogation," and further provides the following definitions of these terms (the definitions have been slightly modified to reflect the discussion of governmental entities other than public entity risk pools):

- *Salvage*—The amount received by a governmental entity other than a pool from the sale of property (usually damaged) on which the entity has paid a total claim to the claimant and has obtained title to the property.
- *Subrogation*—The right of a governmental entity other than a pool to pursue any course of recovery of damages, in its name, against a third party who is liable for costs of an event that have been paid by the governmental entity.

In addition to claims that have not been settled, the governmental entity may also anticipate recoveries from claims that have already been settled. Anticipated recoveries on settled claims should be netted (reduced) against the estimated liability for claims costs.

The accrual for claims costs may be based on a case-by-case review, an overall approach of applying historical experience to all claims outstanding, or a combination of both approaches. GAAP notes that the accrual for IBNR losses must be based on historical experience. When historical experience is used to estimate the accrual, claims should be appropriately categorized by amount and type of claim to ensure that relevant historical experience is applied to similar claims [GASB Cod. Sec. C50.114].

Discounting. The GASB does not specify whether the accrual of claims liabilities should be discounted. Thus, it is acceptable to report the accrual at either a gross amount or a discounted amount, with one exception: structured settlements should be discounted if the amount to be paid to the claimant is fixed by contract and the payment dates are fixed or determinable [GASB Cod. Sec. C50.116].

PRACTICE POINT: For tort claims and similar, structured settlements are most common at state and local governments. If a claim is immaterial, discounting is usually unnecessary.

When claims liabilities are presented in the basic financial statements at discounted amounts, the rate selected to compute the discounted amounts should take into consideration factors such as the following [GASB Cod. Sec. C50.117]:

- Settlement rate (the rate at which a monetary liability with uncertain terms can be settled or a monetary asset [receivable] with uncertain terms can be sold), or
- Investment yield rate (the expected rate of return on investments held by the governmental entity during the period in which the expected payments to the claimant will occur).

> **OBSERVATION:** The discount rate used may be different from other yields, including bond yields and discount rates used for defined benefit pensions and OPEB (Other Postemployment Benefit), respectively. Auditors of the government will want to test the rate used for claims liabilities for reasonableness.

Annuity Contracts. A governmental entity may satisfy its obligation to a claimant by purchasing an annuity in the claimant's name. If the possibility of making additional payments to the claimant is remote, the claim should be removed as a liability. Under this circumstance, the claim would not be presented as a liability and the purchase of the annuity contract would not be presented as an asset.

When claims have been removed from the claims liability account because of the purchase of an annuity contract, the amount removed should be disclosed as a contingent liability. The disclosure should continue if there is a legal possibility that the claimant could demand payment from the governmental entity. Disclosure is not required for annuity contracts purchased if *both* of the following conditions exist [GASB Cod. Sec. C50.118]:

- The claimant has signed an agreement releasing the governmental entity from further obligation, and
- The likelihood of future payments to the claimant is *remote* (see previous **PRACTICE POINT**).

If a claim had been removed from the claims liability account because an annuity contract was purchased in a previous period, but in the current period it was determined that the governmental entity is now primarily liable for the claim, the claim should be reestablished as a claims liability.

Investments. A governmental entity often finances risk through investing. Given the nature of claims, the investments may be maintained separately from other investments (and therefore may be restricted). The investments are valued the same way as all other investments in accordance with GAAP. Investment valuation, accounting and reporting is discussed in Chapter 9 [GASB Cod. Sec. C50.119].

FINANCIAL REPORTING OF RISK MANAGEMENT ACTIVITIES

Government-Wide Financial Statements

The accrual basis of accounting and the economic resources measurement focus should be used to determine which claims and assessments should be presented in a governmental entity's Statement of Net Position. Claims that are *probable* are reported as an expense in the statement of activities and a liability in the Statement of Net Position. Liabilities that are structured and have more than one year of maturities are reported in two components: the amount due within one year and the amount due in more than one year. Claim amounts that are *probable*, but not reasonably estimable or claims that are *reasonably possible* are disclosed in the notes to the basic financial statements. A further discussion of disclosures is presented later in this chapter.

When a claims expense is recorded, the expense must be evaluated to determine how the expense should be presented in the statement of activities. That is, a determination should be made as to whether the claims expense is a direct expense (expenses that are specifically associated with a service, program, or department). In some instances, a claims expense may be an extraordinary item (unusual and infrequent) and therefore should be presented in the lower section of the statement of activities. When a claims expense is either unusual or infrequent, but not both, the item should be disclosed in a note to the basic financial statements [GASB Cod. Secs. C50.120–.121].

Reporting Risk Financing Internal Service Fund Balances and Activity. If an Internal Service Fund is used to account for risk management activities, such activities should be eliminated to avoid "doubling-up" expenses and revenues in the government activities column of the statement of activities. The effect of this approach is to adjust activities in an internal service fund to a break-even balance. That is, if the internal service fund had a "net profit" for the year, there should be a pro rata reduction in the charges made to the funds that used the internal service fund's services for the year. Likewise, a net loss would require a pro rata adjustment that would increase the charges made to the various participating funds. After making these eliminations any residual balances related to the internal service fund's assets and liabilities should be reported in the government activities column in the Statement of Net Position [GASB Cod. Secs. C50.122–.123].

Proprietary and Fiduciary Fund Reporting. The accrual basis of accounting and the economic resources measurement focus should be used to determine which claims should be presented in a proprietary or fiduciary fund. That is, GAAP should be followed to determine the amount of the claim, including recognition of the probability of loss as discussed previously and if an IBNR is present. If a claims liability is incurred, the liability should be presented both in the proprietary or fiduciary fund and in its business activities columns of the Statement of Net Position [GASB Cod. Sec. C50.124].

PRACTICE POINT: Insurance recoveries from theft or embezzlement are reported as nonoperating revenue, or an extraordinary item, as appropriate. Insurance recoveries should be recognized only when realized or realizable. For example, if an insurer has admitted or acknowledged coverage, an insurance recovery would be realizable. If the insurer has denied coverage, the insurance recovery generally would not be realizable. If not otherwise apparent in the basic financial statements, the amount and financial statement classification of insurance recoveries should be disclosed [GASB Cod. Secs. C50.125, 1400.197].

Governmental Fund Reporting. Under current GAAP, the modified accrual basis of accounting and current financial resources measurement focus should be applied to accounting for claims and judgments in governmental funds. Recognition of expenditures and claims liabilities follows the provisions for recognition of a liability as discussed previously (probable, estimable, etc.).

15,010 Specific Accounting and Reporting Issues

As an example of recording a claim liability in a governmental fund, assume that an entity identifies a probable loss and that a reasonable estimate of the loss ranges from $100,000 to $400,000. Assume that the most likely amount of the loss is $150,000. The amount of the claims liability that should be accrued in a governmental fund is based on the application of the modified accrual basis of accounting. If none of the $150,000 estimate is expected to use expendable available financial resources, no claims expenditure (liability) would be accrued, but the full amount ($150,000) would be presented in the government-wide financial statements.

Many governments may allocate the loss expenditures based on an accepted methodology that may align to a budgetary framework, approved cost allocation plan or the nature of the claim. If the total amount charged to the other funds exceeds the total expenditures, the amount(s) is (are) reported as a transfer(s). If excess insurance is available, the claims liabilities are reduced by the amounts expected to be recovered from the insurance. The amounts then charged to other funds are ostensibly interfund reimbursements.

To show how the allocation process may be made to other funds, assume a loss of $500,000 is computed and the loss is allocated to an enterprise fund, capital projects fund, and General Fund, in the amounts of $50,000, $70,000, and $380,000, respectively. To record the recognition and allocation of the loss, the following entries would be made in the affected funds:

	Debit	Credit
GENERAL FUND		
Expenditures – Claims costs	$380,000	
Due from Enterprise Fund	50,000	
Due from Capital Projects Fund	70,000	
Estimated Claims Costs Payable		$500,000
To record risk financing and allocate loss on risk financing.		

	Debit	Credit
ENTERPRISE FUND		
Expenses – Claims costs	50,000	
Due to General Fund		50,000
To record risk financing and allocated loss on risk financing.		

	Debit	Credit
CAPITAL PROJECTS FUND		
Expenditures – Claims costs	70,000	
Due to General Fund		70,000
To record risk financing and allocated loss on risk financing.		

As previously discussed, when the General Fund allocates the loss expenditure or expense to other funds and the total allocation, including the amount allocated to the General Fund, exceeds the accrual computed, the excess amount should be treated as a transfer. To illustrate this requirement, assume the same facts as the previous example except assume that the enterprise fund and capital projects fund are allocated an additional cost of $10,000 each. To record the allocation, the following entries are made:

GENERAL FUND	Debit	Credit
Expenditures – Claims costs	$380,000	
Due from Enterprise Fund	60,000	
Due from Capital Projects Fund	80,000	
Estimated Claims Costs Payable		$500,000
Transfers in – Enterprise Fund		10,000
Transfers in – Capital Projects Fund		10,000

To record risk financing and allocate loss on risk financing along with transfers for funding.

	Debit	Credit
ENTERPRISE FUND		
Expenses – Claims costs	50,000	
Transfers out – General Fund	10,000	
Due to General Fund		60,000

To record risk financing and allocated loss on risk financing and transfers.

	Debit	Credit
CAPITAL PROJECTS FUND		
Expenditures – Claims costs	70,000	
Transfers out – General Fund	10,000	
Due to General Fund		80,000

To record risk financing and allocated loss on risk financing and transfers.

If one fund reimburses another fund for expenditures or expenses paid, the reimbursement should be recorded as a reduction of expenditures or expenses by the reimbursed fund and as an expenditure or expense by the reimbursing fund. This classification problem most often occurs when:

- The General Fund does not allocate loss expenditures or expenses to other funds (or the amount allocated is too small) and another fund reimburses the General Fund for the payment of a claim related to the activities of the other fund, *or*

- The General Fund pays insurance premiums for another fund and, later, the other fund reimburses the general fund for a portion of the premiums paid [GASB Cod. Sec. C50.126].

PRACTICE ALERT: The GASB's *Financial Reporting Model Improvements* Exposure Draft may change this methodology if approved as drafted.

15,012 Specific Accounting and Reporting Issues

Internal Service Fund Used for Risk Financing Activities. Internal service funds commonly are used for risk financing activities, especially in larger governments that also have indirect cost allocation plans for federal grants (see following **OBSERVATION**). When an internal service fund is used to account for a governmental entity's risk financing activities, claims liabilities and the related expenses should be recognized either as discussed previously or based on an actuarial calculation. Any accrual of claims liabilities should be reduced by amounts expected to be paid through excess insurance.

If it is concluded that a loss related to risk financing activities should not be accrued because the occurrence of the loss is *not probable*, or the amount of the loss *is not subject to reasonable estimation*, the loss should be evaluated to determine whether disclosure in the financial statement is necessary [GASB Cod. Sec. C50.127].

An internal service fund is "to account for the financing of goods or services provided by one department or agency to other departments or agencies of the governmental unit, or to other governmental units, on a cost-reimbursement basis." Thus, the risk financing services provided by an internal service fund should be billed to those funds for those services provided. GAAP states that an internal service fund may use any method it considers appropriate to determine the amounts charged to the various other funds if the following guidelines are satisfied:

- The total amount for service charges to other funds is equal to the amount of liability; *or*

- The total amount for service charges to other funds is computed using an actuarial method or historical cost information, and that amount is adjusted over time so that the expenses and revenues of the internal service fund are approximately the same.

If the second approach is used (actuarial method or historical cost information method), an additional charge may be made to other funds that represents a reasonable provision for expected future catastrophic losses.

OBSERVATION: Internal service funds are also used to allocate centralized overhead costs reimbursed by the federal government (either directly or indirectly). The overhead costs are accumulated in the fund, reimbursed by the federal government, and then allocated back to funds based on approved formulas in accordance with *the Uniform Administrative Requirements, Cost Principles, and Audit Requirements for Federal Awards* (Title 2 Code of Federal Regulations, Part 200). Preparers of indirect cost proposals should also review Appendix VII to 2CFR200, *States and Local Government and Indian Tribe Indirect Cost Proposals,* for detailed guidance.

An "actuarial method" can be any of several techniques that actuaries use to determine the amounts and timing of contributions needed to finance claims liabilities so that the total contributions plus compounded earnings on them will equal the amounts needed to satisfy claims liabilities. It may or may not include a provision for anticipated catastrophe losses.

The first method requires that the amount billed to other funds by the internal service fund be equal to the amount of liability recognized under the accrual concepts. Thus, under the first method, the billings to other funds must be based on the incurrence of liabilities based on specific events.

The second method (actuarial method or historical cost information method) is not based on the evaluation of events that have occurred. Under the second method, the amount billed can be based on *projected* claims that *may* occur.

OBSERVATION: GAAP does not allow for "smoothing" of expenses or expenditures as allowed by the second method. A loss contingency is accrued based on the incurrence of a liability as of the date of the Statement of Net Position. It is arguable that the concept of interperiod equity cannot be achieved because U.S. GAAP does not allow for the "averaging of losses" so that any one period would not have a significantly larger value of recognized expenditures than any other period. The GASB provided a solution to the interperiod equity problem by allowing governmental entities to use an actuarial method that results in level charges and to charge an optional amount for expected future catastrophic losses

---

The amount billed by the internal service fund to the other funds should be recognized as revenue, and each fund should recognize either expenditures or an expense based on the amount of the billing. For example, if an internal service fund charged the General Fund and an enterprise fund $400,000 and $50,000, respectively, the following entries would be made [GASB Cod. Sec. C50.128]:

INTERNAL SERVICE FUND	Debit	Credit
Due from General Fund	$400,000	
Due from Enterprise Fund	50,000	
Revenue—Charges for Services		$450,000
To record internal billing for claims and judgments.		

	Debit	Credit
GENERAL FUND		
Expenditures—Payments in Lieu of Insurance Premiums	400,000	
Due to Internal Service Fund		400,000
To record risk financing premiums.		

	Debit	Credit
ENTERPRISE FUND		
Expenses—Payments in Lieu of Insurance	50,000	
Due to Internal Service Fund		50,000
To record risk financing premiums.		

GAAP recognizes that when an actuarial method or historical cost information method is used (with or without an additional charge for expected future catastrophic losses), in any one period, the amount of the claims costs expense recognized and the billings to the other funds may not be the same. The difference between the cumulative claims costs recognized and the cumulative billings does not have to be charged back to the other funds if adjustments are made over a reasonable period to reduce the difference. When a fund balance deficit arises, the deficit should be disclosed in the notes to the governmental entity's financial statements. Any amount in the internal service fund's net position that arose from an optional additional charge for catastrophic losses should be reported as restricted net position equity for future catastrophic losses in notes to the basic financial statements [GASB Cod. Sec. C50.129].

If the internal service fund bills other funds for a total amount that is greater than the total amount as discussed earlier in this section, the excess should be accounted for as interfund transfers by the internal service fund and the other funds. The internal service fund would report a transfer in, and the other funds would report a transfer out.

The amounts billed over time and the amounts of expenses recognized by the internal service fund should be approximately the same over a reasonable period. If the internal service fund incurs a deficit that is not eliminated over a reasonable period, the deficit should be billed to the participating funds to cover the full costs of claims recognized as expenses. When a chargeback occurs, the internal service fund should recognize revenue and the other funds should record either an expenditure or an expense. Long term liabilities for claims may also be reported in internal service funds, depending on the nature of the claim [GASB Cod. Secs. C50.130–.131].

GOVERNMENTS THAT PARTICIPATE IN PUBLIC ENTITY RISK POOLS WITH A TRANSFER OR POOLING OF RISK

PRACTICE POINT: Public entity risk pool accounting and financial reporting is discussed in more detail in Chapter 23.

Premiums (or required contributions) paid by a governmental entity to a public entity risk pool that result in the transfer or sharing of risk should be reported as an expenditure or expense by the governmental entity.

If the governmental entity is subject to supplemental premium assessment (an additional assessment on the members) by the public entity risk pool, consideration should be given to whether an additional expenditure or expense should be accrued or disclosed in the basic financial statements.

An accrual for the supplemental premium assessment should be made if the following conditions exist:

- A supplemental premium assessment will probably be made; and
- A reasonable estimate of the supplemental premium assessment can be made.

When a possible supplemental premium assessment, including a supplemental assessment more than an accrued supplemental assessment, does not satisfy the criteria for accrual (probable and subject to reasonable estimation), the potential supplemental premium assessment should be evaluated to determine whether it should be disclosed in the governmental entity's financial statements.

When a possible supplemental premium assessment is disclosed in the basic financial statements, the following should be part of the disclosure:

- A description of the possible supplemental premium assessment, and
- An estimate (or estimate range) of the assessment (or, if no estimate can be made, disclosure of this fact is required) [GASB Cod. Sec. C50.132].

When a public entity risk pool does not have the authority to assess additional premiums and has incurred a deficit, its economic viability should be evaluated. The governmental entity must be concerned with the possibility that the public entity risk pool will not be able to pay claims as they are settled.

If the following conditions exist, the governmental entity should record a liability for estimated claims costs:

- The public entity risk pool appears not to be able to pay the claims related to the governmental entity as they become due.
- It is probable that the governmental entity will be required to pay its own claims.
- A reasonable estimate of the dollar amount of claims that will be paid by the governmental entity can be made.

When the likelihood of payment of claims that cannot be paid by a public entity risk pool, including any payment for more than an accrued amount, does not satisfy the criteria for accrual (probable and subject to reasonable estimation), the potential payment should be evaluated to determine whether disclosure is appropriate. Any potential payments that can be classified in one of the following categories should be disclosed:

- Potential payment is probable but no reasonable estimate (or estimate range) of the payment can be made, or
- Potential payment is reasonably possible.

When a potential payment is disclosed in the basic financial statements, the following should be disclosed:

- Nature of potential payment; and
- Estimate (or estimate range) of the potential payment (or, if no estimate can be made, disclosure of this fact is required) [GASB Cod. Sec. C50.133].

Capitalization Contributions

When a governmental entity makes a capital contribution to a public entity risk pool where risk has been transferred or pooled, a determination must be made regarding whether to record the contribution as an asset or as an expenditure or expense. The contribution may be accounted for as an asset if "it is probable that the contribution will be returned to the entity upon either the dissolution of or the approved withdrawal from the pool." The judgment as to whether an asset exists should be based on the written contract that governs the relationship between the governmental entity and the public entity risk pool. In addition, an asset exists only if the public entity risk pool has the financial capacity to return the capital contribution to the governmental entity.

When state and local governmental entities join to form a public entity risk pool or when those entities join an established pool and if capitalization contributions are required, they are usually in the form of cash.

The assessment of whether to recognize an asset when a governmental entity makes a capital contribution to a public entity risk pool should not occur only at the date of contribution. If the public entity risk pool's financial condition changes in a period after the contribution, it may be necessary to remove the asset from the governmental entity's basic financial statements and recognize an expenditure or expense.

Contribution Recognition in Government-wide Statements and Proprietary Funds. In government-wide statements, the contribution is reported initially as prepaid insurance (an asset). The related expense is allocated over the periods where the pool is expected to provide coverage. The periods are consistent with the factors used to determine the premiums but should not exceed 10 years (if not readily determinable). Proprietary fund reporting utilizes the same provisions.

Contribution Recognition in Governmental Funds. When the capital contribution made to a public entity risk pool is accounted for as an asset in a governmental fund, the entity's fund balance must be classified as nonspendable to disclose that the asset is not available for expenditure in the following budgetary period. When the contribution is an expenditure, no asset exists for prepaid insurance. Otherwise, if an asset exists, prepaid insurance *is* recognized and allocated and recognized as an expenditure over the coverage period.

If management concludes that it is probable that the contribution to the public entity risk pool will not be returned and the contribution is made by a governmental fund, the contribution may be accounted for using either the allocation method or the non-allocation method. When the allocation method is used, a prepayment is established at the date of the contribution and is subsequently amortized over the period for which it is expected the contribution will be used to determine the amount of premiums the contributor must pay. Again, if the period is not readily determinable, the amortization period should not exceed 10 years. Because the prepayment is not a current financial resource, the fund's fund balance account should be classified as nonspendable by the amount presented for prepaid insurance.

When the non-allocation method of accounting is used in a government fund, the capital contribution is reported immediately as an expenditure. Under this approach no asset is created, and thus there is no need to establish a fund balance reserve at the end of the accounting period [GASB Cod. Secs. C50.134–.138].

Entities Participating in Public Entity Risk Pools, but Without Transfer or Pooling of Risk

A governmental entity may participate in a public entity risk pool when the relationship is not characterized by a transfer or pooling of risk. For example, there is no transfer or pooling of risk in a banking pool or a claims-servicing (account) pool.

When there is no transfer or pooling of risk in the relationship with the public entity risk pool, the governmental entity must evaluate and recognize losses from incurred claims as if there were no participation in the public entity risk pool. Expenditures (or expenses) and claims liabilities are presented in the fund financial statements in the same manner as if the losses and claims were directly borne by the government and not a pool.

Payments made to a public entity risk pool (including capitalization contributions) to which there has been no transfer or pooling of risk should be accounted for as either a deposit or a reduction of the claims liabilities account. A deposit should be recorded when the payment is not expected to be used to pay claims. A reduction of the claims liabilities account should be made when payments to the pool are to be used to pay claims as they are incurred [GASB Cod. Sec. C50.139].

The Impact of Using Public Entity Risk Pools in Comparison with Risk Management

GASB Cod. Sec. Po20.704-1 discusses the factors to determine whether an entity is a public entity risk pool. In making the determination, all the following factors should be considered together defining a risk pool:

- A cooperative group of governmental entities pool resources to finance an exposure, liability, or risk. Risk may include property and liability, workers' compensation, or employee health care. A pool may be a stand-alone entity or included as part of another governmental entity that acts as the pool's sponsor.
- A governmental entity that is a pool's sponsor may also participate in the pool for its own risk management function.
- Stand-alone pools are established under authorizing statute by agreement of any number of state and local governmental entities. Stand-alone pools are sometimes organized or sponsored by municipal leagues, school associations, or other types of associations of governmental entities. Stand-alone pools are frequently operated by a board that has as its membership one member from each participating government. They typically have no publicly elected officials or authority to tax.

If a government provides insurance or risk management coverage separate from its own risk management activities to individuals or organizations outside the governmental reporting entity and there is material transfer or pooling of risk among the participants, that activity should be accounted for as a public-entity risk pool.

If a government provides risk transfer or pooling coverage combined with its own risk management activities to individuals or organizations outside its reporting entity, those activities should continue to be reported in a governmental fund or an internal service fund only if the entity is the predominant participant in the fund. If the entity is not the predominant participant in the fund, then the combined activities should be reported as a public entity risk pool, using an enterprise fund and the accounting and reporting requirements of an enterprise fund.

In summary:

- *Pools should comprise primarily governmental entities.* It was intended that the provisions of GAAP apply to risk financing groups of primarily state and local governments, while recognizing that there may be some cases where a group has a minority of participants—in terms of both representation and risk coverage—that are nongovernmental.

- *Pools should be a cooperative effort.* It was intended that participants would work together to finance risk. Evidence of a cooperative effort may be voluntary participation in the activity, even if participation is a participant's last recourse. If a cooperative effort does not exist, then a governmental program may exist, and contributions from participants may be fees, assessments, or taxes—not premiums (required contributions). A governmental program could be accounted for in the General Fund, a special revenue fund, or an enterprise fund depending on its nature.

OTHER INSURANCE-RELATED TRANSACTIONS

Claims-Made Policies

A governmental entity may purchase a claims-made policy. GAAP defines a "claims-made policy" as follows:

> A type of policy that covers losses from claims asserted (reported or filed) against the policyholder during the policy period, regardless of whether the liability-imposing events occurred during the current or any previous period in which the policyholder was insured under the claims-made contract or other specified period before the policy period (the policy retroactive date).

In a claims-made policy, the risk of loss to which the governmental entity is exposed is not entirely transferred. Specifically, the governmental entity is liable for claims that have occurred but were not reported nor filed during the period covered by the claims-made policy. The exposure to loss resulting from a claims-made policy should be evaluated using the standards discussed on recognizing a liability to determine whether such exposure requires an accrual or disclosure in the basic financial statements.

The risk exposure related to a claims-made policy can be avoided by acquiring a tail-coverage insurance policy. GAAP defines "tail coverage" as follows:

> A type of insurance policy designed to cover claims incurred before, but reported after, cancellation or expiration of a claims-made policy. (The term "extended discovery coverage" is used in the commercial insurance industry.)

When tail coverage is acquired, a governmental entity does not have to evaluate the possible accrual or disclosure of losses arising from claims-made policies [GASB Cod. Sec. C50.140].

Retrospective-Rated Policies and Contracts

A governmental entity may purchase a retrospective-rated policy (or contract). GAAP defines a "retrospective (experience) rating" as follows:

> A method of determining the final amount of an insurance premium by which the initial premium is adjusted based on actual experience during the period of coverage (sometimes subject to maximum and minimum limits). It is designed to encourage safety by the insured and to compensate the insurer if larger-than-expected losses are incurred.

When a retrospective-rated policy is acquired, the minimum premium should be recognized as an expenditure or expense over the period covered by the contract. In addition, the standards discussed regarding recognizing a liability should be used to accrue reported and unreported claims more than the minimum premium. If there is a maximum premium identified in the contract, the accrual should not exceed the amount of the maximum premium [GASB Cod. Sec. C50.141].

In some circumstances, the conditions for recognizing a loss contingency may not exist. If this is the case, no accrual for additional premium payments should be made. However, the governmental entity should refer to the standards for disclosure discussed in this chapter to determine whether the possibility of additional premiums being charged under the retrospective-rated policy should be disclosed in the notes to the basic financial statements.

Some governmental entities purchase retrospective-rated policies based on the experience of a group of policyholders. When a retrospective-rated policy is based on group experience, the initial premium should be amortized as an expenditure or expense over the period covered by the contract. The governmental entity should accrue supplemental premiums or refunds arising from the group's experience to date. The accrual should be based on the ultimate cost of reported and unreported claims as of the date of the basic financial statements. In addition, the following disclosures should be made:

- Insurance coverage is based on retrospective-rated policies, and
- Premiums are accrued based on the experience to date of the ultimate claims cost of the group of which the governmental entity is a participant.

The governmental entity will have to rely on the insurer entity to provide the information necessary to accrue additional premiums or refunds as of the date of the Statement of Net Position.

When an entity cannot accrue estimated losses from reported or unreported claims related to a retrospective-rated policy using group experience because the accrual criteria are not satisfied, the disclosure criteria should be used to determine whether disclosure is appropriate [GASB Cod. Sec. C50.142].

Policyholder or Pool Dividends

A governmental entity may be entitled to a policyholder dividend (or return of contribution) based on the terms of its insurance contract or its participation in a public entity risk pool. GAAP provides the following definition of "policyholder dividends" [GASB Cod. Sec. C50.143]:

> Payments made, or credits extended to the insured by the insurer, usually at the end of a policy year that result in reducing the net insurance cost to the policyholder. These dividends may be paid in cash to the insured or applied by the insured to reduce premiums due for the next policy year.

A policyholder dividend should be recorded by the governmental entity as a reduction of expenditures or expenses as of the date the dividend is declared by the insurer.

Entities Providing Claims Servicing or Insurance Coverage to Others

Governmental entities may provide insurance or risk-management coverage to individuals or entities that are not part of the governmental reporting entity (primary government and all related component units).

For example, a governmental entity may provide insurance coverage under a workers' compensation plan. If there is a material transfer or pooling of risk and the activities are separate from its own risk-management activities, the governmental entity should account for these activities in a public entity risk pool by following the standards discussed in Chapter 23.

However, a governmental entity may provide insurance or risk-management coverage to individuals or entities not part of the governmental reporting entity, but these services may be part of its own risk-management activities. Under this circumstance and assuming the governmental entity is the predominant participant in the fund, all the activities should be accounted for in either the General Fund or an internal service fund, and the standards discussed in this chapter should be followed. If the governmental entity is not the predominant participant, the activities should be accounted for in an enterprise fund, and the standards discussed in Chapter 23 should be followed.

OBSERVATION: Although the General Fund can be used to account for the risk-management activities when the governmental entity is the predominant participant, the author believes it may be preferable to account for such activities in an internal service fund to limit the activities reported in the General Fund to revenues and expenses related to routine governmental transactions Instead, governments should base their fund type classification decisions on the nature of the activity to be reported.

Finally, some governmental entities may service claims and provide no insurance coverage to individuals or entities that are not part of the governmental reporting entities. Under this arrangement, amounts collected or due from, and amounts paid or due to the individuals or other entities should be netted and reported as a net asset or liability determined on an accrual basis. Operating revenue and administrative costs arising from the claims-servicing activities should be accounted for consistently with the standards discussed in Chapter 23 [GASB Cod. Sec. C50.144].

DISCLOSURES

Risk Management Disclosures

Under current GAAP, the following disclosures should be made in the basic financial statements of entities that are not public entity risk pools [GASB Cod. Sec. C50.145]:

- Describe the types of risk to which the governmental entity is exposed (see **PRACTICE ALERT**).
- Identify the methods used for risk financing (such as self-insurance, transfer of risk by purchasing insurance from a commercial enterprise, or transfer to or pooling of risk in a public entity risk pool). If the governmental entity has acquired commercial insurance that is insignificant in relation to the risk exposure, the governmental entity has in substance retained the risk of loss.
- Describe significant reductions in insurance coverage from the previous year, arranged by major category of risk, and indicate whether settlements exceeded insurance coverage for each of the past three years.
- Disclose whether the entity participates in a public entity risk pool and the nature of participation, if any, including rights and obligations of the governmental entity and the pool.
- Disclose whether the governmental entity has retained the risk of loss (risk is not transferred when activities are accounted for in an internal service fund), and describe the following:
  — Basis of estimating liabilities for unpaid claims including the effects of specific, incremental claim adjustment expenditures or expenses, and recoveries related to salvage and subrogation, as well as the effects of other components of the estimated amount, and whether the accrual includes a provision for other allocated or unallocated claim adjustment expenditures or expenses,
  — Carrying amount of unpaid claims liabilities that have been computed on a present-value basis and the range of discount rates used to make the computation, and
  — Total amount of outstanding liabilities that have been removed from the Balance Sheet because of the purchase of annuity contracts from third parties in the name of claimants (amount should not include amounts related to settlements for which claimants have signed an agreement releasing the entity from further obligation and the chance of further payment is remote).
- Present a total claims liabilities reconciliation, including changes in aggregate liabilities for claims in the current year and prior year using the following tabular format:
  — Beginning balance of claims liabilities,
  — Provision for incurred claims expenses for the year and increases or decreases in the provision for events that were incurred in prior years,

- Payments made for claims arising during the current year and prior fiscal years,
- Explanation of other material reconciling items, and
- Ending balance of claims liabilities.

PRACTICE ALERT: As the *Guide* was in the process of publication, the GASB was finalizing deliberations on what may become Statement No. 102 (*Risks and Uncertainties Disclosures*). Language with the standard was being finalized, but the scope of the standard is limited to only certain occurrences of risks including concentrations and constraints common in the governmental environment. Reporting requirements would only be for the current period and forward even if the government presents comparative financial statements.

Level of Disclosure. Professional judgment must be exercised to determine the most appropriate level of disclosure. The notes to the basic financial statements should focus on the primary government (which includes its blended component units) and support the information included in the government-wide financial statements and the fund financial statements.

OBSERVATION: Note disclosures related to discretely presented component units should be presented based on professional judgment. However, unless they are material, the notes to the basic financial statements of a primary government do not carry disclosures on risk from discretely presented component units unless the primary government assumes a contingent portion of the risk (see Component Unit Disclosures, below).

In some situations, it may be appropriate for the governmental entity to make disclosures for the whole reporting entity. Separate or additional disclosures by individual major funds may be appropriate in other situations.

When the basic financial statements of a public entity risk pool are presented separately and included in a primary government's financial report, disclosures in the primary government's basic financial statements should emphasize the nature of the primary government's participation in the pool. The primary government's financial report should note that the public entity risk pool presents separate basic financial statements [GASB Cod. Sec. C50.146].

Component Unit Disclosures. The following disclosures should be made by a component unit that issues separate basic financial statements and participates in its primary government's risk-management internal service fund [GASB Cod. Sec. C50.147]:

- Discuss the risks of loss to which the entity is exposed and the way(s) in which those risks of loss are handled (e.g., purchase of commercial insurance, participation in a public entity risk pool, risk retention).

- Describe significant reductions in insurance coverage from coverage in the prior year by major categories of risk. Also indicate whether the value of settlements exceeded insurance coverage for each of the past three fiscal years.
- Disclose that the component unit participates in the internal service fund.
- Describe the nature of the participation.
- Describe the rights and responsibilities of both the component unit and the primary government.

Subsequent Events. To ensure that the basic financial statements are not misleading, the governmental entity should consider the need to disclose subsequent events, which are events or transactions related to risk management that occur after the date of the Balance Sheet. Disclosure should be made for material items that have one of the following characteristics:

1. The subsequent event resulted in the impairment of an asset or the incurrence of a liability (actual loss, such as damage from an earthquake), or
2. A reasonable possibility exists that a subsequent event resulted in the impairment of an asset or the incurrence of a liability (contingent loss, such as the personal injury claims to parties in which it has been alleged that the governmental entity's negligence contributed to the injuries).

If a governmental entity concludes that a subsequent event should be disclosed, the following information should be presented in the disclosure:

- The nature of the actual loss or loss contingency, and
- An estimate (or range of estimates) of the actual loss or contingent loss (or, if no estimate can be made, disclose appropriately).

In unusual circumstances, a subsequent event may result in the presentation of pro forma financial statements to supplement the historical financial statements. This should be limited to the occurrence of an actual loss that is subject to reasonable estimation. Pro forma statements are prepared by modifying the historical financial statements as if the loss had occurred on the last day of the fiscal year. Usually, only a pro forma Balance Sheet is presented and may be most informative if the pro forma and historical financial statements are presented on a comparative (columnar) basis [GASB Cod. Sec. C50.149].

Disclosure of Loss Contingencies. When a potential future loss, including any loss more than an accrued amount, does not satisfy the criteria for accrual (probable and subject to reasonable estimation), the loss should be evaluated to determine whether it should be disclosed in the governmental entity's financial statements. Any loss that can be classified in one of the following categories should be disclosed:

- Loss is *probable* but no reasonable estimate (or estimate range) of the loss can be made, or
- Loss is *reasonably possible.*

When a loss is disclosed in the basic financial statements, the following should be disclosed:

- Nature of the loss, and
- Estimate (or estimate range) of the loss (or, if no estimate can be made, the disclosure should state so).
- Possible losses arising from unreported claims or unreported assessments do not have to be disclosed unless the following conditions exist:
  — It is *probable* that a claim will be asserted, or an assessment will be made.
  — It is *reasonably possible* that a loss will arise from the asserted claim or assessment.

When a loss is based on a future event whose likelihood of occurring is remote, the loss should not be accrued or disclosed in the financial statements.

There may be a contingency related to a guarantee of indebtedness of others because of an exchange or an exchange-like transaction (but not a nonexchange transaction, which is discussed in Chapter 16). An indirect guarantee of indebtedness may occur when an agreement obligates a government to transfer resources to another entity if certain conditions or events occur. Resources are then legally available to creditors and those creditors may enforce claims against the government. These transactions may occur when revenues, debt service coverage or fund balance or fund net position falls below required amounts. If this contingency exists, it should be disclosed [GASB Cod. Secs. C50.161–.165].

Other Unspecified or General Operations Risks and Gain Contingencies

If there are other risks that do not meet the requirements for accrual, no accrual is made, and no disclosure is made. Contingencies that may result in gains are not presented in the basic financial statements as the entry may be misleading. However, governments may provide disclosure of potential gains in the notes separate from other contingencies that are potential losses. However, care should be exercised as to not to be misleading.

CHAPTER 16
OTHER LIABILITIES

Chapter References:

GASB Statement Nos. 6, 14, 18, 34, 37, 38, 49, 51, 54, 61, 62, 70, 83, 88, 99, 100, 101

GASB Interpretation Nos. 1, 2, 3, 6

GASB Technical Bulletin 2004-2

GASB Technical Bulletin 2020-01

GASB *Implementation Guide*

GASB Concepts Statement No. 6

AICPA Audit and Accounting Guides, *States and Local Governments, Gaming*

NCGA Statement No. 1, Interpretation No. 9

INTRODUCTION

The accounting standards that are used to determine which liabilities should be presented in a governmental entity's basic financial statements vary depending on whether a liability is presented in (1) governmental funds, (2) proprietary funds or fiduciary funds, or (3) the government-wide financial statements.

> **NOTE:** Certain liabilities incurred by state and local governments are specifically addressed in other chapters as follows:
> - Liabilities arising from long-term debt transactions (see Chapter 12),
> - Liabilities arising from defined benefit and defined contribution pension, defined benefit and defined contribution postemployment and other employee benefit transactions (see Chapter 13),
> - Liabilities arising from lease and similar arrangements (see Chapter 14), and
> - Liabilities arising from risk management activities (see Chapter 15).

This chapter discusses other liabilities of governmental funds under current GAAP, such as payables and accruals unique to the modified accrual basis of accounting and current financial resources measurement focus. In addition, the chapter discusses the accounting and reporting of liabilities arising from operation or responsibility for a municipal solid waste landfill, state lottery obligations, pollution remediation obligations, and asset retirement obligations, which may be presented in proprietary funds, governmental funds, or discretely presented component units.

GASB Concepts Statement No. 6 (GASB:CS-6) (*Measurement of Elements of Financial Statements*) addresses both measurement approaches and measurement attributes. A measurement approach determines whether an asset or liability presented in a financial statement should be either:

- Reported at an amount that reflects a value at the date that the asset was acquired, or the liability was incurred, *or*
- Remeasured and reported at an amount that reflects a value at the date of the financial statements.

GASB: CS-6 established the two measurement approaches that are to be used in financial statements, as follows:

- *Initial-Transaction-Date-Based Measurement (Initial Amount)*—This is commonly known as "historical cost." GASB: CS-6 defines the "initial amount" as the transaction price or amount assigned when an asset was acquired, or a liability was incurred, including subsequent modifications to that price or amount, such as through depreciation or impairment.
- *Current-Financial-Statement-Date-Based Measurement* (Remeasured Amount)—This is commonly known as "current value" but may be at fair value, replacement value, or settlement price.

The commonality among the values is that they are defined as the amount assigned when an asset or liability is remeasured as of the financial statement date.

A measurement *attribute* is the feature or characteristic of the asset or liability that is measured. GASB:CS-6 established the four measurement attributes that are to be used in financial statements, as follows:

- *Historical cost* is the price paid to acquire an asset or the amount received pursuant to the incurrence of a liability in an actual exchange transaction.
- *Fair value* is the price that would be received to sell an asset or paid to transfer a liability in an orderly transaction between market participants at the measurement date.
- *Replacement cost* is the price that would be paid to acquire an asset with equivalent service potential in an orderly market transaction at the measurement date.
- *Settlement amount* is the amount at which an asset could be realized, or a liability could be liquidated with the counterparty other than in an active market.

GOVERNMENTAL FUND LIABILITIES

Under current GAAP, the measurement focus for governmental funds is the flow of current financial resources. Liabilities that will consume current financial resources of the fund responsible for payment during the fiscal period are presented in that fund's Balance Sheet. No explicit current liability classification exists on a fund's Balance Sheet (the financial statement is unclassified). (See previous **PRACTICE ALERTS** throughout the *Guide* on the GASB's *Financial*

Reporting Model Improvements Exposure Draft and further discussed in this chapter.)

However, the mere presentation of the liability in the Balance Sheet of a governmental fund implies that the debt is current and will require the use of expendable financial resources. Therefore, the governmental fund's measurement focus is based upon determination of financial position and changes in financial position encompassing sources, uses, and balances of financial resources [GASB Cod. Sec. 1300.102].

The definition of "current liabilities" differs significantly between a governmental fund and a commercial enterprise. GASB Cod. Sec. 1500.106 describes "current liabilities" as obligations whose liquidation is reasonably expected to require the use of existing resources properly classifiable as current assets, or the creation of other current liabilities. GASB Cod. Sec. 1800.109 defines "current assets" as cash or other assets or resources commonly identified as those that are reasonably expected to be realized in cash or sold or consumed within a year.

Thus, the term to maturity of a current liability of a commercial enterprise could be a year or longer, depending on the entity's operating cycle. The liability of a governmental fund is considered current when it is expected to be liquidated with current financial resources. The term to maturity for a government's current liability is much shorter than that for a commercial enterprise.

Long-term liabilities not accounted for in proprietary or fiduciary funds of a governmental reporting entity are presented in the entity's government-wide financial statements [GASB Cod. Sec. 1500.101].

Common governmental fund liabilities include, but are not limited to:

- Accounts payable (to contractors and others),
- Accrued payroll and related liabilities,
- Intergovernmental payables (to other governments beyond the reporting entity),
- Due to other funds,
- Due to component units,
- Advances (federal grants paid in advance of eligible costs), and
- Deposits (usually related to permits and similar).

Debt that has matured and payable as of the reporting date, but unpaid would also be a liability. Short-term debts and similar obligations that arise in the *normal course of operations* that are due should be classified as current liabilities [GASB Cod. Sec. 1500.109]. (The concepts of *"normal"* and *"normally"* are discussed later in this chapter.) As discussed in Chapter 12, a short-term obligation other than a current liability is excluded from current liabilities if:

- The government *intends* to refinance the obligation on a long-term basis and
- The government can consummate the refinancing [GASB Cod. Sec. 1500.110].

Recording Fund Liabilities and Expenditures. As described earlier, governmental funds generally record a liability when it is expected that the liability will be paid from revenues recognized during the current period. Liabilities that are normally expected to be paid with current financial resources should be presented as a fund liability, and liabilities that have been incurred but that are not normally expected to be paid with current financial resources should be considered long-term liabilities. Long-term liabilities are presented in the government-wide financial statements (statement of net position) and not in the Balance Sheet of a fund.

For many years, accountants have criticized the definitions of governmental assets, liabilities, revenues, and expenditures because they are based on circular reasoning. That is, revenue can only be accrued at the end of a period if the revenue will be collected in time to pay accrued liabilities, however, liabilities can be accrued at year-end only when they are paid from revenues recognized during the current period.

GASB Cod. Sec. 1500 provides guidance for determining when liabilities should be accrued specifically for governmental funds (not proprietary funds, fiduciary funds, or the government-wide financial statements).

To address the accrual of liabilities, GASB Cod. Sec. 1500 categorizes governmental fund liabilities as follows:

- Liabilities that *normally* are due and payable in full when incurred,
- The matured portion of general long-term indebtedness (the portion that has come due for payment), and
- Designated accrual modifications reporting certain forms of long-term indebtedness as established in GAAP, including:
  — Debt service on formal debt issues (bonds and capital leases) recognized as governmental fund liabilities and expenditures when due (matured) with optional additional accrual under certain conditions, or
  — Compensated absences,
  — Claims and judgments,
  — Termination benefits,
  — Landfill closure and post-closure care costs,
  — Asset retirement obligations, and
  — Receipts of goods and services for pollution remediation.

These and a slew of other liabilities from operations are recognized as governmental fund liabilities and expenditures to the extent the liabilities are "*normally expected to be liquidated with expendable available financial resources*" [GASB Cod. Secs. 1500.118–.119].

PRACTICE ALERT: The concept of *normally* has been controversial since its introduction in *1982 with NCGA Statement No. 4* with further clarification in 2000 with GASB Interpretation 6. *What is "normal" for one government may not be normal for another.*

Other Liabilities **16,005**

The GASB's *Financial Reporting Model Improvements* Exposure Draft *proposes to clarify this governmental fund issue as follows:*

1. *In applying the proposed short-term financial resources measurement focus and accrual basis of accounting, recognition of elements is based on whether transactions or other events are short term or long term.*
2. *Whether a transaction or other event is short term or long term is determined by the time that elapses between the inception of the transaction and the conclusion of the transaction.*
3. *Short-term transactions and other events are those for which the period from inception to conclusion is one year or less.*
4. *Long-term transactions and other events are those for which the period from inception to conclusion is greater than one year.*

Some have noted that measuring each transaction that may be reported in a governmental fund for the time elapsed between the inception of the transaction to the conclusion of the transaction (or other event) may be difficult to operationalize. However, the GASB is attempting to alleviate much of the "guesswork" in disclosing a governmental fund liability.

The basic guidance for determining when a governmental fund should accrue an expenditure and related liability is found in GASB Cod. Sec. 1600.115, which states:

> Most expenditures and transfers out are measurable and should be recorded when the related liability is incurred.

For governmental funds, a major exception relates to unmatured principal and interest on general long-term debt. Governmental fund liabilities and expenditures for debt service on general long-term debt, inclusive of capital leases, are recognized *when due*—maturing *during the current period*. The provisions of GAAP further explain the process of debt service and recognition of a liability as follows:

> Financial resources usually are appropriated in other funds for transfer to a debt service fund in the period in which maturing debt principal and interest must be paid. Such amounts thus are not current liabilities of the debt service fund as their settlement will not require expenditure of existing fund assets. Further, to accrue the debt service fund expenditure and liability in one period but record the transfer of financial resources for debt service purposes in a later period would be confusing and would result in overstatement of debt service fund expenditures and liabilities and understatement of the fund balance. Thus, disclosure of subsequent-year debt service requirements is appropriate, but they usually are appropriately accounted for as expenditures in the year of payment. On the other hand, if debt service fund resources have been provided during the current year for payment of principal and interest due early in the following year, the expenditure and related liability may be recognized in the debt service fund [GASB Cod. Sec. 1500.122].

Although the term "liability" appears easy to understand, it is often misunderstood, as it contains the concepts of obligations, to determine eligibility, perform services and, the passage of time.

An obligation is a social, legal, or moral requirement, such as a duty, contract, or promise that compels one to follow or avoid a course of action.

Obligations can be legally enforceable as exemplified when a court compels the government to fulfill its obligation. Obligations could arise from legislation or contractual obligations; they may differ, however, based on whether exchange transactions (value for value) or nonexchange transactions take place.

Constructive liabilities may occur in exchange transactions when resources are transferred to a government. In this case, the government must fulfill its obligations. The concept of "little or no discretion to avoid" arises when no power exists to decline sacrificing of resources or penalty/consequences of not doing the action is more than minor. One of the consistent themes in all these nuances is that the parties to an obligation that may be a liability are usually external to the government.

The terms "liability" and "obligation" and matured liabilities in the context of governmental funds are difficult to understand for many practitioners due to these vagaries. As "matured liabilities" in governmental funds only (not associated with proprietary funds) are those that are normally due and payable in full when incurred or the matured portion of general long-term indebtedness (the portion that has come due for payment) [GASB Cod. Sec. 1500.119], practitioners also need to understand that "matured liabilities" also includes debt service on formal debt issued when due (matured) and compensated absences, claims and judgments, special termination benefits, and landfill closure and post-closure care costs, based on facts and circumstances. All of these should be recognized as governmental fund liabilities and expenditures to the extent the liabilities are "normally expected to be liquidated with expendable available financial resources." (See previous **PRACTICE ALERT**).

Most expenditures are measurable and should be recorded when the related fund liability is incurred. As discussed, an exception to this generalization is the treatment of interest and principal payments for general long-term indebtedness. Interest and principal on long-term debt are not recorded as expenditures as they accrue, but when they become due and payable. For example, if a governmental entity issues a 30-year bond, the liabilities would not be reported as a *fund liability* until the debt is due and payable, which would be 30 years after issuance.

Accumulation of Resources to Pay Liabilities. Some governmental entities have established a practice of budgeting obligations on an accrual basis or otherwise funding the eventual payment of these liabilities on something other than a budgetary basis.

For example, prior to implementing GASB Statement No. 101 (*Compensated Absences*), such compensated absences may be reported as a fund expenditure of $100,000 based on the concept of "normally expected to be liquidated with expendable available financial resources" but the governmental entity may budget for and accumulate fund resources in the amount of $300,000, which is the amount of the accrual. (See discussion of GASB Statement No. 101 (*Compensated Absences*) in Chapter 13).

GASB Cod. Sec. 1500.fn. 14 discusses why an accumulation of resources that will be used eventually to pay for unmatured general long-term indebtedness cannot be reported in a governmental fund as an expenditure or obligation of the fund. This is because that funding strategy does not result in the outflow of current financial resources.

Thus, in the previous example the governmental fund would record an expenditure of $100,000 for compensated absences and the additional $200,000 ($300,000 − $100,000) should be reported as part of the assigned fund balance of the governmental (debt service) fund. If appropriate action has been taken by the management of the governmental entity, the assigned fund balance may be identified for the funding of compensated absences, but that transaction does not result in expenditure recognition. However, if the government is legally required to fund these obligations, a committed or a restricted fund balance would be appropriate. A restricted fund balance would be proper if the legal requirement were made by an entity other than the government itself (e.g., a state law or a bond indenture).

Another issue arises when a government sells pension obligation bonds to fund pensions provided to employees. GASB Cod. Sec. 1500.703-1 describes the accounting for the bond sale. Of course, the bonds are reported as a governmental activities liability (bonds payable) in the statement of net position. To the extent a contribution from the proceeds of the bond sale is contributed to a pension plan, the contribution is reported as an addition to the pension plan's fiduciary net position. The employer's net pension liability would be reduced by the amount of the bond proceeds remitted to the pension plan through the measurement date, and a deferred outflow of resources related to pensions would be reported for the proceeds remitted to the pension plan after the measurement date.

If the proceeds are instead used to satisfy a payable to the defined benefit pension plan, the payable would be reduced by amounts remitted to the pension plan through the employer's fiscal year-end. If any proceeds of the bonds have not been remitted to the pension plan, they should be included in the governmental activities assets. Any bond proceeds not used to make benefit payments should be included in the governmental activities assets.

LANDFILL CLOSURE AND POST-CLOSURE CARE COSTS

Many governmental entities are involved with the onerous task of collecting and disposing of an ever-increasing volume of refuse. One method of disposing of this material is through landfill operations. Like other entities, landfills have cash inflows and outflows during their operating lives. However, landfills are unique because when they close, their cash inflows cease but their cash outflows generally must continue to ensure that the surrounding environment is not damaged by tainted water and other residues.

Decades ago, operators and owners were not mandated to provide funds to protect the environment after closing a landfill, but the environmental protection movement fostered legislation that requires such funding. In 1991, the U.S. Environmental Protection Agency (EPA) issued a rule (Solid Waste Disposal Facility Criteria) that applies to municipal solid waste landfills (MSWLFs). The EPA ruling establishes closure requirements for MSWLFs that accept solid waste after October 9, 1991, and "location restrictions, operating criteria, design criteria, groundwater monitoring and corrective action requirements, post-closure care requirements, and financial assurance requirements" for MSWLFs that receive solid waste after October 9, 1993.

The unique character of landfills and the EPA rule raise the accounting issues of how and when costs expected to be incurred after the closing of a landfill should be recorded. Based on research conducted by the GASB, it is apparent that a variety of accounting practices were being used to account for closure and post-closure care costs. GASB Cod. Sec. L10 (*Landfill Closure and Postclosure Care Costs*) was specifically issued to reduce the diversity of acceptable accounting practices in this area. With the issuance of GASB Cod. Sec. L10, the GASB took the position that the EPA rule provided specific requirements and that the time is appropriate to establish accounting standards related to solid waste landfill closure and post-closure care costs.

Although the EPA rule concerning municipal solid waste landfill closure and post-closure care costs applies to private and public owners and operators of landfills, GASB Cod. Sec. L10 does not apply to private entities. GASB Cod. Sec. L10 applies to all governmental MSWLFs irrespective of what type of accounting model they use to account for the activities of a landfill. The costs incurred by the governmental entity may arise from regulations established by a federal, state, or local governmental agency. The guidance established by GASB Cod. Sec. L10 applies to both closure and post-closure care costs [GASB Cod. Sec. L10.101].

GASB Cod. Sec. L10.fn.2 defines *costs* to encompass "both an economic and a financial resources perspective." Under current governmental accounting standards, a proprietary fund recognizes as expenses both economic (e.g., the depreciation of a capital asset) and financial resources (e.g., cash expenditures) used in operations, while a governmental fund's measurement of expenditures is limited to the consumption of financial resources. Thus, because the costing standards established by GASB Cod. Sec. L10 are somewhat different from those associated with governmental funds, the GASB used footnote 2 to clarify the cost recognition approach established in GASB Cod. Sec. L10.

Definition of Closure and Post-Closure Care Costs. The basic objective of GAAP is to recognize all landfill costs by the time a landfill is closed (i.e., it no longer accepts solid waste). Of course, once it is closed, there will be expenditures associated with the landfill (post-closure care), but those costs should have been estimated by the closure date and recognized as such in the governmental entity's financial statements. The degree to which the accounting standards established by GAAP are satisfied is related to a governmental entity's ability to accurately estimate all future costs. These costs could extend over a long time.

The starting point in satisfying the standards established by GAAP is to identify "the estimated total current cost of MSWLF closure and post-closure care." Current cost refers to the cost of buying, in the current year, capital assets and services related to closure and post-closure care, even though those costs will be incurred in future periods.

Specifically, the estimated total current cost of MSWLF closure and post-closure care should include the current cost of:
- Capital assets,
- Final cover, and
- Monitoring and maintenance activities.

Based on the current design plans of the MSWLF, capital asset costs should include expenditures related to the acquisition and installation of equipment and the construction of facilities. Such costs should be limited to capital assets that will be acquired, installed, or built:
- At or near the date the landfill ceases to accept waste, and
- After the landfill ceases to accept waste.

In addition, capital asset costs should include only those assets that will be used exclusively for the MSWLF activity. However, when a capital asset is used by more than one MSWLF, the costs should be allocated between or among the MSWLFs based on usage.

Once the landfill is full, it will generally be necessary to cap the facility. The current cost of the capping should be included as part of the estimated total current cost of the MSWLF [GASB Cod. Sec. L10.103].

Even after the landfill no longer accepts solid waste, the governmental entity will continue to incur costs related to the monitoring and maintenance of facilities and the landfill itself. Federal, state, or local regulations mandate how long the monitoring and maintenance period must last. These ongoing (future) costs are part of the estimated total current cost of the MSWLF. GAAP requires that the estimate be based on the "expected usable landfill area," which is the area expected to receive the solid waste during the life of the MSWLF [GASB Cod. Sec. L10, fn. 4].

However, estimation of the landfill capacity should take into consideration several factors such as MSWLF permit periods (including the probability of renewals) and geological factors. For example, the capacity of the landfill may decrease if, in a subsequent year, it is determined that a portion of the area has geological characteristics that make it unsuitable to accept solid waste.

Federal, state, or local laws and regulations will mandate what measures must be used to ensure that the landfill is properly closed and monitored when solid waste is no longer accepted. These laws and regulations should be the basis for estimating the total current cost of MSWLF closure and post-closure care. Furthermore, the closure and post-closure costs should be based on the laws and regulations that have been approved as of the statement of net position date [GASB Cod. Sec. L10.104].

OBSERVATION: Under specified circumstances, the EPA rule can be modified by allowing state or local landfill requirements to apply to a landfill owner or operator. In this case, state or local requirements would dictate which equipment, facilities, and services must be acquired with respect to closure and post-closure care, and the accounting by the governmental entity should be consistent with the modified requirements.

16,010 Specific Accounting and Reporting Issues

Reporting MSWLFs

Changes in Estimates. At the end of each year, a governmental entity should evaluate its estimate of the total current cost related to closure and post-closure care of a MSWLF. Changes in expected cost may arise from several factors, including inflation or deflation, technological advancements, and modifications to legal requirements at the local, state, or national level. These factors comprise a sizable portion of the amounts of expenses previously recognized and portrayed in the examples in this section [GASB Cod. Sec. L10.105].

Proprietary Funds. When MSWLF activities are accounted for in a proprietary fund, a portion of the estimated total current cost of closure and post-closure care should be recognized each year as an expense. The cost basis for determining the amount of expense to be recognized is based on the definition of "estimated total current cost."

The amortization or allocation period starts the day the landfill accepts solid waste and continues until it no longer accepts waste. The amount of annual expense recognition is based on usage (like the units-of-production depreciation method). If 20% of the landfill is filled during the current year, 20% of the estimated total current cost of closure and post-closure care should be reported as a current expense. If no solid waste is accepted during a period, there should be no expense recognition for that period.

It is likely that cost estimates will change from year to year, and for this reason, the computation of the annual expense must take into consideration the capacity used and the amount of expense recognized in previous years. Thus, the analysis that should be used each year to determine the amount of expense to be recognized is based on the following formula:

$$\left\{\frac{[\text{Estimated total current cost}] \times [\text{Cumulative capacity used}]}{\text{Total estimated capacity}}\right\} - \text{Amount previously recognized} = \text{Current period expenses}$$

For example, if the estimated total current cost is $1,000,000, the cumulative capacity used is 100,000 cubic yards, the total estimated capacity is 500,000 cubic yards, and the amount of expense recognized in all previous years is $125,000, the expense to be recorded in the current year is computed as follows:

$$\frac{[\$1,000,000 \times 100,000 \text{ cubic yards}]}{500,000 \text{ cubic yards}} - \$125,000 = \$75,000 \text{ (current expense)}$$

Since the computation is based on expected or future cost, there is no capital asset on the records of the proprietary fund that can be amortized. For this reason, the current expense related to the estimated total current cost of MSWLF closure and post-closure care is recorded by debiting an expense account and crediting a liability. For example, the expense computed in the previous paragraph would be recognized by making the following journal entry [GASB Cod. Sec. L10.106]:

Other Liabilities **16,011**

LANDFILL ENTERPRISE FUND	Debit	Credit
Expenses—Landfill Closure and Post-Closure Care Costs	75,000	
Estimated Liability for Landfill Closure and Post-Closure Care Costs		75,000
To record landfill closure current costs and liability.		

Acquisitions of equipment and facilities that will occur near or after the date the landfill no longer accepts waste are part of the estimated total current cost of the MSWLF. When these items are purchased (at or near the end of the life of the landfill), they should not be reported as capital assets but rather should be accounted for as a reduction to the estimated liability for landfill closure and post-closure care costs [GASB Cod. Sec. L10.107].

A landfill operator may acquire capital assets used exclusively for a MSWLF that do not meet the definition of "disbursements near or after the date that the MSWLF stops accepting solid waste and during the post-closure period." These capital expenditures are not a component of the estimated total current cost of MSWLF closure and post-closure care and, therefore, must be capitalized and depreciated over the estimated remaining life of the landfill. The total estimated life of the landfill is the period from the date on which waste is first accepted until the date on which waste is no longer accepted. Thus, once the facility is filled, expenditures that have been capitalized must be fully depreciated [GASB Cod. Sec. L10.108]. Exhibit 16-1 contains a complete illustration of the costs and related liabilities.

Governmental Funds. When MSWLF activities are accounted for in a governmental fund, the basic measurement approach used by a proprietary fund should also be used by the governmental fund. Under current GAAP. A portion of the estimated total current cost of closure and post-closure care should be recognized each year using the estimated life of the landfill and the usage of the landfill for a period. However, due to the difference in the measurement focus and basis of accounting of a governmental fund as compared to a proprietary fund, the annual cost recognition related to estimated closure and post-closure care costs generally will not affect a governmental fund's activity statement.

The basic facts used to illustrate the accounting for MSWLF activities in a proprietary fund can be used to illustrate the activity in a governmental fund. As computed earlier, the amount of closure and post-closure care costs recognized was $75,000. This amount must be analyzed to determine whether it is to be paid with current expendable resources of the governmental entity. In almost all instances, it is unlikely that any of the estimated closure and post-closure care costs will use current expendable resources because those costs are based on "disbursements near or after the date that the MSWLF stops accepting solid waste." Assuming none of the $75,000 is due and payable from current expendable resources, the governmental entity will report the total amount of the current cost as a general long-term liability in the governmental activities of the government-wide financial statements.

Capital acquisitions that are included in estimated total current cost should be reported as closure and post-closure care expenditures [GASB Cod. Sec. L10.109].

Government-Wide Financial Statements. Account balances and transactions related to MSWLFs should be reported in government-wide financial statements, like proprietary funds [GASB Cod. Sec. L10.110].

Accounting for Changes in Estimates Related to MSWLFs

Closure and post-closure care costs generally extend over a lengthy period. For this reason, it is likely that there will be several changes in the components used to compute the annual costs of MSWLF closure and post-closure care. For example, the estimated cost of a landfill cap, control facilities, and maintenance services will undoubtedly change from year to year. The accounting for such changes is dependent on the period in which the change takes place. If the change in estimated costs occurs before the landfill is filled, the change is a "change in accounting estimate" and should be reported on a prospective basis. The effect of the change is allocated over the remaining estimated life of the landfill.

For example, in the previous illustration, if it is assumed that in the following year the estimated total current cost is $1,000,000 (no change), the cumulative capacity used is 200,000 cubic yards, the total estimated capacity is 400,000 cubic yards (a change in estimate), and the amount of expense recognized in all previous years is $200,000 ($125,000 + $75,000), the amount of costs to be recognized for the year is computed as follows:

$$\frac{[\$1{,}000{,}000 \times 200{,}000 \text{ cubic yards}]}{400{,}000 \text{ cubic yards}} - \$200{,}000 = \$300{,}000 \text{ (current expense)}$$

The use of the formula takes into consideration changes in accounting estimates [GASB Cod. Sec. L10.111].

When changes in estimates occur after the landfill no longer accepts solid waste, the effects of the changes should be recorded as a current year cost and not allocated over the remaining life of the closed landfill (the number of years mandated by law or regulation that the governmental entity must monitor and maintain the closed landfill). These costs should be recognized when they are probable and subject to reasonable estimation.

Whether those costs are to be reported by a governmental fund as an expenditure on its activity statement depends on whether the cost is due and payable from current expendable resources [GASB Cod. Sec. L10.112].

Some costs may relate to the horizontal expansion of the landfill. Because these costs arise from the expansion of the landfill capacity, they should not affect the factors used to compute the current cost of MSWLF closure and post-closure care for the original landfill. It would be necessary under this circumstance to make two separate computations for estimated total current cost for closure and post-closure care: one for the costs related to the original landfill dimensions, and one for costs related to the (new) expanded landfill area.

PRACTICE ALERT: GASB Cod. Sec. L10.112 was clarified by GASB Statement No. 100 (*Accounting Changes and Error Corrections*), paragraph 12, regarding error corrections. Within GASB Statement No. 100, "an error results from mathematical mistakes, mistakes in the application of accounting principles, or oversight or misuse of facts that existed at the time the financial statements were issued about conditions that existed as of the financial statement date. Facts that existed at the time the financial statements were issued are those facts that could reasonably be expected to have been obtained and (considered) at that time about conditions that existed as of the financial statement date." Errors require retroactive restatement of beginning net position, fund balance and fund net position, as applicable, for the cumulative impact of the error correction on prior periods. For comparative financial statements, all periods are required to be restated. Various note disclosures are also required. Required supplementary information may also need to be restated due to the error. GASB Statement No. 100 became effective for periods beginning after June 15, 2023. A more complete discussion of GASB Statement No. 100 is contained in Chapter 20.

Accounting for Assets Placed in Trust

Under requirements of the EPA rule, some owners or operators of landfills will have to provide financial assurances concerning the future landfill closure and post-closure care costs. The purpose of the EPA requirement is to make sure that landfill owners or operators will have the capability to provide resources to assure that the financial burden of a filled landfill will not become the responsibility of taxpayers. The EPA rule can be achieved by putting assets in various forms of trusts.

When a governmental entity makes payments to the trust, those payments should not be treated as expenditures or expenses, but rather should be reported on the statement of net position as assets with an appropriate title such as "Amounts Held by Trustee." The assets should be reported in the fund that accounts for the landfill activities. Earnings on amounts held by the trustee (or otherwise set aside) should be reported as investment income and not as a reduction to the estimated total current cost of closure and post-closure care [GASB Cod. Sec. L10.113].

OBSERVATION: GAAP comprises accounting and reporting standards for MSWLFs, but the funding strategies must be established by the governmental entity's management team, and those strategies must follow applicable laws and regulations.

Responsibility Assumed by Another Entity

Under some circumstances, the financial obligation related to closure and post-closure care of a landfill may be transferred from the governmental entity to another party, such as a private enterprise. If the responsibility has been legally transferred and the private enterprise is financially capable of meeting the financial obligation imposed by the closure and post-closure care responsibilities, the governmental entity is not required to recognize the annual portion of estimated total current cost of MSWLF closure and post-closure care.

When it is concluded that the financial responsibility for the landfill has been transferred to a private enterprise, the governmental entity should continue to assess the ability of the enterprise to fulfill its obligation. If federal, state, or local laws or regulations require that the governmental entity retain contingent liability for closure and post-closure care costs, and a question regarding the ability of the assuming entity to meet its obligation arises, the governmental entity should determine whether provisions should be made for the closure and post-closure care costs. When it is determined that it is *probable* that the governmental entity will have to assume the financial responsibility because of the poor financial condition of the assuming entity, the related obligation should be recognized on the governmental entity's financial statements. The liability should be computed using the guidelines discussed earlier, depending on whether the landfill activities are accounted for in a proprietary fund or in a governmental fund [GASB Cod. Sec. L10.114].

Note Disclosures

GAAP requires that the following note(s) to a governmental entity's financial statements be presented [GASB Cod. Sec. L10.115]:

- Describe the laws, regulations, etc., that establish requirements for landfill closure and post-closure care.
- State that the liability for landfill closure and post-closure care costs is based on the amount of landfill used to date.
- Disclose the amount of the estimated liability for landfill closure and post-closure care costs (if not presented on the face of a financial statement) and the balance to be recognized in subsequent periods.
- Disclose the percentage of landfill used to date and the estimated remaining life (years) of the landfill.
- Describe how closure and post-closure care costs are being funded (if at all).
- Disclose the amount of assets that have been restricted for the payment of closure and post-closure costs (if not presented on the face of a financial statement).
- Discuss the nature of the estimates used and the potential for changes in estimates that may result from inflation, technological changes, or regulatory changes.

Landfills Reported as Component Units. When landfills are component units of the primary government, preparers should follow professional judgment to determine how the financial statements and related notes of the landfill should be reported. As discussed in Chapter 4, financial information pertaining to the primary government (which could include landfill component units that are blended) and similar information pertaining to discretely presented landfill component units should be distinguishable. This philosophy is extended to disclosures in notes and the presentation of required supplementary information in the financial statements of the financial reporting entity. Determining what should be disclosed in notes to the financial statements is a question of professional judgment. A determination must be made as to which disclosures are essential to the fair presentation of the basic financial statements [GASB Cod. Sec. L10.116].

EXHIBIT 16-1
ILLUSTRATION: LANDFILL CLOSURE AND POST-CLOSURE-CARE COSTS CALCULATIONS

This example is based on GASB Cod. Sec. L10.901, Illustration 1, and is intended to illustrate the application of the standards established in that *Codification* section.

Assume the following information:

According to its operating plan filed with the state, ABC Landfill will open in 20X4 and will operate on a cell basis, opening one cell at a time and installing liners and leachate collection systems before the cell receives any waste. Construction on new cells will begin before older cells reach capacity. When a cell reaches capacity, gas collection wells will be installed, and final cover, including vegetative cover, will be put in place. Water monitoring wells, erosion control systems, and a leachate treatment plant will be constructed during the first and second years of landfill operations.

Other Assumptions:

- Landfill construction begins in 20X6, opens January 1, 20X7.
- Projected landfill life in years: 33.
- The landfill will be operated on a cell basis.
- Total landfill area: 150 acres.
- Initial expected usable landfill area: 100 acres/33 cells.
- Initial estimated capacity based on expected usable landfill area: 4.5 million cubic yards (capacity per cell = 136,364 cubic yards).
- Landfill usage:

Year	Cubic Yards
20X7	90,000
20X8	120,000
20X9	135,000

16,016   Specific Accounting and Reporting Issues

- The post-closure monitoring period required by current state law is 30 years after the entire landfill receives final cover.
- In 20X8, the entity opened an area of the landfill that was subsequently determined to be unusable because of its location on unstable sediment. For this reason, estimated capacity and expected usable landfill area were reduced by approximately 5% to 4,275,000 cubic yards and 31 cells, as of December 31, 20X8. (This reduction also affects expected leachate output from the landfill.)
- Estimates are based on current costs in 20X8, adjusted using the state-provided inflation rate of 1.5% in 20X8 and 1.85% in 20X9.

Estimated Total Current Cost of Closure and Post-Closure Care—20X7

	Element	Amount
1.	**Equipment and Facilities Cost**	
	Near date landfill stops accepting waste during closure/post-closure	$–
	Maintenance and upgrading of on-site leachate treatment facility (costs projected to be paid principally at the end of 30 years)	375,000
	Expected renewals and replacements of storm water and erosion control facilities ($50,000 per year)	1,500,000
	Monitoring well replacements (30 at $25,000 each)	750,000
2.	**Final Cover Cost**	
	(Final cover, including vegetative cover, installed as cells are filled)	–
3.	**Post-Closure Care Cost**	
	Inspection and maintenance of final cover ($75,000 per year)	2,250,000
	Groundwater monitoring ($100,000 per year)	3,000,000
	Gas monitoring ($5,000 per year)	150,000
	On-site leachate pretreatment cost and off-site treatment (30,000,000 gallons total × $.05 per gallon)	1,500,000
	Projected remediation cost based on statistical average at similarly sited landfills	250,000
	Total estimated current cost of closure and post-closure care	**$9,775,000**

Estimated Total Current Cost of Closure and Post-Closure Care—20X8

	Element	Amount
1.	**Equipment and Facilities Cost**	
	Near date landfill stops accepting waste during closure/post-closure	$–
	Maintenance and upgrading of on-site leachate treatment facility (costs projected to be paid principally at the end of 30 years)	380,625
	Expected renewals and replacements of storm water and erosion control facilities ($50,750 per year)	1,522,500
	Monitoring well replacements (30 at $25,375 each)	761,250
2.	**Final Cover Cost**	
	(Final cover, including vegetative cover, installed as cells are filled)	–

Other Liabilities **16,017**

Element	Amount
3. Post-Closure Care Cost	
Inspection and maintenance of final cover ($76,125 per year)	2,283,750
Groundwater monitoring ($101,500 per year)	3,045,000
Gas monitoring ($5,075 per year)	152,250
On-site leachate pretreatment cost and off-site treatment (28,500,000 gallons total × $.05075 per gallon)	1,446,375
Projected remediation cost based on statistical average at similarly sited landfills	253,750
Total estimated current cost of closure and post-closure care	**$9,845,500**

Estimated Total Current Cost of Closure and Post-Closure Care—20X9

Element	Amount
1. Equipment and Facilities Cost	
Near date landfill stops accepting waste during closure/post-closure	$ –
Maintenance and upgrading of on-site leachate treatment facility (costs projected to be paid principally at the end of 30 years)	387,667
Expected renewals and replacements of storm water and erosion control facilities ($51,689 per year)	1,550,670
Monitoring well replacements (30 at $25,844 each)	775,320
2. Final Cover Cost	
(Final cover, including vegetative cover, installed as cells are filled)	–
3. Post-Closure Care Cost	
Inspection and maintenance of final cover ($77,533 per year)	2,325,990
Groundwater monitoring ($103,378 per year)	3,101,340
Gas monitoring ($5,169 per year)	155,070
On-site leachate pretreatment cost and off-site treatment (28,500,000 gallons total × $.05169 per gallon)	1,473,165
Projected remediation cost based on statistical average at similarly sited landfills	258,444
Total estimated current cost of closure and post-closure care	**$10,027,666**

Proprietary Fund Assumption

If it is assumed that the MSWLF activities are accounted for in a proprietary fund, the following entries would be made:

Entry for 20X7

The following entry would be made in 20X7, the first year of operating activity for the landfill.

	Debit	Credit
LANDFILL ENTERPRISES FUND		
Expenses—Landfill Closure and Post-Closure Care Costs	195,500	
Estimated Liability for Landfill Closure and Post-Closure Care Costs		195,500

	Debit	Credit
To record landfill closure current costs and liability changes for 20X7. [$ 9,775,000 × 90,000 cubic yards] ÷ 4,500,000 cubic yards − $0 = $195,500		

Entry for 20X8

The following entry would be made in 20X8. Note that the computation considers two changes in estimates. One change occurs due to the increase in the estimated total current cost of MSWLF closure and post-closure care ($9,845,500), and the other change relates to a reduction in the estimated capacity of the landfill (4,275,000 cubic yards).

	Debit	Credit
LANDFILL ENTERPRISES FUND		
Expenses—Landfill Closure and Post-Closure Care Costs	288,114	
Estimated Liability for Landfill Closure and Post-Closure Care Costs		288,114
To record landfill closure current costs and liability changes for 20X8. [$ 9,845,000 × (90,000 + 120,000) cubic yards ÷ 4,275,000 cubic yards] − $195,500 = $288,114		

Entry for 20X9

The following entry would be made in 20X9. At the end of 20X9, the estimated total current cost of MSWLF closure and post-closure care has been increased to $10,027,666. The $483,614 below is the sum of $195,500 and $288,114.

	Debit	Credit
LANDFILL ENTERPRISE FUND		
Expenses—Landfill Closure and Post-Closure Care Costs	325,636	
Estimated Liability for Landfill Closure and Post-Closure Care Costs		325,636
To record landfill closure current costs and liability changes for 20X9. [$10,027,666 × (90,000 + 120,000 + 135,000) cubic yards ÷ 4,275,000 cubic yards] − [$195,500 + $288,114]		

The estimated liability for landfill closure and post-closure care costs as of December 31, 20X9, would be reported as a long-term liability in the proprietary funds, statement of net position at $809,250.

OBSERVATION: So-called "Financial Assurance Letters" are frequently required by regulatory entities of MSWLFs, including the United States Environmental Protection Agency (EPA). These letters are required to demonstrate that the operator of the MSWLF will be able to pay for the required closure and postclosure care activities, and any corrective action that might become necessary due to releases of contaminants into the surrounding environment. EPA believes that requiring these financial assurance demonstrations ensures proper long-term financial planning by owner/operators so that sites will be closed properly and maintained and monitored in a manner that protects human health and the environment. State and federal government entities are exempt from these requirements.

However, municipal entities are not. Many auditors are engaged to help prepare these letters. They are not an audit function. Rather, they are an agreed-upon procedures engagement. The letters are based upon a site-specific cost estimate. They are prepared at the commencement of operations and adjusted annually during the life of the MSWLF to account for inflation and other factors. Corrective action cost estimates are prepared when a release is detected and must be adjusted annually during the corrective action period.

PRACTICE POINT: Many aspects of GASB Cod. Sec. L10 align to GASB Cod. Sec. P40 and GASB Cod. Sec. A10, which are discussed in the following sections.

POLLUTION REMEDIATION OBLIGATIONS

Governments may face the responsibility of cleaning up or remediating pollution such as asbestos, brownfields, and the like. GASB Cod. Sec. P40 (*Pollution Remediation Obligations*) provides specific guidance on accounting and financial reporting for these obligations.

The GASB describes a pollution remediation obligation as the requirement to address the current or potential detrimental effects of *existing* pollution by participating in pollution remediation activities. Obligations to clean up spills of hazardous wastes or other substances and asbestos contamination removal are common pollution remediation obligations. The activities related to pollution remediation include:

- *Pre-cleanup activities*—The performance of a site assessment, site investigation, and corrective measures feasibility study, and the design of a remediation plan,
- *Cleanup activities*—Neutralization, containment, or removal and disposal of pollutants, and site restoration,
- *External government oversight and enforcement-related activities*—Work performed by an environmental regulatory authority dealing with the site and chargeable to the government, or
- *Operation and maintenance of the remedy*—Required monitoring of the remediation effort (post-remediation monitoring).

In many situations, the above may not be all-encompassing and in others, only one element may be needed. Pollution prevention or control are not pollution remediation obligations as remediation is not occurring, only prevention and control. This includes scrubbers and treatment regimens [GASB Cod. Secs. P40.103–.104].

Distinguishing between what activities should be included in the landfill closure and post-closure care costs discussed in the previous section and pollution remediation discussed in this section involves a degree of professional judgment. GASB Cod. Sec. P40.701-1 directs practitioners to consider the significance and nature of the remediation work. Indeed, pollution remediation is not landfill closure and post-closure. But there could be pollution remediation related to the landfill closure and post-closure activities. If the remedy involves a large and unusual pollution event, the pollution remediation provisions apply.

What Are Outlays for Pollution Remediation?

GASB Cod. Sec. P40 includes the following as pollution remediation direct outlays if attributable to pollution remediation activities:

- Payroll and benefits,
- Equipment and facilities,
- Materials,
- Legal and other professional services (such as engineering, auditing, accounting), and
- Indirect outlays including general overhead.

Natural resource damage remediation costs are only included if related to the pollution remediation. The following are not included:

- Fines,
- Penalties,
- Civil torts, including claims from toxic exposure (although may still be a liability, as discussed in Chapter 15),
- Workplace safety litigation,
- Litigation support for potential recoveries from third parties, and
- Outlays paid by 'society at large' rather than by the reporting government (general taxation or federal funds).

Outlays for operations and maintenance for a pollution remediation that has occurred are different from operations and maintenance related to future service. Monitoring estimates should not be indefinite and are required to be reassessed periodically. The outlays result in liabilities unless a new facility is built, which may result in a capital asset at the time those assets are acquired [GASB Cod. Secs. P40.105–.107].

As an example, GASB Cod. Sec. P40.702-1 discusses a drinking water filtration system. Such systems are not pollution remediation obligations unless the system is part of a pollution remediation *activity*.

On the other hand, GASB Cod. Sec. P40.702-2 discusses maintenance of infrastructure. As an example, removal of lead paint or asbestos from a bridge could cause pollution. Given the detrimental activity of the paint or asbestos removal, the outlays are indeed pollution remediation, including containment or removal and disposal of pollutants. There should be an evaluation for recognition of a liability as part of the commencement of cleanup unless the activity truly is maintenance.

Recognition and Measurement of Pollution Remediation Liabilities

Three activities are required to recognize and measure pollution remediation liabilities, all of which are related:

- *Obligating Events*—Once an obligating event occurs, a government should determine whether one or more components of a pollution remediation obligation are recognizable as a liability.
- *Components and Benchmarks*—Components of a liability (e.g., legal services, site investigation, or required post-remediation monitoring) should be recognized as they become *reasonably estimable.*
- *Measurement, Including the Expected Cash Flow Technique*—Measurement is based on the *current value* of outlays expected to be incurred. The components of the liability should be measured using the expected cash flow technique, which measures the liability as the sum of probability-weighted amounts in a range of possible estimated amounts, or the estimated mean or average [GASB Cod. Sec. P40.108].

Obligation Event Triggers. State and local governments are required to determine whether they should report a liability in their financial statements for pollution remediation obligations if any of the following five events (triggers) has occurred:

- Pollution poses an imminent danger to the public or environment *and* a government has little or no discretion to avoid fixing the problem.
- A government has violated a pollution-prevention permit or license.
- A regulator has identified (or evidence indicates that a regulator will identify) a government as responsible or potentially responsible for cleaning up pollution or has stated that the government must pay all or some of the cleanup costs.
- A government is named, or evidence exists that it will be named in a lawsuit to compel it to address the pollution.
- A government legally obligates itself to or begins to clean up pollution or perform post-cleanup activities [GASB Cod. Sec. P40.109].

If none of the foregoing events has occurred, a government is not required to calculate or report a pollution-remediation liability. However, if one or more of the events has occurred and a range of potential outlays can be reasonably estimated, then a government is required to calculate and report a liability within the financial statements that are reported using the full accrual basis of accounting. The government is only required to estimate and report liabilities for activities that are reasonably estimable. For example, if in the initial stages of pollution remediation, only legal fees and site testing costs were reasonably estimable, then only those costs would be accrued. Once any further remediation costs are reasonably estimated, they will be accrued. Like current landfill closure and post-closure obligation standards discussed in the previous section, the pollution-remediation liabilities would be reevaluated periodically, and estimated liabilities adjusted.

As an example of whether a trigger occurs, an obligating event could be a state law requiring governments within a state to assume pollution remediation obligations when they foreclose on a property. However, GASB Cod. Sec. P40.707-1 discusses how the notion that a government will be named is a high threshold. A policy or practice of foreclosure is not evidence that the government will be named. If the government cannot be compelled by an external party to foreclose on polluted property, no obligating event has occurred. An obligating event occurs when the government forecloses, at which time the state law becomes applicable and <u>names the government</u> as a responsible party or PRP.

PRACTICE POINT: A freight train derailment in eastern Ohio is a case where GASB Cod. Sec. P40 may need to be considered. However, the government where the derailment occurred so far has not been held responsible for the derailment by the National Transportation Safety Board as of the date of publication. The federal government assumed cleanup operations through the United States Environmental Protection Agency, with the presumption that the train operator will ultimately be held as a potentially responsible party. Therefore, the state and local government may initially have an obligating event due to the first and potentially the last triggers above. But once the EPA assumed cleanup operations, recognition and measurement of a liability may no longer be necessary.

Benchmarking and Milestones. Liabilities are recognized as the ranges of their components become reasonably estimable. This is because each component may have a range of potential costs. In other situations, the government may be able to estimate a range of all components of a liability as the situation is more common. Averages and other benchmarks may be available from regulatory entities that may also provide a liability that is estimable.

Throughout the process of remediation, the liability will become more refined. Benchmarks may also change and therefore the liability should change as the benchmarks change. Further evaluation should occur if any of these events occur [GASB Cod. Secs. P40.110–.111]:

Event	Guidance
Receipt of an administrative order	• A government may receive an administrative order compelling it to take a response action at a site or risk penalties. Such response actions may be relatively limited, such as the performance of a remedial investigation and feasibility study (RI/FS) at a Superfund site or performance of a removal action, or they may be broad, such as remediation of a site. The ability to estimate outlays resulting from administrative orders varies with factors such as site complexity and the nature and extent of the work to be performed. The benchmarks that follow should be considered in evaluating the ability to estimate such outlays as far as the actions required by the administrative order involve these benchmarks. (For example, asbestos removal typically would not involve completion of an RI/FS.) • The outlays associated with performing the requisite work generally *are estimable* within a range, and recognition of a remediation liability for this work generally should not be delayed beyond this point.

Event	Guidance
Participation, as a responsible party or a Potentially Responsible Party (PRP), in the site assessment or investigation	• At this stage, the government (and possibly others) has been identified as a responsible party or a PRP and has agreed to pay all or part of a study that will investigate the extent of the environmental impact of the release or threatened release of pollutants and to identify site-remediation alternatives. Further, the total outlay associated with the site assessment or investigation generally is estimable within a reasonable range. In addition, the identification of other PRPs and their agreement to participate in funding the site assessment or investigation typically provide a reasonable basis for determining the government's allocable share of the site assessment or investigation. • At this stage, additional information may be available regarding the extent of environmental impact and possible remediation alternatives. This additional information, however, may or may not be enough to provide a basis for reasonable estimation of the total remediation liability. *At a minimum, the government should recognize its share of the estimated total outlays associated with the site assessment or investigation.* • As the site investigation proceeds, the government's estimate of its share of the site investigation can be refined. Further, additional information may become available based on which the government can refine its estimates of other components of the liability or begin to estimate other components. For example, a government may be able to estimate the extent of environmental impact at a site and to identify existing alternative remediation technologies. A government also may be able to better identify the extent of its involvement at the site relative to other PRPs, the universe of PRPs may be identified, negotiations among PRPs and with federal and state Environmental Protection Agency (EPA) representatives may occur, and information may be obtained that significantly affects the agreed-upon method of remediation.

Other Liabilities **16,025**

Event	Guidance
Completion of a corrective measures' feasibility study.	• At substantial completion of the corrective measures' feasibility study, both a range of the remediation outlays and *the government's allocated share generally will be reasonably estimable.* • The corrective measures feasibility study should be considered substantially complete no later than the point at which the responsible party or PRPs recommend a proposed course of action to the regulatory authority (e.g., the U.S. EPA). If the government had not previously concluded that it could reasonably estimate all components of the remediation liability, recognition should not be delayed beyond this point, even if uncertainties remain (e.g., allocations to individual PRPs and potential recoveries from third parties can be estimated, however, they have not been finalized). Uncertainties about the degree and probabilities of participation by other PRPs should be factored into the measurement of the liability.
Issuance of an authorization to proceed.	• At this point, the regulatory authority has issued its determination (e.g., an EPA record of decision) specifying a preferred remedy. Normally, the government and other PRPs have begun, or perhaps completed, negotiations, litigation, or both for their allocated share of the remediation liability. Accordingly, *the government's estimate normally can be refined based on the specified preferred remedy and a preliminary allocation of the total remediation outlays.*
Remediation design and implementation, through and including operation and maintenance, and post-remediation monitoring.	• During the design phase of the remediation, the government develops a better understanding of the work to be done and *can provide more precise estimates of the total remediation outlays.* Further information likely will become available at various points until site remediation work is completed, subject only to post-remediation monitoring. *The government should continue to refine its estimate of its liability as this additional information becomes available.*

Measurement of the Obligation Based on Expected Outlays at Current Value

As introduced, the remediation obligation is based on the outlays expected to be incurred to settle the liabilities. They are measured at their current value and can involve future events. The current value is based on reasonable and supportable assumptions about future events. The estimates may be based on federal, state, or local laws, court judgments, engineering, and technology assessments, among many other factors expected to be used for the cleanup.

GAAP then uses an "expected cash flow" measurement technique to measure pollution-remediation liabilities using an estimate of ranges of potential outlays required to remediate the pollution [GASB Cod. Secs. P40.112–.114].

Example: Assume a school district has been notified by a regulator that it is responsible for the entire cost of cleaning up asbestos in its school buildings. Also assume the district estimates that there is a 10% chance that cleanup will cost $1,000,000, a 50% chance the cleanup will cost $5,000,000 and a 40% chance the costs will be $10,000,000. The expected cash flow technique would calculate the estimated liability as follows:

Estimated Cost	Probability	Weighted Amount
$1,000,000	10%	$100,000
5,000,000	50%	2,500,000
10,000,000	40%	4,000,000
		$6,600,000

Using this expected cash flow technique, $6,600,000 would be reported by the government as a liability in its financial statements.

PRACTICE POINT: Because a probability measure is used of possible outlays, even a 1% chance of an outlay needs to be accrued. This has been controversial in implementation because the legal community that defends governments against lawsuits was initially wary of a government recording even a 1% possibility of loss and thereby admitting some amount of liability. Care must be taken in these estimations of loss, and in many situations, a professional resource may be needed to give a reliable estimate, if any. In situations where the government cannot reasonably estimate the liability for all portions of the remediation effort, it would only be required to report liabilities for the amounts that can be reasonably estimated.

Remeasuring the Liability and Recoveries

As discussed previously, the liability is adjusted when benchmarks or milestones occur, or added information changes the estimated outlays. An example of this is in GASB Cod. Sec. P40.712-1. In the case, inflation occurs, but no other information indicates a change in the estimated outlays. Remeasurement then is required simply due to inflation.

Recoveries may also occur from other responsible parties. If the expected recoveries are *not yet* realized or realizable, they should reduce the measurement of the liability. If they *are* realized or realizable, they are recognized *separately from the liability* as an asset is recovered. An insurance carrier may be involved. Upon the insurer admitting or acknowledging coverage, realization occurs. Recovery may occur after the remediation is completed, at which time the recovery is recognized as revenue and a receivable (or cash) [GASB Cod. Secs. P40.115–.119].

If the activity is recorded in a proprietary fund, the statement of cash flows would need information related to the recoveries. GASB Cod. Sec. P40.713-1 reminds preparers that the cash flows for pollution remediation activities should be reported gross. Therefore, recoveries should not net against other cash flows.

If a lien is exercised on polluted property, the lien could be considered a recovery. GASB Cod. Sec. P40.713-2 provides guidance that the lien is an expected recovery, and its fair value should reduce the measurement of the remediation expense. Liens are typically realizable and therefore, reduce the expense, but not the overall liability. A lien though is different from a grant providing resources to aid in the remediation. GASB Cod. Sec. P40.713-3 provides guidance that a grant would be recognized in accordance with the revenue recognition provisions of GASB Cod. Sec. N50 if the grantor is not a responsible party. If the payment is from an insurance program operated by a state, the payment is a recovery in accordance with GASB Cod. Sec. P40.713-4.

Capitalization of Outlays

Pollution remediation outlays may result in a capital asset in the government-wide and proprietary fund financial statement when goods and services are acquired for any of these occurrences:

- *Preparing a property for an anticipated sale*, recognize amounts that do not exceed the property's fair value upon completion.
- *Preparing a property for eventual use* even though when acquired, the property had known or suspected pollution remediation. Only the outlays expected to be necessary to place the asset into its intended location and condition for use are included.
- *Performing pollution remediation due to asset impairment*. Only the outlays expected to be necessary to place the asset into its intended location and condition for use are included.
- *To acquire capital assets with a future alternative use*. Capitalization is only to the extent the estimated service utility will exist after remediation activities uses have ceased.

Reporting Pollution Remediation Obligations

Government-Wide and Proprietary Funds. Pollution remediation costs (or revenue) are reported in the Statement of Activities and the Statement of Revenues, Expenses and Changes in Fund Net Position. The activity may be a program revenue, an operating expense (or revenue), special item, or extraordinary item. Liabilities (or capital assets) may be recognized in the Statement of Net Position.

Governmental Funds. The modified accrual basis of accounting applies to pollution remediation obligations. Only amounts that are normally expected to be liquidated with expendable available financial resources should be recognized as liabilities upon receipt of those goods and services under *current GAAP*. (See previous **PRACTICE ALERTS** on the GASB's *Financial Reporting Model Improvements* Exposure Draft.)

The accumulation of resources in a governmental fund for eventual payment of unmatured general long-term indebtedness, including pollution remediation liabilities, does not constitute an outflow of current financial resources and should not result in the recognition of an additional governmental fund liability or expenditure. In the Statement of Revenues, Expenditures, and Changes in

Fund Balances, any facilities and equipment acquisitions for pollution remediation activities should be reported as expenditures. Estimated recoveries of pollution remediation outlays from insurers and other responsible parties or PRPs for which the government is performing remediation activities should reduce any associated pollution remediation expenditures when the recoveries are measurable and available [GASB Cod. Secs. P40.121–.122].

Note Disclosures

GAAP requires certain note disclosures, including the following:

- The nature and source of the pollution-remediation obligation,
- The amount of estimated liabilities for remediation if it is not separately disclosed on the face of the financial statements,
- The methods and assumption used to estimate the liability,
- The potential for estimate changes due to external factors, and
- An estimate of the amount of any expected cost recovery from insurance or other parties.

If a liability was not reasonably estimable, then the government would be required to disclose only the nature of the pollution-remediation activities [GASB Cod. Secs. P40.123–.124].

> **Example:** Assume that a County contracted with a state-licensed contractor to remove specified, nonhazardous solid and liquid industrial waste from its public works and shops for disposal off-site at a state-licensed disposal facility. The contractor complied with all applicable laws and regulations. In 20X6, the County was contacted by EPA, who believed that hazardous materials were on the site. The EPA then listed the site on its National Priorities List. Those materials were generated by the County from various agencies. The County was named as a potentially responsible party (PRP) and directed by EPA to respond to questions and to research its records to further the investigation. The County researched its records and in late 20X6 determined that it had indeed contaminated the site. However, the County could not determine the significance of the waste. Although the County could not reasonably estimate a range of all legal outlays, it estimated that the current value of outlays for legal services to prepare for preliminary negotiations ranged from $50,000 to $80,000. No amounts within this range were better estimates than any other amounts.
>
> Because the County admitted that it was a party to the waste, the legal services need to be accrued, and because no amounts were better estimates than other amounts, the following entry is needed:
>
> | GOVRNMENT-WIDE FINANCIAL STATEMENTS | Debit | Credit |
> |---|---|---|
> | Expenses—Environmental Remediation [(50,000 + 80,000)/2] | 65,000 | |
> | Estimated Liability for Environmental Remediation | | 65,000 |
> | *To record estimated liability for environmental waste disposal from DPW.* | | |
>
> The expense could also be charged to the service or agency that is responsible for the pollution.

During 20X7, the EPA identified other possible transporters and polluters on the site, but little else went on. Therefore, no further entry is needed.

During 20X8, the EPA asserted that there were significant issues with the site and issued an order to the County and other potentially responsible parties to remediate the site. The County initially estimated the outlay that would be incurred to perform the cleanup to be between $1 million and $2 million in current dollars. The County initially estimated that its ultimate share of this outlay would prove to be in the range of 20% to 50%. Stated another way, the County initially estimated that other PRPs would ultimately reimburse 50% to 80% of this outlay. The County also estimated that it would incur outlays for legal services related to the remediation effort ranging from $200,000 to $2 million in current dollars, in addition to any legal service outlays that might be incurred by any PRP group that might be formed. No amounts within any of these ranges were better estimates than any other amounts. Because of a lack of information about the type and extent of the remediation effort that could be required, no range of outlays for the overall remediation effort could be developed at the time.

Due to this activity, the following needs to be accrued:

Element	Amount
Expected Cleanup Costs ($1,000,000 + $2,000,000)/2	$1,500,000
Less, estimated recoveries from third parties [({50% + 80%}/2) × $1,500,000]	(975,000)
Net expected outlays to remediate site	525,000
Expected legal costs [($200,000 + $2,000,000)/2]	1,100,000
Total remediation expense	$1,625,000

As each piece of the remediation is completed, the liability is remeasured and adjusted as needed.

ASSET RETIREMENT OBLIGATIONS

GASB Cod. Sec. A10 contains standards of accounting and financial reporting for *certain* asset retirement obligations (AROs) (*not all* asset retirement obligations).

ARO is defined as a *legally enforceable liability* associated with the retirement of a tangible capital asset. The tangible capital asset must be *permanently* removed from service. Retirement is like other disposals, including sale, abandonment, recycling, or some other manner. The asset impairment provisions of GAAP would apply for a temporary idling.

AROs are a normal occurrence from operations, whether acquired or constructed. There must be a legally enforceable obligation with the retirement of the tangible capital asset or GASB Cod. Sec. A10 does not apply.

GASB Cod. Sec. A10 also does not apply to:
- Obligations that arise solely from a plan to sell or otherwise dispose of a tangible capital asset,

- Obligations associated with the preparation of a tangible capital asset for an alternative use,
- Obligations for pollution remediation, such as asbestos removal, that result from the other-than-normal operation of a tangible capital asset,
- Obligations associated with maintenance, rather than retirement, of a tangible capital asset,
- The cost of a replacement part that is a component of a tangible capital asset,
- Landfill closure and postclosure care obligations, including those not covered by GASB Cod. Sec. L10 (see previous discussion), and
- Conditional obligations to perform asset retirement activities [GASB Cod. Secs. A10.102–.104].

Asbestos removal is within the scope of pollution remediation obligations as it is subject to environmental laws and regulations. The removal of asbestos is not a normal operation of a capital asset.

Recognition of an ARO

Like environmental remediation obligations as discussed in the previous section, GASB Cod. Sec. A10 requires governments to recognize an ARO liability upon incurrence and when reasonably estimable. External and internal obligating events may trigger an ARO, similarly to pollution remediation discussed in the previous section. Such events include:

	Internal Obligating Events	
External Obligating Events	Contamination-Related AROs	Non-Contaminated Related AROs
Approval of federal, state, or local laws or regulations.	The occurrence of contamination that is the result of the normal operation of a tangible capital asset and is not in the scope of the pollution remediation provisions. (For example, a nuclear vessel contamination as part of the normal operation of the plant.)	If the pattern of occurrence of the liability is due to normal use, placing the asset into service and consuming capacity would trigger an ARO.
Creation of a legally binding contract.		If the pattern of incurrence of the liability is not based on the use, just placing the asset into service would trigger an ARO.
Issuance of a court judgment.		If the pattern of incurrence of the liability is not based on the use, just placing the asset into service would trigger an ARO.

An ARO will generate a liability. The offset is a deferred outflow of resources unless the asset is abandoned prior to operation. If abandonment occurs, an expense is recognized [GASB Cod. Secs. A10.105–.110].

Initial Measurement of an ARO

The ARO is determined based on legal requirements relevant to the asset's retirement. It is based on the best estimate of the *current value* of the outlays expected to be incurred. Like the provisions of GASB Cod. Sec. P40, current value is the amount that would be paid if all equipment, facilities, and services included in the estimate were acquired at the end of the current period.

All available evidence should be used to determine the estimate. Also like the provisions of GASB Cod. Sec. P40, a probability weighting is used of potential outcomes when enough evidence is available or can be obtained at reasonable cost. If the cost to obtain the amount is unreasonable, the most likely amount is used.

> **Example:** A public utility is required to establish a liability to retire an electric plant. Assume the ARO related to the plant plant's retirement as of the reporting date has a variety of probabilities. There is a 10% chance the ARO will be $10,000,000, a 50% chance it will be $50,000,000 and a 40% chance it will be $100,000,000. The ARO at the reporting date would be as follows:

Probability (A)	Amount (B)	Total (A × B)
10%	$10,000,000	$1,000,000
50%	$50,000,000	25,000,000
40%	$100,000,000	40,000,000
100%	N/A	$66,000,000

Exception for Minority Interest Owners. It is a common occurrence for a state or local government to be a minority owner in a large-scale plant that would require an ARO. Minority shares are defined in GASB Cod. Sec. A10 as being less than 50% of an ownership interest in an undivided interest arrangement in which:

- The government and one or more other entities jointly own a tangible capital asset to the extent of each entity's ownership interest, and
- Each joint owner is liable for its share of the ARO.

In many cases, the majority owner is not a governmental entity and uses FASB (Financial Accounting Standards Board) standards. Even in the case where no entity has a majority ownership stake, FASB standards may apply where a nongovernmental owner has operational responsibility for the asset.

In these situations, the previous discussion on the initial measurement of the ARO using government GAAP would not apply. Instead, most likely, FASB standards would apply. The measurement of the initial ARO should occur no more than one year and one day prior to the government's reporting date [GASB Cod. Sec. A10.114].

> **Example:** A City is a 10% owner of a large-scale nuclear plant. The City's fiscal year-end is June 30, 202X. The City may use the ARO information from the plant owner or operator if it is measured no earlier than June 29, 20Y9 (one year prior).

Subsequent Measurement of ARO and the Deferred Outflow of Resources. After the initial ARO calculation, recognition of a liability and the related deferred outflow of resources, the ARO should be adjusted at least annually based on the effects of general inflation or deflation. All relevant factors to determine the outlays associated with the ARO should also be remeasured. The factors may have changed since the last measurement due to recent technology, changes in laws or regulations or changes in equipment needed to retire the asset.

Prior to retirement of the asset, any changes in the ARO also increase or decrease the deferred outflow of resources. After retirement of the capital asset, any change in the ARO is either an expense (or revenue). Similar adjustments would occur for minority interest owners.

The deferred outflow of resources would be amortized systematically and rationally upon initial measurement in one of two ways:

- Amortize the deferred outflow of resources over the estimated useful life of the asset.
- Amortize over the *remaining* estimated useful life of an asset for assets placed into operation previously, but implementation of GASB Cod. Sec. A10 or a change in law requires ARO recognition [GASB Cod. Secs. A10.116–.120].

Recognition in Governmental Funds. ARO may occur in a governmental fund. Goods and services may have been provided related to the recognition of the ARO. The amounts normally expected to be liquidated with expendable available financial resources would be declared a liability. Facilities or equipment acquired related to ARO would be an outlay or expenditure [GASB Cod. Sec. A10.121].

Funding and Assurance Provisions

Laws, regulations, judgments, and similar commonly require assets to be restricted for payment of AROs, especially in public utilities. Customers of the utility are billed monthly a rate or charge for the ARO. Amounts received should be placed in a restricted asset account for ARO and additional disclosure is required of the balances. The asset accounts should not offset the ARO in external financial reports [GASB Cod. Secs. A10.122–.123].

Note Disclosure of ARO

GASB Cod. Sec. A10 requires notes to the basic financial statements related to ARO including:

- A general description of the AROs and associated tangible capital assets, as well as the source of the obligations (whether they are a result of federal, state, or local laws or regulations, contracts, or court judgments),
- The methods and assumptions used to measure the liabilities,
- The estimated remaining useful life of the associated tangible capital assets,
- How any legally required funding and assurance provisions associated with AROs are being met; for example, surety bonds, insurance policies,

letters of credit, guarantees by other entities, or trusts used for funding and assurance, and

- The amount of assets restricted for payment of the liabilities, if not separately displayed in the financial statements.

Amounts Cannot Be Reasonably Estimated. If amounts cannot be reasonably estimated and, therefore, no ARO is recognized, the facts and circumstances should be disclosed about what is known on the ARO.

- For minority interest owners, disclosure is limited to:
- A general description of the ARO and associated tangible capital asset, including:
  — The total amount of the ARO shared by the nongovernmental majority owner or the nongovernmental minority owner that has operational responsibility, other minority owners, if any, and the reporting government,
  — The reporting government's minority share of the total amount of the ARO, stated as a percentage, and
  — The dollar amount of the reporting government's minority interest of the ARO,
- The date of the measurement of the ARO produced by the nongovernmental majority owner or the nongovernmental minority owner that has operational responsibility, if that date differs from the government's reporting date,
- How any legally required funding and assurance provisions associated with the government's minority share of an ARO are being met; for example, surety bonds, insurance policies, letters of credit, guarantees by other entities, or trusts used for funding and assurance, and
- The amount of assets restricted for payment of the government's minority share of the ARO, if not separately displayed in the financial statements [GASB Cod. Secs. A10.124–.125].

PRACTICE POINT: The auditing of ARO focuses on the process of estimating the liability, recognition of whether a law, regulation, contract, or judgment exists on triggering ARO and disclosure. The estimation process may require governments to contract a specialist to calculate the ARO. Auditors will likely review the assumptions made by the specialist to determine if the ARO is fairly stated.

STATE LOTTERY OBLIGATIONS AND GAMING

Generally, a state lottery satisfies one or more of the three conditions listed earlier for determining whether an activity should be reported as an enterprise fund. In many lottery games, a fixed percentage of ticket sales must be paid out as winnings. The AICPA's Audit and Accounting Guide *State and Local Governments*, contains guidance that lottery prize costs under this or similar payout arrangements are subject to accrual based on their relationship to total ticket sales and that accrual-based accounting may be appropriate under conditions such as the following:

- Prizes have been won and claimed but have not been paid,
- Prizes have been won but not claimed, or
- Games are in process at the end of the year.

Some lotteries allow a winner to either take an immediate lump sum payment or receive payments over a specified period. If the lottery winner chooses to receive the winnings over a period and the state purchases an annuity from an insurance company in the name of the winner, the AICPA's Audit and Accounting Guide State and Local Governments discusses why no related liability or asset should be reported on the state's financial statements.

Annuity Not Purchased in the Name of the Winner. When the state *does* not purchase an annuity in the name of the winner, the liability should be presented at its present value. When determining the liability to be discounted, the amount should include amounts won as well as amounts won but not yet claimed and amounts that will be won and claimed for games in progress at the end of the year.

Furthermore, the state might decide to finance the periodic payments to the winner by "purchasing U.S.

Treasury securities matched in timing and amount to the future payments." Under this arrangement, the investment in securities should be reported as an asset on the state's financial statements. The lottery liability and the investment cannot be offset against one another. When the state has financed the periodic payments to the lottery winner through the purchase of an annuity from an insurance company, the state should consider whether a contingent liability should be disclosed in its financial statements. A contingent liability may arise if there is some default in payment from the escrow of securities [GASB Cod. Secs. Sp20.801–.804].

Gaming

Gaming has proliferated in many state and local governments in recent years, especially in sports betting. There are revenue recognition issues and compliance issues involved with gaming.

PRACTICE POINT: Even though the state regulatory and compliance issues relating to gaming are beyond the scope of this *Guide*, revenue from the regulatory fees generated by gaming is becoming significant for many states and local governments. Governmental gaming regulators may produce separate fund, departmental, agency or program financial statements which may (or may not) be GAAP-based. The financial statements would include inflows from the regulatory fees and outflows to pay the expenses or expenditures for the department, agency, or program.

Other Liabilities 16,035

Gaming involves activities in which a gaming entity participates in games of chance with customers (players), with both the gaming entity and the customer having the chance to win or lose money or other items of economic value based on the outcome of the game (commonly referred to as *banked games*). Such activities are referred to as *gaming activities* [GASB Cod. Sec. Sp20.805].

Additional examples of banked games and gaming activities are as follows:

Banked Games	Gaming Activities	Gaming Related Activities
Poker and similar games	Slot tournaments in which players play with real money and retain any payouts from machines during the tournament.	Card games
Blackjack		Tournaments
Keno		Lotteries
Sports betting		Pari-mutuel race betting
Non-pari-mutuel race betting		

PRACTICE POINT: The proliferation of states and local governments regulating sports betting has added a further category to "banked games." The AICPA *Gaming Audit and Accounting* Guide paragraph 3.02 treats sports betting similarly to non-pari-mutuel race betting.

Games in which the player has the chance to win or lose money or other items of economic value, with the gaming entity receiving a fee (typically either a fixed fee or a percentage of play) for administering the game, rather than the gaming entity being at risk to win or lose based on the outcome of the game, *are neither banked games nor gaming activities*. Such activities are referred to as gaming-related activities.

Certain games may be either gaming activities or gaming-related activities, depending on the facts and circumstances. For example, gaming activities games include play as part of tournaments in which customers play with real money or equivalents, and the entity is at risk to win or lose based on the outcome of the game.

However, a slot tournament in which customers play with credits or other designated machine input other than cash and cash equivalents and accumulate points that determine their standing in the tournament *but retain no cash or other items of economic value* as payouts from the machine, *is not a banked game* and, therefore, *not a gaming activity* [GASB Cod. Sec. Sp20.806].

For some gaming-related activities, *the entity may have the chance to win or lose money* or other items of economic value based on factors other than the outcome of the game, such as business risk [GASB Cod. Sec. Sp20.807]. For other activities, *the entity has neither business risk nor gaming risk and has no opportunity to make a profit directly from tournament play.* A casino may hold a tournament with no banked games, no entry fee, and prizes that are not directly funded by tournament members. For example, the winner of a tournament with no entry fee and no banked games may receive a cash prize or an automobile. Such activities are neither gaming activities nor gaming–related activities [GASB Cod. Sec. Sp20.808].

Revenue Recognition in Gaming. Revenue recognized and reported by a casino is generally defined as the win from gaming activities, that is, the difference between gaming wins and losses, not the total amount wagered (a net amount). State lotteries that use *video gaming* use similar provisions. However, lotto and instant game ticket sales have revenue separated from prize payouts and expenses, which are reported as expenses *or* deductions from revenue [GASB Cod. Secs. Sp20.809–.810].

Gross gaming revenue, or win, is the difference between:

- Gaming wins from banked games, less
- Gaming losses from banked games, less
- Incentives and adjustments for changes in progressive jackpot liability accruals.

Gross gaming revenue is generally not reported by gaming entities in their external financial statements; rather, net gaming revenue is generally reported [GASB Cod. Sec. Sp20.811]. However, gross gaming revenue is typically a compliance element for regulatory purposes.

Net gaming revenue equals:

- Gross gaming revenue (as defined previously) minus
- Incentives that are charged to gaming revenue, plus or minus
- The change in accrued jackpot liabilities, plus
- Revenue from gaming related activities [GASB Cod. Sec. Sp20.812].

Gaming entities generally report all payouts and prizes related to banked games as a component of net gaming revenue. Accordingly, prizes or payouts resulting from banked games, even if not built into a payout table, should not be reported as marketing or promotional expense. For example, customers hitting a slot machine combination within a specified period may win an automobile in addition to the stated jackpot for the combination. The cost of that automobile should be reported as a component of net gaming revenue [GASB Cod. Sec. Sp20.813].

Special circumstances from certain gaming related activities result in different revenue recognition provisions. Examples are as follows [GASB Cod. Secs. Sp20.814–.816]:

Other Liabilities **16,037**

Fact Pattern	Example	Recognition
Gaming entity is at no risk to win or lose, gaming entity pays out prizes directly funded by tournament members.	Tournament members may each pay $1,000 as an entry fee, with $950 included in the tournament prize pool and $50 as a fee to a casino.	The *prize pool* should be reported as a component of net gaming revenue and the fee to the casino included in net gaming revenue.
Gaming entity has no gaming risk *but has business risk.*	A slot tournament may include no banked games and have a grand prize of $100,000, *regardless of the fees collected from the number of entrants.*	The entity may have the chance to win or lose money, and the gaming entity's *net profit or loss* from such activities should be reported as a component of net gaming revenue.
The gaming entity has no opportunity or intention of making a profit directly from tournament play.	A casino may sponsor a tournament with no banked games, no entry fee, and prizes that are not directly funded by tournament members. The winner of a tournament with no entry fee and no banked games may receive a $100,000 cash prize (or an automobile).	Activities are neither gaming activities nor gaming related activities. Prizes from these types of activities are typically reported as marketing or promotional expenses, rather than as a component of net gaming revenue.

OBSERVATION: According to the AICPA's Audit and Accounting Guide *State and Local Governments*, Chapter 12, lottery activities generally meet the criteria requiring the use of enterprise funds. However, some states report them as a governmental fund as they provide a cash flow mechanism for programs and services of the general government, such as education. Legally separate state lotteries may be reported as discretely presented component units, as they do not meet the criteria for blending in GASB Cod. Sec. 2600.113. This is due to anyone's ability to participate in the lottery by choice and potentially benefit from winnings. Lotteries may also issue fund or departmental financial statements separately from the state. Finally, additional guidance is available in the AICPA's Audit and Accounting Guide *Gaming*, also in Chapter 12. The *Gaming* guide discusses the basic financial statements and required supplementary information that may be presented for lotteries, how resources flow between lotteries and sponsoring governments, assets and liabilities, impairment of capital assets, and segment reporting. Tribal government casinos should also review the *Gaming* guide for additional guidance.

ACCOUNTING AND FINANCIAL REPORTING FOR NONEXCHANGE AND EXCHANGE FINANCIAL GUARANTEE TRANSACTIONS

> **PRACTICE ALERT:** There may be instances of exchange or exchange-like financial guarantees. GASB Statement No. 99 (*Omnibus 2022*) contains guidance for such transactions. Governments that extend an exchange or exchange-like guarantee would follow the same provisions as governments that extend nonexchange financial guarantees. Expense or expenditures relating to the transaction are classified like grants or financial assistance payments. The required note disclosure relating to such transactions follows what is required for nonexchange financial guarantees. If the cumulative amount disclosed as paid by the government related to a guarantee does *not* equal the total amounts paid on the guarantee due to amounts determined prospectively, then the government discloses the dates over which the cumulative value was determined. The requirements for exchange or exchange-like financial guarantees began for reporting periods beginning after June 15, 2023. Earlier application is encouraged. Changes adopted to conform to the provisions are applied retroactively by restating all prior periods presented if practicable. The cumulative effect, if any, of applying the provisions to periods prior to those presented should be reported as a restatement of beginning net position, fund balance, or fund net position, as applicable, of the earliest period presented. Each individual prior period presented should be restated to reflect the period-specific effects of applying the provisions. If restatement for all prior periods presented is not practicable, the cumulative effect, if any, of applying the provisions should be reported as a restatement of beginning net position, fund balance, or fund net position, as applicable, of the earliest period restated (that is, for the earliest period for which it is practicable).

The GASB defines a financial guarantee as a pledge to pay an obligation of a legally separate entity or individual, including a blended or discretely presented component unit, that requires the guarantor to indemnify a third-party obligation holder under specified conditions [GASB Cod. Sec. F30.102].

> **PRACTICE POINT:** Special assessments and financial guarantees that are related to derivative instruments are excluded from the guidance in GASB Cod. Sec. F30. Special assessments are discussed in Chapter 19 and derivative instruments are discussed in Chapter 12.

The GASB requires governments that extend financial guarantees to recognize a liability when qualitative factors or historical data indicate that it is more likely than not that the government will make a payment on the guarantee.

Many governments participate either as a guarantor or a recipient of a guarantee. Guarantees extend to non-governmental entities including not-for-profit and for-profit enterprises. Frequently, these guarantees are exercised by nonfinancial or qualitative events (e.g., violation of an agreement). A common action occurs in nearly every governmental nonexchange guarantee: a government commits to indemnify the holder of the obligation if the entity that issued the obligation does not fulfill its payments.

Qualitative and historical factors must be used to decide whether a payment on the guarantee is *more likely than not* to be made. These factors include, but are not limited to, the following:

- Initiation of the process of entering bankruptcy or a financial reorganization,
- Breach of a debt contract in relation to the guaranteed obligation, such as a failure to meet rate covenants, failure to meet coverage ratios, or default or delinquency in interest or principal payments, and
- Indicators of significant financial difficulty, such as the failure to transfer deposits from debt service funds to paying agents or trustees, the draw on a debt service reserve fund, the initiation of the process by a creditor to intercept receipts to make a debt service payment, debt holder concessions, significant investment losses, loss of a major revenue source, significant increase in noncapital disbursements in relation to operating or current revenues, or commencement of financial supervision by another government [GASB Cod. Sec. F30.104].

If a group of guarantees exists, the government that makes the guarantees as part of a group must review historical data to determine whether a guarantee will be exercised. This may occur in home mortgage guarantees [GASB Cod. Sec. F30.105].

When it is more likely than not (as defined as greater than 50%) that the guaranteeing government will have to make a payment on the guarantee, a liability and an expense in the government-wide financial statements is recognized. The amount recognized should be the best estimate of the discounted present value of the future outflows expected to be incurred because of the guarantee. If a range of estimates is evident and no value in the range is better than another amount, then the minimum amount in the range is used [GASB Cod. Sec. F30.106].

A fund liability may exist if the guarantee is expected to be paid with current financial resources. Liabilities for nonexchange financial guarantees extended are normally expected to be liquidated with expendable available financial resources when payments are due and payable on the guaranteed obligation [GASB Cod. Sec. F30.107].

PRACTICE POINT: The exercise of nonexchange financial guarantees could be very prevalent due to the financial distress because of the COVID-19 pandemic. GAAP requires guarantor governments to disclose a liability if they are more likely than not to make payments on behalf of other governments. GASB Technical Bulletin 2020-1, *Accounting and Financial Reporting Issues Related to Coronavirus Aid, Relief and Economic Security Act (CARES) Act of 2020 and COVID-19*, question 4, discusses when a governmental not-for-profit entity receives a forgivable loan pursuant to the "Paycheck Protection Program" and the entity determines that the loan will be forgiven in a subsequent period based on compliance with the program requirements. Entities in this situation should report a loan until legally released from the debt by the U.S. Treasury. Upon release, an inflow is reported [GASB Cod. Sec. N30.601].

For the government receiving the guarantee, when a government is required to repay a guarantor for payments made on the government's obligations, the government should reclassify that portion of its liability for the guaranteed obligation as a liability to the guarantor, instead of to a debt holder. The government that issued the guaranteed obligation should continue to report the obligation as a liability until all or a portion of the liability is legally released, such as when a plan of adjustment is confirmed by the court in the case of bankruptcy. The release of the obligation triggers revenue for the government receiving the release [GASB Cod. Secs. F30.108–.109].

There could be a situation where debt is recorded twice within the same reporting entity. A component unit may have outstanding debt that is guaranteed by a primary government. The guarantee is exercised, yet the component unit still is obligated to pay the debt. However, GAAP also requires a liability with the primary government for the guarantee. To relieve this problem, GAAP allows a *blended component unit* (not a discreetly presented component unit) to record a receivable when the guarantor records a liability.

As an example of this, GASB Cod. Sec. F30.707-1 contains information when a blended component unit recognizes a receivable from a primary government relating to a financial guarantee. The government that issued the guaranteed obligation would recognize a receivable equal to the amount of the liability recognized by the government extending the guarantee. But the blended component unit would evaluate the collectability of the receivable.

EXAMPLE OF A GUARANTEE BETWEEN GOVERNMENTS: The County Convention Center is a government that is separately reported from County. The State statute allows counties to extend nonexchange financial guarantees on bonds issued by special districts to provide for facilities improvements.

Both the County and the Center have June 30th fiscal year-ends. On November 1, 20X5, the Board of the Center authorized and approved $10 million in general obligation bonds to be issued 30 days later for Center improvements. The bonds mature annually through December 1, 20Y1, with semiannual interest payments.

Also, on November 1, 20X5, the County approved to extend a nonexchange financial guarantee on the issuance with no requirements for the Center to repay the County if there is a default and the guarantee is exercised. During the last half of fiscal year 20X8, the Center's revenue from operations began to decrease due to a new center opened in the neighboring City of Lafayette, in Stone County. A violation of revenue coverage covenants occurred with the Center's bonds. On June 1, 20X8, the semiannual interest payment was made by the Center.

However, the Center had to liquidate the bond reserve account to do so, another violation of a bond covenant. The County determined that as of June 30, 20X8, the Center is more likely than not unable to make any of the remaining required debt service payments on the bonds. The County determined that the present value of the future debt service payments is $4.020 million using a discount rate of 5%, which is equal to the bond's true interest rate. On December 1, 20X8, the County made the entire debt service payment on the bonds.

County's Financial Statements:

GOVERNMENT WIDE FINANCIAL STATEMENTS	Debit	Credit
Expenses – Guarantee on County Convention Center Bonds	4,020,000	
Guarantee Payable – County Convention Center Bonds		4,020,000
To record estimated liability for Convention Center Bonds Guaranteed by the County.		

GAAP requires disclosure in the notes to the basic financial statements by the guaranteeing government (the County) to include the facts and terms of the guarantee, along with the beginning balance, increases, decreases and the ending balance of the debts that are guaranteed. Amounts paid, and amounts expected to be recovered are also disclosed. The Center would have similar, symmetrical disclosure, including amounts owed to the County to repay the guarantee (if any) [GASB Cod. Sec. F30.111].

CHAPTER 17
REVENUES: NONEXCHANGE AND EXCHANGE TRANSACTIONS

Chapter References:

GASB Statement Nos. 24, 33, 34, 36, 38, 62, 65, 77, 84, 85, 99

GASB Implementation Guide

GASB Technical Bulletin 2020-1

GASB Interpretation No. 5

GASB Concepts Statement Nos. 4, 6

NCGA Statement No. 1, Interpretation No. 3

INTRODUCTION

PRACTICE ALERT: The GASB released a *Preliminary Views* (PV) document in the spring of 2020 detailing the Board's initial views on Revenue and Expense Recognition. The project's scope includes classification, recognition, and measurement of revenues and expenses, unless specifically excluded from the project. As of the date of publication, the specific *exclusions* from the project are:

Capital asset (and related debt) activity	Purchases, sales, donations, and nonmonetary exchanges of capital assets, as well as depreciation expense, interest income or expense, and gains and losses derived from impairment or remeasurement of capital assets, inventory, or long-term debt
Certain financial instruments	Investments, financial guarantees, derivative instruments, financings such as leases, and insurance
Postemployment Benefits	All guidance and projects related to pensions, OPEB, compensated absences, and termination benefits

Seven existing GASB statements are currently within scope. More statements could be added as part of further deliberations.

The revenue and expense model in the Board's PV assumes the following:

- Inflows and outflows are of equal importance in resource flows statements.
- Inflows and outflows should be classified independently, and not in relationship to each other.
- The government is an economic entity and not an agent of the citizenry.

Specific Accounting and Reporting Issues

- Symmetrical considerations, to the extent possible, should be included in revenue and expense recognition.
- A consistent viewpoint, from the resource provider perspective, will be applied in the revenue and expense analysis.

The GASB has a preliminary view of two distinct categories of revenue and expense recognition (known as the *AB model*) which are described as follows:

Category	Description	Types of Transactions	Examples of Transactions
A	An acquisition coupled with a sacrifice (or a sacrifice coupled with an acquisition). The acquisition coupled with the sacrifice can be identified as rights and obligations that articulate in equivalent terms, that is, the rights and obligations are dependent on the existence of each other, such that there is a remedy for failure of either party to meet the terms of the arrangement. While the right represents the right to receive consideration in a transaction, the obligation represents the requirement to perform via action or inaction.	May include reciprocal or nonreciprocal transactions. Focus is on a *binding arrangement*. Binding arrangements include: • Mutual assent between the parties of capacity in the transaction, • Identification of rights and obligations, which are substantive, by the parties to the transaction, and • Dependency of the rights and obligations in the binding arrangement on each other's existence.	• Fees for specific services (water, tuition, transit fares, lottery) • Eligibility-driven grants • Research grants • Revolving loans • Medicaid fee for service • Labor/Payroll • Contracts and purchase orders

Category	Description	Types of Transactions	Examples of Transactions
B	A single flow, that is an acquisition without a sacrifice or a sacrifice without an acquisition. The obligation would represent the requirement to provide resources. The right would represent the ability to receive or collect resources.	Binding arrangements, including enabling legislation and purpose-driven grants, along with anything else that is not Category A (most taxation).	• Taxes • Special assessments • Regulatory fees and licenses • Punitive fees, fines, penalties • Donations • Purpose-restricted grants • Medicaid supplementary payments • Capital fees (passenger facility charges, developer fees, impact fees, and similar) • Individual assistance (SNAP) • Certain payments in lieu of taxation • Escheat revenues • Government-mandated transactions

The Board has the preliminary view that the recognition of revenues and expenses utilizes the following flow:

Revenues	Expenses
• Identify if there is an increase in an asset	1. Identify if there is an increase in a liability
• If not an asset, identify if there is a liability	2. If not a liability, identify if there is an asset
• Identify if the asset meets the definition of a deferred inflow of resources	3. Identify if the liability meets the definition of a deferred outflow of resources
• Recognize revenues	4. Recognize expenses

There are many nuances and application issues of the revenues and expense recognition model to categories A and B. Deliberations are continuing with an exposure draft expected for release by March 2025. Any final Statement may not be approved until June 2027.

Most governmental entities are involved in many nonexchange and exchange (and exchange-like) transactions.

This chapter discusses the basic principles that governmental entities should follow to report these sources of revenues in governmental funds, proprietary funds, fiduciary funds, and government-wide financial statements. To provide the framework for establishing accounting principles related to the elements of financial statements and their measurement and recognition within the financial statements, the GASB has issued GASB:CS-4 (*Elements of Financial Statements*) and GASB:CS-6 (*Measurement of Elements of Financial Statements*).

GASB:CS-6 discusses both measurement approaches and measurement attributes. A measurement approach determines whether an asset or liability presented in a financial statement should be:

1. Reported at an amount that reflects a value at the date that the asset was acquired, or the liability was incurred, or

2. Remeasured and reported at an amount that reflects a value at the date of the financial statements.

A measurement attribute is the feature or characteristic of the asset or liability that is measured. Changes in remeasured or initial amounts, as defined here, would potentially be an indicator of an increase of inflows, outflows, deferred inflows of resources, deferred outflows of resources, assets, or liabilities.

There are two measurement approaches in GAAP:

1. *Initial-transaction-date-based measurement (initial amount)*. This is the transaction price or amount assigned when an asset was acquired, or a liability was incurred, including subsequent modifications to that price or amount, such as through depreciation or impairment. This approach is more commonly known as "historical cost" or "entry price," but those terms are not quite accurate.

2. *Current-financial-statement-date-based measurement (remeasured amount)*. This is the amount assigned when an asset or liability is remeasured as of the financial statement date. This is sometimes known as "fair value," "current value," or "carrying value." However, that is also not quite accurate because those values are attributes.

Therefore, there are four measurement attributes that are used in GAAP:

- *Historical cost* is the price paid to acquire an asset or the amount received pursuant to the incurrence of a liability in an actual exchange transaction. The understanding of this attribute is well-known and documented.

- *Fair value* is the price that would be received to sell an asset or paid to transfer a liability in an orderly transaction between market participants at the measurement date.

- *Replacement cost* is the price that would be paid to acquire an asset with equivalent service potential in an orderly market transaction at the measurement date.

- *Settlement amount* is the amount at which an asset could be realized, or a liability could be liquidated with the counterparty, other than in an active market.

"*Acquisition value*" may also be used in certain transactions. Acquisition value is an entry price and is the price that *would be* paid to acquire an asset with equivalent service potential in an orderly market transaction at the acquisition date, or the amount at which a liability could be liquidated with the counterparty at the acquisition date. Acquisition value is limited to donated capital assets, donated works of art, historical treasures and similar assets, or capital assets that a government receives relating to a public-private partnership GASB:CS-4 provides that the revenue element of the "resource flows (change) statements" be defined as an "inflow of resources" resulting in an acquisition of net position by the entity that is applicable to the reporting period.

The acquisition of net position (inflow) is defined as net position coming under the control of the entity or net positions becoming newly available to the entity even if the resources are consumed directly when acquired.

An acquisition of net position results in:

- An increase in assets more than any related increase in liabilities or
- A decrease in liabilities more than any related decrease in assets.

Examples of acquisition of net position include:

- Imposition of a tax (because the resources have newly come under the control of the entity); and
- Performing under the conditions of a grant received in advance (because liabilities of the entity have been satisfied, thereby increasing the entity's net position).

REVENUES: NONEXCHANGE TRANSACTIONS

Overview of the Types of Revenue Transactions

It is important for practitioners to understand the differences between nonexchange and exchange transactions.

Nonexchange Transactions. These may be the most common transactions in states and local governments. They are characterized by the transfer of goods or services that are not equal between parties. For governmental entities, nonexchange transactions range from taxes raised by governmental entities (recipient of the resources) to grants made by one governmental entity (providers of the resources) to another governmental or nongovernmental entity (pass-through grants).

On-behalf payments for fringe benefits and salaries are also nonexchange transactions. Such payments are made by a paying entity or government, such as a state, to a third-party recipient for the employees of a legally separate entity. They may even be paid for volunteers as well as for paid employees. As an example, a state paying for defined benefit pension contributions on behalf of municipal volunteer fire personnel would be an on-behalf payment for fringe benefits and a nonexchange transaction.

Exchange Transactions. These transactions are defined as the simultaneous transfer of approximately equal goods or services between parties. Fees for services, leases, investment revenues, contributions and similar are exchange transactions.

Exchange-like Transactions. These transactions have subtle differences from exchange transactions. GASB Cod. Sec. N50.503 defines an exchange-like transaction as one in which values are exchanged, and though related, *may not be quite equal.* They may also be when direct benefits may not be exclusively for the parties to the transaction. Still, the transaction's exchange characteristics are strong enough to justify treating the transaction as an exchange for accounting purposes.

Examples of exchange-like transactions include the following:

- Fees for professional licenses and building permits,
- Passenger facility charges,
- Certain tap fees,
- Certain developer contributions, and
- Certain grants and donations.

OBSERVATION: A transaction comprising $1 of compensation for a piece of land is not an exchange transaction. Exchange transactions should be those in which each party essentially receives equal values. An exchange-like transaction could be a $10,000 permit to hold a series of summer concerts in a park. Without the permit, the concerts may not be held.

Nonexchange transactions do not include the acquisition of goods and services in an exchange transaction that were funded through a nonexchange transaction. For example, the acquisition of computers from a commercial enterprise is an exchange transaction, even though the governmental entity receives the resources to pay for the computers from a state grant (a nonexchange transaction) [GASB Cod. Sec. N50.103].

OBSERVATION: Revenue recognition in a government is sometimes difficult to understand because of the distinct types of exchanges between citizens and other stakeholders, other governments, and the government itself. Furthermore, many governments have statutory provisions regarding when revenue is recognized for statutory or budgetary purposes, which may be quite different from GAAP. This is highly unlike for-profit enterprises that have exchange transactions between customers, resellers, clients, and the entity. Care must be taken to understand the revenue stream to see if the inflows process has been completed before revenue is recognized.

The Nature of Nonexchange Transactions

The two parties in a nonexchange transaction are the provider of the resources and the receiver of the resources. The provider of the resources could be the federal government, a state or local government, or a nongovernmental entity (such as an individual or a business entity). The receiver of the resources could be a state or local government or a nongovernmental entity. As noted earlier, what distinguishes a nonexchange transaction from an exchange transaction is that in a "nonexchange transaction" a government "either gives value (benefit) to another party without directly receiving equal value in exchange or receives value (benefit) from another party without directly giving equal value in exchange." Ostensibly, these are "one-way" transactions rather than a fee for a good or service.

GAAP provides accounting and reporting standards for the following four categories of nonexchange transactions:

1. Derived tax revenues,
2. Imposed nonexchange revenues (fees, assessments, etc.),
3. Government-mandated nonexchange transactions (grants with performance or eligibility requirements), and
4. Voluntary nonexchange transactions (grants and donations) [GASB Cod. Sec. N50.104].

The extension of a financial guarantee for the obligations of another government, a not-for-profit entity, or a for-profit entity without directly receiving consideration of equal value in exchange is a form of a nonexchange transaction. Had there been consideration, an exchange financial guarantee would have occurred. As a part of either financial guarantee, a government commits to indemnify the holder of the obligation if the entity that issued the obligation does not fulfill its payment requirement. Governments also receive financial guarantees for obligations it has issued in which equal value is not provided by the government in return. However, nonexchange (and exchange) financial guarantees are more the exception rather than the norm for most governments. Further information on nonexchange and exchange financial guarantees is contained in Chapter 16.

PRACTICE ALERT: As discussed in Chapter 16, GASB Statement No. 99 (*Omnibus 2022*) expanded the former nonexchange financial guarantee guidance to exchange financial guarantees. The changes were implemented for fiscal years beginning after June 15, 2023.

Accounting and financial reporting of nonexchange transactions apply based on the four categories of nonexchange transactions and not to specific types of nonexchange transactions. For example, the GASB does not specifically prescribe how sales tax revenue should be measured Instead, GAAP includes general standards for derived tax revenues that apply to all revenues considered to be part of the category, including sales tax revenue. For this reason, the GASB requires a governmental entity to evaluate each of its nonexchange transactions and decide which of the four categories should be used to classify a transaction [GASB Cod. Sec. N50.105].

The GASB established general standards to provide a flexible approach that addresses current implementation problems and future developments in governmental activities. The GASB could not realistically establish recognition standards for every possible type of nonexchange transaction that is currently experienced by a governmental entity. By providing general standards, the GASB enables a specific governmental entity to apply them to all its nonexchange transactions and not just for a few specific situations. Another advantage of general standards is that they apply to "new kinds of transactions that governments may encounter or establish in the future."

In determining which category is appropriate for each nonexchange transaction, a governmental entity must look at the substance of the transaction rather than at its "label." The entity should not group a nonexchange transaction in one of the four categories based on whether the transaction is described as a tax, a grant, or by some other name.

For example, the GASB notes that a grant provided by a governmental entity could be designated as a voluntary contribution (e.g., a voluntary nonexchange transaction). However, another government's grant could be designated as a government-mandated nonexchange transaction.

In a similar fashion, a governmental entity's overreliance on the "label" to name a transaction may result in misclassifying a nonexchange transaction as an exchange transaction, or vice versa. For example, a source of revenue for a governmental entity may be described as a fee (implying an exchange transaction) but the transaction may have the characteristics of a tax (a nonexchange transaction).

To illustrate the difficulty of distinguishing between a nonexchange transaction and an exchange transaction, the GASB uses the example of a "grant" made by a commercial enterprise to a public university. If the university has exclusive rights to any benefits that may derive from the research effort, the transaction is a nonexchange transaction. However, if the commercial enterprise retains the right of first refusal on the results of the research, it is likely that the transaction is an exchange or exchange-like transaction. In other instances, the GASB notes that the relationship between the university and the commercial enterprise may suggest that the transaction should be divided into two separate parts: an exchange transaction portion and a nonexchange transaction portion [GASB Cod. Sec. N50.107].

GASB Cod. Secs. N50.701-1–.701-5 show how difficult certain situations may be in distinguishing between exchange and nonexchange transactions:

Transaction	Exchange or Nonexchange?
Research grants	*Some* are exchange, *some* are nonexchange. *Some may have both* elements. Each grant should be evaluated. Elements that do not have the characteristics of an exchange should be voluntary nonexchange transactions.
Drivers' licenses and business permits	Licenses and permits *are generally exchange or exchange-like transactions.* Many permit and license fees are designed to offset the cost of processing the document. The cost typically does not exceed the value of the services and rights received.
Donated (volunteer) services	*Neither* a nonexchange nor exchange transaction.
Donated food commodities	*Nonexchange transaction* at acquisition value with revenue recognized in the period when all eligibility requirements are met (typically, the period when the commodities are received).
Payment from the federal government to the employer pursuant to the early retiree reinsurance program of the Patient Protection and Affordable Care Act	*Voluntary nonexchange transaction.* Neither the receipt of such payment nor the anticipation of additional payments affects the employer's obligations or expense for OPEB. Contributions of the payment to an OPEB plan are employer contributions.

Recording Nonexchange Transactions

Although the standards contained in GASB Cod. Sec. N50 are written in the context of the accrual basis of accounting, they provide a significant amount of general guidance for nonexchange transactions irrespective of the basis of accounting that is used by a governmental entity. For this reason, the general guidance provided in the GASB Cod. Sec. N50 applies to governmental activities (with the activities usually accounted for in such funds as the general fund and special revenue funds) except that they must be modified to observe the modified accrual basis of accounting under *current GAAP*.

In applying the standards though, the availability criterion must be satisfied when revenue is recognized under the modified accrual basis of accounting. In addition, under both the accrual basis of accounting and the modified accrual basis of accounting, nonexchange transactions are recorded only when transactions are measurable (subject to reasonable estimation), and collection is probable (realizable). GASB Cod. Sec. N50 describes "probable" as likely to occur. Nonexchange transactions that are not recorded because the measurable criterion cannot be satisfied must be disclosed in a governmental entity's financial statements [GASB Cod. Sec. N50.108].

PRACTICE POINT: "Probable" of collection is different than presenting revenue "net of estimated uncollectible amounts." In GASB Cod. Sec. N50.704-1, getting to probable is just the initial step for recognition. After all, the reporting of the transaction would not occur *under current GAAP* if the entire transaction is not probable of collection. As discussed later in this chapter, if there is historical evidence that amounts are partially uncollectible, that amount may need to be presented as an increase to an allowance account (e.g., allowance for doubtful accounts) rather than reducing a related receivable. This might occur relating to taxation.

PRACTICE ALERT: The GASB's *Financial Reporting Model Improvements* Exposure Draft could change the recognition criteria for governmental funds, if approved as proposed. As discussed in previous **PRACTICE ALERTS,** the short-term financial resources measurement focus and accrual basis of accounting would consider short-term transactions to be presented in governmental funds measured based on the time between the inception of a transaction and its conclusion. Recognition of nonexchange transactions in the financial statements would be required unless the transactions are not measurable (reasonably estimable) or are not probable of collection. Transactions that are not recognizable because they are not measurable would be disclosed. Major changes to GASB Cod. Sec. N50 may result if approved as drafted.

Time Requirements and Purpose Restrictions—Two Important Determinations

To determine when nonexchange transactions should be recorded and how those transactions should be presented in the financial statements, the governmental entity needs to consider time requirements and purpose restrictions. Time requirements and purpose restrictions do not have the same effect on the timing of revenue recognition or expense recognition that arises from nonexchange transactions.

Time Requirements. Resources may be provided by one governmental entity or another party to a governmental entity with the requirement that the resources be used in (or begin to be used in) a specified period(s). GASB Cod. Sec. N50 notes that "time requirements specify the period or periods when resources are required to be used or when use may begin."

Time requirements may be imposed by enabling legislation or by a nongovernmental party that provides the resources to governmental entities. For example, legislation may identify the period in which a recipient governmental entity can use a grant, or it may require that resources be used over a specified number of years. In other instances, time requirements imposed by either the provider government or the provider nongovernmental entity may require that the resources provided may never be used (e.g., permanent endowment) or that the resources cannot be used until a specified event has occurred [GASB Cod. Sec. N50.109].

When a nonexchange transaction is subject to a timing requirement, that requirement generally affects the period in which revenue is recognized by the governmental entity. Also, the effect that a timing requirement has on a nonexchange transaction is dependent on whether the transaction is (1) a government-mandated nonexchange transaction or a voluntary nonexchange transaction or (2) an imposed nonexchange revenue transaction. Generally, derived tax revenues (described later in this chapter) are not subject to time requirements [GASB Cod. Sec. N50.110].

Purpose Restrictions. Purpose restrictions relate to the use of resources that arise from a nonexchange transaction. For example, gasoline taxes may be earmarked specifically and exclusively for road maintenance. Because of the nature of purpose restrictions, a governmental entity should recognize assets, liabilities, revenues, and expenses related to nonexchange transactions in its financial statements without taking into consideration purpose restrictions. That is, a purpose restriction does not affect the timing of the recognition of a nonexchange transaction. In fact, the GASB notes that a purpose restriction cannot be met unless a nonexchange transaction has taken place. In summary, a purpose restriction means that a stream of revenue can only be used for a specific activity [GASB Cod. Sec. N50.111].

OBSERVATION: In accordance with GASB Cod. Sec. 1800.168, a purpose, time, or eligibility restriction may be an indicator of a restricted fund balance for any unspent amounts at year-end. Restricted fund balance occurs when resources are externally imposed by creditors, grantors, contributors, or laws and regulations of other governments, or imposed by law through constitutional provisions or enabling legislation.

Reimbursements in Relation to Time and Purpose. Some government-mandated nonexchange transactions (described later in this chapter) are based on a reimbursement arrangement. These transactions are referred to as "reimbursement-type transactions" or "expenditure-driven grant programs." The fundamental characteristic of these types of programs is that the provider government "stipulates that a recipient cannot qualify for resources without first incurring allowable costs under the provider's program." When government-mandated nonexchange transactions are subject to a reimbursement eligibility requirement, the recipient government should not recognize revenue until the recipient has incurred eligible costs that are reimbursable under the program [GASB Cod. Sec. N50.112].

PRACTICE POINT: GASB: TB 2020-1 *Accounting and Financial Reporting Issues Related to the Coronavirus Aid, Relief, and Economic Security Act (CARES Act) and Coronavirus Diseases*, clarifies that resources received from the Coronavirus Relief Fund (CRF) include eligibility requirements as they can only cover costs that are necessary expenditures related to COVID-19. The U.S. Treasury deems these funds as other financial assistance. As such funds are voluntary nonexchange transactions with conditions to be met, resources received from the CRF are liabilities until allowable costs occur, at which time, the liabilities are debited, and revenue credited [GASB Cod. Sec. N50.602].

> **PRACTICE ALERT:** Though not contemplated in GASB: TB 2020-1, American Rescue Plan Act (ARPA) funds and settlement amounts received from the National Opioid Settlement with drug manufacturers, distributors and retail pharmacy chains appear to be nonexchange transactions. However, as of the date of publication, the GASB has not provided definitive guidance to these funds.

Derived Tax Revenue

"Derived tax revenues" are revenues from taxes that are imposed on exchange transactions. Although the tax is imposed on an exchange transaction, the source of revenue is considered revenue from a nonexchange transaction because the exchange transaction is between two parties that do not include a governmental entity.

Derived tax revenue has the following principal characteristics:

- A governmental entity imposes the tax on the provider (the individual or enterprise that acquires the income, goods, or services), and
- The imposition of the tax is based on an exchange transaction.

For example, revenue obtained from a retail sales tax is derived tax revenue because the tax is imposed by the governmental entity on an exchange (the sale) between a retailer (collector of the tax resource) and a customer. Other examples of derived tax revenues include personal income taxes and corporate income taxes.

Under a personal income tax, the governmental entity imposes a tax on an exchange transaction (wages earned from an employer). Likewise, when a corporate income tax is imposed by a governmental entity, the business entity is the provider of the tax resource based on the numerous exchanges that occur with customers and vendors.

A governmental entity should recognize derived tax revenue when:

- The exchange that the tax is based on has occurred,
- The amount is measurable, and
- The tax is expected to be collected (realizable).

For example, when a retail sale occurs, a governmental entity should record the sales tax derived from that sale as revenue, irrespective of when the cash is expected to be received from the retailer. However, to recognize revenue under this concept, a governmental entity will often use estimates to make an appropriate revenue accrual at the end of the year.

As another example, certain retail merchants are required to remit sales tax collections during the month after they collect the tax from customers. Under this circumstance, the governmental entity will have to estimate at the end of its fiscal year the tax collections that it will receive after year-end and that were based on sales that occurred on or before the entity's year-end date.

In other instances, a governmental entity will have to estimate refunds that it must make after its fiscal year-end. For example, a governmental entity that imposes a personal income tax will generally have to make some refunds (due to overpayments) to individuals who file their tax returns after the end of the governmental entity's fiscal year [GASB Cod. Sec. N50.113].

A governmental entity usually cannot collect all taxes that are legally due and, therefore, the government should report as revenue only the estimated tax that it expects to realize. Under this circumstance, the governmental entity will again need to use various estimation methods to report net revenues from derived tax sources. For example, a governmental entity that imposes a personal income tax may use historical trend information (adjusted for current economic and enforcement conditions) to provide an appropriate allowance for uncollectible derived tax receivables.

OBSERVATION: GAAP requires that derived taxes and imposed nonexchange revenues be reported in the statement of activities, net of estimated refunds and estimated uncollectible amounts, respectively. A bad debts expense account should not be used. However, the notes to the basic financial statements would show any amounts receivable net of those uncollectible amounts.

A governmental entity must record an asset arising from a derived tax revenue transaction when the related exchange transaction occurs or when the entity receives resources, whichever comes first. That asset will be recorded as cash when tax receipts are collected during the accounting period, but it will take the form of a receivable when revenue is accrued at the end of the year. However, if the entity collects taxes before the conditions of revenue recognition (as described above) are satisfied, it should record the receipt of cash as tax revenue received in advance (a liability account).

As noted earlier, purpose restrictions do not affect the timing of revenues related to nonexchange transactions. However, because resources are restricted, the governmental entity must disclose that fact in its financial statements. This disclosure requirement may be accomplished by establishing a fund balance restriction (for governmental fund types) or a restriction of net positions (for proprietary or fiduciary fund types). For example, assume that a governmental entity recognizes $100,000 of derived tax revenues (net of uncollectible amounts) during the period (based on exchange transactions covered by the tax legislation) and that the amount is restricted because of a court judgment against the government for the purchase of computers for the entity's library. Such transactions would be recorded in a governmental fund in the following manner:

General Fund	Debit	Credit
Cash (or taxes receivable)	100,000	
Revenue – Derived Taxes		100,000
To record the recognition of derived tax revenues, net of uncollectible amounts.		
Fund Balance – Unassigned (or assigned)	100,000	
Fund Balance Restricted for the Purchase of Computers		100,000
To record the restriction of fund balance due to court judgment.		

> **OBSERVATION:** The purpose restriction does not delay the recognition of the revenue.

The Impact of Tax Audits. Revenues from sales and income tax audits are recorded, if measurable in the same period of the underlying exchange and not dependent upon when they will be collected. If the revenues are unavailable, a deferred inflow of resources is recorded [GASB Cod. Sec. N50.707-1].

Imposed Nonexchange Revenues

"Imposed nonexchange revenues" are based on assessments imposed by a government on a nongovernmental entity (other than assessments that are based on exchange transactions). The principal characteristic of these sources of revenue is that they are "imposed by that government on an act committed or omitted by the provider (such as property ownership or the contravention of a law or regulation) that is not an exchange transaction."

GASB Cod. Sec. N50 identifies the following as imposed nonexchange revenues:

- Property (ad valorem) taxes assessed by a governmental entity,
- Fines and penalties imposed by a governmental entity,
- Property seized by a governmental entity, and
- Property that escheats to a governmental entity.

A governmental entity should recognize imposed nonexchange revenues:

- In the period when use of the resources is required or is first permitted by time requirements,
- When the amount is measurable, and
- When the tax is expected to be collected (realizable).

However, the application of these revenue recognition criteria depends on the revenue source. For example, GASB Cod. Sec. N50.708-1 describes common imposed nonexchange revenue transactions—traffic violations. Undisputed fines are recognized when payments are made or when the statutory time allowed for dispute lapses, whichever occurs first. Disputed fines are recognized when the appropriate legal authority (e.g., traffic court) rules that the fine is valid (legally enforceable) and should be recognized net of estimated refunds from rulings overturned on appeal. Legal enforceability generally occurs when the parties pay their fines, when the statutory time allowed for dispute lapses, or, if disputed, when a court later rules that the fine is enforceable.

Property Taxes (and Other Ad-Valorem Taxes). Generally, the most important example of an imposed nonexchange revenue stream is property taxes. The date that a governmental entity has an enforceable legal claim against a property owner is usually included in the enabling legislation. The legislation may refer to the enforceable legal claim date using a variety of terms, including the lien date, assessment date, or some other descriptive term. The term used in the legislation is not the controlling factor in determining when property tax revenue should be recognized. The basic principle adopted in GAAP is that a "receivable should be recognized as soon as the government has a legal claim to a provider's resources that is enforceable through the eventual seizure of the property." The entity should record the revenue and receivable at that date even if the property owner has the right to appeal the assessment or has other due process rights.

The amount of the property taxes receivable is based on the assessed value of the property and the current property tax rate used by the governmental entity. Even though a governmental entity has an enforceable legal claim against property owners, all property taxes assessed will not be collected, and the entity will need to make a reasonable estimate of the amount of uncollectible property taxes and to provide an appropriate allowance.

OBSERVATION: For revenue recognition, GASB Cod. Sec. N50 emphasizes that the lien date is not the important date. The critical date is the date of an enforceable legal claim. Another key factor is that the enforceable legal claim date does not require that a governmental entity formally place a lien on the property as of that date.

There is one exception to the enforceable legal claim date. In some instances, a governmental entity levies property taxes for one period but the enforceable legal claim date or the payment due date(s) occurs in another period. Under this circumstance, GAAP requires the entity to record the property taxes as revenue in the period in which it levied the taxes, provided that the "available" criteria are met.

For property taxes, "available" is assumed to be collected within the current period or *soon enough thereafter* to be used to pay liabilities of the current period. *Current GAAP* defines "thereafter" to be less than 60 days. A disclosure of this period is required in the notes to the basic financials statements in the summary of significant accounting policies. In unusual circumstances, the period is greater than 60 days, which would require additional disclosure [GASB Cod. Sec. P70.104].

PRACTICE ALERT: As discussed previously, the provision for availability is proposed to change in the GASB's *Financial Reporting Model Improvements* Exposure Draft. The measurement focus and basis of accounting is proposed to convert to the short-term financial resources measurement focus and modified accrual basis of accounting, which has a one-year period of availability.

Property taxes are assessed for a fiscal year and are expected to finance expenditures of the year of assessment. Usually on the assessment date or levy date, the property taxes become a lien against the assessed property (demand date criterion), but the actual amounts paid to the governmental unit may be made on a quarterly or monthly basis during the year covered by the assessment. Property taxes should be recorded as revenue on a modified accrual basis and, therefore, recorded when they are both measurable and available.

During the period between when a governmental entity records a nonexchange transaction that has purpose restrictions and when the entity uses those resources, the entity should indicate in the equity section of its statement of position the value of resources that is restricted. Governmental funds should report the restriction as restricted fund balance, and funds that use proprietary fund accounting should refer to the purpose restriction as a "restriction" of their net position balance.

The amount of the property taxes receivable is based on the assessed value of the property and the current property tax rate used by the governmental unit. All property taxes assessed will not be collected, and the measurability criterion can be satisfied only if the governmental unit can make a reasonable estimate of the amount of uncollectible property taxes [GASB Cod. Secs. N50.114–.115, P70.106].

The recognition date of the receivable for property taxes is the date when an enforceable legal claim to the taxable property arises and is generally stipulated in the applicable legislation. The date is labeled the *"lien date"* or the *"assessment date."* In some cases, the enforceable legal claim does not occur until after the levy period. For example, taxes may be levied in one period, but cannot be used by the government until the next period. As an example, the State of Colorado has this provision in what is known as the "Taxpayer's Bill of Rights" or TABOR [GASB Cod. Sec. P70.105].

In such instances when taxes are levied in one period, but use is restricted until the next period, and when the taxes receivable are recognized or collected in advance of the period of levy, the offset is a deferred inflow of resources. The deferred inflow of resources is then debited, and revenue recognized when the available criterion is met [GASB Cod. Sec. P70.107].

Some governments have property tax rebate programs refunding a portion of property taxes paid, based on income level. GASB Cod. Sec. N50.708-4 requires the rebates to be reported as reductions of property tax revenues of the period in which they become estimable.

When reasonable estimates can be made, the property tax levy may be recorded as follows:

Revenues: Nonexchange and Exchange Transactions 17,017

GENERAL FUND	Debit	Credit
Property Taxes Receivable	400,000	
Revenue – Property Taxes		370,000
Allowance for Uncollectible Property Taxes		30,000
To record the recognition of property taxes receivable, along with allowance for uncollectible accounts.		

The property tax levy revenues are recorded net of the estimated amount of uncollectible property taxes. No bad debts expense account is used because only expenditures, not expenses, are recorded by governmental funds. In the above example, a deferred inflow of resources is recorded as the government may not utilize the funds until after the fiscal year.

The revenue is reported as a net amount because only the net amount is expected to be available during the fiscal period. Since revenues are reported net, it is not appropriate to record a bad debt expense because the expense does not represent an actual expenditure of current financial resources during the period. Reporting revenues on a net basis does not mean that a governmental unit cannot budget for bad debt expense and monitor the expense through its financial accounting system. When this is done, however, the bad debt expense account used for budgeting or internal purposes must be netted against the related gross revenue account and reported as net revenue for financial reporting purposes. In the following illustration, bad debt expense is not recorded, but the example journal entries could easily be modified to accommodate the use of a bad debts expense account for internal reporting purposes.

During the fiscal year, the routine transactions (such as write-offs of accounts and collections on account) affecting the receivables and allowance accounts may be recorded as follows, assuming $350,000 is collected. Interest receivable and revenues for delinquent accounts would be recorded similarly:

GENERAL FUND	Debit	Credit
Cash	350,000	
Property Taxes Receivable – Current		350,000
To recognize property taxes received during the period.		

GASB Cod. Sec. N50.115 states that deferred inflows of resources should be reported when resources associated with imposed nonexchange revenue transactions are received or reported as a receivable before:

1. The period for which property taxes are levied, or
2. The period when resources are required to be used or when use is first permitted for all other imposed nonexchange revenues in which the enabling legislation includes *time requirements* (not purpose requirements).

It may be determined during the fiscal year that the allowance for uncollectible accounts was either over-provided for or underprovided for. When this conclusion is reached, the allowance account and the revenue account are appropriately adjusted to reflect the change in the accounting estimate. For example, in the current illustration, if it were decided that the allowance provision for the year should have been $27,000 and not $30,000, the following entry would be made:

GENERAL FUND	Debit	Credit
Allowance for Uncollectible Property Taxes – Current	3,000	
Property Taxes Receivable – Current		3,000
To record property tax reductions due to amounts that will never be collected.		

At the end of the year, it may be decided to transfer the balance in the current receivables account to a delinquent account for internal control and analysis. The transfer does not substitute for the write-off of an account when a specific account has been identified as uncollectible. In fact, for reporting purposes, the current and delinquent balances are usually combined since they both represent specific accounts that are expected to ultimately be collected. To continue with the illustration, assume that all the remaining net receivables are considered collectible, but they are technically delinquent at the end of the fiscal year. In this case, the following entry would be made, assuming a lien is recorded:

GENERAL FUND	Debit	Credit
Property Taxes Receivable – Delinquent Tax Liens	47,000	
Property Taxes Receivable – Current		47,000
Property Tax Revenue	47,000	
Unavailable Tax Revenue – Tax Liens		47,000
To recognize property taxes that are deemed delinquent with the recording of liens and related reductions in revenue to close the fiscal year.		

The results from the above transactions would show Property Taxes Receivable – Delinquent Tax Liens for $47,000 along with an offsetting Unavailable Tax Revenue – Tax Liens, also for $47,000. The Allowance for Uncollectible Property Taxes – Current account would carry forward to the next year amounting to $20,000. Assuming $30,000 in Tax Liens were collected in the next year, irrespective of interest and penalties, the entry would be as follows:

GENERAL FUND	Debit	Credit
Cash	30,000	
Property Taxes Receivable – Delinquent Tax Liens		30,000
Unavailable Tax Revenue – Tax Liens	30,000	
Revenue – Tax Liens		30,000
To record revenue from payment on delinquent property taxes prior to interest and penalties (separate transaction).		

After this entry, a best practice is to reassess the allowance account.

When it is concluded that assessed property tax revenue will not be available, the revenue cannot be recognized in the current assessment period. Continuing with the current illustration, if it is concluded that $4,000 of the property taxes receivable at the end of the fiscal year will not be collected until more than 60 days after the close of the period, the following entry would be made:

GENERAL FUND	Debit	Credit
Property Tax Revenue	4,000	
Deferred Inflows of Resources – Property Taxes		4,000

To reclassify property tax revenues collected more than 60 days after the close of the fiscal year.

When property taxes are received before the levy or assessment date, the receipt should be recorded as deferred inflows of resources. Subsequently, the revenue is recognized in the period that the tax is levied, assuming the measurable and available criteria are met.

When property taxes are delinquent but are expected to be collected, they should be reported as deferred inflows of resources—property taxes if it is estimated that the taxes will not be available to pay current obligations of the governmental fund. Generally, this would mean that the delinquent property taxes are not expected to be collected within 60 days of the close of the fiscal year. The governmental unit must disclose the important dates associated with assessed property taxes. These dates may include the lien dates, due dates, and collection dates [GASB Cod. Sec. P70.108].

In addition, some units may be prohibited from recognizing property tax revenues based on the measurable and available criteria. When this circumstance exists, the nature of the prohibition should be disclosed in a note to the financial statements. Moreover, the fund balance should be committed or assigned (depending on law) by the amount of the property tax revenue recognized under generally accepted accounting principles, but this is not consistent with the legal requirement that must be observed by the governmental unit.

Other Imposed Nonexchange Revenues. All other imposed nonexchange revenues should be recorded in the governmental entity's financial statements as of the date an enforceable legal claim arises unless the enabling legislation establishes a time requirement. When a time requirement is imposed, the entity should recognize revenue when the resources are permitted and defer the inflows of resources until then.

OBSERVATION: GASB Cod. Sec. N50 notes that the enforceable legal claim date for other imposed nonexchange revenues can generally be determined by the enabling legislation or related regulations.

A governmental entity must record an asset from imposed nonexchange transactions when the entity has an enforceable legal claim to the asset (as explained above) or when the entity receives resources, whichever comes first. That asset will be in the form of cash from tax receipts, fines, and so on, which are collected during the accounting period, but the asset will take the form of a receivable when revenue is accrued at the end of the year. However, if the entity collects imposed nonexchange revenue before the revenue recognition criteria are satisfied, the entity should record the receipt of cash as deferred inflows of resources. In the case of property taxes and other ad-valorem taxes, it is possible for the entity to recognize a receivable before revenue is recognized. That is, it can record property taxes as a receivable and deferred inflow of resources when the entity has an enforceable legal claim (as described earlier) even if it levies the taxes after the date of the enforceable legal claim. Because the entity receives cash before the period for which the taxes were levied, the government reduces the receivable, but its deferred inflow of resources remains the same.

Government-Mandated Nonexchange Transactions and Voluntary Nonexchange Transactions

Government-Mandated Nonexchange Transactions. Revenues from government-mandated nonexchange transactions arise when a governmental entity provides resources to a governmental entity that is at a lower level than the governmental entity that is providing the resources and the provider entity "requires [the recipient] government to use them for a specific purpose or purposes established in the provider's enabling legislation."

The most common example of this is when the federal government (provider government) makes resources available to a state (recipient government), or a state government (provider government) makes resources available to a municipality or other local governmental entity (recipient government). Most grant activity is within this category. GASB Cod. Sec. N50 notes that government-mandated nonexchange revenues have the following principal characteristics:

- The provider government requires that the recipient government institute a specific program (or facilitate the performance of a specific program) conducted by the recipient government or nongovernmental entity (secondary recipient entity or subrecipient(s)).
- Certain performance requirements must be fulfilled (other than the provision of cash or other assets in advance).

Secondary Recipients (Subrecipients) in Government-Mandated Nonexchange Transactions. A secondary recipient in a government-mandated nonexchange transaction can be a governmental entity or a nongovernmental entity. For example, the federal government mandates that states have a drug rehabilitation program and provides some funds to be used directly by the states (recipient government), and some of the funding is passed through the state to counties and certain not-for-profit organizations. In this example, the counties and not-for-profit organizations are secondary recipients.

These secondary recipients are defined as *"subrecipients."* Though beyond the scope of this *Guide*, differentiating between a subrecipient and a contractor is extremely important in federal grant management, compliance auditing and reporting. Title 2, Code of Federal Regulations, Part 200 , subpart A, section 1, defines them as follows:

Term	Definition
Contractor/ Contract	For federal financial assistance, a legal instrument by which a recipient or subrecipient purchases property or services needed to carry out the project or program under a federal award.
Subrecipient	An entity usually but not limited to non-federal entities, that receives a subaward from a pass-through entity to carry out part of a federal award; but does not include an individual that is a beneficiary of such award. A subrecipient may also be a recipient of other federal awards directly from a federal awarding agency.

PRACTICE POINT: There are many compliance requirements for federal awards relating to subrecipients contained in Title 2, Code of Federal Regulations, Part 200. These requirements are detailed within CCH's *Knowledge-Based Audits of Governmental Entities and Knowledge-Based Single Audits* Guide.

Guidance may also be updated annually within the White House Office of Management and Budget's *Compliance Supplement* to Title 2, Code of Federal Regulations, Part 200. Stakeholders that are parties to federal awards, especially signatories of them, must comply with the legal provisions detailed within or referenced in the grant award.

PRACTICE POINT: See section on Pass-Through Grants with the text on administrative involvement later in this chapter.

As the resources received by the recipient government must be used for a singular purpose, such resources always create a purpose restriction. In many instances, the resources are also subject to eligibility requirements, including time restrictions. An example of a government-mandated nonexchange transaction is the federal government requiring a state government to use federal funds to provide educational counseling to certain disadvantaged groups.

In a government-mandated nonexchange transaction, if the two governmental entities that are involved in the transaction are state and local governments, they are both subject to GASB accounting and reporting standards. For this reason, the standards established by GASB Cod. Sec. N50 will apply to the recognition of revenue (by the recipient government) and the recognition of expenditures (by the provider government). However, if the provider government is the federal government or if a secondary recipient of the resources is a nongovernmental entity, then these entities are not subject to the standards established by GASB Cod. Sec. N50.

In a government-mandated nonexchange transaction, the recipient government should recognize revenue when all eligibility requirements (which include time requirements) are satisfied. The eligibility requirements are comprised of one or more of the following elements [GASB Cod. Sec. N50.117]:

Elements	Explanation in GAAP
Required characteristics of recipients	The recipient (and secondary or subrecipients as applicable), have characteristics specified by the provider. GASB Cod. Sec. N50.117(a) provides an example of recipients of a federal program being states and secondary (or subrecipients) being school districts.
Time requirements	Time requirements are specific to enabling legislation or specified by the provider and have been met.
Reimbursements	The provider transfers resources on an expenditure-driven basis and the recipient has incurred allowable costs under the program.
Contingencies (only in voluntary nonexchange transactions)	The provider's offer of resources is contingent upon a specific action of the recipient and that action has occurred. For example, a grant is provided upon the recipient raising the amount of matching funds from donations or transferring funds from other sources.

A prevalent example of when assets would be reported by a provider and liabilities would be reported by a recipient would be in relation to federal grant funds passed from one level of government to another where there would be a potential for disallowed costs.

In an example of special education grants based on student eligibility, there may be an incidence of disallowed costs due to grants being used for students that are found not needing special education as defined in the grant award. If this is the case, a liability would be reported by the receiving government as the funds may have to be returned to the granting government, which may be a state department of education to be passed through to the United States Department of Education (or directly to the United States Department of Education).

In the case of when funds are received during a fiscal year, but before a school year prior to eligibility requirements being met, the funds received prior to the eligibility would be recorded as an asset (advances to school districts) by the providing government and a liability (advances from the state department of education) until eligibility requirements are met by the receiving government.

PRACTICE POINT: GASB: TB 2020-1 contains guidance related to CARES Act resources and the loss of revenue attributable to the impact of COVID-19. The healthcare Provider Relief Fund (PRF) from the U.S. Department of Health and Human Services contains a contingency relating to eligibility and specified actions of the healthcare facility recipient. Until compliance with the eligibility requirement is determined, a liability would be in place. Upon the costs being classified as allowable costs, the liability is debited, and revenue is credited [GASB Cod. Sec. N50.602].

Recognition Requirements: Government-Mandated or Voluntary Nonexchange Transactions

Recognition Requirements: Government-Mandated Nonexchange Transactions. A governmental entity should recognize government-mandated nonexchange transactions and voluntary nonexchange transactions when the entity, or entities involved in the transaction, satisfies all eligibility requirements. The relevant eligibility requirements in a government-mandated nonexchange transaction are generally based on enabling legislation and related regulations.

Those laws and regulations often identify purpose restrictions that apply to the resources provided under the program. The relevant eligibility requirements in a voluntary nonexchange transaction may arise from enabling legislation or from contractual agreements with a nongovernmental entity. For example, a nongovernmental entity, such as a corporation or an individual, may provide resources to a governmental entity but the provisions of those resources may depend on several eligibility factors contained in the donor agreement [GASB Cod. Sec. N50.118].

It is important to remember that a reimbursement eligibility requirement is not a purpose restriction and, therefore, is not subject to financial statement presentation requirements that apply to purpose restrictions. The recognition of revenue by the recipient government and expenditures by the provider government should not be delayed because routine administrative procedures have not been completed. GAAP notes that these procedures could include filing claims for reimbursements under an expenditure-driven program or completing progress reports required by the provider government [GASB Cod. Sec. N50 fn. 9].

However, in practice, most categorical grants require claims to be filed for reimbursement. Furthermore, large governments need to be careful not to receive reimbursement too far in advance of expenditure or else they may be in violation of an agreement with the United States Treasury under the federal Cash Management Improvement Act of 1990 (as amended). If a government draws funds too early, the United States Treasury may be entitled to interest daily between when the funds were received and when the funds were expended.

In some instances, the time requirement may be permanent (e.g., permanent endowment) or the restriction may state that resources may not be spent until the expiration of a specified number of years or until a specified event has occurred. Examples of this include a governmental unit of a local government receiving a permanent addition to its endowment or other trusts, or a local public museum receiving contributions of "works of art, historical treasures, and similar assets to capitalized collections." Often during the interim period, the governmental entity may derive benefits from the resources (investment income or display the artwork or historical relics).

The recipient government should recognize government-mandated nonexchange transactions of this type as revenue when they are received, assuming the recipient government has satisfied all other eligibility requirements. The time requirement is satisfied when "the recipient begins to honor the provider's stipulation not to sell, disburse, or consume the resources and continues to be met for as long as the recipient honors that stipulation." However, during the time restriction period (which means indefinitely for a permanent endowment), the recipient government should note in its statement of position the fund balance restriction for a governmental fund type or net position restriction or similar description for a proprietary or fiduciary fund type [GASB Cod. Sec. N50.119, fn.11].

> **OBSERVATION:** If a governmental entity receives contributions of works of art, historical treasures, or other, similar assets to be added to capitalized collections, the entity should not capitalize those receipts if the collection the assets are being added to has not previously been capitalized. Rather, these amounts are recognized as program expense equal to the amount of revenues recognized. (See previous discussion on acquisition value and donated items.) If the collections are capitalized, then donations are increases in capital assets.

For administrative or practical purposes, a governmental entity may receive resources early from another governmental entity. The receipt of these resources under this circumstance is not considered the receipt of an endowment or other similar receipts as described in the previous paragraph. Therefore, a recipient government should *not* record this type of receipt as revenue until all eligibility requirements that apply to government-mandated nonexchange transactions are satisfied [GASB Cod. Sec. N50.120].

When the provider government does not establish time requirements, the recipient of the resources and the provider of the resources should recognize the government-mandated nonexchange transaction when all other eligibility requirements are satisfied. Assuming no other eligibility requirements exist, both the recipient government and the provider government should recognize revenue and expenditure based on the first day of the fiscal year of the provider government.

For example, the relevant fiscal year of the provider government is generally the first day the appropriation becomes effective. Thus, under that circumstance, both the provider government and the recipient government should record the entire amount related to the government-mandated transaction based on the first day of the provider government's fiscal year (applicable period), unless the provider government has a biennial budgetary process. When the provider government has a biennial budgetary process, each year of the biennial period should be considered a separate year (applicable period), and "the provider and the recipients should allocate one-half of the resources appropriated for the biennium to each applicable period, unless the provider specifies a different allocation" [GASB Cod. Sec. N50.121].

When a secondary recipient government is involved in a government-mandated transaction, the primary recipient government's fiscal year should be used rather than the original provider government's fiscal year. For example, the federal government provides a state government with resources and a local government also receives some of the resources. The local government would use the state government's fiscal year to determine when to recognize revenue; however, the state government would use the federal government's fiscal year to determine when it should recognize revenue under the government-mandated program [GASB Cod. Sec. N50.fn. 12].

GASB Cod. Sec. N50 notes that some grant programs may be established by a state whereby "the required period of disbursement often is specified through the appropriation of resources under the enabling legislation, rather than as part of the legislation or related regulations." In this circumstance an explicit appropriation must be made by state legislature (the existence of the program under the enabling legislation is not enough) and the period to which the appropriation applies must have begun before a local government can recognize revenue (assuming all eligibility criteria are satisfied).

GASB Cod. Sec. N50.710-1 applies this general guidance by noting that a city that receives a grant award (but not the resources) from a state cannot recognize grant revenue unless the state has appropriated resources for the grant. However, in the same question, the GASB notes that, for example, if "state law requires the state treasurer to pay the grant whether the legislature appropriates resources," the city should recognize the grant when it is awarded.

> **PRACTICE POINT:** A common question posed by practitioners involves the belief that grant agreements, acceptances of terms and conditions, delivery of project spending plans and similar, to granting agencies results in the immediate recognition of revenue by the potentially receiving government. This belief is not GAAP in accordance with GASB Cod. Sec. N50, even if allowable costs have occurred, which may be allowable to a prior date in a law. (A backdating provision was allowed in the CARES Act.) GASB Cod. Sec. N50.711-7 reminds practitioners that contractual agreements only provide evidence of the resource recipient government's acceptance of the terms and conditions of the provider government's program, including eligibility requirements in that program. The incurrence of allowable costs in nonexchange transactions that require the existence of a contractual agreement is not enough to fulfill recognition criteria in the absence of an executed contractual agreement in accordance with the grantor's legal requirements. That is the case even if the contractual agreement includes provisions that allow the recipient to be reimbursed allowable costs that are incurred prior to the execution of a contractual agreement.
>
> If the recipient government has eligible costs that are reimbursable once the agreement is approved by the grantor and the recipient, once the costs are filed to the grantor for reimbursement, a receivable may be declared if the eligibility requirements are fulfilled, and the funds are available.

Recognition Requirements: Voluntary Nonexchange Transactions

In contrast to government-mandated nonexchange transactions, *voluntary nonexchange transactions* arise from "legislative or contractual agreements, other than exchanges, entered into willingly by two or more parties." Such transactions are commonly donations to public institutions of education or healthcare. Certain grants and entitlements may also be voluntary nonexchange transactions. A voluntary nonexchange transaction can be based on either a written or an oral agreement, assuming the latter is verifiable. The principal characteristics of voluntary nonexchange transactions are listed below:

- They are not imposed on the provider or the recipient, and
- Satisfaction of eligibility requirements (other than the provision of cash or other assets in advance) is necessary for a transaction to occur.

PRACTICE ALERT: The federal Inflation Reduction Act of 2022 contains provisions for certain payments to state and local governments for a myriad of programs combating climate change. Embedded in the Act was a change to Internal Revenue Code 6417 allowing state and local governments to receive an "applicable credit" even though state and local governments are not subject to taxation. If the government procures clean energy equipment, vehicles, and many other elements which comprise 12 applicable credits, the government may receive a direct payment from the federal government. The programs began on January 1, 2023. Some of the programs extend until 2032. As of the time of publication of this *Guide*, no forms or publications have been finalized from the Internal Revenue Service, nor has the White House Office of Management and Budget ruled if the programs are subject to Title 2, Code of Federal Regulations, Part 200. For accounting and reporting purposes, the programs appear to be voluntary nonexchange transactions. However, no definitive guidance on the payments have been issued by the GASB.

In a voluntary nonexchange transaction, a governmental entity may be the recipient or the provider of the resources, and the second party of the transaction may be another governmental entity or a nongovernmental entity, such as an individual or a not-for-profit organization. Voluntary nonexchange transactions may involve purpose restrictions and/or time requirements, and they often require that resources be returned to the provider if purpose restrictions or eligibility requirements are contravened after the voluntary nonexchange transaction has been recognized by a governmental entity.

NOTE: For convenience, in the following discussion of voluntary nonexchange transactions it is assumed that both parties to the nonexchange transaction are governmental entities. When one of the parties to the nonexchange transaction is not a governmental entity, that nongovernmental entity is not required to follow the standards established by GASB Cod. Sec. N50. The GASB established the same (with one exception) accounting standards for government-mandated nonexchange transactions and voluntary nonexchange transactions. These standards are explained in the previous section. (The accounting standard exception for voluntary nonexchange transactions is that there are four possible eligibility requirements instead of three. The additional requirement—contingency eligibility—is discussed later in this section.)

In a voluntary nonexchange transaction, the provider and the recipient should recognize the nonexchange transaction when all eligibility requirements (which include time requirements) are satisfied. As a reminder, the eligibility requirements are categorized as follows:

- Required characteristics of recipients (discussed earlier),
- Time requirements (discussed earlier),
- Reimbursements (discussed earlier), and
- Contingencies (discussed below).

All eligibility requirements must be satisfied before the parties to a voluntary nonexchange transaction can record an operating transaction. The accounting is as follows:

Activity	Provider	Recipient
Voluntary nonexchange transaction resources transmitted before the eligibility requirements are met (*excluding time requirements*).	Assets	Liabilities
Voluntary nonexchange transaction resources received before time requirements are met but *after all other eligibility requirements have been met.*	Deferred outflows of resources and cash outflows	Deferred inflows of resources and cash inflows

OBSERVATION: In some instances where the provider of the resources is a nongovernmental entity, resources may be made on an installment basis. If there is no time restriction(s) (or other eligibility requirements) that applies to the donation, the GASB requires that the recipient government recognize the full amount of the donation as revenue. If the installments are spread over more than one year, the entity should recognize the amount of revenue as the present value of the future cash flows.

The final possible eligibility requirement for a voluntary nonexchange transaction is based on a contingency imposed by the provider. That is, the right to receive resources by the recipient can occur only if the recipient has performed the specified requirement. For example, a state university has been promised resources by a private donor if the university can persuade its alumni to match dollar-for-dollar the promised gift of the original donor. Under this circumstance, the university can recognize an operating transaction only if the university obtains the appropriate resources from its alumni.

An asset (receivable) must be recorded by the recipient when it has satisfied the revenue criteria for voluntary nonexchange transactions described above. If the recipient collects resources from a voluntary nonexchange transaction before the recipient satisfies the revenue recognition criteria, the recipient should record the receipt of cash as either a deferred inflow of resources or a liability, as explained previously.

Voluntary nonexchange transactions often involve pledges (promises to pay) from nongovernmental entities (e.g., individuals, business enterprises, or not-for-profit organizations). Such promises may involve cash, works of art, and various other assets, and they may or may not involve purpose restrictions or time requirements. The recipient government should record pledges as revenue by the recipient government when "all eligibility requirements are met, provided that the promise is verifiable, and the resources are measurable and probable of collection." The governmental entity may have to establish an allowance account before the entity can recognize pledges as revenue so that the total pledges are reported at their expected realizable value [GASB Cod. Sec. N50.122].

The guidance contained in GASB Cod. Sec. N50.119 previously discussed also applies to pledges. The recipient government should recognize pledges of resources that *cannot* be sold, disbursed, or consumed until after a passage of a specified period or the occurrence of a specified event as revenue when they are received, assuming the government has satisfied all other eligibility requirements. For example, if a government receives a pledge that involves additions to the governmental entity's permanent endowment, term endowments, or contributions of works of art, historical treasures, and similar assets to be included in the entity's collection, the governmental entity should not recognize the pledge as revenue until it receives the pledged property [GASB Cod. Sec. N50.fn.13].

When the provider of resources in a voluntary nonexchange transaction is a government, that government should recognize expenditures based on the same criteria that are used by the recipient government to recognize revenues (as discussed above). If the expenditure recognition criteria are not satisfied and the provider government has made a cash payment to the recipient government, the provider government should record the payment as an advance (asset) or potentially a deferred outflow of resources.

Subsequent Contravention of Eligibility Requirements or Purpose Restrictions

A recipient government may record a nonexchange transaction as an operating transaction, but subsequent events indicate that resources will not be transferred in a manner originally anticipated by both parties, or that resources transferred will have to be returned to the provider. This situation may arise because:

1. Eligibility requirements related to a government-mandated transaction or a voluntary nonexchange transaction are no longer being satisfied, or
2. The recipient will not satisfy a purpose restriction within the period specified (also known as *period of performance*) [GASB Cod. Sec. N50.123].

When it is *probable* (likely to occur) that the recipient will not receive the resources or will be required to return all, or part of the resources already received, the following procedures should be observed:

Provider Government—Revenue	Recipient Government—Expenditures
• The value of resources that will not be provided to the recipient (but that have already been recognized as expenditures by the provider), and/or	• The value of resources that have been promised by the provider (and already recognized as revenue by the recipient), and/or
• The value of resources already provided to the recipient but expected to be returned.	• The amount or resources already received by the recipient but expected to be returned to the provider.

Nonexchange Revenues Administered or Collected by Another Government

A governmental entity may collect derived tax revenues or imposed nonexchange revenues on behalf of a recipient government that imposes the tax. For example, a state government administers a local sales tax (imposed by the locality) with the state sales tax it imposes. In this circumstance, GAAP requires that the recipient government apply the relevant revenue recognition standards that apply to derived tax revenues and imposed nonexchange revenues. The state government would not record revenue for the portion of the tax due to the recipient governmental entity but, rather, would recognize a liability. In some instances, the recipient government may need to estimate the amount of revenue to be accrued in an accounting period. The GASB assumes that the recipient government because it imposes the tax, will have enough information to make an appropriate accrual at the end of the year [GASB Cod. Sec. N50.124].

Derived tax revenues and imposed nonexchange revenues of one governmental entity that are shared with another governmental entity (but not imposed by the recipient government) are based on two transactions, namely:

- Events or actions that give rise to the derived tax revenue or the imposed nonexchange revenue, and
- The sharing of the revenue by one governmental entity (provider government) with another governmental entity (recipient government).

In the first transaction, a governmental entity would record revenue based on the criteria as discussed in this chapter from GASB Cod. Sec. N50, depending on whether the revenue is from derived taxes or imposed nonexchange transactions.

The second transaction results in both the recording of an expenditure or expense (by the provider government) and revenue (by the recipient government) and represents either a government-mandated or a voluntary nonexchange transaction. GAAP requires that both the provider government and the recipient government record the expenditure or expense and revenue, respectively based on the government-mandated nonexchange or voluntary nonexchange criteria. Thus, the two governments would record the sharing of the tax revenue (as an expenditure or expense and revenue in the same period [GASB Cod. Sec. N50.125].

In some instances, shared nonexchange revenues may be based on a continuing appropriation. A continuing appropriation is an "appropriation that, once established, is automatically renewed without further legislative action, period after period, until altered or revoked." When shared revenues are based on continuing appropriations, the eligibility requirement (which is the basis for recording the government-mandated or voluntary nonexchange transaction) is satisfied when either:

- The underlying transaction occurs (for derived tax revenue), or
- The period when resources were required to be used or the first period that use was permitted has occurred (for imposed nonexchange transactions).

For example, when a state shares its sales taxes under the requirements of a continuing appropriation, the recipient should record revenues and receivables when the underlying sales occur, regardless of whether the guidance for derived tax revenues or for government-mandated and voluntary nonexchange transactions applies.

When revenue sharing occurs based on a continuing appropriation, the recipient government should make any accrual of revenue based on information supplied by the provider government. For example, in the case of shared sales taxes, the provider government should make available to the recipient governments information about sales tax revenues that have been earned in the current period but that will not be collected from merchants until the following period. GAAP points out "if notification by the provider government is not available in a timely manner, recipient governments should use a reasonable estimate of the amount to be accrued."

When shared revenue includes allocations of taxes between one level of government and another as a voluntary nonexchange transaction and if at the lower level the allocation is restricted to a program, GASB Cod. Sec. 2200.716-8 discusses how the tax at the lower level should be recognized as general revenue if it is not restricted for any purpose. If the tax revenue contains a purpose restriction for education, for example, then it should be program revenue.

Revenue sharing could occur in a service concession arrangement. If the operator is another government, then the transferor government reports all revenue earned and expenses incurred—including the amount of revenues shared with the transferor—that are associated with the operation of the facility. The transferor government should recognize only its portion of the shared revenue when it is earned in accordance with the arrangement's terms. If revenue-sharing arrangements contain amounts to be paid to the transferor government regardless of revenues earned (e.g., $100,000 annually), then the present value of those amounts should be reported by the transferor and governmental operator as if they were installment payments at the inception of the arrangement.

PRACTICE ALERT: The GASB's *Revenue and Expense Recognition* Preliminary Views document discloses potential changes to the recognition and categorization principles for General Aid to Governments and Shared Revenue Transactions. Both are discussed in Chapter 4 of the Preliminary Views, paragraphs 46 through 51. Both would be Category B transactions as introduced in the **PRACTICE ALERT** in this chapter.

General Aid to Governments transactions would be revenue transactions where legislation or a similar law requires the provision of resources from one government to other governments funding a specific activity or program. Specific formulas may be used to determine the distribution. The legislation or similar law creates a binding arrangement. The GASB provides an example of such transactions in Case 8 of Appendix C to the Preliminary Views, detailing state aid to school districts.

For General Aid to Governments transactions, the GASB's preliminary view is that the resource recipient government would recognize a receivable when payments are due if *both* of the following criteria are met:

- The resource provider has appropriated funds for the provision of resources and the period applicable to the appropriation has begun.
- The resource provider has determined that it intends to provide the resources to the resource recipient.

The offsetting credit would be to revenue.

If the resource provider *cancels the appropriation* and communicates the cancellation to the recipient(s), the receivable will continue to be reported along with the revenue *if the provider intends to provide the payment in a future period.* If not provided, the receivable would be credited, and revenue debited.

Shared Revenue Transactions would be the second subcategory. This would be like current GAAP. The resource provider has two transactions—the imposition of revenue and the sharing of that revenue, both because of the binding arrangement created by the law or ordinance. The GASB's preliminary view is that for shared revenue transactions supported through *periodic appropriations,* the substance of the transaction is general aid as discussed.

For shared revenue transactions supported through *continuing appropriations,* recipients would recognize receivables when the underlying transaction that produces the shared revenue has occurred if:

- The resource provider has appropriated funds for the provision of resources (*if required*), and the period applicable to the appropriation has begun, and
- The resource provider has determined that it intends to provide the resources to the resource recipient.

Revenue Recognition in Governmental Funds Using the Modified Accrual Basis of Accounting

Under *current GAAP,* the standards contained in GASB Cod. Sec. N50 include the fundamental criterion for revenue recognition that applies to the modified accrual basis of accounting, namely that revenue be recorded when it is both available and measurable. In addition, GASB Cod. Sec. N50.108 (and other paragraphs) specifically state that revenue should be recognized only when it is probable (likely to occur) that it will be collected. As discussed below, the same standards for the recognition of revenue under the accrual basis of accounting should be used to record revenue under the modified accrual basis of accounting, except the revenue must be available.

As described above, the availability criterion requires that resources only be recorded as revenue if those resources are expected to be collected or otherwise realized in time to pay liabilities reported in the governmental fund at the end of the accounting period. In practice, the period of collectability has generally ranged from thirty days to as much as a year (see previous **PRACTICE ALERT** s on the GASB's *Financial Reporting Model Improvements* Exposure Draft).

Derived Tax Revenue. GAAP requires that derived tax revenues be recorded in the same period in which the exchange transaction that generates the tax revenue occurs. Thus, once the taxable transaction has occurred, the governmental entity has an enforceable legal claim to the tax resources. If the resources related to the enforceable legal claim are available to the governmental entity, then, under the modified accrual basis of accounting, the governmental entity should record revenue.

Imposed Nonexchange Revenue. For imposed nonexchange revenues that are derived from sources other than property taxes, the government should recognize revenues in the period in which an enforceable legal claim has arisen, *and* resources are available. For property taxes, revenue is reported as a receivable before:

1. The period for which property taxes are levied, *or*
2. The period when resources are required to be used or when use is first permitted for all other imposed nonexchange revenues in which the enabling legislation includes time requirements.

Government-Mandated Nonexchange Transactions. Under the modified accrual basis of accounting, a recipient government should recognize revenues in the period when all applicable eligibility requirements have been met *and* the resources are available.

If there are possible contraventions of eligibility, providers of resources that require the return of those resources should recognize revenue in the period when the returned resources are available [GASB Cod. Secs. N50.126–.127].

Exhibit 17-1 summarizes the assets, deferred outflows of resources, liabilities, deferred inflows of resources, revenue, and expenditure recognition criteria discussed in this section of the chapter.

EXHIBIT 17-1
ASSETS, DEFERRED OUTFLOWS OF RESOURCES, LIABILITIES, DEFERRED INFLOWS OF RESOURCES, REVENUE, AND EXPENDITURE RECOGNITION CRITERIA AS ILLUSTRATED IN GASB Cod. Sec. N50.901

	Derived Tax Revenue	Imposed Nonexchange Revenues	Government-Mandated Nonexchange Transactions	Voluntary Nonexchange Transactions
Assets	Period when the underlying exchange has occurred or when resources are received, whichever comes first.	Period when an enforceable legal claim has arisen or when resources are received, whichever is first.	*Recipients*: Period when *all* eligibility requirements have been met.	*Providers*: Payment of resources *before* eligibility requirements have been met, excluding time requirements.
Deferred Outflows of Resources	Not applicable	Not applicable	Not applicable	*Providers:* Payment of resources before time requirements have been met, but after all other eligibility requirements have been met.

	Derived Tax Revenue	Imposed Nonexchange Revenues	Government-Mandated Nonexchange Transactions	Voluntary Nonexchange Transactions
Liabilities	Not applicable	Not applicable	Receipt of resources before eligibility requirements are met, *excluding time*.	*Providers*: Period when all eligibility requirements have been met.
Deferred Inflows of Resources	Under *current GAAP*, in governmental funds, for resources that are not available.	In governmental funds when resources are not available. Otherwise, when resources are received or reported as a receivable before: 1. The period for which property taxes are levied, *or* 2. The period when resources are required to be used or when use is first permitted for all other imposed nonexchange revenues in which the enabling legislation includes time requirements.(C)	Receipt of resources before time requirements are met, but after all other eligibility requirements are met. Under *current GAAP*, in governmental funds, used for when resources are not available.	Not applicable
Revenue Recognition Criteria(A)	Period when the exchange that the tax is based on has occurred.(B)	When resources are used or the first period is permitted (for property taxes, the levy period). Under *current GAAP*, for governmental funds, resources should also be "available."	When resources become available in governmental funds. Otherwise, when eligibility and time requirements are met.	Period when all eligibility requirements have been met. But when provider precludes the sale, disbursement, or consumption of resources for a specified number of years, until a specified event has occurred or in a permanent or term endowment, revenues when the resources are received, and net position/fund balance is restricted. Under *current GAAP*, for governmental funds, resources should be available.

Specific Accounting and Reporting Issues

	Derived Tax Revenue	Imposed Nonexchange Revenues	Government-Mandated Nonexchange Transactions	Voluntary Nonexchange Transactions
Expenditure Recognition Criteria	Not applicable.	Not applicable.	Not applicable.	*Providers*: Period when all eligibility requirements have been met. When a provider precludes the sale, disbursement, or consumption of resources for a specified number of years, until a specific event has occurred, or with permanent or term endowments, report expenses or expenditures when the resources have been paid.
Impact of a Time Restriction	Generally, not subject to time restrictions	Revenue should not be recognized until the time restriction is satisfied.	Revenue should not be recognized until the time restriction is satisfied.(D)	Revenue should not be recognized until the time restriction is satisfied.(D)
Impact of a Purpose Restriction	For assets, if there are purpose restrictions, net position (or fund balance) is also restricted. Disclose in the notes.			

(A) When revenue is recognized under the modified accrual basis of accounting, the available criterion must be satisfied.
(B) In addition, revenue can be recognized only if the amount is *measurable* (subject to reasonable estimation) and *realizable* (expected to be collected). Nonexchange transactions that are not recognizable because they are not measurable must be disclosed in the governmental entity's financial statements.
(C) When property taxes are levied for one period, but the enforceable legal claim date or the payment due date(s) occurs in another period, GAAP requires that property tax revenue be recorded in the period for which the property tax is levied [GASB Cod. Sec. N50.115].
(D) When the provider of the resources prohibits the sale, disbursement, or consumption of resources for a specified period (or indefinitely, as in permanent endowment), or until a specified event has occurred, revenue should be recorded when the asset is received but the restriction should be disclosed in the entity's financial statements.

PASS-THROUGH GRANTS

Determining Fund Types for Reporting Pass-Through Grant Activity

Pass-through grants are "grants and other financial assistance received by a governmental entity to transfer to or spend on behalf of a secondary recipient." A secondary recipient is "the individual or organization, government or otherwise, that is the ultimate recipient of a pass-through grant, or another recipient organization that passes the grant through to the ultimate recipient." The governmental entity that receives the grant distributed to a secondary recipient is the government. (See also discussion of "subrecipients" previously in this chapter.)

For example, the federal government (the grantor government) may make a grant to a state government (recipient governmental entity) that is to be distributed by the state government to certain municipal governments (secondary recipients) within the state. The secondary recipient does not have to be a governmental entity, but rather could be individuals or nongovernmental organizations.

GASB Cod. Sec. N50.128 requires that cash pass-through grants generally be recorded simultaneously as revenue and expenditures or expenses in a governmental fund under *current GAAP*, or proprietary fund. Only in those instances when the recipient government functions as a cash conduit should a pass-through grant be accounted for in an agency fund. The GASB describes cash conduit activity as transmitting grantor-supplied moneys "without having administrative or direct financial involvement in the program." Applying the standard requires that a governmental entity evaluate its administrative and financial roles in a grant program.

The GASB takes the position that administrative involvement is based on whether the recipient government's role in the grant program constitutes an operational responsibility for the grant program. While there is no attempt to formally define administrative involvement, the GASB notes that the following activities constitute such involvement:

- Monitoring secondary recipients for compliance with specific requirements established by the program;
- Determining which secondary recipients are eligible for grant payments (even if eligibility criteria are established by the provider government), and
- Exercising some discretion in determining how resources are to be allocated.

OBSERVATION: These provisions also occur in determining administrative involvement with a fiduciary activity. For a further discussion on this issue, see Chapter 8.

Administrative involvement may occur before the receipt of the grant by the recipient government or after the grant is received. Both pre-grant activities and post-grant activities should be evaluated to determine whether the recipient government is exercising administrative involvement in the grant program.

A recipient governmental entity's role in a grant program is considered more than custodial when the entity has a direct financial involvement in the program. Direct financial involvement is defined in GASB Cod. Sec. 1300.131(b), footnotes 11 and 12 in the context of fiduciary funds. Footnote 12 refers to the provisions in GASB Cod. Sec. N50.128 as discussed in this section of the chapter. Therefore, similar provisions *could* apply to pass-through grants in suggesting that the entity's role is beyond that of custodial responsibility:

- The recipient government is required to provide matching funds, and
- The recipient government is responsible for disallowed costs.

The GASB does not require a recipient government to consider payments for administrative costs (an indirect financial involvement) when determining whether its role is more than custodial. However, if the indirect financial payments are more than incidental, the recipient government's participation satisfies the administrative involvement criteria described in the standard and, therefore, it would be inappropriate to account for the pass-through grant in a custodial fund.

GASB Cod. Sec. 2200.717-7 states that when a state receives a grant from the federal government and subsequently passes the resources to local governments for capital purposes, the state should report the receipt as an operational grant (program revenue) and not as a capital grant. A capital grant arises only "if it is restricted to the acquisition, construction, or improvement of the state's capital assets." The distributions to the localities are reported as an expenditure.

Fees for Pass-Through Grants. Certain governments may charge administrative fees related to pass-through grants. GASB Cod. Sec. N50.801 (AICPA Literature Cleared by the GASB) states that when a governmental entity receives a fee related to the administration of pass-through grants, the fee should be recorded as revenue.

On-Behalf Payments for Fringe Benefits and Salaries

GASB defines on-behalf payments for fringe benefits and salaries as "direct payments made by one entity (the paying entity or paying government) to a third-party recipient for the employees of another, legally separate entity (the employer entity or employer government)." They include payments made by governmental entities on behalf of nongovernmental entities and payments made by them on behalf of governmental entities and may be made for volunteers and paid employees of the employer entity.

The best example of an on-behalf payment is a pension contribution made by a state government (paying government) to the state's teachers' pension fund (third-party recipient) for employees of a school district (employer government) within the state. On-behalf payments also include payments by a governmental entity to volunteers of another governmental entity. For example, a state government may make pension payments or other fringe benefit payments for individuals who serve as volunteer firefighters for rural fire districts [GASB Cod. Sec. N50.129].

Employer Government Reporting of On-Behalf Payment for Fringe Benefits and Salaries. Employers should recognize revenue and expenditures (or expenses) for these payments. Revenue recognition is subject to the provisions of the pension and/or OPEB standards. For other on-behalf payments, the employer government recognizes revenue equal to the amounts that the third-party recipients of the payments received and that are receivable at year-end for the current fiscal year [GASB Cod. Secs. N50.130–.131].

Expenditures or Expenses. Employers should recognize expenditures or expenses, related assets, or liabilities, also in accordance with the pension and/or OPEB standards. For on-behalf payments for fringe benefits and salaries other than pensions or OPEB:

- If the employer government is not legally responsible for the payment, the employer should recognize expenditures or expenses equal to the amount recognized as revenue.
- If the employer government is legally responsible for the payment, the employer should follow accounting standards for that type of transaction to recognize expenditures or expenses and related liabilities or assets. For example, expenditures or expenses for on-behalf payments for pensions should be recognized and measured using pension accounting standards for state and local governmental employers.

PRACTICE POINT: Additional guidance on employer reporting of pensions and OPEB is in Chapter 13.

Additional Requirements for On-Behalf Payments for Salaries and Fringe Benefits Other than Pensions or OPEB. Employer governments will need to obtain information about the amount of such flows from the paying entity (or the third-party recipient). If cooperation between the entities cannot be achieved, best estimates should be done. Fiscal year adjustments may be necessary with receivables or payables declared based on the adjustment unless the payments occur within the first quarter of the new fiscal year. Allocation to individual funds is not required. However, the employer may choose to allocate to individual funds based on related salaries charged to the funds. Otherwise, the general fund is appropriate for reporting.

For the paying government, expenditures or expenses should be recorded in the same manner as similar cash grants. GASB Cod. Sec. N50.139 provides an example of a state government providing state aid to school districts as education expenditures. On-behalf payments of pension contributions for teachers would be also education expenditures [GASB Cod. Secs. N50.132–.139].

Electronic Benefit Transfers (Supplemental Nutrition Assistance Program)

The supplemental nutrition assistance program (SNAP) (formerly known as food stamps) is defined as "a federal program [Catalog of Federal Domestic Assistance (CFDA) program number 10.551] that is intended to improve the diets of members of low-income households by increasing their ability to purchase food." Currently, transfers of payments are provided by the federal government and are distributed directly to recipients electronically by agents (including local governments) of the state governments. Recipients spend the assistance at retail establishments, and the retailers deposit it with their banks.

REVENUES: EXCHANGE TRANSACTIONS

In an exchange transaction the governmental entity and the other party to the transaction exchange cash, goods, or services that are essentially of the same value. For example, revenue earned from providing water services to customers is an exchange transaction. Unlike nonexchange transactions, the GASB has not provided comprehensive guidance for the recognition of exchange transactions. The GASB has provided guidance for the recognition of investment income for certain investments, see Chapter 9 (see also previous **PRACTICE ALERT** at the introduction to this chapter on the GASB's *Revenue and Expense Recognition* Preliminary Views document).

Recording Exchange Transactions

Governmental Funds. Under *current GAAP,* like nonexchange transactions, exchange transactions should be recorded in a governmental fund when they are measurable, available, and collection is probable. For example, a governmental entity may sell a parcel of land to another party and receive a down payment and a three-year annual note for the balance of the purchase price. The down payment, because it is available to pay current expenditures, would be recorded as revenue of an "other source of financial resources" or a "special item" if it is unusual in nature and/or infrequent in occurrence and under the control of management, however, the subsequent installments would not be recorded as revenue until the cash is received.

Proprietary and Fiduciary Funds. A proprietary or fiduciary fund should recognize revenue on an accrual basis, meaning that revenue is considered realized when:

1. The earning process is complete or virtually complete and
2. An exchange has taken place.

Government-Wide Financial Statements. Revenues related to exchange transactions in a governmental entity's statement of activities should be based on accrual accounting concepts. Governmental activities as presented in the government-wide financial statements should be accounted for and reported based on all applicable pronouncements.

PRACTICE POINT: See discussion of exchange financial guarantees in Chapter 16.

PRACTICE ALERT: One of the main drivers behind the GASB's project on *Revenue and Expense Recognition* was the perceived lack of guidance on exchange and exchange-like transactions. As contained in previous **PRACTICE ALERT**s on the project, many of the transactions comprising what is current GAAP for revenue recognition are similar GAAP to what was in existence prior to the establishment of the GASB and the conceptual framework. In the future, this section of the chapter may expand based on the provisions of an exposure draft (or drafts) because of the project, if issued.

SALES, PLEDGES, AND INTRA-ENTITY TRANSFERS OF ASSETS AND FUTURE REVENUES

States and local governments may sell, pledge or transfer assets (primarily receivables) and specific future revenues. Commitments of future revenues also occur, even though the government does not have the specific resources yet. GAAP includes provisions for these transactions as they present risk to the government [GASB Cod. Sec. S20.101].

The provisions in this section of the chapter do not apply to sales of "rights" such as water access or wastewater capacity. GASB Cod. Sec. S20.701-1 limits the provisions in rights sales only to future cash flows and not access or capacity. Pledges of future revenues to secure bonds are in scope of these provisions in accordance with GASB Cod. Sec. S20.701-2.

Transactions May be Sales or Collateralized Borrowings

Receivables and assets may be sold or collateralized as part of a borrowing transaction. The determination of the accounting is dependent upon whether the government continues to be involved with the receivables or future revenues transferred. An important aspect of the determination is whether the selling or pledging government (the transferor government) retains or gives up control over the receivables or future revenues transferred [GASB Cod. Sec. S20.102].

The GASB provides an example of a sale of advertising revenue in a transit system for displays on busses and similar facilities. The system receives a lump-sum payment during the current year for the rights to semi-annual payments. The system then reports this transaction as a borrowing as there is an active involvement in collecting the advertising revenue. The cash flows from these revenues are not sold and the lump sum received by the district is a liability [GASB Cod. Sec. S20.702-1].

Assessing a Government's Continuing Involvement in Receivables and Future Revenues

The right to future cash flows from receivables should be reported as a sale if the government's continuing involvement with those receivables is terminated. A government no longer has continuing involvement in receivables if all the following criteria are met:

- The receivables are not limited by constraints imposed by the transferor government, such as the transferee's ability to subsequently sell or pledge the receivables.
- The transferor has no options or abilities to unilaterally substitute for or require specific accounts from the receivables transferred. There is no violation of the criterion if there are transfers made of defective accounts.
- The sale agreement is not cancelable by either party.
- The transferor government has been isolated from the receivables and the cash resulting from their collection. The criteria used to determine whether receivables have been isolated from the transferor government

(e.g., a separate legal standing between the transferee and the transferor) is discussed in the following paragraph [GASB Cod. Sec. S20.103].

To determine isolation of receivables, the following criteria should be used based on the provisions of GAAP. In many ways, the creation of a trust could achieve isolation:

- The transferee should have legal standing *separate from the transferor*. Legal separation should be assessed in a manner consistent with the approach for determining whether an organization is a legally separate entity as discussed in Chapter 4.

- Generally, banking arrangements should eliminate access by the transferor and its component units (other than the transferee) to the cash generated by collecting the receivables. Access is eliminated when payments on individual accounts are made directly to a custodial account maintained for the transferee's benefit. However, if the transferor continues to service the accounts or if obligors misdirect their payments on transferred accounts to the transferor:

  — The payments to the transferee should be made only from the resources generated by the specific receivables rather than from the transferor's own resources. The transferor should have no obligation to advance amounts to the transferee before it collects equivalent amounts from the underlying accounts.

  — Cash collected by the transferor on behalf of the transferee should be remitted to the transferee without significant delay. In addition, earnings on invested collections should be passed on to the transferee.

  — The transferor should consider proceeds received from the transferee as satisfaction of individual accounts. The transferor should indicate in its records which accounts have been transferred and which collections pertain to those accounts. For example, in a transaction involving delinquent taxes, the proceeds from the transferee should be accepted by the taxing body as satisfaction of the delinquent taxes owed by the individual property owners. Accordingly, the tax rolls should indicate that those taxes have been paid (or sold, or otherwise settled) and are no longer delinquent.

  — Provisions in the transfer agreement (or provided elsewhere in statutes, charters, or other governing documents or agreements) should protect the transferee from the claims of the transferor's creditors [GASB Cod. Sec. S20.104].

A common example is in GASB Cod. Sec. S20.704-1. In the fact pattern, a housing authority securitizes mortgage receivables it holds and services the accounts for the transferee. The housing authority remits cash after receiving the mortgage payments to the transferee and the housing authority cures delinquencies. The transaction is a sale as the transferor has no obligation to advance amounts to the transferee before collecting the equivalent amounts from the underlying accounts. This is a recourse provision, discussed later in this chapter.

A transaction relating to cash flows from specific future revenues that are exchanged for lump-sum proceeds should be reported as a sale if the government's continuing involvement with those revenues meets all the following criteria:

- The future generation of revenues will not be maintained by active involvement of the transferor government. Active involvement generally requires a substantive action or performance, whereas passive involvement in the generation of future revenues generally requires no substantive actions or performance by the government.
- The transferor government has released and has no restrictions on the transferee government's ability to subsequently sell or pledge the future cash flows.
- The transferor government has been isolated from cash resulting from the collection of the future revenues.
- There is no prohibition on the transfer or assignment of the original resources contained in the contract, agreement, or arrangement between the original resource provider and the transferor government.
- The sale agreement is not cancelable by either party [GASB Cod. Sec. S20.105].

There may be situations where involvement ends in the generation of the specific future revenues. However, the government remains involved with those revenues in some form. The government is actively involved if there is *substantive* performance by the government. Substantive performance in the generation of the specific future revenues is different from incidental activities that are performed to protect the revenue. Active involvement is indicated by the following occurrences:

1. The government produces or provides the goods or services that are exchanged for the revenues.
2. The government levies or assesses taxes, fees, or charges and can directly influence the revenue base or the rate(s) applied to that base to generate the revenues. For example, the revenue bases for property, sales, and income taxes are taxable real estate parcels, taxable retail sales, or taxable income, respectively. The taxing government can directly influence any of those bases by establishing minimum taxable levels, granting exemptions, providing credits, or excluding certain transactions. The taxing government may initiate, activate, or determine tax rates pertaining to each revenue base.
3. The government must submit applications for grants or contributions on an ongoing basis (rather than initial application or qualification), from other governments, organizations, or individuals to obtain the revenues.
4. The government is required to meet grant or contribution performance provisions to qualify for those revenues.

Active involvement in the generation of future revenues does *not* include the following:

- Holding title to revenue-producing assets (for leases, rents, or royalty income, for example);
- Owning a contractual right to a stream of future revenues (rights to tobacco settlement revenues, for example),
- Satisfying the "required characteristics" eligibility criterion discussed previously in this chapter for nonexchange transactions, or
- Agreeing to refrain from specified acts or transactions (e.g., agreeing to noncompetition restrictions) [GASB Cod. Secs. S20.106–.107].

A situation may involve naming rights in a publicly owned stadium. The government has sold the naming of a stadium to a for-profit entity. Annual payments are made to the stadium entity for ten years. The government may receive a lump-sum payment for the payments as well.

In this situation, there is no active involvement in the generation of the naming rights revenue. GASB Cod. Sec. S20.705-1 discusses how the fundamental or primary activity that generates revenues from the sale of public facility naming rights is affixing a specific name on specific facilities. Even though a naming rights agreement may contemplate or assume certain other activities, in this instance, those activities, per se, do not generate the naming rights revenue. They may generate revenues on their own (a contract with a professional sports team and the revenue it generates, for example), and if the cash flows from those revenues were "sold," one would conclude that the government remains actively involved in their generation. However, those revenues are not the subject of the sale of the cash flows in this agreement. As previously discussed, active involvement generally requires a substantive action or performance. Because affixing a name to a facility does not constitute an ongoing substantive action or performance, the public stadium does not remain actively involved in the primary activity that generates naming rights revenues.

The transaction would be reported as a sale of future revenues if the other criteria are met. If those criteria are met, the revenue from the sale would be deferred. Because all naming rights contracts do not include the same terms, obligations, or conditions, each agreement should be examined to determine whether different contract provisions should lead to a different conclusion about active involvement.

Accounting Transactions That Do Not Qualify as Sales

In general terms, when the criteria required for sales reporting are not met, the transaction should be reported as a collateralized borrowing by the transferor. Rather than a sale, these sales and future revenues should be considered for financial statement purposes as pledged rather than sold. If sale criteria are not met, then collateralized borrowing occurs and the following steps are taken by both the transferor and the transferee [GASB Cod. Secs. S20.108–.109]:

Transferor Government in a Collateralized Borrowing	Transferee Government in a Collateralized Borrowing
Does not derecognize receivables.	
Continues recognition of revenues pledged.	Recognizes a receivable for the amounts paid to the pledging government.
Recognizes liability for the proceeds received.	
Makes payments to reduce liability.	

Accounting for Transactions That Meet the Criteria to Be Reported as Sales

If the criteria required for sales reporting are met, the transaction should be reported as a sale:

- *Receivables*—In the sale of receivables, the selling government should remove the individual accounts at their carrying values and no longer recognize as assets the receivables sold.
- *Future revenues*—In the sale of future revenues, the proceeds should be reported by the selling government as either revenue, advances, or deferred inflows of resources in both the fund statements and the government-wide financial statements.

The transactions are handled differently for a transfer of assets within the same financial reporting entity as opposed to when the transferee is a government outside of the selling government's financial reporting entity. If the conditions for sale treatment are met, then the following steps are taken by both the transferor and the transferee government:

1. The transferor government (also known as the selling government) records the following:
   a. The government derecognizes the receivables,
   b. No asset is recognized to derecognize for future revenues, and
   c. The difference between proceeds and carrying value is as follows:
      i. On sale of receivables there is revenue recognition or a gain or loss, and
      ii. On sale of future revenues there is generally deferred inflows of resources.
2. The *transferee government (also known as purchasing government)* records the following:
   a. Intra-entity sale treatment has purchased receivables reported at carrying value and payments to the selling government for rights to future revenues are reported as a deferred outflow of resources.
   b. Outside of the reporting entity the asset (rights) is recorded at cost and amortized over the life of the transfer agreement. The receivables and revenue are reported by the transferee government specific to the type of revenue acquired when met [GASB Cod. Secs. S20.110–.111].

A transferee government should not report an asset and related revenue until recognition criteria appropriate to that type of revenue are met. Instead, the transferee government should report the amount paid as a deferred outflow of resources to be recognized over the duration of the sale agreement. The transferor government should report the amount received from the intra-entity sale as a deferred inflow of resources in its government-wide and fund financial statements and recognize the amount as revenue over the duration of the sale agreement.

Transfers of Capital and Financial Assets and Future Revenues Within the Same Financial Reporting Entity

If assets and future revenues are transferred within the same financial reporting entity, the following accounting occurs when the asset transfers:

- The transferee recognizes the assets or future revenues at the carrying value recorded by the transferor.
- The difference between the amount paid (excluding any amounts that would be refundable) and the carrying value of the receivables transferred are reported as a gain or loss by the transferor and as a revenue (or expenditure or expense) by the transferee in their separately issued financial statements.
- In the financial statements of the reporting entity, the amount is a transfer or a subsidy as appropriate.

GASB Cod. Sec. S20.708-1 reminds practitioners when a capital asset is transferred within the same financial reporting entity, the capital asset is reported at historical cost. The transfer would not result in the historical cost changing. Therefore, the recipient would report the asset at historical cost and the accumulated depreciation. If there are different capitalization thresholds between the entity which would result in a transfer of an asset that was never capitalized, the carryover basis is still applicable in accordance with GASB Cod. Sec. S20.708-2. Therefore, expense and revenue may occur.

Transfers to Defined Benefit Plans (Pensions or OPEB). For transfers to defined benefit plans (pensions or OPEB) within the same reporting entity, any difference between the amount paid by the pension plan or OPEB plan (exclusive of amounts that may be refundable) and the carrying value of the assets transferred should be reported as:

- An *employer* contribution or a nonemployer contributing entity contribution to the pension plan or OPEB plan in accordance with the requirements of GASB Cod. Sec. P20 or GASB Cod. Sec. P50, as applicable, in the separately issued statements of the employer or nonemployer contributing entity and in the financial statements of the reporting entity, and
- An *employer* contribution or a nonemployer contributing entity contribution in accordance with the requirements of GASB Cod. Sec. Pe5 or GASB Cod. Sec. Po50, as applicable, in the stand-alone statements of the pension plan or OPEB plan and in the financial statements of the reporting entity.

> **PRACTICE POINT:** See Chapter 13 on employer reporting of pensions and OPEB, and Chapter 22 for plan reporting.

> **PRACTICE POINT:** These provisions have become highly controversial in some instances. Governments have considered transferring capital assets to defined benefit pension plans to satisfy contribution requirements.

Contributions to plans are required by many state laws to be in cash. GASB Cod. Sec. S20.708-3 contains a fact pattern when a contribution of a government owned building is made to a pension plan that is part of the same reporting entity. The plan would report a capital asset for the carrying value of the building and an addition (a contribution) for the carrying value of the building, less any amount paid by the pension plan). In an extreme case, a government could conceivably contribute infrastructure to a pension plan using the same accounting and achieving the same results.

> *Caution*: Unless the contribution is in cash (and/or generates cash flow), such activity would potentially raise a pension or OPEB liability due to the lack of cash, which would depress the discount rate and increase the liability.

Future Revenue Transfers. If there is an intra-entity sale of future revenues, the transferor government has no carrying value for the rights sold as no assets have been recognized for the revenue. The transferee government has no asset or revenue until the revenue can be recognized. Instead, the transferee government reports a deferred outflow of resources which will then be expensed over the duration of the sale agreement. The transferor government reports a deferred inflow of resources in the government-wide and fund financial statements, recognizing revenue over the duration of the sale agreement.

These provisions apply to both blended and discretely presented component units [GASB Cod. Secs. S20.112 -114].

Other Guidance for Sales

Amortizing Deferred Inflows of Resources and Deferred Outflows of Resources. The deferred inflows of resources and deferred outflows of resources created in the sale agreement are recognized as revenue or expense or expenditure over the life of the sale agreement using a systematic and rational method. Recognition could involve a ratio of proceeds received as a percentage of the total future revenues sold by the transferee. Some governments use the effective interest method if collectability is assured, and the period lasts more than one year [GASB Cod. Sec. S20.115].

Residual Interests from Sales. The transferor government may receive a note for the right to collections that exceed a minimum threshold. The note or right may relate to debt service due from the transferee. The note or right is a residual interest and is an asset. The recognition is based on the type of collection or revenue that is due in the future as follows:

- *Excess receivable collections*: The prime consideration with excess receivable collections is the likelihood of realization. Residual interests recognized in the period in which the sale occurred should be treated as an adjustment of the gain or loss (or revenues in governmental funds). Residual interests recognized in subsequent periods should be reported as revenues.
- *Excess future revenues*: The prime consideration is when the asset recognition criteria appropriate to the specific type of revenue that underlies the note or certificate have been met. Revenue recognition of the residual interest also would occur then.

Recourse and Other Liabilities. A transferee government has a liability for its obligation to remit residual interests from sales. The transferor government recognizes estimated liabilities arising from the purchase and sale agreement (usually involving recourse obligations or repurchase commitments) when the information available prior to the issuance of the financial statements indicates that it is:

- *Probable* that a liability has been incurred at the date of the financial statements, *and*
- The amount of the obligation can be reasonably estimated.

These are the same provisions required to recognize many forms of liabilities [GASB Cod. Sec. S20.116].

Pledges of Future Revenues—But Resources are not Received by the Pledging Government. Charters, statutes, and other requirements may bar (or limit) governments from issuing debt. But the governments may be allowed to create component units or use existing component units for this purpose. In the situation where the debt is issued by the component unit, the government pledges all or a portion of a specific future revenue stream to the debt-issuing component unit without establishing itself as primarily or secondarily obligated for the component unit's debt. The debt-issuing component unit then pledges those future payments from the pledging government as security for its debt.

When the time the pledge agreement is made, the pledging government should not recognize a liability, and the debt-issuing component unit should not recognize a receivable for the future revenues pledged. The pledging government should continue to recognize revenue from the pledged amounts and should recognize a liability to the debt-issuing component unit and an expenditure or expense simultaneously with the recognition of the revenues that are pledged. The debt-issuing component unit should recognize revenue when the pledging government is obligated to make the payments [GASB Cod. Secs. S20.117–.118].

PRACTICE POINT: GASB Statement No. 99 (*Omnibus 2022*) clarified these provisions. The debt-issuing component unit referred to in the previous paragraph be clarified to refer to only *blended* component units. Specifically, when a primary government pledges the future cash flows of specific revenues as security for the debt issued by a *blended component unit*, at the time the pledge agreement is made, the primary government would not recognize a "due to," and the debt-issuing *blended* component unit would not recognize a "due from" in the reporting entity financial statements (or a receivable in the separate financial statements of the component unit) for the future revenues pledged. The pledging government should continue to recognize revenue from the pledged amounts and should recognize a due to the debt-issuing blended component unit and a transfer out simultaneously with the recognition of the revenues that are pledged in the reporting entity financial statements. The debt-issuing blended component unit should recognize a transfer in when the pledging government is obligated to make the payments in the reporting entity financial statements (or revenue in the separate financial statements of the component unit).

Note Disclosure of Future Revenues Sold

In the year of the sale, governments that sell future revenue streams should disclose in the notes to financial statements information about the specific revenues sold, including:

- Identification of the specific revenue sold, including the approximate amount, and the significant assumptions used in determining the approximate amount,
- The period the sale applies to,
- The relationship of the sold amount to the total for the specific revenue, if estimable—that is, the proportion of the specific revenue stream that has been sold, and
- A comparison of the proceeds of the sale and the present value of the future revenues sold, including the significant assumptions used in determining the present value.

Note Disclosure of Future Revenues Pledged

For each period in which the secured debt remains outstanding, GAAP requires the pledging governments to disclose in the notes to financial statements information about specific revenues pledged, including:

- Identification of the specific revenue pledged and the approximate amount of the pledge. Generally, the approximate amount of the pledge would equal the remaining principal and interest requirements of the secured debt,
- Identification of, and general purpose for, the debt secured by the pledged revenue,
- The term of the commitment—that is, the period during which the revenue will not be available for other purposes,
- The relationship of the pledged amount to the total for the specific revenue, if estimable—that is, the proportion of the specific revenue stream that has been pledged, and
- A comparison between the pledged revenues recognized during the period and the principal and interest requirements for the debt that is directly or indirectly collateralized by those revenues. For this disclosure,

pledged revenues recognized during the period may be presented net of specified operating expenses, based on the provisions of the pledge agreement, however, the amounts should not be netted in the financial statements.

The disclosure requirements for pledged future revenues are not required for legally separate entities (such as component units) that report as stand-alone business-type activities whose operations are financed primarily by a single major revenue source. For example, the disclosure requirements would not apply to the stand-alone financial statements of a water utility district whose single major source of revenue (water charges to customers) is pledged for repayment of collateralized debt of the district [GASB Cod. Secs. S20.119–.120].

PRACTICE POINT: Disclosure of asset pledges are discussed in Chapter 12.

Exhibit 17-2 is an example of the reporting of a sale of delinquent receivables.

EXHIBIT 17-2
EXAMPLE: SALE OF DELINQUENT RECEIVABLES

Facts and assumptions: A County (the seller) agrees to sell delinquent taxes due to another governmental entity (the purchaser). The seller County received $2,500,000 in exchange for tax receivables/liens totaling $4,000,000. The County's allowance for uncollectible accounts pertaining to those tax receivables is $1,000,000, resulting in a net carrying value of $3,000,000. The sale agreement stipulates that the liens are sold without recourse except that the County has an obligation with respect to liens found to be defective. For defective liens, the County is required to:

1. Perfect the liens,
2. Reacquire the liens from the purchaser, or
3. Deliver to the purchaser substantially equivalent liens in substitution.

NOTE: Perfected liens are binding with an enforceable claim filed with an appropriate tax or legal entity such as the County clerk's office in this example. The lien is a form of collateral.

Conclusion: This transaction meets the criteria to be recognized as a sale.

Accounting in the year of the sale: The seller County reduces property taxes receivable by $4,000,000, reduces the allowance for uncollectible accounts by $1,000,000, and recognizes a loss on the sale of $500,000 (the carrying value of $3,000,000 less the proceeds of $2,500,000) in the government-wide statement of activities. In its governmental funds prior to the sale, the seller County was reporting a zero-net carrying value for the delinquent taxes receivable because they were either deemed to be uncollectible ($1,000,000) or deferred under the availability criterion ($3,000,000).

Therefore, the entire amount of the proceeds ($2,500,000) is recognized as revenue and the remaining net receivable and related deferred inflows of resource amounts are eliminated.

The seller County has determined that if any liens are found to be defective, it would first attempt to perfect the liens and, if unable to do so, provide acceptable substitutions. The County believes it is not probable that it would repurchase defective liens and therefore does not recognize a liability.

Accounting in future years: If any of the tax liens are subsequently found to be defective and it is probable that the seller county would reacquire those liens, a liability and an expenditure or expense would be recognized, provided that the amount of the repurchase obligation is measurable. At the same time, the county would add back the reacquired tax liens receivable and reduce the expense by the estimated collectible value of those liens. In the governmental funds, either the expenditure would be reduced if the receivable were considered available or related deferred inflow of resources would be established.

TAX ABATEMENT DISCLOSURES

Tax Abatement Disclosures

GASB Cod. Sec. T10 (*Tax Abatements*) focuses on tax abatement *disclosures*, rather than the financial reporting of the effect of tax abatements.

Tax abatements for financial reporting are defined in GASB Cod. Sec. T10.102 as an agreement in which the government promises to forego tax revenues and the individual or entity promises to subsequently take a specific action that contributes to economic development or otherwise benefits the government or its citizens. A common example is a business receiving a tax abatement for years for locating a factory in an area and hiring a specific minimum number of permanent full-time positions.

Many governments produce reports about tax abatement information related to economic development. However, the reports may only provide a small amount of information about how the abatements may affect the government's financial position and results of operations or constrain the ability to raise taxes in the future. Another frequent practice is when a tax abatement is forced on a government by a larger government on the local government's behalf without its consent. Due to law or regulation, a state or a county may force a tax abatement on a city or special district, lowering its tax base temporarily (or permanently), with the hope of raising other forms of local taxation and fees through increased economic activity.

Tax abatements may also be disguised in many forms. They may be contained in a budget, regulation, ordinance, or law as a tax expenditure, tax credit, tax expense, or a similar action by the government. GAAP requires governments to consider a transaction's substance, not its form or title, in determining whether

17,050 *Specific Accounting and Reporting Issues*

the activity meets the definition of a tax abatement for the purposes of disclosure [GASB Cod. Sec. T10.102].

Tax abatements may also be subject to nondisclosure provisions as part of a negotiation process between a business and a government until the agreement becomes final. This is so the government does not lose the business to another competing government.

Various activities of governments may result in disclosure dependent upon the nature of the scenario. GASB Cod. Secs. T10.701-1–.701-9 contain the following fact patterns and results:

Fact Pattern	Tax Abatement or Not a Tax Abatement
Tax increment financing (TIF) to encourage economic development. Bonds in the TIF finance infrastructure improvements. A baseline sales tax is charged in the area and the taxes pay the debt service.	*Not a tax abatement.* It is not an agreement with an individual or entity. Also, it is not a reduction in tax.
A development agreement with a government includes a developer constructing a building, a baseline for property tax revenues in the area being established prior to the start of the project and the developer receives an amount from additional property tax revenues above the baseline based on certain costs incurred related to the building.	*Tax abatement.* However, it may be labeled a TIF. A specific action is occurring for economic development and the developer is receiving revenues above baseline.
In the previous example, the building becomes an asset of the government and not the developer.	*Not a tax abatement.* The taxes are not foregone, and an asset of the government is being improved.
A state agrees with a retailer to open 10 stores in the state. The retailer retains 40% of sales tax revenue for the first five years.	*Tax abatement.* The state is forgoing revenues for five years.
A state shares a portion of the gas tax with local governments. Agreements are also signed with gas stations to retain a portion of the gas tax to pay for ecologically sensitive equipment.	*Tax abatement.* The tax revenue has been reduced. However, only the state government would report the abatement. The local governments only receive shared revenue, not direct tax revenue.
A government agrees with a manufacturer to locate in the jurisdiction. No tax levy occurs for 10 years to the manufacturer. The government has a property tax cap limiting growth. Due to the cap, the overall revenues will not be reduced.	*Tax abatement.* There is a forgoing of revenue under the agreement.
A development authority has been authorized by a local government to agree with individuals and entities that result in the forgoing of tax revenue.	*Tax abatement.* Disclosures are required by the local government and not the authority.
A government agrees with the owner of a property to freeze the property's assessed value for 10 years. The property owner agrees to retain the property's purpose during the period.	*Tax abatement.* Due to the agreement to maintain the property's purpose (and use).

Fact Pattern	Tax Abatement or Not a Tax Abatement
A state government provides tax credits to individuals and entities that benefits the state. The tax credits reduce each party's tax liability. Credits may be sold or transferred to others.	*Tax abatement.* The forgoing of revenue is occurring, even though credits may be utilized by some entity other than the original recipients.

Note Disclosure of Tax Abatements

GAAP requires five broad categories of disclosure related to tax abatements in the notes to the financial statements:

1. Distinguish disclosures resulting from those finalized by the reporting government and those finalized by other governments that reduce the reporting government's tax revenues,
2. Present tax abatements either individually or on an aggregated basis,
3. Organize tax abatement agreements by each major tax abatement program (e.g., economic development, television, and film production),
4. Organize tax abatement agreements by the government that formalized the tax abatement and the specific tax being abated, and
5. Disclose the period in which a tax abatement is entered into and continue until the tax abatement agreement expires, unless there is a commitment made by the government other than to reduce taxes as part of a tax abatement agreement (e.g., a government may commit to improve a highway for better access to a stadium, rather than abating taxes) [GASB Cod. Sec. T10.103].

Governments may choose to disclose information about individual tax abatement agreements or present them in the aggregate. If a government chooses to present individual tax abatement agreements, it should be only those agreements that meet or exceed a quantitative threshold selected by the government. For example, a government may choose to present individual tax abatement agreements that exceed $100,000. This threshold should be disclosed as part of the notes [GASB Cod. Sec. T10.104].

Additional note disclosures will include the following information about tax abatements that governments agree to:

- A brief description, including the names and purposes of tax abatement programs, the specific taxes being abated, the authority under which the agreements are entered into, the criteria of eligibility, the mechanism of reducing taxes (e.g., by reducing assessed value, a specific dollar amount, or percentage of taxes), provisions for recapturing abated taxes, including the conditions when abated taxes become eligible for recapture, and finally the types of commitments made by the recipients of tax abatements,
- The gross dollar amount on an accrual basis that reduced tax revenues during the reporting period because of the tax abatements,
- If amounts are received or are receivable from other governments in association with the abatement, the name(s) of the government(s), the

authority under which the amounts were or will be paid, and the dollar amount received or receivable from other governments),
- If there are commitments made by the government other than to reduce taxes, a description of the types of commitments made and the most significant individual commitments made (this disclosure will be made until the government has fulfilled its commitment),
- As discussed above, the quantitative threshold set by the government used to determine which agreements to disclose individually, and
- If information is legally prohibited from being disclosed, the government would disclose the general nature of the tax abatement information omitted and the specific source of the legal prohibition [GASB Cod. Sec. T10.105].

Similar information will be disclosed for governments that are forced to abate taxes by other governments. Discretely presented component units may also disclose this information. However, the primary government would disclose a discretely presented component unit's tax abatements only when it is essential for fair presentation. Such component units may also force an abatement on a primary government. In these cases, the primary government would disclose the abatements like the description above [GASB Cod. Secs. T10.106–.108].

PRACTICE POINT: Disclosing this information in accordance with GAAP may require a reporting government to analyze records in which such agreements exist, including legal documents, contracts, and similar agreements. These records may not be readily available to preparers due to confidentiality agreements and agreements made by other governments. Coordination within a government and between governments and larger governments may be needed when such coordination has not previously existed. The information required by GAAP may be difficult to obtain from other governments. Empirically, some of this information may already be disclosed in the media or on a website maintained by the government or a larger government. The disclosure of this information may point preparers to the source of where records are maintained for such abatements. Care must also be taken in this disclosure as some tax abatements may be considered politically motivated (favoritism).

CHAPTER 18
EXPENSES AND EXPENDITURES: NONEXCHANGE AND EXCHANGE TRANSACTIONS

Chapter References:

GASB Statement Nos. 6, 24, 33, 34, 36-38, 42, 51, 62, 65, 72, 84, 85, 100

GASB *Implementation Guide*

GASB Technical Bulletin 2020-01

GASB Concepts Statement Nos. 4, 6

NCGA Statement No. 1, Interpretation No. 3

INTRODUCTION

PRACTICE ALERT: The GASB released a *Preliminary Views* (PV) document in the spring of 2020 detailing the Board's initial views on Revenue and Expense Recognition. The project's scope includes classification, recognition, and measurement of revenues and expenses, unless specifically excluded from the project. As of the date of publication, the specific *exclusions* from the project are:

Capital asset (and related debt) activity	Purchases, sales, donations, and nonmonetary exchanges of capital assets, as well as depreciation expense, interest income or expense, and gains and losses derived from impairment or remeasurement of capital assets, inventory, or long-term debt
Certain financial instruments	Investments, financial guarantees, derivative instruments, financings such as leases, and insurance
Postemployment Benefits	All guidance and projects related to pensions, OPEB, compensated absences, and termination benefits

Seven existing GASB statements are currently within scope. More statements could be added as part of further deliberations.

The revenue and expense model in the Board's PV assumes the following:

- Inflows and outflows are of equal importance in resource flows statements.
- Inflows and outflows should be classified independently, and not in relationship to each other.
- The government is an economic entity and not an agent of the citizenry.

- Symmetrical considerations, to the extent possible, should be included in revenue and expense recognition.
- A consistent viewpoint, from the resource provider perspective, will be applied in the revenue and expense analysis.

The GASB has a preliminary view of two distinct categories of revenue and expense recognition (known as the *AB model*) which are described as follows:

Category	Description	Types of Transactions	Examples of Transactions
A	An acquisition coupled with a sacrifice (or a sacrifice coupled with an acquisition). The acquisition coupled with the sacrifice can be identified as rights and obligations that articulate in equivalent terms, that is, the rights and obligations are dependent on the existence of each other, such that there is a remedy for failure of either party to meet the terms of the arrangement. While the right represents the right to receive consideration in a transaction, the obligation represents the requirement to perform via action or inaction.	May include reciprocal or nonreciprocal transactions. Focus is on a *binding arrangement*. Binding arrangements include: • Mutual assent between the parties of capacity in the transaction, • Identification of rights and obligations, which are substantive, by the parties to the transaction, and • Dependency of the rights and obligations in the binding arrangement on each other's existence.	• Fees for specific services (water, tuition, transit fares, lottery) • Eligibility-driven grants • Research grants • Revolving loans • Medicaid fee for service • Labor/Payroll • Contracts and purchase orders

Expenses and Expenditures: Nonexchange and Exchange Transactions 18,003

Category	Description	Types of Transactions	Examples of Transactions
B	A single flow, that is an acquisition without a sacrifice or a sacrifice without an acquisition. The obligation would represent the requirement to provide resources. The right would represent the ability to receive or collect resources.	Binding arrangements, including enabling legislation and purpose-driven grants, along with anything else that is not Category A (most taxation).	• Taxes • Special assessments • Regulatory fees and licenses • Punitive fees, fines, penalties • Donations • Purpose-restricted grants • Medicaid supplementary payments • Capital fees (passenger facility charges, developer fees, impact fees, and similar) • Individual assistance (SNAP) • Certain payments in lieu of taxation • Escheat revenues • Government-mandated transactions

The Board has the preliminary view that the recognition of revenues and expenses utilizes the following flow:

Revenues	Expenses
1. Identify if there is an increase in an asset	1. Identify if there is an increase in a liability
2. If not an asset, identify if there is a liability	2. If not a liability, identify if there is an asset
3. Identify if the asset meets the definition of a deferred inflow of resources	3. Identify if the liability meets the definition of a deferred outflow of resources
4. Recognize revenues	4. Recognize expenses

There are many nuances and application issues of the revenues and expense recognition model to categories A and B. Deliberations are continuing with an exposure draft expected for release by March 2025. Any final Statement may not be approved until June 2027.

Most governmental entities are involved in many nonexchange and exchange (and exchange-like) transactions.

Specific Accounting and Reporting Issues

This chapter discusses the basic principles that governmental entities should follow to report the uses of fund balances in governmental funds resulting in expenditures, and the consumption of net position proprietary funds, fiduciary funds, and government-wide financial statements resulting in expenses. To provide the framework for establishing accounting principles related to the elements of financial statements and their measurement and recognition within the financial statements, the GASB has issued GASB:CS-4 (*Elements of Financial Statements*) and GASB:CS-6 (*Measurement of Elements of Financial Statements*).

GASB:CS-6 discusses both measurement approaches and measurement attributes. A measurement approach determines whether an asset or liability presented in a financial statement should be:

1. Reported at an amount that reflects a value at the date that the asset was acquired, or the liability was incurred, or

2. Remeasured and reported at an amount that reflects a value at the date of the financial statements.

A measurement attribute is the feature or characteristic of the asset or liability that is measured. Changes in remeasured or initial amounts, as defined here, would potentially be an indicator of an increase of inflows, outflows, deferred inflows of resources, deferred outflows of resources, assets, or liabilities.

There are two measurement approaches in GAAP:

1. *Initial-transaction-date-based measurement (initial amount)*. This is the transaction price or amount assigned when an asset was acquired, or a liability was incurred, including subsequent modifications to that price or amount, such as through depreciation or impairment. This approach is more commonly known as "historical cost" or "entry price," but those terms are not quite accurate.

2. *Current-financial-statement-date-based measurement (remeasured amount)*. This is the amount assigned when an asset or liability is remeasured as of the financial statement date. This is sometimes known as "fair value," "current value," or "carrying value." However, that is also not quite accurate because those values are attributes.

Therefore, there are four measurement attributes that are used in GAAP:

1. *Historical cost* is the price paid to acquire an asset or the amount received pursuant to the incurrence of a liability in an actual exchange transaction. The understanding of this attribute is well-known and documented.

2. *Fair value* is the price that would be received to sell an asset or paid to transfer a liability in an orderly transaction between market participants at the measurement date.

3. *Replacement cost* is the price that would be paid to acquire an asset with equivalent service potential in an orderly market transaction at the measurement date.

4. *Settlement amount* is the amount at which an asset could be realized, or a liability could be liquidated with the counterparty, other than in an active market.

"*Acquisition value*" may also be used in certain transactions. Acquisition value is an entry price and is the price that *would be* paid to acquire an asset with equivalent service potential in an orderly market transaction at the acquisition date, or the amount at which a liability could be liquidated with the counterparty at the acquisition date. Acquisition value is limited to donated capital assets, donated works of art, historical treasures and similar assets, or capital assets that a government receives relating to a public-private partnership.

GASB:CS-4 defines seven accounting elements that are to be applied to a government. The seven elements are the fundamental components of financial statements and can be organized by the specific financial statement they relate to.

The concepts statement provides that the expenditure or expense element of the "resource flows (change) statements" is defined as an "outflow of resources" that results in a consumption of net position by the entity that is applicable to the reporting period.

The consumption of net position (outflow) is defined as the using up of net position that result in:

- A decrease in assets exceeding any related decrease in liabilities, or
- An increase in liabilities exceeding any related increase in assets.

Examples of consumption of resources include:

- Using cash resources to make direct aid payments to eligible recipients (because existing cash resources of the entity have been consumed),
- Purchasing of goods and services, and
- Using the labor of employees to provide government services for which payment will be made in the next reporting period (because the entity has consumed employee labor resources that were directly acquired from the employees).

Governmental entities that provide resources that are based on nonexchange transactions must record both expenses (for proprietary and fiduciary funds, and government-wide financial statement purposes) and expenditures (for governmental fund financial statement purposes). The same-timing recognition criteria for determining an expense under the accrual basis of accounting are applicable to determining when expenditures should be recognized under the modified accrual basis of accounting.

This chapter discusses the basic rules that governmental entities should follow to report these transactions in governmental funds, proprietary and fiduciary funds, and the government-wide financial statements.

EXPENSES AND EXPENDITURES: NONEXCHANGE TRANSACTIONS

PRACTICE ALERT: As discussed in previous chapters, the GASB's *Financial Reporting Model Improvements* Exposure Draft proposes to change the measurement focus and basis of accounting for governmental funds to the short-term financial resources measurement focus and modified accrual basis of accounting.

PRACTICE POINT: Readers of this chapter may also want to reach Chapter 17 to fully understand the nature of nonexchange and exchange transactions.

The two parties in a nonexchange transaction are the provider of the resources and the receiver of the resources. The provider of the resources could be the federal governmental, a state or local government, or a nongovernmental entity (such as an individual or business entity). The receiver of the resources could be a state or local government, or a nongovernmental entity. What distinguishes a nonexchange transaction from an exchange transaction is that in a *non exchange* transaction a government "either gives value (benefit) to another party *without* directly receiving equal value in exchange or receives value (benefit) from another party without directly giving equal value in exchange" [GASB Cod. Sec. N50.104].

GASB Cod. Sec. N50 provides accounting and reporting standards for the following four categories of nonexchange transactions of which only two (potentially) have expense and expenditure transactions:

- Government-mandated nonexchange transactions, and
- Voluntary nonexchange transactions.

Derived tax revenue and imposed nonexchange revenues do not give rise to governmental expenses or expenditures. The governmental entity is always the recipient of resources and never the provider of resources under these types of nonexchange transactions.

Nonexchange transactions are fundamentally controlled by legislation, contractual requirements, or both, and this factor is essential in determining when expense and expenditures from nonexchange transactions should be recognized. Thus, expenses and expenditures related to government-mandated nonexchange transactions and voluntary nonexchange transactions should be recognized when all eligibility requirements established by the relevant authority have been satisfied.

The relevant eligibility requirements in a government-mandated nonexchange transaction are generally based on enabling legislation and related regulations. Those laws and regulations often identify purpose restrictions that apply to how the resources provided under the program are to be used. The relevant eligibility requirements in a voluntary nonexchange transaction may arise from enabling legislation or from contractual agreements with a nongovernmental entity. For example, a nongovernmental entity, such as a corporation or an individual, may provide resources to a governmental entity, but the provisions of those resources may depend on several eligibility factors contained in the donor agreement [GASB Cod. Sec. N50.118].

The standards contained in GASB Cod. Sec. N50 generally apply to both revenue and expense recognition at the same time. That is, when both parties to the nonexchange transactions are governmental entities, the same standards that are used to determine whether revenue should be recognized by the recipient government are used to determine when an expense should be recognized by the provider governmental entity.

Time Requirements and Purpose Restrictions

To determine when expenses or expenditures related to nonexchange transactions should be recorded and presented in a governmental entity's financial statements, time requirements and purpose restrictions should be considered. Time requirements and purpose restrictions do not have the same effect on the recognition of expense or expenditure in a governmental entity's financial statements.

Time Requirements. Resources may be provided by one governmental entity to another governmental entity with the requirement that the resources be used in (or begin to be used in) a specified period(s). GASB Cod. Sec. N50 notes that "time requirements specify the period or periods when resources are required to be used or when use may begin."

Time requirements may be imposed by enabling legislation. For example, legislation may identify the period in which a recipient government can use a grant, or it may require that resources be used over a specified number of years. In other instances, time requirements imposed by the provider government may require that the resources provided never be used (permanent endowment) or that they cannot be used until a specified event has occurred.

PRACTICE POINT: The federal Coronavirus Aid, Relief, and Economic Security (CARES) Act of 2020 allowed certain expenses incurred by recipients from prior to when the Act was passed as eligible costs for reimbursement from Coronavirus Act Relief Funds (CRF). It is one of the few times in federal grant operations that costs incurred prior to a grant award were deemed allowable costs. Another time is in the case of a federally declared disaster, which is usually declared prior to when funds are reimbursed from the federal emergency management agency (FEMA). A substantial portion of CRF funds in the CARES Act uses the FEMA mechanism for allowable costs.

When a nonexchange transaction is subject to a timing requirement, that requirement generally affects the period in which expenses and expenditures are recognized by the provider government.

As discussed later, the effect that a timing requirement has on a nonexchange transaction is dependent on whether the transaction is:

- A government-mandated nonexchange transaction or a voluntary nonexchange transaction or
- An imposed nonexchange revenue transaction.

Purpose Restrictions. Purpose restrictions relate to the use of resources that arise from a nonexchange transaction. For example, a party may receive a grant that may be used only to purchase an emergency communication system. Because of the nature of purpose restrictions, expenses, and expenditures (as well as the related liability) related to nonexchange transactions should be recognized in a governmental entity's financial statements without taking into consideration purpose restrictions. That is, a purpose restriction does not affect the timing of the recognition of a nonexchange transaction. In fact, the GASB notes that a purpose restriction cannot be met unless a nonexchange transaction has taken place [GASB Cod. Secs. N50.109–.111].

Although purpose restrictions do not affect the timing of an expense or expenditures by the provider government, a recipient government must disclose the restriction in its financial statements. The discussion of how this is accomplished is detailed in Chapter 17.

Purpose restrictions can be related to both government-mandated nonexchange transactions and voluntary nonexchange transactions.

Government-Mandated Nonexchange Transactions

Expenditures and expenses from government-mandated nonexchange transactions arise when a governmental entity at one level provides resources to another governmental entity at a lower level, and the higher-level governmental entity "requires [the other]government to use them for a specific purpose or purposes established in the provider's enabling legislation."

For example, a state government (provider government) may make resources available to a county government (recipient government). GASB Cod. Sec. N50 notes that government-mandated nonexchange expense or expenditure transactions have the following principal characteristics [GASB Cod. Sec. N50.104]:

- The provider government requires that the recipient government institute a specific program (or facilitate the performance of a specific program) conducted by the recipient government or nongovernmental entity (secondary recipient entity), and
- Certain performance requirements must be fulfilled (other than the provision of cash or other assets in advance).

Because the resources provided by the providing government must be used for a purpose, resources received under a government-mandated nonexchange transaction always create a purpose restriction. In many instances, the resources are also subject to eligibility requirements, including time restrictions. An example of a government-mandated nonexchange transaction includes the requirement by a state government that a local government provide educational counseling to certain disadvantaged groups.

Mandating that a lower-level government entity establish a specific program does not create a government-mandated nonexchange transaction itself. The higher-level government must fund the program. The standards do not apply to unfunded mandates established by a government because these types of programs do not involve the exchange of resources [GASB Cod. Sec. N50.fn. 4].

In a government-mandated nonexchange transaction, when the two governmental entities that are involved in the transaction are the state and a local government, they are both subject to GASB accounting and reporting standards. For this reason, the standards apply to the recognition of revenue (by the recipient government) and the recognition of an expenditure or expense (by the provider government).

In a government-mandated nonexchange transaction, the provider government should recognize an expense or expenditure when all eligibility requirements (which include time requirements) are satisfied. The eligibility requirements are categorized as follows [GASB Cod. Sec. N50.117]:

- Required characteristics of recipients,
- Time requirements, and
- Reimbursements.

These requirements are also discussed in detail in Chapter 17.

GASB Cod. Secs. N50.116, and 118 require resources transmitted *before the eligibility requirements are met* (excluding time requirements) to be reported as assets by the provider, instead of expenses or expenditures.

GASB does not name the account for this transaction, but a caption such as "advances provided to other governments" may be usable. Outflows of resources before time requirements are met but after all other eligibility requirements have been met should be reported as a deferred outflow of resources by the provider government.

Voluntary Nonexchange Transactions

Voluntary nonexchange transactions arise from "legislative or contractual agreements, other than exchanges, entered into willingly by two or more parties." A voluntary nonexchange transaction can be based on either a written or oral agreement, assuming the oral agreement is verifiable. The principal characteristics of voluntary nonexchange transactions are listed below [GASB Cod. Secs. N50.104, N50.fn. 5]:

- They are not imposed on the provider or the recipient.
- Satisfaction of eligibility requirements (other than the provision of cash or other assets in advance) is necessary for a transaction to occur.

In a voluntary nonexchange transaction, a governmental entity may be the recipient or the provider of the resources, and the parties to the transaction may be another governmental entity or a nongovernmental entity, such as an individual or a not-for-profit organization. Examples of voluntary nonexchange transactions include certain grants, some entitlements, and donations. These types of nonexchange transactions may involve purpose restrictions and/or time requirements and often the arrangement requires that resources must be returned to the provider if purpose restrictions or eligibility requirements are contravened after the voluntary nonexchange transaction has been recognized by a governmental entity.

In a voluntary nonexchange transaction, the provider and the recipient should recognize the nonexchange transaction when all eligibility requirements (which include time requirements) are satisfied. The eligibility requirements are categorized as follows [GASB Cod. Sec. N50.117]:

- Required characteristics of recipients,
- Time requirements,
- Reimbursements, and
- Contingencies.

These requirements are also discussed in detail in Chapter 17. Voluntary nonexchange transactions are treated similarly as government-mandated nonexchange transactions. Outflows of resources before time requirements are met but after all other eligibility requirements have been met should be reported as a deferred outflow of resources by the provider.

PRACTICE POINT: Chapter 17, Exhibit 17-1 contains a comprehensive summary of recognition of assets, deferred outflows of resources, liabilities, deferred inflows of resources, revenues, and expenses or expenditures along with various notes related to nonexchange transactions.

PRACTICE POINT: Chapter 17 of the *Governmental GAAP Guide* also contains a discussion regarding GASB Technical Bulletin 2020-1, Accounting and Financial Reporting Issues Related to the Coronavirus Aid, Relief, and Economic Security Act (CARES Act) and Coronavirus Diseases. In many situations, resources may be transmitted to governments prior to eligibility being determined. Many other federal grants also have similar funding transactions. They will be reported as assets by the providing government in the case of transmittal to subrecipients instead of expenses or expenditures until eligibility determination is completed.

SHARING GOVERNMENT-MANDATED AND VOLUNTARY NONEXCHANGE REVENUES

Governments may collect derived tax revenues or imposed nonexchange revenues and share those revenues with other governments. States and counties often collect taxes on behalf of lower levels of government. The state or county transfers the appropriate amount of tax to the local governments as required by law. The ultimate recipients often impose the tax and use the state or the county as a collecting agent. If the imposing entity is the lower government, they can reasonably estimate the accrual-basis information necessary to comply with GAAP for derived tax revenues or imposed nonexchange revenues [GASB Cod. Sec. N50.124].

Another scenario has a government sharing its own derived tax revenues or imposed nonexchange revenues with other governments. Commonly, a sales tax may be provided from one government to another. Both the provider and the recipient governments must comply with the provisions of voluntary or government-mandated nonexchange revenues, as appropriate. The shared revenues are likely received through a continuing periodic appropriation (quarterly, for example). The provider government likely notifies the receiving government of the accrual-basis information necessary for compliance. If the notification is untimely, recipient governments may use a reasonable estimate for the accrual [GASB Cod. Sec. N50.125].

PRACTICE ALERT: The GASB's *Revenue and Expense Recognition* Preliminary Views document discloses potential changes to the recognition and categorization principles for General Aid to Governments and Shared Revenue Transactions. Both are discussed in Chapter 5 of the Preliminary Views, paragraphs 30 through 35. Both would be Category B transactions as introduced in the **PRACTICE ALERT** in this chapter.

General Aid to Governments transactions would be expense transactions where legislation or a similar law requires the provision of resources from one government to other governments funding a specific activity or program. Specific formulas may be used to determine the distribution. The legislation or similar law creates a binding arrangement. The GASB provides an example of such transactions in Case 8 of Appendix C to the Preliminary Views, detailing state aid to school districts.

For General Aid to Governments transactions, the GASB's preliminary view is that the resource providing government would recognize a payable when payments are due if *both* of the following criteria are met:

1. The resource provider has appropriated funds for the provision of resources and the period applicable to the appropriation has begun.
2. The resource provider has determined that it intends to provide the resources to the resource recipient.

18,012 *Specific Accounting and Reporting Issues*

The offsetting credit would be to expenses (see previous **PRACTICE ALERT** on the potential that the term "expenditures" would no longer be used).

If the resource provider *cancels the appropriation* and communicates the cancellation to the recipient(s), the payable will continue to be reported along with the revenue *if the provider intends to provide the payment in a future period*. If not provided, the payable would be debited, and expense credited.

Shared Revenue Transactions would be the second subcategory. This would be like current GAAP. The resource provider has two transactions—the imposition of revenue and the sharing of that revenue, both because of the binding arrangement created by the law or ordinance. The GASB's preliminary view is that for shared revenue transactions supported through *periodic appropriations*, the substance of the transaction is general aid as discussed.

For shared revenue transactions supported through *continuing appropriations*, providers would recognize payables when the underlying transaction that produces the shared revenue has occurred if:

- The resource provider has appropriated funds for the provision of resources (*if required*), and the period applicable to the appropriation has begun, and

- The resource provider has determined that it intends to provide the resources to the resource recipient(s).

Recording Nonexchange Transactions

Governmental Funds. Under *current GAAP*, although the standards are written in the context of the accrual basis of accounting, they provide a significant amount of general guidance for nonexchange transactions irrespective of the basis of accounting that is used by a governmental entity. For this reason, the GASB states that the general guidance applies to governmental funds (activities accounted for in funds such as the general fund and special revenue funds).

Expenditures of governmental funds are accounted for under the current financial resources measurement focus and modified accrual basis of accounting. Expenditures are decreases or outflows of *financial resources* and are recognized in the accounting period in which the fund liability is incurred, if measurable, except for unmatured interest on long-term debt, which is recognized when due.

Government-Wide Financial Statements, Proprietary and Fiduciary Funds. Expenses from nonexchange transactions should be recognized in the government-wide statement of activities and proprietary and fiduciary funds, as applicable, based on accrual accounting concepts and be consistent with the standards.

EXPENSES AND EXPENDITURES: EXCHANGE TRANSACTIONS

In an exchange transaction the governmental entity and the other party to the transaction exchange cash, goods, or services that are essentially of the same value. For example, the purchase of a vehicle by a governmental entity from a car dealer is an exchange transaction. Unlike nonexchange transactions, the GASB has not provided comprehensive guidance for the recognition of exchange transactions.

Recording Exchange Transactions

Governmental Funds. Current GAAP requires that governmental entities produce government-wide financial statements that are based on the accrual accounting basis and the flow of all economic resources. However, GAAP also requires that governmental fund financial statements continue to be presented based on the modified accrual accounting basis and the flow of current financial resources.

The GASB believes that retaining the modified accrual basis of accounting for governmental funds was an important aspect of satisfying financial accountability, which is one of the foundations of governmental financial reporting. In general, a proprietary or fiduciary fund should record an expense when incurred, however, the recognition must be consistent with any relevant standards established by the GASB.

Government-Wide Financial Statements. Expenses related to exchange transactions in a governmental entity's statement of activities should be based on accrual accounting concepts. Governmental activities as presented in the government-wide financial statements should be accounted for and reported based on all applicable pronouncements.

PRACTICE POINT: GASB Statement No. 99 (*Omnibus 2022*) expanded the nonexchange financial guarantee guidance to exchange financial guarantees. These transactions are discussed in Chapters 16 and 17.

PRACTICE ALERT: One of the main drivers behind the GASB's project on *Revenue and Expense Recognition* was the perceived lack of guidance on exchange and exchange-like transactions. As contained in previous **PRACTICE ALERT** s on the project, many of the transactions comprising what is current GAAP for revenue recognition are similar GAAP to what was in existence prior to the establishment of the GASB and the conceptual framework. In the future, this section of the chapter may expand based on the provisions of an exposure draft (or drafts) because of the project, if issued. The GASB's preliminary view on categorizing expenses between categories A and B involves a four-step methodology as follows:

Specific Accounting and Reporting Issues

Step	Discussion	Example(s)
Is there a binding arrangement?	The GASB has proposed that a binding arrangement is an understanding between two or more parties that creates rights, obligations, or both among the parties to a transaction. A binding arrangement would include a *rebuttable presumption of enforceability* and have *economic substance*. The term *binding arrangement* is intended to encompass a broad spectrum of arrangements, which can be written, oral, or implied by the government's existing practices.	Grant agreements, memorandums of understanding, and contracts. Legislation is an example of a binding arrangement that is not contractual. More informal arrangements include the creation of a new customer account for water and sewer service from a public utility, the issuance of a legally enforceable purchase order, or the purchase of a ticket for a bus ride. • *Rebuttable presumption of enforceability* means that the arrangement can be challenged through a change in law or the courts. • *Economic substance* entails economic consequence/benefit between the parties. The notion is different than *significance* or materiality.
Is there mutual assent of the parties?	Per the GASB, all parties to the transaction have *approved* the terms and conditions of the binding arrangement. Furthermore, when the parties approve the terms and conditions of the binding arrangement, they should be able to bind themselves or their entity.	Parties agree to a contract involving terms and conditions to the binding arrangement. But also, may include transactions that do not require mutual assent such as the result of a voter referendum on taxation. Once the provision has been approved by vote, all transactions relating to the vote are deemed approved (unless overturned by future law or court case). Also assumes parties to transaction have capacity (be of legal age, etc.).
Are there identifiable rights and obligations?	Per the GASB, terms and conditions identify and measure rights to receive consideration or compensation in exchange for obligation to provide goods or services.	Where a not-for-profit university agrees to make payments in lieu of taxation (PILOT agreements) to a government in exchange for normal public safety services. Other elements of contracts usually detailed.

Expenses and Expenditures: Nonexchange and Exchange Transactions   18,015

Step	Discussion	Example(s)
Are the rights and obligations interdependent?	Per the GASB, if a government concludes that the rights and obligations in a binding arrangement are interdependent, the obligations will represent *performance obligations*, and the rights would represent the right to *consideration* for that performance.	Where a construction contractor agrees to build a school with various milestones for completion prior to payment. Performance obligations are summarized as "does one party (or parties) have to do something to receive compensation in exchange?" Once the activity has been completed, a receivable or payable results, even if in a series of milestones.

If the government cannot identify a binding arrangement, the transaction would not fit into the GASB's model and may not be recognized as a transaction. If any of the required steps 2 through 4 are not present, then the transaction would be Category B. If satisfying all the steps, the transaction would be Category A.

DEPRECIATION AND AMORTIZATION EXPENSE

Depreciation Expense and Depreciation Periods for Capital Assets. An exchange transaction occurs when a governmental entity acquires capital assets. The expense related to that exchange transaction arises when depreciation expense is recorded in the government-wide financial statements. In proprietary and fiduciary funds and the government-wide financial statements, the cost (net of estimated salvage value) of capital assets (except for certain infrastructure assets, which are discussed later) should be depreciated over their estimated useful lives. Inexhaustible capital assets (such as land, land improvements, and certain infrastructure assets) should not be depreciated [GASB Cod. Sec. 1400.104].

OBSERVATION: Under *current GAAP*, governmental funds report transactions on the modified accrual basis of accounting and current financial resources measurement focus, Due to the basis of accounting, capital assets are not reported as fund assets of governmental funds. Therefore, capital assets are reported as fund expenditures (capital outlay) when acquired and depreciation expense is not applicable to governmental funds.

GASB Cod. Sec. 1400.702-21 discusses, in part, that the estimated useful life of an asset is the period that the governmental entity believes the asset will be used in its activities based upon the government's own experience and plans for the assets. The question further discusses that factors that are relevant to making this determination include the following:

- The asset's present state of condition,
- How the asset will be used,
- Construction type,
- Maintenance policy, and
- Relevant service and technology demands.

The answer to the question does caution governments not to compare with other governments. The GASB notes the experience of other governmental entities is relevant only if the expected experience is anticipated to be the same.

GASB Cod. Sec. 1400.705-11 further discusses that there is not a generally accepted schedule of useful lives that can be used to determine depreciation expense for governmental entities. Although informal schedules or guidance are provided by professional organizations, management is responsible for determining the estimated useful life of a capital asset. Furthermore, the Internal Revenue Service's schedule of lives for property classes related to the Modified Accelerated Cost Recovery System is not based on the actual estimated economic lives of assets.

The GASB suggests that the following may be used to estimate the useful lives of depreciable assets [GASB Cod. Sec. 1400.705-12]:

- General guidelines obtained from professional and industry organizations,
- Information for comparable assets of other governments, and
- Internal information.

These sources are *starting points* and should be modified based on the specific characteristics and expected use of a newly acquired capital asset.

The GASB further discusses, in general, the lives of capital assets should be reviewed each year. In practice, most governments only review those lives that may have changed during the year because of some of the following events that may have occurred:

- Property replacement policies have changed,
- Preventive maintenance policies have changed, and
- Unexpected technological changes have occurred.

If it is concluded that the life of a capital asset should be changed, GASB Cod. Secs. 2250.101–.152, 2300.107 require that the asset's undepreciated cost (less the revised residual value) be allocated over the remaining life of the asset. This is a change in an accounting estimate.

PRACTICE ALERT: The accounting and financial reporting for a change in a useful life for a capital asset was not updated by the issuance of GASB Statement No. 100 (*Accounting Changes and Error Corrections*) [GASB Cod. Sec. 1400.705-13]. A change from a non-depreciable to a depreciable capital asset due to a now definite useful life would also be a change in accounting estimate even after the implementation of GASB Statement No. 100 [GASB Cod. Sec. 1400.720-2].

As with commercial accounting, there is no specific list of acceptable depreciable methods, however, the method selected must be systematic and rational. GASB Cod. Sec. 1400.113 notes that depreciation may be applied in the following manner:

- To a class of assets,
- To a network of assets,
- To a subsystem of a network assets, and
- To individual assets.

OBSERVATION: The composite depreciation method, which is discussed in GAAP in the context of infrastructure assets, can also be used to compute depreciation expense for other capital assets, however, the method should not be applied across classes of assets. In grouping assets for computing depreciation expense, GASB Cod. Secs. 1400.705-14–16 discuss how assets should not be grouped in a manner that would not enable a governmental entity to report depreciation expense as a direct expense for functions as required by GASB Cod. Sec. 2200.132 or note disclosures required by GASB Cod. Secs. 2300.106, 118.

In the rare event when infrastructure assets are sold or the more common event of when infrastructure assets are disposed of excluding a government combination or disposal of operations, GASB Cod. Sec. 1400.702-16 requires the gain or loss to be reported on the statement of activities as the difference between the net book value of the capital asset (original cost or estimated cost minus accumulated depreciation) and the proceeds from the disposition. If the infrastructure is not being depreciated (as allowed under the modified method under certain conditions), the gain or loss is the difference between the original cost (or estimated cost) and the proceeds.

Amortization Expense and Amortization Periods for Intangible and Right-to-Use Assets. Intangible assets are described in GASB Cod. Sec. 1400.118 as those that lack physical substance, are of a nonfinancial nature, and have an *initial* useful life extending beyond a single reporting period. They may be internally or externally generated.

As intangible assets are capital assets, they must be amortized unless they have an indefinite life. GASB Cod. Secs. 1400.151–.152 describe the amortization of intangible assets. Like tangible capital assets, the guidance is based upon service capacity. The useful life of an intangible asset that arises from contractual or other legal rights should not exceed the period to which the service capacity of the asset is limited by contractual or legal provisions. Renewal periods related to contractual or legal rights may be considered in determining the useful life of the intangible asset if there is evidence that the government will be able to renew the contract and that any anticipated outlays incurred as part of achieving the renewal are nominal in relation to the level of service capacity expected to be obtained through the renewal.

As with a tangible capital asset, an intangible asset could have an indefinite useful life if there are no legal, contractual, regulatory, technological, or other factors that limit it. GASB Cod. Sec. 1400.152 prohibits intangible assets with indefinite useful lives to be amortized. If changes in factors and conditions result in the useful life of an intangible asset no longer being indefinite, the asset should be tested for impairment because a change in the expected duration of use of the asset has occurred in accordance with the provisions of impairment in GASB Cod. Sec. 1400. The carrying value of the intangible asset, if any, following the recognition of any impairment loss would then be amortized in subsequent reporting periods over the remaining estimated useful life of the asset.

PRACTICE POINT: Impairment is fully discussed in Chapter 10.

PRACTICE POINT: Chapter 14 describes the lease, public-private and public-public partnerships and the subscription-based information technology arrangements accounting framework. All use a "right-to-use" asset (an intangible asset) for most leases, public-private and public-public partnerships (in the case of a governmental operator) and the holder of a license for a subscription-based information technology arrangement. The amortization of the related right-to-use asset by a lessee, operator or licensee will be systematic and rational over the shorter term or the useful life of the underlying asset, whichever is shorter. If the contract contains a purchase option that the government has determined will be reasonably certain of being exercised, the right-to-use asset would be amortized over the useful life of the underlying asset. In practice, the amortization expense will likely be combined with other forms of depreciation, but captioned "Depreciation and Amortization Expense." As discussed, and illustrated in Chapter 10, right-to-use assets are disclosed in the notes and the basic financial statements as subsets of capital assets.

Right-to-use land should not be amortized. Further, if right-to-use assets involved in a lease, a public-private and public-public partnership or a subscription-based information technology arrangement includes a provision that the underlying right-to-use capital asset be returned to the transferor government in "as good or better" condition than at the date of the arrangement, then theoretically amortization stops.

Infrastructure Depreciation: Modified Approach

The GASB does not require that infrastructure assets that are part of a network or subsystem of a network (referred to as eligible infrastructure assets) be depreciated if the following conditions are satisfied [GASB Cod. Sec. 1400.105]:

- An asset management system is employed that:
  - Has an up-to-date inventory of eligible infrastructure assets,
  - Performs condition assessments of the assets and summarizes the results using a "measurable scale,"
  - Estimates, on an annual basis, the annual amount needed to "maintain and preserve the eligible infrastructure assets at the condition level established and disclosed by the government," and
- The government documents that the eligible infrastructure assets are being "preserved approximately at (or above) a condition level established and disclosed by the government."

A governmental entity that adopts the modified approach may continue to use it if the two conditions listed above are met. GASB Cod. Sec. 1400.703-15 discusses how the second criterion listed refers to the conditions of the asset, not the amount of resources expended to maintain the asset at a specified condition level. For example, if a governmental entity originally estimated that a specific amount was needed to maintain the asset but did not expend those funds, that does not mean that the entity can no longer use the modified approach—if the condition of the asset does not fall below the established condition level.

> **OBSERVATION:** The careful documentation of condition assessments must be made so that their results can be replicated. GASB Cod. Sec. 1400 describes results being subject to replication as "those that are based on sufficiently understandable and complete measurement methods such that different measurers using the same methods would reach substantially similar results."

The condition level must be established and documented by governmental policy or legislative action, and the assessment may be made by the governmental entity directly or by external parties. Professional judgment and good faith are the basis for determining what constitutes acceptable and accurate documentation of the condition of eligible infrastructure assets. However, GASB Cod. Sec. 1400 states that governmental entities should document the following [GASB Cod. Sec. 1400.106]:

- Complete condition assessments of eligible infrastructure assets are performed in a consistent manner at least every three years, and
- The results of the three most recent complete condition assessments provide reasonable assurance that the eligible infrastructure assets are being preserved approximately at (or above) the condition level established and disclosed by the government.

The condition level could be applied to a group of assets by using a condition index or "as the percentage of a network of infrastructure assets in good or poor condition."

If a governmental entity identifies a subsystem of infrastructure assets as "eligible" (and therefore the computation of depreciation is optional), the documentary requirements apply only to the subsystem and not to the entire network of infrastructure assets.

A governmental entity may perform the condition assessment annually or may use a cycle basis. If the entity uses a cyclical basis for networks or subsystems, it must assess all assets of these groups during the cycle. However, rather than apply the condition assessment to all assets, the entity may employ a statistical sample approach in the annual approach or in the cycle approach.

Because eligible infrastructure assets do not have to be depreciated, all expenditures related to their maintenance should be recognized as a current expense when incurred. Expenditures that are capital in nature (additions and improvements) should be capitalized as part of the eligible infrastructure assets because they, by definition, increase the capacity or efficiency of the related infrastructure asset [GASB Cod. Sec. 1400.107].

The adequate maintenance of the condition of eligible infrastructure assets is a continuous process and if the conditions are initially satisfied but subsequently are not, the infrastructure assets are not considered "eligible" and depreciation expense for them must be computed and reported in the statement of activities.

The change in accounting for depreciation expense should be reported as a change in an accounting estimate in accordance with GASB Cod. Secs. 2250.101, .132–.133. A change in estimate is accounted for prospectively. That is, the balances in the infrastructure assets (net of residual values, if any) are to be depreciated over the remaining lives of the assets when the governmental entity no longer qualifies to use the modified approach [GASB Cod. Sec. 1400.108].

While GAAP provides guidance for a change from not depreciating certain infrastructure assets to the recognition of annual depreciation expense on those assets, it does not address how the reverse situation should be reported in a governmental entity's financial statements. A change from depreciating infrastructure assets to not depreciating them could arise for reasons such as the following:

- Business-type activities might decide on a non-depreciating strategy.
- Infrastructure networks or subsystems may be transferred from an enterprise fund to general capital assets.
- A governmental entity may decide to change from depreciating infrastructure assets to the modified approach because it now satisfies the requirements.

GASB Cod. Sec. 1400.fn. 10, requires that a change from the depreciating approach to the non-depreciating approach (modified approach) for certain infrastructure assets be accounted for on a prospective basis (change in an accounting estimate). Thus, when this type of change is made, the carrying amount of the asset remains the same and that amount provides the basis for computing subsequent depreciation expense.

PRACTICE ALERT: GASB Statement No. 100 (*Accounting Changes and Error Corrections*) clarifies the change in approach. Provided that the change is preferable, a change from depreciation to the modified approach would be reported as a change in accounting estimate resulting from a change in measurement methodology [GASB Cod. Secs. 1400.fns. 10–11, 703–16].

GASB Cod. Sec. 1400.703-9 discusses the treatment of maintenance costs (i.e., routine repairs) for the modified approach and the traditional depreciation approach. That is, under both approaches, maintenance costs are expensed.

The treatment of preservation costs is different under the two approaches. Preservation costs are described in GASB Cod. Sec. 1400.703-10 as costs that "generally are considered to be those outlays that extend the useful life of an asset beyond its original estimated useful life, but do not increase the capacity or efficiency of the asset." Some accountants refer to preservation costs as "major repairs."

Under the modified approach preservation costs are expensed, while under the traditional depreciation approach preservation costs are capitalized. Under both approaches additions and improvements are capitalized. Of course, differentiating among these costs (preservation, additions, and improvements) is often difficult. The governmental entity should use "any reasonable approach" to make the cost allocation.

Therefore, the differences between the modified approach and depreciation for maintenance, preservation and general additions and improvements are as follows:

	Modified Approach	Depreciation
Preservation costs	Expense	Capitalize
Additions and improvements	Capitalize	Capitalize

GASB Cod. Sec. 1400.703-11 demonstrates how the above guidance should be applied by raising the question of whether the cost of removing and replacing or resurfacing an existing roadway should be capitalized if the modified approach is used. The results arising from the removing and replacing or resurfacing must be evaluated to determine whether the activity is considered:

- Maintenance or preservation, *or*
- An increase in the capacity or efficiency of the roadway.

If the costs are related to maintenance or preservation, they should be expensed under the modified approach. If the costs increase the capacity or efficiency of the roadway, they must be capitalized. Capacity is increased when a capital asset can provide more services or goods. Efficiency is increased when a capital asset can accomplish the same level of service at a lower cost.

PRACTICE ALERT: The GASB has added a project to the Technical Plan on Infrastructure Assets. The project will address accounting and financial reporting for such assets, including how should infrastructure be recognized and measured in the basic financial statements. The modified approach may or may not be continued to be allowed. Deferred maintenance may be addressed. A Preliminary Views document is expected by July 2024. An Exposure Draft may be released by January 2026, with a final Statement potentially a year later.

PRACTICE ALERT: The analyses of condition of infrastructure reported in accordance with the modified approach currently is summarized in the Management's Discussion and Analysis along with related reporting as part of required supplementary information. The GASB's *Financial Reporting Model Improvements* Exposure Draft would change this to solely report in required supplementary information, along with related note disclosure after that information.

CHAPTER 19
SPECIAL ASSESSMENTS

Chapter References:

  GASB Statement Nos. 6, 33, 34

  GASB *Implementation Guide*

INTRODUCTION

A governmental entity may raise resources assessing only the properties of taxpayers who would directly benefit either from the construction or improvement of a capital asset or from the provision for special services. For example, a city may assess property owners to improve water or sewer lines in a specific location within the city or a local government may assess businesses in a downtown area to provide special sanitation maintenance on an ongoing basis, commonly known as "tax incremental financing" (TIFs). These special assessment activities provided by a governmental entity are generally characterized by their narrow scope and the method by which they are financed.

The costs of providing capital improvements or services within the targeted area are charged specifically to the owners who benefit from those improvements or services in special assessments. Special assessments may also result in the government assuming a portion of the cost through the issuance of debt or by matching resources due to the public benefit received from a special assessment. For example, adding an access road to a new subdivision increases the tax base of all the area, not just the subdivision [GASB Cod. Sec. S40.103].

Due to the provisions of GASB Cod. Sec. S40, fund balance deficits resulting from special assessments are unlikely. This is due to the treatment of special assessment debt like all other debt issued by a governmental unit. The proceeds of the special assessment debt are recorded as another source of financing, and the debt is reported as part of the governmental unit's general long-term debt if the unit is directly liable or in some manner liable for the special assessment debt.

GAAP does not allow separate fund types for special assessments. The rationale for the prohibition is that special assessment transactions and balances are no more unique than capital expenditures, debt service expenditures, and special levies that are accounted for in the other governmental funds or in enterprise funds.

TYPES OF SPECIAL ASSESSMENTS

Services Financed by Special Assessments

Service-type special assessments are used to finance special types of service or special levels of service. They are for operating activities and do not result in a capital asset. Due to the services focus, the assessments should be accounted for in the general fund, a special revenue fund, or an enterprise fund. The GASB provides examples of services commonly financed by special assessments including street lighting, cleaning, and plowing of snow. For most governments, general revenues pay for these services. But if the services are extended to property owners beyond the service area of the government (such as unincorporated areas) or they are provided at a higher level or at more frequent intervals than for the public, assessments may be levied. Only the property owners are charged for the additional services [GASB Cod. Sec. S40.104].

PRACTICE ALERT: The GASB's *Financial Reporting Model Improvements* Exposure Draft proposes to rename special revenue funds to "special resources funds."

For example, a commercial enterprise locates in a government, but the roads are not maintained in the area in which the company wants to locate. The public works fund (a governmental fund) of the government provides for the services just for the company and charges the company a special assessment for the maintenance of the roads so they may be used by the company's vehicles.

In this example, GASB Cod. Sec. 2200.717-8 notes that special assessment activities provided by a governmental entity are generally characterized by their narrow scope and the method by which they are financed. For financial reporting purposes, operating special assessments revenues are not considered general revenues like property taxes.

Operating special assessments are program revenues (charges for services) because they are assessed against those specific parties who are entitled to the specific service. In many cases, revenues are recorded as user fees to indicate that users are directly benefitting from the services financed by special assessments. The public works fund will record the user fees as revenue in accordance with the measurement focus and basis of accounting for governmental funds.

Capital Improvements Financed by Special Assessments

Special assessments often finance capital improvements—infrastructure, sidewalks, parking, water, and sewer systems are commonly financed in this way.

Generally, capital improvements financed by special assessments have two distinct phases: the construction phase and the debt service phase. Construction is usually short—less than a year or two depending on the project. Assessments will need to be levied for the length of time the debt is outstanding, which may be much longer than construction. The assessments are analogous to a mortgage on the properties. A lien is placed on the property so that the owners can pay in installments, or in a lump sum in rare circumstances. The installments are due to a trustee a brief time before paying debt service. Liens are released upon full repayment.

When a governmental unit is directly liable or obligated in some manner (as defined in the section titled "Governmental Liability for Debt") for the special assessment debt, the capital construction and related debt service transactions should be accounted for in a manner like other governmental capital outlays and debt service payments. For this reason, special assessment transactions related to capital improvements may be accounted for in a capital projects fund or debt service fund. If there are no legal or administrative requirements that necessitate the use of a separate capital projects fund or debt service fund, the general fund can be used [GASB Cod. Secs. S40.105–.109].

ACCOUNTING AND REPORTING FOR SPECIAL ASSESSMENTS

Governmental Liability for Debt

Because property owners are generally obligated to finance all or part of the repayment of special assessment debt, a question arises whether the special assessment debt should be reported as debt of the governmental entity. The government is often solely responsible for paying a portion of the project cost based on a perceived public benefit or as a property owner benefiting from the improvement. In those cases, general government sources repay a portion of the debt based on the share.

There may be also a pledge of the government's full faith and credit as security for the bond issue, which may include the assessments of property owners. There may be some other pledge of appropriations or moral obligation even though there might not be a legal obligation to pay the bonds. These acts are done to protect the government's overall credit quality. But pledges such as these are not common. Often, the government has no liability for a special assessment debt issue.

The extent of the "backstop" is contained in laws, regulations, and local debt limitations. Therefore, there are variations in the financing of capital improvements involving special assessments. Distinct types of special assessment debt could be (in decreasing credit quality or security):

- *General obligation debt*—not secured by liens on assessed properties but nevertheless will be repaid in part by special assessment collections. The remainder is paid from government sources.
- *Special assessment debt*—secured by liens on assessed properties and is also backed by the full faith and credit of the government as additional security.
- *Special assessment debt*—secured by liens on assessed properties and is *not* backed by the full faith and credit of the government but is, however, fully, or partially backed by some other type of general governmental commitment.

- *Special assessment debt*—secured by liens on assessed properties, is *not* backed by the full faith and credit of the government and is *not* backed by any other type of general governmental commitment, *the government is not liable under any circumstance for the repayment of this category of debt, should the property owner default.*

If the government owns property that benefits from the improvements in the lowest category of debt (the last bullet), then the government would be obliged to pay the amount assessed against the property, even though it has no liability for the remainder of the debt issue [GASB Cod. Secs. S40.110–.112].

Governmental Fund Reporting. If special assessment revenue is generated, a fund balance remaining at the end of a fiscal year could be restricted if accounted for in a governmental fund. The provisions of the assessment would have to align with the guidance provided in GASB Cod. Secs. 1800.168–.169, because the restriction would occur through a debt covenant or it may occur through enabling legislation. In some instances, depending on local laws, regulations, and ordinances, if the assessment were generated by an action of the government's highest level of decision-making authority, any fund balance would show as a committed fund balance.

Special assessment transactions could be reported within accounts within other funds (again, usually a governmental fund). Additional note disclosure could occur if separate funds are not used to disclose the assessments.

Service-Type Special Assessments. Service-type special assessments that are exchange or exchange-like transactions and related expenditures (expenses) should be recognized on the same basis of accounting as that normally used for that fund type. Both the assessment revenues and the expenditures (expenses) for which the assessments were levied should be recognized on the same basis of accounting as that normally used for that fund type.

In the government-wide financial statements, exchange or exchange-like service type special assessments should be reported as either governmental or business-type activities on the accrual basis. Revenues from service-type special assessment transactions that are nonexchange transactions are reported using the provisions for other nonexchange transactions as discussed in Chapter 17.

Capital Improvement Special Assessments. Given the variability of the government's liability for debt, recognition of a liability varies. The government may be:

- Primarily liable for the debt, or
- It may have no liability whatsoever for special assessment debt *or*
- It may be obligated in some manner to provide a secondary source of funds for repayment of special assessment debt in the event of default by the assessed property owners.

A government is obligated in some manner for special assessment debt if:

- It is legally obligated to assume all or part of the debt in the event of default, or

- The government may take certain actions to assume secondary liability for all or part of the debt—and the government takes, or has given indications that it will take, those actions.

Conditions that indicate that a government is obligated in some manner include:

1. The government is obligated to honor deficiencies to the extent that lien foreclosure proceeds are insufficient.
2. The government is required to establish a reserve, guarantee, or sinking fund with other resources.
3. The government is required to cover delinquencies with other resources until foreclosure proceeds are received.
4. The government must purchase all properties ("sold" for delinquent assessments) that were not sold at public auction.
5. The government is authorized to establish a reserve, guarantee, or sinking fund, and it establishes such a fund. (If a fund is not established, the considerations may nevertheless provide evidence that the government is obligated in some manner.)
6. The government may establish a separate fund with other resources for purchasing or redeeming special assessment debt, and it establishes such a fund. (If a fund is not established, the considerations in the following conditions may nevertheless provide evidence that the government is obligated in some manner.)
7. The government explicitly indicates by contract, such as the bond agreement or offering statement, that in the event of default it may cover delinquencies, although it has no legal obligation to do so.
8. Legal decisions within the state or previous actions by the government related to defaults on other special assessment projects make it probable that the government will assume responsibility for the debt in the event of default.

In summation, *"obligated in some manner"* is intended to include all situations other than those in which:

- The government is prohibited (by constitution, charter, statute, ordinance, or contract) from assuming the debt in the event of default by the property owner *or*
- The government is not legally liable for assuming the debt and makes no statement, or gives no indication, that it will, or may, honor the debt in the event of default [GASB Cod. Secs. S40.114–.115].

Classification of Special Assessment Debt

When property owners are responsible for paying all or a portion of special assessment debt issued to finance capital improvements, the accounting for the special assessment is dependent on whether:

- The debt is general obligation debt,
- The governmental unit is obligated in some manner to repay the debt, or
- The governmental unit is in no way obligated to repay the debt.

General Obligation Debt. General obligation debt is backed by the full faith and credit of a governmental unit. When special assessment debt is backed by a governmental unit, the debt should be reported like any other general obligation debt in the Statement of Net Position.

Obligated in Some Manner. A governmental unit is obligated in some manner to pay special assessment debt when:

- The governmental unit is legally obligated to assume all or part of the special assessment debt *if property owners' default*, or
- The governmental unit may assume secondary responsibility for all, or part of the debt and the unit has either taken such action in the past or indicated that it will take such action.

Special assessment debt that a governmental unit is obligated for in some manner should be reported similarly to any other general obligation debt in the Statement of Net Position, but the debt should be referred to as "Special Assessment Debt with Governmental Commitment" [GASB Cod. Sec. S40.709-1].

The portion of special assessment debt (for which a governmental unit is somewhat obligated) that is a direct obligation of an enterprise fund or is to be repaid from operating revenues of an enterprise fund should be recorded as a liability of the enterprise fund and reported as debt in the business-type activities column in the Statement of Net Position [GASB Cod. Sec. S40.116].

Special Assessment Reserve, Guarantee, or Sinking Fund

A governmental unit may be required or authorized to establish a reserve, guarantee, or sinking fund to accumulate resources in case property owners' default on their special assessments. A debt service fund should be used when resources are accumulated for principal and interest payments due in future years. As a reminder, reserves are not presented on the face of the basic financial statements, because they are components of net position and fund balance [GASB Cod. Sec. S40.117].

Capital Improvements Financed by Special Assessment Debt—Governmental Funds

Under *current GAAP*, construction expenditures should be accounted for in a capital projects fund and the receipt of resources should be reported as "contribution from property owners" rather than described as "bond proceeds." The capital asset should be reported in the governmental activities column in the Statement of Net Position.

PRACTICE ALERT: The GASB's *Financial Reporting Model Improvements* Exposure Draft proposes a change in the recognition of such assessments. At the time of the levy, if the special assessment arises from a short-term transaction, special assessments receivable and inflows of short-term financial resources would be recognized. If the special assessment arises from a long-term transaction, special assessments receivable and inflows of short-term financial resources would only be recognized when payments are due.

When a governmental entity is obligated in some manner to make debt repayments in the case of default by property owners, the expenditures (expenses) "should be reported in the same manner and on the same basis of accounting, as any other capital improvement and financing transaction." Revenues from special assessment capital improvement transactions should be accounted for based on the nonexchange transaction provisions in Chapter 17.

No Obligation to Pay Debt. In some cases, special assessment debt may be issued with the governmental unit having no obligation to repay the debt. Under this circumstance, the special assessment debt would not be reported as an obligation by the governmental entity. However, if a portion of the special assessment is to be paid by the governmental unit based on the public benefit portion of the capital improvement or because the governmental unit owns property that is subject to the special assessment, this portion of the special assessment debt would be recorded as a general long-term debt in the Statement of Net Position.

When a government is in not obligated for the special assessment debt, the debt is not reported in the unit's financial statements. However, transactions related to the financing and construction of the capital asset must be reported by the governmental entity. The receipt of the funds is reported in a custodial fund as discussed in Chapter 8 [GASB Cod. Secs. S40.118–.119].

GASB Cod. Sec. 2200.717-9 discusses how capital special assessments are program revenues (program-specific capital grants and contributions) because the property owners derive a direct benefit from the contributions they make to the program.

Financing Special Assessments with Current Resources

A capital improvement may be initially financed with currently available resources of the governmental unit rather than with proceeds from the issuance of special assessment debt. Payments made directly from a governmental fund (usually the general fund) for capital improvements should be recorded as capital expenditures in the fund making the payments. Resources transferred from a governmental fund to a capital projects fund should be recorded as interfund transfers, and capital outlays eventually made by the capital projects fund should be recorded as capital expenditures.

The levy of the special assessment against property owners should be recorded in the governmental fund that initially provided the resources used to finance the capital improvement. The portion of the special assessment that should be recorded as revenue is the amount that is both measurable and available [GASB Cod. Sec. S40.120].

PRACTICE ALERT: The GASB's *Financial Reporting Model Improvements* Exposure Draft proposes a change in these provisions as well. If an improvement is initially financed with existing governmental fund resources rather than with debt, either a direct capital outflow of short-term financial resources or a transfer to a capital projects fund would be reported. At the time of the levy, if the special assessment arises from a short-term transaction, special assessments receivable and inflows of short-term financial resources would be recognized in the fund that provides the resources. If the special assessment arises from a long-term transaction, special assessments receivable and inflows of short-term financial resources would be recognized as payments are due.

GASB Cod. Sec. N50.708-3 discusses when a government levies amounts in its current property tax levy for future debt service payments. The future amounts are not reported as deferred inflows of resources until those future periods start. Unless a legal requirement specifies otherwise, the period for which these amounts are levied is the same as the period for which the rest of the taxes are levied. If a special assessment is a component of property taxation, then this guidance may be followed for this situation.

Reporting Special Assessments in Proprietary Funds

Capital assets constructed for an enterprise fund and financed by special assessments should be accounted for in a manner like other capital improvements financed by special assessments. However, the capital asset should be recorded both by the enterprise fund and in the business-type activities column of the Statement of Net Position.

The cost of the capital asset should be capitalized, net of special assessment revenues. The special assessment debt related to the construction of the capital asset should be recorded as a liability of the enterprise fund only if one of the following conditions exists:

- The enterprise fund is directly liable for the special assessment debt.
- The enterprise fund is not directly liable for the special assessment debt, but the debt is expected to be repaid from revenues of the enterprise fund.

Debt expected to be repaid by an enterprise fund should be reported as debt of the enterprise fund even though the debt may be backed by the full faith and credit of the governmental unit. The debt must also be reported in the government-wide Statement of Net Position.

Most capital assets constructed for an enterprise fund and financed by special assessments will be accounted for as described in the previous paragraph, it is acceptable to record all special assessment transactions solely in the enterprise fund. Under this approach, the special assessment levy would be recorded as a receivable and contributed capital revenue. Special assessment debt for which the enterprise fund is directly liable or expected to repay from its revenues would be accounted for in the enterprise fund. The accrual basis of accounting should be used to account for special assessments receivable and the related interest income, and special assessment debt and the related interest expense [GASB Cod. Secs. S40.121–.123].

Reporting Capital Assets Financed by Special Assessment Debt in Government-Wide Financial Statements

As noted earlier, capital assets or improvements financed by special assessment debt for which the entity is obligated in some manner must be reported as capital assets in either the governmental or business-type activities column in the Statement of Net Position. The related special assessment revenue and receivables must be accounted for on the accrual basis of accounting.

When the governmental entity is not obligated for the special assessment debt, the capital asset must be reported on the Statement of Net Position and an equal amount of program revenue (capital contributions) should be reported on the statement of activities [GASB Cod. Secs. S40.124–.125].

NOTE DISCLOSURES OF SPECIAL ASSESSMENT DEBT

The disclosures in the governmental unit's financial statements with respect to special assessment debt depend on whether the unit is responsible for the debt.

Government Obligated for Debt. When the government is primarily obligated or obligated in some manner for the repayment of special assessment debt, the following disclosures that are applicable to all general obligation debt should be made in the unit's basic financial statements:

- Nature of government's obligation for special assessment debt,
- Description of individual special assessment debt issues,
- Description of requirements or authorizations for the establishment of guarantees, reserves, or sinking funds if defaults occur,
- Changes in general long-term debt (special assessment debt for which the unit is primarily responsible) and special assessment debt with governmental commitment (special assessment debt for which the unit is obligated in some manner),
- Summary of debt service requirements to maturity, and
- Special assessment debt authorized but unissued.

In addition, the amount of the special assessments receivable that is delinquent should be disclosed on the face of the balance sheet (or the Statement of Net Position as discussed previously) or in a note to the financial statements [GASB Cod. Sec. S40.126].

Government Not Obligated for Debt. When the government is not obligated in any manner for repayment of the special assessment debt, the following disclosures should be made in the unit's financial statements [GASB Cod. Sec. S40.127]:

- Present amount of special assessment debt outstanding,
- Statement that the government is in no manner obligated to repay the special assessment debt, and
- Statement that the government functions as an agent for the property owners by collecting assessments, forwarding collections to special assessment debtholders, and, if appropriate, beginning foreclosure.

GASB Cod. Sec. 2200.704-10 clarifies that GAAP *does not* require governments to include in the management's discussion and analysis (MD&A) a section on special assessment debt for which the government is not obligated. However, the debt may be discussed in connection with capital asset activity if the proceeds are to be used to build or acquire significant infrastructure assets for the government.

Special Assessment Districts of Component Units. A component unit applies the criteria in GASB Cod. Sec. S40 to determine how special assessment transactions and accounts should be reported. When the component unit's financial statements are blended with the primary government's financial statements to form the reporting entity, the component unit's special assessment debt should be reported as a liability in the reporting entity's financial statements based on the criteria even though the primary government may not be responsible in any way for the component unit's special assessment debt [GASB Cod. Sec. S40.128].

> **PRACTICE POINT:** Special assessment debt issued by component units is frequently found in redevelopment agencies or business improvement districts. Depending on the organization of such agencies or districts, if the entities are component units, they are commonly blended, especially if the primary government is the sole corporate entity of the agency or district organized as a not-for-profit organization or the primary government is obligated in some manner for the debt. Additional information is included in Chapter 4 on these types of relationships.

PART IV. FINANCIAL REPORTING BY GENERAL-PURPOSE GOVERNMENTS

CHAPTER 20
FINANCIAL REPORTING

Chapter References:
 GASB Statement Nos. 9–10, 14, 34–35, 37–39, 41–42, 44, 46, 48, 51, 54, 56, 61–63, 69–70, 72–75, 77, 80, 84–85, 90, 98, 100
 GASB *Implementation Guide*
 GASB Concepts Statement No. 4
 AICPA Audit and Accounting Guide, *States and Local Governments*
 NCGA Statement No. 1
 NCGA Interpretation No. 9

INTRODUCTION

The summation of all operations and balances for a reporting period for a state or local government is an annual financial report (AFR). When preparing an AFR, the minimum requirements to comply with GAAP include:

- Management's discussion and analysis (MD&A),
- Basic financial statements, including:
  — Government-wide financial statements,
  — Fund financial statements,
  — Notes to the basic financial statements, and
- Required supplementary information (RSI) in accordance with GAAP other than MD&A.

An Annual Comprehensive Financial Report (ACFR) includes all the elements of an AFR, but adds the following required sections:

- Introductory section,
- Appropriate combining and individual fund statements presented as supplementary information,
- Schedules and narrative explanations presented as section dividers or additional information required for debt or other compliance other than in accordance with GAAP, and
- Statistical section.

Both an AFR and an ACFR include all the entities within the reporting entity, including blended and discretely presented component units and component units that are fiduciary in nature.

Both an AFR and an ACFR present an independent auditor's report. Special-purpose governments presented in Chapters 21 through 24 may have differing schedules and sections, depending on the type of government and whether an

ACFR or an AFR is prepared, or some other special-purpose framework (SPF) is required to be used.

The AFR and the ACFR are presented in accordance with GAAP, or an SPF if required. In many instances, stand-alone reports are prepared for component units, which are then included in a primary government's AFR or ACFR. As discussed in previous chapters, component unit information beyond the balances and results of operations is distinguished from the primary government's information. Note disclosure from component units focuses on whether the information from the component unit is *essential* to the users' understanding of the information about the primary government. All the layers of information from other entities within the reporting entity is applied "from the ground up." At each layer, definitions, display of information and applicable GAAP provisions are all enabled to prepare the AFR or ACFR.

Independent Auditor's Report

Generally accepted auditing standards (GAAS) and, in certain cases, *Government Auditing Standards*, issued by the Comptroller General of the United States of America (GAGAS), are applicable to audits of governmental entities performed by an Independent Auditor. The Independent Auditor's report contains an opinion regarding the fair presentation of the reporting entity's various opinion units as defined in the AICPA's Audit and Accounting Guide *State and Local Governments*. Several types of audit reports may be found in CCH's *Knowledge-Based Audits™ of Governmental Entities*, Chapters 12 (Auditor's Reports), and *Knowledge-Based Single Audits*, Chapter 11 (Auditor's Reports Required by the Single Audit).

This chapter builds on the previous chapters in the *Governmental GAAP Guide* to explain the elements of either the AFR or the ACFR as applicable for the reporting entity.

FINANCIAL REPORTING

Minimum Requirements for ACFRs and AFRs

As summarized above, the ACFR is a superset of an AFR, containing additional information beyond the minimum requirements for general-purpose external financial reporting, which is presented in an AFR. To easily understand the differences and the order of the elements, the following can be reviewed [GASB Cod. Secs. 2200.101–.105]:

Element	GASB Cod. Sec. 2200 subsections	AFR	ACFR
Introductory information, including table of contents, letter(s) of transmittal and other material deemed appropriate by management	.105	Not required	Required
Independent Auditor's Report	Self-evident	Required	Required
MD&A	.106–.109	Required	Required

Financial Reporting **20,003**

Element	GASB Cod. Sec. 2200 subsections	AFR	ACFR
Basic financial statements:	.110–.204	Required	Required
• Government-wide financial statements including —The Statement of Net Position and —The Statement of Activities.		Required for general-purpose governments	Required
• Fund financial statements for major funds and nonmajor funds taken together. Interfund and similar eliminations made in the fund or combining financial statements should be apparent from the headings or disclosed in the notes.		Required for general-purpose governments	Required
• Governmental funds include: —A balance Sheet and —A Statement of Revenues, Expenditures, and Changes in Fund Balances (see **PRACTICE ALERT**).		Required	Required
• Proprietary funds include: —A Statement of Fund Net Position, —A Statement of Revenues, Expenses, changes in Fund Net Position, and —A Statement of Cash Flows prepared using the direct method.		Required	Required
• Fiduciary funds and component units that are fiduciary in nature include: —A Statement of Fiduciary Net Position and —A Statement of Changes in Fiduciary Net Position.		Required	Required
Notes to the Basic Financial Statements	Referenced only—see CCH's *Governmental GAAP Practice and Disclosures Manual*	Required	Required
Required Supplementary Information (RSI) other than MD&A, including schedules, statistical data and other information required by GASB standards due to their essentiality.	.205–.207	Required	Required

Element	GASB Cod. Sec. 2200 subsections	AFR	ACFR
Combining statements for nonmajor funds by fund type of the primary government including blended component units and nonmajor discretely presented component units.	.208–.210	Not required	Required
Individual fund statements and schedules for the funds of the primary government and blended component units.	.208–.211	Not required	Required
Schedules necessary to demonstrate compliance with finance-related legal or contractual provisions, to present information spread throughout the statements that can be brought together in greater detail and/or to present greater detail for information reported in the statements.		Not required unless by law, regulation, grant, bond covenant, etc., or to magnify information from other sections.	Same as AFR
Statistical section.	Referenced only—GASB Cod. Sec. 2800	Not required	Required

PRACTICE ALERT: The GASB's *Financial Reporting Model Improvements* Exposure Draft proposes to make many changes to reporting. In the titles of the fund statements for governmental funds, the GASB proposes:

Current Title	Proposed Title
Balance Sheet	Short-Term Financial Resources Balance Sheet
Statement of Revenues, Expenditures, and Changes in Fund Balance	Statement of Short-Term Financial Resource Flows

The provisions would continue the requirement that the basic financial statements be preceded by MD&A, which is presented as RSI.

The exposure draft also includes proposals that would require that the proprietary fund Statement of Revenues, Expenses, and Changes in Fund Net Position continue to distinguish between operating and nonoperating revenues and expenses. As discussed in Chapter 7, operating revenues and expenses would be defined as revenues and expenses other than nonoperating revenues and expenses. Nonoperating revenues and expenses would include:

- Subsidies received and provided,
- Revenues and expenses related to financing,
- Resources from the disposal of capital assets and inventory, and
- Investment income and expenses.

In addition to the subtotals currently required in a proprietary fund Statement of Revenues, Expenses, and Changes in Fund Net Position, the GASB has proposed requiring that a subtotal for operating income (loss) and noncapital subsidies be presented before reporting other nonoperating revenues and expenses.

In the basic financial statements, each major component unit would be presented in a separate column in the Statement of Net Position and the Statement of Activities, *if it does not reduce the readability of the statements*. If presenting each major component unit in a separate column in the reporting entity's statements of net position and activities reduces the readability of the statements, combining statements of major component units should be included in the reporting entity's basic financial statements after the fund financial statements.

Finally, for those governments that present budgetary comparison schedules as a component of the basic financial statements, the GASB has proposed that those comparison schedules should solely be part of RSI. The analysis of variances formerly presented in the MD&A would be presented as a note to RSI.

The GASB proposed a transition period in a similar fashion to what occurred from 1999 through 2006 (including infrastructure) for the current financial reporting model. GASB has proposed an implementation date based on a government's *total annual revenues in the first fiscal year beginning after June 15, 2022*, as follows:

- Governments with total annual revenues of $75 million or more should apply the requirements of this Statement for fiscal years beginning after June 15, 2024, and all reporting periods thereafter. According to GASB Staff data analyzing the U.S. Census Bureau's 2012 *Census of Governments* data, between 3.02% and 5.96% of the number of all governments would implement the first year, encompassing at least 84.4% of revenues. In scope would be:
    — All 50 states and approximately
    — 19.2% of counties,
    — 2.1% of localities,
    — 8% of independent school districts and
    — Less than 1% of all other governments.
- Governments with total annual revenues of less than $75 million should apply the requirements of this Statement for fiscal years beginning after June 15, 2025, and all reporting periods thereafter, Earlier application would be encouraged.
- However, these dates may be pushed back due to a potential delay. The issuance of a final statement is not expected until March 2024 as of the date of publication of this *Guide*.

Component Unit Implementation. If a primary government chooses early implementation, all the component units also should implement the provisions in the same implementation period. This is irrespective of size or status as a blended or discretely presented component unit.

Determining Appropriate Implementation Period. To determine the appropriate implementation period, revenues include *all revenues* of the primary government's governmental activities and business-type activities, *except for revenue-*

related extraordinary and special items. Fiduciary activities additions would not be included.

Fiduciary Activity Governments. Governments engaged *only in fiduciary activities* should use total annual additions, rather than revenues, to determine the appropriate implementation period.

To implement, changes adopted to conform to the provisions of any final statement would be applied retroactively by restating financial statements, if practicable, for all prior periods presented. If restatement for prior periods is not practicable, the cumulative effect, if any, of applying the provisions would be reported as a restatement of beginning fund balance for the earliest period restated. Also, the reason for not restating prior periods presented should be disclosed. In the first period the provisions would be applied, the notes to financial statements would disclose the nature of the restatement and its effect.

These proposed changes are detailed in sections throughout this chapter.

PRACTICE POINT: Special-purpose governments with only one fund may not present government-wide financial statements. See Chapters 21 through 24 for additional details.

Management's Discussion and Analysis (MD&A)

To some, the MD&A is the most crucial element of the AFR. It is supposed to explain the balances and results of the operations for the reporting period of the reporting entity in comparison with the prior period (or if comparative statements are utilized, the two prior periods). Unfortunately, many preparers leave preparation of the MD&A until the final stage of preparing the AFR.

The basic financial statements should be *preceded* by the MD&A, which the GASB classified as RSI. MD&A information should "provide an objective and easily readable analysis of the government's financial activities based on currently known facts, decisions, or conditions." The MD&A discusses information on all activities of the government, addressing both governmental activities and business-type activities, the major funds activity and results of operations in comparison to prior periods, capital asset and debt transactions, budgetary activity, and other elements.

For the purposes of the MD&A, *currently known facts* generally include information that the government is *aware of* as of the date of the auditor's report. GASB Cod. Sec. 2200.704-11 clarifies that the key word is *known* and, therefore, it should not be speculative. Typically, these events or decisions should have already occurred or have been enacted, adopted, agreed upon, or contracted.

Governments should not discuss in the MD&A the possible effect of events that might happen as that would be speculative. If a government wants to discuss speculative matters, they could be addressed in the letter of transmittal. The question discusses things that might be included in the MD&A that might have a significant effect on financial position or results of operations, if known such as:

- The award and acceptance of a major grant,
- The adjudication of a significant lawsuit,
- A notable change in the property tax base,
- The completion of an agreement to locate a major manufacturing plant in a city,
- An adopted increase in a state's sales tax rate,
- An approved increase in a university's tuition,
- A flood that caused considerable damage to a government's infrastructure, and
- A renegotiated labor contract with government.

Predicting how much sales tax revenues would increase if a planned shopping area is completed or that an Enterprise Resource Planning system under consideration "will pay for itself" over a certain period would be examples of statements that are not based on currently known facts, decisions, or conditions and, therefore, best discussed in a transmittal letter, which is included as part of an ACFR, but not an AFR.

In some instances, issues discussed in the MD&A as "currently known facts" will also be disclosed in the notes to the financial statements as subsequent events or contingencies. The discussion in the MD&A should highlight but not repeat the information required to be disclosed in the notes.

Information in the MD&A should provide a broad overview of both the short-and long-term analyses of the government's activities based on information presented in the financial report and fiscal policies that have been adopted by the governmental entity. Although the analysis provided by management should be directed to current-year results in comparison with the previous year's results, the emphasis should be on the current year.

The MD&A presentation should not be viewed as a public relations opportunity for the governmental entity but rather should be based on facts and incorporate both positive and negative developments. To make the information meaningful and understandable to constituents of the governmental entity, it may be appropriate to use graphs, multiple-color presentations, or other presentation strategies that might provide insight into the analysis [GASB Cod. Secs. 2200.106–.107, fns. 6–7].

The MD&A information should focus on the primary government's activities (both governmental and business-type activities) and distinguish between its activities and the government's discretely presented component units. Professional judgment must be exercised to determine whether the MD&A should include comments related to a specific discretely presented component unit. Factors that may be relevant in making that determination include the relationship between the component unit and the primary government and the significance of the component unit in comparison to all discretely presented component units. In some instances, it may be appropriate to refer readers to the separately presented financial statements of the component unit [GASB Cod. Sec. 2200.108].

Finally, the MD&A should answer the common question through each element: *"why?"* For example, "The overall balance of capital assets increased due to the initiation of construction on the new wing of the County offices, offset by normal end-of-life disposals and accumulated depreciation."

The GASB emphasizes that management of the governmental entity should see the MD&A section of the financial report as an opportunity to communicate with interested parties, and it warns against preparing boilerplate material that adds little insight into the financial position and activity of the government. However, this emphasis on flexibility by the GASB is tempered in that, at a minimum, the following issues should be discussed [GASB Cod. Sec. 2200.109]:

1. Brief discussion of the basic financial statements,
2. Presentation of condensed financial information,
3. Analysis of the overall financial position and results of operations,
4. Analysis of balances and transactions of individual funds,
5. Analysis of significant budget variations,
6. Discussion of significant capital assets and long-term debt activity,
7. Discussion of modified depreciation approach (if employed by the governmental entity), and
8. Description of currently known facts, decisions, or conditions.

PRACTICE POINT: The (a)-(h) listing *contains the minimum*, not the maximum, elements to be included in the MD&A. Governments can provide additional details on the above topics in (a)-(h). Information that does not relate to those topics is likely provided elsewhere, including the transmittal letter or other supplementary information and should not be in the MD&A [GASB Cod. Sec. 2200.fn. 8].

PRACTICE ALERT: The GASB's *Financial Reporting Model Improvements* Exposure Draft contains targeted improvements for the MD&A. The GASB is proposing to require the MD&A to provide an objective and easily readable analysis of the government's financial activities, continuing to focus on currently known facts, decisions, or conditions. "Currently known" is as of the *date the financial statements are issued*, rather than the reporting date. The onus is on financial managers of the government to present the MD&A as they are knowledgeable about the transactions and events that are reflected in the government's financial report, the fiscal policies that govern its operations and decision making, and other conditions that may have a significant effect on financial position or results of operations. MD&A provides financial managers with the opportunity to present both a short- and a long-term analysis of the government's activities. MD&A should be written in a manner that can be understood by readers who may not have a detailed knowledge of governmental accounting and financial reporting. MD&A also should include explanations and interpretations that help users understand the information provided.

Many of the currently presented elements are proposed to be continued. MD&A requirements in general are proposed by the GASB to emphasize that financial managers should report only the most relevant information and should avoid "boilerplate" information. The proposed general information in the MD&A contains five section topics:

- Introduction—brief overview of the financial statements in a manner like current GAAP,

- *Brief* financial summary—contains condensed financial information from government-wide financial statements with supporting information provided as an analysis with similar elements to current GAAP,

- Detailed analysis of the financial position and results of operations, again focusing on the government-wide financial statements, coupled with an analysis of balances and transactions of each major fund and nonmajor funds taken together to make an assessment if fund balances have improved or deteriorated because of the year's operations,

- *Significant* capital asset and long-term debt activity, again containing similar elements to current GAAP, and finally,

- *Currently* known facts, decisions, and conditions. Additional examples will be provided from what is contained in GASB Cod. Sec. 2200 and related implementation guidance.

It is unclear at the time of publication the outcome of these proposed elements until due process is completed by March 2024.

Comparative Data and the MD&A. GASB Cod. Secs. 2200.704-3 and .704-4 discuss when a government with both governmental and business-type activities may present comparative data (inclusive of total reporting entity columns for the current and a previous year) in its basic financial statements. The MD&A is not required for the previous year's presentation because that presentation does not constitute a complete set of financial statements (basic financial statements, notes, and RSI). On the other hand, most governmental entities do not present comparative financial statements (basic financial statements, notes, and RSI for two years) because of the complexity of such presentations, however, if comparative financial statements are presented, the MD&A must be presented for each year.

That does not mean that there must be two separate MD&A presentations. When comparative financial statements are presented, *three years* of comparative information should be presented in the MD&A—the current year, the prior year, and the year preceding the prior year. The analysis only needs to cover two years—from the year preceding the prior year to the prior year and from the prior year to the current year.

Condensed financial information in MD&A for both years could be presented on a comparative basis with the analysis of the overall financial position and results of operations for each year included in the same paragraph or section. Governmental entities that might have the space to present comparative financial statements include governments that have a single program or a business-type-activities-only entity.

> **PRACTICE ALERT:** The transition provisions contained in the *Financial Reporting Model Improvements* Exposure Draft considered the major changes proposed and their impact on MD&A. In the first period that the provisions would be applied, governments would *not* be required to restate prior periods for purposes of providing the comparative data for MD&A. However, governments are encouraged to provide comparative analyses of key elements of governmental activities and business-type activities as reported in the government-wide financial statements in MD&A for that period.

As an MD&A is RSI, the presentations should be limited to the eight elements listed above. For example, service efforts and accomplishments (SEA) or performance data *should not* be presented as a separate category (because it is not listed as such in the "(a)-(h)" listing). However, SEA or performance data could be introduced in a "listed" category if that information helps to explain the required MD&A. That is, performance data could be discussed in the overall analysis of position and results of operations if the SEA information clarifies why certain operating results change from one year to the next. If it is concluded that it is inappropriate to include an item in the MD&A, that information could be included in supplementary information or the letter of transmittal. The degree of detail related to the eight elements will vary from governmental entity to governmental entity. At a minimum, however, the specific requirements addressed in these elements, and described below, must be presented in the MD&A.

> **OBSERVATION:** GASB Cod. Sec. 2200.109 encourages governments to avoid "boilerplate" discussions within the MD&A and only report the most relevant financial information. A frequent complaint of users of financial statements is that boilerplate information is used too often in the MD&A. Preparers of the MD&A should take the MD&A seriously and focus on it as the primary communication tool to users of financial statements and decision-makers.

Discussion of the Basic Financial Statements. This initial section of the MD&A should be the start of the analysis of the balances and results of operations for the government for the period(s). The MD&A information should include a *brief* description of the basic financial statements and how the government-wide financial statements relate to the fund financial statements. This discussion should explain how fund financial statements either "reinforce information in government-wide statements or provide additional information." The explanation assists readers in understanding *why* the statements are different, instead of just stating they are different.

Topics that may be included in this section of the MD&A may include the following:

- The broad scope and overall perspective of government-wide financial statements (Statement of Net Position and the Statement of Activities);

- The nature of major fund financial statements for governmental funds (Balance Sheet and Statement of Revenues, Expenditures, and Changes in Fund Balances) and proprietary fund activities (Statement of Net Position, Statement of Revenues, Expenses, and Changes in Fund Net Position, and Statement of Cash Flows), and
- The fiduciary role of the governmental entity and the nature of the related financial statements (Statement of Fiduciary Net Position and Statement of Changes in Fiduciary Net Position).

GASB Cod. Secs. 2200.704-7 and .730-4 discuss aspects of how the totals in the government-wide financial statements will generally not equal the totals in the fund financial statements. After all, governmental funds are prepared on a different basis of accounting than the government-wide statements. For this reason, GASB Cod. Sec. 2200.160 requires a summary reconciliation between the fund financial statements and the government-wide financial statements at the bottom of the fund financial statements or in a separate schedule.

Specifically, the amount shown as the "total fund balances" in the "total governmental funds" column in the fund balance sheets *must be reconciled* to the "net position" for governmental activities presented in the Statement of Net Position. Also, the amount shown as "net changes in fund balance" in the "total governmental funds" column in the statements of revenues, expenditures, and changes in fund balances must be reconciled to the "changes in net position" for governmental activities presented in the Statement of Activities. The MD&A should provide only an overview of the differences, and that overview should be in a narrative form. If the totals in the government-wide financial statements and fund financial statements are essentially the same, the MD&A should note that they are similar.

Presentation of Condensed Financial Information. The MD&A information should include *condensed* government-wide financial statements and comments on the *significant* changes from the previous year to the current year. This condensed presentation *is not an entire copy of the basic financial statements in the MD&A*. The condensed presentation should include information, *at a minimum*, that supports the analysis of the overall financial position and results of operations (which is the next topic discussed below). GASB Cod. Sec. 2200.109(b) contains a list of the condensed information elements in the MD&A, which includes the following:

- Total assets, distinguishing between capital and other assets,
- Total liabilities, distinguishing between long-term debt outstanding and other liabilities,
- Total net position, distinguishing between amounts presented as the net investment in capital assets, restricted amounts, and unrestricted amounts,
- Total program revenues (by major sources),
- General revenues (by major sources),
- Total revenues,
- Program expenses (by functional category, at a minimum),

- Total expenses,
- Excess (deficiency) before contributions to term and permanent endowments or permanent fund principal, special and extraordinary items, and transfers,
- Contributions,
- Extraordinary and special items,
- Transfers,
- Change in net position, and
- Beginning and ending net position.

OBSERVATION: "Major sources" is undefined in GAAP but is generally construed by preparers to mean greater than 10% of each accounting element.

OBSERVATION: Presentation of a segment does not mean that separate MD&As are presented. The MD&A should present aggregated information. GAAP does not specifically mention aggregation in the MD&A, but presentation of more than one MD&A would lead to confusion.

GASB Cod. Sec. 2200.704-8 encourages the use of charts and graphs in the MD&A. The question reminds practitioners that comparison of condensed financial information should not be presented as charts and graphs. However, charts and graphs may be used to *elaborate* on the presentation of the condensed information.

Analysis of the Overall Financial Position and Results of Operations. The word "analysis" is defined by the Oxford English Dictionary as "a detailed examination of the elements or structure of something." Performing an analysis of the overall financial position and results of operations is a cornerstone of an understandable MD&A. There should be an analysis of the overall improvement or deterioration of financial position and results of operations of the governmental entity based on government-wide financial statements. The analysis should focus on both governmental activities and business-type activities. The emphasis on the comments about the condensed government-wide financial statements should be analytical and not just computational.

For example, percentage changes from the previous year to the current year should be supplemented with a discussion of important economic factors, such as interest rate changes and changes in regional economic activity, which affected the governmental entity's operating results for the year.

Analysis of Balances and Transactions of Individual Funds. Part of the MD&A should concentrate on significant changes in balances and transactions that are related to individual funds. Information concerning the availability of resources for future use should be discussed, taking into consideration restrictions, commitments, and other factors.

Analysis of Significant Budget Variations. The analysis of budgetary information should focus on significant differences between:

- The original budget and the final budget, and
- Actual budgetary results and the final budget.

The commentary should include an analysis of currently known reasons that are expected to have a significant effect on future services or liquidity.

PRACTICE ALERT: As a reminder, a major proposed change in the *Financial Reporting Model Improvements* Exposure Draft is the movement of the budgetary analysis subsection and analysis to a note to RSI along with budgetary schedules discussed later in this chapter.

OBSERVATION: GASB Cod. Sec. 2200.704-9 discusses in part how the MD&A should not merely point out the obvious. For example, stating that there was an increase from the original budget to "cover higher-than-expected expenditures" is not helpful. The analysis should explain what factors led to the increase in expenditures. For example, a reasonable analysis would discuss how a record snowfall total for the year increased the need for snow-and ice-clearing appropriations for the department of public works.

OBSERVATION: The analyses portions of the MD&A should not be taken lightly as the analyses should answer the question "*why*." All too often, practitioners perform the analysis by stating that a balance increased or decreased from the prior year, without answering the question "*why*." In many instances, the practitioner may state a balance increased, when in fact, it decreased or vice versa. In some instances, analysis is copied from a peer government, with editing not performed to remove that government's name, or the text has no bearing on the element being analyzed. Governments should take the time to properly perform the analyses sections of the MD&A as it usually is a focus area of the users of the financial statements.

Discussion of Significant Capital Assets and Long-Term Debt Activity. MD&A information should describe activity that affected capital assets and long-term debt during the period. The discussion should include commitments for capital expenditures, changes in credit ratings, and whether debt limitations may affect future planned activities. In this analysis there is no need to repeat the information that is contained in the notes to the financial statements that relate to capital assets and long-term liabilities. However, the information may be summarized.

PRACTICE POINT: As discussed in Chapter 1 of this *Guide*, the word "significant" is used in many GASB standards. However, it is inconsistently applied. To many practitioners, it is less than "material." However, "material" does not have a definition in GAAP. For auditing purposes, "significant" usually means less than qualitatively material (which is defined as the point where a misstatement is possible relative to size and nature) and more than insignificant (an item of a clearly inconsequential nature).

GASB Cod. Sec. 2200.704-10 exempts special assessment debt from discussion in the MD&A when the governmental entity is not obligated in any manner. However, this *Guide* notes that special assessment debt may be included in the MD&A discussion "if, for example, the proceeds were used to build or acquire significant infrastructure assets for the government." (See Chapter 19.)

PRACTICE POINT: As stated previously, governments often copy information available elsewhere into the MD&A (e.g., tables in the notes to the basic financial statements related to capital assets and long-term debt activity). Again, this is not proper.

PRACTICE POINT: This section's totals for capital assets and debt should reconcile to the amounts in the Statement of Net Position, inclusive of intangible capital assets and all forms of debt as discussed in Chapter 12. Summaries of defeasance and refunding transactions are commonly included in this section, with references to applicable notes to the basic financial statements.

Discussion of Modified Depreciation Approach (If Utilized by the Government). As discussed in Chapters 10 and 18, a governmental entity may choose not to depreciate certain "eligible" infrastructure assets but rather may use the modified approach. For governments that use the modified approach, the MD&A information should discuss the following:

- Any significant changes in the assessed level of condition of eligible infrastructure assets from previous condition assessments,
- A comparison of the current level of asset condition with the condition level that the government has established, and
- Any significant difference between the actual amounts spent to maintain the current level and condition and the estimated annual amount needed to maintain or preserve eligible infrastructure assets at an appropriate level of condition.

OBSERVATION: The nation's aging infrastructure has brought into focus the issue of deferred maintenance disclosure. The modified approach has some aspects of an assessment of deferred maintenance; however, it is not widely used. Many users of financial statements have commented to the GASB that this issue should be explored. For example, common interest realty associations (CIRAs) (commonly known as condominium associations) operate similarly to governments and even use funds. CIRAs often present disclosure of the level of deferred maintenance in the complex and are required to present supplementary information on funding renewals and replacements. For governments, the level of deferred maintenance may be a large unrecorded future obligation. Therefore, it may be beneficial to the users of the government's financial statements to disclose estimates of deferred maintenance by type of infrastructure (roads, dams, bridges, etc.) that are disclosed elsewhere in engineering reports to decision-makers. This may be accomplished by a table in the MD&A.

Description of Currently Known Facts, Decisions, or Conditions. The MD&A should describe currently known facts, decisions, or conditions that are expected to have a significant effect on the entity's financial position (net position) and operations results (revenues, expenses, and other changes in net position). GAAP emphasizes that currently known facts do not constitute prospective information, such as forecasted financial statements.

OBSERVATION: GASB Cod. Sec. 2200.704-11 clarifies how currently known facts must be based on events that have taken place. This aspect is also the most overlooked requirement in an MD&A. Many preparers insert that the government has passed a budget for the next fiscal period. Nearly every government has some currently known facts and conditions at the date of the financial statements that are qualitative as well as quantitative. For example, gain or loss of a major employer, restructuring of operations, pension or OPEB plan, major change in taxation or other revenues, status of a large construction project or the anticipated level of deferred maintenance are all potential currently known facts and conditions that could be inserted into an MD&A.

Basic Financial Statements

As introduced in this chapter, the following are the components of a governmental entity's basic financial statements [GASB Cod. Sec. 2200.105]:

- Government-wide financial statements,
- Fund financial statements, and
- Notes to the basic financial statements.

Under current GAAP, budgetary comparison schedules may be presented as a component of the basic financial statements rather than as RSI. In practice, most practitioners include budgetary information as part of RSI. When the budgetary comparison schedules are presented as a basic financial statement, the schedules should be reported within the governmental fund financial statements, and they are subjected to a different level of auditing than as RSI (see previous **PRACTICE ALERT** on the *Financial Reporting Model Improvements* Exposure Draft).

GOVERNMENT-WIDE FINANCIAL STATEMENTS

The focus of government-wide financial statements is on the overall financial position and activities of the reporting entity. These financial statements are constructed around the concept of a primary government as detailed in Chapter 4. Due to the provisions of GAAP, the government-wide statements encompass the primary government and its component units, except for fiduciary funds of the primary government and component units that are fiduciary in nature.

Exclusion of Fiduciary Activities. Financial statements of fiduciary funds and component units that are fiduciary in nature *are not* presented in the government-wide financial statements but *are included in the fund financial statements*. Fiduciary funds are excluded from government-wide financial statements because resources of these funds cannot be used to finance a governmental entity's activities. The financial statements of a Fiduciary Fund are included in the entity's fund financial statements because the governmental entity is financially accountable for those resources even though they belong to other parties [GASB Cod. Secs. 2200.110–.111].

PRACTICE POINT: The presentation of fiduciary fund statements is discussed later in this chapter. For a complete discussion of fiduciary activities, see Chapter 8.

The government-wide financial statements should accomplish the following:
- Present financial information about the overall government without presenting information about individual funds or fund types,
- Exclude financial information about fiduciary activities,
- Differentiate between financial information that applies to the primary government and that of discretely presented component units,
- Differentiate between the primary government's governmental activities and business-type activities, and
- Measure and present all financial balances and activities based on the economic resources measurement focus and the accrual basis of accounting.

PRACTICE POINT: A governmental entity cannot just issue government-wide financial statements or only fund financial statements and deem them a complete set of financial statements. However, the reporting requirements for certain special-purpose governments differ. In addition, generally, governments cannot combine the government-wide and fund financial statements. An exception is made in GAAP for single-program governments. Such governments may combine the government-wide and fund financial statements. These exceptions are discussed in Chapters 21 through 24 [GASB Cod. Secs. Sp20.107–.108].

To achieve some of the objectives listed above, GAAP requires that government-wide financial statements be formatted following these guidelines [GASB Cod. Secs. 2200.112–.113]:
- Separate rows and columns should be used to distinguish between the primary government's governmental activities and business-type activities.
- A total column should be used for the primary government.
- Separate rows and columns should distinguish between the total primary government (governmental activities plus business-type activities) and its discretely presented component units.

- A total column may be used for the reporting entity (primary government and discretely presented component units), but this is optional.
- A total column may be used for prior-year information, but this is optional.

Governmental activities are "generally financed through taxes, intergovernmental revenues, and other nonexchange revenues," and business-type activities are financed to some degree by charging external parties for the goods or services they acquire. Activities are not required to be segregated into governmental and proprietary funds beyond what is reported by management, unless the activity is required to be in an enterprise fund as discussed in Chapter 7 and described in GASB Cod. Sec. 1300.109. Governmental activities are generally accounted for in governmental funds and internal service funds. Business-type activities are usually reported in enterprise funds.

A total column should be used to combine the governmental activities and the business-type activities of a governmental entity. A separate column that combines the government and its component units (discretely presented) may or may not be used. However, if a separate column is used, the column *should not* be titled "memorandum only." The "memorandum only" columnar heading is appropriate only when columns with different measurement focuses and bases of accounting are added together. The government-wide financial statements are based on a single measurement focus and basis of accounting.

The government-wide financial statements have separate columns for governmental activities and business-type activities. In general, governmental funds are combined to form the governmental activities column and enterprise funds are combined to form the business-type activities column; however, an activity and a fund are not the same. An "activity" refers to a program or service but a "fund" is an accounting and reporting vehicle. For this reason, an activity (governmental or business-type) could be performed in one or more funds, and a fund could perform one or more activities.

For example, an enterprise fund could report an activity that is governmental, rather than business, in nature and that activity should be presented in the governmental activities column in the government-wide financial statements. If this occurs, the activity will represent a reconciling item between the fund financial statements and the government-wide financial statements [GASB Cod. Sec. 2200.160].

GASB Cod. Sec. 2200.706-3 does not require that comparative prior-year data be presented Many governments do present *summarized* prior-year data. For this reason, GASB Cod. Sec. 2200.112 provides no guidelines for the presentation of prior-year data. Presenting comparative data in governmental financial statements, as opposed to corporate financial statements, is problematic because of the complicated structure of governmental statements. For example, reporting a comparative Statement of Net Position for many governmental entities requires eight columns or more. Trying to format a Statement of Activities for many governmental entities would probably be too unwieldy.

If a governmental entity is not a complex reporting entity (e.g., if it has only governmental activities and no component units), presenting prior-year data might not be cumbersome. For more complicated reporting entities, the best way to present prior-year data may be by reproducing the prior-year financial statements in the current year's financial statements. (See further discussion on *comparative* financial statements later in this chapter.)

PRACTICE POINT: Some of these presentation provisions are not applicable to entities that are subjected to regulatory accounting, such as public utilities and insurance entities. The provisions of GASB Cod. Sec. Re10 include provisions for entities subject to regulatory accounting provisions. The provisions primarily stem from Financial Accounting Standards Board (FASB) Accounting Standards Codification® (ASC) Topic 980, *Regulated Operations*, Regulatory accounting is discussed in Chapter 24.

The government-wide statements are prepared using accrual accounting. Under the flow of economic resources measurement focus and accrual basis of accounting, revenues are recognized when earned and expenses are recorded when incurred when these activities are related to exchange and exchange-like activities. In addition, capital assets (such as infrastructure buildings and equipment) are capitalized and depreciated over their estimated economic lives [GASB Cod. Sec. 2200.114].

Unlike commercial enterprises, much of the revenue received by governments is not based on an exchange or an exchange-like transaction (i.e., the selling of a product or service and receiving something of approximate equal value) but rather arises from the entity's taxing powers or as grants from other governmental entities or individuals (nonexchange transactions). For these nonexchange transactions, the standards contained in GASB Cod. Sec. N50 and discussed in Chapter 17 and Chapter 18 are used.

The government-wide financial statements include the following:

- Statement of Net Position, and
- Statement of Activities.

A government-wide Statement of Cash Flows is not required.

Statement of Net Position

The formula for deriving a Statement of Net Position is as follows:

$$\begin{array}{r}\text{Assets}\\ \text{+ Deferred Outflows of Resources}\\ \text{− Liabilities}\\ \text{− Deferred Inflows of Resources}\\ \hline \text{= Net Position}\end{array}$$

Net position is comprised of:

- Net investment in capital assets,
- Restricted net position, and
- Unrestricted net position (which may or may not be a deficit).

Although the GASB recommends that the net position format be adopted for the Statement of Net Position, it allows formatting the statement so that a net position section (equity) is presented whereby total assets plus deferred outflows of resources equal total liabilities plus deferred inflows of resources plus the residual balance. Irrespective of how the Statement of Net Position is formatted, the difference between total assets and total liabilities must be referred to as "net position" rather than as "fund balance" or "equity" [GASB Cod. Sec. 2200.115].

Presentation of Assets, Deferred Outflows of Resources, Liabilities, and Deferred Inflows of Resources. Assets, deferred outflows of resources, liabilities, and deferred inflows of resources should be presented in the Statement of Net Position based on their relative liquidity. The liquidity of assets is determined by their ability to be converted to cash and the absence of any restriction that might limit their conversion to cash. The liquidity of liabilities is based on maturity dates or expected payment dates. Because of the significant degree of aggregation used in the preparation of government-wide financial statements, the GASB notes that the liquidity of an asset or liability account presented in the Statement of Net Position should be determined by assessing the average liquidity of the class of assets or liabilities to which it belongs, "even though individual balances may be significantly more or less liquid than others in the same class and some items may have both current and long-term element" [GASB Cod. Sec. 2200.116].

Most governmental entities prepare an unclassified Statement of Net Position that lists assets based on their liquidity. Alternatively, GASB Cod. Sec. 2200 notes that assets, deferred outflows of resources, liabilities, and deferred inflows of resources may be presented in the Statement of Net Position using a classified financial statement format whereby accounts are grouped in current and noncurrent categories like the presentation used by business enterprises [GASB Cod. Sec. 2200.fn.13].

If prepared by the government, a *classified* Statement of Net Position format would be organized as follows (with elements as applicable):

Assets
- Current assets:
   - Cash and cash equivalents
   - Investments
   - Receivables
   - Internal balances
   - Inventories
   - Other
- Total current assets
- Noncurrent assets:
   - Restricted assets
   - Capital assets
- Categories of capital assets, net of accumulated depreciation and amortization, as applicable

- Total noncurrent assets
- **Total Assets**

  Deferred Outflows of Resources
  — Categories of deferred outflows of resources
- **Total Deferred Outflows of Resources**
- **Total Assets and Deferred Outflows of Resources**

Liabilities
- Current liabilities:
  — Accounts payable and accrued expenses
  — Internal balances
  — Advances
  — Current portion of long-term obligations
- Total current liabilities
- Noncurrent liabilities:
  — Categories
  — Noncurrent portion of long-term obligations
- **Total noncurrent liabilities**
- **Total Liabilities**

  Deferred Inflows of Resources
  — Categories of deferred inflows of resources
- **Total Deferred Inflows of Resources**

Net Position
- Net investment in capital assets
- Restricted—nonexpendable
- Restricted for:
  — Categories of restricted net position
- Unrestricted (deficit if if necessary)
- **Total Net Position**
- **Total Liabilities, Deferred Inflows of Resources, and Net Position**

Neither GASB Cod. Sec. 2200, nor GASB:CS-4 discuss whether there is a possibility of a current portion of a deferred outflow of resources or a deferred inflow of resources. Because these are presented in separate sections in the Statement of Net Position, it is not proper to commingle these with other assets or liabilities even if a classified Statement of Net Position is used.

When a governmental entity presents a classified Statement of Net Position, the question arises as to whether the amount that represents restricted net position (in the equity section) requires that specific assets be identified as "restricted assets" (in the asset section).

When preparing financial statements, no general requirements are in GAAP specifying which equity accounts are required to be traceable to specific assets. Therefore, when a classified Statement of Net Position is presented, there is no need to establish a subcategory of assets identified as restricted. However, a financial statement preparer should carefully evaluate the ramifications of restrictions to determine whether they are a determinant in categorizing an asset as current or noncurrent.

Current assets should *not* include "cash and claims to cash that are restricted as to withdrawal or use for other than current operations, are designated for expenditure in the acquisition or construction of noncurrent assets or are segregated for the liquidation of long-term debt." GASB Cod. Sec. 2200.708-2 states that "resources accounted for in the General Fund, special revenue funds, and debt service funds are generally expected to be used in current operations or to liquidate current obligations and thus generally would be considered current assets." On the other hand, cash presented in a capital projects fund or a permanent fund, due to the nature of each fund type, should be evaluated to determine whether the amount or a portion of the amount should be reported as a current or noncurrent asset.

Capital assets are reported in the Statement of Net Position, based on their original historical cost, plus ancillary charges such as transportation, installation, and site preparation costs. Capital assets that have been donated to a governmental entity must be capitalized at their estimated fair value (plus any ancillary costs) at the date of receipt. Capital assets are discussed in Chapter 10.

PRACTICE ALERT: As discussed in Chapters 10 and 14 of this *Guide*, the GASB is in the process of a major project on the *classification* of nonfinancial assets, but not the recognition and measurement of such assets. In scope are the following types of assets, excluding investments discussed in Chapter 9 of this *Guide*:

- Tangible capital assets held for sale and tangible capital assets used for service,
- Intangible capital assets and tangible capital assets,
- Intangible lease assets and tangible owned assets, and
- Contracts for the right-to-use intangible assets and leases of tangible assets.

Tangible capital assets held for sale tentatively may be required to be classified separately from tangible capital assets used for service by requiring them to be reported as a major class of capital asset. Intangible capital assets would be classified separately from tangible capital assets by requiring them to be reported by major class separate from major classes of tangible capital assets.

Right-to-use assets would be required to be recognized for subscription-based information technology arrangements separately from other capital assets. Assets representing the right-to-use intangible underlying assets, other than subscription-based information technology arrangements, should not be classified separately from assets representing the right-to-use tangible underlying assets. Assets representing the right-to-use intangible underlying assets would be classified separately from owned intangible assets.

The exposure draft is expected to define the term *held for sale*. Such capital assets held for sale would be required to be reclassified as used for service if the usage of the asset changes over time.

An exposure draft was being released as this edition of the *Guide* was slated for publication. A final standard is expected by June 2024.

The liquidity of assets is determined by their ability to be converted to cash and the absence of any restriction that might limit their conversion to cash. If an asset is restricted, the nature of the restriction must be evaluated to determine the appropriate location within the asset classification. The following are common examples of how restrictions would affect asset presentation:

- *Cash restricted for the servicing of debt.* If the cash is expected to be used to pay "current maturities," the cash could be reported with unrestricted cash.

- *Permanently restricted assets.* If assets are permanently restricted, they are not available to pay a governmental entity's expenses and are, therefore, as illiquid as capital assets.

- *Term restrictions.* The term of the restriction determines where assets subject to term restrictions are presented. If the restriction ends within a brief period after the date of the financial statements, the assets would be liquid. On the other hand, if the time restriction is longer than one year, the assets are as illiquid as long-term receivables that have a similar "maturity" date.

Once individual liabilities are grouped into titles for financial statement presentation, account groupings that have an average maturity of greater than one year must be reported in two components—the portion due within one year and the portion due beyond one year. For example, if several individual general ledger accounts have been grouped for financial statement purposes in the account titled "notes payable" and, on average, this grouping has an average maturity greater than one year, the presentation in the Statement of Net Position could appear as follows:

Partial Statement of Net Position	
Liabilities	
Notes Payable:	
Due within one year	$1,000,000
Due beyond one year	6,000,000

If several liability groupings have an average maturity life beyond one year, detailed information by account title (e.g., notes payable, bonds payable) does not have to be made on the face of the Statement of Net Position but rather may be presented in a note to the financial statements with appropriate reference.

GASB Cod. Sec. 2200.708-4 discusses how a governmental entity must make an estimate of compensated absences that may be paid within one year based on factors such as:

- Historical experience,
- Budgeted amounts, and
- Personnel policies concerning the length of accumulation.

> **PRACTICE ALERT:** See Chapter 13 for a full discussion of GASB Statement No. 101 (*Compensated Absences*).

In the government-wide financial statements, both short-and long-term liabilities of a governmental entity are presented as described earlier. Long-term liabilities may include debts such as notes, mortgages, bonds, and obligations related to capitalized lease agreements. In addition, operating liabilities related to activities such as compensated absences, claims and assessments must be reported in the Statement of Net Position.

Presentation of Components of Net Position. Net position represents the difference between a governmental entity's total assets plus its deferred outflows and its total liabilities plus its deferred inflows. The Statement of Net Position must identify the components of net position, namely:

- Net investment in capital assets,
- Restricted net position, and
- Unrestricted net position.

> **PRACTICE POINT:** GASB Cod. Sec. 2200.708-6 reminds practitioners that GAAP does not allow other terms, such as "equity," "net worth," and "fund balance," to be used in the Statement of Net Position.

> **PRACTICE POINT:** The GASB Statement No. 99 (*Omnibus 2022*) contains a further emphasis of this, including removal of the terms "fund equity," "balance sheet," "as a whole" and "basis of accounting" improperly presented in many places in the *Codification*.

Net Investment in Capital Assets. The portion of net position consisting of net investment in capital assets includes capital assets of the government, net of accumulated depreciation. Accumulated depreciation also includes the amortization of intangible assets. The amount is further reduced by the outstanding balances of all forms of debt attributable to the improvement of those assets. Forms of debt issued for construction of assets for other governments or other operating borrowings are excluded.

Deferred outflows of resources and deferred inflows of resources that are attributable to the acquisition, construction, or improvement of those assets or related debt also should be included in this component of net position. If there are significant unspent related debt proceeds or deferred inflows of resources at the end of the reporting period, the portion of the debt or deferred inflows of resources attributable to the unspent amount should not be included in the calculation of net investment in capital assets. Instead, that portion of the debt or deferred inflow of resources should be included in the same net position component (restricted or unrestricted) as the unspent amount [GASB Cod. Sec. 2200.118, fn. 14].

GASB Cod. Secs. 2200.708-9–12, .709-10–15 make the following observations about net investment in capital assets:

- All capital assets, regardless of any restrictions (e.g., federal surplus property) must be considered in the computation of net investment in capital assets. The purpose of identifying net position as restricted and unrestricted is to provide insight into the availability of *financial*, not capital, resources.

- To further explain, the net investment in capital assets component of net position consists of:

Element	Operation
Capital asset balance, including tangible, intangible and right-to-use assets relating to leases, public-private and public-public partnerships, and availability payment arrangements (P3s) and subscription-based information technology arrangements (SBITAs).	Less
Accumulated depreciation (as well as accumulated amortization of intangible capital assets and right-to-use assets).	Subtotaled to arrive at capital assets, net of accumulated depreciation. *Plus*
Deferred outflows of resources that are capital-related (not related to postemployment benefit plans).	Less
Outstanding balances of bonds, mortgages, notes, leases, P3s, SBITAs, or other borrowings that are attributable to the acquisition, construction, or improvement of those assets.	Less
Deferred inflows of resources that are capital-related (not related to postemployment benefit plans).	*Equals* **Net Investment in Capital Assets**

If there are significant unspent related debt proceeds or deferred inflows of resources at the end of the reporting period, the portion of the debt or deferred inflows of resources attributable to the unspent amount should not be included in the calculation of net investment in capital assets. Instead, that portion of the debt or deferred inflows of resources should be included in the same net position component (restricted or unrestricted) as the unspent amount—for example: *restricted for capital projects*.

Many governmental entities create a capital projects fund to account for capital debt proceeds to be used to acquire, construct, or improve infrastructure assets and buildings (including land) and then specific accounts in the General Fund or other funds for capital debt proceeds to be used to acquire capital assets other than infrastructure assets. When these approaches are used, it is relatively simple to identify the unspent portion of capital debt proceeds. For those governmental entities that do not use these two approaches and commingle funds, they must "use their best estimates—in a manner that can be documented—to determine the unspent portion." according to GAAP. The equity interest in capital assets of a joint venture would also be excluded from this calculation.

Refunding Bonds and Net Investment in Capital Assets. When debt is issued to refund existing capital-related debt, the newly issued debt is considered capital-related and is used to compute the net investment in capital assets component.

> **OBSERVATION:** GASB Cod. Sec. 2200.709-6 discusses the effect of refunding existing capital-related debt on net investment in capital assets. Even though the direct connection between the capital assets and the debt issued to finance the construction or acquisition has been eliminated, the replacement debt assumes the capital characteristics of the original issue. However, if the new issue is refunding capital appreciation debt, only the portion of the new debt that refunds the original principal of the old debt should be considered capital related.
>
> - When a governmental entity has capital assets but no related debt, the net position component should be simply identified as "investment in capital assets" (the "net" is dropped).
> - When a general-purpose government issues bonds to construct school buildings for its independent school districts and the repayment of the bonds is the responsibility of the general-purpose government because the debt was not used to acquire, construct, or improve capital assets for the governmental entity, the outstanding debt is not capital-related and is not used to compute the amount of net investment in capital assets of the general-purpose government. The effect is to reduce unrestricted net position. If doing so has a significant effect on the unrestricted net position component, the circumstances may be further explained in a note to the financial statements.

With the inclusion of deferred inflows of resources or deferred outflows of resources in the calculation of net investment in capital assets, borrowings become more important. For example, in a debt refunding transaction, the borrowing portion presumably is now included as a part of related debt. Unamortized positions of up-front payments in hybrid derivative instruments related to debt issued to fund capital assets are also included in the calculation of net investment in capital assets. Some view securities lending transactions as borrowings; however, they would not be germane in the calculation of net investment in capital assets. The borrowings related to sales of future revenues would also not be germane, because they also do not involve capital assets—they involve receivables.

Restricted Net Position. Restricted net position arises if either of the following conditions exists [GASB Cod. Sec. 2200.119]:

- Externally imposed by creditor (such as through debt covenants), grantors, contributors, or laws or regulations of other governments, or
- Imposed by law through constitutional provisions or enabling legislation.

Enabling legislation "authorizes the government to assess, levy, charge, or otherwise mandate payment of resources (from external resource providers)" and includes a legally enforceable requirement that those resources be used only for the specific purposes stipulated in the legislation. Enabling legislation also commonly places restrictions on asset use in governmental utility operations if the utility reports in accordance with a regulatory framework [GASB Cod. Sec. 2200.fn.16]. Regulatory frameworks are discussed in Chapter 24.

GAAP defines "legal enforceability" as an action when a government can be compelled by an external party—citizens, public interest groups, or the judiciary—to use resources created by enabling legislation only for the purposes specified by the legislation. However, enforceability cannot ultimately be proven unless tested through the judicial process, therefore, professional judgment must be exercised [GASB Cod. Sec. 2200.120].

When a state legislature passes a law to earmark a percentage of specific tax proceeds (e.g., a percentage of its sales taxes) for a specific purpose, this is different from enabling legislation. The enabling-legislation criterion is satisfied only when the same law creates both the tax and the restriction on how the resulting resources may be used.

The specific purpose of the enabling legislation may be changed from time to time by the government. *From the point of change forward*, the resources accumulated under the new enabling legislation should be reported as restricted to the purpose specified by the new enabling legislation. Professional judgment should be used to determine if remaining balances accumulated under the original enabling legislation should continue to be reported as restricted to the original purpose, restricted to the purpose specified in the new legislation, or unrestricted [GASB Cod. Sec. 2200.121].

If there is a violation of the restriction established in the enabling legislation, or if the government reconsiders, the restriction needs to be reevaluated as it may no longer be enforceable. If it is determined that the restriction is no longer enforceable, then the balances are reclassed to unrestricted net position *from the beginning of the period* [GASB Cod. Sec. 2200.122].

Restricted net position should be identified based on major categories that make up the restricted balance. These categories could include items such as net position restricted for capital projects and net position restricted for debt service. Supporting details of restricted net position should be presented in the body of the financial statements and not in the notes to the financial statements.

Restricted Assets and Restricted Net Position. The liabilities related to restricted assets must be considered in determining restricted net position as presented in the Statement of Net Position. For example, the Statement of Net Position would generally identify net assets restricted for capital projects. To determine that amount, the starting point would be to identify total net position (total assets and deferred outflows of resources, less total liabilities, and deferred inflows of resources) in all capital projects funds. Additionally, because a capital projects fund is on the modified accrual basis and the Statement of Net Position is on the accrual basis, it would be necessary to take into consideration any "conversion" adjustments that would increase or decrease the liabilities in the capital projects funds. However, a negative (deficit) balance in restricted net position cannot be displayed on the Statement of Net Position. Any negative amount would be used to reduce the unrestricted net position balance.

In some instances, net position may be restricted on a permanent basis (in perpetuity). Under this circumstance, the restricted net position must be subdivided into expendable and nonexpendable restricted net position. This is common with permanent endowments such as land trusts, permanent fund principal amounts, minority interests in component units, and similar [GASB Cod. Sec. 2200.123].

Generally, the amount of net position identified as restricted in the Statement of Net Position will not be the same as the amount of restricted fund balance in a governmental fund Balance Sheet and potentially restricted fund net position in a proprietary fund Statement of Net Position because:

- The financial statements are based on different measurement focuses and bases of accounting under *current GAAP* and
- There are different definitions for restricted net position and restricted fund balance. (Fund financial statements are discussed later in this chapter.)

GASB Cod. Secs. 2200.710-2-16, .711-1, .712-1-8 have the following common themes about restricted net position:

- GASB Cod. Sec. 2200.119 is the starting point for determining whether net position is restricted. In addition, to be considered restricted net position, the restriction must be narrower than the "reporting unit in which it is reported." For example, if the resources are restricted to "public safety," then the resources are restricted. On the other hand, if the resources are to be used "for the benefit of the citizens," that restriction is as broad as the governmental entity and there is effectively no restriction on net position.
- The requirements of GASB Cod. Sec. 2200.123 apply only to permanent endowments or permanent fund principal because restrictions imposed on term endowments will at some point be expendable.
- The liabilities related to restricted assets must be considered in determining restricted net position.
- Earmarking an existing revenue source is different from enabling legislation. The enabling-legislation criterion is satisfied only when the same law creates a tax or other source of revenue and the restriction on how the resulting resources may be used.

A state legislature may change an existing law that previously restricted the use of tax revenue to a type of expenditure. GASB Cod. Sec. 2200.712-2 clarifies that although "the new restriction is not established by the original enabling legislation, the net position arising from the changed legislation is nonetheless restricted for purposes of financial statement disclosure even though the new tax revenues are to be used for a purpose different from that identified in the original legislation."

In some instances, a state statute may exist that requires that "revenues derived from a fee or charge shall not be used for any purpose other than that for which the fee or charge was imposed." Therefore, if a local government has imposed such a fee or charge (e.g., for the replacement of infrastructure assets), the unspent resources accumulated from the fee or charge represents a restricted net position.

Unrestricted Net Position. Assets that are not classified as net investment in capital assets or restricted are included in the category unrestricted net position. Portions of the entity's net position may be identified by management to reflect tentative plans or commitments of governmental resources. The tentative plans or commitments may be related to items such as plans to retire debt at some future date or to replace infrastructure or specified capital assets.

Designated amounts are different from restricted amounts because designations represent planned actions, not actual commitments. For this reason, designated amounts should not be classified with restricted net position but rather should be reported as a part of the unrestricted net position component. In addition, designations cannot be disclosed as such on the face of the Statement of Net Position [GASB Cod. Secs. 2200.124–.125].

OBSERVATION: A frequent problem occurred when governments implemented the defined benefit pension and postemployment benefit other than pension standards. An unrestricted net deficit occurred (negative unrestricted net position), which required explanation to non-accountants. Preparers should be careful in the language that is used to explain the unrestricted net deficit. GASB Cod. Sec. 2200.708-12 discusses, in part, how a preparer should notify users of the financial statements information related to such amounts that may mask other information due to the magnitude of the amounts. If the effect of the implementation of a GASB standard is significant, the GASB encourages additional details of unrestricted net position in the notes to the financial statements to isolate its effect. The government may also address these circumstances in the MD&A as part of either the net position or, in this case, the liabilities discussions. The author of this volume encourages governments to include this disclosure in both the notes to the financial statements and the MD&A if the effect is significant.

A fund with restrictions may include an asset balance that exceeds the requirements of the related restriction. Under this circumstance, the excess amount should be used to compute the amount of unrestricted net position. Furthermore, in this example involving a special revenue fund *under current GAAP*, the fund itself would likely have a restricted fund balance, as well as either a committed or assigned fund balance for the excess portion (see previous **PRACTICE ALERT** s on the GASB's *Financial Reporting Model Improvements* Exposure Draft).

A special revenue fund may include resources that are unrestricted (e.g., a transfer from the General Fund) and resources that are restricted (e.g., revenues from a state shared motor fuel tax that must be used for street repair and maintenance). Because the resources (cash) are fungible, a revenue flow assumption must be made by the governmental entity to identify whether unrestricted or restricted resources are used first. GAAP allows either approach, however, the financial statements must disclose the accounting policy adopted.

In some instances, a governmental entity may specifically restrict assets that are to be used to pay the current portion of bonds that were issued to finance the acquisition of capital assets. Even though the restricted assets are used to determine the amount of restricted net position, the related current portion of the maturing debt must be used to determine the amount of net investment in capital assets rather than restricted net position.

Costs related to the issuance of debt must be expensed and gains and losses related to the refunding of debt must be amortized. For reporting purposes, the unamortized portion of these accounts is used to determine the amount of the related net position based on the purpose of issuing the debt. For example, if debt was issued to finance the construction of a capital asset, any unamortized balances are used to compute the reported amount of net investment in capital assets. On the other hand, if debt was issued for a specific purpose and the proceeds have not been expended, the unamortized balances are used to determine the amount of restricted net position. If the debt was issued and the proceeds were not restricted, the unamortized balances are used to compute unrestricted net position.

Finally, GASB Cod. Sec. 2200.708-13 clarifies the effect of an equity interest in a joint venture in unrestricted net position. The investment does not reflect capital assets:

- Held directly by the governmental entity or
- Restricted as defined in GASB Cod. Sec. 2200.119.

Therefore, the unrestricted net position category is the default category. If an item does not qualify for classification as net investment in capital assets or restricted net position, then it must be classified as unrestricted net position.

The Statement of Net Position illustrated in this chapter (Exhibit 20-1) is classified and presented in accordance with GASB Cod. Sec. 2200.

NOTE: The Exhibits in this chapter are based on the Commonwealth of Massachusetts fiscal year ended June 30, 2021, Annual Comprehensive Financial Report. Certain elements were updated to generalize the information and to implement GASB statements where necessary. The author thanks Comptroller William McNamara and Ms. Pauline Lieu, Director of Financial Reporting and Analysis for the use of this material.

EXHIBIT 20-1
STATE OF BAY STATEMENT OF NET POSITION
As of June 30, 20Y4
(Amounts expressed in thousands)

	Primary Government			
	Governmental Activities	Business-Type Activities	Government-Wide Total	Discretely Presented Component Units

ASSETS AND DEFERRED OUTFLOWS OF RESOURCES
Current assets:

Cash and cash equivalents	$16,813,248	$4,849,496	$21,662,744	$4,795,788
Restricted cash with fiscal agent	248,690	–	248,690	–
Short-term investments	304,140	783,464	1,087,604	–
Assets held in trust	–	–	–	130,188
Receivables, net of allowance for uncollectible amounts:				
Taxes	4,087,398	–	4,087,398	–
Federal grants and reimbursements receivable	2,307,778	60,616	2,368,394	355,578
Loans	6,859	6,876	13,735	513,696
Other receivables	1,242,332	1,022,349	2,264,681	380,493
Due from other governments	21,263	–	21,263	–
Due from component units	597	352	949	–
Due from primary government	–	–	–	634,205
Other current assets	–	59,863	59,863	91,359
Total current assets	**25,032,305**	**6,783,016**	**31,815,321**	**6,901,307**
Noncurrent assets:				
Cash and cash equivalents—restricted	–	247,256	247,256	905,862
Long-term investments	–	1,438,047	1,438,047	1,563,299

	Primary Government			Discretely Presented Component Units
	Governmental Activities	Business-Type Activities	Government-Wide Total	
Investments, restricted investments, and annuity contracts	1,832,078	1,110	1,833,188	84,338
Receivables, net of allowance for uncollectible amounts:				
Taxes	435,544	–	435,544	–
Federal grants and reimbursements receivable	380	–	380	–
Loans	73,366	31,011	104,377	4,284,897
Other receivables	162,253	16,874	179,127	47,559
Due from component units	6,198	–	6,198	–
Due from primary government	–	–	–	3,906
Non-depreciable capital assets	1,849,740	668,361	2,518,101	15,798,496
Depreciable capital and right-to-use assets, net	3,204,074	7,325,749	10,529,823	25,007,308
Other noncurrent assets	–	126,957	126,957	46,154
Other noncurrent assets—restricted	3,003	–	3,003	–
Total noncurrent assets	**7,566,636**	**9,855,365**	**17,422,001**	**47,741,819**
TOTAL ASSETS	**32,598,941**	**16,638,381**	**49,237,322**	**54,643,126**
Deferred outflows of resources relating to:				
Change in fair value of interest rate swaps	88,793	1,204	89,997	114,666
Bond refundings	95,806	169,076	264,882	216,950
Defined benefit pensions	8,709,458	277,125	8,986,583	384,224
Defined benefit OPEB	3,013,735	362,691	3,376,426	434,446
Certain asset retirement obligations	–	1,158	1,158	–

Financial Reporting by General-Purpose Governments

	Primary Government			Discretely Presented Component Units
	Governmental Activities	Business-Type Activities	Government-Wide Total	
Other deferred outflows of resources	–	479	479	–
Total deferred outflows of resources	**11,907,792**	**811,733**	**12,719,525**	**1,150,286**
TOTAL ASSETS AND DEFERRED OUTFLOWS OF RESOURCES	**$44,506,733**	**$17,450,114**	**$61,956,847**	**$55,793,412**
LIABILITIES AND DEFERRED INFLOWS OF RESOURCES				
Current liabilities:				
Accounts payable and other liabilities	4,109,262	699,386	4,808,648	1,465,512
Accrued payroll	179,478	239,716	419,194	2,835
Compensated absences	530,368	168,861	699,229	36,769
Accrued interest payable	441,358	21,345	462,703	188,770
Tax refunds and abatements payable	1,453,334	693,390	2,146,724	–
Due to component units	673,272	7	673,279	–
Due to primary government	–	–	–	949
Due to federal government	506,638	152,226	658,864	–
Claims and judgments	13,271	–	13,271	–
Advances	6,134,899	37,409	6,172,308	347,327
Prizes payable	124,362	–	124,362	–
Deposits	–	138,229	138,229	–
Other grants payable	141,370	–	141,370	–
Lease and similar contracts current liabilities	3,231	2,952	6,183	–
Other borrowings and unamortized premiums	186,651	–	186,651	–
Bonds payable and unamortized premiums	1,440,282	2,444,606	3,884,888	1,144,459

	Primary Government			Discretely Presented Component Units
	Governmental Activities	Business-Type Activities	Government-Wide Total	
Environmental remediation liability	8,290	–	8,290	–
Total current liabilities	**15,946,066**	**4,598,127**	**20,544,193**	**3,186,621**
Noncurrent liabilities:				
Compensated absences	223,779	61,927	285,706	23,111
Accrued interest payable	–	–	–	171,456
Due to component units	3,906	–	3,906	–
Due to primary government	–	–	–	6,198
Due to federal government—grants	–	3,887	3,887	–
Claims and judgments	20,000	–	20,000	–
Advances	–	–	–	35,941
Prizes payable	631,016	–	631,016	–
Lease and similar contracts noncurrent liabilities	11,029	5,772	16,801	72,796
Bonds payable and unamortized premiums	30,789,031	4,397,824	35,186,855	10,116,576
Other borrowings and unamortized premiums	6,321,734	–	6,321,734	–
Construction grants payable to other governments	37,929	–	37,929	–
Environmental remediation liability	586,985	–	586,985	–
Liability for hedging derivative instruments	88,793	1,204	89,997	143,041
Net pension liability	46,159,763	982,015	47,141,778	2,299,007
Net OPEB liability	18,434,733	1,259,744	19,694,477	3,200,799
Other noncurrent liabilities	**337,040**	**157,252**	**494,292**	**232,782**
Total noncurrent liabilities	**103,645,738**	**6,869,625**	**110,515,363**	**16,301,707**
TOTAL LIABILITIES	**119,591,804**	**11,467,752**	**131,059,556**	**19,488,328**

| | Primary Government ||| Discretely Presented Component Units |
	Governmental Activities	Business-Type Activities	Government-Wide Total	
Deferred inflows of resources relating to:				
Public-Private Partnerships	–	13,585	13,585	296
Refunding bonds	1,084,179	7,957	1,092,136	64,191
Defined benefit pensions	480,355	72,150	552,505	185,472
Defined benefit OPEB	2,406,295	631,573	3,037,868	693,978
Taxation	–	59,333	59,333	–
Other	–	111	111	–
Total deferred inflows of resources	3,970,829	784,709	4,755,538	943,937
TOTAL LIABILITIES AND DEFERRED INFLOW OF RESOURCES	123,562,633	12,252,461	135,815,094	20,432,265
NET POSITION				
Net investment in capital assets	(1,658,414)	3,861,405	2,202,991	34,512,326
Restricted for:	–	–	–	–
Family and employment security	–	1,596,367	1,596,367	–
Retirement of indebtedness	918,907	–	918,907	–
Higher education endowment funds	–	22,925	22,925	–
Higher education academic support and programs	–	5,553	5,553	–
Higher education scholarships and fellowships:	–	–	–	–
Nonexpendable	–	3,142	3,142	–
Expendable	–	20,878	20,878	–
Higher education capital projects—expendable purposes	–	1,706	1,706	–
Grants and gifts	401,886	257,777	659,663	–

	Primary Government			Discretely Presented Component Units
	Governmental Activities	Business-Type Activities	Government-Wide Total	
Other purposes	–	–	–	4,693,134
Unrestricted (deficits)	(78,718,279)	(572,100)	(79,290,379)	(3,844,313)
TOTAL NET POSITION	**$(79,055,900)**	**$5,197,653**	**$(73,858,247)**	**$35,361,147**

The notes to the basic financial statements are an integral part of this statement.

Statement of Activities

The format for the government-wide Statement of Activities is significantly different from an income statement used by for-profit entities. The focus of the Statement of Activities is on the net cost of various activities provided by the governmental entity. The statement begins with a column that identifies the cost of each governmental activity. Another column identifies the revenues that are specifically related to the classified governmental activities. The difference between the expenses and revenues related to specific activities computes the net cost or benefits of the activities, which "identifies the extent to which each function of the government draws from the general revenues of the government or is self-financing through fees and intergovernmental aid" [GASB Cod. Sec. 2200.126].

The GASB established the unique presentation format for the Statement of Activities in part because it believes that format provides an opportunity to provide feedback on a typical budgetary question that is asked when a program is adopted; namely, "What will the program cost and how will it be financed?" Due to this presentation format, expenses and revenues should be reported "gross" or "broad" in the Statement of Activities.

The governmental entity must determine the level at which governmental activities are to be presented, however, the level of detail must be at least as detailed as that required in the governmental fund financial statements (which are discussed later). Generally, activities would be aggregated and presented at the functional category level, however, entities are encouraged to present activities at a more detailed level, such as by programs. Due to the size and complexities of some governmental entities, it may be impractical to expand the level of detail beyond that of functional categories. (The discussion that follows assumes that the level of detail presented in the Statement of Activities is at the functional category level.)

The minimum level of detail for expenses presented in the Statement of Activities is, for governmental activities, by function (e.g., "public safety," "public health"), and for business-type activities by different identifiable activities (e.g., "water," "sewer," "refuse collection"). The level of detail for presentation in the Statement of Activities is the required minimum level and not the actual level of detail used to prepare the fund financial statements. That is, fund financial statements could be prepared at a more detailed level than the minimum required, and the Statement of Activities could reflect a lesser level (e.g., the minimum level required). There is no specific level of detail that is required for all governments given the variations between the types of governments.

PRACTICE POINT: Many governments align the presentation of functions based on the sections of the government's budget. As an example, as complex as the State of California is, the State's Statement of Activities reports only the following programs in governmental activities:

- General government,
- Education,
- Health and human services,
- Natural resources and environmental protection,
- Business,
- Consumer services and housing,
- Transportation and
- Corrections and rehabilitation.

Programs of business-type activities include:

- Electric power,
- Water resources,
- State lottery,
- Unemployment programs (unique to states),
- The State University system,
- Water pollution control revolving,
- Housing loans, and
- Other.

Segments versus Business-Type Activities. GAAP requires that business-type activities be separately reported at least by segment in the Statement of Activities (government-wide financial statement). Rather than define a segment in the context of the Statement of Activities, GAAP used the definition of a segment, which is reproduced as follows, established for the presentation of segment information in a note to the financial statements for enterprise funds:

> [A] segment is considered to exist when "an identifiable activity reported as or within an Enterprise Fund or another stand-alone entity for which one or more revenue bonds or other revenue-backed debt instruments (such as certificates of participation) are outstanding." A segment has a specific identifiable revenue stream pledged in support of revenue bonds or other revenue-backed debt and has related expenses, gains and losses, assets, and liabilities that can be identified [GASB Cod. Sec. 2500.101].

Segments are different than business-type activity reporting as the reporting in a Statement of Activities is not specifically tied to bonds or other revenue-backed debt instruments. An activity within an enterprise fund is identifiable if it has a specific revenue stream and related expenses and gains and losses that are accounted for separately. Determining whether an activity is different may require the use of professional judgment, but is generally based on the goods, services, or programs provided by an activity [GASB Cod. Secs. 2200.127–.128].

GASB Cod. Sec. 2200.714-2 discusses potential criteria for reporting separate activities in the Statement of Activities presented for an Enterprise Fund. "Generally, the difference between activities in the goods, services or programs provided" is obvious, but in some circumstances professional judgment must be used to determine which activities should be reported separately.

For example, as introduced in the **PRACTICE POINT** above regarding the Statement of Activities for the State of California, unemployment compensation (for a state) is reported differently from a housing loan program of the state and, therefore, they should be separate activities. But for public institutions of higher education, an athletic program may be separate or integrated, depending upon the school's operations. Ultimately, the question gives guidance to preparers to present the level of detail that provides the most meaningful information to meet user needs.

The GASB's objective is "to present a level of detail that will provide useful information to meet the needs of users of the financial statements." As an example, an enterprise fund may be used to account for water services and electric services as shown above. Although both services are considered "utility services," they are different activities and should be presented as such on the Statement of Activities if separate assets and liabilities can be identified for each activity. On the other hand, a public university accounted for as an enterprise fund would likely have revenues from residence halls, athletics, food services, and a bookstore. For the most part, these revenue-producing functions would generally not be considered separate activities because they are all related to the single activity of providing the higher education service.

Expenses—Direct and Indirect. Once the level of detail is determined, the primary government's expenses for each governmental activity should be presented. It should be noted that these are expenses and not expenditures and are based on the concept of the flow of economic resources, which includes depreciation expense. As noted earlier, the minimum level of detail allowed is functional program categories, such as general government, public safety, parks and recreation, and public works. At a minimum, each functional program should include "direct expenses," which are defined as "those that are specifically associated with a service, program, or department and, thus, are clearly identifiable to a function" [GASB Cod. Sec. 2200.129].

Some functional categories, namely, general government and administrative support, are by their very nature indirect expenses. GAAP does not require that these indirect expenses be allocated to other functional categories. However, if these indirect expenses are in fact allocated (either partially allocated or fully allocated) to the other functional expense categories, the Statement of Activities must be expanded to include separate columns for direct and indirect expenses so that the presentation format provides a basis for comparison with other governmental entities that choose not to allocate their indirect expenses [GASB Cod. Sec. 2200.130].

When a governmental entity allocates part or all its indirect costs (and, therefore, presents columns for direct and indirect costs), a column that presents the total of these two columns may be presented in the Statement of Activities, but a total column is not required.

In some instances, a governmental entity will charge (through the General Fund or an internal service fund) other funds or programs an overhead rate that is based on general administrative expenses. The GASB states that under this circumstance it is not necessary to identify and eliminate these charges from the various direct program expenses presented in the Statement of Activities, however, the summary of significant accounting policies should state that the direct program expenses include such charges [GASB Cod. Sec. 2200.131]. A common example of an item in an overhead rate charged to programs would be pension expense.

GASB Cod. Sec. 2200.715-5 discusses how indirect expenses could be allocated to business-type activities as well as governmental activities assuming there is a reasonable basis for doing so. However, if those expenses are allocated to business-type activities, the allocation creates an additional item that must be disclosed as a reconciling item between the fund financial statements and the government-wide financial statements. For example, there may be no basis to allocate interest on long-term debt to business-type activities if the business-type activity is not expected to pay the principal on the long-term debt.

At the other extreme, the indirect expenses of the "general government" functional category presented in the Statement of Activities may be allocable to both governmental and business-type activities. But in the allocation, there may be an inappropriate change to the net positions in both types of activities. As a result, a transfer from governmental activities to business-type activities would be required to balance the effect on net position, even though there is no expectation of internal reimbursements for indirect-expense allocations, nor may the transfer be lawful in some jurisdictions.

An example of the alternative presentation of indirect expenses in a Statement of Activities is as follows:

Functions/Programs	Expenses	Indirect Expenses Allocation	Charges for Services	Operating Grants and Contributions	Capital Grants and Contributions	Governmental Activities	Program Revenues Business-Type Activities	Total	Component Units
Primary Government									
Governmental Activities:									
General Government	Positive amount	Negative amount							
Programs	Positive amounts	Positive amounts							
Total governmental activities	Total	Net Zero	Total	Total	Total	Total	NOT totaled	Total	No amounts
Business-type activities									
Activities:	Amounts	No Amounts	Amounts	Amounts	Amounts	No Amounts	Amounts	Total	No amounts
Total Business-Type Activities	Amounts	No Amounts	Amounts	Amounts	Amounts	No Amounts	Amounts	Total	No amounts

				Program Revenues			Net (Expense) Revenue and Changes in Net Position		
Functions/Programs	Expenses	Indirect Expenses Allocation	Charges for Services	Operating Grants and Contributions	Capital Grants and Contributions	Governmental Activities	Program Revenues Business-Type Activities	Total	Component Units
Total primary government	Total	No amounts	Total	Total	Total	Total	Total	Total	No Amounts
Component units									
Activities:	Amounts	No amounts	Total	Total	Total	No amounts	No Amounts	No Amounts	Total
Total component units	Total	No amounts	Total	Total	Total	No amounts	No Amounts	No Amounts	Total
General Revenues:									
					Details:	Amounts	Amounts	Total	Amounts
			Total General Revenues, special items, and transfers			Total	Total	Total	Total
					Change in Net position	Total	Total	Total	Total
					Net position – beginning	Amount	Amount	Amount	Amount
					Net position – ending	Total	Total	Total	Total

When a governmental entity performs a common support activity (e.g., vehicle maintenance) for a variety of programs (public safety, streets, etc.), to the extent possible the common activity costs should be allocated as a direct expense of the specific programs. GASB Cod. Sec. 2200.715-2 notes that any costs that cannot be allocated to a specific function should be reported as "general government or a similar indirect cost center" in the Statement of Activities.

GAAP requires that each functional program include direct expenses, which are defined as "those that are specifically associated with a service, program, or department and, thus, are clearly identifiable to a particular function." GAAP requires that non-enterprise fund employee benefit costs (such as pension costs, vacation pay, etc.) should be allocated to functional programs (such as public safety, streets, etc.) if the employee's wage is also considered a direct expense.

A governmental entity may negotiate indirect costs rates under various federal governmental grants and contracts whereby those rates are used to transfer the costs (reimbursement) from the General Fund to specific governmental funds that administer the federal awards. As the rates are based on indirect costs, they cannot be reported as direct expenses of a function but, rather, must be reported as "general government" expenses (or an equivalent caption) in the Statement of Activities.

Depreciation and Amortization. Generally, the cost (net of estimated salvage value) of capital assets should be depreciated over their estimated useful lives. Right-to-use assets are amortized over the *shorter* of their useful lives or the related contract. (For a discussion of depreciation and amortization expense, see Chapter 18.)

PRACTICE POINT: The term "depreciation" also incorporates amortization of intangible assets by reference per GASB Cod. Sec. 2200, fn. 14. Most practitioners combine depreciation and amortization in one number, captioning the entry "depreciation and amortization" if reported as a direct expense. The related contra-asset is frequently captioned "accumulated depreciation and amortization." GAAP allows amortization only to the period to which the service capacity of the asset is available or to the contractual or legal provisions, whichever is shorter. If additional service capacity is available on a renewal, an update to the amortization may occur, which would be presented as a change in accounting estimate. Intangible assets with indefinite periods are not amortized. The asset impairment provisions of GAAP do apply to intangible assets and rights [GASB Cod. Secs. 1400.135–.136]. A further discussion on these issues is presented in Chapter 10.

Depreciation and amortization expense should be reported as a direct expense of the specific functional category if the related capital asset can be identified with the functional category. For example, depreciation expense related to a police vehicle should be reported, along with other direct expenses, at the appropriate functional expense category (e.g., public safety). Depreciation on capital assets that are shared by two or more functions should be reported as a direct expense based on a pro rata allocation to the appropriate functional expense categories. For example, if a building houses the administrative office of the police department and the public assistance department, the depreciation expense for the office building would be allocated on an appropriate basis to the two functional expense categories (e.g., public safety and health and welfare) [GASB Cod. Sec. 2200.132].

Depreciation expense for infrastructure should not be allocated to the various functions of government and should be reported as a direct expense. For example, streets, highways, and related infrastructure assets may be reported as a part of public works or transportation. Water and sewer mains or electrical lines may be reported as a part of a utility department. The reporting is generally associated with the function where the capital outlay occurs, or the maintenance of the infrastructure is recorded [GASB Cod. Sec. 2200.133].

Depreciation and amortization expense related to capital assets that are not identified with a functional category (such as the depreciation of a city hall) does not have to be reported as a direct expense to specific functions but rather may be presented as a separate line item in the Statement of Activities or included in the general government functional category. However, when unallocated depreciation expense is reported as a separate line in the Statement of Activities, it should be indicated on the face of the statement that the amount reported as depreciation expense represents only unallocated depreciation expense and not total depreciation expense.

GASB Cod. Sec. 2200.715-9 requires unallocated depreciation expense to be on the face of the Statement of Activities. That can be achieved by using an appropriate description of the line item, such as "Unallocated Depreciation Expense," or by labeling the line item "Depreciation Expense" with a reference (such as an asterisk) to the bottom of the statement that states that "the amount represents only unallocated depreciation expense and not total depreciation expense."

Interest Expense. Generally, interest expense on general long-term debt is considered an indirect expense and should not be allocated as a direct expense to specific functional categories but rather should be presented as a single line item, appropriately labeled. However, "when borrowing is essential to the creation or continuing existence of a program and it would be misleading to exclude the interest from direct expenses of that program," the related interest expense should be reported as a direct expense with the appropriate functional classification [GASB Cod. Sec. 2200.134].

GASB Cod. Sec. 2200.715-11 provides the following example of a financing arrangement whereby interest expense is considered a direct expense and allocated to a function or program:

> A state government has a program to make reduced-rate loans to school districts in the state. The initial funding for the program was provided by a large bond issue. Since the bond issue is fundamental to the school district loan program and is an integral part of the cost of providing the program to local districts, the interest expense should be allocated to this activity.

If part of interest expense is reported as a direct expense of a functional line item, it should be indicated on the face of the statement if the amount reported as interest expense represents only unallocated interest expense and not total interest expense. The amount of total interest expense must be determinable on the face of the Statement of Activities or it must be disclosed in a note to the financial statements.

OBSERVATION: The GASB takes the position that treating interest expense as a direct expense is inconsistent with the nature of financing projects. For example, a capital asset related to one project may be purchased with existing funds, and a similar asset for another project may be financed. Under a direct allocation approach, one project would have more expenses than the other even though the determination of the interest expense is based on management discretion rather than on the nature of each project.

Regarding reporting interest expense in the Statement of Activities, GAAP requires under most circumstances, interest on general long-term liabilities is not reported as a direct expense. Therefore, using the caption "interest on long-term debt" is enough to indicate that all interest expense is indirect. The amount of total interest expense must be determinable on the face of the Statement of Activities, or it must be disclosed in a note to the financial statements.

Similarly, interest expense for enterprise funds and component units does not have to be reported as a separate line item in the business-type activities section of the Statement of Activities because the expense is a direct expense for each of these operating units.

A state's constitution might not allow for the issuance of debt except by a constitutional amendment approved by voters. Under this circumstance, the debt is issued only for a specific activity. However, the interest on the debt is still considered indirect and should not be allocated to the specific function or activity. If the state government is concerned that a functional activity should in fact include interest expense, the alternative format for the Statement of Activities may be used whereby indirect expenses are allocated (either partially allocated or fully allocated) to the other functional expense categories. Under this format, the Statement of Activities must be expanded to include separate columns for direct and indirect expenses so that the presentation format provides a basis for comparison with other governmental entities that choose not to allocate their indirect expenses.

Revenues and Other Resource Inflows. A fundamental concept in the formatting of the Statement of Activities, as described above, is the identification of resource inflows to the governmental entities that are related to specific programs and those that are general in nature. Governmental programs are generally financed from the following sources of resource inflows:

Source of Revenue	Examples	Reporting
Parties who purchase, use, or directly benefit from goods and services provided through the program.	Fees for garbage collections, transportation fares, and fees for using recreational facilities, building permits and hunting permits.	Always *program revenue.*
Outside parties (other governments and nongovernmental entities or individuals) who provide goods and services to the governmental entity.	Intergovernmental grants (federal to state, state to local), subsidies.	*Program revenues* if they are restricted to a specific program or programs. Otherwise, they are general revenue.
The reporting government's constituencies.	Property taxes and similar taxation.	*General revenue,* even if restricted to a specific program.
The governmental entity.	Investment income.	Usually, *general revenue.*

Using this classification process, the governmental entity should format its Statement of Activities based on the following broad categories of resource inflows [GASB Cod. Sec. 2200.135] (as also shown above in the example of indirect expenses):

- Program revenues, consisting of:
    — Charges for services,
    — Operating grants and contributions, and
    — Capital grants and contributions,
- General revenues,
- Contributions to permanent funds,
- Extraordinary items,
- Special items, and
- Transfers.

PRACTICE ALERT: The GASB's *Financial Reporting Model Improvements* Exposure Draft proposes to combine extraordinary items and special items in the

Statement of Activities (as well as the governmental fund and proprietary fund statements). The proposed caption would be *Unusual or Infrequent Items* and would be presented prior to the net change in resource flows. The definitions of each item would not change. Since the presentation would be aggregated, the notes to the basic financial statements would present the disaggregated amounts and explanatory information, including the program or function or identifiable activity to which the item was related and whether the item was within the control of management.

The definitions for the several types of revenues are mutually exclusive and, therefore, a source of revenue can only meet the definition of one type of revenue [GASB Cod. Secs. 2200.136–.140]:

Type of Revenue		Definition in GAAP
Program Revenues	•	Those that are derived directly from the program itself or from parties outside the reporting government's taxpayers or citizenry, as a whole; they reduce the net of the function to be financed from the general government's general revenues.
Charges for services	•	Revenues based on exchange or exchange-like transactions. These revenues arise from charges to customers or applicants who purchase, use, or directly benefit from the goods, services, or privileges provided. Revenues in this category include fees charged for specific services, such as:
		— Water use,
		— Garbage collection,
		— Licenses and permits (dog licenses, liquor licenses, and building permits); and
		— Operating special assessments, such as for street cleaning or special street lighting, and any other amounts charged to service recipients.
	•	Payments from other governments that are exchange transactions—for example, when County A reimburses County B for boarding County A's prisoners—also should be reported as charges for services.
Program-specific grants and contributions (operating and capital)	•	Revenues arising from mandatory and voluntary nonexchange transactions with other governments, organizations, or individuals that are restricted for use in a program. Some grants and contributions consist of capital assets or resources that are restricted for capital purposes—to purchase, construct, or renovate capital assets associated with a specific program. These should be reported separately from grants and contributions that may be used either for operating expenses or for capital expenditures of the program at the discretion of the reporting government. These categories of program revenue are specifically attributable to a program and reduce the net expense of that program to the reporting government. For example, a state may provide an operating grant to a county sheriff's department for a drug-awareness-and-enforcement program or a capital grant to finance construction of a new jail.

Type of Revenue	Definition in GAAP
	• Multipurpose grants (those that provide financing for more than one program) should be reported as program revenue if the amounts restricted to each program are specifically identified in either the grant award or the grant application. Multipurpose grants that do not provide for specific identification of the programs and amounts should be reported as general revenues. Preparers of the financial statements should review the terms and conditions of the grant award contained in the grant application or award letter to determine the ultimate purpose of a grant.

Program Revenues

Program revenues arise because the specific program with which they are identified exists, otherwise the revenues would not flow to the governmental entity. Program revenues are presented in the Statement of Activities as a subtraction from the related program expense to identify the net cost (or benefit) of a program.

This formatting scheme enables a reader of a governmental entity to identify those programs that are providing resources that may be used for other governmental functions or those that are being financed from general revenues and other sources of resources.

Lotteries and Revenue Classification. Lotteries generate distinct types of revenues for states. As discussed in the AICPA's Audit & Accounting Guide *State and Local Governments*, the activities may be a part of the primary government or a component unit. Generally, lotteries use enterprise funds. However, they may not meet the criteria to use an enterprise fund and, therefore, are a governmental activity.

If the lottery is a component unit, the lottery may *not* meet the criteria for blending. When state lotteries are created to primarily generate revenue for a state, the services provided by a lottery result in the opportunity for financial gain to *anyone* who chooses to participate. When prizes occur, the lottery operation does not exclusively, or almost exclusively, benefit the primary government. Therefore, if a lottery is a component unit, it is likely discretely presented [GASB Cod. Sec. 2600.706-17].

Questions routinely occur about how revenues raised by one function or activity but used by another function or activity should be classified in the Statement of Activities. Continuing in the previous example of a lottery, if revenue generated by a state lottery (one function or activity) must be used to finance education (another function or activity), should the proceeds from the lottery be reported as revenue for the lottery or for education? The following factors are to be used to determine which revenue should be related to a program [GASB Cod. Secs. 2200.136–.137, 2200.717-1 and .717-12]:

- For charges for services, the determining factor is which function generates the revenue.

- For grants and contributions, the determining factor is the function to which the revenue is restricted.

Thus, in the lottery example, the proceeds from the lottery would be reported as charges for services of the lottery activity because the educational activity used the resources but did not charge for the services.

Other Program Revenue Classification Issues. In some instances, it is impractical to classify the program that should report an item of program revenue, in which case the governmental entity may establish a policy for classifying the program revenue if the policy is consistently applied.

The language used in GAAP strongly implies that only three categories could be used to identify program revenues, namely:

1. Charges for services,

2. Operating grants and contributions, and

3. Capital grants and contributions.

However, the formatting of the Statement of Activities is more flexible. For example, more than one column could be included under one of the three program revenue columns. Furthermore, the columnar heading may be modified to be more descriptive. For example, a program revenue column could be labeled "operating grants, contributions, and restricted interest."

PRACTICE POINT: Identifying revenues with a function does not mean that revenues must be allocated to a function. Revenues are related to a function only when they are related to the function. If no direct relationship is obvious, the revenue is general revenue, not program revenue.

A governmental entity that classifies its expenses by *function* may receive a state grant (which meets the definition of program revenue) that is to be used for specified programs. The fact that the grant is based on one classification scheme and a governmental entity's Statement of Activities is based on another does not change the original character of the revenue. That is, the grant is still classified as program revenue (not general revenue) even though it must be allocated to a variety of functions in the Statement of Activities.

The following illustrates how potential program revenues should be evaluated [GASB Cod. Secs. 2200.717-12–16, .720-2–3]:

Fact Pattern	Suggested Guidance
State law requires that 20% of the state's lottery sales revenue be used for elementary and secondary education programs in the state. Should the 20% be allocated to the education function as program revenue?	**No.** The proceeds from the sales of lottery tickets are related to the "lottery" program and not to the education program. Presenting the net revenues of a program in a Statement of Activities does not imply that those net proceeds are used for that program. In this instance, the net revenue from the lottery program is a "profit" that reduces the governmental entity's need to finance other programs (including educational programs) through general revenues.
State gas taxes are shared with eligible local governments. The local governments have discretion over when and how the money is spent if it is for road and highway projects. Even though a high percentage of the revenue will likely be spent for capital purposes, maintenance and repair expenses are also allowable. How should the revenue (grants and contributions) be reported by the local governments—capital, operating, or some combination?	GASB Cod. Sec. 2200.138 notes that if a grant or contribution can be used either for operating or capital purposes, at the discretion of the governmental entity, it should be reported as an operating contribution.
A government charges indirect expenses to its human services program through an indirect cost plan and is reimbursed by the federal and state grant agencies for the costs of the program. However, in the Statement of Activities, the government does not allocate the indirect expenses to the human services program, but rather, reports them in the general government function. Should the portion of the grant that reimburses the indirect expense be reported as program revenues of the human services or general government function?	In this instance, there should be a "matching" of program revenues and program expenses. If the indirect expenses are allocated to the human services program, the portion of the grant that reimburses the indirect expenses should be reported as program revenues. If the indirect expenses are not allocated to the human services program, the portion of the grant that reimburses the indirect expenses should be reported as program revenues for the general government function.

Investment revenue that qualifies as program revenues (legally restricted for a purpose) should be reported as program revenue. Depending on the nature of the restriction, the restricted investment revenue should be reported either as operating, or capital grants and contributions in the Statement of Activities.

Charges for services revenues that are characterized as charges for services are based on exchange or exchange-like transactions and arise from charges for providing goods, services, and privileges to customers or applicants who acquire goods, services, or privileges directly from a governmental entity. Generally, these and similar charges are intended to cover, at least to some extent, the cost of goods and services provided to various parties.

In some instances, a state law might prohibit the use of fines for specific purposes (e.g., public safety expenses and other expenses that are related to the generation of the fine revenue). Even though the uses of the fine revenues (or in general, all charges for services) are somewhat limited, they are nonetheless program revenues and not general revenues.

The size or importance of a program's revenue does not change the character of the revenue for classification purposes in the Statement of Activities. For example, a community that has many distinct types of fines that are used to fund a variety of programs do not make the fine revenue general revenue. The net cost of a function or program is the difference between (1) expenses and (2) the charges, fees, and fines that derive directly from it and the grants and contributions that are restricted to it. A function may also generate a "profit" that can be used in a variety of ways. That fact does not make the revenue general.

Some public schools charge tuition fees for programs such as out-of-District students, vocational education, and adult educational programs where the fee is intended to cover the direct instructional cost of the program plus indirect administrative and support services. Therefore, the tuition revenue should be classified with the appropriate program revenue classification in the Statement of Activities. None of the revenue should be allocated to the indirect functional classification.

Governmental entities may receive mandatory and voluntary grants or contributions (nonexchange transactions) from other governments or individuals that must be used for a governmental activity. For example, a state government may provide grants to localities that are to be used to reimburse costs related to adult literacy programs. These and other similar sources of assets should be reported as program-specific grants and contributions in the Statement of Activities, but they must be separated into those that are for operating purposes and those that are for capital purposes. If a grant or contribution can be used either for operating or capital purposes, at the discretion of the governmental entity, it should be reported as an operating contribution.

Grants and contributions that are provided to finance more than one program (multipurpose grants) should be reported as program-specific grants "if the amounts restricted to each program are specifically identified in either the grant award or the grant application." (The grant application should be used in this manner only if the grant was based on the application.) If the amount of the multipurpose grants cannot be identified with a specific program, the revenue should be reported as general revenue rather than as program-specific grants and contributions.

Earnings related to endowments or permanent fund investments are considered program revenues if they are restricted to a specific program use, however, the restriction must be based on either an explicit clause in the endowment agreement or contract. Likewise, earnings on investments that do not represent endowments or permanent fund arrangements are considered program revenues if they are legally restricted to a specific program. Investment earnings on endowments or permanent fund investments that are not restricted and, therefore, are available for general operating expenses are not program revenues but rather should be reported as general revenues in the "lower" section of the Statement of Activities.

A permanent fund may be managed and controlled by one function (such as the transportation function) but a portion of the investment income may be restricted for use in another function (such as the public safety function). The portion of the investment income restricted to the other function should be reported as program revenue for the other function and not the function that is managing the permanent fund. Earnings on invested accumulated resources of a specific program that are legally restricted to the specific program should be reported as program revenues. That is, the restricted resources are program revenues of the function to which they are restricted [GASB Cod. Sec. 2200.717-11].

Grants and contributions may or may not be program revenues. Differing facts could result in different postings in the Statement of Activities as follows: [GASB Cod. Secs. 2200.716-4–.716-10]:

Fact Pattern	Suggested Guidance
A school district is awarded an operating grant from the state department of education. The grant agreement states that the department will reimburse the school district for all eligible expenses of three specific programs. The grant award, however, does not specifically identify the amounts restricted to each program, because they will not be known until the school district submits its after-the-fact request for funding. Can the school district report the grant as program revenues for the three programs, or should it be reported as general revenue?	The grant should be reported by the school district as program revenue and allocated to specific functions based on the amounts of reimbursable expenses incurred for each program. Since the reimbursements are known (even though they were not known at the time of the state grant) before the financial statements are prepared, the state grants do relate to a specific program.
A local government is awarded a categorical grant that finances many programs. The grant award lists the programs covered but does not restrict any specific amounts to specific programs. Should the government allocate the grant amount to covered programs and report it as program revenue?	Grants and contributions that are provided to finance more than one program (multipurpose grants) should be reported as program-specific grants "if the amounts restricted to each program are specifically identified in either the grant award or the grant application." The grant application should be used in this manner only if the grant was based on the application. If the amount of the multipurpose grants cannot be identified with a program (or programs), the revenue should be reported as general revenues rather than as program-specific grants and contributions. In this case, the grants must be reported as general revenues.

Fact Pattern	Suggested Guidance
State law allocates a percentage of the state's sales tax revenues to local governments. A portion of the local share is restricted to education. At the local level, is the sales tax allocation to education program or general revenue?	The local government should classify the shared sales tax revenue as a voluntary contribution and not as a tax, as required by GASB Cod. Sec. N50. The portion of the shared revenue for a local school district would be reported as a general revenue because the resources are available for "education" and not for an individual program within the educational activities.
A local government receives a large bequest from the estate of a wealthy benefactor. The corpus of the donation cannot be spent, but instead is required to be invested to provide earnings that are restricted to an exclusive use. Because the principal amount can never be spent, how should it be reported?	The receipt of the gift should be accounted for in a permanent fund and reported as revenue in the fund's Statement of Revenues, Expenditures, and Changes in Fund Balances. The principal amount would be reported as restricted in the fund's balance sheet. When a governmental entity receives contributions to its term and permanent endowments or to permanent fund principal, those contributions should be reported as separate items in the lower portion of the Statement of Activities. These receipts are not considered to be program revenues (such as program specific grants), because in the case of permanent contributions, the principal can never be expended. In the Statement of Net Position, the principal would be reported as restricted.

OBSERVATION: GASB Cod. Sec. 2200.716-7 discusses revenue recognition from pass-through grants, on-behalf payments and supplemental nutritional assistance program (SNAP) revenues, along with revenue recognized because of a special funding situation in accordance with GASB Cod. Sec. P20, P21, P22 or P24 (the *Codification Sections* for pensions and postemployment benefits other than pensions). Revenues should be recognized as program revenues because they are specifically attributable to a program and reduce the net cost of that program to the reporting government.

All investment income, including changes in the fair value of investments (gains or losses), should be recognized as revenue in the operating statement (or other Statement of Activities). When identified separately as an element of investment income, the change in the fair value of investments should be captioned "net increase (decrease) in the fair value of investments." Realized gains and losses should not be displayed separately from the net increase (decrease) in the fair value of investments in the financial statements, except that realized gains and losses may be separately displayed in the separate reports of governmental external investment pools. Similar treatment occurs when a hedging derivative instrument become ineffective.

Changes in fair value, including losses, be reported as an offset to program revenues when the earnings from the investments are restricted for a specific purpose. If no restriction exists, the losses would be reported as a loss or an offset to investment income in the general revenue section of the Statement of Activities.

> **OBSERVATION:** GAAP requires donated capital assets, works of art, historical treasures, and similar assets to be recorded at acquisition value at the acquisition date, rather than at fair value. Acquisition value is defined as the price that would be paid to acquire an asset with equivalent service potential in an orderly market transaction at the acquisition date, or the amount at which a liability could be liquidated with the counterparty. Capital assets that a government receives in a service concession arrangement or a life interest in real estate because of an irrevocable split-interest agreement would also be at acquisition value [GASB Cod. Secs. 1400.109, S30.105, I70.121, N50.711-5].

General Revenues. General revenues should be reported in the "lower" portion of the Statement of Activities. Such revenues include resource flows related to all forms of taxation. The various significant types of revenue should be separately identified in the Statement of Activities. Nontax sources of resources that are not reported as program revenues must be reported as general revenues. This latter group includes unrestricted grants, unrestricted contributions, and unrestricted investment income [GASB Cod. Sec. 2200.140].

General revenues are used to offset the net (expense) revenue amounts computed in the "upper" portion of the presentation, and the resulting amount is labeled as excess (deficiency) of revenues over expenses before extraordinary items and special items. (See previous **PRACTICE ALERT** on the combining of extraordinary items and special items in the Statement of Activities.)

> **OBSERVATION:** All taxes, including dedicated taxes (e.g., motor fuel taxes), are considered general revenues rather than program revenues. The GASB takes the position that only charges to program customers or program-specific grants and contributions should be characterized as reducing the net cost of a governmental activity.

Careful analysis is sometimes needed to properly classify a revenue source as either program revenue or general revenue. For example, GASB Cod. Sec. 2200.718-5 provides an illustration where a developer is required to make a one-time contribution to a municipality based on the assessed value of a recently completed project and those resources are to be used to help maintain the infrastructure related to the project. The revenue source is not a program revenue but, rather, a general revenue because it "arises from an imposed nonexchange transaction that is, in substance, a tax." Therefore, the contribution would be presented in the lower portion of the Statement of Activities and could be labeled as "restricted for infrastructure maintenance."

In some instances, a governmental entity may establish a prerequisite fee or license that must be paid before a business or other party is subject to another charge or tax. The character of each revenue source must be evaluated independently to determine whether it is program revenue or a tax (general revenue). For example, a local governmental entity may require a business to obtain a business license and to maintain the license, the business must also pay a "business license tax" that is based on the entity's gross receipts. The license and any license renewal fee are program revenues (charges for services), whereas the business license tax is general revenue (gross receipts tax) even though it is related to maintaining the business license.

Not all program revenues create restricted net position. By their nature, grants, and contributions (both operational and capital) give rise to restricted net position, but charges for services may be unrestricted, restricted to the program that gave rise to the charge, or restricted to a program that is unrelated to the revenue-generated service. On the other hand, a tax revenue could be restricted for a use (e.g., taxes levied specifically to pay debt service) but nonetheless reported as general revenue, perhaps under a heading that identifies it as restricted for a specific purpose.

Taxes and General Revenues. Taxes imposed by another government are not a tax receipt (by the recipient government) but, rather, a nonexchange transaction. The characteristics of the shared tax revenue must be examined to determine whether it is a program revenue or general revenue.

All taxes are considered general revenues rather than program revenues with the following illustrations (in each case the tax receipt is reported as general revenue):

- A county government imposes a separate sales tax, the proceeds of which are required to be used for public safety or health and welfare programs. Because of the restrictions on use, these taxes are not "discretionary" revenues.
- A city levies a special tax that is restricted for use within a specific program or function (a separate property tax levied to pay debt service costs, for example).
- A county government has enacted a transient occupancy (hotel, motel) tax, a percentage of which is required to be used for "tourism" programs in the county. The county has significant tourism activity and reports it as a separate function in its Statement of Activities. The county maintains that the revenue comes from "those who directly benefit from the goods or services of the program," and consequently should be reported as charges for services.

GAAP requires that derived taxes and imposed nonexchange revenues (both general revenues) be reported net of estimated refunds and estimated uncollectible amounts, respectively. Uncollectible exchange transactions revenues related to governmental activities in the Statement of Activities should also be recorded net of any uncollectible amounts. That is, a bad-debts expense account should not be used for presentation purposes.

When a governmental entity receives contributions to its term and permanent endowments or to permanent fund principal, those contributions should be reported as separate items in the lower portion of the Statement of Activities.

These receipts are not considered program revenues (such as program-specific grants) because, in the case of term endowments, there is an uncertainty of the timing of the release of the resources from the term restriction and, in the case of permanent contributions, the principal can never be expended [GASB Cod. Sec. 2200.141].

Earnings of a permanent fund that are required to be used for a specific purpose but are not distributed in the current year are earnings that should be reported as program revenues, even though they are not distributed or spent in the current year.

Exhibit 20-2 illustrates a Statement of Activities. An alternative format creates a separate column for indirect activities. For example, if a government has a cost allocation plan for indirect costs, they may prefer to present these in a separate column from direct costs. This alternative format is not shown in this chapter, because the presentation is self-evident.

Alternative presentation for Statement of Activities. As shown in Exhibit 20-2, the format of the Statement of Activities is unwieldy. When an entity has only governmental activities and a few functions, it may be possible to simplify the presentation of the statement by starting with a total column and then adding columns to the right of the total column that identify expenses and program revenues. The formatted statement could look something like the following:

	Total	Function #1	Function #2	Function #3
Expenses:				
Details	$XXX	$XXX	$XXX	$XXX
Total expenses	XXX	XXX	XXX	XXX
Program revenues:				
Charges for services	XXX	XXX	XXX	XXX
Operating grants and contributions	XXX	XXX	XXX	XXX
Capital grants and contributions	XXX	XXX	XXX	XXX
Net Program expense	XXX	$XXX	$XXX	$XXX
General revenues:				
Taxes:	XXX			
Real estate	XXX			
Others	XXX			
Unrestricted grants and contributions	XXX			
Unrestricted investment earnings	XXX			
Total general revenues	XXX			
Change in net position	XXX			
Net position—beginning	XXX			
Net position—ending	$XXX			

EXHIBIT 20-2
STATE OF BAY STATEMENT OF ACTIVITIES
For the Year Ended June 30, 20Y4
(Amounts expressed in thousands)

		Program Revenues			Net (Expenses) Revenues and Changes in Net Position			
					Primary Government			
Functions/Programs	Expenses	Charges for Services	Operating Grants and Contributions	Capital Grants and Contributions	Governmental Activities	Business-type Activities	Total	Discretely Presented Component Units
Primary government:								
Governmental Activities:								
General government	$3,522,506	$747,288	$2,419,259	$24,582	$(331,377)	$–	$(331,377)	$–
Judiciary	1,429,817	59,074	3,812	–	(1,366,931)	–	(1,366,931)	–
Municipal aid	6,499,305	–	–	–	(6,499,305)	–	(6,499,305)	–
Medicaid	20,208,100	1,272,228	12,319,582	–	(6,616,290)	–	(6,616,290)	–
Group health insurance	1,710,258	860,726	–	–	(849,532)	–	(849,532)	–
Energy and environmental affairs	900,326	319,315	46,033	–	(534,978)	–	(534,978)	–
Housing and economic development	2,963,819	242,815	885,052	–	(1,835,952)	–	(1,835,952)	–
Health and human services	11,658,328	1,576,692	4,583,792	52,677	(5,445,167)	–	(5,445,167)	–
Transportation and public works	3,283,352	627,594	–	–	(2,655,758)	–	(2,655,758)	–
Early elementary and secondary education	7,687,798	6,624	1,519,899	–	(6,161,275)	–	(6,161,275)	–
Public safety and homeland security	3,716,834	345,917	594,003	–	(2,776,914)	–	(2,776,914)	–
Labor and workforce development	428,225	56,603	240,033	–	(131,589)	–	(131,589)	–
Lottery	4,617,789	5,827,632	–	–	1,209,843	–	1,209,843	–
Interest (unallocated)	1,510,178	–	–	–	(1,510,178)	–	(1,510,178)	–
Total governmental activities	**70,136,635**	**11,942,508**	**22,611,465**	**77,259**	**(35,505,403)**	**–**	**(35,505,403)**	**–**
Business-Type Activities:								
Unemployment Compensation	19,438,890	1,608,603	17,208,485	–	–	(621,802)	(621,802)	–
Family and Employment Security Trust	236,361	1,005,102	1,164	–	–	769,905	769,905	–
Higher Education:	–	–	–	–	–	–	–	–
Flagship University	3,417,854	1,635,792	846,694	62,592	–	(872,776)	(872,776)	–
State Universities	1,050,949	502,827	156,155	51,980	–	(339,987)	(339,987)	–
Community Colleges	900,836	200,278	333,593	60,279	–	(306,686)	(306,686)	–
Total business-type activities	**25,044,890**	**4,952,602**	**18,546,091**	**174,851**	**–**	**(1,371,346)**	**(1,371,346)**	**–**
Total primary government	**95,181,525**	**16,895,110**	**41,157,556**	**252,110**	**(35,505,403)**	**(1,371,346)**	**(36,876,749)**	**–**
Discretely Presented Component Units:								
Transportation Authority	6,008,439	906,314	3,366,666	3,584,255	–	–	–	1,848,796
Health Insurance Exchange	1,087,062	883,408	206,669	–	–	–	–	3,015
State Revolving Fund	130,940	92,945	26,571	99,151	–	–	–	87,727
Other nonmajor component units	1,197,025	425,980	762,140	41,225	–	–	–	32,320
Total discretely presented component units	**8,423,466**	**2,308,647**	**4,362,046**	**3,724,631**	**–**	**–**	**–**	**1,971,858**

Financial Reporting by General-Purpose Governments

	Primary Government			
	Governmental Activities	Business-Type Activities	Total	Discretely Presented Component Units
General revenues:				
Taxes:				
Income	20,120,712	–	20,120,712	–
Sales taxes	7,626,572	–	7,626,572	–
Corporate taxes	3,652,060	–	3,652,060	–
Motor and special fuel taxes	666,730	–	666,730	–
Other taxes	2,881,261	–	2,881,261	–
Miscellaneous:				
Investment earnings/(loss)	22,388	148,569	170,957	293,610
Tobacco settlement	225,892	–	225,892	–
Contribution from municipalities	53,819	–	53,819	–
Other revenue (expense)	395,033	225,680	620,713	–
Transfers	(1,517,599)	1,517,599	–	–
Total general revenues and transfers	34,126,868	1,891,848	36,018,716	293,610
Change in net position	(1,378,535)	520,502	(858,033)	2,265,468
Net position/(deficits)—beginning, *as restated* (see **PRACTICE ALERT**)	(77,677,365)	4,677,151	(73,000,214)	33,095,679
Net position/(deficits)—ending	$(79,055,900)	$5,197,653	$(73,858,247)	$35,361,147

The notes to the basic financial statements are an integral part of this statement.

PRACTICE ALERT: The beginning balance restatement above is from the implementation of a new GASB standard in accordance with GASB Statement No. 100 (*Accounting Changes and Error Corrections*). Other than error corrections, three types of accounting changes are contained within GASB-100:

Type of Accounting Change	How Occurs
Change in Accounting Principle	Results from either: • A change from one GAAP pronouncement to another on the basis that the new GAAP is preferable to the old. The change enhances qualitative aspects of financial reporting. *Or*, • A new GASB pronouncement was issued requiring the change.
Change in Accounting Estimate	Occurs due to changes in inputs such as data, assumptions, and measurement methods as a result of changes in information, experience, or circumstances. These changes are common as they occur in the valuation of investments, capital assets and defined benefit pensions and postemployment benefits other than pensions. The change is justified as the new method is preferable to the prior method, *except* when a change is required by a new GASB pronouncement.

Type of Accounting Change	How Occurs
Change to or within the Financial Reporting Entity	Results from: • The addition or removal of a fund that results from the movement of *continuing operations* within the primary government, including its blended component units. **PRACTICE POINT:** The phrase *continuing operations* include an "integrated set of activities, assets and liabilities." The phrase in GASB-100, footnote 1, is primarily excerpted from GASB Cod. Sec. Co10.102 (GASB-69, par. 4). • A change in a fund's presentation as major or nonmajor. *Or*, • With certain exceptions, the addition of a component unit to the financial reporting entity *or* the removal of a component unit from the financial reporting entity. *Or*, • A change in a component unit's presentation as blended or discretely presented.

Single period financial statements will still require a retroactive restatement of beginning net position, fund balance, and fund net position for the cumulative impact of the change. Comparative financial statement changes will still require restatement of all prior periods presented, if practicable. If restatement of all periods is impracticable, the cumulative impact is made to the earliest period practicable for the change.

The requirements in GASB-100 for notes to the basic financial statements for changes in accounting principle are also minor changes from existing GAAP. They include:

- The nature of the change in accounting principle, including the financial statement line items impacted by the change in accounting principle and the identification of the new pronouncement that was implemented,
- The reason for the change and why it was preferable, unless the change occurred due to implementation of a new GASB pronouncement, and
- For comparative statements, if prior periods are not restated, the reason why the restatement is not practicable.

The impact of the change on beginning net position, fund balance or fund net position is then disclosed.

Like current GAAP, *changes in accounting estimates* will be reported *prospectively* upon implementing GASB-100. The notes to the financial statements for changes in accounting estimates include for each circumstance where the change has a significant impact:

- The nature of the change, including the financial statement line items impacted, and
- The reason for the change unless the change is *required* by a GASB pronouncement and why the change is preferable.

Changes to or within the financial reporting entity will be reported just like changes in accounting principles. The only piece that would not require note disclosure would be a change between a major fund presentation and nonmajor or vice versa as discussed previously.

GASB Statement No. 100 was implemented for periods beginning after June 15, 2023. Further details of GASB-100 are discussed later in this chapter, specifically changes impacting RSI.

Special and Extraordinary Items. The next section of the Statement of Activities includes a category where special items and extraordinary items (gains or losses) are to be presented. An event is unusual in nature if it possesses a high degree of abnormality and therefore is not related to the entity's normal operations. An event is infrequent in occurrence if it is not expected to occur again in the near future. These concepts must be applied in the context of the characteristics of each individual governmental entity, and their application is highly judgmental. Thus, what is considered unusual or frequent for one governmental entity may not be unusual or frequent for another governmental entity.

Special items are described as "significant transactions or other events within the control of management that are either unusual in nature or infrequent in occurrence." Special items should be reported separately and before extraordinary items. If a significant transaction or other event occurs but is not within the control of management and that item is either unusual or infrequent, the item is not reported as a special item, but the nature of the item must be described in a note to the financial statements [GASB Cod. Sec. 2200.144].

The following may qualify as special items:
- Sales of certain general governmental capital assets.
- Special termination benefits resulting from workforce reductions due to sale of utility operations.
- Early-retirement program offered to all employees.
- Significant forgiveness of debt, other than within an order of municipal bankruptcy.
- Sale of a large governmental asset that resulted in a minimal gain or loss.

In the above example of a Statement of Activities, a construction project was terminated resulting in a loss to a state. That is an example of a special item. It was under the control of management, and it was unusual or infrequent.

An item can only satisfy the criteria of either an extraordinary item or a special item, but not both. For example, if an item is both unusual and infrequent, it must be reported as an extraordinary item regardless of whether it was subject to management control.

There is no comprehensive list of extraordinary items, because that determination must be made on a case-by-case basis using professional judgment. The following *may* qualify as extraordinary items:

- Costs related to an environmental disaster caused by a large chemical spill in a train derailment in a small city.
- Considerable damage to the community or destruction of government facilities by natural disaster (tornado, hurricane, flood, earthquake, and so forth) or terrorist act. Geographic location of the government may determine if a weather-related natural disaster is infrequent. For example, hurricanes in Florida are not unusual nor infrequent.
- Restoration of an impaired capital asset financed by insurance proceeds, which may be reported in the governmental fund financial statements as another financing source or an extraordinary item.
- A large bequest to a small government by a private citizen.
- Remeasurement of assets and liabilities resulting in gains or losses from municipal bankruptcy under the provisions of Chapter 9 of the United States Bankruptcy Code, as are adjustment of new payment terms that result in adjustment of fund liabilities (or assets) [GASB Cod. Sec. Bn5].

PRACTICE POINT: GASB Technical Bulletin 2020-1, Accounting and Financial Reporting Issues Related to the Coronavirus Aid, Relief, and Economic Security Act (CARES Act) and *Coronavirus Diseases*, contains a question clarifying that outflows of resources that have been incurred in response to the COVID-19 pandemic are deemed by the GASB not to be extraordinary items nor special items. GASB Cod.Secs.1800.145,and.148 require extraordinary items to be both unusual in nature and infrequent in occurrence. The GASB believes viruses are not unusual.

The following transactions that should not be extraordinary items [GASB Cod. Secs. 1800.151, 2200.149]:

- Write-down or write-off of receivables, inventories, equipment leased to others, or intangible assets,
- Gains or losses from exchange or translation of foreign currencies, including those relating to major devaluations and revaluations,
- Other gains or losses from sale or abandonment of capital assets used in operations,
- Effects of a strike, including those against major suppliers, and
- Adjustment of accruals on long-term contracts.

Transfers. Transfers between governmental activities and business-type activities often occur. Internal transfers should be reported in the lower portion of the Statement of Activities [GASB Cod. Sec. 2200.141]. In the previous example of a Statement of Activities, $1,517,599,000 was shown as transfers prior to a total of general revenues, contributions, payments, special items, and transfers.

Gains and losses arising from the disposition of capital assets that are related to specific programs should be reported as either general revenues (gains) or general government-type expenses (losses) because they are peripheral activities and not derived directly from a program. If the gains or losses are insignificant, they could be offset against depreciation expense for the period. Governmental entities that use group or composite depreciation methods would generally close disposition gains and losses to accumulated depreciation.

Eliminations and Reclassifications. As suggested earlier, the preparation of government-wide financial statements is based on a consolidating process (like corporate consolidations) rather than on a combining process. Eliminations and reclassifications related to the consolidation process are based on (1) internal balances—Statement of Net Position, (2) internal activities—Statement of Activities, (3) intra-entity activity, and (4) internal service fund balances [GASB Cod. Sec. 2200.151].

PRACTICE ALERT: One of the changes in GASB-100 was the elimination of "boilerplate" language regarding note disclosure of reclassifications. Many governments prior to implementation of GASB-100 disclosed in the notes a sentence similar to: "Certain prior year amounts were reclassified to conform to the current year's presentation." This will no longer be presented upon implementation. Instead, the nature of the reclassification, the line items impacted and an explanation as to why the reclassification is preferable will be required. Comparative financial statement change provisions would also have to be disclosed. The nature of the reclassification and the line items affected will also be required even if balances or net positions did not change.

Internal Balances. The government-wide financial statements present the governmental entity and its blended component units as a single reporting entity. Based on this philosophy, most balances between funds that are initially recorded as interfund receivables and payables at the individual fund level should be eliminated in the preparation of the Statement of Net Position within each of the two major groups of the primary government (the governmental activities and business-type activities). The purpose of the elimination is to avoid the grossing-up effect on assets and liabilities presented in the Statement of Net Position.

For example, if there is an interfund receivable or payable between the General Fund and a special revenue fund, those amounts would be eliminated to determine the balances that would appear in the governmental-activities column. Likewise, if there is an interfund receivable or payable between two proprietary funds of the primary government, those amounts would also be eliminated in the business-type activities column. However, the net residual interfund receivable or payable between governmental and business-type activities should not be eliminated but, rather, should be presented in each column (governmental activities and business-type activities) and labeled as "internal balances" or a similar description. These amounts will be the same and will, therefore, cancel out when they are combined (horizontally) in the Statement of Net Position to form the column for total primary governmental activities [GASB Cod. Sec. 2200.152].

If internal balances are presented in a Statement of Net Position, funds are owed from governmental activities to business-type activities, or vice versa. Even though it seems unusual to have a negative amount in the asset section of the statement, the total would not be $0 had the amount been shown in liabilities.

OBSERVATION: Generally, a governmental entity will maintain its accounting transactions using the conventional fund approach and convert this information to a government-wide basis using the flow of economic resources and accrual basis of accounting. Thus, at the fund level, the internal balance between a governmental fund (modified accrual basis) may not equal the related balance with a proprietary fund (accrual basis), however, once the governmental fund is adjusted (through a worksheet) to the government-wide (accrual) basis, those adjusted amounts will equal the amounts presented in the proprietary funds.

There also may be interfund receivables or payables that arise because of transactions between the primary government and its fiduciary funds. These amounts should not be eliminated but rather should be reported in the Statement of Net Position as receivables from and payables to external parties. As a reminder, the financial statements of fiduciary funds are not consolidated (or combined) as part of the government-wide financial statements.

Internal Activities. To avoid the "doubling-up" effect of internal activities among funds, interfund transactions should be eliminated so that expenses and revenues are recorded only once. For example, a fund (generally the General Fund or an internal service fund) may charge other funds for services provided (such as insurance coverage and allocation of overhead expenses) on an internal basis. When these funds are consolidated to present the functional expenses of governmental activities in the Statement of Activities, the double counting of the expense (with an offset to revenue recorded by the provider fund) should be eliminated in a manner so that "the allocated expenses are reported only by the function to which they were allocated" [GASB Cod. Sec. 2200.153].

Internal activities should not be eliminated when they are classified as "interfund services provided and used." For example, when a municipal water company charges a fee for services provided to the general government, the expense and revenues related to those activities should not be eliminated [GASB Cod. Sec. 2200.154]. This type of internal activity is more fully discussed later in the section titled "Fund Financial Statements."

Intra-entity Activity. Transactions (and related balances) between the primary government and its blended component units should be reclassified based on the guidance discussed later in the section titled "Fund Financial Statements."

Transactions (and related balances) between the primary government and its discretely presented component units should not be eliminated in the government-wide perspective financial statements. That is, the two parties to the transactions should report revenue and expense accounts as originally recorded in those respective funds. Amounts payable and receivable between the primary government and its discretely presented component units should be reported as a separate line item in the Statement of Net Position. Likewise, payables and receivables among discretely presented component units must also be reported separately [GASB Cod. Sec. 2200.155].

Internal Service Fund Balances. As described above (see "internal activities" [Statement of Activities]), internal service fund and similar activities should be eliminated to avoid doubling up expenses and revenues in preparation of the government activities column of the Statement of Activities. The effect of this approach is to adjust activities in an internal service fund to a break-even balance. That is, if the internal service fund had a "net profit" for the year, there should be a pro rata reduction in the charges made to the funds that used the internal service fund's services for the year. Likewise, a net loss would require a pro rata adjustment that would increase the charges made to the various participating funds. After making these eliminations, any residual balances related to the internal service fund's assets and liabilities should be reported in the governmental activities column in the Statement of Net Position [GASB Cod. Sec. 2200.156].

In some instances, an internal service might not be accounted for in an internal service fund but, rather, is accounted for in another governmental fund (probably the General Fund or a special revenue fund).

Furthermore, the internal-service transaction might not cut across functional expense categories. That is, there is a "billing" between different departments but the expenses of those departments are all included in the same functional expenses. Conceptually, the same break-even approach as described earlier should be applied so as not to gross up expenses and program revenues of a particular functional expense; however, the GASB does not require that an elimination be made (unless the amounts are material), because the result of this non-elimination is that direct expenses and program revenues are overstated by equal amounts, but net (expense) revenue related to the function is not overstated.

OBSERVATION: The GASB takes the position that activities conducted with an internal service fund are generally governmental activities rather than business-type activities even though an internal service fund uses the flow of economic resources and the accrual basis of accounting. However, when enterprise funds account for all or the predominant activities of an internal service fund, the internal service fund's residual assets and liabilities should be reported in the business-type activities column of the Statement of Net Position.

FUND FINANCIAL STATEMENTS

Reporting Major Funds in Governmental and Proprietary Fund Financial Statements

Separate financial statements are presented for governmental and proprietary fund statements. The basis for reporting these funds is not by fund type but, rather, by *major funds*. GAAP requires that a governmental fund or enterprise fund be presented in a separate column in the fund financial statements if the fund is considered a major fund.

A major fund is one that satisfies *both* of the following criteria [GASB Cod. Secs. 2200.157–.159]:

1. **10% Threshold**—Total assets and deferred outflows of resources, liabilities and deferred inflows of resources, revenues, or expenditures or expenses (excluding extraordinary items) of the individual governmental or enterprise fund are equal to or greater than 10% of the corresponding element total (assets, liability, and so forth) for all funds that are considered governmental funds or enterprise funds.

2. **5% Threshold**—The same element that met the 10% criterion in is also at least 5% of the corresponding element total for all governmental and enterprise funds combined.

GAAP intends that a major fund arises when an individual accounting element (assets, for example) of a fund meets *both* the 10% and the 5% threshold. That is, a single element must satisfy *both* criteria. Revenue, net of discounts and allowance (rather than gross revenues) should be used in applying the major fund criteria to governmental fund and enterprise fund activities. Also, in determining total revenues and expenditures or expenses, extraordinary items should be excluded. GASB Cod. Sec. 2200.159 does allow some latitude if the government's officials believe that presentation of a fund is particularly important to financial statement users even if mathematically it wouldn't be considered a major fund.

PRACTICE POINT: In some instances, a governmental entity may account for all its activities in only governmental funds or, alternatively, may use only Enterprise Funds. Under either of these two circumstances, only the 10% test is *relevant* because if the 10% test is satisfied, obviously the 5% test will also be satisfied.

The General Fund is always considered a major fund and, therefore, must be presented in a separate column. Major fund reporting requirements do not apply to internal service funds.

The major fund concept is a minimum threshold. If a governmental entity believes that a fund that is not considered a major fund is important to readers of the financial statements, the entity should present that fund in a separate column.

A governmental entity must apply the major fund criteria each year to determine which funds are major funds. Thus, for example, an individual capital projects fund might be reported as a major fund one year and the next year considered a nonmajor fund. However, if a fund does not satisfy the conditions for a major fund, it can still be presented as a major fund if the governmental entity believes that for consistency it is important to do so.

Internal service funds cannot be presented as major funds. They should be aggregated and presented in a separate column on the face of the proprietary fund financial statements, just to the right of the total column for enterprise funds. If a governmental entity wants to present additional detail about internal service funds, that information can be presented in combining statements, but those statements are supplementary information and, therefore, are optional for

AFRs. They are not considered to be part of the basic external financial statements. However, they are a part of an ACFR.

All other funds that are not considered major funds must be aggregated in a separate column and labeled as nonmajor funds. Therefore, more than one column cannot be used to present nonmajor funds, for example, by fund type.

Interfund balances and activities are not required to be eliminated when nonmajor funds are aggregated, however, a governmental entity may choose to do so.

PRACTICE POINT: The decision and calculations on major funds should not be taken lightly. The more major funds, the more "opinion units" involved in the government's independent audit. For example, if a government has eight major governmental funds plus the General Fund, along with four major proprietary funds, chances are most funds and transactions may be fully audited. After all, over 90% of governmental fund activity may be part of the major governmental funds (eight funds plus the General Fund exceeding the 10% threshold). The calculation is typically performed with prior-year audited information at the start of the current-year audit or current-year interim information "trued up" for the entire year and adjusted for any known material flows. Materiality thresholds may also be low in comparison to peer governments. As a result, the audit costs may be much higher than peer governments. Care must be taken to follow the guidelines in GAAP in coordination with the government's independent auditor.

Many of the questions in GASB Cod. Secs. 2200.729-11–24 provide the following illustrations for identifying major funds to assist the preparer in determining what is and what is not a major fund and processes to utilize in calculations:

Financial Reporting **20,063**

Fact Pattern	Suggested Guidance
A city has a component unit that meets the criteria for blending and is included with its special revenue funds. Do the major fund reporting requirements apply to blended component units?	**Yes.** The concept of blending is based on the notion that certain component units are so closely related to the primary government that they are, in substance, the same as the primary government. The component unit's balances and transactions should be reported in a manner like the balances and transactions of the primary government itself. Therefore, if a component unit is blended into the reporting entity's financial statements as a special revenue fund, for example, it would be evaluated against the major fund criteria with the reporting entity's other governmental funds.
[GAAP] states that governments should apply the 10% criterion for one element (total assets, liabilities, revenues, or expenses or expenditures), and major fund criterion to all funds of that category or type. When should "category" be used and when should "type" be used?	The major fund requirement applies to all funds in the governmental category; thus, the 10% criterion should be applied to the governmental funds *category*. The major funds reporting requirements apply to enterprise funds but do not apply to internal service funds, thus, the 10% criterion should only be applied to the enterprise fund *type* rather than to the proprietary fund *category*.
If an individual governmental or Enterprise Fund meets the initial 10% criterion for one element (total assets, deferred outflows of resources, liabilities, deferred inflows of resources, revenues, or expenses or expenditures), and meets the 5% benchmark for a different element, is that fund required to be presented as a major fund?	**No.** A fund is considered a major fund when the element satisfies both the 10% and the 5% criteria, not just one of the criteria.
In applying the major fund criteria to enterprise funds, should the government consider both operating and nonoperating revenues and expenses?	**Yes.** The application of the tests requires that both operating and nonoperating revenues and expenses be considered for an enterprise fund.
For determining major governmental funds, are other financing sources and uses included in the calculations?	**No.** In performing the criteria tests for governmental funds, other financing sources and uses would be excluded.

Fact Pattern	Suggested Guidance
Can the budgetary basis (non-GAAP) of accounting be used to determine major funds?	**No.** The budgetary basis might be useful in making an initial assessment, but ultimately, the major fund calculations should be done using GAAP bases of accounting. Governmental funds should be evaluated based on modified accrual measurements; enterprise funds should be tested using accrual-basis measurements.
If a government uses only governmental funds and has no enterprise funds, should both the major fund percentages (10% and 5%) be applied to the fund element totals?	**No.** Determining which funds should be reported as major funds normally is a two-step process. The first step should always be to compare individual fund assets plus deferred outflows of resources, liabilities plus deferred inflows of resources, revenues, and expenditures against 10% of the combined element totals for the relevant fund type or category (enterprise or governmental funds). An individual fund is required to first exceed the 10% criterion before the second step, the 5% test, is undertaken. If an individual element does not surpass the 10% cutoff, the 5% comparison is not required. Therefore, the government in this question need not make the 5% calculation because the category totals do not change and any element that exceeds 10% will automatically also exceed 5%.
For determining major funds, should revenue be at gross, or net of discounts and allowances?	Major funds are determined based on revenues reported using the measurement focus and basis of accounting required by GAAP for governmental or enterprise funds, as appropriate. Therefore, because revenues are required to be reported net of discounts and allowances, the major fund determination should be based on **net**, rather than on gross, revenues.
For major fund determination, should total assets plus deferred outflows of resources, liabilities plus deferred inflows of resources, revenues, or expenditures or expenses include the effects of the items in the reconciliation of the fund statements to the government-wide statements?	**No.** The totals to be used for major fund determination should be the *unreconciled* combined amounts. An individual fund's significance is measured by its status among *funds*, this comparison against government-wide amounts would not be appropriate.

Fact Pattern	Suggested Guidance
Are interfund balances and transactions required to be eliminated from the totals in the major fund test?	**No.** Adjustments (are not required) to the combined totals for assets plus deferred outflows of resources, liabilities plus deferred inflows of resources, revenues, and expenditures/expenses. However, because the major fund criteria focus on assets plus deferred outflows of resources and liabilities plus deferred inflows of resources *separately*, significant interfund balances could influence the outcome of the major fund test. Interfund balances should not be eliminated, but if there are significant interfund receivables and payables, governments may adopt a policy (and use it consistently from year to year) to use a single "net" amount for each fund. Those changes would carry over to the respective total columns so that the governmental and enterprise fund totals would include the combined "net" amounts from the individual funds. Use of the "netting" process discussed in this answer should be limited to the determination of major funds. It should not be used for fund financial statement reporting purposes. In the fund operating statements, transfers in and transfers out are not included in the major fund calculation (revenues and expenditures or expenses) and do not affect the major funds determination because they are reported as other financing sources (uses). Interfund services provided and used are not distinguished from other revenues or expenditures or expenses.

PRACTICE POINT: An illustration of the major fund determination is contained in the *Governmental GAAP Practice and Disclosures Manual*, Chapter 13.

Required Reconciliation to Government-wide Statements. The totals in the government-wide financial statements for governmental activities will not equal the totals in the governmental fund financial statements because different measurement focus and bases of accounting are used to prepare the financial statements. For this reason, the GASB requires that, at the bottom of the fund financial statements *or* in a separate schedule, a summary reconciliation between the fund financial statements and the government-wide financial statements be provided. That is, the amount shown as the "total fund balances" in the column "total governmental funds" in the fund balance sheets must be reconciled to the "net position" column for governmental activities presented in the Statement of Net Position. Also, the amount shown as "net changes in fund balance" in the column "total governmental funds" in the statements of revenues, expenditures, and changes in fund balances, must be reconciled to the "changes in net position" column, for governmental activities presented in the Statement of Activities [GASB Cod. Sec. 2200.160].

PRACTICE ALERT: As discussed in throughout this *Guide*, the GASB's *Financial Reporting Model Improvements* Exposure Draft proposes to change the measurement focus and basis of accounting for governmental funds to the short-term financial resources measurement focus and modified accrual basis of accounting. Should the proposal be approved extant, this change may greatly impact the reconciliation, as well as the preparation of the amounts presented in the statements.

In many instances, the GASB believes that summary reconciliation can achieve the objective of tying the financial statements together with simple explanations that appear on the face of the fund financial statements or in an accompanying schedule. However, the GASB points out that "if the aggregated information in the summary reconciliation obscures the nature of the individual elements of a reconciling item, governments should provide a more detailed explanation in the notes to the financial statements."

GASB Cod. Sec. 2200.730-4 discusses how this could occur when a reconciling item is "a combination of several similar balances or transactions or is a net adjustment." For example, the reconciling item could be described as arising because liabilities are reported in the fund financial statements only when they are due and payable in the current period but appear in the government-wide financial statements when they are incurred. If this reconciling item includes a variety of liabilities (such as compensated absences, bonds, litigation, and accrued interest), a governmental entity may decide to further explain the nature of the reconciling item and its components in a note.

The financial statement preparer must be careful not to present lengthy explanations on the face of the financial statements or in the accompanying schedules that detract from the financial statements themselves. For this reason, it is best to present the detailed explanations in a note to the financial statements.

OBSERVATION: The summary reconciliation provides a "crosswalk" between government-wide financial statements and fund financial statements to facilitate an understanding by financial statement readers who may be concerned that two different measurement approaches are reflected in a governmental entity's financial report.

GASB Cod. Sec. 2200.730-2 discusses the issue of whether the accounting records for governmental funds should include the adjustment necessary to report governmental activities on an accrual basis because it is usually assumed that financial statements should be derived from account balances in the accounting records.

The formal accounting records should not include adjustments of this nature. Governmental funds are typically accounted for on a cash, modified accrual, or budgetary basis of accounting, and, if necessary, worksheet adjustments are made to convert these balances to a GAAP basis (modified accrual) for financial reporting purposes. The modified accrual-based financial statements are the basis for preparing the fund financial statements required by GAAP. Once the governmental funds have been converted to the modified accrual-basis, they are combined for internal purposes, and various worksheet conversion adjustments are made to convert them to an accrual basis for reporting governmental activities in the government-wide financial statements.

A governmental entity may apply the major fund criteria to its activities (governmental or enterprise funds) and determine that all its funds are major funds except one. For example, a government may have a single special revenue fund that is a major fund, a single capital projects fund that is a major fund, a General Fund (which is always a major fund) and a remaining permanent fund that is not a major fund. Based on the reporting requirements, there will be a separate column that reports the permanent fund even though it is not a major fund. However, GASB Cod. Sec. 2200.729-18 reminds practitioners that GAAP *requires* the financial statements to "clearly distinguish between major and nonmajor funds." This could be accomplished by providing (1) a super-heading labeled "Major Funds" and placing beneath it the separate columns for the General Fund, the special revenue fund, and the capital projects fund and (2) a super-heading labeled "Other Fund" and placing beneath it a single separate column for the permanent fund.

Required Financial Statements: Governmental Funds. The measurement focus and basis of accounting used to prepare financial statements for governmental funds is the current financial resources measurement focus and the modified accrual basis of accounting.

Based on the fundamental concepts discussed above, the following financial statements must be prepared for governmental funds [GASB Cod. Sec. 2200.161] (See the following **PRACTICE ALERT**.):

- Balance Sheet, and
- Statement of Revenues, Expenditures, and Changes in Fund Balances.

PRACTICE ALERT: As previously discussed, the GASB's *Financial Reporting Model Improvements* Exposure Draft proposes to change the titles to "Short-term financial resources balance sheet" and "Statement of short-term financial resource flows," respectively. The Short-term financial resources balance sheet would contain many of the same elements as the current Balance Sheet, adjusted for the change in the measurement focus and basis of accounting.

Balance Sheet. A governmental fund's balance sheet should be prepared using the "balance sheet format," where assets and deferred outflows of resources equal liabilities, deferred inflows of resources and fund balances. A total of assets and deferred outflows of resources may be included. A total of liabilities and deferred inflows of resources may be included. The balance sheet should report the governmental entity's current financial resources and the claims to those resources for each major governmental fund and for the nonmajor funds. A total column should be used to combine all the major funds and nonmajor funds taken together [GASB Cod. Sec. 2200.162].

PRACTICE POINT: Deferred outflows of resources are rare in governmental funds as of the date of this publication due to the measurement focus and basis of accounting for such funds. Deferred inflows of resources are far more common due to the revenue recognition provisions for taxes and grants.

Fund Balance Classifications. The fund balance of a governmental fund should be identified as nonspendable, restricted, committed, assigned, or unassigned amounts. The restricted fund balances of the combined nonmajor funds must be presented in appropriate detail to inform the reader of the nature of the restrictions and to identify the amount of the other current financial resources that are available for future appropriation.

For example, the fund balance for nonmajor debt service funds may be described as restricted for debt service. In addition, the remaining fund balances for nonmajor funds must be at least identified by fund type on the face of the balance sheet, or if aggregated, disaggregated in the notes to the basic financial statements [GASB Cod. Sec. 2200.163].

As noted earlier, there must be a summary reconciliation between the total fund balances in the balance sheet and the total net position as presented in the Statement of Net Position for governmental activities (government-wide financial statement). Some of the typical items that may be needed to reconcile the two amounts are as follows [GASB Cod. Sec. 2200.164]:

- The difference between reporting capital assets (net of accumulated depreciation) in the Statement of Net Position and the non-recognition of those assets in the fund balance sheets.
- The difference between reporting long-term liabilities in the Statement of Net Position and the non-recognition of those liabilities in the fund balance sheets.
- The difference between the recognition of other liabilities in the Statement of Net Position when they are incurred and the recognition in the fund balance sheets of only those liabilities that are payable with current financial resources.
- The difference between reporting the net position balances of internal service funds in the Statement of Net Position and the non-recognition of those net position in the fund balance sheets.

Exhibit 20-3 provides an illustration of a governmental fund Balance Sheet under *current GAAP*.

Financial Reporting **20,069**

EXHIBIT 20-3
STATE OF BAY
Balance Sheet Governmental Funds
As of June 30, 20Y4
(Amounts expressed in thousands)

	General	Lotteries	Building Authority	Special Revenue Fund 1	Special Revenue Fund 2	Other Governmental Funds	Total
ASSETS							
Cash and cash equivalents	$7,571,342	$47,857	$636,735	$534,558	$4,891,987	$3,130,769	$16,813,248
Restricted cash	—	—	—	—	—	248,690	248,690
Investments	304,140	755,378	1,076,700	—	—	—	2,136,218
Receivables, net:							
Taxes	4,327,157	—	53,993	—	—	141,792	4,522,942
Due from federal government	1,408,708	—	—	—	—	899,450	2,308,158
Loan receivable	—	—	68,012	—	—	12,213	80,225
Other receivables	1,271,311	5,798	5,162	—	—	90,807	1,373,078
Due from municipalities	21,263	—	—	—	—	—	21,263
Due from other funds	328,813	—	—	—	—	89,751	418,564
Due from component units	597	—	—	—	—	—	597
TOTAL ASSETS	**$15,233,331**	**$809,032**	**$1,840,602**	**$534,558**	**$4,891,987**	**$4,613,472**	**$27,922,983**
LIABILITIES, DEFERRED INFLOWS OF RESOURCES AND FUND BALANCES							
Liabilities:							
Accounts payable	$2,779,393	$46,620	$9,862	$58,289	$—	$1,195,133	$4,089,297
Accrued payroll	163,843	—	—	16	—	15,619	179,478
Tax refunds	1,452,680	—	288	—	—	366	1,453,334
Due to other funds	—	—	—	—	—	418,564	418,564
Due to component units	35,070	—	—	—	—	638,202	673,272
Due to federal government	506,638	—	—	—	—	—	506,638
Advances	—	—	—	476,253	4,891,987	766,658	6,134,899
Claims and judgments	13,271	—	—	—	—	—	13,271
Grants payable	—	—	46,743	—	—	—	46,743
Other accrued liabilities	831	—	—	—	—	19,134	19,965
Total liabilities	4,951,726	46,620	56,893	534,558	4,891,987	3,053,676	13,535,461
Deferred inflows of resources	539,292	5,712	—	—	—	25,173	570,177
Total liabilities and deferred inflows of resources	5,491,018	52,332	56,893	534,558	4,891,987	3,078,849	14,105,638
Fund balances:							
Nonspendable	—	755,378	—	—	—	—	755,378
Restricted	—	—	971,301	—	—	349,492	1,320,793
Committed	4,626,419	—	—	—	—	2,179,151	6,805,570
Assigned	1,070,523	1,322	812,408	—	—	162,744	2,046,997
Unassigned (deficits)	4,045,371	—	—	—	—	(1,156,764)	2,888,607
Fund balances	**9,742,313**	**756,700**	**1,783,709**	**—**	**—**	**1,534,623**	**13,817,345**
TOTAL LIABILITIES, DEFERRED INFLOWS OF RESOURCES AND FUND BALANCES	**$15,233,331**	**$809,032**	**$1,840,602**	**$534,558**	**$4,891,987**	**$4,613,472**	**$27,922,983**

A reconciliation between the total fund balances balance sheet under *current GAAP* and the governmental activities net position as portrayed in the Statement of Net Position is as follows:

STATE OF BAY
Reconciliation of the Governmental Funds
Balance Sheet to the Statement of Net Position
June 30, 20Y4
(Amounts expressed in thousands)

Total Fund Balances—Governmental Funds		$13,817,345
Amounts reported in governmental activities in the Statement of Net Position are different due to the following transactions:		
Capital assets used in governmental activities are not financial resources and, therefore, are not reported in the funds. These assets consist of:		
Capital not being depreciated or amortized	$1,849,740	
Capital and right-to-use assets being depreciated and amortized	3,204,074	
Capital assets, net		5,053,814
Revenues are not available soon enough after year-end to pay for current period's expenditures and therefore are deferred inflows of resources in the governmental funds		570,177
Other deferred inflows of resources:		
Gain on refunding bonds	(1,084,179)	
Defined benefit pensions	(480,355)	
Defined benefit OPEB	(2,406,295)	
Total other deferred inflows of resources		(3,970,829)
Deferred outflows of resources not reported in governmental funds:		
Fair value of hedging derivatives	88,793	
Loss on refunding bonds	95,806	
Defined benefit pensions	8,709,458	
Defined benefit OPEB	3,013,735	
Total other deferred outflows of resources		11,907,792
Building authority assets		6,511
Long-term receivables		28,000
Due from component units		6,198
Certain liabilities, including bonds payable, are not due and payable in the current period and therefore are not reported in the funds. These liabilities include:		
Net pension liability	(46,159,763)	
Net OPEB liability	(18,434,733)	
Bonded debt	(29,048,457)	
Unamortized bond premiums	(3,180,856)	
Accrued interest on bonds	(441,358)	
Building authority bonds	(6,508,385)	
Grants to municipalities	(132,556)	
Lottery prizes payable	(755,378)	
Leases, public-private partnerships, and subscription-based information technology arrangements	(14,260)	

Environmental remediation liability	(595,275)
Claims and judgments	(20,000)
Hedging derivative instruments	(88,793)
Employee benefits and compensated absences	(1,095,094)
Total other long-term liabilities	**(106,474,908)**
Total Net Position (deficit) of Governmental Activities	**$(79,055,900)**

Statement of Revenues, Expenditures, and Changes in Fund Balances. This operating statement for governmental funds measures the flow of current financial resources and, therefore, would essentially follow the current standards used to prepare governmental financial statements. The operating statement would have columns for each major fund, one for all (combined) nonmajor funds and a total column. The following format is used [GASB Cod. Sec. 2200.165]:

	General Fund	Major Fund #2	Nonmajor Funds	Total
Revenues (detailed)	$XXX	$XXX	$XXX	$XXX
Total Revenues				
Expenditures (detailed)	XXX	XXX	XXX	XXX
Total Expenditures				
Excess (deficiency) of revenues over (under) expenditures	XXX	XXX	XXX	XXX
Other financing sources and uses, including transfers (detailed)	XXX	XXX	XXX	XXX
Total Other financing sources and uses				
Special and extraordinary items (detailed)	XXX	XXX	XXX	XXX
Net change in fund balances	XXX	XXX	XXX	XXX
Fund balances—Beginning of period	XXX	XXX	XXX	XXX
Fund balances—End of period	$XXX	$XXX	$XXX	$XXX

PRACTICE ALERT: The Statement of Short-Term Financial Resource Flows as proposed in the *Financial Reporting Model Improvements* Exposure Draft has the following elements in comparison to the above:

Statement of Revenues, Expenditures, and Changes in Fund Balances (Current GAAP)	Statement of Short-Term Financial Resource Flows (Proposed GAAP)
Revenues (detailed)	Inflows of resources for current activities (detailed)
Total Revenues	Total inflows of resources for current activities
Expenditures (detailed)	Outflows of resources for current activities (detailed)

Statement of Revenues, Expenditures, and Changes in Fund Balances (Current GAAP)	Statement of Short-Term Financial Resource Flows (Proposed GAAP)
Total Expenditures	Total outflows of resources for current activities
Excess (deficiency) of revenues over (under) expenditures	Net flows for current activities
Other financing sources and uses, including transfers (detailed)	Net flows for noncurrent activities (detailed)
Total Other financing sources and uses	Total net flows for noncurrent activities
Special and extraordinary items (detailed)	Unusual or infrequent items (detailed)
Net change in fund balances	Net change in fund balances
Fund balances—Beginning of period	Fund balances—Beginning of period
Fund balances—End of period	Fund balances—End of period

The above format is selected because the GASB believes that most readers of the financial statements focus on (1) the excess (deficiency) of revenues over expenditures and (2) the overall change in the fund balance. Also, the GASB noted that the format is one of the formats most used by governmental entities. The fund balance portion of the statement should articulate to the Balance Sheet fund balances [GASB Cod. Sec. 2200.fn30].

Revenues and expenditures presented in the Statement of Revenues, Expenditures, and Changes in Fund Balances are classified consistent with GAAP as discussed in Chapter 5 [GASB Cod. Sec. 1800.131]. Governmental fund expenditures are classified by function at a minimum.

> **PRACTICE POINT:** Like the Statement of Activities, many governments present the Statement of Revenues, Expenditures, and Changes in Fund Balances with functions and programs in alignment to the budget.

Debt issuance costs paid out of the proceeds of debt issuance should be reported as expenditures rather than netted against the proceeds (and presented as an other financing source). Debt issuance costs paid from resources other than debt proceeds should be recorded as expenditures at the same time the related debt proceeds are recorded [GASB Cod. Sec. 2200.166].

Other Financing Sources and Uses. Under *current GAAP*, the category "other financing sources and uses" includes items such as

- Sale of long-term debt (including the effects of premiums and discounts),
- Certain payments to escrow agents related to bond refundings,
- Proceeds from new leases that are not short-term,
- Proceeds from the sale of capital assets (unless these items are special items), and
- Transfers [GASB Cod. Sec. 2200.167].

GAAP does not allow governments to combine other financing sources and uses as one element. GAAP also does not allow other financing sources to be combined with revenues and other financing uses with expenditures. GASB Cod. Sec. 2200.735-1 reminds practitioners that the presentation of the Statement of Revenues, Expenditures and Changes in Fund Balances is limited to the prescribed format.

To understand what is presented in the other financing sources and uses section of the Statement of Revenues, Expenditures and Changes in Fund Balances, if debt with a face amount of $1,000,000 was issued for $1,100,000, the transaction would be presented as follows in a governmental fund's operating statement:

Portion of Statement of Revenues, Expenditures, and Changes in Fund Balances	
Other financing sources and uses:	
Long-term debt issued	$1,000,000
Premium on long-term debt issued	100,000

Special and extraordinary items (defined earlier) are presented after the category titled "other financing sources and uses." If a governmental entity has both special items and extraordinary items, they should be reported under the single heading labeled "special and extraordinary items." That is, there should not be separate broad headings for each item type [GASB Cod. Sec. 2200.168] (see previous **PRACTICE ALERT** on the GASB's *Financial Reporting Model Improvements* Exposure Draft and unusual and infrequent items).

When a significant transaction or other event occurs that is either unusual or infrequent, but not both, and is not under the control of management, that item should be reported in one of the following ways:

- Presented and identified as a separate line item in either the "revenue" category or "expenditures" category.

- Presented but not identified as a separate line item in either the "revenue" category or "expenditures" category and described in a note to the financial statements.

OBSERVATION: An extraordinary gain or loss related to the early extinguishment of debt cannot occur on a Statement of Revenues, Expenditures, and Changes in Fund Balances because this statement presents only the changes in current financial resources (as part of other financing sources and uses) and not gains and losses from events and transactions.

There must be a summary reconciliation between the total net change in fund balances (total governmental funds) as shown in the Statement of Revenues, Expenditures, and Changes in Fund Balances and the change in net position as presented in the governmental activities column of the Statement of Activities. Some of the typical items that will be needed to reconcile the two amounts are [GASB Cod. Sec. 2200.169]:

- The difference between reporting revenues and expenses on the accrual basis in the Statement of Activities and the reporting of revenues and expenditures on the modified accrual basis in the Statement of Revenues, Expenditures, and Changes in Fund Balances.
- The difference between reporting depreciation expense in the Statement of Activities and reporting the acquisition of capital assets as an expenditure in the Statement of Revenues, Expenditures, and Changes in Fund Balances.
- The difference between reporting proceeds from the issuance of long-term liabilities as another source of financing in the Statement of Revenues, Expenditures, and Changes in Fund Balances and the non-recognition of those proceeds in the Statement of Activities.
- The difference between reporting the repayment of the principal of long-term liabilities as an expenditure in the Statement of Revenues, Expenditures, and Changes in Fund Balances and the non-recognition of those payments in the Statement of Activities.
- The difference between reporting the net revenue (expenses) of internal service funds in the Statement of Activities and the non-recognition of those activities in the Statement of Revenues, Expenditures, and Changes in Fund Balances.

Exhibit 20-4 illustrates a Statement of Revenues, Expenditures, and Changes in Fund Balances for governmental funds under *current GAAP*.

EXHIBIT 20-4
STATE OF BAY
Statement of Revenues, Expenditures, and Changes in Fund Balances
Governmental Funds for the Year Ended June 30, 20Y4
(Amounts in thousands)

	General	Lotteries	Building Authority	Special Revenue Fund 1	Special Revenue Fund 2	Other Governmental Funds	Total
REVENUES							
Taxes	$30,644,106	$20	$1,071,686	$—	$—	$3,238,876	$34,954,688
Assessments	396,914	—	—	—	—	952,917	1,349,831
Federal grants and reimbursements	13,777,958	—	—	1,308,908	—	7,866,356	22,953,221
Fees and other charges	3,919,261	5,827,985	—	—	—	1,374,927	11,122,173
Miscellaneous	500,388	653	7,180	—	—	493,035	1,001,256
TOTAL REVENUES	**$49,238,627**	**$5,828,658**	**$1,078,866**	**$1,308,908**	**$—**	**$13,926,111**	**$71,381,169**
EXPENDITURES							
Legislature	72,682	$—	$—	$—	$—	$—	$72,682
Judiciary	1,017,350	—	—	—	—	5,522	1,022,872
Inspector General	5,747	—	—	—	—	7	5,754
Governor and Lieutenant Governor	8,921	—	—	—	—	78	8,999
Secretary of State	58,444	—	—	—	—	19,237	77,681
Treasurer	235,097	4,721,164	15,240	11,208	—	1,600,693	6,583,402
Auditor	19,825	—	—	—	—	—	19,825
Attorney General	54,103	—	—	—	—	57,727	111,830
Ethics Commission	2,489	—	—	—	—	—	2,489
District Attorney	145,969	—	—	—	—	7,820	153,789
Campaign and Political Finance	1,660	—	—	—	—	—	1,660
Sheriff's Departments	686,640	—	—	—	—	11,957	698,597
Disabled Persons Protection Commission	5,464	—	—	—	—	1,203	6,667
Commission on Status of Women	206	—	—	—	—	3	209
Library Commissioners	33,821	—	—	—	—	3,274	37,095
Gaming Commission	—	—	—	—	—	45,591	45,591
Comptroller	19,689	—	—	—	—	1,951	21,640
Administration and Finance	2,048,335	—	—	297,275	—	564,656	2,910,266
Energy and Environmental Affairs	289,805	—	—	416	—	170,307	460,528
Health and Human Services	6,930,871	—	—	12,211	—	3,759,376	10,702,458
Technology Services	147,316	—	—	257	—	8,015	155,588
Transportation	—	—	—	3,280	—	2,905,855	2,909,135
Office of the Child Advocate	1,723	—	—	—	—	—	1,723
Commission Against Discrimination	6,824	—	—	—	—	—	6,824
Cannabis Control Commission	—	—	—	—	—	11,334	11,334
Education	3,539,520	—	—	251,756	—	1,257,618	5,048,894
Health and Information Analysis	21,284	—	—	—	—	—	21,284
Building Assistance	—	—	751,521	—	—	—	751,521
Public Safety and Homeland Security	1,463,381	—	—	388	—	305,612	1,769,381
Peace Officer Standards	23	—	—	—	—	—	23
Housing and Economic Development	807,481	—	—	728,925	—	903,588	2,439,994
Labor and Workforce Development	62,497	—	—	2,467	—	291,068	356,032
Medicaid	18,214,658	—	2,731	—	—	1,993,441	20,208,099

Financial Reporting by General-Purpose Governments

	General	Lotteries	Building Authority	Special Revenue Fund 1	Special Revenue Fund 2	Other Governmental Funds	Total
Postemployment benefits	1,641,918	—	—	—	—	12,271	1,656,920
Municipal aid	6,369,568	—	—	—	—	129,737	6,499,305
Capital Outlay	—	—	—	—	—	1,307,695	1,307,695
Debt service	—	—	600,064	—	—	2,507,945	3,108,009
Principal on current refundings	—	—	—	—	—	1,064,644	1,064,644
TOTAL EXPENDITURES	43,913,311	4,721,164	1,369,556	1,308,184	-	18,948,225	70,260,439
EXCESS/(DEFICIENCY) OF REVENUES OVER/(UNDER) EXPENDITURES	5,325,316	1,107,494	(290,690)	724	-	(5,022,114)	1,120,730
OTHER FINANCING SOURCES:							
Bonds premium	—	—	93,521	—	—	692,595	786,116
Issuance of general obligation bonds	—	—	1,834,375	—	—	2,382,048	4,216,423
Issuance of current refunding bonds	—	—	—	—	—	865,115	865,115
Issuance of advance refunding bonds	—	—	—	—	—	900,775	900,775
Issuance of leases, public-private and public-public partnerships, and subscription-based information technology arrangements	2,126	—	—	—	—	—	2,126
Transfers in for debt service	—	—	—	—	—	2,458,994	2,458,994
Other transfers in	2,065,944	—	—	—	—	2,043,604	4,109,548
TOTAL OTHER FINANCING SOURCES	2,068,071	—	1,927,896	—	—	9,343,131	13,339,097
OTHER FINANCING USES:							
Payments to refunding bond escrow agent	—	—	1,570,822	—	—	898,359	2,469,181
Transfers out	839,845	1,207,661	—	724	—	1,863,195	3,911,125
Transfers of appropriations	1,543,381	—	—	—	—	4,718	1,548,099
Transfers of bond proceeds	—	—	—	—	—	167,923	167,923
Transfers out for debt service	1,198,237	—	—	—	—	1,260,757	2,458,994
TOTAL OTHER FINANCING USES	3,581,163	1,207,661	1,570,822	724	—	4,194,952	10,555,322
TOTAL OTHER FINANCING SOURCES AND (USES)	(1,513,092)	(1,207,661)	357,074	(724)	—	5,148,179	2,783,776
NET CHANGE IN FUND BALANCES/(DEFICITS)	3,812,224	(100,167)	66,384	—	—	126,065	3,904,506
FUND BALANCES AT BEGINNING OF YEAR, AS RESTATED **(SEE PREVIOUS PRACTICE POINT)**	5,930,089	856,867	1,717,325	—	—	1,408,558	9,912,839
FUND BALANCES AT END OF YEAR	$9,742,313	$756,700	$1,783,709	$—	$—	$1,554,623	$13,817,345

The notes to the basic financial statements are an integral part of this statement.

The required reconciliation between the net change in fund balance and the net change in governmental activities contained in the Statement of Activities would be as follows:

STATE OF BAY
Reconciliation of the Statement of Revenues, Expenditures, and Changes in Fund Balances to the Statement of Activities
For the Year Ended June 30, 20Y4
(Amounts in thousands)

Total Change in Fund Balances—governmental funds	$3,904,506
Amounts reported for governmental activities in the Statement of Activities are different due to the following adjustments:	
Capital outlays are reported as expenditures in the governmental funds. However, in the Statement of Activities, the cost of capital assets is capitalized and then depreciated (or amortized) over the estimated useful lives as depreciation (or amortization) expense. In the current period, the amount of capital outlay, construction in process and similar:	347,759
Depreciation (amortization) expense	(216,784)
Amounts presented in the Statement of Activities, but not in the governmental fund statements of revenues, expenditures, and changes in fund balances due to different bases of accounting	(250,388)
The issuance of long-term debt provides current financial resources to governmental funds, while the repayment of principal of long-term debt consumes the current financial resources of governmental funds. Neither transaction has any effect on net position. Also, governmental funds report the effect of premiums, discounts, and similar items when debt is first issued, whereas these amounts are deferred and amortized as part of the statement of activities. This amount is the net effect of these differences in the treatment of long-term debt and related items	(1,806,965)
New leases, public-private and public-public partnerships, and subscription-based information technology arrangements	2,854
Building authority activity, net	(5,099)
Net pension expense	(2,873,279)
Net OPEB expense	(484,523)
Other governmental activities expenses in the Statement of Activities, but not in governmental funds	3,384
Net Change in Net Position—Governmental Activities	**$(1,378,535)**

The notes to the basic financial statements are an integral part of this statement.

Financial statements for proprietary funds should be based on the flow of economic resources (measurement focus) and the accrual basis of accounting. The proprietary fund category includes enterprise funds and internal service funds. Proprietary fund activities should be accounted for and reported based on all applicable GASB pronouncements.

Based on the fundamental concepts discussed above, the following financial statements must be prepared for proprietary funds:

- Statement of Net Position,
- Statement of Revenues, Expenses, and Changes in Fund Net Position, and
- Statement of Cash Flows.

The major fund reporting requirement does not apply to internal service funds even though they are proprietary funds. However, all internal service funds should be combined into a single column and presented on the face of the proprietary funds' financial statements. This column must be presented to the right of the total column for all enterprise funds. The internal service funds column and the enterprise funds total column should not be added together [GASB Cod. Secs. 2200.170–.171].

Statement of Net Position. Assets and liabilities presented in the Statement of Net Position of a proprietary fund should be classified as current and long-term, just like a for-profit entity. Assets and liabilities are not permitted to be offset unless a right of offset is in place. If deferred outflows of resources are allowable for the transaction in accordance with GAAP, they are presented in the Statement of Net Position following the asset section. Deferred inflows of resources are presented after liabilities. Like governmental funds, assets may be added to deferred outflows of resources and liabilities may be added to deferred inflows of resources, providing subtotals.

The Statement of Net Position may be presented in either one of the following formats:

- Net position format (where assets plus deferred outflows of resources, less liabilities less deferred inflows of resources equal net position), or
- Balance sheet format (where assets and deferred outflows equal liabilities and deferred inflows plus net position).

Many practitioners favor the net position format versus the balance sheet format as it is easier to transfer information to the government-wide Statement of Net Position.

Net position should be identified as (1) net investment in capital assets, (2) restricted, and (3) unrestricted. The guidance discussed earlier (in the context of government-wide financial statements) should be used to determine what amounts should be related to these three categories of net position. Capital contributions should not be presented as a separate component of net position. Also, designations of net position cannot be identified on the face of the Statement of Net Position [GASB Cod. Secs. 2200.172–.173].

Many practitioners prepare statements of net position for proprietary funds using a classified presentation. The provisions for a classified presentation are in the following subsections [GASB Cod. Sec. 2200.174].

Current Assets. The term *current assets* is used to apportion cash and other assets and resources commonly identified as those that are *reasonably* expected to be realized in cash or sold or consumed within one year.

Current assets may be inclusive of:

1. Cash available for current operations and items that are the equivalent of cash,
2. Inventories of merchandise, raw materials, goods in process, finished goods, operating supplies, and ordinary maintenance material and parts,
3. Trade accounts, notes, and acceptances receivable,

4. Receivables from taxpayers, other governments, vendors or contractors, customers, beneficiaries, and employees, if collectible within a year,
5. Installment or accounts and notes receivable if they conform generally to normal trade practices and terms within the business-type activity,
6. Marketable securities representing the investment of cash available for current operations, and
7. Prepayments such as insurance, interest, rents, unused royalties, current paid advertising service not yet received, and operating supplies.

Prepayments are current assets due to the requirement to use the current assets within a year, but not ostensibly the conversion into cash within a year [GASB Cod. Sec. 2200.175].

Current assets do not include cash and claims to cash when they are restricted under the following conditions [GASB Cod. Sec. 2200.176]:

- Amounts cannot be used for current operations.
- Amounts are to be used to acquire noncurrent assets.
- Amounts are to be used to pay long-term debts.

GASB Cod. Sec. 2200.fn32 further comments that even though they are not actually set aside in special accounts, resources that are clearly to be used soon for the liquidation of long-term debts, payments to sinking funds, or for similar purposes should also, under this concept, be excluded from current assets. However, where such resources are considered to offset maturing debt that has properly been set up as a current liability, they may be included within the current asset classification.

Unearned discounts, finance charges, and interest on receivables are shown as reductions of the related receivables. Asset valuation allowances for losses, similarly to those on receivables, are deducted from the assets or groups they relate, with disclosure [GASB Cod. Secs. 2200.177–.178].

If there is a change in an allowance for uncollectable accounts, a reclassification may occur. GASB Cod. Sec. 2200.745-1 discusses a change in an uncollectable loan receivable account. The change would be reported as an expense as there is no related revenue account to reduce. The guidance states that a forgiven or uncollectible loan becomes like a gift, grant or contribution and is properly reported as an expense.

In a proprietary fund it is assumed that assets (especially current assets) are unrestricted in that there are no conditions that would prevent the governmental entity from using the resources for unrestricted purposes. Generally, assets are reported as restricted assets when the nature and amount of those assets satisfy applicable legal or contractual provisions or when restrictions on asset use change the nature or normal understanding of the availability of the asset.

For example, cash and cash equivalents are normally considered unrestricted current assets available to pay current liabilities. However, an amount of cash may be restricted pursuant to a debt covenant to be a debt service reserve that must be maintained throughout the life of the outstanding bonds at a specific contractual amount, therefore, it would be misleading to report this restricted cash with all other cash (classified as current asset). Under this circumstance, the cash should be reported as restricted cash in the financial statement category labeled "noncurrent assets."

If the name of the asset account does not adequately explain the normally perceived availability of that asset, the item should be identified as a restricted asset in the Statement of Net Position. On the other hand, although equipment is not available to pay liabilities, the title of the account adequately describes the availability (or lack of liquidity) of the asset and, therefore, there is no need to identify the asset as restricted [GASB Cod. Sec. 2200.179].

Many governmental entities have assets that are restricted to specific purposes, but if those purposes are related to current operations, they should be reported as current assets.

OBSERVATION: Regarding net position (equity) classifications, restricted net positions arise only when assets are (1) externally imposed by a creditor (such as through debt covenants), grantors, contributors, or laws or regulations of other governments or (2) imposed by law through constitutional provisions or enabling legislation. These provisions are the same as utilized in the government-wide Statement of Net Position.

Current Liabilities. Current liabilities are principally obligations whose liquidation is expected to require the use of existing resources that are classified as current assets, or the creation of other current liabilities. Typically, current liabilities include, but are not limited to:

- Payables incurred in the acquisition of materials and supplies to be used in providing services,
- Collections received in advance of the performance of services, and
- Debts that arise from operations related to the operating cycle, such as accruals for wages, salaries, commissions, rentals, and royalties.

If the liability's regular and ordinary liquidation is expected to occur within one-year, current liabilities may also include:

- Short-term debts arising from the acquisition of capital assets,
- Serial maturities of long-term obligations,
- Amounts required to be expended within one year under sinking fund provisions, and
- Certain agency obligations arising from the collection or acceptance of cash or other assets for the account of third parties.

There may be many other elements of current liabilities, including long-term obligations that are (or will be) callable by a creditor due to covenant violations as of the date of the financial statements and not cured within a grace period. They may also include advance ticket sales for entertainment facilities (stadiums), security deposits (unless for long-term deliveries of service), and many other potential transactions [GASB Cod. Secs. 2200.180–.181].

There is no requirement that there be a specific one-to-one relationship between assets and liabilities presented and the amounts presented in the three categories of net position. In other words, a reader will not generally be able to look at the Statement of Net Position and identify the specific assets and liability accounts that are reported as, for example, unrestricted net assets.

Short-Term Obligations Expected to be Refinanced. Like other current liabilities, short-term obligations that are scheduled to mature within one year after the date of the government's financial statements are classified as current liabilities with a major exception. If the government is refinancing a short-term obligation and replacing it with a long-term obligation, or renewing, extending, or replacing it with ongoing short-term obligations for an uninterrupted period beyond one year, the obligation should be classified as a long-term obligation. This is because the refinancing is not expected to require the use of unrestricted net position during the following period.

The government must intend to refinance the obligation on a long-term basis, and it must have the ability to complete the refinancing. The ability and intent are demonstrated in either of two ways:

- After the date of the financial statements, but prior to their issuance, the long-term obligation has been issued and has refinanced the short-term obligation on a long-term basis, *or*
- Before the financial statements have been issued, a financing agreement has been signed that permits the government to refinance, with determinable terms and with all the following conditions:
  — The agreement does not expire within one year, nor is it cancelable by the lender (or the perspective lender), unless there is a compliance violation,
  — No violation exists at the date of the financial statements or prior to the issuance of the financial statements. If one exists, a waiver has been obtained, and
  — The lender is expected to honor the agreement.

If a new long-term obligation has been issued, the amount of the short-term obligation excluded from current liabilities in the Statement of Net Position must be less than the proceeds of the new long-term obligation. If there is a financing agreement in place meeting the terms and conditions above, the amount of the short-term obligation excluded from current liabilities is the amount available for refinancing under the agreement if the amount is less than the amount of the short-term obligation. Reasonable estimates should be made in the case of fluctuating amounts or potential violations. If no reasonable estimate can be made, the short-term obligation should continue to be included in current liabilities [GASB Cod. Secs. 2200.182–.189].

Exhibit 20-5 illustrates a Statement of Net Position for proprietary funds.

EXHIBIT 20-5
STATE OF BAY
Statement of Net Position
Proprietary Funds
As of June 30, 20Y4
(Amounts in thousands)

	Unemployment Compensation Trust Fund	Family and Employment Security Trust Fund	Flagship University	State Universities	Community Colleges	Total
ASSETS AND DEFERRED OUTFLOWS OF RESOURCES:						
Current assets:						
Cash and cash equivalents	$2,714,565	$1,342,587	$143,864	$366,003	$282,477	$4,849,496
Short-term investments	—	—	639,163	73,993	70,308	783,464
Receivables, net:						
Federal grants and reimbursements receivable	—	—	26,377	24,698	9,541	60,616
Loans	—	—	5,667	1,209	—	6,876
Other receivables	336,213	293,948	284,206	26,030	64,676	1,005,073
Due from affiliates	—	—	17,028	65	183	17,276
Due from foundation	—	—	—	168	184	352
Other current assets	—	—	48,356	6,396	5,111	59,863
Total current assets	3,050,778	1,636,535	1,164,661	498,562	432,480	6,783,016
Noncurrent assets:						
Cash and cash equivalents— restricted	—	—	210,070	37,150	36	247,256
Long-term investments	—	—	1,163,887	204,780	69,380	1,438,047
Restricted investments	—	—	—	1,110	—	1,110
Other receivables, net	—	—	16,625	249	—	16,874
Loans receivable, net	—	—	27,692	3,319	—	31,011
Non-depreciable capital assets	—	—	448,925	106,706	112,730	668,361
Depreciable capital assets, net	—	—	4,795,044	1,791,975	738,730	7,325,749
Other noncurrent assets	—	—	115,863	9,925	1,169	126,957
Total noncurrent assets	—	—	6,778,106	2,155,214	922,045	9,855,365
Total assets	3,050,778	1,636,535	7,942,767	2,653,776	1,354,525	16,638,381
Deferred outflows of resources:						
Related to hedging derivatives	—	—	—	—	1,204	1,204
Defined benefit pensions	—	—	185,335	60,674	31,116	277,125
Defined benefit OPEB	—	—	239,859	84,270	38,562	362,691
Debt refunding	—	—	125,201	43,875	—	169,076
Certain asset retirement obligations	—	—	1,158	—	—	1,158
Other	—	—	—	479	—	479
Total deferred outflows of resources	—	—	551,553	189,298	70,882	811,733
Total assets and deferred outflows	3,050,778	1,636,535	8,494,320	2,843,074	1,425,407	17,450,114
LIABILITIES AND DEFERRED INFLOWS:						
Current liabilities:						
Accounts payable and other liabilities	365,985	31,315	217,459	42,693	41,934	699,386
Accrued payroll	—	119	162,296	47,517	29,784	239,716
Compensated absences	—	—	97,562	36,304	34,995	168,861
Accrued interest payable	—	—	21,103	105	137	21,345
Tax refunds and abatements payable	684,656	8,734	—	—	—	693,390

	Unemployment Compensation Trust Fund	Family and Employment Security Trust Fund	Flagship University	State Universities	Community Colleges	Total
Advances	—	—	—	25,024	12,385	37,409
Student deposits	—	—	96,685	7,006	34,538	138,229
Due to foundation	—	—	—	—	7	7
Leases, public-private and public-public partnerships, and subscription-based information technology arrangements	—	—	904	1,139	909	2,952
Due to federal government	152,226	—	—	—	—	152,226
Bonds, notes payable and other obligations	2,268,015	—	136,055	35,726	4,810	2,444,606
Total current liabilities	**3,470,882**	**40,168**	**732,064**	**195,514**	**159,499**	**4,598,127**
Noncurrent liabilities:						
Compensated absences	—	—	23,878	20,854	17,195	61,927
Due to federal government grants	—	—	—	3,887	—	3,887
Leases, public-private and public-public partnerships, and subscription-based information technology arrangements	—	—	1,289	3,188	1,295	5,772
Bonds, notes payable and other obligations	—	—	3,121,428	1,231,967	44,429	4,397,824
Hedging derivative instruments	—	—	—	—	1,204	1,204
Net pension liability	—	—	644,879	235,434	101,702	982,015
Net OPEB liability	—	—	829,808	299,071	130,865	1,259,744
Other noncurrent liabilities	—	—	140,455	10,213	6,584	157,252
Total noncurrent liabilities	—	—	**4,761,737**	**1,804,614**	**303,274**	**6,869,625**
Total liabilities	**3,470,882**	**40,168**	**5,493,801**	**2,000,128**	**462,773**	**11,467,752**
Deferred inflows of resources:						
Public-private and public-public partnerships	—	—	—	13,418	167	13,585
Pensions	—	—	18,297	22,356	31,497	72,150
OPEB	—	—	338,233	176,554	116,786	631,573
Grants and donations	—	—	54,921	—	4,412	59,333
Bond refundings	—	—	—	7,957	—	7,957
Other	—	—	—	111	—	111
Total deferred inflows of resources	—	—	**411,451**	**220,396**	**152,862**	**784,709**
Total liabilities and deferred inflows	**3,470,882**	**40,168**	**5,905,252**	**2,220,524**	**615,635**	**12,252,461**
NET POSITION:						
Net investment in capital assets	—	—	2,306,226	755,109	800,070	3,861,405
Restricted for:						
Family and employment benefits	—	1,596,367	—	—	—	1,596,367
Higher education endowment funds	—	—	22,378	40	507	22,925
Higher education academic support and programs	—	—	—	1,358	4,195	5,553
Higher education scholarships and fellowships:						
Nonexpendable	—	—	—	3,142	—	3,142
Expendable	—	—	—	10,225	10,653	20,878
Higher Education capital projects—expendable purposes	—	—	—	1,252	454	1,706
Grants and gifts	—	—	232,756	23,722	1,299	257,777
Unrestricted	(420,104)	—	27,708	(172,298)	(7,406)	(572,100)
Total net position	**$(420,104)**	**$1,596,367**	**$2,589,068**	**$622,550**	**$809,772**	**$5,197,653**

The notes to the basic financial statements are an integral part of this statement.

Statement of Revenues, Expenses, and Changes in Fund Net Position

The operating statement of a proprietary fund is the Statement of Revenues, Expenses, and Changes in Fund Net Position. In preparing this statement, the following standards should be observed [GASB Cod. Sec. 2200.190]:

- Revenues should be reported by major source,
- Revenues that are restricted for the payment of revenue bonds should be identified,
- Operating and nonoperating revenues should be reported separately,
- Operating and nonoperating expenses should be reported separately,
- Separate subtotals should be presented for operating revenues, operating expenses, and operating income,
- Nonoperating revenues and expenses should be reported after operating income,
- Capital contributions and additions to term and permanent endowments should be reported separately.
- Special and extraordinary items should be reported separately,
- Transfers should be reported separately.

The Statement of Revenues, Expenses, and Changes in Fund Net Position should be presented in the following sequence [GASB Cod. Sec. 2200.191]:

	Major Fund #1	Major Fund #2	Nonmajor Funds	Total
Operating revenues (detailed)	$XXX	$XXX	$XXX	$XXX
Total operating revenues	XXX	XXX	XXX	XXX
Operating expenses (detailed)	XXX	XXX	XXX	XXX
Total operating expenses	XXX	XXX	XXX	XXX
Operating income (loss)	**XXX**	**XXX**	**XXX**	**XXX**
Nonoperating revenues and expenses (detailed)	XXX	XXX	XXX	XXX
Income before other revenues, expenses, gains, losses, and transfers	XXX	XXX	XXX	XXX
Capital contributions, additions to permanent and term endowments, special and extraordinary items (detailed), and transfers	XXX	XXX	XXX	XXX
Change in net position	**XXX**	**XXX**	**XXX**	**XXX**
Net position—Beginning of period	XXX	XXX	XXX	XXX
Net position—End of period	**$XXX**	**$XXX**	**$XXX**	**$XXX**

GASB Cod. Sec. 2200.191 only requires the presentation of operating and nonoperating expenses as "detailed."

GASB Cod. Sec. 2200.751-3 further says that there is no specific type or level of detail. Under *current GAAP*, governments are not required to report expenses by natural (object) classification. Some governments (particularly public colleges and universities—PCUs) may use natural classification and others use functions. Natural classifications include such categories as salaries, benefits, depreciation, supplies, interest, and others. Functional classifications are by operating area. For PCUs, operating areas would include academics, housing, ancillary services, and others.

PRACTICE ALERT: The GASB's *Financial Reporting Model Improvements* Exposure Draft presents the following sequence of information for within a Statement of Revenues, Expenses, and Changes in Fund Net Position:

- Operating revenues (detailed)
  - Total operating revenues
- Operating expenses (detailed)
  - Total operating expenses
  - Operating income (loss)
- Noncapital subsidies (detailed)
  - Total noncapital subsidies
  - Operating income (loss) and noncapital subsidies
- Other nonoperating revenues and expenses (detailed)
  - Total other nonoperating revenues and expenses
  - Income (loss) before unusual or infrequent items
- Unusual or infrequent items (detailed)
- Increase (decrease) in net position
- Net position–beginning of period
- Net position–end of period

Operating revenues and expenses are revenues and expenses *other than* nonoperating revenues and expenses. Nonoperating revenues and expenses are proposed by the GASB to be:

- Subsidies received and provided,
- Revenues and expenses related to financing,
- Resources from the disposal of capital assets and inventory, and
- Investment income and expenses.

Revenues and expenses normally classified as nonoperating in most proprietary fund financial statements may be classified as operating revenues and expenses in those transactions constitute the proprietary fund's principal ongoing operations. As an example, interest revenues, and expenses should be reported as operating revenues and expenses by a proprietary fund established to provide housing financed by bonds and rents. Consistent with the classifications in the Statement of Cash Flows, revenues, and expenses of certain loan program as described in GASB Cod. Sec. 2450.116 should be reported as operating revenues and expenses.

As proposed by the GASB, subsidies are resources received from another party or fund to keep rates lower than otherwise would be necessary to support the level of good and service to be provided or resources provided to another party or fund that results in higher rates than otherwise would be established for the level of good and services to be provided.

OBSERVATION: Revenues should be reported net of related discounts or allowances. The amount of the discounts or allowances must be presented in the operating statement (either parenthetically or as a subtraction from gross revenues) or in a note to the financial statements. Furthermore, if there is a right of return, GAAP requires that revenue should be recognized only if prices are fixed, if the sale is not contingent on another sale, if there is no recourse if there is a theft of the item, if the sale was at more than an "arm's length," there are no future obligations between the parties, and the value of returns can be reasonably estimated [GASB Cod. Secs. 1600.134–.136, 2200.fn.44].

Operating Versus Nonoperating Revenues and Expenses. As introduced above, a principal element of the Statement of Revenues, Expenses, and Changes in Fund Net Position is that there must be a differentiation between operating revenues and nonoperating revenues, and operating expenses and nonoperating expenses *based on policies established by the governmental entity.* Those policies should be disclosed in the entity's summary of significant accounting policies and must be applied consistently from period to period.

In general, differentiations between operating and nonoperating transactions should follow the broad guidance established by GASB Cod. Sec. 2450. For example, transactions related to (1) capital and related financing activities, (2) noncapital financing activities, (3) investing activities, and (4) nonexchange revenues, such as tax revenues, generally would be considered nonoperating transactions for purposes of preparing the Statement of Revenues, Expenses, and Changes in Fund Net Position [GASB Cod. Sec. 2200.192].

PRACTICE ALERT: The ability for an entity to make this policy determination may no longer be available if the provisions in the GASB's *Financial Reporting Model Improvements* Exposure Draft is ultimately approved. The policy flexibility in current GAAP was primarily due to the differences in activities reporting in proprietary funds and the variability in bond covenants. If indeed the provisions are approved, one might imagine a supplementary schedule for bond covenant compliance purposes being necessary.

In addition, current GAAP provides the following guidance on operating versus nonoperating flows:

Revenue and expense transactions normally classified as other operating cash flows from operations in most proprietary funds should be classified as operating revenues and expenses if those transactions constitute the reporting proprietary fund's principal ongoing operations. For example, interest revenue and expense transactions should be reported as operating revenue and expenses by a proprietary fund established to provide loans to first-time homeowners [GASB Cod. Sec. 2200.fn.45].

PRACTICE POINT: GASB Cod. Secs. 2450.113–.116 provides general concepts of operating activities that will vary dependent upon the government's operations. The definition is also used to delineate operating versus nonoperating activities for proprietary funds under current GAAP. The definition utilized by the reporting entity should be disclosed in the summary of significant accounting policies section of the notes to the basic financial statements.

In the question, property taxes are levied by a hospital district for care of indigent patients. The property taxes would *not* be an operating activity unless they are levied for capital purposes. The operating activity of a hospital involves patient care. However, the GASB concludes that even if the amount levied is calculated to finance estimated care of the indigent, it is not a charge for services. Instead, property taxpayers are financing the care of the indigent, which is a subsidy as defined in GASB Cod. Sec. 2450.118(d) and presentation as a noncapital financing inflow. For the Statement of Revenues, Expenses, and Changes in Fund Net Position purposes, the tax revenue may indeed be defined as operating per the hospital's policies and procedures.

However, it would be reclassified in the Statement of Cash Flows to noncapital financing.

The Statement of Revenues, Expenses, and Changes in Fund Net Position must reflect the "all-inclusive" concept. That is, except for prior-period adjustments and the effects of certain changes in accounting principles, all resources inflows (except for liabilities) must be reported in a proprietary fund's operating statement. Thus, additions to permanent and term endowments are not shown as direct additions to a fund's net position. The guidance for determining when these items should be recognized is based on GASB Cod. Sec. N50 [GASB Cod. Sec. 2200.193].

The fact that capital contributions are reported in a proprietary fund's operating statement does not mean that the contribution results in an increase in unrestricted net position. The transactions must be evaluated to determine whether the amount is appropriately presented as a part of net investment in capital assets.

As described earlier, there must be reconciliations between the government-wide financial statements and the governmental fund financial statements. Generally, there is no need for a similar reconciliation between the government-wide financial statements and proprietary fund financial statements because both sets of financial statements are based on the same measurement focus and basis of accounting [GASB Cod. Sec. 2200.194].

Typically, there are no reconciling items between business-type activities as they appear in the government-wide financial statements and the proprietary fund financial statements because both statements are prepared on the accrual basis of accounting and economic resources measurement focus.

If there are reconciling items, the following may be present between business-type activities and government-wide financial statements:

- When enterprise funds are the only or predominant participants in an internal service fund, the balances related to the internal service fund must be included in the business-type activities column (not the governmental activities column, which is the typical presentation). Because internal service funds are not included in the totals of the enterprise funds (but, rather, are presented in a column to the right of those funds) in the fund financial statements, a reconciling item arises.

- When enterprise funds participate in an internal service fund and the internal service fund is not at a "break-even" position, a look-back adjustment must modify the expenses in the business-type activities column. This creates a difference between the expenses as presented in the fund financial statements and the expenses presented in the government-wide financial statements.

- When a governmental activity is performed in an enterprise fund (or vice versa), the results of the activity are presented in an enterprise fund financial statement, but those same results are also presented in the governmental activity column of the government-wide financial statements. This creates a difference between the two financial statements.

Exhibit 20-6 illustrates a Statement of Revenues, Expenses, and Changes in Fund Net Position for proprietary funds.

EXHIBIT 20-6
STATE OF BAY
Statement of Revenues, Expenses, and Changes in Fund Net Position
Proprietary Funds
For the Year Ended June 30, 20Y4
(Amounts in thousands)

	Unemployment Compensation Trust Fund	Family and Employment Security Trust Fund	Flagship University	State Universities	Community Colleges	Total
Operating revenues:						
Unemployment compensation contribution	$ 1,565,470	$ —	$ —	$ —	$ —	$ 1,565,470
Family and employment security contribution	—	1,005,102	—	—	—	1,005,102
Net tuition and fees	—	—	930,613	373,444	179,474	1,483,531
Grants and reimbursements	—	—	667,149	94,793	216,785	978,727
Auxiliary enterprises	—	—	163,812	72,077	2,355	238,244
Sales and services	—	—	415,781	34,976	5,446	456,203
Miscellaneous	43,133	—	125,586	22,330	13,003	204,052
Total operating revenues	1,608,603	1,005,102	2,302,941	597,620	417,063	5,931,329
Operating expenses:						
Unemployment compensation	19,438,890	—	—	—	—	19,438,890
Family and employment security	—	236,361	—	—	—	236,361
Instruction	—	—	934,793	340,588	300,765	1,576,146
Research	—	—	552,472	222	16	552,710
Academic support	—	—	199,897	100,336	103,767	404,000
Student services	—	—	141,160	111,672	133,544	386,376
Scholarships and fellowships	—	—	85,500	57,709	78,891	222,100
Public service	—	—	90,363	5,008	4,494	99,865
Operation and maintenance of plant	—	—	226,965	109,933	73,269	410,167
Institutional support	—	—	314,676	118,611	139,098	572,385
Other operating expenses	—	—	314,182	3,033	2,062	319,277
Depreciation and amortization	—	—	300,201	107,429	47,368	454,998
Auxiliary operations	—	—	218,370	94,102	2,761	315,233
Total operating expenses	19,438,890	236,361	3,378,579	1,048,643	886,035	24,988,508
Operating income/(loss)	(17,830,287)	768,741	(1,075,638)	(451,023)	(468,972)	(19,057,179)
Nonoperating revenues/ (expenses):						
Other federal revenues	17,200,114	—	179,545	61,362	116,808	17,557,829
Other revenues	—	—	209,799	15,881	—	225,680
Other expenses	—	—	(39,275)	(2,306)	(14,801)	(56,382)
Investment income/(loss)	8,371	1,164	133,393	(5,434)	20,610	158,104
Total nonoperating revenues/ (expenses)	17,208,485	1,164	483,462	69,503	122,617	17,885,231
Income/(loss) before capital grants and contributions and transfers	(621,802)	769,905	(592,176)	(381,520)	(346,355)	(1,171,948)
Capital grants and contributions	—	—	62,592	51,980	60,279	174,851
Transfers, net	—	(3,252)	685,885	390,390	444,576	1,517,599
Total capital grants and contributions and transfers	—	(3,252)	748,477	442,370	504,855	1,692,450
Change in net position	(621,802)	766,653	156,301	60,850	158,500	520,502

	Unemployment Compensation Trust Fund	Family and Employment Security Trust Fund	Flagship University	State Universities	Community Colleges	Total
Total net position—beginning	201,698	829,714	2,432,767	561,700	651,272	4,677,151
Total net position—ending	$ (420,104)	$ 1,596,367	$ 2,589,068	$ 622,550	$ 809,772	$ 5,197,653

The notes to the basic financial statements are an integral part of this statement.

Statement of Cash Flows

Proprietary funds should prepare a Statement of Cash Flows based on the guidance contained in GASB Cod. Sec. 2450, except the Statement of Cash Flows should be prepared based on the direct method in computing cash flows from operating activities. The Statement of Cash Flows is required to be supplemented with a reconciliation of operating cash flows and operating income [GASB Cod. Sec. 2200.195].

Even if an entity has no operating income or expense, a Statement of Cash Flows is still required. GASB Cod. Sec. 2200.755-1 discusses that there still may be nonoperating flows. A reconciliation of operating income to net cash flow would start with zero, given no operating income. Adjusting and reconciling items would then be presented.

Exhibit 20-7 illustrates a Statement of Cash Flows for proprietary funds.

Financial Reporting **20,091**

EXHIBIT 20-7
STATE OF BAY
Statement of Cash Flows Proprietary Funds
For the Year Ended June 30, 20Y4
(Amounts in thousands)

	Unemployment Compensation Trust Fund	Family and Employment Security Trust Fund	Flagship University	State Universities	Community Colleges	Total
CASH FLOWS FROM OPERATING ACTIVITIES						
Collection of unemployment contributions	$ 1,823,332	$ —	$ —	$ —	$ —	$ 1,823,332
Collection of family and employment security contributions	—	958,454	—	—	—	958,454
Tuition, residence, dining, and other student fees	—	—	1,025,916	367,938	176,296	1,570,150
Research grants and contracts	—	—	650,603	132,878	229,683	1,013,164
Payments to suppliers	—	—	(834,725)	(228,662)	(139,241)	(1,202,628)
Payments to employees	—	—	(2,061,084)	(506,065)	(508,720)	(3,075,869)
Payments to students	—	—	(89,267)	(42,813)	(78,891)	(210,971)
Payments for unemployment benefits	(18,687,125)	—	—	—	—	(18,687,125)
Payments for family and employment security benefits	—	(215,327)	—	—	—	(215,327)
Collection of loans to students and employees	—	—	8,661	1,182	—	9,843
Income from contract services	—	—	421,292	1,878	500	423,670
Maintenance costs	—	—	—	(1,820)	—	(1,820)
Auxiliary enterprise charges	—	—	163,585	37,696	90	201,371
Other receipts/(payments)	43,133	—	(556,909)	(379,932)	(427,897)	(1,321,605)
Net cash provided by/(used in) operating activities	(16,820,660)	743,127	(1,271,928)	(617,720)	(748,180)	(18,715,361)
CASH FLOW FROM NON-CAPITAL FINANCING ACTIVITIES						
State appropriations	—	—	845,481	300,454	316,380	1,462,315
Grants and contracts	17,200,114	—	220,922	58,914	114,544	17,594,494
Student organizations	—	—	818	—	—	818
Net transfers in/(out)	—	(3,252)	685,885	390,390	444,576	1,517,599
Assignment of Perkins loans	—	—	—	(219)	—	(219)
Net cash provided by/(used in) non-capital financing activities	17,200,114	(3,252)	1,753,106	749,539	875,500	20,575,007
CASH FLOWS FROM CAPITAL AND RELATED FINANCING ACTIVITIES						
Capital appropriations	—	—	62,592	32,293	13,105	107,990
Purchases of capital assets	—	—	(322,341)	(56,350)	(24,597)	(403,288)
Proceeds/(loss) from sales of capital assets	—	—	7,734	2,734	—	10,468
Proceeds from debt issuance	2,108,108	—	792,956	43,972	—	2,945,036
Other capital asset activity	—	—	8,413	(772)	324	7,965
Principal paid on capital debt and leases	—	—	(708,067)	(49,801)	(5,394)	(763,262)
Payment of debt issuance costs and mortgage insurance premium	—	—	(54,930)	—	—	(54,930)

	Unemployment Compensation Trust Fund	Family and Employment Security Trust Fund	Flagship University	State Universities	Community Colleges	Total
Interest paid on capital debt and leases	—	—	(153,367)	(46,327)	(2,073)	(201,767)
Net cash provided by/(used in) capital financing activities	2,108,108	—	(367,010)	(74,251)	(18,635)	1,648,212
CASH FLOWS FROM INVESTING ACTIVITIES						
Proceeds from sales and maturities of investments	—	—	1,048,212	118,885	24,547	1,191,644
Purchases of investments	—	—	(1,325,603)	(115,645)	(35,347)	(1,476,595)
Investment earnings	8,371	1,164	54,561	8,993	1,134	74,223
Net cash provided by/(used in) investing activities	8,371	1,164	(222,830)	12,233	(9,666)	(210,728)
Net increase/(decrease) in cash and cash equivalents	2,495,933	741,039	(108,662)	69,801	99,019	3,297,130
Cash and cash equivalents, restricted cash, and cash equivalents at the beginning of the fiscal year	218,632	601,548	462,596	333,352	183,494	1,799,622
Cash and cash equivalents, restricted cash, and cash equivalents at the end of the fiscal year	$ 2,714,565	$ 1,342,587	$ 353,934	$ 403,153	$ 282,513	$ 5,096,752
Reconciliation of net operating revenues and expenses to cash used by operating activities:						
Operating income/(loss)	$ (17,830,287)	$ 768,741	$ (1,075,638)	$ (451,023)	$ (468,972)	$ (19,057,179)
Adjustments to reconcile operating income/(loss) to net cash provided by/(used in) operating activities:						
Depreciation and amortization expense	—	—	300,201	107,429	47,368	454,998
Fringe benefits paid by the primary government	—	—	—	96,456	110,262	206,718
Changes in assets and liabilities:						
Accounts receivable, prepaids and other assets	59,882	(55,382)	(678,619)	(397,800)	(447,947)	(1,519,866)
Accounts payable, accrued liabilities and benefits	751,765	29,768	85,044	11,308	14,243	892,128
Student deposits and other unearned and deferred revenues	—	—	6,881	20,894	9,667	37,442
Other noncurrent assets—restricted and liabilities	197,980	—	90,203	(4,984)	(12,801)	270,398
Net cash provided by/(used in) operating activities	$ (16,820,660)	$ 743,127	$ (1,271,928)	$ (617,720)	$ (748,180)	$(18,715,361)

Non-cash investing, capital, and financing activities: The Flagship University, the State Universities and Community Colleges had $38.0 million, $173.2 million, and $171.5 million, respectively, of non-cash activities.

The notes to the basic financial statements are an integral part of this statement.

Required Financial Statements: Fiduciary Funds and Component Units That Are Fiduciary in Nature

Assets held by a governmental entity for other parties (either as a trustee or as an agent) and that cannot be used to finance the governmental entity's own operating programs should be reported in the entity's fiduciary fund financial statement category. The financial statements for fiduciary funds should be based on the flow of economic resources measurement focus and the accrual basis of accounting. Fiduciary fund financial statements are not reported by major fund (which is required for governmental funds and proprietary funds) but must be reported based on the following fund types [GASB Cod. Sec. 2200.197]:

- Pension (and other employee benefit) trust funds,
- Private-purpose trust funds,
- Investment trust funds, and
- Custodial funds.

The financial statements of a fiduciary component unit should be included in one of the four fund types listed above. GASB Cod. Sec. 2200.729-8 emphasizes that a fiduciary fund that a governmental entity believes is particularly important cannot be presented in a separate column in the fund financial statements. If a governmental entity wants to present additional detail about its fiduciary funds, that information can be presented in combining statements. However, those statements are optional and are not considered to be a part of the basic external financial statements. They are a part of the ACRF.

Pension and OPEB plans that are administered through trusts that meet the criteria for an irrevocable trust as discussed in Chapter 8 are presented within the notes to the financial statements of the primary government if separate GAAP-based financial reports have not been issued. If separate GAAP financial reports have been issued, the notes may reflect information about how to obtain those reports.

The following financial statements should be included for fiduciary funds:

- Statement of Fiduciary Net Position, and
- Statement of Changes in Fiduciary Net Position.

Statement of Fiduciary Net Position. The assets, liabilities, and net position of fiduciary funds should be presented in the Statement of Fiduciary Net Position. There is no need to divide net position into the three categories (net investment in capital assets, restricted net position, and unrestricted net position) that must be used in the government-wide financial statements as all net position is ultimately in trust for beneficiaries [GASB Cod. Sec. 2200.198].

If deferred outflows of resources and deferred inflows of resources are presented as part of fiduciary activities, the deferred outflows follow assets and deferred inflows follow liabilities, respectively. Subtotals then may be used. Further details on pension and OPEB plans, and external investment trust funds are contained in Chapters 22 and 9, respectively [GASB Cod. Sec. 2200.198].

Statement of Changes in Fiduciary Net Position. The Statement of Changes in Fiduciary Net Position should summarize the additions to, deductions from, and net increase or decrease in net position for the year. GAAP also requires the statement to provide information "about significant year-to-year changes in net position." Except for custodial fund reporting, the Statement of Changes in

Fiduciary Net Position should disaggregate additions by source and deductions by type and, if applicable, separate display of administrative costs.

Investment Flow Reporting. The Statement of Changes in Fiduciary Net Position's section on additions includes as applicable, separate display of:

- Investment earnings,
- Investment costs, and
- Net investment earnings (the net of the two).

Investment costs consists of investment management fees, custodial fees, and all other investment-related costs if such costs are separable from investment earnings and investment costs [GASB Cod. Sec. 2200.198].

Custodial Fund Reporting. Governments may report a single aggregated total for additions and a separate single aggregated total for deductions solely for custodial funds if resources within the funds are to be held for three months or less. The descriptions of the aggregated totals should be understandable and relate to the nature of the flows [GASB Cod. Sec. 2200.200].

Exhibit 20-8 is a Statement of Fiduciary Net Position and Exhibit 20-9 is a Statement of Changes in Fiduciary Net Position.

EXHIBIT 20-8
STATE OF BAY
FIDUCIARY FUNDS
STATEMENT OF FIDUCIARY NET POSITION
As of June 30, 20Y4
(Amounts in thousands)

	Pension and Other Employee Benefits Trust Funds	Investment Trust Funds	Private-Purpose Trust Funds	Custodial Funds
ASSETS				
Cash and cash equivalents	$289,585	$5,713,259	$1,216	$517,657
Short-term investments	—	33,680	—	—
Net investment in pension investment board at fair value	74,585,737	21,107,131	—	—
Investments, restricted investments	—	—	—	527,160
Receivables, net:				
Taxes	—	—	—	28,742
Other receivables	187,063	2,105	—	174,984
Due from federal government	—	—	—	2,203
Other assets	361	—	—	—
Total assets	**75,062,746**	**26,856,175**	**1,216**	**1,250,746**
LIABILITIES				
Accounts payable and other accrued liabilities	24,211	421	—	7,509
Due to municipalities	—	—	—	56,768
Other liabilities	—	—	—	6,559
Total liabilities	**24,211**	**421**	**—**	**70,836**
NET POSITION				
Restricted for:				
Employees' pension	73,127,595	—	—	—
Employees' postemployment benefits	1,910,940	—	—	—
External investment trust fund participants	—	26,855,754	—	—
Individuals, organizations, and other governments	—	—	1,216	1,179,910
Total net position	**$75,038,535**	**$26,855,754**	**$1,216**	**$1,179,910**

The notes to the basic financial statements are an integral part of this statement.

EXHIBIT 20-9
STATE OF BAY
FIDUCIARY FUNDS
STATEMENT OF CHANGES IN FIDUCIARY NET POSITION
For the Year Ended June 30, 20Y4
(Amounts in thousands)

	Pension and Other Employee Benefits Trust Funds	Investment Trust Funds	Private-Purpose Trust Funds	Custodial Funds
ADDITIONS				
Contributions:				
Employer contributions	$1,675,827	$—	$—	$—
Nonemployer contributions	1,790,446	—	—	—
Employer contributions—other employers	13,352	—	—	—
Employee contributions	1,486,147	—	—	—
Early Retirement Incentive Program contributions	28,449	—	—	—
Teachers' contributions from State	162,976	—	—	—
Proceeds from sale of units	—	20,436,971	—	—
Sales tax collections for other governments	—	—	—	296,188
Child support collections	—	—	—	678,362
Other additions	183,006	1,290,068	1	1,910,726
Total contributions	5,340,203	21,727,039	1	2,885,276
Net investment earnings/(loss):				
Investment earnings/(loss)	17,427,125	5,207,583	—	24,537
Less: investment cost	(327,762)	(337,294)	—	(29,626)
Net investment earnings/(loss)	17,099,363	4,870,289	—	(5,089)
Total additions	22,439,566	26,597,328	1	2,880,187
DEDUCTIONS				
Administration	43,714	—	—	—
Retirement benefits and refunds	6,421,640	1,112,598	—	—
Payments to other Retirement System from State	162,976	—	—	—
Cost of units redeemed	—	20,996,377	—	—
Distributions to unit holders	—	7,834	—	—
Sales tax payments to other governments	—	—	—	296,188
Child support payments to individuals	—	—	—	691,905
Other deductions	72,310	—	—	1,914,472
Total deductions	6,700,640	22,116,809	—	2,902,565
Change in fiduciary net position	15,738,926	4,480,519	1	(22,378)
Fiduciary Net position—beginning	59,299,609	22,375,235	1,215	1,202,288
Fiduciary Net position—ending	$75,038,535	$26,855,754	$1,216	$1,179,910

The notes to the basic financial statements are an integral part of this statement.

Comparative Financial Statements

Comparative financial statements are presented when a *complete set* of financial statements is included in an annual financial report, covering one (or more) preceding periods, along with the current period. This is different from including only prior-year *summary* information along with the current year. Summary information is including only a total column for the prior year's Statement of Net Position and a column for the prior year's net (expense) revenue and changes in net position in the Statement of Activities. Summarized information presentations are more common than presenting a complete set of financial statements for one or more preceding periods.

To have a comparative set of financial statements, the following is required to be presented for one (or more) preceding periods from the current period:
- Government-wide Statement of Net Position and Statement of Activities,
- Proprietary Fund Statements of Fund Net Position and Statements of Revenues, Expenses, and Changes in Fund Net Position, and
- The notes to the Basic Financial Statements for the preceding period(s) repeated to the *extent* they continue to be of significance.

If there are reclassifications, restatements or changes that occurred since the earliest financial statement presented, information should be furnished to explain the change. This is to enhance comparability [GASB Cod. Secs. 2200.201–.203].

The required information for a comparative set of financial statements does not include the prior MD&A, nor the other applicable RSI. GASB Cod. Sec. 2200.704-3 reminds practitioners that the current year's MD&A should already provide data that is inclusive of (in this case) three years' comparative data, for the current year, the preceding year, and the year preceding the prior year. The related analysis includes all three years. The RSI should already be in the form of trends, inclusive of prior years.

NOTES TO THE BASIC FINANCIAL STATEMENTS

The notes to the financial statements should focus on the primary government (which includes its blended component units) and support the information included in the government-wide financial statements and the fund financial statements [GASB Cod. Secs. 2300.102, 106, 2600.123, C50.146, D20.116].

OBSERVATION: Note disclosures of discretely presented or blended component units should only be those that are essential to fair presentation in the reporting government's basic financial statements. Deciding what is "essential" is based on the government's professional judgment and should be done on a component-unit-by-component-unit basis. A specific type of disclosure might be essential for one component unit but not for another depending on the individual component unit's relationship with the primary government. For example, if a primary government is obligated in some manner for the debt of a component unit, it is likely that debt-related disclosures should be made for that component unit.

PRACTICE POINT: *CCH's Governmental GAAP Practice and Disclosures Manual* contains the entirety of required disclosures contained in GASB statements as of the date of publication and examples. Included with the manual is a financial statement disclosures checklist from the perspective of the preparer and a suggested disclosure sequence.

The following is a *nonauthoritative* sequence of note disclosures [GASB Cod. Sec. 2300.901]:

I. Summary of Significant Accounting Policies (including departures from GAAP, if any).

> **PRACTICE POINT:** If budgetary comparison information is reported in a budgetary comparison statement as part of the basic financial statements, rather than as RSI, the following should be inserted after subparagraph I.E:
>
> F. Budgetary data.
> 1. Budget basis of accounting.
> 2. Excess of the expenditures over appropriations. [NCGAI 6, Appendix, as modified]

   A. Description of the government-wide financial statements and exclusion of fiduciary activities and similar component units.
   B. A brief description of the component units of the financial reporting entity and their relationships to the primary government. This should include a discussion of the criteria for including component units in the financial reporting entity and how the component units are reported. Also include information about how the separate financial statements for the individual component units may be obtained. In component unit separate reports, identification of the primary government in whose financial report the component unit is included and a description of its relationship to the primary government.
   C. Basis of presentation—Government-wide financial statements.
      1. Governmental and business-type activities, major component units.
      2. Policy for eliminating internal activity.
      3. Effect of component units with differing fiscal year-ends.
   D. Basis of presentation—fund financial statements.
      1. Major and nonmajor governmental and enterprise funds, internal service funds, and fiduciary funds by fund type.
      2. Descriptions of activities accounted for in the major funds, internal service fund type, and fiduciary fund types.
      3. Interfund eliminations in fund financial statements not apparent from headings.
   E. Basis of accounting.
      1. Accrual—government-wide financial statements.
      2. Modified accrual—governmental fund financial statements, including the length of time used to define *available* for purposes of revenue recognition.
      3. Accrual—proprietary and fiduciary fund statements.
   F. Assets, liabilities, and net position and fund balances described in the order of appearance in the statements of net assets/balance sheet.

1. Definition of cash and cash equivalents used in the proprietary fund statement of cash flows.
2. Disclosure of valuation bases.
3. Capitalization policy—estimated useful lives of capital assets.
4. Description of the modified approach for reporting infrastructure assets (if used).
5. Significant or unusual accounting treatment for material account balances or transactions.
6. Policy regarding whether to first apply restricted or unrestricted resources when an expense is incurred for purposes for which both restricted and unrestricted net assets are available.

G. Revenues, expenditures/expense.
1. Types of transactions included in program revenues in the government-wide statement of activities.
2. Policy for allocating indirect expense to functions in the government-wide statement of activities.
3. Unusual or significant accounting policy for material revenue, expenditures, and expenses.
4. Property tax revenue recognition.
5. Vacation, sick leave, and other compensated absences.
6. Policy for defining operating revenues and operating expenses in proprietary fund statements of revenues, expenses, and changes in fund net position.

II. **Stewardship, Compliance, and Accountability.**
A. Significant violations of finance-related legal and contractual provisions and actions taken to address such violations.
B. Deficit fund balance or fund net assets of individual funds.

III. **Detail Notes on All Activities and Funds.**

PRACTICE POINT: If aggregated information in the summary reconciliations to government-wide statements obscures the nature of individual elements of a particular reconciling item, a more detailed explanation should be inserted after the Summary of Significant Accounting Policies.

A. Assets.
1. Cash deposits and pooling of cash and investments.
2. Investments.
3. Reverse repurchase agreements.
4. Securities lending transactions.
5. Receivable balances.
6. Property taxes.
7. Due from other governments—grants receivable.
8. Required disclosures about capital assets.

B. Liabilities.
　　1. Payable balances.
　　2. Pension plan obligations and postemployment benefits other than pension benefits.
　　3. Other employee benefits.
　　4. Construction and other significant commitments.
　　5. Claims and judgments.
　　6. Lease obligations.
　　7. Short-term debt and liquidity.
　　8. Long-term debt.
　　　　a. Description of individual bond issues and leases outstanding.
　　　　b. Required disclosures about long-term liabilities.
　　　　c. Summary of debt service requirements to maturity.
　　　　d. Terms of interest rate changes for variable-rate debt.
　　　　e. Disclosure of legal debt margin.
　　　　f. Bonds authorized but unissued.
　　　　g. Synopsis of revenue bond covenants.
　　　　h. Special assessment debt and related activities.
　　　　i. Debt refundings and extinguishments.
　　　　j. Demand bonds.
　　　　k. Bond, tax, and revenue anticipation notes.
　　9. Landfill closure and postclosure care.
C. Interfund receivables and payables and interfund eliminations.
D. Revenues and expenditures/expenses.
　　1. On-behalf payments for fringe benefits and salaries.
　　2. Significant transactions that are either unusual or infrequent, but not within the control of management.
E. Donor-restricted endowment disclosures.
F. Interfund transfers.
G. Encumbrances outstanding.

IV. Segment Information—Enterprise Funds.

V. Individual Major Component Unit Disclosures (if not reported on the face of the government-wide statements or in combining statements).

VI. The Nature of the Primary Government's Accountability for Related Organizations.

VII. Joint Ventures and Jointly Governed Organizations.

VIII. Related Party Transactions.

IX. Summary Disclosure of Significant Contingencies.

A. Litigation.

B. Federally assisted programs—compliance audits.

X. Significant Effects of Subsequent Events.

PRACTICE POINT: The item on pensions references the alignment of the bases of accounting between the government and the plan(s). The bases of accounting may not be in alignment when the government (or the plans) use(s) a special-purpose framework. If a government uses a special-purpose framework, a reconciliation between the framework and the plan's information would be inserted in the subsection. An example disclosure in the Summary of Significant Accounting Policies is as follows:

For purposes of measuring the net pension and OPEB liabilities, deferred outflows of resources and deferred inflows of resources related to pensions and OPEB, and pension and OPEB expense, information about the fiduciary net position of the State Employees' Pension and OPEB Plan (SEPOP) and additions to/deductions from the SEPOP's fiduciary net positions have been determined on the same basis as they are reported by the SEPOP. For this purpose, benefit payments (including refunds of employee contributions) are recognized when due and payable in accordance with the benefit terms. Investments are reported at fair value.

GASB Cod. Sec. 2300.703-4 discusses the use of restricted resources disclosure. Governments are required to state their policy for *when* they use restricted resources. That is, are restricted resources used only after unrestricted resources have been spent for a purpose or are restricted resources assumed to be spent first?

This sort of disclosure should be in a policy and, if significant, discussed in the summary of significant accounting policies.

Reporting Component Units

The reporting of component units in a primary government's basic external financial statements is discussed in Chapter 4.

Required Supplementary Information Other Than MD&A

Required supplementary information (RSI) is not a part of the basic financial statements, but the GASB considers RSI to be an important part of a governmental entity's financial report. All RSI (except for the MD&A) must be presented immediately after the notes to the basic financial statements [GASB Cod. Sec. 2200.205].

Current GAAP requires the following RSI for general-purpose governments, as applicable:

- MD&A (see earlier discussion in this chapter),
- Budgetary comparison schedules (see the following discussion),
- Reporting infrastructure assets under the modified approach (see Chapter 10), and
- Employee-benefit-related information as detailed in Chapter 13 for defined benefit pensions and postemployment benefits other than pensions.

For special-purpose governments, RSI is also required, including the MD&A with specific guidance for:

- Defined benefit pensions and postemployment benefits other than pensions (see Chapter 22), and
- Public entity risk pools revenue and claims development information (see Chapter 23).

Budgetary Comparison Schedules

GAAP requires that the budgetary comparison schedules for the General Fund and each major special revenue fund that has a legally adopted annual budget be presented as RSI or as a basic financial statement. The schedule should include columns for the following [GASB Cod. Sec. 2200.206]:

- The original budget,
- The final appropriated budget, and
- Actual results (presented on the government's budgetary basis).

PRACTICE ALERT: The GASB's *Financial Reporting Model Improvements* Exposure Draft is proposing to eliminate the reporting of budgetary information as basic financial statements and only report as RSI. Expanded reporting is proposed including variances between final budget and actual amounts and original budget and final budget amounts as a part of the budgetary comparison schedule.

GASB Cod. Sec. 2200.763-12 discusses the issue of governments that budget on a biennial basis. There is no exemption from reporting RSI. The phrase *legally adopted* also applies to the General Fund as well as to major special revenue funds. As explained in GASB Cod. Sec. 2200.763-15, if a special-purpose government maintains a General Fund (or its equivalent), but it is not legally required to adopt or does not legally adopt a budget, the budgetary comparison schedule would not be presented in the basic financial statements or RSI. Nonmajor special revenue funds, capital projects and debt service funds are *not required* to be presented but may be presented as *supplementary information* to comply with laws or regulations or to increase transparency. Such schedules are required when an ACFR is produced [GASB Cod. Sec. 2400.105].

The following budgetary descriptions are as follows [GASB Cod. Sec. 2200.206]:

- *Original budget*—The first complete appropriated budget. The original budget may be adjusted by reserves, transfers, allocations, supplemental appropriations, and other legally authorized legislative and executive changes before the beginning of the fiscal year. The original budget should also include actual appropriation amounts automatically carried over from prior years by law.
- *Final budget*—The original budget adjusted by all reserves, transfers, allocations, supplemental appropriations, and other legally authorized legislative and executive changes applicable to the fiscal year, whenever signed into law or otherwise legally authorized.
- *Appropriated budget*—The expenditure authority created by the appropriation bills or ordinances which are signed into law and related estimated revenues.

The GASB encourages (but does not require) governmental entities to present an additional column that reflects the differences between the final budget and the actual amounts. An additional column may present the differences between the original budget and the final budget. (See previous **PRACTICE ALERT**.)

The comparative budgetary information described above can be presented as a basic financial statement rather than as RSI (schedule presentation). When the information is presented as a basic financial statement, the information should be reported with fund financial statements after the statement of changes in revenues, expenditures, and changes in fund balances. All the budgetary information must be presented in one place.

A governmental entity may not present budgetary comparison information for its General Fund as a basic financial statement and present similar information related to its major special revenue funds as RSI. In some instances, a governmental entity might not be required to legally adopt an annual budget for its General Fund or a special revenue fund that is a major fund and, therefore, there is no requirement to present the budgetary comparison information. If that is the case, GAAP requires that the fact that budgetary comparison information is not presented for a fund be included in the notes to RSI.

The comparative budgetary information may be presented "using the same format, terminology, and classifications as the budget document, or using the format, terminology, and classifications in a Statement of Revenues, Expenditures, and Changes in Fund Balances." In either case, there must be a reconciliation (presented in a separate schedule or in notes to RSI) between the budgetary information and GAAP information. Any excess of expenditures over appropriations in an individual fund must be disclosed in a note to the RSI. If the governmental entity presents the comparative budgetary information as a basic financial statement, the note related to the excess of expenditures over appropriations must be reported as a note to the financial statements rather than as a note to RSI [GASB Cod. Sec. 2200.207].

Some other factors need to be weighed in the disclosure of original and final budgets:

- Some governmental entities initially use an interim budget (e.g., three months) that provides temporary spending authority. The original budget (as described above) must cover the entire fiscal period.

- GASB Cod. Sec. 2200.206(a) specifically states that "the original budget includes actual appropriation amounts automatically carried over from prior years by law." If prior-year encumbrances are rolled forward by law, the current (original) budget includes those items. The amount of the encumbrances will be known or a reasonable estimate of them can be made in time to prepare the financial information.

- GASB Cod. Sec. 2200.206(b) specifically states that amendments (such as transfers of appropriations between line items) must be included in the final budget, regardless of when they are "signed into law or otherwise legally authorized."

In some instances, a governmental entity is, for budgetary purposes, required to account for an activity in a fund type by law, but based on the definitions contained in GAAP must report that activity in another fund type. The reporting and disclosure requirements established by GAAP apply to the fund type that is used to report the activity and not to the fund type required for internal budgetary purposes.

Disclosure of Budgetary Policies. Most governments include a description of general budgetary policies in the summary of significant accounting policies. To comply with this recommendation, some governmental entities disclose their budgetary calendar and the legal level of budgetary control. Where financial statements prepared in conformity with GAAP do *not* demonstrate finance-related legal and contractual compliance, additional schedules, and explanations in the ACFR may be necessary to report legal compliance responsibilities and accountabilities. In many cases, a separate budgetary (or legal) basis report is produced by the government which contains a separate independent auditor's report (if audited) [GASB Cod. Sec. 2400.104].

Excess of Expenditures over Appropriations. GAAP requires that budgetary comparison schedules be presented only for the General Fund and each major special revenue fund that has a legally adopted annual budget. One of the requirements states that any excess of expenditures over appropriations in an individual fund must be disclosed in the notes to RSI. However, GASB Cod. Sec. 2300.106(h) requires disclosure in the notes to the financial statements of significant violations of finance-related legal and contractual provisions. Therefore, the disclosure of an excess of expenditures over appropriations is required for all funds, including all nonmajor governmental funds if the excess constitutes a significant violation of finance-related legal and contractual provisions. Disclosure is also required of actions taken to address those violations.

Reconciling Budget and GAAP Information

Budgetary comparison schedules should be accompanied by information that reconciles GAAP information and budgetary information. These differences may arise because of:

- Entity differences,
- Perspective differences,
- Basis differences,
- Timing differences, or
- Other differences [GASB Cod. Secs. 2200.207, 2400.109].

Entity Differences. The reporting entity may include component units whose activities are not a part of the appropriated budget. For example, a blended component unit may be subject to a legal non-appropriated budget and, thus, be excluded from the appropriated budget. But based on the criteria discussed in Chapter 4, the component unit may be a part of the overall reporting entity.

Perspective Differences. The structure of the budget itself determines its perspective. The financial information contained in the budget may be constructed to reflect various points of view including the governmental unit's organizational structure, fund structure, or program structure. For example, budgetary information may be prepared on a program basis whereby all expenditures associated with an objective may be grouped irrespective of which organizational unit or fund makes the expenditure.

The fund structure used by a government may also establish accounting element differences based on law or regulation. Assets, liabilities, fund balances, revenues, and expenditures may have different recognition in law in comparison to GAAP. Even the organizational structure may show differences [GASB Cod. Secs. 2400.113–.116].

OBSERVATION: When there is a difference between the perspective for budgeting purposes and for financial reporting purposes, it is often difficult to reconcile the two sets of financial information. For example, if the budgetary system uses a program basis and the financial reporting system uses the fund basis, it is unlikely that a meaningful reconciliation can be prepared. In this case, the reconciliation between the GAAP-basis financial statements and the budgeted financial statements would be limited to entity, basis, and timing differences.

In most instances, perspective differences are minor and can easily be isolated to prepare the necessary reconciliation between the budgetary and GAAP information. However, some governmental entities have budgetary structures that prevent them from associating the estimated revenues and appropriations from their legally adopted budget to the major revenue sources and functional expenditures that they report in their General Fund and major special revenue funds and, therefore, are not able to prepare budgetary comparison schedules (or statements) required by GAAP. For example, assume that a governmental entity's budgetary focus (not related to the data elsewhere in this chapter) is referred to as the "Comprehensive Statutory Budget" and its budget is as follows:

	Budgeted per Statutory (In thousands of dollars) Ordinance
REVENUES:	
Taxes	$ 121,434
Licenses and permits	2,695
Intergovernmental revenues	8,343
Charges for services	22,387
Fines and forfeits	127
Investment earnings	640
Rental income	795
Miscellaneous	19,303
Total Revenues	175,724
EXPENDITURES:	
General government	54,955
Public safety	89,791
Highways and Streets	4,145
Culture and leisure	1,166
Interdepartmental	27,088
Non-departmental health	5,868
Intergovernmental	2,606
Total Expenditures	185,619
Estimated Surplus (Deficit)	$ (9,895)

In this case, the government only passes a budget for the General Fund, like many other governments. A legally adopted budget schedule should be presented for any fund where a budget is passed. Within each category may be many other categories. For example, taxes may have separate entries for property, automobile excise, interest and penalties, gasoline, and other categories. Charges for services may have budgeted revenues from every type of charge that the government assesses. Every category of expenditures may be disaggregated in a way the government operates.

For example, general government may have each department within general government and then further delineated by personnel services, supplies, other services and charges and even more detail, depending upon how the government manages its operations. There is no specific requirement in GAAP for specific categories of revenues and expenditures in the schedule, other than compliance with the definitions of *original budget*, *final budget*, and actual amounts as discussed previously. However, GASB Cod. Sec. 2200.207 allows a government to present the budgetary comparison schedule using the same format, terminology, and classifications as the budget document in a comparable manner to the

Statement of Revenues, Expenditures, and Changes in Fund Balances for the General Fund and each major special revenue fund. In practice, governments include a schedule that is in enough detail necessary for the users of the schedule.

If a budgetary comparison schedule is prepared that compares the above Comprehensive Statutory Budget to a Statement of Revenues, Expenditures, and Changes in Fund Balances, reconciling items are needed to explain the differences between budgetary inflows and outflows on an actual basis and those amounts reported in the General Fund on a GAAP basis.

A governmental entity that has perspective differences of the nature described above may prepare a budgetary comparison schedule as RSI based on the fund organization, or program structure that the entity uses as a basis for the legally adopted budget. The foundation for this exception is that the focus of the comparison schedule will be based on activities that are reported in the entity's General Fund or in a special revenue fund. That is, when an activity (or collection of activities) is not presented as a part of the General Fund or a special revenue fund, the budgetary unit that includes various activities cannot be the focus for presenting budgetary comparison schedules.

PRACTICE POINT: The exception perspective that is allowed for comparative budgetary information can only be in the form of budgetary comparison schedules presented as RSI and not as financial statements.

Under the alternative comparison schedule focus approach, most of the items on the reconciliation would be similar to other reconciliations, but the following two items (based on the example presented above) would be used to remove the budgetary amounts for the various other funds (it is assumed in this example that the special revenue fund is not a major fund and, therefore, does not require a separate budgetary comparison schedule) from the actual amounts reported in the budgetary comparison schedule.

Basis Differences. The budgeting basis may differ from the accounting basis. For example, the governmental unit may be required by law to use the cash basis for budgeting purposes but may be required by financial reporting purposes to use the modified accrual basis [GASB Cod. Secs. 2400.110–.111].

Timing Differences. There may be differences between the budgetary amounts and the GAAP basis amounts due to the different treatment of items such as continuing appropriations and biennial budgeting. For example, a governmental unit may treat encumbrances that are outstanding at the end of the year as expenditures of the current period for budgetary purposes, but, for reporting purposes, they cannot be classified as expenditures of the current period [GASB Cod. Sec. 2400.112].

Other Differences. Any other differences not classified in the previous four categories also should be included in the reconciliation between the entity's budgetary practices and GAAP.

Additional Reporting. The prior discussion has been concerned exclusively with budgetary reporting on a comparative basis with actual results for funds that adopt an annual appropriated budget. Governmental units may be subject to control through the implementation of other types of budgets, including a *nonappropriated* budget, which is a financial plan for an organization, program, activity, or function approved in a manner authorized by constitution, charter, statute, or ordinance but not subject to appropriation and therefore outside the boundaries of the definition of "appropriated budget" [GASB Cod. Sec. 2400.108].

GAAP takes the position that "more comprehensive budget presentations are generally to be preferred over the minimum standards." Thus, the existence of the minimum presentation requirements should not inhibit a reporting entity from presenting additional budgetary information. Even if additional budgetary disclosures are not made, there should be a disclosure in notes to the financial statements describing budgetary controls, including appropriated budgets and other budget or financial control plans used by the reporting entity [GASB Cod. Sec. 2400.120].

Exhibit 20-10 illustrates a budget-to-actual comparison schedule.

EXHIBIT 20-10
STATE OF BAY
REQUIRED SUPPLEMENTARY INFORMATION
BUDGETARY COMPARISON SCHEDULE
For the Year Ended June 30, 20Y4
(Amounts in thousands)

	Original Budget	Final Budget	Actual	Variance
REVENUES AND OTHER FINANCING SOURCES				
Revenues:				
Taxes	$24,716,800	$24,716,800	$30,302,388	$5,585,588
Assessments	430,650	430,650	399,848	(30,802)
Federal grants and reimbursements	13,868,076	13,868,076	13,440,226	(427,850)
Tobacco settlement revenue	261,482	261,482	245,636	(15,846)
Departmental	3,034,358	3,034,358	3,534,235	499,877
Miscellaneous	467,178	467,178	292,625	(174,553)
Total revenues	42,778,544	42,778,544	48,214,958	5,436,414
Other financing sources:				
Fringe benefit cost recovery	—	—	453,299	453,299
Lottery reimbursement	—	—	105,986	105,986
Lottery distributions	—	—	1,090,040	1,090,040
Operating transfers in	1,871,154	1,871,154	203,049	(1,668,105)
Rainy Day Fund transfer	—	17,106	1,115,597	1,098,491
Other transfers	—	—	1,460,324	1,460,324
Total other financing sources	1,871,154	1,888,260	4,428,295	2,540,035
Total revenues and other financing sources	44,649,698	44,666,804	52,643,253	7,976,449
EXPENDITURES AND OTHER FINANCING USES				
Expenditures:				
Legislature	120,148	120,011	72,682	47,329
Judiciary	1,077,142	1,074,157	1,016,437	57,720
Inspector General	6,059	6,059	5,747	312
Governor and Lieutenant Governor	10,863	10,864	9,385	1,479
Secretary of State	60,905	61,404	58,444	2,960
Treasurer	2,324,395	281,209	220,935	60,274
Auditor	21,243	21,243	19,825	1,418
Attorney General	57,321	57,414	54,951	2,463
Ethics Commission	2,584	2,584	2,489	95
District Attorney	148,905	148,905	145,969	2,936
Office of Campaign & Political Finance	1,840	1,840	1,660	180
Sheriff's	695,002	694,877	686,626	8,251
Disabled Persons Protection Commission	7,897	7,897	5,464	2,433
Commission on the Status of Women	206	206	206	1
Gaming Commission	721	—	—	—
Board of Library Commissioners	34,018	34,018	33,821	197
Comptroller	66,551	66,551	19,689	46,862
Administration and Finance	10,186,385	2,832,745	2,337,693	495,052
Energy and Environmental Affairs	315,535	316,906	289,802	27,104
Health and Human Services	25,755,295	7,406,305	6,875,935	530,370
Technology Services and Security	195,918	195,918	146,520	49,398
Office of the Child Advocate	2,999	2,999	1,723	1,276
Executive Office of Education	3,021,817	3,151,219	2,833,844	317,375
Health Information and Analysis	33,588	23,588	23,330	258
Commission Against Discrimination	8,349	8,349	6,824	1,525
Public Safety and Homeland Security	1,530,399	1,552,568	1,463,381	89,187

20,110 *Financial Reporting by General-Purpose Governments*

	Original Budget	Final Budget	Actual	Variance
Peace Officer Standards and Training	250	250	23	227
Housing and Economic Development	899,102	898,489	807,492	90,997
Labor and Workforce Development	95,346	79,662	59,672	19,990
Municipal aid	—	6,355,436	6,352,585	2,851
Medicaid	—	18,280,385	18,122,376	158,009
Postemployment benefits Debt service:	—	3,739,620	3,739,584	36
Principal retirement	35,605	660,586	628,828	31,758
Interest and fiscal charges	—	597,633	569,410	28,223
Total expenditures	46,716,388	48,691,897	46,613,352	2,078,546
Other financing uses:				
Fringe benefit cost assessment	—	—	8,730	(8,730)
Operating transfers out	—	311,738	318,688	(6,950)
Medical assistance transfer	—	537,187	505,250	31,937
Rainy Day Fund transfer	—	1,098,140	1,098,139	1
Other transfers	—	—	1,151,006	(1,151,006)
Other fund deficit support	—	—	23,699	(23,699)
Total other financing uses	—	1,947,065	3,105,512	(1,158,447)
Total expenditures and other financing uses	46,716,388	50,638,962	49,718,864	920,099
Excess/(deficiency) of revenues and other financing sources over expenditures and other financing uses	$(2,066,690)	$(5,972,158)	2,924,389	$8,896,547
Fund balances/(deficits) at beginning of year			4,232,877	
Fund balances/(deficits) at end of year			$7,157,266	

See independent auditors' report and notes to the required supplementary information.

Exhibit 20-11 illustrates a budget-to-GAAP reconciliation.

EXHIBIT 20-11
BUDGET-TO-GAAP RECONCILIATION
For the Year Ended June 30, 20Y4
(Amounts in thousands)

REVENUES

Actual amounts (budgetary basis) "revenues" from the budgetary comparison schedules	$48,214,958
Adjustments for amounts budgeted for on a cash basis, rather than on the modified accrual basis:	
Tax receivable, net	473,798
Tax refunds and abatements payable, net	(132,079)
Federal reimbursements and other receivables	704,770
Reclassifications:	
Higher education revenue is reclassified for GAAP reporting	(94,910)
Inflows from component units and other miscellaneous financing sources	87,675
Certain revenue is reclassified to fiduciary funds for GAAP reporting	(15,585)
Total revenues as reported on the Statement of Revenues, Expenditures and Changes in Fund Balances—Governmental Funds	**$49,238,627**

OTHER FINANCING SOURCES

Actual amounts (budgetary basis) "other financing sources" from the budgetary comparison schedule	$4,428,295
Adjustments and Reclassifications:	
Higher education revenue is reclassified for GAAP reporting	(3)
Proceeds of capital lease on GAAP basis	2,126
Consolidation of transfers between funds	(2,262,726)
Inflows from component units and other miscellaneous financing sources	(99,621)
Total other financing sources as reported on the Statement of Revenues, Expenditures and Changes in Fund Balances—Governmental Funds	**$2,068,071**

EXPENDITURES

Actual amounts (budgetary basis) "expenditures" from the budgetary comparison schedule	$46,613,352
Adjustments for amounts budgeted for on a cash basis, rather than on the modified accrual basis:	
Medicaid payments	(19,967)
Compensated absences and other accrued liabilities	151,040
Reclassifications:	
Capital lease additions are additions to expenditures for GAAP purposes on a fund perspective	2,126

Budgetary debt service is reclassified to transfers out to a debt service fund for GAAP purposes as the Commonwealth does not have a statutory debt service fund	(1,198,237)
Higher education expenditures are reclassified for GAAP reporting	(1,638,294)
Expenditures to component units reported on a GAAP basis	18,877
Certain expenditures are reclassified to fiduciary funds for GAAP reporting	(15,586)
Total expenditures as reported on the Statement of Revenues, Expenditures and Changes in Fund Balances—Governmental Funds	**$43,913,311**

OTHER FINANCING USES

Actual amounts (budgetary basis) "other financing uses" from the budgetary comparison schedule	$3,105,512
Adjustments and Reclassifications:	
Consolidation of transfers between funds	(2,262,726)
Budgetary higher education amounts are reclassified to transfers under the modified accrual basis	1,543,382
Budgetary debt service is reclassified to transfers out to a debt service fund for GAAP purposes as the Commonwealth does not have a statutory debt service fund	1,198,237
Transfers to component units reported on a GAAP basis	(3,242)
Total other financing uses as reported on the Statement of Revenues, Expenditures and Changes in Fund Balances—Governmental Funds	**$3,581,163**

See independent auditors' report and notes to the required supplementary information.

Notes to the RSI—Budgetary Reporting

The State passes a combined budget for all budgeted operations. State finance law requires that a balanced budget be approved by the Governor and the Legislature. The Governor presents an annual budget to the Legislature, which includes estimates of revenues and other financing sources, and recommended expenditures and other financing uses.

The Legislature, which has full authority to amend the budget, adopts an expenditure budget by appropriating monies at the individual appropriation account level in an annual appropriations act. Generally, expenditures may not exceed the level of spending authorized for an appropriation account.

Before signing the appropriations act, the Governor may veto or reduce any specific item, subject to legislative override. Further changes to the budget established in the annual appropriations act may be made via supplemental appropriation acts or other legislative acts. These must also be signed by the Governor and are subject to the line-item veto.

In addition, General Laws authorize the Secretary of Administration and Finance, with the approval of the Governor, upon determination that available revenues will be insufficient to meet authorized expenditures, to withhold allotments of appropriated funds which effectively reduce the account's expenditure budget. The majority of the State's appropriations are noncontinuing accounts which lapse at the end of each fiscal year. Others are continuing accounts for which the Legislature has authorized that an unspent balance from the prior year be carried forward and made available for spending in the current fiscal year. In addition, the Legislature may direct certain revenues be retained and made available for spending within an appropriation. Fringe benefits, pension costs, and certain other costs which are mandated by state finance law are not itemized in the appropriation process and are not separately budgeted.

Because revenue budgets are not updated subsequent to the original appropriation act, the comparison of the initial revenue budget to the subsequent, and often modified, expenditure budget can be misleading. Also, these financial statements portray fund accounting with gross inflows and outflows, thus creating a difference to separately published budget documents, which eliminate some interfund activity. In conducting the budget process, the Commonwealth excludes those interfund transactions that by their nature have no impact on the combined fund balance of the budgeted funds.

The FY04 Budget Act (Chapter Y6, Section AB7 of the Acts of 19Y3), amended section ABC, directing the Governor to notify the Legislature in writing as to the reasons for and the effect of any reductions in spending. Alternatively, the Governor may propose specific additional revenues to fund the deficiency. The Governor may also propose to transfer funds from the Rainy-Day Fund to cure the deficiency. This proposal must be delivered to the Legislature 15 days before any reductions take effect.

> **PRACTICE POINT:** GASB requires RSI for the following additional information, mostly 10 years in length, in addition to the budget to actual schedule above and the MD&A, as applicable:
> - Public entity risk pools—certain revenue and claims development information,
> - Schedules of assessed condition, estimated and actual maintenance and preservation costs for governments that use the modified approach for infrastructure assets (not required to be 10 years),
> - Various detailed schedules for defined benefit pension plans,
> - Various detailed employers' schedules for defined benefit pension plans,
> - Various employers' schedules for defined benefit pension plans not held in trust,
> - Various detailed schedules for defined benefit other postemployment benefit plans, and
> - Various detailed employers' schedules for defined benefit other postemployment benefit plans.
>
> For expediency, these are not portrayed in the *Governmental GAAP Guide*. Many are contained in CCH's *Governmental GAAP Practice and Disclosures Manual*.

PRACTICE ALERT: Errors and restatements do occur in RSI. GASB Statement No. 100 (*Accounting Changes and Error Corrections*), contains guidance on reporting accounting changes and error corrections not only in RSI, but also in supplementary information (SI). Such changes are not fully considered in current GAAP. GASB-100 requires consistency between what is presented in the basic financial statements and what is presented in applicable RSI and SI. The 10-year RSI schedules above do not require restatements for *accounting changes*. The MD&A will also not have to be changed for accounting changes. However, the inconsistency should be explained and the notes relating to the accounting change should be referenced.

In the case when an *error correction* impacts prior RSI, including the MD&A, *all impacted periods by the error will be required to be restated*, if practicable. An explanation of the nature of the error should be provided in RSI (or SI), in the notes to RSI. For SI, it is unclear from the provisions of GASB-100 where the explanation would be, other than perhaps as a footnote to the SI schedule.

This guidance would also apply to Statistical Section information discussed later in this chapter.

COMBINING FINANCIAL STATEMENTS IN ACFRs

Although it is not required in the minimum presentation to be in accordance with GAAP, an ACFR should include combining statements presented as supplementary information in the financial section for the following situations:

- Combining financial statements by fund type for the primary government when there is more than one nonmajor fund, and
- Combining financial statements for discretely presented component units when the reporting entity has more than one nonmajor component unit (fund financial statements for individual component units are required if the financial information is not available to readers in separately issued reports).

Each of the individual financial statements in the combining financial statements is in the same format and contains the same content as its respective fund type as previously discussed in this Chapter.

More Than One Nonmajor Fund. The focus of the fund statements included in the basic financial statements is on the major funds. As noted earlier, each major fund is presented in the fund statements in a separate column. Nonmajor funds are aggregated and presented in a single column. There is no requirement to present combining statements for nonmajor funds in the basic external financial statements, but the information may be presented as supplementary information to the financial statements. If the nonmajor funds are not presented as supplementary information they must be presented as a part of the ACFR in the combining financial statements by fund type for the primary government.

The combining financial statements could have a section for all special revenue funds, capital projects funds, and so on. For instance, a governmental unit may have five nonmajor special revenue funds and three nonmajor capital projects funds. The combining financial statements would include a separate column for each of the eight nonmajor funds and a total column that can be traced into the fund financial statements that present major funds and aggregated nonmajor funds. In addition, the overall format and terminology used in the fund financial statements and the combining financial statements should be able to provide a basis for easy cross-reference between the two sets of information.

The concept of a major fund does not apply to an internal service fund. For this reason, all internal service funds are presented in the combining financial statements as a part of the ACFR rather than as a part of the basic external financial statements in a manner like the presentation described in the previous paragraph.

OBSERVATION: If a governmental entity has only a single internal service fund, it is presented in the fund financial statements as a separate column and there would be no need to present its financial information in a combining financial statement.

Individual Fund Financial Statements. The ACFR should include individual fund statements for the following situations:

- When the primary government has a single nonmajor fund of a given fund type; and
- When it is necessary to present comparative budgetary information about the previous year and the current year if it is not presented in RSI.

Content of Combining Statements and Individual Fund Statements. As discussed, GAAP requires that a primary government present its major governmental and major enterprise and combined internal service funds on the face of the fund financial statements. In addition, the following combining, and individual fund statements must be included in the financial section of an ACFR. Combining balance sheets for governmental funds are presented just like major governmental funds, with fund balances segregating nonspendable, restricted, committed, assigned, and unassigned balances. Required statements are as follows unless the entity presents only the basic financial statements [GASB Cod. Sec. 2200.208]:

- Nonmajor governmental funds, usually grouped by fund type and potentially with a summary grouping that reconciles to the nonmajor funds column in the major fund statements:
    — Combining Balance Sheets.
    — Combining Statements of Revenues, Expenditures, and Changes in Fund Balances.
    — Individual fund Balance Sheets and Statements of Revenues, Expenditures, and Changes in Fund Balances and schedules necessary to demonstrate compliance with finance-related legal and contractual provision of governmental funds.

- Internal service funds and nonmajor enterprise funds:
  — Combining Statements of Fund Net Position.
  — Combining Statements of Revenues, Expenses, and Changes in Fund Net Position.
  — Combining Statements of Cash Flows.
  — Individual Statements of Revenues, Expenses, and Changes in Fund Net Position and individual Statements of Cash Flows and schedules necessary to demonstrate compliance with finance-related legal and contractual provisions.
- Fiduciary Funds:
  — A combining Statement of Fiduciary Net Position.
  — A combining Statement of Changes in Fiduciary Net Position.

PRACTICE POINT: Many state and local laws, regulations and ordinances require presentation of all funds. If an AFR is prepared, the additional funds would be supplementary information.

PRACTICE POINT: Combining statements may be prepared for multiple pension and postemployment benefit other than pension trust funds to provide additional transparency.

More Than One Nonmajor Discretely Presented Component Unit. The financial statements of the reporting entity should allow users to distinguish between the primary government and its component units by communicating information about the component units and their relationships with the primary government rather than creating the perception that the primary government and all its component units are one legal entity [GASB Cod. Secs. 2100.142, 2600.105].

In addition, GASB Cod. Sec. 2600.108 requires that information related to each major component unit be presented in the reporting entity's basic financial statements. To satisfy this standard, any one of the following approaches can be used:

- Present each major component unit in a separate column in the government-wide financial statements,
- Present combining statements (with a separate column for each major unit and a single column for the aggregated nonmajor units), or
- Present condensed financial statements in a note to the financial statements (with a separate column for each major unit and a single column for the aggregated nonmajor units).

OBSERVATION: The requirement for major component unit information does not apply to component units that are fiduciary in nature.

> **PRACTICE ALERT:** The GASB's *Financial Reporting Model Improvements* Exposure Draft proposes to eliminate the option to present condensed financial statements in the notes. The GASB has proposed presentation of each major component unit in a separate column in the reporting entity's statements of net position and activities, if readable. If presenting each major component unit in a separate column in the reporting entity's Statements of Net Position and Statements of Activities reduces the readability of the statements, combining statements of major component units should be included in the reporting entity's basic financial statements after the fund financial statements.

Each of these three presentation methods creates information that is a part of the basic external financial statements, however, if there is more than one nonmajor component unit, the information concerning these nonmajor units must be presented in combining financial statements.

The data presented in the combining schedules should be the entity totals derived from the component units' Statements of Net Position and Statements of Activities. If the component units are engaged only in business-type activities, the disclosure is taken from the Statements of Revenues and Expenses and Changes in Fund Net Position instead of the Statements of Activities. Presentation of individual funds of component units is not required unless the component unit does not produce separately available financial statements.

The combining statements of the component units follow the same format and methodology as discussed for nonmajor funds [GASB Cod. Sec. 2200.209].

Under current GAAP, if the government presents condensed component unit information in the notes, the minimum details to be presented are:

- *Condensed* Statement of Net Position:
  - Total assets—distinguishing between current assets, capital assets, and other assets. Amounts receivable from other funds or component units should be reported separately.
  - Total deferred outflows of resources.
  - Total liabilities—distinguishing between current liabilities and long-term liabilities. Amounts payable to other funds or component units should be reported separately.
  - Total deferred inflows of resources.
  - Total net position—distinguishing among net investment in capital assets, restricted (separately reporting expendable and nonexpendable components), and unrestricted.
- *Condensed* Statement of Activities:
  - Expenses (by major functions and for depreciation expense, if separately reported).
  - Program revenues (by type).
  - Net program (expense) revenue.
  - Tax revenues.

— Other nontax general revenues.
— Contributions to endowments and permanent fund principal.
— Special and extraordinary items.
— Change in net position.
— Beginning net position.
— Ending net position.

In addition to the financial statement information, the notes to the financial statements should disclose, for each major component unit, the nature and value of significant transactions with the primary government and other component units [GASB Cod. Secs. 2200.213–.217].

Other Supplementary Schedules

The ACFR should include other schedules for the following situations:

- When it is necessary to demonstrate compliance with finance-related legal and contractual provisions,
- When it is useful to bring together information that is spread throughout the financial statements and present the information in more detail, and
- When it is useful to present more detail for a line item that is presented in a financial statement.

Under certain circumstances, these schedules may be used to present data that is on a legally or contractually prescribed basis that is different from GAAP and/or may include data that management wants to present that is not required by GAAP. A common schedule may be used to comply with bond covenants [GASB Cod. Sec. 2200.210].

Narrative descriptions that facilitate the understanding of information in combining financial statements, individual fund and component unit financial statements, and schedules may be included directly on divider pages, the financial statements, or schedules, or in an accompanying section appropriately labeled [GASB Cod. Sec. 2200.211].

PRACTICE POINT: The Government Finance Officers Association (GFOA) Certificate of Achievement for Excellence in Financial Reporting (COA) program includes additional supplementary schedules as a part of the program for diverse types of entities. For postemployment benefit plans as well as cash and investment pools, schedules of administrative expenses, investment expenses and payments to consultants for fees paid to other professionals other than investment providers are included. Postemployment benefit plans also include an investment section and an actuarial section. In addition, some governments that are required to have a single audit performed may include a section attached to their financial reports with a schedule of expenditures of federal awards, required reporting and other schedules. Finally, state, and local governments may have additional schedules presented that are required by law, regulation, or bond indenture. Unless a GASB statement requires these schedules, they are not RSI, they are supplementary information only.

STATISTICAL SECTION

Information included in the statistical tables section is *not* a part of the governmental unit's basic financial statements even though the material is a part of the ACFR. Statistical tables may include non-accounting information and often cover 10 years or more information. In general, the purpose of presenting statistical tables is to give the user a historical perspective that will enhance the analysis of the governmental unit's financial condition [GASB Cod. Sec. 2200.212].

GASB Cod. Sec. 2800 contains the reporting requirements for the statistical section of governments' annual reports *when an ACFR is presented.*

The objectives of reporting statistical section information are as follows:

> To provide financial statement users with additional historical perspective, context, and detail to assist in using the information in the financial statements, notes to financial statements, and required supplementary information to understand and assess a government's economic condition [GASB Cod. Sec. 2800.104].

The statistical information is separated into five categories [GASB Cod. Sec. 2800.105]:

- *Financial trends information* is intended to assist users in understanding and assessing how a government's financial position has changed over time. Examples for general-purpose governments are:
  — Net position by component and changes in net position by component for the last 10 fiscal years, and
  — Fund balances for governmental funds and changes in fund balances for governmental funds for the last 10 fiscal years.

> **PRACTICE POINT:** Many of these schedules may change with the implementation of any GAAP standard that requires a beginning balance restatement or a change in accounting practice.

> **PRACTICE ALERT:** The GASB's *Financial Reporting Model Improvements* Exposure Draft contains an update for this section specifically for governments engaged only in business-type activities or in business-type activities as well as fiduciary activities. Revenues would be presented by major source for their business-type activities, distinguishing between operating, noncapital subsidy, and other nonoperating revenues and expenses. This proposal is the sole provision in the Exposure Draft that would be implemented prospectively, if approved as drafted.

- *Revenue capacity information* is intended to assist users in understanding and assessing the factors that affect a government's ability to generate its own revenues. Examples for general-purpose governments include, but are not limited to, the following:

- Assessed and actual values of taxable property for the last 10 fiscal years,
- Direct and overlapping property tax rates for the last 10 fiscal years,
- Principal property taxpayers for the current year and nine years ago, and
- Property tax levies and collections for the last 10 fiscal years.

- *Debt capacity information* is intended to assist users in understanding and assessing a government's debt burden and its ability to issue additional debt. Examples for general-purpose governments are:
  - Ratios of outstanding debt by type for the last 10 fiscal years,
  - Ratios of general bonded debt outstanding for the last 10 fiscal years,
  - Direct and overlapping governmental activities debt as of current year-end,
  - Legal debt margin for the last 10 fiscal years, and
  - Pledged revenue coverage for the last 10 fiscal years.

- *Demographic and economic information* is intended to assist users in understanding the socioeconomic environment that a government operates within, and it provides information that facilitates comparisons between governments over time. Examples for general-purpose governments are:
  - Demographic and economic statistics for the last 10 calendar years, and
  - Principal employers for the current year and nine years ago.

- *Operating information* is intended to provide contextual information about a government's operations and resources for users to understand and assess its economic condition. Examples for general-purpose governments are:
  - Full-time equivalent employees by function or program for the last 10 fiscal years,
  - Operating indicators by function or program for the last 10 fiscal years, and
  - Capital asset statistics by function or program for the last 10 fiscal years.

Comprehensive illustrated examples of statistical schedules for both general-purpose governments and special-purpose governments. Many of the schedules are *optional*. These are further expanded in GASB Cod. Sec. 2800.901, including dozens of schedules for:

- General-purpose local governments,
- General-purpose county governments,
- General-purpose state governments,
- School districts,
- Governments engaged only in business-type activities, including universities, airports, and water and sewer systems,

- Retirement systems, and
- A library district.

Professional judgment should be used to determine whether statistical tables other than the ones listed should be presented in the ACFR.

The statistical tables should include information for blended component units by combining the primary governmental statistics and the component units' statistics. Professional judgment should be used to determine whether statistical data related to discretely presented component units should be presented.

> **PRACTICE POINT:** Some of these schedules are contained in CCH's *Governmental GAAP Practice and Disclosures Manual*.

BASIC FINANCIAL STATEMENTS REQUIRED FOR SPECIAL-PURPOSE GOVERNMENTS

The standards discussed throughout this chapter are written in the context of general-purpose governmental entities, such as state and local governments. However, these standards also apply, with some modification, to special-purpose governments that are "legally separate entities and may be component units or other stand-alone governments." GAAP provides the following definitions of these entities [GASB Cod. Secs. Ca5.101, Co5.101, Ho5.101, In3.101, Sp20.101, Ut5.101]:

> *Component units* are legally separate organizations for which elected officials of the primary government are financially accountable. In addition, a component unit can be another organization for which the nature and significance of its relationship with a primary government are such that exclusion would cause the reporting entity's financial statements to be misleading or incomplete.
>
> An *"other stand-alone government"* is a legally separate governmental organization that (a) does not have a separately elected governing body and (b) does not meet the definition of a component unit. Other stand-alone governments include some special-purpose governments, joint ventures, jointly governed organizations, and pools.

GAAP does not provide a definition of special-purpose governments However, GASB Cod. Sec. Sp20.701-1 notes that such governments "generally provide a limited (or sometimes a single) set of services or programs, for example, fire protection, library services, mosquito abatement, and drainage." It is important to distinguish between a general government and a special-purpose government because under certain circumstances, not all the reporting standards must be observed by special-purpose governments due to their operations. (See Chapters 21 through 24 for further discussion and examples of financial statements for certain special-purpose governments.)

PART V. STAND-ALONE FINANCIAL REPORTING BY SPECIAL-PURPOSE GOVERNMENTS

CHAPTER 21
PUBLIC COLLEGES AND UNIVERSITIES

Chapter References:

GASB Statement Nos. 14, 34, 35, 61, 80, 84, 90, 92, 97

GASB *Implementation Guide*

INTRODUCTION

GAAP is primarily written from the viewpoint of general-purpose governments. The preceding chapters of the *Governmental GAAP Guide* do focus on states, municipal governments and similar. However, many of the provisions can apply to public colleges and universities (PCUs).

As discussed in GASB Cod. Sec. Co5.101, many PCUs are legally separate entities. They can be component units of a primary government or a stand-alone government. Component units were described in Chapter 4, Other stand-alone governments are legally separate, but do not have a separately elected governing body and do not meet the definition of a component unit. Other stand-alone governments may include joint ventures and jointly governed organizations, in addition to some PCUs.

PCUs commonly are reported as business-type activities. Some have governmental activities due to their taxing authority, grant activities and other nonexchange transactions. Such activities would be reported in governmental funds and internal service funds. PCUs that are business-type activities would have enterprise and internal-service funds. Both models may use fiduciary funds [GASB Cod. Sec. Co5.102].

> **PRACTICE POINT:** Those who work in large, multi-campus PCUs understand that such institutions are complex entities. In addition to instruction, they provide housing, medical care, research, have public safety functions, provide transportation and recreation, may provide utilities, may have complex investments, have licensed media outlets, and perform operations on a similar scale to large cities or states.

BASIC REPORTING PROVISIONS

PCUs Engaged in Governmental Activities

For PCUs engaged in governmental activities, all the previous applicable guidance to governmental funds and governmental activities would apply. The presentation would include governmental fund financial statements and government-wide financial statements, along with required supplementary information (RSI) including the management's discussion and analysis, as applicable.

Relief from potentially complex financial reporting is available for PCUs that only engage in a single governmental program. The fund financial statements and the government-wide financial statements could be combined using a format that includes a column to reconcile individual line items of each element from the fund statements to the government-wide information. As an alternative, the Statement of Activities could be presented with expenses at the top of a page and revenues at the bottom in a single column. The difference is net revenues. Following net revenues would be contributions to permanent endowments and other non-recurring transactions, which would adjust beginning net position to ending net position. The required descriptions of the reconciling items would be on the face of the financial statements, in an accompanying schedule or in the notes to the basic financial statements. In practice, such a presentation would only occur in highly simplified, small PCUs that happen to have governmental activities. A preclusion to such a presentation would occur if the PCU budgets for more than one program [GASB Cod. Secs. Co5.103–.105].

PCUs Engaged in Only Business-Type Activities

The most common presentation for PCUs would be utilizing the same accounting and financial reporting for proprietary funds (see Chapter 7), The financial reporting for proprietary funds discussed in Chapter 20, also applies to these PCUs, including:

- Management's discussion and analysis (MD&A),
- Enterprise fund financial statements, including:
  — Statement of Net Position,
  — Statement of Revenues, Expenses, and Changes in Fund Net Position,
  — Statement of Cash Flows,
- Notes to the basic financial statements, and
- Required Supplementary Information (RSI) other than MD&A as applicable [GASB Cod. Sec. Co5.106].

PRACTICE POINT: See Chapter 8 on reporting of fiduciary funds which are prevalent in PCUs. Endowments are usually fiduciary activities. All applicable provisions as discussed in Chapter 8 would apply to foundations and other fiduciary activities at PCUs.

As a reminder, an enterprise fund must be used to account for an activity if *any one* of the following criteria is satisfied:

- The activity is financed with debt that is secured solely by a pledge of the net revenues from fees and charges of the activity.
- Laws or regulations require that the activity's costs of providing services, including capital costs (such as depreciation or capital debt service), be recovered with fees and charges rather than with taxes or similar revenues.

- The pricing policies of the activity establish fees and charges designed to recover its costs, including capital costs (such as depreciation, debt service or amortization of intangible assets) [GASB Cod. Sec. 1300.109].

The first condition refers to debt secured solely by fees and charges. If that debt is secured by a pledge of fees and charges from the activity and the full faith and credit of the PCU or the component unit, this arrangement does not satisfy the "sole source of debt security" criterion and the activity does not have to be accounted for (assuming the other two criteria are not satisfied) in an enterprise fund. This conclusion is not changed even if it is anticipated that the PCU or the component unit is not expected to make debt payments under the arrangement. On the other hand, debt that is secured partially by a portion of its own proceeds does satisfy the "sole source of debt security" criterion.

Although the criteria established above identify those conditions under which an activity must be accounted for in an enterprise fund, GAAP also states that an enterprise fund may be used to "report any activity for which a fee is charged to external users for goods or services." The GASB believes that many PCUs can report as an enterprise fund because they charge tuition fees and various other fees for their educational services.

PCUs That Are Component Units or PCUs That Have Component Units

PCUs are commonly component units of general-purpose governments, primarily states, counties, and other municipal governments. All the provisions of component unit reporting would apply as discussed in Chapter 4. This includes the "layering effect" of reporting from the bottom up. The separately issued financial statements of the PCU should disclose the PCU is a component unit of another government and the component units of the PCU should do the same. The notes would identify the relationship as well [GASB Cod. Sec. Co5.107]. An additional discussion of nongovernmental component units of PCUs is included later in this chapter.

OBSERVATION: GASB Cod. Sec. 2100.fn3 discusses how component units and other related entities to a government may be organized as not-for-profit or for-profit entities. Not-for-profit entities (e.g., foundations) are typically related to public healthcare and higher education institutions. For-profit component units may be limited liability corporations related to the public healthcare, higher education, or postemployment benefit fund entities. GASB Cod. Sec. 2100.143 requires governments to apply "the definition and display provisions of this section." To accomplish this, translation may have to occur between the basis of accounting of the component units and the primary government. GASB Cod. Secs. 2600.701-3, 704-12-14 discuss translation between the bases of accounting and presentation. However, there is no requirement to change the recognition, measurement, or disclosure standards applied in the separately issued financial statements of a nongovernmental component unit.

PCUs as an Other-Stand-Alone Government

A PCU may be its own primary government as it is a stand-alone entity. Such PCUs are required to apply all provisions of GAAP, including when they have their own component units. The component unit reporting within a PCU's annual financial report can be in a single fund, or several fund types, just like any other primary government. The component units can be blended or discreetly presented. If blended, the component unit's financial data is reported within the single column of the PCU and inclusive of condensed information in the notes as discussed in Chapter 20.

FINANCIAL REPORTING BY PCUs

Statement of Net Position

Assets and liabilities presented in the statement of net position of a PCU are reported as an enterprise fund

Exhibit 21-1 is an illustration of a Statement of Net Position.

EXHIBIT 21-1
STATEMENT OF NET POSITION
College Statement of Net Position as of June 30, 20XX

	College	Foundation
Assets		
Current Assets		
Cash and cash equivalents	$19,251,737	$244,559
Restricted cash and cash equivalents—current	3,073,652	—
Investments in marketable securities	7,771,848	7,369,720
Accounts receivable, net	1,584,213	—
Contributions receivable, net	—	72,377
Loans receivable—current portion	4,591	—
Other Current Assets	268,387	19,976
Total Current Assets	31,954,428	7,706,632
Noncurrent Assets		
Restricted cash and cash equivalents	11,009,502	—
Endowment investments	—	1,332,859
Investments in marketable securities	20,211,799	—
Contributions receivable, net	—	155,215
Loans receivable—net of current portion	2.303.011	—
Capital assets, net	88,197,783	—
Total Noncurrent Assets	121,722,095	1,488,074
Total Assets	$153,676,523	$9,194,706

Public Colleges and Universities **21,005**

	College	Foundation
Liabilities		
Current Liabilities		
Accounts payable and accrued liabilities	$2,499,980	$104,441
Accounts payable—construction	991,141	—
Accrued workers' compensation—current portion	114,499	—
Compensated absences—current portion	2,932,979	—
Faculty payroll accrual	2,502,575	—
Advances	2,760,910	—
Deposits	365,885	—
Other current liabilities	366,117	—
Long-term debt—current	1,589,046	—
Total Current Liabilities	**14,123,132**	**104,441**
Noncurrent Liabilities		
Long-term debt (Note XX)	40,380,931	—
Accrued workers' compensation—net of current portion	441,461	—
Compensated absences, net of current portion	1,636,695	—
Loans payable—federal financial assistance program	1,877,907	—
Total Noncurrent Liabilities	**44,336,994**	—
Total Liabilities	**58,460,126**	—
Deferred Inflows of Resources		
Public-Private Partnership	468,589	—
Total Deferred Inflows of Resources	**468,589**	—
Net Position		
Net Investment in Capital Assets	$52,034,054	—
Restricted for:		
Non-expendable—scholarships and academic purposes	1,970,057	—
Expendable non-scholarship amounts	1,332,859	—
Expendable scholarships	1,434,327	359,465
Academic purposes	—	2,448,404
Research	209,259	—
Loans	452,043	—
Debt service	82,880	—
Other	1,727,090	—
Unrestricted	36,838,098	4,951,537
Total Net Position	**$94,747,808**	**$9,092,265**

Statement of Revenues, Expenses, and Changes in Fund Net Position

The operating or change statement of an enterprise fund is the Statement of Revenues, Expenses, and Changes in Fund Net Position.

When a PCU has only business-type activities, the formatting of its Statement of Revenues, Expenses, and Changes in Fund Net Position must differentiate between operating and nonoperating transactions and events.

PRACTICE POINT: Federal grant funds relating to the Coronavirus Aid, Relief, and Economic Security (CARES) Act as well as similar federal awards such as those in the American Rescue Plan Act are received by PCUs. Funds such as those received through the Higher Education Emergency Relief Fund in the CARES Act are reported as nonoperating revenues as they are subsidies from the federal government. PCUs may have also received Provider Relief Funds if they operate healthcare entities. Provider Relief Funds are subject to eligibility requirements and are recognized as liabilities if received before eligibility. Upon eligibility being confirmed, the liability is reclassed to nonoperating revenue.

Exhibit 21-2 is an illustration of a Statement of Revenues, Expenses, and Changes in Fund Net Position for a PCU.

EXHIBIT 21-2
STATEMENT OF REVENUES, EXPENSES, AND CHANGES IN FUND NET POSITION

Castle Rock College Statement of Revenues, Expenses, and Change in Fund Net Position For the Year Ended June 30, 20XX

	College	Foundation
Operating Revenues		
Student tuition and fees	$41,218,000	—
Less: Scholarship allowances	(7,576,655)	—
Net Student Tuition and Fees	**33,641,345**	—
Federal grants and contracts	6,278,275	—
State and local grants and contracts	1,005,846	—
Private grants	196,023	—
Sales and services of educational department	692,883	—
Gifts and contributions	—	191,209
Auxiliary enterprises: Residential life	13,739,521	—
Other operating revenues	1,394,650	33,231
Total Operating Revenues	**56,948,543**	**224,440**

Public Colleges and Universities

	College	Foundation
Operating Expenses		
Education and General:		
Instruction	24,274,404	—
Academic support	9,241,661	—
Student services	9,656,265	—
Institutional support	11,635,665	402,109
Operations and maintenance of plant	12,063,644	—
Depreciation	3,986,967	—
Scholarships	155,356	404,875
Auxiliary enterprises: Residential life	11,907,599	—
Total Operating Expenses	82,921,561	806,984
Operating Income (Loss)	(25,972,998)	(582,544)
Nonoperating Revenues (Expenses)		
State appropriations	30,676,068	—
Gifts	809,513	—
Investment income, net of investment expense	3,637,537	1,309,149
Interest expense on debt	(628,616)	—
Debt issuance costs	(16,533)	—
Net nonoperating revenues before capital and endowment additions (reductions)	34,477,969	1,309,149
Income before capital and endowment additions (reductions)	8,504,971	726,605
Capital and Endowment Additions (reductions)		
State capital appropriations	—	—
Capital grants	8,400,165	—
Transfers (to)/from state agencies	(1,315,343)	—
Private gifts to endowment	—	146,846
Total capital and endowment additions (reductions)	7,084,822	146,846
Increase/(Decrease) in Net Position	15,589,793	873,451
Net Position—Beginning of Year	79,158,015	8,218,814
Net Position—End of Year	**$94,747,808**	**$9,092,265**

PRACTICE ALERT: As discussed in earlier chapters of the *Guide*, the GASB's *Financial Reporting Model* Exposure Draft proposes a definition of operating and nonoperating activities. This may change the way that the foregoing Statement of Revenues, Expenses, and Changes in Fund Net Position may be reported with respect to the elements of operating and nonoperating activities. As proposed, the above schedule could be:

EXHIBIT 21-2—PROPOSED STATEMENT OF REVENUES, EXPENSES, AND CHANGES IN FUND NET POSITION—GASB EXPOSURE DRAFT

Castle Rock College Statement of Revenues, Expenses, and Change in Fund Net Position For the Year Ended June 30, 20XX

	College	Foundation
Operating Revenues		
Student tuition and fees	$41,218,000	—
Less: Scholarship allowances	(7,576,655)	—
Net Student Tuition and Fees	**33,641,345**	—
Federal grants and contracts (**See Note**)	6,278,275	—
State and local grants and contracts (**See Note**)	1,005,846	—
Private grants (**See Note**)	196,023	—
Sales and services of educational department	692,883	—
Gifts and contributions	—	191,209
Auxiliary enterprises: Residential life	13,739,521	—
Other operating revenues	1,394,650	33,231
Total Operating Revenues	**56,948,543**	**224,440**
Operating Expenses		
Education and General:		
Instruction	24,274,404	—
Academic support	9,241,661	—
Student services	9,656,265	—
Institutional support	11,635,665	402,109
Operations and maintenance of plant	12,063,644	—
Depreciation	3,986,967	—
Scholarships	155,356	404,875
Auxiliary enterprises: Residential life	11,907,599	—
Total Operating Expenses	**82,921,561**	**806,984**
Income (Loss) Generated by Operations	*(25,972,998)*	*(582,544)*
Noncapital Subsidies:		
State appropriations	30,676,068	—
Gifts	809,513	—
Total Noncapital Subsidies	**31,485,581**	—
Operating Income (Loss) and Noncapital Subsidies	*5,512,583*	*(582,544)*

	College	Foundation
Financing and Investing Activities:		
Investment income, net of investment expense (**See Note**)	3,637,537	1,309,149
Interest expense on debt	(628,616)	—
Debt issuance costs	(16,533)	—
Total Financing and Investing Activities	2,992,388	1,309,149
Income before Other Items	8,504,971	726,605
Other Items:		
State capital appropriations	—	—
Capital grants	8,400,165	—
Transfers (to)/from state agencies (**See Note**)	(1,315,343)	—
Private gifts to endowment	—	146,846
Total Other Items	7,084,822	146,846
Increase/(Decrease) in Net Position	15,589,793	873,451
Net Position—Beginning of Year	79,158,015	8,218,814
Net Position—End of Year	**$94,747,808**	**$9,092,265**

NOTE: It will be unclear if these items would be operating or nonoperating without further analysis and upon finalization of the GASB's project. Each could very easily be both. The investment expense though would be reported separately from investment income.

As discussed in Chapter 20 and amplified in GASB Cod. Sec. Co5.703-3, a PCU that is a special-purpose government engaged only in business-type activities *may* report its expenses using either natural or functional classifications. GASB Cod. Sec. 2200.109 lists the specific components that should comprise MD&A, and one of the components relates to condensed institution-wide financial statements and comments on the significant changes from the prior year to the current year. Furthermore, the condensed presentation should include information that, at a minimum, supports the analysis of the overall financial position and results of operations. One of the specific items that must be presented as condensed financial information is "program expenses, at a minimum by function."

Thus, it may appear that there is a conflict between the requirements of GASB Cod. Sec. 2200 regarding the reporting program expenses and the statement that a PCU could report its expenses using a natural rather than a functional classification. GAAP requires special-purpose governments engaged only in business-type activities to follow the requirements for MD&A [GASB Cod. Secs. 2200.106–.109] *only as appropriate*. Thus, a PCU could report its expenses on a natural basis, but if it does so, the MD&A related to condensed expenses should also be based on a natural classification discussion rather than on a program basis.

Statement of Cash Flows

A PCU should prepare a Statement of Cash Flows based on the direct method of computing cash flows from operating activities. The Statement of Cash Flows should be supplemented with a reconciliation of operating cash flows and operating income (the indirect method).

Exhibit 21-3 provides an illustration of a Statement of Cash Flows. Note that the College Foundation reported in the previous exhibits is a fiduciary activity and, therefore, is not required to present a Statement of Cash Flows.

EXHIBIT 21-3
STATEMENT OF CASH FLOWS
Castle Rock College
Statement of Cash Flows
For the Year Ended June 30, 20XX

Castle Rock College
Statement of Cash Flows
For the Year Ended June 30, 20XX

	College
Cash Flows from Operating Activities	
Tuition and fees	$32,699,610
Research grants and contracts	8,048,517
Private grants	279,306
Payments to suppliers	(25,492,422)
Payments to utilities	(3,076,039)
Payments to employees	(41,238,727)
Payments for benefits	(2,250,968)
Payments for scholarships	(443,336)
Loans issued to students	(462,593)
Collections of loans to students	350,778
Auxiliary enterprise receipts—Residential life	13,739,521
Receipts from sales and services of educational departments	677,175
Room and parking fees	34,535
Other receipts	1,345,072
Net Cash Provided (Used) by Operating Activities	**(15,789,571)**
Cash Flows from Noncapital Financing Activities	
State appropriations	25,785,452
Tuition remission to the State	(1,511,564)
Gifts from grants for other than capital purposes	371,034
Net Cash Flows Provided (Used) by Noncapital Financing Activities	**24,644,922**

	College
Cash Flows from Capital and Related Financing Activities	
Perkins loan program net funds received	6,918
Purchases of capital assets	(15,041,600)
Proceeds from debt issuances	3,560,863
Principal repayments	(1,540,340)
Interest payments	(1,566,476)
Transfer of funds to State Agencies	(1,315,343)
Debt issuance costs	(16,533)
Net Cash Provided (Used) by Capital and Related Financing Activities	**(15,912,511)**
Cash Flows from Investing Activities	
Proceeds from sales of investments	2,482,275
Interest and other income	897,957
Purchases of securities investments	(7,228,231)
Net Cash Provided (Used) by Investing Activities	**(3,847,999)**
Net Increase (Decrease) in cash and cash equivalents	(10,905,159)
Cash and cash equivalents—Beginning of Year	44,240,050
Cash and cash equivalents—End of Year	**$33,334,891**
Cash and cash Equivalents at End of Year Include:	
Cash and cash equivalents—current	$19,251,737
Restricted cash and cash equivalents—current	3,073,652
Restricted cash and cash equivalents	11,009,502
Cash and cash equivalents—End of Year	**$33,334,891**

Noncash Investing and Financing Activities

During the year, the College had significant noncash investing and financing activities, including $23,990,403 in the acquisition of capital assets and payments made by a state agency on behalf of the College for $8,400,165. An additional $2,739,580 resulted from fair value changes in securities. $6,402,180 was paid for fringe benefits on the College's behalf by the State. The College's service concession arrangement deferred inflow of resources position was amortized by $468,595 during the year.

	College
Reconciliation of Net Operating Income (loss) to Net Cash Provided (Used) by Operating Activities:	
Net operating income (loss)	$(25,971,998)
Adjustments to reconcile net operating income (loss) to net cash provided (used) by operating activities:	
Depreciation expense	3,986,967
Bad debt expense realized on student loans	21,775
On-behalf fringe benefit payments made by the State	6,402,180

	College
Changes in assets, liabilities, and deferred inflows of resources:	
Receivables, net	(371,031)
Other current assets	(384)
Accounts payable and accrued liabilities	93,152
Compensated absences	100,188
Accrued faculty payroll	(28,591)
Advances	(456,987)
Student deposits	34,535
Other current liabilities	(42,320)
Student loans	(111,815)
Net Cash Provided (Used) by Operating Activities	**$(15,789,571)**

> **PRACTICE POINT:** GASB Cod. Sec. 2450.105 discusses how the total amounts of cash and cash equivalents at the beginning and end of the period shown in the Statement of Cash Flows should be easily traceable to similarly titled line items or subtotals shown in the Statement of Net Position as of those dates. As the College has multiple amounts for cash and cash equivalents, a reconciliation is included in the schedule. Otherwise, if only one line item for cash and cash equivalents is in the Statement of Net Position, the reconciliation included above is not necessary if the amounts agree.

PCU COMPONENT UNIT REPORTING—SPECIAL ISSUES

Nongovernmental Component Units

PCUs may have nongovernmental component units. GASB Cod. Secs. 2600.701-3, .704-12–14 discuss the reporting of nongovernmental component units of primary governments, including PCUs. It is likely these entities prepare their financial statements based on the not-for-profit reporting model described in the FASB ASC™ 958 (*Not-for-Profit Entities*) and in limited circumstances, for-profit reporting. Although the models are based on accrual accounting concepts (component units are presented only in the government-wide financial statements), there are differences.

Initially, the PCU would need to apply the guidance in GASB Cod. Sec. 2600.701-3 which directs preparers to GASB Cod. Sec. 2100 to apply all applicable criteria to determine if a component unit relationship exists and further, what type of component unit.

The display of the nongovernmental component unit's information in the PCU would then be determined. GASB Cod. Sec. 2600.704-12 provides guidance that the component units that use other GAAP reporting models would be incorporated into the PCU's financial statements like governmental component units. Due to the provisions of GASB Cod. Sec. 2600.106, all component units are required to apply the definition and display provisions before they are combined with the primary government.

Therefore, some reclassifications may need to occur, but this is discussed in a follow-up question. In the PCU's Statement of Net Position, a discretely presented component unit's financial data may be presented in a separate discrete column or combined with the financial data of other discretely presented component units. Similarly, in the PCU's Statement of Activities, a nongovernmental component unit's financial data may be presented on a separate line or combined with the financial data of other component units.

The financial data of a nongovernmental component unit would be arrayed based on the same display considerations as those discussed for component units engaged only in business-type activities. If the reporting entity's financial statements do not include a Statement of Activities, the nongovernmental component unit's financial statement data should be reconfigured into a display that is compatible with the reporting entity's change statement format and be presented in a discrete column to the right of the financial statement data of the primary government. However, if it is impractical to reformat the nongovernmental component unit's change statement data, they need not be reported on the same page as that of the primary government but may be reported on a separate following page.

GASB Cod. Sec. 2600.704-13 discusses the extent that the financial statements of a nongovernmental component unit of a PCU would need to be converted to GASB provisions. There are no requirements to change the recognition, measurement, or disclosure standards applied in a nongovernmental component unit's separately issued financial statements. However, as discussed previously, the provisions of this section should be applied to the financial statements of a nongovernmental component unit when those statements are incorporated into a governmental financial reporting entity. That is, a nongovernmental component unit should include *component units of its own*. In addition, the financial statements of a nongovernmental component unit *may need to be reformatted to comply with the classification and display requirements* in GAAP.

Reformatting Nongovernmental Component Unit Financial Statements. GASB Cod. Sec. 2600.704-14 presents information when a PCU is reported as a business-type activity with a foundation reporting in accordance with FASB standards, in an equivalent manner to a comparably displayed financial statements. If the foundation's Statement of Net Assets is not presented in a classified format, its assets and liabilities should be reclassified into their current and noncurrent components. Also, the foundation's net assets should be redistributed among the three net position components—net investment in capital assets, restricted (distinguishing between expendable and nonexpendable and between major categories of restrictions), and unrestricted. The data in the foundation's Statement of Activities may need to be realigned to distinguish between operating and nonoperating revenues and expenses and relocated to their appropriate positions in the GASB's required format. Also, because the university can present its operating expenses by either natural classification or functional categories, the foundation's expenses may need to be reconfigured to conform to the approach used by the university. In addition, the foundation's revenues may need to be reduced by related discounts and allowances, if reported separately as expenses, to be consistent with the university's presentation.

In addition, the summary of significant accounting policies could be disclosed in a section on the PCU's reporting entity as follows [GASB Cod. Sec. 2600.908]:

> The foundation is a private nonprofit organization that reports under FASB standards, including Topic 958. As such, certain revenue recognition criteria and presentation features are different from GASB revenue recognition criteria and presentation features. No modifications have been made to the foundation's financial information in the PCU's financial reporting entity for these differences.

Equity Interests and Majority Equity Interests. PCUs may have equity interests in for-profit entities that the PCU establishes with a student (or a professor, private corporation, etc.) with the goal of investment return. If the PCU owns most of the equity interest in a legally separate organization (e.g., through acquisition of its voting stock), the PCU's intent for owning the equity interest should determine whether the organization should be presented as a component unit or an investment of the PCU. If the PCU's intent for owning a majority equity interest is to directly enhance its ability to provide services, the organization should be reported as a component unit.

For example, a PCU that purchases 100% of the stock of an energy plant to provide a controlled source of energy for its capital assets should report the energy company as a component unit. When such a component unit is discreetly presented, the equity interest should be reported as an asset of the fund that has the equity interest. If the interest is reported in a governmental fund, it may be reported as a joint venture. Changes in the equity interest should be reported pursuant to the requirements of either governmental funds or proprietary funds, depending on how the interest is reported. When such a component unit is blended, in the period of acquisition the purchase typically should be reported as an outflow of the fund that provided the resources for the acquisition and, in that and subsequent reporting periods, the component unit should be reported pursuant to the blending requirements of GASB Cod. Sec. 2100, as discussed in Chapter 4, If, however, the PCU owns the equity interest for obtaining income or profit rather than to directly enhance its ability to provide services, it should report its equity interest as an investment, regardless of the extent of its ownership. For many research institutions, there is an equity interest as an investment, rather than to provide services.

Majority Equity Interest Held by the PCU. In some cases, the PCU can own or acquire most of the equity interest in a legally separate organization (e.g., through acquisition of voting stock of a corporation or acquisition of interest in a partnership).

Solely for this purpose, an equity interest is a financial interest in a legally separate organization evidenced by the ownership of shares of the organization's stock or by otherwise having *an explicit, measurable right to the net resources of the organization that is usually based on an investment of financial or capital resources by a government.* An equity interest is explicit and measurable if the PCU has a present or future claim to the net resources of the entity and the method for measuring the PCU's share of the entity's net resources is determinable.

The definition of equity interest is not intended to include a PCU's residual interest in assets that may (on dissolution) revert to the PCU for lack of another equitable claimant.

If a PCU's holding of that *majority* equity interest meets the definition of an investment, the equity interest should be reported as an investment and measured using the equity method.

- If a PCU's holding of that equity interest meets the definition of an investment, the legally separate organization should not be reported as a component unit of the government.

- If the endowment of a PCU (or similar) holds a majority equity interest in a legally separate organization that meets the definition of an investment, that majority equity interest should be measured at fair value.

If a PCU's holding of a majority equity interest in a legally separate organization does not meet the definition of an investment, the holding of the majority equity interest results in the PCU being financially accountable for the organization and, therefore, the PCU should report the legally separate organization as a component unit. The majority equity interest should be reported as an asset of the government or fund that holds the equity interest, measured using the equity method.

However, if the component unit is blended, the asset and net position associated with the equity interest held by the PCU or fund should be eliminated in the blending process. In financial statements prepared using the current financial resources measurement focus, the asset representing the PCU's equity interest should be limited to amounts appropriately reported under the current financial resources measurement focus in a governmental fund *under current GAAP* [GASB Cod. Sec. 2600.116, fn. 7]

An example of holding a majority equity interest would be if a Public Hospital were affiliated with the College, discussed in Exhibits 21-1 through 21-3, which is a common occurrence with PCUs. Medical Centers often create a separate corporation to assist in funding breakthroughs in medical technology, thereby allowing the research physicians to potentially capitalize on the research while potentially sheltering the PCU from liability. Care must be taken in the accounting and financial reporting of the research center.

For example, if the center produces or obtains patents, if the patents were to be used in the center's operations, the patents may be recorded as intangible assets. However, if the patents were produced or obtained for income or profit, they would be recorded as investments and would need to be valued annually at fair value.

OTHER MEASUREMENT AND REPORTING ISSUES

Grants and Lending

Pell Grants. GASB Cod. Sec. Co5.702-1 discusses whether Pell Grants can be reported in a custodial fund (see **PRACTICE POINT** below).

GASB Cod. Sec. N50.128 contains guidance that pass-through grants should be reported as revenues and expenses (or expenditures) in the recipient government's financial statements *if the government has any administrative or direct financial involvement in the program.* A recipient government has administrative involvement if it determines eligible secondary recipients or projects, even if using grantor-established criteria. Therefore, because of their administrative involvement with Pell Grant requirements and because Pell Grants are nonexchange transactions, PCUs should record Pell Grant receipts as *nonoperating revenues* in their financial statements, and any amounts applied to student receivable accounts should be recorded as scholarship discounts or allowances.

This is different than if the PCU was a cash conduit for Pell Grants. The GASB describes cash conduit activity as transmitting grantor-supplied moneys "without having administrative or direct financial involvement in the program."

Administrative involvement is based on whether the recipient government's role in the grant program constitutes an operational responsibility for the grant program, such as the following:

- Monitoring secondary recipients for compliance with specific requirements established by the program,
- Determining which secondary recipients are eligible for grant payments (even if eligibility criteria are established by the provider government), and
- Exercising some discretion in determining how resources are to be allocated.

PRACTICE POINT: For fiduciary activities, one of the key determinants of a non-pension or OPEB (Other Post-Employment Benefit) potential fiduciary component unit is whether the assets within the organization are for the benefit of individuals and the government does not have administrative involvement or direct financial involvement with the assets. A non-component unit activity could be fiduciary in nature if the assets associated with the activity are not derived from government-mandated nonexchange transactions or voluntary nonexchange transactions except for pass-through grants for which the government does not have administrative involvement or direct financial involvement. Further discussion of administrative involvement is contained in Chapter 8.

Due to the administrative involvement with Pell Grant requirements and because Pell Grants are nonexchange transactions, public institutions should record Pell Grant receipts as nonoperating revenues in their financial statements, and any amounts applied to student receivable accounts should be recorded as scholarship discounts or allowances. However, most other student loans are operational in nature and, therefore, are shown in the operating activities section of a Statement of Cash Flows.

Furthermore, in GASB Cod. Sec. 2450.116, the GASB concluded that certain "loan programs" are the operating activities of a governmental enterprise. The loans are not typical investments because they are not necessarily intended to earn a profit. There are only two examples of qualifying loan programs, including student loan programs. In the examples provided, loans are made to individuals who might not otherwise qualify for loans. The program is intended to directly benefit the individuals receiving the loans. Usually, the interest rate on a loan provided by this type of program is below the market rate. A student loan program provides direct benefits to individuals: students in need of financing their education.

The GASB expected few types of loan programs or finance authorities to meet the spirit of the exception provided, even if making and collecting loans are the primary operations of the enterprise. A finance authority that facilitates financing by serving as an intermediary or conduit would not usually qualify even if the project to be financed indirectly benefits the institution or its students. For example, an authority created to finance institution building projects (such as classroom buildings or dormitories) would not qualify, because the direct beneficiary is the institution rather than individual students. Debt is issued by the authority and the proceeds are loaned to universities for their building or dormitory construction projects. Although the students who eventually live in the dorms will benefit from the activity, the direct beneficiary of the dormitory authority is the university itself, which is part of the governmental financial reporting entity. Such an arrangement merely facilitates the government's financing process. The substance of the arrangement is that the institution issued bonds to serve its own needs.

Other Forms of Lending. Student loans are integral to most PCU operations. GASB Cod. Sec. L30 describes the accounting and financial reporting for nonrefundable fees and costs associated with lending activities and loan purchases. Lending, committing to lend, refinancing, or restructuring loans, which many PCUs arrange are "lending activities." If the PCU is only an indirect recipient of the loan, rather than making the loan to the student, then GASB Cod. Sec. L30 *does not apply.*

If the PCU does make direct loans, then the PCU should use the applicable provisions, which are from for-profit standards. In summary, the following are the accounting and financial reporting standards for activities that are likely to occur at PCUs:

Item	Accounting and Financial Reporting Principles	GASB Codification Sections
Loan Origination Fees and Costs	Loan origination fees except for the portion related to points should be recognized as revenue in the period received. Likewise, direct loan origination costs should be expensed.	GASB Cod. Secs. L30.105–.107
Loan Commitment Fees	Fees received for a commitment to originate a loan or group of loans should be recorded as a liability and, if the commitment is exercised, recognized as revenue in the period of exercise. If the commitment expires unexercised, the commitment fees should be recognized as revenue upon expiration of the commitment. Exceptions to this are: • If the PCU's experience with similar arrangements indicates that the likelihood that the commitment will be exercised is remote, the commitment fee should be recognized as revenue in the period received. • If the amount of the commitment fee is determined retrospectively as a percentage of the line of credit available but unused in a previous period, if that percentage is nominal in relation to the stated interest rate on any related borrowing, and if that borrowing will bear a market interest rate at the date the loan is made, the commitment fee should be recognized as revenue as of the determination date.	GASB Cod. Secs. L30.108 and .501, .502, .506, and .509.

In the unlikely occurrence that a PCU is engaged in mortgage banking activities, GASB Cod. Secs. L30.101–.138 discusses the accounting and financial reporting for those activities.

Scholarship Allowances and Discounts. As discussed in Chapter 7, GAAP requires proprietary funds to report revenues net of allowances and discounts [GASB Cod. Sec. 2200.fn. 44]. The discounts and allowances appear in one of two ways in the Statements of Revenues, Expenses, and Changes in Fund Net Position:

- As a parenthetical amount on the tuition and fees line, offsetting the gross tuition and fees, *or*
- Revenues are reported gross with the value of allowances and discounts shown below the revenues.

GASB Cod. Sec. 2200.717-17 discusses that consistent with the provisions of GASB Cod. Secs. N50 and 2200.fn. 44, exchange revenues for governmental activities should be reported net of uncollectible accounts.

Research and Development

For many PCUs, federal, state, local, and private grants are a large source of revenue as easily seen in the Statements of Revenues, Expenses, and Changes in Fund Net Position presented earlier in this chapter. The expenses for research and development usually have complex compliance requirements as well. As shown in the above Statements, such revenues from contracts are operating revenues in accordance with GASB Cod. Sec. 2200.752-1.

For reporting in the Statements of Cash Flows, GASB Cod. Sec. 2200.fn. 45 applies the guidance in GASB Cod. Sec. 2450.116 to define operating revenues and expenses. If the nature of an enterprise would fall under a financing or investing cash flows category, the revenues and expenses may be considered 'operating.' Given that most research and development are like a contract for services, reporting operating revenues and expenses would be proper.

Appropriations from Other Governments

Many PCUs rely on appropriations from other governments, particularly states. GASB Cod. Sec. Co5.702-3 does not allow a PCU to establish a policy to include state appropriations in operating revenues. The objective of GASB Cod. Sec. 2200.192 in disclosing the policy (under current GAAP) is to disclose the differences between operating and nonoperating revenues and expenses. As the appropriations are not generated by the PCU and are instead provided to the PCU to subsidize operating expenses, appropriations are nonoperating revenues.

Split-Interest Agreements—GASB Cod. Sec. I70

A PCU may receive a gift from a donor structured as a split-interest agreement, where the PCU acts as the trustee A split-interest agreement takes one of two forms: (1) an annuity trust or (2) a unitrust. Under an annuity trust, the donor receives an annual fixed payment during the period covered by the trust agreement. Under a unitrust, the donor receives an annual payment based on a specified percentage of the fair value of the market value of the trust's assets.

GASB Cod. Sec. I70 requires that a government that receives resources pursuant to an irrevocable split-interest agreement recognize assets, liabilities, and deferred inflows of resources. GASB Cod. Sec. I70 also requires that a government recognize assets representing its beneficial interests in irrevocable split-interest agreements that are administered by a third party if those beneficial interests are under the control of the government and embody present service capacity.

The following is an example of accounting for an irrevocable split-interest agreement involving a life interest in real estate that may be common in a PCU:

> **Example:** In the beginning of 20X8, Mrs. Mary Smith, a widowed graduate of State College in 19S7, decided to contact the Chief Endowment Officer of the College seeking to donate her house to the College. Her house is adjacent to the State College campus. Mrs. Smith seeks to retain the right to use the house until she passes away. The Chief Endowment Officer presented this offer to the College Board of Trustees, which quickly accepted the gift. The Board intends to use the house as the new President of the College's house.
>
> The house will be used for official functions and meetings. Therefore, State College's Chief Financial Officer documented that the house should be classified as a capital asset in accordance with the provisions of GASB Cod. Sec. I70. An appraisal was done and an acquisition value of $2,500,000 was determined in

accordance with the provisions of GASB Cod. Sec. 3100. As Mrs. Smith is elderly, the College agreed to pay to insure the house and for regular maintenance and necessary repairs. The Chief Financial Officer calculates the liability for such expenses for the next five years (her estimated remaining life) to be $500,000. The following is then entered into the books and records of the College on the day of closing of the irrevocable split-interest agreement:

ENDOWMENT FUND	Debit	Credit
Capital Asset – Smith House (ISIA)	$2,500,000	
Estimated Liability- Insurance, Maintenance, Repairs – Smith House (ISIA)		$500,000
Deferred Inflow of Resources – Smith House (ISIA)		$2,000,000

At the end of 20X8, $100,000 had been paid for the insurance, maintenance, and repairs on the Smith House. Depreciation occurred as well, using a 40-year estimated useful life, per the State College's policy. The following is then entered:

ENDOWMENT FUND	Debit	Credit
Depreciation Expense – Smith House (ISIA)	$62,500	
Estimated Liability – Insurance, Maintenance, Repairs – Smith House (ISIA)	100,000	
Deferred Inflow of Resources – Smith House (ISIA) ($2,000,000/40 years)	50,000	
Cash (assumed)		$100,000
Accumulated depreciation – Smith House (ISIA)		62,500
Revenue – Smith House		50,000

Five years after the signing of the ISIA, Mrs. Smith dies. All liabilities had been paid before her death. $250,000 had been amortized to revenue from the deferred inflow of resources, leaving $1,750,000 to recognize as follows:

ENDOWMENT FUND	Debit	Credit
Deferred Inflow of Resources – Smith House (ISIA)	$1,750,000	
Revenue – Smith House (ISIA) Termination		$1,750,000

PRACTICE POINT: For a further discussion on Irrevocable Split-Interest Agreements and GASB Cod. Sec. I70, see Chapter 9.

Investment Income Restricted to Permanent or Term Endowments

When a PCU receives contributions to its term and permanent endowments or to permanent fund principal, those contributions should be reported as separate items in the lower portion of the Statement of Activities or Statement of Revenues, Expenses, and Changes in Fund Net Position (depending upon which reporting model is used by the PCU). These receipts are not considered to be program revenues (such as program-specific grants) because, in the case of term endowments, there is an uncertainty of the timing of the release of the resources from the term restriction and, in the case of permanent contributions the principal can never be expended.

A question arises as to whether investment income that is restricted to permanent or term endowments could be reported as additions to permanent and term endowments.

GASB Cod. Sec. 2200.753-3 discusses how investment income of this nature should not be reported as additions to permanent and term endowments. If the PCU reports as a special-purpose governmental entity and reports only business-type activities (enterprise fund model), investment income restricted to permanent, or term endowments should be reported as nonoperating revenue. If the PCU reports governmental activities and therefore prepares a statement of activities, the income should be reported as general revenues in the lower portion of the financial statement.

Investments in Land and Other Real Estate Held by Endowments

A PCU may acquire or receive from a donor income-producing real estate (or a partial interest in such real estate) as a permanent or term endowment. Many PCUs were formed by grants of land from the federal government (also known as "land grant institutions"). GASB Cod. Sec. I50 requires that land and other real estate held as investments by endowments be reported at fair value at the reporting date. Any changes recorded in fair value during the period should be reported as investment income [GASB Cod. Secs. I50.108, .124].

Disclosures should include the methods and significant assumptions used to determine the fair value of such investments and provide other information that is currently presented for other investments reported at fair value [GASB Cod. Sec. I50.101].

Facilities Financed by Conduit Debt Obligations

> **PRACTICE POINT:** As discussed in Chapter 12, conduit debt obligation accounting and financial reporting is subject to GASB Statement No. 91 (*Conduit Debt Obligations*) (CDOs). PCUs commonly finance construction of capital assets as obligors of CDOs from entities beyond the PCU's reporting entity—typically a state college building authority or similar. In some cases, the issuer may retain title to the capital asset(s) constructed or acquired from the proceeds of the CDO. In other cases:
>
> - The issuer relinquishes the title to the capital asset at the end of the arrangement, coinciding with the retirement of the CDO, or
> - The issuer *does not* relinquish the title to the capital asset at the end of the arrangement, but the PCU has exclusive use of the entire capital asset until the end of the arrangement, or
> - The issuer does not relinquish title and the PCU has exclusive use of portion of the capital asset until the end of the arrangement.

Nonexchange financial guarantees may also be involved with the CDO. Assuming the provisions of a CDO are met, different accounting and financial reporting may result. For a further discussion of these differences, see Chapter 12.

Accrual of Tuition and Fees Revenue

PCUs often receive revenues for tuition and fees in one year for services that must be delivered across more than one fiscal year. GASB Cod. Sec. 2200.751-6 states that tuition and fees should be reported as revenue in the period they are earned. This is further magnified if the academic term encompasses two fiscal years. Allocation is required per GASB Cod. Sec. Co5.702-2.

Federal Unrelated Business Income Taxes

PCUs *may* be subject to federal unrelated business income taxation (UBIT). UBIT is a tax on any trade or business that is operational and "not substantially related to the organization's tax-exempt purpose or function." For accounting purposes, any UBIT paid is an expense (or expenditure) in accordance with GAAP as discussed in other chapters of this *Guide*.

Accounting for Joint Activities including Fundraising (AICPA (American Institute of Certified Public Accountants) Guidance Cleared by the GASB)

The AICPA released Statement of Position 98-2 discussing the accounting for the costs of a joint activity. If the criteria of purpose, audience, and content are met, the costs of a joint activity that are identifiable with a function should be charged to that function and joint costs should be allocated between fund-raising and the appropriate program or management and general function. If any of the criteria are not met, all costs of the joint activity should be reported as fund-raising costs, including costs that otherwise might be considered program or management and general costs if they had been incurred in a different activity, subject to the exception in the following sentence. Costs of goods or services provided in exchange transactions that are a part of joint activities, such as costs of direct donor benefits of a special event (e.g., a meal), should not be reported as fund raising [GASB Cod. Sec. Co5.801].

Detailed guidance of allocation methodologies is presented in GASB Cod. Secs. Co5.802–.813 describing the identification of purpose criterion, program functions, program and management and general functions, audience, content, allocation methods, incidental activities, and disclosures. Much of the emphasis in the practice area is on fund-raising costs. These elements are highly specialized and beyond the scope of this *Guide*. Furthermore, the guidance has not been updated since before the current reporting model was implemented in the early 2000s. Practitioners at PCUs required to perform these allocations should review GASB Cod. Secs. Co5.801–.813 and the related glossary.

22,001

CHAPTER 22
PENSION AND OTHER POSTEMPLOYMENT BENEFIT PLANS

Chapter References:

GASB Statement Nos. 67, 73, 74, 82, 84, 85, 92, 97

GASB Implementation Guide

AICPA Audit and Accounting Guide, *States and Local Governments,* Chapters 13 and 14

INTRODUCTION

State and local governments often control or have a component unit that is fiduciary in nature that may include pension and other employee benefit plans Governments may report such plans in stand-alone special-purpose reports or as fiduciary funds within the financial statements of the sponsoring government. The employee benefit plans addressed in this chapter are follows:

- Most defined benefit pension plans and public employee retirement systems,
- Defined contribution and deferred compensation plans presented as stand-alone statements, and
- Most defined benefit postemployment benefit plans other than pensions.

The primary function of a plan is to administer benefits and invest contributions into the plan to fund benefits currently and in the future. The administration of the benefits entails an actuarial valuation, investing in accordance with approved allocation methodology, and compliance with the plan provisions, laws, and regulations in a particular jurisdiction.

PENSION PLANS AND PUBLIC EMPLOYEE RETIREMENT SYSTEMS

The Scope of GASB's Pension Plan Guidance

GASB Cod. Sec. Pe5, *(Pension Plans Administered Through Trusts that Meet Specified Criteria—Defined Benefit)* is applicable for defined benefit pension plans that are administered through trusts or equivalent arrangements. To have a trust or equivalent arrangement, the following must be present:

- Contributions from employers and nonemployer contributing entities to the pension plan and earnings on those contributions must be irrevocable. In some situations, payments are made by the employer to satisfy contribution requirements, identified in the plan provisions as *plan member contributions*. (See section on employer-paid member contributions later in this chapter, at "Communication Issues from the Plan to Employers or Sponsors.") Such amounts are classified by the plan as plan member contributions.

- Plan assets must provide pensions to plan members in accordance with benefit terms.
- Pension plan assets are legally protected from the creditors of the employers, the nonemployer contributing entities, plan members, and the pension plan administrator [GASB Cod. Sec. Pe5.101].

PRACTICE POINT: If a trust *is not in place*, many of the defined benefit disclosures and schedules discussed in this chapter are also applicable in the disclosure of such arrangements. Pension plans may also provide that a defined benefit plan contain *both* assets held in trust *and* assets that are not held in trust. This may occur if employer reserves for future rate increases (as an example) are held by a plan, but not held in trust [GASB Cod. Sec. Pe5.102].

These provisions are applicable if the plan issues a stand-alone financial report (usually from a public employee retirement system) (PERS) or the plan is included as part of a pension trust fund of an employer (typical for single-employer plans).

Additional provisions are discussed later in this chapter for other postemployment benefit plans (mainly retiree health care or OPEB). However, when such benefits are not paid from a plan separate from the pension plan, the term "pensions" also include the contributions, benefits, assets and liabilities for retirement income and death, insurance, and disability benefits since they are administered through the pension plan. If they are provided separately from the pension plan, they are OPEB.

In some cases, the effects of a termination benefit may increase the liability for pensions or OPEB. A typical scenario is discussed in GASB Cod. Sec. Pe5.726-10. In this case, a pension is provided to eligible retirees who are age 65 or older. The government offers an early retirement incentive in the form of additional service credits to any employee with at least 20 years of service. Acceptance of the offer increases the pension paid to the employee. Therefore, the termination benefit is included as part of the net pension liability. Termination benefits are also discussed from the employer's perspective in Chapter 13 [GASB Cod. Secs. Pe5.103–.105].

An important distinction to understand is the difference between a defined benefit and a defined contribution. In a defined benefit, an employee contributes and is matched by an employer based on a formula approved in advance. In many cases, the employer pays the majority or even 100% of the employee contribution. The pensions due to the employee upon retirement may be stated as a specified dollar amount or as an amount that is calculated based on one or more factors such as age, years of service, and compensation.

In a defined contribution plan, an account is established for the employee. The employer may or may not contribute to the account based on service or some other formula. Earnings then are held in the employee's account, net of fees [GASB Cod. Sec. Pe5.106].

PRACTICE POINT: Due to the provisions of GASB Statement No. 97 (*Certain Component Unit Criteria, and Accounting and Financial Reporting for Internal Revenue Code Section 457 Deferred Compensation Plans—an Amendment of GASB Statements No. 14 and No. 84, and a Supersession of GASB Statement No. 32*), and as clarified by GASB Cod. Sec. 1300.716-33 (GASBIG 2021-1 Q4.6), if the participant employees can choose investment options, the participant employees *have control* of the employee benefit plan. This is even the case when the employer or sponsor selects a set of investment options. The employer or sponsor's process of selecting a set of investment options is not directing the use, exchange, or employment of the assets in a manner that provides benefits to the participant employees. The participant employees can change one asset for another and even borrow against those assets, directing the employer or sponsor to garnish future wages to repay the loan (along with other provisions). In these cases, many defined contribution plans and nearly all deferred compensation plans, regardless of type of plan, may not be reported in general-purpose government external financial reports. For public employee retirement systems (PERS plans) (discussed further in this chapter), inconsistent presentation may result. Some Boards may want to present such plans, with a subset of PERS plans fully administering such assets and in control. For those PERS plans that want to present plans where they do not have control in accordance with GAAP, stand-alone reporting is an ideal situation. Presenting in a stand-alone report will not be a departure from GAAP. The chapter section titled "Defined Contribution and Deferred Compensation Plans Presented as Stand-Alone Statements" discusses this reporting.

Obligations to employees may be pooled and sent to a single-employer plan, a larger plan that is a separate entity that invests and administers the pensions on behalf of the employers and employees while maintaining separate accounts for each employer, or to a plan that pools not only the investments but also the liabilities.

These types of plans are single-employer plans, agent multiple-employer plans, or cost-sharing multiple-employer plans, respectively. Types of plans are as follows:

Type of Plan	Definition and Example
Single-employer pension plans	Pensions provided to employees of one employer and that employer's component units (if they are part of the plan). Example: City Fire and Police Retirement Plan.
Agent multiple-employer pension plans	Plans where plan assets are pooled for investment purposes, but separate accounts are maintained for each individual employer so that each employer contributions *must be only for each employer's employee benefits*. Example: State and Municipalities of Bay Public Employees Retirement System.
Cost-sharing multiple-employer pension plans	Plans where assets are pooled for investment purposes and can also be used to pay for benefits of *any employer* within the plan. Example: State of Bay Employees Retirement Association (includes the State, Cities, and Special Districts within the State).

There are many variations of these certain large statewide entities may have an agent multiple-employer plan or multiple-agent multiple-employer plans along with cost-sharing multiple-employer plan or plans. Decisions on the type of plan or plans in use are predicated on enabling statutes and other provisions of contracts and other laws.

A government may act as a fiduciary, serving as an administrator for one or more pension plans and even multiple types of plans. When more than one plan is administered by a government that is a fiduciary, GAAP applies separately to each plan administered, with full consideration of the number of plans as discussed in the next section [GASB Cod. Secs. Pe5.107–.110].

Variations Due to Numbers of Plans. If all assets accumulated in a defined benefit pension plan for the payment of benefits may legally be used to pay benefits (including refunds of plan member contributions) to *any* of the plan members, the total assets should be reported as assets of one defined benefit pension plan even if:

- Administrative policy requires that separate reserves, funds, or accounts for specific groups of plan members, employers, or types of benefits be maintained (e.g., a reserve for plan member contributions, a reserve for disability benefits), or

- Separate accounts for the contributions of state government versus local government employers, or

- Separate actuarial valuations are performed for different classes of plan members (e.g., general employees and public safety employees), or

- Diverse groups of plan members because different contribution rates may apply for each class or group depending on the applicable benefit structures, benefit formulas, or other factors.

These variations are especially prevalent in governments at all levels, which may have different structures, classes, benefits, etc. If any of the plan members may receive assets to pay benefits irrespective of class, etc., *then one plan is present with different classes.*

The only situation where multiple plans may exist is when the members are not allowed to receive assets to pay benefits outside of their class, structure, or similar [GASB Cod. Sec. Pe5.111].

PRACTICE POINT: This issue is commonly misunderstood by practitioners. Even if separate actuarial valuations are performed due to separate collective bargaining agreements, only one plan exists if those agreements do not stipulate that the members of that bargaining unit can only receive specific assets accumulated for that bargaining unit and only that bargaining unit (or similar).

Defined Benefit Plan Financial Reporting

GAAP requires the following accrual basis of accounting financial statements in the same manner as fiduciary funds [GASB Cod. Sec. Pe5.112]:

Statement	Elements
Statement of Fiduciary Net Position	• Assets, deferred outflows of resources, liabilities, deferred inflows of resources, and fiduciary net position, as applicable, as of the end of the pension plan's reporting period.
Statement of Changes in Fiduciary Net Position	• Additions to, deductions from, and net increase (or decrease) in fiduciary net position for the pension plan's reporting period.

Statement of Fiduciary Net Position. Within each of the elements presented in each Statement, the following may be included, as applicable [GASB Cod. Secs. Pe5.113–.119].

Statement of Fiduciary Net Position Elements	Transactions that may be Included in Each Element
Assets	The major categories of assets, including, but not limited to: • Cash and cash equivalents, • Receivables, • Investments, and assets used in pension plan operations, and • The principal components of the receivables and investments categories.

Statement of Fiduciary Net Position Elements	Transactions that may be Included in Each Element
Receivables	Receivables are only short-term amounts due from employers, nonemployer contributing entities, and plan members, and investments. Amounts recognized as receivables for contributions should include only those due pursuant to legal requirements and investments. Amounts due in more than one year should be recognized as the receivable arises. Discounting and the effective interest method may be used if the receivable is due in more than one year.
Investments	Investments are reported on a *trade date basis* at fair value in accordance with the provisions of GASB Cod. Secs. I50 and 3100 as applicable (see Chapter 9). Unallocated insurance contracts should be reported as interest-earning investment contracts. Synthetic guaranteed investment contracts that are fully benefit responsive are reported at contract value.
Liabilities	Liabilities are only benefits (including refunds of plan member contributions) due to plan members and accrued investment and administrative expenses.
Fiduciary Net Position	Assets + Deferred outflows of resources − Liabilities − Deferred inflows of resources = Net position restricted for pensions at the end of a reporting period.

OBSERVATION: Note that the classes of assets do not include capital assets such as buildings. Many plans purchase the building where the administrative offices are and attempt to deem it an asset. However, if the building was purchased with contributions, then the asset really is an investment in a title as the benefits of ownership (and sale) will inure to the beneficiary, not to the plan. But the provisions of GASB Cod. Secs. I50.101–.105, in defining an investment, specifically exclude capital assets *held for sale*. If the plan holds the real estate as part of its portfolio, ultimately, the highest and best use of the building may be for income or profit and, therefore, would be an investment. Most plans do include real estate as part of their portfolios. The administrative building, and its contents may be included as part of that investment, especially if there are portions of the building leased to third parties. In other cases, the building where the plan is located was purchased by a separate government or private entity and leased to the plan. Care must be taken to present these transactions properly.

PRACTICE POINT: Many PERS plans (and similar) report other types of plans, including OPEB and defined contribution plans, in common trusts in accordance with IRC Section 115. Even though the participants in defined contribution plans may have the ability to asset allocate or chose investments. See previous **PRACTICE POINT** on GASB-97. A best practice may be to present such plans in stand-alone reports.

PRACTICE POINT: Deferred outflows of resources and deferred inflows of resources rarely would be presented in a Statement of Fiduciary Net Position. As discussed in Chapter 11, the GASB defines when deferred outflows of resources (and deferred inflows of resources) are presented.

The example of a Statement of Fiduciary Net Position is in Exhibit 22-1.

PRACTICE POINT: The Statement of Fiduciary Net Position shown below also includes OPEB and defined contribution information as it is for a PERS. Note that the following has no relationship to the exhibits in Chapter 20.

EXHIBIT 22-1
STATE OF SILVER PUBLIC EMPLOYEES' RETIREMENT SYSTEM
STATEMENT OF FIDUCIARY NET POSITION
AS OF JUNE 30, 20Y1
(Amounts in thousands)

	Base Plan	Firefighters Retirement	Judges Retirement	Retiree Health Benefits	20XX Total
Assets					
Cash and cash equivalents	$2,671	$66	$292	$54	$3,083
Investments, at fair value:					
Fixed income – domestic	3,713,963	91,345	20,122	127,507	3,952,937
Fixed income – international	10,450	257	59	-	10,766
Commercial mortgages	645,620	15,879	3,498	-	664,997
Short-term	220,071	5,413	1,192	-	226,676
Real estate	606,993	14,929	3,289	-	625,211
Domestic stocks	6,019,999	148,063	32,619	271,898	6,472,579
Global stocks	3,132,891	77,054	16,976	69,082	3,296,003
Private equities	905,712	22,276	4,907	-	932,895
Total investments	15,258,370	375,282	82,954	468,541	16,185,147
Receivables	121,540	-	-	-	121,540
Other assets including prepaid benefits	80,429	-	-	3,473	83,902
Total assets	15,460,339	375,282	82,954	472,014	16,390,589
Liabilities					
Accrued liabilities	11,193	270	59	44	11,566
Benefits and refunds payable	376	9	-	-	385
In transit amounts	2,072	51	-	-	2,123
Investments purchased	110,752	2,724	600	-	114,076
Total liabilities	124,393	3,054	659	44	128,150

	Base Plan	Firefighters Retirement	Judges Retirement	Retiree Health Benefits	20XX Total
Net Position Restricted for Pensions and Postemployment Benefits Other Than Pensions	$15,335,946	$372,228	$82,295	$471,970	$16,262,439

PRACTICE POINT: The above portrays a defined benefit pension and a defined benefit OPEB plan held in trust by a PERS. Using "Fiduciary Net Position" is also acceptable as a heading with separate lines following for "Net Position Restricted for Pensions" and "Net Position Restricted for OPEB (or Postemployment Benefits Other than Pensions)" [GASB Cod. Secs. Pe5.119, Po50.121].

Statement of Changes in Fiduciary Net Position. A pension plan should prepare an operating statement that reports the net increase or decrease in fiduciary net position from the beginning of the year until the end of the year. The Statement of Changes in Fiduciary Net Position should be prepared on the same basis of accounting used to prepare the pension plan's Statement of Fiduciary Net Position.

The two financial statements are interrelated (in a manner like an income statement and a balance sheet) in that:

- The net increase as reported in the Statement of Changes in Fiduciary Net Position, when added to
- The beginning balance of fiduciary net position in the Statement of Fiduciary Net Position, is equal to
- The net plan assets as reported at the end of the year in the Statement of Fiduciary Net Position.

The components of the inflows and outflows are as follows [GASB Cod. Secs. Pe5.120–.125]:

Statement of Changes in Fiduciary Net Position Elements	Transactions that may be Included in Each Element
Additions	• Contributions from employers, • Contributions from nonemployer contributing entities (e.g., state government contributions to a local government pension plan), • Contributions from plan members, including those transmitted by the employers, and • Net investment earnings as described below.

Statement of Changes in Fiduciary Net Position Elements	Transactions that may be Included in Each Element
Investment Earnings	• Investment earnings includes: — Changes in the fair value of investments, — Interest, — Dividends, and — Other income that is displayed separately or aggregated if immaterial. • The net increase (decrease) in the fair value of investments should include realized gains and losses on investments that were both bought and sold during the period. • Realized and unrealized gains and losses should not be separately displayed in the financial statements. Realized gains and losses, computed as the difference between the proceeds of sale and the original cost of the investments sold, *may be disclosed in notes to the basic financial statements*. The disclosure also should state that the calculation of realized gains and losses is independent of the calculation of the net change in the fair value of pension plan investments and the realized gains and losses on investments that had been held in more than one reporting period and sold in the current period were included as a change in the fair value reported in the prior period(s) and the current period. Interest income is reported at the stated rate without including amortized premiums and discounts.
Investment Costs	Includes the following *if they are separable from investment earnings and administrative costs*: • Investment management fees, • Custodial fees, and • All other significant investment-related costs.
Net Investment Earnings	The net of investment earnings and investment costs.
Deductions	At a minimum: • Benefit payments to plan members (including refunds of plan member contributions) and • Total administrative expense. Some plans may disaggregate benefit payments to retirees and survivors. If matching amounts are refunded along with accumulated interest, the refund caption may state this. Disability payments and claims may also be paid out of a defined benefit plan.
Net increase (or decrease) in Fiduciary Net Position	Additions – Deductions = Net Increase (Decrease) in Fiduciary Net Position

Various Issues Regarding Additions and Deductions. Two issues may affect additions and deductions due to recent clarified guidance from the GASB In GASB Cod. Sec. Pe5.711-1 , a PERS administers multiple defined benefit plans for state employees. The plans remit money to an investment pool for operating expenses of the pool. Also, movements of member account asset balances occur between plans when members change employment from one state department or agency to another and, therefore, between plans. In the plan's Statement of Changes in Fiduciary Net Position, all changes should be reported as either additions or deductions. The changes are not reported as *transfers* as transfers are internal to an entity.

From the standpoint of GASB Cod. Sec. Pe5, each defined benefit plan is effectively a separate entity. Thus, with the exceptions discussed in the next paragraph, for purposes of financial reporting, movements between plans are external transactions rather than transfers. The investment pool expense is an investment expense, and the movement of member account asset balances may be reported as separate line items within the deductions and additions sections of each plan.

PRACTICE POINT: GASB Cod. Sec. S20.112 clarifies transfers of capital or financial assets between a government employer or nonemployer contributing entity and a defined benefit pension or OPEB plan within the same reporting entity. Any difference between the amount paid by the plan, excluding amounts that may be refundable, is reported by the plan as an employer contribution or a nonemployer contributing entity contribution in accordance with GASB Cod. Sec. Pe5 or Po50, as applicable, in the stand-alone statements of the pension or OPEB plan and in the financial statements of the reporting entity.

Employer Paid Member Contributions. Commonly, payments are made by employers to satisfy contribution requirements identified by the plan terms as plan member contribution requirements (EPMCs). For GASB Cod. Sec.Pe5 or Po50 purposes, those amounts should remain as plan member contributions. However, for the employer and employer reporting, such reporting of EPMCs may be different.

Unrealized Gains and Losses. Unrealized gains and losses must be recorded as part of investment income because fair value is the basis for measuring investments held by the pension plan. When debt securities are held by the pension plan, any related discount or premium should not be amortized as part of investment income, and interest income should be based on the stated interest rate. If the plan has a net investment loss for the year, the caption in the statement of changes in plan net position might be labeled "net investment (loss) earnings." Some plans segregate the unrealized portion of investment income (loss) from the realized portion for analysis and trend information.

The example of a Statement of Changes in Plan Net Position is shown in Exhibit 22-2. As a reminder, the Statement also includes OPEB and defined contribution information as it is for a PERS.

EXHIBIT 22-2
STATE OF SILVER PUBLIC EMPLOYEES' RETIREMENT SYSTEM
STATEMENT OF CHANGES IN FIDUCIARY NET POSITION
FOR THE FISCAL YEAR ENDED JUNE 30, 20Y0
(Amounts in thousands)

	Base Plan	Firefighters Retirement	Judges Retirement	Retiree Health Benefits	20XX Total
Additions					
Contributions from members	$237,033	$4	$630	$-	$237,667
Contributions from employers	356,367	7,453	3,947	21,900	389,667
Total contributions	593,400	7,457	4,577	21,900	627,334
Investment earnings:					
Net appreciation in fair value	1,411,349	34,527	7,613	54,697	1,508,186
Interest, dividends and other	330,011	8,074	1,781	-	339,866
Less: investment costs	(45,467)	(1,112)	(240)	(190)	(47,009)
Net Investment Earnings	1,695,893	41,489	9,155	54,507	1,801,043
Other – net	29	-	5	2	37
Total Additions	2,289,322	48,946	13,736	76,409	2,428,414
Deductions					
Benefits and refunds	865,272	19,294	6,173	18,166	908,905
Administrative expenses	8,810	43	74	104	9,031
Total Deductions	874,082	19,337	6,247	18,270	917,936
Increase/(Decrease) in Net Position	1,415,240	29,609	7,489	58,139	1,510,478
Beginning of Year	13,920,706	342,619	74,806	413,831	14,751,961
Net Position Restricted for Pensions and Postemployment Benefits Other Than Pensions – End of Year	$15,335,946	$372,228	$82,295	$471,970	$16,262,439

Notes to the Basic Financial Statements

The following should be disclosed by all defined benefit pension plans as applicable [GASB Cod. Sec. Pe5.126]:

Plan Description. The basic elements of the plan are required to be disclosed as follows:

- Type of pension plan (single-employer, agent multiple-employer, or cost-sharing multiple-employer),
- Number of governmental employers participating in the plan and other entities contributing to the plan,
- Information regarding the Board's composition, including the number of trustees by source of selection and the types of constituencies or credentials applicable to the selection,

- Type of governmental employees covered by the plan and their plan status (such as active members, retirees and beneficiaries receiving benefits, and terminated employees not yet receiving benefits, who some plans term "inactives") (when the plan is closed to new entrants, that fact should be disclosed),
- Description of plan provisions such as types of benefits provided and policies concerning cost-of-living adjustments (automatic or discretionary),
- Authority under which benefits are provided or may be amended, and
- Descriptions of contribution requirements, including the authority under which contribution requirements of employers, nonemployer contributing entities, if any, and plan members are established or may be amended and the contribution rates (in dollars or as a percentage of covered payroll) of those entities for the reporting period. If the pension plan or the entity that administers the pension plan has the authority to establish or amend contribution requirements, disclose the basis for determining contributions (e.g., statute, contract, actuarial basis, or some other manner).

Summary of Significant Accounting Policies—Pension Plan Investments. Required disclosures regarding the investments of the plan include:

- The investment policies of the plan, including the following:
  — Procedures and authority for establishing and amending investment policy decisions,
  — The policies pertaining to asset allocation,
  — A description of any significant investment policy changes during the reporting period,
  — A brief description of how the fair value of investments is determined, including the methods and significant assumptions used to estimate the fair value of investments if that fair value is based on other than quoted market prices,
  — Identification of investments (other than those issued or explicitly guaranteed by the U.S. government) in any one organization that represent 5% or more of the pension plan's fiduciary net position (concentrations), and
  — The annual money-weighted rate of return on pension plan investments.

OBSERVATION: The money-weighted return on investments is the internal rate of return on pension plan investments, net of pension plan investment expense, adjusted for the changing amounts invested. Pension plan investment expense should be measured on the accrual basis of accounting. Inputs to the internal rate of return calculation should be determined at least monthly. The use of more frequently determined inputs is encouraged.

PRACTICE ALERT: The financial markets are under tremendous stress due to inflation and global uncertainty. Investment valuations may be impacted for transactions that are no longer orderly due to a significant decline in market activity, potentially adjusting the long-term estimated rate of return for defined benefit plans.

> **PRACTICE POINT:** The applicable investment disclosures required by GAAP are also required, if not already included in the notes to the basic financial statements. For further information, see Chapter 9.

Receivables. Policies and information on receivables to be disclosed will consist of any long-term contracts for contributions to the pension plan between (1) an employer or nonemployer contributing entity and (2) the pension plan, and the balances outstanding on any such long-term contracts at the end of the pension plan's reporting period.

Allocated Insurance Contracts That Are Omitted from Plan Net Position. The notes to the basic financial statements should include the amount reported in benefit payments in the current period that is attributable to the purchase of allocated insurance contracts, a brief description of the pensions for which allocated insurance contracts were purchased in the current period, and the fact that the obligation for the payment of benefits covered by allocated insurance contracts has been transferred to one or more insurance companies. This information is only inserted if allocated insurance contracts are in use during the year or at year-end.

Reserves. Required disclosures of reserves include (as applicable):

- A description of the policy related to the reserve(s),
- Authority under which pension plan funding sources are established and may be amended,
- The policy and conditions under which the reserves may be used, and
- Balances reported as legally required reserves at the reporting dates, their purposes, and whether they are fully funded. (Balances reported as "designations" also may be utilized by the plan's administrator, but they should not be reported as reserves.)

> **OBSERVATION:** Reserve accounts have many distinct aspects They are not required by GAAP, but they are used by management to segment operations. The largest reserves tend to be the summation of amounts contributed by member employees and those funded by amounts contributed by member employers. There may be contribution credit reserves, where any excess contributions are reserved for periods when member employers cannot fully fund or decide not to fully fund required contributions. There may be other reserves to fund benefits, including cost of living adjustments. Other reserves may be for contingencies, differentials between market value and historical cost of investments and other items. These reserves should be approved by the plan's governing board or in statute and they should reconcile to the plan's net position. In practice, there may be some assets that are not a part of an actuarial valuation, meaning that they are not a part of the actuarially calculated value of assets to be used to pay benefits due to some governing board's decision.

However, those "non-valuation" assets will become a part of those assets to pay benefits. A statute or trust agreement as well as market value smoothing patterns may cause some instances where the market value of the entirety of assets does not equate to those in reserves to pay plan benefits.

Deferred Retirement Option Programs (DROPs). These programs are prevalent. DROPs are programs that permit a plan member to elect a calculation of benefit payments based on service credits and salary, as applicable, as of the DROP entry date. The plan member continues to provide service to the employer and is paid for that service by the employer after the DROP entry date, however, the pensions that would have been paid to the plan member (if the plan member had retired and not entered the DROP) are credited to an individual member account within the defined benefit pension plan until the end of the DROP period. If a DROP is used as a part of the plan, then the notes to the basic financial statements should include a description of the DROP terms and conditions and the balance of the amounts held by the pension plan pursuant to the DROP.

Disclosures Specific to Single-Employer and Cost-Sharing Multiple-Employer Plans (but not Agent Multiple-Employer Plans)

In addition to the above, the following items are added to the notes to the basic financial statements for single-employer pension plans and cost-sharing multiple-employer pension plans, but not agent multiple-employer plans [GASB Cod. Sec. Pe5.127]:

- The components of the liability of the employers and nonemployer contributing entities to plan members for benefits provided through the pension plan, including the total pension liability, the pension plan's fiduciary net position and the pension plan's fiduciary net position as a percentage of the total pension liability (formerly known as the "funded ratio").

- Significant assumptions and other inputs used to measure the total pension liability, including assumptions about inflation, salary changes, and ad-hoc postemployment benefit changes (including ad-hoc COLAs).

- Regarding mortality assumptions, the source of the assumptions (e.g., the published tables on which the assumption is based or that the assumptions are based on a study of the experience of the covered group) should be disclosed.

- The dates of experience studies on which significant assumptions are based also should be disclosed. If different rates are assumed for different periods, information should be disclosed about what rates are applied to the different periods of the measurement.

- Discount rate information, including:

    — The discount rate applied in the measurement of the total pension liability and the change in the discount rate since the pension plan's prior fiscal year-end, if any,

- Assumptions made about projected cash flows into and out of the pension plan, such as contributions from employers, nonemployer contributing entities, and plan members,
- The long-term expected rate of return on pension plan investments and a description of how it was determined, including significant methods and assumptions used for that purpose,
- If the discount rate incorporates a municipal bond rate, the municipal bond rate used and the source of that rate,
- The periods of projected benefit payments to which the long-term expected rate of return and, if used, the municipal bond rate applied to determine the discount rate,
- The assumed asset allocation of the pension plan's portfolio, the long-term expected real rate of return for each major asset class, and whether the expected rates of return are presented as arithmetic or geometric means, if not otherwise disclosed,
- Sensitivity measures of the net pension liability calculated using a discount rate that is 1-percentage-point higher than that required and a discount rate that is 1-percentage-point lower than that required by GASB Cod. Sec. Pe5, and
- The date of the actuarial valuation on which the total pension liability is based and, if applicable, the fact that update procedures were used to roll forward the total pension liability to the pension plan's fiscal year-end.

Required Supplementary Information (RSI)

OBSERVATION: GASB Cod. Sec. Pe5.fn. 8, emphasizes that RSI should include all information whether the basic financial statements are presented in a stand-alone report or solely in the financial report of another government as a pension trust fund. No duplication is necessary for a government that presents similar information in accordance with GASB Cod. Sec. P20 (see Chapter 13).

RSI for Single-Employer and Cost-Sharing Multiple-Employer Plans. The RSI for plans extends to 10 years of information. The first two schedules discussed below can be combined if practical. The schedules should be as of a fiscal year-end and, for cost-sharing plans, the information disclosed should be for the entire plan.

The RSI should include the following 10-year schedules [GASB Cod. Sec. Pe5.128]:

- A Schedule of Changes in the Net Pension Liability, with:
  - Annual beginning and ending balances of the total pension liability,
  - The pension plan's fiduciary net position, and
  - The net pension liability.

These amounts are then shown with the effects on those items during the year for:

- Service costs,
- Interest on the total pension liability,
- Changes of benefit terms,
- Differences between expected and actual experience regarding economic or demographic factors in the measurement of the total pension liability,
- Changes of assumptions about future economic or demographic factors or of other inputs, and
- Contributions from all sources, delineated by source (including from nonemployer contributing entities, pension plan net investment income, benefit payments, including refunds of plan member contributions, pension plan administrative expense, and, finally, other changes, separately identified if individually significant).

If possible, the above schedule can be combined with a similar 10-year schedule showing the total pension liability, the pension plan's fiduciary net position, the net pension liability, the pension plan's fiduciary net position as a percentage of the total pension liability, and, finally, the covered payroll and the net pension liability as a percentage of covered payroll.

Covered payroll is defined to be the portion of compensation paid to active employees on which contributions to a pension plan are based. The measure should also be used by employers.

If an Actuarially Determined Contribution is Calculated. The second schedule is a 10-year schedule presenting information *only if an actuarially determined contribution* is calculated for employers or nonemployer contributing entities. The schedule should identify whether the information relates to the employers, or to the nonemployer contributing entities, or both. The schedule should include:

- The actuarially determined contributions of employers or nonemployer contributing entities. These may include long-term receivables recognized for contractually deferred contributions with separate payment schedules, and cash receipts or long-term receivables for amounts assessed to an individual employer upon joining a multiple-employer pension plan or for increases in the total pension liability for changes of benefit terms specific to an employer in a multiple-employer pension plan.
- For cost-sharing pension plans, the contractually required contribution of employers or nonemployer contributing entities would be included.
- The value of contributions recognized during the fiscal year by the pension plan in relation to the actuarially determined contribution should also be disclosed. For purposes of this schedule, contributions should include only amounts recognized as additions to the pension plan's fiduciary net position resulting from cash contributions and from contributions recognized by the pension plan as current receivables.
- The difference between the actuarially determined contribution in and the value of contributions recognized by the pension plan in relation to the actuarially determined contribution is then calculated.

- Covered-employee payroll is then disclosed along with the amounts of contributions recognized by the pension plan in relation to the actuarially determined contribution as a percentage of covered payroll.

The final presentation is a 10-year schedule presenting for each fiscal year the annual money-weighted rate of return on pension plan investments.

> **PRACTICE POINT:** The 10-year schedule only presents information when an actuarially determined contribution is used. If a statutory rate is used (e.g., a percentage of taxation) for contributions to the pension plan, no comparison is made.

> **PRACTICE POINT:** The schedules should exclude amounts, if any, associated with payables to the pension plan that arose in a prior fiscal year and those associated with separately financed specific liabilities of the individual employer or nonemployer contributing entity, as applicable, to the pension plan.

RSI Only for Agent Multiple-Employer Plans. The only RSI for Agent Multiple-Employer Plans is a 10-year schedule presenting for each fiscal year the annual money-weighted rate of return on pension plan investments [GASB Cod. Sec. Pe5.129].

Notes to the RSI. The notes to the RSI should include significant methods and assumptions used in calculating the actuarially determined contributions, if any. In addition, for each of the schedules, information should be presented about factors that significantly affect trends in the amounts reported (e.g., changes of benefit terms, changes in the size or composition of the population covered by the benefit terms, or the use of different assumptions). (The amounts presented for prior years should not be restated for the effects of changes—for example, changes of benefit terms or changes of assumptions—that occurred after the end of the fiscal year for which the information is reported.) [GASB Cod. Sec. Pe5.130].

> **PRACTICE POINT:** Investment-related factors that significantly affect trends in the amounts reported should be limited to those factors over which the pension plan or participating governments have influence (e.g., changes in investment policies). Information about external, economic factors (e.g., changes in market prices) should not be presented.

The example of a Schedule of Changes in the Employers' Net Pension Liability is presented in Exhibit 22-3. Exhibit 22-4 is a Schedule of Employer Contributions. Exhibit 22-5 is a Schedule of Investment Returns using a money-weighted rate of return. **Note: The amounts in the following exhibits are not meant to agree to those contained in Exhibits 22-1 and 22-2 as they are examples for content and formatting purposes.**

EXHIBIT 22-3
SCHEDULE OF CHANGES IN THE EMPLOYERS' NET PENSION LIABILITY AND RELATED RATIOS

Last 10 fiscal years (Amounts in Thousands) (only 2 years shown)

	20X8	20X7
Total Pension Liability		
Service cost	$75,864	$74,276
Interest	216,515	205,038
Changes in benefit terms	—	—
Differences between actual and expected experience	(37,539)	(15,211)
Changes in assumptions	—	—
Benefit payments, including refunds of member contributions	(119,434)	(112,603)
Net Change in Pension Liability	135,406	151,500
Total Pension Liability—Beginning	48,868,199	48,716,699
Total Pension Liability—Ending - (a)	**$49,003,605**	**$48,868,199**
Plan Fiduciary Net Position		
Contributions—employer	$1,015,397	$1,024,426
Contributions—member	690,355	886,525
Net investment income	4,702,603	724,563
Benefit payments, refunds	(3,707,349)	(3,885,835)
Administrative expense	(28,669)	(48,527)
Other	(15,217)	6,691
Net change in plan fiduciary net position	**2,657,120**	**(1,292,157)**
Plan fiduciary net position—Beginning	37,222,014	38,514,171
Plan fiduciary net position—Ending (b)	**$39,879,134**	**$37,222,014**
Employers' Net Pension Liability (a-b)	**$9,124,471**	**$11,646,185**
Plan's fiduciary net position as a Percentage of the Total Pension Liability	81.38%	76.17%
Covered Payroll	$4,492,930	$4,364,240
Employers' Net Pension Liability as a Percentage of Covered Payroll	203.09%	266.85%

The notes to the schedule explain any differences and changes from previous years' estimates.

EXHIBIT 22-4
SCHEDULE OF EMPLOYER CONTRIBUTIONS

Last 10 fiscal years (Dollar Amounts in Thousands) (only 2 years shown)

	20X8	20X7
Actuarially Determined Contributions	$1,705,752	$1,910,951
Contributions in relation to the Actuarially Determined Contribution	1,705,752	1,910,951
Contribution Deficiency (Excess)	$—	$—
Covered Payroll	$4,492,930	$4,364,240
Contributions as a Percentage of covered payroll	37.97%	43.79%

EXHIBIT 22-5
SCHEDULE OF INVESTMENT RETURNS

Last 10 fiscal years (only 2 years shown)

	20X8	20X7
Annual Money-Weighted Rate of Return, Net of Investment Expense	8.19%	11.23%

PRACTICE ALERT: Errors and restatements do occur in RSI. GASB Statement No. 100 (*Accounting Changes and Error Corrections*), contains guidance on reporting accounting changes and error corrections not only in RSI, but also in supplementary information (SI). Such changes are not fully considered in current GAAP. GASB-100 requires consistency between what is presented in the basic financial statements and what is presented in applicable RSI and SI. The 10-year RSI schedules above do not require restatements for *accounting changes*. The PERS' MD&A will also not have to be changed for accounting changes. However, the inconsistency should be explained and the notes relating to the accounting change should be referenced.

In addition, the notes to the required supplementary information are included for the year ended (in this case December 31, 20X8). The notes would include any changes between years that may affect comparability, including, at a minimum, descriptions of changes in benefit terms, assumptions, and methods and assumptions used in calculating actuarially determined contributions.

Additional Items in Postemployment Benefit Plan ACFRs

ACFRs are frequently released for separately issued defined benefit postemployment benefit plans, although they are not required by GAAP. Should a plan prepare an ACFR, the components of the document are like those of general-purpose governments. They include the following:

- Introductory section (letter of transmittal and various other introductory items).
- Financial section (report of the independent auditor, management's discussion and analysis, basic financial statements, and notes to basic financial statements).
- Required supplementary information (other than management's discussion and analysis).
- Supplementary information (schedules of administrative, investment, and consultant's expenses).
- An investment section detailing the plan's investments at fair value, investment return, investment allocation and other items.

PRACTICE POINT: The investment section amounts need to reconcile to the investments on the Statement of Fiduciary Net Position because both are presented at fair value as of fiscal year-end.

- An actuarial section presenting the actuarial valuation of the plan with amounts that apportioned to members, assumptions, and other items, including an actuary's certification letter.
- The statistical section.

ACFR preparation for defined benefit plans is important as the information contained in them may help management make better decisions. An ACFR for a plan may inform users of the financial statements even more than a general-purpose government's ACFR. However, care must be taken that the information contained within a defined benefit plan ACFR is timely and succinct because a sizable portion of the information may be needed to produce a timely ACFR in a member general purpose government's ACFR.

OTHER ASPECTS OF DEFINED BENEFIT PENSION PLANS

Separately Financed Liabilities to the Plan

Many plans are subject to state laws and regulations that allow for new employers to join the plan and, in some cases, leave the plan. In most cases, leaving a plan is not economically feasible as most plans are subject to laws and regulations that require employers who want to leave a plan, to "buy out" at the risk-free rate of return, thereby inflating any liability.

If an employer joins a plan, a liability is established at the employer based on the plan provisions for the existing employees that are subject to those conditions. Assets are usually required to be contributed to fund the liability either immediately or through a payment plan. If a payment plan is established, they are excluded from the RSI schedule of actuarially determined contributions to the pension plan as they are separate payment schedules from normal contributions [GASB Cod. Sec. Pe5.128].

The resulting contributions to the plan to finance such separately financed specific liabilities during the measurement period are recognized as follows:

- For cost-sharing employer, the amount of the employer's proportionate share of the total of such contributions (excluding nonemployer contributions) reduces the employer's pension expense.
- For a governmental nonemployer contributing entity in a special funding situation (e.g., a state contributing to a teacher's retirement plan on behalf of school districts), the amount of the governmental nonemployer contributing entity's proportionate share would also have its pension expense reduced [GASB Cod. Secs. P20.156, .195, .207].

The Actuarial Valuation Process

The timing of the actuarial valuations for nearly every plan was established upon implementation of GASB Cod. Sec. Pe5. Any change in the valuation date would trigger a remeasurement and a beginning balance restatement for the employer(s)/sponsor(s) of the plan.

GAAP requires that the actuarial valuation be performed either as of the pension plan's most recent fiscal year-end or the use of an update to "roll forward" to the most recent fiscal year-end from an actuarial valuation no more than 24 months earlier than the pension plan's most recent fiscal year-end.

Example	Date Requirements
Pension Plan's most recent fiscal year-end	December 31, 2024
Actuarial Valuation Date can be as of	December 31, 2024 *or*
The Actuarial Valuation Date can be between	January 1, 2022, and December 31, 2024, with Roll-forward procedures in between.

Note that the employers' fiscal year-end is not considered. If update procedures are used and *significant* changes occur between the actuarial valuation date and the pension plan's fiscal year-end, professional judgment should be used to determine the extent of procedures needed to roll forward the measurement from the actuarial valuation to the pension plan's fiscal year-end, and consideration should be given to whether a new actuarial valuation is needed. Significant changes could include the effects of changes in the discount rate resulting from changes in the pension plan's fiduciary net position or from changes in the municipal bond rate [GASB Cod. Sec. Pe5.133].

The GASB also left the establishment of assumptions that are used in developing the total pension liability up to the plan in consultation with the actuary. The selection of all assumptions used in determining the total pension liability should be made in conformity with Actuarial Standards of Practice issued by the Actuarial Standards Board. However, the plan and all member employer(s) in the plan should use the same assumptions or else the valuation would not be relevant [GASB Cod. Sec. Pe5.134].

PRACTICE POINT: GAAP requires the selection of assumptions used in determining the total pension liability to be in conformity with the provisions in GAAP for financial reporting purposes. A *deviation*, as the term is used in Actuarial Standards of Practice issued by the Actuarial Standards Board, from the guidance in Actuarial Standards of Practice should not be considered in conformity with GAAP. Management of the plan may utilize a deviation for projection purposes, but the deviation must be discarded for external financial reporting.

Benefits are projected, including all benefits measured in accordance with the benefit terms of the plan and all legal or contractual agreements that are in place as of the pension plan's fiscal year-end (not the employers'). Projected benefit payments should include the effects of automatic postemployment benefit changes (service credits, for example), including automatic cost of living adjustments (COLAs).

If benefits have adjustments that are made more on an ad-hoc basis, including benefit changes or COLAs, they are also included to the extent that they are "substantially automatic." GASB Cod. Sec. Pe5.fn10 explains that "substantially automatic" is somewhat up to professional judgment, but relevant considerations may include the historical pattern of granting the changes, the consistency in the amounts of the changes or in the amounts of the changes relative to a defined cost-of-living or inflation index, and whether there is evidence to conclude that changes might not continue to be granted in the future despite what might otherwise be a pattern that would indicate such changes are substantively automatic.

Benefit changes should be projected, including projected salary changes (in circumstances in which the pension formula incorporates future compensation levels), and projected service credits (both in determining a plan member's probable eligibility for benefits and in the projection of benefit payments in circumstances in which the pension formula incorporates years of service). Excluded from the calculation would be any benefits to be paid from allocated insurance contracts [GASB Cod. Sec. Pe5.135].

As previously stated, the discount rate to be used is derived through a cash flow model. It is a single rate that initially uses the long-term expected rate of return on pension plan investments that are expected to be used to finance the payment of benefits, to the extent that the pension plan's fiduciary net position is projected to be sufficient to make projected benefit payments and pension plan assets are expected to be invested using a strategy to achieve that return. This rate is then matched to a yield or an index rate for 20-year, tax-exempt general obligation municipal bonds with an average rating of AA/Aa or higher (or equivalent quality on another rating scale), to the extent that the conditions are such that the plan cannot finance its benefits through the pension plan's fiduciary net position. The point of "crossover," therefore, becomes important because after that point, an AA/Aa index is used [GASB Cod. Secs. Pe5.136 and .140].

PRACTICE POINT: The discount rate aspect was a large point of discussion in the development of current GAAP. Many users of governmental financial statements desired a "risk-free" rate of return as a discount rate like that for for-profit defined benefit plans. However, use of a "risk-free" rate of return would have two effects:

1. The liability would have been far larger than what is being presented today because it would assume that all benefits would be due and payable immediately to the extent that no funds would be available to pay the liability and
2. The discount rate would not have assumed the long-term aspect of governmental operations and the long-term aspect of the employer-employee relationship to fund the liability.

The issue continues to be deliberated. Many stakeholders continue to advocate to require pension systems to file annual reports with the United States Treasury using an assumed rate of return adjusted to a United States Treasury rate—a rate that is far different than most discount rates in use. Many state and local government groups have voiced opposition to this plan as it has become politicized. A compromise may be to voluntarily disclose the differences in the management's discussion and analysis as the differences in the liability is a currently known fact in accordance with GASB Cod. Sec. 2200.109(h).

OBSERVATION: Due to the provisions of certain laws, many plans may never hit a "crossover point," because there are strong laws that force employers to fund contributions or else the plan may seize tax revenues or similar elements. If that is the case, a higher discount rate might be able to be used. Professional judgment should be used, but an indicator of sufficiency may include the most recent five-year contribution history of the employers and nonemployer contributing entities as a key indicator of future contributions from those sources and should reflect all other known events and conditions GASB Cod. Sec. Pe5.138. The GASB included this provision to smooth out any contribution "spikes" due to pension obligation bond proceeds funding current cash flows.

The discount rate should be calculated annually or with each valuation. The cash flows to be included in the calculation would not only include the employer's and the employee's contributions and benefit payments, but also any nonemployer contributions intended to finance benefits of current active and inactive plan members (status at the pension plan's fiscal year-end). Future cash inflows from all sources are only used to the extent that they are projected to exceed service costs for those plan members. The application of the cash flows is then matched to service costs of plan members in the current period (as there is no ability to fund future costs if service costs exceed cash inflows). Then, past service costs are funded with any remaining balance unless the effective pension plan terms related to contributions indicate that a different relationship between contributions to the pension plan from nonemployer contributing entities and service costs should be applied. Contributions from members should be applied to service costs before contributions from employers and nonemployer contributing entities [GASB Cod. Sec. Pe5.137].

Finally, the GASB concluded that the entry age actuarial cost method should be used to attribute the actuarial present value of projected benefit payments of each plan member to periods. The attribution is made on an individual plan-member-by-plan-member basis. Each plan member's service costs should be level as a percentage of that member's projected pay. For purposes of this calculation, if a member does not have projected pay, the projected inflation rate should be used in place of the projected rate of change in salary. The beginning of the attribution period should be the first period in which the member's service accrues pensions under the benefit terms, notwithstanding vesting or other similar terms. The service costs of all pensions should be attributed through all assumed exit ages, through retirement. In pension plans in which the benefit terms include a DROP, the date of entry into the DROP is the plan member's retirement date (see previous discussion on DROPs) [GASB Cod. Sec. Pe5.142].

COMMUNICATION ISSUES FROM THE PLAN TO EMPLOYERS OR SPONSORS

Agent Multiple-Employer Plans. For agent multiple-employers, receiving the information from an agent multiple-employer plan to record in the basic financial statements, notes to the basic financial statements, and required supplementary information might be a challenge. The plans need to present each employer with a financial statement, the note disclosure, and required supplementary information discussed therein. If the plan has hundreds of employers and performs allocations of investment revenues and administrative expenses to the various employers, the timely presentation of this information is a challenge.

The AICPA includes a "best practice" requiring the information to be transmitted from the plans to the employers to be audited separately from the audit of the plan's financial statements. A separate internal controls engagement may also ensue in accordance with AT-C Section 320 (*Reporting on an Examination of Controls at a Service Organization Relevant to User Entities' Internal Control Over Financial Reporting*).

Controls may be required to be tested based on management's assertion that internal controls are suitably designed and have been operating effectively for an entire year under audit (also known as a Type 2 report).

Single-Employer Plans. For single-employer plans, testing on census data and the information transfer is required. Therefore, in both cases, time should be increased to prepare this data, unless it can be prepared "off-cycle" to the date of the basic financial statements.

Cost-Sharing Multiple-Employer Plans. The AICPA is also concerned with the ability to audit the transfer of information from a cost-sharing multiple-employer plan to the employers in the plan. The state and local government expert panel has released a set of white papers detailing schedules that the plan should produce as "best practices." Additionally, a set of auditing interpretations have been released including these schedules and additional guidance for evidence gathering. The schedules would be separately audited. The AICPA provides an example of a *"Schedule of Employer Allocations"* detailed by employer of the allocation percentages based on contributions, including when a nonemployer funds a portion of the liability in a special funding situation. The schedule contained in the AICPA interpretation is as follows:

	20X7 Contributions	Allocation
Employer 1	$2,143,842	36.3748%
Employer 2	268,425	4.5544%
Employer 3	322,142	5.4658%
Employer 4	483,255	8.1994%
Employer 5	633,125	10.7423%
Employer 6	144,288	2.4481%
Employer 7	95,365	1.6181%
Employer 8	94,238	1.5989%
Employer 9	795,365	13.4950%
Employer 10	267,468	4.5382%
Employer 11	403,527	6.8467%
Employer 12	165,886	2.8146%
Employer 13	68,454	1.1615%
Employer 14	6,240	0.1059%
Employer 15	2,144	0.0364%
Total	**$5,893,764**	**100.00%**

PRACTICE POINT: As previously introduced, the classification of employer-paid member contributions (EPMCs) is a prominent issue. Commonly, payments are made by employers to satisfy contribution requirements that are identified by the plan terms as plan member contribution requirements. For the plan's purposes, those amounts should remain as plan member contributions. However, for the employer, the reporting may be different. Therefore, the allocation percentages above need to address employer-paid member contributions, depending upon the treatment of such contributions at the employer.

A *"Schedule of Pension Amounts by Employer"* contains two alternative presentations. Alternative 1 lists all employers in the plan and the allocation for every accounting element that needs to be transferred to the employers, based on the allocations in the previous schedule. For large cost-sharing multiple-employer plans with more than a handful of employers, Alternative 1 may yield a very onerous schedule. A second alternative contains just the aggregated amounts for each accounting element, including:

- Net pension liability,
- Deferred Outflows of Resources, including, but not limited to:
  — Differences between Expected and Actual Experience,
  — Net Difference between Projected and Actual Investment Earnings on Pension Plan Investments,
  — Changes of Assumptions,

- Changes in Proportion and Differences between Employer Contributions and Proportionate Share of Contributions, and
- Total Deferred Outflows of Resources.
* Deferred Inflows of Resources, including, but not limited to:
  - Differences between Expected and Actual Experience,
  - Changes of Assumptions,
  - Changes in Proportion and Differences between Employer Contributions and Proportionate Share of Contributions, and
  - Total Deferred Inflows of Resources.
* Proportionate Share of Plan Pension Expense,
* Net Amortization of Deferred Amounts from Changes in Proportion and Differences between Employer Contributions and Proportionate Share of Contributions, and
* Total Employer Pension Expense.

It is then up to the employer to use the information in the allocation schedule and multiply the allocation against the aggregated amounts for each element. Upon receipt of each of the schedules, the employers can then rely on this information to be placed in their basic financial statements, notes to the basic financial statements, and required supplementary information because it will contain an audit opinion. Like agent multiple-employer plan information, time should be increased to prepare this data, unless it can be prepared "off-cycle" to the date of the basic financial statements.

PRACTICE POINT: Should EPMCs be present as described previously, the "Schedule of Pension Amounts by Employer" from a cost-sharing multiple-employer plan to its employers may change. Added information may be included, as applicable:

- A column to reflect pension expense related to specific liabilities of individual employers due to their joining the plan or leaving the plan, and
- Revisions to the column headings to be clear as to whether the pension expense includes or excludes the effect of employer-paid member contributions as follows:
  - "Proportionate Share of Pension Expense" is changed to "Proportionate Share of Allocable Pension Expense"; and
  - "Pension Expense" is changed to "Pension Expense Excluding That Attributable to Employer-Paid Member Contributions."

DEFERRED COMPENSATION PLANS AND DEFINED CONTRIBUTION PLANS PRESENTED AS STAND-ALONE STATEMENTS

Due to the provisions of GASB Statement No. 97 (*Certain Component Unit Criteria, and Accounting and Financial Reporting for Internal Revenue Code Section 457 De-*

ferred Compensation Plans—an Amendment of GASB Statements No. 14 and No. 84, and a Supersession of GASB Statement No. 32), and as clarified by GASB Cod. Sec. 1300.716-33 (GASBIG 2021-1, Q4.6), if the participant employees can choose investment options, the participant employees *have control* of the employee benefit plan. This is even the case when the employer or sponsor selects a set of investment options.

The employer or sponsor's process of selecting a set of investment options is not directing the use, exchange, or employment of the assets in a manner that provides benefits to the participant employees. The participant employees can change one asset for another and even borrow against those assets, directing the employer or sponsor to garnish future wages to repay the loan (along with other provisions). In these cases, many defined contribution plans and nearly all deferred compensation plans, regardless of type of plan, may not be reported in general-purpose government external financial reports.

For public employee retirement systems (PERS plans) (discussed further in this chapter), inconsistent presentation may result. Some Boards may want to present such plans, with a subset of PERS plans fully administering such assets and in control. For those PERS plans that want to present plans where they do not have control in accordance with GAAP, stand-alone reporting is an ideal situation. Presenting in a stand-alone report will not be a departure from GAAP.

In many cases, due to the provisions of GASB-84 and GASB-97, a state or local government may not be in control of these plans as the participants can choose investments, even from an investment slate determined by the employer(s). The only reporting at the state or local government may be the outflows to these arrangements from governmental and business-type activities.

In some cases, the state or local government (or the PERS plan) may desire reporting of these plans. As discussed, stand-alone reporting is acceptable.

As previously discussed, in a *defined contribution* plan, an account is established for the employee. The employer may or may not contribute to the account based on service or some other formula. Earnings then are held in the employee's account, net of fees.

- The members of the plan receive a pension dependent on the following:
- Contributions (or credits) to the member's account,
- The actual earnings on investments of those contributions (or credits),
- The effects of forfeitures of contributions or credits made for other plan members, and
- Plan administrative costs that are allocated to the member's account.

Other types of plans could also be administered, such as deferred compensation plans (in accordance with IRC Section 457 (see next section) or Section 403 as examples). If the financial report of a PERS or other government includes one or more plans, each plan applies these provisions as applicable [GASB Cod. Secs. Pe6.105–.106].

Notes to the Basic Financial Statements of Defined Contribution Plans

The notes to basic financial statements of a defined contribution pension plan should include all disclosures required by below, as applicable, when the financial statements are presented in a stand-alone pension plan financial report or solely in the financial report of another government (as a pension trust fund). If a defined contribution pension plan is included in the financial report of a government that applies the requirements for defined benefit plans, the government should present the information in a manner that avoids unnecessary duplication. The following should be included for defined contribution plans [GASB Cod. Sec. Pe6.107]:

- Identification of the pension plan as a defined contribution pension plan,
- Classes of plan members covered (e.g., general employees or public safety employees), the number of plan members, participating employers (if the pension plan is a multiple-employer pension plan), and, if any, nonemployer contributing entities, and
- The authority under which the pension plan is established or may be amended.

IRC SECTION 457(b) DEFERRED COMPENSATION PLANS

PRACTICE POINT: This subsection assumes the government or plan has implemented GASB Statement No. 97 (*Certain Component Unit Criteria, and Accounting and Financial Reporting for Internal Revenue Code Section 457 Deferred Compensation Plans—an Amendment of GASB Statements No. 14 and No. 84, and a Supersession of GASB Statement No. 32*) and desires to continue reporting such plans.

Internal Revenue Code (IRC) Section 457(b) Deferred Compensation Plans are employee benefit plans. In certain rare circumstances, they meet the definition of a pension plan. They are widely used by states and local governments as an additional benefit for employees that participate.

To be a pension plan, an IRC Section 457(b) plan must be an arrangement through which pensions are determined, assets dedicated for pensions are accumulated and managed, and benefits are paid as they come due [GASB Cod. Secs. Pe5.527, P23.509]. If the 457(b) plan meets this definition, then it is a pension plan for accounting and financial reporting purposes. It may or may not be held in trust. All previous elements as discussed for defined benefit plans would then apply, including the need for an actuarial valuation and a balance restatement to the date that the government implemented GASB Statement No. 68.

In most situations, 457(b) plans are merely other employee benefit plans. The assets included in such plans are *deferred compensation* [GASB Cod. Sec. D25.101].

The employer or sponsor would then apply the provisions of GASB Cod. Sec. 1300 specific to fiduciary activities, including reporting. All accounting and financial reporting elements relating to fiduciary activities would be used in the stand-alone financial statements of the 457(b) plan [GASB Cod. Sec. D25.102].

457(b) Plan Meets the Definition of a Pension Plan. In the rare circumstance that the 457(b) plan meets the definition of a pension plan and issues a stand-alone financial statement, the plan would provide financial statements like what is shown above for a PERS. The plan may be a defined benefit plan, in which case all actuarial information would be needed. If the plan is a defined contribution plan, more limited information may be needed [GASB Cod. Secs. D25.103–.104].

PRACTICE POINT: Other employee benefit plans may also be reported in a stand-alone fashion from PERS plans including the following plans:

- *Internal Revenue Code Section 403(b) plans.* These tax-deferred annuity plans (or mutual funds) are funded by salary reductions. They are usually found in public institutions of higher education and hospitals. However, some governments use them to receive lump-sum payments at retirement from defined benefit plans. The risk of having enough funds at retirement then shifts to the retiree. Elementary and secondary public and private school systems also often offer Internal Revenue Code (IRC) Section 403(b) plans to their employees. *Caution:* These plans are *not* required to be held in trust due to IRC provisions. However, the benefits are restricted to beneficiaries of the plan. Due to the restriction, the plan may be deemed an "equivalent arrangement." GAAP has no specific definition of the phrase "equivalent arrangement" however.

- *Cash Balance Plan*—A plan with hypothetical accounts maintained for participants. The employer credits participants' accounts with funds annually and promises earnings at a specified rate. However, the rate may be different from actual earnings. Therefore, the risk is on the employer, unless the employer changes the formula for posting earnings.

- *Retirement Savings Plan (IRC § 401(k) Plan)*—A plan only offered to certain tribal governments and rural cooperatives that established such plans prior to the 1986 Tax Act. Contributions are usually from employees on a pre-tax basis or can be post-income tax basis utilizing a Roth mechanism. Employers can match, but it is not required. Investment options are usually selected by the employer, but many 401(k) plans are self-directed. Trusts are required.

- *Target Benefit Plan*—A plan where employees make contributions on an actuarial basis knowing a certain date of retirement in the future. There are no guarantees of balance or return.

- *IRC § 401(h) Retiree Health Accounts*—Accounts established to help employees fund OPEB amounts. Contributions can be made by the employer or the employee or both. They can be fixed or a variable amount if they are below IRC limits that adjust annually. Investments in such accounts are usually target-date oriented based on the employee's expected retirement date. Benefits can only be drawn at retirement and only for qualifying medical expenses. Trusts are *not* required, and benefits are subordinated to other plans. In many situations, IRC Section 401(h) accounts are coupled with defined benefit pension or OPEB plans (see also OPEB subsection).

- *IRC § 420 Excess Pension Asset Accounts*—Accounts established to facilitate the qualified transfer of excess pension assets to retiree health accounts. Only one transfer annually is permitted, and the transfer is limited to the amount which is estimated to be the amount the employer maintaining the plan will pay for pension liabilities. In general, the fair value of the assets in the pension plan must be 125% of the sum of the funding target and the target normal cost in any year. The recipient accounts are IRC *§ 401(h) Retiree Health Accounts.* These accounts will sunset on December 31, 2025, unless extended by Congress and approved by the President.

PRACTICE POINT: Internal Revenue Code (IRC) Sections 401(h) and 420 accounts are used to pay current retiree health benefits which are obligations of a separate plan. Although the assets may be invested together with assets that are available to pay pension benefits, separate accounting must be maintained for all flows and balances. Stringent provisions are in place within the IRC regarding transfers of pension assets to fund Sections 401(h) and 420 accounts and ongoing contribution and benefit provisions. Tax advice should be sought from counsel as much of Sections 401(h) and 420 accounts are beyond the scope of this *Guide.*

PRACTICE ALERT: On December 29, 2022, the federal Consolidation Appropriations Act of 2023 was approved. Within the Act was the Setting Every Community Up for Retirement Enhancement Act (SECURE) 2.0. The original SECURE 1.0 Act was passed in 2019. Accounting and operational aspects in SECURE 2.0 that impact governments include, but are not limited to:

Change	Effective Date
Optional higher "catch up" contribution limits for older employees to 401(k), 403(b) and 457(b) plans if age 60 through 63 by the end of the year. The limits are the greater of $10,000 *or* an amount equal to 150% of the normal limit in 2024 ($11,250 in 2023). The $10,000 is indexed to inflation beginning after 2025.	Taxable years beginning after 2024.
Government employers may make matching contributions in the participant's names in 457(b), 401(a) or 403(b) plans equaling the amount the employee pays for student loans. The employee would certify to the employer that the loan amount was paid.	Plan years beginning after 2023.
Allows small financial incentives such as gift cards, to induce employees to participate in 401(k) and 403(b) plans.	Plan years beginning after December 29, 2022.

Change	Effective Date
Mandatory automatic enrollment to 401(k) plans for part-time workers if the employee completes one year of service at half time (deemed to be 1,000 hours) or three years with 500 hours. Employees subject to collective bargaining are ineligible.	Effective for plan years beginning after 2024. 403(b) plans are also required if they are *not* subject to the Employee Retirement and Income Security Act (ERISA).
Optional expansion of investment options in 403(b) plans beyond annuities.	Immediately effective upon passage.
Small account balances (over $1,000) of terminated participants may be rolled to an IRA if the participant does not elect otherwise. The IRA can then be transferred to a new employer's plan with a sixty-day notice.	Effective on December 29, 2023.
Disability payments from accounts of first responders who become disabled will be excluded from income tax.	Effective for plan years beginning after 2026.
Penalty free distributions from accounts if below age $59^{1}/_{2}$ if repaid and meet certain expenses such as personal or family emergencies, birth or adoption expenses, victim of domestic abuse, illness, residence in a disaster area, long-term care, distributions for public safety officers and other first responders.	Varying years from immediate through 2025.

POSTEMPLOYMENT BENEFIT PLANS OTHER THAN PENSION PLANS

Postemployment healthcare benefits include medical, dental, vision, and other health-related benefits (OPEB) provided to terminated or retired employees and their dependents and beneficiaries. Many of the elements of defined benefit pension plan accounting and financial reporting are also present in OPEB plans.

As an example, to have an irrevocable trust or equivalent arrangement in a defined benefit OPEB plan, the plan must have characteristics in which:

- Contributions from employers and nonemployer contributing entities and earnings on those contributions are irrevocable. Like defined benefit pension plans, but more prevalent than pension plans, EPMCs may be in place and if in place, they are classified as plan member contributions,

- OPEB plan assets must provide OPEB benefits to plan members in accordance with benefit terms. Refunds to an employer or nonemployer contributing entity of the non-vested portion of contributions that are forfeited by plan members in a defined contribution OPEB plan also satisfy this criterion, and, finally,

- OPEB plan assets are legally protected from the creditors of the employers, nonemployer contributing entities, the OPEB plan administrator, and plan members.

Like defined benefit pension plans, OPEB plans may be part of a PERS, and reports may be included in a stand-alone report, or in the case of single-employer OPEB plans, included as part of another government. All applicable GAAP for investments and reporting apply, just like defined benefit pension plans. Where OPEB plans diverge in practice include the following commonalities:

- Single-employer OPEB plans are very prevalent.
- Often, OPEB plans lack a trust or equivalent arrangement, affording the employer(s) flexibility in administration.
- OPEB plan provisions are much less defined than pension plan provisions. During economic downturns, legislative bodies will seek ways to restructure OPEB.
- OPEB liabilities are based on expected *claims* as a driver of costs in addition to service costs and interest.
- OPEB plans usually have little assets in comparison to pensions.

The plan may be insured. However, they are often misunderstood. To have an insured plan, benefits must be financed through an arrangement where premiums are paid to an insurance company while employees are in active service. The insurance company then *unconditionally* obligates itself to pay the OPEB of those employees as defined in the OPEB plan terms [GASB Cod. Secs. Po50.101–.104]. Contracting with an insurance provider to manage benefits does not signify an insured plan.

PRACTICE POINT: Many governments believe that if a third-party insurance entity is involved with their OPEB plan, they are unconditionally absolved from payment of OPEB benefits. This could not be further from reality. In most cases, third-party insurance entities merely manage or administer the claims process for the government and have no further obligation. In these situations, the government is uninsured or "self-insured." Therefore, an OPEB liability may be present.

OPEB may be provided in a defined benefit OPEB plan or a defined contribution plan with the same provisions of defined benefits or defined contributions as pensions. A defined benefit OPEB plan has "terms that specify the value of benefits to be provided at a future date or after a certain period. The amount specified usually is a function of one or more factors such as age, years of service, and compensation." A defined contribution plan is an OPEB plan that has "terms that specify how contributions to a plan member's account are to be determined, rather than the amount of benefit the member is to receive. The amounts received by a member will depend only on the amount contributed to the member's account, earnings on investments of those contributions, and forfeitures of contributions made for other members that may be allocated to the member's account."

Some OPEB plans have characteristics of both defined benefit OPEB plans and defined contributions plans. GASB Cod. Sec. Po50.107 defaults to a defined benefit OPEB plan unless all three of the following characteristics are met, which would be indicative of a defined contribution plan. A defined contribution plan has these characteristics:

- Provides an individual account for each plan member,
- Defines the contributions that an employer or nonemployer contributing entity is required to make (or credits that it is required to provide) to an active plan member's account for periods in which that member renders service, and
- Provides that the OPEB a plan member will receive will depend only on the contributions (or credits) to the plan member's account, actual earnings on investments of those contributions (or credits), and the effects of forfeitures of contributions (or credits) made for other plan members, as well as OPEB plan administrative costs that are allocated to the plan member's account.

Like pensions, the defined benefit OPEB standards proposed apply to single-employer, agent multiple-employer, and cost-sharing multiple-employer plans, which are defined as follows:

- *Single-employer plan*—A plan that covers the current and former employees, including beneficiaries, of only one employer (and component units in the employer's reporting entity that are part of the same plan).
- *Agent multiple-employer plan*—An aggregation of single-employer plans, with pooled administrative and investment functions. Separate accounts are maintained for each employer so that the employer's contributions provide benefits only for its employees. A separate actuarial valuation is performed for each individual employer's plan to determine the employer's period contribution rate and other information for the individual plan, based on the benefit formula selected by the employer and the individual plan's proportionate share of the pooled assets. The results of the individual valuations are aggregated at the administrative level.
- *Cost-sharing multiple-employer plan*—A single plan with pooling (cost-sharing) arrangements for the participating employers. All risks, rewards, and costs, including benefit costs, are shared, and are not attributed individually to the employers. A single actuarial valuation covers all plan members, and the same contribution rate(s) applies for each employer. In practice, there are few cost-sharing multiple-employer OPEB plans in comparison to the predominance of cost-sharing multiple-employer pension plans.

In some cases, assets are accumulated in trust and non-trust situations. The non-trust portion is typically a reserve for future rate increases. If the non-trust assets are held by the plan with a trust, then a trust is present as the trust is separate from the employer(s). If the assets are held by the employer(s), they are the employer's assets [GASB Cod. Secs. Po50.108–.111].

Administering Public Employee OPEB Systems

As discussed, a PERS may administer numerous defined benefit pension plans as well as OPEB plans. They may also serve as a pass-through to defined contribution and deferred compensation plans which would be reported as stand-alone statements.

Defined benefit OPEB plans (other than insured plans) are classified first according to the number of employers whose employees are provided with OPEB through the OPEB plan. Like pensions, a primary government and its component units are one employer. If a defined benefit OPEB plan is used to provide OPEB to the employees of only one employer, the OPEB plan should be classified for financial reporting purposes as a single-employer defined benefit OPEB plan (single-employer OPEB plan) as described above. If a defined benefit OPEB plan is used to provide OPEB to the employees of more than one employer, the OPEB plan should be classified for financial reporting purposes as a multiple-employer defined benefit OPEB plan.

If the financial statements of more than one defined OPEB are included in the PERS report, the standards must be applied separately to each plan. The financial statements for each plan should be presented separately in the combining financial statements of the PERS along with appropriate schedules and other required disclosures. Thus, the standards apply to the individual plans administered by the PERS, but the PERS itself must follow all applicable standards to prepare its financial statements. Specifically, the PERS would report as a special-purpose government engaged only in fiduciary activities.

To determine whether a PERS is administering a single OPEB plan or two or more OPEB plans (thus requiring separate reporting), the custody of the assets held must be analyzed to determine whether they are (1) available to pay benefits for all the members of the OPEB plans or (2) available to pay benefits only to certain plan members.

401(h) Account Management. Some PERS manage both pensions and OPEB plans. In many situations, a single contribution is paid from the employer(s) (and/or employees) to the plan. Assets should be allocated between the pension plan and the OPEB plan. This requires, in part, allocation of the employer's total contribution between the pension plan and the OPEB plan and separate reporting of each plan's fiduciary net position. GAAP does not specify how the allocations should be made because that depends on the specific circumstances, including the benefit structure and terms and the method(s) of financing the pension and postemployment healthcare benefits. Therefore, an accounting policy should be adopted and applied consistently from period to period [GASB Cod. Sec. Po50.701-18].

Separate reporting is required for pension and postemployment healthcare plan that meets the criteria of a trust and is administered by a plan [GASB Cod. Sec. Po50.701-2].

Number of OPEB Plans

Assets Available to All Plan Members. If assets held by the PERS are legally available to pay benefits for all the plan members, the OPEB plan is a single plan, and only a single set of financial statements needs to be prepared. GASB Cod. Sec. Po50 notes that an OPEB plan is a single employer plan even if the following circumstances exist:

- Legally or because of administrative policy, the OPEB plan must maintain separate accounts based on such factors as specified groups, specific employers, or benefits provided by the plan.
- Separate actuarial valuations are made for classes or groups of covered employees.

Assets Available Only to Certain Plan Members. If any portion of the assets held by the PERS can be paid legally only to certain classes of employees (e.g., public safety officers) or employees of certain employers (e.g., only to state government employees), more than one plan is being administered and separate financial statements must be prepared for each plan [GASB Cod. Sec. Po50.113].

The assets availability criterion must also be applied to a governmental employer's ACFR. Separate reporting is required in the governmental employer's (or sponsor's) ACFR when more than one OPEB plan is being presented in the ACFR.

OPEB Plan Financial Reporting

GAAP requires that the following financial statements be presented by a defined benefit OPEB plan, just like pension plans [GASB Cod. Sec. Po50.114]:

- Statement of Fiduciary Net Position, and
- Statement of Changes in Fiduciary Net Position.

Statement of Fiduciary Net Position for an OPEB Plan. The statement of fiduciary net position is prepared on an accrual basis and reports the plan's assets, liabilities, and net position. The statement should identify the major assets of the OPEB plan (e.g., cash, receivables, investments, and operating assets), and the receivables and investments categories should be further divided into their significant components. Reported liabilities should be subtracted from total assets and the difference reported as "net position held in trust for OPEB" [GASB Cod. Secs. Po50.115–.117].

Exhibits 22-1 and 22-2 include GASB Cod. Sec. Po50 compliant information.

Investments reported in the statement should be recorded on a trade-date basis, applying all the other applicable GAAP provisions regarding investments. Allocated insurance contracts are excluded from plan assets, like pension reporting, if the following are present [GASB Cod. Secs. Po50.118–.119]:

- The contract irrevocably transfers to the insurer the responsibility for providing the benefits,
- All required payments to acquire the contracts have been made, and

- The likelihood is remote that the employer, nonemployer contributing entities, or OPEB plan will be required to make additional payments to satisfy the benefit payments covered by the contract.

Statement of Changes in Fiduciary Net Position for an OPEB Plan. An OPEB plan should prepare an operating statement that reports the net increase or decrease in net plan position from the beginning of the year until the end of the year, like pension plans. The Statement of Changes in Plan Net Position should be prepared on the same basis of accounting used to prepare the OPEB plan's Statement of Fiduciary Net Position. This is the same as the financial reporting for other fiduciary activities discussed in previous chapters.

The Statement of Changes in Fiduciary Net Position should present separate categories for additions and deductions in fiduciary net position for the year. The additions section of the Statement of Changes in Fiduciary Net Position should include the following components:

- Contributions received from an employer(s),
- Contributions received from employees (including those received via the employer),
- Contributions received from those other than employer(s) and employees,
- Net investment income for the year (includes the net appreciation or depreciation of the fair value of the plan assets) and investment income and other increases not reported as net appreciation or depreciation (these two components of investment income may be separately reported or reported as a single amount), and
- Total investment expenses (including investment fees, custodial fees, and "all other significant investment-related costs") [GASB Cod. Secs. Po50.122–.124].

As above, payments to an insurance company for an allocated insurance contract that is excluded from OPEB plan assets, including purchases of annuities with amounts allocated from existing investments with the insurance company, should be included in amounts recognized as benefit payments. Dividends from an allocated insurance contract should be recognized as a reduction of benefit payments recognized in the period. Benefit payments should not include benefits paid by an insurance company in accordance with such a contract.

Deductions on the Statement of Changes in Plan Net Position should include OPEB payments to retirees and beneficiaries, and administrative expenses. These items should not be combined but separately presented in the statement. Administrative expenses, such as depreciation expense and operating expenses, should be measured using accrual accounting and reported as deductions from net position [GASB Cod. Secs. Po50.125–.127].

Notes to the Basic Financial Statements for a Defined Benefit OPEB Plan

If a defined benefit OPEB plan is included in the financial report of a government that also applies the requirements of GAAP for benefits provided through the

OPEB plan and similar information is required by the information below specifically for OPEB plans, the government *should not duplicate the disclosures*. Many of the aspects in this section are duplicative of the disclosures required for defined benefit pensions [GASB Cod. Sec. Po50.fn. 7].

The following should be disclosed in the notes, as applicable:

Plan Description. The basic information about the plan is required to be disclosed, including:

- The name of the OPEB plan, identification of the entity that administers the OPEB plan, and identification of the OPEB plan as a single-employer, agent, or cost-sharing OPEB plan.
- The number of participating employers (if the OPEB plan is an agent or cost-sharing OPEB plan) and the number of nonemployer contributing entities, if any.
- Information regarding the OPEB plan's board and its composition (e.g., the number of trustees by source of selection or the types of constituency or credentials applicable to selection).
- The number of plan members, separately identifying numbers of the following:
  — Inactive plan members currently receiving benefit payments,
  — Inactive plan members entitled to but not yet receiving benefit payments,
  — Active plan members, and
  — If the OPEB plan is closed to new entrants, that fact should be disclosed.
- The authority under which benefit terms are established or may be amended, the types of benefits provided through the OPEB plan, and the classes of plan members covered.
- If the OPEB plan or the entity that administers the OPEB plan has the authority to establish or amend benefit terms:
  — A brief description should be provided of the benefit terms, including the key elements of the OPEB formulas and the terms or policies, if any, with respect to automatic postemployment benefit changes, including automatic cost-of-living adjustments (automatic COLAs), and
  — Ad hoc postemployment benefit changes, including ad hoc cost-of-living adjustments (ad hoc COLAs), and the sharing of benefit-related costs with inactive plan members.
- A brief description of contribution requirements, including:
  — Identification of the authority under which contribution requirements of employers, nonemployer contributing entities, if any, and plan members are established or may be amended,
  — The contribution rates (in dollars or as a percentage of covered payroll) of the employer, nonemployer contributing entities, if any, and plan members for the reporting period, and

— Legal or contractual maximum contribution rates, if applicable. If the OPEB plan or the entity that administers the OPEB plan has the authority to establish or amend contribution requirements, disclose the basis for determining contributions (e.g., statute, contract, actuarial basis, or some other manner).

OPEB Plan Investments. The basic elements of investment disclosure for the OPEB plan include:

- Investment policies, including:
  — Procedures and authority for establishing and amending investment policy decisions,
  — Policies pertaining to asset allocation, and
  — Description of significant investment policy changes during the reporting period.
- Identification of investments (other than those issued or explicitly guaranteed by the U.S. government) in any one organization that represent 5% or more of the OPEB plan's fiduciary net position (concentrations).
- Disclosure of the money-weighted rate of return on OPEB plan investments. The annual money-weighted rate of return on OPEB plan investments calculated as:
  — The internal rate of return on OPEB plan investments, net of
  — OPEB plan investment expense, and
  — An explanation that a money-weighted rate of return expresses investment performance, net of OPEB plan investment expense, adjusted for the changing amounts with funds invested.

OPEB plan investment expense should be measured on the accrual basis of accounting. Inputs to the internal rate of return calculation should be determined at least monthly. The use of more frequently determined inputs is encouraged.

Receivables. The plan should disclose the terms of any long-term contracts for contributions to the OPEB plan between:

- An employer or nonemployer contributing entity and
- The OPEB plan, and
- The balances outstanding on any such long-term contracts at the end of the OPEB plan's reporting period.

Allocated Insurance Contracts Excluded from OPEB Plan Assets. If the OPEB plan holds *allocated* insurance contracts, disclosure should include:

- The amount reported in benefit payments in the current period that is attributable to the purchase of allocated insurance contracts.
- A brief description of the OPEB for which allocated insurance contracts were purchased in the current period.
- The fact that the obligation for the payment of benefits covered by allocated insurance contracts has been transferred to one or more insurance companies.

Reserves. In circumstances in which there is a policy of setting aside, for purposes such as benefit increases or reduced employer contributions, a portion of the OPEB plan's fiduciary net position that otherwise would be available for existing OPEB or for OPEB plan administration:
- A description of the policy related to such reserves.
- The authority under which the policy was established and may be amended.
- The purposes for and conditions under which the reserves are required or permitted to be used.
- The balances of the reserves [GASB Cod. Sec. Po50.128].

Specific Required Disclosures for Single-Employer and Cost-Sharing OPEB Plans. For single-employer and cost-sharing OPEB plans, additional information is needed in the notes as follows:
- The components of the liability of the employers and nonemployer contributing entities to plan members for benefits provided through the OPEB plan (net OPEB liability) calculated in accordance with the provisions of GASB Cod. Sec. Po50, including:
  — The total OPEB liability (TOL),
  — The OPEB plan's fiduciary net position,
  — The net OPEB liability (NOL), and
  — The OPEB plan's fiduciary net position as a percentage of the TOL.

The notes should also describe significant assumptions and other inputs used to measure the TOL, including assumptions about:
- Inflation,
- Healthcare cost trend rates,
- Salary changes,
- Ad hoc postemployment benefit changes (including ad hoc COLAs), and
- Sharing of benefit-related costs with inactive plan members.

Regarding the sharing of benefit-related costs, if projections are based on an established pattern of practice, that fact should be disclosed.

The following is required disclosure of mortality assumptions:
- The source of the assumptions (e.g., the published tables on which the assumptions are based or that the assumptions are based on a study of the experience of the covered group),
- The dates of experience studies on which significant assumptions are based,
- For all significant assumptions, if different rates are assumed for different periods, information should be disclosed about what rates are applied to the different periods of the measurement,
- In addition, if the alternative measurement method (see later section) is used to measure the total OPEB liability, the source or basis for all significant assumptions should be disclosed.

A sensitivity analysis is also presented in two different tables:
- For the healthcare cost trend rate and
- For the discount rate.

Regarding the healthcare cost trend rate, measures of the NOL calculated using (a) a healthcare cost trend rate that is 1-percentage-point higher than the assumed healthcare cost trend rate and (b) a healthcare cost trend rate that is 1-percentage-point lower than the assumed healthcare cost trend rate, should be disclosed.

For the discount rate, like defined benefit pensions, the discount rate applied in the measurement of the TOL and the change in the discount rate since the OPEB plan's prior fiscal year-end, if any, should be disclosed. This portion of the notes should include assumptions made about projected cash flows into and out of the OPEB plan:

- Such as contributions from employers, nonemployer contributing entities, and plan members,
- The long-term expected rate of return on OPEB plan investments (if any),
- A description of how the expected rate of return was determined, including significant methods and assumptions used for that purpose,
- If the discount rate incorporates a municipal bond rate, the municipal bond rate used and the source of that rate,
- The periods of projected benefit payments to which the long-term expected rate of return and, if used, the municipal bond rate that is applied in determining the discount rate, and, finally,
- The assumed asset allocation of the OPEB plan's portfolio, the long-term expected real rate of return for each major asset class, and whether the expected rates of return are presented as arithmetic or geometric means.

After this note disclosure on the discount rate, the second sensitivity analysis table is included with measures of the NOL calculated using a discount rate that is 1-percentage- point higher and 1-percentage-point lower.

Finally, the note should conclude with the date of the actuarial valuation or alternative measurement method calculation on which the TOL is based and, if applicable, the fact that update procedures were used to roll forward the TOL to the OPEB plan's fiscal year-end. If the alternative measurement method is utilized based on the provisions of GASB Cod. Sec. Po50 to measure the TOL, the fact that this alternative method was used in place of an actuarial valuation also should be disclosed [GASB Cod. Sec. Po50.129].

Required Supplementary Information for OPEB Plans

Defined Benefit Single-Employer and Cost-Sharing OPEB Plans. Except as noted in the following paragraph, GASB Cod. Sec. Po50 requires a schedule of changes in the net OPEB liability and a schedule of contributions (if applicable) along with notes to the required supplementary information (RSI). The RSI should be presented immediately after the notes to the financial statements.

Information for each year should be measured as of the OPEB plan's most recent fiscal year-end. Information about cost-sharing OPEB plans should be presented for the entire OPEB plan [GASB Cod. Sec. Po50.130].

Schedule of Changes in the Net OPEB Liability. This schedule will be presented for 10 years, presenting each year the beginning, and ending balances of the TOL, the OPEB plan's fiduciary net position and the NOL, along with the effects of the following items, as applicable:

- Service cost,
- Interest on the TOL,
- Changes of benefit terms,
- Differences between actual and expected experience regarding economic or demographic factors in the measurement of the TOL,
- Changes of assumptions about future economic or demographic factors or other inputs,
- Contributions from employers, including amounts for OPEB benefits come due that will not be reimbursed to the employers using OPEB plan assets,
- Contributions from nonemployer contributing entities, including amounts for OPEB as the benefits come due that will not be reimbursed to the nonemployer contributing entities using OPEB plan assets,
- The total of contributions from active plan members and inactive plan members not yet receiving benefit payments,
- OPEB plan net investment income, and
- Benefit payments (including refunds of plan member contributions and amounts from employers or nonemployer contributing entities for OPEB as the benefits come due).

OPEB plan administrative expense and other changes, separately identified if individually significant, finish the initial part of the schedule.

If the alternative measurement method is used, differences between expected and actual experience about economic or demographic factors in the measurement of the TOL and changes of assumptions about the future economic or demographic factors or other inputs may be combined.

The schedule then is continued, again for 10 years, presenting the following each year, like pensions:

- The TOL,
- The OPEB plan's fiduciary net position,
- The NOL,
- The OPEB plan's fiduciary net position as a percentage of the TOL,
- The *covered-employee payroll,* and
- The NOL as a percentage of the *covered-employee payroll* (see **PRACTICE POINT**).

> **PRACTICE POINT:** For single-employer defined benefit OPEB plans, and cost-sharing multiple-employer defined benefit OPEB plans, the measure of payroll required to be presented should be *covered payroll*. Covered payroll is the payroll on which contributions to the OPEB plan are based. If contributions to the OPEB plan *are not based on a measure of pay, no measure of payroll should be presented*. Many OPEB plans receive a percentage of taxation or similar for their contributions. As such, no measure of pay would be presented. No measure of pay should be presented for plans involving volunteers as well.

Schedule of Employer Contributions. A 10-year schedule of employer contributions will be presented for each year *if an actuarially determined contribution* is calculated for employers or nonemployer contributing entities.

The schedule includes, the actuarially determined contributions of employers or nonemployer contributing entities. For purposes of this schedule, actuarially determined contributions should exclude amounts, if any, associated with payables to the OPEB plan that arose in a prior fiscal year and those associated with separately financed specific liabilities to the OPEB plan.

For cost-sharing multiple-employer OPEB plans, the statutorily or contractually required contribution of employers or nonemployer contributing entities, if different. For purposes of this schedule, statutorily or contractually required contributions should include amounts from employers or nonemployer contributing entities for OPEB as the benefits come due that will not be reimbursed to the employers or nonemployer contributing entities using OPEB plan assets and should exclude amounts, if any, associated with payables to the OPEB plan that arose in a prior fiscal year and those associated with separately financed specific liabilities to the OPEB plan.

Other disclosures include:

- The value of contributions, including amounts from employers or nonemployer contributing entities for OPEB as the benefits come due that will not be reimbursed to the employers or nonemployer contributing entities using OPEB plan assets, recognized during the fiscal year by the OPEB plan in relation to the actuarially determined contribution. For purposes of this schedule, contributions should exclude amounts resulting from contributions recognized by the OPEB plan as noncurrent receivables.
- The difference between the actuarially determined contribution and the value of contributions recognized by the OPEB plan in relation to the actuarially determined contribution.
- *The covered-employee payroll* (see previous **PRACTICE POINT**).
- The value of contributions recognized by the OPEB plan in relation to the actuarially determined contribution as a percentage of *covered-employee payroll* (see previous **PRACTICE POINT**).

> **PRACTICE POINT:** EPMCs may be more prevalent for OPEB than for pensions. If payments are made by the employer to satisfy contribution requirements that are identified by the OPEB plan terms as plan member requirements, they remain as plan member contributions. Employer reporting will change including for the purposes of determining a cost-sharing employer's proportion. For the employer, those amounts will be employee contributions.

Finally, a 10-year schedule is included each year presenting the annual *money-weighted* return on OPEB plan investments. This is the only required schedule *for agent multiple-employer OPEB plans* [GASB Cod. Sec. Po50.131].

Notes to the Required Schedules. The notes to RSI are like those required for pension plans. Significant methods and assumptions used in calculating the actuarially determined contributions, if any, should be presented as notes to the schedule.

In addition, for each of the schedules, information should be presented about factors that significantly affect trends in the amounts reported (e.g., changes of benefit terms, changes in the size or composition of the population covered by the benefit terms, or the use of different assumptions).

Information about investment-related factors that significantly affect trends in the amounts reported should be limited to those factors over which the OPEB plan or the participating governments have influence (e.g., changes in investment policies).

Information about external, economic factors (e.g., changes in market prices) should not be presented. (The amounts presented for prior years should not be restated for the effects of changes—for example, changes of benefit terms or changes of assumptions—that occurred after the end of the fiscal year for which the information is reported.) [GASB Cod. Sec. Po50.132].

Differences between Pension Valuations and OPEB Valuations for Defined Benefit Plans

For OPEB, the actuarial valuation is like that used for pensions including the issues regarding deviations, which may be more prevalent for OPEB. Only the entry-age normal actuarial method is allowed.

> **PRACTICE POINT:** Unlike pensions, few OPEB plans have considerable amounts of assets. Therefore, the "crossover" point will occur much sooner than in pensions (and in many cases immediately). Therefore, the same discount rate as a pension plan might not be able to be used.

Unlike pensions, projected benefit payments also should include taxes or other assessments expected to be imposed on benefit payments using the rates in effect at the OPEB plan's fiscal year-end. If different rates have been approved by the assessing government to be applied in future periods, the rates approved by the assessing government associated with the periods in which the assessments on the benefit payments will be imposed. This aspect will include any effect a required conversion of a retiree to Medicare may have on the valuation.

A major difference from defined benefit pensions is how projected benefit payments should be based on claims costs, or *age adjusted premiums* approximating claims costs, in accordance with actuarial standards of practice. (This is the former *implicit rate subsidy* used in accordance with the provisions of superseded GAAP.) For OPEB plans, the predominant costs are retiree healthcare claims, which are more variable and ascend more frequently as a beneficiary matures. Therefore, the testing of this claims data and the location of the claims data become important for audit purposes.

Other differences between defined benefit pensions and defined benefit OPEB regarding the actuarial valuation process include:

Assumptions	Pensions	OPEB
Long-term rate of return on plan assets	Main component of discount rate due to the availability of fiduciary net position.	Not a major issue, especially if there are no assets.
Mortality	*Vital.* How long a beneficiary is estimated to live (and if spouses and dependents are eligible, their lives) are a major component of the liability.	Important, but not as much as in pensions. Furthermore, many plans require conversion to Medicare upon eligibility.
Inflation and salary	Another key component of the calculation of benefits.	Since the liability is based on projected claims and not likely salary, not a large issue.
Retirement age and rate of retirement	Key component.	Could be crucial for projecting cash flow and liability.
COLAs and Healthcare Cost Trend Rate differences	Important only if offered.	Healthcare cost trend rate is more important than discount rates for OPEB and usually ascending faster than inflation.
Options to benefits	May not be offered in plan provisions.	Many plans only subsidize a portion of premiums or only pay for a certain number of years (prior to Medicare eligibility for example).
Utilization	Not an issue as once someone is vested, they will likely stay in the plan.	Particularly important as the older a beneficiary is, the more he or she will need healthcare.
Participation rate	Not an issue as once someone is vested, they will likely stay in the plan.	Retirees often pay into the plan. Also, if the plan has higher premiums than other plans, such as Medicare, the beneficiary may choose the other plan.
Taxation	Not an issue under current tax law.	Dependent on plan provisions and federal law.

A legal or contractual cap on benefit payments for OPEB will also be considered in projecting benefit payments. A consideration must be made if the cap has been enforced in the past and other relevant factors and circumstances [GASB Cod. Secs. Po50.139–.141].

Alternative Measurement Method: Small Plans

In general, the measurement standards required by GASB Cod. Sec. Po50 apply to all defined benefit OPEB plans, however, the GASB did attempt to simplify the implementation of OPEB standards for a single-employer plan that has fewer than 100 plan members (active and retired). For such plans, the OPEB plan may (1) apply all the measurement standards without modification or (2) apply the measurement standards with one or more of the following modifications:

- *Assumptions in general*—Assumptions should be based on actual experience but grouping techniques may be used where assumptions may be based on combined experience data for similar plans as explained below (see "use of grouping").
- *Expected point in time at which benefits will begin to be provided*—This assumption may be based on a single assumed retirement age or that all employees will receive benefits at an established service years attainment.
- *Expected point in time at which plan members will exit from active service*—This reflects future assumptions for members and again, could be a single age or based on years of service.
- *Health-care cost trend rate*—This assumption should be based on an objective source.
- *Marital and dependency status*—This assumption may be based on the current marital status of employees or historical demographic data for the covered group.
- *Mortality*—This assumption should reflect current published mortality tables.
- *Turnover*—This assumption is made based on how long a member will remain employed until the age when benefits will be made, or the active employee will be eligible for benefits, based on historical data.
- *Plans with coverage options*—Employers with postemployment benefit plans where the employee has coverage options should base the coverage option on experience but also take into consideration the choices of pre- and post-Medicare-eligible members.
- *Qualification for benefits assumption*—This assumption, when experience data are not available, may be based on the simplifying assumption that the longer an employee works, the greater the probability he or she will work long enough to qualify for benefits. For example, if an employee must work for 10 years to qualify for benefits, then the probability of qualification increases 10% for each year the employee works.
- *Use of grouping*—Rather than consider each participant, participants may be grouped into categories based on such factors as an age range or length-of-service range.
- *Use of health insurance premiums*—Employers that have postemployment healthcare plans where the employer makes premium payments to an insurer may use the current premium structure to project future healthcare benefit payments [GASB Cod. Secs. Po50.150–.151].

> **PRACTICE POINT:** Except for the very smallest plans, the alternative measurement method is a difficult calculation. Furthermore, some believe the method is not reliable. An actuarial valuation may be beneficial assuming the costs do not outweigh the benefits.

Medicare Part D Retiree Drug Subsidy Payments from the Federal Government

Prescription drug benefits are a principal element of claims and, therefore, a large component of an OPEB liability. A retiree drug subsidy (RDS) was approved by the federal government as part of the Medicare Prescription Drug, Improvement, and Modernization Act of 2003. Two alternatives for RDS occur in practice:

- An RDS payment is made from the federal government to *an employer*. Therefore, the transaction *does not affect* accounting for employer contributions or the presentation by an OPEB plan. Accordingly, there is no reduction of the OPEB plan liability due to the RDS received by the employer.

- An RDS payment is made from the federal government *directly to an OPEB plan*. The plan will report this amount in the Statement of Changes in Fiduciary Net Position separately from member contributions and from employer contributions. The reporting is an on-behalf payment from the federal government. For single-employer and cost-sharing OPEB plans, benefit payments are required to be projected *without reduction for RDS payments*. The information is also presented in RSI [GASB Cod. Sec. Po50.601].

Plans That Are Not Administered as Trusts or Equivalent Arrangements

For plans not administered as trusts or equivalent arrangements, any assets accumulated for OPEB purposes should continue to be reported as assets of the employer or nonemployer contributing entity. If an OPEB plan is not administered through a trust, a government that holds assets accumulated for OPEB purposes in a fiduciary capacity should report the assets in a custodial fund. The amount of assets accumulated more than liabilities for benefits due to plan members and accrued investment and administrative expenses should be reported as a liability to participating employers or nonemployer contributing entities. If the agency fund (custodial fund) is included in the financial report of an employer whose employees are provided with benefits through the OPEB plan or a nonemployer contributing entity that makes benefit payments as OPEB comes due, balances reported by the agency fund should exclude amounts that pertain to the employer or nonemployer contributing entity that reports the custodial fund [GASB Cod. Secs. P53.107–.108, 2200.199].

Defined Contribution OPEB Plans

When an OPEB is a defined contribution plan, it should prepare its financial statements based on the general guidance for fiduciary funds in the same manner as defined contribution pension funds. The Retirement Health Savings Account reported in the exhibits earlier in this chapter is an example of a defined contribution OPEB plan. If the plan is administered as a trust or equivalent arrangement, it should disclose:

- Identification of the OPEB plan as a defined contribution OPEB plan,
- The authority under which the OPEB plan is established or may be amended,
- The classes of members covered, and
- The number of plan members, participating employers (if a multiple-employer plan) and, if any, nonemployer contributing entities [GASB Cod. Sec. Po51.106].

PRACTICE POINT: Care must be taken not to confuse flexible spending and similar dependent care accounts with defined contribution OPEB plans as they are for current employees. See also the previous section on Defined Contribution and Deferred Compensation Plans Presented as Stand-Alone Statements.

CHAPTER 23
PUBLIC ENTITY RISK POOLS

Chapter References:
- GASB Statement Nos. 1, 10, 30, 34, 53, 65, 72, 92, 99
- GASB Interpretation No. 4
- GASB *Implementation Guide*

INTRODUCTION

As discussed in Chapter 15, state and local governments encounter the same accounting and reporting issues as commercial enterprises that provide insurance coverage (insurer) and that purchase insurance coverage (insured). When a governmental entity is organized as a public entity risk pool, it may take on many of the characteristics of an insurer.

A *public entity risk pool* is a cooperative group of governmental entities that join to finance an exposure, liability, or risk. Risk may include property and liability, workers' compensation, and employee healthcare that is *separate from postemployment benefits provided to current and future retirees, their beneficiaries and dependents based on an OPEB (Other Post-Employment Benefit) plan.* (See Chapter 22.) A public entity risk pool also does not include Medicaid insurance plans provided to low-income state residents under Title XIX of the federal Social Security Act [GASB Cod. Sec. Po20.102].

A pool may be a stand-alone entity or be included as part of a larger governmental entity that acts as the pool's sponsor. The activities of a public entity risk pool vary, but in general they can be classified as follows:

Type of Pool	Definition	Example
Risk-sharing pool	Governmental entities join to share in the cost of losses.	Statewide municipal league intergovernmental risk pool.
Insurance-purchasing pool (risk-purchasing group)	Governmental entities join to acquire commercial insurance coverage.	Counties excess insurance authority (that contracts with a commercial insurance entity through a competitive bid process).
Banking pool	Governmental entities can borrow funds from a pool to pay losses.	Statewide deposit insurance trust fund.
Claims-servicing or account pool	Governmental entities join to administer the separate account of each entity in the payment of losses.	Municipal health trust administered by a state as a claims-paying agent for employees not eligible for OPEB.

An individual public entity risk pool can perform one or more of the above activities, but the latter two activities (banking pool and claims-servicing or account pool) do not result in the transfer of risk from the participating governmental entity to the public entity risk pool.

A public entity risk pool must be evaluated to determine the rights and responsibilities of the pool and the governmental entities that participate in the pool. The agreement between a public entity risk pool and the governmental entity may transfer a part or all the risk of loss to the risk pool or may retain all the risk.

In addition to the agreement between the pool and the participants, the laws of a particular jurisdiction and the economic resources of the ultimate insurer should be taken into consideration when determining to what extent, if any, there has been a transfer of risk to the public entity risk pool from a governmental entity. For example, if a public entity risk pool has insufficient resources to pay claims as incurred, the risk of loss is retained by the individual governmental entity, irrespective of the agreement between the two parties. On the other hand, if an agreement has a deductible amount clause per claim, only the risk related to the amount of the loss more than the deductible amount is transferred to the public entity risk pool [GASB Cod. Secs. Po20.103–.112].

> **PRACTICE POINT:** The concept of insurance is full of jargon and public entity risk pool accounting and reporting is no exception. Unfortunately, if practitioners are involved in public entity risk pools, the language must be utilized. The chapter includes many definitional elements commonly used in public entity risk pools so that practitioners understand the nuances of the procedures.

PUBLIC ENTITY RISK POOL ACCOUNTING AND REPORTING

Public entity risk pools can either have a transfer or pooling (sharing) of risk or a pool may not involve a transfer of risk. The following subject areas of the chapter pertain to the each of the alternatives:

	Some Transfer or Pooling (Sharing) of Risk	Not Involving Transfer or Pooling of Risk
Required Financial Statements	Yes	Yes
Fund Type	Yes	Yes
Premium Revenue	Yes	No
Claim Costs	Yes	No
Loss Contingencies	Yes	No
Acquisition and Other Costs	Yes	No
Policyholder Dividends and Experience Refunds	Yes	No
Premium Deficiency Calculation	Yes	No
Reinsurance	Yes	No
Capitalization Contributions Made to Other Public Entity Risk Pools	Yes	No
Capitalization Contributions Received	Yes	No

	Some Transfer or Pooling (Sharing) of Risk	Not Involving Transfer or Pooling of Risk
Investments	Yes	No
Lending Assets	Yes	No
Real Estate Used in Pool Operations	Yes	No
Disclosures	Yes	No
Required Supplementary Information (RSI)	Yes	No
Pools Not Involving Transfer or Pooling of Risk	No	Yes

Required Financial Statements for All Pools

Public entity risk pools are enterprise funds. Pools may also present an Annual Comprehensive Financial Report (ACFR). At the very least, the basic financial statements should consist of:

- Management's discussion and analysis,
- Enterprise fund financial statements including a Statement of Net Position, a Statement of Revenues, Expenses and Changes in Net Position and a Statement of Cash Flows (see Chapters 7, and 20),
- Notes to the basic financial statements (see section titled "Required Note Disclosures later in this chapter), and
- RSI other than MD&A as applicable, but not required if there is not a transfer or pooling of risk.

Fund Type. As discussed in the previous paragraph, Enterprise Funds are required to be used for all public entity risk pools and utilizing all applicable accounting and financial reporting [GASB Cod. Secs. Po20.114–.115].

Premium Revenue

A public entity risk pool should recognize premium revenue (or required contributions) over the contract period based on the amount of risk protection provided to the insured entity. In those instances where the risk protection for each period is the same, premium revenue should be recognized on a straight-line basis.

For example, if a public entity risk pool charges $110,000 to a participating governmental entity for $5,000,000 of coverage for losses over a two-year period, the amount of premium revenue recognized each year is $55,000. On the other hand, if coverage for losses is $5,000,000 in year 1 and $6,000,000 in year 2, premium revenue is computed as follows:

	Premium Revenue	
	Year 1	Year 2
($110,000 × $5,000,000) ÷ $11,000,000	$50,000	—
($110,000 × $6,000,000) ÷ $11,000,000	—	$60,000

In most instances, the period of risk and the contract period are the same; however, when they are significantly different, the premium revenue should be recognized over the period of risk [GASB Cod. Sec. Po20.116].

It may not be possible to determine the premium until after the contract period ends. For example, a premium may be based on the dollar value of actual claims incurred during a period. An example of an experience-based premium contract is a contract that uses "retrospective (experience) rating," which is defined as a method of determining the final amount of an insurance premium by which the initial premium is adjusted based on actual experience during the period of coverage (sometimes subject to maximum and minimum limits). It is designed to encourage safety by the insured and to compensate the insurer if larger-than-expected losses are incurred.

In other instances, the premium may be based on the value of property covered during a contract period. An example of a value-based contract is a "reporting-form contract," which is a contract or policy in which the policyholder is required to report the value of property insured to the insurer at certain intervals. The final premium on the contract is determined by applying the contract rate to the average of the values reported [GASB Cod. Sec. Po20.117].

In most instances of experience-based or valuation-based premiums, the public entity risk pool should be able to determine a reasonable estimate of the total premium. In this case, the premium revenue should be recognized over the contract period, based on the amount of risk protection provided. Estimates of the total premium should be revised as the public entity risk pool accumulates experience statistics from participants or receives revised property valuation reports from participants.

Any adjustment to estimated total premiums would be reflected in any current and future financial statements in which the premium revenue is recognized as the adjustment is a change in accounting estimate. The adjustment is made prospectively.

For example, assume that a premium of $150,000 for fire insurance is charged for a three-year period, given that the amount of property covered by the contract is expected to be $20,000,000 in year 1, $25,000,000 in year 2, and $30,000,000 in the final year (year 3) of the contract. The amount of premium revenue to be recognized in each of the three years under a reporting-form contract that is retrospectively rated is computed as follows:

	Premium Revenue		
	Year 1	Year 2	Year 3
($150,000 × $20,000,000) ÷ $75,000,000	$40,000	—	—
($150,000 × $25,000,000) ÷ $75,000,000	—	$50,000	—
($150,000 × $30,000,000) ÷ $75,000,000	—	—	$60,000

During year 2, assume that the estimated amounts of property covered in years 2 and 3 increase to $28,000,000 and $33,000,000, respectively, and that the total premium is estimated to be $172,000. In this circumstance, the amount of premium revenue to be recognized in years 2 and 3 would be as follows:

	Premium Revenue	
	Year 2	Year 3
([$172,000 − $40,000] × $28,000,000) ÷ $61,000,000	$60,590	—
([$172,000 − $40,000] × $33,000,000) ÷ $61,000,000	—	$71,410

If the public entity risk pool cannot reasonably estimate the total premium, premium revenue should be recognized using either the cost-recovery method or the deposit method. GAAP describes these two methods as follows:

- *Cost recovery method*—Under the cost recovery method, premiums are recognized as revenue in an amount equal to estimated claims costs as insured events occur until the ultimate premium is reasonably estimable, and recognition of income is postponed until that time.
- *Deposit method*—Under the deposit method, premiums are not recognized as revenue and claims costs are not charged to expense until the ultimate premium is reasonably estimable, recognition of revenue is postponed until that time.

To illustrate the cost-recovery method and the deposit method, assume that a public entity risk pool decides to bill a governmental entity the following amounts, but the billings are tentative because the total premium is based on retrospective rating and is not subject to reasonable estimation at the end of year 1:

Year	Amount
Year 1	$100,000
Year 2	110,000
Year 3	130,000
	$340,000

If estimated claims costs are $90,000 at the end of year 1, the following entries would be made by the risk pool under each of the two revenue recognition methods:

INSURANCE FUND	Debit	Credit
COST-RECOVERY METHOD (YEAR 1):		
Premiums Receivable	100,000	
Premium Revenue		90,000
Unearned Premium Revenue		10,000
Expenses—Claims Costs	90,000	
Estimated Claims Costs Payable		90,000
DEPOSIT METHOD (YEAR 1):		
Premiums Receivable	100,000	
Unearned Premium Revenue		100,000
Expenses—Claims Costs	90,000	
Estimated Claims Costs Payable		90,000

OBSERVATION: The use of the term "unearned" is limited in GAAP to insurance activities. A search of the *Codification* only results in the use of "unearned" relating to these activities.

Assume that during year 2, the following reasonable estimates of premium revenue are made:

Year	Amount
Year 1	$130,000
Year 2	150,000
Year 3	170,000
	$450,000

As the public entity risk pool can reasonably estimate premium revenues, the following entries would be made in year 2:

INSURANCE FUND	Debit	Credit
COST-RECOVERY METHOD (YEAR 2):		
Premiums Receivable ($130,000 + $150,000 − $100,000)	180,000	
Unearned Premium Revenue	10,000	
Premium Revenue		190,000
DEPOSIT METHOD (YEAR 2):		
Unearned Premium Revenue	100,000	
Premiums Receivable	180,000	
Premium Revenue ($130,000 + $150,000)		280,000
Expenses—Claims Costs	90,000	
Estimated Claims Costs Payable		90,000

A public entity risk pool may collect a premium (or required contribution) that is specifically identified for coverage of future catastrophic losses. GAAP defines "catastrophe" as a conflagration, earthquake, windstorm, explosion, or similar event resulting in substantial losses *or* an unusually considerable number of unrelated and unexpected losses occurring in a single period [GASB Cod. Sec. Po20.118].

The accounting problem with respect to premiums related to catastrophic loss protection is that it is difficult to match the recognition of premium revenues and the recognition of losses that arise from future catastrophic losses. Specifically, should the premium related to catastrophic losses be recorded as unearned revenue until the actual loss occurs? The GASB states that premiums specifically related to future catastrophic losses should be recognized as premium revenue over the period covered by the contract. However, premium revenue related to catastrophic losses should be separately reported in the Statement of Net Position as a restriction of net position if either one of the following conditions exists:

- The premium is contractually restricted for catastrophic losses, or
- The premium is legally restricted for catastrophic losses by an outside organization or individual (for instance, by pool participants).

OBSERVATION: Although GAAP refers specifically to the conditions necessary for the identification of a reservation of public entity risk pool equity, in the absence of such conditions, a pool could designate a portion of its equity for future catastrophic losses.

Claim Costs

Claim costs to be paid by a public entity risk pool should be evaluated using the fundamental criteria for loss contingencies [GASB Cod. Secs. C50.151–.168]. Thus, claim costs should be accrued at the end of the accounting period if the following conditions exist:

- Information available prior to issuance of the financial statements indicates that it is probable (the occurrence of the future event(s) that confirms that a loss has occurred) that a liability has been incurred at the date of the financial statements.
- The amount of the loss can be reasonably estimated.

Estimated claims costs become liabilities for the public entity risk pool when the covered event occurs. The occurrence of a fire or the injury of an individual covered by an agreement with the pool represents the critical date for determining a liability. In addition, some coverage (and, therefore, the recognition of a liability) is based on claims-made policies. A *claims-made policy or contract* is a type of policy that covers losses from claims asserted (reported or filed) against the policyholder during the policy period, regardless of whether the liability-imposing events occurred during the current or any previous period in which the policyholder was insured under the claims-made contract or other specified period before the policy period (the policy retroactive date).

Using the criteria for loss contingencies and the critical event (date of occurrence or claims-made policy criterion) for liability recognition, the public entity risk pool must estimate a liability for unpaid claims costs. The "liability for unpaid claims costs" is the amount needed to provide for the estimated ultimate cost of settling claims for events that have occurred on or before a date (ordinarily, the Statement of Net Position date). The estimated liability includes the amount of money that will be needed for future payments on *both*

- Claims that have been reported and
- Incurred but not reported (IBNR) claims.

The above definition includes estimates for costs related to filed claims and IBNR claims. "IBNR claims" are claims for insured events that have occurred but have not yet been reported to the governmental entity, public entity risk pool, insurer, or reinsurer as of the date of the financial statements. IBNR claims include:

- Known loss events that are expected to later be presented as claims,
- Unknown loss events that are expected to become claims, and
- Expected future development on claims already reported.

The estimated liability for unpaid claims costs must be evaluated periodically to determine whether current factors make it necessary to adjust the liability for unpaid claims costs. For example, recent settlements may suggest that claims that have not been settled are understated. Adjustments of this nature are a change in an accounting estimate and, therefore, the resulting adjustment should be accounted for as an increase (or decrease) to current expenses of the public entity risk pool.

The estimated liability for unpaid claims costs should be reduced by estimated recoveries that may arise from unsettled claims. GAAP provides the following examples and definitions of recoveries [GASB Cod. Sec. Po20.119]:

- *Salvage*—The amount received by a public entity risk pool from the sale of property (usually damaged) on which the pool has paid a total claim to the insured and has obtained title to the property.
- *Subrogation*—The right of an insurer to pursue any course of recovery of damages, in its name or in the name of the policyholder, against a third party who is liable for costs of an insured event that have been paid by the insurer.

When a liability for unpaid claims is recognized, a related accrual should also be made for claim adjustment expenses. Claim adjustment expenses should include an estimate for all future adjustment expenses that arise in connection with the settlement of unpaid claims. Both allocated and unallocated claim adjustment expenses should be part of the accrual.

Allocated claim adjustment expenses are related to the settlement or processing of specific claims and include expenses such as fees paid to adjusters and legal fees. Unallocated claim adjustment expenses are related to the settlement and processing of claims but are not traceable to a specific claim. Overhead costs of the public entity risk pool's claims department, such as administrative personnel salaries, allocations of depreciation, and utilities costs, are examples of unallocated claim adjustment expenses [GASB Cod. Sec. Po20.120].

The requirement to include unallocated expenses in the accrual for claim adjustment expenses presents a difficult allocation problem for most public entity risk pools. For example, what portion of the forthcoming year's overhead costs for the claims department should be included in the accrual? In addition, should only the future unallocated expenses of a single year be considered if it is likely that it may take years to settle some claims?

A practical solution to the allocation problem is to estimate the percentage of claims identified and settled in one year and consider the balance to be the basis for the portion of overhead costs to be included in the year-end accrual. To illustrate, assume that a public entity risk pool has budgeted $500,000 for its overhead costs during the forthcoming year, and it is estimated that about 80% of the claims processed are identified and settled in the same year. In this illustration, the liability for claim adjustment expenses should include an accrual of $100,000 ($500,000 × 20%) for unallocated claim adjustment expenses. Other more sophisticated allocation schemes are possible, but it is unlikely that the difference in amounts accrued between another allocation scheme and the one described here would have a material effect on the entity's financial statements.

In part, the accrual for claims liabilities represents estimates of cash flows that may occur several months or years into the future. The existence of such deferred payments raises the question of whether future cash flows related to the settlement of claims should be reported at gross value or at a discounted amount. The

GASB does not take a position on whether future cash flows should be discounted. Thus, the accrual for claims liabilities can be reported either at a gross amount or at a discounted value.

OBSERVATION: The public entity risk pool should disclose the method (gross method or discounting method) used to measure the accrual for claims liabilities.

The GASB provides one exception to its neutral position with respect to discounting. Structured settlements should be discounted if the payout values and payment dates are fixed by contract. A "structured settlement" is a means of satisfying a claim liability, consisting of an initial cash payment to meet specific present financial needs combined with a stream of future payments designed to meet future financial needs, generally funded by annuity contracts [GASB Cod. Sec. Po20.121].

To illustrate a structured settlement, assume that a public entity risk pool agrees in a written settlement to pay $100,000 immediately and to purchase three annuities of $200,000 (representing various payments to the claimant spread over a period of years) at the end of year 2, year 4, and year 5. If a 10% discount rate is assumed, the claims liability should be recorded for $526,000 as follows:

Year	Future Cash Flows As Required by Contract	10% Present Value Factor	Present Value
1	$100,000	1.000	$100,000
2	200,000	0.826	165,200
4	200,000	0.683	136,600
5	200,000	0.621	124,200
			$526,000

The following entry would be made to record the structured settlement:

INSURANCE FUND	Debit	Credit
Expenses—Claims Costs	526,000	
Estimated Claims Costs Payable		526,000

At the end of each year, it is necessary to record the amount of increase in the estimated liability because of discounting. For example, at the end of year 1, the following entry should be made:

INSURANCE FUND	Debit	Credit
Expenses—Claims Costs	42,600	
Estimated Claims Costs Payable ($526,000−$100,000) × 10%		42,600

If the public entity risk pool uses the discounting technique to measure claims liabilities, the GASB recommends that factors such as the pool's settlement rate and its investment yield rate be considered in establishing a discount rate. The "settlement rate" is the rate at which a monetary liability with uncertain terms can be settled or a monetary asset (receivable) with uncertain terms can be sold. The investment yield rate is the rate that the public entity risk pool is earning or expects to earn on its portfolio of investments over the period covered by the structured settlement [GASB Cod. Sec. Po20.122].

Some claims against the public entity risk pool may be settled by the purchase of an annuity contract. An "annuity contract" is "a contract that provides fixed or variable periodic payments made from a stated or contingent date and continuing for a specified period, such as for a number of years or for life."

When a claim is settled by the purchase of an annuity contract, the claim should be removed from the accrued liability account if the possibility of additional payments to the claimant are remote (likelihood of future payment is slight). Thus, neither the claim nor the investment in the annuity contract is reported in the public entity risk pool's Statement of Net Position. Under this arrangement, the claim is accounted for as an in-substance defeasance of the debt. Thus, the responsibility for payment of the claim has been met, although the claim is still legally an outstanding obligation.

To illustrate the in-substance payment of a claim through the purchase of an annuity contract, assume that a claim with a recorded value of $250,000 is settled with the purchase of an annuity contract at a cost of $260,000. To record the purchase of the annuity contract, the following entry would be made:

INSURANCE FUND	Debit	Credit
Estimated Claims Costs Payable	250,000	
Expenses—Claims Costs	10,000	
Cash		260,000

OBSERVATION: It is unlikely that the cost of purchasing an annuity will equal the recorded value of the claim. For example, a difference will arise if the public entity risk pool does not use discounting to measure its claims. Even when discounting is used (e.g., in a structured settlement), the rate used to discount a claim is not likely to be the rate that will be charged by the commercial enterprise from which the annuity is acquired. Any difference should be accounted for as an increase (decrease) in the claims costs expense for the year.

When claims have been removed from the claims liability account due to settlement by the purchase of an annuity contract, there is still a contingent liability. If the commercial enterprise could not fulfill its contractual requirements, the responsibility for payment would revert to the public entity risk pool. For this reason, GAAP requires the disclosure of the dollar value of claims removed from the claims liability account due to settlement by the purchase of annuity contracts, and that this disclosure continue for as long as the pool's contingent liability exists. Disclosure is not required if both of the following conditions exist [GASB Cod. Sec. Po20.123]:

- The claimant has signed an agreement releasing the public entity risk pool from further obligation.
- The likelihood of future payments to the claimant is remote.

Loss Contingencies

The conditions for recording a claim are that it is probable (likely to occur) that a liability has been incurred and a reasonable estimate of the liability can be made. If either of these conditions does not exist and there is at least a reasonable possibility (more than remote but less than probable) that a loss or an additional loss may have been incurred, the claim must be disclosed. The disclosure should include the following:

- Nature of the claim, and
- Estimate of the possible loss or range of loss (or state that an estimate cannot be made).

Similar disclosures should be made for any excess over amounts of claims accrued, if there is a reasonable possibility that an amount more than the accrued amount may have to be paid by the public entity risk pool [GASB Cod. Sec. Po20.124].

Acquisition Costs

Acquisition costs represent costs that arise from the acquisition of new contracts or the renewal of new contracts, including commissions, inspection fees, and salaries of employees involved in the underwriting process. Underwriting includes selecting, classifying, evaluating, rating, and assuming risks. Acquisition costs are expensed in the period incurred [GASB Cod. Secs. Po20.125–.126].

Other Costs

Other costs should be expensed as incurred. Costs subject to immediate expense include gains or losses related to the management of the pool's portfolios of investments, administrative costs, and policy maintenance. "Policy maintenance costs" are "costs associated with maintaining records relating to insurance contracts and with the processing of premium collections and commissions" [GASB Cod. Sec. Po20.127].

Policyholder Dividends and Experience Refunds

A public entity risk pool may return a portion of the original premium paid based on the experience of the pool or a class of policies issued by the pool. A policyholder dividend (or return of contributions), as distinguished from an experience refund, is not determined based on the actual experience of an individual policyholder or pool participant but is instead *based on the experience of the pool or of a class of policies.*

Policyholder dividends should be accrued as dividends expense using an estimate of the amount to be paid. Dividends used by policyholders to reduce premiums should also be reported as premium income. Policyholder dividends include amounts returned to pool participants from excess premiums for future catastrophe losses. Alternatively, experience refunds are based on the experience of individual policyholders or pool participants. If experience refund arrangements exist under experience-rated contracts, a separate liability should be accrued for those amounts, based on experience and the provisions of the contract. Instead, revenue should be reduced by amounts that are expected to be paid in the form of experience refunds (a credit) [GASB Cod. Secs. Po.128–.129].

For example, assume that an experience refund of $5,000 for a policyholder is estimated. To record the estimate, the following entry would be made:

INSURANCE FUND	Debit	Credit
Premium Revenue	5,000	
Estimated Liability for Experience Refunds		5,000

Premium Deficiency Calculation

GAAP requires that a net realizable value test be made to determine whether there is a loss on existing contracts. If future expenses, plus any unamortized acquisition costs, exceed future premiums, then a loss or expense should be recognized [GASB Cod. Sec. Po20.130].

Contracts should be grouped and evaluated to determine whether the public entity risk pool has incurred a premium deficiency. The contracts should be grouped based on common characteristics, such as the manner of acquisition, policy servicing, and measuring the revenue and expense related to the contracts. A premium deficiency is recognized if the following formula results in an amount greater than zero:

Element	Operation
Total expected claims costs including IBNR	+
Expected claim adjustment expenses	+
Expected dividends to policyholders or pool participants	=
Subtotal	Sum
Less: Related unearned premiums	-
If net amount is greater than zero, then premium deficiency is recognized	>0

To illustrate a premium deficiency calculation, assume the following nonauthoritative example from the GASB [GASB Cod. Sec. Po20.901]:

- For the premium deficiency calculation, policies are grouped consistent with the manner of acquiring, servicing, and measuring revenue and expense elements of the policies in the pool.
- Policyholder dividends are based on the experience of the entire pool, not on groups of policies. Therefore, if the overall pool experience is favorable, it is possible that dividends may be paid to policyholders with policies in a group in which a premium deficiency exists.
- Anticipation investment income is included in the determination and all amounts are in thousands. All accrued amounts are reported in the financial statements prior to the effect of the premium deficiency. Expected or anticipated amounts are related to events that are expected to occur (e.g., claims filed against a claims-made policy or claims against an occurrence-based policy) after the Statement of Net Position date and through the expiration of policy terms.

Element	Accrued Amounts	Expected or Anticipated Amount
Unearned premium	$100	$-
Unpaid claims costs (including IBNR claims costs)	110	105
Claim adjustment expense	7	5
Policyholder dividends	-	5
Investment income	4	5

Therefore, the following would be the deficiency:

Element	Calculation	
Unearned premium		$100
Less:		
Expected claims costs	$105	
Expected claim adjustment expense	5	
Expected policyholder dividends	5	
Investment income	(5)	
Total costs		(110)
Premium deficiency expense		$10

If the premium deficiency is reasonably estimable, the pool has a legal and enforceable right to assess policyholders for the deficiency, and the collectability is probable and reasonably estimable, revenues and receivables should be declared by the pool for the assessments.

GAAP does not provide guidance as to whether expected investment income related to the grouping of contracts should be used to determine a premium deficiency. If expected investment income is used as part of the determination of a premium deficiency, the calculation should be disclosed [GASB Cod. Sec. Po20.131].

If a premium deficiency exists, then the unamortized acquisition costs are expensed as shown above.

Deficiencies more than the amount are recognized as a liability as of the reporting date and as an expense. The liability adjusts in future periods as expected costs are incurred so that no liability exists by the end of the insurance contract. If deficiencies exist because of risk-sharing pool participation contracts, the deficiency is reported as revenue and assessments receivable if [GASB Cod. Sec. Po20.132]:

- A reasonable estimate of the additional contributions due can be made.
- The public entity risk pool has a legally enforceable claim to additional contributions.
- The collectability of the additional contributions is probable.

Reinsurance

A public entity risk pool may engage in reinsurance contracts. "Reinsurance" is a transaction in which an assuming enterprise (reinsurer), for a consideration (premium), assumes all or part of a risk undertaken originally by another insurer (ceding enterprise). However, the legal rights of the insured are not affected by the reinsurance transaction, and the ceding enterprise issuing the original insurance contract remains liable to the insured for payment of policy benefits.

The purpose of reinsurance is to spread the risk of loss, especially unusual losses that may occur, to more than one insurer. The public entity risk pool must evaluate the terms of the reinsurance contract to determine how certain accounts should be presented in its financial statements.

When the public entity risk pool (ceding enterprise) can recover amounts from reinsurers (or excess insurers) based on paid claims and claim adjustment expenses, a receivable should be recorded and claims costs expense should be reduced. If the total amount due from reinsurers will not be collected, an allowance for estimated uncollectible amounts should be established.

When amounts due from reinsurers are related to unpaid claims and claim adjustment expenses, the estimated amount due should be netted against the estimated claims costs liability and the claims costs expense should be reduced.

To account for the premium given by the public entity risk pool to the reinsurer, the portion (or all) of the unearned ceded premiums should be offset against the unearned premiums received from policyholders or pool participants. For example, assume a public entity risk pool receives unearned premiums of $700,000 from policyholders and 40% of these premiums are due to the reinsurer. These two transactions are recorded as follows:

INSURANCE FUND	Debit	Credit
Cash	700,000	
Unearned Premium Revenue		700,000
To record premiums received from policyholder.		
Unearned Premium Revenue Ceded	280,000	
Ceded Premiums Payable ($700,000 × 40%)		280,000
To record ceded premiums due to reinsurer.		

For financial reporting purposes, receivables due from and payables due to the same reinsurer should be netted. In addition, (1) reinsurance premiums paid and related earned premiums and (2) reinsurance recoveries on claims and incurred claims costs, may be netted on the public entity risk pool's operating statements [GASB Cod. Sec. Po20.133].

OBSERVATION: GASB Statement No. 92 (*Omnibus 2020*), par. 11, amended these provisions slightly to clear up inconsistent language. The GASB noted that the provisions required amounts that are recoveries from reinsurers or excess insurers to be reported as reductions of expenses by public entity risk pools. However, the paragraph also allowed that recoveries be netted—an inconsistency. The initial provisions were amended to not require that recoveries from reinsurers or excess insurances be reported as reductions of expenses. These provisions became effective immediately upon issuance.

Amounts received from reinsurance transactions that represent the recovery of acquisition costs incurred by the public entity risk pool should be netted against the unamortized acquisition costs. The net amount of acquisition costs (original acquisition costs less recoveries related to reinsurance transactions) should be expensed. The public entity risk pool may agree to service all the ceded insurance contracts while being reasonably compensated by the reinsurer. Under this circumstance, an accrual should be made for the estimated future (excess) maintenance costs related to the ceded contracts [GASB Cod. Sec. Po20.134].

Some agreements may be a reinsurance transaction in form but not in substance. The risk of economic loss may not be shifted from the public entity risk pool to the reinsurer. In this case, amounts paid to the reinsurer should be treated as a deposit. If the amount received from a reinsurer exceeds the amount of the deposit, a net liability should be presented on the public entity risk pool's statement of net position [GASB Cod. Sec. Po20.135].

Capitalization Contributions Made to Other Public Entity Risk Pools

A public entity risk pool may have a relationship with another public entity risk pool that is like the relationship between a governmental entity and a public entity risk pool (as described earlier). For example, a public entity risk pool (the participant pool) may share a portion of its risk with another public entity risk pool (the excess pool). When this arrangement exists, and the participant pool makes a capitalization contribution to the excess pool, the participant pool should observe the following accounting standards:

- If the pooling agreement does *not* include additional member assessments and the pool reports a deficit for its operations, the participant pool should consider the financial capacity or stability of the pool to meet its obligations when they are due. If it appears that the pool is insolvent, and it is *probable* that the participant will be required to pay its own obligations upon failure, the obligations are reported as an expense or expenditure and as a liability (if it can be estimated).
- Capitalization contributions to the public entity risk pool with a transfer or a pooling of risk are reported as deposits if it is *probable* that the contribution will be returned upon dissolution or withdrawal from the pool. The probability is based on the pool agreement and the pool's financial capacity. In governmental funds, the deposit is nonspendable fund balance.
- In the government-wide statements, the contribution is prepaid insurance (an asset) and allocated to expense systematically and rationally for the coverage period, but no more than 10 years if the period is not determinable.

In addition, the participant pool must also observe the accounting standards that relate to reinsurance contracts. The guidance related to reinsurance may require the participant pool to net some balances related to the excess pool, or to treat certain payments to the excess pool as a deposit.

The initial capitalization contracts to form a pool or to join a pool are usually established by statute, regulation, or agreement. The contributions are generally in cash [GASB Cod. Secs. Po20.136, fn. 6, J50.113, C50.133–.134, .136].

Capitalization Contributions Received

If it is *probable* that a capitalization contribution made to a public entity risk pool will be returned to the participant in the pool, the public entity risk pool (with transfer or pooling of risk) should account for the receipt of the contribution as a liability.

If it is as probable that the contribution will *not* be returned, the receipt of the contribution should be reported as unearned premiums (a liability). The unearned premiums should be amortized and reported as premium revenue over the period for which it is expected that the capital contribution will be used to determine the amount of premiums the contributor must pay. However, if the period for which it is expected that the capital contribution will be used to determine the amount of premiums is not readily determinable, the amortization period cannot exceed 10 years [GASB Cod. Secs. Po20.137–.138].

GAAP requires that all capitalization contributions received by a public entity risk pool that had previously been recorded as a component of capital be reclassified as a liability. Any capitalization contribution that had previously been recorded as revenue should be accounted for as a prior-period adjustment, with the restatement of the beginning balance of retained earnings for each period reported on a comparative basis.

Investments

Public entity risk pools, like commercial insurance companies, acquire a variety of investments to partially finance their costs of operations. A discussion of the method of accounting for these investments and other related issues is provided in Chapter 9.

The following are common instruments held by public entity risk pools:

- *Mortgage loans*—If they are not investments, they are reported at outstanding principal balances if acquired at par or at amortized cost if purchased at a discount or premium. Allowances for uncollectible accounts may be present. If they are investments, they are measured at fair value. Changes in fair value and all other related amortizations and costs are netted to investment income.

- *Investment derivative instruments*—Measured and reported at fair value.

- *Loan origination and commitment fees*—Excluding points, origination and commitment fees are recognized as revenue. Points received by a lender in relation to a loan origination are deferred inflows of resources and recognized as revenue systematically and rationally over the life of the loan. Direct loan origination costs are expensed. Loan commitment fees are liabilities until the commitment is exercised and then recognized as revenue. If the commitment is unexercised, the borrower loses the fee and revenue is also recognized. Purchase premiums and discounts may be present and are recognized as an adjustment of yield using the effective interest method [GASB Cod. Secs. Po20.139–.142].

Lending Assets

With limited exceptions discussed in Chapter 9 for investments measured at cost or net asset value (NAV), lending assets held as investments are measured at fair value. All investment income, including changes in the fair value, are a component of other income in the Statement of Revenues, Expenses and Changes in Net Position [GASB Cod. Secs. Po20.143–.144].

Real Estate Used in the Pools Operations

Real estate is classified as an investment or as a capital asset, depending on whether the real estate is held for income or profit. Real estate operating costs are investment or operating expenses accordingly [GASB Cod. Sec. Po20.145].

REQUIRED NOTE DISCLOSURES

The following additional information should be disclosed in the public entity risk pool's financial statements [GASB Cod. Sec. Po20.146]:

- A description of the nature of risk transfer or the pooling agreement, including the rights and responsibilities assumed by both the public entity risk pool and its participants,
- A description of the number and types of participants,
- An explanation of the basis used to estimate the liabilities for unpaid claims and claim adjustment expenses, and an explicit statement that the estimate of the liabilities is based on the ultimate cost of settling the claims and includes the effects of inflation and other societal and economic factors,
- A description of the nature of acquisition costs that are capitalized, the method used to amortize such costs, and the amount of acquisition costs amortized for the period,
- Disclosure of the face (gross) amounts and carrying amounts of liabilities for unpaid claims and claim adjustment expenses presented on a present-value basis and the range of annual interest rates used to determine their present value,
- A statement of whether the public entity risk pool takes into consideration estimated investment income when determining if premium deficiencies exist,
- A description of the importance of excess insurance or reinsurance transactions to the public entity risk pool, including the following:
  — Type of coverage,
  — Reinsurance premiums ceded, and
  — Estimated amounts recoverable from excess insurers and reinsurers as of the statement of net position date that reduce the unpaid claims and claim adjustments expenses,
- A presentation of a total claims liabilities reconciliation, including changes in aggregate liabilities for claims and claim adjustment expenses from the prior year to the current year, using the following tabular format (see the example in Exhibit 23-2):
  — Beginning balance of liabilities for unpaid claims and claim adjustment expenses,
  — Incurred claims and claim adjustment expenses for the year (with separate disclosure for the provision for insured events related to the

current year and increases or decreases in the provision for events that were incurred in prior years),

— Payments made (with separate disclosure for payments of claims and claim adjustment expenses related to insured events of the current year and payments of claims and claim adjustment expenses related to incurred events of prior years),

— Explanation for other material reconciling items, and

— Ending balance of liabilities for unpaid claims and claim adjustment expenses, and

- Disclosure of the total amount of outstanding liabilities that have been settled by purchasing annuity contracts from third parties in the name of claimants and the amount of liabilities that have been omitted from the statement of net position. (The disclosure should not include amounts related to settlements in which claimants have signed agreements releasing the pool from further obligation and the chance of further payment is remote.)

PRACTICE POINT: GASB Statement No. 99 (*Omnibus 2022*) removed old terminology referring to *balance sheet* and *balance sheet date*. Such terminology was replaced by *statement of net position* and *statement of net position date* (as well as plural forms of the phrases).

REQUIRED SUPPLEMENTARY INFORMATION

GAAP requires reporting premium or required contribution revenue and claims development information [GASB Cod. Sec. Po20.147].

When a public entity risk pool presents separate financial statements, the revenue and claims development information should be presented as required supplementary information immediately after the notes to the financial statements. When a public entity risk pool does not present separate financial statements, but presents its statements as part of another general governmental reporting entity's financial report, the revenue and claims development information may be presented as statistical information in the combined entity's ACFR.

The presentation provides a basis for interested parties to identify and track trends related to current claims and developments in prior years' claims. In addition, the presentation provides a basis for determining the success of a pool's underwriting function and its ability to estimate its loss reserve over time.

Example of RSI Including Claims Development Information. The required supplementary information should be presented in a 10-year schedule (including the latest fiscal year) and include seven components (seven separate lines). The seven components are discussed in the following section and are cross-referenced to Exhibit 23-1, which is part of a nonauthoritative illustration in GASB Cod. Sec. Po20.901.

Item	Explanation
Line 1	The first line of the schedule of required supplementary information for revenue and claims development information focuses on revenues. A public entity risk pool should present: 1. The amount of gross premium (or required contributions) revenue and reported investment revenue, 2. The amount of premium (or required contributions) revenue ceded, and 3. The amount of net reported premium (or required contributions) revenues (net of excess insurance or reinsurance) and reported investment revenue.
Line 2	The second line in the required supplementary information schedule discloses the amount of reported unallocated claim adjustment expenses and other costs. **OBSERVATION:** Allocated claim adjustment expenses are related to the settlement or processing of specific claims, and they include expenses such as fees paid to adjusters and legal fees. Unallocated claim adjustment expenses are related to the settlement and processing of claims but are not traceable to a specific claim. Overhead costs of the public entity risk pool's claims department, such as administrative personnel salaries, allocations of depreciation, and utilities costs, are examples of unallocated claim adjustment expenses. **OBSERVATION:** Other costs that are not capitalized as acquisition costs for new contracts or renewed contracts should be expensed as incurred. Costs subject to immediate expense include gains or losses related to the management of the pool's portfolios of investments, administrative costs, and policy maintenance costs. "Policy maintenance costs" are "costs associated with maintaining records relating to insurance contracts and with the processing of premium collections and commissions."

Item	Explanation
Line 3	The third line in the schedule should present: 1. The gross dollar value of incurred claims and allocated claim adjustment expenses, 2. The loss assumed by excess insurers or reinsurers, and 3. The net dollar value of incurred claims and allocated claim adjustment expenses. These three disclosures should include both paid and accrued amounts. Incurred claims and allocated claim adjustment expenses may be internally developed by a public entity risk pool using various reporting methods. GAAP allows a public entity risk pool to present its claims information on an accident-year basis for occurrence-based policies, and a report-year basis for claims-made policies. Alternatively, the information may be presented on a *policy-year basis*. A *claims-made policy* is a type of policy that covers losses from claims asserted (reported or filed) against the policyholder during the policy period, regardless of whether the liability-imposing events occurred during the current or any previous period in which the policyholder was insured under the claims-made contract or other specified period before the policy period (the policy retroactive date). The *policy-year basis* is a method that assigns incurred losses and claim adjustment expenses to the year in which the event that triggered coverage under the pool insurance policy or participation contract occurred. For occurrence-based coverage for which all members have a common contract renewal date, the policy-year basis is the same as the accident-year basis. For claims-made coverage, the policy-year basis is the same as the report-year basis. Amounts included in incurred claims and allocated claim adjustment expenses for a year should result only from events that triggered coverage under the policy or participation contract. Once a method of developing the incurred claims and allocated claim adjustment expenses is adopted by a public entity risk pool, the method should be used consistently throughout each period. **OBSERVATION:** The acceptability of more than one reporting basis (accident-year basis, report-year basis, and policy-year basis) raises the question of whether required supplementary information presented by public entity risk pools will be comparable. The GASB states that since the information is presented on a 10-year basis, trends for one public entity risk pool can be identified and compared to trends for other public entity risk pools. Furthermore, the GASB noted that some public entity risk pools have already developed trend information on an accident-year basis for statutory reporting and, therefore, it is not necessary to require these pools to develop the information on another basis.
Line 4	The fourth line in the 10-year trend schedule relates to the dollar value of incurred claims and allocated expense amounts recognized for a year and actual subsequent payments related to those amounts. The amounts should be presented on a cumulative basis from year to year and should extend out for up to 10 years. For example, in Exhibit 23-1, the net amount that was originally estimated in 20W9 ($287,000) resulted in actual cash payments in 20W9 of $118,000, and actual cash payments over the 10-year period of $473,000.
Line 5	The fifth line in the schedule discloses the re-estimated amount for losses assumed by excess insurers or reinsurers based on the information available as of the end of the most current year. For example, in Exhibit 23-1, the original estimated ceded claims and expenses made in 20W9 was $52,000, but the most recent estimate of that amount (as of 20X8) is $104,000.

Item	Explanation
Line 6	The sixth line in the schedule presents the re-estimated net incurred claims and expenses based on the information available as of the end of the most current year. For example, in Exhibit 23-1, the original estimate of net incurred claims and expenses made in 20W9 was $235,000, however, the estimates change in subsequent years as the public entity risk pool gains more experience (settlement of actual claims) with the policies. By the seventh year of experience, the estimated net incurred claims and expenses are equal to the net amount paid ($473,000), which suggests that the public entity risk pool follows that no additional liability exists related to policy claims initiated in 20W9.
Line 7	The seventh line in the 10-year schedule provides insight into the public entity risk pool's ability to estimate claims and expenses by relating the original estimate of claims and expenses to the most recent estimate. For example, in Exhibit 23-1, the original estimate of estimated claims and expenses was $235,000 (Line 3) for 20W9, but the most recent re-estimated amount as of 20X8 was $473,000 (Line 6). The difference of $238,000 ($473,000 − $235,000) is presented in Line 7 and labeled as the "increase in estimated net incurred claims and expenses from end of policy year." **OBSERVATION:** The information developed for Line 4, Line 5, Line 6, and Line 7 should be based on the same reporting method(s) used in Line 3 (accident year, report year, or policy year).

The dollar amounts presented in the 10-year required supplementary information by public entity risk pools may be supplemented by the presentation of the same information on a percentage basis, although the latter presentation is not required. Also, percentage presentations cannot be substituted for dollar amount presentations (dollar amounts are illustrated only in Exhibit 23-1). GAAP notes that the presentation of percentage information "should not obscure or distort required elements of the table."

EXHIBIT 23-1
TEN-YEAR CLAIMS DEVELOPMENT INFORMATION
Fiscal and Policy Year Ended (In Thousands of Dollars)

	20W9	20X0	20X1	20X2	20X3	20X4	20X5	20X6	20X7	20X8
1. Required contribution and investment revenue:										
Earned	$908	$957	$1,357	$1,493	$1,479	$1,595	$1,811	$1,993	$2,192	$2,411
Ceded	366	387	559	615	624	686	754	830	913	1,004
Net earned	542	570	798	878	855	909	1,057	1,163	1,279	1,407
2. Unallocated expenses	64	68	81	91	70	81	92	110	123	131
3. Estimated claims and expenses, end of policy year:										
Incurred	287	303	453	503	569	651	780	909	1,092	1,512
Ceded	52	54	96	111	129	148	168	186	210	251
Net incurred	235	249	357	392	440	503	612	723	882	1,261
4. Net paid (cumulative) as of:										
End of policy year	118	124	179	196	220	251	306	361	450	641
One year later	177	186	268	294	330	377	459	542	675	
Two years later	254	268	385	422	474	542	660	779		
Three years later	304	321	461	506	568	649	790			
Four years later	359	379	545	597	671	766				
Five years later	404	427	614	673	756					

Six years later	445	469	674	740					
Seven years later	473	499	717						
Eight years later	473	499							
Nine years later	473								
5. Re-estimated ceded claims and expenses	104	109	160	174	184	195	211	217	234	251
6. Re-estimated net incurred claims and expenses:										
End of policy year	235	249	357	392	440	503	612	723	882	1,261
One year later	294	311	447	490	550	628	765	898	1,102	
Two years later	338	357	513	563	632	722	874	1,028		
Three years later	380	401	577	632	710	811	982			
Four years later	422	446	641	703	789	902				
Five years later	449	474	682	748	840					
Six years later	468	494	710	779						
Seven years later	473	499	717							
Eight years later	473	499								
Nine years later	473									
7. Increase in estimated net incurred claims and expenses from end of policy year	238	250	360	387	400	399	370	305	220	0

EXHIBIT 23-2
NOTE DISCLOSURE FOR UNPAID CLAIMS LIABILITIES

Note X **Unpaid Claims Liabilities**

As discussed in Note A, the Fund establishes a liability for both reported and unreported insured events, which includes estimates of both future payments of losses and related claim adjustment expenses, both allocated and unallocated. The following represents changes in those aggregate liabilities for the Fund during the past two years (in thousands):

	20X8	20X7
Unpaid claims and claim adjustment expenses at beginning of year	$1,421	$1,189
Incurred claims and claim adjustment expenses:		
Provision for insured events of current year	1,282	900
Increases in provision for insured events of prior years	649	540
Total incurred claims and claim adjustment expenses	1,931	1,440
Payments:		
Claims and claim adjustment expenses attributable to insured events of current year	641	450
Claims and claim adjustment expenses attributable to insured events of prior years	904	758
Total payments	1,545	1,208
Total unpaid claims and claim adjustment expenses at end of year	**$1,807**	**$1,421**

At year-end 20X8, $718,000 of unpaid claims and claim adjustment expenses are presented at their net present value of $576,000. These claims are discounted at annual rates ranging from 8 1/2% to 11%. Unpaid claims expenses of $249,000 are not reported in the 20X8 year-end balances because the Fund has purchased annuities in claimants' names to settle those claims.

EXHIBIT 23-3
REQUIRED SUPPLEMENTARY INFORMATION FOR RECONCILIATION OF CLAIMS LIABILITIES BY TYPE OF CONTRACT

Reconciliation of Claims Liabilities by Type of Contract

The schedule below presents (in thousands) the changes in claims liabilities for the past two years for the Fund's two types of contracts: property and casualty and employee health and accident benefits.

	Property and Casualty 20X8	Property and Casualty 20X7	Employee Health and Accident 20X8	Employee Health and Accident 20X7	Totals 20X8	Totals 20X7
Unpaid claims and claim adjustment expenses at beginning of year	$762	$716	$659	$473	$1,421	$1,189
Incurred claims and claim adjustment expenses:						
Provision for insured events of current year	513	360	769	540	1,282	900
Increases in provision for insured events of prior fiscal years	389	324	260	216	649	540
Total incurred claims and claim adjustment expenses	902	684	1,029	756	1,931	1,440
Payments:						
Claims and claim adjustment expenses attributable to insured events of current fiscal year	256	180	385	270	641	450
Claims and claim adjustment expenses attributable to insured events of prior fiscal years	542	455	362	303	904	758
Total payments	798	635	747	573	1,545	1,208
Total unpaid claims and claim adjustment expenses at end of fiscal year	$866	$765	$941	$656	$1,807	$1,421

Pools Not Involving Transfer or Pooling of Risks

As a result of the arrangement between the public entity risk pool and participants, there may be no risk transfer or risk pooling among the participants. Under this arrangement, the public entity risk pool does not assume the role of an insurer but rather takes on the role of an agent for participants by performing the administrative duties of a claims servicer. Furthermore, under this arrangement, each participant is responsible for its own incurred claims.

When there is no transfer or pooling of risks, standards established in the previous section do not apply. Although the transactions and events related to the public entity risk pool (claims-servicing pool) are accounted for in an Enterprise Fund, no liability for incurred claims costs is reported. The pool's statement of net position reflects amounts due from participants as receivables and amounts due to participants as payables. In addition, GAAP states that the receipt of a capitalization contribution should be netted against any related amount and a single asset or liability should be reported.

The pool's Statement of Net Position reflects amounts due from participants as receivables and amounts due to participants as payables, after the amount of the capitalization contribution is taken into consideration. The Statement of Revenues, Expenses and Changes in Net Position includes revenue from performing claims-servicing activities and related administrative expenses [GASB Cod. Sec. Po20.148].

24,001

CHAPTER 24
OTHER SPECIAL-PURPOSE GOVERNMENTS

Chapter References:
    GASB Statement Nos. 14, 34, 37, 51, 61, 62, 65, 72, 87, 89
    GASB Technical Bulletin 2020-1
    GASB *Implementation Guide*
    AICPA Audit and Accounting Guide, *Health Care Entities*
    AICPA Statement of Position 98-2

INTRODUCTION

The majority of the *Governmental GAAP Guide* focuses on general-purpose governments, which were introduced in Chapter 1, as those entities provide a wide range of services (often including both governmental and business-type activities). They include states, counties, cities, towns, villages, and similar governmental entities. Although recognized Indian tribes may not specifically meet the criteria to be defined as a governmental entity, most Tribal Nations prepare their financial statements in accordance with the principles applicable to general-purpose state and local governments. Also included in the description of general-purpose governments are U.S. territories and the District of Columbia.

Special-purpose governments also were introduced in Chapter 1 as legally separate governmental entities that perform only one or a few activities and include colleges and universities, school districts, water and other utility districts or authorities, fire protection districts, cemetery districts, public employee retirement systems, public entity risk pools, governmental hospital or health-care organizations, public housing authorities, airport authorities, and similar entities.

In the previous chapters to the *Guide*, the focus has been on:

- Public Colleges and Universities (PCUs) (Chapter 21),
- Pension and Other Postemployment Benefit Plans (Chapter 22), and
- Public Entity Risk Pools (Chapter 23).

In addition, specific transactions were discussed in Chapter 16, regarding state lotteries and gaming entities. These are all common operations. However, other special-purpose governments have specific GAAP.

Special-purpose governments with specific GAAP provisions discussed in this chapter include:

- Public broadcasters and cable systems,
- Public hospitals and other healthcare providers,

- Insurance entities, other than public entity risk pools, and
- Regulated entities.

Each has slightly different GAAP based upon the provisions of various GASB *Codification* sections. For example, GASB Cod. Sec. A10 *(Asset Retirement Obligations)* is likely applicable to public utilities more than to other governments and may be subject to regulatory accounting. Specific provisions are also in GAAP for customer and developer deposits at utilities. GASB Cod. Sec. I70 *(Irrevocable Split-Interest Agreements)* is likely more applicable to public hospitals and public colleges and universities with endowments more than to general-purpose governments.

OTHER SPECIAL-PURPOSE GOVERNMENTS

Public Broadcasters and Cable Systems

PCUs and some general-purpose governments own broadcast facilities. In certain areas of the country, cable television systems may be owned by governments.

Beyond the capital assets of the broadcast facility generally including technology, transmitters, the intangible asset of a license to broadcast and other elements which would be accounted for and reported similarly to other governments, broadcast facilities may license program material. They may also barter time blocks for programming. They likely also pay various fees for network programming (such as from the Public Broadcasting System—PBS). The facility may also have a related foundation for fundraising.

GAAP requires a broadcast licensee to report an asset and liability for a broadcast license agreement either:

- At the present value of the liability using an imputed interest cost, or
- At the gross amount of the liability.

If the present value of the liability is used, the difference between the gross and the net liability is accounted for as interest [GASB Cod. Sec. Br10.102].

PRACTICE POINT: It is common for broadcasters to lease transmitter tower space. Public broadcasters are therefore subject to the provisions of GASB Cod. Sec. L20. Further, for television broadcasters, the federal communications commission in 2017 began the process of "repacking" the television spectrum. Large segments of the spectrum were no longer needed due to the prevalence of high-definition television. After repacking, the spectrum was auctioned to cellular and other companies for "5G" service (and future services). Some broadcasters took the opportunity of the repack to return their licenses, only broadcasting on cable systems (or not at all). However, the broadcaster may have been still subject to a lease contract for the no longer needed tower space. The broadcaster may have subleased that space to third parties. The leasing transactions would be subject to the provisions of GASB Cod. Sec. L20 as further detailed in Chapter 14. Had a liability for the broadcast license been unamortized at the point of returning to the FCC, a gain would have resulted. Had the license been returned to the FCC in exchange for compensation from the FCC, the difference between that compensation and the unamortized value of the license would also be a gain. An independent third party may have also bought the license as part of the repack process, resulting in a similar treatment.

As an example, radio station KLMN is a discretely presented component unit of State University. KLMN signs an agreement to broadcast a two-hour daily program of news from the national news service for seven years, paying $1,000 per month. The agreement is noncancelable unless one of the parties ceases broadcasting. The present value of the liability is $68,453, using a discounted interest rate of 6% in accordance with similar lease contracts of the University. The lease contracts were signed within three months of the broadcast agreement and were for the same noncancelable period. The radio station's comptroller would make the following entry:

KLMN Fund	Debit	Credit
Right to broadcast national news	$68,453	
Broadcast rights obligation		$68,453

To record asset for intangible right to broadcast nightly news and liability for rights fees due monthly for next seven years.

The first monthly installment would be as follows, including amortization of the right:

KLMN Fund	Debit	Credit
Broadcast rights obligation ($1,000 – interest expense)	$658	
Interest expense	342	
Cash		$1,000
Amortization Expense	815	
Amortization Expense – broadcast rights		815

To record monthly payment for nightly news and amortize right to broadcast using the effective interest method.

Bartering. It is common for broadcasting stations to barter time blocks or advertising segments. For example, a station may have a promotion for concert tickets received as a barter from a recording company. The station would then run a contest with winners going to the concert.

In other situations, unused blocks of time are bartered with companies. For example, a CPA (Certified Public Accountant) firm wants to promote its financial advisory services. The CPA firm barters the time on the station, receiving calls from listeners for financial advice. The CPA firm promotes its business, and the station utilizes time not normally used. In other situations, the station exchanges advertising time for network programming. The affiliated broadcast station does not sell the related advertising time, but since it licenses the time from the federal communications commission, it has a cost. Therefore, the network pays for the services in accordance with the agreement. This arrangement is common in sports programming.

GAAP requires all barter transactions *except those involving the exchange of advertising time for network programming* to be reported at the estimated fair value of the product or service received, as a nonmonetary exchange.

PRACTICE POINT: Nonmonetary exchanges are discussed in detail in Chapter 1 of the *Governmental GAAP Practice and Disclosures Manual*.

PRACTICE POINT: GASB Statement No. 99 (*Omnibus 2022*) clarifies guidance on disclosure of nonmonetary transactions. As many broadcast stations are governments, if there are one or more nonmonetary transactions during a period *and* GASB Cod. Sec. N70 (*Nonmonetary Transactions*) applies, then the notes to the basic financial statements are required to include the measurement attribute(s) applied to the assets transferred, rather than the basis of accounting for those assets. In the Basis for Conclusions in GASB-99, the GASB believed that the use of the phrase *basis of accounting* in GASB Cod. Sec. N70 is not consistent with earlier accounting guidance clarifying that basis of accounting refers to when financial statement elements are recognized. The GASB believes that the requirement in GASB Cod. Sec. N70 was intended to provide information about the measurement attributes of the assets transferred, which are identified in Concepts Statement No. 6 (*Measurement of Elements of Financial Statements*). These provisions were implemented immediately upon issuance.

Barter revenue is reported when commercials are broadcast, and merchandise or services received should be reported when received or used. If the merchandise or services are received prior to the commercial, a liability is reported. If the opposite is true, a receivable is reported [GASB Cod. Sec. Br10.103].

Cable Systems. Cable television services may be provided by a general government or a special-purpose government. They may utilize governmental activities or business-type activities (or both). For a governmental activity, either taxation or intergovernmental revenues utilizing an internal service fund is used. For example, a special district also operates a cable television service in a small village. The board meetings are broadcast on the system. The cost of the broadcast is likely in an internal service fund.

More likely though, external fees are charged to ratepayers. The monthly fees are a business-type activity usually reported in an enterprise fund. GAAP accounting for the system operated as an enterprise fund would be the same for any other enterprise fund. The financial statements required for business-type activities would also be required GASB Cod. Secs. Ca5.102–.104].

If the system engaged in both governmental and business-type activities, a complete set of financial statements, including required reconciliations, would be required. If the system were a component unit, all component unit provisions would apply [GASB Cod. Secs. Ca5.105–.109].

Specific transactions unique to cable television systems include recognition of revenue during the "prematurity period," recognition of subscriber-related costs, depreciation of capitalized costs, and proper recording of hookup revenue and related costs.

Management of the system must establish the beginning and the end of the prematurity period which usually lasts less than two years. This period may last longer in cities due to the complexity of wiring a system. During this period, the system is partially under construction and partially in service. Like other capital assets being placed in service, the achievement of a predetermined subscriber level ends the prematurity period. At that time, no additional investment is required other than for cable television plants. The government that operates the system must clearly distinguish the periods and in some cases areas of the system may be in the prematurity period while other areas may be fully operational. The areas may have:

- Geographic differences,
- Mechanical differences (utilizing different "head-ends" or plants),
- Timing differences, likely based on construction elements or marketing,
- Different break-even points or return on investment decisions that will start or stop construction, or
- Separate accounting and reporting records [GASB Cod. Sec. Ca5.112].

Like other capital assets, during the prematurity period, the costs of the cable television plant, materials, direct labor, and overhead are capitalized. Subscriber-related costs and other general and administrative costs are period costs. Programming costs that benefit the prematurity period and fully operational periods are allocated [GASB Cod. Sec. Ca5.113].

The allocation of costs during the prematurity period is based on a formula determining a fraction. The numerator is *the greater of*:

- The average number of subscribers expected that month as of the beginning of the prematurity period, *or*
- The average number of subscribers that would be attained using at least equal (i.e., straight-line) monthly progress in adding new subscribers toward the estimate of subscribers at the end of the prematurity period, *or*
- The average number of actual subscribers.

The denominator is the total number of subscribers expected at the end of the prematurity period. In practice, this is like the percentage of completion method for construction accounting. The fraction then derives depreciation and amortization expense during the prematurity period. Costs that have been capitalized should be depreciated over the same period used to depreciate the plant [GASB Cod. Secs. Ca5.114–.115, .117]. Initial hookup revenue is recognized as revenue to the extent of direct selling costs incurred. Any remainder is recognized as a deferred inflow of resources and amortized to revenue over the estimated average remaining period that subscribers are expected to remain connected to the system. The individual subscriber installation costs (labor, materials, overhead) are capitalized similarly. Any costs of disconnecting and reconnecting a subscriber are expensed [GASB Cod. Secs. Ca5.118–.119].

Public Hospitals and Other Healthcare Providers

Hospitals and other healthcare providers are commonly governments. Such facilities may be engaged in either governmental or business-type activities or both. Governmental activities are generally financed through taxes, intergovernmental revenues, and other nonexchange revenues. They are usually reported in governmental funds and internal service funds. Business-type activities are financed in whole or in part by fees charged to external users for goods or services. They are usually reported in enterprise funds [GASB Cod. Sec. Ho5.102]. Hospitals may be component units, likely to shield the primary government from liability.

If organized as a governmental activity, a business-type activity and/or as a component unit, all related GAAP accounting and financial reporting applies.

PRACTICE POINT: The GASB's Technical Bulletin 2020-1 contains clarifications for hospitals that may have received Provider Relief Funds from the CARES Act as discussed in previous chapters. Losses of revenue attributable to the effects of COVID-19 are contingent on eligibility. Funds received in advance of those specific Provider Relief Fund eligibility requirements are liabilities and not revenue until the law's eligibility requirements are met [GASB Cod. Secs. Ho5.601–.602].

PRACTICE POINT: The following sections on charity care, accounting for joint activities, purpose, audience, content, allocation methods, incidental activities, and disclosures of allocated joint costs are from the AICPA *Audit and Accounting Guide* - Healthcare Entities and the AICPA Statement of Position 98-2, which have been cleared by the GASB and included in the GASB *Codification*. Only the *Codification* references are included in these sections as the individual paragraphs in the AICPA literature change.

Charity Care. Charity care includes healthcare services provided to patients, but never expected to result in cash flows. No revenue is recognized. For financial reporting purposes, gross service revenue does not include charity care and net service revenue is reported net of contractual and other adjustments in the statement of revenues, expenses, and changes in net position [GASB Cod. Sec. Ho5.802].

Governmental healthcare entities are required to disclose management's policy for providing charity care and the level of charity care provided, based on some measure of the entity's costs, units of service, or some other measure [GASB Cod. Sec. Ho5.803].

> **PRACTICE POINT:** Public healthcare and hospital entities are likely to have leases, public-private partnerships, and subscription-based information technology arrangements. These are discussed in Chapter 14.

Accounting for Joint Activities – Fundraising versus Program or Management and General. Joint activities are allocable between fundraising and an appropriate program or management and general function. Joint activities have criteria of *purpose, audience,* and *content*. If any of the criteria are *not* met, all joint costs are fundraising, including those that are usually management and general functions. The exception is costs of goods or services provided in exchange transactions that are part of joint activities, such as costs of direct donor benefits of a special event (e.g., a meal), which should not be reported as fundraising [GASB Cod. Sec. Ho5.804].

The criteria are complex and are only applicable if fundraising costs of the healthcare entity are also required to be allocated to programmatic functions [GASB Cod. Secs. Ho5.805–.812]. Any cost allocation should be systematic and rational, resulting in a reasonable joint cost that can be applied consistently given similar facts and circumstances [GASB Cod. Sec. Ho5.813].

Disclosures of Allocations of Joint Costs. Entities that allocate joint costs should disclose the following in the notes in addition to all other applicable GAAP disclosure:

- The types of activities for which joint costs have been incurred,
- A statement that such costs have been allocated, and
- The total amount allocated during the period and the portion allocated to each functional expense category [GASB Cod. Sec. Ho5.815].

Insurance Entities – Other Than Public Entity Risk Pools

> **PRACTICE POINT:** Public Entity Risk Pools are discussed in Chapter 23.

Like the other entities discussed in this chapter, insurance entities may be engaged in either governmental or business-type activities or both. Governmental activities are financed primarily through taxes, intergovernmental revenues, and other nonexchange revenues. They are generally reported in governmental funds and internal service funds. Business-type activities are financed in whole or in part by fees charged to external users for goods or services. They are usually reported in enterprise funds [GASB Cod. Sec. In3.102].

All GAAP apply to insurance entities as applicable, including if the entity is a component unit and/or produces a stand-alone financial statement.

In general, such insurance entities initiate short-duration insurance contracts [GASB Cod. Sec. In3.110].

> **PRACTICE POINT:** This section does not apply to contracts for providing coverage for OPEB (Other Post Employment Benefit). Such contracts are discussed in Chapter 13 and Chapter 22. Also see the following section, titled "Regulated Operations."

General Principles Insurance contracts are classified as *short-duration* if the contract provides insurance protection for a fixed period of short duration and enables the insurer to cancel the contract or to adjust the provisions of the contract at the end of any contract period, such as adjusting the amount of premiums charged or coverage provided.

Examples of short-duration contracts include most property and liability insurance contracts and workers' compensation programs, as well as certain government credit enhancement and mortgage guaranty contracts. Accident and health insurance contracts may be short-duration or long-duration depending on whether the contracts are expected to remain in force for an extended period.

For example, individual and group insurance contracts that are noncancelable or guaranteed renewable (renewable at the option of the insured), or collectively renewable (individual contracts within a group are not cancelable), ordinarily are *long-duration contracts* [GASB Cod. Secs. In3.111–.112].

Premium Revenue. Like public entity risk pools, premiums from short-duration insurance contracts are recognized as revenue over the period of the contract in proportion to the amount of insurance protection provided. A liability for unpaid claims (including estimates of costs for claims relating to insured events that have occurred but have not been reported to the insurer) and a liability for claim adjustment expenses should be accrued when insured events occur. Variable costs related to acquiring the contracts are capitalized and charged to expense in proportion to the premium revenue recognized. Other investment, administrative, and policy-related costs are expensed [GASB Cod. Secs. In3.113–.114].

If premiums are subject to adjustment (e.g., retrospectively rated, or other experience-rated insurance contracts for which the premium is determined after the period of the contract based on claim experience or reporting-form contracts for which the premium is adjusted after the period of the contract based on the value of insured property), premium revenue should be recognized as follows:

1. If, as is usually the case, the ultimate premium is reasonably estimable, the estimated ultimate premium should be recognized as revenue over the period of the contract. The estimated ultimate premium should be revised to reflect current experience.
2. If the ultimate premium *cannot be reasonably estimated*, the cost recovery method or the deposit method may be used until the ultimate premium becomes reasonably estimable [GASB Cod. Secs. In3.115–.116].

Recognizing Claims Costs. Liabilities for unpaid claims costs related to insurance contracts, including estimates of incurred but not reported claims, are accrued when insured events occur. The liability for unpaid claims is based on the estimated ultimate cost of settling the claims (including the effects of inflation and other societal and economic factors), using experience adjusted for current trends, and any other factors that would modify experience rating provisions. Changes in estimates of claim costs resulting from the continuous review process and differences between estimates and payments for claims should be recognized in the period in which the estimates are changed, or payments are made.

Estimated recoveries on unsettled claims, such as salvage, subrogation, or a potential ownership interest in real estate, are evaluated in terms of their estimated realizable value and deducted from the liability for unpaid claims. Estimated recoveries on settled claims other than mortgage guaranty claims are also deducted from the liability for unpaid claims [GASB Cod. Secs. In3.117–.118].

A liability for all costs expected to be incurred in connection with the settlement of unpaid claims (*claim adjustment expenses*) is accrued when the related liability for unpaid claims is accrued. Claim adjustment expenses include costs associated directly with specific claims paid or in the process of settlement, such as legal and adjusters' fees. Claim adjustment expenses also include other costs that cannot be associated with specific claims but are related to claims paid or in the process of settlement, such as internal costs of the claims function. Other costs that do not vary and not primarily related to acquisition are expensed as incurred. Commissions and other costs (e.g., salaries of certain employees involved in the underwriting and policy issue functions, and medical and inspection fees) that are primarily related to insurance contracts issued or renewed during the period in which the costs are incurred should be considered acquisition costs and are expensed [GASB Cod. Secs. In3.119–.123].

Premium Deficiencies. A premium deficiency is recognized as a liability if the sum of expected claim costs, claim adjustment expenses, and expected dividends to policyholders exceeds related unearned premiums. Disclosure is required if the insurance entity considers investment revenue in the determination of a premium deficiency. The liability is adjusted in future periods as costs incur so that no liability remains at the end of the contract period [GASB Cod. Secs. In3.124–.126, fn. 12].

Reinsurance. Like public entity risk pool operations, any amount that is recoverable from reinsurers relating to *paid* claims and claims adjustments expenses are recorded as assets, adjusted for estimated uncollectible amounts. If amounts recoverable relate to *unpaid* claims, they are netted against such liabilities. Ceded unearned premiums should also be netted against unearned premiums. Any amounts from the same reinsurer that result in net receivables and net payables are netted as well. Reinsurance premiums ceded and related recoveries on claims are also netted against the related premiums and incurred claims costs in either the statement of activities or the statement of revenues, expenses, and changes in fund net position. Further adjustments may be made for estimated excess future servicing costs under the reinsurance contract and the effects of indemnification [GASB Cod. Secs. In3.127–.129, fn.13].

Policyholder Dividends. Policyholder dividends are accrued using an estimate of the amounts to be paid. Dividends declared or paid to policyholders reduce the related liability. Any amounts paid more than the dividend liability are expensed [GASB Cod. Secs. In3.130–.131].

Investments and Mortgage Loans, Real Estate Used in Operations. Insurers may hold mortgage loans as investments or not as investments. Such loans that are *not* investments are reported at outstanding balances of principal, if at par, or at amortized cost if acquired at a discount or premium, adjusting for uncollectible amounts. All other mortgage loans that are investments are reported at fair value. Changes in fair value, amortizations, related charges, and credits are also reported at fair value. Real estate that is held as an investment is also reported at fair value. Loan origination and commitment fees may also occur and are recorded similarly to other lending activities. Finally, real estate used in operations are recorded as capital assets with related depreciation occurring [GASB Cod. Secs. In3.132–.137].

Disclosures. Required disclosures for insurance entities other than public entity risk pools include the following:

- The basis for estimating the liabilities for unpaid claims and claim adjustment expenses,
- The carrying amount of liabilities for unpaid claims and claim adjustment expenses relating to contracts that are presented at present value in the financial statements and the range of interest rates used to discount those liabilities,
- Whether the insurance enterprise considers anticipated investment revenue in determining if a premium deficiency exists,
- The nature and significance of reinsurance transactions to the insurance enterprise's operations, including reinsurance premiums assumed and ceded, and estimated amounts that are recoverable from reinsurers and that reduce the liabilities for unpaid claims and claim adjustment expenses,
- The relative percentage of participating insurance, the method of accounting for policyholder dividends, the dollar value of dividends, and the amount of any additional revenue allocated to participating policyholders, and
- The fair value disclosures similarly to other investments, as applicable [GASB Cod. Sec. In3.138].

REGULATED OPERATIONS

Regulatory accounting and financial reporting is common for entities such as public utilities or insurance entities that are subject to a third-party regulator, typically a state or a federal entity. The basis of accounting is a special-purpose framework.

PRACTICE POINT: Should an entity be required to report using regulatory provisions, a modified independent auditor's report is produced as the underlying balances and results of operations are not presented in accordance with GAAP as promulgated by the GASB. If there are no other issues with the entity requiring a modified report, the report will be issued unmodified regarding the regulatory provisions and an adverse opinion in accordance with GAAP.

PRACTICE POINT: This section does not apply to governmental entities required or allowed to elect a statutory framework. Such frameworks are approved in legislation by a state and are primarily budgetary, cash, modified cash, or some other statutory basis of accounting which is not GAAP. A similar auditor's report to regulated operations is presented for such entities.

Applicability of Regulatory Accounting and Reporting

Regulated operations are usually business-type activities that meet *all* the following criteria:

1. The regulated business-type activity's rates for regulated services provided to its customers are established by or are subject to approval by an independent, third-party regulator or by its own governing board empowered by statute or contract to establish rates that bind customers.
2. The regulated rates are designed to recover the specific regulated business-type activity's costs of providing the regulated services.
3. In view of the demand for the regulated services or products and the level of competition, direct and indirect, it is reasonable to assume that rates set at levels that will recover the regulated business-type activity's costs can be charged to and collected from customers. This criterion requires consideration of anticipated changes in levels of demand or competition during the recovery period for any capitalized costs (see **PRACTICE POINT** on capitalization of interest later in this chapter).

Entities may have partially regulated operations and partially unregulated operations. These are usually utility enterprise funds contained within a general-purpose government. Should this occur, the regulatory provisions continue to apply to those regulated operations. All other provisions in GAAP apply to the unregulated operations. Price controls or inflationary accounting are not regulatory accounting. If an entity is required to report using contractual accounting (which is a special-purpose framework), regulatory accounting applies. Contractual accounting may be required by certain grants [GASB Cod. Secs. Re10.101–.103].

General Standards for Regulatory Accounting

Assets and Capitalization of Costs. Regulatory provisions require recognition of an asset based on certain conditions and rate actions. A regulated business-type activity should capitalize all or part of an incurred cost that otherwise would be charged to expense if both of the following criteria are met:

1. It is probable that future revenue in an amount at least equal to the capitalized cost will result from inclusion of that cost in allowable costs for rate-making purposes. The term "probable" is utilized similarly to the measurement of other contingencies, and

2. Based on available evidence, the future revenue will be provided to permit recovery of the previously incurred cost rather than to provide for expected levels of similar future costs. If the revenue will be provided through an automatic rate-adjustment clause, this criterion requires that the regulator's intent clearly be to permit recovery of the previously incurred cost.

Regulators also can reduce or eliminate the value of an asset by disallowing rates and charges. If a regulator excludes all or part of a cost from allowable costs and it is *not probable* that the cost will be included as an allowable cost in a future period, the cost cannot be expected to result in future revenue through the rate-making process. Accordingly, the carrying amount of any related asset is reduced to the extent that the asset has been impaired. Whether the asset has been impaired should be judged the same as for governments in general [GASB Cod. Secs. Re10.105–.106].

Liabilities and Deferred Inflows of Resources. Regulators can also impose liabilities or deferred inflows of resources. Liabilities are usually obligations to the regulated business-type activity's customers and deferred inflows of resources represent an acquisition of net position from the regulated business-type activity's customers that is applicable to a future reporting period. The usual ways in which a transaction results in a liability or a deferred inflow of resources and the resulting accounting are as follows:

- A regulator may require refunds to customers. Refunds that meet the criteria for the accrual of loss contingencies should be recorded as liabilities and as reductions of revenue or as expenses of the regulated business-type activity.

- A regulator can provide current rates intended to recover costs that are expected to be incurred in the future with the understanding that if those costs are not incurred, future rates will be reduced by corresponding amounts. If current rates are intended to recover such costs and the regulator requires the regulated business-type activity to remain accountable for any amounts charged pursuant to such rates and not yet expended for the intended purpose, the regulated business-type activity should not recognize as revenues amounts charged pursuant to such rates. Those amounts are reported as a deferred inflow of resources and recognized as revenue when the associated costs are incurred.

- A regulator can require that a gain or other reduction of net allowable costs be given to customers over future periods. That would be accomplished, for rate-making purposes, by allocating in a systematic and rational manner, the gain or other reduction of net allowable costs over those future periods and adjusting rates to reduce revenues in approximately the amount of the allocation. If a gain or other reduction of net allowable costs is to be allocated over future periods for rate-making purposes, the regulated business-type activity should not recognize that gain or other reduction of net allowable costs in the current period. Instead, it should be reported as a deferred inflow of resources for future reductions of charges to customers that are expected to result.

The actions of a regulator can eliminate a liability only if the liability was imposed by actions of the regulator [GASB Cod. Secs. Re10.107–.108].

PRACTICE POINT: Certain regulators may not recognize deferred inflows of resources. Practitioners should understand the regulatory language prior to utilizing these provisions.

Derivatives instruments and Hedging. Utilities may utilize hedging activities in its operations. GASB Cod. Sec. Re10.701-2 discusses regulatory accounting and hedging. Non-regulated utilities should test potential hedging derivative instruments for effectiveness and if effective, apply hedging.

To apply the regulatory accounting provisions, a regulated utility is required to determine the amount that otherwise should be reported as revenue or expense. That determination occurs only after consideration of whether a derivative instrument is a hedging derivative instrument; that is, only after the derivative instrument is determined to be effective in significantly reducing an identified risk.

For example, a regulated gas utility purchases futures contracts to hedge price risk associated with a future natural gas purchase. Whether the futures contracts are effective hedges of future natural gas purchases should first be evaluated, for example, by employing the synthetic instrument method. If the futures contracts are effective, any fair value increases and decreases on the futures contracts should be reported as deferred inflows of resources or deferred outflows of resources, having no impact on the statement of revenues, expenses, and changes in fund net position.

Customer Deposits Relating to Public Utilities. Many electric, water, gas, sewer, and other utility operations require customer deposits to assure timely payment for services. Customer deposits to secure service payments normally are required before service starts and are refunded when service is terminated. Utility operations also may require land developers or individual property owners to make deposits as advance payments of system development fees to extend utility service lines to their properties. Utility operations generally are reported in enterprise funds (and may be regulated). Unearned customer and developer deposits initially are recorded as liabilities in those funds and in the government-wide financial statements. Customer deposits remain as liabilities until they are applied against unpaid billings or refunded to customers. Developer deposits remain as liabilities until they are recognized as revenue from system development fees [GASB Cod. Sec. Ut5.801].

PRACTICE POINT: This provision is from AICPA literature cleared by the GASB.

Specific Regulated Operations Standards Based on General Standards

Costs of Construction. A regulator may require capitalization of the cost of financing construction as part of the cost of capital assets. The cost may be financed partially by borrowings and partially by fund equity. A computed interest cost and a designated cost of equity funds are capitalized, and the change in net position for the current period is increased by a corresponding amount. After the construction is completed, the resulting capitalized cost is the basis for depreciation and unrecovered investment for rate-making purposes. In such cases, the amounts capitalized for rate-making purposes as part of the cost of acquiring the assets should be capitalized for financial reporting purposes instead of the amount of interest that would be capitalized. Those amounts should be capitalized only if their subsequent inclusion in allowable costs for rate-making purposes is probable. The statement of revenues, expenses, and changes in fund net position (or the statement of activities or the regulatory equivalent) should include an item of other revenue, a reduction of interest expense, or both, in a manner that indicates the basis for the amount capitalized [GASB Cod. Sec. Re10.110].

> **PRACTICE POINT:** As a reminder, these provisions are specific only to regulated operations. Capitalized interest is not a part of construction in process for GAAP purposes. Interest cost though may be part of a rate established for regulatory purposes. In such cases, the amounts capitalized for rate-making purposes as part of the cost of acquiring the assets will be capitalized as a regulatory asset for financial reporting purposes.

Intra-Entity Profit. Profit on intra-entity sales to other entities that are in the same reporting entity as the regulated business-type activity *should not* be eliminated in general-purpose external financial statements if *both* of the following criteria are met:

1. The sales price is reasonable.
2. It is probable that, through the rate-making process, future revenue *approximately equal* to the sales price will result from the regulated business-type activity's use of the services.

The sales price usually should be considered reasonable if the price is accepted or not challenged by the regulator that governs the regulated affiliate. Otherwise, reasonableness should consider the circumstances. For example, reasonableness might be judged by the return on investment earned by operations or by a comparison of the transfer prices with prices available from other sources [GASB Cod. Secs. Re10.111–.112].

Asset Impairment. When an operating asset or an asset under construction of a regulated business-type entity becomes impaired, the impairment should be accounted for in accordance with GASB Cod. Sec. 1400 as discussed in Chapter 10 of this *Guide*. In addition, the regulated business-type activity should determine whether recovery of any allowed cost is likely to be provided with either of two scenarios:

1. Full return on investment *during the period* from the time the asset is impaired to the time when recovery is completed or
2. Partial or no return on investment *during that period.*

Determination of which scenario applies should focus on the facts and circumstances related to the specific impairment should consider the past practice and current policies of the applicable regulatory jurisdiction on impairment situations. Based on that determination, the regulated business-type activity should account for the impairment as follows [GASB Cod. Secs. Re10.113–.116]:

Element	Full Return on Investment Likely to be Provided	Partial or No Return on Investment Likely to Be Provided
Cost of the impaired plant	Any disallowance of all or part of the cost of the impaired plant that is *both probable* and *reasonably estimable* (similarly to other loss contingencies) should be recognized as a loss, and the carrying basis of the recorded asset should be correspondingly reduced. The remainder of the cost of the impaired plant should be reported as a separate new asset.	Any disallowance of all or part of the cost of the impaired plant that is both probable and reasonably estimable (similarly to other loss contingencies) should be recognized as a loss. The present value of the future revenues expected to be provided to recover the allowable cost of that impaired plant and return on investment, if any, should be reported as a separate new asset. Any excess of the remainder of the cost of the impaired plant over that present value also should be recognized as a loss. The discount rate used to compute the present value should be the regulated business-type activity's incremental borrowing rate; that is, the rate that the regulated business-type activity would have to pay to borrow an equivalent amount for a period equal to the expected recovery period. In determining the present value of expected future revenues, the regulated business-type activity should consider such matters as: • The probable period before such recovery is expected to begin, *and* • The probable period over which recovery is expected to be provided. If the estimate of either period is a range, the loss contingency guidance should be applied to determine the loss to be recognized. Accordingly, the most likely period within that range should be used to compute the present value. If no period within that range is a better estimate than any other, the present value should be based on the minimum period within that range.
Adjustment of Asset Carrying Amount— Change in Rates	A rate equal to the allowed overall cost of capital in the jurisdiction in which recovery is expected to be provided should be used.	The rate that was used to compute the present value should be used.

Element	Full Return on Investment Likely to be Provided	Partial or No Return on Investment Likely to Be Provided
New Asset Amortization during Recovery Period	The asset should be amortized in the same manner as that used for rate-making purposes.	The asset should be amortized in a manner that will produce a constant return on the unamortized investment in the new asset equal to the rate at which the expected revenues were discounted.

Disallowed Costs of Construction. Regulators will likely audit material construction projects subject to regulation. When it becomes *probable* that part of the cost of a recently completed plant will be disallowed for rate-making purposes and a reasonable estimate of the amount of the disallowance can be made, the estimated amount of the probable disallowance should be deducted from the reported cost of the plant and recognized as a loss. If part of the cost is explicitly, but indirectly, disallowed (e.g., by an explicit disallowance of return on investment on a portion of the plant), an equivalent amount of cost should be deducted from the reported cost of the plant and recognized as a loss [GASB Cod. Sec. Re10.117].

Sale-leaseback Transactions-Regulated Operations Only. Sale-leaseback transaction accounting may result in a difference between the timing of revenue and expense relating to such transactions. The timing of revenue and expense recognition related to the sale-leaseback transaction should be modified as necessary to conform to this section. That modification is required for a transaction accounted for by the deposit method or as a financing.

If a sale-leaseback transaction is accounted for by the deposit method but the sale is recognized for rate-making purposes, the amortization of the asset should be modified to equal the total of the rental expense and the gain or loss allowable for rate-making purposes. Similarly, if the sale-leaseback transaction is accounted for as a financing and the sale is recognized for rate-making purposes, the total of interest imputed under the interest method for the financing and the amortization of the asset should be modified to equal the total rental expense and the gain or loss allowable for rate-making purposes.

The difference between the amount of revenue or expense recognized for a transaction that is accounted for by the deposit method or as a financing and the amount of revenue or expense included in allowable cost for rate-making purposes is capitalized or accrued as a separate regulatory-created asset or liability, as appropriate, if that difference meets the criteria of the regulatory provisions [GASB Cod. Secs. Re10.118–.120].

> **PRACTICE POINT:** See Chapter 14 for a complete discussion of GASB Cod. Sec. L20 (*Leases*) and related arrangements.

Refunds. For refunds that are recognized in a period other than the period in which the related revenue was recognized, the regulated business-type activity should disclose the effect on the change in net position and indicate the years in which the related revenue was recognized. Such effect may be disclosed by including it as a line item in the statement of revenues, expenses and changes in fund net position or the statement of activities, as applicable [GASB Cod. Sec. Re10.121].

Recovery without Return on Investment. In some cases, a regulator may permit a regulated business-type activity to include a cost that would be charged to expense by an unregulated business-type activity as an allowable cost over a period by amortizing that cost for rate-making purposes, but the regulator does not include the unrecovered amount in the rate base. That procedure does not provide a return on investment during the recovery period. If recovery of such major costs is provided without a return on investment during the recovery period, the regulated business-type activity discloses the remaining amounts of such assets and the remaining recovery period applicable to them [GASB Cod. Sec. Re10.122].

Discontinuation of Regulatory Accounting – (Deregulation)

Discontinuance of regulatory accounting may be caused by:

1. Deregulation,
2. A change in the regulator's approach to setting rates from cost-based rate making to another form of regulation,
3. Increasing competition that limits the regulated business-type activity's ability to sell utility services at rates that will recover costs, or
4. Regulatory actions resulting from resistance to rate increases that limit the regulated business-type activity's ability to sell utility services at rates that will recover costs if the regulated business-type activity is unable to obtain (or chooses not to seek) relief from prior regulatory actions through appeals to the regulator or the courts.

These instances must be reported in the basic financial statements as they may be a material change in operations.

When a regulated business-type activity determines that its operations in a regulatory jurisdiction no longer meet the criteria for application of regulated operations, that regulated business-type activity should discontinue these accounting provisions to its operations in that jurisdiction immediately. Similar actions should occur if the portion that fails to meet the criteria is separable from other operations that demonstrably continue to meet the criteria.

When a regulated business-type activity discontinues regulatory accounting to all or part of its operations, that regulated business-type activity should eliminate from its Statement of Net Position prepared for general-purpose external financial reporting the effects of any actions of regulators that had been recognized as assets and liabilities as discussed in this section but would not have been recognized as assets and liabilities by business-type activities in general.

However, the carrying amounts of capital assets and inventory measured and reported in accordance with the regulatory provisions should not be adjusted unless those assets are impaired, in which case the carrying amounts of those assets should be reduced to reflect that impairment. Whether those assets have been impaired should be judged in the same manner as for business-type activities in general. The net effect of the adjustments should be recognized in the period in which the discontinuation occurs and should be classified as a special or extraordinary item if they meet the criteria for such elements.

The carrying amounts of capital assets and inventory for regulated business-type activities applying regulatory accounting differ from those for business-type activities in general only because of the allowance for resources used during construction, intra-entity profit, and disallowances of costs of recently completed plants. If any other amounts that would not be includable in the carrying amounts of capital assets or inventory by business-type activities in general are included in or netted against the carrying amounts of capital assets or inventory, those amounts should be accounted for as part of the deregulation action.

Finally, a regulated business-type activity that discontinues application of regulatory accounting should no longer recognize the effects of actions of a regulator as assets or liabilities unless the right to receive payment or the obligation to pay exists resulting from past events or transactions and regardless of future transactions [GASB Cod. Secs. Re10.124–.127, fn.11].

Disclosure of Deregulation. In a discontinuance of regulatory accounting involving all or a portion of operations, disclosure is required of the reasons and identification of which portion (or all) of the operations the deregulation applies [GASB Cod. Sec. Re10.128].

CHAPTER 25
CROSS-REFERENCE

INTRODUCTION

The introduction to each chapter of the *Governmental GAAP Guide* contains references to GASB, NCGA or AICPA guidance. This chapter cross-references that guidance to *Codification* sections and chapters in the *Guide*.

Original Pronouncement	Title	Codification References [GASB Cod. Secs.]	Governmental GAAP Guide Chapters
NCGA-1	Governmental Accounting and Financial Reporting Principles	1100, 1200, 1300, 1400, 1500, 1600, 1700, 1800, 2200, 2300, 2400, 2600, 2700, 2900, P70	1, 2, 3, 5, 10, 16, 20
NCGA-2	Superseded	Superseded	Superseded
NCGA-3	Superseded	Superseded	Superseded
NCGA-4	Accounting and Financial Reporting Principles for Claims and Judgments and Compensated Absences	1600, C50	6, 15
NCGA-5	Superseded	Superseded	Superseded
NCGA-6	Superseded	Superseded	Superseded
NCGA-7	Superseded	Superseded	Superseded
NCGA Interpretation 1	Superseded	Superseded	Superseded
NCGA Interpretation 2	Superseded	Superseded	Superseded
NCGA Interpretation 3	Revenue Recognition—Property Taxes	P70	17
NCGA Interpretation 4	Superseded	Superseded	Superseded
NCGA Interpretation 5	Superseded	Superseded	Superseded
NCGA Interpretation 6	Notes to Financial Statements Disclosure	2300, 2400	20
NCGA Interpretation 7	Superseded	Superseded	Superseded
NCGA Interpretation 8	Superseded	Superseded	Superseded
NCGA Interpretation 9	Certain Fund Classifications and Balance Sheet Accounts	1300, B50, U50	5, 6, 20, 24
NCGA Interpretation 10	State and Local Government Budgetary Reporting	1700, 2400	2

25,002 Stand-Alone Financial Reporting by Special-Purpose Governments

Original Pronouncement	Title	Codification References [GASB Cod. Secs.]	Governmental GAAP Guide Chapters
NCGA Interpretation 11	Superseded	Superseded	Superseded
GASB-1	Authoritative Status of NCGA Pronouncements and AICPA Industry Audit Guide	P80, Po20	1
GASB-2	Superseded	Superseded	Superseded
GASB-3	Deposits with Financial Institutions, Investments (including Repurchase Agreements), and Reverse Repurchase Agreements	C20, I50, I55	9
GASB-4	Superseded	Superseded	Superseded
GASB-5	Superseded	Superseded	Superseded
GASB-6	Accounting and Financial Reporting for Special Assessments	1300, 1400, 1500, 1600, S40	19
GASB-7	Advance Refundings Resulting in Defeasance of Debt	D20	12
GASB-8	Superseded	Superseded	Superseded
GASB-9	Reporting Cash Flows of Proprietary and Nonexpendable Trust Funds and Governmental Entities That Use Proprietary Fund Accounting	2450	7, 20
GASB-10	Accounting and Financial Reporting for Risk Financing and Related Insurance Issues	2200, C50, Po20	15, 23
GASB-11	Superseded	Superseded	Superseded
GASB-12	Superseded	Superseded	Superseded
GASB-13	Superseded	Superseded	Superseded
GASB-14	The Financial Reporting Entity	1100, 2100, 2600, C20, C50, D20, I50, I55, J50, L20, Ca5, Co5, Ho5, In3, Sp20, Ut5	4, 8, 20, 24
GASB-15	Superseded	Superseded	Superseded
GASB-16	Accounting for Compensated Absences **PRACTICE ALERT**: This will be superseded upon the implementation of GASB Statement No. 101 (*Compensated Absences*) for reporting periods beginning after December 15, 2023.	1600, C60	13
GASB-17	*Superseded*	Superseded	Superseded

Cross-Reference **25,003**

Original Pronouncement	Title	Codification References [GASB Cod. Secs.]	Governmental GAAP Guide Chapters
GASB-18	Accounting for Municipal Solid Waste Landfill Closure and Postclosure Care Costs	L10	16
GASB-19	Superseded	Superseded	Superseded
GASB-20	Superseded	Superseded	Superseded
GASB-21	Accounting for Escheat Property	E70	11
GASB-22	Superseded	Superseded	Superseded
GASB-23	Accounting and Financial Reporting for Refundings of Debt Reported by Proprietary Activities	D20	12
GASB-24	Accounting and Financial Reporting for Certain Grants and Other Financial Assistance	N50	17
GASB-25	Superseded	Superseded	Superseded
GASB-26	Superseded	Superseded	Superseded
GASB-27	Superseded	Superseded	Superseded
GASB-28	Accounting and Financial Reporting for Securities Lending Transactions	I60	9
GASB-29	Superseded	Superseded	Superseded
GASB-30	Risk Financing Omnibus—an amendment of GASB Statement No. 10	2800, C50, Po20	15, 23
GASB-31	Accounting and Financial Reporting for Certain Investments and for External Investment Pools	1600, 2600, I50, J50, In5	9
GASB-32	Superseded	Superseded	Superseded
GASB-33	Accounting and Financial Reporting for Nonexchange Transactions	1600, N50	17
GASB-34	Basic Financial Statements—and Management's Discussion and Analysis—for State and Local Governments	1100, 1200, 1300, 1400, 1500, 1600, 1700, 1800, 2100, 2200, 2250, 2300, 2400, 2450, 2500, 2600, 2700, Ca5, Co5, Ho5, In3, Sp20, Ut5, B50, C20, C50, C60, D20, I50, I55, I60, J50, L10, L20, P80, S40	All, especially 20

25,004 *Stand-Alone Financial Reporting by Special-Purpose Governments*

Original Pronouncement	Title	Codification References [GASB Cod. Secs.]	Governmental GAAP Guide Chapters
GASB-35	Basic Financial Statements—and Management's Discussion and Analysis—for Public Colleges and Universities—an amendment of GASB Statement No. 34	2450, Co5, D20	21
GASB-36	Recipient Reporting for Certain Shared Nonexchange Revenues—an amendment of GASB Statement No. 33	N50	17, 18
GASB-37	Basic Financial Statements—and Management's Discussion and Analysis—for State and Local Governments: Omnibus—an amendment of GASB Statements No. 21 and No. 34	1100, 1300, 1400, 1800, 2200, 2500, E70	All, especially 20
GASB-38	Certain Financial Statement Note Disclosures	1300, 1500, 1600, 2300, C20, I50, L20	2, 11, 14, 16, 17, 19
GASB-39	Determining Whether Certain Organizations Are Component Units—an amendment of GASB Statement No. 14	2100, 2600	4
GASB-40	Deposit and Investment Risk Disclosures—an amendment of GASB Statement No. 3	C20, I50, I55, I60	9
GASB-41	Budgetary Comparison Schedules—Perspective Differences—an amendment of GASB Statement No. 34	2200, 2400	2, 20
GASB-42	Accounting and Financial Reporting for Impairment of Capital Assets and for Insurance Recoveries	1100, 1400, 2300, C50	10, 24
GASB-43	Superseded	Superseded	Superseded
GASB-44	Economic Condition Reporting: The Statistical Section—an amendment of NCGA Statement 1	2800	20
GASB-45	Superseded	Superseded	Superseded
GASB-46	Net Assets Restricted by Enabling Legislation—an amendment of GASB Statement No. 34	1800, 2200, 2300	5
GASB-47	Accounting for Termination Benefits	T25	13
GASB-48	Sales and Pledges of Receivables and Future Revenues and Intra-Entity Transfers of Assets and Future Revenues	2300, S20	17

Cross-Reference **25,005**

Original Pronouncement	Title	Codification References [GASB Cod. Secs.]	Governmental GAAP Guide Chapters
GASB-49	Accounting and Financial Reporting for Pollution Remediation Obligations	1500, P40	16
GASB-50	Superseded	Superseded	Superseded
GASB-51	Accounting and Financial Reporting for Intangible Assets	1100, 1300, 1400 1800, 2200, 2300, 2600, L10, Ca5, Ho5, In3, Sp20, Ut5	10
GASB-52	Land and Other Real Estate Held as Investments by Endowments	I50	9
GASB-53	Accounting and Financial Reporting for Derivative Instruments	D40, I50, In5	9, 12
GASB-54	Fund Balance Reporting and Governmental Fund Type Definitions	1100, 1300, 1800, 2200, 2300	1, 5, 6
GASB-55	Superseded	Superseded	Superseded
GASB-56	Codification of Accounting and Financial Reporting Guidance Contained in the AICPA Statements on Auditing Standards	2250, 2300, L20	1
GASB-57	Superseded	Superseded	Superseded
GASB-58	Accounting and Financial Reporting for Chapter 9 Bankruptcies	Bn5	1
GASB-59	Financial Statements Omnibus	C50, D40, I50	9
GASB-60	Superseded	Superseded	Superseded
GASB-61	The Financial Reporting Entity: Omnibus—an amendment of GASB Statements No. 14 and No. 34	2100, 2300, 2600, C20, C50, I50, I55, J50, Co5, Ho5, Sp20, Ut5	4
GASB-62	Codification of Accounting and Financial Reporting Guidance Contained in Pre-November 30, 1989 FASB and AICPA Pronouncements	1400, 1500, 1600, 1800, 2200, 2250, 2300, C50, C55, C75, D20, F70, I30, I40, I50, L20, L30, N70, R30, R50, Br10, Ca5, In3, Re10	All, especially 24
GASB-63	Financial Reporting of Deferred Outflows of Resources, Deferred Inflows of Resources and Net Position	1800, 2200, 2300	5, 12, 20, 22

25,006 *Stand-Alone Financial Reporting by Special-Purpose Governments*

Original Pronouncement	Title	Codification References [GASB Cod. Secs.]	Governmental GAAP Guide Chapters
GASB-64	Derivative Instruments: Application of Hedge Accounting Termination Provisions—an Amendment of GASB Statement No. 53	D40	9, 12
GASB-65	Items Previously Reported as Assets and Liabilities	1800, 2200, 2250, 2450, D20, F60, I30, L20, L30, N50, P80, S20, Po20, Re10	1, 14, 17, 18
GASB-66	Technical Corrections—2012—an amendment of GASB Statements No. 10 and No. 62	C50, L20, L30, Po20	12, 23
GASB-67	Financial Reporting for Pension Plans—an amendment of GASB Statement No. 25	I50, Pe5, Pe6	8, 13, 22
GASB-68	Accounting and Financial Reporting for Pensions—an amendment of GASB Statement No. 27	P20, P21, T25	8, 13
GASB-69	Government Combinations and Disposals of Government Operations	Co10, T25, 2300	4, 10
GASB-70	Accounting and Financial Reporting for Nonexchange Financial Guarantees	2300, N30 **PRACTICE ALERT:** GASB Cod. Sec. N30 will be replaced by GASB Cod. Sec. F30 (*Financial Guarantees*) after including GASB Statement No. 99 (*Omnibus 2022*), pars. 4–7, containing guidance on financial guarantees that are exchange and exchange-like transactions, upon implementation, for reporting periods beginning after June 15, 2023.	16, 19

Original Pronouncement	Title	Codification References [GASB Cod. Secs.]	Governmental GAAP Guide Chapters
GASB-71	Pension Transition for Contributions Made Subsequent to the Measurement Date—an amendment of GASB Statement No. 68	Not Codified—See GASB-68	8, 13
GASB-72	Fair Value Measurement and Application	1100, 1400, 1600, 2300, 3100, C55, D40, I50, I60, L30, In3, In5, Po20	9
GASB-73	Accounting and Financial Reporting for Pensions and Related Assets That Are Not within the Scope of GASB Statement 68, and Amendments to Certain Provisions of GASB Statements No. 67 and No. 68	2200, P22, P23, P24, T25, Pe5	8, 13
GASB-74	Financial Reporting for Postemployment Benefit Plans Other Than Pension Plans	2200, P53, Po50, Po51, P53	8, 13, 22
GASB-75	Accounting and Financial Reporting for Postemployment Benefits Other Than Pensions	2300, C60, P50, P51, P52, P54, T25	8, 13
GASB-76	The Hierarchy of Generally Accepted Accounting Principles for State and Local Governments	1000	1
GASB-77	Tax Abatement Disclosures	T10, 2300	17
GASB-78	Pensions Provided through Certain Multiple-Employer Defined Benefit Pension Plans	P20	13, 22
GASB-79	Certain External Investment Pools and Pool Participants	1100, 1300, 1600, 2100, 2200, 2300, 2600, 3100, D40, F70, I50, N50, P23, P53, S20, Ca5, Co5, Co10, Ho5, In3, Po20, Sp20, Ut5	9
GASB-80	Blending Requirements for Certain Component Units—an amendment of GASB Statement No. 14	I50, In5, 2600	4, 21
GASB-81	Irrevocable Split-Interest Agreements	I70	17, 21
GASB-82	Pension Issues—an amendment of GASB Statements No. 67, No. 68, and No. 73	2200, P20, P21, P22, P23, P24, T25, Pe5	13, 22

Stand-Alone Financial Reporting by Special-Purpose Governments

Original Pronouncement	Title	Codification References [GASB Cod. Secs.]	Governmental GAAP Guide Chapters
GASB-83	Certain Asset Retirement Obligations	1500, 1600, A10, C50, P40	10
GASB-84	Fiduciary Activities	1100, 1300, 1400, 1500, 1600, 1800, 2100, 2200, 2300, 2450, 2500, 2600, 2800, 3100, C20, C50, D25, E70, I50, I55, L20, N50, P23, P50, P52, P53, S40, Ca5, Co5, Ho5, In3, In5, Pe5, Pe6, Po20, Po50, Po51, Sp20, Ut5	1, 8, 13, 20
GASB-85	Omnibus 2017	2600, I50, P20, P21, P22, P24, Co5, Co10, In3, Pe6, Po20, Po50, Sp20, 2300, N50, P50, P51, P52, P54, Ho5, Ut5	4, 9, 13, 15, 17, 18, 21, 22, 23, 24
GASB-86	Certain Debt Extinguishment Issues	1500, 2300, C20, D20, D40, I50, I55	12
GASB-87	Leases	1200, 1400, 1500, 1600, 1800, 2100, 2200, 2300, 2450, 2600, 2800, C50, D20, D40, J50, L20, L30, R30, Bn5, Re10	14
GASB-88	Certain Disclosures Related to Debt Including Direct Borrowings and Direct Placements	1500, 2300, D30	12
GASB-89	Accounting for Interest Incurred before the End of a Construction Period	1100, 1400, 2200, I30, Re10	10, 24
GASB-90	Majority Equity Interests—an Amendment of GASB Statements No. 14 and No. 61	2100, 2600, I50, In5	4, 9
GASB-91	Conduit Debt Obligations	1500, 2450, C50, C65, L20, N30, S20, S30, In5	12, 16

Cross-Reference **25,009**

Original Pronouncement	Title	Codification References [GASB Cod. Secs.]	Governmental GAAP Guide Chapters
GASB-92	Omnibus 2020	1100, 1300, 1600, 2100, 2200, 2300, 2600, 3100, D40, F70, I50, N50, P23, P53, S20, Ca5, Co5, Co10, Ho5, In3, Po20, Sp20, Ut5, C50, C65, N30, S20, In5, L20	1, 4, 8, 9, 12, 22, 23
GASB-93	Replacement of Interbank Offered Rates	D20, D40, F70, I50, I55, L20, Re10	9, 12, 14
GASB-94	Public-Private and Public-Public Partnerships and Availability Payment Arrangements	1200, 1400, 1500, 2300, A90, C65, D20, L20, P90, Bn5	10, 14
GASB-95	Postponement of the Effective Dates of Certain Authoritative Guidance	Not codified	Introduction, all other chapters
GASB-96	Subscription-Based Information Technology Arrangements	1200, 1400, 1500, 1800, 2300, D20, L20, S80, Bn5, Pe5, Po50	10, 14
GASB-97	Certain Component Unit Criteria, and Accounting and Financial Reporting for Internal Revenue Code Section 457 Deferred Compensation Plans	1300, 2100, 2600, D25, I50, P20, P21, P22, P24, Ca5, Co5, Ho5, In3, Pe5, Pe6, Sp20, Ut5	8, 9, 13, 22
GASB-98	The Annual Comprehensive Financial Report	1100, 1200, 2100, 2200, 2300, 2400, 2600, 2700, 2800, P80, S40, Po20	Introduction, 20

25,010 *Stand-Alone Financial Reporting by Special-Purpose Governments*

Original Pronouncement	Title	Codification References [GASB Cod. Secs.]	Governmental GAAP Guide Chapters
GASB-99	Omnibus 2022	1100, 1400, 1500, 1600, 1800, 2100, 2200, 2300, 2600, 3100, A90, C20, C50, D30, D40, F30, F60 (deleted), I50, L20, N30 (to be merged into F30 and then deleted), N50, N70, P90, R30, S20, S80, Po20, Re10	All
GASB-100	Accounting Changes and Error Corrections	1400, 1800, 2200, 2250, 2300, 2450, 2600, D40, I50, L10, R30, P80, Co10, In5, Po20	Introduction, 3, 4, 6, 7, 16, 18, 20, 22
GASB-101	Compensated Absences (see GASB-16, above)	1600, C60	13
GASB Interpretation 1	Demand Bonds Issued by State and Local Governmental Entities—an interpretation of NCGA Statement 1 and NCGA Interpretation 9	1500, 1800, D30	12
GASB Interpretation 2	Superseded	Superseded	Superseded
GASB Interpretation 3	Financial Reporting for Reverse Repurchase Agreements—an interpretation of GASB Statement No. 3	1300, I55	9
GASB Interpretation 4	Accounting and Financial Reporting for Capitalization Contributions to Public Entity Risk Pools—an interpretation of GASB Statements No. 10 and No. 14	C50, J50, Po20	23
GASB Interpretation 5	Property Tax Revenue Recognition in Governmental Funds—an interpretation of NCGA Statement 1 and an amendment of NCGA Interpretation 3	P70	17

Cross-Reference **25,011**

Original Pronouncement	Title	Codification References [GASB Cod. Secs.]	Governmental GAAP Guide Chapters
GASB Interpretation 6	Recognition and Measurement of Certain Liabilities and Expenditures in Governmental Fund Financial Statements—an interpretation of NCGA Statements 1, 4, and 5; NCGA Interpretation 8; and GASB Statements No. 10, No. 16, and No. 18	1500, 1600, C50, C60, L10	16
GASB Technical Bulletin 84-1	Purpose and Scope of GASB Technical Bulletins and Procedures for Issuance	Not codified	1
GASB Technical Bulletins between 1984 and 2004	Superseded	Superseded	Superseded
GASB Technical Bulletin 2004-1	Tobacco Settlement Recognition and Financial Reporting Entity Issues	2100, 2600, T50	17
GASB Technical Bulletin 2004-2	Recognition of Pension and Other Postemployment Benefit Expenditures/Expense and Liabilities by Cost-Sharing Employers	P20, P50	13, 22
GASB Technical Bulletin 2006-1	Accounting and Financial Reporting by Employers and OPEB Plans for Payments from the Federal Government Pursuant to the Retiree Drug Subsidy Provisions of Medicare Part D	P50, P52, Po50	13, 22
GASB Technical Bulletin 2008-1	Superseded	Superseded	Superseded
GASB Technical Bulletin 2020-1	Accounting and Financial Reporting Issues Related to Coronavirus Aid and Economic Security Act (CARES) Act of 2020 and COVID-19	1800, 2200, 2250, N30, N50, P80, Ho5	1, 16, 17, 18, 20, 24
GASB Implementation Guides	Self-evident	All	All
GASB and remaining NCGA Concepts Statements	Self-evident—not authoritative for preparers and auditors	Appendix B and Appendix C	1
AICPA Statements of Position prior to 1998	Superseded	All superseded as applicable to governments	Superseded

Stand-Alone Financial Reporting by Special-Purpose Governments

Original Pronouncement	Title	Codification References [GASB Cod. Secs.]	Governmental GAAP Guide Chapters
AICPA SOP 98-2	Accounting for Costs of Activities of Not-for-Profit Organizations and State and Local Governmental Entities That Include Fund Raising	Co5, Ho5	21, 24
AICPA Audit and Accounting Guide, *State and Local Governments*	Self-Evident	1000, 1500, 1600, 1700, 1800, 2200, 2300, 2400, D20, N50, P80	All
AICPA Audit and Accounting Guide, *Gaming*	Self-Evident	1400, P80, Sp20	17, 24
AICPA Audit and Accounting Guide, *Health Care Entities*	Self-Evident	1000, P80, Ho5	24

GASB Exposure Draft at the Time of Publication in Process:

Exposure Draft Project No.	Title	Codification References [GASB Cod. Secs.]	Governmental GAAP Guide Chapters
3–25	Financial Reporting Model Improvements	All	All

In addition, the *Risks and Uncertainties Disclosures* proposal was in the process of release at the time of publication. Should they be finalized by the time of the release of the 2025 *Guide*, the previous table will be updated, along with any Exposure Drafts that have become GASB pronouncements.

Glossary

This glossary has been developed to assist users of the *Governmental GAAP Guide* to understand terms that are commonly used in state and local governments. It is not meant to be all-inclusive, nor is it meant to be authoritative. The GASB Standard referenced is the latest GASB Statement that includes the definition in a glossary or in the text of the Statement.

PRACTICE POINT: This glossary does not include definitions contained in *Government Auditing Standards* as issued by the General Accountability Office (GAO). Those definitions are on ARM at the link for Government Auditing Standards, pages 211-221. Though they may be of interest to preparers, those definitions are more of interest to auditors.

PRACTICE POINT: This is the only chapter in the *Guide* that references GASB Standards where applicable.

Item	GASB Pronouncement[1]	Definition
2a7-like pool	GASB-59	An external investment pool that is not registered with the SEC as an investment company, but nevertheless has a policy that it will, and does, operate in a manner consistent with the SEC's Rule 2a-7 of the Investment Company Act of 1940 (17 *Code of Federal Regulations* § 270.2a-7). Rule 2a-7 allows SEC-registered mutual funds to use amortized cost rather than market value to report net assets to compute share prices if certain conditions are met. Those conditions include restrictions on the types of investments held, restrictions on the term-to-maturity of individual investments and the dollar-weighted average of the portfolio, requirements for portfolio diversification, and requirements for divestiture considerations in the event of security downgrades and defaults and required actions if the market value of the portfolio deviates from amortized cost by a specified amount. (See "External Investment Pool" and "Qualified External Investment Pool.")
AAA general obligations index	GASB-53	An index published by Municipal Market Data composed of interest rates of the highest quality state and local debt issuers.

26,002 Glossary

Item	GASB Pronouncement[1]	Definition
Accountability (accountable)	GASB-14	The relationship that results from the appointment of a voting majority of an organization's governing board.
Accounting change	GASB-100	A change in (a) accounting principles, (b) accounting estimates, or (c) to or within the reporting entity.
Accounting estimates	GASB-100	Outputs determined based on inputs such as data, assumptions, and measurement methodologies. As outputs, accounting estimates are amounts subject to measurement uncertainty that are recognized or disclosed in the basic financial statements. A change in an accounting estimate results from changes to the inputs of that estimate. Changes to inputs result from a change in circumstance, new information, or more experience.
Accounting principle	GASB-62	Accounting principles and practices but also the methods of applying them.
ACFR	GASB-98	Abbreviation for Annual Comprehensive Financial Report. (See further explanation under "Annual Comprehensive Financial Report.")
Acquisition costs (government combinations)	GASB-69	Acquisition costs are the costs the acquiring government incurs to affect a government acquisition. Acquisition costs include, but are not limited to, fees for legal, accounting, valuation, professional, or consulting services.
Acquisition costs (insurance entities other than public entity risk pools)	GASB-62	Costs incurred in the acquisition of new and renewal insurance contracts. Acquisition costs include those costs that vary with and are primarily related to the acquisition of insurance contracts (for example, agent and broker commissions, certain underwriting and policy issue costs, and medical and inspection fees).
Acquisition value	GASB-72	The price that would be paid to acquire an asset with equivalent service potential in an orderly market transaction at the acquisition date, or the amount at which a liability could be liquidated with the counterparty at the acquisition date.

Glossary **26,003**

Item	GASB Pronouncement[1]	Definition
Act of God	GASB-10	An event beyond human origin or control, natural disasters. Lighting, windstorms, and earthquakes are examples.
Active employees	GASB-75	Individuals employed at the end of the reporting or measurement period, as applicable.
Active market	GASB-72	A market in which transactions for an asset or liability take place with enough frequency and volume to provide pricing information on an ongoing basis.
Active plan members	GASB-74	Employees in active service that are covered under the terms of an OPEB plan.
Actual contributions	GASB-68	Cash contributions recognized as additions to a pension plan's fiduciary net position.
Actual synthetic rate	GASB-53	If the hedged item is an existing financial instrument or an expected transaction that is intended to be a financial instrument, the rate achieved by a synthetic instrument considering its cash flows for a period.
Actuarial accrued liability (AAL)		That portion, as determined by a particular Actuarial Cost Method, of the Actuarial Present Value of pension plan benefits and expenses which is not provided for by future Normal Costs. *No longer utilized for general purpose external financial reporting.*
Actuarial assumptions		Assumptions as to the occurrence of future events affecting pension costs, such as: mortality, withdrawal, disablement, and retirement, changes in compensation and government-provided pension benefits, rates of investment earnings and asset appreciation or depreciation, procedures used to determine the Actuarial Value of Assets, characteristics of future entrants for Open Group Actuarial Cost Methods, and other relevant items.
Actuarial cost method		A procedure for determining the Actuarial Present Value of pension plan benefits and expenses and for developing an actuarially equivalent allocation of such value to time periods, usually in the form of a Normal Cost and an Actuarial Accrued Liability.

Glossary

Item	GASB Pronouncement[1]	Definition
Actuarial experience gain and loss		A measure of the difference between actual experience and that expected based upon a set of Actuarial Assumptions, during the period between two Actuarial Valuation dates, as determined in accordance with a particular Actuarial Cost Method.
Actuarial method	GASB-10	Any of several techniques that actuaries use to determine the amounts and timing of contributions needed to finance claims liabilities so that the total contributions plus compounded earnings on them will equal the amounts needed to satisfy claims liabilities. It may or may not include a provision for anticipated catastrophe losses.
Actuarial present value of projected benefit payments	GASB-75	Projected benefit payments discounted to reflect the expected effects of the time value (present value) of money and the probabilities of payment.
Actuarial valuation	GASB-75	The determination, as of a point in time (the actuarial valuation date), of the service cost, total pension or OPEB liability, and related actuarial present value of projected benefit payments for pensions performed in conformity with Actuarial Standards of Practice unless otherwise specified by the GASB.
Actuarial valuation date	GASB-75	The date as of which an actuarial valuation is performed.
Actuarial value of assets		The value of cash, investments and other property belonging to a pension plan, as used by the actuary for an Actuarial Valuation. *No longer utilized for general purpose external financial reporting as assets are at market value.*
Actuarially determined contribution	GASB-75	A target or recommended contribution to a defined benefit pension or OPEB plan for the reporting period, determined in conformity with Actuarial Standards of Practice based on the most recent measurement available when the contribution for the reporting period was adopted.
Actuarially equivalent		Of equal Actuarial Present Value, determined as of a given date with each value based on the same set of Actuarial Assumptions.

Glossary

Item	GASB Pronouncement[1]	Definition
Ad hoc cost-of-living adjustments (ad hoc COLAs)	GASB-75	Cost-of-living adjustments that require a decision to grant by the authority responsible for making such decisions.
Ad hoc postemployment benefit changes	GASB-75	Postemployment benefit changes that require a decision to grant by the authority responsible for making such decisions
Administrative involvement	GASB-84	With regard to fiduciary activities, a government has administrative involvement with the assets if, for example, it (a) monitors compliance with the requirements of the activity that are established by the government or by a resource provider that does not receive the direct benefits of the activity, (b) determines eligible expenditures that are established by the government or by a resource provider that does not receive the direct benefits of the activity, or (c) has the ability to exercise discretion in how assets are allocated.
Advance refunding (of bonds) (could also occur in leases).	GASB-7	In an *advance refunding* transaction, new debt is issued to provide monies to pay interest on old, outstanding debt as it becomes due, and to pay the principal on the old debt either as it matures or at an earlier call date. An advance refunding occurs before the maturity or call date of the old debt, and the proceeds of the new debt are invested until the maturity or call date of the old debt. Most advance refundings result in defeasance of debt. Defeasance of debt can be either legal or in substance. **PRACTICE POINT:** Advance refunding transactions are taxable due to the provisions of the Tax Cuts and Jobs Act of 2017 (PL 115-97).
Agent employer	GASB-75	An employer whose employees are provided with pensions or OPEB through an agent multiple-employer defined benefit pension or OPEB plan.
Agent fees	GASB-28	Amounts paid by a lender to its securities lending agent as compensation for managing its securities lending transactions.

Glossary

Item	GASB Pronouncement[1]	Definition
Agent multiple-employer defined benefit pension or OPEB plan (agent pension or OPEB plan)	GASB-75	A multiple-employer defined benefit pension (or OPEB) plan in which pension plan assets are pooled for investment purposes but separate accounts are maintained for each individual employer so that each employer's share of the pooled assets is legally available to pay the benefits of only its employees.
Aggregate actuarial cost method		A method under which the excess of the Actuarial Present Value of Projected Benefits of the group included in an Actuarial Valuation over the Actuarial Value of Assets is allocated on a level basis over the earnings or service of the group between the valuation date and assumed exit. This allocation is performed for the group, not as a sum of individual allocations. That portion of the Actuarial Present Value allocated to a valuation year is called the Normal Cost. The Actuarial Accrued Liability is equal to the Actuarial Value of Assets. *No longer utilized for general purpose external financial reporting.*
AICPA		American Institute of Certified Public Accountants (also known as the American Institute of CPAs)
Allocated insurance contract	GASB-74	A contract with an insurance company under which related payments to the insurance company are currently used to purchase immediate or deferred annuities for individual employees. Also, may be referred to as an annuity contract.
Allotment (or allot)	NCGAI-10	Where spending authority is apportioned for a period by an approving authority.
Amenities (real estate)	GASB-62	Examples of amenities include golf courses, utility plants, clubhouses, swimming pools, tennis courts, indoor recreational facilities, and parking facilities.
Amortization	GASB-51	Depreciation of an intangible asset.
Amortization (of unfunded actuarial accrued liability)		Systematic and rational manner of allocating liability amounts to future periods, based upon an accepted methodology. Amortization payments include payments of interest on and to amortize a liability.

Glossary **26,007**

Item	GASB Pronouncement[1]	Definition
Annexation	GASB-69	Changes in the territorial boundaries of governments. An annexation may also be known as reorganization. In a government annexation arrangement, one government extends the bounds of its geographic footprint to include new incorporated or unincorporated areas. Often, annexations result only in changes in boundaries, and the annexed governments generally do not give up assets or gain relief from liabilities. However, in annexations in which assets, deferred outflows of resources, liabilities, and deferred inflows of resources comprising an operation are transferred, those items are required to be recognized at the carrying amounts reported by the transferring government.
Annual OPEB cost		An accrual-basis measure of the periodic cost of an employer's participation in a defined benefit OPEB plan. No longer utilized for general purpose external financial reporting.
Annual required contributions of the employer(s) (ARC)		The employer's periodic required contributions to a defined benefit OPEB plan, calculated in accordance with the parameters. *No longer utilized for general purpose external financial reporting.*
Annuity contract	GASB-10	A contract that provides fixed or variable periodic payments made from a stated or contingent date and continuing for a specified period, such as for several years or for life.
Annual Financial Report (AFR)	Self-evident	The annual report of a reporting entity government focusing on the basic financial statements required by GAAP. (See ACFR.)

26,008 *Glossary*

Item	GASB Pronouncement[1]	Definition
Annual Comprehensive Financial Report (ACFR)	GASB-98	Formerly, the Comprehensive Financial Report. In both cases, detailed report containing the basic financial statements and other information and are intended for users who need a broad range of information. ACFRs may include such nonfinancial information as statistical data, analytical data, demographic information, forecasts, economic and service delivery statistics, legally required data, narrative explanations, and graphic displays. It includes introductory, financial, and statistical sections (actuarial section on postemployment benefit plans), and other combining information on funds.
Appoint	GASB-14	To select members of a governing body (if the ability to do so is not severely limited by a nomination process) or confirm appointments made by others (provided that the confirmation is more than a formality or part of a ministerial responsibility).
Appropriated budget	NCGAI-10	The expenditure authority created by a bill or ordinance that is in law. It may also include revenues, transfers, allocations, allotments, and program changes. It may be for a single period or for multiple years and for capital or for operating purposes or both.
Appropriation	NCGAI-10	A line item giving spending authority in a budget.
ARPA	PL 117-2	Federal American Rescue Plan Act of 2021.
Asset impairment	GASB-42	A significant, unexpected decline in the service utility of a capital asset.
Asset-backed securities	GASB-31	Assets that are composed of, or collateralized by, loans or receivables. Collateralization can consist of liens on real property, leases, or credit card debt.
Asset retirement obligation (ARO)	GASB-83	A legally enforceable liability associated with the retirement of a tangible capital asset.
Assets	GASB-65 (also GASB:CS-4)	Resources with present service capacity that the government presently controls.

Item	GASB Pronouncement[1]	Definition
Assigned fund balance	GASB-54	Amounts that are constrained by the government's *intent* to be used for specific purposes but are neither restricted nor committed. Intent should be expressed by (a) the governing body itself or (b) a body (a budget or finance committee, for example) or official to which the governing body has delegated the authority to assign amounts to be used for specific purposes.
Assignment	GASB-64	An assignment occurs when a swap agreement is amended to replace an original swap counterparty, or the swap counterparty's credit support provider, but all the other terms of the swap agreement remain unchanged.
At the market	GASB-53	The prevailing market price or rate. For example, an at-the-market swap is entered into at no cost to the government.
Attained age actuarial cost method		A method under which the excess of the Actuarial Present Value of Projected Benefits over the Actuarial Accrued Liability in respect of everyone included in an Actuarial Valuation is allocated on a level basis over the earnings or service of the individual between the valuation date and assumed exit. The portion of this Actuarial Present Value which is allocated to a valuation year is called the Normal Cost. The Actuarial Accrued Liability is determined using the Unit Credit Actuarial Cost Method. *No longer utilized for general purpose external financial reporting.*
Authoritative GAAP	GASB-76	Category A GAAP and Category B GAAP. Authoritative GAAP is incorporated periodically into the *Codification of Governmental Accounting and Financial Reporting Standards* (Codification), and when presented in the Codification, it retains its authoritative status.

26,010 Glossary

Item	GASB Pronouncement[1]	Definition
Automatic cost-of-living adjustments (automatic COLAs)	GASB-75	Cost-of-living adjustments that occur without a requirement for a decision to grant by a responsible authority, including those for which the amounts are determined by reference to a specified experience factor (such as the earnings experience of the pension or OPEB plan) or to another variable (such as an increase in the consumer price index).
Automatic postemployment benefit changes	GASB-75	Postemployment benefit changes that occur without a requirement for a decision to grant by a responsible authority, including those for which the amounts are determined by reference to a specified experience factor (such as the earnings experience of the pension or OPEB plan) or to another variable (such as an increase in the consumer price index).
Availability Payment Arrangement	GASB-94	An arrangement in which a government compensates an operator for services that may include designing, constructing, financing, maintaining, or operating an underlying nonfinancial asset for a period of time in an exchange or exchange-like transaction.
Available (property taxes)	GASBI-5	Collected within the current period or expected to be collected soon enough thereafter to be used to pay liabilities of the current period.
Balance sheet	GASB-34	Report of information about the current financial resources (assets, liabilities, and fund balances) of each major governmental fund and for nonmajor governmental funds in the aggregate and totaled as of the reporting date.
Bank holding company	GASB: TB 97-1	A company that controls one or more banks and may contain subsidiaries with operations related to banking.
Bankers' acceptances	GASB-3	Bankers' acceptances generally are created based on a letter of credit issued in a foreign trade transaction. Bankers' acceptances are short-term, non-interest-bearing notes sold at a discount and redeemed by the accepting banks at maturity for face value.
Banking pool	GASB-10	Risk financing arrangement in which monies are loaned to pool members in the event of a loss.

Glossary **26,011**

Item	GASB Pronouncement[1]	Definition
Bargain purchase option (leases)	GASB-62	A provision allowing the lessee the option to purchase the leased property for a price that is sufficiently lower than the expected fair value of the property at the date the option becomes exercisable such that exercise of the option appears, at the inception of the lease, to be reasonably assured. *No longer used for general purpose external financial reporting due to* implementation of GASB-87, but still used in practice.
Bargain renewal option (leases)	GASB-62	A provision allowing the lessee the option to renew the lease for a rental sufficiently lower than the fair rental of the property at the date the option becomes exercisable such that exercise of the option appears, at the inception of the lease, to be reasonably assured. *No longer used for general purpose external financial reporting due to implementation of GASB-87, but still used in practice.*
Barter (broadcasting)	GASB-62	The exchange of unsold advertising time for products or services. The broadcaster benefits (providing the exchange does not interfere with its cash sales) by exchanging otherwise unsold time for such things as programs, fixed assets, merchandise, other media advertising privileges, travel and hotel arrangements, entertainment, and other services or products.
Basic financial statements	GASB-34	The core required financial statements of a government including management's discussion and analysis, government-wide financial statements, fund financial statements, notes to the financial statements and required supplementary information other than the management's discussion and analysis.
Basis differences	NCGAI-10	Differences that may arise when the basis of budgeting is different than GAAP.
Basis risk	GASB-53	The risk that arises when variable rates or prices of a hedging derivative instrument and a hedged item are based on different reference rates.

Item	GASB Pronouncement[1]	Definition
Benchmark interest rate	GASB-53	A widely recognized and quoted rate in an active financial market that is broadly indicative of the overall level of interest rates attributable to high-credit-quality obligors in that market. It is a rate that is widely used in a financial market as a basis for determining the interest rates of financial instruments and commonly referenced in interest-rate-related transactions.
Beneficial interest	GASB-81	The right to a portion of benefits from donated resources pursuant to split-interest agreements in which the interest is placed into a trust or other legally enforceable agreement with characteristics that are equivalent to an irrevocable split interest agreement and transfers the resources to an intermediary.
Blending (blended)	GASB-14	The method of reporting the financial data of a component unit that presents the component unit's balances and transactions in a manner like the presentation of the balances and transactions of the primary government.
Book entry	GASB-3	A system that eliminates the need for physically transferring bearer-form paper or registering securities by using a central depository facility.
Borrower	GASB-28	A broker-dealer or other entity that transfers collateral to a governmental entity in a securities lending transaction.
Borrower rebate	GASB-28	Payments from the lender to the borrower as compensation for the use of cash collateral provided by the borrower.
Broadcaster	GASB-62	An entity or an affiliated group of entities that transmits radio or television program material.

Item	GASB Pronouncement[1]	Definition
Brokered market	GASB-72	A market in which brokers attempt to match buyers with sellers but do not stand ready to trade for their own account. In other words, brokers do not use their own capital to hold an inventory of the items for which they make a market. The broker knows the prices bid and asked by the respective parties, but each party is typically unaware of another party's price requirements. Prices of completed transactions are sometimes available. Brokered markets include electronic communication networks, in which buy and sell orders are matched, and commercial and residential real estate markets.
Budgetary comparison schedules	GASB-34	Schedules presented as required supplementary information for the general fund and for each major special revenue fund that has a legally adopted annual budget. The budgetary comparison schedule should present both (a) the original and (b) the final appropriated budgets for the reporting period as well as (c) actual inflows, outflows, and balances, stated on the government's budgetary basis. A separate column to report the variance between the final budget and actual amounts is encouraged but not required. Governments may also report the variance between original and final budget amounts.
Business enterprise capital assets	GASB-42	Assets that are used to produce revenues by selling goods or services. They are established as, and are expected to be, a self-supporting enterprise. Revenues produced are subject to market influences. Examples include power generation and transmission and casino enterprises.
Business-type activities	GASB-34	Activities financed in whole or in part by fees charged to external parties for goods and services.
Cable television plant	GASB-62	The cable television plant required to render service to the subscriber includes the following equipment:

26,014 *Glossary*

Item	GASB Pronouncement[1]	Definition
		• *Head-end*—This includes the equipment used to receive signals of distant television or radio stations, whether directly from the transmitter or from a microwave relay system. It also includes the studio facilities required for operator-originated programming, if any.
		• *Cable*—This consists of cable and amplifiers (which maintain the quality of the signal) covering the subscriber area, either on utility poles or underground.
		• *Drops*—These consist of the hardware that provides access to the main cable, the short length of cable that brings the signal from the main cable to the subscriber's television set, and other associated hardware, which may include a trap to block channels.
		• *Converters and descramblers*—These devices are attached to the subscriber's television sets when special services are provided, such as "pay cable" or two-way communication.
Call option	GASB-53	An option that gives its holder the right but not the obligation to purchase a financial instrument or commodity at a certain price for a period of time.
Capital and related financing activities	GASB-9	The (a) acquiring and disposing of capital assets used in providing services or producing goods, (b) borrowing money for acquiring, constructing, or improving capital assets and repaying the amounts borrowed, including interest, and (c) paying for capital assets obtained from vendors on credit.
Capital assets	GASB-34	Assets including land, improvements to land, easements, buildings, building improvements, vehicles, machinery, equipment, works of art and historical treasures, infrastructure, and all other tangible or intangible assets that are used in operations and that have initial useful lives extending beyond a single reporting period.

Glossary

Item	GASB Pronouncement[1]	Definition
Capital improvement assessment	GASB-6	Increase on taxes for capital asset acquisition or construction for a specific amount of time, for specific debts for specific property owners.
Capital projects funds	GASB-54	Funds used to account for and report financial resources that are restricted, committed, or assigned to expenditure for capital outlays, including the acquisition or construction of capital facilities and other capital assets. Capital projects funds exclude those types of capital-related outflows financed by proprietary funds or for assets that will be held in trust for individuals, private organizations, or other governments.
Capping	GASB 18	The cost of final cover expected to be applied near or after the date that the landfill stops accepting solid waste.
CARES Act	GASB TB 2020-1	Federal Coronavirus Aid, Relief, and Economic Security Act of 2020.
Carrying amount (book value)	GASB-3	The amount at which assets and liabilities are reported in the financial statements.
Cash	GASB-9	Currency.
Cash balance plan		A form of hybrid pension plan. In these plans, hypothetical accounts are maintained for participants. The government then credits the accounts with funds annually and promises earnings at an established rate. The rate may be different than actual earnings and the formula may be changed annually.
Cash conduit	GASB-24	A grantee that transmits grantor-supplied monies to subrecipients without having administrative or direct financial involvement in the program.
Cash equivalents	GASB-9	Cash equivalents are defined as short-term, highly liquid investments that are both: • Readily convertible to known amounts of cash. • So near their maturity that they present insignificant risk of changes in value because of changes in interest rates.

Glossary

Item	GASB Pronouncement[1]	Definition
Cash flow hedge	GASB-53	A hedge that protects against the risk of either changes in total variable cash flows or adverse changes in cash flows caused by variable prices, costs, rates, or terms that cause future prices to be uncertain.
Catastrophe	GASB-10	A conflagration, earthquake, windstorm, explosion, or similar event resulting in substantial losses *or* an unusually large number of unrelated and unexpected losses occurring in a single period.
Category A GAAP	GASB-76	Officially established accounting principles—Governmental Accounting Standards Board (GASB) Statements.
Category B GAAP	GASB-76	GASB Technical Bulletins, GASB Implementation Guides, and literature of the AICPA cleared by the GASB.
Cede	GASB-10	To transfer all or part of an insurance risk to another enterprise through reinsurance.
CFDA		Catalog of Federal Domestic Assistance
Change in accounting estimate	GASB-100	A change in an accounting estimate results from changes to the inputs that determine estimates. Changes to inputs result from a change in circumstance, new information, or more experience.
Change in accounting principle	GASB-100	A change in accounting principle results from either: a. A change from one generally accepted accounting principle to another generally accepted accounting principle that is justified on the basis that the newly adopted accounting principle is preferable to the accounting principle applied before the change. The qualitative characteristics of financial reporting—understandability, reliability, relevance, timeliness, consistency, and comparability—should be the basis for determining whether a new accounting principle would be preferable. b. The implementation of new authoritative accounting or financial reporting pronouncements.

Item	GASB Pronouncement[1]	Definition
Change in the fair value of investments	GASB-31	The difference between the fair value of investments at the beginning of the year and at the end of the year, taking into consideration investment purchases, sales, and redemptions.
Chapter 9 (U.S. Bankruptcy Code)	GASB-58	Section of the Uniform Commercial Code (UCC) intended to protect a financially distressed government from its creditors while it develops and negotiates a plan for adjusting its debts. Chapter 9 must be approved by a state prior to usage by a government. In states where Chapter 9 is not approved, other mechanisms may be used including fiscal oversight.
Charges for services	GASB-37	Term used for a broad category of program revenues that arise from charges to customers, applicants, or others who purchase, use, or directly benefit from the goods, services, or privileges provided, or are otherwise directly affected by the services. Revenues in this category include fees charged for specific services, such as water use or garbage collection, licenses and permits, such as dog licenses, liquor licenses, and building permits, operating special assessments, such as for street cleaning or special street lighting, and any other amounts charged to service recipients. Fines and forfeitures are also included in this category because they result from direct charges to those who are otherwise directly affected by a program or service, even though they receive no *benefit*. Payments from other governments for goods or services—for example, when County A reimburses County B for boarding County A's prisoners—also should be reported in this category.
Charity Care	GASB-76 (GASB Cod Sec 1000.802)	Charity care represents health care services that are provided but never expected to result in cash flows, therefore, charity care does not qualify for recognition as revenue.

Glossary

Item	GASB Pronouncement[1]	Definition
Claim (insurance entities other than public entity risk pools)	GASB-62	A demand for payment of a policy benefit because of the occurrence of an insured event, such as the death or disability of the insured, the incurrence of hospital or medical bills, the destruction or damage of property and related deaths or injuries, defects in or liens on real estate, or the occurrence of a surety loss.
Claim adjustment expenses	GASB-62	Expenses incurred while investigating and settling claims. Claim adjustment expenses include any legal and adjusters' fees, and the costs of paying claims and all related expenses. Unallocated claim adjustment expenses include other costs that cannot be associated with specific claims but are related to claims paid or in the process of settlement, such as salaries and other internal costs of the pool's claims department.
Closed amortization period (closed basis) (the opposite is an open amortization period)		A specific number of years that is counted from one date and, therefore, declines to zero with the passage of time. For example, if the amortization period initially is 30 years on a closed basis, 29 years remain after the first year, 28 years after the second year, and so forth. In contrast, an open amortization period (open basis) is one that begins again or is recalculated at each actuarial valuation date. Within a maximum number of years specified by law or policy (for example, 30 years), the period may increase, decrease, or remain stable. *No longer utilized for general purpose external financial reporting.*
Closed period	GASB-75	A specific number of years that is counted from one date and declines to zero with the passage of time. For example, if the recognition period initially is five years on a closed basis, four years remain after the first year, three years after the second year, and so forth.
Closed-end mutual fund	GASB-31	An SEC-registered investment company that issues a limited number of shares to investors which are then traded as an equity security on a stock exchange. See also Open-end mutual fund.

Item	GASB Pronouncement[1]	Definition
Collateral	GASB-28	The cash, securities, or letters of credit received by the lender from the borrower as protection against the borrower's failure to return the underlying securities.
Collateral investment pool	GASB-28	An agent-managed pool that for investment purposes commingles the cash collateral provided on the securities lending transactions of more than one lender.
Collective deferred outflows of resources and deferred inflows of resources related to pensions or OPEB	GASB-75	Deferred outflows of resources and deferred inflows of resources related to pensions arising from certain changes in the collective net pension or OPEB liability.
Collective net pension liability (Collective net OPEB liability)	GASB-75	The net pension or OPEB liability for benefits provided through: • A cost-sharing pension plan or • A single-employer or agent pension or OPEB plan in circumstances in which there is a special funding situation.
Collective pension or OPEB expense	GASB-75	Pension or OPEB expense arising from certain changes in the collective net pension or OPEB liability.
Collective total OPEB liability	GASB-75	The total OPEB liability for benefits provided through a defined benefit OPEB plan that is *not administered* through a trust and: • Is used to provide benefits to the employees of a primary government and its component units or • In which there is a special funding situation.
Collective total pension liability	GASB-73	The total pension liability for benefits provided through: • A pension plan that is used to provide pensions to the employees of a primary government and its component units or • A pension plan in circumstances in which there is a special funding situation.

Item	GASB Pronouncement[1]	Definition
		• There are at least three parties involved:
— An issuer,
— A third-party obligor, and
— A debtholder *or* a debt trustee.
• The issuer and the third-party obligor are not within the same financial reporting entity.
• The debt obligation is not a parity bond of the issuer, nor is it cross-collateralized with other debt of the issuer.
• The third-party obligor or its agent, not the issuer, ultimately receives the proceeds from the debt issuance.
• The third-party obligor, not the issuer, is primarily obligated for the payment of all amounts associated with the debt obligation (debt service payments).
• The issuer's commitment related to the debt service payments is limited.
Consistent critical terms method	GASB-53	A method of evaluating effectiveness by qualitative consideration of the uniformity of the significant terms of the hedgeable item with the terms of the potential hedging derivative instrument.
Contamination	GASB-83	An event or condition normally involving a substance that is deposited in, on, or around a tangible capital asset in a form or concentration that may harm people, equipment, or the environment due to the substance's radiological, chemical, biological, reactive, explosive, or mutagenic nature.
Contingency	GASB-62	An existing condition, situation, or set of circumstances involving uncertainty as to possible gain (referred to as a gain contingency) or loss (referred to as a loss contingency) to a government that will ultimately be resolved when one or more future events occur or fail to occur. Resolution of the uncertainty may confirm the acquisition of an asset or the reduction of a liability or the loss or impairment of an asset or the incurrence of a liability.

Glossary **26,023**

Item	GASB Pronouncement[1]	Definition
Contingent rentals	GASB-62	The increases or decreases in lease payments that result from changes occurring after the inception of the lease in the factors (other than the passage of time) on which lease payments are based, except as provided in the following sentence. Any escalation of minimum lease payments relating to increases in construction or acquisition cost of the leased property or for increases in some measure of cost or value during the construction or pre-construction period should be excluded from contingent rentals. Lease payments that depend on a factor directly related to the future use of the leased property, such as machine hours of use or sales volume during the lease term, are contingent rentals and, accordingly, are excluded from minimum lease payments in their entirety. However, lease payments that depend on an existing index or rate, such as the consumer price index or the prime interest rate, should be included in minimum lease payments based on the index or rate existing at the inception of the lease, any increases or decreases in lease payments that result from subsequent changes in the index or rate are contingent rentals and thus affect the determination of revenue or expense/expenditure as accruable. *No longer used for general purpose external financial reporting due to implementation of GASB-87, but still used in practice.*
Contract value		The value of an unallocated contract that is determined by the insurance company in accordance with the terms of the contract.
Contribution deficiencies (excess contributions)		The difference between the annual required contributions of the employer(s) (ARC) and the employer's actual contributions in relation to the ARC. *No longer utilized for general purpose external financial reporting.*

Item	GASB Pronouncement[1]	Definition
Contributions	GASB-75	Additions to a pension or OPEB plan's fiduciary net position for amounts from employers, nonemployer contributing entities (for example, state government contributions to a local government pension or OPEB plan), or employees.
Control (of assets)	GASB-84	A government controls the assets of an activity if the government: • Holds the assets or • Can direct the use, exchange, or employment of the assets in a manner that provides benefits to the specified or intended recipients. Restrictions from legal or other external restraints that stipulate the assets can be used only for a specific purpose do not negate a government's control of the assets.
Correction of an error	GASB-62	Changes to previously issued financial statements after discovering mathematical mistakes, mistakes in the application of accounting principles, or oversight or misuse of facts that existed at the time the financial statements were prepared.
COSO		Committee of Sponsoring Organizations
Cost approach	GASB-72	A valuation technique that reflects the amount that would be required currently to replace the service capacity of an asset (often referred to as current replacement cost).

Item	GASB Pronouncement[1]	Definition
Cost method (investments in common stock)	GASB-62	When an investor records an investment in the stock of an investee at cost and recognizes as revenue dividends received that are distributed from net accumulated earnings of the investee since the date of acquisition by the investor. The net accumulated earnings of an investee after the date of investment are recognized by the investor only to the extent distributed by the investee as dividends. Dividends received more than earnings after the date of investment are considered a return of investment and are recorded as reductions of cost of the investment. A series of operating losses of an investee or other factors may indicate that a decrease in value of the investment has occurred that is other than temporary and should accordingly be recognized.
Cost recovery method (insurance entities other than public entity risk pools)	GASB-62	Under the cost recovery method, premiums are recognized as revenue in an amount equal to estimated claim costs as insured events occur until the ultimate premium is reasonably estimable, and recognition of revenue is postponed until that time.
Cost-of-living adjustments	GASB-75	Postemployment benefit changes intended to adjust benefit payments for the effects of inflation.
Costs incurred to rent real estate projects	GASB-62	Examples of such costs include costs of model units and their furnishings, rental facilities, semi-permanent signs, rental brochures, advertising, "grand openings," and rental overhead including rental salaries.
Costs incurred to sell real estate projects	GASB-62	Examples of such costs include costs of model units and their furnishings, sales facilities, sales brochures, legal fees for preparation of prospectuses, semi-permanent signs, advertising, "grand openings," and sales overhead including sales salaries.
Cost-sharing employer	GASB-75	An employer whose employees are provided with pensions or OPEB through a cost-sharing multiple-employer defined benefit pension or OPEB plan.

Glossary

Item	GASB Pronouncement[1]	Definition
Cost-sharing multiple-employer defined benefit pension or OPEB plan (cost-sharing pension or OPEB plan)	GASB-75, GASB-78	A multiple-employer defined benefit pension or OPEB plan that is administered through an irrevocable trust and which the pensions or OPEB obligations to the employees of more than one employer are pooled and pensions or OPEB assets can be used to pay the benefits of the employees of any employer that provides pensions or OPEB through the pension or OPEB plan. (**NOTE:** As used solely in GASB-78, it is a multiple-employer defined benefit pension plan in which the pension obligations to the employees of more than one employer are pooled and pension plan assets can be used to pay the benefits of the employees of any employer that provides pensions through the pension plan.)
Counterparty		The party that pledges collateral or repurchase agreement securities to the government or that sells investments to or buys them for the government. Also used as the other party in a contractual agreement.
Coverage ratio	GASB-44	A measure of the magnitude of resources available to pay the interest on and repay the principal of debt backed by pledged revenues. For each type of debt backed by pledged revenues, a coverage ratio is generally calculated by dividing gross pledged revenues or pledged revenues net of specific operating expenses by the sum of interest expenses and principal repayments.
Covered group		Plan members included in an actuarial valuation.
Covered-employee payroll	GASB-75	The payroll of employees that are provided with pensions or OPEB through the pension or OPEB plan, respectively.
Covered payroll	GASB-82	The portion of compensation paid to active employees on which contributions to a pension plan are based.
CPA		Certified public accountant
Credit risk	GASB-72	The risk that a counterparty will not fulfill its obligations.

Item	GASB Pronouncement[1]	Definition
Critical term	GASB-53	A significant term of the hedgeable item and potential hedging derivative instrument that affects whether their changes in cash flows or fair values substantially offset. Examples are the notional or principal amounts, payment dates, and, in some cases, fair values at inception, indexes, rates, and options.
Crossover refunding bonds	GASBIG 2015-1 Q 7.23.15	In a crossover refunding, both the refunded debt and the refunding issued debt are reported on the statement of net position until the crossover date. Like other refunding bonds, gains and losses are deferred. May result in a taxable debt issuance, which would allow the issuer government to arbitrage the proceeds, but also encounter risk.
Current (normal) servicing fee rate (mortgage banking)	GASB-62	A servicing fee rate that is representative of servicing fee rates most commonly used in comparable servicing agreements covering similar types of mortgage loans.
Current assets	GASB-62	For accounting and financial reporting purposes, the term *current assets* is used to designate cash and other assets or resources commonly identified as those that are reasonably expected to be realized in cash or sold or consumed within a year. Therefore, current assets generally include such resources as: • Cash available for current operations and items that are the equivalent of cash, • Inventories of merchandise, raw materials, goods in process, finished goods, operating supplies, and ordinary maintenance material and parts, • Trade accounts, notes, and acceptances receivable, • Receivables from taxpayers, other governments, vendors, customers, beneficiaries, and employees, if collectible within a year, • Installment or deferred accounts and notes receivable if they conform generally to normal trade practices and terms within the business-type activity,

Item	GASB Pronouncement[1]	Definition
		<ul><li>Marketable securities representing the investment of cash available for current operations, and</li><li>Prepayments such as insurance, interest, rents, unused royalties, current paid advertising service not yet received, and operating supplies.</li></ul>Prepayments are not current assets in the sense that they will be converted into cash but in the sense that, if not paid in advance, they would require the use of current assets within a year. Therefore, current assets *exclude* such resources as:<ul><li>Cash and claims to cash that are restricted as to withdrawal or use for other than current operations, that are designated for disbursement in the acquisition or construction of noncurrent assets, or that are segregated for the liquidation of long-term debts,</li><li>Receivables arising from unusual transactions (such as the sale of capital assets) that are not expected to be collected within 12 months,</li><li>Cash surrender value of life insurance policies,</li><li>Land and other natural resources,</li><li>Depreciable assets, and</li><li>Long-term prepayments that are applicable to the operations of several years, or deferred outflows such as bonus payments under a long-term lease.</li></ul>

Item	GASB Pronouncement[1]	Definition
Current liabilities	GASB-62	Used principally to designate obligations whose liquidation is reasonably expected to require the use of existing resources properly classifiable as current assets, or the creation of other current liabilities. As a category in the statement of net [position], the classification is intended to include obligations for items that have occurred during the operating cycle, such as payables incurred in the acquisition of materials and supplies to be used in providing services, collections received in advance of the performance of services, and debts that arise from operations directly related to the operating cycle, such as accruals for wages, salaries, commissions, rentals, and royalties. Other liabilities whose regular and ordinary liquidation is expected to occur within one year also are intended for inclusion, such as short-term debts arising from the acquisition of capital assets, serial maturities of long-term obligations, amounts required to be expended within one year under sinking fund provisions, and certain agency obligations arising from the collection or acceptance of cash or other assets for the account of third parties. The current liability classification also is intended to include obligations that, by their terms, are due on demand or will be due on demand within one year from the date of the financial statements, even though liquidation may not be expected within that period. It also is intended to include long-term obligations that are or will be callable by the creditor either because the debtor's violation of a provision of the debt agreement at the date of the financial statements makes the obligation callable or because the violation, if not cured within a specified grace period, will make the obligation callable. Accordingly, such callable obligations should be classified as current liabilities unless one of the following conditions is met:

26,030 *Glossary*

Item	GASB Pronouncement[1]	Definition
		• The creditor has waived or subsequently lost the right to demand repayment for more than one year from the date of the financial statements.
		• For long-term obligations containing a grace period within which the debtor may cure the violation, it is probable that the violation will be cured within that period, thus preventing the obligation from becoming callable.
Current refunding	GASB-23	Refunding transaction when the issuance of new debt immediately replaces previously outstanding issued debt.
Current value	GASB-83	The amount that would be paid if all equipment, facilities, and services included in the estimate were acquired during the current period.
Current-financial-statement-date-based measurement (remeasured amount)	GASB:CS-6	The amount assigned when an asset or liability is remeasured as of the financial statement date.
Custodial agreement	GASB-3	A written contract establishing the responsibilities of a custodian holding collateral for deposits with financial institutions, investment securities, or securities underlying repurchase agreements.
Custodial credit risk	GASB-40	The custodial credit risk for *deposits* is the risk that, in the event of the failure of a depository financial institution, a government will not be able to recover deposits or will not be able to recover collateral securities that are in the possession of an outside party. The custodial credit risk for *investments* is the risk that, in the event of the failure of the counterparty to a transaction, a government will not be able to recover the value of investment or collateral securities that are in the possession of an outside party.

Item	GASB Pronouncement[1]	Definition
Custodial funds	GASB-84	Used to report fiduciary activities that are *not* required to be in pension (and other employee benefit) trust funds, investment trust funds, or private-purpose trust funds. The external portion of external investment pools that are *not held in a trust* should be reported in a separate *external investment pool fund* column under the custodial funds classification.
Daily liquid assets	GASB-79	For purposes of GASB-79, only the following are daily liquid assets: • Cash, including demand deposits and certificates of deposit that mature within one business day • U.S. government securities that are direct obligations • Securities that will mature within one business day, with maturity determined without considering the maturity shortening features • Securities subject to a demand feature that is exercisable and payable within one business day • Amounts receivable and due unconditionally within one business day on pending sales of portfolio securities.

Item	GASB Pronouncement[1]	Definition
Dealer market	GASB-72	A market in which dealers stand ready to trade (either buy or sell for their own account), providing liquidity by using their capital to hold an inventory of the items for which they make a market. Typically, bid and ask prices (representing the price at which the dealer is willing to buy and the price at which the dealer is willing to sell, respectively) are more readily available than closing prices. Over-the-counter markets (for which prices are publicly reported, for example, by the National Association of Securities Dealers Automated Quotations systems or by OTC Markets Group, Inc.) are dealer markets. The market for U.S. Treasury securities is another example of a dealer market. Dealer markets also exist for some other assets and liabilities, including other financial instruments, commodities, and physical assets (for example, used equipment).
Debt	GASB-88	A liability that arises from a contractual obligation to pay cash (or other assets that may be used in lieu of cash) in one or more payments to settle an amount that is fixed at the date the contractual obligation is established. For disclosure purposes, debt does not include leases, except for contracts reported as a financed purchase of the underlying asset, or accounts payable. For purposes of this determination, interest to be accrued and subsequently paid (such as interest on variable-rate debt) or interest to be added to the principal amount of the obligation (such as interest on capital appreciation bonds) does not preclude the amount to be settled from being considered fixed at the date the contractual obligation is established.

Glossary

Item	GASB Pronouncement[1]	Definition
Debt security	GASB-31	Any security that represents a creditor relationship with an entity. It also includes (a) preferred stock that either is required to be redeemed by the issuing entity or is redeemable at the option of the investor and (b) a collateralized mortgage obligation (CMO) or other instrument that is issued in equity form but is accounted for as a nonequity instrument. However, it excludes option contracts, financial futures contracts, and forward contracts.
		• Thus, the term *debt security* includes, among other items, U.S. Treasury securities, U.S. government agency securities, municipal securities, corporate bonds, convertible debt, commercial paper, negotiable certificates of deposit, securitized debt instruments (such as CMOs and real estate mortgage investment conduits—REMICs), and interest-only and principal-only strips.
		• Trade accounts receivable arising from sales on credit and loans receivable arising from real estate lending activities of proprietary activities are examples of receivables that do not meet the definition of a security, thus, those receivables are not debt securities. (If, however, they have been securitized, they then meet the definition.)
Debt service funds	GASB-54	Funds used to account for and report financial resources that are restricted, committed, or assigned to expenditure for principal and interest. Debt service funds should be used to report resources if legally mandated. Financial resources that are being accumulated for principal and interest maturing in future years also should be reported in debt service funds.
Deferred compensation (plan)	GASB-97	Under Internal Revenue Code Section 457(b), an other employee benefit plan that usually does not meet the definition of a pension plan. Contributions commonly are solely deferrals from employees and the employees have control over the investments.

Glossary

Item	GASB Pronouncement[1]	Definition
Deferred inflow(s) of resources	GASB-65 (also GASB:CS-4)	An acquisition of net assets by the government that is applicable to a future reporting period. A deferred inflow of resources has a negative effect on net position, like liabilities.
Deferred outflow(s) of resources	GASB-65 (also GASB:CS-4)	A consumption of net assets by the government that is applicable to a future reporting period. A deferred outflow of resources has a positive effect on net position, like assets.
Deferred retirement option program (DROP)	GASB-73	A program that permits an employee to elect a calculation of benefit payments based on service credits and salary, as applicable, as of the DROP entry date. The employee continues to provide service to the employer and is paid for that service by the employer after the DROP entry date, however, the pensions that would have been paid to the employee (if the employee had retired and not entered the DROP) are credited to an individual employee account within the defined benefit pension plan until the end of the DROP period.
Defined benefit pension plans (or OPEB)	GASB-75	Pension or OPEB plans that are used to provide defined benefit pensions or OPEB.
Defined benefit pensions (or OPEB)	GASB-75, GASB-78	Pensions or OPEB for which the income or other benefits that the employee will receive at or after separation from employment are defined by the benefit terms. The pensions or OPEB may be stated as a specified dollar amount or as an amount that is calculated based on one or more factors such as age, years of service, and compensation. (**NOTE:** Solely as used in GASB-78, pensions for which the income or other benefits that the employee will receive at or after separation from employment are defined by the benefit terms. The pensions may be stated as a specified dollar amount or as an amount that is calculated based on one or more factors such as age, years of service, and compensation.)
Defined contribution pension plans (or OPEB)	GASB-75	Pension or OPEB plans that are used to provide defined contribution pensions or OPEB.

Glossary

Item	GASB Pronouncement[1]	Definition
Defined contribution pensions (or OPEB)	GASB-75	Pensions or OPEB having terms that: • Provide an individual account for each employee, • Define the contributions that an employer is required to make (or the credits that it is required to provide) to an active employee's account for periods in which that employee renders service, and • Provide that the pensions an employee will receive will depend only on the contributions (or credits) to the employee's account, actual earnings on investments of those contributions (or credits), and the effects of forfeitures of contributions (or credits) made for other employees, as well as pension plan administrative costs, that are allocated to the employee's account.
Deflated depreciated replacement cost approach	GASB-42	Regarding accounting for impaired capital assets, this approach replicates the historical cost of the service produced. A current cost for a capital asset to replace the current level of service is estimated. This estimated current cost is depreciated to reflect the fact that the capital asset is not new, and then is deflated to convert it to historical cost dollars.
Demand bond	GASBI-1	Long-term debt issuances with demand ("put") provisions that require the issuer to repurchase the bonds upon notice from the bondholder at a price equal to the principal plus accrued interest. To assure its ability to redeem the bonds, issuers of demand bonds frequently enter into short-term standby liquidity agreements and long-term "take out" agreements.
Deposit	GASB-10	Money placed with a banking or other institution or with a person, sometimes for a specific purpose.

Item	GASB Pronouncement[1]	Definition
Deposit method (insurance entities other than public entity risk pools)	GASB-62	Under the deposit method, premiums are not recognized as revenue and claim costs are not charged to expense until the ultimate premium is reasonably estimable.
Depository institution	GASB-79	A bank, credit union, or savings institution.
Depository insurance	GASB-40	Depository insurance includes: • Federal depository insurance funds, such as those maintained by the Federal Deposit Insurance Corporation (FDIC or FDICIA). • State depository insurance funds. • Multiple financial institution collateral pools that insure public deposits. In such a pool, a group of financial institutions holding public funds pledge collateral to a common pool.

Derivative instrument	GASB-53	A derivative instrument is a financial instrument or other contract that has all the following characteristics:
		a. *Settlement factors.* It has:
		  (1) one or more reference rates and
		  (2) one or more notional amounts or payment provisions or both. Those terms determine the amount of the settlement or settlements and, in some cases, whether a settlement is required.
		b. *Leverage.* It requires no initial net investment or an initial net investment that is smaller than would be required for other types of contracts that would be expected to have a similar response to changes in market factors.
		c. *Net settlement.* Its terms require or permit net settlement, it can readily be settled net by a means outside the contract, or it provides for delivery of an asset that puts the recipient in a position not substantially different from net settlement.

Item	GASB Pronouncement[1]	Definition
Derived tax revenues	GASB-33	Assessments imposed on exchange transactions (for example, income taxes, sales taxes, and other assessments on earnings or consumption).
Deviation (Actuarial Standards of Practice)	GASB-82	As used in actuarial standards of practice, a selection of assumptions that deviate from the guidance in an actuarial standard of practice as released by the Actuarial Standards Board.
Difference	GASB-62	In an extinguishment of debt, the excess of the reacquisition price over the net carrying amount or the excess of the net carrying amount over the reacquisition price.
Direct debt	GASB-44	The outstanding long-term debt instruments—including bonds, notes, certificates of participation, loans, and capital leases—of the government preparing the statistical section.
Direct administrative involvement	GASB-84	For fiduciary activities, a recipient government has administrative involvement if, for example, it: • Monitors secondary recipients for compliance with program-specific requirements, • Determines eligible secondary recipients or projects, even if using grantor-established criteria, or • Can exercise discretion in how funds are allocated. A recipient government has direct financial involvement if, for example, it finances some direct program costs because of a grantor-imposed matching requirement or is liable for disallowed costs.
Direct borrowing	GASB-88	A government that enters into a loan agreement with a lender.
Direct financial involvement	GASB-84	For fiduciary activities, a government has direct financial involvement with the assets if, for example, it provides matching resources for the activities.
Direct placement	GASB-88	A government that issues a debt security directly to an investor.

Glossary

Item	GASB Pronouncement[1]	Definition
Direct rate	GASB-44	An amount or percentage applied to a unit of a specific revenue base by the government preparing the statistical section information—for example, a property tax rate of $1 per $1,000 of assessed property value, a sales tax rate of 5% of a retail sale, or a water charge of a certain amount per 100 gallons of water used.
Direct selling costs (cable television systems)	GASB-62	Direct selling costs include commissions, the portion of a salesperson's compensation other than commissions for obtaining new subscribers, local advertising targeted for acquisition of new subscribers, and costs of processing documents related to new subscribers acquired. Direct selling costs do not include supervisory and administrative expenses or indirect expenses, such as rent and costs of facilities.
Direct the "use"	GASB-84	See "Use."
Discount rate (investment return assumption)	GASB-75	The single rate of return that, when applied to all projected benefit payments, results in an actuarial present value of projected benefit payments equal to the total of the following: a. The actuarial present value of benefit payments projected to be made in future periods in which: (1) The amount of the pension plan's fiduciary net position is projected to be greater than the benefit payments that are projected to be made in that period and (2) Pension plan assets up to that point are expected to be invested using a strategy to achieve the long-term expected rate of return, calculated using the long-term expected rate of return on pension plan investments. b. The actuarial present value of projected benefit payments not included in (a), calculated using the municipal bond rate.

Item	GASB Pronouncement[1]	Definition
Discount rate (as used in GASB-73)	GASB-73	A yield or index rate for 20-year tax-exempt general obligation municipal bonds with an average rating of AA/Aa or higher (or equivalent quality on another rating scale).
Discount rate (non-trust arrangements)	GASB-75	The municipal bond rate for defined benefit plans. For all other uses, the interest rate charged in the contract, based on risk.
Discounting	GASB-10	A method used to determine the present value of a future cash payment or series of payments that takes into consideration the time value of money.
Discrete presentation (discretely presented)	GASB-14	The method of reporting financial data of component units in a column(s) separate from the financial data of the primary government. An integral part of this method of presentation is that individual component unit supporting information is required to be provided either in condensed financial statements within the notes to the reporting entity's basic financial statements or in combining statements in the basic financial statements.
Dividends to policyholders (insurance entities other than public entity risk pools)	GASB-62	Amounts distributable to policyholders of participating insurance contracts as determined by the insurer. Under various state insurance laws, dividends are apportioned to policyholders on an equitable basis. The dividend allotted to any contract often is based on the amount that the contract, as one of a class of similar contracts, has contributed to the changes in net assets available for distribution as dividends.
Dollar purchase–reverse repurchase agreement	GASB-3	A repurchase–reverse repurchase agreement that involves the transfer of securities in which the parties agree that the securities returned usually will be of the same issuer but will not be the same certificates. Fixed coupon and yield maintenance agreements are the most common types of dollar agreements.

Glossary

Item	GASB Pronouncement[1]	Definition
Dollar-offset method	GASB-53	A quantitative method of evaluating effectiveness that compares the changes in expected cash flows or fair values of the potential hedging derivative instrument with the changes in expected cash flows or fair values of the hedgeable item.
DTC	GASB: TB 87-1	Depository Trust Company
Duration	GASB-40	A measure of a debt investment's exposure to fair value changes arising from changing interest rates. It uses the present value of cash flows, weighted for those cash flows as a percentage of the investment's full price.
EFFR	GASB-93	Effective Federal Funds Rate. EFFR is calculated by the Federal Reserve Bank of New York as the weighted average of the rate for transactions in which institutions with surplus balances lend the balances to institutions in need of larger balances.
Embedded derivative instrument	GASB-53	A derivative instrument that is an element of a hybrid instrument. A hybrid instrument consists of a companion instrument and an embedded derivative instrument. When separated, an embedded derivative instrument, such as an interest rate swap, is measured at fair value. May be an embedded option.
Embedded lease	GASB-87	Within a contract, components that are leases in accordance with the definition of a lease per GASB-87, even though the word "lease" may not appear in the contract (usually due to law or regulation).
Employer entity	GASB-24	The entity that employs the individuals for whom a paying entity makes on-behalf payments for fringe benefits and salaries. The employer entity may be governmental or nongovernmental.
Employer's contributions		Contributions made in relation to the annual required contributions of the employer (ARC). An employer has contributed in relation to the ARC if the employer has: a. made payments of benefits directly to or on behalf of a retiree or beneficiary, b. made premium payments to an insurer, or

Item	GASB Pronouncement[1]	Definition
		c. irrevocably transferred assets to a trust, or an equivalent arrangement, in which plan assets provide benefits to retirees and their beneficiaries in accordance with the terms of the plan and are legally protected from creditors of the employer(s) or plan administrator. Measures related to the ARC are no longer utilized for general purpose external financial reporting.
Employer-paid member contributions	GASB-82	Payments made by the employer to satisfy contribution requirements that are identified by the pension plan terms as plan member contributions. For the pension plan, these amounts are classified as plan member contributions. For the employer, these amounts are classified as employee contributions, including for determining a cost-sharing employer's proportion and deferred outflows of resources related to employer contributions after the measurement date. An employer's expense and expenditures for those amounts should be included in the salaries and wages of the period for which the contribution is assessed. If an employer makes payments to satisfy employee contribution requirements (for example, if an employer "picks up" employee contributions in connection with an election made in accordance with IRC Section 414(h)(2) and Revenue Ruling 2006-43), the employer does not include such amounts in salaries and wages of the employee. (See also "pick-ups.")
Enabling legislation	GASB-54	Authorization for a government to assess, levy, charge, or otherwise mandate payment of resources (from external resource providers) and includes a legally enforceable requirement that those resources be used only for the specific purposes stipulated in the legislation.

Item	GASB Pronouncement[1]	Definition
Enterprise funds	GASB-34	Used to report any activity for which a fee is charged to external users for goods or services. Activities are required to be reported as enterprise funds if any one of the following criteria is met. Governments should apply each of these criteria in the context of the activity's principal revenue sources: a. The activity is financed with debt that is secured solely by a pledge of the net revenues from fees and charges of the activity. Debt that is secured by a pledge of net revenues from fees and charges and the full faith and credit of a related primary government or component unit—even if that government is not expected to make any payments—is not payable solely from fees and charges of the activity. (Some debt may be secured, in part, by a portion of its own proceeds but should be considered as payable "solely" from the revenues of the activity.) b. Laws or regulations require that the activity's costs of providing services, including capital costs (such as depreciation or debt service), be recovered with fees and charges, rather than with taxes or similar revenues. c. The pricing policies of the activity establish fees and charges designed to recover its costs, including capital costs (such as depreciation or debt service).

Item	GASB Pronouncement[1]	Definition
Entry age actuarial cost method	GASB-75	A method under which the actuarial present value of the projected benefits of everyone included in an actuarial valuation is allocated on a level basis over the earnings or service of the individual between entry age and assumed exit age(s). The portion of this actuarial present value allocated to a valuation year is called the normal cost. The portion of this actuarial present value not provided for at a valuation date by the actuarial present value of future normal costs is called the actuarial accrued liability.
Equity interest	GASB-90	A financial interest in a legally separate organization evidenced by the ownership of shares of the organization's stock or by otherwise having an explicit, measurable right to the net resources of the organization that is usually based on an investment of financial or capital resources by a government. An equity interest is explicit and measurable if the government has a present or future claim to the net resources of the entity and the method for measuring the government's share of the entity's net resources is determinable. This does not include a government's residual interest in assets that may (on dissolution) revert to the government for lack of another equitable claimant. That type of interest is like escheat. (See also "Majority equity interest.")

26,044 Glossary

Item	GASB Pronouncement[1]	Definition
Equity method (investment in common stock)	GASB-62	When an investor initially records an investment in the stock of an investee at cost and adjusts the carrying amount of the investment to recognize the investor's share of the earnings or losses of the investee after the date of acquisition. The amount of the adjustment is included in the determination of the changes in net assets by the investor. Such amount reflects adjustments including adjustments to eliminate inter-entity gains and losses, and to amortize, if appropriate, any difference between investor cost and underlying equity in net assets of the investee at the date of investment. The investment of an investor is also adjusted to reflect the investor's share of changes in the investee's capital. Dividends received from an investee reduce the carrying amount of the investment. A series of operating losses of an investee or other factors may indicate that a decrease in value of the investment has occurred that is other than temporary and that should be recognized even though the decrease in value is in excess of what would otherwise be recognized by application of the equity method. The equity method of accounting for an investment in common stock should be followed by a government whose investment in voting stock gives it the ability to exercise significant influence over operating and financial policies of an investee even though the government holds 50 % or less of the voting stock.
Equity security	GASB-31	Any security that represents an ownership interest in an entity, including common, preferred, or other capital stock, unit investment trusts, and closed-end mutual funds. However, the term equity security does not include convertible debt or preferred stock that either is required to be redeemed by the issuing entity or is redeemable at the option of the investor.

Item	GASB Pronouncement[1]	Definition
Equivalent arrangement	GASB-84	For the purposes of implementing GASB-84 only, one that, although not a trust by name, has the same characteristics required of a trust: a. Assets provide benefits to recipients in accordance with the benefit terms and b. Assets are legally protected from the creditors of the government that is acting as a fiduciary.
Equivalent single amortization period		The weighted average of all amortization periods used when components of the total unfunded actuarial accrued liability are separately amortized, and the average is calculated in accordance with the parameters.
Escheat (abandoned) property	GASB-21	The reversion of property to a governmental entity in the absence of legal claimants or heirs. The laws of many governmental entities provide that a rightful owner or heir can reclaim escheat property into perpetuity, provided the claimant can establish his or her right to the property. This does not necessarily mean that governments hold all escheat property into perpetuity. Because large portions of escheat property are never reclaimed, most governments use some of the property to help finance either their general or specific operations.
Estimated actual value of taxable property	GASB-44	The fair value of taxable real or personal property or a surrogate measure of fair value if actual fair value information is not available. In practice, fair value is often referred to as market value. The estimated actual value of taxable property may be determined in a variety of manners, such as through a system that tracks changes in market values by monitoring property sales or by dividing the assessed value of property by an assumed assessment percentage.

Item	GASB Pronouncement[1]	Definition
Estimated economic life of leased property	GASB-62	The estimated remaining period during which the property is expected to be economically usable by one or more users, with normal repairs and maintenance, for the purpose for which it was intended at the inception of the lease, without limitation by the lease term. No longer used for external financial reporting upon implementation of GASB-87, but may be used in practice.
Estimated residual value of leased property	GASB-62	The estimated fair value of the leased property at the end of the lease term.
Excess insurance (insurer)	GASB-10	The transfer of risk of loss from one party (the insured) to another (the excess insurer) in which the excess insurer provides insurance (as defined in this glossary) more than a certain, typically large amount. For example, a public entity risk pool may purchase excess insurance to transfer risk of aggregate losses above $5 million by its pool participants.
Exchange (or exchange-like) financial guarantee	GASB-99	A guarantee of an obligation of a legally separate entity or individual, including a blended or discretely presented component unit, that requires the guarantor to indemnify a third-party obligation holder under specified conditions, in exchange for which the guarantor receives consideration. (See nonexchange financial guarantee.)
Exchange-like transaction	GASB-33	Transactions between a government and another party(ies) where the values may not be equal, or the direct benefits of the exchange may not be exclusive to the parties to the exchange. These tend to be licenses, permits, or similar documents.
Exchange (or exchange transaction)	GASB-62	A reciprocal transfer between a government and another entity that results in the government acquiring assets or services or satisfying liabilities by surrendering other assets or services or incurring other obligations.

Item	GASB Pronouncement[1]	Definition
Exchange-like transaction	GASB-33	Transactions between a government and another party(ies) where the values may not be equal, or the direct benefits of the exchange may not be exclusive to the parties to the exchange. These tend to be licenses, permits, or similar documents.
Exchange market	GASB-72	A market in which closing prices are both readily available and generally representative of fair value. An example of such a market is the New York Stock Exchange.
Exit price	GASB-72	The price that is received to sell an asset or paid to transfer a liability.
Expected cash flow technique	GASB-72	The probability-weighted average (that is, mean of the distribution) of possible future cash flows.
Expected transaction	GASB-53	A transaction that is probable of occurring that exposes a government to the risk of adverse changes in cash flows or fair values. An expected transaction also may be a firm commitment—a binding agreement for the exchange of a specified quantity of resources at a specified price on a specified future date or dates.
External investment pool	GASB-31	An arrangement that commingles (pools) the moneys of more than one legally separate entity and invests, on the participants' behalf, in an investment portfolio, one or more of the participants is not part of the sponsor's reporting entity. An external investment pool can be sponsored by an individual government, jointly by more than one government, or by a nongovernmental entity. An investment pool that is sponsored by an individual state or local government is an external investment pool if it includes participation by a legally separate entity that is not part of the same reporting entity as the sponsoring government. If a government-sponsored pool includes only the primary government and its component units, it is an internal investment pool and not an external investment pool. (See also "Qualified External Investment Pool.")

Glossary

Item	GASB Pronouncement[1]	Definition
Extinguishment of debt	GASB-62	Using financial resources that did not arise from debt proceeds, the debtor pays the creditor and is relieved of all its obligations with respect to the debt. This includes the debtor's reacquisition of its outstanding debt securities in the public securities markets, regardless of whether the securities are cancelled or held as so-called treasury bonds. The debtor is legally released from being the primary obligor under the debt, either judicially or by the creditor, and it is probable that the debtor will not be required to make future payments with respect to that debt under any guarantees.
Extraordinary items	GASB-34	Transactions or other events that are both unusual in nature and infrequent in occurrence not within the control of management.
Fair value	GASB-72	The price that would be received to sell an asset or paid to transfer a liability in an orderly transaction between market participants at the measurement date.
Fair value (CAUTION: real estate only)	GASB-62	The amount in cash or cash equivalent value of other consideration that a real estate parcel would yield in a current sale between a willing buyer and a willing seller (selling price), that is, other than in a forced or liquidation sale. The fair value of a parcel is affected by its physical characteristics, its probable ultimate use, and the time required for the buyer to make such use of the property considering access, development plans, zoning restrictions, and market absorption factors.
Fair value hedge	GASB-53	A hedge that protects against the risk of either total changes in fair value or adverse changes in fair value caused by fixed terms, rates, or prices.
Fair value of the leased property	GASB-62	The price for which the property could be sold in an arm's-length transaction between willing parties, that is, other than in a forced or liquidation sale. The following are examples of the determination of fair value:

Item	GASB Pronouncement[1]	Definition
		a. The fair value of the property at the inception of the lease, in some cases, will be its normal selling price, reflecting any volume or trade discounts that may be applicable. However, the determination of fair value should be made considering market conditions prevailing at the time, which may indicate that the fair value of the property is less than the normal selling price and, in some instances, less than the cost of the property.
		b. The fair value of the property at the inception of the lease, in some cases, will be its cost, reflecting any volume or trade discounts that may be applicable.
		However, when there has been a significant lapse of time between the acquisition of the property by the lessor and the inception of the lease, the determination of fair value should be made considering market conditions prevailing at the inception of the lease, which may indicate that the fair value of the property is greater or less than its cost or carrying amount, if different. No longer used for general purpose external financial reporting due to implementation of GASB-87, but still used in practice. May also be used as part of the process of imputing a discount rate used in a lease.
Federal Deposit Insurance Corporation (FDIC or FDICIA)	GASB-40	A corporation created by the federal government that insures deposits in banks and savings associations.
Federal Home Loan Mortgage Corporation (FHLMC) (Freddie Mac) (mortgage banking)	GASB-62	FHLMC is a private corporation authorized by Congress to assist in the development and maintenance of a secondary market in conventional residential mortgages. FHLMC purchases mortgage loans and sells mortgages principally through mortgage participation certificates (PCs) representing an undivided interest in a group of conventional mortgages. FHLMC guarantees the timely payment of interest and the collection of principal on the PCs.

26,050 *Glossary*

Item	GASB Pronouncement[1]	Definition
Federal National Mortgage Association (FNMA) (Fannie Mae) (mortgage banking)	GASB-62	FNMA is an investor-owned corporation established by Congress to support the secondary mortgage loan market by purchasing mortgage loans when other investor resources are limited and selling mortgage loans when other investor resources are available.
Fiduciary activity	GASB-84	For activities other than fiduciary component units or pension or OPEB arrangements that are not component units, when all of the following criteria are met: the assets associated with the activity are controlled by the government, the assets associated with the activity are not derived either solely from the government's own source revenues or from government-mandated nonexchange transactions or voluntary nonexchange transactions with the exception of pass-through grants for which the government does not have administrative or direct financial involvement, the assets associated with the activity have one or more of the following characteristics: the assets are: a. Administered through a trust agreement or equivalent arrangement in which the government itself is not a beneficiary, b. Dedicated to providing benefits to recipients in accordance with the benefit terms, and c. Legally protected from the creditors of the government, the assets are for the benefit of individuals and the government does not have administrative involvement with the assets or direct financial involvement over the assets. In addition, the assets are not derived from the government's provision of goods or services to those individuals, the assets are for the benefit of organizations or other governments that are not part of the financial reporting entity and the assets are not derived from the government's provisions of goods or services to those organizations or other governments.

Item	GASB Pronouncement[1]	Definition

Fiduciary component unit	GASB-84	An organization that meets the component unit criteria and is either a pension or an OPEB plan administered through a trust or a circumstance in which assets that are not part of the reporting entity are accumulated for pensions or OPEB. In determining whether legally separate entities are component units, a primary government is considered to have a financial burden if it is legally obligated or has otherwise assumed the obligation to make contributions to the pension or OPEB plan. A component unit that is not a pension or OPEB arrangement is also a fiduciary activity if the assets have one or more of the following characteristics:
		
		a. The assets are
		
		   (1) administered through a trust or equivalent arrangement in which the government itself is not a beneficiary,
		
		   (2) dedicated to providing benefits to recipients in accordance with benefit terms, and
		
		   (3) legally protected from the creditors of the government, or
		
		b. The assets are for the benefit of individuals and the government does not have administrative involvement with the assets or direct financial involvement with the assets, nor are the assets derived from the government's provision of goods or services to those individuals, or
		
		c. The assets are for the benefit of organizations or other governments not part of the reporting entity, nor are the assets derived from the provisions of goods or services to those organizations or other governments.
		
		In determining whether a component unit is a fiduciary component unit, control of the assets of the component unit by the primary government is not a factor that is considered.

Glossary

Item	GASB Pronouncement[1]	Definition
Fiduciary funds (and similar component units)	GASB-84	Funds consisting of pension (and other employee benefit) trust funds, investment trust funds, private-purpose trust funds, and custodial funds. The funds are used to report assets held in a fiduciary capacity for others and therefore cannot be used to support the government's own programs.
Final budget	GASB-34	The original budget adjusted by all reserves, transfers, allocations, supplemental appropriations, and other legally authorized legislative and executive changes applicable to the fiscal year, whenever signed into law or otherwise legally authorized.
Financial accountability (financially accountable)	GASB-14	The level of accountability that exists if a primary government appoints a voting majority of an organization's governing board and is either able to impose its will on that organization or there is a potential for the organization to provide specific financial benefits to, or impose specific financial burdens on, the primary government. A primary government may also be financially accountable for governmental organizations with a separately elected governing board, a governing board appointed by another government, or a jointly appointed board that is fiscally dependent on the primary government.
Financial asset	GASB-72	Cash, evidence of ownership interest in an entity, or a contract that conveys to one entity a right to do either of the following: a. Receive cash or another financial instrument from a second entity. b. Exchange other financial instruments on potentially favorable terms with the second entity (for example, an option).
Financial benefit	GASB-14	Legal entitlement to, or the ability to otherwise access, the resources of an organization.
Financial burden	GASB-14	An obligation, legal or otherwise, to finance the deficits of, or provide financial support to, an organization, an obligation in some manner for the debt of an organization.

Item	GASB Pronouncement[1]	Definition
Financial instrument	GASB-72	A financial instrument is cash, evidence of an ownership interest in an entity, or a contract that both: • Imposes on one entity a contractual obligation to deliver cash or another financial instrument to a second entity or exchange other financial instruments on potentially unfavorable terms with the second entity (for example, an option). • Conveys to that second entity a contractual right to receive cash or another financial instrument from the first entity or to exchange other financial instruments on potentially favorable terms with the first entity (for example, an option).
Financial liability	GASB-72	A contract that imposes on one entity an obligation to do either of the following: a. Deliver cash or another financial instrument to a second entity, or b. Exchange other financial instruments on potentially unfavorable terms with the second entity (for example, an option).
Financial reporting entity	GASB-14	A primary government, organizations for which the primary government is financially accountable, and other organizations for which the nature and significance of their relationship with the primary government are such that exclusion would cause the reporting entity's financial statements to be misleading or incomplete. The nucleus of a financial reporting entity usually is a primary government. However, a governmental organization other than a primary government (such as a component unit, a joint venture, a jointly governed organization, or other stand-alone government) serves as the nucleus for its own reporting entity when it issues separate financial statements.
Fiscal accountability	GASB-34	Compliance with public decisions concerning the raising and spending of public funds within a reporting period.

Item	GASB Pronouncement[1]	Definition
Fiscal funding clause (lease)	NCGA-5	Provision in a lease that allows a cancellation if a governing body does not appropriate funds to pay for a lease each period. No longer used for external financial reporting upon implementation of GASB-87 but may be used in practice.
Fiscally independent/ fiscally dependent government	GASB-14	A government is fiscally independent if it can: a. Determine its budget without another government having the substantive authority to approve and modify that budget, b. Levy taxes or set rates or charges without substantive approval by another government, and c. Issue bonded debt without substantive approval by another government. A government is fiscally dependent if it is unable to complete one or more of these procedures without the substantive approval of another government.
Fixed coupon repurchase-reverse repurchase agreement	GASB-3	A dollar repurchase—reverse repurchase agreement in which the parties agree that the securities returned will have the same stated interest rate as, and maturities like, the securities transferred.
Foreign currency risk	GASB-53	The risk that changes in exchange rates will adversely affect the cash flows or fair value of a transaction.
Foreign currency transactions	GASB-62	Transactions whose terms are denominated in a currency other than the U.S. dollar. Foreign currency transactions arise when a government: a. Buys or sells on credit goods or services whose prices are denominated in a foreign currency, b. Borrows or lends resources and the amounts payable or receivable are denominated in a foreign currency, or

Item	GASB Pronouncement[1]	Definition
		c. For other reasons, acquires or disposes of assets, or incurs or settles liabilities denominated in a foreign currency.
Form over substance	GASB-56	Consideration of the underlying economic effect of a transaction, which may be different than the legal justification or organization of a transaction.
Forward contract	GASB-53	A contractual agreement to buy or sell a security, commodity, foreign currency, or other financial instrument, at a certain future date for a specific price. An agreement with a supplier to purchase a quantity of heating oil at a certain future time, for a certain price, and a certain quantity is an example of a forward contract. Forward contracts are not securities and are not exchange-traded. Some forward contracts, rather than taking or making delivery of the commodity or financial instrument, may be settled by a cash payment that is equal to the fair value of the contract.
Frozen attained age actuarial cost method		A method under which the excess of the Actuarial Present Value of Projected Benefits of the group included in an Actuarial Valuation, over the sum of the Actuarial Value of Assets plus the Unfunded Frozen Actuarial Accrued Liability, is allocated on a level basis over the earnings or service of the group between the valuation date and assumed exit. This allocation is performed for the group, not as a sum of individual allocations. The Unfunded Frozen Actuarial Accrued Liability is determined using the Unit Credit Actuarial Cost Method. The portion of this Actuarial Present Value allocated to a valuation year is called the Normal Cost. *No longer utilized for general purpose external financial reporting.*

Item	GASB Pronouncement[1]	Definition
Frozen entry age actuarial cost method		A method under which the excess of the Actuarial Present Value of Projected Benefits of the group included in an Actuarial Valuation, over the sum of the Actuarial Value of Assets plus the Unfunded Frozen Actuarial Accrued Liability, is allocated on a level basis over the earnings or service of the group between the valuation date and assumed exit. This allocation is performed for the group, not as a sum of individual allocations. The Frozen Actuarial Accrued Liability is determined using the Entry Age Actuarial Cost Method. The portion of this Actuarial Present Value allocated to a valuation year is called the Normal Cost. *No longer utilized for general purpose external financial reporting.*
Fund balance	GASB-54	In a governmental fund, the residual of assets, less liabilities and deferred inflows of resources (if applicable). Fund balance has five components: nonspendable, restricted, committed, assigned, and unassigned.
Fund financial statements	GASB-34	Display of information about major funds individually and nonmajor funds in the aggregate for governmental and enterprise funds. Fiduciary statements should include financial information for fiduciary funds and similar component units. Each of the three fund categories should be reported using the measurement focus and basis of accounting required for that category.
Funded ratio (OPEB only)		The actuarial value of assets expressed as a percentage of the actuarial accrued liability. *No longer utilized for general purpose external financial reporting.*
Funding excess		The excess of the actuarial value of assets over the actuarial accrued liability. *No longer utilized for general purpose external financial reporting.*
Funding policy		The program for the amounts and timing of contributions to be made by plan members, employer(s), and other contributing entities (for example, state government contributions to a local government plan) to provide the benefits specified by an OPEB plan.

Glossary **26,057**

Item	GASB Pronouncement[1]	Definition
Futures contract	GASB-53	An exchange-traded security to buy or sell a security, commodity, foreign currency, or other financial instrument at a certain future date for a specific price. A futures contract obligates a buyer to purchase the commodity or financial instrument and a seller to sell it unless an offsetting contract is entered into to offset one's obligation. The resources or obligations acquired through these contracts are usually terminated by offsetting contracts.
GAAP		Generally accepted accounting principles
GAAS		Generally accepted auditing standards
GAGAS		Generally accepted government auditing standards
GAN		Grant anticipation note
GAO		General Accountability Office
GASB		Governmental Accounting Standards Board
GASB *Implementation Guides*	GASB-76	GASB Implementation Guides are used to provide guidance that is limited to clarifying, explaining, or elaborating on GASB Statements (or GASB Interpretations). GASB Implementation Guides provide the GASB with a mechanism to address a wide range of detailed issues in a single document.
GASB *Interpretations*	GASB-76	GASB Interpretations provide a means for the Board to clarify, explain, or elaborate on GASB Statements as an aid to understanding those Statements. **(NOTE**: GASB concluded in GASB-76 that GASB Interpretations are no longer needed.)
GASB *Statements*	GASB-76	The primary communication method for accounting and financial reporting standards for state and local governmental entities. GASB Statements meet a fundamental need in the application of GAAP.
GASB *Technical Bulletins*	GASB-76	GASB Technical Bulletins provide a means to a. issue timely guidance to clarify, explain, or elaborate on GASB Statements and b. address areas not directly covered by GASB Statements.

26,058 *Glossary*

Item	GASB Pronouncement[1]	Definition
		GASB Technical Bulletins can be subjected to a shorter period of broad public exposure than proposed Statements and are issued when a majority of the Board does not object to their issuance.
Gaming (governmental gaming)	GASB-76 (Cod. Sec. 1000.811)	Gaming includes activities in which a gaming entity participates in games of chance with customers, with both the gaming entity and the customer having the chance to win or lose money or other items of economic value based on the outcome of the game (commonly referred to as banked games). Such activities are referred to as gaming activities. Examples of games that typically are played as banked games include, but are not limited to, table games, machines, keno, bingo, and sports and non-pari-mutuel race betting.
General Fund	GASB-54	The primary operating fund of a government. The General Fund accounts for and reports all financial resources not accounted for and reported in another fund.
General obligation debt	GASB-6	Debt paid by and secured by general taxation, generally income or property taxation. The full faith and credit of the government secures the debt.
General purpose external financial reporting	GASB:CS-3	A means of communicating financial information to meet the common information needs of the primary users of a government's financial report.
General purpose government	GASB-34	States, Tribal Nations, cities, counties, towns, and villages (and so on).

Item	GASB Pronouncement[1]	Definition
General revenues	GASB-34	All revenues are *general revenues* unless they are required to be reported as program revenues. All taxes, even those that are levied for a specific purpose, are general revenues and should be reported by type of tax—for example, sales tax, property tax, franchise tax, income tax. All other nontax revenues (including interest, grants, and contributions) that do not meet the criteria to be reported as program revenues should also be reported as general revenues. General revenues should be reported after total net expense of the government's functions.
GIC		Guaranteed investment contract.
Going concern	GASB-56	Significant information that is available raising doubts whether a legally separate entity can continue to meet its obligations as they become due without substantial disposal of assets outside the ordinary course of business, restructuring of operations and debts, oversight of a financial assistance, oversight or review board or similar intervention.
Government	GASB-76 (Cod. Sec. 1000.801)	Public corporations and bodies corporate and politic [are governmental entities]. Other entities are governmental entities if they have one or more of the following characteristics: • Popular election of officers or appointment (or approval) of a controlling majority of the members of the entity's governing body by officials of one or more state or local governments, • The potential for unilateral dissolution by a government with the net assets reverting to a government, and • The power to enact and enforce a tax levy.

26,060 *Glossary*

Item	GASB Pronouncement[1]	Definition
		Furthermore, entities are presumed to be governmental if they can issue directly (rather than through a state or municipal authority) debt that pays interest exempt from federal taxation. However, entities possessing only that ability (to issue tax-exempt debt) and none of the other governmental characteristics may rebut the presumption that they are governmental if their determination is supported by compelling, relevant evidence.
Government acquisitions	GASB-69	A government combination in which a government acquires another entity, or the operations of another entity, in exchange for significant consideration. The consideration provided should be significant in relation to the assets and liabilities acquired. The acquired entity or operation becomes part of the acquiring government's legally separate entity.
Government combinations	GASB-69	A variety of arrangements including mergers and acquisitions. Government combinations also include transfers of operations that do not constitute entire legally separate entities and in which no significant consideration is exchanged. Transfers of operations may be present in shared service arrangements, reorganizations, redistricting, annexations, and arrangements in which an operation is transferred to a new government created to provide those services.
Government mergers	GASB-69	A government merger is a government combination of legally separate entities in which no significant consideration is exchanged and either: a. Two or more governments (or one or more governments and one or more nongovernmental entities) cease to exist as legally separate entities and are combined to form one or more new governments, or b. One or more legally separate governments or nongovernmental entities cease to exist, and their operations are absorbed into, and provided by, one or more continuing governments.

Item	GASB Pronouncement[1]	Definition
Government National Mortgage Association (GNMA) (also known as Ginnie Mae) (mortgage banking)	GASB-62	GNMA is a U.S. governmental agency that guarantees certain types of securities (mortgage-backed securities) and provides resources for and administers certain types of low-income housing assistance programs.
Governmental capital assets	GASB-42	Assets that directly or indirectly are used in providing services that are not directly associated with fees or other revenues. Examples include roads, bridges, schools, and equipment used for fire protection.
Governmental funds	GASB-34	Funds (emphasizing major funds) consisting of the General Fund, Special Revenue Funds, Capital Projects Funds, Debt Service Funds and Permanent Funds, as applicable. The funds focus primarily on the sources, uses, and balances of current financial resources and often has a budgetary orientation.
Government-mandated nonexchange transactions	GASB-33	When a government at one level provides resources to a government at another level and requires the recipient to use the resources for a specific purpose (for example, federal programs that state or local governments are mandated to perform).
Government-wide financial statements	GASB-34	Display of information about the reporting government as a whole, except for its fiduciary activities. The statements should include separate columns for the governmental and business-type activities of the primary government as well as for its component units. Government-wide financial statements should be prepared using the economic resources measurement focus and the accrual basis of accounting. They consist of a statement of net [position] and a statement of activities.
Grants and other financial assistance	GASB-24	Transactions in which one governmental entity transfers cash or other items of value to (or incurs a liability for) another governmental entity, an individual, or an organization as a means of sharing program costs, subsidizing other governments or entities, or otherwise reallocating resources to the recipients.

Item	GASB Pronouncement[1]	Definition
Group insurance (insurance entities other than public entity risk pools)	GASB-62	Insurance protecting a group of persons, usually employees of an entity and their dependents. A single insurance contract is issued to their employer or other representative of the group. Individual certificates often are given to each insured individual or family unit. The insurance usually has an annual renewable contract period, although the insurer may guarantee premium rates for two or three years. Adjustments to premiums relating to the actual experience of the group of insured persons are common.
Hazardous wastes or hazardous substances	GASB-49	Wastes and substances that are toxic, corrosive, ignitable, explosive, or chemically reactive, or appear on special U.S. Environmental Protection Agency lists. This includes wastes and substances listed in 33 U.S.C. § 2701(23), and 42 U.S.C. § 6903(5) and § 9601(14). The definition of hazardous *substance* under the Superfund law is broader than the definition of hazardous *wastes* under the federal Resource Conservation and Recovery Act (RCRA). As used in this GASB-49, the terms *hazardous waste* and *hazardous substance* also include materials designated by state environmental regulators.
Healthcare cost trend rates	GASB-74	The rates of change in per capita health claims costs over time because of factors such as medical inflation, utilization of health care services, plan design, and technological developments.
Hedge accounting	GASB-53	The financial reporting treatment for hedging derivative instruments that requires that the changes in fair value of hedging derivative instruments be reported as either deferred inflows or deferred outflows.
Hedgeable item	GASB-53	An asset or liability or expected transaction that may be associated with a potential hedging derivative instrument.

Item	GASB Pronouncement[1]	Definition
Hedging derivative instrument	GASB-53	A derivative instrument that is associated with a hedgeable item and significantly reduces an identified financial risk by substantially offsetting changes in cash flows or fair values of the hedgeable item.
Highest and best use	GASB-72	The use of a nonfinancial asset by market participants that maximizes the value of the asset or the group of assets and liabilities within which the asset is used.
Historical cost	GASB:CS-6	The price paid to acquire an asset, or the amount received pursuant to the incurrence of a liability in an actual exchange transaction.
Hybrid instrument	GASB-53	An instrument that is composed of an embedded derivative instrument and a companion instrument.
Hybrid (pension plan)		Plan having both defined benefit and defined contribution characteristics. May (or may not) be reported in general purpose external financial reports due to the provisions of GASB-84 and GASB-97.
Hypothetical derivative instrument	GASB-53	An assumed derivative instrument designed to have terms that exactly match the critical terms of the hedged item, other than its maturity date, which would be the same as that of the potential hedging derivative instrument.
Immediate family(ies) (related parties)	GASB-62	Family members whom an elected or appointed official or a member of management might influence or by whom they might be influenced because of the family relationship.
Imposed nonexchange revenues	GASB-33	Assessments imposed on nongovernmental entities, including individuals, other than assessments on exchange transactions (for example, property taxes and fines).
Imposition of will (impose its will)	GASB-14	The ability to significantly influence the programs, projects, activities, or level of services performed or provided by an organization.

Glossary

Item	GASB Pronouncement[1]	Definition
Imputation (*Imputation of Interest Rates*)	GASB-62	If an established exchange price is not determinable and if the note has no ready market, to estimate the present value of a note, an applicable interest rate should be approximated, which may differ from the stated or coupon rate. The choice of a rate may be affected by the credit standing of the issuer, restrictive covenants, collateral, payment, and other terms pertaining to the debt. The prevailing rates for similar instruments of issuers with similar credit ratings will normally help determine the appropriate interest rate for determining the present value of a specific note at its date of issuance. In any event, the rate used for valuation purposes should be the rate at which the debtor can obtain financing of a similar nature from other sources at the date of the transaction. The objective should be to approximate the rate that would have resulted if an independent borrower and an independent lender had negotiated a similar transaction under comparable terms and conditions with the option to pay the cash price upon purchase or to give a note for the purchase, which bears the prevailing rate of interest to maturity.
Inactive employees	GASB-75	Individuals no longer employed by an employer in the pension or OPEB plan or the beneficiaries of those individuals. Inactive employees include individuals who have accumulated benefits under the terms of a pension or OPEB plan but are not yet receiving benefits and individuals currently receiving benefits.
Inactive plan members	GASB-74	Employees no longer in active service (or their beneficiaries) who have accumulated benefits under the terms of an OPEB plan.

Item	GASB Pronouncement[1]	Definition
Inception of the lease	GASB-62	The date of the lease agreement or commitment, if earlier. For purposes of this definition, a commitment should be in writing, signed by the parties in interest to the transaction, and should specifically set forth the principal provisions of the transaction. If any of the principal provisions are yet to be negotiated, such a preliminary agreement or commitment does not qualify for purposes of this definition. *Upon implementation of GASB-87, the inception of the lease may be different than the date that the lessee has control over the underlying asset.*
Incidental operations	GASB-62	Revenue-producing activities engaged in during the holding or development period to reduce the cost of developing the property for its intended use, as distinguished from activities designed to generate income or a return from the use of the property.
Income approach	GASB-72	A valuation technique that converts future amounts (for example, cash flows or income and expenses) to a single current (discounted) amount.
Income distributions	GASB-28	Interest, dividends, stock splits, and other distributions made by an issuer of securities. Income distributions on underlying securities are payable from the borrower to the lender, and income distributions on collateral securities are payable from the lender to the borrower.
Incremental borrowing rate		The rate of interest a government pays to borrow to secure collateralized assets during a similar term equal to payments in a similar economic environment. Used for leases and bond discount rate assumptions. Defined in FASB GAAP, but not in GASB.
Incremental costs of incidental operations	GASB-62	Costs that would not be incurred except in relation to the conduct of incidental operations. Interest, insurance, security, and similar costs that would be incurred during the development of a real estate project regardless of whether incidental operations were conducted are not incremental costs.

Item	GASB Pronouncement[1]	Definition
Incremental direct costs (lending activities)	GASB-62	Costs to originate a loan that: a. Result directly from and are essential to the lending transaction and b. Would not have been incurred by the lender had that lending transaction not occurred.
Incremental revenues from incidental operations	GASB-62	Revenues that would not be produced except in relation to the conduct of incidental operations.
Incurred but not reported claims (IBNR)	GASB-62	Claims relating to insured events that have occurred but have not yet been reported to the insurer or reinsurer as of the date of the financial statements. IBNR claims include: a. Known loss events that are expected to later be presented as claims, b. Unknown loss events that are expected to become claims, and c. Expected future development on claims already reported.
Incurred claims	GASB-10	Claims (losses) paid or unpaid for which the entity has become liable.
Indemnification	GASB-28	A securities lending agent's (or other agent's) guarantee that it will protect the lender from certain losses.
Indirect expenses	GASB-34	Expenses that are not program-specific and are usually allocated based upon a systematic and rational formula.
Indirect project costs	GASB-62	Costs incurred after the acquisition of the property, such as construction administration (for example, the costs associated with a field office at a project site and the administrative personnel that staff the office), legal fees, and various office costs, that clearly relate to projects under development or construction. Examples of office costs that may be considered indirect project costs are cost accounting, design, and other departments providing services that are clearly related to real estate projects.

Item	GASB Pronouncement[1]	Definition
Individual investment accounts	GASB-31	An investment service provided by a governmental entity for other, legally separate entities that are not part of the same reporting entity. With individual investment accounts, specific investments are acquired for individual entities and the income from and changes in the value of those investments affect only the entity for which they were acquired.
Inflows of resources	GASB-65 (also GASB:CS-4)	An acquisition of net position by the government that is applicable to the reporting period (revenues).
Infrastructure (or infrastructure assets)	GASB-34	Long-lived capital assets that normally are stationary in nature and normally can be preserved for a significantly greater number of years than most capital assets. Examples of infrastructure assets include roads, bridges, tunnels, drainage systems, water and sewer systems, dams, and lighting systems. Buildings, except those that are an ancillary part of a network of infrastructure assets, should not be considered infrastructure assets.
Initial direct costs (lease)	GASB-62	Only those costs incurred by the lessor that are: • Costs to originate a lease incurred in transactions with independent third parties that: • Result directly from and are essential to acquire that lease and • Would not have been incurred had that leasing transaction not occurred, and • Certain costs directly related to specified activities performed by the lessor for that lease.

Item	GASB Pronouncement[1]	Definition
		Those activities are evaluating the prospective lessee's financial condition, evaluating and recording guarantees, collateral, and other security arrangements, negotiating lease terms, preparing and processing lease documents, and closing the transaction. The costs directly related to those activities should include only that portion of the employees' total compensation and payroll-related fringe benefits directly related to time spent performing those activities for that lease and other costs related to those activities that would not have been incurred but for that lease. Initial direct costs should not include costs related to activities performed by the lessor for advertising, soliciting potential lessees, servicing existing leases, and other ancillary activities related to establishing and monitoring credit policies, supervision, and administration. Initial direct costs should not include administrative costs, rent, depreciation, any other occupancy and equipment costs and employees' compensation and fringe benefits related to activities described in the previous sentence, unsuccessful origination efforts, and idle time. *No longer used for external financial reporting upon implementation of GASB-87 but used in practice.*
Initial-transaction date-based measurement (initial amount)	GASB:CS-6	The transaction price or amount assigned when an asset was acquired, or a liability was incurred, including subsequent modifications to that price or amount that are derived from the amount at which the asset or liability was initially reported.
Inputs	GASB-72	The assumptions that market participants would use when pricing an asset or liability, including assumptions about risk, such as the following: • The risk inherent in a valuation technique used to measure fair value (such as a pricing model), and • The risk inherent in the inputs to the valuation technique.

Item	GASB Pronouncement[1]	Definition
		Inputs may be observable or unobservable.
In-substance assignment	GASB-64	An in-substance assignment occurs when all the following criteria are met: • The original swap counterparty, or the swap counterparty's credit support provider, is replaced. • The original swap agreement is ended, and the replacement swap agreement is initiated on the same date. • The terms that affect changes in fair values and cash flows in the original and replacement swap agreements are identical. These terms include, but are not limited to, notional amounts, terms to maturity, variable payment terms, reference rates, time intervals, fixed-rate payments, frequencies of rate resets, payment dates, and options, such as floors and caps. • Any difference between the original swap agreement's exit price and the replacement swap's entry price is attributable to the original swap agreement's exit price being based on a computation specifically permitted under the original swap agreement. Exit price represents the payment made or received because of terminating the original swap. Entry price represents the payment made or received because of initiating a replacement swap.

Glossary

Item	GASB Pronouncement[1]	Definition
In-substance defeasance	GASB-86	Debt is considered defeased in substance for accounting and financial reporting purposes if the government irrevocably places cash and other monetary assets acquired with only existing resources—that is, resources other than the proceeds of refunding debt—with an escrow agent in a trust to be used solely for satisfying scheduled payments of both interest and principal of the defeased debt, and the possibility that the government will be required to make future payments on the debt is remote. The trust is restricted to owning only monetary assets that are essentially risk-free as to the amount, timing, and collection of interest and principal. The monetary assets should be denominated in the currency in which the debt is payable. For debt denominated in U.S. dollars, essentially risk-free monetary assets are limited to: • Direct obligations of the U.S. government, • Obligations guaranteed by the U.S. government, and • Securities backed by U.S. government obligations as collateral and for which interest and principal payments on the collateral generally flow immediately through to the security holder. In addition, the monetary assets held by the trust are required to provide cash flows (from interest and maturity of those assets) that approximately coincide, as to timing and amount, with the scheduled interest and principal payments on the defeased debt. However, some securities described above can be paid before their scheduled maturities and so are not essentially risk-free as to the timing of the collection of interest and principal. As a result, they do not qualify for defeasance purposes.

Item	GASB Pronouncement[1]	Definition
Insurance	GASB-10	The transfer of risk of loss from one party (the insured) to another party (the insurer) in which the insurer promises (usually specified in a written contract) to pay the insured (or others on the insured's behalf) an amount of money (or services, or both) for economic losses sustained from an unexpected (accidental) event during a period of time for which the insured makes a premium payment to the insurer.
Insured benefits	GASB-75	Defined benefit provisions provided through an insured plan.
Insured plan	GASB-75	Defined benefit pension (or OPEB) plans in which benefits are financed through an arrangement where premiums are paid or other payments are made to an insurance company while employees are in active service, in return for which the insurance company unconditionally undertakes an obligation to pay the pensions (or OPEB) of those employees as defined in the pension (or OPEB) plan terms.
Intangible asset	GASB-51	An asset that possesses all the following characteristics: a. Lack of physical substance. An asset may be contained in or on an item with physical substance, for example, a compact disc in the case of computer software. An asset also may be closely associated with another item that has physical substance, for example, the underlying land in the case of a right-of-way easement. These modes of containment and associated items should not be considered when determining whether an asset lacks physical substance. b. Nonfinancial nature. In the context of this Statement, an asset with a nonfinancial nature is one that is not in a monetary form like cash and investment securities, and it represents neither a claim or right to assets in a monetary form like receivables, nor a prepayment for goods or services.

26,072 Glossary

Item	GASB Pronouncement[1]	Definition
		c. Initial useful life extending beyond a single reporting period.
IBOR	GASB-93	Interbank Offered Rate (Replacement of LIBOR). An interest rate used for lending between banks for short timeframes. Used as a reference rate for financial instruments.
Interest rate implicit in a lease	GASB-62	The discount rate that, when applied to: 1. The minimum lease payments, excluding that portion of the payments representing executory costs to be paid by the lessor, together with any gain thereon, and 2. The unguaranteed residual value accruing to the benefit of the lessor, causes the aggregate present value at the beginning of the lease term to be equal to the fair value of the leased property to the lessor at the inception of the lease, minus any investment tax credit retained by and expected to be realized by the lessor. *No longer used for external financial reporting purposes upon implementation of GASB-87 but may be used in practice, especially when imputing rates.*
Interest rate risk	GASB-53	The risk that changes in interest rates will adversely affect the fair values of a government's financial instruments or a government's cash flows.
Interest rate swap	GASB-53	A swap that has a variable payment based on the price of an underlying interest rate or index.
Interest-earning investment contract	GASB-31	A direct contract, other than a mortgage or other loan, that a government initiates as a creditor of a financial institution, broker-dealer, investment company, insurance company, or other financial services company and for which it receives, directly or indirectly, interest payments. Interest-earning investment contracts include time deposits with financial institutions (such as certificates of deposit), repurchase agreements, and guaranteed and bank investment contracts (GICs and BICs).

Item	GASB Pronouncement[1]	Definition
Intermediary	GASB-81	The trustee, fiscal agent, government, or any other legal or natural person that is holding and administering donated resources pursuant to a split-interest agreement. For the purposes of GASB-81, an intermediary is not required to be a third party.
Internal activities (interfund transfers)	GASB-34	Transfers between funds or activities of a government during a period.
Internal balances (interfund loans)	GASB-34	Receivables or payables between funds or activities of a government that exist at the reporting date.
Internal investment pool	GASB-31	An arrangement that commingles (pools) the moneys of more than one fund or component unit of a reporting entity. Investment pools that include participation by legally separate entities that are not part of the same reporting entity as the pool sponsor are not internal investment pools, but rather are external investment pools.
Internal reserve method (mortgage banking)	GASB-62	A method for making payments to investors for collections of principal and interest on mortgage loans by issuers of GNMA securities. An issuer electing the internal reserve method is required to deposit in a custodial account an amount equal to one month's interest on the mortgage loans that collateralize the GNMA security issued.
Internal Revenue Code (IRC)		26 U.S. Code (US Code Title 26). Law establishing the Federal Tax Code.

Glossary

Item	GASB Pronouncement[1]	Definition
Internal Revenue Code Section 403(b) plans		These tax deferred annuity plans (or mutual funds) are funded by salary reductions. They are usually found in public institutions of higher education and hospitals. However, some governments use them to receive lump-sum payments at retirement from defined benefit plans. The risk of having enough funds at retirement then shifts to the retiree. Elementary and secondary public and private school systems also often offer Internal Revenue Code (IRC) Section 403(b) plans to their employees. *Caution*: These plans are *not* required to be held in trust due to IRC provisions. However, the benefits are restricted to beneficiaries of the plan. Due to the restriction, the plan may be deemed an "equivalent arrangement."
Internal Revenue Code Section 457(b) plans		See Deferred Compensation Plans. A plan administrator invests plan assets at the direction of plan participants. Due to the provisions of the plan, the participant has the risk of loss of value.
Internal Revenue Service		Federal taxation agency.
Internal service funds	GASB-34	Used to report any activity that provides goods or services to other funds, departments, or agencies of the primary government and its component units, or to other governments, on a cost-reimbursement basis. Internal service funds should be used only if the reporting government is the predominant participant in the activity. Otherwise, the activity should be reported as an enterprise fund.
Internally generated intangible asset	GASB-51	An intangible asset that is created or produced by the government or an entity contracted by the government, or if it is acquired from a third party but requires more than minimal incremental effort on the part of the government to begin to achieve its expected level of service capacity. Computer software is a common type of internally generated intangible asset.

Item	GASB Pronouncement[1]	Definition
In-the-money	GASB-53	In the case of a call option, an option that has a market price above its strike price. In the case of a put option, an option that has a market price below its strike price.
Intra-entity activity	GASB-34	Resource flows between a primary government and blended component units during a period.
Intrinsic value	GASB-53	The value of an option if the option is exercised immediately. An option that has intrinsic value is in-the-money.
Inventory	GASB-62	The aggregate of those items of tangible personal property that: • Are held for sale in the ordinary course of operations, • Are in process of production for such sale, or • Are to be currently consumed in the production of goods or services to be available for sale. Operating materials and supplies (for example, property held for installation or use in the provision of services) of certain business-type activities usually are treated as inventory.
Investee	GASB-72	An entity that issued an equity instrument of which all or a portion is held by an investor.
Investing activities	GASB-9	Making and collecting loans and acquiring and disposing of debt or equity instruments.
Investment	GASB-72	A security or other asset that: a. A government holds primarily for income or profit and b. Has present service capacity based solely on its ability to generate cash or to be sold to generate cash.
Investment derivative instrument	GASB-53	A derivative instrument that is entered primarily for obtaining income or profit, or a derivative instrument that does not meet the criteria of a hedging derivative instrument.
Investment trust funds	GASB-84	Used to report the fiduciary activities from the external portion of investment pools and individual accounts that are held in a trust that are

26,076　*Glossary*

Item	GASB Pronouncement[1]	Definition
		a. Administered through a trust agreement or equivalent arrangement in which the government itself is *not* a beneficiary,
		b. Dedicated to providing benefits to recipients in accordance with the benefit terms, and
		c. Legally protected from the creditors of the government.
Irrevocable split-interest agreement	GASB-81	A split-interest agreement in which the donor has not reserved, or conferred to another person, the right to terminate the agreement at will and have the assets returned to the donor or a third party.
Irrevocable trust	GASB-75	For defined benefit and defined contribution plans, where contributions from employers and nonemployer contributing entities to the plan and earnings on those contributions are irrevocable, where plan assets provide benefits to plan members in accordance with benefit terms and plan assets are legally protected from the creditors of employers, nonemployer contributing entities and the plan administrator. If the plan is a defined benefit plan, plan assets are also legally protected from creditors of the plan members.
Issuer	GASB-40	An issuer is the entity that has the authority to distribute a security or other investment. A *bond issuer* is the entity that is legally obligated to make principal and interest payments to bond holders. In the case of mutual funds, external investment pools, and other pooled investments, *issuer* refers to the entity invested in, not the investment company-manager or pool sponsor.
Joint venture	GASB-14	A legal entity or other organization that results from a contractual arrangement and that is owned, operated, or governed by two or more participants as a separate and specific activity subject to joint control, in which the participants retain: • An ongoing financial interest or • An ongoing financial responsibility.

Glossary

Item	GASB Pronouncement[1]	Definition
Jointly governed organizations	GASB-14	A regional government or other multi-governmental arrangement that is governed by representatives from each of the governments that create the organization, but that is not a joint venture because the participants do not retain an ongoing financial interest or responsibility.
Lead interest	GASB-81	The right (a type of beneficial interest) to all or a portion of the benefits of resources during the term of a split-interest agreement.
Lease	GASB-87	A contract that conveys control of the right to use another entity's nonfinancial asset (the underlying asset) as specified in the contract for a period in an exchange or exchange-like transaction. Examples of nonfinancial assets include buildings, land, vehicles, and equipment.
Lease – Leaseback	GASB-87	In a lease-leaseback transaction, an asset is leased by one party (first party) to another party and then leased back to the first party.
Lease term	GASB-87	The lease term is defined as the period during which a lessee has a noncancelable right to use an underlying asset, plus the following periods, if applicable: a. Periods covered by a lessee's option to extend the lease if it is reasonably certain, based on all relevant factors, that the lessee will exercise that option. b. Periods covered by a lessee's option to terminate the lease if it is reasonably certain, based on all relevant factors, that the lessee will not exercise that option. c. Periods covered by a lessor's option to extend the lease if it is reasonably certain, based on all relevant factors, that the lessor will exercise that option. d. Periods covered by a lessor's option to terminate the lease if it is reasonably certain, based on all relevant factors, that the lessor will not exercise that option.
Legal defeasance (of bonds)	GASB-7	When debt is legally satisfied based on certain provisions in the debt instrument even though the debt is not actually paid.

Item	GASB Pronouncement[1]	Definition
Legal enforceability	GASB-54	When a government can be compelled by an external party—such as citizens, public interest groups, or the judiciary—to use resources created by enabling legislation only for the purposes specified by the legislation.
Legally responsible entity	GASB-24	For on-behalf payments for fringe benefits and salaries, the entity required by legal or contractual provisions to make the payment. Legal provisions include those arising from constitutions, charters, ordinances, resolutions, governing body orders, and intergovernmental grant or contract regulations.
Legally separate organization (separate legal standing)	GASB-14	An organization created as a body corporate or a body corporate and politic (also known as "separate body politic") or otherwise possessing similar corporate powers. An organization that has separate legal standing has an identity of its own as an "artificial person" with a personality and existence distinct from that of its creator and others.
Lender	GASB-28	A governmental entity that transfers its securities to a broker-dealer or other entity in a securities lending transaction.
Lessee	GASB-87	Party signing a contract to lease property from a lessor.
Lessee's incremental borrowing rate	GASB-62	The rate that, at the inception of the lease, the lessee would have incurred to borrow over a similar term the resources necessary to purchase the leased asset.
Lessor	GASB-87	Party that owns property that is leased by a lessee.
Level 1 inputs	GASB-72	Quoted prices (unadjusted) in active markets for identical assets or liabilities that the government can access at the measurement date.
Level 2 inputs	GASB-72	Inputs other than quoted prices included within Level 1 that are observable for an asset or liability, either directly or indirectly.
Level 3 inputs	GASB-72	Unobservable inputs for an asset or liability.

Glossary

Item	GASB Pronouncement[1]	Definition
Level dollar amortization method		The amount to be amortized is divided into equal dollar amounts to be paid over a given number of years, part of each payment is interest and part is principal (like a mortgage payment on a building). Because payroll can be expected to increase because of inflation, level dollar payments generally represent a decreasing percentage of payroll, in dollars adjusted for inflation, the payments can be expected to decrease over time. *No longer used for general purpose external financial reporting.*
Level of utilization	GASB-42	The portion of usable capacity of a capital asset being used.
Level percentage of projected payroll amortization method		Amortization payments are calculated so that they are a constant percentage of the projected payroll of active plan members over a given number of years. The dollar amount of the payments generally will increase over time as payroll increases due to inflation, in dollars adjusted for inflation, the payments can be expected to remain level.
Leverage	GASB-53	The means of enhancing changes in fair value while minimizing or eliminating an initial investment. A leveraged investment has changes in fair value that are disproportionate to the initial net investment. An unleveraged investment requires a far greater initial investment to replicate similar changes in fair values. Derivative instruments are leveraged instruments because their changes in fair value are disproportionate to the initial net investment. For example, an interest rate swap that has a notional value of $100 million is entered with no initial net investment. Thereafter, as interest rates change, the swap produces changes in fair value consistent with a $100 million fixed-rate financial instrument.
Liabilities	GASB-65 (also GASB:CS-4)	Present obligations to sacrifice resources that the government has little or no discretion to avoid.

Glossary

Item	GASB Pronouncement[1]	Definition
Liability for claim adjustment expenses	GASB-62	The amount needed to provide for the estimated ultimate cost required to investigate and settle claims relating to insured events that have occurred on or before a date (ordinarily, the financial statement date), regardless if reported to the insurer at that date.
Liability for unpaid claims	GASB-62	The amount needed to provide for the estimated ultimate cost of settling claims relating to insured events that have occurred on or before a date (ordinarily, the financial statement date). The estimated liability includes the amount of money that will be required for future payments on both: (a) Claims that have been reported to the insurer and (b) Claims relating to insured events that have occurred but have not been reported.
Lien	GASB-33	An enforceable legal claim by a government. The date of the lien may be known as a lien date or an assessment date.
Life-contingent term	GASB-81	A term specifying that the termination of a split-interest agreement is contingent upon the occurrence of a specified event, commonly the death of either the donor or other lead interest beneficiary.
Loan commitment	GASB-53	Formal offer for a defined period by a lender to extend a loan to a borrower according to specified terms such as the amount of the borrowing and repayment terms, including interest rates.
Loan premium or fee	GASB-28	Payments from the borrower to the lender as compensation for the use of the underlying securities when the borrower provides securities or letters of credit as collateral.
Long-term obligations	GASB-62	Obligations scheduled to mature beyond one year from the date of a government's financial statements.
Maintenance costs (insurance entities other than public entity risk pools)	GASB-62	Costs associated with maintaining records relating to insurance contracts and with the processing of premium collections and commissions.

Item	GASB Pronouncement[1]	Definition
Major fund	GASB-34	The general fund or its equivalent and any other fund where: a. Total assets, liabilities, revenues, or expenditures/expenses of that individual governmental or enterprise fund are at least 10% of the corresponding total (assets, liabilities, and so forth) for all funds of that category or type (that is, total governmental or total enterprise funds), *and* b. Total assets, liabilities, revenues, or expenditures/expenses of the individual governmental fund or enterprise fund are at least 5% of the corresponding total for all governmental and enterprise funds combined. In addition to funds that meet the major fund criteria, any other governmental or enterprise fund that the government's officials believe is particularly important to financial statement users (for example, because of public interest or consistency) may be reported as a major fund.
Majority equity interest	GASB-90	Holding most voting stock of a legally separate entity.
Management	GASB-62	Persons who are responsible for achieving the objectives of the government and who have the authority to establish policies and make decisions by which those objectives are to be pursued. Management normally includes the chief executive officer (for example, city manager), directors or secretaries in charge of principal government departments or functions (such as service provision administration or finance), and other persons who perform similar policymaking functions. Persons without formal titles also may be members of management.

26,082 *Glossary*

Item	GASB Pronouncement[1]	Definition
Management's discussion and analysis (MD&A)	GASB-34	A component of required supplementary information, an introduction to the basic financial statements providing an analytical overview of the government's financial activities. The MD&A should provide an objective and easily readable analysis of the government's financial activities based on currently known facts, decisions, or conditions. MD&A should discuss the current-year results in comparison with the prior year, with emphasis on the current year. This fact-based analysis should discuss the positive and negative aspects of the comparison with the prior year. The use of charts, graphs, and tables is encouraged to enhance the understandability of the information. MD&A should focus on the primary government. Comments in MD&A should distinguish between information pertaining to the primary government and that of its component units. Determining whether to discuss matters related to a component unit is a matter of professional judgment and should be based on the individual component unit's significance to the total of all discretely presented component units and that component unit's relationship with the primary government. When appropriate, the reporting entity's MD&A should refer readers to the component unit's separately issued financial statements.
Margin	GASB-3	The excess of the market value including accrued interest of the securities underlying a repurchase—reverse repurchase, or a fixed coupon repurchase—reverse repurchase agreement over the agreement amount, including accrued interest. It is common practice for a margin to be built into an agreement to protect against declines in the market value of the underlying securities.
Market approach	GASB-72	A valuation technique that uses prices and other relevant information generated by market transactions involving identical or comparable (similar) assets, liabilities, or groups of assets and liabilities.

Item	GASB Pronouncement[1]	Definition
Market maker	GASB-72	An entity or individual that provides both a bid and ask price and is willing and able to transact at those prices.
Market multiples	GASB-72	A valuation technique that relies on the use of ratios as an expression of market price relative to a key statistic, such as earnings, book value, or cash flows.

Market participants	GASB-72	Buyers and sellers that:
		
		 1. Are in the principal (or most advantageous) market for an asset or liability, and
		 2. Have all the following characteristics:
		     a. They are independent of each other. That is, they are not related parties, although the price in a related-party transaction may be used as an input to a fair value measurement if the government has evidence that the transaction was entered into at market terms.
		     b. They are knowledgeable, having a reasonable understanding about the asset or liability and the transaction using all available information, including information that might be obtained through due diligence efforts that are usual and customary.
		     c. They can engage in a transaction for the asset or liability.
		     d. They are willing to engage in a transaction for the asset or liability. That is, they are motivated but not forced or otherwise compelled to do so.

Market risk	GASB-72	The risk that changes in market prices will reduce the fair value of an asset, increase the fair value of a liability, or adversely affect the cash flows of an expected transaction. Market risk comprises the following: a. Interest rate risk, b. Currency risk, and c. Other price risks.

Glossary

Item	GASB Pronouncement[1]	Definition
Market-access risk	GASB-53	The risk that a government will not be able to enter credit markets or that credit will become costlier. For example, to complete a derivative instrument's objective, an issuance of refunding bonds may be planned in the future. If at that time the government is unable to enter credit markets, expected cost savings may not be realized.
Market-corroborated inputs	GASB-72	Inputs that are derived principally from or corroborated by observable market data by correlation or other means.
Market-related value of plan assets		A term used with reference to the actuarial value of assets. A market-related value may be fair value, market value (or estimated market value), or a calculated value that recognizes changes in fair value or market value over a period of, for example, three to five years.
Master agreement	GASB-3	A written contract covering all future transactions between the parties to repurchase—reverse repurchase agreements that establishes each party's rights in the transactions. A master agreement will often specify, among other things, the right of the buyer-lender to liquidate the underlying securities in the event of default by the seller-borrower.

Item	GASB Pronouncement[1]	Definition
Master Settlement Agreement (MSA)	GASB: TB 2004-1	In 1998, the U.S. tobacco industry reached an agreement (referred to as the Master Settlement Agreement, or MSA) with state governments releasing the tobacco companies from present and future smoking-related claims that had been, or potentially could be, filed by the states. In exchange, the tobacco companies agreed to make annual payments *in perpetuity* to the states, subject to certain conditions and adjustments. The states of California and New York entered into additional agreements with their county governments and selected major cities to allocate a specific portion of their ongoing annual settlement payments to those local governments. The states and the California and New York local governments are referred to in this Technical Bulletin as "settling governments." Some settling governments have created legally separate entities (referred to as Tobacco Settlement Authorities, or TSAs) to issue debt and to obtain the rights to all or a portion of the settling governments' future tobacco settlement resources (TSRs). TSRs are exchange transactions.
Matched position	GASB-3	A condition existing when reverse repurchase agreement proceeds are invested in securities that mature at or almost at the same time as the reverse repurchase agreement and the proceeds from those securities will be used to liquidate the agreement.
Matrix pricing	GASB-72	A valuation technique used to value securities based on their relationship to benchmark quoted prices.
Matured liabilities	GASBI-6	Liabilities that normally are due and payable in full when incurred or the matured portion of general long-term indebtedness (the portion that has come due for payment).
Measurement date	GASB-72	The date when the fair value of an asset or liability is determined.
Measurement period	GASB-75	The period between the prior and the current measurement dates.

Item	GASB Pronouncement[1]	Definition
Minimum lease payments	GASB-62	From the standpoint of the lessee: The payments that the lessee is obligated to make or can be required to make in connection with the leased property. However, a guarantee by the lessee of the lessor's debt and the lessee's obligation to pay (apart from the rental payments) executory costs such as insurance and maintenance in connection with the leased property should be excluded. If the lease contains a bargain purchase option, only the minimum rental payments over the lease term and the payment called for by the bargain purchase option should be included in the minimum lease payments. Otherwise, minimum lease payments include the following: • The minimum rental payments called for by the lease over the lease term. • Any guarantee by the lessee of the residual value at the expiration of the lease term, whether payment of the guarantee constitutes a purchase of the leased property. When the lessor has the right to require the lessee to purchase the property at termination of the lease for a certain or determinable amount, that amount should be considered a lessee guarantee. When the lessee agrees to make up any deficiency below a stated amount in the lessor's realization of the residual value, the guarantee to be included in the minimum lease payments should be the stated amount, rather than an estimate of the deficiency to be made up.

Glossary **26,087**

Item	GASB Pronouncement[1]	Definition
		• Any payment that the lessee is required to make or can be required to make upon failure to renew or extend the lease at the expiration of the lease term, whether the payment would constitute a purchase of the leased property. In this connection, it should be noted that the definition of lease term includes "all periods, if any, for which failure to renew the lease imposes a penalty on the lessee in an amount such that renewal appears, at the inception of the lease, to be reasonably assured." If the lease term has been extended because of that provision, the related penalty should not be included in minimum lease payments.
		From the standpoint of the lessor: The payments described above plus any guarantee of the residual value or of rental payments beyond the lease term by a third party unrelated to either the lessee or the lessor, provided the third party is financially capable of discharging the obligations that may arise from the guarantee. Will no longer be used for external financial reporting upon implementation of GASB-87 but *may be used in practice.*
Modified approach (to infrastructure financial reporting)	GASB-34	Alternative to depreciation of infrastructure assets if two requirements are met. First, the government manages the eligible infrastructure assets using an asset management system that has the characteristics set forth below. Second, the government documents that the eligible infrastructure assets are being preserved approximately at (or above) a condition level established and disclosed by the government. To meet the first requirement, the asset management system should:
		a. Have an up-to-date inventory of eligible infrastructure assets,
		b. Perform condition assessments of the eligible infrastructure assets and summarize the results using a measurement scale, and

Item	GASB Pronouncement[1]	Definition
		c. Estimate each year the annual amount to maintain and preserve the eligible infrastructure assets at the condition level established and disclosed by the government.
Monetary assets and liabilities	GASB-62	Assets and liabilities whose amounts are fixed in terms of units of currency by contract or otherwise. Examples are cash, short- or long-term accounts and notes receivable in cash, and short- or long-term accounts and notes payable in cash.
Money purchase plans		Hybrid defined contribution plan. In these plans, contributions are determined for and allocated for specific individuals as a percentage of compensation. The employer's contributions are based on a formula.
Money-weighted rate of return	GASB-74	A method of calculating period-by-period returns on pension or OPEB plan investments that adjusts for the changing amounts invested. Money-weighted rate of return is calculated as the internal rate of return on pension or OPEB plan investments, net of pension or OPEB plan investment expense.
Money market investment	GASB-31	A short-term, highly liquid debt instrument, including commercial paper, banker's acceptances, and U.S. Treasury and agency obligations. Asset-backed securities, derivatives, and structured notes are not included in this term.
More likely than not	GASB-101	A likelihood of more than 50%.
Mortgage banking activity	GASB-62	An activity that is engaged primarily in originating, marketing, and servicing real estate mortgage loans for other than its own account. Mortgage banking activities, as local representatives of institutional lenders, act as correspondents between lenders and borrowers.
Most advantageous market	GASB-72	The market that maximizes the amount that would be received to sell an asset or minimizes the amount that would be paid to transfer a liability, after considering transaction costs and transportation costs.

Item	GASB Pronouncement[1]	Definition
MSWLF	GASB-18	Municipal solid waste landfill.
Multi-period excess earnings technique	GASB-72	A valuation technique based on prospective financial information (for example, revenues, expenses, or cash flows) associated with a collection of assets. The initial amount is reduced for the contributions of supporting assets, with the residual amount being the excess earnings associated with the asset being valued.
Multiple-employer defined benefit pension or OPEB plan	GASB-78	A defined benefit pension or OPEB plan that is used to provide pensions or OPEB to the employees of more than one employer.
Net asset value per share	GASB-72	The amount of net assets attributable to each share of capital stock (other than senior equity securities, that is preferred stock) outstanding at the close of the period. It excludes the effects of assuming conversion of outstanding convertible securities, whether their conversion would have a diluting effect. Also used in external investment pool valuation.
Net carrying amount	GASB-62	In an extinguishment of debt, the amount due at maturity, adjusted for unamortized premium, discount and cost of issuance.

26,090 *Glossary*

Item	GASB Pronouncement[1]	Definition
Net investment in capital assets	GASB-63	Capital assets, net of accumulated depreciation, reduced by the outstanding balances of bonds, mortgages, notes, or other borrowings that are attributable to the acquisition, construction, or improvement of those assets. Deferred outflows of resources and deferred inflows of resources that are attributable to the acquisition, construction, or improvement of those assets or related debt also should be included in this component of net position. If there are significant unspent related debt proceeds or deferred inflows of resources at the end of the reporting period, the portion of the debt or deferred inflows of resources attributable to the unspent amount should not be included in the calculation of net investment in capital assets. Instead, that portion of the debt or deferred inflows of resources should be included in the same net position component (restricted or unrestricted) as the unspent amount.
Net OPEB liability	GASB-75	The liability of employers and nonemployer contributing entities to plan members for benefits provided through a defined benefit OPEB plan that is administered through an irrevocable trust. Calculated based on the total OPEB liability, less fiduciary net position. (If amount is positive, a net OPEB *asset* is the result.)
Net pension liability	GASB-68	The liability of employers and nonemployer contributing entities to employees for benefits provided through a defined benefit pension plan. Calculated based on the total pension liability, less fiduciary net position. (If amount is positive, a net pension *asset* is the result.)
Net position	GASB-63 (also GASB:CS-4)	The residual of assets, plus deferred outflows of resources, less liabilities, less deferred inflows of resources. Fiduciary activities net to *fiduciary net position*. Net position is displayed in three components—*net investment in capital assets*, *restricted* (distinguishing between major categories of restrictions), and *unrestricted*.

Item	GASB Pronouncement[1]	Definition
Net realizable value	GASB-62	The estimated selling price in the ordinary course of operations less estimated costs of completion (to the stage of completion assumed in determining the selling price), holding, and disposal.
Network affiliation agreement (broadcasting)	GASB-62	A broadcaster may be affiliated with a network under a network affiliation agreement. Under the agreement, the station receives compensation for the network programming that it carries based on a formula designed to compensate the station for advertising sold on a network basis and included in network programming. Program costs, a major expense of television stations, generally are lower for a network affiliate than for an independent station because an affiliate does not incur program costs for network programs.
Nonauthoritative accounting literature	GASB-76	Sources of nonauthoritative accounting literature include GASB Concepts Statements, pronouncements and other literature of the Financial Accounting Standards Board, Federal Accounting Standards Advisory Board, International Public Sector Accounting Standards Board, and International Accounting Standards Board, and AICPA literature not cleared by the GASB, practices that are widely recognized and prevalent in state and local government, literature of other professional associations or regulatory agencies, and accounting textbooks, handbooks, and articles. (**AUTHOR'S NOTE**: This book is another example.)
Noncapital financing activities	GASB-9	The borrowing of money for purposes other than to acquire, construct, or improve capital assets and repaying those amounts borrowed, including interest. This category includes proceeds from all borrowings (such as revenue anticipation notes) not clearly attributable to acquisition, construction, or improvement of capital assets, regardless of the form of the borrowing. Also included are certain other interfund and intergovernmental receipts and payments.

Glossary

Item	GASB Pronouncement[1]	Definition
Nonemployer contributing entities	GASB-75	Entities that make contributions to a pension or OPEB plan that is used to provide pensions or OPEB to the employees of other entities, that is administered through a trust. Employees are not considered nonemployer contributing entities. For arrangements in which pensions are provided through a pension plan that is *not administered through a trust*, entities that make defined benefit payments directly as pensions come due for employees of other entities, including using the entity's assets held by others for providing benefits. Employees are *not* considered nonemployer contributing entities.
Nonexchange financial guarantee	GASB-70	A nonexchange financial guarantee is a guarantee of an obligation of a legally separate entity or individual, including a blended or discretely presented component unit, which requires the guarantor to indemnify a third-party obligation holder under specified conditions.
Nonexchange transaction	GASB-33	When a government gives (or receives) value without directly receiving (or giving) equal value in return. Four classes of nonexchange transactions are used: 1. Derived tax revenues, 2. Imposed nonexchange revenues, 3. Government-mandated nonexchange transactions, and 4. Voluntary nonexchange transactions.
Nonmonetary assets and liabilities	GASB-62	Assets and liabilities other than monetary ones. Examples are inventories, investments in common stocks, capital assets, and liabilities for rent collected in advance.
Nonperformance risk	GASB-72	The risk that an entity will not fulfill an obligation. Nonperformance risk includes, but may not be limited to, the government's own credit risk.
Nonspendable fund balance	GASB-54	The nonspendable fund balance classification includes amounts that cannot be spent because they are either (a) not in spendable form or

Item	GASB Pronouncement[1]	Definition
		(b) legally or contractually required to be maintained intact.

The "not in spendable form" criterion includes items that are not expected to be converted to cash, for example, inventories and prepaid amounts. It also includes the long-term amount of loans and notes receivable, as well as property acquired for resale. However, if the use of the proceeds from the collection of those receivables or from the sale of those properties is restricted, committed, or assigned, then they should be included in the appropriate fund balance classification (restricted, committed, or assigned), rather than nonspendable fund balance. The corpus (or principal) of a permanent fund is an example of an amount that is legally or contractually required to be maintained intact. |
Normal cost (also known as service cost)		That portion of the Actuarial Present Value of pension plan benefits and expenses which is allocated to a valuation year by the Actuarial Cost Method. Normal cost is no longer used for general purpose external financial reporting, but service cost is.
Notes to the financial statements (notes to the basic financial statements)	GASB-34	Notes explaining the governments balances and results of operations, presented in accordance with GAAP.
Notional amount	GASB-53	The number of currency units, shares, bushels, pounds, or other units specified in the derivative instrument. It is a stated amount on which payments depend. The notional amount is like the principal amount of a bond.
Obligating event (pollution remediation)	GASB-49	An event that triggers the recognition of a liability for pollution remediation.
Observable inputs	GASB-72	Inputs that are developed using market data, such as publicly available information about actual events or transactions, and which reflect the assumptions that market participants would use when pricing an asset or liability.

Glossary

Item	GASB Pronouncement[1]	Definition
Off-market term	GASB-53	A provision in a derivative instrument, such as a rate, price, or term, that is not consistent with the current market for that type of contract.
OMB		White House Office of Management and Budget
On-behalf payments for fringe benefits and salaries	GASB-24	Direct payments made by one entity (the paying entity or paying government) to a third-party recipient for the employees of another, legally separate entity (the employer entity or employer government). They include payments made by governmental entities on behalf of nongovernmental entities and payments made by nongovernmental entities on behalf of governmental entities and may be made for volunteers as well as for paid employees of the employer entity.
Ongoing financial interest	GASB-14	An equity interest or any other arrangement that allows a participating government to have access to a joint venture's resources.
Ongoing financial responsibility	GASB-14	• A participating government is obligated in some manner for the debts of a joint venture. Or, • When the joint venture's existence depends on continued funding by the participating government.
OPEB Plans	GASB-74	Arrangements through which OPEB is determined, assets dedicated for OPEB (if any) are accumulated and managed, and benefits are paid as they come due.
Open group/closed group		Terms used to distinguish between two classes of Actuarial Cost Methods. Under an Open Group Actuarial Cost Method, Actuarial Present Values associated with expected future entrants are considered, under a Closed Group Actuarial Cost Method, Actuarial Present Values associated with future entrants are not considered.

Item	GASB Pronouncement[1]	Definition
Open-end mutual fund	GASB-31	An SEC-registered investment company that issues shares of its stock to investors, invests in an investment portfolio on the shareholders' behalf, and stands ready to redeem its shares for an amount based on its current share price. An open-end mutual fund creates new shares to meet investor demand, and the value of an investment in the fund depends directly on the value of the underlying portfolio. Open-end mutual funds include governmental external investment pools that are registered as investment companies with the SEC and that operate as open-end funds.
Operating activities (cash flows)	GASB-9	Cash flows resulting from providing services and producing and delivering goods and include all transactions and other events that are not defined as capital and related financing, noncapital financing, or investing activities. Cash flows from operating activities generally are the cash effects of transactions and other events that initiate the determination of operating income.
Operation	GASB-69	An integrated set of activities conducted and managed for providing identifiable services with associated assets or liabilities. For example, an operation may include the assets and liabilities specifically associated with the activities conducted and managed by the fire department in a general-purpose government. Conversely, fire engines donated to or acquired by a fire department would constitute only a portion of that activity and, therefore, would not constitute an operation.

Item	GASB Pronouncement[1]	Definition
Opinion Unit		As best described in the AICPA Audit and Accounting Guide *State and Local Governments*, due to the unique nature of governmental financial reporting, the basis at which the auditor considers the basic financial statements to be presented fairly, in all material respects, in accordance with GAAP. Opinion units may or may not align to reporting units. Separate materiality determinations are made for each opinion unit for the purposes of planning, performing, evaluating the results of, and reporting on the audit of a government's basic financial statements. Some governments may only have one opinion unit, including governments engaged only in fiduciary activities. A special-purpose government may have one (or more) discretely presented component units. The component units of the special-purpose government is an opinion unit separate from the special-purpose government's other opinion unit(s), unless the aggregate component units meet the conditions for combining with the aggregate remaining fund information of the primary government.
Option	GASB-53	A contract that gives its holder the right but not the obligation to buy or sell a financial instrument or commodity at a certain price for a period.
Option pricing model	GASB-72	A valuation technique used to value an option contract that is based on the critical terms of the contract and implied volatility.
Orderly transaction	GASB-72	A transaction that assumes exposure to the market for a period before the measurement date to allow for marketing activities that are usual and customary for transactions involving such assets or liabilities. It is not a forced transaction (for example, a forced liquidation or distress sale).

Item	GASB Pronouncement[1]	Definition
Original budget	GASB-34	The first complete adopted budget of a government. The original budget may be adjusted by reserves, transfers, allocations, supplemental appropriations, and other legally authorized legislative and executive changes *before* the beginning of the fiscal year. The original budget should also include actual appropriation amounts automatically carried over from prior years by law. For example, a legal provision may require the automatic rolling forward of appropriations to cover prior-year encumbrances.
Origination fees (lending activities)	GASB-62	Costs to originate a loan that: a. Result directly from and are essential to the lending transaction and b. Would not have been incurred by the lender had that lending transaction not occurred.
Other postemployment benefits (OPEB)	GASB-75	Benefits other than retirement income (such as death benefits, life insurance, disability, and long-term care) that are paid in the period after employment and that are provided separately from a pension plan, as well as postemployment health care benefits paid in the period after employment (if any), regardless of the way they are provided. Other postemployment benefits do not include termination benefits or termination payments for sick leave.
Other stand-alone government	GASB-14	A legally separate governmental organization that: • Does not have a separately elected governing body and • Does not meet the definition of a component unit. Other stand-alone governments include some special-purpose governments, joint ventures, jointly governed organizations, and pools.
Outflow of resources (or outlays)	GASB-65 (also GASB:CS-4)	A consumption of net position by the government that is applicable to the reporting period (expenses or expenditures).

Glossary

Item	GASB Pronouncement[1]	Definition
Overlapping debt	GASB-44	The outstanding long-term debt instruments—including bonds, notes, certificates of participation, loans, and capital leases—of governments that overlap geographically, at least in part, with the government preparing the statistical section information.
Overlapping rate	GASB-44	An amount or percentage applied to a unit of a specific revenue base by governments that overlap geographically, at least in part, with the government preparing the statistical section information.
Own-source revenues	GASB-84	Revenues that are generated by a government itself, such as tax revenues and water and sewer charges. Investment income is also an own-source revenue. Intergovernmental aid and shared revenues are not own-source revenues.
Parameters		The set of requirements for calculating actuarially determined OPEB information included in financial reports.
Participation	GASB-31	The ability of an investment to capture market (interest rate) changes through the investment's negotiability or transferability, or redemption terms that consider market rates.
Participation contract	GASB-10	A formal written contract between a public entity risk pool and a pool participant describing, among other things, the period, the amount of risk coverage the pool will provide for the participating governmental entity, and the required contribution the participant must pay for that coverage. (The term *policy* is used in the commercial insurance industry.)
Pass-through grants	GASB-24	Grants and other financial assistance received by a governmental entity to transfer to or spend on behalf of a secondary recipient.
Pay-as-you-go (PAYGO)		A method of financing a pension plan under which the contributions to the plan are generally made at about the same time and in about the same amount as benefit payments and expenses becoming due.

Item	GASB Pronouncement[1]	Definition
Paying entity	GASB-24	The entity that makes on-behalf payments for fringe benefits and salaries for the employees of another employer entity. The paying entity may be governmental or nongovernmental.
Payroll growth rate		An actuarial assumption with respect to future increases in total covered payroll attributable to inflation, used in applying the level percentage of projected payroll amortization method.
Penalty (leases)	GASB-62	Any requirement that is imposed or can be imposed on the lessee by the lease agreement or by factors outside the lease agreement to disburse cash, incur or assume a liability, perform services, surrender or transfer an asset or rights to an asset or otherwise forego an economic benefit, or suffer an economic detriment. Factors to consider when determining if an economic detriment may be incurred include, but are not limited to, the uniqueness of purpose or location of the property, the availability of a comparable replacement property, the relative importance or significance of the property to the continuation of the lessee's operations or service to its customers, the existence of leasehold improvements or other assets whose value would be impaired by the lessee vacating or discontinuing use of the leased property, adverse tax consequences, and the ability or willingness of the lessee to bear the cost associated with relocation or replacement of the leased property at market rental rates or to tolerate other parties using the leased property.
Pension (and other employee benefit) trust funds	GASB-84	Used to report resources require to be held in trust for the members and beneficiaries of defined benefit pension plans, defined contribution plans, or other employee benefit plans, where the assets are: • Administered through a trust agreement or equivalent arrangement in which the government itself is not a beneficiary,

26,100 *Glossary*

Item	GASB Pronouncement[1]	Definition
		• Dedicated to providing benefits to recipients in accordance with the benefit terms, and
		• Legally protected from the creditors of the government.
Pension plans	GASB-78	Arrangements through which pensions are determined, assets dedicated for pensions are accumulated and managed, and benefits are paid as they come due.
Pensions	GASB-78	Retirement income and, if provided through a pension plan, postemployment benefits other than retirement income (such as death benefits, life insurance, and disability benefits). Pensions do not include postemployment healthcare benefits and termination benefits.
Percentage-of-completion method (construction contracts)	GASB-62	The percentage-of-completion method recognizes revenue as work on a contract progresses. The recognized revenue should be that percentage of estimated total revenue that either:
		• Incurred costs to date bear to estimated total costs after giving effect to estimates of costs to complete based upon most recent information, or
		• May be indicated by such other measure of progress toward completion as may be appropriate, having due regard to work performed.

Glossary **26,101**

Item	GASB Pronouncement[1]	Definition
Perfected security interest	GASB-3	An interest in property, including securities, that is superior to the interests of the general creditors. Possession of the security by the secured party or its agent is generally needed to create a perfected security interest. In addition, a perfected security interest can be created without taking possession of the security if the transferor of the security interest has signed a security agreement that contains a description of the collateral and the secured party pays for the investment. Such a security interest is perfected for a period of 21 days. However, the secured party risks loss or impairment of its security interest during the 21-day period, because the Uniform Commercial Code provides that a holder in due course of a negotiable instrument or a bona fide purchaser of the instrument will take priority over the secured party. After 21 days, the security interest becomes unperfected unless the secured party takes possession of the security.
Period-certain term	GASB-81	A term specifying that the termination of a split-interest agreement occurs after a specified number of years.
Permanent funds	GASB-54	Funds used to account for and report resources that are restricted to the extent that only earnings, and not principal, may be used for purposes that support the reporting government's programs—that is, for the benefit of the government or its citizenry. Permanent funds do not include private-purpose trust funds, which should be used to report situations in which the government is required to use the principal or earnings for the benefit of individuals, private organizations, or other governments.
Phase (real estate)	GASB-62	A parcel on which units are to be constructed concurrently.

26,102 *Glossary*

Item	GASB Pronouncement[1]	Definition
Pick-ups	GASB-82	If an employer makes payments to satisfy employee contribution requirements to a pension plan (for example, in connection with an election made in accordance with Internal Revenue Code Section 414(h)(2) and Revenue Ruling 2006-43), the employer does not include such amounts in salaries and wages of the employee. (See also "Employer-paid member contributions.")
Plan assets		Resources, usually in the form of stocks, bonds, and other classes of investments, that have been segregated and restricted in a trust, or in an equivalent arrangement, in which: • Employer contributions to the plan are irrevocable, • Assets provide benefits to retirees and their beneficiaries, and • Assets are legally protected from creditors of the employer(s) or plan administrator, for the payment of benefits in accordance with the terms of the plan.
Plan liabilities		Obligations payable by the plan at the reporting date, including, primarily, benefits and refunds due and payable to plan members and beneficiaries, and accrued investment and administrative expenses. Plan liabilities do not include actuarial accrued liabilities for benefits that are not due and payable at the reporting date.
Plan members	GASB-75	Individuals that are covered under the terms of a pension or OPEB plan. Plan members generally include • Employees in active service (active plan members) and • Employees no longer in active service (or their beneficiaries) who have accumulated benefits under the terms of a pension plan (inactive plan members).
Plan net position (plan net position held in trust for OPEB)		The difference between total plan assets and total plan liabilities at the reporting date. If held in an irrevocable trust, it is termed Fiduciary Net Position.

Item	GASB Pronouncement[1]	Definition
Plan of adjustment	GASB-58	Plan submitted to a bankruptcy judge that separates the government's claims and liabilities into classes that may or may not be adjusted as part of the bankruptcy.
Pledged receivables	GASB-48	Taxes or other types of receivables used to secure either a collateralized borrowing or sold to a third party in exchange for cash.
Pledged revenues	GASB-48	Revenues to be collected in the future securing either a collateralized borrowing or sold to a third party in exchange for cash.
Policy	GASB-10	A formal written contract of insurance between an insurer and an insured describing, among other things, the period and amount of risk coverage the insurer agrees to provide the insured.
Policyholder	GASB-10	The party to whom an insurance policy is issued and who pays a premium to an insurer for the insurer's promise to provide insurance protection.
Policyholder dividends	GASB-10	Payments made, or credits extended to the insured by the insurer, usually at the end of a policy year, that result in reducing the net insurance cost to the policyholder. These dividends may be paid in cash to the insured or applied by the insured to reduce premiums due for the next policy year.
Policy-year basis	GASB-10	For disclosure purposes, a method that assigns incurred losses and claim adjustment expenses to the year in which the event that triggered coverage under the pool insurance policy or participation contract occurred. For occurrence-based coverage where all members have a common contract renewal date, the policy-year basis is the same as the accident-year basis. For claims-made coverages, policy-year basis is the same as the report-year basis.

Item	GASB Pronouncement[1]	Definition
Pollution	GASB-49	The U.S. Environmental Protection Agency provides the following discussion of the term *pollution* on its website: "Generally, the presence of a substance in the environment that because of its chemical composition or quantity prevents the functioning of natural processes and produces undesirable environmental and health effects. Under the Clean Water Act, for example, the term has been defined as the man-made or man-induced alteration of the physical, biological, chemical, and radiological integrity of water and other media."
Pollution remediation obligation	GASB-49	An obligation to address the current or potential detrimental effects of existing pollution by participating in pollution remediation activities. For example, obligations to clean up spills of hazardous wastes or hazardous substances and obligations to remove contamination such as asbestos are pollution remediation obligations.
Popular reports	GASB:CS-1	Less detailed reporting intended for users whose financial reporting needs are better satisfied through more condensed information.
Postemployment	GASB-75	The period after employment ceases.
Postemployment benefit changes	GASB-75	Adjustments to the pension of an inactive employee (or plan member).
Postemployment healthcare benefits	GASB-75	Medical, dental, vision, and other health-related benefits paid after the termination of employment.
Potential hedging derivative instrument	GASB-53	A derivative instrument that is associated with a hedgeable item prior to the determination that the derivative instrument is effective in significantly reducing the identified financial risk.
Potentially responsible party (PRP)	GASB-49	An individual or entity—including owners, operators, transporters, or generators—that is held potentially responsible for pollution at a site. The term refers to a party that is held by law as potentially responsible for pollution at any site. It is not limited to parties associated with Superfund sites.

Item	GASB Pronouncement[1]	Definition
Pre-acquisition costs (real estate)	GASB-62	Costs related to a property that are incurred for the express purpose of, but prior to, obtaining that property. Examples of pre-acquisition costs may be costs of surveying, zoning or traffic studies, or payments to obtain an option on the property.
Prematurity period (cable television systems)	GASB-62	During the prematurity period, the cable television system is partially under construction and partially in service. The prematurity period begins with the first earned subscriber revenue. Its end will vary with circumstances of the system but will be determined based on plans for completion of the first major construction period or achievement of a specified predetermined subscriber level at which no additional investment will be required other than for cable television plants. The length of the prematurity period varies with the franchise development and construction plans.
Premium (insurance)	GASB-10	The consideration paid for an insurance contract.
Premium deficiency	GASB-10	The amount by which expected claims costs (including IBNR) and all expected claim adjustment expenses, expected dividends to policyholders or pool participants, unamortized acquisition costs, and incurred policy maintenance costs exceed related unearned premium revenue.
Preparer	GASB:CS-3	Those who are responsible for producing financial reports that recognize relevant events in the financial statements or that disclose or present messages about such events elsewhere in the financial report.
Present value	GASB-72	A valuation technique used to link future amounts (cash flows or values) to a present amount by employing a discount rate (an application of the income approach).

Item	GASB Pronouncement[1]	Definition
Primary dealers	GASB-3	A group of government securities dealers included in the "List of Government Securities Dealers Reporting to the Market Reports Division of the Federal Reserve Bank of New York [NY Fed]" that submit daily reports of market activity and positions and monthly financial statements to the NY Fed and are subject to its informal oversight. Primary dealers include SEC-registered securities broker-dealers, banks, and a few unregulated firms.
Primary government	GASB-14	A state government or general purpose local government. Also, a special-purpose government that has a separately elected governing body, is legally separate, and is fiscally independent of other state or local governments.
Principal market	GASB-72	The market with the greatest volume and level of activity for an asset or liability.
Principal-to-principal market	GASB-72	A market in which transactions, both originations and resales, are negotiated independently with no intermediary. Little information about those transactions may be made available publicly.
Private-purpose trust funds	GASB-84	Used to report escheat property or all other trust arrangements under which principal and income benefit individuals, private organizations, or other governments, that are *not* pension arrangements, OPEB arrangements, or activities required to be reported in investment trust funds and are held in a trust that meets the following criteria. The assets are: (a) Administered through a trust agreement or equivalent arrangement (hereafter jointly referred to as a trust) in which the government itself is not a beneficiary, (b) Dedicated to providing benefits to recipients in accordance with the benefit terms, and (c) Legally protected from the creditors of the government.

Item	GASB Pronouncement[1]	Definition
Probable	GASB-62	Classification of a loss contingency where the future event or events are likely to occur.
Productive assets	GASB-62	Assets held for or used in the production of goods or services by the government. Productive assets include an investment in another entity if the investment is accounted for by the equity method but exclude an investment not accounted for by that method.
Program revenues	GASB-34	Revenues derived directly from the program itself or from parties outside the reporting government's taxpayers or citizenry, as a whole, they reduce the net cost of the function to be financed from the government's general revenues. The statement of activities should separately report three categories of program revenues: a. Charges for services, b. Program-specific operating grants and contributions, and c. Program-specific capital grants and contributions.
Program-specific grants and contributions (operating and capital)	GASB-34	Revenues arising from mandatory and voluntary nonexchange transactions with other governments, organizations, or individuals that are restricted for use in a program.
Project costs	GASB-62	Costs clearly associated with the acquisition, development, and construction of a real estate project.
Projected benefit payments	GASB-75	All benefits estimated to be payable through the pension or OPEB plan to current active and inactive employees because of their past service and their expected future service.
Projected salary increase assumption		An actuarial assumption with respect to future increases in the individual salaries and wages of active plan members, used in determining the actuarial present value of total projected benefits when the benefit amounts are related to salaries and wages. The expected increases commonly include amounts for inflation, enhanced productivity, and employee merit and seniority.

Glossary

Item	GASB Pronouncement[1]	Definition
Projected unit credit actuarial cost method (PUC)		A method under which the benefits (projected or unprojected) of everyone included in an Actuarial Valuation are allocated by a consistent formula to valuation years. The Actuarial Present Value of benefits allocated to a valuation year is called the Normal Cost. The Actuarial Present Value of benefits allocated to all periods prior to a valuation year is called the Actuarial Accrued Liability. *No longer used for general purpose external financial reporting.*
Property and liability insurance	GASB-10	Insurance contracts that provide protection against (a) damage to, or loss of, property caused by various perils, such as fire and theft, or (b) legal liability resulting from injuries to other persons or damage to their property. Property and liability insurance companies also may issue accident and health insurance contracts. There is a broad insurance distinction between companies writing life and health insurance and those writing the property insurance or "nonlife" lines of fire, marine, casualty, and surety. Although no one definition has been fully established, some use the generic title "property and casualty" insurance, whereas others use "property and liability" insurance.
Proprietary funds	GASB-34	Funds consisting of enterprise funds (emphasizing major funds) and internal service funds. The funds focus on the determination of operating income, changes in net [position] (or cost recovery), financial position and cash flows.
Public Benefit Corporation		Entity created by state law, usually associated with not-for-profit entities.

Item	GASB Pronouncement[1]	Definition
Public Corporation (See also "Component Units")	GASB-76 (Cod. Sec. 1000.801, fn. 4)	*Black's Law Dictionary* defines a public corporation as: "An artificial person (for example, [a] municipality or a governmental corporation) created for the administration of public affairs. Unlike a private corporation it has no protection against legislative acts altering or even repealing its charter. Instrumentalities created by [the] state, formed and owned by it in [the] public interest, supported in whole or part by public funds, and governed by managers deriving their authority from [the] state." *Sharon Realty Co. v. Westlake, Ohio Com. Pl., 188 N.E. 2d 318, 323, 25 O.O.2d 322* (Ct. Com. Pl. 1961). A public corporation is an instrumentality of the state, founded and owned in the public interest, supported by public funds and governed by those deriving their authority from the state. *York County Fair Ass'n v. South Carolina Tax Commission, 249 S.C. 337, 154 S.E. 2d 361, 362 (1967).*
Public employee retirement system (PERS)	GASB-68	A special-purpose government that administers one or more pension plans, also, may administer other types of employee benefit plans, including postemployment healthcare plans and deferred compensation plans.
Public entity risk pool	GASB-10	A cooperative group of governmental entities joining together to finance an exposure, liability, or risk. Risk may include property and liability, workers' compensation, or employee health care. A pool may be a stand-alone entity or included as part of a larger governmental entity that acts as the pool's sponsor.

Glossary

Item	GASB Pronouncement[1]	Definition
Public-Private Partnership (or Public-Public Partnership) (PPP)	GASB-94	An arrangement in which a government (the transferor) contracts with (an operator) to provide public services by conveying control of the right to operate or use a nonfinancial asset, such as infrastructure or other capital asset (the underlying PPP asset) for a period of time in an exchange or exchange-like transaction. The operator may be a governmental entity (public-public partnership) or a nongovernmental entity (public-private partnership). Underlying PPP assets include existing assets of a transferor, assets that are newly purchased or constructed by the operator, or existing assets of a transferor that have been improved by the operator. Some PPPs are service concession arrangements.
Purpose restriction (eligibility)	GASB-33	The purpose for which resources are required to be used. All other purposes other than those required are unallowed (or disallowed).
Put option	GASB-53	An option that gives its holder the right but not the obligation to sell a financial instrument or commodity at a certain price for a period of time.
Qualified External Investment Pool	GASB-79	An external investment pool that elects (and maintains) measurement for financial reporting purposes all investments at amortized cost, if it meets *all the following criteria:* • The pool transacts with participants at a stable net asset value per share (for example, all contributions and redemptions are transacted at $1 net asset value per share), • Portfolio maturity requirements are met, • Portfolio quality requirements are met, • Portfolio diversification requirements are met, • Portfolio liquidity requirements are met, and • Shadow pricing requirements are met.

Item	GASB Pronouncement[1]	Definition
		If an external investment pool is noncompliant with any of the criteria during the reporting period, it should measure investments at fair value in accordance with GASB-31, as amended, except for investments with remaining maturities that are 90 days or less, which may remain at amortized cost.
Quantitative method	GASB-53	A method of evaluating effectiveness using a mathematical relationship. Synthetic instrument, dollar-offset, and regression analysis are the quantitative methods specifically addressed in this Statement.
RAN		Revenue anticipation note
Reacquisition price	GASB-62	In extinguishments of debt, the amount paid on extinguishment, including a call premium and miscellaneous costs of reacquisition. If extinguishment is achieved by a direct exchange of new securities, the reacquisition price is the total present value of the new securities.
Readily determinable fair value	GASB-72	An equity security has a readily determinable fair value if it meets any of the following conditions: a. The fair value of an equity security is readily determinable if sales prices or bid-and-asked quotations are currently available on a securities exchange registered with the U.S. Securities and Exchange Commission or in the over-the-counter market, provided that those prices or quotations for the over-the-counter market are publicly reported by the National Association of Securities Dealers Automated Quotations systems or by OTC Markets Group, Inc. Restricted stock meets that definition if the restriction terminates within one year. b. The fair value of an equity security traded only in a foreign market is readily determinable if that foreign market is of a breadth and scope comparable to one of the U.S. markets referred to in (a).

Item	GASB Pronouncement[1]	Definition
		c. The fair value of an investment in a mutual fund is readily determinable if the fair value per share (unit) is determined and published and is the basis for current transactions.
Real rate of return	GASB-75	The rate of return on an investment after adjustment to eliminate inflation.
Reasonably possible	GASB-62	Classification of a loss contingency where the change of the future event or events occurring is more than remote but less than likely.
Recipient government	GASB-24	In a pass-through grant, a governmental entity that receives grants and other financial assistance to transfer to or spend on behalf of a secondary recipient.
Redistricting	GASB-69	Redrawing of the territorial boundaries usually within a government and usually for political, census or other demographic purposes. For example, redistricting may be used in a school district's enrollment rebalancing efforts. Sometimes, however, redistricting may involve the transfer of operations from one district to another.
Reference rate	GASB-93	A specified interest rate, security price, commodity price, foreign exchange rate, index of prices or rates, or other variable (including the occurrence or nonoccurrence of a specified event such as a scheduled payment under a contract). A reference rate may be a price or rate of an asset or a liability but is not the asset or liability itself. A reference rate is a variable that, along with either a notional amount or a payment provision, determines the settlement of a derivative instrument. Other accounting literature may refer to a reference rate as a *reference index* or an *underlying*.
Refunding	GASB-23	Issuance of new debt when proceeds are used to repay previously outstanding debt. The proceeds may be used currently (current refunding) or placed in escrow until a later date (advance refunding).

Item	GASB Pronouncement[1]	Definition
Registered security	GASB-3	A security that has the name of the owner written on its face. A registered security cannot be negotiated except by the endorsement of the owner.
Regression analysis method	GASB-53	A statistical technique that measures the relationship between a dependent variable and one or more independent variables. The future value of the dependent variable is predicted by measuring the size and significance of each independent variable in relation to the dependent variable. Regression analysis included in the text of this Statement uses only one independent variable.
Regulated lease	GASB-87	Lease subject to external laws, regulations or legal rulings. A common regulated lease involves aviation.
Reinsurance	GASB-62	A transaction in which a reinsurer (assuming enterprise), for a consideration (premium), assumes all or part of a risk undertaken originally by another insurer (government). However, the legal rights of the insured are not affected by the reinsurance transaction and the insurance enterprise issuing the insurance contract remains liable to the insured for payment of policy benefits.
Related organization	GASB-14	An organization for which a primary government is not financially accountable (because it does not impose will or have a financial benefit or burden relationship) even though the primary government appoints a voting majority of the organization's governing board.

Item	GASB Pronouncement[1]	Definition
Related parties	GASB-62	A government's related organizations, joint ventures, and jointly governed organizations, as defined in Statement No. 14 *(The Financial Reporting Entity)*, as amended, elected and appointed officials of the government, its management, members of the immediate families of elected or appointed officials of the government and its management, and other parties with which the government may deal if one party can significantly influence the management or operating policies of the other to an extent that one of the transacting parties might be prevented from fully pursuing its own separate interests. Another party also is a related party if it can significantly influence the management or operating policies of the transacting parties (for example, through imposition of will as discussed in Statement 14, as amended) or if it has an ownership interest in one of the transacting parties and can significantly influence the other to an extent that one or more of the transacting parties might be prevented from fully pursuing its own separate interests.
Relative fair value before construction (real estate)	GASB-62	The fair value of each land parcel in a real estate project in relation to the fair value of the other parcels in the project, exclusive of value added by on-site development and construction activities.
Relative liquidity	GASB-34	Organization of the assets and liabilities in a statement of net position with the elements "closest to cash" placed at the top of each category, followed by elements by descending liquidity.

Item	GASB Pronouncement[1]	Definition
Relief from royalty technique	GASB-72	A valuation technique used to value certain intangible assets (for example, trademarks and trade names) based on the premise that the only value that a purchaser of the assets receives is the exemption from paying a royalty for its use. Application of this method usually involves estimating the fair value of an intangible asset by quantifying the present value of the stream of market-derived royalty payments that the owner of the intangible asset is exempted from or "relieved" from paying.
Remainder interest	GASB-81	The right (a type of beneficial interest) to receive all or a portion of the resources remaining at the end of a split-interest agreement's term.
Remeasured amounts	GASB:CS-6	Remeasured amounts reflect the conditions in effect at the financial statement date and may be determined using several methods. Remeasurement changes the amount reported for an asset or liability from an initial amount or previous remeasured amount to an amount indicative of a value at the financial statement date. Remeasured amounts establish a new carrying value for the asset or liability that is determined without reference to previously reported amounts.
Remedial investigation and feasibility study (RI/FS)	GASB-49	Extensive technical studies to investigate the scope of site impacts (RI) and determine the remedial alternatives (FS) that, consistent with the National Contingency Plan provisions of the federal Superfund law or similar state laws, may be implemented at a polluted site. An RI/FS may include a variety of on- and off-site activities, such as monitoring, sampling, and analysis.
Remote	GASB-62	Classification of a loss contingency where the chance of the future event or events occurring is slight.
Replacement cost	GASB:CS-6	The price paid to acquire an asset with equivalent service potential in an orderly market transaction at the measurement date.

Item	GASB Pronouncement[1]	Definition
Reporting date		The date of the financial statements, the last day of the fiscal year. Also known as the financial reporting date.
Reporting form contract	GASB-10	A contract or policy in which the policyholder is required to report the value of property insured to the insurer at certain intervals. The final premium on the contract is determined by applying the contract rate to the average of the values reported.
Reporting Unit	GASB:CS-3	A reporting unit may be a governmental unit (that is, it has separate legal standing), part of a governmental unit (such as governmental activities or business-type activities, a major fund, an aggregation of funds (a group of nonmajor funds), or a segment), or an aggregation or consolidation of two or more governmental units (such as a primary government and its component units). When the reporting unit is only part of a governmental unit, the assets, liabilities, residual balances, and changes in those amounts that are included in the reporting unit's financial statements have been assigned by the governmental unit to that reporting unit for control, management, or financial reporting purposes.
Repurchase agreement (repo)	GASB-3	a. An agreement in which a governmental entity (buyer-lender) transfers cash to a broker-dealer or financial institution (seller-borrower), the broker-dealer or financial institution transfers securities to the entity and promises to repay the cash plus interest in exchange for the *same* securities.
		b. A generic term for an agreement in which a governmental entity (buyer-lender) transfers cash to a broker-dealer or financial institution (seller-borrower), the broker-dealer or financial institution transfers securities to the entity and promises to repay the cash plus interest in exchange for the same securities (as in definition (a) above) or for different securities.

Item	GASB Pronouncement[1]	Definition
Required contribution	GASB-10	The consideration a pool participant pays a public entity risk pool for a participation contract. (The term *premium* is used in the commercial insurance industry.)
Required supplementary information (RSI)		Schedules, statistical data, and other information that are an essential part of financial reporting and should be presented with, but are not part of, the basic financial statements of a governmental entity. RSI is required by GAAP.
Reset date	GASB-40	The time, frequently quarterly or semiannually, that a bond's variable coupon is repriced to reflect changes in a benchmark index.
Resource Conservation and Recovery Act (RCRA)	GASB-49	A federal law that provides comprehensive regulation of hazardous wastes from point of generation to final disposal. All generators of hazardous waste, transporters of hazardous waste, and owners and operators of hazardous waste treatment, storage, or disposal facilities must comply with the applicable requirements of the statute.
Restoration cost approach	GASB-42	About an impaired capital asset, the amount of impairment is derived from the estimated costs to restore the utility of the capital asset. The estimated restoration cost can be converted to historical cost either by restating the estimated restoration cost using an appropriate cost index or by applying a ratio of estimated restoration cost over estimated replacement cost to the carrying value of the capital asset.
Restricted fund balance	GASB-54	Fund balance with constraints placed on the use of resources that are either: a. Externally imposed by creditors (such as through debt covenants), grantors, contributors, or laws or regulations of other governments, or b. Imposed by law through constitutional provisions or enabling legislation.

Item	GASB Pronouncement[1]	Definition
Restricted net position	GASB-63	Restricted assets reduced by liabilities and deferred inflows of resources related to those assets. Generally, a liability relates to restricted assets if the asset results from a resource flow that also results in the recognition of a liability or if the liability will be liquidated with the restricted assets reported.
Restricted stock	GASB-31	Equity securities whose sale is restricted at acquisition by legal or contractual provisions (other than in connection with being pledged as collateral) except if that restriction terminates within one year or if the holder has the power by contract or otherwise to cause the requirement to be met within one year. Any portion of the security that can reasonably be expected to qualify for sale within one year, such as may be the case under SEC Rule 144 (17 *Code of Federal Regulations* § 230.144) or similar rules of the SEC, is not considered restricted.
Retirement of a tangible capital asset	GASB-83	The permanent removal of a tangible capital asset from service.
Retrospective (experience) rating	GASB-10	A method of determining the final amount of an insurance premium by which the initial premium is adjusted based on actual experience during the period of coverage (sometimes subject to maximum and minimum limits). It is designed to encourage safety by the insured and to compensate the insurer if larger-than-expected losses are incurred.

Glossary **26,119**

Item	GASB Pronouncement[1]	Definition
Return of contribution	GASB-10	Payments made, or credits extended to the participant by a public entity risk pool, usually at the end of a participation contract year, that result in reducing the participant's net participation contribution. These returns may be paid in cash to the participant or applied by the pool to reduce participation contributions due for the next participation contract year. (The term *dividend* is used in the commercial insurance industry.) Returns of contributions are distinguished from experience refunds in that returns are not determined based on the actual experience of an individual pool participant but, instead, on the experience of the entire pool or of a class of participants.
Revenue obligation debt (also known as special obligation debt)	GASB-48	Debt issued secured by a stream of revenues. The debt may or may not be backed by the full faith and credit of the government.
Reverse repurchase agreement (reverse repo)	GASB-3	An agreement in which a broker-dealer or financial institution (buyer-lender) transfers cash to a governmental entity (seller-borrower), the entity transfers securities to the broker-dealer or financial institution and promises to repay the cash plus interest in exchange for the *same* securities. A generic term for an agreement in which a broker-dealer or financial institution (buyer-lender) transfers cash to a governmental entity (seller-borrower), the entity transfers securities to the broker-dealer or financial institution and promises to repay the cash plus interest in exchange for the same securities or for different securities.
Risk	GASB-10	Defined variously as uncertainty of loss, chance of loss, or the variance of actual from expected results. Also, the subject matter of an insurance contract (for example, the insured property or liability exposure).
Risk adjustment	GASB-72	See "Risk premium."

Glossary

Item	GASB Pronouncement[1]	Definition
Risk management	GASB-10	The process of managing an organization's activities to minimize the adverse effects of certain types of losses. The main elements of risk management are risk control (to minimize the losses that strike an organization) and risk financing (to obtain finances to restore the economic damages of those losses).
Risk premium	GASB-72	Compensation sought by risk-averse market participants for bearing the uncertainty inherent in the cash flows of an asset or a liability. Also referred to as a risk adjustment.
Rollover risk	GASB-53	The risk that a hedging derivative instrument associated with a hedgeable item does not extend to the maturity of that hedgeable item. When the hedging derivative instrument terminates, the hedgeable item will no longer have the benefit of the hedging derivative instrument. An example is an interest rate swap that pays the government a variable-rate payment that is designed to match the term of the variable-rate interest payments on the government's bonds. If the hedging derivative instrument's term is 10 years and the hedged debt's term is 30 years, after 10 years the government will lose the benefit of the swap payments.
Sabbatical leave	GASB-101	Compensated leave of absence earned during a minimum service period (unrestricted). Is not a compensated absence if the employee performs duties during the sabbatical that are different from normal duties.
Salary–related payment	GASB-101	Additional obligations that a government incurs related to paying an employee for services rendered. (The term *salary* in *salary-related payments* represents any pay provided to the employee, whether it is a fixed amount or an hourly wage.) Examples of salary-related payments include the employer share of Social Security and Medicare taxes.
Sale–leaseback	GASB-87	Transactions that involve the sale of an underlying asset by the owner and a lease of the property back to the seller (original owner).

Item	GASB Pronouncement[1]	Definition
Salvage	GASB-62	The amount received by an insurer from the sale of property (usually damaged) on which the insurer has paid a total claim to the insured and has obtained title to the property.
Secondary recipient (sub-recipient)	GASB-24	The individual or organization, governmental or otherwise, which is the ultimate recipient of a pass-through grant, or another recipient organization that passes the grant through to the ultimate recipient. All rights and responsibilities of the grant award are still with the recipient government which must monitor [and hold accountable] the secondary recipient (sub-recipient) for compliance with the terms and conditions of the grant award. (Sub-recipient monitoring.)
SEC-registered broker-dealer	GASB-3	A securities broker-dealer regulated by the Securities and Exchange Commission under the Securities Exchange Act of 1934. Broker-dealers may be "carrying" (holding depositors funds) or "non-carrying" (not holding depositors funds but regulated by the SEC).
Securities Industry and Financial Markets Association (SIFMA) swap index	GASB-53	An index sponsored by the Securities Industry and Financial Markets Association of seven-day high-grade tax-exempt variable-rate demand obligations, formerly known as The Bond Market Association swap index.
Securities lending agent	GASB-28	An entity that arranges the terms and conditions of loans, monitors the market values of securities lent and the collateral received, and often directs the investment of cash collateral.
Securities lending transactions	GASB-28	Transactions in which governmental entities transfer their securities to broker-dealers and other entities for collateral—which may be cash, securities, or letters of credit—and simultaneously agree to return the collateral for the same securities in the future.
Securitization	GASB-48	The pledging of all or a portion of a revenue stream to provide early access to future cash flows.

Glossary

Item	GASB Pronouncement[1]	Definition
Security	GASB-31	A transferrable financial instrument that evidences ownership or creditorship, whether in physical or book entry form.
Segment	GASB-37	An *identifiable activity* (or grouping of activities), reported as or within an enterprise fund or another stand-alone entity that has one or more bonds or other debt instruments (such as certificates of participation) outstanding, with a revenue stream pledged in support of that debt. In addition, the activity's revenues, expenses, gains and losses, assets, and liabilities are required to be accounted for separately.
Segmented time distributions	GASB-40	Segmented time distributions group investment cash flows into sequential time periods in tabular form.
Select and ultimate rates		Actuarial assumptions that contemplate different rates for successive years. Instead of a single assumed rate with respect to, for example, the investment return assumption, the actuary may apply different rates for the early years of a projection and a single rate for all subsequent years. For example, if an actuary applies an assumed investment return of 8% for year 20W0, 7.5% for 20W1, and 7% for 20W2 and thereafter, then 8% and 7.5% are select rates, and 7% is the ultimate rate.
Self-insurance	GASB-10	A term often used to describe an entity's retention of risk of loss arising out of the ownership of property or from some other cause, rather than transferring that risk to an independent third party through the purchase of an insurance policy. It is sometimes accompanied by the setting aside of assets to fund any related losses. Because no insurance is involved, the term *self-insurance* is a misnomer.

Item	GASB Pronouncement[1]	Definition
Separately financed specific liabilities to the pension (or OPEB) plan	GASB-75	Specific contractual liabilities to a defined benefit Pension or OPEB plan for one-time assessments to an individual employer or nonemployer contributing entity of amounts resulting from, for example, increases in the total pension or OPEB liability due to an individual employer joining a Pension or OPEB plan or changes of benefit terms specific to an individual employer, or a contractual commitment for a nonemployer contributing entity to make a one-time contribution for purposes of reducing the net pension or OPEB liability. The term *separately* financed is intended to differentiate these payables to the Pension or OPEB plan from payables to the Pension or OPEB plan that originate from the portion(s) of the total Pension or OPEB liability that is pooled by two or more employers (or by a single, agent, or cost-sharing employer and a nonemployer contributing entity in a special funding situation) for financing purposes. Payables to the pension or OPEB plan for unpaid (legal, contractual, or statutory) financing obligations associated with the pooled portion of the total pension or OPEB liability are not considered to be separately financed specific liabilities, even if separate payment terms have been established for those payables.

Item	GASB Pronouncement[1]	Definition
Service assessments	GASB-6	Service-type special assessment projects are for operating activities and do not result in the purchase or construction of fixed assets. Often the assessments are for services that are normally provided to the public as general governmental functions and that would otherwise be financed by the general fund or a special revenue fund. Those services include street lighting, street cleaning, and snow plowing. Financing for these routine services typically comes from general revenues. However, when routine services are extended to property owners outside the normal service area of the government or are provided at a higher level or at more frequent intervals than for the public, special assessments are sometimes levied. Only the affected property owners are charged for the additional services.
Service concession arrangement	GASB-94	An arrangement between a transferor (a government) and an operator (governmental or nongovernmental entity) in which: • The transferor conveys to an operator the right and related obligation to provide services using infrastructure or another public asset (a "facility") in exchange for significant consideration and • The operator collects and is compensated by fees from third parties.(See also "Public-Private Partnership.")
Service continuation	GASB-69	Where a new or continuing government intends to provide services like the formerly separate governments, organizations, or operations.
Service cost(s) (see also "Normal cost")	GASB-75	The portion(s) of the actuarial present value of projected benefit payments that are attributed to valuation years.

Glossary

Item	GASB Pronouncement[1]	Definition
Service units approach	GASB-42	About accounting for an impaired capital asset, the isolation of the historical cost of the service utility of the capital asset that cannot be used due to the impairment event or change in circumstances. The amount of impairment is determined by evaluating the service provided by the capital asset—either maximum estimated service units or total estimated service units throughout the life of the capital asset—before and after the event or change in circumstance.
Servicing (mortgage banking)	GASB-62	Mortgage loan servicing includes collecting monthly mortgagor payments, forwarding payments and related accounting reports to investors, collecting escrow deposits for the payment of mortgagor property taxes and insurance, and paying insurance from escrow resources when due.
Settlement amount	GASB:CS-6	The amount at which an asset could be realized or a liability could be liquidated with the counterparty, other than in an active market.
Settlement rate	GASB-10	The rate at which a monetary liability with uncertain terms can be settled or a monetary asset (receivable) with uncertain terms can be sold.
Shadow price	GASB-79	The net asset value per share of a qualifying external investment pool, calculated using total investments measured at fair value at the calculation date.
Shared service arrangements	GASB-69	In a shared service arrangement, two or more governments agree to consolidate similar operations. For example, two governments may agree to consolidate the separate fire departments of each government into a single shared activity serving the constituents of both governments. The shared service arrangement could be in the form of a separate government, joint venture, jointly governed organization, joint operation, or cost-sharing arrangement.

Item	GASB Pronouncement[1]	Definition
Short-term lease	GASB-87	A lease that, at the commencement of the lease term, has a maximum possible term under the lease contract of 12 months (or less), including any options to extend, regardless of their probability of being exercised. For a lease that is cancelable by either the lessee or the lessor, such as a rolling month-to-month lease or a year-to-year lease, the maximum possible term is the noncancelable period, including any notice periods.
Short-term obligations	GASB-62	Obligations that are scheduled to mature within one year after the date of a government's financial statements.
Similar productive assets	GASB-62	Productive assets that are of the same general type, that perform the same function, or that are employed in the same line of operations.
Simulation models	GASB-40	Simulation models estimate changes in an investment's or a portfolio's fair value, given hypothetical changes in interest rates. Various models or techniques may be used, such as "shock tests" or value-at-risk.
Single employer	GASB-75	An employer whose employees are provided with pensions or OPEB through a single-employer defined benefit pension or OPEB plan.
Single-employer defined benefit pension or OPEB plan (single-employer pension or OPEB plan)	GASB-75	A defined benefit pension or OPEB plan that is used to provide pensions or OPEB to employees of only one employer.
Site Assessment	GASB-49	A site-specific baseline risk assessment that identifies hazards, assesses exposure to the hazards and their toxicity, and characterizes and quantifies the potential risks posed by the site. A site assessment may be noninvasive, involving inquiry into previous uses of a site, site reconnaissance, and interviews (a Phase I site assessment), or may involve invasive testing for pollution (a Phase II site assessment).

Item	GASB Pronouncement[1]	Definition
SLGS	GASB-7	State and local government securities issued by the U.S. Treasury to provide state and local governments with required cash flows at yields that do not exceed Internal Revenue Service (IRS) arbitrage limits.
Special assessments (special assessment debt)	GASB-6	Capital improvements or services provided by local governments are intended primarily to benefit a property owner or group of property owners rather than the general citizenry. The benefitting owners pay a regular assessment to the government through a lien on their property to pay the debt. The liens on assessed properties secure the debt which may or may not be also backed by the full faith and credit of the government as additional security.
Special funding situations	GASB-75	Circumstances in which a nonemployer entity is legally responsible for making contributions directly to a pension or OPEB plan that is used to provide pensions or OPEB to the employees of another entity or entities and either of the following criteria is met: a. The amount of contributions for which the nonemployer entity legally is responsible is *not* dependent upon one or more events or circumstances unrelated to the pensions. b. The nonemployer entity is the only entity with a legal obligation to make contributions directly to a pension or OPEB plan.
Special item	GASB-62	Events and transactions that are distinguished either by their unusual nature or by the infrequency of their occurrence, or both, *within the control of management*.
Special purpose government	GASB-34	Governments engaged usually in a single (or small number of) governmental program(s).

Item	GASB Pronouncement[1]	Definition
Special revenue fund	GASB-54	Funds are used to account for and report the proceeds of specific revenue sources that are restricted or committed to expenditure for specified purposes other than debt service or capital projects. The term *proceeds of specific revenue sources* establishes that one or more specific restricted or committed revenues should be the foundation for a special revenue fund. Those specific restricted or committed revenues may be initially received in another fund and subsequently distributed to a special revenue fund. Those amounts should not be recognized as revenue in the fund initially receiving them, however, those inflows should be recognized as revenue in the special revenue fund in which they will be expended in accordance with specified purposes. Special revenue funds should not be used to account for resources held in trust for individuals, private organizations, or other governments.
Special termination benefits		Benefits offered by an employer for a short period of time as an inducement to employees to hasten the termination of services. For example, to reduce payroll and related costs, an employer might offer enhanced pension benefits or OPEB to employees as an inducement to take early termination, for employees who accept the offer within a 60-day window of opportunity.
Specific identification	GASB-40	In the context of interest rate risk disclosures, the specific identification method does not compute a disclosure measure but presents a list of each investment, its amount, its maturity date, and any call options.
SPF		Special purpose framework (formerly known as OCBOA).

Item	GASB Pronouncement[1]	Definition
Split-interest agreement	GASB-81	Agreements in which the donor enters into a trust or other legally enforceable agreement (with characteristics that are equivalent to split-interest agreements) under which the donor transfers resources to an intermediary to administer for the unconditional benefit of at least two beneficiaries, one of which can be a government.
Sponsor		The entity that established the plan. The sponsor generally is the employer or one of the employers that participate in the plan to provide benefits for their employees. Sometimes, however, the sponsor establishes the plan for the employees of other entities but does not include its own employees and, therefore, is not a participating employer of that plan. An example is a state government that establishes a plan for the employees of local governments within the state, but the employees of the state government are covered by a different plan.
Sponsoring government	GASB-31	A governmental entity that provides investment services—whether an investment pool or individual investment accounts—to other entities and that therefore has a fiduciary responsibility for those investments.
Spot price	GASB-53	Current delivery price of a commodity trading in the spot market at a specified location or pricing point. In the spot market, commodities sold or purchased for cash are immediately delivered.

Glossary

Item	GASB Pronouncement[1]	Definition
Stabilization arrangements (or stabilization funds or rainy-day funds)	GASB-54	Amounts for use in emergency situations or when revenue shortages or budgetary imbalances arise. Those amounts are subject to controls that dictate the circumstances under which they can be spent. Many governments have formal arrangements to maintain amounts for budget or revenue stabilization, working capital needs, contingencies or emergencies, and other similarly titled purposes. The authority to set aside those amounts generally comes from statute, ordinance, resolution, charter, or constitution. Stabilization amounts may be expended only when certain specific circumstances exist. The formal action that imposes the parameters for spending should identify and describe the specific circumstances under which a need for stabilization arises. Those circumstances should be such that they would not be expected to occur routinely. For example, a stabilization amount that can be accessed "in an emergency" would not qualify to be classified within the committed category because the circumstances or conditions that constitute an emergency are not sufficiently detailed, and it is not unlikely that an "emergency" of some nature would routinely occur. Similarly, a stabilization amount that can be accessed to offset an "anticipated revenue shortfall" would not qualify unless the shortfall was quantified and was of a magnitude that would distinguish it from other revenue shortfalls that occur during the normal course of governmental operations.
Stand-alone pension or OPEB plan financial report (stand-alone plan financial report)	GASB-74	A report that contains the financial statements of a pension plan and is issued by the pension or OPEB plan or by the public employee retirement system that administers the plan. The term *stand-alone* is used to distinguish such a financial report from pension plan financial statements that are included as a pension or OPEB trust fund of another government.

Item	GASB Pronouncement[1]	Definition
Statement of activities	GASB-34	Report of the results of operations of the reporting government presented in a format that reports the net (expense) revenue of its individual functions. An objective of using the net (expense) revenue format is to report the relative financial burden of each of the reporting government's functions on its taxpayers. This format identifies the extent to which each function of the government draws from the general revenues of the government or is self-financing through fees and intergovernmental aid. General revenues, contributions to term and permanent endowments, contributions to permanent fund principal, special and extraordinary items, and transfers should be reported separately after the total net expenses of the government's functions, ultimately arriving at the "change in net [position]" for the period.
Statement of cash flows	GASB-34	Required statement for proprietary funds directly showing the cash inflows and outflows of a period and reconciling operating cash flows to operating income.
Statement of net [position] (statement of fiduciary net position)	GASB-63	Report of all financial and capital resources. Governments are encouraged to present the statement in a format that displays assets plus deferred outflows of resources less liabilities plus deferred inflows of resources equal net [position], although the traditional balance sheet format (assets plus deferred outflows of resources equal liabilities plus deferred inflows of resources plus net position) may be used. Regardless of the format used, however, the statement of net [position] should report the difference between assets plus deferred outflows of resources and liabilities plus deferred inflows of resources as net position, not fund balances or equity.

Item	GASB Pronouncement[1]	Definition
Statement of revenues, expenditures, and changes in fund balances	GASB-34	A report of information about the inflows, outflows, and balances of current financial resources of each major governmental fund and for the nonmajor governmental funds in the aggregate. A total column should be presented as of the period ended by the reporting date.
Statement of revenues, expenses, and changes in fund net position or fund equity (statement of revenues, expenses, and changes in fiduciary net position)	GASB-34	The operating statement for proprietary funds (or fiduciary funds).
Stock rights	GASB-31	Rights given to existing stockholders to purchase newly issued shares in proportion to their holdings at a specific date.
Stock warrants	GASB-31	Certificates entitling the holder to acquire shares of stock at a certain price within a stated period. Warrants often are made part of the issuance of bonds or preferred or common stock.
Strike price	GASB-53	In the case of a call option, the price at which the holder of a call option may purchase a financial instrument or commodity. In the case of a put option, it is the price at which the holder may sell a financial instrument or commodity. The strike price also is known as the exercise price.
Structured notes	GASB-31	Debt securities whose cash flow characteristics (coupon, redemption amount, or stated maturity) depend on one or more indexes, or that have embedded forwards or options.
Structured Overnight Financing Rate (SOFR)	GASB-93	Rate published by the Federal Reserve Bank of New York as an alternative to U.S. Dollar LIBOR. Reflects the financing rate on overnight repurchase transactions secured by U.S. Treasury securities.

Item	GASB Pronouncement[1]	Definition
Structured settlement	GASB-10	A means of satisfying a claim liability, consisting of an initial cash payment to meet specific present financial needs combined with a stream of future payments designed to meet future financial needs, generally funded by annuity contracts.
Sublease	GASB-87	Lease that involves three parties: the original lessor, the original lessee (who is the lessor in the sublease), and the new lessee.
Subrogation	GASB-62	The right of an insurer to pursue any course of recovery of damages, in its name or in the name of the policyholder, against a third party who is liable for costs relating to an insured event that have been paid by the insurer.
Subscriber related costs (cable television systems)	GASB-62	These are costs incurred to obtain and retain subscribers to the cable television system and include costs of billing and collection, bad debts, and mailings, repairs and maintenance of taps and connections, franchise fees related to revenues or number of subscribers, general and administrative system costs, such as salary of the system manager and office rent, programming costs for additional channels used in the marketing effort or costs related to revenues from, or number of subscribers to, per channel or per program service, and direct selling costs.
Subscription Based Information Technology Arrangement (SBITA)	GASB-96	A contract that conveys control of the right to use another party's (a SBITA vendor) hardware, software, or both, including information technology infrastructure (the underlying hardware or software), as specified in the contract for a period of time in an exchange or exchange-like transaction.
Subsequent event	GASB-56	Events or transactions that affect the financial statements after the reporting date. Recognized events require adjustment to the financial statements as they existed prior to the reporting date. Non-recognized events may require disclosure.

Item	GASB Pronouncement[1]	Definition
Subsidized capital assets	GASB-42	Assets that are used to produce revenues through charges for services or fees, but that a government would subsidize, if needed, because the service provided by the capital assets is a public benefit. The revenues produced are set by the management of the government, perhaps based upon cost of services or political considerations, rather than set with consideration of market influences. Examples include water and sewer systems, stadiums, convention centers, metropolitan transportation systems, hospitals, and toll roads.
Substantive plan		The terms of an OPEB plan as understood by the employer(s) and plan members.
Superfund	GASB-49	A federal law (the Comprehensive Environmental Response, Compensation, and Liability Act of 1980 [CERCLA], as amended by the Superfund Amendments and Reauthorization Act of 1986 [SARA], which together are referred to as Superfund) that provides the U.S. Environmental Protection Agency with broad authority to order liable parties to remediate polluted sites or use Superfund money to remediate them and then seek to recover its costs and additional damages.
Supporting (or supplementary) information (SI)	GASB:CS-3	Supporting information that is useful for placing basic financial statements and notes to basic financial statements in an appropriate operational, economic, or historical context. SI is presented with the basic financial statements, notes to basic financial statements, and RSI in a government's general purpose external financial report. Although the GASB does not require SI to be presented, preparers of governmental financial reports who elect to present SI (or are otherwise required by law or regulations to present SI) with their basic financial statements, notes to basic financial statements, and RSI should follow any applicable GASB-issued or GASB-cleared guidance regarding the format and content of that information.

Item	GASB Pronouncement[1]	Definition
Susceptible to accrual	NCGA-1	Revenues of governmental funds that are collected or collectible within the current period or soon enough thereafter to be used to pay liabilities of the current period.
Swap	GASB-53	A type of derivative instrument in which there is an agreement to exchange future cash flows. These cash flows may be either fixed or variable and may be either received or paid. Variable cash flows depend on a reference rate.
Swaption	GASB-53	An option to engage in a swap. When a swaption is an interest rate option, it may be used to hedge long-term debt. When a government sells a swaption (also called writing a swaption), a cash payment may be received. Option pricing theory, including time and volatility measures, is used to value swaptions.
Synthetic instrument method	GASB-53	A method of evaluating effectiveness that combines a hedged item and a potential hedging derivative instrument into a hypothetical financial instrument to evaluate whether the hypothetical financial instrument pays a substantively fixed rate.
Synthetic price	GASB-53	The price of the existing or expected commodity transaction as adjusted by the effect of the potential hedging derivative instrument. That is, the net price considering both the actual price of the existing or expected commodity transaction and the effect of the potential hedging derivative instrument.

Item	GASB Pronouncement[1]	Definition
Taft-Hartley Plan	GASB-78	A type of multiple-employer defined benefit plan, where a state or local government may be an employer with employees provided pensions. As used in GASB-78, these types of plans utilize irrevocable trusts or equivalent arrangements, but are not managed by a state or local government, are used to provide defined benefit pensions both to employees of state or local governmental employers and to employees of employers that are not state or local government employers and there are no predominant state or local governmental employer, either individually or collectively with other state or local governmental employers that provide pensions through the pension plan. Typically, these plans are managed by labor unions, are subject to the provisions of ERISA and may have reporting to the Pension Benefit Guarantee Corporation (a U.S. government agency). Such plans have been in existence since the Taft-Hartley Act of 1947.
Tail	GASB-10	The length of time between the occurrence of an event giving rise to a claim and the actual reporting and eventual settlement of that claim.
Tail coverage	GASB-10	A type of insurance policy designed to cover claims incurred before, but reported after, cancellation or expiration of a claims-made policy. (The term *extended discovery coverage* is used in the commercial insurance industry.)
Take out agreement	GASBI-1	Used to provide long-term financing in the event the remarking agent is unable to sell demand bonds within a specified period after the exercise of the demand by bondholders.
TAN		Tax anticipation note
Target Benefit Plans		Hybrid pension plan where employees contribute on an actuarial basis knowing a certain date of retirement. There is no guarantee of a balance or return. Many mutual funds sell these types of plans (in which case they are known as "target date funds").

Item	GASB Pronouncement[1]	Definition
Tax abatement	GASB-77	A reduction in tax revenues that results from an agreement between one or more governments and an individual or entity in which (a) one or more governments promise to forgo tax revenues to which they are otherwise entitled and (b) the individual or entity promises to take a specific action after the agreement has been entered into that contributes to economic development or otherwise benefits the governments or the citizens of those governments.
Tax deductions	GASB-77	Tax deductions are subtractions from the tax base (for example, gross income). Thus, deductions indirectly affect the amount of tax due by making the tax base smaller. In general, tax credits are directly applied to the amount of tax due. Therefore, tax credits are generally "more valuable" than deductions, they provide a dollar-for-dollar reduction in the amount of tax due.
Tax expenditure(s)	GASB-77	Governmental programs employed to lower the taxes of broad classes of taxpayers, or the taxes of individuals or entities based on the performance of specific actions. Tax expenditures include tax exemptions, tax deductions, and tax abatements, among other programs. Governments exempt certain individuals, entities, or activities from taxation. Common examples of tax exemptions include the exclusion of income earned on municipal bonds from income taxes and the full or partial exemption of senior citizens and military veterans from property taxes.
Terminal funding		A method of funding a pension plan under which the entire Actuarial Present Value of benefits for everyone is contributed to the plan's fund at the time of withdrawal, retirement or benefit commencement.

Item	GASB Pronouncement[1]	Definition
Termination benefits	GASB-75	Inducements offered by employers to active employees to hasten the termination of services, or payments made in consequence of the early termination of services. Termination benefits include early-retirement incentives, severance benefits, and other termination-related benefits.
Termination risk	GASB-53	The risk that a hedging derivative instrument's unscheduled end will affect a government's asset and liability strategy or will present the government with potentially significant unscheduled termination payments to the counterparty. For example, a government may be relying on an interest rate swap to insulate it from the possibility of increasing interest rate payments. If the swap has an unscheduled termination, that benefit would not be available.
Third-party recipient	GASB-24	For purposes of on-behalf payments for fringe benefits and salaries, the individual or organization that receives the payment. For example, an employee who receives a salary supplement or a pension plan that receives pension contributions.
Time requirements	GASB-33	Specification of • The period when resources are required to be used (sold, disbursed, or consumed) or when use may begin (for example, operating or capital grants for a specific period) or • That the resources are required to be maintained intact in perpetuity or until a specified date or event has occurred (for example, permanent endowments, term endowments, and similar agreements). Time requirements affect the timing of recognition of nonexchange transactions.

Item	GASB Pronouncement[1]	Definition
Time value of an option	GASB-53	The portion of an option's fair value that is attributable to the time remaining on the option before expiration. An option with time value but no intrinsic value is out-of-the-money or at-the-market. Time value is the difference between an option's fair value and its intrinsic value.
Tort	GASB-10	A wrongful act, injury, or damage (not involving a breach of contract) for which a civil action can be brought.
Total direct rate	GASB-44	The weighted average of all individual direct rates applied by the government preparing the statistical section information.
Total OPEB liability	GASB-75	The portion of the actuarial present value of projected benefit payments that is attributed to past periods of member service in conformity with the requirements of GAAP. The total OPEB liability is the liability of employers and nonemployer contributing entities to plan members for benefits provided through a defined benefit OPEB plan that *is not* administered through a trust.
Total pension liability	GASB-73	The portion of the actuarial present value of projected benefit payments that is attributed to past periods of employee service.
Transaction costs	GASB-72	The costs to sell an asset or transfer a liability in the principal (or most advantageous) market for the asset or liability that: • Are directly attributable to the disposal of the asset or the transfer of the liability and • Meet both of the following criteria: — They result directly from and are essential to that transaction. — They would not have been incurred by the entity had the decision to sell the asset or transfer the liability not been made.

Glossary

Item	GASB Pronouncement[1]	Definition
Transaction date	GASB-62	The date at which a transaction (for example, a sale or purchase of merchandise or services) is recorded in accounting records in conformity with GAAP. A long-term commitment may have more than one transaction date (for example, the due date of each progress payment under a construction contract is an anticipated transaction date).
Transaction gain or loss (foreign currency transaction)	GASB-62	Transaction gains or losses result from a change in exchange rates between the U.S. dollar and the currency in which a foreign currency transaction is denominated. They represent an increase or decrease in: • The actual U.S. dollar cash flows realized upon settlement of foreign currency transactions and • The expected U.S. dollar cash flows on unsettled foreign currency transactions.
Transfers of operations	GASB-69	A government combination involving the operations of a government or nongovernmental entity, rather than a combination of legally separate entities, in which no significant consideration is exchanged. Operations may be transferred to another existing entity or to a new entity.
Transition year		The fiscal year in which a new GAAP statement is first implemented.
Transportation costs	GASB-72	The costs that would be incurred to transport an asset from its current location to its principal (or most advantageous) market.
Troubled debt restructuring	GASB-62	When a creditor for economic or legal reasons related to the debtor's financial difficulties grants a concession to the debtor that it would not otherwise consider. That concession either stems from an agreement between the creditor and the debtor or is imposed by law or a court.
Trust (or equivalent arrangement)	GASB-84	Specifically, for the purposes of implementation of GASB-84, where assets are: • Administered through an agreement or equivalent arrangement (hereafter jointly referred to as a trust) in which the government itself is not a beneficiary,

Item	GASB Pronouncement[1]	Definition
		• Dedicated to providing benefits to recipients in accordance with the benefit terms, and
		• Legally protected from the creditors of the government.
Type of contract	GASB-10	Classification of policies or participation contracts based on the nature of the coverages provided that distinguishes them as an identifiable class of contract. For example, types of contracts may include general liability, property, automobile liability, automobile physical damage, multi-peril, and workers' compensation.
Unallocated insurance contracts	GASB-67	Contracts with an insurance company under which payments to the insurance company are accumulated in an unallocated pool or pooled account (not allocated to specific plan members) to be used either directly or through the purchase of annuities to meet benefit payments when plan members retire. Monies held by the insurance company under an unallocated contract may be withdrawn and otherwise invested.
Unassigned fund balance	GASB-54	The residual classification for the general fund. This classification represents fund balance that has not been assigned to other funds and that has not been restricted, committed, or assigned to specific purposes within the general fund. The general fund should be the only fund that reports a positive unassigned fund balance amount. In other governmental funds, if expenditures incurred for specific purposes exceeded the amounts restricted, committed, or assigned to those purposes, it may be necessary to report a negative unassigned fund balance.
Uncollateralized deposit	GASB-40	An uncollateralized deposit does not have securities pledged to the depositor-government.
Unconditional benefit	GASB-81	A right belonging to the government that cannot be taken away without the government's consent, such as an unconditional beneficial interest.

Item	GASB Pronouncement[1]	Definition
Underlying securities	GASB-28	The securities lent by the lender to the borrower.
Underlyings	GASB-53	A specified interest rate, security price, commodity price, foreign exchange rate, index of prices or rates, or other variable (including the occurrence or nonoccurrence of a specified event such as a scheduled payment under a contract). An underlying may be a price or rate of an asset or liability but is not the asset or liability itself.
Underlying asset	GASB-87	The asset leased as a lessee or lessor.
Underwriting	GASB-10	The process of selecting, classifying, evaluating, rating, and assuming risks.
Undivided interest (joint operation)	GASB-14	An arrangement that resembles a joint venture, but no entity or organization is created by the participants. An undivided interest is an ownership arrangement in which two or more parties own property in which title is held individually to the extent of each party's interest. Implied in that definition is that each participant is also liable for specific, identifiable obligations (if any) of the operation. Because an undivided interest is not a legal entity, borrowing to finance its operations often is done individually by each participant. An additional consequence of the absence of a formal organizational structure is that there is no entity with assets, liabilities, expenditures/expenses, and revenues—and thus, *equity*—to allocate to participants. A government participating in this type of arrangement should report its assets, liabilities, expenditures/expenses, and revenues that are associated with the joint operation.
Unfunded actuarial accrued liability (unfunded actuarial liability)		The excess of the Actuarial Accrued Liability over the Actuarial Value of Assets. *No longer used for general purpose external financial reporting.*

Item	GASB Pronouncement[1]	Definition
Unguaranteed residual value (leases)	GASB-62	The estimated residual value of the leased property exclusive of any portion guaranteed by the lessee or by a third party unrelated to the lessor.
Unit of account	GASB-72	The level at which an asset or a liability is aggregated or disaggregated for recognition or disclosure purposes.
Unmatured long-term indebtedness	GASBI-6	The portion of general long-term indebtedness that is not yet due for payment reported as general long-term liabilities of the government, rather than as governmental fund liabilities. Applies not only to formal debt issues such as bonds, but also to other forms of general long-term indebtedness, including capital leases, compensated absences, claims and judgments, pensions, special termination benefits, landfill closure and postclosure obligations, and "other commitments that are not current liabilities properly recorded in governmental funds."
Unobservable inputs	GASB-72	Inputs for which market data are not available and that are developed using the best information available about the assumptions that market participants would use when pricing an asset or liability.
Unrestricted net position	GASB-63	The net amount of the assets, deferred outflows of resources, liabilities, and deferred inflows of resources that are not included in the determination of net investment in capital assets or the restricted component of net position.
Usable capacity	GASB-42	The service utility of a capital asset that at acquisition was expected to be used to provide service. Current usable capacity of a capital asset is the capacity in a current period. Original usable capacity was the capacity of a capital asset at inception. Maximum service capacity is a rate of use where the capital asset is utilized to its maximum potential. Surplus capacity is the difference between maximum service capacity and usable capacity.

Item	GASB Pronouncement[1]	Definition
Use (direct the use of assets)	GASB-84	Expending or consuming an asset for the benefit of individuals, organizations, or other governments, outside of the government's provision of services to them.
Users (of financial reports)	GASB:CS-1	Recipients of a government's financial information, including, but not limited to: • Those to whom government is primarily accountable (the citizenry), • Those who directly represent the citizens (legislative and oversight bodies), and • Those who lend or who participate in the lending process (investors and creditors). The needs of intergovernmental grantors and other users are encompassed within the needs of the three primary user groups. Internal managers in the executive branch of government who have ready access to financial data through *internal* reporting are not considered *primary* users.
Valuation technique	GASB-72	A specific method or combination of methods used to determine the fair value of an asset or liability.
Variable rate investment	GASB-40	An investment with terms that provide for the adjustment of its interest rate on set dates (such as the last day of a month or calendar quarter) and that, upon each adjustment until the final maturity of the instrument or the period remaining until the principal amount can be recovered through demand, can reasonably be expected to have a fair value that will be unaffected by interest rate changes.
Variance power	GASB-81	The unilateral power to redirect the use of the transferred resources to another beneficiary, overriding the donor's instructions. This transfer would occur without the approval of the donor, specified beneficiaries, or any other interested party.

Item	GASB Pronouncement[1]	Definition
Vesting method	GASB-16	An estimate of accrued sick leave liability based on the sick leave accumulated at the balance sheet date by those employees who currently are eligible to receive termination payments as well as other employees who are expected to become eligible in the future to receive such payments. To calculate the liability, these accumulations should be reduced to the maximum amount allowed as a termination payment. Accruals for those employees who are expected to become eligible in the future should be based on assumptions concerning the probability that individual employees or classes or groups of employees will become eligible to receive termination payments. (To be discontinued for general purpose external financial reporting purposes upon implementation of GASB-101 but may continue to be used for budgetary purposes.)
Voluntary nonexchange transaction	GASB-33	Legislative or contractual agreements, other than exchanges, entered into willingly by the parties to the agreement (for example, certain grants and private donations).
Voting majority	GASB-14	When the number of a government's appointees to a component unit's board is sufficient to exhibit control.
Weekly liquid assets	GASB-79	For purposes of GASB-79, only the following are weekly liquid assets: • Cash, including demand deposits and certificates of deposit that mature within five business days and are expected to be held to maturity, • U.S. government securities that are direct obligations, • Securities that: — are U.S. government securities that are not direct obligations, — are issued at a discount without provision for the payment of interest, and — have a remaining maturity of 60 days or less,

Item	GASB Pronouncement[1]	Definition
		• Securities that will mature within five business days, with maturity determined without considering the maturity shortening features,
		• Securities subject to a demand feature that is exercisable and payable within five business days, and
		• Amounts receivable and due unconditionally within five business days on pending sales of portfolio securities.
Weighted average maturity (WAM)	GASB-40	A weighted average maturity measure expresses investment time horizons—the time when investments become due and payable—in years or months, weighted to reflect the dollar size of individual investments within an investment type.
Wrap contract	GASB-53	A contract in which the issuer provides assurance that the adjustments to the interest crediting rate of a synthetic guaranteed investment contract will not result in a future interest crediting rate that is less than zero.
Written option	GASB-53	An option sold by a government. The purchaser of the option becomes the holder of it.
Yellow Book		GAGAS issued by GAO
Yield-maintenance repurchase–reverse repurchase agreement	GASB-3	A dollar repurchase—reverse repurchase agreement in which the parties agree that the securities returned will provide the seller-borrower with a yield as specified in the agreement.
Zero fair value	GASB-53	Value of a derivative instrument that is either initiated or exited with no consideration being exchanged. A zero-fair value should be within a dealer's normal bid/offer spread.

---

[1] Latest GASB standard referencing the term. Certain reference remain from standards that are no longer effective as the replacement standard does not update the definition or the term is in common use (e.g., references contain terms in common use, despite being rescinded by newer GASB Standards).

27,001

Accounting Resources on the Web

Presented here are World Wide Web URLs of interest to practitioners. Because of the constantly changing nature of the Internet, addresses change and new resources become available every day. To find additional resources, use search engines such as Bing (http://www.bing.com/), Google (http://www.google.com/), and Yahoo! (http://search.yahoo.com).

PRACTICE POINT: The GASB has issued the full text of all of its pronouncements freely on the Internet, at www.gasb.org (click on "Pronouncements"). The full text can be accessed along with summaries and status. Interpretations and technical bulletins are also available. Text is offered as PDF files, but can be copied and pasted.

Accounting Research Manager® http://www.AccountingResearchManager.com
Accounting Today magazine http://www.accountingtoday.com
AICPA http://www.aicpa.org
AICPA Government Audit Quality Center http://www.aicpa.org/gaqc
American Accounting Association http://aaahq.org
American Legal Publishing Corp. https://codelibrary.amlegal.com/
American Public Power Association (APPA) https://www.publicpower.org/
American Water Works Association http://www.awwa.org
Association for Budgeting and Financial Management (ABFM) http://www.abfm.org
Association of Certified Fraud Examiners (ACFE) http://www.acfe.com/
Association of College and University Auditors (ACUA) http://www.acua.org/ACUA/College_University_Auditors.asp
Association of Financial Guaranty Insurers (AFGI) http://www.afgi.org
Association of Government Accountants (AGA) http://www.agacgfm.org
Association of Latino Professionals in Finance and Accounting (ALPFA) http://www.alpfa.org
Association of Local Government Auditors http://www.GovernmentAuditors.org
Association of Public Pension Fund Auditors (APPFA) http://www.appfa.org
Association of School Business Officials International http://www.asbointl.org
Automated Clearing House https://fiscal.treasury.gov/ach/
Bloomberg News on Municipal Bonds http://www.bloomberg.com/news/municipal-bonds
BoardSource http://www.boardsource.org
Bond Buyer (including municipal bond indexes) http://www.bondbuyer.com
Bureau of Labor Statistics http://www.bls.gov

Bureau of the Fiscal Service (Treasury Dept.) http://www.fiscal.treasury.gov

CCH Publications www.cchcpelink.com/books

Center for Retirement Research at Boston College http://crr.bc.edu/

Check Payment Systems Association http://www.cpsa-checks.org

Chief Financial Officers Council—2CFR200 *Uniform Administrative Requirements, Cost Principles, and Audit Requirements for Federal Awards* **(Uniform Guidance)** https://cfo.gov/grants/

Code of Federal Regulations http://www.gpo.gov/fdsys/browse/collectionCfr.action

Committee of Sponsoring Organizations of the Treadway Commission (COSO) http://www.coso.org

Congress.gov https://www.congress.gov/

Council of State Governments (CSG) http://www.csg.org

Council of the Inspectors General on Integrity & Efficiency (CIGIE) http://www.ignet.gov

CPE www.cchcpelink.com

Department of Education OIG's Non-Federal Audit Team https://www2.ed.gov/about/offices/list/oig/index.html

Electronic Municipal Market Access (EMMA) http://emma.msrb.org

Electronic Privacy Information Center http://epic.org

FASB http://www.fasb.org

Federal Accounting Standards Advisory Board (FASAB) http://www.fasab.gov

Federal Audit Clearinghouse http://harvester.census.gov/facweb

Federal Digital System (FDsys) http://www.govinfo.gov

Federal Register http://www.gpo.gov/fdsys/browse/collection.action?collectionCode=FR

GASB http://www.gasb.org

General Services Administration http://www.gsa.gov

Governing **magazine** http://www.governing.com

Government Accountability Office http://www.gao.gov

Government Accounting Standards http://gao.gov/yellowbook/overview

Government Finance Officers Association (GFOA) http://www.gfoa.org

Government Publishing Office http://www.gpo.gov

Grants Portal http://www.grants.gov/

GuideStar http://www.guidestar.org

Harvard John F. Kennedy School of Government Executive Education https://exed.hks.harvard.edu/

Health and Human Services (HHS) Grants/Funding http://www.hhs.gov/grants

HUD Audit Guidance links https://www.hudoig.gov/reports-publications/audit-guides

Accounting Resources on the Web **27,003**

HUD Office of Public and Indian Housing (PIH) https://www.hud.gov/program_offices/public_indian_housing

HUD Real Estate Assessment Center (REAC) https://www.hud.gov/program_offices/public_indian_housing/reac

Information for Tax-Exempt Organizations https://www.irs.gov/charities-non-profits/exempt-organizations-help-from-the-irs#:~:text=You%20may%20direct%20technical%20and,(toll%2Dfree%20number)

Institute of Internal Auditors, The (IIA) http://www.theiia.org

Institute of Management Accountants (IMA) http://www.imanet.org

IntelliConnect® http://IntelliConnect.cch.com

Intergovernmental Audit Forums http://www.auditforum.org

Internal Revenue Service (IRS) http://www.irs.gov

International City/County Managers Association http://www.icma.org

International Institute of Municipal Clerks (IIMC) http://www.iimc.com

Investment Company Institute (ICI) http://www.ici.org

Legal Information Institute (Cornell Law School) http://www.law.cornell.edu/statutes.html

Minority Business Development Agency http://www.mbda.gov

Municipal Code Corporation (MCC) http://www.municode.com

Municipal Securities Rulemaking Board (MSRB) http://www.msrb.org

NACHA—The Electronic Payments Association http://www.nacha.org

National Association of Asian American Professionals (NAAAP) http://www.naaap.org

National Association of Black Accountants, Inc. http://www.nabainc.org

National Association of Bond Lawyers http://www.nabl.org

National Association of College and University Business Officers (NACUBO) http://www.nacubo.org

National Association of Counties (NACO) http://www.naco.org

National Association of Housing and Redevelopment Officials (NAHRO) http://www.nahro.org

National Association of Regional Councils http://www.narc.org

National Association of State Agencies for Surplus Property http://www.nasasp.org

National Association of State Auditors, Comptrollers, and Treasurers (NASACT) http://www.nasact.org

National Association of State Boards of Accountancy (NASBA) http://www.nasba.org

National Association of State Budget Officers http://www.nasbo.org

National Association of State Retirement Administrators http://www.nasra.org

National Conference of State Legislatures (NCSL) http://www.ncsl.org

National Federation of Municipal Analysts (NFMA) http://www.nfma.org
National Governors Association (NGA) http://www.nga.org
National Labor Relations Board https://www.nlrb.gov
National League of Cities (NLC) http://www.nlc.org
National Rural Development Partnership http://www.rd.usda.gov
Native American Finance Officers Association (NAFOA) http://www.nafoa.org
North American Industry Classification System (NAICS) http://www.census.gov/eos/www/naics
Occupational Employment Statistics http://stats.bls.gov/oes/home.htm
Office of Federal Contract Compliance Programs (OFCCP) http://www.dol.gov/ofccp
Office of Management and Budget http://www.whitehouse.gov/omb
Office of Women's Business Ownership (SBA) http://www.sba.gov/offices/headquarter/wbo
Privacy Foundation http://www.privacyfoundation.org
Prompt Payment Act Interest Rate http://www.fms.treas.gov/prompt/rates.html
Public Pension Financial Forum (P2F2) http://www.P2F2.org
Securities and Exchange Commission http://www.sec.gov
Securities Industry and Financial Markets Association (SIFMA) http://www.sifma.org
Software and Information Industry Association (SIIA) http://www.siia.net
Standards for Internal Control in the Federal Government (the Green Book) http://gao.gov/greenbook/overview
The Library of Congress http://www.loc.gov
USA CityLink http://www.usacitylink.com
USA.gov http://www.usa.gov
USA.gov for Nonprofits http://www.usa.gov/Business/Nonprofit.shtml
USA Spending.Gov http://www.usaspending.gov
U.S. Census Bureau: Federal, State, and Local Government Page http://www.census.gov/govs/
U.S. Code Search http://uscode.house.gov
U.S. Conference of Mayors http://www.usmayors.org
U.S. Department of Agriculture http://www.usda.gov
U.S. Department of Commerce http://www.commerce.gov
U.S. Department of Defense http://www.defense.gov
U.S. Department of Education http://www.ed.gov
U.S. Department of Energy http://www.energy.gov
U.S. Department of Health and Human Services http://www.hhs.gov

U.S. Department of Housing and Urban Development http://www.hud.gov

U.S. Department of Labor http://www.dol.gov

U.S. Department of State http://www.state.gov

U.S. Department of the Interior http://www.doi.gov

U.S. Department of the Treasury's Listing of Approved Sureties http://www.fiscal.treasury.gov/fsreports/ref/suretyBnd/c570.htm

U.S. Department of Transportation http://www.dot.gov

U.S. Department of Treasury Bureau of the Fiscal Service http://www.fiscal.treasury.gov

U.S. Department of Veterans Affairs http://www.va.gov

U.S. Environmental Protection Agency http://www.epa.gov

U.S. GAO Bid Protest Decisions http://www.gao.gov/decisions/bidpro/bidpro.htm

U.S. Government Forms http://www.gsa.gov/forms

U.S. House of Representatives http://www.house.gov

U.S. House of Representatives Current Floor Proceedings http://clerk.house.gov/floorsummary/floor.aspx

U.S. HUD Client Information and Policy System http://portal.hud.gov/hudportal/HUD?src=/program_offices/administration/hudclips

U.S. HUD Office of Inspector General http://www.hudoig.gov

U.S. Postal Service http://www.usps.com

U.S. Senate http://www.senate.gov

U.S. Small Business Administration http://www.sba.gov

U.S. Transportation and Safety Administration http://www.tsa.gov

U.S. Treasury http://www.treasury.gov

Wolters Kluwer www.taxna.wolterskluwer.com

INDEX

A

Accountability . . . 1027-1029, 3001. *See also* Financial accountability

Accounting and Financial Reporting Issues Related to Coronavirus Aid, Relief and Economic Security Act (CARES) Act of 2020 and Coronavirus Diseases (GASB:TB 2020-1) . . . 7016, 16,039-16,040, 17,011-17,012, 18,010-18,011, 20,057

Accounting and reporting issues
. acquisitions . . . 4065-4066
. capabilities . . . 1042
. capital assets . . . 10,020-10,029, 19,009
. combinations . . . 4061-4066
. consideration, defined . . . 4065
. derivatives . . . 9016-9021
. . assumptions . . . 12,028-12,029
. . early termination journal entries, . . . 12,035
. . fair value of swap, . . . 12,028-12,029
. . hedge effectiveness, . . . 12,029
. . pro forma financial statement balances . . . 12,031-12,032
. . sample journal entries . . . 12,029-12,031
. . standards . . . 9020-9021
. financing special assessments with current resources . . . 19,007-19,008
. governmental liability for debt . . . 19,003-19,004
. grants and other financial assistance . . . 17,034-17,037
. infrastructure assets . . . 10,004-10,006
. intangible assets . . . 10,012-10,015
. items constructed but not ultimately owned by government . . . 10,018-10,019
. liabilities . . . 6016-6021
. mergers of governments, . . . 4062
. nonexchange and exchange financial guarantee transactions . . . 16,038-16,041
. nonexchange revenues administered or collected by another government . . . 17,028-17,031
. proprietary funds . . . 7007-7009

Accounting and reporting issues—continued
. recording nonexchange transactions . . . 17,009-17,010
. government-wide financial statements
. revenue and expense recognition criteria . . . 17,032-17,034
. revenue recognition using modified accrual basis of accounting . . . 17,031-17,034
. service concession agreements . . . 10,015
. special assessment debt . . . 19,003-19,009
. special assessment districts of component units . . . 19,010
. special assessment reserve, guarantee, or sinking fund . . . 19,006
. subsequent contravention of eligibility requirements or purpose restrictions . . . 17,028
. transfers and disposals of operations . . . 4066

Accounting hierarchy, proprietary funds . . . 1011-1013

Accounting literature, . . . 1010

Account pool . . . 23,002

Accrual basis of accounting . . . 3003-3011. *See also* Converting from modified accrual to accrual basis

ACFR. *See* Annual comprehensive financial report

Acquisitions . . . 4065-4066

Activity classification, . . . 5021-5022

Acts of God . . . 15,001

Actuarial method . . . 15,012-15,014

Advanced refunding. *See* Extinguishment of debt

Agent multiple-employer plans . . . 13,017

AICPA. *See* American Institute of Certified Public Accountants

Allocation method of prepaid amounts . . . 11,005-11,006

ALL

Index

American Institute of Certified Public Accountants (AICPA)
. Code of Professional Conduct, . . . 1001-1002
. Industry Audit and Accounting Guides, . . . 1010
. not-for-profit model . . . 1013

Amortization
. expenses . . . 18,015-18,021
. long-term debt . . . 12,041-12,042
. unamortized debt issuance costs . . . 20,029

Amortization expense
. amortization periods for intangible assets . . . 18,017-18,018
. expenses and expenditures . . . 18,015-18,021
. modified (depreciation) approach
. . exchange transactions . . . 18,015-18,021

Annual comprehensive financial report (ACFR). *See* Financial reporting

Annual financial report. *See* AFR

Annuity contracts . . . 15,008

Anticipation notes . . . 12,006-12,008

Appointment of voting majority . . . 4015-4017

Appropriated budget . . . 2002-2003, 2005, 20,103

Appropriations
. budgets . . . 2002-2004
. lapsing . . . 2008-2009
. nonlapsing . . . 2010-2012

Appropriations control account, . . . 2005-2006

Arbitrage liability . . . 6017, 12,035-12,036

ARC. *See* Annual required contribution

Artwork . . . 10,006-10,007

ASC™ 958 . . . 1013

ASC™ . . . 980, 1012

Assessment of accountability . . . 1027-1029

Assessment of fiscal potential . . . 1030

Assets
. capital assets. *See* Capital assets
. current assets . . . 7010
. fiduciary funds . . . 8001-8002, 11,010
. governmental funds . . . 6014-6016, 11,010
. government-wide financial statements. *See* Government-wide financial statements
. infrastructure. *See* Infrastructure assets

Assets—continued
. invested in capital assets, net of related debt . . . 5034-5039
. proprietary funds . . . 7010-7012, 11,010
. reporting restrictions on use . . . 7010-7011
. restricted net assets . . . 5039-5043
. unrestricted net assets . . . 5043

Asset retirement obligations
. generally . . . 16,029-16,030
. deferred outflow of resources . . . 16,031-16,032
. funding and assurance provisions . . . 16,032
. governmental funds . . . 16,032
. measurement of . . . 16,031-16,032
. minority interest owners, exception for . . . 16,031
. note disclosure . . . 16,032-16,033
. recognition of . . . 16,030

Assigned fund balance . . . 5045-5046

Auditor's report . . . 20,002

B

Balance sheets . . . 20,067-20,071

Banking pool . . . 23,002

Bankruptcy
. of municipal governments . . . 1006

Basic governmental accounting principles
. accounting and reporting capabilities, . . . 1042
. annual comprehensive financial reports . . . 1055-1056
. annual financial reports . . . 1055-1056
. basis of accounting . . . 1052-1053
. budgeting and budgetary reporting, . . . 1053-1054
. common terminology and classification, . . . 1055
. depreciation of capital assets . . . 1050-1051
. fund accounting systems, . . . 1042-1043
. fund type . . . 1043-1050
. going-concern considerations, . . . 1060-1061
. interim financial reporting, . . . 1057
. measurement focus . . . 1052-1053
. number of funds, . . . 1050
. related-party transactions . . . 1057-1059
. reporting capital assets . . . 1050-1051
. reporting long-term liabilities, . . . 1052
. subsequent events, . . . 1059

AME

Index

Basic governmental accounting principles—continued
. summary . . . 1041-1057
. transfer, revenue and expenditure classification . . . 1054-1055
. valuation of capital assets . . . 1050-1051

Basis of accounting . . . 3003-3011
. generally . . . 3001-3003
. basic governmental accounting principles . . . 1052-1053
. fiduciary funds . . . 3017
. fund financial statements . . . 3018-3019
. governmental funds . . . 3016-3017, 6011
. government-wide financial statements . . . 3016-3019
. proprietary funds . . . 3017, 7007-7009

Basis risk, hedging derivative instruments . . . 12,022

Blending . . . 4006, 4036-4039

Body politic, . . . 4007

Bond anticipation notes . . . 12,006-12,008

Books, rare and historical . . . 10,006-10,007

Budgetary accounting . . . 2001-2015
. generally, . . . 2001
. additional reporting . . . 20,108
. appropriations . . . 2002-2004
. basis differences . . . 20,107
. budgetary accounting system . . . 2003-2004
. budgetary comparison schedules . . . 20,102-20,104, 20,108-20,110
. budgetary control and authority . . . 2002-2003
. budgets . . . 2002-2006
. . levels of operations . . . 2006
. . recording of . . . 2005-2012
. . time span of . . . 2002
. closure of budget period . . . 2012-2013
. comparison schedules . . . 20,102-20,104
. disclosure of budgetary policies . . . 20,104
. encumbrances . . . 2006-2012
. entity differences . . . 20,105
. estimated revenues . . . 2005
. excess of expenditures over appropriations . . . 20,104-20,105
. fiduciary funds, . . . 2014
. final budget, . . . 2003
. by fund type . . . 2013-2015
. GAAP reconciliation . . . 20,110-20,112
. governmental funds . . . 2004-2005
. original budget, . . . 2003

Budgetary accounting—continued
. operations and accountabilty . . . 2002-2013
. other differences . . . 20,107
. perspective differences . . . 20,105-20,107
. proprietary funds . . . 2013-2014
. reconciling budget and GAAP information . . . 20,105-20,114
. reporting . . . 2014-2015
. timing differences . . . 20,107

Budget, defined, . . . 2001

Business interruptions . . . 15,001

C

Calls and puts, . . . 9019

Capital assets . . . 10,001-10,038
. accounting and financial reporting . . . 10,020-10,029, 19,009
. acquired through special assessments . . . 10,017
. art and historical treasures . . . 10,006-10,007
. capitalization policies . . . 10,016-10,017
. defined . . . 10,002-10,004
. discretely-presented component unit disclosures . . . 10,012
. fiduciary funds . . . 10,009-10,010, 11,010
. funded by federal grants, contributions, nonexchange transactions . . . 10,017
. governmental funds . . . 10,008-10,009, 11,010
. government-wide financial statements . . . 10,007-10,008, 11,010
. impairment accounting and reporting . . . 10,020-10,029
. infrastructure assets, modified approach for . . . 10,004-10,006
. intangible assets . . . 10,012-10,015, 10,020
. invested in capital assets, net of related debt . . . 5034-5039
. items constructed but not ultimately owned by government . . . 10,018-10,019
. modified approach . . . 10,004-10,006
. notes to financial statements, disclosure in . . . 10,010-10,012
. proprietary funds . . . 11,010
. reporting . . . 1050-1051, 10,018
. . unclear ownership . . . 10,018
. special assessments . . . 19,008
. types of . . . 10,001

Capitalization policy . . . 10,016-10,017

Capital projects funds
- generally ... 6006-6007
- arbitrage, ... 6017
- bond issuance, ... 6019
- budgetary accounts unnecessary, ... 2004
- leases, ... 6017-6018
- long-term debt ... 6018

CARES Act grant programs ... 7016

Cash balance plan ... 8018

Cash flow statement. *See* Statement of cash flows

Cash Management Improvement Act of 1990 ... 17,023

Category A of public-sector accounting hierarchy ... 1010, 1018-1020

Category B of public-sector accounting hierarchy ... 1010, 1020-1021

Certificates of deposit, ... 9055

Chapter 9 filings (municipal bankruptcies) ... 1006

Character classification, ... 5022

Charges for services ... 5027

Claims and judgments ... 15,001-15,024. *See also* Public entity risk pools
- annuity contracts ... 15,008
- capital contributions ... 15,015-15,016
- claims-made policies ... 15,018, 23,021
- component unit disclosures ... 15,022-15,023
- disclosures ... 15,021-15,024
- discounting ... 15,007-15,008
- entities providing services to others ... 15,020
- fiduciary funds ... 15,009
- governmental funds ... 15,009-15,011
- government-wide financial statements ... 15,008-15,009
- IBNR claims ... 15,005-15,006
- insurance related transactions ... 9017, 15,018-15,020
- internal service fund ... 15,009, 15,011-15,014
- investments ... 15,008
- level of disclosure ... 15,022
- liability recognition ... 15,003-15,008
- loss contingencies ... 15,023-15,024
- participation in public entity risk pools ... 15,014-15,018
- policyholder dividends ... 15,019-15,020

Claims and judgments—continued
- proprietary funds ... 15,009
- public entity risk pools in comparison with risk management ... 15,016-15,018
- retrospective-related policies ... 15,019
- risk management disclosures ... 15,021-15,022
- salvage or subrogation ... 15,007
- subsequent events ... 15,023
- transferring risk ... 15,003
- valuation of claims cost liabilities ... 15,006-15,007

Claims-made policies ... 15,018, 23,021

Claims-servicing pool ... 23,002

Classification. *See* Terminology and classification

Collateral investment pool, ... 9044

Colleges and universities. *See* Public colleges and universities (PCUs)

Combining financial statements ... 4034-4035, 20,114-20,118

Committed fund balance ... 5045

Commodity swaps, ... 12,019

Communication Methods in General Purpose External Financial Reports That Contain Basic Financial Statements (GASB:CS-3) ... 1024, 1032-1036

Communication Methods in General Purpose External Financial Reports That Contain Basic Financial Statements—Notes to Financial Statements (GASB:CS-7) ... 1024, 1032-1036

Compensated absences ... 13,006-13,013, 13,072-13,081
- generally ... 13,006-13,007
- defined ... 13,007
- governmental funds ... 13,013
- notes to basic financial statements ... 13,013
- recognition and measurement criteria ... 13,008-13,013
- pay rate ... 13,012
- sabbatical leave ... 13,007
- salary-related payments ... 13,012-13,013
- sporadic leave and other exceptions ... 13,011

Component units ... 4003-4004
- ACFR ... 20,092, 20,101
- blending ... 4006, 4036-4039

CAP

Component units—continued
- combining statements . . . 4034
- condensed statements . . . 4034-4035
- defined . . . 4011-4012
- disclosures . . . 4049-4053, 15,022-15,023
- economic resources . . . 4028-4030
- fiduciary component units . . . 4039-4041
- financial accountability . . . 4014-4026
- governmental entities . . . 4012-4043
- investments in for-profit corporations . . . 4042-4043
- issues presenting component unit information in primary government . . . 4051
- jointly appointed boards, . . . 4025-4026
- with joint venture characteristics . . . 4059-4060
- landfills . . . 16,015
- majority equity interests, . . . 4026
- nature and significance of relationship . . . 4027-4032
- nongovernmental . . . 4041-4043
- potential for dual inclusion . . . 4026-4027
- presentation . . . 4032-4035
- public colleges and universities . . . 21,012-21,015
- - equity interests and majority equity interests . . . 21,014-21,015
- - nongovernmental component units . . . 21,012-21,015
- - reporting . . . 21,012-21,015
- reporting . . . 4032-4039, 20,101
- revenues pledged . . . 17,047-17,048
- scope of services . . . 4037-4038
- separate columns, . . . 4033-4034
- significant economic support . . . 4030-4031
- similar governing bodies . . . 4036-4037
- special assessment districts . . . 19,010
- Tobacco Settlement Authorities (TSAs) . . . 4039

Computer software, accounting for . . . 10,013

Concept Statements . . . 1023-1041

Condensed statements . . . 4034-4035

Conduit debt obligations . . . 12,012-12,017, 12,053-12,054
- capital assets, construction (or acquisition) of . . . 12,016-12,017
- commitments made by issuers associated . . . 12,013-12,015
- generally . . . 12,012-12,013
- liabilities . . . 12,015

Conduit debt obligations—continued
- recognition and measurement of . . . 12,015-12,016

Confirmation process, . . . 4015-4016

Consideration, defined . . . 4065

Constitutional limitations on debt . . . 20,041-20,042

Construction projects and risk mitigation . . . 15,002

Consumption method . . . 11,003

Contributions to permanent funds, . . . 5029

Cost allocation plan, . . . 5028

Cost recovery method . . . 23,005

Cost-sharing arrangements . . . 4061

Cost-sharing multiple-employer pension plan . . . 13,017

Credit quality
- declines in, . . . 9052
- features . . . 9053

Credit risk
- concentration of, . . . 9064
- custodial . . . 9063-9064
- defined, . . . 9058
- disclosures related to investments . . . 9063-9064
- hedging derivative instruments . . . 9058
- investment derivative instruments . . . 12,021

Crossover refunding . . . 12,037

Current liabilities . . . 16,003

Custodial funds . . . 1048-1049, 8023-8024

D

Damage to assets . . . 15,001

Debt
- extinguishment. *See* Extinguishment of debt
- invested in capital, assets, net of related debt . . . 5034-5039
- long-term. *See* Long-term debt

Debt issuance proceeds . . . 5016-5017

Debt refunding
- generally . . . 12,037
- accounting and financial reporting of refunding . . . 12,039
- cash flow requirements . . . 12,045
- economic gain or loss . . . 12,045-12,046

Debt refunding—continued
. governmental funds . . . 12,039-12,041
. refunding disclosures . . . 12,046-12,047

Debt service funds
. generally . . . 6007-6008
. budgetary accounts unnecessary, . . . 2003
. debt extinguishment, . . . 6020
. debt issuance costs . . . 6019, 6025
. expenditures . . . 6025
. leases, . . . 6017-6018
. unmatured principal and interest . . . 6019-6020
. zero-interest-rate bonds . . . 6020-6021

Defeased debt. *See* Extinguishment of debt

Deferrals . . . 11,010

Deferred compensation plans . . . 13, 018, 22,026-22,028

Deferred inflows . . . 14,018, 14,022-14,023

Deferred outflows of resources . . . 11,007-11,010

Deferred retirement option programs (DROPS) . . . 22,013-22,014

Defined benefit pension plans . . . 13,018-13,019
. agent multiple-employer plan . . . 8018, 13,017
. ARC. *See* Annual required contribution
. cost-sharing employers . . . 8018, 13,017, 13,034-13,042
. PERS. *See* Public employee retirement system
. pension valuations and OPEB valuations, compared . . . 22,043-22,044
. postemployment health care plans . . . 22,001
. required supplementary information . . . 13,041-13,042
. single-employer plan . . . 8017, 13,028

Defined contribution plans . . . 8018-8020, 13,016

Demand bonds
. governmental funds . . . 6017, 12,008-12,012
. government-wide financial statements . . . 12,049
. proprietary funds . . . 12,048-12,049
. reporting . . . 5018
. take-out agreements . . . 12,009

Deposit and investment portfolio disclosures . . . 9056-9057

Deposit and investment portfolio disclosures—continued
. cash deposits with financial institutions . . . 9056
. credit risk . . . 9063-9064
. duration . . . 9066-9067
. equity method investments, . . . 9061
. fair value . . . 9068-9070
. foreign currency risk, . . . 9067
. interest rate risk, . . . 9064
. investment policies . . . 9062-9063
. investment risk, . . . 9062
. investment types, . . . 9062
. irrevocable split interest agreements, . . . 9075
. legal or contractual provisions . . . 9014-9015
. level of, . . . 9062
. qualifying external investment pools . . . 9070-9072, 9075
. realized gains and losses, . . . 9060-9061
. reverse repurchase agreements . . . 9036-9038, 9072-9073
. . generally . . . 9037-9038
. . legal or contractual provisions for . . . 9072-9073
. . other agreements . . . 9073
. . repurchase agreements, compared . . . 9036-9037
. . yield maintenance agreement . . . 9073
. securities lending transactions, . . . 9073-9074
. segmented time distributions, . . . 9064-9065
. simulation model, . . . 9067
. specific identification, . . . 9065
. weighted average maturity, . . . 9065-9066

Deposit method . . . 23,005

Deposits and investments . . . 9001-9086
. generally . . . 9001-9002
. basis of accounting and measurement focus, . . . 9022-9024
. cash deposits with financial institutions . . . 9013-9015
. . legal or contractual provisions for deposits . . . 9014-9015
. . risks of deposits . . . 9015-9016
. cost method . . . 9027
. disclosures. *See* Deposit and investment portfolio disclosures
. endowments . . . 9029
. equity method . . . 9024-9027

Index

Deposits and investments—continued
. fair value hierarchy . . . 9007-9013
. for-profit corporations, investments in . . . 4042-4043
. generate cash, ability to . . . 9022
. held primarily for income or profit . . . 9021-9022
. individual investment accounts . . . 9036
. irrevocable split-interest agreements . . . 9044-9049
. life settlement contracts . . . 9028
. markets . . . 9004-9005
. market participants . . . 9005
. open-end mutual funds . . . 9029
. present service capacity . . . 9021
. pooled cash . . . 9027-9028
. recognition and reporting
. . irrevocable split-interest agreements . . . 9044-9049
. . other investments . . . 9030-9035
. sponsor external investment pools . . . 9035-9036
. transaction costs in pricing, role of . . . 9005-9006
. 2a7-like pools . . . 9003, 9023
. valuation
. . approaches . . . 9006-9007
. . techniques . . . 9006

Depreciation expense
. business-type activities . . . 7030-7032
. capital assets . . . 1050-1051
. enterprise funds, . . . 7017
. expenses and expenditures . . . 18,015-18,021
. infrastructure assets . . . 10,005
. modified (depreciation) approach
. . capital assets . . . 10,005-10,006
. . exchange transactions . . . 18,018-18,021
. statement of activities . . . 7030, 20,035-20,060

Derivatives
. accounting and reporting . . . 9016-9021
. . assumptions . . . 12,028-12,029
. . pro forma financial statement balances . . . 12,031-12,032
. . sample journal entries . . . 12,029-12,031
. . standards . . . 9020-9021
. commodity swaps, . . . 9019
. credit quality
. . declines in, . . . 9052
. . features . . . 9053

Derivatives—continued
. defined . . . 9016-9018
. disclosures
. . general disclosures . . . 9057-9058
. . hedging derivative instruments, . . . 12,054-12,058
. . investment derivative instruments, . . . 9057-9060
. . other disclosures, . . . 12,055-12,056
. early termination, . . . 12,035
. fair value determination, . . . 9020-9021
. forward contracts, . . . 9019
. futures contracts, . . . 9019
. guaranteed securities, . . . 9052
. hedge accounting . . . 12,021-12,022
. . cash flow hedges . . . 12,022-12,024
. . fair value hedges . . . 12,024
. . forward contracts . . . 12,024
. . termination events . . . 12,032-12,035
. hedging derivative instruments
. . basis risk . . . 12,022
. . credit risk . . . 12,021
. . disclosure . . . 9058
. . foreign currency risk . . . 12,022
. . interest rate risk . . . 12,021
. . market-access risk, . . . 12,022
. . risk . . . 12,021-12,022
. . rollover risk . . . 12,022
. . termination risk . . . 12,021
. interest rate locks, . . . 9019
. interest rate swaps, . . . 9019
. investment derivative instruments, . . . 9020
. . credit risk . . . 9020
. . defined, . . . 9020
. . disclosure . . . 9057-9060
. . foreign currency risk . . . 9020, 9060
. . interest rate risk . . . 9020
. . types of . . . 9018-9020
. participating governments, qualifying external investment pools . . . 9070-9072
. qualifying external investment pools . . . 9070-9072
. specific investment derivative disclosure, . . . 9057-9058
. types of . . . 9018-9020

Derived tax revenue . . . 17,012-17,014

Direct expenses . . . 20,037-20,039

Disaggregation of receivables and payables . . . 11,010-11,012

Disclosures. *See also* Note disclosures

28,007

DIS

Disclosures.—continued
- component units . . . 4049-4053, 15,022-15,023
- conduit debt . . . 12,053-12,054
- deposits and investments. *See* Deposit and investment portfolio disclosures
- derivatives . . . 9057-9060
  - general disclosures . . . 9057-9058
  - hedging derivative instruments . . . 12,054-12,058
  - investment derivative instruments . . . 9057-9060
  - other disclosures . . . 12,055-12,056
- fund balance disclosure requirements . . . 5048-5049
- future revenues pledged . . . 17,047-17,048
- future revenues sold . . . 17,047
- hedging derivative instruments . . . 12,054-12,058
- investment derivative instruments . . . 9057-9060
- joint ventures . . . 4054-4059
- level of disclosure . . . 15,022
- loss contingencies . . . 15,023-15,024
- public entity risk pools . . . 23,018-23,019
  - unpaid claims liabilities . . . 23,025
- refundings . . . 12,050
  - cash flow requirements differences . . . 12,045
  - computing required refunding disclosures . . . 12,046-12,047
  - economic gain or loss . . . 12,045-12,046
- risk management . . . 15,021-15,022
- subsequent events . . . 15,023
- tax abatement . . . 17,049-17,052
- variable interest rate . . . 12,056

Discrete presentation . . . 4006, 4032-4035

Disposals of operations . . . 4066

Dollar repurchase-reverse repurchase agreements, . . . 9037

Dual inclusion . . . 4026-4027

E

Early termination, . . . 12,035

Economic resources . . . 4028-4030

Electronic benefits transfers (EBTs) . . . 17,066

"Elements of Financial Statements" (GASB:CS-4)
- generally . . . 1024, 1025

"Elements of Financial Statements" (GASB:CS-4)—continued
- deferred, advance or unearned vs deferred revenue, use of . . . 1037-1039
- financial position statements . . . 1037-1041
- purpose of concepts statements . . . 1036-1041
- resource flow statements, . . . 6023
  - generally . . . 1039-1040
  - assets . . . 6014
  - expenditures, . . . 6025
  - fund equity or net position, . . . 6021
  - liabilities . . . 6016-6021, 7012-7013
  - revenues . . . 6024
- terminology and classification . . . 5020

Eliminations and reclassifications
- ACFR . . . 20,058
- date of reclassification . . . 12,012
- government-wide financial statements . . . 5008-5012
- internal activities (statement of activities) . . . 5010-5011
- internal balances (statement of net position) . . . 5008-5010
- internal service fund balances . . . 5011-5012
- intra-entity activity . . . 5011
- overdrawn funds . . . 5010

Employee Retirement Income Security Act of 1974 (ERISA) . . . 1005

Encumbrances . . . 2006-2012

Endowments . . . 9029

Enterprise funds
- generally . . . 1045
- activities . . . 7004
- financial statements . . . 21,002-21,003
- proprietary funds . . . 7001-7005
- segment information . . . 7018-7020
- state lotteries and gaming . . . 16,033-16,037

Entity classification . . . 1013-1015

Entry age actuarial cost method . . . 13,022, 13,024-13,025

Errors and omissions . . . 15,001

Estimated revenues control account . . . 2005

Evaluation of operating results . . . 1029-1030

Excess pension asset accounts . . . 8019

Exchange-like transactions . . . 17,006-17,007

Exchange transactions . . . 17,005

Index

Exchange transactions—continued
. accounting and reporting issues . . . 16,038-16,041
. expenses and expenditures . . . 18,013
. fiduciary funds . . . 17,038
. governmental funds . . . 17,038, 18,013
. government-wide financial statements . . . 17,038, 18,013
. proprietary funds . . . 17,038
. revenues . . . 17,038

Expenditure-driven grant programs . . . 17,011

Expenses and expenditures . . . 18,001-18,021
. generally . . . 18,001-18,006
. depreciation expense . . . 7017, 18,015-18,021
. exchange transactions . . . 18,013-18,015
. nonexchange transactions . . . 18,006-18,011
. operating . . . 7014
. payments in lieu of taxes (PILOT payments) . . . 7018
. pension and employee benefits . . . 7018
. proprietary funds . . . 7016-7018
. purpose restrictions . . . 18,008
. time requirements . . . 18,007-18,008
. uncollectible accounts related to nonrevenue transactions . . . 7018
. voluntary nonexchange transactions . . . 18,010-18,011

Experience-based premium contract . . . 23,003

Experience refunds . . . 23,012

Exposure Draft . . . 1016-1017

External investment pools . . . 9049-9056, 9070-9072. *See also* Investment trust funds

Externally imposed restrictions . . . 5036, 5039

Extinguishment of debt . . . 12,036-12,047
. advance refundings
. . governmental funds . . . 12,039-12,041
. . proprietary funds . . . 12,041-12,042
. amortization . . . 12,041-12,042
. computing the required disclosures . . . 12,045-12,047
. current and advance refunding . . . 12,037, 12,042
. defeasance . . . 12,038-12,039
. governmental funds . . . 12,039-12,041
. in-substance defeasance of debt using only existing resources . . . 12,038-12,039
. proprietary funds . . . 12,041-12,042
. refunding debt previously refunded . . . 12,042-12,044

Extinguishment of debt—continued
. refunding transactions . . . 12,037

Extraordinary items . . . 5030-5033, 20,056-20,057

F

FAF (Financial Accounting Foundation) . . . 1003

Fair value
. generally . . . 9002-9013
. derivatives . . . 9020-9021

FASAB (Federal Accounting Standards Advisory Board) . . . 1002, 1010

FASB (Financial Accounting Standards Board) . . . 1002

Federal Accounting Standards Advisory Board (FASAB) . . . 1002, 1010

Fiduciary funds . . . 8001-8028
. assets . . . 8001-8002
. basis of accounting and measurement focus . . . 3016-3017
. budgetary system and accounting . . . 2014, 8024
. claims and judgments . . . 15,009
. custodial funds . . . 8023-8024
. defined . . . 8001-8002
. exchange transactions . . . 17,038
. fiduciary activities, identification of . . . 8002-8014
. . generally . . . 8002
. . accounting and treasury services . . . 8011
. . alumni and booster clubs . . . 8014
. . cemeteries . . . 8010-8011
. . clearing accounts . . . 8012-8013
. . component units . . . 8002-8005
. . control, key decision to determining . . . 8011-8014
. . decisions that may need to be made for other fiduciary activities . . . 8010
. . identifying other activities . . . 8007-8011
. . inmates accounts . . . 8010
. . own-source revenues . . . 8014-8015
. . payroll . . . 8012-8013
. . pension and OPEB arrangements . . . 8007
. . non-pension or OPEB component units . . . 8005-8006
. . retainage, performance bonds, and deposits . . . 8012
. . seized property . . . 8013
. . student activity accounts . . . 8008-8010

FID

28,010 Index

Fiduciary funds—continued
. fiduciary activities, identification of—continued
.. college tuition savings and ABLE plans . . . 8013-8014
. fund financial statements . . . 8024-8028
.. additions . . . 8027-8028
.. accumulated assets . . . 8026-8027
.. assets . . . 8025-8026
.. deductions . . . 8028
.. external investment pool information . . . 8024-8025
.. fiduciary net position . . . 8026-8027
.. liabilities . . . 8026
.. plan information not separately issued . . . 8024
.. plan information separately issued . . . 8024
.. statement of changes in fiduciary net position, . . . 8027
.. statement of fiduciary net position . . . 8025
. fund types . . . 1046-1050
. government-wide financial statements . . . 8028
. insured plans . . . 13,069-13,070
. investment trust funds . . . 8020-8022
. materials and supplies . . . 11,010
. nonexchange transactions . . . 18,012
. pension (and other employee benefit) trust funds . . . 8015-8020
. PERS. See Public employee retirement system
. prepayments and deferrals . . . 11,010
. private-purpose trust funds . . . 8022-8023
. required financial statements . . . 20,092-20,093
. statement of fiduciary net position . . . 20,093-20,096

Final budget . . . 20,103

Financial accountability . . . 4014-4026
. access to other entity's resources . . . 4020-4021
. appointment of voting majority . . . 4015-4017
. defined . . . 4006-4007
. financial benefit to or burden on primary government . . . 4019-4024
. financial guarantee of debt . . . 4022-4024
. fiscal dependency . . . 4024-4026
. governing entities with jointly appointed boards . . . 4025-4026

Financial accountability—continued
. governmental organizations with boards appointed by other government . . . 4025
. imposition of will . . . 4017-4019
. responsibility for debt . . . 4021-4022
. responsibility for deficits or support . . . 4021
. special-purpose governments . . . 4024-4025

Financial Accounting Foundation (FAF) . . . 1002

Financial Accounting Standards Board (FASB) . . . 1002, 1003

Financial assistance. See Grants and other financial assistance

Financial benefit . . . 4019

Financial burden . . . 4019

Financial position statement elements . . . 1037

Financial reporting . . . 20,001-20,121
. generally . . . 20,001-20,002
. ACFRs and AFRs, minimum requirements for . . . 20,002-20,006
. auditor's report . . . 20,002
. basic financial statements . . . 20,015, 20,097-20,114
. combining financial statements . . . 20,114-20,118
. comparative financial statements . . . 20,096-20,097
. component units . . . 20,092-20,093
. fiduciary funds and similar component units . . . 20,092-20,093
. financial reporting . . . 20,002-20,121
. fund financial statements . . . 20,060-20,097
. government-wide financial statements . . . 20,015-20,121
. independent auditor's report . . . 20,002
. individual fund statements . . . 20,115
. MD&A . . . 20,006-20,015
. post-employment benefit plans . . . 22,019-22,020
. required supplementary information (RSI) . . . 20,102-20,105
. schedules . . . 20,118
. special purpose governments . . . 20,121
. statement of activities . . . 20,035-20,060 See also Statement of activities
. statement of cash flows . . . 20,090-20,092
. statistical section . . . 20,119-20,121
. supplementary information . . . 20,102-20,105

FIN

Index

Financial reporting entity . . . 4006-4007
Financial reporting objectives . . . 1025-1027
Financial statements
. custodial funds . . . 1048-1049
. disclosure in notes . . . 1033-1034
. elements. *See* "Elements of Financial Statements"
. enterprise funds . . . 1045
. fiduciary funds . . . 1046-1050
. fund financial statements. *See* Fund financial statements
. governmental . . . 1043-1044, 1049-1050
. government-wide. *See* Government-wide financial statements
. internal service funds . . . 1045-1046, 7021-7035
. measurement of elements . . . 1040-1041
. postemployment benefit plans . . . 22,035-22,036
. proprietary funds . . . 1044, 1049-1050, 1055
. recognition . . . 1033, 1041
. required . . . 20,067
. terminology and classification. *See* Terminology and classification
. trust funds . . . 1047-1048

Fiscal independence or dependence . . . 4010-4011, 4024-4026

Flexible budget . . . 2013-2014

Flow of current financial resources . . . 3012-3013

Flow of economic resources . . . 3011-3012

Foreign currency risk, . . . 9067
. hedging derivative instruments . . . 12,022, 12,055
. investment derivative instruments . . . 9020, 9060

For-profit versus governmental entities, . . . 1005-1006

Forward contracts . . . 9019

Function classification . . . 5021

Fund accounting systems, . . . 1042-1043

Fund balance
. assigned fund balance . . . 5045-5046
. classifications . . . 5044-5047
. committed fund balance . . . 5045
. non-spendable fund balance . . . 5044
. reporting . . . 5044-5047, 6001
. restricted fund balance . . . 5044-5045
. unassigned fund balance . . . 5046-5047

Fund equity . . . 6021
Fund financial statements
. ACFR . . . 20,093
. balance sheets . . . 20,067-20,071
. basis of accounting and measurement focus . . . 3016-3019
. current assets . . . 20,078-20,080
. current liabilities . . . 20,080-20,081
. fiduciary funds . . . 8024-8028
. . statement of changes in fiduciary net position, . . . 8027
. . statement of fiduciary net position . . . 8025
. governmental funds . . . 6013-6025, 20,067-20,078
. major funds in governmental and proprietary funds . . . 20,060-20,065
. operating versus nonoperating revenues and expenses . . . 20,086-20,090
. reporting major funds . . . 20,060-20,065
. required reconciliation to government-wide statements . . . 20,065-20,067
. revenues, expenditures, and changes . . . 20,071-20,078, 20,084-20,086
. statement of net position . . . 20,078, 20,084-20,086

Funds
. fiduciary funds. *See* Fiduciary funds
. governmental funds. *See* Governmental funds
. proprietary funds. *See* Proprietary funds

Future revenues
. pledged . . . 17,047-17,048
. sold . . . 17,047

Futures contracts . . . 9019

G

GAAP (Generally accepted accounting principles) . . . 1001-1061

Gaming . . . 16,033-16,037
. revenue recognition . . . 16,036-16,037

GARS (Governmental Accounting Research System), . . . 1022

GASAC (Governmental Accounting Standards Advisory Council) . . . 1022

GASB. *See* Governmental Accounting Standards Board; *specific GASB Statements*

GASB-62 . . . 1011-1012

GASB-68 . . . 13,026

Index

GASB-94 . . . 10,003, 10,015
GASB-99 . . . 16,038, 24,004
GASB-100 . . . 4013-4014, 5004, 6012, 7008, 16,013, 20,054-20,056, 22,019
GASB-101 . . . 13,001, 13,006
GASB:CS-1 (Objectives of Financial Reporting)
. generally . . . 1017-1018, 1025-1027
. basis of accounting and measurement focus . . . 3001
GASB:CS-2 (Service Efforts and Accomplishments) . . . 1024, 1030-1032
GASB:CS-3 (Communication Methods in General Purpose External Financial Reports That Contain Basic Financial Statements) . . . 1024, 1032-1036
GASB:CS-4. See "Elements of Financial Statements"
GASB:CS-5 (Service Efforts and Accomplishments Reporting) . . . 1024, 1031-1032
GASB:CS-6 (Measurement of Elements of Financial Statements)
. generally . . . 1024
. expenses and expenditures . . . 18,004-18,005
. financial statements, elements of . . . 1040-1041
. liabilities . . . 16,001-16,002
. revenues . . . 17,004
GASB:CS-7 (Communication Methods in General Purpose External Financial Reports That Contain Basic Financial Statements—Notes to Financial Statements) . . . 1024, 1032-1036
GASB:TB 84-1 (Purpose and Scope of GASB Technical Bulletins and Procedures for Issuance) . . . 1020
GASB:TB 2020-1 (Accounting and Financial Reporting Issues Related to Coronavirus Aid, Relief and Economic Security Act (CARES) Act of 2020 and Coronavirus Diseases) . . . 7016, 16,039-16,040, 17,011-17,012, 18,010-18,011, 20,057
General funds
. generally, . . . 6002-6003
Generally accepted accounting principles (GAAP) . . . 1001-1061

General obligation bonds . . . 7012-7013, 12,003-12,006
General obligation debt . . . 19,003
General-purpose governmental entities . . . 1014-1015
General revenues . . . 5029, 20,050-20,052
Going-concern considerations, . . . 1060-1061
Government acquisitions . . . 4062
Governmental Accounting and Financial Reporting Principles (NCGA-1). See NCGA-1 (Governmental Accounting and Financial Reporting Principles)
Governmental Accounting Research System (GARS), . . . 1022
Governmental Accounting Standards Advisory Council (GASAC) . . . 1022
Governmental Accounting Standards Board (GASB). See also specific GASB Statements
. authority of . . . 1003
. Concept Statements . . . 1023-1041, 3001. See also specific GASB Concept Statement
. Implementation Guides . . . 1007, 1010, 1021
. Interpretations . . . 1021
. principle setting . . . 1015-1023
. . exposure draft stage . . . 1016-1017
. . Governmental Accounting Standards Advisory Council (GASAC) . . . 1022
. . invitation to comment, . . . 1016
. . Post-Implementation Review Process (PIR) . . . 1021-1022
. . pre-agenda research stage . . . 1015-1016
. . preliminary views stage . . . 1016
. . pronouncements . . . 1018-1021
. . resource aids . . . 1022-1023
. . standard-setting stage, . . . 1017-1018
. pronouncements . . . 1018-1021
. resource aids . . . 1022-1023
. Service Efforts and Accomplishments (SEA) reporting . . . 1017-1018
. Statements . . . 1017
. Technical Bulletins
. . Category B GAAP, . . . 1020-1021
. . issuance . . . 1007-1008
Governmental entities
. generally . . . 4001-4005
. combinations and disposals of government operations . . . 4061-4066
. component units . . . 4012-4032
. different reporting periods . . . 4048-4049

Index

Governmental entities—continued
. financial reporting entity concept . . . 4005-4006
. guarantees between . . . 16,038-16,041
. note disclosures . . . 4049-4053
. 100 percent equity interest, . . . 4052
. primary governments . . . 4002, 4004, 4007-4012
. reporting component units . . . 4032-4041
. reporting intra-entity transactions and balances . . . 4043-4047
. reporting relationships with organizations other than component units . . . 4053-4060
. stand-alone government financial statements, . . . 4052-4053
. "sub-government" entities . . . 4005

Governmental funds
. generally . . . 1043-1044, 1049-1050, 6001-6025, 11,001-11,012
. accounting and reporting . . . 6011-6012
. advance refundings . . . 12,039-12,041
. arbitrage . . . 6017
. assets . . . 6014-6016, 10,008-10,009
. . classifications of . . . 6014-6016
. balance sheets . . . 6013-6014, 20,067-20,071
. basis of accounting and measurement focus . . . 3016-3017, 6011
. bond premium, discount, and bond issuance costs . . . 6019
. bonds issued between interest payment dates, . . . 6018-6019
. bond, tax and revenue anticipation notes, . . . 6017
. budgeting . . . 2004-2005
. capital assets . . . 6015-6016, 10,008-10,009
. capital projects funds. *See* Capital projects funds
. claims and judgments . . . 15,009-15,011, 15,016. *See also* Claims and judgments
. classification and disclosure . . . 6025
. debt extinguishment . . . 6020
. debt service funds. *See* Debt service funds
. defeasance with existing resources . . . 12,048
. demand bonds . . . 6017, 12,008-12,012, 12,048
. disaggregation of receivables and payables . . . 11,010-11,012
. establishing and operating . . . 6009
. exchange transactions . . . 17,038, 18,013

Governmental funds—continued
. expenditures and other financing uses . . . 6025
. extinguishment of debt . . . 12,036-12,047
. fund balance, defined . . . 6001
. fund equity, . . . 6021
. fund financial statements . . . 6014-6025
. general funds, . . . 6002-6003
. investments . . . 6014
. joint ventures . . . 4058
. landfills . . . 16,011-16,012
. leases, . . . 6017-6018
. lease transactions reported, . . . 5019
. liabilities . . . 6016-6021. *See also* Liabilities—governmental funds
. long-term debt . . . 6018-6019, 12,006
. long-term receivables . . . 6014-6015
. major funds reporting in financial statements . . . 6014-6025, 20,060-20,065
. materials and supplies . . . 11,002-11,005
. net position, . . . 6021
. nonexchange transactions . . . 17,038, 18,012
. other financing sources . . . 6024-6025
. other financisng uses . . . 6025
. pension obligation. *See* Pension obligation
. permanent funds . . . 6008-6009
. prepayments and deferred outflows of resources . . . 11,005-11,007
. recording fund liabilities and expenditures . . . 16,004-16,006
. refunded debt . . . 12,048
. reporting fund balances . . . 5044-5047
. revenues . . . 6024
. revenues and other financing sources . . . 6022-6025
. special and extraordinary items . . . 5032-5033
. special revenue funds . . . 6003-6006
. statement of revenues, expenditures, and changes in fund balances . . . 6021-6022
. terminology and classification . . . 5016-5023
. types of . . . 6001
. unmatured principal and interest . . . 6019-6020
. zero-interest-rate bonds . . . 6020-6021

Governmental reporting entity . . . 4001-4005

Government-construction or acquisition of asset . . . 10,018-10,019

Government investment pools . . . 9043

GOV

Index

Government-mandated nonexchange transactions
. expense or liability recognition . . . 17,032
. expenses and expenditures . . . 18,008-18,009
. revenues . . . 17,020-17,022
. secondary recipients . . . 17,020-17,022

Government mergers, . . . 4062

Government-wide financial statements
. ACFR . . . 20,015-20,060
. activities that support predominately governmental funds . . . 7033-7035
. assets . . . 10,007-10,008
. . art and historical treasures . . . 10,006-10,007
. . capital assets . . . 10,007-10,008
. . capitalization policies . . . 10,016-10,017
. . intangible assets . . . 10,012-10,015
. . unclear ownership . . . 10,018
. basis of accounting and measurement focus . . . 3016-3019
. bond, tax, and revenue anticipation notes . . . 12,049
. business-type activities . . . 7022, 7030-7032
. claims and judgments . . . 15,016
. defeasance with existing resources . . . 12,050
. demand bonds . . . 12,049
. eliminations and reclassifications. *See* Eliminations and reclassifications
. exchange transactions . . . 17,038, 18,013
. exclusively government activities . . . 7022, 7027-7030
. external parties . . . 7022-7024
. fiduciary funds . . . 7024, 8028, 11,010
. hedging derivatives . . . 12,049-12,050
. integrating internal service funds into . . . 7025-7027
. joint ventures . . . 4058
. landfills . . . 16,012
. liabilities . . . 12,049-12,050
. long-term debt . . . 12,049-12,050
. nonexchange transactions . . . 17,038, 18,012
. proprietary funds . . . 7025-7027, 11,010
. refunded debt . . . 12,050
. special and extraordinary items . . . 5033
. terminology and classification . . . 5013-5016

Grants and contributions . . . 5028, 20,042-20,049

Grants and other financial assistance
. on-behalf payments for fringe benefits and salaries . . . 17,036-17,037
. pass-through grants . . . 17,034-17,037
. SNAP . . . 17,037

Guarantee contracts . . . 9017

Guaranteed securities . . . 9052

H

Hedging derivative instruments . . . 12,017-12,036
. accounting and reporting standards overview for . . . 12,022
. consistent critical terms method . . . 12,023-12,025
. defined . . . 12,017-12,019
. dollar-offset method . . . 12,026
. illustration of . . . 12,028-12,035
. measurement of hedge effectiveness, other methods of . . . 12,026-12,027
. regression analysis method . . . 12,026
. risk . . . 12,021-12,022
. synthetic instrument method . . . 12,025-12,026
. types of . . . 12,019-12,021

Hierarchy of objectives . . . 1029

Historical cost information method . . . 15,012-15,013

Historical treasures . . . 10,006-10,007

I

IASB (International Accounting Standards Board) . . . 1002

IBNR (Incurred but not reported) claims . . . 15,005-15,006, 23,008

IFRS (International Financial Reporting Standards) . . . 1004

Impairment of capital assets . . . 10,020-10,029
. combinations, resulting from . . . 10,028-10,029
. definition of . . . 10,020-10,021
. deflated depreciated replacement cost approach . . . 10,024-10,025
. insurance recoveries . . . 10,025-10,026
. intangible capital assets . . . 10,026-10,027
. measurement of . . . 10,022
. regulated operation asset impairment . . . 10,027-10,028

GOV

Index

Impairment of capital assets—continued
. reporting impairment write-down . . . 10,026
. restoration cost approach . . . 10,023-10,024
. service units approach . . . 10,024
. temporary impairments . . . 10,025-10,026
. two-step test process . . . 10,021-10,022

Implementation Guides . . . 1007, 1010, 1021

Imposed nonexchange revenues . . . 17,014-17,020

Imposition of will . . . 4017-4019
. fiscal dependency, compared . . . 4018

Incurred but not reported (IBNR) claims . . . 15,005-15,006, 23,008

Individual investment accounts . . . 8022, 9036

Infrastructure assets. *See also* Capital assets
. modified approach . . . 10,004-10,006
. proprietary fund . . . 7011

In-substance defeasance of debt . . . 12,038-12,039

Insurance. *See also* Claims and judgments; Public entity risk pools
. contracts . . . 9019-9020
. entities . . . 24,007-24,010
. . disclosures . . . 24,010
. . general principles . . . 24,008
. . investments and mortgage loans, real estate used in operations . . . 24,009-24,010
. . policyholder dividends . . . 24,009
. . premium deficiencies . . . 24,009
. . premium revenue . . . 24,008
. . recognizing claims costs . . . 24,008-24,009
. . reinsurance . . . 24,009
. insurance-purchasing pool . . . 23,001
. recoveries . . . 10,025-10,026
. . impairment of capital assets . . . 10,020-10,029

Intangible assets . . . 10,012-10,015
. generally . . . 10,012-10,013
. internally generated . . . 10,013-10,015
. right-to-use, amortization of . . . 10,020
. Service Concession Arrangements . . . 10,015

Integrating internal service funds into government-wide financial statements . . . 7025-7027
. activities that support predominantly governmental funds . . . 7033-7035

Integrating internal service funds into government-wide financial statements—continued
. activities with external parties . . . 7022-7024
. activities with fiduciary funds, . . . 7024
. exclusively business-type activities . . . 7030-7032
. exclusively government activities . . . 7027-7030

Interest capitalization . . . 7011

Interest-earning investment contracts . . . 9029

Interest expense . . . 7029-7030, 7032, 20,040-20,042

Interest rate locks . . . 9019

Interest rate risk
. disclosure requirements for investment derivatives, . . . 9059-9060
. risk disclosures, basics and examples of, . . . 9064

Interest rate swaps . . . 9019

Interfund activity
. receivables and payables . . . 11,010
. terminology and classification . . . 5002-5012
. transfers . . . 7030, 7033

Internal investment pools . . . 9032-9033
. fund overdrafts . . . 9033-9034

Internal service funds
. activities . . . 7006
. financial statements . . . 7025
. integrating, into government-wide financial statements . . . 7025-7027
. proprietary funds . . . 1044
. rate setting and enterprise funds . . . 7021-7022
. risk financing activities . . . 15,011-15,014
. statement of activities . . . 20,059-20,060

International Accounting Standards Board (IASB) . . . 1002

International Financial Reporting Standards (IFRS) . . . 1004

International Public Sector Accounting Standards Board (IPSASB) . . . 1004

International Public Sector Accounting Standards (IPSAS) . . . 1004

Internet
. online technical inquiry system . . . 1022

INT

Index

Internet—continued
. web sites . . . 1023

Intra-entity activity . . . 20,059

Intra-entity transactions and balances . . . 4043-4047
. blended component unit reporting . . . 4043-4045
. discretely presented component unit reporting . . . 4045-4046
. leasing arrangements . . . 4047
. primary governments and pension plans, transfers between . . . 4046-4047

Inventories . . . 11,002-11,005

Invested in capital assets, net of related debt . . . 5034-5039

Investment Company Act of 1940 . . . 9049

Investment derivative instruments
. credit risk . . . 9020
. defined . . . 9020
. foreign currency risk . . . 9020
. interest rate risk . . . 9020

Investment earnings, . . . 5028-5029

Investment income . . . 7027-7028, 7032

Investment pools . . . 4060, 9032-9034, 9038, 9042-9043

Investments. *See* Deposits and investments

Investment trust funds
. fiduciary funds . . . 8020-8022
. individual investment accounts . . . 8022
. sponsoring governments, . . . 8021-8022

IPSASB (International Public Sector Accounting Standards Board) . . . 1004

IPSAS (International Public Sector Accounting Standards) . . . 1004

IRC section 403(b) plan . . . 8018-8019

IRC section 457 plan . . . 8019

IRC section 457(b) plan . . . 22,028-22,031

Irrevocable Split-Interest Agreements (ISIA)
. governments are beneficiaries of . . . 9044-9049
. recognition and reporting . . . 9044-9049
. statement of cash flows impact . . . 9045

J

Job-related illnesses or injuries . . . 15,001

Joint building or finance authorities . . . 4058-4059

Jointly appointed boards . . . 4025-4026

Jointly governed organizations . . . 4059

Joint ventures . . . 4054-4060
. defined . . . 4054
. disclosure requirements . . . 4058
. equity interest . . . 4056
. governmental funds . . . 4058
. government-wide financial statements . . . 4058
. joint building or finance authorities . . . 4058-4059
. joint control . . . 4055
. ongoing financial interest . . . 4055
. ongoing financial responsibility . . . 4055-4056
. organizations with characteristics of . . . 4059-4060
. proprietary funds . . . 4057
. reporting joint ventures with equity interest . . . 4056

L

Landfills . . . 16,007-16,019
. assets placed in trusts . . . 16,013
. changes in estimates . . . 16,010, 16,012-16,013
. closure and post-closure care costs . . . 16,008-16,010
. component units . . . 16,015
. disclosures . . . 16,014
. estimated total current cost of MSWLF closure or post-closure care . . . 16,010-16,012
. governmental funds . . . 16,011-16,012
. government-wide financial statements . . . 16,012
. illustration . . . 16,015-16,018
. note disclosures . . . 16,014
. proprietary funds . . . 16,010-16,011
. responsibility assumed by another entity . . . 16,014

Lapsing appropriations . . . 2008-2009

Large governments and self-insurance . . . 15,002

Leases . . . 14,001-14,044
. generally . . . 14,001
. availability payment arrangements . . . 14,033-14,038
. combinations . . . 14,028
. contracts that transfer ownership . . . 14,011
. easements and rights . . . 14,003

INT

Index

Leases—continued
- exchange and exchange-like transactions, compared . . . 14,002-14,003
- exclusions from . . . 14,004-14,005
- financial asset . . . 14,004
- intra-entity leases . . . 14,032
- lease term . . . 14,005-14,009
  - bargain renewals and lease terms . . . 14,007-14,008
  - generally . . . 14,005-14,006
  - lease inception, control and month-to-month leasing . . . 14,006
  - options . . . 14,006
  - relevant factors . . . 14,008
  - reassessment of . . . 14,008-14,009
- lease incentives . . . 14,024-14,026
- lease-leaseback transactions . . . 14,032
- lessee accounting . . . 14,011-14,018
  - amortization . . . 14,014
  - asset amortization . . . 14,015-14,018
  - discount rate . . . 14,013-14,014
  - example of . . . 14,017-14,018
  - governmental funds . . . 14,016
  - incentives, . . . 14,026
  - lease liability calculation . . . 14,012-14,013
  - leased asset . . . 14,015
  - note disclosure . . . 14,016-14,017
  - remeasurement triggers . . . 14,014-14,015
- lessor accounting . . . 14,018-14,024
  - asset . . . 14,023
  - deferred inflow . . . 14,022-14,023
  - discount amortization, . . . 14,021
  - discount rate, . . . 14,021
  - example of, . . . 14,024
  - external laws, regulations, court rulings . . . 14,019-14,020
  - governmental funds . . . 14,023
  - incentives, . . . 14,024-14,026
  - initial direct costs . . . 14,018-14,019
  - investments, . . . 14,018-14,019
  - note disclosure . . . 14,023-14,024
  - receivable calculation . . . 14,020-14,021
  - receivable remeasurement triggers, . . . 14,022
- special provisions for entities that primarily leasing operations (public housing), . . . 14,024
- liabilities . . . 6017-6018
- nonfinancial asset . . . 14,001
- modifications and terminations . . . 14,028-14,030
- multiple components . . . 14,026-14,028

special provisions for entities that primarily leasing operations (public housing),—continued
- public-private and public-public partnerships . . . 14,033-14,038
- qualifying sales . . . 14,031
- related party leases . . . 14,031
- sale-leaseback transactions . . . 14,031-14,032
- short-term leases . . . 14,009-14,011
  - lessees . . . 14,009
  - lessors . . . 14,009
- subleases . . . 14,030-14,031
- subscription-based information technology arrangements . . . 14,038-14,043

Lessee accounting . . . 14,011-14,018

Lessor accounting . . . 14,018-14,024

Liabilities . . . 16,001-16,041
- generally . . . 16,001-16,002
- arbitrage liability . . . 12,035-12,036
- asset retirement obligations . . . 16,029-16,033
- claims and judgments . . . 15,003-15,008
- conduit debt obligations . . . 12,012-12,017
- governmental funds. *See* Liabilities—governmental funds
- government-wide financial statements . . . 12,049-12,050
- landfill closure and postclosure care costs . . . 16,007-16,019
- long-term . . . 12,001-12,058
- pollution remediation obligations . . . 16,019-16,029
- proprietary funds . . . 7012-7013, 12,048-12,049
- state lottery obligations and gaming . . . 16,033-16,037

Liabilities—governmental funds
- generally . . . 16,002-16,003
- accounting and reporting . . . 6016-6021
- accumulation of resources to pay liabilities . . . 16,006-16,007
- asset retirement obligations . . . 16,029-16,033
- bond anticipation notes . . . 12,006-12,008
- bond issuance costs, . . . 6019
- bond premium costs . . . 6019
- demand bonds . . . 12,008-12,012
- discount costs . . . 6019
- landfill closure and postclosure care costs . . . 16,007-16,019

LIA

Liabilities—governmental funds—continued
. long-term debt . . . 12,007
. pollution remediation obligations . . . 16,019-16,029
. revenue anticipation notes . . . 12,006-12,008
. state lottery obligations and gaming . . . 16,033-16,037
. tax anticipation notes . . . 12,006-12,008

Loan commitments . . . 9018

Long-term debt . . . 12,001-12,058
. generally . . . 12,001-12,003
. arbitrage liability . . . 12,035-12,036
. determining required refunding disclosures . . . 12,046-12,047
. extinguishment of debt and debt refunding or defeasance . . . 12,036-12,047
. governmental funds . . . 12,006
. government-wide financial statements . . . 12,049-12,050
. note disclosure of debt, . . . 12,050-12,058
. proprietary funds . . . 12,048-12,049
. specific debt-related issues . . . 12,017-12,036
. types of . . . 12,003-12,017

Long-term liabilities . . . 1051-1052, 16,003

Long-term receivables . . . 6014-6015

Lotteries . . . 7004, 16,033-16,037

M

Maintenance and preservation costs, exchange transactions . . . 18,020-18,021

Major funds . . . 20,060-20,065

Majority equity interests, . . . 4026

Management's discussion and analysis (MD&A) . . . 20,006-20,015
. analysis of balance and transactions of individual funds . . . 20,012
. analysis of budget variations . . . 20,013
. analysis of overall financial position . . . 20,012
. capital assets and long-term debt activity . . . 20,013-20,014
. condensed information section . . . 20,011-20,012
. currently known facts . . . 20,015
. discussion of basic financial statements . . . 20,010-20,011
. modified depreciation approach . . . 20,014-20,015

Materials and supplies . . . 11,002-11,005

MD&A. *See* Management's discussion and analysis (MD&A)

"Measurement and Recognition Attributes" (GASB) . . . 1040-1041

Measurement and reporting issues . . . 21,016-21,022
. accrual of tuition and fees revenue . . . 21,022
. federal unrelated business income taxes . . . 21,022
. grants and lending . . . 21,016-21,018
. investment income restricted to permanent or term endowments . . . 21,021
. other forms of lending . . . 21,017-21,018
. Pell grants . . . 21,016-21,017
. scholarship allowances and discounts . . . 21,018
. split-interest agreements . . . 21,019-21,020

Measurement focus . . . 3011-3019
. generally . . . 3001-3003
. basic governmental accounting principles . . . 1052-1053
. deposits and investments . . . 9027-9028
. fiduciary funds . . . 3017
. flow of current financial resources . . . 3012-3013
. flow of economic resources . . . 3011-3012
. fund financial statements . . . 3017-3018
. governmental funds . . . 3016-3017, 6011
. government-wide financial statements . . . 3016-3019
. illustration . . . 3013-3016
. proprietary funds . . . 3017, 7007-7009

Measurement of Elements of Financial Statements (GASB:CS-6)
. generally . . . 1024
. expenses and expenditures . . . 18,004-18,005
. financial statements, elements of . . . 1040-1041
. liabilities . . . 16,001-16,002
. revenues . . . 17,004

Mergers of governments, . . . 4062

Modified accrual basis of accounting . . . 3004-3011. *See also* Converting from modified accrual to accrual basis
. property taxes . . . 17,014-17,020
. revenue recognition . . . 17,031-17,034

Index

Modified (depreciation) approach
. capital assets ... 10,019-10,020
. exchange transactions ... 18,015

Money market funds ... 9029

Money purchase plan ... 8018

Municipal solid waste landfills (MSWLFs). *See* Landfills

N

Nature and significance of relationship ... 4027-4032
. access to economic resources ... 4029-4030
. closely related or financially integrated, examples of ... 4031-4032
. direct benefit of economic resources ... 4028
. significant economic support ... 4030-4031

NCGA-1 (Governmental Accounting and Financial Reporting Principles)
. basic principles ... 1041-1042
. basis of accounting ... 3003-3010
. demand bond disclosures ... 12,052-12,053
. fund, defined ... 7001
. GAAP overview ... 1023-1041
. object classification ... 5022-5023
. recording fund liabilities and expenditures ... 16,004-16,006
. service efforts and accomplishments ... 1030-1032

Net position, ... 6021

Nomination process ... 4015

Non-allocation method ... 11,006-11,007

Nonappropriated budget ... 2002-2003, 20,105

Nonexchange transactions ... 17,001-17,052
. generally ... 17,001-17,005
. accounting and reporting issues ... 16,038-16,041
. customer system development fees ... 7011-7012
. derived tax revenue ... 17,012-17,014
. enabling legislation ... 5039-5040
. expenses and expenditures ... 18,006-18,011
. fiduciary funds ... 17,038, 18,012
. governmental funds ... 17,038, 18,012
. government-mandated nonexchange transactions ... 17,020-17,022, 18,008-18,009

Nonexchange transactions—continued
. government-wide financial statements ... 17,038, 18,012
. imposed nonexchange revenues ... 17,014-17,020
. mandatory and voluntary, defined, ... 5028
. measurement focus and basis ... 1052-1053, 3016
. nature of ... 17,007-17,009
. property taxes ... 17,014-17,020
. proprietary funds ... 17,038, 18,012
. purpose restrictions ... 17,010-17,012, 18,008
. recording ... 17,009-17,010
. . fiduciary funds ... 17,038
. . government-wide financial statements ... 17,038
. . governmental funds ... 17,038
. . proprietary funds ... 17,038
. revenues ... 17,006-17,038
. time requirements ... 17,010-17,012, 18,007-18,008
. types of revenue transactions ... 17,006-17,007
. voluntary nonexchange transactions. *See* Voluntary nonexchange transactions

Nongovernmental component units ... 4041-4043

Nonlapsing appropriations ... 2010-2012

Nonperformance guarantees on contracts ... 9017

Nonreciprocal interfund activity ... 4045, 5005-5008

Non-spendable fund balance ... 5044

Note disclosures ... 4049-4053
. anticipation notes and other forms of short-term debt ... 12,052
. claims and judgments ... 15,021-15,024
. combinations, ... 4066
. component units ... 4049-4053, 15,022-15,023
. condensed financial statements ... 4034-4035
. conduit debt obligations ... 12,053-12,054
. demand bonds ... 12,052-12,053
. deposits and investments. *See* Deposit and investment portfolio disclosures
. derivatives ... 12,054-12,058
. disaggregation of receivables and payables ... 11,010-11,012

Note disclosures—continued
. focus of . . . 4050
. landfills . . . 16,014
. level of disclosure . . . 15,022
. long-term debt . . . 12,050-12,058
. loss contingencies . . . 15,023-15,024
. public entity risk pools . . . 23,018-23,019
. refunding . . . 12,050-12,058
. required supplementary information . . . 4050
. risk management . . . 15,021-15,022
. securities lending transactions . . . 9038-9044
. short-term debt . . . 12,052
. single and agent-multiple-employers . . . 13,025-13,033
. separately issued (stand-alone) financial statements of component units . . . 4051-4052
. subsequent events . . . 15,023
. unpaid claims liabilities . . . 23,025

Number of funds . . . 1050

O

Object classification . . . 5022-5023

Objectives of Financial Reporting (GASB:CS-1)
. generally . . . 1017-1018, 1025-1027
. basis of accounting and measurement focus . . . 3001

OCIP (Owner-controlled insurance program) . . . 15,002

On-behalf payments for fringe benefits and salaries . . . 17,036-17,037

Online technical inquiry system . . . 1022

OPEB. See Other postemployment benefits

Open-end mutual funds . . . 9049

Operations, transfers of . . . 4066

Options contracts . . . 9019

Organizational unit classification . . . 5021

Original budget . . . 20,103

Other postemployment benefits (OPEB) . . . 13,055-13,072
. alternative measurement method . . . 13,062, 13,066, 13,068
. cost sharing employers . . . 13,066
. defined . . . 13,056

Other postemployment benefits (OPEB)—continued
. defined benefit plans
. . for cost-sharing employers . . . 13,066
. . types of . . . 13,057-13,058
. defined contribution OPEB plan . . . 13,057, 13,070-13,072
. employer reporting . . . 13,055-13,072
. GAAP provisions . . . 13,056-13,059
. insured plans . . . 13,069-13,070
. measurement of liability . . . 13,064-13,065
. note disclosure . . . 13,063-13,064, 13,069
. reporting assets accumulated for . . . 13,070
. required supplementary information . . . 13,064-13,065, 13,066, 13,069
. retiree drug subsidies (RDS) . . . 13,067
. single and agent employers . . . 13,060-13,065
. special funding situations . . . 13,058-13,059, 13,067
. types of . . . 13,057-13,058

Overdrawn funds . . . 5010

Owner-controlled insurance program (OCIP) . . . 15,002

P

Paid within a reasonable time . . . 5004-5005

Pass-through grants . . . 17,034-17,037

Payables and receivables, disaggregation . . . 11,010-11,012

PCUs. See Public colleges and universities

Pell grants . . . 21,016-21,017

Pension and other form of pension benefit . . . 13,013-13,055
. generally . . . 13,013-13,014
. allocations of pension elements . . . 13,045-13,047
. basic provisions of . . . 13,015-13,020
. cost sharing employers . . . 13,034-13,048
. defined benefit pension plans. See Defined benefit pension plans
. defined contribution plans . . . 8018-8020, 13,013-13,015, 13,052-13,055
. employer contributions to nongovernmental plans . . . 13,047
. expenses and expenditures . . . 7018
. non-trust situations . . . 13,049-13,052
. note disclosure and RSI . . . 13,048
. single and agent-multiple-employers . . . 13,025-13,033

Index

Pension and other form of pension benefit—continued
. special funding situations . . . 13,042-13,045, 13,058-13,059
. separately financed specific liabilities . . . 13,046-13,047
. trust or equivalent arrangement, requirements for . . . 13,015-13,016
. valuations
. . actuarial . . . 13,021-13,025

Pension trust funds . . . 8015-8020. *See also* Public employee retirement system (PERS)

Permanent funds . . . 6008-6009

PERS. *See* Public employee retirement system

Plain language articles . . . 1023

Pledges
. future revenues pledged . . . 17,047-17,048
. nonexchange transactions . . . 17,027-17,028

Policyholder dividends . . . 15,019-15,020, 23,012

Pollution remedial obligations . . . 16,019-16,029
. capitalization of outlays . . . 16,027
. disclosures . . . 16,028-16,029
. generally . . . 16,019-16,020
. liability and recoveries . . . 16,026-16,027
. measurement . . . 16,025-16,026
. outlays . . . 16,020
. recognition and measurement . . . 16,021-16,025
. reporting . . . 16,027-16,028

Pools . . . 4060

Postemployment benefits. *See also* Other postemployment benefits (OPEB)
. generally . . . 22,001, 22,031-22,033
. ACFR . . . 22,019-22,020
. defined benefit Single Employer and Cost-Sharing OPEB plans . . . 22,040-22,041
. defined contribution OPEB plans . . . 22,047
. financial reporting . . . 22,035-22,036
. notes . . . 22,036-22,037
. OPEB plan investments . . . 22,0387
. plan description . . . 22,037-22,038
. plans that not administered as trusts or equivalent arrangements . . . 22,046
. public employee OPEB plans . . . 22,034
. receivables . . . 22,038
. reserves . . . 22,039
. single-employer and cost-sharing OPEB plans, specifically for . . . 22,039-22,040

Postemployment benefits.—continued
. small plans . . . 22,045-22,046
. statement of changes in plan net position . . . 22,036

Post-Implementation Review Process (PIR) . . . 1021-1022

Potential for dual inclusion . . . 4026-4027

Pre-agenda research stage . . . 1015-1016

Preliminary Views Document . . . 1016

Prepayments and deferrals . . . 11,010

Prepayments and deferred outflows of resources . . . 11,005-11,007

Primary governments . . . 4002, 4007-4012, 4051
. different reporting periods, component units with . . . 4048-4049

Principles. *See* Basic governmental accounting principles

Principle setting . . . 1015-1023

Private-purpose trust funds . . . 1048, 8022-8023

Program classification . . . 5021

Program revenues . . . 5027, 20,044-20,050

Property taxes . . . 17,015-17,020

Proprietary funds . . . 7001-7035
. accounting and reporting . . . 7007-7009, 12,048-12,049
. accounting hierarchy . . . 1011-1012
. advance refundings . . . 12,041-12,042
. anticipation notes . . . 12,049
. assets . . . 7009-7012, 10,001-10,007
. basis of accounting and measurement focus . . . 3016-3017, 7007-7009
. blended component units . . . 7005
. budgetary accounting . . . 2013-2015, 7007
. capital assets . . . 10,001-10,007
. capital contributions from governmental funds . . . 7015-7016
. CARES Act grant programs . . . 7016
. claims and judgments . . . 15,011-15,014
. current with an effective hedge that is terminated . . . 12,050
. customer system development fees . . . 7011-7012
. demand bonds . . . 12,049
. depreciation expense . . . 7017
. enterprise funds . . . 7001-7006. *See also* Enterprise funds

PRO

Proprietary funds—continued
- exchange transactions . . . 17,038
- expenses . . . 7016-7018
- fund equity or net position . . . 6021
- fund financial statements . . . 7009-7035
- fund types . . . 1043-1050
- infrastructure assets . . . 7011
- interest capitalization . . . 7011
- internal service funds . . . 7006-7007. *See also* Internal service funds
- joint ventures . . . 4054-4060
- landfills . . . 16,010-16,011
- liabilities . . . 7012-7013, 12,048-12,049
- long-term debt . . . 12,048-12,049
- major funds, focus on . . . 7007-7008
- major funds reporting in financial statements . . . 20,060-20,065
- materials and supplies . . . 11,010
- nonexchange transactions . . . 17,038, 18,012
- pension obligation . . . 7018
- PILOT payments . . . 7018
- prepayments and deferrals . . . 11,010
- public entity risk pools. *See* Public entity risk pools
- rate setting and enterprise funds . . . 7021-7022
- reconciliations, . . . 7008-7009
- reporting restrictions on use . . . 7010-7011
- restrictions in . . . 5044
- revenues, . . . 7014-7016
- segment information . . . 7018-7020
- special and extraordinary items . . . 5033
- special assessment debt . . . 7005-7006
- statement of cash flows. *See* Statement of cash flows
- statement of revenues, expenses, and change fund net assets . . . 7013-7016
- terminology and classification . . . 5023-5024
- uncollectible accounts related to nonrevenues . . . 7018
- uncollectible accounts related to revenues . . . 7015
- utility deposits, . . . 7011

Public broadcasters and cable systems . . . 24,002-24,005
- bartering . . . 24,003-24,004
- cable television services . . . 24,004-24,005

Public colleges and universities (PCUs) . . . 21,001-21,022
- generally . . . 21,001

Public colleges and universities (PCUs)—continued
- accrual of tuition and fees revenue . . . 21,022
- appropriations from other governments . . . 21,019
- business-type activities . . . 21,002-21,003
- component units . . . 21,003, 21,012-21,015
- - equity interests and majority equity interests . . . 21,014-21,015
- - majority equity interest held by . . . 21,014-21,015
- - nongovernmental component units . . . 21,012-21,015
- - reporting . . . 21,012-21,015
- conduit debt obligations . . . 21,021-21,022
- engaged in governmental activities . . . 21,001-21,002
- engaged in only business-type activities . . . 21,002-21,003
- federal unrelated business income taxes . . . 21,022
- financial reporting by . . . 21,004-21,012
- joint activities, accounting for . . . 21,022
- other forms of lending . . . 21,017-21,018
- other-stand-alone government . . . 21,004
- Pell grants . . . 21,016-21,017
- research and development . . . 21,018-21,019
- restricted investment income . . . 21,020-21,021
- scholarship allowances and discounts . . . 21,018
- split-interest agreements . . . 21,019-21,020
- statement of cash flows . . . 21,010-21,012
- statement of net position . . . 21,004-21,005, 21,012
- statement of revenues, expenses, and changes in fund net position . . . 21,006-21,009

Public employee retirement system (PERS) . . . 22,001-22,047
- actuarial valuation process . . . 22,021-22,024
- agent multiple-employer plans . . . 22,024-22,026
- allocated insurance contracts . . . 22,012-22,013
- assets available only to certain plan members . . . 22,035
- assets available to all plan members . . . 22,035

Index

Public employee retirement system (PERS)—continued
- communication issues from plan to employers/sponsors ... 22,024-22,026
- cost-sharing multiple-employer plans ... 22,024-22,025
- deferred compensation plans ... 22,028-22,031
- defined contribution pension plans ... 22,028
- deferred retirement option programs (DROPS) ... 22,013-22,014
- defined benefit financial reporting ... 22,005-22,020
- defined contribution plans ... 22,028
- disclosures ... 22,014-22,015
- fiduciary funds ... 8015-8020
- financial reporting framework ... 22,035
- Medicare Part D retiree drug subsidy payments ... 22,046
- net OPEB liability, schedule of changes in ... 22,041
- net pension liability ... 22,014
- notes ... 22,011-22,015, 22,036-22,040, 22,043
- OPEB plan investments ... 22,038
- pension plan investments ... 22,011-22,012
- plan description ... 22,011, 22,037-22,038
- receivables ... 22,012, 22,038
- required supplementary information ... 22,015-22,020
- reserves ... 22,013, 22,039
- schedule of employer contributions ... 22,019, 22,042
- schedule of investment returns ... 22,019
- separately financed liabilities to plan ... 22,020-22,021
- single-employer plans ... 22,024
- statement of changes in fiduciary net position ... 22,007-22,011, 22,036
- statement of fiduciary net position ... 22,005-22,007, 22,036
- valuation ... 22,021-22,024

Public entity risk pools ... 23,001-23,027. *See also* Claims and judgments
- acquisition costs ... 23,012
- capitalization contributions received ... 23,016-23,017
- capitalization contributions to other pools ... 23,016
- claims costs ... 23,007-23,011

Public entity risk pools—continued
- claims development information ... 23,019-23,022
- classification of activities ... 23,002
- defined ... 23,001
- disclosures ... 23,018-23,019
- - unpaid claims liabilities ... 23,025
- experience refunds ... 23,012
- investments ... 23,017
- lending assets ... 23,017
- loss contingencies ... 23,011
- other costs ... 23,012
- policyholder dividends ... 23,012
- premium deficiency calculation ... 23,012-23,014
- premium revenue ... 23,003-23,007
- reconciliation of claims liabilities ... 23,026
- reinsurance ... 23,014-23,016
- real estate ... 23,018
- required financial statements ... 23,003
- required supplementary information ... 23,019-23,027
- salvage or subrogation ... 23,008
- single-employer and cost-sharing OPEB plans ... 22,039-22,040
- structured settlement ... 23,009-23,011

Public hospitals and other healthcare providers ... 24,006-24,007
- charity care ... 24,006
- joint activities, accounting for ... 24,007
- joint costs, disclosures of allocations of ... 24,007

Purchase method ... 11,003-11,004

Purpose and Scope of GASB Technical Bulletins and Procedures for Issuance (GASB:TB 84-1) ... 1020

R

"Rainy day" funds ... 5047-5048

Rare books ... 10,006

Reasonable time for loan repayment ... 5005

Receivables and payables
- disaggregation ... 11,010-11,012
- government's continuing involvement ... 17,039-17,042
- interfund ... 11,010
- sales ... 17,039-17,049

Reciprocal interfund activity ... 4044, 5004-5005

REC

Reclassifications. *See* Eliminations and reclassifications

Recognition and Measurement of Certain Liabilities and Expenditures in Governmental Fund Financial Statements (GASBI-6)
. liabilities . . . 16,004-16,006

Refundings
. advance refundings . . . 12,037-12,047
. . governmental funds . . . 12,039-12,041
. . proprietary funds . . . 12,041-12,042
. crossover refunding . . . 12,037
. current . . . 12,037, 12,042-12,044
. current with an effective hedge that is terminated . . . 12,043
. debt previously refunded . . . 12,042-12,044
. disclosures . . . 12,050-12,058
. . cash flow requirements differences . . . 12,057-12,058
. . computing required refunding disclosures . . . 12,045-12,047
. . economic gain or loss . . . 12,045-12,047

Reimbursement-type transactions . . . 17,023

Related organizations . . . 4053-4054, 4059-4060

Related-party transactions . . . 1057-1059

Relationship nature, component units . . . 4027-4032

Reporting component units . . . 4032-4041

Reporting-form contract . . . 23,004

Reporting periods . . . 4048-4049

Repurchase and reverse repurchase agreements
. accounting and reporting . . . 9036-9038
. comparison . . . 9036-9037
. generally . . . 9037-9038
. investment pools . . . 9038
. legal or contractual provisions . . . 9072-9073
. reporting . . . 9038

Required supplementary information (RSI) . . . 20,102-20,105
. actuarially determined contribution . . . 22,016
. agent multiple-employer plans . . . 22,016-22,017
. communication methods . . . 1034-1036
. cost sharing employers . . . 13,034-13,048

Required supplementary information (RSI)—continued
. MD&A. *See* Management's discussion and analysis
. note . . . 22,017
. note disclosures . . . 4050, 13,048
. public entity risk pools . . . 23,019-23,027
. single-employer and cost-sharing multiple-employer plans only . . . 22,015-22,016
. single and agent-multiple-employers . . . 13,025-13,034

Resource flow statement elements . . . 1039-1040

Restoration cost approach . . . 10,023-10,024

Restricted fund balance . . . 5044-5045

Restricted net position . . . 5039-5043, 20,025-20,028

Retainage . . . 5036

Retiree health accounts . . . 8019

Retirement systems. *See* Public employee retirement system

Retrospective (experience) rating . . . 23,004

Retrospective-rated policies . . . 15,019

Revenue anticipation notes . . . 12,006-12,008, 12,049

Revenue-based contracts . . . 9018

Revenue bonds and notes . . . 12,003-12,006

Revenues
. future revenues
. . pledged . . . 17,047-17,048
. . sold . . . 17,042-17,043
. government's continuing involvement . . . 17,039-17,042
. nonexchange transactions. *See* Nonexchange transactions
. operating . . . 7014
. resource inflows . . . 5027, 20,042-20,060
. transfers to defined benefit plans . . . 17,044-17,045

Reverse repurchase agreements. *See* Repurchase and reverse repurchase agreements

Risk management liabilities . . . 15,003-15,014

Risk-sharing pool . . . 23,001

Roads . . . 10,003

RSI. *See* Required supplementary information

Index

S

Sabbatical leave, defined . . . 13,007

Sales
. accounting for transactions that do not qualify as sales . . . 17,042-17,043
. accounting for transactions to be reported as sales . . . 17,043-17,044
. amortizing deferred inflows and outflows of resources . . . 17,045
. future revenues sold . . . 17,043
. government's continuing involvement in future revenues . . . 17,039-17,042
. government's involvement in receivables . . . 17,039-17,042
. residual interests from sales . . . 17,045-17,046
. sale of delinquent receivables . . . 17,048-17,049
. transactions may be sales/collateralized borrowings . . . 17,039
. transfers of assets and future revenues . . . 17,039-17,042

Salvage . . . 15,007, 23,008

SEC Rule 2a7 . . . 9049

Securities lending transactions . . . 9038-9044
. accounting standards . . . 9038-9044
. cash collateral held as deposits . . . 9044
. collateral securities and underlying securities . . . 9044
. defined . . . 9038
. investment pools . . . 9042-9043
. receipt of cash . . . 9039-9040
. receipt of letters of credit . . . 9042
. receipt of securities . . . 9040-9042
. risks . . . 9043
. securities lending agent, defined . . . 9038-9039
. transaction costs . . . 9042

Segmented time distributions . . . 9064-9065

Self-insurance . . . 15,002

Separate legal standing . . . 4007-4008

Service concession agreements . . . 10,015

Service Efforts and Accomplishments (GASB:CS-2) . . . 1024, 1030-1032

Service Efforts and Accomplishments Reporting (GASB:CS-5) . . . 1024, 1030-1032

SNAP (Supplemental Nutrition Assistance Program) . . . 17,037

SOP . . . 78-10

Special and extraordinary items . . . 5030-5033

Special assessments . . . 19,001-19,010
. generally . . . 19,001
. capital assets . . . 19,009
. capital improvements . . . 19,002-19,003, 19,006-19,007
. classification of debt . . . 19,005-19,006
. component units . . . 19,010
. disclosures . . . 19,009-19,010
. financing, with current resources . . . 19,007-19,008
. governmental fund reporting . . . 19,004
. governmental funds . . . 19,006-19,007
. governmental liability for debt . . . 19,003-19,005
. governmental obligations for debt . . . 19,009
. no governmental obligations for debt . . . 19,007, 19,009-19,010
. proprietary funds . . . 19,008
. reserve, guarantee, sinking fund . . . 19,006
. services . . . 19,002

Special items . . . 5030-5033, 20,056-20,057

Special purpose frameworks (SPFs) . . . 3010-3011

Special-purpose governmental entities . . . 1015, 20,121, 24,001-24,018
. generally . . . 24,001-24,002
. deregulation . . . 24,017-24,018
. insurance entities . . . 24,007-24,010
. . disclosures . . . 24,010
. . general principles . . . 24,008
. . investments and mortgage loans, real estate used in operations . . . 24,009-24,010
. . policyholder dividends . . . 24,009
. . premium deficiencies . . . 24,009
. . premium revenue . . . 24,008
. . recognizing claims costs . . . 24,008-24,009
. . reinsurance . . . 24,009
. public broadcasters and cable systems . . . 24,002-24,005
. public hospitals and other healthcare providers . . . 24,006-24,007
. regulated operations . . . 24,010-24,018
. regulatory accounting
. . assets and capitalization of costs . . . 24,011-24,012
. . customer deposits . . . 24,013

SPE

Special-purpose governmental entities—continued
. regulatory accounting—continued
.. deferred inflows of resources . . . 24,012-24,013
.. derivatives and hedging . . . 24,013
.. discontinuation of . . . 24,017-24,018
.. liabilities . . . 24,012-24,013
.. reporting and, applicability of . . . 24,011
. specific regulated operations standards
.. asset impairment . . . 24,014-24,016
.. costs of construction . . . 24,013-24,014
.. disallowed costs of construction . . . 24,016
.. intra-entity profit . . . 24,014
.. recovery without return on investment . . . 24,017
.. refunds . . . 24,016-24,017
.. sale-leaseback transactions . . . 24,016

Special-purpose governments . . . 4024-4025

Special revenue funds . . . 6003-6006

Speeches . . . 1023

SPFs (Special purpose frameworks) . . . 3010-3011

Split-interest agreements . . . 21,019-21,020

Stabilization arrangements . . . 5047-5048

Standard-setting stage, . . . 1017-1018

State and local government accounting hierarchy . . . 1007-1011
. application guidance . . . 1010-1011
. category A . . . 1007-1008, 1010, 1018-1020
. category B . . . 1007-1010, 1020-1021
. special purpose framework . . . 1011

State lotteries. *See* Lotteries

Statement of activities . . . 20,035-20,060
. alternative presentation . . . 20,052-20,056
. charges for services . . . 20,045, 20,046
. classification of revenues and expenses . . . 5025-5030
. depreciation expense . . . 7030, 20,039-20,040
. eliminations and reclassifications . . . 20,058
. expenses . . . 20,037-20,042
. extraordinary items . . . 20,056-20,057
. general revenues . . . 20,050-20,052
. government-wide financial statements . . . 20,035-20,060
. grants and contributions . . . 20,042-20,049
. interest expense . . . 7029-7030, 20,040-20,042

Statement of activities—continued
. interfund transfers . . . 7030
. internal activities . . . 20,059
. internal balances . . . 20,058-20,059
. internal service fund balances . . . 20,059-20,060
. intra-entity activity . . . 20,059
. investment income . . . 7032
. program revenues . . . 20,044-20,060
. revenues and resource inflows . . . 20,042-20,060
. special items . . . 20,056-20,057
. taxes . . . 20,050

Statement of cash flows . . . 20,090-20,092
. proprietary funds
.. generally . . . 7018
. public colleges and universities . . . 21,010-21,012

Statement of net position
. ACFR . . . 20,018-20,029
. assets and liabilities . . . 20,019-20,023
. capital assets . . . 20,023-20,025
. classification of . . . 5013-5016
. components of net assets . . . 20,023
. current liabilities . . . 5014
. illustration . . . 20,029-20,035
. net investment in capital assets . . . 20,023-20,025
. public colleges and universities . . . 21,004-21,005
. restricted assets . . . 20,022
. restrictions . . . 20,025-20,028
. revenue flow assumption . . . 20,028-20,029
. short-term obligations expected to be refinanced . . . 5015-5016
. unrestricted net position . . . 20,028-20,035

Statistical section . . . 20,119-20,121

Structured settlement . . . 23,009-23,011

Subrogation . . . 15,007, 23,008

Subscription-based information technology arrangements . . . 14,038-14,043

Subsequent events, . . . 1059

Supplemental Nutrition Assistance Program (SNAP) . . . 17,037

Supplementary information
. combining financial statements . . . 20,114-20,118
. defined . . . 1035-1036
. individual fund financial statements . . . 20,115

SPE

Index 28,027

Supplementary information—continued
. presentation . . . 1035-1036
. required supplementary information. *See* Required supplementary information (RSI)
. schedules . . . 20,118

Supplies . . . 11,002-11,005

T

Tail coverage . . . 15,018

Take-out agreements . . . 12,009, 12,048

Target benefit plan . . . 8018

Tax Abatement Disclosures (GASB-77) . . . 17,049-17,052

Tax anticipation notes . . . 12,006-12,008, 12,049

Tax incremental financing (TIF) . . . 19,001

Tax sheltered annuity plans . . . 13,018

Technical Bulletins. *See also specific Bulletin*
. Category B GAAP, . . . 1020-1021
. issuance . . . 1010

Temporary impairments of capital assets . . . 10,025-10,026

Termination benefits . . . 13,001-13,006
. generally . . . 13,002-13,003
. disclosures . . . 13,006
. employer's defined benefit pension or OPEB, effect on . . . 13,006
. involuntary . . . 13,002-13,003
. measurement and recognition . . . 13,003-13,006
. voluntary . . . 13,002

Terminology and classification . . . 5001-5049
. capital asset sales . . . 5019
. debt issuance proceeds . . . 5016-5017
. demand bonds . . . 5018
. designations, . . . 5043-5044
. eliminations and reclassifications . . . 5008-5012
. extraordinary and special items . . . 5030-5033
. governmental fund financial statements . . . 5016-5023
. government-wide financial statements . . . 5013-5016, 5025-5030
. interfund activity . . . 5004-5012

Terminology and classification—continued
. invested in capital assets, net of related debt . . . 5034-5039
. lease transactions reported in governmental funds, . . . 5019
. net assets in government-wide statements and proprietary fund statements . . . 5033-5039
. other debt issuance transactions . . . 5017-5018
. proprietary fund financial statements . . . 5013-5016, 5023-5024
. restricted net position . . . 5039-5043
. revenue and expenditure classification . . . 5019-5023
. . activity classification, . . . 5021-5022
. . character classification . . . 5022
. . expenditures, . . . 5019-5023
. . function (or program) classification . . . 5021
. . object classification . . . 5022-5023
. . organizational unit classification . . . 5021
. . revenues, . . . 5020
. statement of activities (expenses and revenues) . . . 5025-5030
. statement of net position . . . 5013-5016
. unrestricted net assets . . . 5044

Theft of assets . . . 15,001

Torts . . . 15,001

Transfers . . . 5030

Transfers of operations . . . 4062-4063, 4066

Trust funds . . . 1047-1048

Tunnels . . . 10,003

2a7-like pools . . . 9049

U

Unassigned fund balance . . . 5046-5047

Undivided interests . . . 4061

Unemployment compensation funds . . . 1045-1050

Universities. *See* Public colleges and universities (PCUs)

Unmatured long-term indebtedness . . . 16,006-16,007

Unrestricted net assets . . . 5043

User guides . . . 1023

Utility deposits, . . . 7011

UTI

V

Valuation
. actuarial . . . 13,021-13,025
. of derivatives . . . 9020-9021
. fair value . . . 9002-9013
. . derivatives . . . 9020-9021

Voluntary nonexchange transactions . . . 17,022-17,028
. contingencies . . . 17,027
. expense and liability recognition . . . 17,034
. expenses and expenditures . . . 18,010-18,011
. grants . . . 17,034-17,037
. modified accrual basis of accounting . . . 17,032-17,034

nonexchange revenues administered or collected by another government . . . 17,028-17,031
. pledges . . . 17,027-17,028
. revenue recognition . . . 17,027, 17,028-17,031
. subsequent contravention of eligibility requirements . . . 17,028

W

Water and sewer systems . . . 10,003

Web sites . . . 1023

Weighted average maturity . . . 9065-9066

"Why Government Accounting and Financial Reporting is—and Should Be—Different" (GASB) . . . 1004-1005

Worksheet conversion entries. *See* Converting from modified accrual to accrual basis

Works of art . . . 10,006-10,007

Y

Yield maintenance agreements . . . 9073

Z

Zero-interest-rate bonds . . . 6020-6021